Accounting Information Systems

NINTH EDITION

JAMES A. HALL
Peter E. Bennett Chair in Business and Economics
Lehigh University

Australia • Brazil • Mexico • Singapore • United Kingdom • United States

Accounting Information Systems, Ninth Edition

James A. Hall

Vice President, General Manager, Social Science & Qualitative Business: Balraj Kalsi

Product Director: Mike Schenk

Senior Product Manager: Matt Filmonov

Content Developer: Ted Knight

Senior Product Assistant: Adele Scholtz

Senior Marketing Manager: Robin LeFevre

Manufacturing Planner: Doug Wilke

Art and Cover Direction, Production Management, and Composition: Lumina Datamatics, Inc.

Cover Image: © Color Symphony/ Shutterstock

Intellectual Property

Analyst: Christina Ciaramella

Project Manager: Betsy Hathaway

Library of Congress Control Number: 2014954894

ISBN: 978-1-133-93440-0

Cengage Learning
20 Channel Center Street
Boston, MA 02210
USA

Cengage Learning is a leading provider of customized learning solutions with office locations around the globe, including Singapore, the United Kingdom, Australia, Mexico, Brazil, and Japan. Locate your local office at: **www.cengage.com/global**

Cengage Learning products are represented in Canada by Nelson Education, Ltd.

To learn more about Cengage Learning Solutions, visit **www.cengage.com**

Purchase any of our products at your local college store or at our preferred online store **www.cengagebrain.com**

Printed in the United States of America
Print Number: 01 Print Year: 2014

DEDICATION

To my wife Eileen, and my children Elizabeth and Katie

BRIEF CONTENTS

CONTENTS

Chapter 7 The Conversion Cycle 291

Chapter 8 Financial Reporting and Management Reporting Systems 331

PREFACE

Welcome to the Ninth Edition

The ninth edition *of Accounting Information Systems* includes a range of new and revised homework assignments and up-to-date content changes, as well as several reorganized chapters. All of these changes add up to more student and instructor enhancements than ever before. As this preface makes clear, we have made these changes to keep students and instructors as current as possible on issues such as business processes, systems development methods, IT governance and strategy, security, internal controls, and relevant aspects of Sarbanes-Oxley legislation.

Focus and Flexibility in Designing Your AIS Course

Among accounting courses, accounting information systems (AIS) courses tend to be the least standardized. Often, the objectives, background, and orientation of the instructor, rather than adherence to a standard body of knowledge, determine the direction the AIS course takes. Therefore, we have designed this text for maximum flexibility:

- This textbook covers a **full range of AIS topics** to provide instructors with flexibility in setting the direction and intensity of their courses.
- At the same time, for those who desire a **structured model,** the first nine chapters of the text, along with the chapters on electronic commerce and general IT controls, provide what has proven to be a **successful template for developing an AIS course.**
- Previous editions of this book have been used successfully in **introductory-, advanced-, and graduate-level AIS courses.**
- The **topics in this book are presented from the perspective of the managers' and accountants' AIS-related responsibilities under the Sarbanes-Oxley Act.**
- Although this book was written primarily to meet the needs of accounting majors about to enter the modern business world, we have also developed it to be an **effective text for general business, industrial engineering, and computer science students who seek a thorough understanding of AIS and internal control issues as part of their professional education.**

Key Features

CONCEPTUAL FRAMEWORK

This book employs a conceptual framework to emphasize the professional and legal responsibility of accountants, auditors, and management for the design, operation, and control of AIS applications. This responsibility pertains to business events that are narrowly defined as financial transactions. Systems that process nonfinancial transactions are not subject to the standards of internal control under Sarbanes-Oxley legislation. Supporting the information needs of all users in a modern organization, however, requires systems that integrate both accounting and nonaccounting functions. While providing the organization with unquestioned benefit, a potential consequence of such integration is a loss of control due to the blurring of the lines that traditionally separate AIS from non-AIS functions. **The conceptual framework presented in this book distinguishes AIS applications that are legally subject to specific internal control standards.**

EVOLUTIONARY APPROACH

Over the years, accounting information systems have been represented by a number of different approaches or models. Each new model evolved because of the shortcomings and limitations of its predecessor. An interesting feature in this evolution is that older models are not immediately replaced by the newest technique. Thus, at any point in time, various generations of legacy systems exist across different organizations and often coexist within a single enterprise. Modern accountants need to be familiar with the operational characteristics of all AIS approaches that they are likely to encounter. **Therefore, this book presents the salient aspects of legacy and state-of-the-art systems.**

EMPHASIS ON INTERNAL CONTROLS

The book presents a conceptual model for designing and assessing internal controls based on the Committee of Sponsoring Organizations of the Treadway Commission (COSO) framework. We use the COSO model to explore control issues related to both the manual and the IT aspects of AIS. In addition to the classic controls designed to influence human behavior, such as segregation of duties, independent verification, and supervision, special emphasis is placed on controls that address the following IT risks and concerns:

- Computer application integrity
- Operating systems security
- Database management systems security
- Electronic data interchange (EDI)
- Electronic commerce and network security
- Enterprise resource planning (ERP) systems
- Systems development and program change procedures
- Organization of the corporate IT function
- IT outsourcing and cloud computing
- Data center security

EXPOSURE TO SYSTEMS DESIGN AND DOCUMENTATION TOOLS

IT professionals employ a number of documentation tools to communicate the key features of information systems. Among these tools are data flow diagrams (DFDs), systems flowcharts, entity relationship diagrams (ERDs), and program logic flowcharts. Modern accountants, whether in the conduct of an audit or the provision of advisory services, work closely with IT professionals and must master the use of IT documentation tools and techniques This book contains numerous systems design and documentation cases and assignments intended to develop students' competency in this area.

Significant Changes in the Ninth Edition

End-of-Chapter Material

The end-of-chapter material in the ninth edition has undergone significant revision. Most of the multiple choice questions and problems, and all of the cases have been revised or replaced. This important body of material is tailored to the chapters' contents, and the solutions provided in the solutions manual accurately reflect the problem requirements. In particular, great attention was given to internal control case solutions to ensure consistency in appearance and an accurate reflection of the cases in the text. All case solution flowcharts are numerically coded and cross-referenced to text that explains the internal control issues. This approach, which has been classroom tested, facilitates effective presentation of internal control case materials.

Chapter 3, "Ethics, Fraud, and Internal Control"

This chapter has been revised to include the most recent research results published by the Association of Certified Fraud Examiners (ACFE). The ACFE study provides estimates of losses due to fraud, categorizes fraud by various factors, and creates a profile of fraud perpetrators.

Chapter 4, "The Revenue Cycle"; Chapter 5, "The Expenditure Cycle Part I: Purchases and Cash Disbursements Procedures"; Chapter 6, "The Expenditure Cycle Part II: Payroll Processing and Fixed Asset Procedures"; Chapter 7, "The Conversion Cycle"; and Chapter 8, "Financial Reporting and Management Reporting Systems"

These chapters have been significantly revised to reflect a risk-based approach to AIS design and audit. The approach taken in each chapter is to examine the risks from errors and fraud that are inherent to the particular cycle being studied. Based on the risk analysis, and the level of technology in place, specific physical and IT controls are described to mitigate the risks. Since the purpose of internal controls is to mitigate risk, this risk-based approach fits more logically into a classroom discussion. Furthermore, challenging students to think about what can go wrong encourages classroom discussion and supports the notion of brainstorming as recommended by Statement on Auditing Standards (SAS) 109.

Chapter 9, "Database Management Systems"

At one time, an accountant in the conduct of an audit could pull an invoice from a filing cabinet. Today that invoice is most likely stored in various pieces on several normalized database tables and accessing it requires an understanding of relational database structures. The chapter has been extensively rewritten to address this growing need for modern accountants to have a working understanding of data modeling techniques. The chapter begins with an overview of database technology and describes in detail the functions and relationship between its primary elements. It then presents the key characteristics of the relational database model including data modeling, deriving relational tables from entity relationship (ER) diagrams, the creation of user views, and data normalization techniques. The chapter concludes with a discussion of distributed database issues.

Chapter 15, "Auditing IT Controls Part I: Sarbanes-Oxley and IT Governance"

This chapter was revised to provide an introduction to IT auditing. It opens with an overview of auditing in which the key components of an audit are discussed. Topics in this revised section include auditing standards, the structure of an audit, management assertions, and the audit risk model. Next, the chapter turns to internal control and audit issues related to Sections 302 and 404 of SOX including IT control and computer fraud issues. The body of the chapter is basically unchanged from the eighth edition, which deals with the risks and controls related to IT governance including the structure of the IT function within an organization, computer center threats, and key elements of a disaster recovery planning. The final section of the chapter has been revised to examine the current issues surrounding the growing trend toward IT outsourcing. In particular, it reviews the theories underlying outsourcing and the expected benefits. IT outsourcing is also associated with significant risks, which are addressed. The chapter concludes with a discussion of audit issues related to outsourcing including the Statement on Standards for Attestation Engagements (SSAE) 16 reporting standard.

Organization and Content

PART I: OVERVIEW OF ACCOUNTING INFORMATION SYSTEMS

Chapter 1, "The Information System: An Accountant's Perspective"

Chapter 1 places the subject of accounting information systems in perspective for accountants. It is divided into three major sections, each dealing with a different aspect of information systems.

- The first section explores the information environment of the firm. It identifies the types of information used in business, describes the flows of information through an organization, and presents a framework for viewing AIS in relation to other information systems components. The section concludes with a review of the key elements of the general model for AIS.
- The second section deals with the impact of organization structure on AIS. It presents the business organization as a system of interrelated functions. Extensive attention is given the IT and accounting segments, which play collaborative roles as the purveyors of financial information for the rest of the organization.
- The third section discusses the role of accountants as designers and auditors of AIS. The nature of the responsibilities shared by accountants and computer professionals for developing AIS applications is examined.

Chapter 2, "Introduction to Transaction Processing"

Chapter 2 divides the treatment of transaction processing systems into six major sections.

- The first section provides an overview of transaction processing, showing its vital role as an information provider for financial reporting, internal management reporting, and the support of day-to-day operations. Three transaction cycles account for most of a firm's economic activity: the revenue cycle, the expenditure cycle, and the conversion cycle.
- The second section describes the relationship among accounting records, both hard copy and digital, in forming an audit trail.
- The third section describes the key features of flat file and database structures used to store accounting data.
- The fourth section presents an overview of documentation techniques used to describe the key features of systems. This section presents several documentation techniques for representing manual procedures and computer operations. These include data flow diagrams, entity relationship diagrams, system flowcharts, program flowcharts, and record layout diagrams.
- The fifth section addresses alternative transaction processing approaches. It reviews the fundamental features of batch and real-time technologies, and their implication for transaction processing.
- The final section examines data coding schemes, their role in transaction processing and AIS as a means of coordinating and managing a firm's transactions, and the advantages and disadvantages of the major types of numeric and alphabetic coding schemes.

Chapter 3, "Ethics, Fraud, and Internal Control"

Chapter 3 deals with the related topics of ethics, fraud, and internal control.

- The first section examines ethical issues related to business and specifically to computer systems. The questions raised are intended to stimulate class discussions.
- The second section deals with the subject of fraud and its implications for accountants. Although the term *fraud* is very familiar in today's financial press, it is not always clear what constitutes fraud. This section distinguishes between management fraud and employee fraud. This section presents techniques for identifying unethical and dishonest management and for assessing the risk of management fraud. Employee fraud can be prevented and detected by a system of internal controls. The section discusses the results of a research study conducted by the Association of Certified Fraud Examiners.
- The final section describes the internal control structure and control activities specified in the COSO framework. The controls presented in this chapter, both physical and IT controls, are applied to specific applications in chapters that follow.

PART II: TRANSACTION CYCLES AND BUSINESS PROCESSES

Chapter 4, "The Revenue Cycle"; Chapter 5, "The Expenditure Cycle Part I: Purchases and Cash Disbursements Procedures"; and Chapter 6, "The Expenditure Cycle Part II: Processing and Fixed Asset Procedures"

The approach taken in these three chapters is similar. First, the respective cycle is reviewed conceptually using data flow diagrams to present key features and control points of each major subsystem. We then examine physical systems with two objectives in mind: (1) illustrate how system functionality changes under different levels of technology, and (2) demonstrate how the internal control focus shifts as the mix between technology and manual procedures changes. To accomplish this, we review examples of systems at different points on the technology continuum. The first examples are basic technology systems that use independent PCs, which function primarily as record keeping devices. We then move on to examples of advanced technologies that integrate key business functions.

Under each technology, the risks from errors and fraud are examined and the controls to mitigate risks are discussed. This approach provides the student with a solid understanding of the business tasks in each cycle and an awareness of how different technologies influence changes in the operation and control of the systems.

Chapter 7, "The Conversion Cycle"

Manufacturing systems represent a dynamic aspect of AIS. **Chapter 7** discusses the technologies and techniques used in support of two alternative manufacturing environments: traditional mass production (batch) processing and lean manufacturing. These environments are driven by information technologies, such as materials requirements planning (MRP), manufacturing resources planning (MRP II), and enterprise resource planning (ERP). The chapter addresses the shortcomings of the traditional cost accounting model as it compares to two alternative models: activity-based costing (ABC) and value stream accounting.

Chapter 8, "Financial Reporting and Management Reporting Systems"

Chapter 8 examines an organization's nondiscretionary and discretionary reporting systems.

- First, it focuses on the general ledger system (GLS) and on the files that constitute a GLS database.
- Next, it examines how financial statement information is provided to both external and internal users through a multistep reporting process. The emerging technology of Extensible Business Reporting Language (XBRL) is changing traditional financial reporting for many organizations. The key features of XBRL and the internal control implications of this technology are considered.
- The chapter then looks at discretionary reporting systems that constitute the management reporting system (MRS). Discretionary reporting is not subject to the professional guidelines and legal statutes that govern nondiscretionary financial reporting. Rather, it is driven by several factors, including

management principles; management function, level, and decision type; problem structure; responsibility accounting; and behavioral considerations. The impact of each factor on the design of the management reporting system is investigated.

PART III: ADVANCED TECHNOLOGIES IN ACCOUNTING INFORMATION

Chapter 9, "Database Management Systems"

Chapter 9 addresses the design and management of an organization's data resources.

- The first section demonstrates how problems associated with traditional flat-file systems are resolved under the database approach.
- The second section describes in detail the functions and relationships among four primary elements of the database environment: the users, the database management system (DBMS), the database administrator (DBA), and the physical database.
- The third section is devoted to an in-depth explanation of the characteristics of the relational database model.
- The fourth section examines database design topics including data modeling, deriving relational tables from ER diagrams, the creation of user views, and data normalization techniques.
- The chapter concludes with a discussion of distributed database issues. It examines three possible database configurations in a distributed environment: centralized, partitioned, and replicated databases.

Chapter 10, "The REA Approach to Database Modeling"

Chapter 10 presents the resources, events, and agents (REA) model as a means of specifying and designing accounting information systems that serve the needs of all users within an organization. The chapter is composed of three major sections.

- The chapter begins by defining the key elements of REA. The basic model employs a unique form of ER diagram called an REA diagram. The diagram consists of three entity types (resources, events, and agents) and a set of associations linking them.
- Next, the rules for developing an REA diagram are explained and illustrated in detail. An important aspect of the model is the concept of economic duality, which specifies that each economic event must be mirrored by an associated economic event in the opposite direction. The section illustrates the development of an REA database for a hypothetical firm, following a multistep process called view modeling. The result of this process is an REA diagram for a single organizational function.
- The chapter's third section explains how multiple REA diagrams (revenue cycle, purchases, cash disbursements, and payroll) are integrated into a global or enterprise-wide model. The enterprise model is then implemented into a relational database structure, and user views are constructed. The section concludes with a discussion of how REA modeling can improve competitive advantage by allowing management to focus on the value-added activities of their operations.

Chapter 11, "Enterprise Resource Planning Systems"

Chapter 11 presents a number of issues related to the implementation of enterprise resource planning (ERP) systems. It is composed of five major sections.

- The first section outlines the key features of a generic ERP system by comparing the function and data storage techniques of a traditional flat-file or database system to that of an ERP.
- The second section describes various ERP configurations related to servers, databases, and bolt-on software.
- Data warehousing is the topic of the third section. A data warehouse is a relational or multidimensional database that supports online analytical processing (OLAP). Issues discussed include data modeling, data extraction from operational databases, data cleansing, data transformation, and loading data into the warehouse.
- The fourth section examines risks associated with ERP implementation. These include "big bang" issues, opposition to change within the organization, choosing the wrong ERP model, choosing the wrong consultant, cost overrun issues, and disruptions to operations.
- The fifth section reviews several control and auditing issues related to ERPs. The discussion follows the COSO framework.

Chapter 12, "Electronic Commerce Systems"

Driven by the Internet revolution, electronic commerce is dramatically expanding and undergoing radical changes. Although electronic commerce has brought enormous opportunities for consumers and businesses, its effective control present challenges to organization management teams and accountants. To properly evaluate the potential exposures and risks in this environment, the modern accountant must be familiar with the technologies and techniques that underlie electronic commerce. **Chapter 12** and its associated appendix deal with several aspects of electronic commerce.

- The body of the chapter examines Internet commerce including business-to-consumer and business-to-business relationships. It presents the risks associated with electronic commerce, including hardware failures, software errors, unauthorized access from remote locations, and denial of service attacks that can prevent an organization from conducting business.
- The chapter also reviews security and assurance techniques to reduce risk and promote trust.
- The chapter concludes with a discussion of how Internet commerce impacts the accounting and auditing profession.
- The internal usage of networks to support distributed data processing and traditional business-to-business transactions conducted via EDI systems are presented in the appendix.

PART IV: SYSTEMS DEVELOPMENT ACTIVITIES

Chapter 13, "Managing the Systems Development Life Cycle," and Chapter 14, "Construct, Deliver, and Maintain Systems Projects"

The chapters in Part IV examine the accountant's role in the systems development process.

- **Chapter 13** begins with an overview to the systems development life cycle (SDLC). This multistage process guides organization management through the development and/or purchase of information systems.
- Next, Chapter 13 presents the key issues pertaining to developing a systems strategy, including its relationship to the strategic business plan, the current legacy situation, and feedback from the user community. The chapter provides a methodology for assessing the feasibility of proposed projects and for selecting individual projects to go forward for construction and delivery to their users.
- The chapter concludes by reviewing the role of accountants in managing the SDLC.
- **Chapter 14** covers the many activities associated with in-house development, which fall conceptually into two categories: (1) constructing the system and (2) delivering the system. Through these activities, systems selected in the project initiation phase (discussed in Chapter 13) are designed in detail and implemented. This involves creating input screen formats, output report layouts, database structures, and application logic. Finally, the completed system is tested, documented, and rolled out to the user.
- The chapter then examines the increasingly important option of using commercial software packages. Conceptually, the commercial software approach also consists of construct and delivery activities. The chapter examines the pros, cons, and issues involved in selecting off-the-shelf systems.
- The chapter also addresses the important activities associated with systems maintenance and the associated risks that are important to managers, accountants, and auditors.

Several comprehensive cases designed as team-based systems development projects are available online at www.cengagebrain.com. These cases have been used effectively by groups of three or four students working as a design team. Each case has sufficient details to allow analysis of user needs, preparation of a conceptual solution, and the development of a detailed design, including user views (input and output), processes, and databases.

PART V: COMPUTER CONTROLS AND IT AUDITING

Chapter 15, "Auditing IT Controls Part I: Sarbanes-Oxley and IT Governance"

Chapter 15 opens with an overview of IT auditing in which the key components of an audit are discussed including auditing standards, the structure of an audit, management assertions, and the audit risk model. Next, the chapter examines management and auditor responsibilities under Sections 302 and 404 of the Sarbanes-Oxley Act (SOX). The design, implementation, and assessment of IT controls form the central theme for this chapter and the two chapters that follow. This chapter presents risks, controls, and tests of controls related to IT governance, including organizing the IT function, controlling computer center operations, designing an adequate disaster recovery plan, and IT outsourcing.

Chapter 16, "Auditing IT Controls Part II: Security and Access"

Chapter 16 continues the treatment of IT controls as described by the COSO control framework. The focus of the chapter is on SOX compliance regarding the security and control of operating systems, database management systems, and communication networks. This chapter examines the risks, controls, audit objectives, and tests of controls that may be performed to satisfy either compliance or attest responsibilities.

Chapter 17, "Auditing IT Controls Part III: Systems Development, Program Changes, and Application Auditing"

Chapter 17 concludes the examination of general IT controls as outlined in the COSO control framework. The chapter focuses on SOX compliance regarding systems development and program change procedures. It examines the risks, controls, audit objectives, and tests of controls that may be performed to satisfy compliance or attest responsibilities. The chapter also examines several computer-assisted audit tools and techniques (CAATTs) for testing IT application controls and for performing substantive tests.

SUPPLEMENTS

Product Website

Additional teaching and learning resources, including access to additional internal control and systems development cases, are available by download from the book's website at www.cengagebrain.com.

Accessing CengageBrain

1. Use your browser to go to www.CengageBrain.com.
2. The first time you go to the site, you will need to register. It's free. Click on "Sign Up" in the top right corner of the page and fill out the registration information. (After you have signed in once, whenever you return to CengageBrain, you will enter the user name and password you have chosen and you will be taken directly to the companion site for your book.)
3. Once you have registered and logged in for the first time, go to the "Search for Books or Materials" bar and enter the author or ISBN for your textbook. When the title of your text appears, click on it and you will be taken to the companion site. There you can choose among the various folders provided on the Student side of the site. NOTE: If you are currently using more than one Cengage textbook, the same user name and password will give you access to all the companion sites for your Cengage titles. After you have entered the information for each title, all the titles you are using will appear listed in the pull-down menu in the "Search for Books or Materials" bar. Whenever you return to CengageBrain, you can click on the title of the site you wish to visit and go directly there.

PowerPoint® Slides

Completely updated PowerPoint® slides provide colorful lecture outlines of each chapter of the text, incorporating text graphics and flowcharts where needed. The PowerPoint® presentation is available for download from the text website.

Test Bank

The *Test Bank,* available in Word, contains true/false, multiple-choice, short answer, and essay questions. The files are available for download from the text website.

Solutions Manual

The *Solutions Manual* contains solutions to all end-of-chapter problems and cases. Adopting instructors may download the *Solutions Manual* under password protection at the Instructor's Resource page of the book's website.

ACKNOWLEDGMENTS

I am grateful to the following people for reviewing the book in recent editions and for providing helpful comments:

Beth Brilliant
Kean University

Sarah Brown
Southern Arkansas University

Stephen Burd
University of New Mexico

David M. Cannon
Grand Valley State University

Meir Fischer
Post University

James Holmes
University of Kentucky

Alan Levitan
University of Louisville

Andrew D. Luzi
California State University, Fullerton

Sakthi Mahenthiran
Butler University

Gerald Myers
Pacific Lutheran University

John Nader
Grace Bible College

Jeff L. Payne
University of Kentucky

H. Sam Riner
University of North Alabama

Kirsten Rosacker
University of Wisconsin-Lacrosse

Helen M. Savage
Youngstown State University

Jerry D. Siebel
University of South Florida

Richard M. Sokolowski
Teikyo Post University

Dennis Stovall
Grand Valley State University

Jerry Turner
Texas Christian University

Patrick Wheeler
University of Missouri-Columbia

Srini Ragothaman
University of South Dakota

James A. Hall
Lehigh University

PART

I

Overview of Accounting Information Systems

CHAPTER

1

The Information System: An Accountant's Perspective

Learning Objectives

After studying this chapter, you should:

- Recognize the primary information flows within the business environment.
- Understand the difference between accounting information systems and management information systems.
- Understand the difference between financial transactions and nonfinancial transactions.
- Know the principal features of the general model for information systems.
- Understand the organizational structure and functional areas of a business.
- Be able to distinguish between external auditing, internal auditing, and advisory services as they relate to accounting information systems.

Unlike many other accounting subjects, such as intermediate accounting, **accounting information systems (AIS)** lacks a well-defined body of knowledge. Much controversy exists among college faculty as to what should and should not be covered in the AIS course. To some extent, however, the controversy is being resolved through legislation. The Sarbanes-Oxley Act (SOX) of 2002 established new corporate governance regulations and standards for public companies registered with the Securities and Exchange Commission (SEC). This wide-sweeping legislation impacts public companies, their management, and their auditors. Of particular importance to AIS students is the impact of SOX on internal control standards and related auditing procedures. Although SOX does not define the entire content of the AIS course, it does identify critical areas of study that need to be included. These topics and more are covered in the chapters of this text.

The purpose of this chapter is to place the subject of AIS in perspective for accountants. Toward this end, the chapter is divided into three major sections, each dealing with a different aspect of information systems. The first section explores the information environment of the firm. It identifies the types of information used in business, describes the flow of information through an organization, and presents a framework for viewing AIS in relation to other information systems components. The section concludes with a review of the key elements of the general model for AIS. The second section of the chapter deals with the impact of organizational structure on AIS. Here we examine the business organization as a system of interrelated functions. Extensive attention is given the IT and accounting segments, which play collaborative roles as the purveyors of financial information for the rest of the organization. The final section discusses the unique responsibility of accountants as domain experts in the design of AIS and as auditors of AIS.

The Information Environment

We begin the study of AIS with the recognition that information is a business resource. Like other business resources such as raw materials, capital, and labor, information is vital to the survival of the contemporary business organization. Every business day, vast quantities of information flow to decision makers and other users to meet a variety of internal needs. In addition, information flows out from the organization to external users, such as customers, suppliers, and stakeholders who have an interest in the firm. Figure 1-1 presents an overview of these internal and external **information flows**.

The pyramid in Figure 1-1 shows the business organization divided horizontally into several levels of activity. Business operations form the base of the pyramid. These activities consist of the product-oriented work of the organization, such as manufacturing, sales, distribution, billing, and cash receipts. Above the base level, the organization is divided into three management tiers: operations management, middle management, and top management. Operations management is directly responsible for controlling day-to-day operations. Middle management is accountable for the short-term planning and coordination of activities necessary to accomplish organizational objectives. Top management is responsible for longer-term planning and setting organizational objectives. Every individual in the organization, from business operations to top management, needs information to accomplish his or her tasks.

Notice in Figure 1-1 how information flows in two directions within the organization: horizontally and vertically. The horizontal flow supports operations-level tasks with highly detailed information about the many business transactions affecting the firm. This includes information about events such as the sale and shipment of goods, the use of labor and materials in the production process, and internal transfers of resources from one department to another. The vertical flow

FIGURE 1-1 INTERNAL AND EXTERNAL FLOWS OF INFORMATION

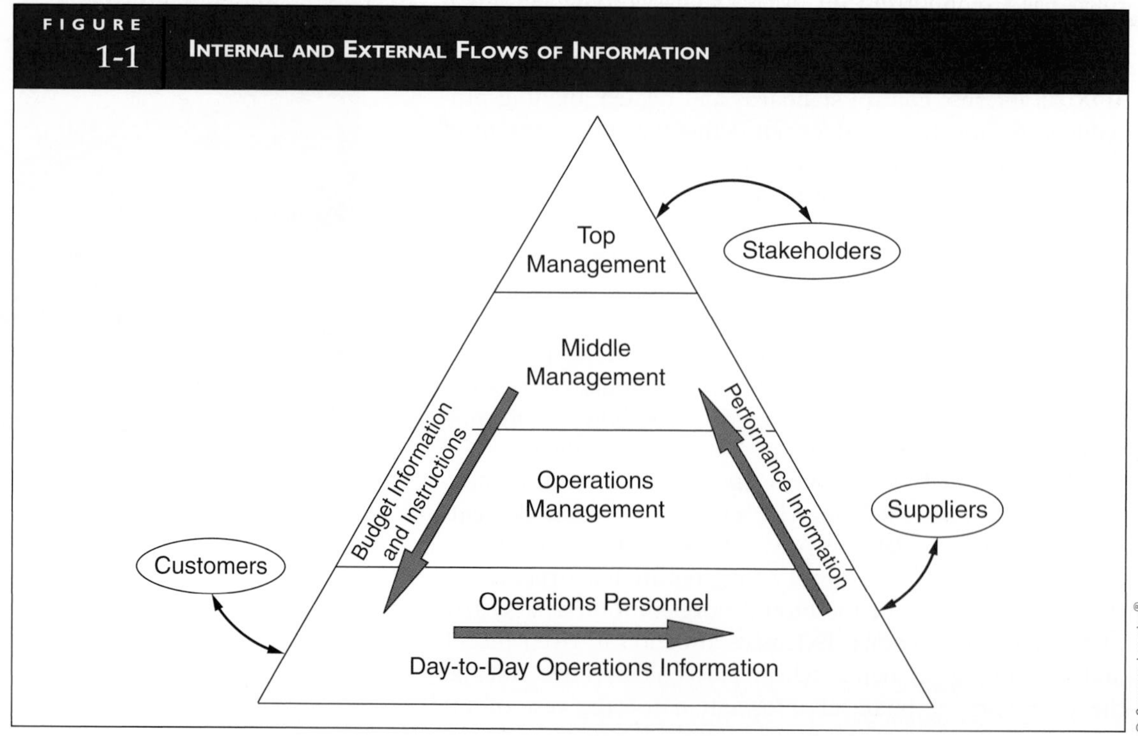

distributes information downward from senior managers to junior managers and operations personnel in the form of instructions, quotas, and budgets. In addition, summarized information pertaining to operations and other activities flows upward to managers at all levels. Management uses this information to support its various planning and control functions.

A third flow of information depicted in Figure 1-1 represents exchanges between the organization and users in the external environment. External users fall into two groups: **trading partners** and **stakeholders**. Exchanges with trading partners include customer sales and billing information, purchase information for suppliers, and inventory receipts information. Stakeholders are external entities with a direct or indirect interest in the firm. Stockholders, financial institutions, and government agencies are examples of external stakeholders. Information exchanges with these groups include financial statements, tax returns, and stock transaction information.

INFORMATION OBJECTIVES

Specific information objectives will differ from firm to firm as specific user needs vary. Three fundamental objectives are, however, common to all organizations:

1. *To support the firm's day-to-day operations.* Operations personnel use information to assist them in the efficient and effective discharge of their daily tasks.
2. *To support management decision making.* Managers use information to assist them in planning and control decisions related to their areas of responsibility.
3. *To support the stewardship function of management.* Stewardship refers to managers' responsibility to properly manage the resources of the firm and to report on their activities. External users receive stewardship information through traditional financial statements and other mandated reports. Internally, managers receive stewardship information from various responsibility reports.

These objectives call for information sets that are diverse in their level of detail and nature. For example, managers cannot effectively employ the finely detailed information needed to support day-to-day operations. Management decision information tends to be highly summarized and oriented toward reporting on overall performance and trends rather than routine tasks. Similarly, accrual-based financial statement information, which is prepared for stakeholders, is unsuitable for most internal uses. The information needed to satisfy these diverse needs is the product of the information system.

AN INFORMATION SYSTEMS FRAMEWORK

The **information system** is the set of formal procedures by which data are collected, stored, processed into information, and distributed to users.

Figure 1-2 shows the information system of a hypothetical manufacturing firm decomposed into its elemental subsystems. Notice that two broad classes of systems emerge from the decomposition: the accounting information system (AIS) and the **management information system (MIS)**. We will use this framework to identify the domain of AIS and distinguish it from MIS. Keep in mind that Figure 1-2 is a conceptual view; physical information systems are not typically organized into such discrete packages. More often, MIS and AIS functions are integrated within physical systems to achieve operational efficiency.

The distinction between AIS and MIS centers on the concept of a transaction, as illustrated by Figure 1-3. The information system accepts input, called transactions, which are converted through various processes into output information that goes to users. Transactions fall into two classes: financial transactions and nonfinancial transactions. Before exploring this distinction, let's first define the term *transaction*:

> *A* **transaction** *is an event that affects or is of interest to the organization and is processed by its information system as a unit of work.*

FIGURE 1-2 A FRAMEWORK FOR INFORMATION SYSTEMS

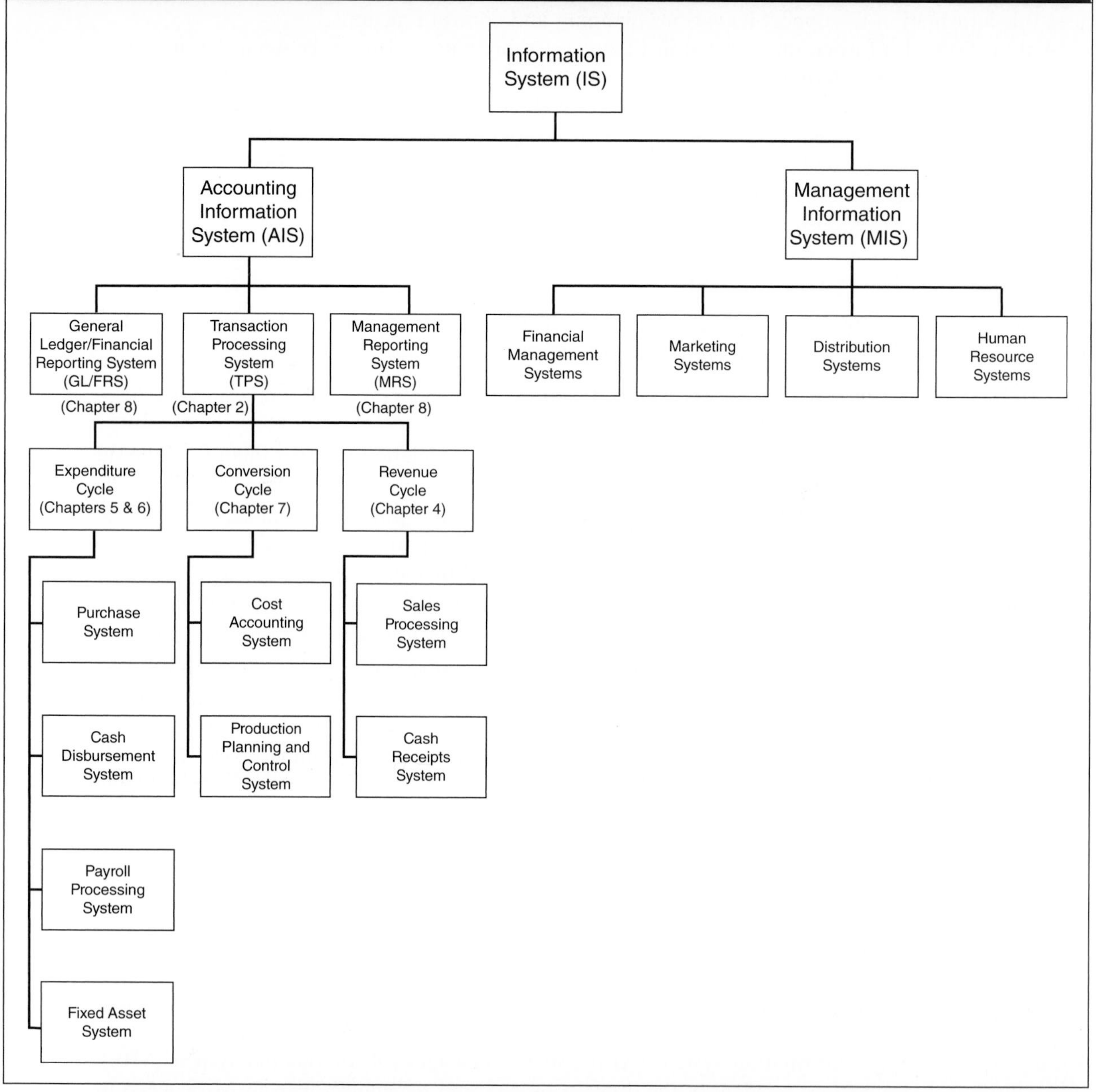

Information System (IS)
Accounting Information System (AIS)
Management Information System (MIS)
General Ledger/Financial Reporting System (GL/FRS)
(Chapter 8)
Transaction Processing System (TPS)
(Chapter 2)
Management Reporting System (MRS)
(Chapter 8)
Financial Management Systems
Marketing Systems
Distribution Systems
Human Resource Systems
Expenditure Cycle (Chapters 5 & 6)
Conversion Cycle (Chapter 7)
Revenue Cycle (Chapter 4)
Purchase System
Cash Disbursement System
Payroll Processing System
Fixed Asset System
Cost Accounting System
Production Planning and Control System
Sales Processing System
Cash Receipts System

FIGURE 1-3 TRANSACTIONS PROCESSED BY THE INFORMATION SYSTEM

Financial Transactions
Nonfinancial Transactions
Information System
Information
User Decisions

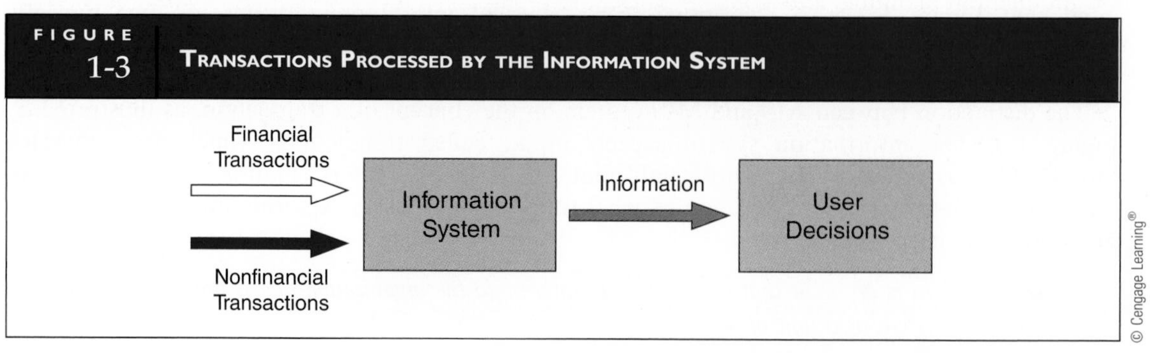

This definition encompasses both financial and nonfinancial events. Because financial transactions are of particular importance to the accountant's understanding of information systems, we need a precise definition for this class of transaction:

> *A* **financial transaction** *is an economic event that affects the assets and equities of the organization, is reflected in its accounts, and is measured in monetary terms.*

Sales of products to customers, purchases of inventory from vendors, and cash disbursements and receipts are examples of financial transactions. Every business organization is legally bound to correctly process these types of transactions.

Nonfinancial transactions are events that do not meet the narrow definition of a financial transaction. For example, adding a new supplier of raw materials to the list of valid suppliers is an event that may be processed by the enterprise's information system as a transaction. Important as this information obviously is, it is not a financial transaction, and the firm has no legal obligation to process it correctly—or at all.

Financial transactions and nonfinancial transactions are closely related and are often processed by the same physical system. For example, consider a financial portfolio management system that collects and tracks stock prices (nonfinancial transactions). When the stocks reach a threshold price, the system places an automatic buy or sell order (financial transaction). Buying high and selling low is bad for business, but it is not against the law. Therefore, no law requires company management to design optimal buy-and-sell rules into their system. Once the order is placed, however, the processing of this financial transaction must comply with legal and professional guidelines.

The Accounting Information System

AIS subsystems process financial transactions and nonfinancial transactions that directly affect the processing of financial transactions. For example, changes to customers' names and addresses are processed by the AIS to keep the customer file current. Although not technically financial transactions, these changes provide vital information for processing future sales to the customer.

The AIS is composed of three major subsystems: (1) the **transaction processing system (TPS)**, which supports daily business operations with numerous reports, documents, and messages for users throughout the organization; (2) the **general ledger/financial reporting system (GL/FRS)**, which produces the traditional financial statements, such as the income statement, balance sheet, statement of cash flows, tax returns, and other reports required by law; and (3) the **management reporting system (MRS)**, which provides internal management with special-purpose financial reports and information needed for decision making such as budgets, variance reports, and responsibility reports. We examine each of these subsystems in the following sections of this chapter.

The Management Information System

Management often requires information that goes beyond the domain of AIS. As organizations grow in size and complexity, specialized functional areas emerge, requiring additional information for production planning and control, sales forecasting, inventory warehouse planning, market research, and so on. The MIS processes nonfinancial transactions that are not normally processed by traditional AIS. Table 1-1 gives examples of typical MIS applications related to functional areas of a firm.

The Need to Distinguish between AIS and MIS

SOX legislation requires that corporate management design and implement internal controls over the entire financial reporting process. This includes the financial reporting system, the general ledger system, and the transaction processing systems that supply the data for financial reporting. SOX further requires that management certify these controls and that the external auditors express an opinion on control effectiveness. Because of the highly integrative nature of modern

TABLE 1-1 EXAMPLES OF MIS APPLICATIONS IN FUNCTIONAL AREAS

Function	Examples of MIS Applications
Finance	Portfolio management systems Capital budgeting systems
Marketing	Market analysis New product development Product analysis
Distribution	Warehouse organization and scheduling Delivery scheduling Vehicle loading and allocation models
Personnel	Human resource management systems ■ Job skill tracking system ■ Employee benefits system

information systems, management and auditors need a conceptual view of the information system that clearly distinguishes key processes and areas of risk and legal responsibility from other (non-legally binding) aspects of the system. Without such a model, mandated management and audit responsibilities under SOX may not be efficiently or adequately met.

AIS SUBSYSTEMS

We devote separate chapters to an in-depth study of each AIS subsystem depicted in Figure 1-2. At this point, we briefly outline the role of each subsystem.

Transaction Processing System

The TPS is central to the overall function of the information system. It converts economic events into financial transactions, records financial transactions in the accounting records (journals and ledgers), and distributes essential financial information to operations personnel to support their daily operations.

The TPS deals with business events that occur frequently. In a given day, a firm may process thousands of transactions. To deal efficiently with such volume, similar types of transactions are grouped into transaction cycles. The TPS consists of three transaction cycles: the revenue cycle, the expenditure cycle, and the conversion cycle. Each cycle captures and processes different types of financial transactions. Chapter 2 of this text provides an overview of transaction processing. Chapters 4, 5, 6, and 7 examine in detail the revenue, expenditure, and conversion cycles.

General Ledger/Financial Reporting Systems

The general ledger system (GLS) and the financial reporting system (FRS) are two closely related subsystems. Because of their operational interdependency, however, they are generally viewed as a single integrated system—the GL/FRS. The bulk of the input to the GL portion of the system comes from transaction cycle subsystems. Summaries of transaction activity are processed by the GLS to update the general ledger control accounts. Other, less common and infrequent, events such as stock transactions, mergers, and lawsuit settlements, for which there may be no formal processing cycle in place, enter the GLS through alternate sources. The FRS measures the status of financial resources and the changes in those resources and communicates this information to external users. This type of reporting is called **nondiscretionary reporting** because the organization has few or no choices in the information it provides. Much of this information consists of traditional financial statements, tax returns, and other reports demanded by law.

Management Reporting System

Managers must respond rapidly to many day-to-day business problems, as well as plan and control their operations. The MRS provides the internal financial information needed to manage a business. Typical reports produced by the MRS include budgets, variance reports, cost-volume-profit analyses, and reports using current (rather than historical) cost data. This type of reporting is called **discretionary reporting** because the organization can choose what information to report and how to present it.

A GENERAL MODEL FOR AIS

Figure 1-4 presents the **general model for AIS**. This is a *general* model because it applies to all accounting information systems, regardless of their underlying technologies. The model depicts the relationship between the key elements that constitute an AIS application: end users, data sources, data collection, data processing, database management, information generation, and feedback. Each of these is discussed next.

End Users

End users fall into two general groups: external and internal. **External users** include creditors, stockholders, potential investors, regulatory agencies, tax authorities, suppliers, and customers. **Internal users** include management at all levels of the organization, as well as operations personnel. In contrast to their more structured external reporting responsibilities, organizations have a great deal of latitude when it comes to internal reporting, which is driven by what best gets the job done. Internal reporting is, however, characterized by frequent changes in the information needs of internal users. This volatility poses a significant challenge to system designers who must balance the information requests and needs of internal users against legal, economic, internal control, and security issues. Frequent changes in information requirements necessitate information system changes, which in turn expose systems to material errors and, as we shall see later in this text, the potential for fraud.

FIGURE 1-4 GENERAL MODEL FOR ACCOUNTING INFORMATION SYSTEMS

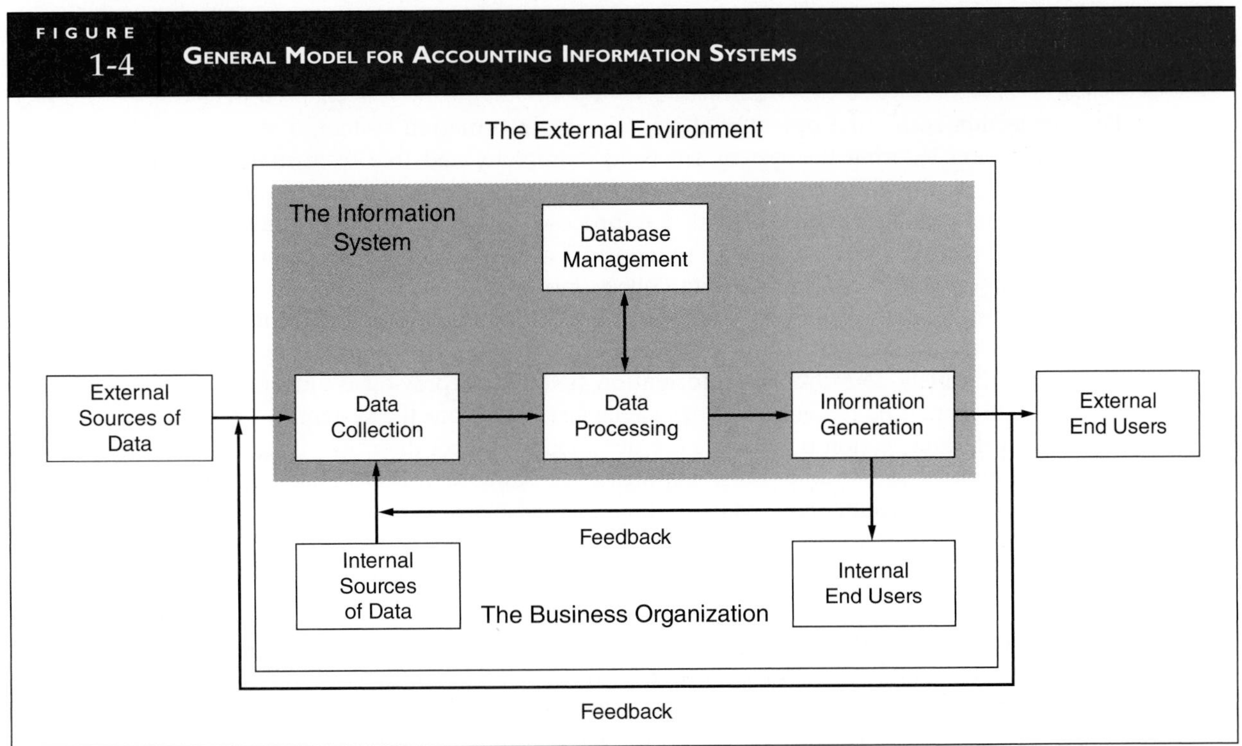

DATA VERSUS INFORMATION. Before discussing the data sources portion of Figure 1-4, we need to make an important distinction between the terms *data* and *information*. **Data** are facts, which may or may not be processed (edited, summarized, or refined) and have no direct effect on a user's actions. By contrast, **information** causes the user to take an action that he or she otherwise could not, or would not, have taken. Information is often defined simply as processed data, but this definition is inadequate. Information is determined by the effect it has on the user, not by its physical form. For example, a purchasing agent receives a daily report listing raw material inventory items that are at low levels. This report causes the agent to place orders for more inventories. The facts in this report have information content for the purchasing agent. This same report in the hands of the personnel manager, however, is a mere collection of facts, or data, causing no action and having no information content.

In other words, one person's information is another person's data. Thus, information is not just a set of processed facts arranged in a formal report. Information triggers users to take actions that support their day-to-day business tasks, resolve conflicts, and plan for the future. We should note that action does not necessarily mean a physical act. For instance, a purchasing agent who receives a report showing that inventory levels are adequate will respond by ordering nothing. The agent's action to do nothing is a conscious decision, triggered by information and different from doing nothing because of being uninformed. The distinction between data and information has pervasive implications for the study of information systems. If output from the information system fails to cause users to act, the system serves no purpose.

Data Sources

Data sources are financial transactions that enter the information system from either internal or external sources. External financial transactions are the most common source of data. These are economic exchanges with other business entities and individuals outside the firm. Examples include the sale of goods and services, the purchase of inventory, the receipt of cash, and the disbursement of cash (including payroll). Internal financial transactions involve the exchange or movement of resources within the organization. Examples include the movement of raw materials into work-in-process (WIP), the application of labor and overhead to WIP, the transfer of WIP into finished goods inventory, and the depreciation of plant and equipment.

Data Collection

Data collection is the first operational stage in the information system. The objective is to ensure that event data entering the system are valid, complete, and free from material errors. In many respects, this is the most important stage in the system. Should transaction errors pass through data collection undetected, the system may process the errors and generate erroneous and unreliable output. This, in turn, could lead to incorrect actions and poor decisions by the users.

Two rules govern the design of data collection procedures: relevance and efficiency. The information system should capture only relevant data. A fundamental task of the system designer is to determine what is and what is not relevant. He or she does so by analyzing the user's needs. Only data that ultimately contribute to information (as defined previously) are relevant. The data collection stage should be designed to filter irrelevant facts from the system.

Efficient data collection procedures are designed to collect data only once. These data can then be made available to multiple users. Capturing the same data more than once overloads facilities and leads to data redundancy, which causes inconsistencies among the redundant elements and reduces overall system effectiveness.

Data Processing

Once collected, data usually require processing to produce information. **Data processing** tasks range from simple to complex. Examples include mathematical algorithms (such as linear programming models) used for production scheduling applications, statistical techniques for sales forecasting, and posting and summarizing procedures used for accounting applications.

FIGURE 1-5 THE DATA HIERARCHY

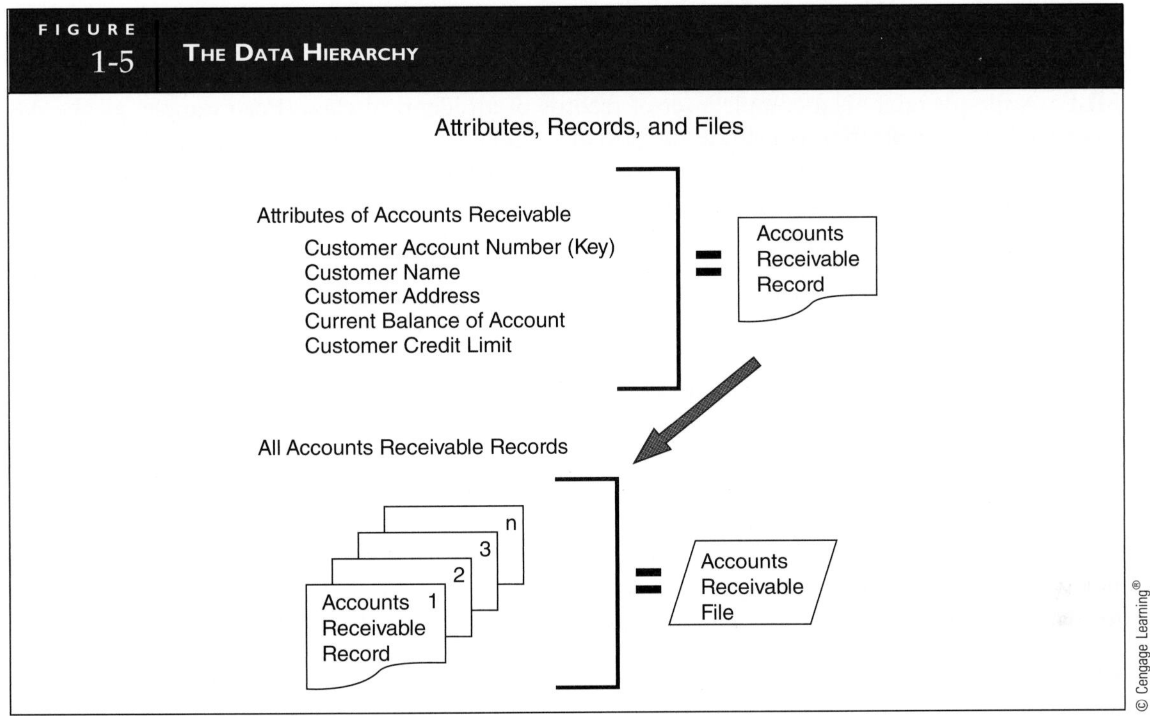

Database Management

The organization's **database** is its physical repository for financial and nonfinancial data. We use the term *database* in the generic sense. The term could apply to a filing cabinet or a computer disk. Regardless of the database's physical form, business data are organized in a logical hierarchy. The levels in the data hierarchy—attribute, record, and file—are illustrated in Figure 1-5.

DATA ATTRIBUTE. The data attribute is the most elemental piece of potentially useful data in the database. An attribute is a logical and relevant characteristic of an entity about which the firm captures data. The attributes shown in Figure 1-5 are logical because they all relate to a common entity—accounts receivable (AR). Each attribute is also relevant because it contributes to the information content of the entire set of attributes. As proof of this, the absence of any single relevant attribute diminishes or destroys the information content of the set. The addition of irrelevant or illogical attributes would not enhance the information content of the set.

RECORD. A record is a complete set of attributes for a single occurrence within an entity class. For example, a particular customer's name, address, and account balance is one occurrence (or record) within the AR class. To find a particular record within the database, we must be able to identify it uniquely. Therefore, every record in the database must be unique in at least one attribute.[1] This unique identifier attribute is called the primary key. Because no natural attribute (such as customer name) can guarantee uniqueness, we typically assign artificial keys to records.

The key for the AR records in Figure 1-5 is the customer account number. This is the only unique identifier in this record class. The other attributes possess values that may also exist in other records. For instance, multiple customers may have the same name, sales amounts, credit limits, and balances. Using any one of these as a key to find a specific record would not work efficiently. These nonunique attributes are, however, often used as secondary keys for categorizing

1 When we get into more advanced topics, we will see how a combination of nonunique attributes can be used as a unique identifier.

data. For example, the account balance attribute can be used to prepare a list of customers with balances greater than $10,000.

FILE. A file (or table) is a complete set of records of an identical class. For example, all the AR records of the organization constitute the AR file. Similarly, files are constructed for other classes of records such as inventory, accounts payable, and payroll. The organization's database is the entire collection of such files.

DATABASE MANAGEMENT TASKS. **Database management** involves three fundamental tasks: storage, retrieval, and deletion. The storage task assigns keys to new records and stores them in their proper location in the database. Retrieval is the task of locating and extracting an existing record from the database for processing. After processing is complete, the storage task restores the updated record to its place in the database. Deletion is the task of permanently removing obsolete or redundant records from the database.

Information Generation

Information generation is the process of compiling, arranging, formatting, and presenting information to users. Information can be an operational document such as a sales order, a structured report, or a message on a computer screen. Regardless of physical form, useful information has the following characteristics: relevance, timeliness, accuracy, completeness, and summarization.

RELEVANCE. The contents of a report or document must serve a purpose. This could be to support a manager's decision or a clerk's task. We have established that only data relevant to a user's action have information content. Therefore, the information system should present only relevant data in its reports. Reports containing irrelevancies waste resources and may be counterproductive to the user. Irrelevancies detract attention from the true message of the report and may result in incorrect decisions or actions.

TIMELINESS. The age of information is a critical factor in determining its usefulness. Information must be no older than the time frame of the action it supports. For example, if a manager makes decisions daily to purchase inventory from a supplier based on an inventory status report, then the information in the report should be no more than a day old.

ACCURACY. Information must be free from material errors. Materiality is, however, a difficult concept to quantify. It has no absolute value; it is a problem-specific concept. This means that, in some cases, information must be perfectly accurate. In other instances, the level of accuracy may be lower. A material error exists when the amount of inaccuracy in information causes the user to make poor decisions or to fail to make necessary decisions. We sometimes must sacrifice absolute accuracy to obtain timely information. Often, perfect information is not available within the user's decision time frame. Therefore, in providing information, system designers seek a balance between information that is as accurate as possible, yet timely enough to be useful.

COMPLETENESS. No piece of information essential to a decision or task should be missing. For example, a report should provide all necessary calculations and present its message clearly and unambiguously.

SUMMARIZATION. Information should be aggregated in accordance with the user's needs. Lower-level managers tend to need information that is highly detailed. As information flows upward through the organization to top management, it becomes more summarized.

Feedback

Feedback is a form of output that is sent back to the system as a source of data. Feedback may be internal or external and is used to initiate or alter a process. For example, an inventory status report signals the inventory control clerk that items of inventory have fallen to, or below, their minimum allowable levels. Internal feedback from this information will initiate the inventory ordering process to replenish the inventories. Similarly, external feedback about the level of uncollected customer accounts can be used to adjust the organization's credit-granting policies.

Organizational Structure and AIS

In later chapters we see how the design and/or audit of accounting information systems require an understanding of the functional segments and activities that constitute an organization's structure. Physical accounting information systems are comprised of technologies of various types and configurations, as well as people and tasks from across the organization. Indeed, the so-called accounting information system actually involves diverse accounting and nonaccounting activities and personnel. For example, the sales processing system, which is a subsystem of the revenue cycle (refer to Figure 1-2), includes the following organization functions: sales, credit, inventory control, warehousing, shipping, billing, accounts receivable, general ledger, and data processing. Figure 1-6 depicts these and other typical business functions for a hypothetical manufacturing firm. The shaded functions in Figure 1-6 (those associated with processing sales orders) emphasize the entity-wide impact of AIS.

FUNCTIONAL SEGMENTATION

Segmentation by business function is a common method of organizing a business entity. Functional **segments** derive from the flow of resources through the firm. For example, assume a manufacturing firm that employs the following resources: materials, labor, financial capital, and information. Table 1-2 shows the relationship between these resources and the functional segments that manage them.

The segments and the functions within them will vary among organizations, depending on their size and lines of business. A public water company, for example, does not need to market its product and probably will have little in the way of advertising or market research functions. Also, a service organization with no inventories to manage will not need an inventory control function. The remainder of this section outlines the functional areas for the hypothetical firm represented in Figure 1-6.

Materials Management

The objective of materials management is to plan and control the materials inventory of the company. A manufacturing firm must have sufficient inventories on hand to meet its production needs and yet avoid excessive inventory levels. Every dollar invested in inventory is a dollar that is not earning a return. Furthermore, idle inventory can become obsolete, lost, or stolen. Ideally, a firm would coordinate inventory arrivals from suppliers such that they move directly into the production process. As a practical matter, however, most organizations maintain safety stocks to carry them through the lead time between placing the order for inventory and its arrival. We see from Figure 1-6 that materials management has three sub-functions:

1. *Purchasing* is responsible for ordering inventory from vendors when inventory levels fall to their reorder points. The nature of this task varies among organizations. In some cases, purchasing requires no more than sending a purchase order to a designated vendor. In other cases, this task involves soliciting bids from a number of competing vendors. The nature of the business and the type of inventory determine the extent of the purchasing function.
2. *Receiving* is the task of accepting the inventory previously ordered by purchasing. Receiving activities include counting and checking the physical condition of these items. This is an organization's first, and perhaps only, opportunity to detect incomplete deliveries and damaged merchandise before they move into the production process.
3. *Stores* takes physical custody of the inventory received and releases these resources into the production process as needed.

FIGURE 1-6 FUNCTIONAL AREAS OF A FIRM

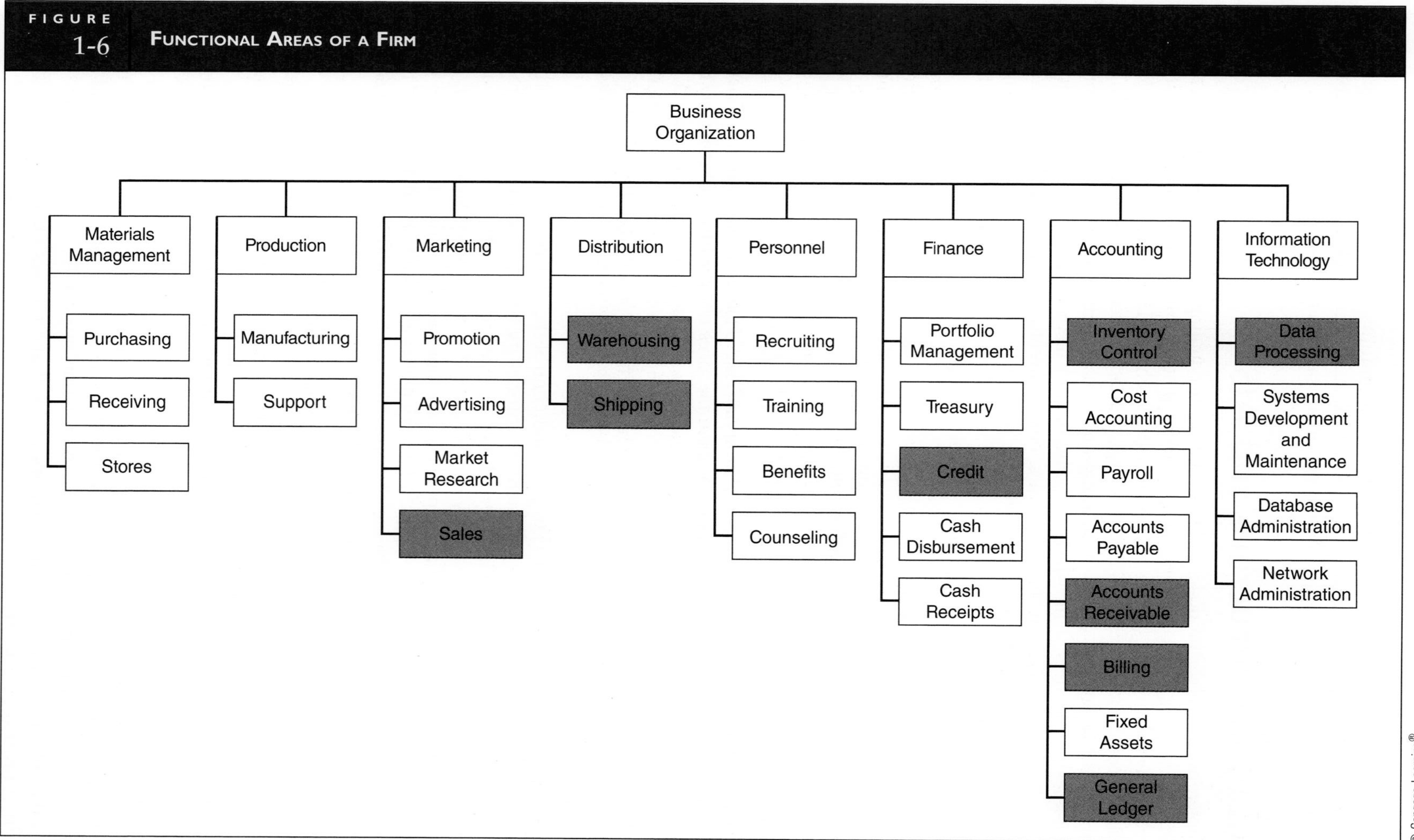

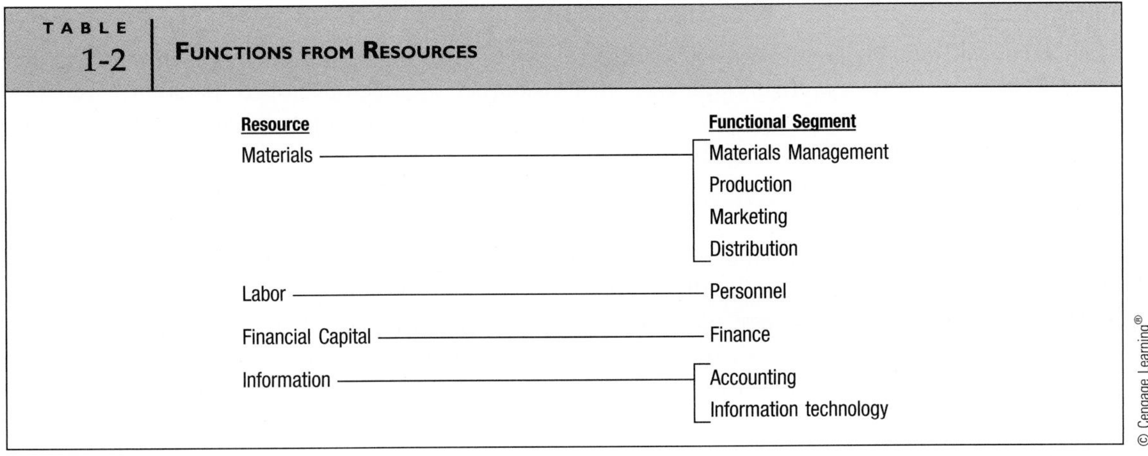

TABLE 1-2 **FUNCTIONS FROM RESOURCES**

Resource	Functional Segment
Materials	Materials Management
	Production
	Marketing
	Distribution
Labor	Personnel
Financial Capital	Finance
Information	Accounting
	Information technology

Production

Production activities occur in the conversion cycle in which raw materials, labor, and plant assets are used to create finished products. The specific activities are determined by the nature of the products being manufactured. In general they fall into two broad classes: (1) primary manufacturing activities and (2) production support activities. Primary manufacturing activities shape and assemble raw materials into finished products. Production support activities ensure that primary manufacturing activities operate efficiently and effectively. These include, but are not limited to, the following types of activities:

Production planning *involves scheduling the flow of materials, labor, and machinery to efficiently meet production needs. This requires information about the status of sales orders, raw materials inventory, finished goods inventory, and machine and labor availability.*

Quality control *monitors the manufacturing process at various points to ensure that the finished products meet the firm's quality standards. Effective quality control detects problems early to facilitate corrective action. Failure to do so may result in excessive waste of materials and labor.*

Maintenance *keeps the firm's machinery and other manufacturing facilities in running order. The manufacturing process relies on its plant and equipment and cannot tolerate breakdowns during peak production periods. Therefore, the key to maintenance is prevention—the scheduled removal of equipment from operations for cleaning, servicing, and repairs. Many manufacturers have elaborate preventive maintenance programs. To plan and coordinate these activities, maintenance engineers need extensive information about the history of equipment usage and future scheduled production.*

Marketing

The marketplace needs to know about, and have access to, a firm's products. The marketing function deals with the strategic problems of product promotion, advertising, and market research. On an operational level, marketing performs such daily activities as sales order entry.

Distribution

Distribution is the activity of getting the product to the customer after the sale. This is a critical step since much can go wrong before the customer takes possession of the product. Incorrect shipments, damaged merchandise, or excessive lags between taking and filling of orders can result in customer dissatisfaction and lost sales. Ultimately, success depends on filling orders accurately in the warehouse, packaging goods correctly, and shipping them quickly to the customer.

Personnel

Competent and reliable employees are a valuable resource to a business. The objective of the personnel function is to effectively manage this resource. A well-developed personnel function includes recruiting, training, continuing education, counseling, evaluating, labor relations, and compensation administration.

Finance

The finance function manages the financial resources of the firm through banking and treasury activities, portfolio management, credit evaluation, cash disbursements, and cash receipts. Because of the cyclical nature of business, many firms swing between positions of excess funds and cash deficits. In response to these cash flow patterns, financial planners seek lucrative investments in stocks and other assets, and low-cost lines of credit from banks. The finance function also administers the daily flow of cash in and out of the firm.

THE ACCOUNTING FUNCTION

Accounting manages the financial information resource of the firm. In this regard, it plays two important roles in transaction processing. First, accounting captures and records the financial effects of the economic events that constitute the firm's transactions. These include events such as the movement of raw materials from the warehouse into production, shipments of the finished products to customers, cash flows into the firm and deposits in the bank, the acquisition of inventory, and the discharge of financial obligations. Second, accounting distributes transaction information to operations personnel to coordinate many of their key tasks. The following accounting functions contribute directly to business operations: inventory control, cost accounting, payroll, accounts payable, accounts receivable, billing, fixed asset accounting, and the general ledger. We deal with each of these specifically in later chapters. For the moment, however, we need to maintain a broad view of accounting to understand its functional role in the organization.

The Value of Information

The value of information to a user is determined by its **reliability**. We saw earlier that the purpose of information is to lead the user to a desired action. For this to happen, information must possess certain attributes—relevance, accuracy, completeness, summarization, and timeliness. When these attributes are consistently present, information has reliability and provides value to the user. Unreliable information has no value. At best, it is a waste of resources; at worst, it can lead to dysfunctional decisions. Consider the following example:

> *A marketing manager signed a contract with a customer to supply a large quantity of product by a certain deadline. He made this decision based on information about finished goods inventory levels. Because of faulty record keeping, however, the information was incorrect. The actual inventory levels of the product were insufficient to meet the order, and the necessary quantities could not be manufactured by the deadline. Failure to comply with the terms of the contract resulted in litigation.*

This poor sales decision was a result of flawed information. Effective decisions require information that has a high degree of reliability.

Accounting Independence

Information reliability rests heavily on the concept of accounting **independence**. Simply stated, accounting activities must be separate and independent of the functional areas that manage and maintain custody of physical resources. For example, accounting monitors and records the movement of raw materials into production and the sale of finished goods to customers. Accounting authorizes purchases of raw materials and the disbursement of cash payments to vendors and employees. Accounting supports these functions with information, but does not participate in the physical activities.

INFORMATION TECHNOLOGY

Figure 1-6 depicts four information technology (IT) functions: (1) data processing, (2) systems development and maintenance, (3) database administration, and (4) network administration. Although an organization may have many additional IT functions, these four are included in this discussion because they hold specific internal control concerns for management and auditors that we will investigate in detail in later chapters. Below, we outline the key features of each of them.

Data Processing

The data processing function brings to bear IT personnel, computer hardware, application programs (software), and corporate data to support user information needs through transaction processing and information reporting. Data processing configurations vary among different types of business entities. At one end of a continuum of options is the centralized data processing model, and at the other end is the distributed data processing model. Many organizations employ a combination of centralized and distributed processing.

CENTRALIZED DATA PROCESSING. Under the **centralized data processing** model, all data processing is performed by one or more large computers housed in a common data center that serves users throughout the organization. Figure 1-7 illustrates the centralized approach. End users process transactions from terminals in their respective departments, which are connected to the central computer and database. Because the computing resources (IT personnel, hardware, software, and data) are centrally located and accessible by all authorized users, the centralized data processing configuration lends itself to intra-organization communication and data sharing between user departments.

DISTRIBUTED DATA PROCESSING. Figure 1-8 depicts the **distributed data processing (DDP)** model, in which users process their transactions locally. Under this configuration each user segment possesses the IT personnel, facilities, hardware, software, and data they need to support

FIGURE 1-7 CENTRALIZED DATA PROCESSING MODEL

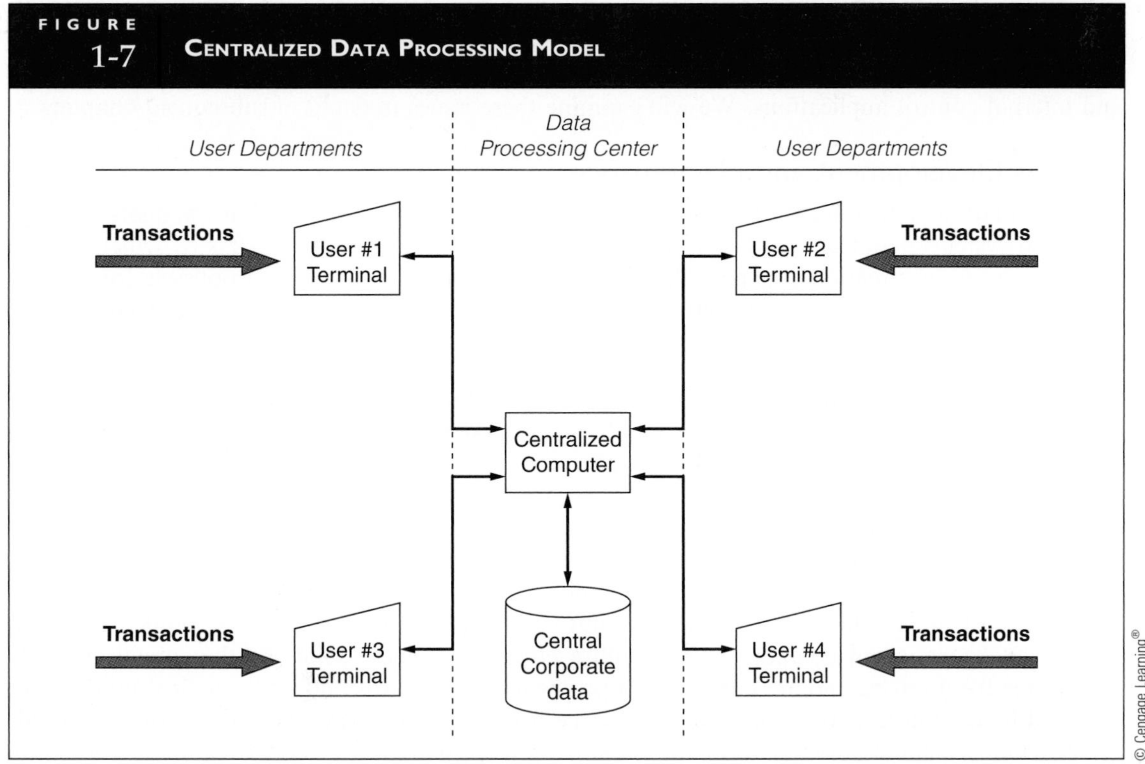

FIGURE 1-8 DISTRIBUTED DATA PROCESSING MODEL

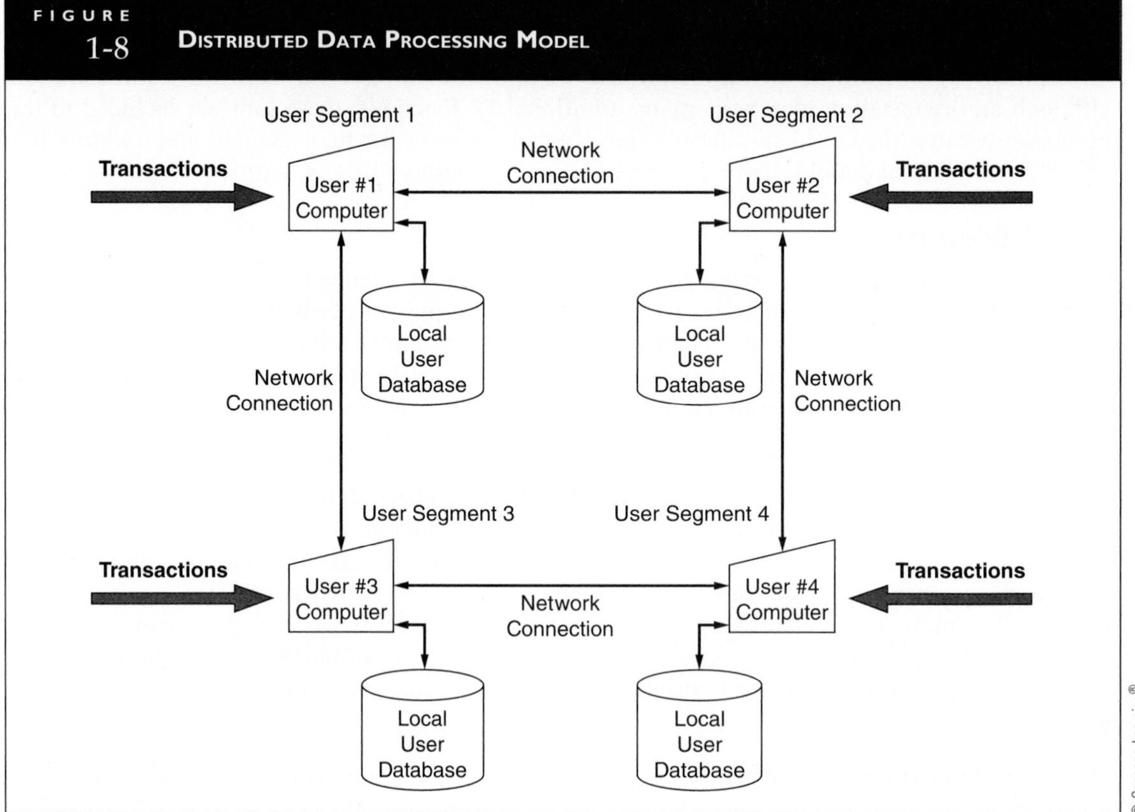

their operations. Unlike in the centralized approach, users in a DDP environment function independently and tend not to share data and information. Any necessary sharing, however, is accomplished through network connections between the users.

Both the centralized and distributed data processing models have their respective benefits, risks, and internal control implications. We will examine these issues in detail in subsequent chapters.

Systems Development and Maintenance

The information system needs of organizations are met by two related functions: systems development and systems maintenance. The systems development function is the process by which organizations acquire information systems. The systems maintenance function is responsible for making changes to existing systems to accommodate changes in user needs. We examine each of these functions separately below.

SYSTEMS DEVELOPMENT. Organizations acquire information systems in two ways: they purchase commercial software and/or they build custom systems in-house from scratch. **Commercial software** is available for both general accounting use and for industry-specific applications, such as medical billing. Commercial software packages are sometimes called **turnkey systems** because they can often be implemented by the user with little or no modification.

The business community has recognized the many advantages of buying commercial systems. Software vendors such as Microsoft, Oracle, and SAP design their products to appeal to a large community of users, which keeps down the unit cost to the customer. Also, by purchasing commercial packages, client companies can acquire effective business solutions that are thoroughly tested, free from errors, and are current with professional standards and technological innovations designed by domain experts. Both small and large firms that have standardized information needs are potential customers for commercial software. Larger organizations with unique information needs often develop **custom software** through a formal process called the **systems development life cycle**. Creating custom software requires the organization to have an in-house team of qualified and experienced IT professionals consisting of systems analysts, programmers, and database designers. The IT team works with corporate users to assess their information needs, design computer solutions, and physically implement them.

Custom systems are more expensive than commercial packages because the organization must absorb all the development costs, which commercial vendors are able to spread across the entire user population. For example, companies in competitive, fast-moving industries such as telecommunications, pharmaceuticals, and financial services invest hundreds of millions of dollars in custom software. When information needs are unique, however, and no commercial package adequately meets them, custom software is often the only option.

To fill this void some commercial software vendors design their systems in modules that allow flexibility through numerous processing options. Large scale **enterprise resource planning (ERP)** systems are an example of this approach. The base ERP system is comprised of thousands of small program modules. From this vast array of options the IT team selects those modules that support the organization's specific information and data-processing needs. Configuring the system in this way often takes many months, but the result is a customized system with the advantages of a commercial system. ERP key features, benefits, risks, and control issues are discussed in Chapter 11.

SYSTEMS MAINTENANCE. Over the course of the system's life (often several years), a system may be modified many times as user needs change and evolve. Maintenance changes may be trivial, such as modifying the system to produce an additional report, or significant, such as modifying it to execute new accounting rules that impact many different system modules. Between 80 and 90 percent of a system's total cost may be incurred because of maintenance activities.

Systems development and maintenance activities constitute material financial investments in hardware, software, and personnel for many organizations. These activities also represent significant risks that need to be controlled and, consequently, are of concern to management and accountants. We deal with these issues in detail in Chapters 13, 14, and 17.

Database Administration

Centrally organized companies maintain their data resources in a central location that is shared by all authorized end users (refer to Figure 1-7). In this shared-data arrangement, a special independent group—database administration—headed by the database administrator is responsible for the security and integrity of the database. We explore the database concept and the role of the database administrator in Chapter 9.

Network Administration

A **network** is a collection of interconnected computers and communications devices that allows users to communicate, access data and applications, and share information and resources. **Network administration** is responsible for the effective functioning of the software and hardware that constitute the organization's network. This involves configuring, implementing, and maintaining network equipment. In addition, network administration is responsible for monitoring network activity to ensure that the network is being used in accordance with company policies and that it is secure from attack by hackers from outside the organization as well as unauthorized individuals within the organization. Network technologies, security issues, and control techniques are the topics of Chapters 12 and 16.

Outsourcing the IT Function

From this brief discussion we see that the IT segment of an organization comprises highly technical, dynamically changing, and expensive activities. Corporate management has long complained about the administrative burden and high cost associated with managing and maintaining the IT function. In an effort to bring costs under control and to escape their IT headaches, many corporate executives look to **IT outsourcing**. Under this practice the organization sells its IT resources (hardware, software, and facilities) to a third-party outsourcing vendor such as HP Enterprise Services (formally EDS). The outsourcing organization then leases back IT services from the vendor for a contract period of typically between five and ten years. The company's IT employees are often transferred in such deals and become employees of the outsourcing vendor. Of course, when the vendor takes the IT function off shore, employee transfers are not possible.

A variant of IT outsourcing, called **cloud computing**, is location-independent computing, where shared data centers deliver hosted IT services over the Internet. These services fall into three categories: **software as a service (SaaS)**, **infrastructure as a service (IaaS)**, and **platform as a service (PaaS)**. The concept can be equated to the way in which electricity is delivered to a private home. The homeowner enters into a contract with the local public utility company to deliver electricity as needed. The public utility company may generate some of this electricity, but during high demand periods it will go to the national electric grid to tap into the production of other electricity generators across the country. Similarly, an organization pursuing cloud computing signs a contract with an IT service provider to provide computing resources. When demand exceeds the provider's IT capacity, it acquires additional capacity from data centers in the "cloud" that are connected via the Internet. A potential risk to the client firm is that it does not necessarily know where its data are actually being processed, just as the homeowner does not know where his or her electricity is being generated. The advantage to the client organization is access to whatever computing power it needs, while it pays only for what it uses. Also, cloud computing contracts are flexible and relatively short term. In contrast, traditional outsourcing contracts tend to be fixed price, inflexible, and much longer term.

IT outsourcing is a rapidly growing phenomenon. The departure from tradition that it represents carries both advantages and risks that management and auditors need to recognize. In Chapter 15 we explore these issues in detail.

The Role of Accountants in AIS

Accountants are involved in both the design and the audit of accounting information systems. The final section of this chapter briefly outlines key areas of responsibility; these issues are expanded upon in subsequent chapters.

ACCOUNTANTS AS SYSTEM DESIGNERS

Accountants play a prominent role on systems development teams as **domain experts**. In that capacity they are responsible for many aspects of the conceptual system. This involves specifying certain operational rules, reporting requirements, and framing internal control objectives that the system must achieve. The IT professionals on the team are responsible for the physical system including system architecture, programming, and database design. To illustrate the distinction between conceptual and physical systems, consider the following example:

> *The credit department of a retail business requires information about delinquent accounts from the AR department. This information is used to support decisions made by the credit manager regarding the credit-worthiness of customers.*

The design of the **conceptual system** involves specifying the criteria for identifying delinquent customers and the information that needs to be reported. As the domain expert, the accountant determines the nature of the information required, its sources, its destination, and the accounting rules that need to be applied. The **physical system** includes the **data storage** medium to be used and the method for capturing and presenting the information. IT professionals determine the most economical and effective technologies for accomplishing the task. Hence, systems design is a collaborative effort. Because of the specificity of accounting rules, the implications of material error, and the potential for fraud, the accountant's involvement in systems design is essential and pervasive throughout the development process.

ACCOUNTANTS AS SYSTEM AUDITORS

Accountant's perform audits of business organizations for various reasons, which typically involve the accounting information system. The most common audits are external (attestation) audits, internal (operational) audits, and fraud audits. Each type of audit requires that the **auditor** have a thorough understanding of AIS functions and internal controls.

An external audit is an independent attestation performed by an expert—the auditor—who expresses an opinion in the form of a formal **audit report** regarding the presentation of financial statements. This task, known as the **attest function**, is performed by Certified Public Accountants (CPAs) who work for public accounting firms that are independent of the client organization being audited. The audit objective is to assure the fair presentation of corporate financial statements. This requires auditors to perform tests of the information system's internal controls as well as **substantive tests** of data that reside in the system's databases. External audits are often referred to as *financial audits* and the SEC requires all publicly traded companies to undergo a financial audit annually. CPAs conducting such audits are acting on behalf of outsiders such as stockholders, creditors, government agencies, and the general public.

A critical element in the relationship between auditors and their constituents is the concept of auditor **independence**. Within the context of an audit, independence means that the auditor is free from factors that might influence the auditors' report regarding the financial position of the client firm. Such factors include, but are not limited to, financial interests in the client firm including stock holding or employment outside of the attest service, family ties or other personal relationships with the client, or provision of nonaudit (advisory) services to audit clients. In the absence of independence, the auditor's report would be of little value to its users.

Attest Service versus Advisory Services

An important distinction needs to be made regarding the external auditor's attestation function and the rapidly growing field of advisory services, which many public accounting firms offer. Advisory services are professional services offered by public accounting firms to improve their client organizations' operational efficiency and effectiveness. The domain of advisory services is intentionally unbounded so that it does not inhibit the growth of future services that are currently unforeseen. As examples, advisory services include actuarial advice, business advice, fraud investigation services, information system design and implementation, and internal control assessments for compliance with SOX.

Prior to the passage of SOX, accounting firms were permitted to provide advisory services and attest services concurrently to clients. SOX legislation, however, greatly restricts the types of nonaudit services that auditors may render audit clients. It is now unlawful for a registered public accounting firm that is currently providing attest services for a client to provide the following services:

- bookkeeping or other services related to the accounting records or financial statements of the audit client
- financial information systems design and implementation
- appraisal or valuation services, fairness opinions, or contribution-in-kind reports
- actuarial services
- internal audit outsourcing services
- management functions or human resources
- broker or dealer, investment adviser, or investment banking services
- legal services and expert services unrelated to the audit
- any other service that the Board determines, by regulation, is impermissible.

The IT advisory services units of public accounting firms have different names in different firms, but they all engage in tasks generally known as risk management. These groups often play a dual role within their respective firms; they provide nonaudit clients with IT advisory services and also work with their firm's financial audit staff to perform IT-related **tests of controls** (often called **IT auditing**) as part of the attestation function. Keep in mind that in many cases the purpose of the task, rather than the task itself, defines the service being rendered. For example, a risk management professional may perform a test of IT controls as an advisory service for a nonaudit client who is preparing for a financial audit by a different public accounting firm. The same professional may perform the same test for an audit client as part of the attest function.

Internal Audits

Internal auditing is an independent appraisal function established within an organization to examine and evaluate its activities. Internal auditors perform a wide range of activities including conducting financial audits, performing IT audits examining an operation's compliance with organizational policies and legal obligations, evaluating operational efficiency, and detecting and pursuing fraud within the firm.

An internal audit is typically conducted by auditors who work for the organization, but this task may be outsourced to other organizations. Internal auditors are often certified as a Certified Internal Auditor (CIA) or a Certified Information Systems Auditor (CISA). While internal auditors self-impose independence to perform their duties effectively, they are employed by the organization and represent its interests. These auditors generally answer to executive management of the organization or the audit committee of the board of directors. The standards, guidance, and certification of internal audits are governed mainly by the Institute of Internal Auditors (IIA) and, to a lesser degree, by the Information Systems Audit and Control Association (ISACA).

External versus Internal Auditors

The characteristic that conceptually distinguishes external auditors from internal auditors is their respective constituencies: while external auditors represent outsiders, internal auditors represent the interests of the organization. Nevertheless, in this capacity, internal auditors often cooperate with and assist external auditors in performing aspects of financial audits. This cooperation is done to achieve audit efficiency and reduce audit fees. For example, a team of internal auditors can perform tests of computer controls under the supervision of a single external auditor.

The independence and competence of the internal audit staff determine the extent to which external auditors may cooperate with and rely on work performed by internal auditors. Some internal audit departments report directly to the controller. Under this arrangement, the internal auditor's independence is compromised, and the external auditor is prohibited by professional standards from relying on evidence provided by them. In contrast, external auditors can rely in part on evidence gathered by internal audit departments that are organizationally independent and report to the board of directors' audit committee (discussed later). A truly independent internal audit staff adds value to the audit process. For example, internal auditors can gather audit evidence throughout a fiscal period, which external auditors may then use at year end to conduct more efficient, less disruptive, and less costly audits of the organization's financial statements.

Fraud Audits

In recent years fraud audits have, unfortunately, increased in popularity as a corporate governance tool. They have been thrust into prominence by a corporate environment in which both employee theft of assets and major financial frauds by management (e.g., Enron, WorldCom) have become rampant. The objective of a fraud audit is to investigate anomalies and gather evidence of fraud that may lead to criminal conviction. Sometimes fraud audits are initiated when corporate management suspects employee fraud. Alternatively, boards of directors may hire fraud auditors to investigate their own executives if theft of assets or financial fraud is suspected. Organizations victimized by fraud usually contract with specialized fraud units of public accounting firms or with companies that specialize in forensic accounting. Typically, fraud auditors have earned the Certified Fraud Examiner (CFE) certification, which is governed by the Association of Certified Fraud Examiners (ACFE).

The Role of the Audit Committee

The boards of directors of publicly traded companies form a subcommittee known as the audit committee that has special responsibilities regarding audits. This committee is usually composed of three people who should be outsiders (not associated with the families of executive management nor former officers, etc.). With the advent of the SOX, at least one member of the audit committee must be a "financial expert." The audit committee serves as an independent "check and balance" for the internal audit function and liaison with external auditors. One of the most significant changes imposed by SOX has been to the relationship between management and the external auditors. Prior to SOX, external auditors were hired and fired by management. Many believe, with some justification, that this relationship erodes auditor independence when disputes over audit practices arise. SOX mandates that external auditors now report to the audit committee, which hires and fires auditors and resolves disputes.

To be effective, the audit committee must be willing to challenge the internal auditors (or the entity performing that function) as well as management when necessary. Part of the role of committee members is to look for ways to identify risk. For instance, they might serve as a sounding board for employees who observe suspicious behavior or spot fraudulent activities. In general, they become an independent guardian of the entity's assets by whatever means is appropriate. Corporate frauds often have some relationship to audit committee failures. These include lack of independence of audit committee members, lack of experienced members on the audit committee, inactive audit committees, and the total absence of an audit committee.

Designer/Auditor Duality

The accountant's dual roles of designer and auditor draw upon a common skill set. An accountant cannot effectively conduct an audit if he or she does not understand the principles of systems design. The functions involved in a system, the tasks performed by it, and the internal controls that are, or should be, in place are design issues about which auditors routinely gather evidence. Similarly, an accountant cannot properly design a system without a thorough understanding of audit issues and concerns. For example, the designer must understand the nature of a particular audit risk before he or she can plan the design of internal control techniques needed to mitigate the risk. Also, the designer must understand audit objectives regarding evidence gathering so he or she may create a system that facilitates the subsequent extraction of audit evidence.

The accountant's dual responsibility for systems design and auditing has greatly influenced the organization and approach taken in this text. Although primarily an AIS design text, chapter topics are presented from the auditor's perspective. Human activities, manual procedures, and information technologies such as networks, databases, and computer applications that constitute the AIS are presented and discussed within the context of the audit risks they pose and how those risks can be mitigated through internal controls. This approach is followed throughout the remaining chapters of the book.

Summary

The first section of this chapter introduced basic systems concepts and presented a framework for distinguishing between accounting information systems and management information systems. This distinction is related to the types of transactions these systems process. AIS applications process financial transactions, and MIS applications process nonfinancial transactions. The section then presented a general model for accounting information systems. The model is composed of four major tasks that exist in all AIS applications: data collection, data processing, database management, and information generation.

The second section examined the relationship between organizational structure and the information system. It focused on functional segmentation as the predominant method of structuring a business and examined the functions of a typical manufacturing firm. The section presented two general methods of organizing the IT function: the centralized approach and the distributed approach.

The final section of this chapter examined the dual roles of accountants as (1) designers of AIS and (2) auditors of AIS. The IT function is responsible for designing the physical system, and the accounting function is responsible for specifying the conceptual system. An audit is an independent attestation performed by the auditor, who expresses an opinion about the fairness of a company's financial statements. A distinction was drawn between attestation and financial services. Both external and internal auditors conduct IT audits.

Key Terms

accounting information systems (AIS) (3)
attest function (21)
auditor (21)
centralized data processing (17)
cloud computing (20)
commercial software (18)
conceptual system (20)
custom software (19)
data (10)
data collection (10)
data processing (10)
data sources (10)
data storage (20)
database (11)
database management (12)
discretionary reporting (9)
distributed data processing (DDP) (17)
end users (9)
enterprise resource planning (ERP) (19)
feedback (12)
financial transaction (7)
general ledger/financial reporting system (GL/FRS) (7)
general model for AIS (9)
independence (16)
information (10)
information flows (4)
information generation (12)
information system (5)
infrastructure as a service (IaaS) (20)
internal auditing (22)
IT auditing (21)
IT outsourcing (20)
management information system (MIS) (5)
management reporting system (MRS) (7)
network (19)
network administration (19)
nondiscretionary reporting (8)
nonfinancial transactions (7)
physical system (20)
platform as a service (PaaS) (20)
reliability (16)
segments (13)
software as a service (SaaS) (20)
stakeholders (5)
substantive tests (21)
systems development life cycle (19)
tests of controls (21)
trading partners (5)
transaction (5)
transaction processing system (TPS) (7)
turnkey systems (18)

Review Questions

1. What are the four levels of activity in the pyramid representing the business organization? Distinguish between horizontal and vertical flows of information.
2. What is the relationship among data, information, and an information system?
3. Distinguish between AIS and MIS.
4. What are the three cycles of transaction processing systems?
5. What is discretionary reporting?
6. What are the characteristics of good or useful information?
7. What rules govern data collection?
8. What are the levels of data hierarchy?
9. What are the three fundamental tasks of database management?
10. What is feedback, and how is it useful in an information system?
11. What are the fundamental objectives of all information systems?
12. What does stewardship mean, and what is its role in an information system?
13. List five functional areas and their sub-functions.
14. Distinguish the roles of internal and external auditors.
15. What is the role of a database administrator?
16. What is the role of the accounting function in an organization?
17. Distinguish between the centralized and distributed approaches to organizing the IT function.
18. What is distributed data processing?
19. What is an ERP system?
20. What two roles are played by accountants with respect to the information system?

21. Define the term *attest function*.
22. Define the term *financial services*.
23. What is IT auditing?
24. Distinguish between conceptual and physical systems.
25. What is the role of the audit committee of the board of directors?
26. Who initiates a fraud audit within the organization?
27. When can external auditors rely on the work performed by internal auditors?
28. Name the tests that auditors perform to gather evidence.
29. What characteristic conceptually distinguishes internal and external auditing?
30. What is the role of network administration?
31. What is cloud computing?
32. Name the two ways in which organizations acquire information systems.
33. Why are custom systems more expensive than commercial systems?
34. What types of companies are potential customers for commercial software?
35. Briefly explain accounting independence.
36. Why do systems designers need to know anything about auditing?

Discussion Questions

1. Discuss the differences between internal and external users of information and their needs and demands on an information system. Historically, which type of user has the firm catered to most?
2. Comment on the level of detail necessary for operations management, middle management, and stockholders.
3. Distinguish between financial and nonfinancial transactions. Give three examples of each.
4. An information system must meet three fundamental objectives. Discuss why these objectives cannot effectively be met by a common set of information.
5. Do you think transaction processing systems differ significantly between service and manufacturing industries? Are they equally important to both sectors?
6. Discuss the difference between the financial reporting system and general ledger system.
7. Examine Figure 1-4 and discuss where and how problems can arise that can cause the resulting information to be bad or ineffective.
8. Discuss how the elements of efficiency, effectiveness, and flexibility are crucial to the design of an information system.
9. Discuss what is meant by the statement, "The accounting system is a conceptual flow of information that represents physical personnel, machinery, and flows of raw materials and cash through the organization."
10. Discuss the importance of accounting independence in accounting information systems. Give an example of where this concept is important (use an example other than inventory control).
11. Discuss why it is crucial that internal auditors report solely to the audit committee of the board of directors and answer to no other group.
12. Contrast centralized data processing with distributed data processing. How do the roles of end users differ between the two approaches?
13. Discuss how conceptual and physical systems differ and which functions are responsible for each of these systems.
14. Why is an active board of directors audit committee important to an organization?
15. Do you agree with the statement, "The term *IT auditor* should be considered obsolete because it implies a distinction between regular auditors and auditors who examine computerized AIS"? Why or why not?
16. Describe cloud computing and explain how it is similar to obtaining a commodity product.
17. Why is it important to organizationally separate the accounting function from other functions of the organization?
18. What is an external financial audit, and what are the sources of audit evidence?
19. Why do firms outsource their IT functions? Explain the options of traditional IT outsourcing and cloud computing, and how they differ.

Multiple-Choice Questions

1. Which of the following is NOT a financial transaction?
   a. purchase of products
   b. cash receipts
   c. update valid vendor file
   d. sale of inventory
2. The following are subsystems of the accounting information system, EXCEPT the
   a. transaction processing system.
   b. human resources system.
   c. general ledger/financial reporting system.
   d. management reporting system.
3. Which of the following is NOT a purpose of the transaction processing system?
   a. managing and reporting on the status of financial investments
   b. converting economic events into financial transactions
   c. distributing essential information to operations personnel to support their daily operations
   d. recording financial transactions in the accounting records
4. The objectives of the data collection activity of the general model for accounting information systems are to collect data that are
   a. relevant and redundant.
   b. efficient and objective.
   c. efficient and redundant.
   d. efficient and relevant.
5. Which of the following is NOT a characteristic of effective information?
   a. relevance
   b. accuracy
   c. summarization
   d. precision
6. Which of the following is NOT a database management task?
   a. retrieval
   b. storage
   c. summarization
   d. deletion
7. When viewed from the highest to most elemental level, the data hierarchy is
   a. attribute, record, file.
   b. record, attribute, key.
   c. file, record, attribute.
   d. file, record, key.
   e. key, record, file.
8. Which is NOT a source of evidence for an external auditor?
   a. work performed by internal auditors who organizationally report to the controller
   b. tests of controls
   c. substantive tests
   d. work performed by internal auditors who report to the audit committee of the BOD
9. Which of the following is NOT an objective of all information systems?
   a. support for the stewardship function of management
   b. support for management decision making
   c. support for the day-to-day operations of the firm
   d. all of the above are objectives
10. Which of the following best describes the activities of the materials management function?
    a. purchasing, receiving, and inventory control
    b. receiving, sales, distribution, and purchasing
    c. receiving, storage, purchasing, and accounts payable
    d. purchasing, receiving, and storage
    e. purchasing, storage, and distribution
11. Which of the following best describes the activities of the production function?
    a. maintenance, inventory control, and production planning
    b. production planning, quality control, manufacturing, and cost accounting
    c. quality control, production planning, manufacturing, and payroll
    d. maintenance, production planning, storage, and quality control
    e. manufacturing, quality control, and maintenance

12. Which of the following best describes the activities of the accounting function?
    a. inventory control, accounts payable, fixed assets, and payroll
    b. fixed assets, accounts payable, cash disbursements, and cost accounting
    c. purchasing, cash receipts, accounts payable, cash disbursements, and payroll
    d. inventory control, cash receipts, accounts payable, cash disbursements, and payroll
    e. inventory control, cost accounting, accounts payable, cash disbursements, and payroll
13. Which statement about cloud computing is most true?
    a. Cloud computing involves long-term contracts.
    b. Cloud computing is location-independent computing.
    c. Cloud computing involves an organization selling its IT resources to a vendor and leasing back IT services from the vendor.
    d. Cloud computing involves fixed price contracts.
    e. Cloud computing involves signing entering into multiple contracts with each IP service provider to create a cloud of resources.
14. Which of the following statements is most accurate?
    a. ERP systems are commercial software packages that are sometimes called turnkey systems because they can be implemented by the user with little or no modification.
    b. Substantive tests provide evidence focused on the system controls.
    c. Public accounting firms that provide attest services are not allowed under SOX to offer IT advisory services.
    d. Both small and large firms that have standardized information needs are potential customers for commercial software.
    e. External auditors may rely on the work of internal auditors only if they report to the controller or the CEO of the client company.

Problems

1. USERS OF INFORMATION

Classify the following users of information as either:

I—internal user
T—external user: trading partner
S—external user: stakeholder

a. Internal Revenue Service
b. Inventory control manager
c. Board of directors
d. Customers
e. Lending institutions
f. Securities and Exchange Commission
g. Stockholders
h. Chief executive officer
i. Suppliers
j. Bondholders

2. GENERAL MODEL FOR AIS

Redraw the diagram presented in Problem 2. Label each element in the diagram and briefly describe its role and key features.

3. ACCOUNTING INFORMATION SYSTEM ACQUISITION

What is the most likely system acquisition method—commercial software, custom software, or ERP—for each of the following situations? Explain your answers.

- A heating and air-conditioning supply company with 20 employees that sells standard off-the-shelf products to wholesale customers in a local community needs a system to manage its affairs.
- A major oil company with diverse holdings, complex oil leases, and esoteric accounting practices needs a system that can coordinate its many enterprises.
- A large organization with multiple divisions needs an information system to support its operations. The information needs of the various divisions are diverse, but standard within their respective industries.

4. INFORMATION SYSTEM CATEGORIZATION

Classify the following as tasks performed by either:

TPS—transaction processing system

PROBLEM 2

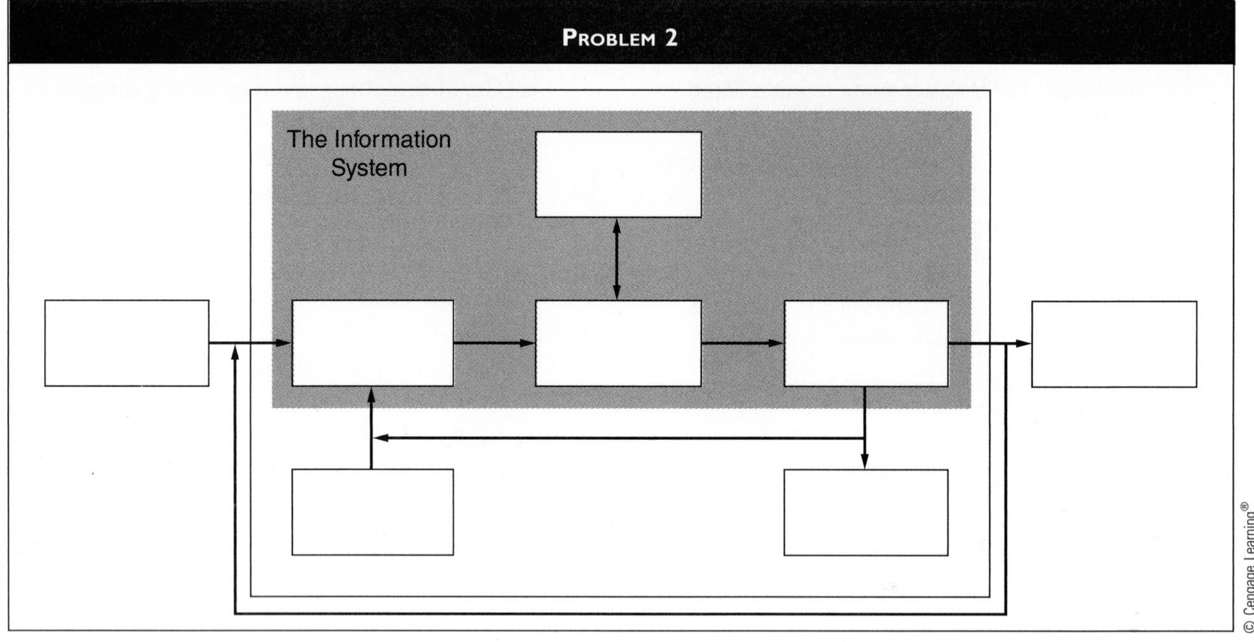

FRS—financial reporting system
MRS—management reporting system

a. Preparation of balance sheet
b. Capture customer sales order
c. Preparation of variance reports
d. Preparation of budgets
e. Purchase order preparation
f. Summary of inventory purchases by vendor
g. Preparation of comparative sales report by division
h. Preparation of cash disbursements to vendors
i. Annual report preparation
j. Customer billing process
k. Cost-volume-profit analysis

5. ORGANIZATION FUNCTIONS

Based on Figure 1-6 in the text, draw a diagram of functional segments for an oil company that has the following operations:

a. A head office in New York City responsible for international and national marketing, acquisition of leases and contracts, and corporate reporting.
b. Two autonomous regional facilities in Tulsa, Oklahoma, and New Orleans, Louisiana. These facilities are responsible for oil exploration,drilling, refining, storage, and the distribution of petroleum products to corporate service stations throughout the country and abroad.

6. ORGANIZATION FUNCTIONS

Based on Figure 1-6 in the text, draw a diagram of functional segments for a manufacturer of diversified products. The general characteristics of the firm are as follows:

a. The organization produces three unrelated products: lawn and garden furniture for sale in home improvement centers and department stores, plastic packaging products for the electronics and medical supply industries, and paper products (e.g., plates, cups, and napkins) for the fast-food industry.
b. Although the manufacturing facilities are located within a single complex, none of the three products shares the same suppliers, customers, or physical production lines.
c. The organization's functional activities include design, production, distribution, marketing, finance, human resources, and accounting.

7. FUNCTIONAL SEGMENTATION

The current organizational structure of Blue Sky Company, a manufacturer of small sailboats, is presented below.

Required

a. What operational problems (e.g., inefficiency, errors, or fraud) do you think Blue Sky could experience because of this structure?
b. Draw a new diagram reflecting an improved structure that solves the problems you identified. If necessary, you may add up to two new positions.

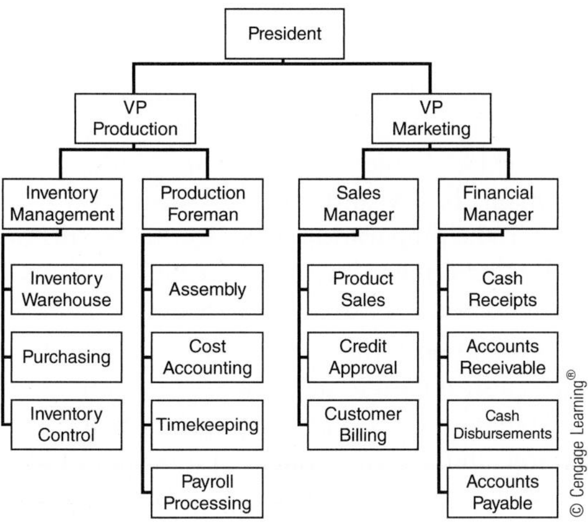

8. COMMUNICATIONS

Before the mid-1970s, systems programmers and businesspeople (including accountants) did not communicate well with one another. The programmers were criticized for using too much jargon, and the businesspeople were criticized for not adequately expressing their needs. Efforts have been made to overcome this communication gap, but room for improvement still exists. What problems do you think may result from this communication gap? What can you do to help further close the gap when you enter the workforce?

9. CHARACTERISTICS OF USEFUL INFORMATION

All records in a file must be uniquely identifiable in at least one attribute, which is its primary key. Drawing on your general knowledge of accounting, identify the primary key for the following types of accounting records. To illustrate, the first record is done for you.

Record Type	Primary Key
Accounts Receivable	Customer Number
Accounts Payable	
Inventory	
Customer Sales Orders	
Purchase Orders to vendors	
Cash Receipts (checks) from Customers	
Cash Disbursements (checks) to vendors	
Employee Payroll Earnings Records	

10. DATA ATTRIBUTES

Drawing from your basic accounting knowledge, list the relevant data attributes that constitute the record types below. Identify which attribute is the primary key for the record.

Accounts Payable record
Inventory record
Customer Sales Orders record
Purchase Orders to vendors
Cash Receipts (checks) from customers
Employee Payroll Earnings records

11. ROLE OF INTERNAL AUDIT FUNCTION

Nano Circuits Inc, is a publicly traded company that produces electronic control circuits, which are used in many products. In an effort to comply with SOX, Nano is in the process of establishing an in-house internal audit function, which previously had been outsourced. The company began this process by hiring a Director of Internal Audits. Nano Circuits' CEO recently called a planning meeting to discuss the roles of key corporate participants regarding the implementation and maintenance of internal controls. Central to this decision is the organizational placement of the future internal audit function and to whom the new Director of Internal Audit should report. In addition, Nano Circuits considered the need to reconstitute its Board of Directors Audit Committee. Participants at the meeting included the company president, the chief financial officer, a member of the audit committee, a partner from Nano Circuits external audit firm, and the Director of Internal Audits. Expectations and concerns presented by the meeting participants are summarized below.

CEO: The CEO expressed concern that Nano Circuits complies with SOX and PCAOB requirements and recommendations. The internal audit function should strengthen the organization's internal control system by developing control policies and procedures and by detecting violations of policies and procedures.

CFO: The CFO saw the role of the internal audit function as one that should be focused primarily on financial issues and therefore, the director of Internal Audits should report to the CFO.

Audit committee member: The committee member felt strongly that the Audit Committee as currently constituted is appropriate and no changes need to be made. Although none of the committee members are trained accountants they all have extensive industry experience, they have all been associated with Nano Circuits in various capacities for many years, and are well qualified to fulfill their policy-oversight responsibilities.

External audit partner: The external audit partner pointed out that the internal audit function should be organized such that it supports a close working relationship with the external auditors. This would include monitoring internal control systems on a continuing basis to provide a body of evidence on which the external auditor can rely.

Director of Internal Audits: The Director of Internal Audits argued that the new IA function should focus more on operational auditing issues, but it also should play a role in the review of internal controls over financial reporting.

Required

a. Describe the role that each of the following areas has in the establishment, maintenance, and evaluation of internal control:
   i. Management
   ii. External auditor
   iii. Internal audit
b. To whom should the Director of Internal Audits report? Explain your answer.
c. Comment on the audit committee member's perspective as to the committee's current composition.

12. INTERNAL AUDITOR INDEPENDENCE

Technical Solutions Inc, is expanding and reorganizing its Internal Audit (IA) function. Currently the Director of Internal Audit, Sharon Kalafut, reports to the corporate controller, who receives and reviews all internal audit reports. Kalafut forwards copies of the internal audit reports to the audit committee of the board of directors and to the manager directly responsible for the function being audited.

An issue of contention among the management team pertains to which department or function the Director of Internal Audits should report. Martin Stevens the CEO wants to ensure that Technical Solutions complies with the SOX and that the internal audit department is structured such that it strengthens the company's internal control system. Also, an overarching objective for the reorganized audit function is that the external auditors are able to rely on the work performed by the internal audit department to a substantial degree. Arguments put forth by interested parties as to where the IA department should be organizationally located are presented below:

- **Chief Operations Officer (COO).** John Sweeney, the COO of Technical Solutions, believes that the Director of IA should report to him. Under this arrangement the IA staff members would be involved in the preparation of policy statements on internal control regarding safeguarding of assets and in the design of business processes.
- **Chief Information Officer (CIO).** Larry Rich, the CIO, has pushed hard to have the IA function report to him and take on an active role in the design, installation, and initial operation of a new computerized systems. IA staff will be primarily concerned with the design and implementation of internal accounting controls and conduct the evaluation of these controls during the test runs and audits.
- **Corporate Controller.** The controller Linda Johnson, believes the IA group should remain within her functional area. Currently the IA staff performs a number of controller related tasks. These include:
  - Internal auditors reconcile bank statements of the corporation each month. The controller believes this strengthens the internal control function because the internal auditor is not involved in either the receipt or the disbursement of cash.
  - Internal auditors review the annual budget each year for relevance and reasonableness before the budget is approved. At the end of each month, the controller's staff analyzes the variances from budget and prepares explanations of these variances. These variances and explanations are then reviewed by the internal audit staff.
  - Finally, the internal auditors make accounting entries for complex transactions when employees of the accounting department are

not adequately trained to handle such transactions. The controller believes this gives an added measure of assurance to the accurate recording of such transactions.

Required

a. Define independence as it relates to the internal audit function.

b. For each of the proposed tasks to be performed by the IA function, explain whether Technical Solutions' internal audit independence will be materially impaired. Consider each manager's arguments independently.

c. To maintain independence, where should the Director of Internal Audits report? Explain your answer.

CHAPTER 2

Introduction to Transaction Processing

Chapter 1 introduced the transaction processing system (TPS) as an activity consisting of three major subsystems called cycles: the revenue cycle, the expenditure cycle, and the conversion cycle. Even though each cycle performs different specific tasks and supports different objectives, they share common characteristics. For example, all three TPS cycles capture financial transactions, record the effects of transactions in accounting records, and provide information about transactions to users in support of their day-to-day activities. In addition, transaction cycles produce much of the raw data from which management reports and financial statements are derived. Because of their financial impact on the firm, transaction cycles command much of the accountant's professional attention.

The purpose of this chapter is to present some preliminary topics that are common to all three transaction processing cycles. In subsequent chapters, we will draw heavily from this material as we examine the individual subsystems of each cycle in detail. This chapter is organized into six major sections. The first is an overview of transaction processing. This section defines the broad objective of the three transaction cycles and specifies the roles of their individual subsystems. The second section describes the relationship among accounting records, both traditional and digital, in forming an audit trail. The third section describes the key features of flat file and database structures used to store accounting data. The fourth section examines several documentation techniques used to represent systems including manual procedures and the computer components of system. The fifth section addresses alternative transaction processing approaches. It reviews the fundamental features of batch and real-time technologies and their implication for transaction processing. The final section examines data coding schemes and their role in transaction processing.

Learning Objectives

After studying this chapter, you should:

- Understand the broad objectives of transaction cycles.
- Recognize the types of transactions processed by each of the three transaction cycles.
- Know the basic accounting records used in transaction processing systems.
- Understand the relationship between traditional accounting records and their digital equivalents in computer-based systems.
- Be familiar with the documentation techniques used for representing manual procedures and the computer components of systems.
- Understand the differences between batch and real-time processing and the impact of these technologies on transaction processing.
- Be familiar with data coding schemes used in accounting information systems.

An Overview of Transaction Processing

TPS applications process financial transactions. A financial transaction was defined in Chapter 1 as

> *An economic event that affects the assets and equities of the firm, is reflected in its accounts, and is measured in monetary terms.*

The most common financial transactions are economic exchanges with external parties. These include the sale of goods or services, the purchase of inventory, the discharge of financial obligations, and the receipt of cash on account from customers. Financial transactions also include certain internal events such as the depreciation of fixed assets; the application of labor, raw materials, and overhead to the production process; and the transfer of inventory from one department to another.

Financial transactions are common business events that occur regularly. For instance, thousands of transactions of a particular type (sales to customers) may occur daily. To deal efficiently with such volume, business firms group similar types of transactions into transaction cycles.

TRANSACTION CYCLES

Three transaction cycles process most of the firm's economic activity: the expenditure cycle, the conversion cycle, and the revenue cycle. These cycles exist in all types of businesses—both profit-seeking and not-for-profit types. For instance, every business (1) incurs expenditures in exchange for resources (expenditure cycle), (2) provides value added through its products or services (conversion cycle), and (3) receives revenue from outside sources (revenue cycle). Figure 2-1 shows the relationship of these cycles and the resource flows between them.

FIGURE 2-1 RELATIONSHIP BETWEEN TRANSACTION CYCLES

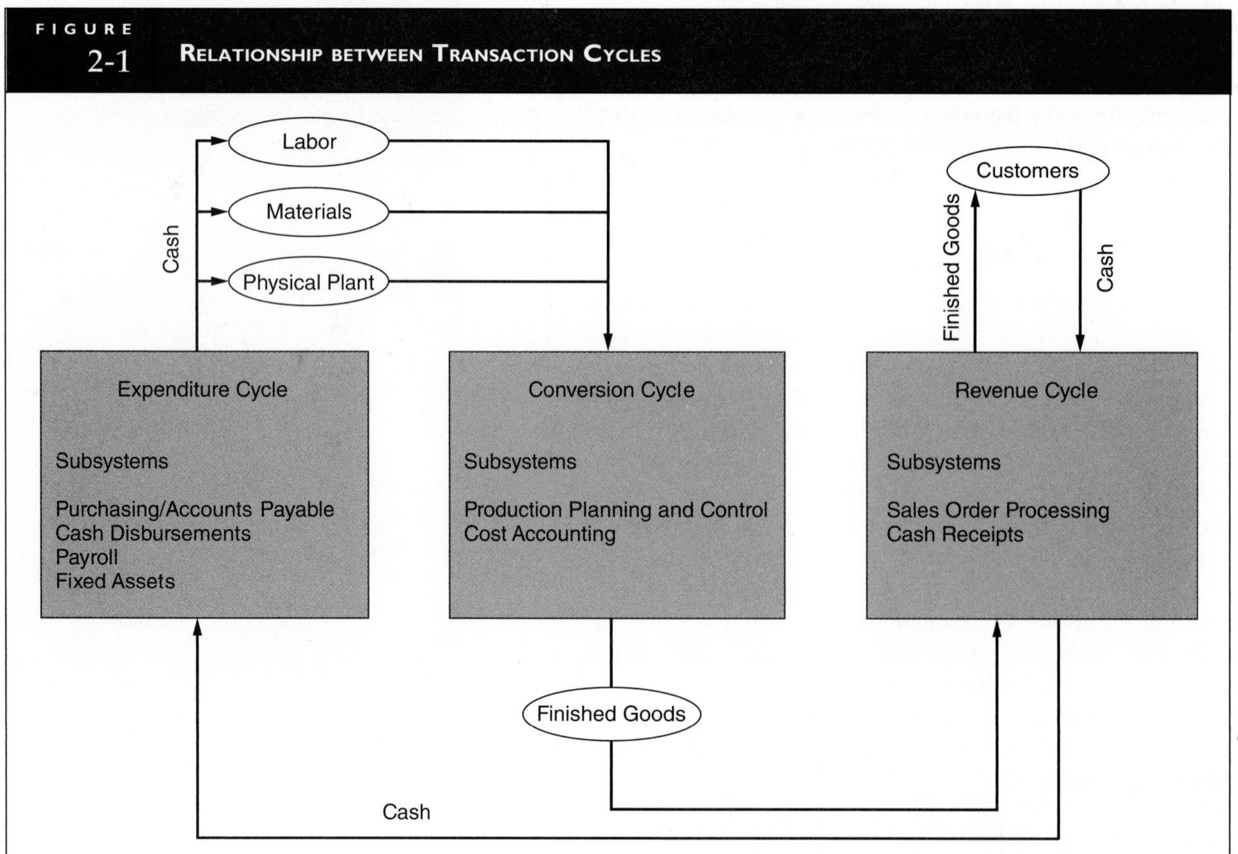

The Expenditure Cycle

Business activities begin with the acquisition of materials, property, and labor in exchange for cash—the **expenditure cycle**. Figure 2-1 shows the flow of cash from the organization to the various providers of these resources. Most business-to-business (B2B) expenditure transactions are based on a credit relationship between the trading parties. The actual disbursement of cash takes place at some point after the receipt of the goods or services. Days or even weeks may pass between these two events. Thus, from a systems perspective, this transaction has two parts: a physical component (the acquisition of the goods or services) and a financial component (the cash disbursement to the supplier). A separate subsystem of the cycle processes each component. The primary expenditure cycle subsystems are outlined next. Because of the extent of this body of material, two chapters are devoted to a detailed examination. Purchases/accounts payable and cash disbursements systems are the topics of Chapter 5. Payroll and fixed asset systems are examined in Chapter 6.

Purchases/accounts payable (AP) system. *This system recognizes the need to acquire physical inventory (such as raw materials) and places an order with the vendor. When the goods are received, the purchases system records the event by increasing inventory and establishing an account payable to be paid at a later date.*

Cash disbursements system. *When the obligation created in the purchases system becomes due, the cash disbursements system authorizes the payment, disburses the funds to the vendor, and records the transaction by reducing the cash and accounts payable accounts.*

Payroll system. *The payroll system collects labor usage data for each employee, computes the payroll, and disburses paychecks to the employees. Conceptually, payroll is a special-case purchases and cash disbursements system. Because of accounting complexities associated with payroll, most firms have a separate system for payroll processing.*

Fixed asset system. *A firm's fixed asset system processes transactions pertaining to the acquisition, maintenance, and disposal of its fixed assets. These are relatively permanent assets that collectively often represent the organization's largest financial investment. Examples of fixed assets include land, buildings, furniture, machinery, and motor vehicles.*

The Conversion Cycle

The **conversion cycle** is comprised of two major subsystems: the production system and the cost accounting system. The production system involves the planning, scheduling, and control of the physical product through the manufacturing process. This includes determining raw material requirements, authorizing the work to be performed and the release of raw materials into production, and directing the movement of the work-in-process through its various stages of manufacturing. The cost accounting system monitors the flow of cost information including labor, overhead and raw materials related to production. Information this system produces is used for inventory valuation, budgeting, cost control, performance reporting, and management decisions, such as make-or-buy decisions. We examine the basic features of these systems in Chapter 7.

Manufacturing firms convert raw materials into finished products through formal, physical, and observable conversion cycle operations. The conversion cycle in service and retailing establishments, however, may not be formal and observable. Nevertheless, these firms still engage in value added conversion cycle activities that culminate in the development of a salable product or service. These activities include the readying of products and services for market and allocating resources such as depreciation, building amortization, and prepaid expenses to the proper accounting period. Unlike manufacturing firms, merchandising companies do not account for these activities through formal conversion cycle subsystems that track and allocate costs to specific goods. In contrast, some service organizations such as public accounting firms, law firms, and consulting firms do track specific costs (primarily labor) to client accounts in much the same way as a manufacturing cost accounting system would track labor and raw materials to the products they produce.

The Revenue Cycle

Firms sell their goods and services to customers through the **revenue cycle**, which involves processing cash sales, credit sales, and the receipt of cash following a credit sale. Revenue cycle transactions also have a physical and a financial component, which are processed separately. The primary subsystems of the revenue cycle, which are the topics of Chapter 4, are briefly outlined below.

Sales order processing. *The majority of business sales are made on credit and involve tasks such as preparing sales orders, granting credit, shipping products (or rendering of a service) to the customer, billing customers, and recording the transaction in the accounts (accounts receivable, inventory, expenses, and sales).*

Cash receipts. *For credit sales, some period of time (days or weeks) passes between the point of sale and the receipt of cash. Cash receipts processing includes collecting cash, depositing cash in the bank, and recording these events in the accounts (accounts receivable and cash).*

Accounting Records

MANUAL SYSTEMS

This section describes the purpose of each type of **accounting record** used in transaction cycles. We begin with traditional records used in manual systems (documents, journals, and ledgers) and then examine their digital counterparts in computer-based systems.

Documents

Documents serve several purposes in transaction processing. Documents may initiate transaction processing or be the output of a process. They also provide auditors with evidence of economic events. In this section we examine three types of documents: source documents, product documents, and turnaround documents.

SOURCE DOCUMENTS. Economic events result in the creation of some documents at the beginning (the source) of the transaction. These are called **source documents** and are used to capture and formalize transaction data that the transaction cycle uses for processing. Figure 2-2 shows the creation of a source document.

The economic event (in this case the sale) causes the sales clerk to prepare a multipart sales order, which is formal evidence that a sale occurred. Copies of this source document enter the sales system and are used to convey information to various functions, such as billing, shipping, and accounts receivable. The information contained in the sales order triggers specific activities in each of these functions.

PRODUCT DOCUMENTS. Product documents are the result of transaction processing rather than the triggering mechanism for the process. For example, a payroll check to an employee is a product document of the payroll system. Figure 2-3 extends the example in Figure 2-2 to illustrate that the customer's bill is a product document of the sales system. We will study many other examples of product documents in later chapters.

TURNAROUND DOCUMENTS. Turnaround documents are product documents of one system that become source documents for another system. This is illustrated in Figure 2-4. The customer receives a perforated two-part bill or statement. One portion is the actual bill, and the other portion is the remittance advice. Customers remove the remittance advice and return it to the company along with their payment (typically a check). The remittance advice is a turnaround document that contains important information about a customer's account to help the cash receipts system process the payment. One of the problems designers of cash receipts systems face is matching customer payments to the correct customer accounts. Providing this needed information as a product of the sales system ensures accuracy when the cash receipts system processes it.

FIGURE 2-2 CREATION OF A SOURCE DOCUMENT

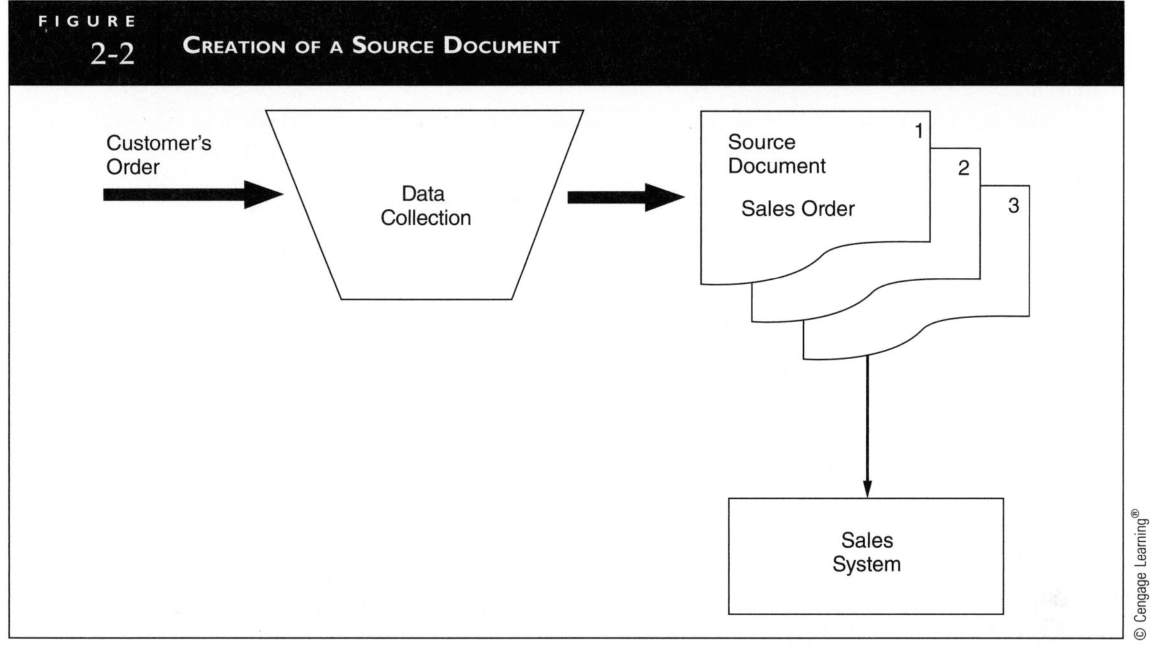

FIGURE 2-3 A PRODUCT DOCUMENT

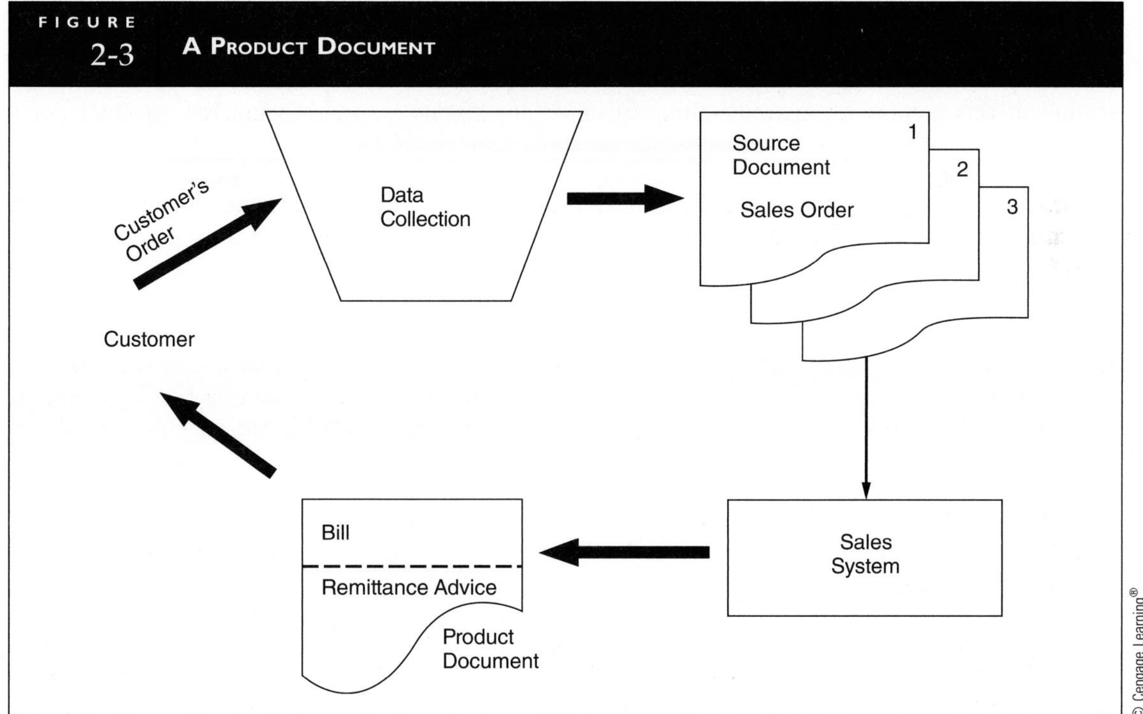

Journals

A **journal** is a chronological record of a transaction. At some point in the transaction process, when all relevant facts about the transaction are known, the event is recorded in a journal in chronological order. Documents are the primary data source for journals. Figure 2-5 shows a sales order being recorded in the sales journal (see the following discussion on special journals). Each transaction requires a separate journal entry, reflecting the accounts affected and the amounts to be debited

FIGURE 2-4 A TURNAROUND DOCUMENT

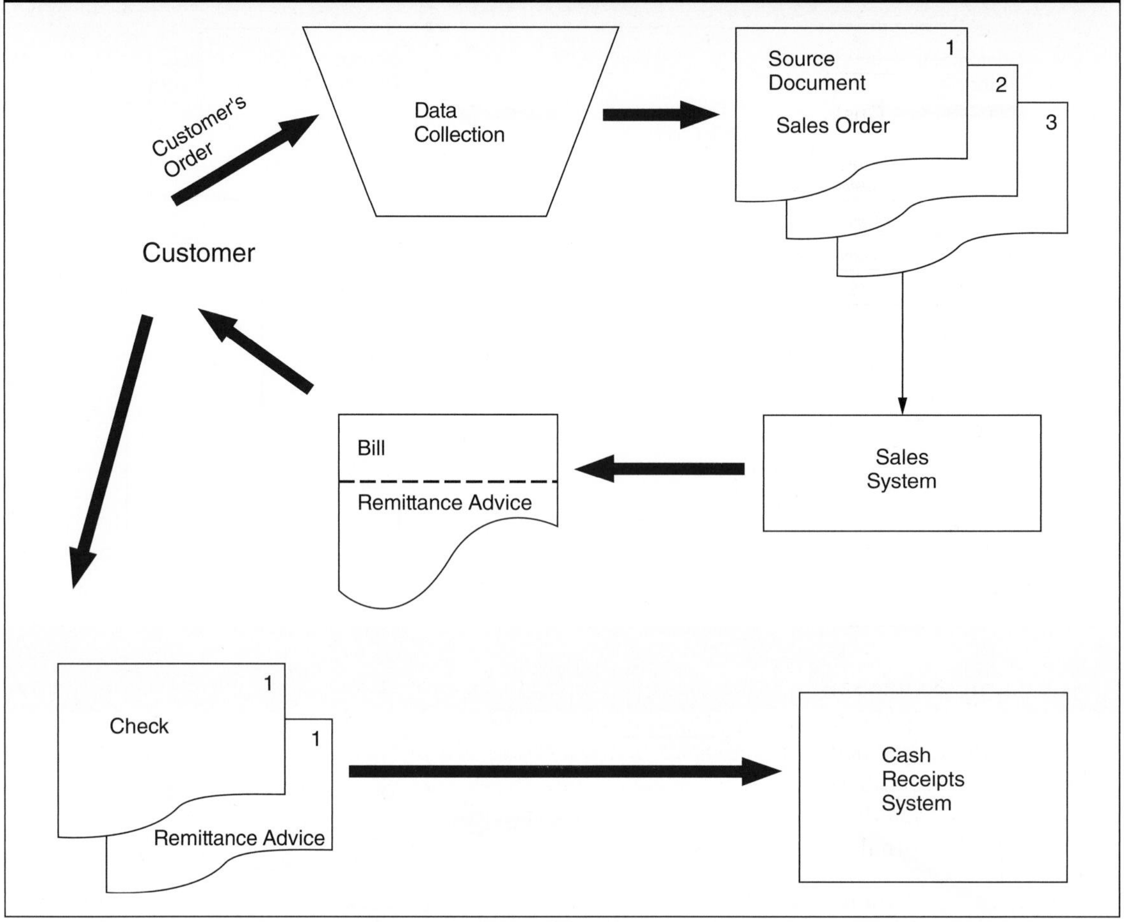

Customer's Order
Data Collection
Source Document
Sales Order
1
2
3
Customer
Bill
Remittance Advice
Sales System
Check
1
1
Remittance Advice
Cash Receipts System

FIGURE 2-5 SALES ORDER RECORDED IN SALES JOURNAL

Economic Event
Capture Event
Record Event
Customer's Order
1
Sales Order
Sales Journal

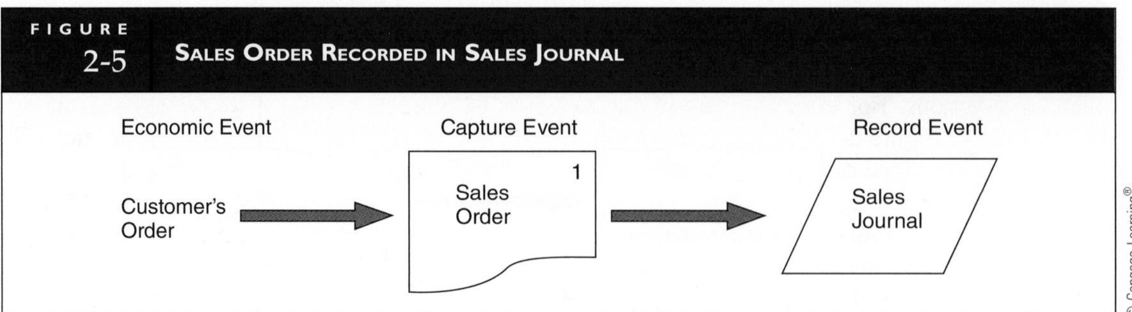

and credited. There is often a time lag between initiating a transaction and recording it in the accounts. The journal holds a complete record of transactions and thus provides a means for posting to accounts. There are two primary types of journals: special journals and general journals.

SPECIAL JOURNALS. Special journals are used to record specific classes of transactions that occur in high volume. Such transactions can be grouped together in a special journal and processed more efficiently than a general journal permits. Figure 2-6 shows a special journal for recording sales transactions.

FIGURE 2-6 SALES JOURNAL

Date	Customer	Invoice Num.	Acct. Num.	Post	Debit Acct. Rec. #102	Credit Sales #401
Sept. 1	Hewitt Co.	4523	1120		3300	3300
15	Acme Drilling	8821	1298		6825	6825
Oct. 3	Buell Corp.	22987	1030		4000	4000
10	Check Ltd.	66734	1110		8500	8500

As you can see, the sales journal provides a specialized format for recording only sales transactions. At the end of the processing period (month, week, or day), a clerk posts the amounts in the columns to the ledger accounts indicated (see the discussion of ledgers in this chapter). For example, the total sales will be posted to account number 401. Most organizations use several other special journals, including the cash receipts journal, cash disbursements journal, purchases journal, and the payroll journal.

REGISTER. The term **register** is often used to denote certain types of special journals. For example, the payroll journal is often called the payroll register. We also use the term *register*, however, to denote a log. For example, a receiving register is a log of all receipts of raw materials or merchandise ordered from vendors. Similarly, a shipping register is a log that records all shipments to customers.

GENERAL JOURNALS. Firms use the general journal to record nonrecurring, infrequent, and dissimilar transactions. For example, we usually record periodic depreciation and closing entries in the general journal. Figure 2-7 shows one page from a general journal. Note that the columns are nonspecific, allowing any type of transaction to be recorded. The entries are recorded chronologically.

As a practical matter, most organizations have replaced their general journal with a journal voucher system. A journal voucher is actually a special source document that contains a single journal entry specifying the general ledger accounts that are affected. Journal vouchers are used to record summaries of routine transactions, nonroutine transactions, adjusting entries, and closing entries. The total of journal vouchers processed is equivalent to the general journal. Subsequent chapters discuss the use of this technique in transaction processing.

Ledgers

A **ledger** is a book of accounts that reflects the financial effects of the firm's transactions after they are posted from the various journals. While journals show the chronological effect of business activity, ledgers show activity by account type. A ledger indicates the increases, decreases, and current balance of each account. Organizations use this information to prepare financial statements, support daily operations, and prepare internal reports. Figure 2-8 shows the flow of financial information from the source documents to the journal and into the ledgers.

FIGURE 2-7 GENERAL JOURNAL

GENERAL JOURNAL PAGE

	DATE	DESCRIPTION	POST. REF.	DEBIT	CREDIT	
1	Sept. 1, 2009	Depreciation Expense	520	5 0 0 0		1
2		Accumulated Depreciation	210		5 0 0 0	2
3						3
4	Sept. 2, 2009	Insurance Expense	525	1 2 0 0		4
5		Prepaid Insurance	180		1 2 0 0	5
6						6
7	Sept. 3, 2009	Cash	101	1 1 0 0 0		7
8		Capital Stock	310		1 1 0 0 0	8
9						9
10						10
11						11
12						12

FIGURE 2-8 FLOW OF INFORMATION FROM THE ECONOMIC EVENT TO THE GENERAL LEDGER

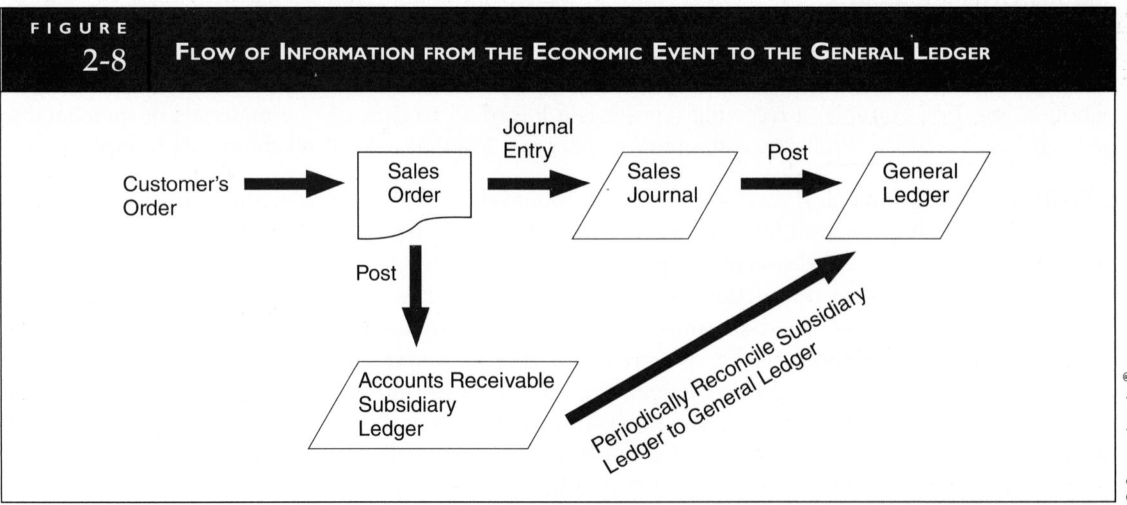

There are two basic types of ledgers: (1) general ledgers, which contain the firm's account information in the form of highly summarized control accounts, and (2) subsidiary ledgers, which contain the details of the individual accounts that constitute a particular control account.[1]

1 Not all accounts in the general ledger have corresponding subsidiary accounts. Accounts such as sales and cash typically have no supporting details in the form of a subsidiary ledger.

GENERAL LEDGERS. The general ledger (GL) summarizes the activity for each of the organization's accounts. The general ledger function updates these records from journal vouchers prepared from special journals and other sources located throughout the organization. The general ledger presented in Figure 2-9 shows the beginning balances, the changes, and the ending balances as of a particular date for several different accounts.

FIGURE 2-9 GENERAL LEDGER

Cash ACCOUNT NO. *101*

DATE		ITEM	POST. REF.	DEBIT	CREDIT	BALANCE	
						DEBIT	CREDIT
Sept.	10		S1	3300		3300	
	15		S1	6825		10125	
Oct.	3		S1	4000		14125	
	10		CD1		2800	11325	

Accounts Receivable ACCOUNT NO. *102*

DATE		ITEM	POST. REF.	DEBIT	CREDIT	BALANCE	
						DEBIT	CREDIT
Sept.	1		S1	1400		1400	
	8		S1	2605		4005	
	15		CR1		1650	2355	

Accounts Payable ACCOUNT NO. *201*

DATE		ITEM	POST. REF.	DEBIT	CREDIT	BALANCE	
						DEBIT	CREDIT
Sept.	1		P1		20500		20500
	10		CD1	2800			17700

FIGURE 2-9 GENERAL LEDGER (CONTINUED)

Purchases ACCOUNT NO. *502*

DATE		ITEM	POST. REF.	DEBIT	CREDIT	BALANCE	
						DEBIT	CREDIT
Sept.	*1*		P1	*2 0 5 0 0*		*2 0 5 0 0*	

The general ledger provides a single value for each control account, such as accounts payable, accounts receivable, and inventory. This highly summarized information is sufficient for financial reporting, but it is not useful for supporting daily business operations. For example, for financial reporting purposes, the firm's total accounts receivable value must be presented as a single figure in the balance sheet. This value is obtained from the accounts receivable control account in the general ledger. To actually collect the cash this account represents, however, the firm must have certain detailed information about customers that this summary figure does not provide. It must know customers' addresses, which customers owe money, how much each customer owes, when certain customers last made payment, when the next payment is due, and so on. The accounts receivable subsidiary ledger contains these essential details.

SUBSIDIARY LEDGERS. Subsidiary ledgers are kept in various accounting departments of the firm, including inventory, accounts payable, payroll, and accounts receivable. This separation provides better control and support of operations. Figure 2-10 illustrates that the total of account balances in a subsidiary ledger should equal the balance in the corresponding general ledger control account. Thus, in addition to providing financial statement information, the general ledger is a mechanism for verifying the overall accuracy of accounting data that separate accounting departments have processed. Any event incorrectly recorded in a journal or subsidiary ledger will cause an out-of-balance condition that should be detected during the general ledger update. By periodically reconciling summary balances from subsidiary accounts, journals, and control accounts, the completeness and accuracy of transaction processing can be formally assessed.

THE AUDIT TRAIL

The accounting records described previously provide an **audit trail** for tracing account balances contained in the financial statements back to source documents and the economic events that created them. An audit trail is of utmost importance in the conduct of a financial audit.

The external auditor's responsibility involves, in part, the review of selected accounts and transactions to determine their validity, accuracy, and completeness. Let's assume an auditor wishes to verify the accuracy of a client's AR balance as published in its annual financial statements. The auditor can trace the AR value on the balance sheet to the general ledger AR control account. This balance can then be reconciled with the total for the accounts receivable

FIGURE 2-10 RELATIONSHIP BETWEEN THE SUBSIDIARY LEDGER AND THE GENERAL LEDGER

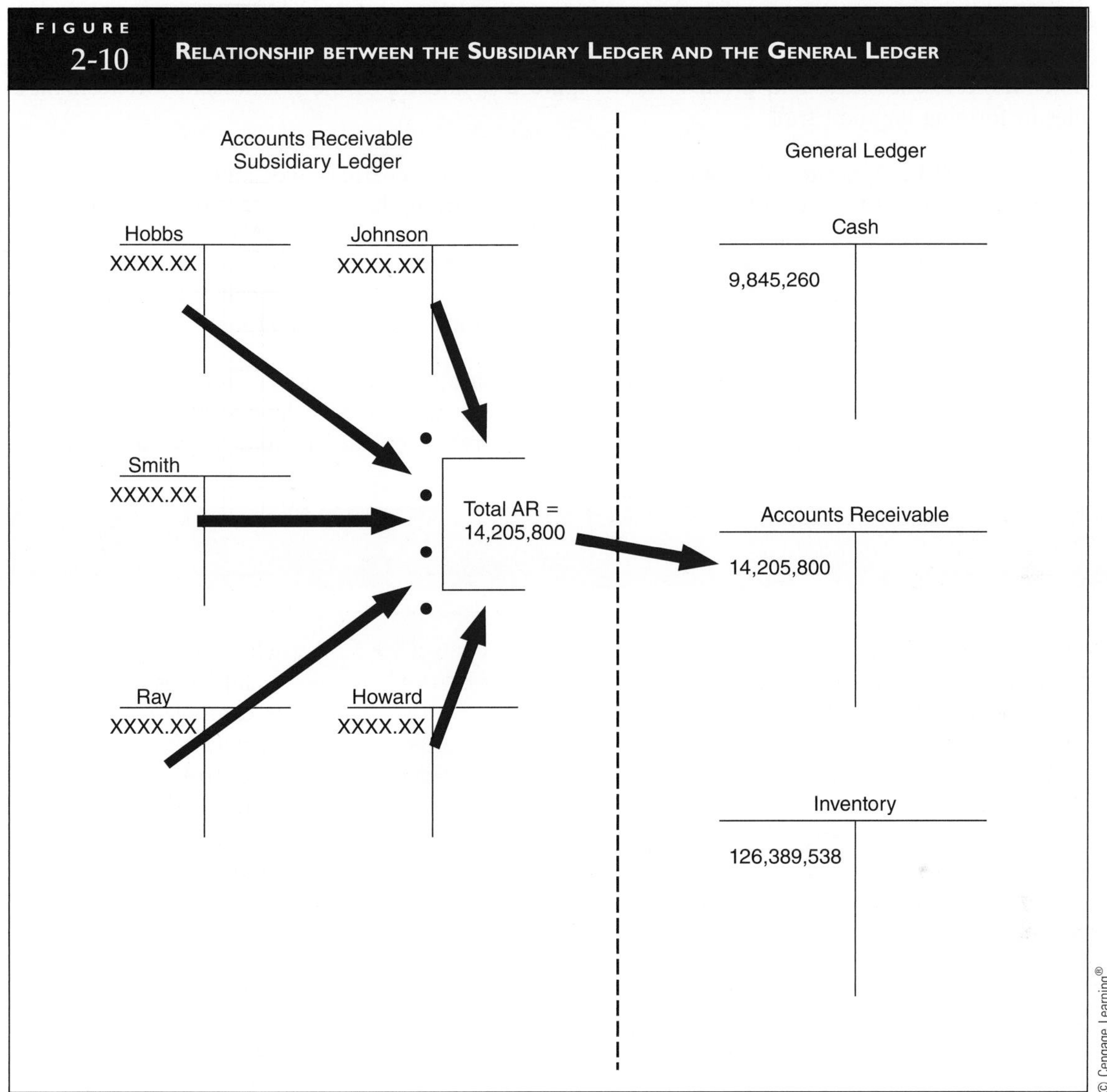

subsidiary ledger. Rather than examining every transaction that affected the AR account, the auditor will use a sampling technique to examine a representative subset of transactions. Following this approach, the auditor can select a number of accounts from the AR subsidiary ledger and trace these back to the sales journal. From the sales journal, the auditor can identify the specific source documents that initiated the transactions and pull them from the files to verify their validity and accuracy.

The audit of AR often includes a procedure called confirmation. This involves contacting selected customers to determine if the transactions recorded in the accounts actually took place and if customers agree with the recorded balance. Information contained in source documents and subsidiary accounts enables the auditor to identify and locate customers chosen for confirmation. The results from reconciling the AR subsidiary ledger with the control account and from confirming customers' accounts help the auditor form an opinion about the accuracy of accounts receivable as reported on the balance sheet. The auditor performs similar tests on all of the client firm's major accounts and transactions to arrive at an overall opinion about the fair presentation of the financial statement. The audit trail plays an important role in this process.

DIGITAL ACCOUNTING RECORDS

Modern accounting systems store data in four types of digital computer files: master files, transaction files, reference files, and archive files. Figure 2-11 illustrates the relationship between these files in forming an audit trail.

MASTER FILE. A **master file** contains account data. The general ledger and subsidiary ledgers are examples of master files. Data values in master files are updated (changed) by transactions.

TRANSACTION FILE. A **transaction file** is a temporary file of transaction records used to update data in a master file. Sales orders, inventory receipts, and cash receipts are examples of transaction files. The actual file update process is explained later in the chapter.

REFERENCE FILE. A **reference file** stores data that are used as standards for processing transactions. For example, the payroll program may refer to a tax table to calculate the proper amount of withholding taxes for payroll transactions. Other reference files include price lists used for

FIGURE 2-11 DIGITAL ACCOUNTING RECORDS IN A COMPUTER-BASED SYSTEM

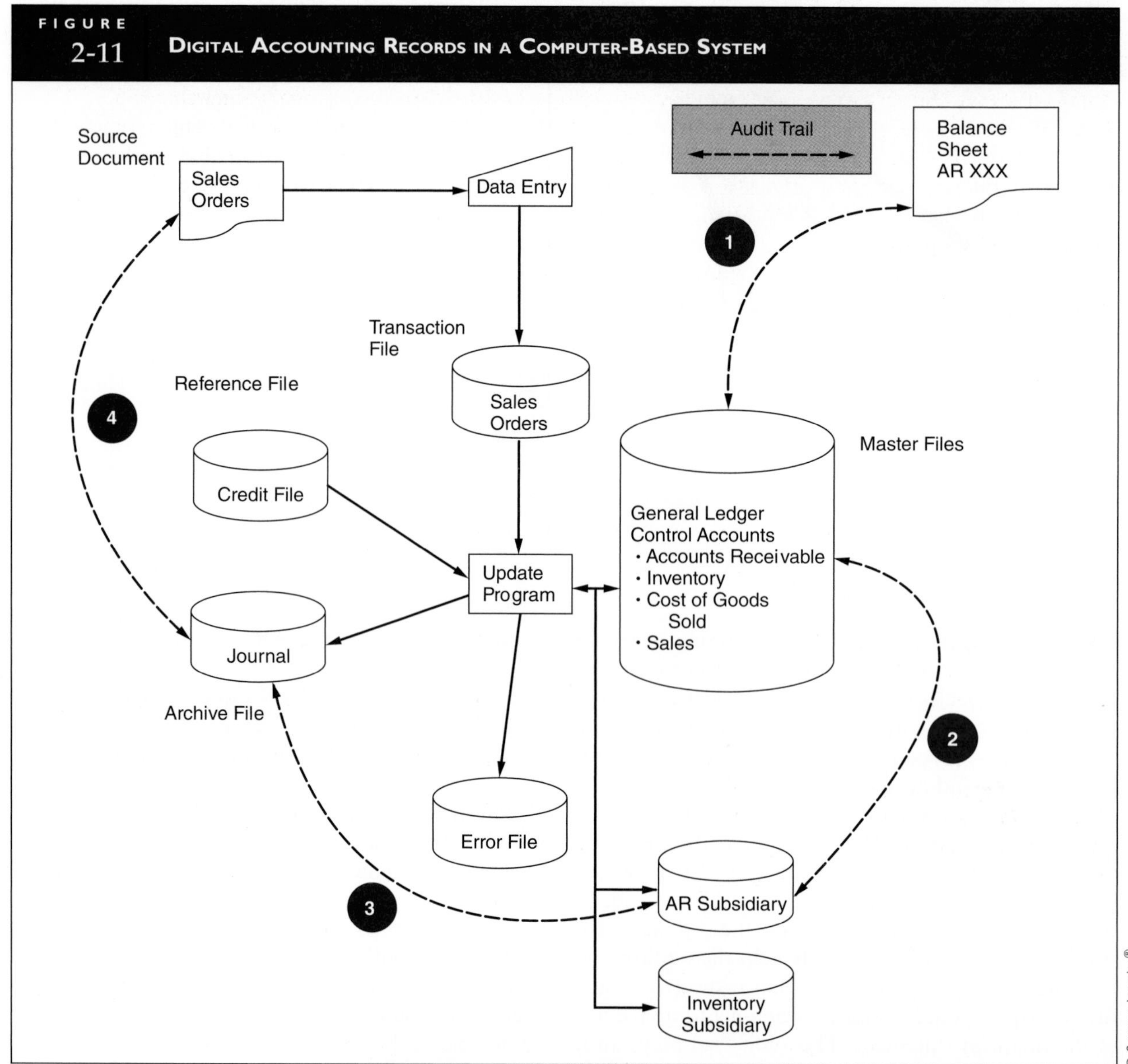

preparing customer invoices, lists of authorized suppliers, employee rosters, and customer credit files for approving credit sales. The reference file in Figure 2-11 is a credit history file.

ARCHIVE FILE. An **archive file** contains records of past transactions that are retained for future reference and form an important part of the audit trail. Archive files include journals, prior-period payroll information, lists of former employees, records of accounts written off, and prior-period ledgers.

The Digital Audit Trail

Audit trails among digital records are less observable than those between hard-copy documents, but they still exist. Let's walk through the system represented in Figure 2-11 to illustrate how digital files provide an audit trail. We begin with the capture of the economic event. In this example, sales are recorded manually on source documents. The next step in this process is to convert the source documents to digital form. This is done in the data-entry stage, where the transactions are edited for correctness and a transaction file of sales orders is produced. Some computer systems do not use physical source documents. Instead, transactions are captured directly on digital media.

The next step is to update the various master file subsidiary and GL control accounts that are affected by the transaction. During the update procedure, additional editing of transactions takes place. Some transactions may prove to be in error or invalid for such reasons as incorrect account numbers, insufficient quantities on hand, or customer credit problems. In this example, the system determines the available credit for each customer from the credit file before processing the sale. Any records that are rejected for credit problems are transferred to the error file. The remaining good records are used to update the master files. Only these valid transactions are added to the archive file, which serves as the sales journal. By copying the valid transactions to the journal, the original transaction file is not needed for audit trail purposes. This file can now be erased (scratched) in preparation for the next batch of sales orders.

Like the paper audit trail, this digital audit trail allows transaction tracing. Again, an auditor attempting to evaluate the accuracy of the AR figure published in the balance sheet could do so via the following steps, which are identified in Figure 2-11 with the dotted arrows.

1. Compare the accounts receivable balance in the balance sheet with the master file AR control account balance.
2. Reconcile the AR control figure with the AR subsidiary account total.
3. Select a sample of updated entries made to accounts in the AR subsidiary ledger and trace these to transactions in the sales journal (archive file).
4. From these journal entries, identify specific source documents that can be pulled from their files and verified. If necessary, the auditor can confirm the accuracy and propriety of these source documents by contacting the customers in question.

File Structures

Digital file structures and storage techniques vary widely among transaction processing systems. This is because each file structure was designed to serve a particular task. Some structures are most effective for processing large portions of a master file. For example, on payday, every employee record in the employee payroll master file needs to be processed, because all (or most) employees get paid. Some file structures are better for directly locating and processing a single record in a large file, without having to search through thousands of other records on the file. For example, selecting a specific customer's record, in response to a customer query over the phone, from a customer master file that contains a million records requires a direct access file structure. Unfortunately, no single structure works optimally in all applications; therefore, selecting a data management file structure often involves compromise. The appendix to this chapter presents several examples of file structures and discusses their respective advantages and disadvantages.

File technologies broadly fall into two classes: (1) flat files and (2) databases. The sections that follow examine the general characteristics of each class and illustrate the evolution of data management systems. The flat-file approach is often associated with so-called **legacy systems**, which are large mainframe systems that were commonplace in the 1960s and 1970s, but still exist today. Most modern system implementations employ database technologies, although flat-file systems are still implemented in special applications. In addition, database technology has been with us since the 1960s, and some legacy systems use early database technologies. Eventually, flat files will probably succumb to databases, but in the meantime, accountants and auditors must deal with both.

THE FLAT-FILE MODEL

The **flat-file model** describes an environment in which individual data files are not related to other files. End users in this environment own their data files rather than share them with other users. Thus, stand-alone applications rather than integrated systems perform data processing.

When multiple users need the same data for different purposes, they must obtain separate data sets structured to their specific needs. Figure 2-12 illustrates how customer sales data might be presented to three different users in a durable goods retailing organization. The accounting function needs customer sales data organized by account number and structured to show outstanding balances. This is used for customer billing, AR maintenance, and financial statement preparation. Marketing needs customer sales history data organized by demographic keys. Marketing uses this for targeting new product promotions and for selling product upgrades. The product services group needs customer sales data organized by products and structured to show scheduled service dates. Such information is used for making after-sales contacts with customers to schedule preventive maintenance and to solicit sales of service agreements.

The data redundancy demonstrated in this example contributes to three significant problems in the flat-file environment: **data storage**, **data updating,** and **currency of information**. These and other problems associated with flat files are discussed in the following sections.

Data Storage

An efficient information system captures and stores data only once and makes this single source available to all users who need it. In the flat-file environment, this is not possible. To meet the private data needs of users, organizations must incur the costs of both multiple collection and multiple storage procedures. Some commonly used data may be duplicated dozens, hundreds, or even thousands of times.

Data Updating

Organizations have a great deal of data stored in files that require periodic updating to reflect changes. For example, a change to a customer's name or address must be reflected in the appropriate master files. When users keep separate files, all changes must be made separately for each user. This adds significantly to the task and the cost of data management.

Currency of Information

In contrast to the problem of performing multiple updates is the problem of failing to update all the user files affected by a change in status. If update information is not properly disseminated, the change will not be reflected in some users' data, resulting in decisions based on outdated information.

Task-Data Dependency

Another problem with the flat-file approach is the user's inability to obtain additional information as his or her needs change. This problem is called **task-data dependency**. The user's information set is constrained by the data that he or she possesses and controls. Users act independently rather than as members of a user community. In such an environment, it is difficult to establish a mechanism for the formal sharing of data. Therefore, new information needs tend to be satisfied by procuring new data files. This takes time, inhibits performance, adds to data redundancy, and drives data management costs even higher.

FIGURE 2-12 FLAT-FILE MODEL

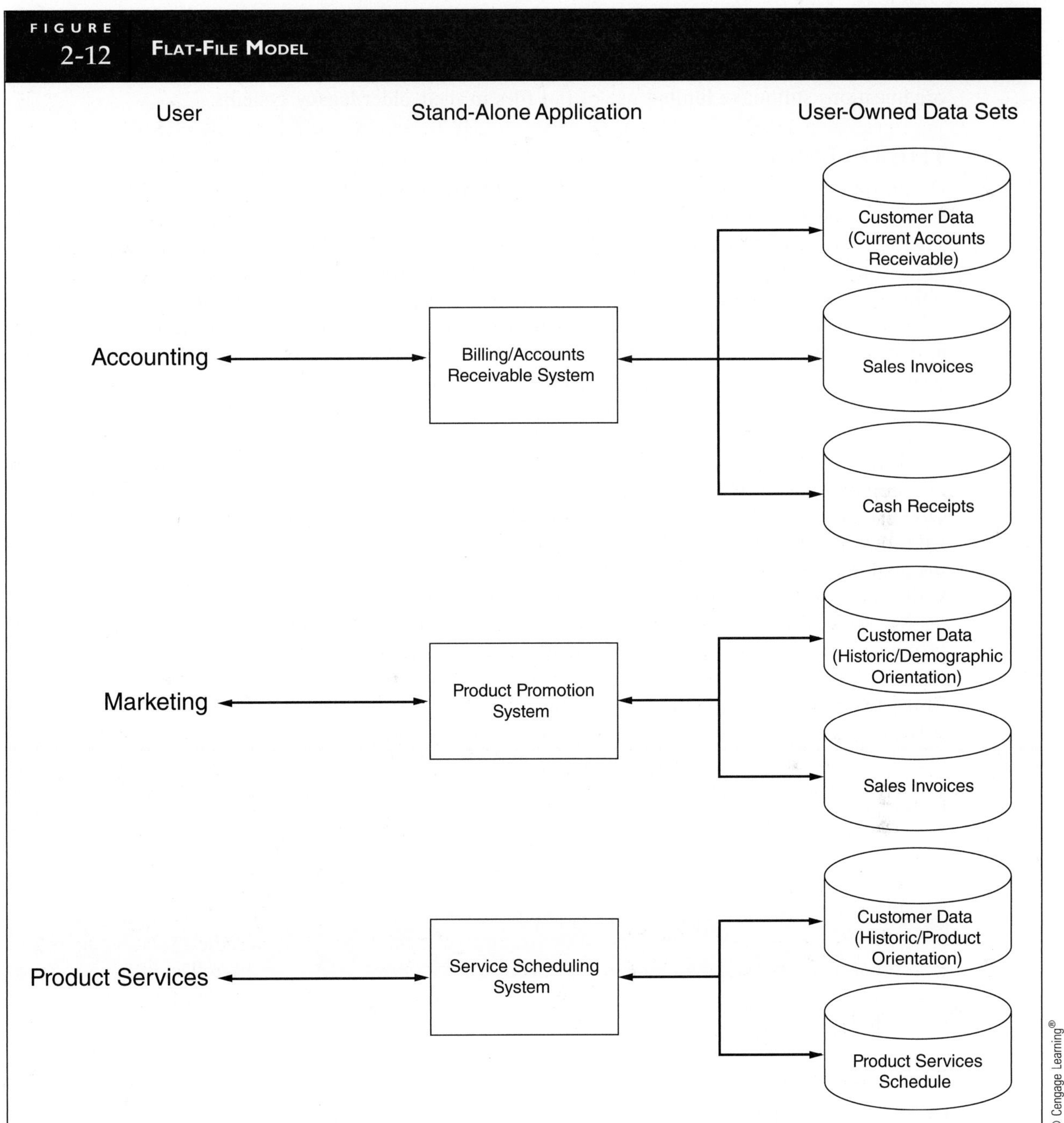

Flat Files Limit Data Integration

The flat-file approach is a single-view model. Files are structured, formatted, and arranged to suit the specific needs of the owner or primary user of the data. Such structuring, however, may exclude data needed by other users, thus preventing successful integration of data across the organization. For example, because the accounting function is the primary user of accounting data, these data are often captured, formatted, and stored to accommodate financial reporting and generally accepted accounting principles (GAAP). This structure, however, may be useless to the organization's other (nonaccounting) users of accounting data such as the marketing, finance, production, and engineering functions. These users are presented with three options: (1) do not use accounting data to support decisions, (2) manipulate and massage the existing data structure to suit their unique needs, or (3) obtain additional private sets of the data and incur the costs and operational problems associated with data redundancy. In spite of these inherent limitations some organizations still make limited use of flat files in their older legacy systems.

THE DATABASE MODEL

Organizations have overcome some of the problems associated with flat files by implementing the **database model** to data management. Figure 2-13 illustrates how this approach centralizes the organization's data into a common database that is shared by other users. With the organization's data in a central location, all users have access to the data they need to achieve their respective objectives. Access to the data resource is controlled by a **database management system (DBMS)**. The DBMS is a software system that permits users to access authorized data only. The user's application program sends requests for data to the DBMS, which validates and authorizes access to the database in accordance with the user's level of authority. If the user requests data that he or she is not authorized to access, the request is denied. Clearly, the organization's procedures for assigning user authority is an important control issue for auditors to consider.

The most striking difference between the database model and the flat-file model is the pooling of data into a common database that all organizational users share. With access to the full domain of entity data, changes in user information needs can be satisfied without obtaining additional private data sets. Users are constrained only by the limitations of the data available to the entity and the legitimacy of their need to access it. Through data sharing, the traditional problems associated with flat-file systems described previously can be eliminated.

We devote Chapters 9 and 10 to a detailed examination of the relational database model and the process and control issues unique to it. Until then, to simplify discussion in the transaction processing chapters that follow, we make no references to the specific file technology that may be used in the systems presented. The specific file structure employed, whether flat file or databases, is for the most part irrelevant to the process and control issues that are the focus of those chapters. Instead, we will refer to digital data files in generic terms such as *AR subsidiary ledger*, *Accounts Payable Control*, or *Customer Order file*. Similarly, the digital data storage symbols depicted in system flowcharts that follow in this chapter and in subsequent chapters represent generic data files.

FIGURE 2-13 DATABASE MODEL

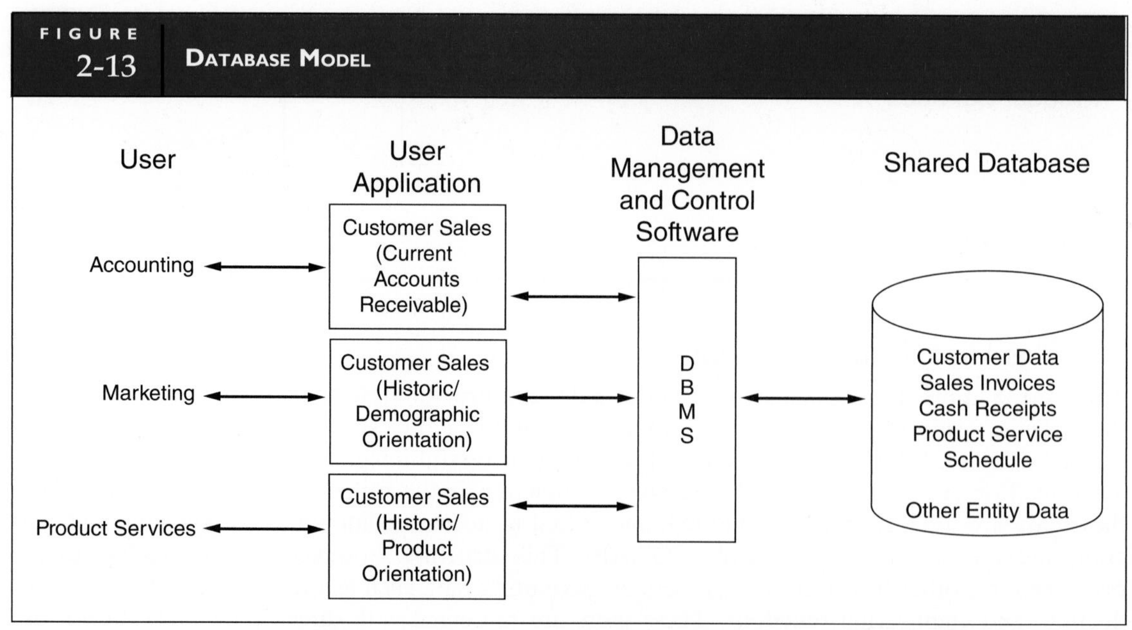

Documentation Techniques

The old saying that a picture is worth a thousand words is very applicable when it comes to documenting accounting information systems. A written description of a system can be wordy and difficult to follow. Experience shows that visual images convey vital system information more effectively and efficiently than words. Accountants use system documentation routinely, as both systems designers and auditors. The ability to document systems in graphic form is therefore an important skill for accountants to master. Five basic documentation techniques are introduced in this section: data flow diagrams, entity relationship diagrams, system flowcharts, program flowcharts, and record layout diagrams.

DATA FLOW DIAGRAMS AND ENTITY RELATIONSHIP DIAGRAMS

Two commonly used systems design and documentation techniques are the entity relationship diagram and the data flow diagram. This section introduces the principal features of these techniques, illustrates their use, and shows how they are related.

Data Flow Diagrams

The **data flow diagram (DFD)** uses symbols to represent the entities, processes, data flows, and data stores that pertain to a system. Figure 2-14 presents the most commonly used symbol set. DFDs are used to represent systems at different levels of detail from very general to highly

FIGURE 2-14 DATA FLOW DIAGRAM SYMBOL SET

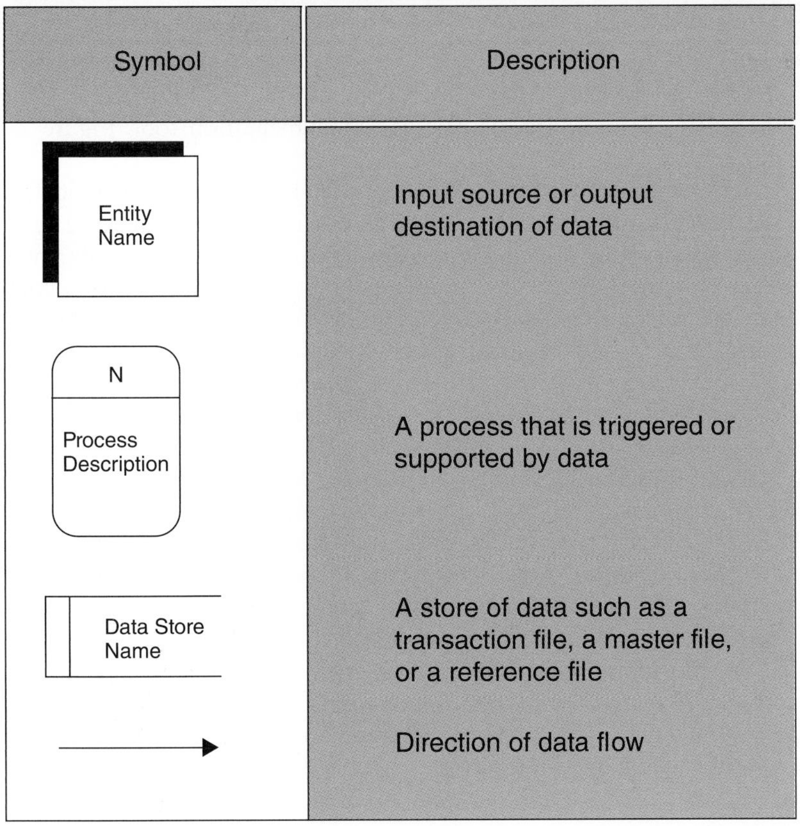

Symbol	Description
Entity Name	Input source or output destination of data
N / Process Description	A process that is triggered or supported by data
Data Store Name	A store of data such as a transaction file, a master file, or a reference file
→	Direction of data flow

FIGURE 2-15 DATA FLOW DIAGRAM OF PURCHASES SYSTEM

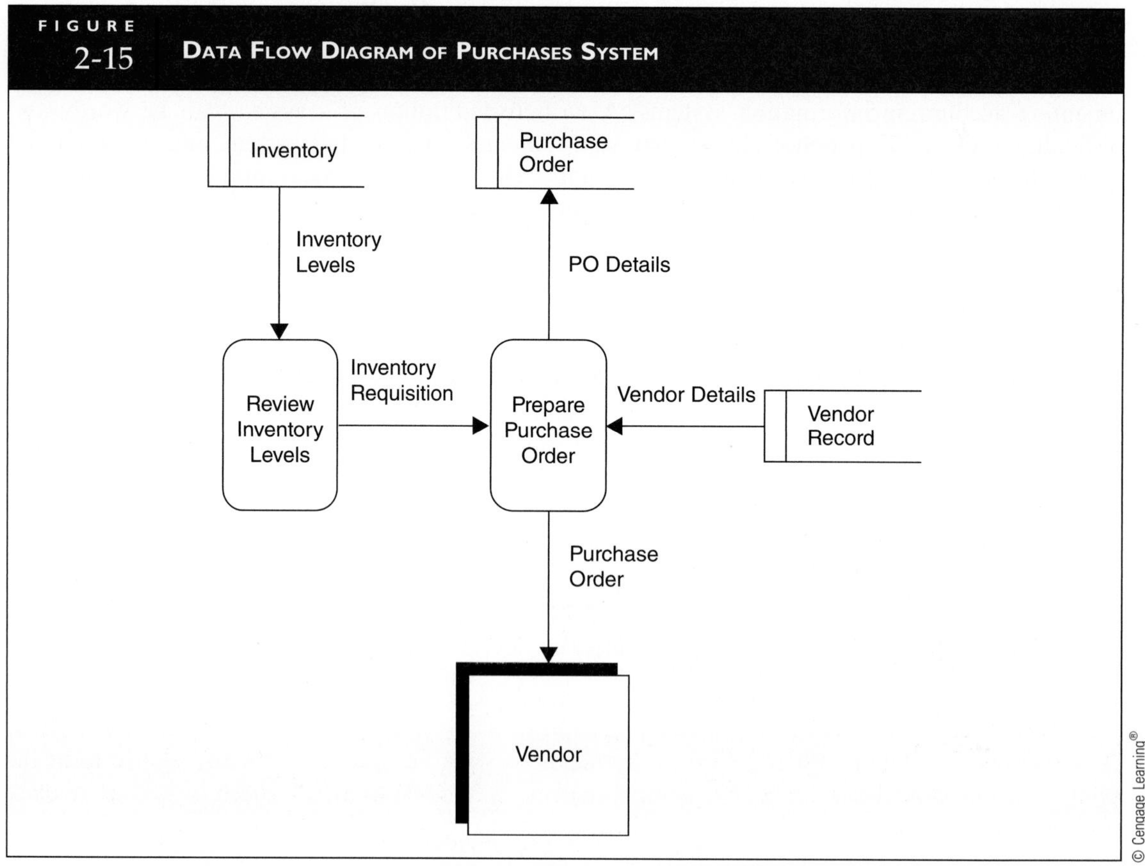

detailed. In Chapter 14, we will study the construction of multilevel DFDs. At this point, a single-level DFD is sufficient to demonstrate its role as a documentation tool. Figure 2-15 provides an example of this.

Entities in a DFD represent objects that lie outside the system being modeled. They are the sources of and destinations for data. These may be other interfacing systems or entities external to the organization. As a matter of convention, entities are labeled as singular nouns on a DFD, such as *customer* or *supplier*. Data stores represent the accounting files and records used in each process, and the labeled arrows represent data flows between processes, data stores, and entities.

Processes in the DFD should be labeled with a descriptive verb such as *Review Inventory Levels*, *Prepare Purchase Order*, *Receive Customer Order*, or *Update Accounts Receivable*. Processes should not be represented as nouns like Inventory Warehouse, Purchases Dept., or Sales Dept. The arrows connecting the DFD objects should be labeled to represent specific flows of data such as Inventory Requisition, Purchase Order, or Sales Order. In addition, each data flow label should be uniquely named; the same label should not be attached to two different flow lines in the same DFD. When data flow into a process and out again (to another process), the data have, in some way, been changed. This is true even if the data have not been physically altered. For example, consider the approval process for a purchase order: A purchase order flows into the process, is reviewed for correctness, approved, and flows out to the next process. While physically the same document, the approved PO is different, as a matter of information content, from the unapproved PO that entered the process. Otherwise, the process serves no purpose.

Systems analysts use DFDs extensively to represent the logical elements of the system. This technique does not, however, depict the physical system. In other words, DFDs show what logical tasks are being performed, but not how they are performed or who (or what) is performing them. For example, the DFD in Figure 2-15 does not show whether the Review Inventory Levels process is separated physically from the Prepare Purchase Order process, which compliance with internal control objectives would require.

Entity Relationship Diagrams

An **entity relationship (ER) diagram** is a documentation technique used to represent the relationship between business entities. In this context, the term **entity** applies to anything about which the organization captures data. An entity may be a physical resource (automobile, cash, or inventory), an event (customer order, purchase inventory, or receive payment), or an agent (salesperson, customer, or vendor). One common use for ER diagrams is to model an organization's database, which we examine in detail in Chapters 9 and 10.

Figure 2-16 shows the symbol set used in an ER diagram. The square symbol represents entities in the system. The labeled connecting line represents the nature of the relationship between two entities. The degree of the relationship, called **cardinality**, is the numeric mapping between entities such as one-to-one (1:1), one-to-many (1:M), or many-to-many (M:M).[2] Cardinality reflects normal business rules as well as organizational policy. For instance, the 1:1 cardinality in the first example in Figure 2-16 suggests that each salesperson in the organization is assigned one automobile. If instead the organization's policy were to assign a single (one) automobile to more than one (many) salespersons who share it, this policy would be reflected by a 1:M relationship. Similarly, the M:M relationship between vendor and inventory in Figure 2-16 implies that the organization buys the same type of products from one or more vendors. A company policy to buy particular items from a single vendor only would be represented by a 1:M cardinality.

System designers identify organization entities and prepare a model of them, similar to the one presented in Figure 2-17. This **data model** is the blueprint for what ultimately will become the physical database. The data model presented in our example is not, however, sufficiently refined to be the plan for a workable database. Constructing a realistic data model is an advanced topic that involves understanding and applying techniques and rules that are presented in Chapters 9 and 10.

FIGURE 2-16 ENTITY RELATIONSHIP DIAGRAM SYMBOLS

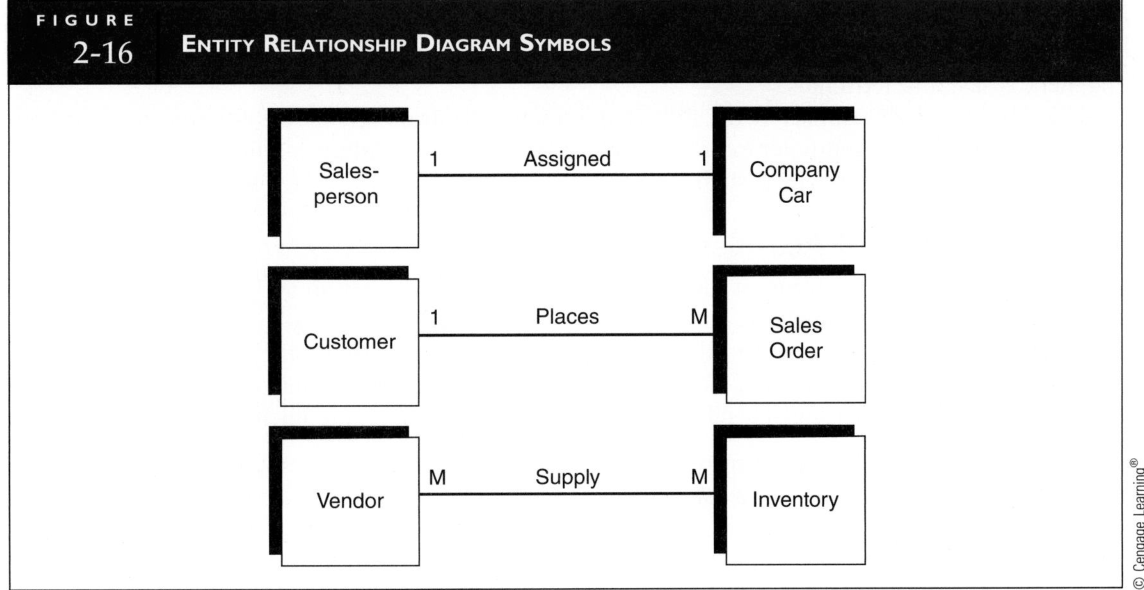

2 We will study variants of these three basic cardinalities in Chapter 9 when we examine data modeling in greater detail. At that time a more precise documentation technique for representing cardinality called *crow's foot notation* will be introduced.

FIGURE 2-17 DATA MODEL

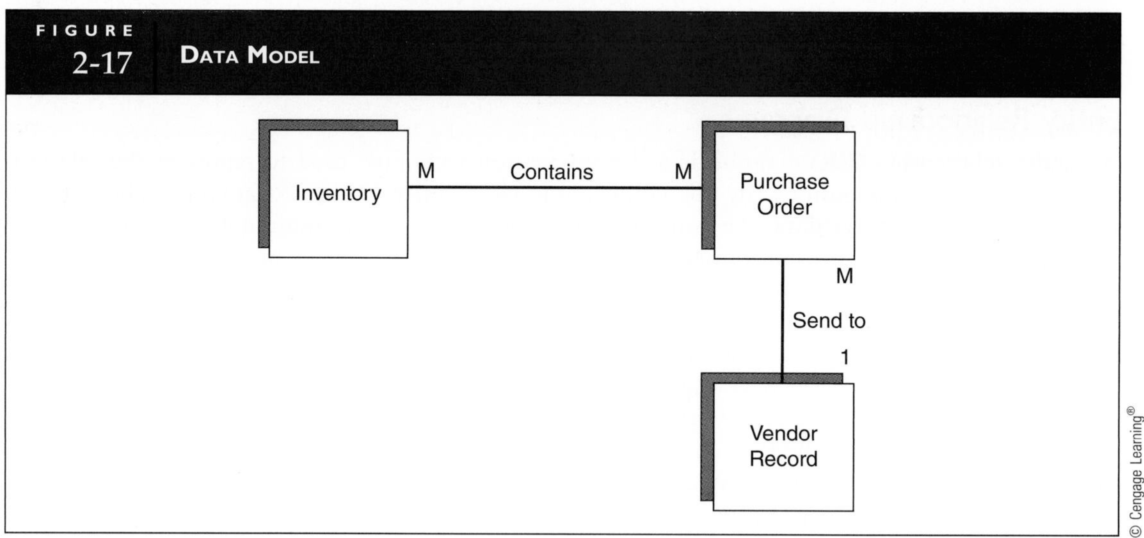

Relationship between ER Diagrams and Data Flow Diagrams

DFDs and ER diagrams document different aspects of systems, but they are related. DFDs model system processes while ER diagrams model the data used in systems. Each data store in a DFD is represented as an entity in a corresponding ER diagram. Figure 2-17 presents the ER diagram for the DFD in Figure 2-15.

SYSTEM FLOWCHARTS

A **system flowchart** is the graphical representation of the *physical* relationships among key elements of a system. These elements may include organizational departments, manual activities, computer programs, hard-copy accounting records (documents, journals, ledgers, and files), and digital records (reference files, transaction files, archive files, and master files).[3] System flowcharts also describe the physical computer media being employed in the system, such as magnetic tape, magnetic disks, and terminals.

The flowcharting examples in the following sections illustrate techniques for representing both manual activities and computer processes. We begin by documenting manual activities and will add computer processes to the system later.

Flowcharting Manual Activities

To demonstrate the flowcharting of manual activities, let's assume that an auditor needs to flowchart a sales order system to evaluate its internal controls and procedures. The auditor will begin by interviewing individuals involved in the sales order process to determine what they do. This information will be captured in a set of written facts similar to those below. Keep in mind that the purpose here is to demonstrate flowcharting. Therefore, for clarity, the system facts are intentionally simplistic.

1. A clerk in the sales department receives a hard-copy customer order by mail and manually prepares four hard copies of a sales order.

---

3 This terminology is a slight departure from the accounting convention that I have followed in earlier editions of this text in which a distinction is drawn between *document flowcharts* and *system flowcharts*. The term *document flowchart* was coined at a time when systems that exclusively employed manual recording and posting activities, and paper (hard copy) documents, journals, and ledgers were commonplace. Today, few functional systems fall into this category; even basic modern accounting systems incorporate both manual and computer operations. Apart from being obsolete, I have found that the term document flowchart can be misleading for students attempting to master flowcharting. Therefore, in this text we will use the term system flowchart or simply *flowchart* for representing the physical accounting system, whether it is manual, computer-based, or has elements of both.

2. The clerk sends Copy 1 of the sales order to the credit department for approval. The other three copies and the original customer order are filed temporarily, pending credit approval.
3. The credit department clerk validates the customer's order against hard-copy credit records kept in the credit department. The clerk signs Copy 1 to signify approval and returns it to the sales clerk.
4. When the sales clerk receives credit approval, he or she files Copy 1 and the customer order in the department. The clerk sends Copy 2 to the warehouse and Copies 3 and 4 to the shipping department.
5. The warehouse clerk picks the products from the shelves, records the transfer in the hard-copy stock records, and sends the products and Copy 2 to the shipping department.
6. The shipping department receives Copy 2 and the goods from the warehouse, attaches Copy 2 as a packing slip, and ships the goods to the customer. Finally, the clerk files Copies 3 and 4 in the shipping department.

Based on these facts, the auditor can create a flowchart of this partial system. It is important to note that flowcharting is as much an art form as it is a technical skill, giving the flowchart author a great deal of license. Nevertheless, the primary objective should be to provide an unambiguous description of the system. With this in mind, certain rules and conventions need to be observed:

1. The flowchart should be labeled to clearly identify the system that it represents.
2. The correct symbols should be used to represent the various entities in the system.
3. All symbols on the flowchart should be labeled.
4. Lines should have arrowheads to clearly show the process flow direction and sequence of events.
5. If complex processes need additional explanation for clarity, a text description should be included on the flowchart or in an attached document referenced by the flowchart.

LAY OUT THE PHYSICAL AREAS OF ACTIVITY. Remember that a flowchart reflects the physical system, which is represented as vertical columns of events and actions separated by lines of demarcation. Generally, each of these areas of activity is a separate column with a heading. From the written system facts, we see that there are four distinct areas of activity: sales department, credit department, warehouse, and shipping department. The first step in preparing the flowchart is to lay out these areas of activity and label each of them. This step is illustrated in Figure 2-18.

TRANSCRIBE THE WRITTEN FACTS INTO VISUAL FORMAT. At this point we are ready to start visually representing the system facts. The symbols used for this purpose will be selected from the set presented in Figure 2-19. We begin with the first stated fact:

1. *A clerk in the sales department receives a hard-copy customer order by mail and manually prepares four hard copies of a sales order.*

Figure 2-20 illustrates how this fact is represented. The customer is the source of the order but is not part of the system. The oval object is typically used to convey a data source or destination that is separate from the system being flowcharted. The document symbol entering the sales department signifies the hard-copy customer order and is labeled accordingly. The bucket-shaped symbol represents a manual process. In this case, the clerk in the sales department prepares four copies of the sales order. Notice that the clerk's task, not the clerk, is depicted. The arrows between the objects show the direction of flow and the sequence of events.

By transcribing each fact in this way, we systematically construct a flowchart. See how the second and third facts restated below add to the flowchart in Figure 2-21.

2. *The clerk sends Copy 1 of the sales order to the credit department for approval. The other three copies and the original customer order are filed temporarily, pending credit approval.*
3. *The credit department clerk validates the customer's order against hard-copy credit records kept in the credit department. The clerk signs Copy 1 to signify approval and returns it to the sales clerk.*

FIGURE 2-18 FLOWCHART SHOWING AREAS OF ACTIVITY

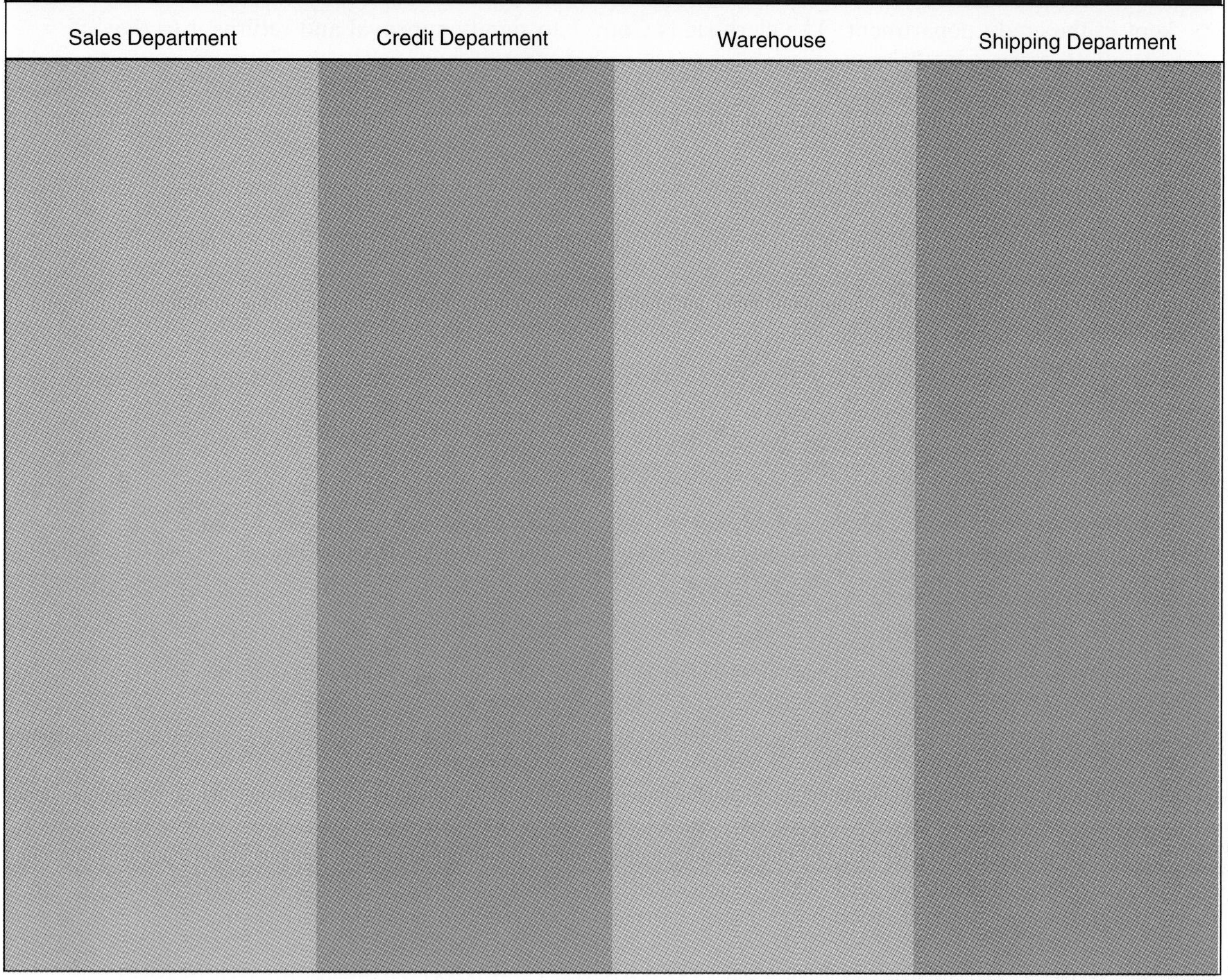

Sales Department	Credit Department	Warehouse	Shipping Department

Two new symbols are introduced in this figure. First, the inverted triangle symbol represents the temporary file mentioned in Fact 2. This is a physical file of paper documents such as a drawer in a filing cabinet or desk. Such files are typically arranged according to a specified order. To signify the filing system used, the file symbol will usually contain an "N" for numeric (invoice number), "C" for chronological (date), or "A" for alphabetic order (customer name). Secondly, the parallelogram shape represents the credit records mentioned in Fact 3. This symbol is used to depict many types of hard-copy accounting records, such as journals, subsidiary ledgers, general ledgers, and shipping logs.

Having laid these foundations, let's now complete the flowchart by depicting the remaining facts.

4. *When the sales clerk receives credit approval, he or she files Copy 1 and the customer order in the department. The clerk sends Copy 2 to the warehouse and Copies 3 and 4 to the shipping department.*
5. *The warehouse clerk picks the products from the shelves, records the transfer in the hard-copy stock records, and sends the products and Copy 2 to the shipping department.*
6. *The shipping department receives Copy 2 and the goods from the warehouse, attaches Copy 2 as a packing slip, and ships the goods to the customer. Finally, the clerk files Copies 3 and 4 in the shipping department.*

FIGURE 2-19 **Symbol Set for Representing Manual Procedures**

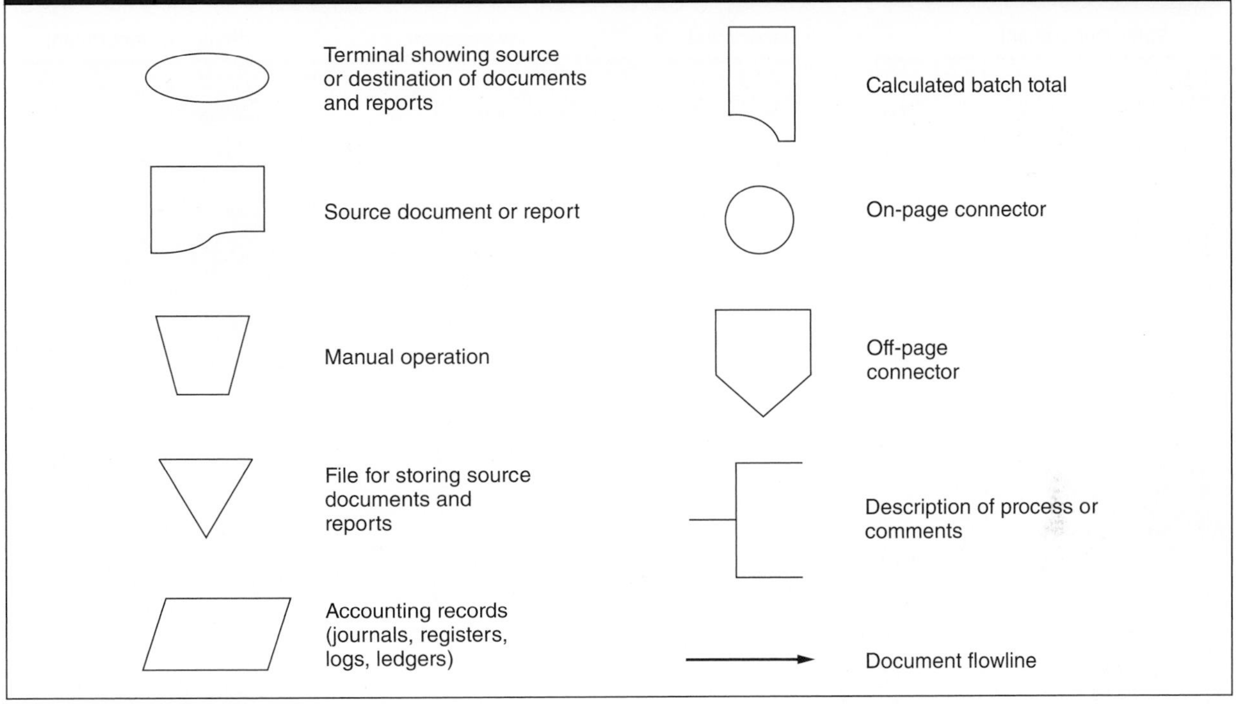

FIGURE 2-20 **Flowchart Showing Stated Fact 1 Translated into Visual Symbols**

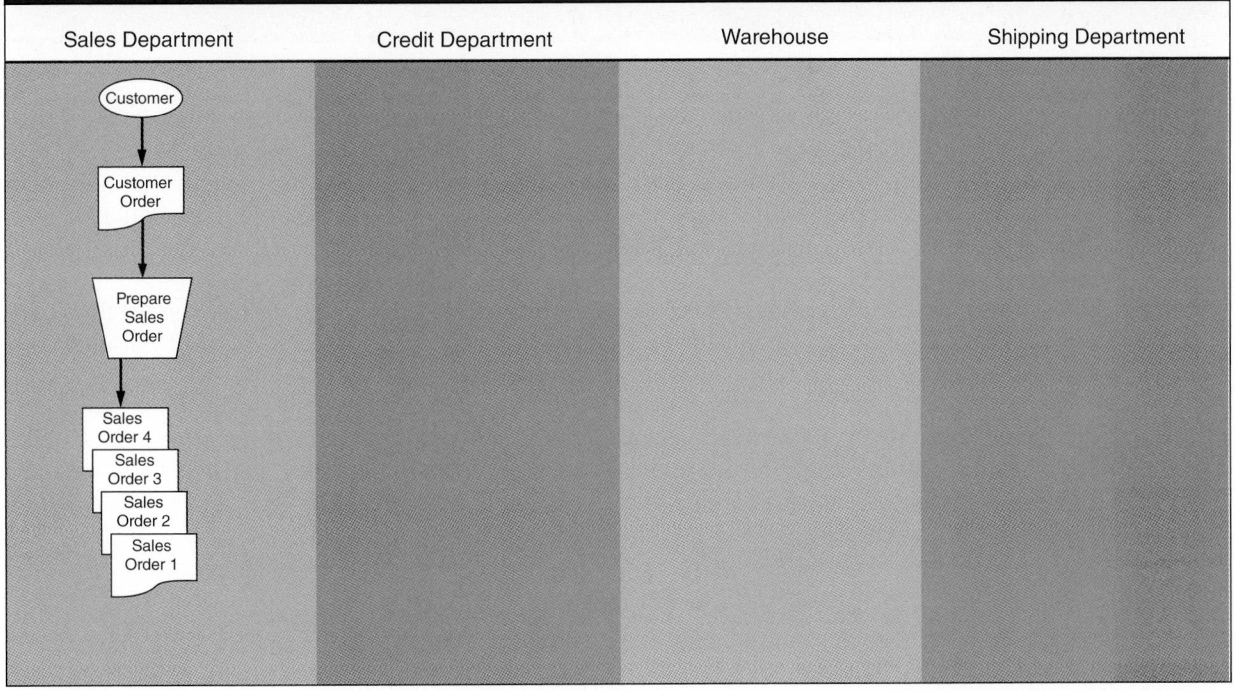

FIGURE 2-21 FLOWCHART SHOWING STATED FACTS 1, 2, AND 3 TRANSLATED INTO VISUAL SYMBOLS

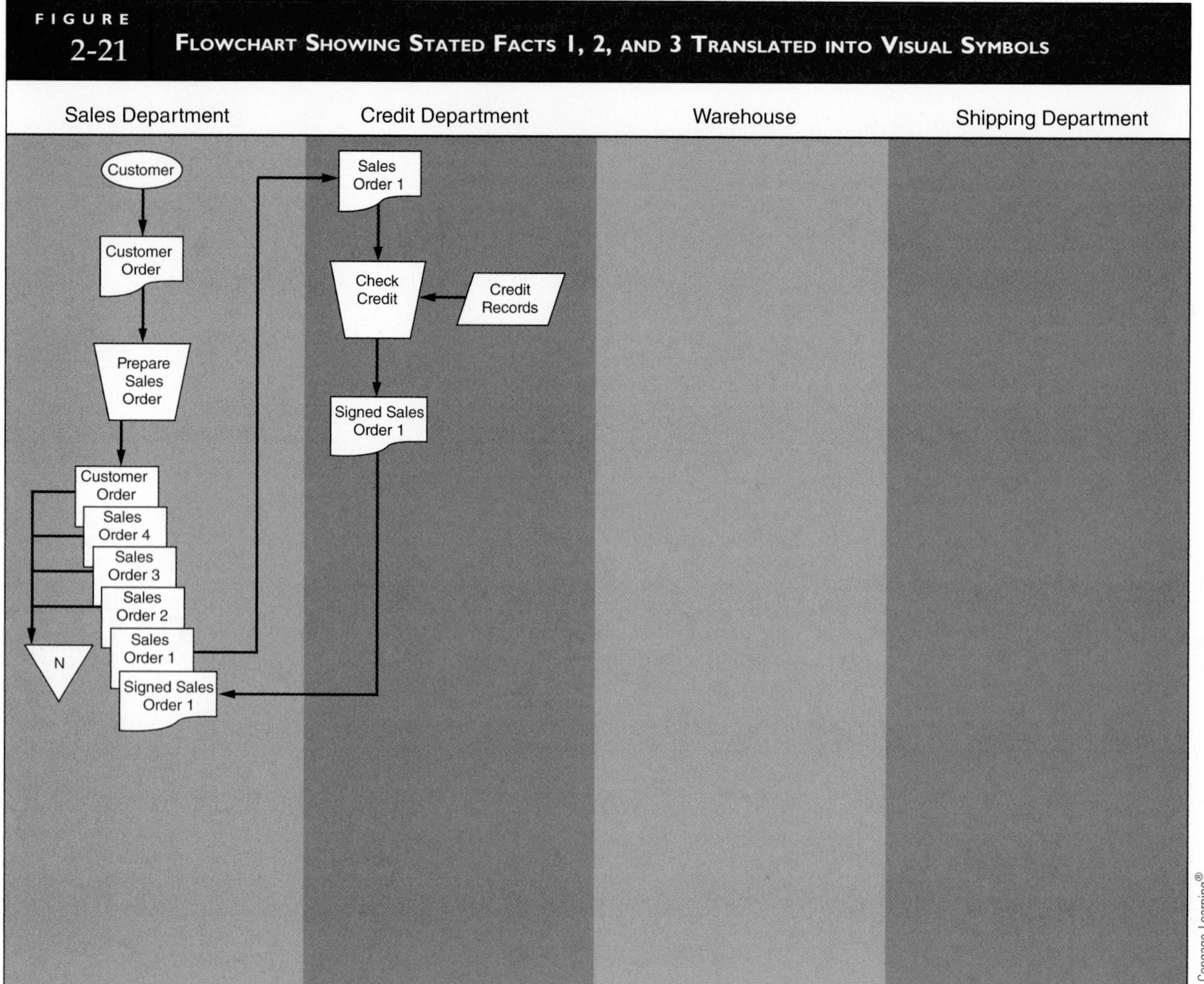

The completed flowchart is presented in Figure 2-22. Notice the circular symbol labeled "A." This is an on-page connector used to replace flow lines that otherwise would cause excessive clutter on the page. In this instance, the connector replaces the lines that signify the movement of Copies 3 and 4 from the sales department to the shipping department. Lines should be used whenever possible to promote clarity. Restricted use of connectors, however, can improve the readability of the flowchart.

Notice also that the physical products or goods mentioned in Fact 5 are not shown on the flowchart. The document (Copy 2) that accompanies and controls the goods, however, is shown. Typically, a system flowchart shows only the flow of documents, not physical assets.

Finally, for visual clarity, system flowcharts show the processing of a single transaction only. You should keep in mind, however, that transactions may flow through a system in batches (groups) rather than as single events. Batch processing involves gathering together large numbers of similar transactions and processing them as a single unit of work. This provides for certain operational efficiencies that are discussed in a later section of this chapter.

Flowcharting Computer Processes

We now examine flowcharting techniques to represent a system that employs both manual and computer processes. The symbol set used to construct this system flowchart will come from both

FIGURE 2-22 FLOWCHART SHOWING ALL STATED FACTS TRANSLATED INTO VISUAL SYMBOLS

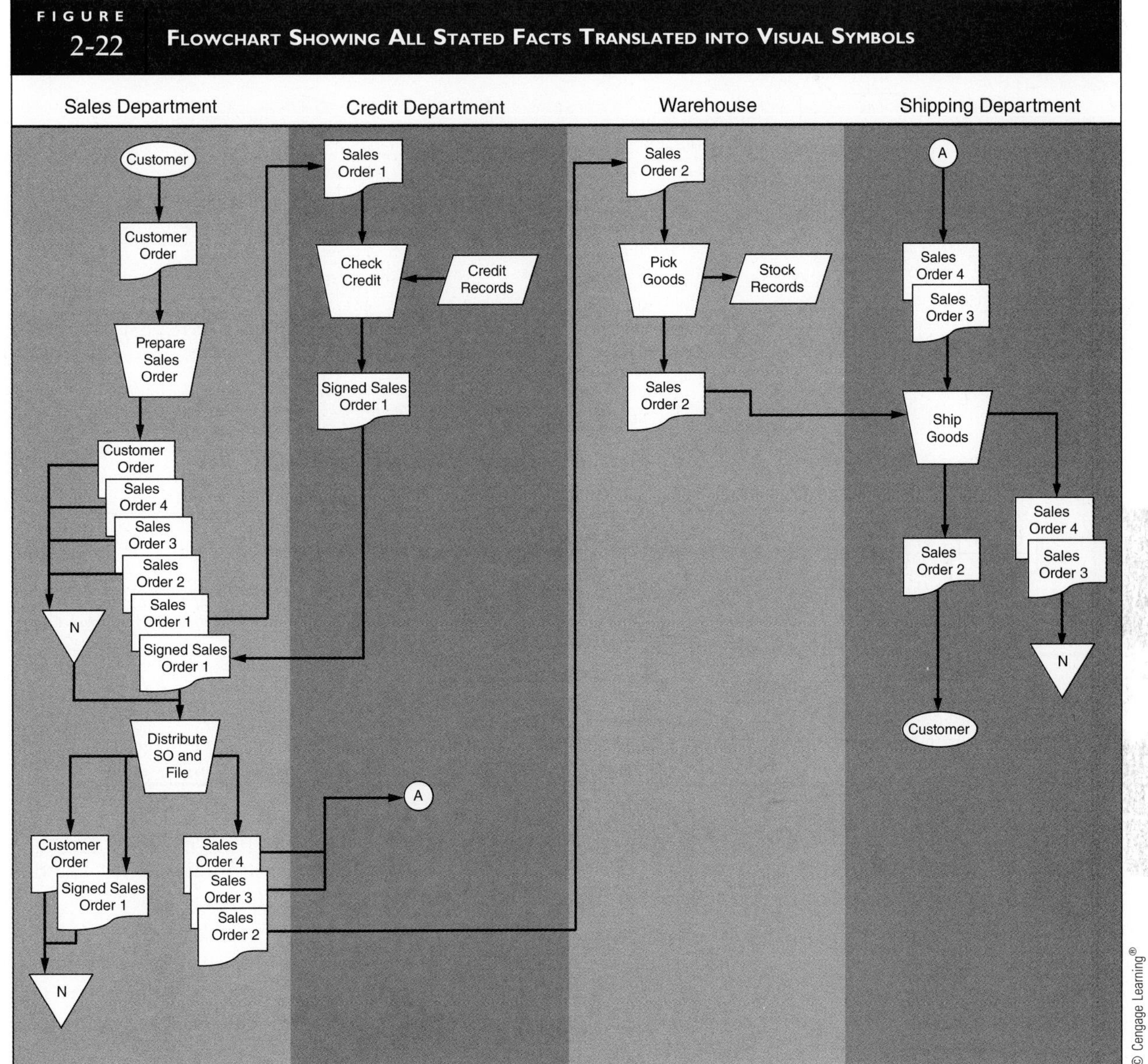

Figure 2-19 and Figure 2-23. Again, our example is based on a sales order system with the following facts:

1. *A clerk in the sales department receives a customer order by mail and enters the information into a computer terminal that is networked to a centralized computer program in the computer operations department. The original customer order is filed in the sales department.*

   Facts 2, 3, and 4 relate to activities that occur in the computer operations department.

2. *A computer program edits the transactions for data entry errors, checks the customers' credit by referencing a credit history file, and produces a transaction file of sales orders.*
3. *The sales order transaction file is then processed by an update program that posts the transactions to corresponding records in AR and inventory files.*
4. *Finally, the update program produces three hard copies of the sales order. Copy 1 is sent to the warehouse, and Copies 2 and 3 are sent to the shipping department.*

FIGURE 2-23 Symbol Set for Representing Computer Processes

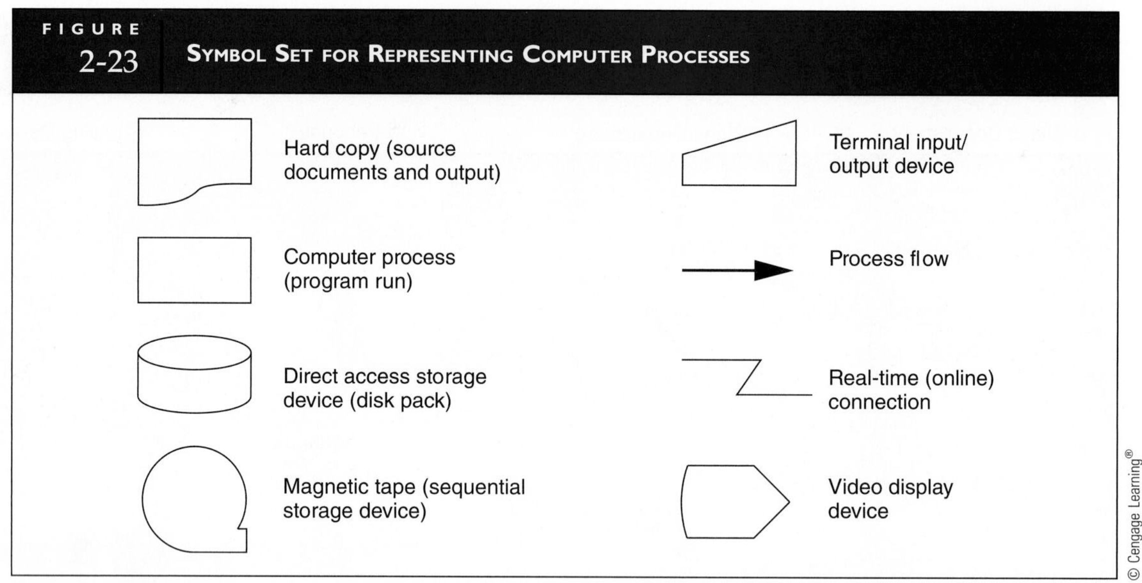

5. *On receipt of Copy 1, the warehouse clerk picks the products from the shelves. Using Copy 1 and the warehouse personal computer (PC), the clerk records the inventory transfer in the digital stock records that are kept on the PC. Next, the clerk sends the physical inventory and Copy 1 to the shipping department.*
6. *The shipping department receives Copy 1 and the goods from the warehouse. The clerk reconciles the goods with Copies 1, 2, and 3 and attaches Copy 1 as a packing slip. Next, the clerk ships the goods (with Copy 1 attached) to the customer. Finally, the clerk records the shipment in the hard-copy shipping log and files Copies 2 and 3 in the shipping department.*

LAY OUT THE PHYSICAL AREAS OF ACTIVITY. The flowcharting process begins by creating a template that depicts the areas of activity similar to the one shown in Figure 2-18. The differences in this case are that this system has a computer operations department and does not have a credit department.

TRANSCRIBE THE WRITTEN FACTS INTO VISUAL FORMAT. As with the manual system example, the next step is to systematically transcribe the written facts into visual objects. Figure 2-24 illustrates how Facts 1, 2, and 3 translate visually.

The customer, customer order, and file symbols in this flowchart are the same as in the previous example. The sales clerk's activity, however, is now automated, and the manual process symbol has been replaced with a computer terminal symbol. Also, because this is a data-input operation, the arrowhead on the flowchart line points in the direction of the edit and credit check program. If the terminal was also used to receive output (the facts do not specify such an operation), arrowheads would be on both ends of the line.

Recall that the emphasis in flowcharting is on the physical system. For example, the terminal used by the sales clerk to enter customer orders is physically located in the sales department, but the programs that process the transactions and the files that it uses and updates are stored in a separate computer operations department.

Notice how the flow line points from the credit history file to the edit program. This indicates that the file is read (referenced) but not changed (updated) by the program. In contrast, the interactions between the update program and the AR and inventory files are in the opposite direction. The relevant records in these files have been changed to reflect the transactions. The file update process is explained later in the chapter.

Let's now translate the remaining facts into visual symbols. Fact 4 states that the update program produces three hard-copy documents in the computer operations department, which are

FIGURE 2-24 FLOWCHART SHOWING THE TRANSLATION OF FACTS 1, 2, AND 3 INTO VISUAL SYMBOLS

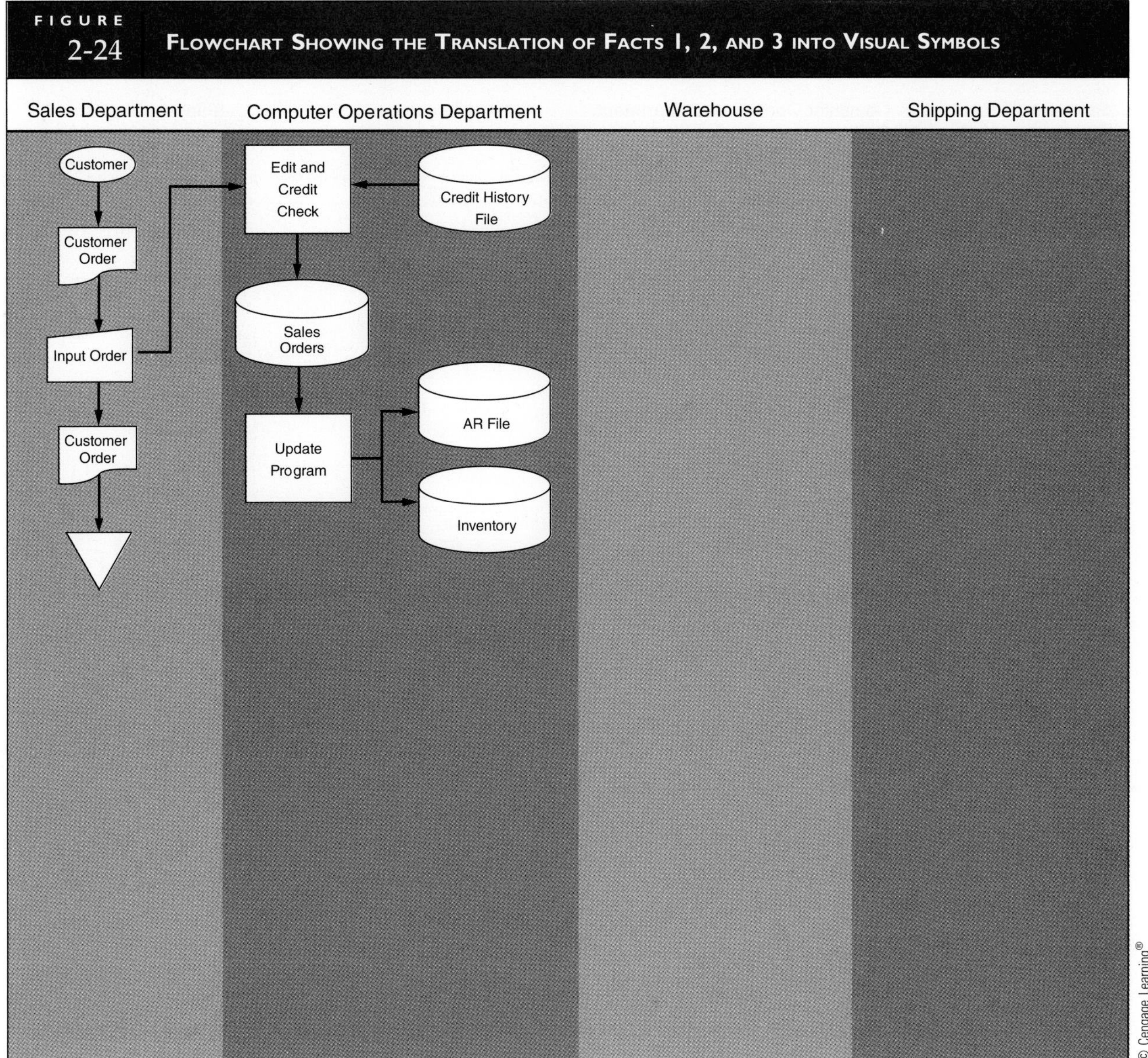

then distributed to the warehouse and shipping departments. The translation of this fact is illustrated in Figure 2-25.

Fact 5 states that the warehouse clerk updates the stock records on the department PC and then sends the physical inventory and Copy 1 to the shipping department. Notice on Figure 2-25 how this computer activity is represented; the warehouse PC is a stand-alone computer system that is not networked into the computer operations department like the terminal in the sales department. The PC, the stock record update program, and the stock records themselves are all physically located in the warehouse. As with manual procedures, when documenting computer operations the flowchart author must accurately represent the physical arrangement of the system components. As we will see in later chapters, the physical arrangement of system components (both manual and computer) often plays an important role in the auditor's assessment of internal control.

Finally, Fact 6 describes how the shipping department clerk reconciles the goods with the supporting documents, sends the goods and the packing slip to the customer, updates the shipping log, and files two copies of the sales order. This is entirely a manual operation, as evidenced by the symbols in Figure 2-25. Note that the shipping log uses the same symbol that is used for representing journals and ledgers.

FIGURE 2-25 FLOWCHART SHOWING ALL FACTS TRANSLATED INTO VISUAL SYMBOLS

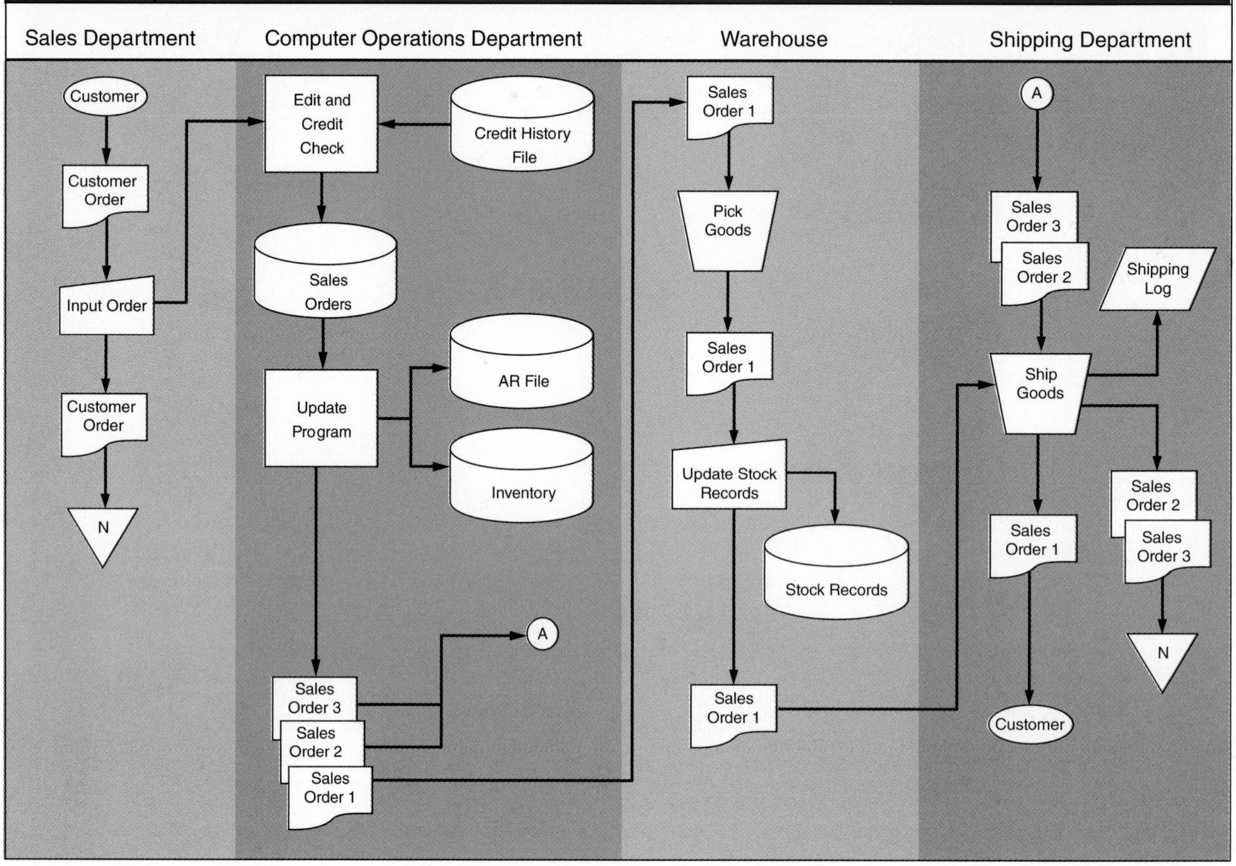

Sales Department
Computer Operations Department
Warehouse
Shipping Department
Customer
Customer Order
Input Order
Customer Order
N
Edit and Credit Check
Credit History File
Sales Orders
Update Program
AR File
Inventory
A
Sales Order 3
Sales Order 2
Sales Order 1
Sales Order 1
Pick Goods
Sales Order 1
Update Stock Records
Stock Records
Sales Order 1
A
Sales Order 3
Sales Order 2
Shipping Log
Ship Goods
Sales Order 2
Sales Order 3
Sales Order 1
N
Customer

PROGRAM FLOWCHARTS

The system flowchart in Figure 2-25 shows the relationship between computer programs, the files they use, and the outputs they produce. This high-level documentation, however, does not provide all the operational details that are sometimes needed. For example, an auditor wishing to assess the correctness of the edit program's logic cannot do so from the system flowchart. This requires a **program flowchart**. The symbol set used for program flowcharts is presented in Figure 2-26.

FIGURE 2-26 PROGRAM FLOWCHART SYMBOLS

Logical process
Terminal start or end operation
Input/output operation (read and write records)
Decision
Flow of logical process

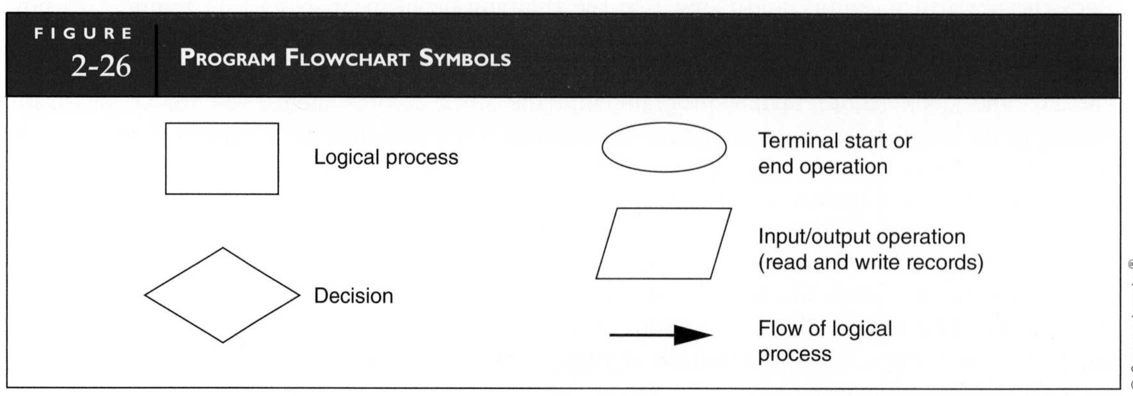

Every program represented in a system flowchart should have a supporting program flowchart that describes its logic. Figure 2-27 presents the logic of the edit program shown in Figure 2-28. A separate symbol represents each step of the program's logic, and each symbol represents one or more lines of computer program code. The connector lines between the symbols establish the logical order of execution. Tracing the flowchart downward from the start symbol, we see that the program performs the following logical steps in the order listed:

1. The program retrieves a single record from the unedited transaction file and stores it in memory.
2. The first logical test is to see if the program has reached the end-of-file (EOF) condition for the transaction file. Most file structures use a special record or marker to indicate an EOF condition. When EOF is reached, the edit program will terminate and the next program in the system (in this case, the update program) will be executed. As long as there is a record in the unedited transaction file, the result of the EOF test will be "no" and process control is passed to the next logical step in the edit program.
3. Processing involves a series of tests to identify certain clerical and logical errors. Each test, represented by a decision symbol, evaluates the presence or absence of a condition. For example, an edit test could be to detect the presence of alphabetic data in a field that should contain only numeric data. We examine specific edit and validation tests in Chapter 3.
4. Error-free records are sent to the edited transaction file.
5. Records containing errors are sent to the error file.
6. The program loops back to Step 1, and the process is repeated until the EOF condition is reached.

FIGURE 2-27 PROGRAM FLOWCHART FOR EDIT PROGRAM

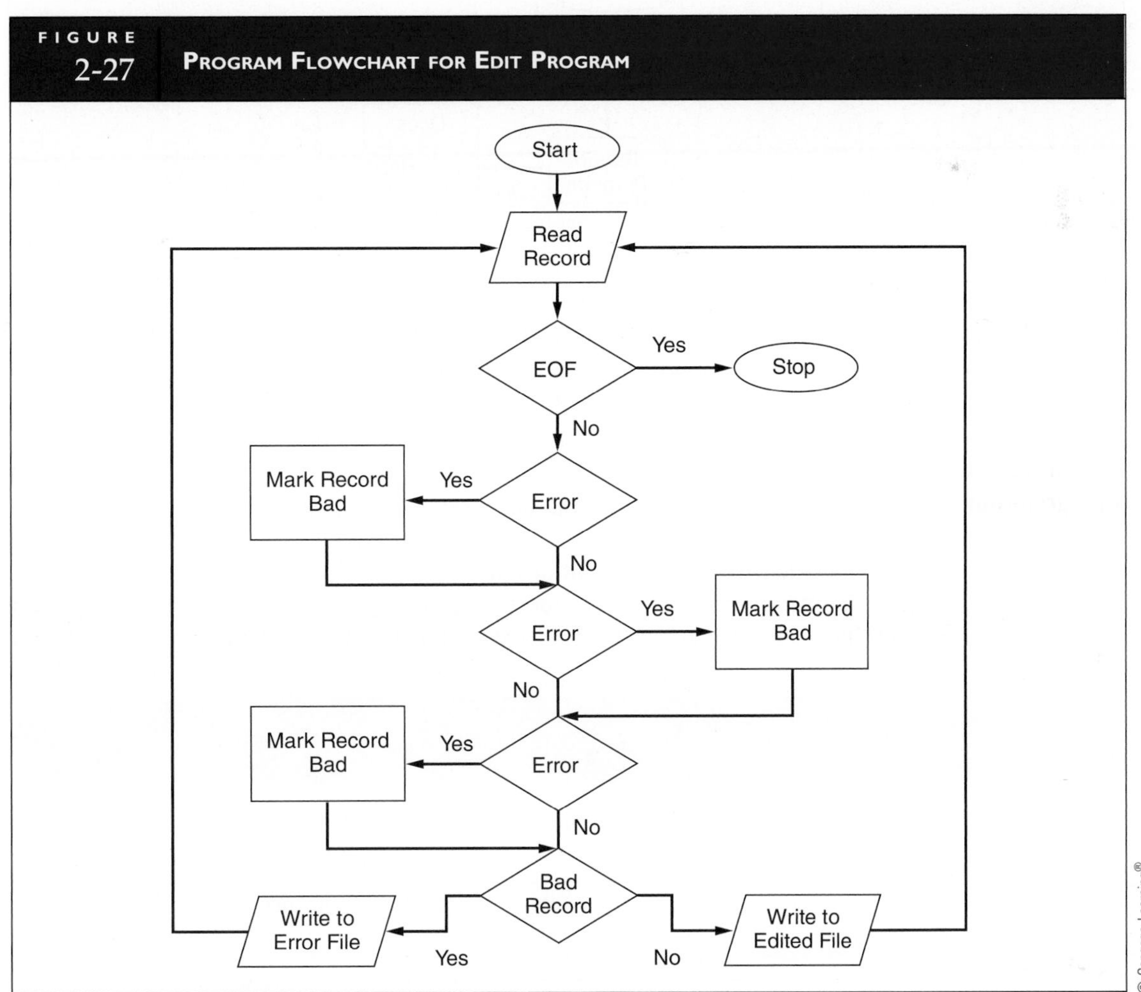

FIGURE 2-28 SYSTEM FLOWCHART

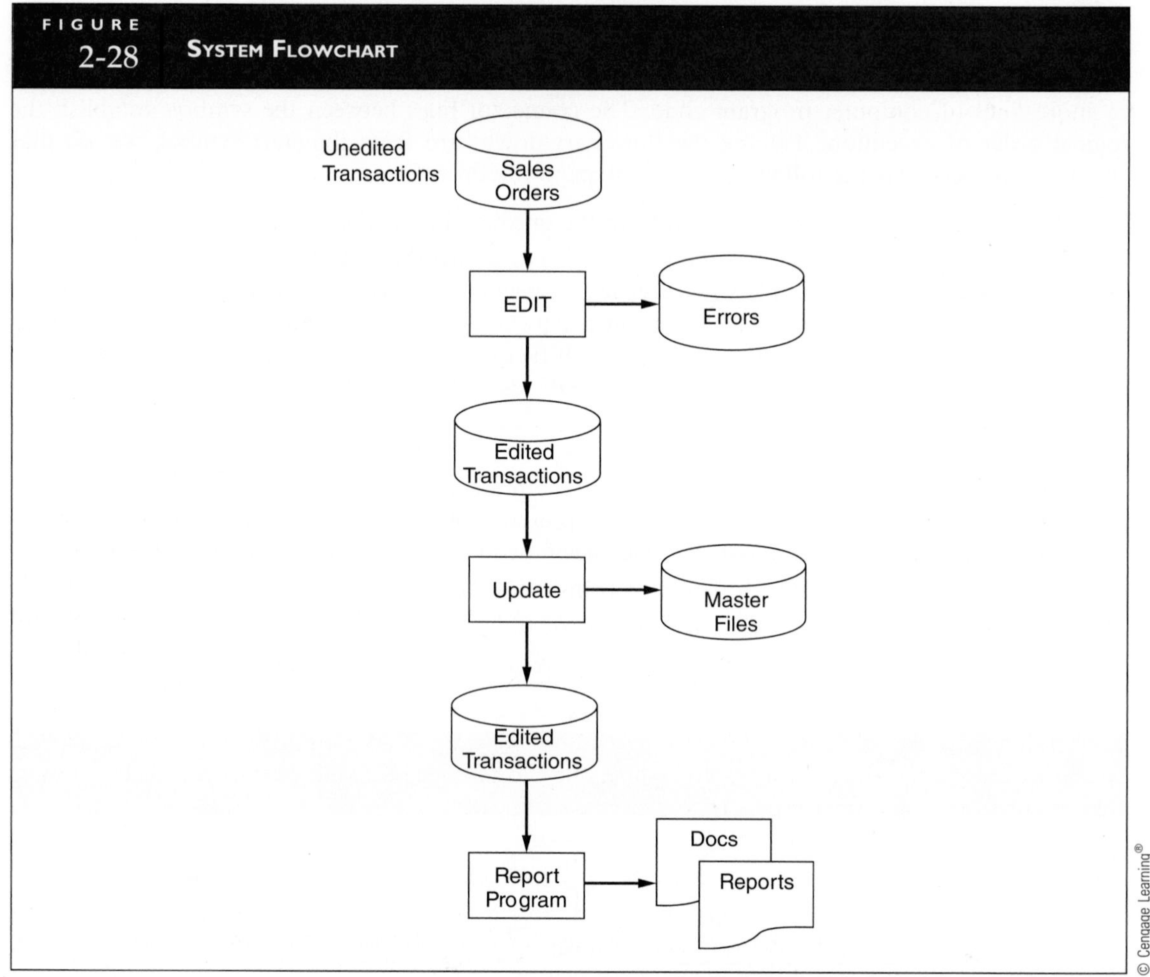

Accountants sometimes use program flowcharts to verify the correctness of program logic. They compare flowcharts to the actual program code to determine whether the program is actually doing what the documentation describes. Program flowcharts provide essential details for conducting IT application audits, which we examine in Chapter 17.

RECORD LAYOUT DIAGRAMS

Record layout diagrams are used to reveal the internal structure of digital records in a flat-file or database table. The layout diagram usually shows the name, data type, and length of each attribute (or field) in the record. Detailed data structure information is needed for such tasks as identifying certain types of system failures, analyzing error reports, and designing tests of computer logic for debugging and auditing purposes. A simpler form of record layout, shown in Figure 2-29, suits our

FIGURE 2-29 RECORD LAYOUT DIAGRAM FOR CUSTOMER FILE

Customer File

Key

Customer Number	Customer Name	Street Address	City	State	Zip Code	Credit Limit

purposes best. This type of layout shows the content of a record. Each data attribute and key field is shown in terms of its name and relative location in the record.

Transaction Processing Models

This section in the chapter examines alternative transaction processing models, which fall broadly into two types: (1) batch processing and (2) real-time processing. Batch processing involves gathering transactions into groups or batches and then processing the entire batch as a single event. Real time processing systems process individual transactions continuously as they occur. Many systems incorporate both real-time and batch processing features. Systems designers base their configuration choices on a variety of considerations. Table 2-1 summarizes some of the distinguishing characteristics of batch and real-time processing that feature prominently in these decisions.

DIFFERENCES BETWEEN BATCH AND REAL-TIME SYSTEMS

Information Time Frame

Because **batch systems** assemble transactions into groups for processing, a time lag will always exist between the point at which an economic event occurs and the point at which it is processed by the system and reflected in the firm's accounts. The length of lag (minutes or weeks) depends on the frequency of batch processing. For example, payroll processing is typically a batch system with long lag times. The economic events—the application of employee labor—occur continuously throughout the pay period. At the end of the period (a week or a month), the paychecks for all employees are prepared together as a batch. On the other hand, **real-time systems** process transactions individually at the moment the event occurs; therefore, no time lags exist between occurrence and processing. An example of real-time processing is an airline reservations system, which processes transactions from one traveler at a time while he or she waits.

Resources

Generally, batch systems demand fewer organization resources (such as programming costs, computer time, and user training) than real-time systems. For example, because the programming logic of batch systems is generally simpler than that of equivalent real-time systems, they tend to have shorter development periods and are easier for programmers to maintain. On the other hand, a large portion of total programming costs for real-time systems are incurred in designing user interfaces. Real-time systems must be user-friendly, forgiving, and easy to work with. Pop-up menus, online tutorials, and special help features require additional programming and add to the cost of the system.

In addition, real-time systems require dedicated processing capacity because they must deal with transactions as they occur. Some real-time systems need to be available 24 hours a day whether they are being used or not. The computer capacity dedicated to such systems cannot be used for other purposes. Thus, implementing a real-time system may require either the purchase

TABLE 2-1 CHARACTERISTIC DIFFERENCES BETWEEN BATCH AND REAL-TIME PROCESSING

	Data Processing Methods	
Distinguishing Feature	Batch	Real-Time
Information time frame	Lag exists between time when the economic event occurs and when it is recorded.	No time lag exists. Processing takes place when the economic event occurs.
Resources	Generally, fewer resources (e.g., hardware, programming, training) are required.	More resources are required than for batch processing.
Operational efficiency	Certain records are processed after the event to avoid operational delays.	Operational delays are not an issue. All records pertaining to the event are processed immediately.

of a dedicated computer or an investment in additional computer capacity. In contrast, batch systems use computer capacity only when the program is being run. When the batch job completes processing, the freed capacity can be reallocated to other applications.

Operational Efficiency

Real-time processing of large volumes of transactions can create operational inefficiencies. A single transaction may affect several different accounts. Some of these accounts, however, may not need to be updated in real time, and the task of doing so takes time that, when multiplied by thousands of transactions, can cause significant processing delays. Batch processing of noncritical accounts, however, improves operational efficiency by eliminating unnecessary activities at critical points in the process.

Efficiency versus Effectiveness

In selecting a transaction processing mode, the designer must consider the trade-off between efficiency and effectiveness. When immediate access to current information is critical to the user's needs, real-time processing is the logical choice. When time lags in information have no detrimental effects on the user's performance, and operational efficiencies can be achieved by processing data in batches, batch processing may be the best choice.

UPDATING MASTER FILES FROM TRANSACTIONS

Whether batch or real-time processing is being used, updating a master file record involves changing the value of one or more of its variable fields to reflect the effects of a transaction. Figure 2-30 presents record structures for a sales order transaction file and two associated master files, AR subsidiary ledger and inventory subsidiary ledger. The primary key (PK)—the unique identifier—for the inventory file is INVENTORY NUMBER. The primary key for AR is ACCOUNT NUMBER. Notice that the record structure for the sales order file contains a primary key (SALES ORDER NUMBER) and two secondary key (SK) fields, ACCOUNT NUMBER and

FIGURE 2-30 RECORD STRUCTURES FOR SALES, INVENTORY, AND ACCOUNTS RECEIVABLE FILES

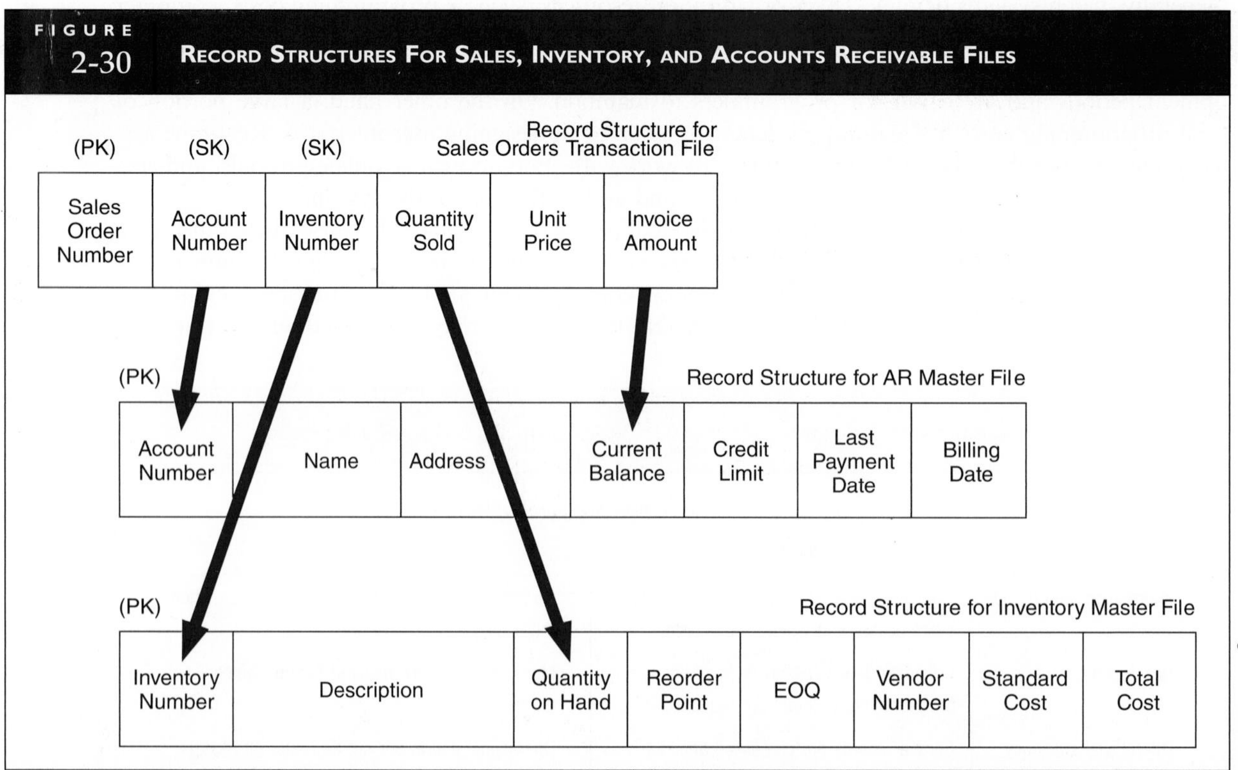

INVENTORY NUMBER. These secondary keys are used for locating the corresponding records in the master files. To simplify the example, we assume that each sale is for a single item of inventory only.[4] The update procedure in this example involves the following steps:

1. The computer update program reads a sales order record.
2. ACCOUNT NUMBER is used to search the AR master file and retrieve the corresponding AR record.
3. The update program calculates the new customer balance by adding the value stored in the INVOICE AMOUNT field of the sales order record to the CURRENT BALANCE field value in the AR master record.
4. Next, INVENTORY NUMBER is used to search for the corresponding record in the inventory master file.
5. The update program reduces inventory levels by deducting the QUANTITY SOLD value in a transaction record from the QUANTITY ON HAND field value in the inventory record.
6. A new sales order record is read, and the process is repeated.

Master File Backup Procedures

Master file backup is a standard procedure in transaction processing systems to maintain master file integrity in the event that any of the following problems should occur:

1) An update program error corrupts the master files being updated.
2) Undetected errors in the transaction data result in corrupted master file balances.
3) A disaster such as a fire or flood physically destroys current master files.

If the current master file becomes corrupted or is destroyed, corporate IT professionals can retrieve the most current backed-up file from the archives and use it to reconstruct the current version of the master file. Backup procedures will vary depending on whether batch or real-time processing is being used. File backup is an important IT control issue that we examine in Chapter 3.

BATCH PROCESSING USING REAL-TIME DATA COLLECTION

A popular data processing approach, particularly for large operations, is to digitally capture and process aspects of the transaction at the source as they occur, and process other aspects of the transaction in batch mode. Figure 2-31 illustrates this approach with a sales order system such as that used in a department store. Note that although only one sales department is represented in the system flowchart, such a system could have dozens or even hundreds of sales locations all connected to the same central system. Key steps in the process are the following:

- The sales department clerk captures customer sales data pertaining to the item(s) being purchased and the customer's account.
- The system then checks the customer's credit limit from data in the customer record (account receivable subsidiary file) and updates his or her account balance to reflect the amount of the sale.
- Next the system updates the quantity-on-hand field in the inventory record (inventory subsidiary file) to reflect the reduction in inventory. This provides up-to-date information to other clerks as to inventory availability.
- A record of the sale is then added to the sales order file (transaction file), which is processed in batch mode at the end of the business day. This batch process records each transaction in the sales journal and updates the affected general ledger accounts.

You may be wondering at this point why the sales journal and general ledger accounts are being processed in batch mode. Why not update them in real time along with the subsidiary accounts? The answer is to achieve operational efficiency by avoiding potential processing delays. We examine this issue next.

---

4 Chapter 9 examines database structures that permit more complex and realistic business transactions.

FIGURE 2-31 BATCH PROCESSING WITH REAL-TIME DATA COLLECTION

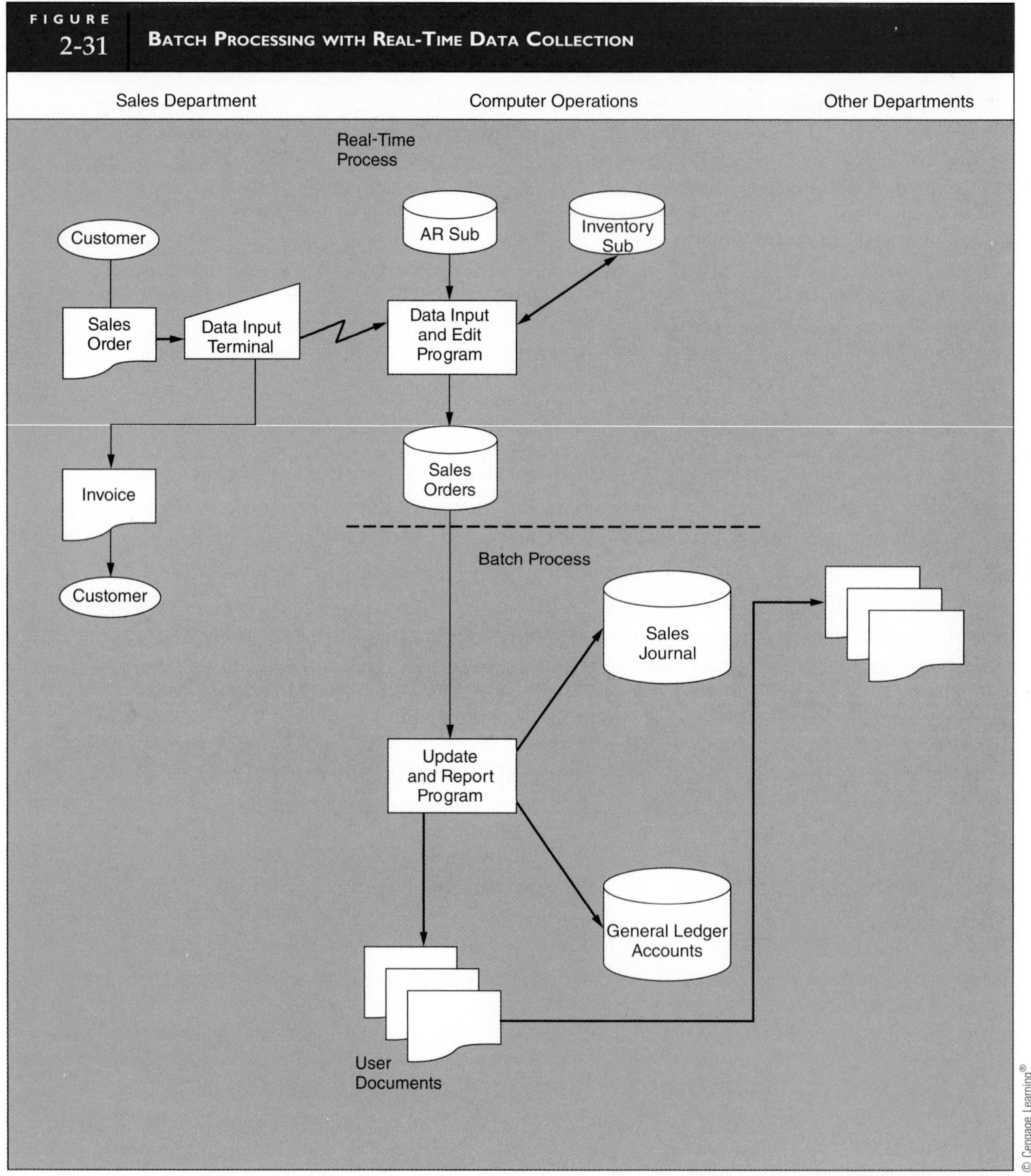

Assume that an organization employs a high volume sales order system, similar to the one in Figure 2-31, which is capable of processing thousands of concurrent transactions from distributed terminals throughout its many large departments.

Each customer sales transaction will affect a change in the following six accounting records:

- Customer account receivable (Subsidiary unique to the customer)
- Inventory item (Subsidiary almost unique)
- Inventory control (GL common to all customers)

- Account receivable control (GL common)
- Sales (GL common)
- Cost of goods sold (GL common)

To maintain the integrity of accounting data, once a particular record is accessed for updating, it is locked by the system and made unavailable to other processes (customer transactions) until the current process is complete. Using the six records here as an example, consider the implications that this data-locking rule has on the customers using the system.

When processing a customer AR subsidiary record, the rule has no implications for other users of the system. Each user accesses only his or her unique record. For example, accessing John Smith's account does not prevent Mary Jones from accessing her account. Updating the inventory subsidiary record is almost unique. Because it is possible, however, that both Mary Jones and John Smith are independently purchasing the same item at the same time, Mary Jones may be kept waiting a few seconds until John Smith's transaction releases the lock on the inventory account, but such rare conflicts will be of little inconvenience to customers. In general, therefore, master file records that are unique to a transaction such as customer accounts and individual inventory records may be updated in real time without causing operational delays.

In high volume data processing systems, however, updating general ledger records in real time may cause data access delays. The general ledger accounts listed above are common to all the customer transactions being processed by the system and would need to be updated by each transaction before it can be completed. If the processing of John Smith's transaction in real time begins before that of Mary Jones, then she will wait only a few seconds until all four general ledger records have been updated before her transaction can proceed. This short delay time, however, when multiplied by hundreds or thousands of users who are processing transactions simultaneously, can result in long delays for customers whose transactions are placed on hold until they can access the GL accounts needed to complete the process.

Also, depending on how record locks are assigned by the system, a disruptive condition called a **deadlock** may result. This happens when one process places a lock on one or more of the records it needs for processing, but has not locked all of them. At the same time a second process places a lock on the remaining record(s) needed by the first. Neither transaction can be completed; they are in a deadlock as both processes wait for the locks to be removed by the other. For example, assume process #1 has a lock on the AR Control - GL record, process #2 has a lock on the Sales- GL record, process #3 has a lock on the Inventory Control GL record, and process #4 has a lock on the CGS GL record. None of these processes can finish updating the GL accounts to complete their transactions. This situation creates a standoff that can bring processing to a halt because a deadlock will never resolve itself without outside intervention. Typically after a period of time when the deadlock is detected the system will terminate the transactions that are furthest from completion and make them restart.

To avoid these problems and to achieve internal control benefits associated with batch processing (discussed in Chapter 3) general ledger accounts are often updated periodically in batch mode. Batch processing may be performed as end-of-day procedures or more frequently throughout the day.

REAL-TIME PROCESSING

Real-time systems process the entire transaction as it occurs. For example, a sales order processed by the system in Figure 2-32 can be captured, filled, and shipped the same day. Such a system has many potential benefits, including improved productivity, reduced inventory, increased inventory turnover, decreased lags in customer billing, and enhanced customer satisfaction. Because transaction information is transmitted electronically, physical source documents can be eliminated or greatly reduced.

Real-time processing is well suited to systems that process lower transaction volumes and those that do not share common records. These systems make extensive use of local area network and wide area network technology. Terminals at distributed sites throughout the organization are used for receiving, processing, and sending information on the status of current transactions. These are linked in a network arrangement so users can communicate. The operational characteristics of networks are examined in Chapter 12.

FIGURE 2-32 REAL-TIME PROCESSING OF SALES ORDERS

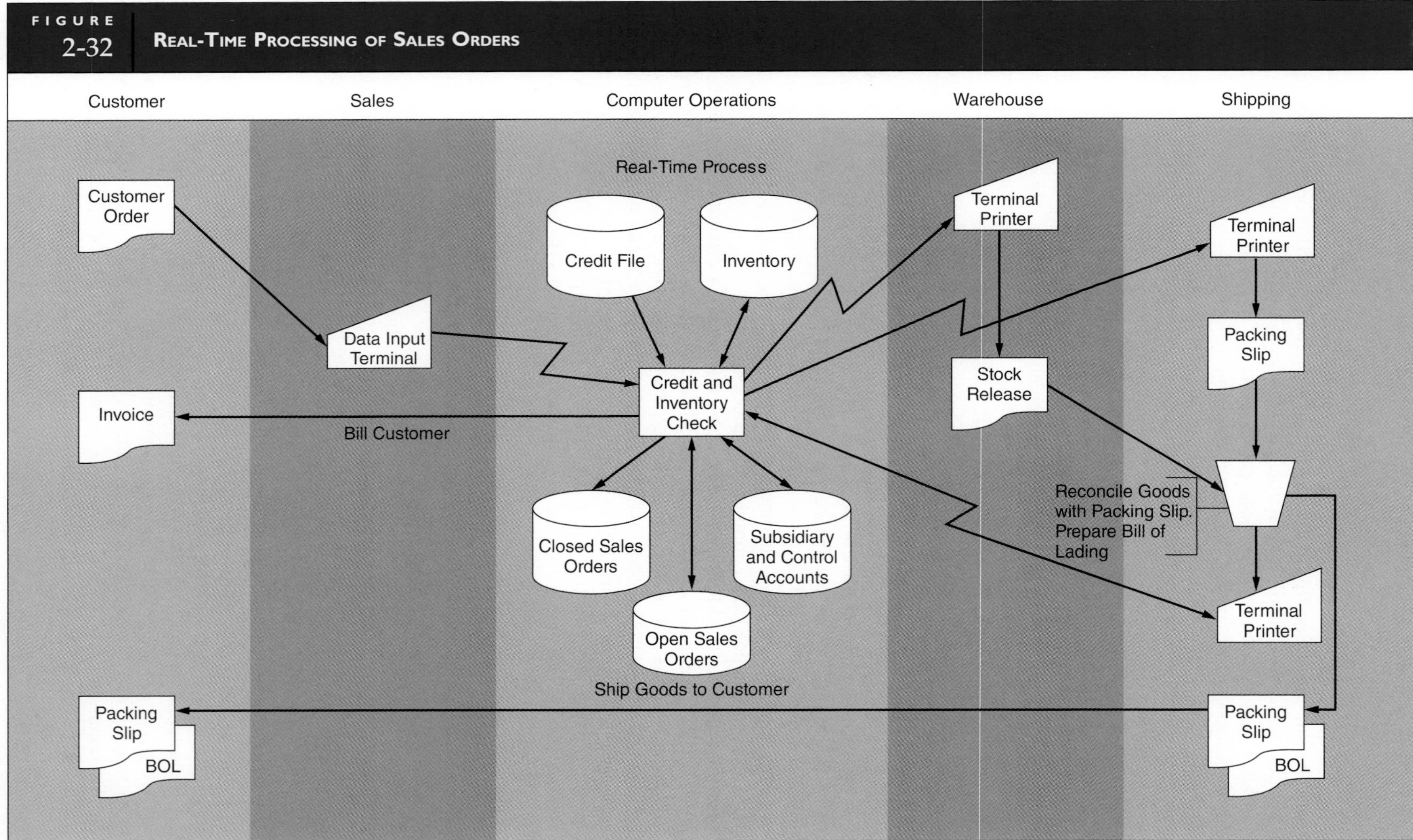

Data Coding Schemes

Data coding involves creating simple numeric or alphabetic codes to represent complex economic phenomena that facilitate efficient data processing. In Figure 2-30, for example, we saw how the secondary keys of transaction file records are linked to the primary keys of master file records. The secondary and primary keys in the example are instances of data coding. In this section we explore several data coding schemes and their application in AIS. To emphasize the importance of data codes, we first consider a hypothetical system that does not use them.

A SYSTEM WITHOUT CODES

Business organizations process large volumes of transactions that are similar in their basic attributes. For instance, a firm's AR file may contain accounts for several different customers with the same name and similar addresses. To process transactions accurately against the correct accounts, the firm must be able to distinguish one John Smith from another. This task becomes particularly difficult as the number of similar attributes in an item class increases.

Consider the most elemental item that a machine shop wholesaler firm might carry in its inventory—a machine nut. Assume that the total inventory of nuts has only three distinguishing attributes: size, material, and thread type. As a result, this entire item class of inventory must be distinguished on the basis of these three features, which are as follows:

1. The size attribute falls within a range of ¼ inch to 1¾ inches in diameter in increments of $^1/_{64}$ of an inch, giving 96 nut sizes.
2. For each size subclass, four materials are available: brass, copper, mild steel, and case-hardened steel.
3. Each of these size and material subclasses come in three different threads: fine, standard, and coarse.

Under these assumptions, this class of inventory could contain 1,152 separate items (96 × 4 × 3). The identification of a single item in this class thus requires a description featuring these distinguishing attributes. To illustrate, consider the following journal entry to record the receipt of $1,000 worth of half-inch, case-hardened steel nuts with standard threads supplied by Industrial Parts Manufacturer of Cleveland, Ohio.

	DR	CR
Inventory—nut, ½ inch, case-hardened steel, standard thread	1,000	
AP—Industrial Parts Manufacturer, Cleveland, Ohio		1,000

This uncoded entry takes a great deal of recording space, is time-consuming to record, and is obviously prone to many types of errors. The negative effects of this approach may be seen in many parts of the organization:

1. *Sales staff.* Properly identifying the items sold requires the transcription of large amounts of detail onto source documents. Apart from the time and effort involved, this tends to promote clerical errors and incorrect shipments.
2. *Warehouse personnel.* Locating and picking goods for shipment are impeded and shipping errors will likely result.
3. *Accounting personnel.* Postings to ledger accounts will require searching through the subsidiary files using lengthy descriptions as the key. This will be painfully slow, and postings to the wrong accounts will be common.

A SYSTEM WITH CODES

These problems are solved, or at least greatly reduced, by using codes to represent each item in the inventory and supplier accounts. Let's assume the inventory item in our previous example had been assigned the numeric code 896, and the supplier in the AP account is given the code number 321. The coded version of the previous journal entry can now be greatly simplified:

ACCOUNT	DR	CR
896	1,000	
321		1,000

This is not to suggest that detailed information about the inventory and the supplier is of no interest to the organization. Obviously it is! These facts will be kept in reference files and used for such purposes as the preparation of parts lists, catalogs, bills of material, and mailing information. The inclusion of such details, however, would clutter the task of transaction processing and could prove dysfunctional, as this simple example illustrates. Other advantages of data coding in AIS are:

1. Concisely representing large amounts of complex information that would otherwise be unmanageable.
2. Providing a means of accountability over the completeness of the transactions processed.
3. Identifying unique transactions and accounts within a file.
4. Supporting the audit function by providing an effective audit trail.

The following discussion examines some of the more commonly used coding techniques and explores their respective advantages and disadvantages.

NUMERIC AND ALPHABETIC CODING SCHEMES

Sequential Codes

As the name implies, **sequential codes** represent items in some sequential order (ascending or descending). A common application of numeric sequential codes is the prenumbering of source documents. At printing, each hard-copy document is given a unique sequential code number. This number becomes the transaction number that allows the system to track each transaction processed and to identify any lost or out-of-sequence documents. Digital documents are similarly assigned a sequential number by the computer application when they are created.

ADVANTAGES. Sequential coding supports the reconciliation of a batch of transactions, such as sales orders, at the end of processing. If the transaction processing system detects any gaps in the sequence of transaction numbers, it alerts management to the possibility of a missing or misplaced transaction. By tracing the transaction number back through the stages in the process, management can eventually determine the cause and effect of the error. Without sequentially numbered documents, problems of this sort are difficult to detect and resolve.

DISADVANTAGES. Sequential codes carry no information content beyond their order in the sequence. For instance, a sequential code assigned to a raw material inventory item tells us nothing about the attributes of the item (type, size, material, warehouse location, and so on). Also, sequential coding schemes are difficult to change. Inserting a new item at some midpoint requires renumbering the subsequent items in the class accordingly. In applications where record types must be grouped together logically and where additions and deletions occur regularly, this coding scheme is inappropriate.

Block Codes

A numeric **block code** is a variation on sequential coding that partly remedies the disadvantages just described. This approach can be used to represent whole classes of items by restricting each class to a specific range within the coding scheme. A common application of block coding is the construction of a **chart of accounts**.

A well-designed and comprehensive chart of accounts is the basis for the general ledger and is thus critical to a firm's financial and management reporting systems. The more extensive the chart of accounts, the more precisely a firm can classify its transactions and the greater the range of

FIGURE 2-33 CHART OF ACCOUNTS

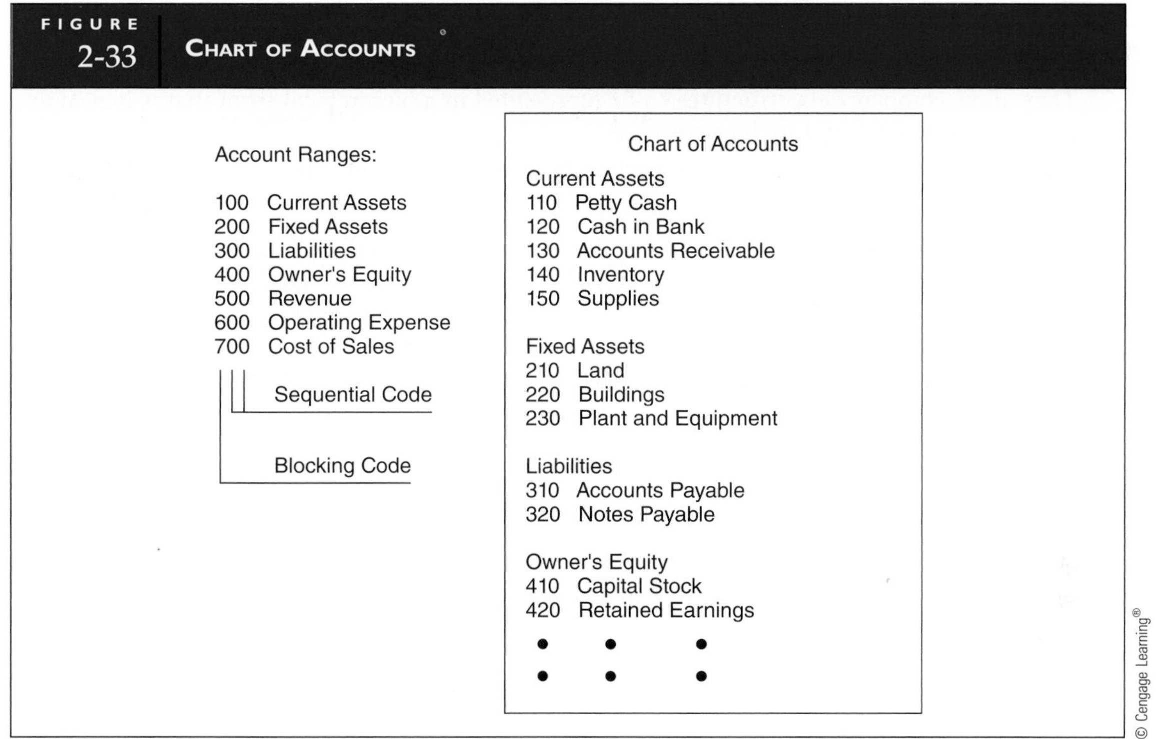

information it can provide to internal and external users. Figure 2-33 shows an example of accounts using block codes.

Notice that each account type is represented by a unique range of codes or blocks. Thus, balance sheet and income statement account classifications and subclassifications can be presented. In this example, each of the accounts consists of a three-digit code. The first digit is the blocking digit and represents the account classification; for example, current assets, liabilities, or operating expense. The other digits in the code are sequentially assigned.

ADVANTAGES. Block coding allows for the insertion of new codes within a block without having to reorganize the entire coding structure. For example, if advertising expense is account number 626, the first digit indicates that this account is an operating expense. As new types of expense items are incurred and have to be specifically accounted for, they may be added sequentially within the 600 account classification. This three-digit code accommodates 100 individual items (X00 through X99) within each block. Obviously, the more digits in the code range, the more items that can be represented.

DISADVANTAGES. As with the sequential codes, the information content of the block code is not readily apparent. For instance, account number 626 means nothing until matched against the chart of accounts, which identifies it as advertising expense.

Group Codes

Numeric **group codes** are used to represent complex items or events involving two or more pieces of related data. The code consists of zones or fields that possess specific meaning. For example, a department store chain might code sales order transactions from its branch stores as follows:

Store Number	Dept. Number	Item Number	Salesperson
04	09	476214	99

ADVANTAGES. Group codes have a number of advantages over sequential and block codes.

1. They facilitate the representation of large amounts of diverse data.
2. They allow complex data structures to be represented in a hierarchical form that is logical and more easily remembered by humans.
3. They permit detailed analysis and reporting both within an item class and across different classes of items.

Using the previous example to illustrate, Store Number 04 could represent the Hamilton Mall store in Allentown; Dept. Number 09 represents the sporting goods department; Item Number 476214 is a hockey stick; and Salesperson 99 is Jon Innes. With this level of information, a corporate manager could measure profitability by store, compare the performance of similar departments across all stores, track the movement of specific inventory items, and evaluate sales performance by employees within and between stores.

DISADVANTAGES. Ironically the primary disadvantage of group coding results from its success as a classification tool. Because group codes can effectively present diverse information, they tend to be overused. Unrelated data may be linked simply because it can be done. This can lead to unnecessarily complex group codes that cannot be easily interpreted. Finally, overuse can increase storage costs, promote clerical errors, and increase processing time and effort.

Alphabetic Codes

Alphabetic codes are used for many of the same purposes as numeric codes. Alphabetic characters may be assigned sequentially (in alphabetic order) or may be used in block and group coding techniques.

ADVANTAGES. The capacity to represent large numbers of items is increased dramatically through the use of pure alphabetic codes or alphabetic characters embedded within numeric codes (**alphanumeric codes**). The earlier example of a chart of accounts using a three-digit code with a single blocking digit limits data representation to only 10 blocks of accounts—0 through 9. Using alphabetic characters for blocking, however, increases the number of possible blocks to 26—A through Z. Furthermore, while the two-digit sequential portion of that code has the capacity of only 100 items (10^2), a two-position alphabetic code can represent 676 items (26^2). Thus, by using alphabetic codes in the same three-digit coding space, we see a geometric increase in the potential for data representation:

$$(10 \text{ blocks} \times 100 \text{ items each}) = 1{,}000 \text{ items}$$

to

$$(26 \text{ blocks} \times 676 \text{ items each}) = 17{,}576 \text{ items}$$

DISADVANTAGES. The primary drawbacks with alphabetic coding are (1) as with numeric codes, there is difficulty rationalizing the meaning of codes that have been sequentially assigned, and (2) users tend to have difficulty sorting records that are coded alphabetically.

Mnemonic Codes

Mnemonic codes are alphabetic characters in the form of acronyms and other combinations that convey meaning. For example, a student enrolling in college courses may enter the following course codes on the registration form:

Course Type	*Course Number*
Acctg	101
Psyc	110
Mgt	270
Mktg	300

This combination of mnemonic and numeric codes conveys a good deal of information about these courses; with a little analysis, we can deduce that Acctg is accounting, Psyc is psychology, Mgt is management, and Mktg is marketing. The sequential number portion of the code indicates the level of each course. Another example of the use of mnemonic codes is assigning state codes in mailing addresses:

Code	*Meaning*
NY	New York
CA	California
OK	Oklahoma

ADVANTAGES. The mnemonic coding scheme does not require the user to memorize meaning; the code itself conveys a high degree of information about the item that is being represented.

DISADVANTAGES. Although mnemonic codes are useful for representing classes of items, they have limited ability to represent items within a class. For example, the entire class of accounts receivable could be represented by the mnemonic code AR, but we would quickly exhaust meaningful combinations of alphabetic characters if we attempted to represent the individual accounts that make up this class. These accounts would be represented better by sequential, block, or group coding techniques.

Summary

This chapter divided the treatment of transaction processing systems into five major sections. The first section provided an overview of transaction processing, showing its vital role as an information provider for financial reporting, internal management reporting, and the support of day-to-day operations. To efficiently deal with large volumes of financial transactions, business organizations group together transactions of similar types into transaction cycles. Three transaction cycles account for most of a firm's economic activity: the revenue cycle, the expenditure cycle, and the conversion cycle. The second section described the relationship among accounting records in both manual and computer-based systems. We saw how both hardcopy and digital documents form an audit trail. The third section of the chapter presented an overview of documentation techniques used to describe the key features of systems. Accountants must be proficient in using documentation tools to perform their professional duties. Five types of documentation are commonly used for this purpose: data flow diagrams, entity relationship diagrams, system flowcharts, program flowcharts, and record layout diagrams. The fourth section presented two approaches to transaction processing: (1) batch processing and (2) real-time processing. The section also examined the operational efficiency issues associated with each configuration. Finally, we examined data coding schemes and their role in transaction processing and AIS as a means of coordinating and managing a firm's transactions. In examining the major types of numeric and alphabetic coding schemes, we saw how each has certain advantages and disadvantages.

Appendix

Data Structures

Data structures represent the physical and logical arrangement of data in files and databases. Data structures have two fundamental components: organization and access method. **Organization** refers to the way records are physically arranged on the secondary storage device (for example, a disk). This may be either sequential or random. The records in sequential files are stored in contiguous locations that occupy a specified area of disk space. Records in random files are stored without regard for their physical relationship to other records

TABLE 2-2 TYPICAL FILE PROCESSING OPERATIONS

1. Retrieve a record from the file based on its primary key value.
2. Insert a record into a file.
3. Update a record in the file.
4. Read a complete file of records.
5. Find the next record in a file.
6. Scan a file for records with common secondary keys.
7. Delete a record from a file.

of the same file. In fact, random files may have records distributed throughout a disk. The **access method** is the technique used to locate records and to navigate through the database or file.

No single structure is best for all processing tasks, and selecting a structure involves a trade-off between desirable features. The file operation requirements that influence the selection of the data structure are listed in Table 2-2.

In the following section, we examine several data structures that are used in flat-file systems. Recall from the chapter that the flat-file model describes an environment in which individual data files are not integrated with other files. End users in this environment own their data files rather than share them with other users. Data processing is thus performed by stand-alone applications rather than integrated systems. The **flat-file approach** is a single-view model that characterizes legacy systems in which data files are structured, formatted, and arranged to suit the specific needs of the owner or primary user of the system. Such structuring, however, may omit or corrupt data attributes that are essential to other users, thus preventing successful integration of systems across the organization.

SEQUENTIAL STRUCTURE

Figure 2-34 illustrates the **sequential structure**, which is typically called the **sequential access method**. Under this arrangement, for example, the record with key value 1875 is placed in the physical storage space immediately following the record with key value 1874. Thus, all records in the file lie in contiguous storage spaces in a specified sequence (ascending or descending) arranged by their primary key.

FIGURE 2-34 SEQUENTIAL STORAGE AND ACCESS METHOD

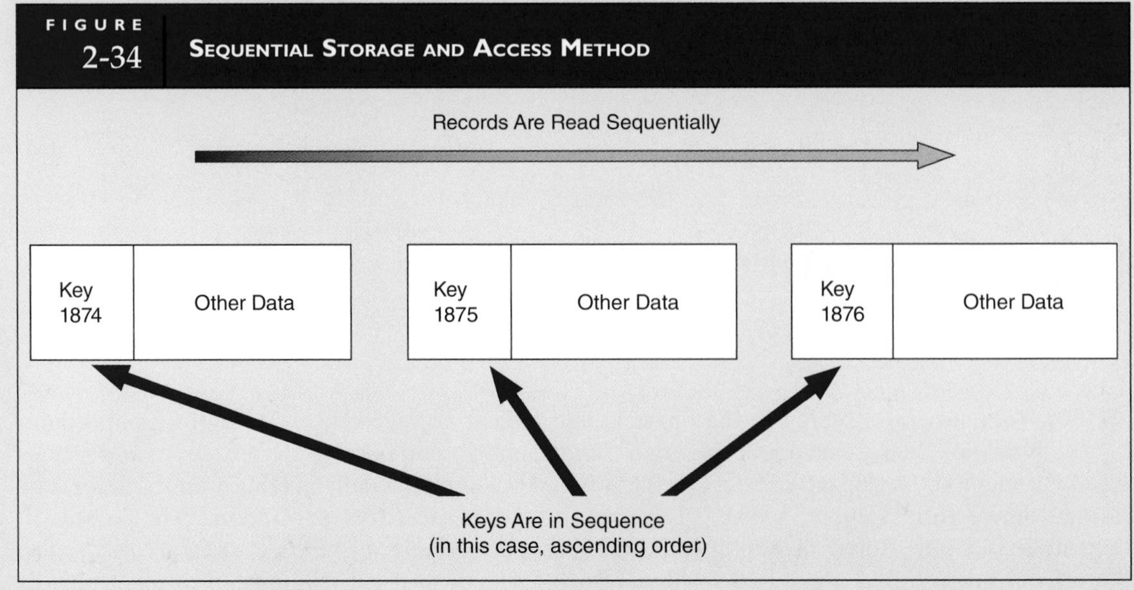

Sequential files are simple and easy to process. The computer application starts reading the data at the beginning of the file and processes each record in sequence. Of the file processing operations in Table 2-2, this approach is efficient for Operations 4 and 5, which are, respectively, reading an entire file and finding the next record in the file. Also, when a large portion of the file (perhaps 20 percent or more) is to be processed in one operation, the sequential structure is efficient for record updating (Operation 3 in Table 2-2). Sequential files are not efficient when the user is interested in locating only one or a few records on a file. An example of a sequential file application is payroll processing, where 100 percent of the employee records on the payroll file are processed each payroll period. Magnetic tape is a cheap, effective, and commonly used storage medium for sequential files. Sequential files may also be stored on magnetic disks.

The sequential access method does not permit accessing a record directly. Applications that require direct access operations need a different data structure. The techniques described next address this need.

DIRECT ACCESS STRUCTURES

Direct access structures store data at a unique location, known as an address, on a disk. The operating system uses this address to store and retrieve the data record for processing. The direct access approach is similar to the way songs are stored on a CD. If the listener chooses, he or she can select a specific song directly without searching through all the other songs.

An important part of the direct access approach is in determining the disk address, which is based on the record's primary key. Bank account numbers, social security numbers, credit card numbers, and license plate numbers are examples of primary keys that are translated into addresses to store and retrieve data by different business applications. The following techniques are examples of data structures that have direct access capability.

INDEXED STRUCTURE

An **indexed structure** is so named because, in addition to the actual data file, there exists a separate index that is itself a file of record addresses. This index contains the numeric value of the physical disk storage location (cylinder, surface, and record block) for each record in the associated data file. The data file itself may be organized either sequentially or randomly. Figure 2-35 presents an example of an indexed random file.

Records in an **indexed random file** are dispersed throughout a disk without regard for their physical proximity to other related records. In fact, records belonging to the same file may reside on different disks. A record's physical location is unimportant as long as the operating system software can find it when needed. Searching the index for the desired key value, reading the corresponding storage location (address), and then moving the disk read/write head to the address location accomplish this. When a new record is added to the file, the data management software selects a vacant disk location, stores the record, and adds the new address to the index.

The physical organization of the index itself may be either sequential (by key value) or random. Random indexes are easier to maintain, in terms of adding records, because new key records are simply added to the end of the index without regard to their sequence. Indexes in sequential order are more difficult to maintain because new record keys must be inserted between existing keys. One advantage of a sequential index is that it can be searched rapidly. Because of its logical arrangement, algorithms can be used to speed the search through the index to find a key value. This becomes particularly important for large data files with associated large indexes.

The principal advantage of indexed random files is in operations involving the processing of individual records (Operations 1, 2, 3, and 6 in Table 2-2). Another advantage is their efficient use of disk storage. Records may be placed wherever there is space without concern for maintaining contiguous storage locations. Random files, however, are not efficient structures for operations that involve processing a large portion of a file. A great deal of access time may be required to access an entire file of records that are randomly dispersed throughout the storage device. Sequential files are more efficient for this purpose.

FIGURE 2-35 INDEXED RANDOM FILE STRUCTURE

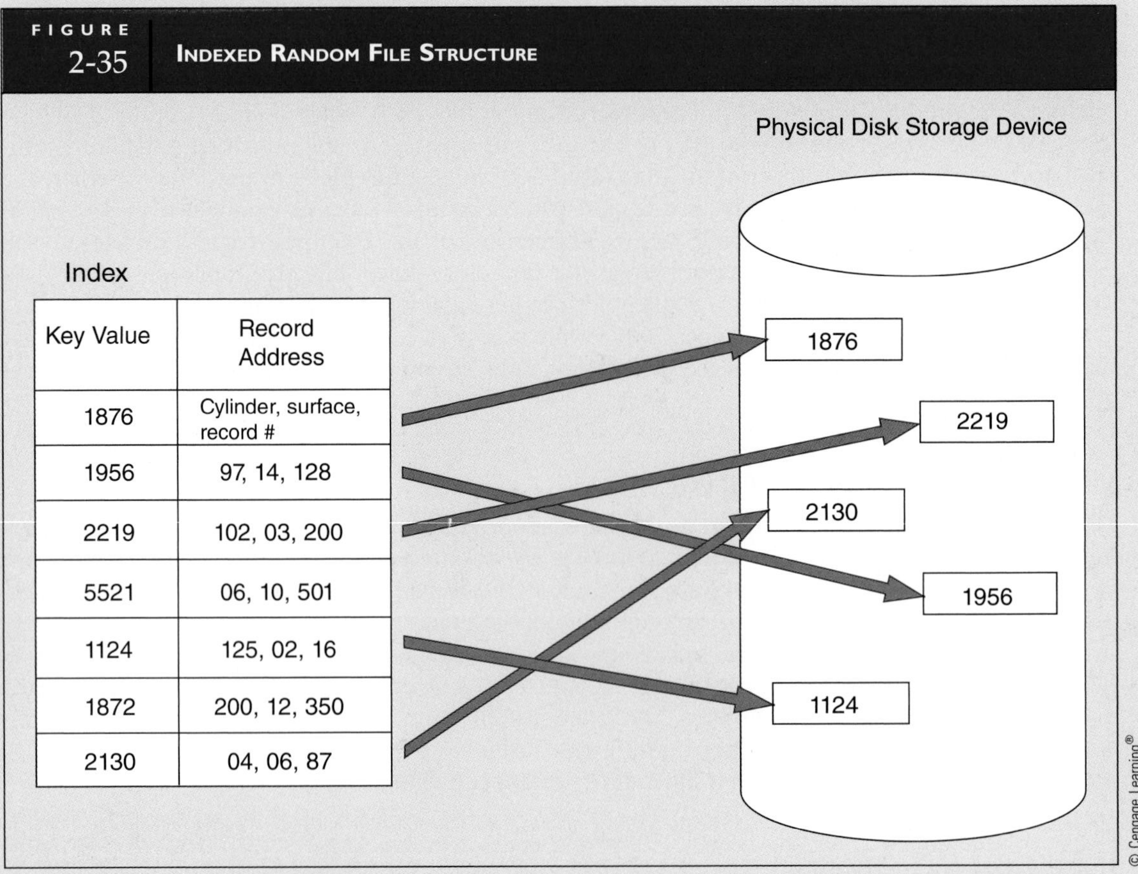

VIRTUAL STORAGE ACCESS METHOD STRUCTURE

The **virtual storage access method (VSAM)** structure is used for very large files that require routine batch processing and a moderate degree of individual record processing. For instance, the customer file of a public utility company will be processed in batch mode for billing purposes and directly accessed in response to individual customer queries. Because of its sequential organization, the VSAM structure can be searched sequentially for efficient batch processing. Figure 2-36 illustrates how VSAM uses indexes to allow direct access processing.

The VSAM structure is used for files that often occupy several cylinders of contiguous storage on a disk. To find a specific record location, the VSAM file uses a number of indexes that describe in summarized form the contents of each cylinder. For example, in Figure 2-36, we are searching for a record with the key value 2546. The access method goes first to the overall file index, which contains only the highest key value for each cylinder in the file, and determines that Record 2546 is somewhere on Cylinder 99. A quick scan of the surface index for Cylinder 99 reveals that the record is on Surface 3 of Cylinder 99. VSAM indexes do not provide an exact physical address for a single record. Instead, they identify the disk track on which the record in question resides. The last step is to search the identified track sequentially to find the record with key value 2546.

The VSAM structure is moderately effective for Operations 1 and 3 in Table 2-2. Because VSAM must read multiple indexes and search the track sequentially, the average access time for a single record is slower than that of the indexed sequential or indexed random structures. Direct access speed is sacrificed to achieve very efficient performance in Operations 4, 5, and 6.

FIGURE 2-36 VIRTUAL STORAGE ACCESS METHOD (VSAM) USED FOR DIRECT ACCESS

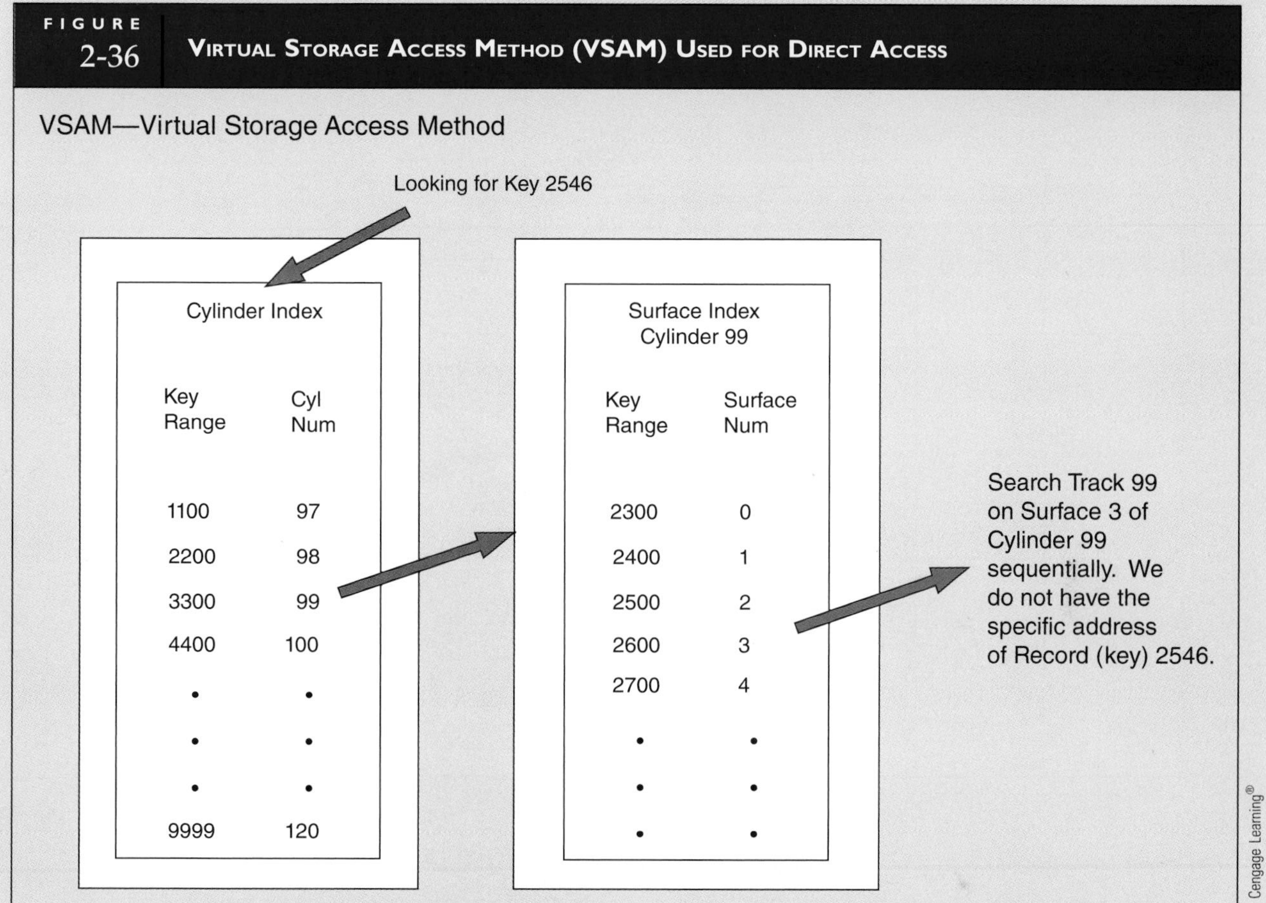

The greatest disadvantage with the VSAM structure is that it does not perform record insertion operations (Operation 2) efficiently. Because the VSAM file is organized sequentially, inserting a new record into the file requires the physical relocation of all the records located beyond the point of insertion. The indexes that describe this physical arrangement must, therefore, also be updated with each insertion. This is extremely time-consuming and disruptive. One method of dealing with this problem is to store new records in an overflow area that is physically separate from the other data records in the file. Figure 2-37 shows how this is done.

A VSAM file has three physical components: the indexes, the prime data storage area, and the overflow area. Rather than inserting a new record directly into the prime area, the data management software places it in a randomly selected location in the overflow area. It then records the address of the location in a special field (called a pointer) in the prime area. Later, when searching for the record, the indexes direct the access method to the track location on which the record *should* reside. The pointer at that location reveals the record's *actual* location in the overflow area. Thus, accessing a record may involve searching the indexes, searching the track in the prime data area, and finally searching the overflow area. This slows data access time for both direct access and batch processing.

Periodically, the VSAM file must be reorganized by integrating the overflow records into the prime area and then reconstructing the indexes. This involves time, cost, and disruption to operations. Therefore, when a file is highly volatile (records are added or deleted frequently), the maintenance burden associated with the VSAM approach tends to render it impractical. For large, stable files that need both direct access and batch processing, however, the VSAM structure is an option.

FIGURE 2-37 INSERTING A RECORD INTO A VIRTUAL STORAGE ACCESS METHOD FILE

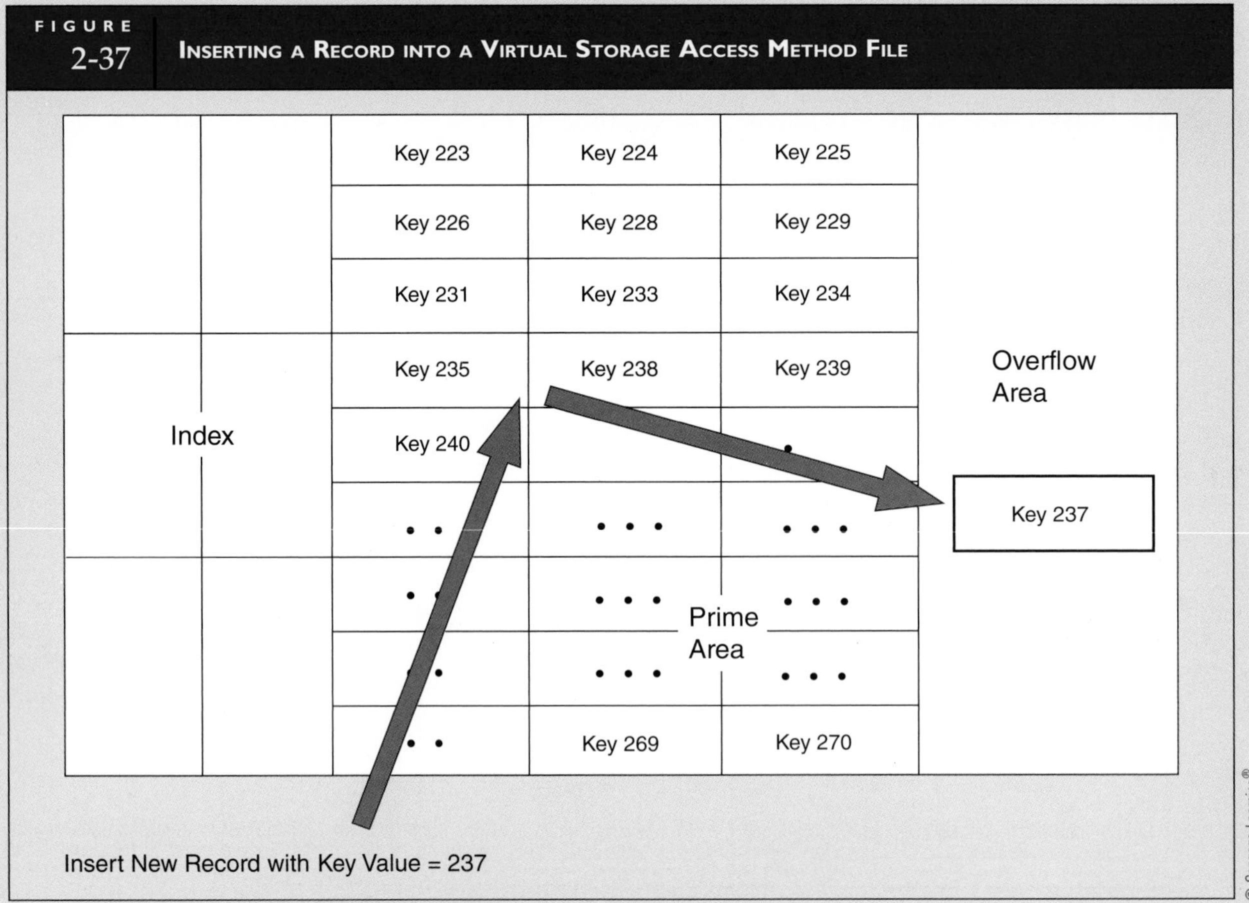

HASHING STRUCTURE

A **hashing structure** employs an algorithm that converts the primary key of a record directly into a storage address. Hashing eliminates the need for a separate index. By calculating the address, rather than reading it from an index, records can be retrieved more quickly. Figure 2-38 illustrates the hashing approach.

This example assumes an inventory file with 100,000 inventory items. The algorithm divides the inventory number (the primary key) into a prime number. Recall that a prime number is one that can be divided only by itself and 1 without leaving a residual value. Thus, the calculation will always produce a value that can be translated into a storage location. Hence, the residual 6.27215705 becomes Cylinder 272, Surface 15, and Record 705. The hashing structure uses a random file organization because the process of calculating residuals and converting them into storage locations produces widely dispersed record addresses.

The principal advantage of hashing is access speed. Calculating a record's address is faster than searching for it through an index. This structure is suited to applications that require rapid access to individual records in performing Operations 1, 2, 3, and 6 in Table 2-2.

The hashing structure has two significant disadvantages. First, this technique does not use storage space efficiently. The storage location chosen for a record is a mathematical function of its primary key value. The algorithm will never select some disk locations because they do not correspond to legitimate key values. As much as one-third of the disk pack may be wasted.

The second disadvantage is the reverse of the first. Different record keys may generate the same (or similar) residual, which translates into the same address. This is called a collision because two records cannot be stored at the same location. One solution to this problem is to randomly select a

FIGURE 2-38 HASHING TECHNIQUE WITH POINTER TO RELOCATE THE COLLISION RECORD

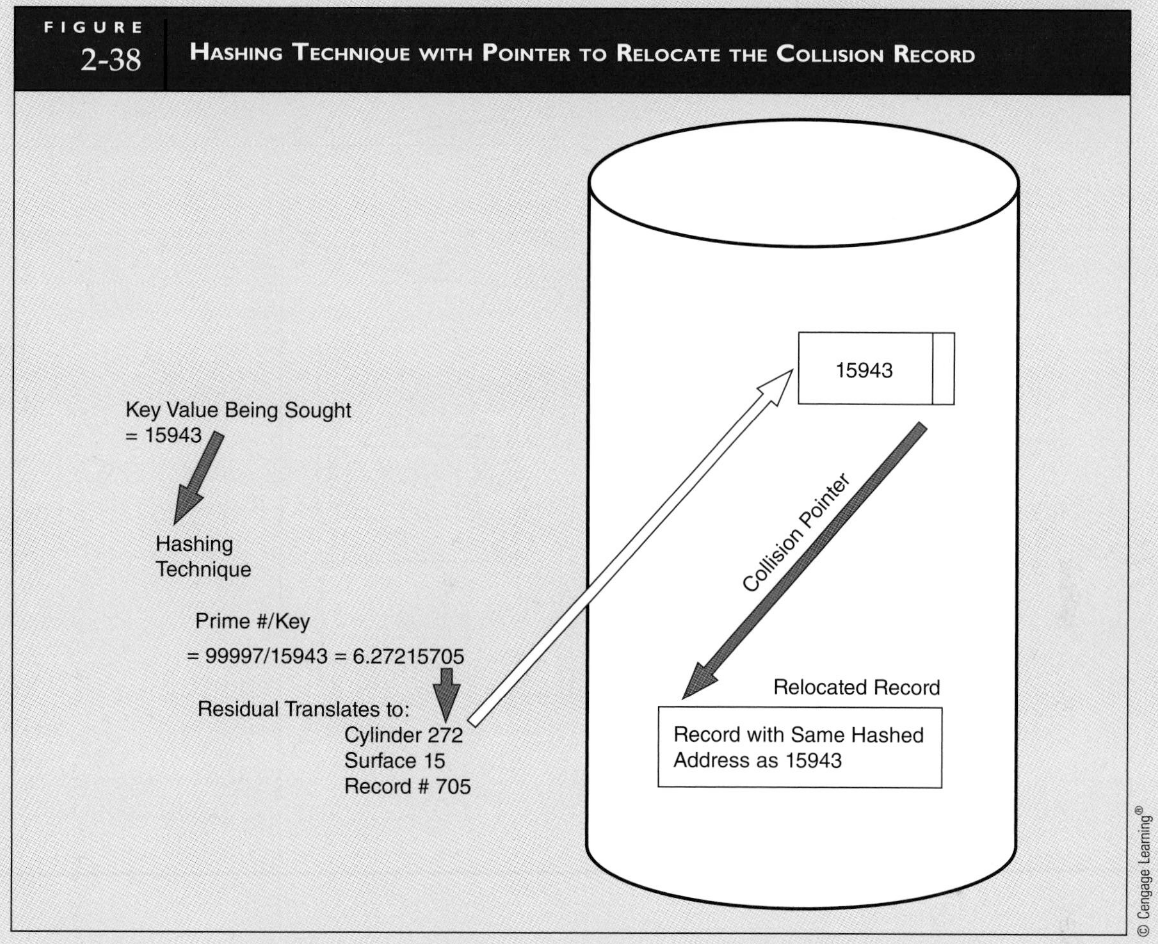

location for the second record and place a pointer to it from the first (the calculated) location. The dark arrow in Figure 2-38 represents this technique.

The collision problem slows access to records. Locating a record displaced in this manner involves first calculating its theoretical address, searching that location, and then determining the actual address from the pointer contained in the record at that location. This has an additional implication for Operation 7 in Table 2-2—deleting a record from a file. If the first record is deleted from the file, the pointer to the second (collision) record will also be deleted and the address of the second record will be lost. This can be dealt with in two ways: (1) after deleting the first record, the collision record can be physically relocated to its calculated address, which is now vacant, or (2) the first record is marked deleted but is left in place to preserve the pointer to the collision record.

POINTER STRUCTURE

Figure 2-39 presents the **pointer structure**, which in this example is used to create a linked-list file. This approach stores in a field of one record the address (pointer) of a related record. The pointers provide connections between the records. In this example, Record 124 points to the location of Record 125; Record 125 points to 126; and so on. As each record is processed, the computer program reads the pointer field to locate the next one. The last record in the list contains an EOF marker. The records in this type of file are spread over the entire disk without concern for their physical proximity with other related records. Pointers used in this way make

FIGURE 2-39 A LINKED-LIST FILE

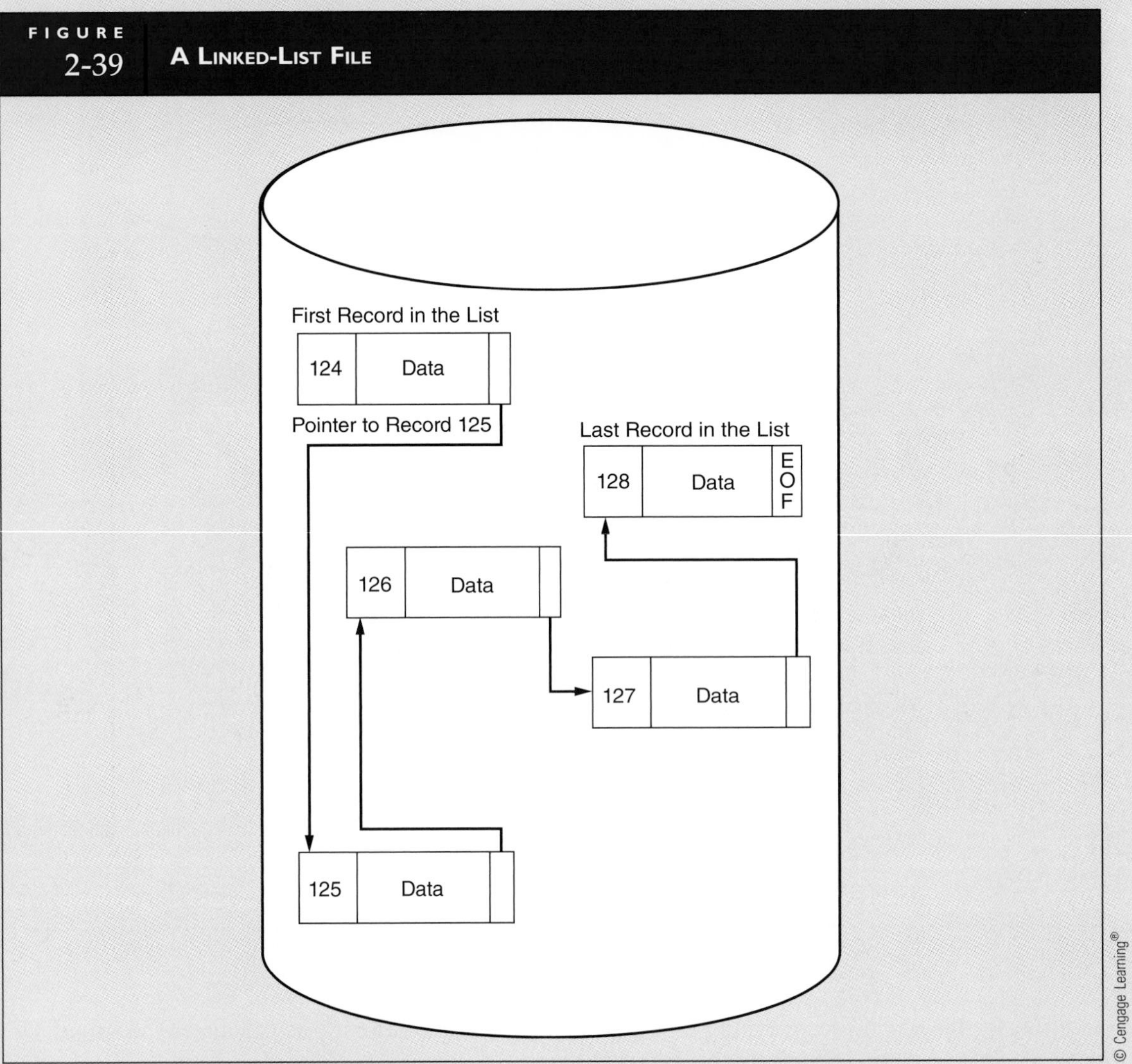

efficient use of disk space and are efficient structures for applications that involve Operations 4, 5, and 6 in Table 2-2.

Types of Pointers

Figure 2-40 shows three types of pointers: physical address, relative address, and logical key pointers. A **physical address pointer** contains the actual disk storage location (cylinder, surface, and record number) that the disk controller needs. This physical address allows the system to access the record directly without obtaining further information. This method has the advantage of speed because it does not need to be manipulated further to determine a record's location. It also has two disadvantages: first, if the related record is moved from one disk location to another, the pointer must be changed. This is a problem when disks are periodically reorganized or copied. Second, the physical pointers bear no logical relationship to the records they identify. If a pointer is lost or destroyed and cannot be recovered, the record it references is also lost.

A **relative address pointer** contains the relative position of a record in the file. For example, the pointer could specify the 135th record in the file. This must be further manipulated to convert it to

FIGURE 2-40 TYPES OF POINTERS

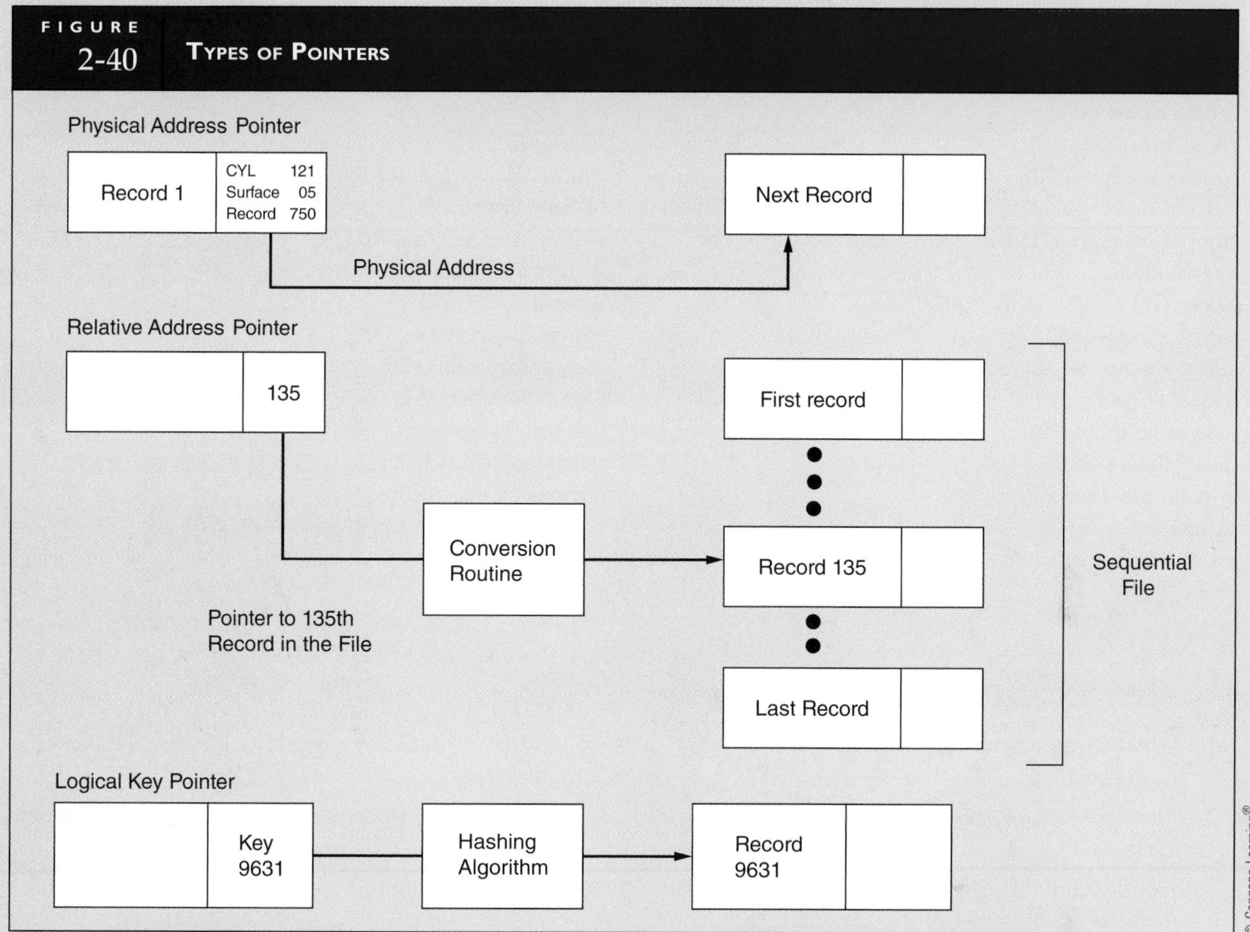

the actual physical address. The conversion software calculates this by using the physical address of the beginning of the file, the length of each record in the file, and the relative address of the record being sought.

A **logical key pointer** contains the primary key of the related record. This key value is then converted into the record's physical address by a hashing algorithm.

Key Terms

access method (74)
accounting record (36)
alphabetic codes (72)
alphanumeric codes (72)
archive file (45)
audit trail (42)
batch systems (63)
block code (70)
cardinality (51)
chart of accounts (70)
conversion cycle (35)
currency of information (46)
data flow diagram (DFD) (49)
data model (51)
data storage (46)
data structures (73)
data updating (46)
database management system (DBMS) (48)
database model (48)
direct access structures (75)

entity relationship (ER) diagram (51)
expenditure cycle (35)
flat-file approach (74)
flat-file model (46)
group codes (71)
hashing structure (78)
indexed random file (75)
indexed structure (75)
journal (37)
ledger (39)
legacy systems (46)
logical key pointer (81)
master file (44)
mnemonic codes (72)
organization (73)
physical address pointer (80)
pointer structure (79)
product documents (36)
program flowchart (60)
real-time systems (63)
record layout diagrams (62)
reference file (44)
register (39)
relative address pointer (80)
revenue cycle (36)
sequential access method (74)
sequential codes (70)
sequential files (75)
sequential structure (74)
source documents (36)
system flowchart (52)
task-data dependency (46)
transaction file (44)
turnaround documents (36)
virtual storage access method (VSAM) (76)

Review Questions

1. What three transaction cycles exist in all businesses?
2. Name the major subsystems of the expenditure cycle.
3. Identify and distinguish between the physical and financial components of the expenditure cycle.
4. Name the major subsystems of the conversion cycle.
5. Name the major subsystems of the revenue cycle.
6. Name the three types of documents.
7. Name the two types of journals.
8. Distinguish between a general journal and journal vouchers.
9. Name the two types of ledgers.
10. What is an audit trail?
11. What is the confirmation process?
12. Computer-based systems employ four types of files. Name them.
13. Give an example of a record for each of the four file types found in a computer-based system.
14. What is the purpose of a digital audit trail?
15. Give an example of how cardinality relates to business policy.
16. Distinguish between entity relationship diagrams, data flow diagrams, and system flowcharts.
17. What is meant by cardinality in entity relationship diagrams?
18. For what purpose are entity relationship diagrams used?
19. What is an entity?
20. Distinguish between batch and real-time processing.
21. What is the flat-file model?
22. Is a data flow diagram an effective documentation technique for identifying who or what performs a particular task? Explain.
23. Is a flowchart an effective documentation technique for identifying who or what performs a particular task? Explain.
24. How may batch processing be used to improve operational efficiency?
25. Why might an auditor use a program flowchart?
26. How are system flowcharts and program flowcharts related?
27. What are the three general problems associated with data redundancy?
28. What is task-data dependency?
29. What is the database model?
30. What information is provided by a record layout diagram?

31. In one sentence, what does updating a master file record involve?
32. What is the purpose of the DBMS?
33. Flat files limit data integration. Explain.
34. What factor influences the decision to employ real-time data collection with batch updating rather that purely real-time processing? Explain.
35. What are the advantages of real-time data processing?
36. What are the advantages of real-time data collection?
37. What are some of the more common uses of data codes in accounting information systems?
38. Compare and contrast the relative advantages and disadvantages of sequential, block, group, alphabetic, and mnemonic codes.

Discussion Questions

1. Discuss the flow of cash through the transaction cycles. Include in your discussion the relevant subsystems and any time lags that may occur.
2. Explain whether the cost accounting system primarily supports internal or external reporting.
3. Discuss the role of the conversion cycle for service and retailing entities.
4. Can a turnaround document contain information that is subsequently used as a source document? Why or why not?
5. Would the writing down of obsolete inventory be recorded in a special journal or the general journal? Why?
6. Are both registers and special journals necessary?
7. Discuss the relationship between the balance in the accounts payable general ledger control account and what is found in the accounts payable subsidiary ledger.
8. What role does the audit trail play in the task of confirmation?
9. Explain how the magnetic audit trail functions.
10. Are large batch sizes preferable to small batch sizes? Explain.
11. Discuss why an understanding of legacy system technologies is of some importance to auditors.
12. If an organization processes large numbers of transactions that use common data records, what type of system would work best (all else being equal)?
13. If an organization processes transactions that have independent (unique) data needs, what type of system would work best (all else being equal)?
14. What is the most striking difference between the database model and the flat-file model?
15. What is meant by the term *single user view* as it applies to flat files, and why is this a problem?
16. Explain the similarity and difference between the data update and information currency problems associated with flat files.
17. Should an auditor wishing to assess the adequacy of separation of functions examine a data flow diagram or a system flowchart? Why?
18. Discuss some of the problems associated with general ledger systems that do not have data coding schemes.
19. For each of the following items, indicate whether a sequential, block, group, alphabetic, or mnemonic code would be most appropriate (you may list multiple methods; give an example and explain why each method is appropriate):

    a. state codes
    b. check number
    c. chart of accounts
    d. inventory item number
    e. -bin number (inventory warehouse location)
    f. sales order number
    g. vendor code
    h. invoice number
    i. customer number

Multiple-Choice Questions

1. The production subsystem of the conversion cycle includes all of the following EXCEPT
   a. determining raw materials requirements.
   b. make or buy decisions on component parts.
   c. release of raw materials into production.
   d. scheduling the goods to be produced.
2. Which of the following files is a temporary file?
   a. transaction file
   b. master file
   c. reference file
   d. none of the above
3. Which statement is NOT true?
   a. Manufacturing firms have a conversion cycle but retail firms do not.
   b. The conversion cycle includes the task of determining raw materials requirements.
   c. A payroll check is an example of a product document of the payroll system.
   d. A journal voucher is actually a special source document.
   e. Business activities begin with the acquisition of materials, property, and labor in exchange for cash
4. Which of the following statements is NOT true?
   a. Sorting records that are coded alphabetically tends to be more difficult for users than sorting numeric sequences.
   b. Mnemonic codes are limited in their ability to represent items within a class.
   c. Sequential codes carry no information content beyond their order in the sequence.
   d. Mnemonic coding requires the user to memorize codes.
5. Which of the following is NOT an advantage of real-time processing of files over batch processing?
   a. shorter transaction processing time
   b. reduction of inventory stocks
   c. improved customer service
   d. all are advantages
6. Which statement is NOT true Batch processing
   a. permits data to be edited in a separate computer run.
   b. is subject to deadlocks when processing common accounts.
   c. can use databases and flat files.
   d. can be initiated from a terminal.
7. Which is least appropriate type of transaction for a real-time system.
   a. airline reservations.
   b. payroll.
   c. point-of-sale transactions.
   d. air traffic control systems.
   e. all of these applications typically utilize real time processing.
8. Which of the following statements is not correct?
   a. Database systems resolve task data dependency.
   b. The flat-file model encourages data redundancy.
   c. A primary goal of database systems is to mini mize data redundancy.
   d. Database systems provide increased accessibility to data and data integration.
   e. The database approach uses one common data base to promote the concept of single user view.
9. Which of the following is NOT true of a turn around document?
   a. They may reduce the number of errors made by external parties.
   b. They are commonly used by utility companies (gas, power, water).
   c. They are documents used by internal parties only.
   d. They are both input and output documents.
10. A documentation tool used to represent the logical elements of a system is a(n)
    a. programming flowchart.
    b. entity relationship diagram.
    c. system flowchart.
    d. data flow diagram.

11. Which of the following is NOT a true statement?
    a. Transactions are recorded on ledgers and are posted to journals.
    b. Transactions are recorded in journals and are posted to ledgers.
    c. Infrequent transactions are recorded in the general journal.
    d. Frequent transactions are recorded in special journals.
12. Which of the following is true of the relationship between subsidiary ledgers and general ledger accounts?
    a. The two contain different and unrelated data.
    b. The relationship between the two constitute part of the audit trail.
    c. All general ledger accounts have subsidiaries.
    d. The total of subsidiary ledger accounts usually exceeds the total in the related general ledger account.
13. A documentation tool that depicts the physical flow of information relating to a particular trans action through an organization is a (n)
    a. ER diagram.
    b. program flowchart.
    c. decision table.
    d. data flow diagram.
    e. system flowchart.
14. A database Deadlock
    a. is a lock placed on a record to prevent it from being accessed by other processes.
    b. occurs when two records are accidentally assigned the same primary key
    c. occurs when a unique record is accessed by several different processes simultaneously.
    d. is none of the above.
15. An invoice file would best be coded using a(n) coding ____________ scheme.
    a. alphabetic
    b. mnemonic
    c. block
    d. sequential
16. Which statement is NOT correct?
    a. Legacy systems may process financially significant transactions.
    b. Mainframes are exclusive to legacy systems, while modern systems use only the client-server model.
    c. Legacy systems may use database technology.
    d. All the above are true.
17. A coding scheme in the form of acronyms and other combinations that convey meaning is a(n)
    a. sequential code.
    b. mnemonic code.
    c. alphabetic code.
    d. block code.
18. (Appendix Question) In a hashing structure
    a. two records can be stored at the same address.
    b. pointers are used to indicate the location of all records.
    c. pointers are used to indicate location of a record with the same address as another record.
    d. all locations on the disk are used for record storage.
19. (Appendix Question) An advantage of a physical address pointer is that
    a. it points directly to the actual disk storage location.
    b. it is easily recovered if it is inadvertently lost.
    c. it remains unchanged when disks are reorganized.
    d. all of the above are advantages of the physical address pointer.
20. (Appendix Question) Which statement is NOT correct? The Virtual storage Access Method
    a. is used for very large files that need both direct access and batch processing.
    b. may use an overflow area for records.
    c. provides an exact physical address for each record.
    d. is appropriate for files that require few insertions or deletions.
21. (Appendix Question) Which statement is true about a hashing structure?
    a. The same address could be calculated for two different records.
    b. Storage space is used efficiently.
    c. Records cannot be accessed rapidly.
    d. A separate index is required.
22. (Appendix Question) Which statement is NOT correct?
    a. Indexed random files are dispersed throughout the storage device without regard for physical proximity with related records.
    b. Indexed random files use disk storage space efficiently.
    c. Indexed random files are efficient when processing a large portion of a file at one time.
    d. Indexed random files are easy to maintain in terms of adding records.

Problems

1. TRANSACTION CYCLE IDENTIFICATION

Categorize each of the following activities into the expenditure, conversion, or revenue cycles, and identify the applicable subsystem.

a. preparing the weekly payroll for manufacturing personnel
b. releasing raw materials for use in the manufacturing cycle
c. recording the receipt of payment for goods sold
d. recording the order placed by a customer
e. ordering raw materials
f. determining the amount of raw materials to order

2. TYPES OF FILES

For each of the following records, indicate the appropriate related file structure: master file, transaction file, reference file, or archive file.

a. customer ledgers
b. purchase orders
c. list of authorized vendors
d. records related to prior pay periods
e. vendor ledgers
f. hours each employee has worked during the current pay period
g. tax tables
h. sales orders that have been processed and recorded

3. SYSTEM FLOWCHART

Figure 2-4 in the text illustrates how a customer order is transformed into a source document, a product document, and a turnaround document. Develop a similar flowchart for the process of paying hourly employees. Assume time sheets are used and the payroll department must total the hours. Each hour worked by any employee must be charged to some account (a cost center). Each week, the manager of each cost center receives a report listing the employee's name and the number of hours charged to this center. The manager is required to verify that this information is correct by signing the form and noting any discrepancies, then sending this form back to the payroll department. Any discrepancies noted must be corrected by the payroll department.

4. SYSTEM FLOWCHART

Using the format presented in Figure 2-4 in the text develop a flowchart for the process of paying vendor accounts payable. Assume that vendor invoices are received and sent to the AP department where they are reviewed and approved for payment. Once approved the invoice and a cash disbursement voucher are sent to the cash disbursement department, where a check is prepared and sent to the vendor. A copy of the check, the invoice, and the voucher are returned to the AP Department.

5. RECORD STRUCTURES FOR INVENTORY RECEIPT PROCESS

Refer to Figure 2-30 in the text and the discussion about updating master files from transaction files. The discussion pertains to the record structures for a sales transaction. Prepare a diagram (similar to Figure 2-30) that presents the record structure for the receipt of inventory items that had been ordered previously. Assume that a purchase order file exists and will be updated through information collected via a receiving report, which is the transaction record. Further, assume that the purchase was made on account, and the vendor AP record needs to be updated. Do not show the general ledger records in your diagram. Explain each step in the update process.

6. RECORD STRUCTURES FOR RECEIPT OF CASH ON ACCOUNT

Refer to Figure 2-30 and the discussion about updating master files from transaction files. The discussion presents the record structures for a sales transaction. Prepare a diagram (similar to Figure 2-30) that presents the record structures for the receipt of cash from customers who are paying their outstanding accounts receivable. Assume a cash receipts file exists, which contains the transaction records to be processed. Show the subsidiary and general ledger files. Explain each step in the update process.

7. SYSTEM FLOWCHART

Using the diagram for Problem 7, answer the following questions:

- What do Symbols 1 and 2 represent?
- What does the operation involving Symbols 3 and 4 depict?
- What does the operation involving Symbols 4 and 5 depict?
- What does the operation involving Symbols 6, 8, and 9 depict?

PROBLEM 7: SYSTEM FLOWCHART

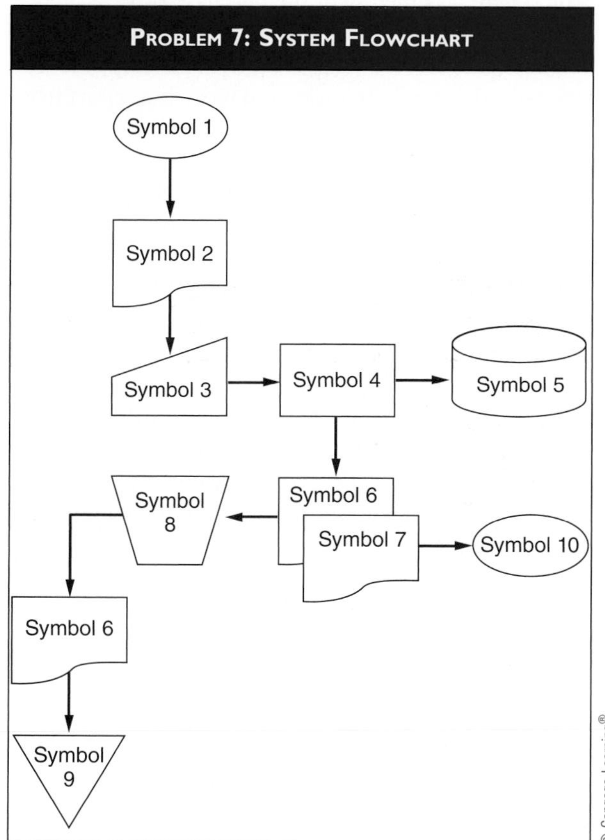

8. SYSTEM FLOWCHART

Analyze the system flowchart in Problem 8, and describe in detail the processes that are occurring.

PROBLEM 8: SYSTEM FLOWCHART

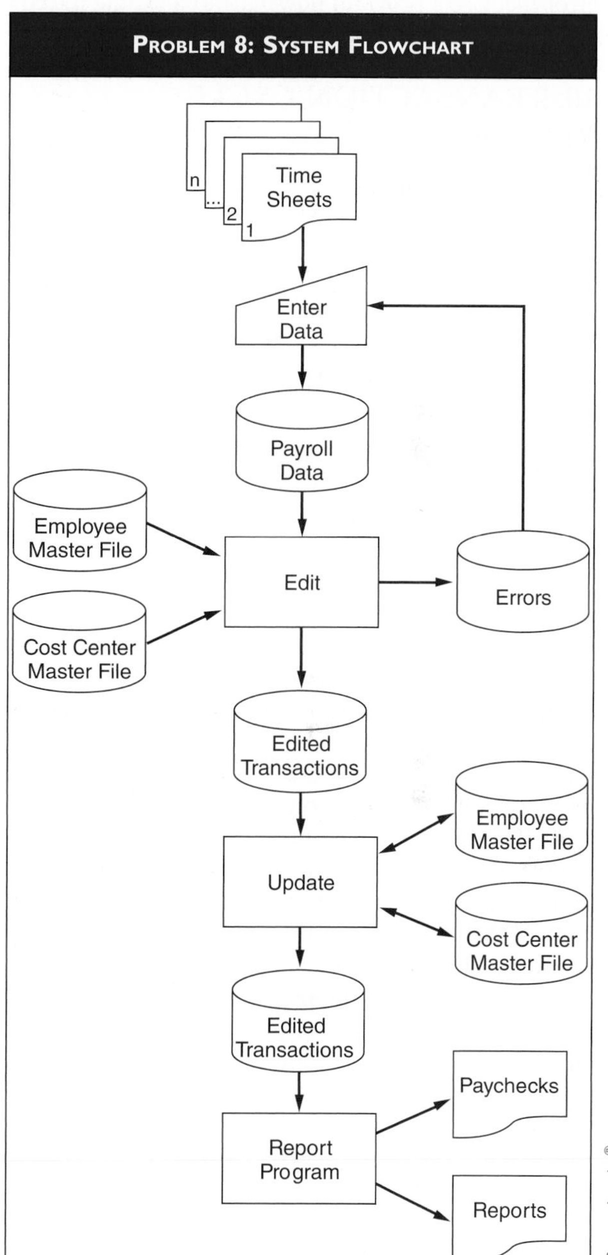

9. SYSTEM FLOWCHARTS AND PROGRAM FLOWCHART

From the diagram in Problem 8, identify three types of errors that may cause a payroll record to be placed in the error file. Use a program flowchart to illustrate the edit program.

10. TRANSACTION CYCLE RELATIONSHIP

Refer to Figure 2-1 in the text, which provides a generic look at relationships between transaction cycles. Modify this figure to reflect the transaction cycles you might find at a dentist's office.

11. SYSTEM FLOWCHART MANUAL SALES PROCEDURES

The following describes the sales procedures for a hypothetical company. All procedures are manual and use hard-copy documents.

The sales department clerk receives a customer orders from the customers and prepares a three-part sales order. The three copies are sent to the credit department for approval, where the clerk reviews the Customer Credit Records. After approval, the credit department clerk returns one copy of the sales order to the Sales Department, where it is reviewed and filed. The remaining two copies are sent to the warehouse. The Warehouse clerk picks the goods from the shelves and sends them along with one copy of the sales order to the shipping Department. The third copy of the sales order is filed in the warehouse. Upon receipt if the goods, the shipping clerk prepares a shipping notice and sends the goods and one copy of the sales order to the customer. The clerk then sends the shipping notice to the Billing Department. Upon receipt of the shipping notice the billing clerk updates the customer's account receivable and files the shipping notice in the department.

Required

Prepare a system flowchart of the sales procedures previously described.

12. SYSTEM DOCUMENTATION—EXPENDITURE CYCLE (MANUAL PROCEDURES)

The following describes the expenditure cycle manual procedures for a hypothetical company.

The inventory control clerk examines the inventory records for items that must be replenished and prepares a two-part purchase requisition. Copy 1 of the requisition is sent to the purchasing department, and Copy 2 is filed.

Upon receipt of the requisition, the purchasing clerk selects a supplier from the valid vendor file (reference file) and prepares a three-part purchase order. Copy 1 is sent to the supplier, Copy 2 is sent to the accounts payable department where it is filed temporarily, and Copy 3 is filed in the purchases department.

A few days after the supplier ships the order, the goods arrive at the receiving department. They are inspected, and the receiving clerk prepares a three-part receiving report describing the number and quality of the items received. Copy 1 of the receiving report accompanies the goods to the stores, where they are secured. Copy 2 is sent to inventory control, where the clerk posts it to the inventory records and files the document. Copy 3 is sent to the accounts payable department, where it is filed with the purchase order.

A day or two later, the accounts payable clerk receives the supplier's invoice (bill) for the items shipped. The clerk pulls the purchase order and receiving report from the temporary file and compares the quantity ordered, quantity received, and the price charged. After reconciling the three documents, the clerk enters the purchase in the purchases journal and posts the amount owed to the accounts payable subsidiary account.

On the payment due date, the accounts payable clerk posts to the accounts payable subsidiary account to remove the liability and prepares a voucher authorizing payment to the vendor. The voucher is then sent to the cash disbursements clerk. Upon receipt of the voucher, the cash disbursements clerk prepares a check and sends it to the supplier. The clerk records the check in the check register and files a copy of the check in the department filing cabinet.

Required

Prepare a data flow diagram and a system flowchart of the expenditure cycle procedures previously described.

13. SYSTEM DOCUMENTATION CASH RECEIPTS PROCEDURES (MANUAL AND COMPUTER)

The Mailroom receives checks and remittance advices from customers in payment of their accounts receivable. The clerk reviews the documents for completeness and correctness, sends the checks to the Cash Receipts department, and sends the remittance advices to the Accounts Receivable department. The

AR clerk receives the remittance advices and updates the customers' AR records from the PC in the AR department. The cash receipts clerk receives the checks and post them to the cash receipts journal from the PC in the department. The clerk then sends the checks to the bank for deposit.

Required
Prepare a system flowchart of the procedures described above.

14. SYSTEM DOCUMENTATION—PAYROLL

The following describes the payroll procedures for a hypothetical company.

Every Thursday, the timekeeping clerk sends employee time cards to the payroll department for processing. Based on the hours worked reflected on the time cards, the employee pay rate and withholding information in the employee file, and the tax rate reference file, the payroll clerk calculates gross pay, withholdings, and net pay for each employee. The clerk then manually prepares paychecks for each employee, files hard copies of the paychecks in the payroll department, and posts the earnings to the hard-copy employee records. Finally, the clerk manually prepares a payroll summary and sends it and the paychecks to the cash disbursements department.

The cash disbursements clerk reconciles the payroll summary with the paychecks and manually records the transaction in the hard-copy cash disbursements journal. The clerk then files the payroll summary and sends the paychecks to the treasurer for signing.

The signed checks are then sent to the paymaster, who distributes them to the employees on Friday morning.

Required
Prepare a data flow diagram and a system flowchart of the payroll procedures previously described.

15. SYSTEM DOCUMENTATION—PAYROLL

Required
Assuming the payroll system described in Problem 14 uses database files and computer processing procedures, prepare a data flow diagram, an entity relationship diagram, and a systems flowchart.

16. SYSTEM DOCUMENTATION—REVENUE CYCLE MANUAL AND COMPUTER PROCESSES

The following describes the revenue cycle procedures for a hypothetical company.

The sales department clerk receives hard-copy customer orders and manually prepares a six-part hard-copy sales order. Copies of the sales order are distributed to various departments as follows: Copies 1, 2, and 3 go to the shipping department, and Copies 4, 5, and 6 are sent to the billing department where they are temporarily filed by the billing clerk.

Upon receipt of the sales order copies, the shipping clerk picks the goods from the warehouse shelves and ships them to the customer. The clerk sends Copy 1 of the sales order along with the goods to the customer. Copy 2 is sent to the billing department, and Copy 3 is filed in the shipping department.

When the billing clerk receives Copy 2 from the warehouse, she pulls the other copies from the temporary file and completes the documents by adding prices, taxes, and freight charges. Then, using the department PC, the billing clerk records the sale in the digital Sales Journal, sends Copy 4 (customer bill) to the customer, and sends Copies 5 and 6 to the AR and inventory control departments, respectively.

Upon receipt of the documents from the billing clerk, the accounts receivable and inventory control clerks post the transactions to the AR Subsidiary and Inventory Subsidiary ledgers, respectively, using their department PCs. Each clerk then files the respective sales order copies in the department.

On the payment due date, the customer sends a check for the full amount and a copy of the bill (the remittance advice) to the company. These documents are received by the mailroom clerk who distributes them as follows:

1. The check goes to the cash receipts clerk, who manually records it in the hard-copy cash receipts journal and prepares two deposit slips. One deposit slip and the check are sent to the bank; the other deposit slip is filed in the cash receipts department.
2. The remittance advice is sent to the AR clerk, who posts to the digital subsidiary accounts and then files the document.

Required
Prepare a data flow diagram and a system flowchart of the revenue cycle procedures previously described.

17. SYSTEM DOCUMENTATION—EXPENDITURE CYCLE (MANUAL AND COMPUTER PROCEDURES)

The following describes the expenditure cycle for a hypothetical company.

The company has a centralized computer system with terminals located in various departments. The terminals are networked to a computer application, and digital accounting records are hosted on a server in the data processing department.

Each day, the computer in the data processing center scans the inventory records looking for items that must be replenished. For each item below its reorder point, the system creates a digital purchase order and prints two hard copies. A technician in the data center sends the purchase orders to the purchasing department clerk.

Upon receipt of the purchase orders, the purchasing clerk reviews and signs them. He sends Copy 1 to the supplier and files Copy 2 in the purchases department.

A few days later, the supplier ships the order and the goods arrive at the receiving department. The receiving clerk reviews the digital purchase order from his terminal, inspects the goods, creates a digital Receiving Report record, and prints two hard copies of the receiving report. The system automatically updates the inventory records to reflect the receipt of goods. The clerk sends Copy 1 of the receiving report with the goods to the stores, where they are secured. Copy 2 is filed in the receiving department.

A day or two later, the accounts payable clerk receives a hard-copy supplier's invoice (bill) for the items shipped. The clerk accesses the digital receiving report and purchase order from her terminal. She then reconciles these documents with the supplier's invoice. If all aspects of the order reconcile, the clerk records the purchase in the digital purchases journal and posts the amount owed to the accounts payable subsidiary account from her terminal.

Each day, the computer application in the data processing department automatically scans the accounts payable subsidiary file for items that are due for payment and prints a two-part check. The system closes out the accounts payable record and creates a record in the digital cash disbursements journal. A data processing clerk then sends the check to the Cash Disbursement department where it is approved, signed, and distributed to the supplier. The check copy is filed in the Cash Disbursements department.

Required
Prepare a data flow diagram and a system flowchart of the expenditure cycle procedures previously described.

18. SYSTEM DOCUMENTATION—CASH RECEIPTS PROCEDURES CENTRALIZED COMPUTER)

This system employs a central computer and data to which users connect from their departments via terminals.

The Mailroom receives checks and remittance advices from customers in payment of their accounts receivable. The clerk reviews the documents for completeness and correctness, and manually prepares two copies of a remittance list for control purposes. The clerk sends the checks and one copy of the remittance list to the Cash Receipts department. He sends the remittance advices and the second copy of the remittance list to the Accounts Receivable department. The cash receipts clerk receives the checks and post them to the cash receipts journal from the terminal in the department. The clerk then prepared three copies of a deposit slip. The check and two copies of the deposit slip go to the bank. The third copy is filed in the department. Finally, the clerk sends the remittance list to the Controller's Office. When the AR clerk receives the remittance advices and the remittance list she updates the customers' AR records from the terminal in the AR department. The clerk then files the remittance advices and the remittance list in the department. The controller's office clerk receives the remittance list from cash receipts and a copy of the deposit slip from the bank. The clerk reconciles the documents to make sure that all checks were deposited and files both documents in the department.

Required
Prepare a system flowchart of the procedures described above.

19. SYSTEM DOCUMENTATION—PURCHASES AND AP PROCEDURES (CENTRALIZED COMPUTER)

This system employs a central computer and data to which users connect from their departments via terminals.

The purchases system monitors inventory levels in the inventory file. When an item of inventory falls to its predetermined reorder point the system automatically creates a records in the digital purchase order file and prepares a hard-copy purchase order, which is sent to the vendor.

The inventories arrive in the receiving department with a packing slip attached. The receiving clerk inspects and counts the items to verify that they are correct and undamaged and then records the receipt in the Receiving Report file from the terminal in the department. The system automatically updates the inventory records, and the clerk files the packing slip in the department.

The hard-copy vendor's invoice arrives at the Accounts Payable department a few days later. The AP clerk accesses the purchases system from her terminal and reviews the digital purchase order and receiving report to ensure that the items ordered were received and that the bill is correct. The clerk then records the invoice in the digital Vendor Invoice file, and sets up an account payable record in the digital AP file. Finally, the clerk files the hard-copy invoice in the department.

Required

Prepare a system flowchart of the procedures described above.

20. SYSTEM DOCUMENTATION—CASH DISBURSEMENT PROCEDURES (CENTRALIZED COMPUTER)

This system employs a central computer and data files to which users connect from their departments terminals. Access to the files is through a central Purchases System

Previous procedures created a purchase order record and a receiving report record which are stored on respective files in the data center.

A few days later, a hard-copy vendor's invoice arrives at the Accounts Payable department. The AP clerk accesses the purchases system from her terminal and reviews the digital purchase order and receiving report to ensure that the items ordered were received and that the bill is correct. The clerk then records the invoice in the digital Vendor Invoice file, and sets up an account payable record in the digital AP file. The AP is assigned a due date when it will be paid. Finally, the clerk files the hard-copy invoice in the department.

The Cash Disbursement reviews the AP file for items that are due and approves payment. The system automatically records the disbursement in the digital Cash Disbursement Journal and prints a hard-copy check, which is sent to the vendor. The clerk prints a summary of all cash disbursements made and files it in the department.

Required

Prepare a system flowchart of the procedures described above.

21. CODING SCHEME

Devise a coding scheme using block and sequential codes for the following chart of accounts for Jensen Camera Distributors.

Cash
Accounts Receivable
Office Supplies Inventory
Prepaid Insurance
Inventory
Investments in Marketable Securities
Delivery Truck
Accumulated Depreciation—Delivery Truck
Equipment
Accumulated Depreciation—Equipment
Furniture and Fixtures
Accumulated Depreciation—Furniture and Fixtures
Building
Accumulated Depreciation—Building
Land
Accounts Payable
Wages Payable
Taxes Payable
Notes Payable
Bonds Payable
Common Stock
Paid-In Capital in Excess of Par
Treasury Stock
Retained Earnings
Sales
Sales Returns and Allowances

Dividend Income
Cost of Goods Sold
Wages Expense
Utility Expense
Office Supplies Expense
Insurance Expense
Depreciation Expense
Advertising Expense
Fuel Expense
Interest Expense

22. CODING SCHEME

Devise a coding scheme for the warehouse layout shown in Problem 22. Be sure to use an appropriate coding scheme that allows the inventory to be located efficiently from the picking list.

23. FLAT-FILE VERSUS DATABASE MODEL

Outline the traditional problems associated with the flat-file model that are resolved by the database model.

PROBLEM 22: CODING SCHEME

WAREHOUSE LAYOUT

Three warehouse locations—Warehouses 1, 2, and 3
Each warehouse is organized by aisles.

Aisle A

Aisle B

Aisle C

Aisle D

Aisle E

WAREHOUSE LAYOUT

Each aisle is separated into a right and left side, with 7 shelves of goods and 17 partitions, with each storage area called a "bin."

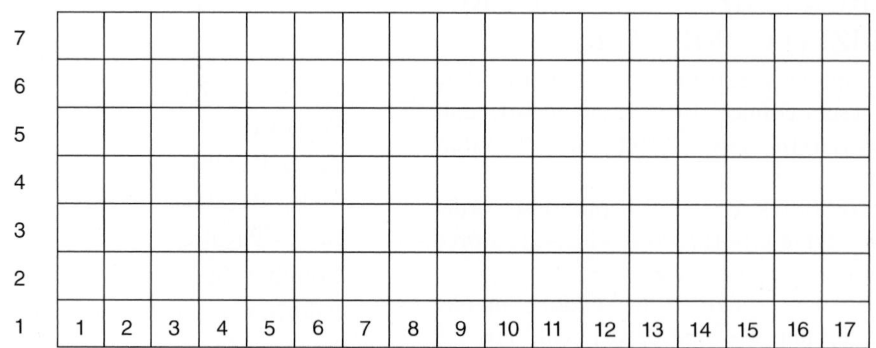

Appendix–File Structure Problems

24. ACCESS METHODS

For each of the following file processing operations, indicate whether a sequential file, indexed random file, virtual storage access method, hashing, or pointer structure would work best. You may choose as many as you wish for each step. Also, indicate which would perform the least optimally.

a. Retrieve a record from the file based on its primary key value.
b. Update a record in the file.
c. Read a complete file of records.
d. Find the next record in a file.
e. Insert a record into a file.
f. Delete a record from a file.
g. Scan a file for records with secondary keys.

25. FILE ORGANIZATION

For the following situations, indicate the most appropriate type of file organization. Explain your choice.

a. A local utility company has 80,000 residential customers and 10,000 commercial customers. The monthly billings are staggered throughout the month and, as a result, the cash receipts are fairly uniform throughout the month. For 99 percent of all accounts, one check per month is received. These receipts are recorded in a batch file, and the customer account records are updated biweekly. In a typical month, customer inquiries are received at the rate of about 20 per day.
b. A national credit card agency has 12 million customer accounts. On average, 30 million purchases and 700,000 receipts of payments are processed per day. Additionally, the customer support hotline provides information to approximately 150,000 credit card holders and 30,000 merchants per day.
c. An airline reservations system assumes that the traveler knows the departing city. From that point, fares and flight times are examined based on the destination. When a flight is identified as being acceptable to the traveler, the availability is checked and, if necessary, a seat is reserved. The volume of transactions exceeds one-half million per day.
d. A library system stocks over 2 million books and has 30,000 patrons. Each patron is allowed to check out five books. On average, there are 1.3 copies of each title in the library. Over 3,000 books are checked out each day, with approximately the same amount being returned daily. The checked-out books are posted immediately, as well as any returns of overdue books by patrons who wish to pay their fines.

CHAPTER

3

Ethics, Fraud, and Internal Control

This chapter examines three closely related areas of concern, which are specifically addressed by the Sarbanes-Oxley Act (SOX) and are important to accountants and management. These are ethics, fraud, and internal control. We begin the chapter by surveying ethical issues that highlight the organization's conflicting responsibilities to its employees, shareholders, customers, and the general public. Organization managers have an ethical responsibility to seek a balance between the risks and benefits to these constituents that result from their decisions. Management and accountants must recognize the new implications of information technologies for such historic issues as working conditions, the right to privacy, and the potential for fraud. The first section concludes with a review of the code of ethics requirements mandated by SOX.

The second section deals with the subject of fraud and its implications for accountants. Although the term *fraud* is very familiar in today's financial press, it is not always clear what constitutes fraud. In this section, we discuss the nature and meaning of fraud, differentiate between employee fraud and management fraud, explain fraud-motivating forces, review some common fraud techniques, and outline the key elements of the reform framework that SOX legislates to remedy these problems.

The final section in this chapter examines the subject of internal control. Both managers and accountants should be concerned about the adequacy of the organization's internal control structure as a means of deterring fraud and preventing errors. In this section, internal control issues are first presented on a conceptual level. We then discuss internal control within the context of the Committee of Sponsoring Organizations (COSO) framework recommended for SOX compliance.

Learning Objectives

After studying this chapter, you should:

- Understand the broad issues pertaining to business ethics.
- Have a basic understanding of ethical issues related to the use of information technology.
- Be able to distinguish between management fraud and employee fraud.
- Be familiar with common types of fraud schemes.
- Be familiar with the key features of the COSO internal control framework.
- Understand the objectives and application of both physical and IT control activities.

Ethical Issues in Business

Ethical standards are derived from societal mores and deep-rooted personal beliefs about issues of right and wrong that are *not* universally agreed upon. It is quite possible for two individuals, both of whom consider themselves to be acting ethically, to be on opposite sides of an issue. Often, we confuse ethical issues with legal issues. When the Honorable Gentleman from the state of ——, who is charged with ethical misconduct, stands before Congress and proclaims that he is "guilty of no wrongdoing," is he really saying that he did not break the law?

We have been inundated with scandals in the stock market, stories of computer crimes and viruses, and almost obscene charges of impropriety and illegalities by corporate executives. Using covert compensation schemes, Enron's Chief Financial Officer (CFO) Andy Fastow managed to improve his personal wealth by approximately $40 million. Similarly, Dennis Kozowski of Tyco, Richard Scrushy of Health-South, and Bernie Ebbers of WorldCom all became wealthy beyond imagination while driving their companies into the ground. Indeed, during the period from early 1999 to May 2002, the executives of 25 companies extracted $25 billion worth of special compensation, stock options, and private loans from their organizations while their companies' stock plummeted 75 percent or more.[1]

A thorough treatment of ethics issues is impossible within this chapter section. Instead, the objective of this section is to heighten the reader's awareness of ethical concerns relating to business, information systems, and computer technology.

BUSINESS ETHICS

Ethics pertains to the principles of conduct that individuals use in making choices and guiding their behavior in situations that involve the concepts of right and wrong. More specifically, **business ethics** involves finding the answers to two questions: (1) How do managers decide what is right in conducting their business? and (2) once managers have recognized what is right, how do they achieve it?

Ethical issues in business can be divided into four areas: equity, rights, honesty, and the exercise of corporate power. Table 3-1 identifies some of the business practices and decisions in each of these areas that have ethical implications.

Making Ethical Decisions

Business organizations have conflicting responsibilities to their employees, shareholders, customers, and the public. Every major decision has consequences that potentially harm or benefit these constituents. For example, implementing a new computer information system within an organization may cause some employees to lose their jobs, while those who remain enjoy the benefit of improved working conditions. Seeking a balance between these consequences is the managers' **ethical responsibility**. The following ethical principles provide some guidance in the discharge of this responsibility.[2]

PROPORTIONALITY. The benefit from a decision must outweigh the risks. Furthermore, there must be no alternative decision that provides the same or greater benefit with less risk.

Justice. The benefits of the decision should be distributed fairly to those who share the risks. Those who do not benefit should not carry the burden of risk.

Minimize risk. Even if judged acceptable by the principles, the decision should be implemented so as to minimize all of the risks and avoid any unnecessary risks.

COMPUTER ETHICS

The use of information technology in business has had a major impact on society and thus raises significant ethical issues regarding computer crime, working conditions, privacy, and more. **Computer ethics** is "the analysis of the nature and social impact of computer technology and the

1 Robert Prentice, *Student Guide to the Sarbanes-Oxley Act* (Thomson Publishing, 2005): p. 23.

2 M. McFarland, "Ethics and the Safety of Computer System," *Computer* (February 1991).

TABLE 3-1 Ethical Issues in Business

Category	Issues
Equity	Executive Salaries Comparable Worth Product Pricing
Rights	Corporate Due Process Employee Health Screening Employee Privacy Sexual Harassment Diversity Equal Employment Opportunity Whistle-Blowing
Honesty	Employee and Management Conflicts of Interest Security of Organization Data and Records Misleading Advertising Questionable Business Practices in Foreign Countries Accurate Reporting of Shareholder Interests
Exercise of Corporate Power	Political Action Committees Workplace Safety Product Safety Environmental Issues Divestment of Interests Corporate Political Contributions Downsizing and Plant Closures

Source: The Conference Board, "Defining Corporate Ethics," in P. Madsen and J. Shafritz, *Essentials of Business Ethics* (New York: Meridian, 1990): 18.

corresponding formulation and justification of policies for the ethical use of such technology.... [This includes] concerns about software as well as hardware and concerns about networks connecting computers as well as computers themselves."[3]

One researcher has defined three levels of computer ethics: pop, para, and theoretical.[4] Pop computer ethics is simply the exposure to stories and reports found in the popular media regarding the good or bad ramifications of computer technology. Society at large needs to be aware of such things as computer viruses and computer systems designed to aid handicapped persons. Para computer ethics involves taking a real interest in computer ethics cases and acquiring some level of skill and knowledge in the field. All systems professionals need to reach this level of competency so they can do their jobs effectively. Students of accounting information systems should also achieve this level of ethical understanding. The third level, theoretical computer ethics, is of interest to multidisciplinary researchers who apply the theories of philosophy, sociology, and psychology to computer science with the goal of bringing some new understanding to the field.

A New Problem or Just a New Twist on an Old Problem?

Some argue that all pertinent ethical issues have already been examined in some other domain. For example, the issue of property rights has been explored and has resulted in copyright, trade secret, and patent laws. Although computer programs are a new type of asset, many believe that

3 J. H. Moor, "What Is Computer Ethics?" *Metaphilosophy* 16 (1985): 266–75.

4 T. W. Bynum, "Human Values and the Computer Science Curriculum" (Working paper for the National Conference on Computing and Values, August 1991).

these programs should be considered no differently from other forms of property. A fundamental question arising from such debate is whether computers present new ethical problems or just create new twists on old problems. Where the latter is the case, we need only to understand the generic values that are at stake and the principles that should then apply.[5] However, a large contingent vociferously disagrees with the premise that computers are no different from other technologies. For example, many reject the notion of intellectual property being the same as real property. There is, as yet, no consensus on this matter.

Several issues of concern for students of accounting information systems are discussed in the following section. This list is not exhaustive, and a full discussion of each of the issues is beyond the scope of this chapter. Instead, the issues are briefly defined, and several trigger questions are provided. Hopefully, these questions will provoke thought and discussion in the classroom.

Privacy

People desire to be in full control of what and how much information about themselves is available to others, and to whom it is available. This is the issue of **privacy**. The creation and maintenance of huge, shared databases make it necessary to protect people from the potential misuse of data. This raises the issue of **ownership** in the personal information industry.[6] Should the privacy of individuals be protected through policies and systems? What information about oneself does the individual own? Should firms that are unrelated to individuals buy and sell information about these individuals without their permission?

Security (Accuracy and Confidentiality)

Computer **security** is an attempt to avoid such undesirable events as a loss of confidentiality or data integrity. Security systems attempt to prevent fraud and other misuse of computer systems; they act to protect and further the legitimate interests of the system's constituencies. The ethical issues involving security arise from the emergence of shared, computerized databases that have the potential to cause irreparable harm to individuals by disseminating inaccurate information to authorized users, such as through incorrect credit reporting.[7] There is a similar danger in disseminating accurate information to persons unauthorized to receive it. However, increasing security can actually cause other problems. For example, security can be used both to protect personal property and to undermine freedom of access to data, which may have an injurious effect on some individuals. Which is the more important goal? Automated monitoring can be used to detect intruders or other misuse, yet it can also be used to spy on legitimate users, thus diminishing their privacy. Where is the line to be drawn? What is an appropriate use and level of security? Which is most important: security, accuracy, or confidentiality?

Ownership of Property

Laws designed to preserve real property rights have been extended to cover what is referred to as *intellectual property*, that is, software. The question here becomes what an individual (or organization) can own. Ideas? Media? Source code? Object code? A related question is whether owners and users should be constrained in their use or access. Copyright laws have been invoked in an attempt to protect those who develop software from having it copied. Unquestionably, the hundreds of thousands of program development hours should be protected from piracy. However, many believe the copyright laws can cause more harm than good. For example, should the look and feel of a software package be granted copyright protection? Some argue that this flies in the face of the original intent of the law. Although

5 G. Johnson, "A Framework for Thinking about Computer Ethics," in J. Robinette and R. Barquin (eds), *Computers and Ethics: A Sourcebook for Discussions* (Brooklyn: Polytechnic Press, 1989): 26–31.

6 W. Ware, "Contemporary Privacy issues" (Working Paper for the National Conference on Computing and Human Values, August 1991).

7 K. C. Laudon, "Data Quality and Due Process in Large Interorganizational Record Systems," *Communications of the ACM* (1986): 4–11.

the purpose of copyrights is to promote the progress of science and the useful arts, allowing a user interface the protection of copyright may do just the opposite. The best interest of computer users is served when industry standards emerge; copyright laws work against this. Part of the problem lies in the uniqueness of software, its ease of dissemination, and the possibility of exact replication. Does software fit with the current categories and conventions regarding ownership?

Equity in Access

Some barriers to access are intrinsic to the technology of information systems, but some are avoidable through careful system design. Several factors, some of which are not unique to information systems, can limit access to computing technology. The economic status of the individual or the affluence of an organization will determine the ability to obtain information technology. Culture also limits access, for example, when documentation is prepared in only one language or is poorly translated. Safety features, or the lack thereof, have limited access to pregnant women, for example. How can hardware and software be designed with consideration for differences in physical and cognitive skills? What is the cost of providing equity in access? For what groups of society should equity in access become a priority?

Environmental Issues

Computers with high-speed printers allow for the production of printed documents faster than ever before. It is probably easier just to print a document than to consider whether it should be printed and how many copies really need to be made. It may be more efficient or more comforting to have a hard copy in addition to the electronic version. However, paper comes from trees, a precious natural resource, and ends up in landfills if not properly recycled. Should organizations limit nonessential hard copies? Can *nonessential* be defined? Who can and should define it? Should proper recycling be required? How can it be enforced?

Artificial Intelligence

A new set of social and ethical issues has arisen out of the popularity of expert systems. Because of the way these systems have been marketed—that is, as decision makers or replacements for experts—some people rely on them significantly. Therefore, both knowledge engineers (those who write the programs) and domain experts (those who provide the knowledge about the task being automated) must be concerned about their responsibility for faulty decisions, incomplete or inaccurate knowledge bases, and the role given to computers in the decision-making process.[8] Further, because expert systems attempt to clone a manager's decision-making style, an individual's prejudices may implicitly or explicitly be included in the knowledge base. Some of the questions that need to be explored are: Who is responsible for the completeness and appropriateness of the knowledge base? Who is responsible for a decision made by an expert system that causes harm when implemented? Who owns the expertise once it is coded into a knowledge base?

Unemployment and Displacement

Many jobs have been and are being changed as a result of the availability of computer technology. People unable or unprepared to change are displaced. Should employers be responsible for retraining workers who are displaced as a result of the computerization of their functions?

Misuse of Computers

Computers can be misused in many ways. Copying proprietary software, using a company's computer for personal benefit, and snooping through other people's files are just a few obvious examples.[9] Although copying proprietary software (except to make a personal backup copy) is

---

8 R. Dejoie, G. Fowler, and D. Paradice (eds), *Ethical Issues in Information Systems* (Boston: Boyd & Fraser, 1991).

9 K. A. Forcht, "Assessing the Ethic Standards and Policies in Computer-Based Environments," in R. Dejoie, G. Fowler, and D. Paradice (eds), *Ethical Issues in Information Systems* (Boston: Boyd & Fraser, 1991).

clearly illegal, it is commonly done. Why do people think that it is not necessary to obey this law? Are there any good arguments for trying to change this law? What harm is done to the software developer when people make unauthorized copies? A computer is not an item that deteriorates with use, so is there any harm to the employer if it is used for an employee's personal benefit? Does it matter if the computer is used during company time or outside of work hours? Is there a difference if some profit-making activity takes place rather than, for example, using the computer to write a personal letter? Does it make a difference if a profit-making activity takes place during or outside working hours? Is it okay to look through paper files that clearly belong to someone else? Is there any difference between paper files and computer files?

SARBANES-OXLEY ACT AND ETHICAL ISSUES

Public outcry surrounding ethical misconduct and fraudulent acts by executives of Enron, Global Crossing, Tyco, Adelphia, WorldCom, and others spurred Congress into passing the American Competitiveness and Corporate Accountability Act of 2002. This wide-sweeping legislation, more commonly known as the **Sarbanes-Oxley Act (SOX)**, is the most significant securities law since the Securities and Exchange Commission (SEC) Acts of 1933 and 1934. SOX has many provisions designed to deal with specific problems relating to capital markets, corporate governance, and the auditing profession. Several of these are discussed later in the chapter. At this point, we are concerned primarily with Section 406 of the act, which pertains to ethical issues.

Section 406—Code of Ethics for Senior Financial Officers

Section 406 of SOX requires public companies to disclose to the SEC whether they have adopted a code of ethics that applies to the organization's chief executive officer (CEO), CFO, controller, or persons performing similar functions. If the company has not adopted such a code, it must explain why. A public company may disclose its code of ethics in several ways: (1) by including the code as an exhibit to its annual report, (2) by posting the code to the company website, or (3) by agreeing to provide copies of the code upon request.

Although Section 406 applies specifically to executive and financial officers of a company, a company's code of ethics should apply equally to all employees. Top management's attitude toward ethics sets the tone for business practice, but it is also the responsibility of lower-level managers and nonmanagers to uphold a firm's ethical standards. Ethical violations can occur throughout an organization from the boardroom to the receiving dock. Methods must therefore be developed for including all management and employees in the firm's ethics schema. The SEC has ruled that compliance with Section 406 necessitates a written code of ethics that addresses the following ethical issues.

CONFLICTS OF INTEREST. The company's code of ethics should outline procedures for dealing with actual or apparent conflicts of interest between personal and professional relationships. Note that the issue here is in dealing with conflicts of interest, not prohibiting them. Although avoidance is the best policy, sometimes conflicts are unavoidable. Thus, one's handling and full disclosure of the matter become the ethical concern. Managers and employees alike should be made aware of the firm's code of ethics, be given decision models, and participate in training programs that explore conflict of interest issues.

FULL AND FAIR DISCLOSURES. This provision states that the organization should provide full, fair, accurate, timely, and understandable disclosures in the documents, reports, and financial statements that it submits to the SEC and to the public. Overly complex and misleading accounting techniques were used to camouflage questionable activities that lie at the heart of many recent financial scandals. The objective of this rule is to ensure that future disclosures are candid, open, truthful, and void of such deceptions.

LEGAL COMPLIANCE. Codes of ethics should require employees to follow applicable governmental laws, rules, and regulations. As stated previously, we must not confuse ethical issues with legal issues. Nevertheless, doing the right thing requires sensitivity to laws, rules, regulations, and societal expectations. To accomplish this, organizations must provide employees with training and guidance.

INTERNAL REPORTING OF CODE VIOLATIONS. The code of ethics must provide a mechanism to permit prompt internal reporting of ethics violations. This provision is similar in nature to Sections 301 and 806, which were designed to encourage and protect whistle-blowers. Employee ethics hotlines are emerging as the mechanism for dealing with these related requirements. Because SOX requires this function to be confidential, many companies are outsourcing their employee hotline service to independent vendors.

ACCOUNTABILITY. An effective ethics program must take appropriate action when code violations occur. This will include various disciplinary measures, including dismissal. Employees must see an employee hotline as credible, or they will not use it. Section 301 directs the organization's audit committee to establish procedures for receiving, retaining, and treating such complaints about accounting procedures and internal control violations. Audit committees will also play an important role in the oversight of ethics enforcement activities.

Fraud and Accountants

Perhaps no major aspect of the independent auditor's role has caused more controversy than the auditor's responsibility for detecting fraud during an audit. In recent years, the structure of the U.S. financial reporting system has become the object of scrutiny. The SEC, the courts, and the public, along with Congress, have focused on business failures and questionable practices by the management of corporations that engage in alleged fraud. The question often asked is, "Where were the auditors?" The passage of SOX has had a tremendous impact on the external auditor's responsibilities for fraud detection during a financial audit. It requires the auditor to test controls specifically intended to prevent or detect fraud likely to result in a material misstatement of the financial statements. The current authoritative guidelines on fraud detection are presented in **Statement on Auditing Standards (SAS) No. 99, *Consideration of Fraud in a Financial Statement Audit*.** The objective of SAS 99 is to seamlessly blend the auditor's consideration of fraud into all phases of the audit process. In addition, SAS 99 requires the auditor to perform new steps such as a brainstorming during audit planning to assess the potential risk of material misstatement of the financial statements from fraud schemes.

DEFINITIONS OF FRAUD

Although *fraud* is a familiar term in today's financial press, its meaning is not always clear. For example, in cases of bankruptcies and business failures, alleged fraud is often the result of poor management decisions or adverse business conditions. Under such circumstances, it becomes necessary to clearly define and understand the nature and meaning of fraud.

Fraud denotes a false representation of a material fact made by one party to another party with the intent to deceive and induce the other party to justifiably rely on the fact to his or her detriment. According to common law, a fraudulent act must meet the following five conditions:

1. *False representation.* There must be a false statement or a nondisclosure.
2. *Material fact.* A fact must be a substantial factor in inducing someone to act.
3. *Intent.* There must be the intent to deceive or the knowledge that one's statement is false.
4. *Justifiable reliance.* The misrepresentation must have been a substantial factor on which the injured party relied.
5. *Injury or loss.* The deception must have caused injury or loss to the victim of the fraud.

Fraud in the business environment has a more specialized meaning. It is an intentional deception, misappropriation of a company's assets, or manipulation of a company's financial data to the advantage of the perpetrator. In accounting literature, fraud is also commonly known as *white-collar crime, defalcation, embezzlement,* and *irregularities.* Auditors encounter fraud at two levels: *employee fraud and management fraud.* Because each form of fraud has different implications for auditors, we need to distinguish between the two.

Employee fraud, or fraud by nonmanagement employees, is generally designed to directly convert cash or other assets to the employee's personal benefit. Typically, the employee circumvents the company's internal control system for personal gain. If a company has an effective system of internal control, defalcations or embezzlements can usually be prevented or detected.

Employee fraud usually involves three steps: (1) stealing something of value (an asset), (2) converting the asset to a usable form (cash), and (3) concealing the crime to avoid detection. The third step is often the most difficult. It may be relatively easy for a storeroom clerk to steal inventories from the employer's warehouse, but altering the inventory records to hide the theft is more of a challenge.

Management fraud is more insidious than employee fraud because it often escapes detection until the organization has suffered irreparable damage or loss. Management fraud usually does not involve the direct theft of assets. Top management may engage in fraudulent activities to drive up the market price of the company's stock. This may be done to meet investor expectations or to take advantage of stock options that have been loaded into the manager's compensation package. The Commission on Auditors' Responsibilities calls this performance fraud, which often involves deceptive practices to inflate earnings or to forestall the recognition of either insolvency or a decline in earnings. Lower-level management fraud typically involves materially misstating financial data and internal reports to gain additional compensation, to garner a promotion, or to escape the penalty for poor performance. Management fraud has three defining characteristics: [10]

1. The fraud is perpetrated at levels of management above the one to which internal control structures generally relate.
2. The fraud frequently involves using the financial statements to create an illusion that an entity is healthier and more prosperous than, in fact, it is.
3. If the fraud involves misappropriation of assets, it frequently is shrouded in a maze of complex business transactions, often involving related third parties.

The preceding characteristics of management fraud suggest that management can often perpetrate irregularities by overriding an otherwise effective internal control structure that would prevent similar irregularities by lower-level employees.

THE FRAUD TRIANGLE

The **fraud triangle** consists of three factors that contribute to or are associated with management and employee fraud. These are (1) *situational pressure,* which includes personal or job-related stresses that could coerce an individual to act dishonestly; (2) *opportunity,* which involves direct access to assets and/or access to information that controls assets, and; (3) *ethics,* which pertains to one's character and degree of moral opposition to acts of dishonesty. Figure 3-1 graphically depicts the interplay among these three forces. The figure suggests that an individual with a high level of personal ethics, who is confronted by low pressure and limited opportunity to commit fraud, is more likely to behave honestly than one with weaker personal ethics who is under high pressure and is exposed to greater fraud opportunities.

Research by forensic experts and academics has shown that the auditor's evaluation of fraud is enhanced when the fraud triangle factors are considered. Obviously, matters of ethics and personal stress do not lend themselves to easy observation and analysis. To provide insight into these factors, auditors often use a *red-flag* checklist consisting of the following types of questions:[11]

- Do key executives have unusually high personal debt?
- Do key executives appear to be living beyond their means?
- Do key executives engage in habitual gambling?

10 R. Grinaker, "Discussant's Response to a Look at the Record on Auditor Detection of Management Fraud," *Proceedings of the 1980 Touche Ross University of Kansas Symposium on Auditing Problems* (Kansas City: University of Kansas, 1980).

11 Ibid

FIGURE 3-1 FRAUD TRIANGLE

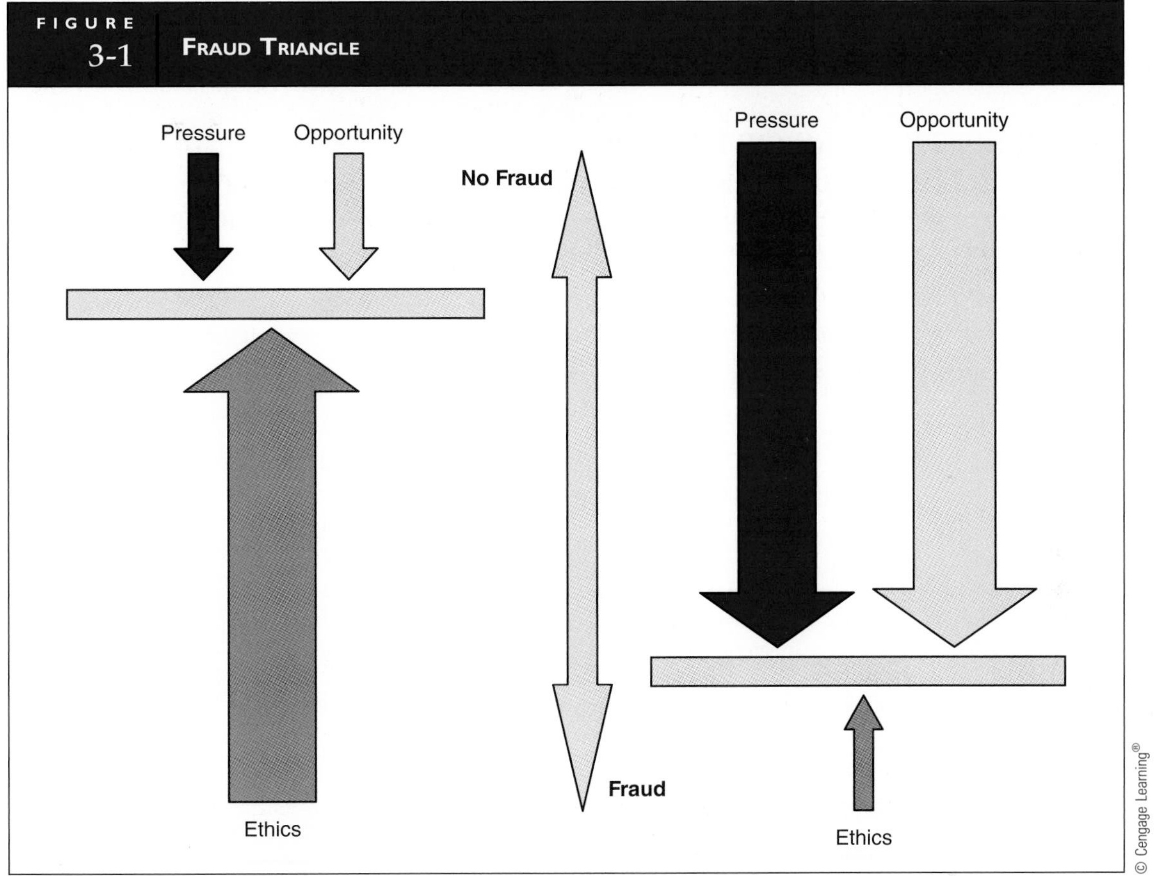

- Do key executives appear to abuse alcohol or drugs?
- Do any of the key executives appear to lack personal codes of ethics?
- Are economic conditions unfavorable within the company's industry?
- Does the company use several different banks, none of which sees the company's entire financial picture?
- Do any key executives have close associations with suppliers?
- Is the company experiencing a rapid turnover of key employees, either through resignation or termination?
- Do one or two individuals dominate the company?

A review of some of these questions shows that contemporary auditors may need to use professional investigative agencies to run confidential background checks on key managers of existing and prospective client firms.

FINANCIAL LOSSES FROM FRAUD

A research study published by the Association of Certified Fraud Examiners (ACFE) in 2010 estimated losses from fraud and abuse to be 5 percent of annual revenues. This translates to approximately $3.5 trillion in fraud losses for 2012. The actual cost of fraud is, however, difficult to quantify for a number of reasons: (1) not all fraud is detected; (2) of that detected, not all is reported; (3) in many fraud cases, incomplete information is gathered; (4) information is not properly distributed to management or law enforcement authorities; and (5) too often, business organizations decide to take no civil or criminal action against the perpetrator(s) of fraud. In addition to the direct economic loss to the organization, indirect costs, including reduced productivity, the cost of legal action, increased unemployment, and business disruption due to investigation of the fraud, need to be considered.

Of the 1388 occupational fraud cases examined in the ACFE study, the median loss from fraud was $140,000, while almost 20 percent of the organizations experienced losses of $1 million or more. The distribution of dollar losses is presented in Table 3-2.

THE PERPETRATORS OF FRAUDS

The ACFE study examined a number of factors that profile the perpetrators of the frauds, including position within the organization, collusion with others, gender, age, and education. The median financial loss was calculated for each factor. The results of the study are summarized in Tables 3-3 through 3-7.[12]

TABLE 3-2 Distribution of Losses

Amount of Loss ($)	Percent of Frauds
1–200,000	55.5
200,000–400,000	12.8
400,000–600,000	5.7
600,000–800,000	3.5
800,000–1,000,000	1.9
1,000,000 and above	20.6

Source: Association of Certified Fraud Examiners World Headquaters "The Gregor Building 716 West Avenue" Austin, TX, 2012.

TABLE 3-3 Losses from Fraud by Position

Position	Percent of Frauds	Loss ($)
Owner/Executive	18.5	723,000
Manager	34.3	150,000
Employee	43	50,000
Other	4.2	86,000

TABLE 3-4 Losses from Fraud by Collusion

Perpetrators	Loss ($)
Two or more (33%)	175,000
One (67%)	100,000

TABLE 3-5 Losses from Fraud by Gender

Gender	Loss ($)
Male (55%)	200,000
Female (45%)	91,000

12 *Report to the Nation on Occupational Fraud & Abuse* (Association of Certified Fraud Examiners, 2010): 159–243.

TABLE 3-6 **Losses from Fraud by Age**

Age Range	Loss ($)
<26	25,000
26–30	50,000
31–35	100,000
36–40	150,000
41–45	183,000
46–50	200,000
51–55	600,000
56–60	232,000
>60	250,000

TABLE 3-7 **Losses from Fraud by Educational Level**

Education Level	Loss ($)
High School	75,000
College	200,000
Postgraduate	300,000

Fraud Losses by Position within the Organization

Table 3-3 shows that 43 percent of the reported fraud cases were committed by non-managerial employees, 34 percent by managers, and 18 percent by executives or owners. Although the reported number of frauds perpetrated by employees is higher than that reported for managers and more than twice that reported for executives, the average losses per category are inversely related.

Fraud Losses and the Collusion Effect

Collusion among employees in the commission of a fraud is difficult to both prevent and detect. This is particularly true when the collusion is between managers and their subordinate employees. Management plays a key role in the internal control structure of an organization. Managers are relied upon to prevent and detect fraud among their subordinates. When they participate in fraud with the employees over whom they are supposed to provide oversight, the organization's control structure is weakened, or completely circumvented, and the company becomes more vulnerable to losses.

Table 3-4 compares the median losses from frauds committed by individuals acting alone (regardless of position) and frauds involving collusion. This includes both internal collusion and schemes in which an employee or manager colludes with an outsider such as a vendor or a customer. Although frauds involving collusion are less common (33 percent of cases), the median loss is $175,000 as compared to $100,000 for frauds perpetrated by individuals working alone.[13]

Fraud Losses by Gender

Table 3-5 shows that the median fraud loss per case caused by males ($200,000) was more than twice that caused by females ($91,000).

Fraud Losses by Age

Table 3-6 indicates that perpetrators younger than 26 years of age caused median losses of $25,000, while those perpetrated by individuals 50 and older were many times larger.

13 The results in Table 3-4 came from the 2008 ACFE report.

Fraud Losses by Education

Table 3-7 shows the median loss from frauds relative to the perpetrator's education level. Frauds committed by high school graduates averaged only $75,000, while those with bachelor's degrees averaged $200,000. Perpetrators with advanced degrees were responsible for frauds with a median loss of $300,000.

Conclusions to be Drawn

Although the ACFE fraud study results are interesting, they appear to provide little in the way of anti-fraud decision-making criteria. Upon closer examination, however, a common thread appears. Notwithstanding the importance of personal ethics and situational pressures in inducing one to commit fraud, opportunity is the factor that actually facilitates the act. Opportunity was defined previously as access to assets and/or the information that controls assets. No matter how intensely driven by situational pressure one may become, even the most unethical individual cannot perpetrate a fraud if no opportunity to do so exists. Indeed, the opportunity factor explains much of the financial loss differential in each of the demographic categories presented in the ACFE study:

- *Position.* Individuals in the highest positions within an organization are beyond the internal control structure and have the greatest access to company funds and assets.
- *Gender.* Women are not fundamentally more honest than men, but men occupy high corporate positions in greater numbers than women. This affords men greater access to assets.
- *Age.* Older employees tend to occupy higher-ranking positions and therefore generally have greater access to company assets.
- *Education.* Generally, those with more education occupy higher positions in their organizations and therefore have greater access to company funds and other assets.
- *Collusion.* One reason for segregating occupational duties is to deny potential perpetrators the opportunity they need to commit fraud. When individuals in critical positions collude, they create opportunities to control or gain access to assets that otherwise would not exist.

FRAUD SCHEMES

Fraud schemes can be classified in a number of different ways. For purposes of discussion, this section presents the ACFE classification format. Three broad categories of fraud schemes are defined: fraudulent statements, corruption, and asset misappropriation.[14]

Fraudulent statements

Fraudulent statements are associated with management fraud. While all fraud involves some form of financial misstatement, to meet the definition under this class of fraud scheme, the financial statement misrepresentation must itself bring direct or indirect financial benefit to the perpetrator. In other words, the statement is not simply a vehicle for obscuring or covering a fraudulent act. For example, misstating the cash account balance to cover the theft of cash is not financial statement fraud. On the other hand, understating liabilities to present a more favorable financial picture of the organization, to drive up stock prices, does fall under this classification.

Table 3-8 shows that while fraudulent statements account for only 7.6 percent of the fraud cases covered in the ACFE fraud study, the median loss from this type of fraud scheme is significantly higher than losses from corruption and asset misappropriation.

Appalling as this type of fraud loss appears on paper, these numbers fail to reflect the human suffering that parallels them in the real world. How does one measure the impact on stockholders as they watch their life savings and retirement funds evaporate after news of the fraud breaks? The underlying problems that permit and aid these frauds are found in the boardroom, not the mail

14 *Report to the Nation on Occupational Fraud & Abuse.* (Austin, TX: Association of Certified Fraud Examiners, 200810, p.0: 731.

TABLE 3-8 **Losses from Fraud by Scheme Type**

Scheme Type	Percentage of Frauds*	Loss ($)
Fraudulent statements	7.6	1,000,000
Corruption	33.4	250,000
Asset misappropriation	86.7	120,000

*The sum of the percentages exceeds 100 because some of the reported frauds in the ACFE study involved more than one type of fraud scheme.

room. In this section, we examine some prominent corporate governance failures and the legislation to remedy them.

THE UNDERLYING PROBLEMS. The series of events symbolized by the Enron, WorldCom, and Adelphia debacles caused many to question whether our existing federal securities laws were adequate to ensure full and fair financial disclosures by public companies. The following underlying problems are at the root of this concern.

1. *Lack of Auditor Independence.* Auditing firms that are also engaged by their clients to perform nonaccounting activities, such as actuarial services, internal audit outsourcing services, and consulting, lack independence. The firms are essentially auditing their own work. The risk is that as auditors they will not bring to management's attention the detected problems that may adversely affect their consulting fees. For example, Enron's auditors—Arthur Andersen—were also their internal auditors and their management consultants.
2. *Lack of Director Independence.* Many boards of directors are composed of individuals who are not independent. Examples of lack of independence are directors who have a personal relationship by serving on the boards of other directors' companies; have a business trading relationship as key customers or suppliers of the company; have a financial relationship as primary stockholders or have received personal loans from the company; or have an operational relationship as employees of the company.

   A notorious example of corporate inbreeding is Adelphia Communications, a telecommunications company. Founded in 1952, it went public in 1986 and grew rapidly through a series of acquisitions. It became the sixth largest cable provider in the United States before an accounting scandal came to light. The founding family (John Rigas, CEO and chairman of the board; Timothy Rigas, CFO, chief administrative officer, and chairman of the audit committee; Michael Rigas, vice president for operation; and J.P. Rigas, vice president for strategic planning) perpetrated the fraud. Between 1998 and May 2002, the Rigas family successfully disguised transactions, distorted the company's financial picture, and engaged in embezzlement that resulted in a loss of more than $60 billion to shareholders.

   Although it is neither practical nor wise to establish a board of directors that is totally void of self-interest, popular wisdom suggests that a healthier board of directors is one in which the majority of directors are independent outsiders, with the integrity and the qualifications to understand the company and objectively plan its course.
3. *Questionable Executive Compensation Schemes.* A Thomson Financial survey revealed the strong belief that executives have abused stock-based compensation.[15] The consensus is that fewer stock options should be offered than currently is the practice. Excessive use of short-term stock options to compensate directors and executives may result in short-term thinking and strategies aimed at driving up stock prices at the expense of the firm's long-term health.

15 H. Stock, "Institutions Prize Good Governance: Once Bitten, Twice Shy, Investors Seek Oversight and Transparency." *Investor Relations Business* (November 4, 2002).

In extreme cases, financial statement misrepresentation has been the vehicle to achieve the stock price needed to exercise the option.

As a case in point, Enron's management was a firm believer in the use of stock options. Nearly every employee had some type of arrangement by which he or she could purchase shares at a discount or were granted options based on future share prices. At Enron's headquarters in Houston, televisions were installed in the elevators so employees could track Enron's (and their own portfolio's) success. Before the firm's collapse, Enron executives added millions of dollars to their personal fortunes by exercising stock options.

4. *Inappropriate Accounting Practices.* The use of inappropriate accounting techniques is a characteristic common to many financial statement fraud schemes. Enron made elaborate use of special-purpose entities to hide liabilities through off-balance-sheet accounting. Special-purpose entities are legal, but their application in this case was clearly intended to deceive the market. Enron also employed income-inflating techniques. For example, when the company sold a contract to provide natural gas for a period of two years, the company would recognize all the future revenue in the period when the contract was sold.

   WorldCom was another culprit of improper accounting practices. In April 2001, WorldCom management decided to transfer transmission line costs from current expense accounts to capital accounts. This allowed them to defer some operating expenses and report higher earnings. Also, through acquisitions, they seized the opportunity to raise earnings. WorldCom reduced the book value of hard assets of MCI by $3.4 billion and increased goodwill by the same amount. Had the assets been left at book value, they would have been charged against earnings over four years. Goodwill, on the other hand, was amortized over a much longer period. In June 2002, the company declared a $3.8 billion overstatement of profits because of falsely recorded expenses over the previous five quarters. The size of this fraud increased to $9 billion over the following months as additional evidence of improper accounting came to light.

SARBANES-OXLEY ACT AND FRAUD. To address plummeting institutional and individual investor confidence triggered in part by business failures and accounting restatements, Congress enacted SOX into law in July 2002. This landmark legislation was written to deal with problems related to capital markets, corporate governance, and the auditing profession, and has fundamentally changed the way public companies do business and how the accounting profession performs its attest function.

The act establishes a framework to modernize and reform the oversight and regulation of public company auditing. Its principal reforms pertain to (1) the creation of an accounting oversight board, (2) auditor independence, (3) corporate governance and responsibility, (4) disclosure requirements, and (5) penalties for fraud and other violations. These provisions are discussed in the following section.

1. *Accounting Oversight Board.* SOX created a **Public Company Accounting Oversight Board (PCAOB)**. The PCAOB is empowered to set auditing, quality control, and ethics standards; to inspect registered accounting firms; to conduct investigations; and to take disciplinary actions.
2. *Auditor Independence.* The act addresses auditor independence by creating more separation between a firm's attestation and nonauditing activities. This is intended to specify categories of services that a public accounting firm cannot perform for its client. These include the following nine functions:
   a. Bookkeeping or other services related to the accounting records or financial statements
   b. Financial information systems design and implementation
   c. Appraisal or valuation services, fairness opinions, or contribution-in-kind reports
   d. Actuarial services
   e. Internal audit outsourcing services
   f. Management functions or human resources
   g. Broker or dealer, investment adviser, or investment banking services

h. Legal services and expert services unrelated to the audit
i. Any other service that the PCAOB determines is impermissible

Although SOX prohibits auditors from providing these services to their audit clients, they are not prohibited from performing such services for nonaudit clients or privately held companies.

3. *Corporate Governance and Responsibility.* The act requires all audit committee members to be independent and requires the audit committee to hire and oversee the external auditors. This provision is consistent with many investors who consider the board composition to be a critical investment factor. For example, a Thomson Financial survey revealed that most institutional investors want corporate boards to be composed of at least 75 percent independent directors.[16]

   Two other significant provisions of the act relating to corporate governance are (1) public companies are prohibited from making loans to executive officers and directors, and (2) the act requires attorneys to report evidence of a material violation of securities laws or breaches of fiduciary duty to the CEO, CFO, or the PCAOB.
4. *Issuer and Management Disclosure.* SOX imposes new corporate disclosure requirements, including:

   a. Public companies must report all off-balance-sheet transactions.
   b. Annual reports filed with the SEC must include a statement by management asserting that it is responsible for creating and maintaining adequate internal controls and asserting to the effectiveness of those controls.
   c. Officers must certify that the company's accounts "fairly present" the firm's financial condition and results of operations.
   d. Knowingly filing a false certification is a criminal offense.

5. *Fraud and Criminal Penalties.* SOX imposes a range of new criminal penalties for fraud and other wrongful acts. In particular, the act creates new federal crimes relating to the destruction of documents or audit work papers, securities fraud, tampering with documents to be used in an official proceeding, and actions against whistle-blowers.

Corruption

Corruption involves an executive, manager, or employee of the organization in collusion with an outsider. The ACFE study identifies four principal types of corruption: bribery, illegal gratuities, conflicts of interest, and economic extortion. Corruption accounts for about 10 percent of occupational fraud cases.

BRIBERY. Bribery involves giving, offering, soliciting, or receiving things of value to influence an official in the performance of his or her lawful duties. Officials may be employed by government (or regulatory) agencies or by private organizations. Bribery defrauds the entity (business organization or government agency) of the right to honest and loyal services from those employed by it. For example, the manager of a meat-packing company offers a U.S. health inspector a cash payment. In return, the inspector suppresses his report of health violations discovered during a routine inspection of the meat-packing facilities. In this situation, the victims are those who rely on the inspector's honest reporting. The loss is salary paid to the inspector for work not performed and any damages that result from failure to perform.

ILLEGAL GRATUITIES. An **illegal gratuity** involves giving, receiving, offering, or soliciting something of value because of an official act that has been taken. This is similar to a bribe, but the transaction occurs after the fact. For example, the plant manager in a large corporation uses his influence to ensure that a request for proposals is written in such a way that only one contractor will be able to submit a satisfactory bid. As a result, the favored contractor's proposal is accepted

16 Ibid

at a noncompetitive price. In return, the contractor secretly makes a financial payment to the plant manager. The victims in this case are those who expect a competitive procurement process. The loss is the excess costs the company incurs because of the noncompetitive pricing of the construction.

CONFLICTS OF INTEREST. Every employer should expect that his or her employees will conduct their duties in a way that serves the interests of the employer. A **conflict of interest** occurs when an employee acts on behalf of a third party during the discharge of his or her duties or has self-interest in the activity being performed. When the employee's conflict of interest is unknown to the employer and results in financial loss, then fraud has occurred. The preceding examples of bribery and illegal gratuities also constitute conflicts of interest. This type of fraud can exist, however, when bribery and illegal payments are not present, but the employee has an interest in the outcome of the economic event. For example, a purchasing agent for a building contractor is also part owner in a plumbing supply company. The agent has sole discretion in selecting vendors for the plumbing supplies needed for buildings under contract. The agent directs a disproportionate number of purchase orders to his company, which charges above-market prices for its products. The agent's financial interest in the supplier is unknown to his employer.

ECONOMIC EXTORTION. Economic extortion is the use (or threat) of force (including economic sanctions) by an individual or organization to obtain something of value. The item of value could be a financial or economic asset, information, or cooperation to obtain a favorable decision on some matter under review. For example, a contract procurement agent for a state government threatens to blacklist a highway contractor if he does not make a financial payment to the agent. If the contractor fails to cooperate, the blacklisting will effectively eliminate him from consideration for future work. Faced with a threat of economic loss, the contractor makes the payment.

Asset Misappropriation

The most common fraud schemes involve some form of asset misappropriation in which assets are either directly or indirectly diverted to the perpetrator's benefit. Almost 90 percent of the frauds included in the ACFE study fall in this general category. Certain assets are, however, more susceptible than others to misappropriation. Transactions involving cash, checking accounts, inventory, supplies, equipment, and information are the most vulnerable to abuse. Table 3-9 shows the percentage of occurrence and the median value of fraud losses in eight subcategories of asset misappropriation. The following sections provide definitions and examples of the fraud schemes listed in the table.

Skimming

Skimming involves stealing cash from an organization before it is recorded on the organization's books and records. One example of skimming is an employee who accepts payment from a

TABLE 3-9 **Losses from Asset Misappropriation Schemes**

Scheme Type	Percentage of Frauds*	Loss ($)
Skimming	14.6	58,000
Cash Larceny	11	54,000
Billing	24.9	100,000
Check Tampering	11.9	143,000
Payroll	9.3	48,000
Expense Reimbursement	14.5	26,000
Theft of Cash	11.8	20,000
Non-Cash Misappropriations	17.2	58,000

*The sum of percentage exceeds 100 percent because some fraud cases in the ACFE study involved multiple schemes from more than one category.

customer but does not record the sale. Another example is **mail room fraud** in which an employee opening the mail steals a customer's check and destroys the associated remittance advice. By destroying the remittance advice, no evidence of the cash receipt exists. This type of fraud may continue for several weeks or months until detected. Ultimately the fraud will be detected when the customer complains that his account has not been credited. By that time, however, the mail room employee will have left the organization and moved on.

Cash Larceny

Cash larceny involves schemes in which cash receipts are stolen from an organization after they have been recorded in the organization's books and records. An example of this is **lapping**, in which the cash receipts clerk first steals and cashes a check from Customer A. To conceal the accounting imbalance caused by the loss of the asset, Customer A's account is not credited. Later (the next billing period), the employee uses a check received from Customer B and applies it to Customer A's account. Funds received in the next period from Customer C are then applied to the account of Customer B, and so on.

Employees involved in this sort of fraud often rationalize that they are simply borrowing the cash and plan to repay it at some future date. This kind of accounting cover-up continues indefinitely or until the employee returns the funds. Lapping is usually detected when the employee leaves the organization or becomes sick and must take time off from work. Unless the fraud is perpetuated, the last customer to have funds diverted from his or her account will be billed again, and the lapping technique will be detected. Employers can deter lapping by periodically rotating employees into different jobs and forcing them to take scheduled vacations.

Billing Schemes

Billing schemes, also known as **vendor fraud**, are perpetrated by employees who cause their employer to issue a payment to a false supplier (vendor) by submitting invoices for fictitious goods or services, inflated invoices, or invoices for personal purchases. Three examples of billing scheme are presented here.

A **shell company** fraud first requires that the perpetrator establish a false supplier on the books of the victim company. The fraudster then manufactures false purchase orders, receiving reports, and invoices in the name of the vendor and submits them to the accounting system, which creates the illusion of a legitimate transaction. Based on these documents, the system will set up an account payable and ultimately issue a check to the false supplier (the fraudster). This sort of fraud may continue for years before it is detected.

A **pass through fraud** is similar to the shell company fraud with the exception that a transaction actually takes place. Again, the perpetrator creates a false vendor and issues purchase orders to it for inventory or supplies. The false vendor then purchases the needed inventory from a legitimate vendor. The false vendor charges the victim company a much higher than market price for the items, but pays only the market price to the legitimate vendor. The difference is the profit that the perpetrator pockets.

A **pay-and-return** scheme involves a clerk with check-writing authority who intentionally pays a vendor twice for the same invoice for the purchase of inventory or supplies. The vendor, recognizing that its customer made a double payment issues a reimbursement check to the victim company, which the clerk intercepts and cashes.

Check Tampering

Check tampering involves forging or changing in some material way a check that the organization has written to a legitimate payee. One example of this is an employee who steals an outgoing check to a vendor, forges the payee's signature, and cashes the check. A variation on this is an employee who steals blank checks from the victim company and makes them out to himself or to an accomplice.

Payroll Fraud

Payroll fraud is the distribution of fraudulent paychecks to existent and/or nonexistent employees. For example, a supervisor keeps an employee on the payroll who has left the organization. Each week, the supervisor continues to submit time cards to the payroll department as if the employee were still working for the victim organization. The fraud works best in organizations in which the supervisor is responsible for distributing paychecks to employees. The supervisor may thus intercept the paycheck, forge the former employee's signature, and cash it. Another example of payroll fraud is to inflate the hours worked on an employee time card so that he or she will receive a larger than deserved paycheck. This type of fraud often involves collusion with the supervisor or timekeeper.

Expense Reimbursements

Expense reimbursement frauds are schemes in which an employee makes a claim for reimbursement of fictitious or inflated business expenses. For example, a company salesperson files false expense reports, claiming meals, lodging, and travel that never occurred.

Thefts of Cash

Thefts of cash are schemes that involve the direct theft of cash on hand in the organization. An example of this is an employee who makes false entries on a cash register, such as voiding a sale, to conceal the fraudulent removal of cash. Another example is a bank employee who steals cash from the vault.

Non-Cash Misappropriations

Non-cash fraud schemes involve the theft or misuse of the victim organization's non-cash assets. One example of this is a warehouse clerk who steals inventory from a warehouse or storeroom. Another example is a customer services clerk who sells confidential customer information to a third party.

Computer Fraud

Because computers lie at the heart of modern accounting information systems, the topic of **computer fraud** is of importance to auditors. Although the fundamental structure of fraud is unchanged by computers—fraudulent statements, corruption, and asset misappropriation—computers do add complexity to the fraud picture. To fully appreciate these complexities requires an awareness of technology and internal control issues that are discussed in subsequent chapters. Computer fraud is therefore deferred to Chapter 15, where we examine a number of related topics.

Internal Control Concepts and Techniques

With a backdrop of ethics and fraud in place, let's now examine internal control concepts and techniques for dealing with these problems. The **internal control system** comprises policies, practices, and procedures employed by the organization to achieve four broad objectives:

1. To safeguard assets of the firm.
2. To ensure the accuracy and reliability of accounting records and information.
3. To promote efficiency in the firm's operations.
4. To measure compliance with management's prescribed policies and procedures.[17]

---

17 American Institute of Certified Public Accountants, *AICPA Professional Standards*, Vol. 1. AU Sec. 320. (New York: AICPA, 1987): 30–35.

Modifying Assumptions

Inherent in these control objectives are four modifying assumptions that guide designers and auditors of internal controls.[18]

MANAGEMENT RESPONSIBILITY. This concept holds that the establishment and maintenance of a system of internal control is a **management responsibility**. This point is made eminent in SOX legislation.

REASONABLE ASSURANCE. The internal control system should provide **reasonable assurance** that the four broad objectives of internal control are met in a cost-effective manner. This means that no system of internal control is perfect and the cost of achieving improved control should not outweigh its benefits.

METHODS OF DATA PROCESSING. Internal controls should achieve the four broad objectives regardless of the data processing method used. The control techniques used to achieve these objectives will, however, vary with different types of technology.

LIMITATIONS. Every system of internal control has limitations on its effectiveness. These include (1) the possibility of error—no system is perfect, (2) circumvention—personnel may circumvent the system through collusion or other means, (3) management override—management is in a position to override control procedures by personally distorting transactions or by directing a subordinate to do so, and (4) changing conditions—conditions may change over time and render existing controls ineffective.

Exposures and Risk

Figure 3-2 portrays the internal control system as a shield that protects the firm's assets from numerous undesirable events that bombard the organization. These include attempts at unauthorized access to the firm's assets (including information); fraud perpetrated by persons both inside and outside the firm; errors due to employee incompetence, faulty computer programs and corrupted input data; and mischievous acts, such as unauthorized access by computer hackers and threats from computer viruses that destroy programs and databases.

The absence or weakness of a control is called an **exposure**. Exposures, which are illustrated as holes in the control shield in Figure 3-2, increase the firm's risk to financial loss or injury from undesirable events. A weakness in internal control may expose the firm to one or more of the following types of risks:

1. Destruction of assets (both physical assets and information).
2. Theft of assets.
3. Corruption of information or the information system.
4. Disruption of the information system.

The Preventive-Detective-Corrective Internal Control Model

Figure 3-3 illustrates that the internal control shield is composed of three levels of control: preventive controls, detective controls, and corrective controls. This is the preventive-detective-corrective (PDC) control model.

PREVENTIVE CONTROLS. Prevention is the first line of defense in the control structure. **Preventive controls** are passive techniques designed to reduce the frequency of occurrence of

18 American Institute of Certified Public Accountants, Committee on Auditing Procedure, *Internal Control—Elements of a Coordinated System and Its Importance to Management and the Independent Public Accountant*, Statement on Auditing Standards No. 1, Sec. 320 (New York: AICPA, 1973).

FIGURE 3-2 INTERNAL CONTROL SHIELD

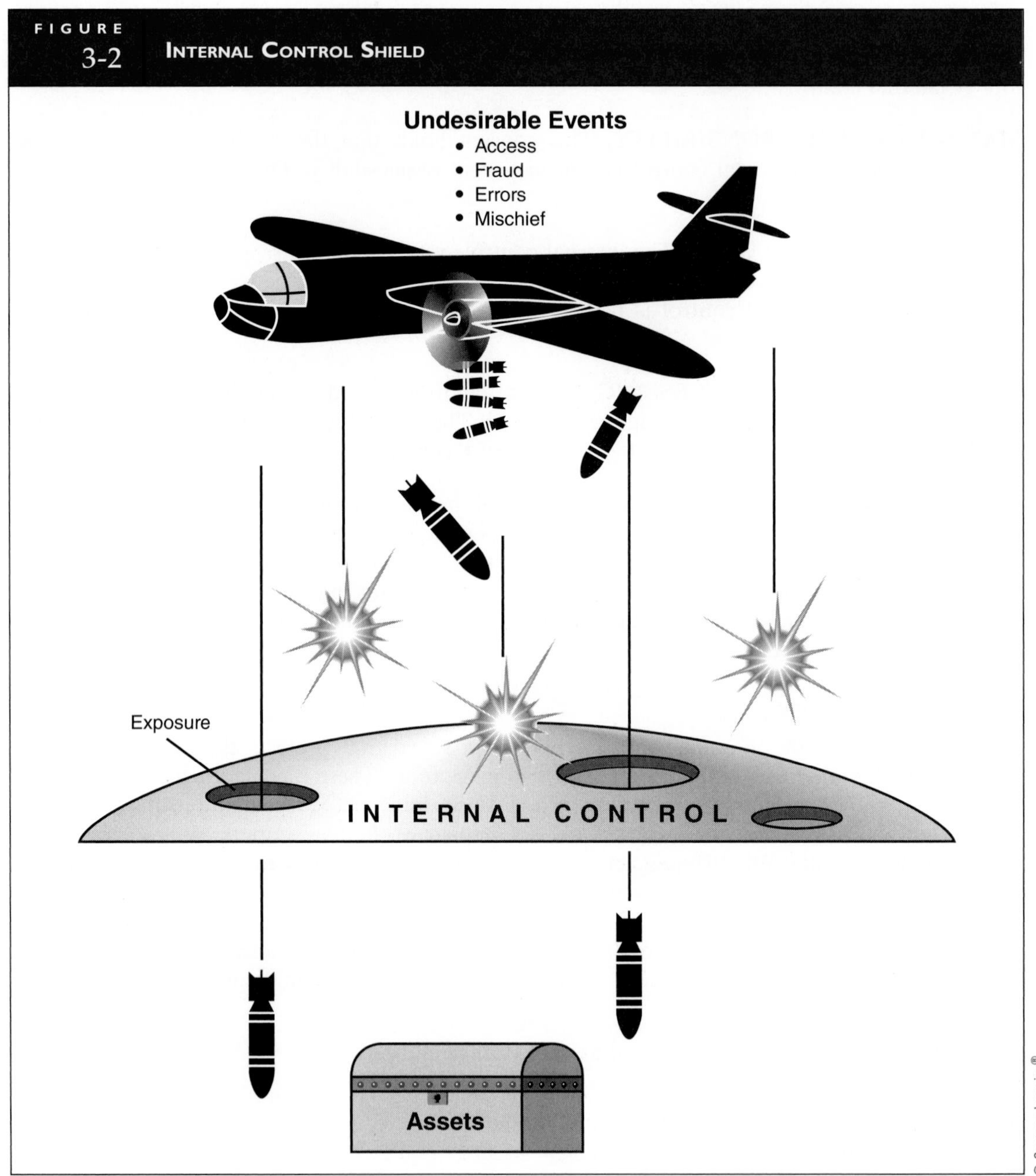

undesirable events. Preventive controls force compliance with prescribed or desired actions and thus screen out aberrant events. When designing internal control systems, an ounce of prevention is most certainly worth a pound of cure. Preventing errors and fraud is far more cost-effective than detecting and correcting problems after they occur. The vast majority of undesirable events can be blocked at this first level. For example, a well-designed source document is an example of a preventive control. The logical layout of the document into zones that contain specific data, such as customer name, address, items sold, and quantity, forces the clerk to enter the necessary data. The source documents can therefore prevent necessary data from being omitted. However, not all problems can be anticipated and prevented. Some will elude the most comprehensive network of preventive controls.

FIGURE 3-3 PREVENTIVE, DETECTIVE, AND CORRECTIVE CONTROLS

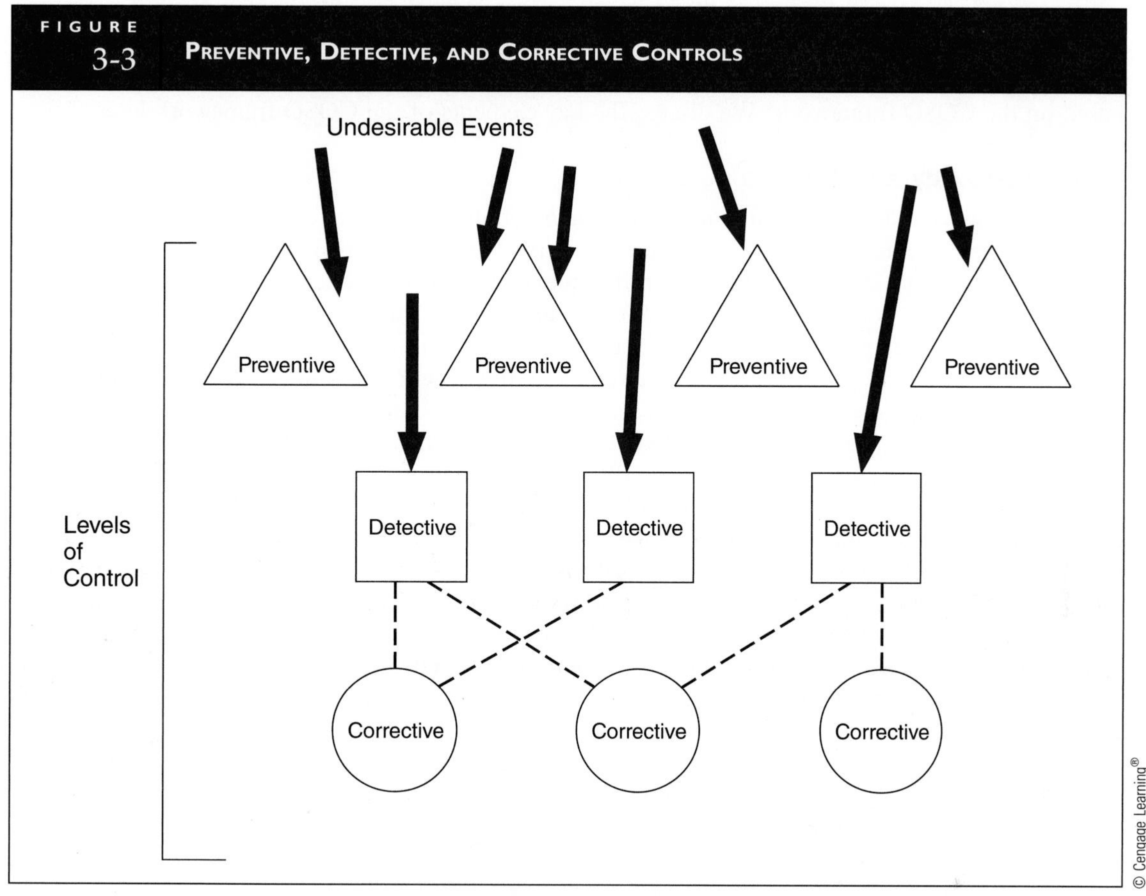

DETECTIVE CONTROLS. Detective controls form the second line of defense. These are devices, techniques, and procedures designed to identify and expose undesirable events that elude preventive controls. Detective controls reveal specific types of errors by comparing actual occurrences to pre-established standards. When the detective control identifies a departure from standard, it sounds an alarm to attract attention to the problem. For example, assume a clerk entered the following data on a customer sales order:

Quantity	Price	Total
10	$10	$1,000

Before processing this transaction and posting to the accounts, a detective control should recalculate the total value using the price and quantity, and expose the error.

CORRECTIVE CONTROLS. Corrective controls are actions taken to reverse the effects of errors detected in the previous step. There is an important distinction between detective controls and corrective controls. Detective controls identify anomalies and draw attention to them; corrective controls actually fix the problem. For any detected error, however, there may be more than one feasible corrective action, and the best course of action may not always be obvious. For example, in viewing the error above, your first inclination may have been to change the total value from $1,000 to $100 to correct the problem. This presumes that the quantity and price values on the document are correct; they may not be. At this point, we cannot determine the real cause of the problem; we know only that one exists.

Linking a corrective action to a detected error, as an automatic response, may result in an incorrect action that causes a worse problem than the original error. For this reason, error correction should be viewed as a separate control step that should be taken cautiously. The PDC control model is conceptually pleasing but offers little practical guidance for designing specific controls. For this, we need a more precise framework. The current authoritative document for specifying internal control objectives and techniques is **Statement on Auditing Standards (SAS) No. 109**,[19] which is based on the COSO framework. We discuss the key elements of the COSO framework later.

Sarbanes-Oxley and Internal Control

Sarbanes-Oxley legislation requires management of public companies to implement an adequate system of internal controls over their financial reporting process. This includes controls over transaction processing systems that feed data to the financial reporting systems. Management's responsibilities for this are codified in Sections 302 and 404 of SOX. Section 302 requires that corporate management (including the CEO) certify the organization's internal controls on a quarterly and annual basis. In addition, Section 404 requires the management of public companies to assess the effectiveness of the organization's internal controls. This entails providing an annual report addressing the following points: (1) a statement of management's responsibility for establishing and maintaining adequate internal control, (2) an assessment of the effectiveness of the company's internal controls over financial reporting, (3) a statement that the organization's external auditors have issued an attestation report on management's assessment of the company's internal controls, (4) an explicit written conclusion as to the effectiveness of internal control over financial reporting,[20] and (5) a statement identifying the framework used in the assessment of internal controls.

Regarding the control framework to be used, both the PCAOB and the SEC have endorsed the framework put forward by the **Committee of Sponsoring Organizations of the Treadway Commission (COSO)**. Further, they require that any other framework used should encompass all of COSO's general themes.[21] The COSO framework was the basis for SAS 109, which was developed for auditors and describes the complex relationship between a firm's internal controls, the auditor's assessment of risk, and the planning of audit procedures. The key elements of the COSO framework are presented in the following section.

COSO INTERNAL CONTROL FRAMEWORK

The COSO framework consists of five components: the control environment, risk assessment, information and communication, monitoring, and control activities.

The Control Environment

The **control environment** is the foundation for the other four control components. The control environment sets the tone for the organization and influences the control awareness of its management and employees. Important elements of the control environment are:

- The integrity and ethical values of management.
- The structure of the organization.
- The participation of the organization's board of directors and the audit committee, if one exists.
- Management's philosophy and operating style.
- The procedures for delegating responsibility and authority.
- Management's methods for assessing performance.
- External influences, such as examinations by regulatory agencies.
- The organization's policies and practices for managing its human resources.

19 SAS 109, *Understanding the Entity and Its Environment and Assessing the Risks of Material Misstatement*, New York: AICPA March 2006.

20 Management may not conclude that internal controls are effective if one or more material weaknesses exist. In addition, management must disclose all material weaknesses that exist as of the end of the most recent fiscal year.

21 A popular competing control framework is Control Objectives for Information and related Technology (COBIT®) published by the IT Governance Institute (ITGI). This framework maps into COSO's general themes.

SAS 109 requires that auditors obtain sufficient knowledge to assess the attitude and awareness of the organization's management, board of directors, and owners regarding internal control. The following paragraphs provide examples of techniques that may be used to obtain an understanding of the control environment.

1. Auditors should assess the integrity of the organization's management and may use investigative agencies to report on the backgrounds of key managers. Some of the "Big Four" public accounting firms employ former FBI agents whose primary responsibility is to perform background checks on existing and prospective clients. If cause for serious reservations comes to light about the integrity of the client, the auditor should withdraw from the audit. The reputation and integrity of the company's managers are critical factors in determining the auditability of the organization. Auditors cannot function properly in an environment in which client management is deemed unethical and corrupt.
2. Auditors should be aware of conditions that would predispose the management of an organization to commit fraud. Some of the obvious conditions may be lack of sufficient working capital, adverse industry conditions, bad credit ratings, and the existence of extremely restrictive conditions in bank or indenture agreements. If auditors encounter any such conditions, their examination should give due consideration to the possibility of fraudulent financial reporting. Appropriate measures should be taken, and every attempt should be made to uncover any fraud.
3. Auditors should understand a client's business and industry and should be aware of conditions peculiar to the industry that may affect the audit. Auditors should read industry-related literature and familiarize themselves with the risks that are inherent in the business.
4. The board of directors should adopt, as a minimum, the provisions of SOX. In addition, the following guidelines represent established best practices.
   - *Separate CEO and chairman.* The roles of CEO and board chairman should be separate. Executive sessions give directors the opportunity to discuss issues without management present, and an independent chairman is important in facilitating such discussions.
   - *Set ethical standards.* The board of directors should establish a code of ethical standards from which management and staff will take direction. At a minimum, a code of ethics should address such issues as outside employment conflicts, acceptance of gifts that could be construed as bribery, falsification of financial and/or performance data, conflicts of interest, political contributions, confidentiality of company and customer data, honesty in dealing with internal and external auditors, and membership on external boards of directors.
   - *Establish an independent audit committee.* The audit committee is responsible for selecting and engaging an independent auditor, for ensuring that an annual audit is conducted, for reviewing the audit report, and for ensuring that deficiencies are addressed. Large organizations with complex accounting practices may need to create audit subcommittees that specialize in specific activities.
   - *Compensation committees.* The compensation committee should not be a rubber stamp for management. Excessive use of short-term stock options to compensate directors and executives may result in decisions that influence stock prices at the expense of the firm's long-term health. Compensation schemes should be carefully evaluated to ensure that they create the desired incentives.
   - *Nominating committees.* The board nominations committee should have a plan to maintain a fully staffed board of directors with capable people as it moves forward for the next several years. The committee must recognize the need for independent directors and have criteria for determining independence. For example, under its newly implemented governance standards, General Electric (GE) considers directors independent if the sales to, and purchases from, GE total less than 1 percent of the revenue of the companies for which they serve as executives. Similar standards apply to charitable contributions from GE to any

organization on which a GE director serves as officer or director. In addition, the company has set a goal that two-thirds of the board will be independent nonemployees.[22]

- *Access to outside professionals.* All committees of the board should have access to attorneys and consultants other than the corporation's normal counsel and consultants. Under the provisions of SOX, the audit committee of an SEC reporting company is entitled to such representation independently.

Risk Assessment

Organizations must perform a **risk assessment** to identify, analyze, and manage risks relevant to financial reporting. Risks can arise or change from circumstances such as:

- Changes in the operating environment that impose new or changed competitive pressures on the firm.
- New personnel who have a different or inadequate understanding of internal control.
- New or reengineered information systems that affect transaction processing.
- Significant and rapid growth that strains existing internal controls.
- The implementation of new technology into the production process or information system that impacts transaction processing.
- The introduction of new product lines or activities with which the organization has little experience.
- Organizational restructuring resulting in the reduction and/or reallocation of personnel such that business operations and transaction processing are affected.
- Entering into foreign markets that may impact operations (that is, the risks associated with foreign currency transactions).
- Adoption of a new accounting principle that impacts the preparation of financial statements.

SAS 109 requires that auditors obtain sufficient knowledge of the organization's risk assessment procedures to understand how management identifies, prioritizes, and manages the risks related to financial reporting.

Information and Communication

The accounting information system consists of the records and methods used to initiate, identify, analyze, classify, and record the organization's transactions and to account for the related assets and liabilities.

The quality of information the accounting information system generates impacts management's ability to take actions and make decisions in connection with the organization's operations and to prepare reliable financial statements. An effective accounting information system will:

- Identify and record all valid financial transactions.
- Provide timely information about transactions in sufficient detail to permit proper classification and financial reporting.
- Accurately measure the financial value of transactions so their effects can be recorded in financial statements.
- Accurately record transactions in the time period in which they occurred.

SAS 109 requires that auditors obtain sufficient knowledge of the organization's information system to understand:

- The classes of transactions that are material to the financial statements and how those transactions are initiated.

22 Rachel E. Silverman, "GE Makes Changes in Board Policy," *The Wall Street Journal* (November 8, 2002).

- The accounting records and accounts that are used in the processing of material transactions.
- The transaction processing steps involved from the initiation of a transaction to its inclusion in the financial statements.
- The financial reporting process used to prepare financial statements, disclosures, and accounting estimates.

Monitoring

Management must determine that internal controls are functioning as intended. **Monitoring** is the process by which the quality of internal control design and operation can be assessed. This may be accomplished by separate procedures or by ongoing activities.

An organization's internal auditors may monitor the entity's activities in separate procedures. They gather evidence of control adequacy by testing controls and then communicate control strengths and weaknesses to management. As part of this process, internal auditors make specific recommendations for improvements to controls.

Ongoing monitoring may be achieved by integrating special computer modules into the information system that capture key data and/or permit tests of controls to be conducted as part of routine operations. Embedded modules thus allow management and auditors to maintain constant surveillance over the functioning of internal controls. In Chapter 17, we examine a number of embedded module techniques.

Another technique for achieving ongoing monitoring is the judicious use of management reports. Timely reports allow managers in functional areas such as sales, purchasing, production, and cash disbursements to oversee and control their operations. By summarizing activities, highlighting trends, and identifying exceptions from normal performance, well-designed management reports provide evidence of internal control function or malfunction. In Chapter 8, we review the management reporting system and examine the characteristics of effective management reports.

Control Activities

Control activities are the policies and procedures used to ensure that appropriate actions are taken to deal with the organization's identified risks. Control activities are grouped into two distinct categories: information technology (IT) controls and physical controls.

IT CONTROLS. IT controls relate specifically to the computer environment. They fall into two broad groups: general controls and application controls. **General controls** pertain to entity-wide IT concerns such as controls over the data center, organization databases, network security, systems development, and program maintenance. These control issues need to be discussed within the context of specific technologies that are the topics of several chapters of this book. Therefore, we defer treatment of general IT controls to Chapters 15, 16, and 17, which deal with this extensive body of material. **Application controls** ensure the integrity of specific computer systems such as sales order processing, accounts payable, and payroll applications. We examine application control issues and techniques later in this chapter.

PHYSICAL CONTROLS. This class of controls relates to the human activities employed in accounting systems. These activities may be purely manual, such as the physical custody of assets, or they may involve the physical use of computers to record transactions or update accounts. Physical controls do not relate to the computer logic that actually performs accounting tasks. Rather, they relate to the human activities that trigger those tasks or utilize the results of those tasks. In other words, physical controls focus on people, but are not restricted to an environment in which clerks update paper accounts with pen and ink. Virtually all systems, regardless of their sophistication, employ human activities that need to be controlled.

Our discussion will address issues pertaining to six categories of physical control activities: transaction authorization, segregation of duties, supervision, accounting records, access control, and independent verification.

FIGURE 3-4 SEGREGATION OF DUTIES OBJECTIVES

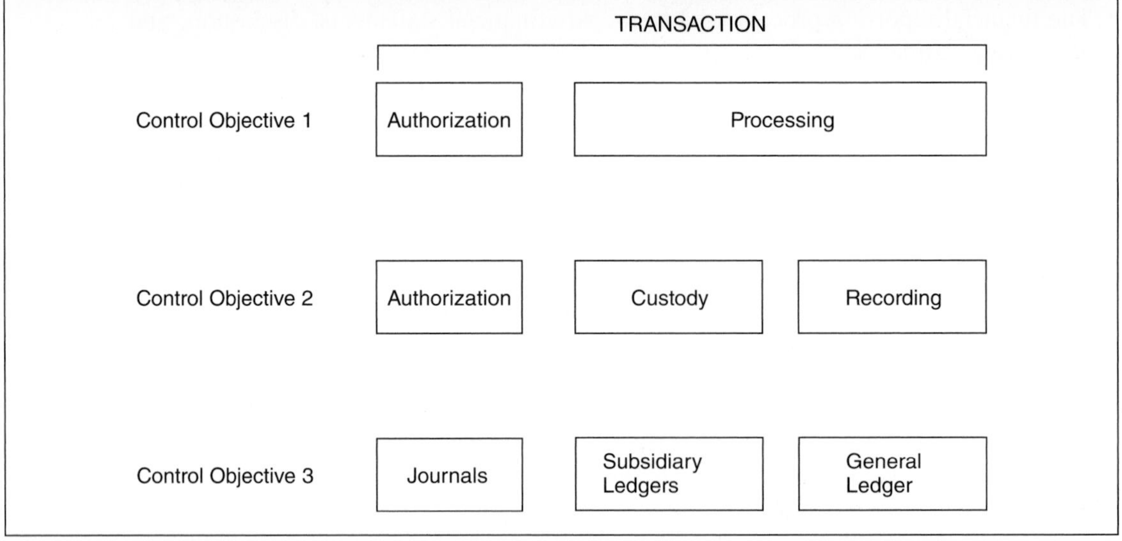

TRANSACTION AUTHORIZATION. The purpose of **transaction authorization** is to ensure that all material transactions processed by the information system are valid and in accordance with management's objectives. Authorizations may be general or specific. General authority is granted to operations personnel to perform day-to-day operations. An example of general authorization is the procedure to authorize the purchase of inventories from a designated vendor only when inventory levels fall to their predetermined reorder points. This is called a programmed procedure (not necessarily in the computer sense of the word) in which the decision rules are specified in advance, and no additional approvals are required. On the other hand, specific authorizations deal with case-by-case decisions associated with nonroutine transactions. An example of this is the decision to extend a particular customer's credit limit beyond the normal amount. Specific authority is usually a management responsibility.

SEGREGATION OF DUTIES. One of the most important control activities is the segregation of employee duties to minimize incompatible functions. **Segregation of duties** can take many forms, depending on the specific duties to be controlled. However, the following three objectives provide general guidelines applicable to most organizations. These objectives are illustrated in Figure 3-4.

Objective 1. *The segregation of duties should be such that the authorization for a transaction is separate from the processing of the transaction. For example, the purchasing department should not initiate purchases until the inventory control department gives authorization. This separation of tasks is a control to prevent individuals from purchasing unnecessary inventory.*

Objective 2. *Responsibility for the custody of assets should be separate from the record-keeping responsibility. For example, the department that has physical custody of finished goods inventory (the warehouse) should not keep the official inventory records. Accounting for finished goods inventory is performed by inventory control, an accounting function. When a single individual or department has responsibility for both asset custody and record keeping, the potential for fraud exists. Assets can be stolen or lost, and the accounting records falsified to hide the event.*

Objective 3. *The organization should be structured so that a successful fraud requires collusion between two or more individuals with incompatible responsibilities. For example, no individual should have sufficient access to accounting records to perpetrate a fraud. Thus, journals, subsidiary ledgers, and the general ledger are maintained separately. For most people, the thought of approaching another employee with the proposal to collude in a fraud presents an insurmountable psychological barrier. The fear of rejection and subsequent disciplinary action discourages solicitations of this sort. However, when employees with incompatible responsibilities work together daily in close quarters, the resulting familiarity tends to erode this barrier. For this reason, the segregation of incompatible tasks should be physical as well as organizational. Indeed, concern about personal familiarity on the job is the justification for establishing rules prohibiting nepotism.*

SUPERVISION. Implementing adequate segregation of duties requires that a firm employ a sufficiently large number of employees. Achieving adequate segregation of duties often presents difficulties for small organizations. Obviously, it is impossible to separate five incompatible tasks among three employees. Therefore, in small organizations or in functional areas that lack sufficient personnel, management must compensate for the absence of segregation controls with close **supervision**. For this reason, supervision is often called a compensating control.

An underlying assumption of supervision control is that the firm employs competent and trustworthy personnel. Obviously, no company could function for long on the alternative assumption that its employees are incompetent and dishonest. The competent and trustworthy employee assumption promotes supervisory efficiency. Firms can thus establish a managerial span of control where a single manager supervises several employees. In manual systems, maintaining a span of control tends to be straightforward because both manager and employees are at the same physical location.

ACCOUNTING RECORDS. The **accounting records** of an organization consist of source documents, journals, and ledgers. These records capture the economic essence of transactions and provide an audit trail of economic events. The audit trail enables the auditor to trace any transaction through all phases of its processing from the initiation of the event to the financial statements. Organizations must maintain audit trails for two reasons. First, this information is needed for conducting day-to-day operations. The audit trail helps employees respond to customer inquiries by showing the current status of transactions in process. Second, the audit trail plays an essential role in the financial audit of the firm. It enables external (and internal) auditors to verify selected transactions by tracing them from the financial statements to the ledger accounts, to the journals, to the source documents, and back to their original source. For reasons of both practical expedience and legal obligation, business organizations must maintain sufficient accounting records to preserve their audit trails.

ACCESS CONTROL. The purpose of **access controls** is to ensure that only authorized personnel have access to the firm's assets. Unauthorized access exposes assets to misappropriation, damage, and theft. Therefore, access controls play an important role in safeguarding assets. Access to assets can be direct or indirect. Physical security devices, such as locks, safes, fences, and electronic and infrared alarm systems, control against direct access. Indirect access to assets is achieved by gaining access to the records and documents that control the use, ownership, and disposition of the asset. For example, an individual with access to all the relevant accounting records can destroy the audit trail that describes a particular sales transaction. Thus, by removing the records of the transaction, including the accounts receivable balance, the sale may never be billed and the firm will never receive payment for the items sold. The access controls needed to protect accounting records will depend on the technological characteristics of the accounting system. Indirect access control is accomplished by controlling the use of documents and records and by segregating the duties of those who must access and process these records.

INDEPENDENT VERIFICATION. Verification procedures are independent checks of the accounting system to identify errors and misrepresentations. Verification differs from supervision because it takes place after the fact, by an individual who is not directly involved with the transaction or task being verified. Supervision takes place while the activity is being performed, by a supervisor with direct responsibility for the task. Through independent verification procedures, management can assess (1) the performance of individuals, (2) the integrity of the transaction processing system, and (3) the correctness of data contained in accounting records. Examples of independent verifications include:

- Reconciling batch totals at points during transaction processing.
- Comparing physical assets with accounting records.
- Reconciling subsidiary accounts with control accounts.
- Reviewing management reports (both computer and manually generated) that summarize business activity.

The timing of verification depends on the technology employed in the accounting system and the task under review. Verifications may occur several times an hour or several times a day. In some cases, verification may occur daily, weekly, monthly, or annually.

IT APPLICATION CONTROLS

Management and auditors are required under SOX to consider IT application controls relevant to financial reporting. Application controls are associated with specific applications, such as payroll, purchases, and cash disbursements systems, and fall into three broad categories: **input controls**, **processing controls**, and **output controls**.

Input Controls

Input controls are programmed procedures, often called edits, which perform tests on transaction data to ensure that they are free from errors. Edit routines are designed into systems at different points, depending on whether processing is real time or batch. Edit controls in real-time systems are placed at the data collection stage to monitor data as they are entered from terminals. Batch systems collect data in transaction files, where they are temporarily held for subsequent processing. In that case, edit tests are performed in a separate procedure (the edit run) prior to the master file update process.

Whatever the edit method used, transaction data should never update master files until the transactions have been tested for validity, accuracy, and completeness. If a record fails an edit test, it is flagged as an "error" record and rejected. Later, we will see how to deal with these records. The following are examples of input edit controls.

CHECK DIGIT. Data codes are used extensively in transaction processing systems for representing such things as customer accounts, items of inventory, and general ledger accounts in the chart of accounts. If the data code of a particular transaction is entered incorrectly and goes undetected, then a transaction processing error will occur, such as posting to the wrong account. These processing problems are caused by two common types of data input errors: transcription errors and transposition errors.

Transcription errors are divided into three categories:

1. Addition errors occur when an extra digit or character is added to the code. For example, inventory item number 83276 is recorded as 832766.
2. Truncation errors occur when a digit or character is removed from the end of a code. In this type of error, the inventory item above would be recorded as 8327.
3. Substitution errors are the replacement of one digit in a code with another. For example, code number 83276 is recorded as 83266.

Transposition errors are of two types.

1. Single transposition errors occur when two adjacent digits are reversed. For instance, 83276 is recorded as 38276.
2. Multiple transposition errors occur when nonadjacent digits are transposed. For example, 83276 is recorded as 87236.

These problems are controlled by using a **check digit** edit. A check digit is a control digit (or digits) that is added to the data code when it is originally assigned. This allows the integrity of the code to be established during subsequent processing. The check digit can be located anywhere in the code, as a prefix, a suffix, or embedded someplace in the middle. The simplest form of check digit is to sum the digits in the code and use this sum as the check digit. For example, for the customer account code 5372, the calculated check digit would be

$$5 + 3 + 7 + 2 = 17$$

By dropping the tens column, the check digit 7 is added to the original code to produce the new code 53727. The entire string of digits (including the check digit) becomes the customer account number. During data entry, the system can recalculate the check digit to ensure that the code is correct. This technique will detect only transcription errors. For example, if a substitution error occurred and the above code were entered as 52727, the calculated check digit would be 6 ($5 + 2 + 7 + 2 = 16 = 6$) and the error would be detected. However, this technique would fail to identify transposition errors. For example, transposing the first two digits yields the code 35727, which still sums to 17 and produces the check digit 7. This error would go undetected.

A popular check digit technique for dealing with transposition errors is modulus 11. Using the code 5372, the steps in this technique are outlined next.

1. Assign weights. Each digit in the code is multiplied by a different weight. In this case, the weights used are 5, 4, 3, and 2, shown as follows:

Digit		Weight
5	×	5 = 25
3	×	4 = 12
7	×	3 = 21
2	×	2 = 4

2. Sum the products: ($25 + 12 + 21 + 4 = 62$).
3. Divide by the modulus. We are using modulus 11 in this case, giving $62/11 = 5$ with a remainder of 7.
4. Subtract the remainder from the modulus to obtain the check digit: ($11 - 7 = 4$ [check digit]).
5. Add the check digit to the original code to yield the new code: 53724.

Using this technique to recalculate the check digit during processing, a transposition error in the code will produce a check digit other than 4. For example, if the code above was incorrectly entered as 35724, the recalculated check digit would be 6.

MISSING DATA CHECK. This edit identifies blank or incomplete input fields that should contain data that are required to process the transaction.

NUMERIC-ALPHABETIC CHECK. This edit identifies when data in a particular field are in the wrong form. For example, a customer's account balance should not contain alphabetic data, and the presence of it will cause a data processing error. Therefore, if alphabetic data are detected, the error record flag is set.

LIMIT CHECK. Limit checks are used to identify field values that exceed an authorized limit. For example, assume the firm's policy is that no employee works more than 44 hours per week. The payroll system input control program can test the HOURS WORKED field in the weekly payroll records for values greater than 44.

RANGE CHECK. Many times, data have upper and lower limits to their acceptable values. For example, if the range of pay rates for hourly employees in a firm is between \$18 and \$30, this control can examine the pay rate field of all payroll records to ensure that they fall within this range.

The purpose of this control is to detect keystroke errors by data entry clerks. It would not detect an error where a correct pay rate of, say, $19 is incorrectly entered as $29.

REASONABLENESS CHECK. The error above may be detected by a test that determines if a value in one field, which has already passed a limit check and a range check, is reasonable when considered along with data in other fields of the record. For example, an employee's pay rate of $28 per hour falls within an acceptable range. This rate is excessive, however, when compared to the employee's job skill code of 693; employees in this skill class should not earn more than $20 per hour.

VALIDITY CHECK. A validity check compares actual field values against known acceptable values. This control is used to verify such things as transaction codes, state abbreviations, or employee job skill codes. If the value in the field does not match one of the acceptable values, the record is flagged as an error.

This is a frequently used control in cash disbursements systems. One form of cash disbursement fraud involves manipulating the system into making a fraudulent payment to a nonexistent vendor. To prevent this, the firm may establish a list of valid vendors with whom it does business exclusively. Thus, before payment of any trade obligation, the validation program matches the vendor number on the cash disbursement voucher against the valid vendor list. If the code does not match, payment is denied, and management reviews the transaction.

Processing Controls

After input data have been edited, the transactions enter the processing stage of the application. Processing controls are programmed procedures to ensure that an application's logic is functioning properly. In this section we review some common examples of processing controls, but the list is not exhaustive. As we examine specific applications in later chapters, we will review the specific processing controls that apply to them.

Batch controls are used to manage the flow of high volumes of transactions through batch processing systems. The objective of batch control is to reconcile system output with the input originally entered into the system. This control ensures that:

- All records in the batch are processed.
- No records are processed more than once.
- An audit trail of transactions is created from input through processing to the output stage of the system.

Batch control begins at the data input stage and continues through all data processing phases of the application. To achieve this, a batch control record is created when the batch of transactions is entered into the system. The control record contains relevant information about the batch, such as:

- A unique batch number.
- A batch date.
- A transaction code (indicating the types of transactions, such as a sales order or cash receipt).
- The number of records in the batch (record count).
- The total dollar value of a financial field (batch control total).
- The total of a unique nonfinancial field (hash total).

Figure 3-5 depicts a batch control record in relation to the batch of transactions it describes. The data in the control record are used to assess the integrity of the batch during all subsequent processing. For example, the batch control record in the figure shows a batch of 50 sales order records with a total dollar value of $122,674.87 and a hash total of 4537838.

Run-to-run controls use the values in the batch control record to monitor the batch as it moves from one programmed procedure (run) to another. Thus, at various points throughout processing

FIGURE 3-5 BATCH CONTROL RECORD

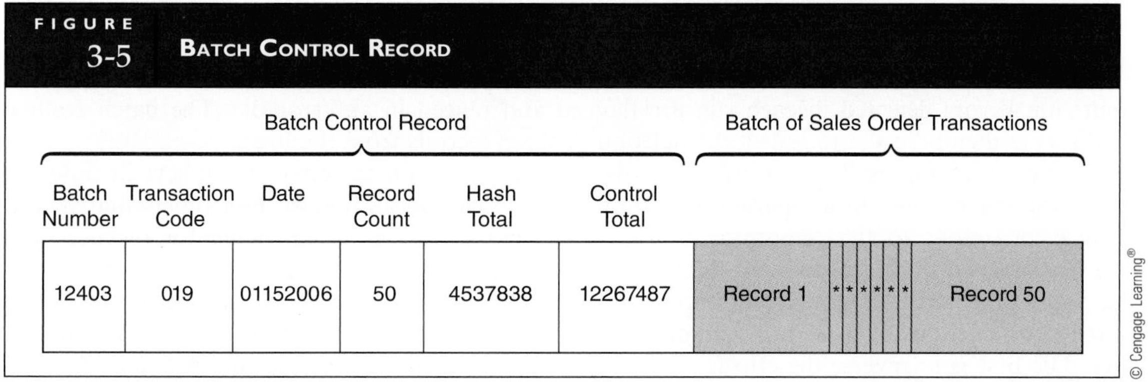

and at the end of processing, the batch totals are recalculated and compared to the batch control record. This ensures that each run in the system processes the batch correctly and completely.

Figure 3-6 illustrates the use of run-to-run controls in a sales order system. This application comprises four runs: (1) data input, (2) accounts receivable update, (3) inventory update, and

FIGURE 3-6 RUN-TO-RUN CONTROLS

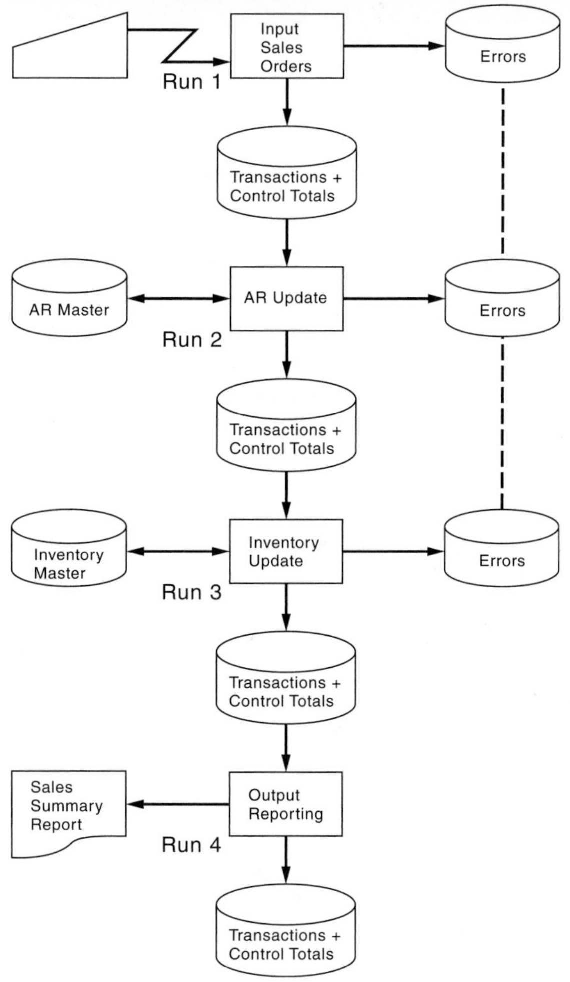

(4) output. At the end of the accounts receivable run, batch control figures are recalculated and reconciled with the control totals passed from the data input run. These figures are then passed to the inventory update run, where they are again recalculated, reconciled, and passed to the output run. Errors detected in each run are flagged and placed in an error file. The batch control values are then adjusted to reflect the deletion of these records from the batch.

Notice from Figure 3-6 that error records may be placed on the error file at several different points in the process. In a separate procedure (not shown), an authorized user representative will make corrections to the error records and resubmit them as a special batch for reprocessing. Errors detected during processing require careful handling because these records may already be partially processed. Simply resubmitting corrected records into the data input stage may result in processing portions of these transactions twice. Two methods are used to deal with this complexity. The first is to reverse the effects of the partially processed transactions and resubmit the corrected records to the data input stage. The second method is to reinsert corrected records into the processing stage at which the error was detected.

The term **hash total**, which was used in the preceding discussion, is the summation of a nonfinancial field to keep track of the records in a batch. Any numeric field, such as a customer's account number, a purchase order number, or an inventory item number, may be used to calculate a hash total. In the following example, the sales order number (SO#) field for an entire batch of sales order records is summed to produce a hash total.

SO#	
14327	
67345	
19983	
•	
•	
•	
88943	
96543	
4537838	(hash total)

Let's see how we use this seemingly meaningless number. Assume that after this batch of records is created, someone replaced one of the sales orders in the batch with a fictitious record of the same dollar amount. How would the batch control procedures detect this irregularity? Both the record count and the dollar amount control totals would still balance. However, the hash total that the batch control procedures calculated would not balance. The irregularity would thus be detected.

Audit Trail Controls

Audit trail controls in an IT environment ensure that every transaction can be traced through each stage of processing from its economic source to its presentation in financial statements. The following are examples of audit trail control.

TRANSACTION LOGS. Every transaction the system successfully processes should be recorded on a transaction log, which serves as a journal. Figure 3-7 shows this process. Three reasons underscore the importance of this log. First, the transaction log is a permanent record of transactions, although the input transaction file is typically a temporary file. Once processed, the records on the input file are erased to make room for the next batch of transactions. Second, not all of the records in the input file may be successfully processed. Some of them will fail tests during subsequent processing and will be passed to an error file. A transaction log contains only successful transactions—those that have changed master file account balances. The transaction log and error files combined should account for all the transactions in the batch. The validated transaction file may then be scratched with no loss of data. Finally, as we will see later, the transaction logs facilitate master file backup procedures.

FIGURE 3-7 TRANSACTION LOG TO PRESERVE THE AUDIT TRAIL

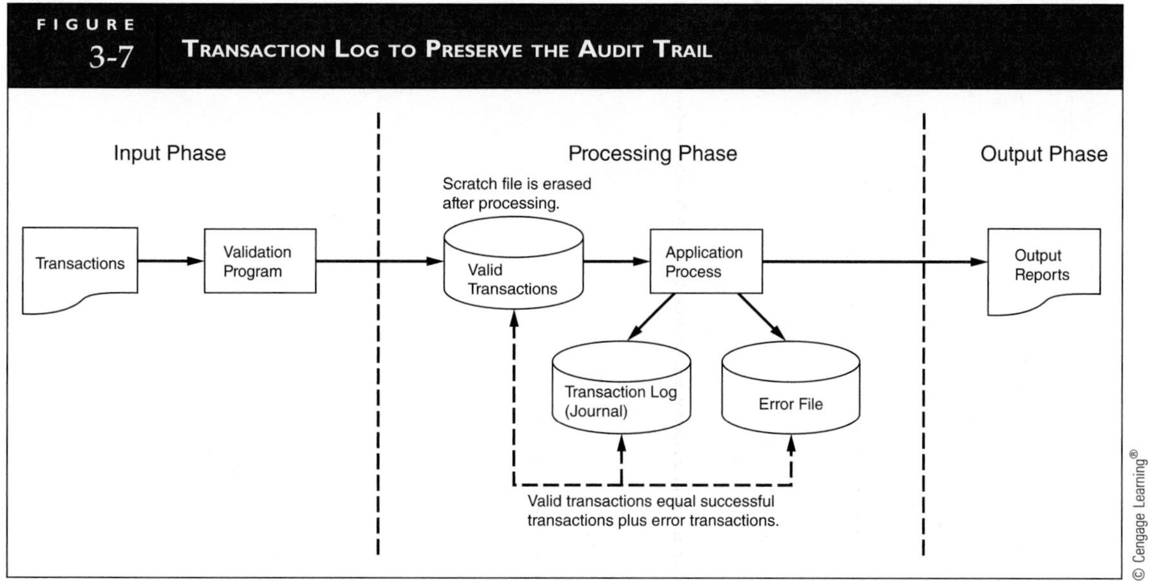

LOG OF AUTOMATIC TRANSACTIONS. The system triggers some transactions internally. For example, when inventory drops below the reorder point, the system automatically generates a purchase requisition. To maintain an audit trail of these activities, all internally generated transactions must be placed in a transaction log.

Master File Backup Controls

Depending on the type of system in place, master file backup procedures may be viewed as either a general control or an application control. In a database environment, the database supports all corporate users, and database backup procedures apply to all applications. Therefore, backup in a databases environment is a general control. In Chapter 16, we review database backup as a general control that impacts the entire IT function. In a flat-file environment, corporate users do not share data files and therefore, individual backup procedures need to be designed specifically for each user's application. Viewed in this context, backup is an application control. The discussion that follows presents the master file backup procedures for three types of flat-file systems: batch processing using sequential files, batch processing using direct access files, and real-time processing systems.

GFS BACKUP TECHNIQUE

Systems that use sequential master files (whether tape or disk) employ a backup technique called **grandfather-father-son (GFS)**, which is an integral part of the master file update process. Figure 3-8 illustrates the GFS backup technique, which begins when the current master file (the father) is processed against the transaction file to produce a new updated master file (the son). Note that the son is a physically different file from the father. With the next batch of transactions, the son becomes the current master file (the new father), and the original father becomes the backup file (grandfather). This procedure is continued with each new batch of transactions, creating several generations of backup files. When the desired number of backup copies is reached, the oldest backup file is erased (scratched). If the current master file is destroyed or corrupted, it is reconstructed by processing the most current backup file against the corresponding transaction file.

The systems designer determines the number of backup master files needed for each application. Two factors influence this decision: (1) the financial significance of the system and (2) the degree of file activity. For example, a master file that is updated several times a day may require 30 or 40 generations of backup, while a file that is updated only once each month may need only four or five backup versions. This decision is important because certain types of system failures can result in the destruction of large numbers of backup versions within the same family of files.

FIGURE 3-8 GRANDFATHER-FATHER-SON APPROACH

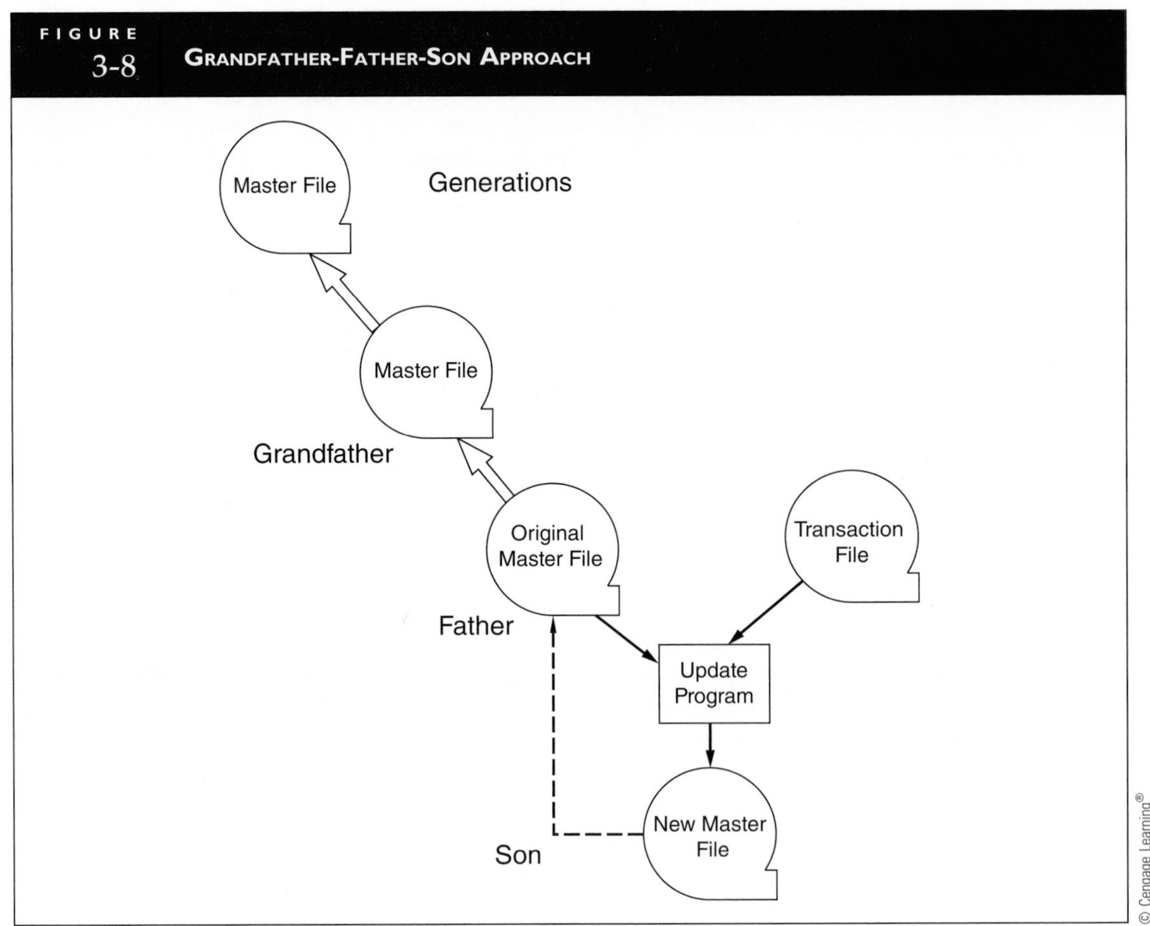

BACKUP PROCESS IN BATCH SYSTEM USING DIRECT ACCESS FILES

Each record in a direct access file is assigned a unique disk location or address (see Chapter 2 appendix for examples of direct access file structures) that is determined by its primary key value. Because only a single valid location exists for each record, updating the record must occur in place. Figure 3-9 shows this technique.

In this example, an AR record with a $100 current balance is being updated by a $50 sales transaction. The master file record is permanently stored at a disk address designated Location A. The update program reads both the transaction record and the master file record into memory. The account receivable is recalculated to reflect the new current balance of $150 and then returned to Location A. The original AR balance value of $100 is destroyed when replaced by the new value of $150. This technique is called *destructive update*.

The destructive update approach leaves no backup copy of the original master file. Only the current value is available to the user. To back up the master, a separate procedure that is shown in Figure 3-10 must be implemented. Prior to each scheduled update run, the master file being updated is copied to create a backup version. Should the original be destroyed or corrupted, reconstruction is possible in two stages. First, a special recovery program uses the backup master file to reconstruct a new master file. Second, the file update process is repeated using the previous batch of transactions to restore the master to current status.

BACKUP OF MASTER FILES IN A REAL-TIME SYSTEM

Real-time systems pose a more difficult problem because transactions are being processed continuously. Backup procedures are therefore scheduled at pre-specified intervals throughout the day (e.g., every 15 minutes). If the current version of the master file is destroyed through a disk failure

FIGURE 3-9 DESTRUCTIVE UPDATE APPROACH

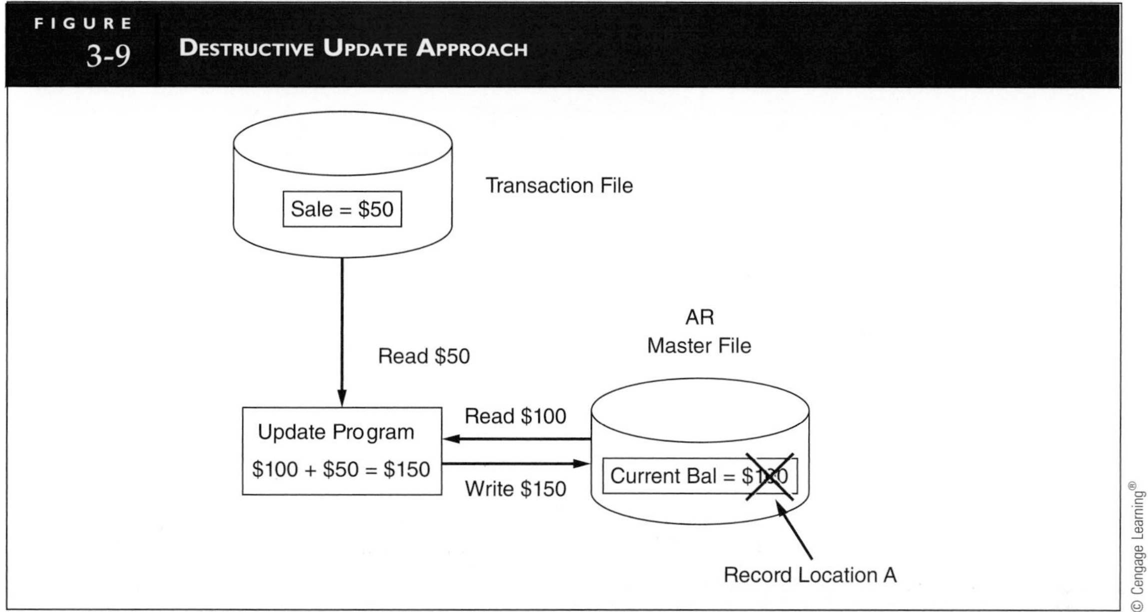

FIGURE 3-10 BACKUP PROCEDURES FOR BATCH SYSTEMS USING DIRECT ACCESS FILES

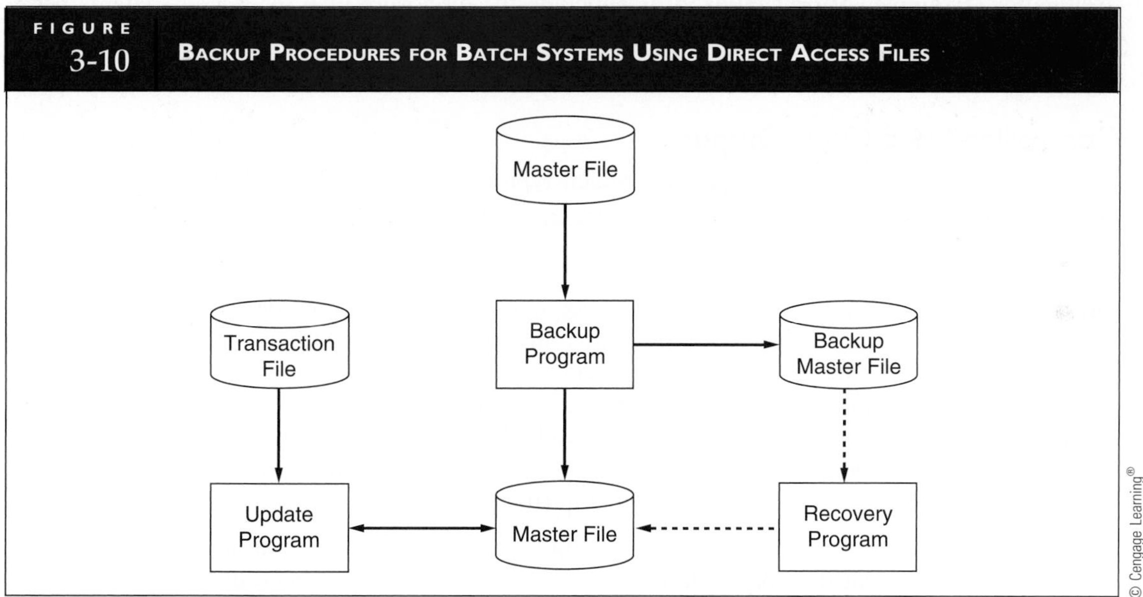

or corrupted by a program error, it can be reconstructed from the most current backup file. The transactions processed since the last backup, however, need to be reprocessed to bring the master file to current status. These records are retrieved from the transaction log, which is created continuously in real time. This procedure is illustrated in Figure 3-11.

OUTPUT CONTROLS

Output controls are a combination of programmed routines and other procedures to ensure that system output is not lost, misdirected, or corrupted and that privacy is not violated. Exposures of this sort can cause serious disruptions to operations and may result in financial losses to a firm. For example, if the checks that a firm's cash disbursements system produces are lost, misdirected, or destroyed, trade accounts and other bills may go unpaid. This could damage the firm's credit rating and result in lost discounts, interest, or penalty charges. If the privacy of certain types of output is violated, a firm could have its business objectives compromised or could become exposed

FIGURE 3-11 BACKUP PROCEDURES FOR REAL-TIME PROCESSING SYSTEM

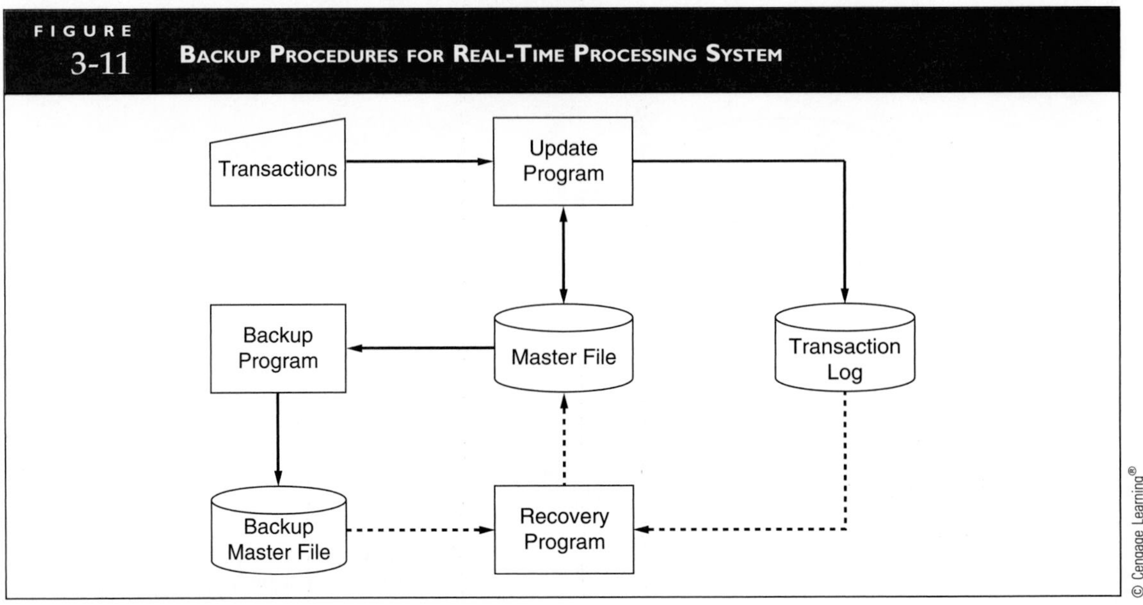

to litigation. Examples of privacy exposures include the disclosure of trade secrets, patents pending, marketing research results, and patient medical records. This section examines output risks and controls for both hard-copy and digital output.

Controlling Hard-Copy Output

Batch systems usually produce hard copy, which typically requires the involvement of intermediaries in its production and distribution. Figure 3-12 shows the stages in this output process and serves as the basis for this section.

OUTPUT SPOOLING. In large-scale data processing operations, output devices such as line printers can become backlogged with many programs simultaneously demanding limited resources. This can cause a bottleneck and adversely affect system throughput. To ease this burden, applications are often designed to direct their output to a magnetic disk file rather than print it directly. This is called **spooling**. Later, when printer resources become available, the output files are printed.

The creation of an output file as an intermediate step in the printing process presents an added exposure. A computer criminal may use this opportunity to:

1. Access the output file and change critical data values (such as dollar amounts on checks). The printer program will then print the fallacious output as if the system produced it.
2. Access the file and change the number of copies of output to be printed. The extra copies may then be removed without notice during the printing stage.
3. Make a copy of the output file to produce illegal output reports.
4. Destroy the output file before output printing takes place.

The management and auditors need to be aware of these potential exposures and ensure that proper access and backup procedures are in place to protect output files.

PRINT PROGRAMS. When a printer becomes available, the print run program produces hard-copy output from the output file. Print programs are often complex systems that require operator intervention. Four common types of operator actions are:

1. Pausing the print program to load the correct type of output documents (check stocks, invoices, or other special forms).

FIGURE 3-12 STAGES IN THE OUTPUT PROCESS

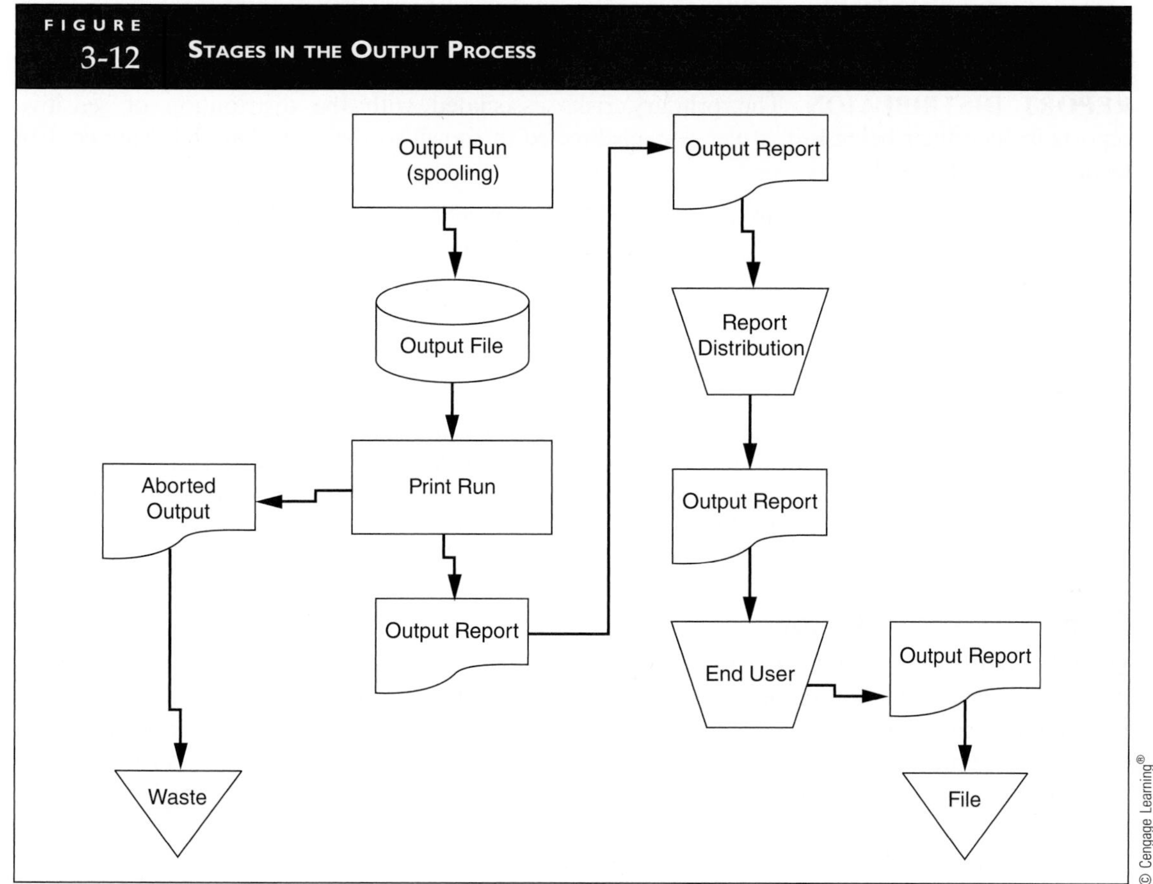

2. Entering parameters that the print run needs, such as the number of copies to be printed.
3. Restarting the print run at a prescribed checkpoint after a printer malfunction.
4. Removing printed output from the printer for review and distribution.

Print program controls should be designed to deal with two types of exposures present in this environment: (1) the production of unauthorized copies of output and (2) employee browsing of sensitive data. Some print programs allow the operator to specify more copies of output than the output file calls for, which allows for the possibility of producing unauthorized copies of output. One way to control this is to employ output document controls. This is most effective when dealing with prenumbered invoices for billing customers or prenumbered check stock. At the end of the run, the number of copies specified by the output file should be reconciled with the actual number of output documents used.

To prevent operators and others from viewing sensitive output, special multipart paper can be used, with a grayed-out top copy to prevent the print from being read. This type of product is often used for payroll check printing. An alternative privacy control is to direct the output to a special remote printer that can be closely supervised.

WASTE. Computer output waste is a potential source of exposure. Aborted reports and the carbon copies from multipart paper need to be disposed of properly. Computer criminals disguised as janitorial staff have been known to sift through trash cans searching for carelessly discarded output that is presumed to be of no value. From such trash, computer criminals may obtain information about a firm's market research, credit ratings of its customers, or even trade secrets, which they can sell to a competitor. Computer waste is also a source of passwords that a perpetrator may use to access the firm's computer system. To control against this threat, all sensitive computer output should be passed through a paper shredder.

REPORT DISTRIBUTION. The primary risks associated with the distribution of sensitive reports include their being lost, stolen, or misdirected in transit to the user. The following control techniques can be used:

1. The reports may be placed in a secure mailbox to which only the user has the key.
2. The user may be required to appear in person at the distribution center and sign for the report.
3. A security officer or special courier may deliver the report to the user.

END-USER CONTROLS. Once in the hands of the user, output reports should be examined for correctness. Errors the user detects should be reported to the appropriate IT management. Such errors may be symptoms of an improper systems design, incorrect procedures, errors accidentally inserted during systems maintenance, or unauthorized access to data files or programs. Once a report has served its purpose, it should be stored in a secure location until its retention period has expired and then it should be shredded.

Controlling Digital Output

Digital output can be directed to the user's computer screen or printer. The primary output threat is the interception, disruption, destruction, or corruption of the output message as it passes across the communications network. This threat comes from two types of exposures: (1) exposures from equipment failure and (2) exposures from subversive acts. We discuss network security issues in Chapter 16.

Summary

This chapter began by examining ethical issues that societies have pondered for centuries. It is increasingly apparent that good ethics is a necessary condition for the long-term profitability of a business. This requires that ethical issues be understood at all levels of the firm, from top management to line workers. In this section, we identified several ethical issues of direct concern to accountants and managers. SOX legislation has directly addressed these issues.

The next section examined fraud and its relationship to auditing. Fraud falls into two general categories: employee fraud and management fraud. Employee fraud is generally designed to convert cash or other assets directly to the employee's personal benefit. Typically, the employee circumvents the company's internal control structure for personal gain. However, if a company has an effective system of internal control, defalcations or embezzlements can usually be prevented or detected. Management fraud typically involves the material misstatement of financial data and reports to attain additional compensation or promotion or to escape the penalty for poor performance. Managers that perpetrate fraud often do so by overriding the internal control structure. The underlying problems that permit and aid these frauds are frequently associated with inadequate corporate governance. In this section, we examined some prominent corporate governance failures and outlined the key elements of SOX, which was legislated to remedy them. Finally, several well-documented fraud techniques were reviewed.

The third section examined the subject of internal control. The adequacy of the internal control structure is an issue of great importance to both management and accountants. Internal control was examined first using the PDC control model that classifies controls as preventive, detective, and corrective. Next, the COSO framework recommended for compliance with SOX was examined. This consists of five levels: control environment, risk assessment, information and communication, monitoring, and control activities. In this section, we examined both physical and IT control activities.

Key Terms

access controls (121)
accounting records (121)
application controls (119)
audit trail controls (126)
batch controls (124)
billing schemes (111)
bribery (109)
business ethics (96)
cash larceny (111)
check digit (123)
check tampering (111)
Committee of Sponsoring Organizations of the Treadway Commission (COSO) (116)
computer ethics (96)
computer fraud (112)
conflict of interest (110)
control activities (119)
control environment (116)
corrective controls (115)
corruption (109)
detective controls (115)
economic extortion (110)
employee fraud (102)
ethical responsibility (96)
ethics (96)
expense reimbursement frauds (112)
exposure (113)
fraud (101)
fraud triangle (102)
fraudulent statements (106)
general controls (119)
grandfather-father-son (GFS) (127)
hash total (126)
illegal gratuity (109)
input controls (122)
internal control system (112)
lapping (111)
mail room fraud (111)
management fraud (102)
management responsibility (113)
monitoring (119)
non-cash fraud (112)
output controls (122)
ownership (98)
pass through fraud (111)
pay-and-return (111)
payroll fraud (112)
preventive controls (113)
privacy (98)
processing controls (122)
Public Company Accounting Oversight Board (PCAOB) (108)
reasonable assurance (113)
risk assessment (118)
run-to-run controls (124)
Sarbanes-Oxley Act (SOX) (100)
security (98)
segregation of duties (120)
shell company (111)
skimming (110)
spooling (130)
Statement on Auditing Standards (SAS) No. 109 (116)
Statement on Auditing Standards (SAS) No. 99, *Consideration of Fraud in a Financial Statement Audit* (101)
supervision (121)
thefts of cash (112)
transaction authorization (120)
transcription errors (122)
transposition errors (122)
vendor fraud (111)
verification procedures (121)

Review Questions

1. What is ethics?
2. What is business ethics?
3. What are the four areas of ethical business issues?
4. What are the main issues to be addressed in a business code of ethics required by the Securities and Exchange Commission?
5. What are the three ethical principles that may provide some guidance for ethical responsibility?
6. What is computer ethics?
7. How do the three levels of computer ethics—pop, para, and theoretical—differ?

8. Are computer ethical issues new problems or just a new twist on old problems?
9. What are the computer ethical issues regarding privacy?
10. What are the computer ethical issues regarding security?
11. What are the computer ethical issues regarding ownership of property?
12. What are the computer ethical issues regarding equity in access?
13. What are the computer ethical issues regarding the environment?
14. What are the computer ethical issues regarding artificial intelligence?
15. What are the computer ethical issues regarding unemployment and displacement?
16. What are the computer ethical issues regarding misuse of computers?
17. What is the objective of Statement on Auditing Standards No. 99?
18. What are the five conditions that constitute fraud under common law?
19. Name the three fraud-motivating forces.
20. What is employee fraud?
21. What is management fraud?
22. What three forces constitute the triangle of fraud?
23. How can external auditors attempt to uncover motivations for committing fraud?
24. What is lapping?
25. What is collusion?
26. What is bribery?
27. What is economic extortion?
28. What is conflict of interest?
29. Define check tampering.
30. What is billing (or vendor) fraud?
31. Define cash larceny.
32. What is skimming?
33. What are the four broad objectives of internal control?
34. What are the four modifying assumptions that guide designers and auditors of internal control systems?
35. Give an example of a preventive control.
36. Give an example of a detective control.
37. Give an example of a corrective control.
38. What are management's responsibilities under Sections 302 and 404?
39. What are the five internal control components described in the COSO framework?
40. What are the six broad classes of physical control activities defined by COSO?
41. What is the purpose of a valid vendor file?
42. Give one example of an error that a check digit control detects.
43. What are the primary objectives of a batch control?
44. If all of the inputs have been validated before processing, then what purpose do run-to-run controls serve?
45. What is the objective of a transaction log?
46. How can spooling present an added exposure?
47. What is the purpose of a limit check?
48. What is the purpose of a range check?
49. What is a validity check?
50. What information would a batch control record contain?

Discussion Questions

1. Distinguish between ethical issues and legal issues.
2. Some argue against corporate involvement in socially responsible behavior because the costs incurred by such behavior place the organization at a disadvantage in a competitive market. Discuss the merits and flaws of this argument.
3. Although top management's attitude toward ethics sets the tone for business practice, sometimes it is the role of lower-level managers to uphold a firm's ethical standards. John, an operations-level manager, discovers that the company is illegally dumping toxic materials and is in violation of environmental regulations. John's immediate supervisor is involved in the dumping. What action should John take?

4. When a company has a strong internal control structure, stockholders can expect the elimination of fraud. Comment on the soundness of this statement.
5. Distinguish between employee fraud and management fraud.
6. The estimates of losses annually resulting from computer fraud vary widely. Why do you think obtaining a good estimate of this figure is difficult?
7. How has the Sarbanes-Oxley Act had a significant impact on corporate governance?
8. Discuss the concept of exposure and explain why firms may tolerate some exposure.
9. If detective controls signal error flags, why shouldn't these types of controls automatically make a correction in the identified error? Why are corrective controls necessary?
10. Discuss the nonaccounting services that external auditors are no longer permitted to render to audit clients.
11. Discuss whether a firm with fewer employees than there are incompatible tasks should rely more heavily on general authority than specific authority.
12. An organization's internal audit department is usually considered an effective control mechanism for evaluating the organization's internal control structure. The Birch Company's internal auditing function reports directly to the controller. Comment on the effectiveness of this organizational structure.
13. According to COSO, the proper segregation of functions is an effective internal control procedure. Comment on the exposure (if any) caused by combining the tasks of paycheck preparation and distribution to employees.
14. Explain the five conditions necessary for an act to be considered fraudulent.
15. Distinguish between exposure and risk.
16. Explain the characteristics of management fraud.
17. The text identifies a number of personal traits of managers and other employees that might help uncover fraudulent activity. Discuss three traits.
18. Give two examples of employee fraud, and explain how the thefts might occur.
19. Discuss the fraud schemes of bribery, illegal gratuities, and economic extortion.
20. Distinguish between skimming and cash larceny.
21. Distinguish between a shell company fraud and pass through fraud.
22. Why are the computer ethics issues of privacy, security, and property ownership of interest to accountants?
23. A profile of fraud perpetrators prepared by the Association of Certified Fraud Examiners revealed that adult males with advanced degrees commit a disproportionate amount of fraud. Explain these findings.
24. Explain why collusion between employees and management in the commission of a fraud is difficult to both prevent and detect.
25. Because all fraud involves some form of financial misstatement, how is fraudulent statement fraud different?
26. Explain the problems associated with lack of auditor independence.
27. Explain the problems associated with lack of director independence.
28. Explain the problems associated with questionable executive compensation schemes.
29. Explain the problems associated with inappropriate accounting practices.
30. Explain the purpose of the Public Company Accounting Oversight Board.
31. Why is an independent audit committee important to a company?
32. What are the key points of the "Issuer and Management Disclosure" of the Sarbanes-Oxley Act?
33. In this age of high technology and computer-based information systems, why are accountants concerned about physical (human) controls?
34. What are the classes of transcription errors?
35. What is the purpose of a check digit?
36. Does a hash total need to be based on a financial data field? Explain.
37. Explain the GFS backup technique. Is it used for sequential files or direct access techniques? Explain.

Multiple-Choice Questions

1. Which of the following is not an example of preventive control?
   a. separation of responsibilities for the recording, custodial, and authorization functions
   b. sound personnel practices
   c. documentation of policies and procedures
   d. password authentication software and hardware
   e. source documents for capturing sales data
2. A control designed to validate a transaction at the point of data entry is
   a. recalculation of a batch total.
   b. a record count.
   c. a check digit.
   d. checkpoints.
   e. recalculation of hash total.
3. Application controls are classified as
   a. input, processing, and output.
   b. input, processing, output, and storage.
   c. input, processing, output, and control.
   d. input, processing, output, storage, and control.
   e. collecting, sorting, summarizing, and reporting.
4. Which of the following is NOT an element of the fraud triangle?
   a. ethics
   b. justifiable reliance
   c. situational pressure
   d. opportunity
5. How are individual transactions edited in a real-time file processing system?
   a. in a separate computer run
   b. in online mode as transactions are entered
   c. during a backup procedure
   d. not edited due to time constraints
   e. editing of real-time transactions is not necessary
6. In an automated payroll processing environment, a department manager substituted the time card for a terminated employee with a time card for a fictitious employee. The fictitious employee had the same pay rate and hours worked as the terminated employee. The best control technique to detect this action using employee identification numbers would be to use a:
   a. batch total.
   b. record count.
   c. hash total.
   d. subsequent check.
   e. financial total.
7. The underlying assumption of reasonable assurance regarding implementation of internal control means that
   a. auditors are reasonably assured that fraud has not occurred in the period.
   b. auditors are reasonably assured that employee carelessness can weaken an internal control structure.
   c. implementation of the control procedure should not have a significant adverse effect on efficiency or profitability.
   d. management assertions about control effectiveness should provide auditors with reasonable assurance.
   e. a control applies reasonably well to all forms of computer technology.
8. Ensuring that all material transactions processed by the information system are valid and in accordance with management's objectives is an example of
   a. transaction authorization.
   b. supervision.
   c. accounting records.
   d. independent verification.
9. Which of the following journal entries would a bookkeeper make to conceal the theft of cash receipts from customers in payment of their accounts?

	DR	CR
a.	Miscellaneous Expense	Cash
b.	Petty Cash	Cash
c.	Cash	Accounts Receivable
d.	Sales Returns	Accounts Receivable
e.	None of the above	

10. What name is given to computer programs that are used for checking the validity and accuracy of transaction data?
    a. operating system programs.
    b. edit programs.
    c. compiler programs.
    d. integrated test programs.
    e. interrogation programs.

11. Which of the following situations is NOT a segregation of duties violation?
    a. The treasurer has the authority to sign checks but gives the signature block to the assistant treasurer to run the check-signing machine.
    b. The warehouse clerk, who has custodial responsibility over inventory in the warehouse, selects the vendor and authorizes purchases when inventories are low.
    c. The sales manager has the responsibility to approve credit and the authority to write-off accounts.
    d. The department time clerk is given the undistributed payroll checks to mail to absent employees.
    e. The accounting clerk who shares the record-keeping responsibility for the accounts receivable subsidiary ledger performs the monthly reconciliation of the subsidiary ledger and the control account.

12. An employee in the receiving department keyed in a shipment from a remote terminal and inadvertently omitted the purchase order number. The best application control to detect this error would be a
    a. batch total.
    b. missing data check.
    c. completeness check.
    d. reasonableness test.
    e. compatibility test.

13. Which of the following controls would best prevent the lapping of accounts receivable?
    a. Segregate duties so that the clerk responsible for recording in the accounts receivable subsidiary ledger has no access to the general ledger.
    b. Request that customers review their monthly statements and report any unrecorded cash payments.
    c. Separate the tasks of depositing cash receipts and posting to the AR sub ledger.
    d. Request that customers make checks payable to the company.

14. Which of the following is often called a compensating control?
    a. transaction authorization
    b. supervision
    c. accounting records
    d. segregation of duties

15. Which of the following is an example of an input control?
    a. making sure that reports are distributed to the proper people
    b. monitoring the work of data entry clerks
    c. collecting accurate statistics of historical transactions while gathering data
    d. performing a check-digit test on a customer account number.
    e. having another person review the design of a business form

16. Providing timely information about transactions in sufficient detail to permit proper classification and financial reporting is an example of
    a. the control environment.
    b. risk assessment.
    c. information and communication.
    d. monitoring.

17. The fraud scheme that is similar to the concept of "borrowing from Peter to pay Paul" is
    a. expense account fraud.
    b. bribery.
    c. lapping.
    d. transaction fraud.

18. What is the process for posting to accounting records in a computer system?
    a. master file is updated to a transaction file
    b. master file is updated to an index file
    c. transaction file is updated to a master file
    d. master file is updated to a year-to-date file
    e. current balance file is updated to an index file

19. Which of the following benefits is least likely to result from a system of internal controls?

a. reduction of cost of an external audit

b. prevention of employee collusion to commit fraud

c. availability of reliable data for decision-making purposes

d. some assurance of compliance with the Foreign Corrupt Practices Act of 1977

e. some assurance that important documents and records are protected

Problems

1. FRAUD SCHEME

A city health inspector threatens to close down a restaurant by issuing a fake health violation notice if the owner does not make a financial payment to the inspector. If the restaurant owner does not cooperate, he will not be able to open for business and the publicity will drive away his customers permanently. Faced with a threat of economic loss, the owner makes the payment.

Required

What type of fraud is this, and what controls can be implemented to prevent or detect the fraud?

2. FRAUD SCHEME

A purchasing agent for a large hardware retailer has sole discretion in selecting vendors for the parts and supplies sold by the company. The agent directs a disproportionate number of purchase orders to a supply company owned by the agent's brother in law, which charges above-market prices for its products. The agent's relationship with the supplier is unknown to his employer.

Required

What type of fraud is this, and what controls can be implemented to prevent or detect the fraud?

3. MAIL ROOM FRAUD AND INTERNAL CONTROL

Sarat Sethi, a professional criminal, took a job as a mail room clerk at Benson & Abernathy and Company, a large department store. The mail room was an extremely hectic work environment consisting of a supervisor and 45 clerks. The clerks were responsible for handling promotional mailings, catalogs, and interoffice mail, as well as receiving and distributing a wide range of outside correspondence to various internal departments. One of Sethi's jobs was to open cash receipts envelopes from customers making payments on their credit card balances. He separated the remittance advices (the bills) and the checks into two piles. He then sent remittance advices to the accounts receivable department, where the customer accounts were updated to reflect the payment. He sent the checks to the cash receipts department, where they were recorded in the cash journal and then deposited in the bank. Batch totals of cash received and accounts receivable updated were reconciled each night to ensure that everything was accounted for. Nevertheless, over a one-month period Sethi managed to steal $100,000 in customer payments and then left the state without warning.

The fraud occurred as follows: Because the name of the company was rather long, some people had adopted the habit of making out checks simply to Benson. Sethi had a false identification prepared in the name of John Benson. Whenever he came across a check made out to Benson, he would steal it along with the remittance advice. Sometimes people would even leave the payee section on the check blank. He also stole these checks. He would then modify the checks to make them payable to J. Benson and cash them. Because the accounts receivable department received no remittance advice, the end-of-day reconciliation with cash received disclosed no discrepancies.

Required

a. This seems like a foolproof scheme. Why did Sethi limit himself to only one month's activity before leaving town?

b. What controls could Benson & Abernathy implement to prevent this from happening again?

4. SEGREGATION OF DUTIES

Explain why each of the following combinations of tasks should or should not be separated to achieve adequate internal control.

a. Approval of bad debt write-offs and the reconciliation of the accounts receivable subsidiary ledger and the general ledger control account.

b. Distribution of payroll checks to employees and approval of employee time cards.
c. Posting of amounts from both the cash receipts and the cash disbursements journals to the general ledger.
d. Writing checks to vendors and posting to the cash account.
e. Recording cash receipts in the journal and preparing the bank reconciliation.

5. EXPENSE ACCOUNT FRAUD

While auditing the financial statements of Petty Corporation, the certified public accounting firm of True Blue and Smith discovered that its client's legal expense account was abnormally high. Further investigation of the records indicated the following:

- Since the beginning of the year, several disbursements totaling $15,000 had been made to the law firm of Swindle, Fox, and Kreip.
- Swindle, Fox, and Kreip were not Petty Corporation's attorneys.
- A review of the canceled checks showed that they had been written and approved by Mary Boghas, the cash disbursements clerk.
- Boghas's other duties included performing the end-of-month bank reconciliation.
- Subsequent investigation revealed that Swindle, Fox, and Kreip are representing Mary Boghas in an unrelated embezzlement case in which she is the defendant. The checks had been written in payment of her personal legal fees.

Required

a. What control procedures could Petty Corporation have employed to prevent this unauthorized use of cash? Classify each control procedure in accordance with the COSO framework (authorization, segregation of functions, supervision, and so on).
b. Comment on the ethical issues in this case.

6. SEGREGATION OF FUNCTIONS

Comment on the specific risks (if any) that are caused by the following combination of tasks.

a. A sales manager, who works on commission based on gross sales, approves credit and has the authority to write off uncollectible accounts.
b. The warehouse clerk, who has custodial responsibility over inventory in the warehouse, updates the inventory subsidiary ledger and prepares an inventory summary for the general ledger department.
c. The billing clerk bills customers and records sales in the sales journal
d. The shop foreman approves and submits time cards to timekeeping and distributes paychecks to employees.
e. The accounting clerk posts to individual account receivable subsidiary accounts and performs the reconciliation of the subsidiary ledger and the general ledger control account.

7. FRAUD-MOTIVATING FACTORS

Research has shown that situational pressures and opportunity are factors that contribute to fraudulent behavior.

Required

a. Identify two situational pressures in a public company that would increase the likelihood of fraud.
b. Identify three opportune moments that would increase the likelihood of fraud.

8. FINANCIAL AID FRAUD

Harold Jones, the financial aid officer at a small university, manages all aspects of the financial aid program. Jones receives requests for aid from students, determines whether the students meet the aid criteria, authorizes aid payments, notifies the applicants that their request has been either approved or denied, writes the financial aid checks on the account he controls, and requires that the students come to his office to receive the checks in person. For years, Jones has used his position of authority to perpetrate the following fraud.

Jones encourages students who clearly will not qualify to apply for financial aid. Although the students do not expect aid, they apply on the off chance that it will be awarded. Jones modifies the financial information in the students' applications so that it falls within the established guidelines for aid. He then approves aid and writes aid checks payable to the students. The students, however, are informed that aid was denied. Because the students expect no aid, the checks in Jones's office are never collected. Jones forges the students' signatures and cashes the checks.

Required

Identify the internal control procedures (classified per COSO) that could prevent or detect this fraud.

9. KICKBACK FRAUD

The kickback is a form of fraud often associated with purchasing. Most organizations expect their purchasing agents to select the vendor that provides the best products at the lowest price. To influence the purchasing agent in his or her decision, vendors may grant the agent financial favors (cash, presents, football tickets, and so on). This activity can result in orders being placed with vendors that supply inferior products or charge excessive prices.

Required

Describe the controls that an organization can employ to deal with kickbacks. Classify each control as preventive, detective, or corrective.

10. ASSESSING INTERNAL CONTROL

The following describes the cash receipts procedures for a medium-sized online and catalogue-based retailer.

Customer payments come directly to the general mail room along with other mail items. The customer payments mail constitutes about 20 percent of the total mail received each day. The mailroom clerks sort through the mail, open the customer payment envelopes, remove the customer checks and remittance advices, and reconcile the two documents. The mailroom supervisor then sends the reconciled checks and remittance advices to the Accounts Receivable clerk, who posts the amounts received to the customer AR subsidiary ledger and the cash receipts journal from her computer terminal. The AR clerk then manually prepares a remittance list of all checks received, endorses the checks "for deposit only" and sends the checks and remittance list to the Treasurer. Finally, the clerk files the remittance advices in the AR department.

Once the checks and remittance list arrive at the Treasury department, the treasurer reconciles the documents, and manually prepares three hard copies of the deposit slip. Next, he sends the checks and two copies of the deposit slip to the bank. Finally, he files the third copy of the deposit slip and the remittance in the department.

Required

a. Identify the internal control weaknesses in the cash receipts process.
b. For each weakness, describe the associated risks.
c. For each weakness provide a possible control activity.

11. ASSESSING INTERNAL CONTROL

The following describes the cash disbursement procedures for a wholesale building supply company.

When the accounts payable clerk receives the supplier's invoice she records the purchase in the purchases journal, records the liability in the AP subsidiary ledger, and sets a due date based on the terms specified on the invoice. The clerk then updates the inventory control and accounts payable control accounts in the general ledger. The invoice is then filed in the department.

Each day, the clerk visually searches the AP subsidiary ledger from her terminal for invoices that are due to be paid. From her computer terminal, the clerk prepares the check and records it in the check register. The negotiable portion of the check is mailed to the vendor and a check copy is filed. The clerk then closes the liability in the AP subsidiary ledger and updates the accounts payable control and cash accounts in the general ledger.

Required

a. Identify the internal control weaknesses in the cash receipts process.
b. For each weakness, describe the associated risks.
c. For each weakness provide a possible control activity.

12. EVALUATION OF INTERNAL CONTROLS

The Never Sink Canoe (NSC) Company is a small manufacturer of high-quality canoes, pontoons, and fishing craft. It sells its products to sporting good stores throughout the northeast United States and parts of Canada. NSC began as a small family owned company that served a local market. Over the years it expanded its market through the use of seasonal sales force employees. The sales staff work on straight commission and travel extensively while taking orders from customers at sporting outlets and trade shows during the water sports and fishing season. All sales are on credit and payment is due within 30 days after being billed. In late fall when the season ends, the temporary sales personnel are laid off until the following spring. Employee turnover is high with approximately 50 percent of the laid-off sales staff returning the following year.

NSC's revenue and expense procedures associated with their sales force activities are as follows:

The salesperson takes an order, reviews the customer's credit worthiness, and submits the approved order to the accounting clerk at the main office who calculates the sales commission to be remitted and promptly writes a check to the salesperson. The clerk then sets up an account receivable for the customer. The clerk also receives cash in payment of customer accounts and updates the related customer AR records.

The order is then sent to the billing department, where the sale is recorded and the customer is billed. Finally, the order is sent to the warehouse where the items are selected, packaged and shipped to the customer. The warehouse clerk then updates the inventory subsidiary ledger to reflect the shipment.

Sales staff periodically submit travel expense reimbursement claims on hard copy forms to the accounting clerk. NSC policy requires sales staff to keep receipts, but they are not required to submit them with the reimbursement forms. The clerk prepares an account payable for each salesperson based on their reimbursement form and twice each month writes checks them for the amount indicated in their individual AP account.

After the end of the past season, and after the temporary employees had been laid off, NSC financials showed a substantial rise in sales compared to previous years. These increases were, however, offset to a great extent by a high rate of product returns. Furthermore, travel expenses were disproportionately high compared with previous years.

Required

a. Using the COSO internal control model for control activities (e.g., transaction authorization, segregation of duties) identify any potential internal control weaknesses in the NSC system.
b. For each weakness discuss the potential for fraud in the system
c. Make recommendations for correcting each identified control weakness.

13. DOCUMENTING SYSTEM AND EVALUATING CONTROLS

The following section describes the warehouse and shipping procedures for a company:

The warehouse clerk receives two copies of a stock release document from the sales department. The stock release document describes the items that were sold, the quantities to be picked from the shelves, and the warehouse locations of the items. The clerk then picks the items and sends them with one copy of the stock release document to the shipping department. Using the second copy of the stock release, the clerk accesses the inventory subsidiary ledger from the PC in the warehouse and updates the inventory to reflect the items shipped. The clerk also looks for Items that have fallen below their reorder points, selects a vendor, prepares a purchase order, and sends it to the vendor.

Upon receipt of the goods and a copy of the stock release document the shipping clerk prepares the items for shipment, records the shipment in the hard copy shipping log, and sends the items sold along with the stock release document to the carrier.

a. Prepare a systems flowchart of the procedures previously described.
b. Identify any control problems in the system.
c. What sorts of fraud are possible in this system?

14. ANALYSIS OF FLOWCHART, INTERNAL CONTROLS

The flowchart labeled Problem 14 depicts the responsibilities of an accounting clerk in a small company.

Required

a. Identify any control problems in the system.
b. What sorts of fraud are possible in this system?

15. EVALUATING INTERNAL CONTROLS

Gaurav Mirchandaniis is the warehouse manager for a large office supply wholesaler. Mirchandaniis receives two copies of the customer sales order from the sales department. He picks the goods from the shelves and sends them and one copy of the sales order to the shipping department. He then files the second copy in a temporary file. At the end of the day, Mirchandaniis retrieves the sales orders from the temporary file and updates the inventory subsidiary ledger from a terminal in his office. At that time, he identifies items that have fallen to low levels, selects a supplier, and prepares three copies of a purchase order. One copy is sent to the supplier, one is sent to the accounts payable clerk, and one is filed in the warehouse. When the goods arrive from the supplier, Mirchandaniis reviews the attached packing slip, counts and inspects the goods, places

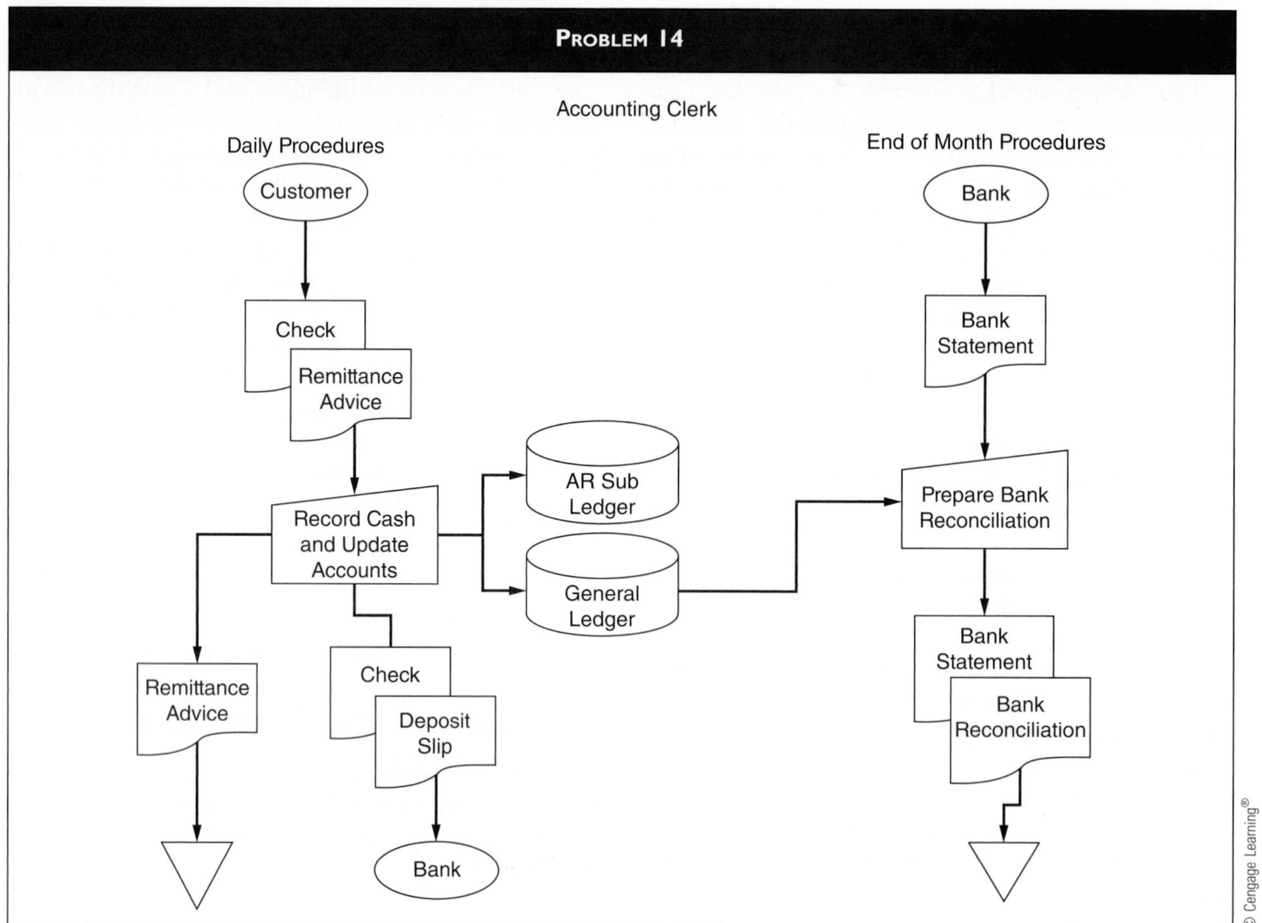

them on the shelves, and updates the inventory ledger to reflect the receipt. He then prepares a receiving report and sends it to the accounts payable department.

Required

a. Prepare a systems flowchart of the procedures previously described.
b. Identify any control problems in the system.
c. What sorts of fraud are possible in this system?

16. EVALUATION OF PAYROLL CONTROLS

A Forman of a construction company is responsible for a construction crew comprised of many unskilled workers. Their tasks consist of mixing cement, digging foundations, and loading onto trucks. The work is hard, and employee turnover rate is high and individuals often leave without notice. Throughout the work week employees record their attendance on separate time cards, which the foreman approves and submits to the payroll department at the end of week. Based on the time cards, the payroll department prepares the paychecks, sends them to the foreman who then distributes the checks to his work crew.

Required

a. Prepare a systems flowchart of the procedures described here.
b. Identify any control problems in the system.
c. What sorts of fraud are possible in this system?

17. EVALUATION OF CONTROLS

Mary Jane Smith has been a highly regarded employee of the Brier Corporation for almost 20 years. Her loyalty to the company is reflected in her dedication to her job as general accounting clerk from which she has not taken a vacation in almost 12 years. Because of her dedication and long tenure, she has acquired many related responsibilities, which has allowed the Brier Corp to reduce its work force through attrition, control salary expenses and become more efficient and competitive. The following describes Mary Jane's responsibilities.

Mary Jane receives copies of credit sales orders from the sales department. From these documents she accesses the AR subsidiary ledger from her office computer and records the AR. She then records the sale in the sales journal and posts the transactions to the general ledger accounts. Cash receipts in payment of customer accounts receivable come directly to her office. She records the cash receipts in the GL cash and AR accounts and updates the AR subsidiary ledger. She then endorses the checks "for deposit only" and deposits them in the bank at the end of each day.

a. Identify any control problems in the procedures described above.
b. What sorts of fraud are possible in this system?
c. What controls are needed to reduce the risk of fraud?

18. INPUT VALIDATION

Describe the types of input edits used for the following data in a payroll system.

a. Employee name
b. Employee number
c. Social Security number
d. Rate per hour or salary
e. Marital status
f. Number of dependents
g. Cost center
h. Regular hours worked
i. Overtime hours worked

19. APPLICATION CONTROLS

Application controls are classified as (1) input controls, (2) processing controls, and (3) output controls.

Required

For each of the three control categories listed, provide two specific controls and explain how each contributes to ensuring the reliability of data. Use the following format.

Control Category	Specific Controls	Contribution to Data Reliability

20. INPUT CONTROLS SALES ORDER SYSTEM

A vintage car parts and accessories company needs to design a new sales order processing system to handle phone and e-mail orders. The company currently has a web page where customers can browse their catalog but cannot order directly on-line. The majority of the orders are placed by phone, and the rest are placed via e-mail. All sales are via credit card or check. The phone orders need to be entered into the system as they are received. The e-mail orders, however, can be batched and submitted for data entry at the end of the day. The following information will be collected for each order:

- Customer number (if customer does not have one, one needs to be assigned)
- Customer name
- Address
- Payment method (credit card or check)
- Credit card number and expiration date
- Items ordered and quantity
- Unit price

Required

Describe application input controls needed to ensure that orders are entered accurately into the system. Also, discuss any differences in control measures between the batch and the real-time processing.

PART

II

Transaction Cycles and Business Processes

CHAPTER 4

The Revenue Cycle

Economic enterprises, both for-profit and not-for-profit, generate revenues through business processes that constitute their revenue cycle. In its simplest form, the revenue cycle is the direct exchange of finished goods or services for cash in a single transaction between a seller and a buyer. More complex revenue cycles process sales on credit. Many days or weeks may pass between the point of sale and the subsequent receipt of cash. This time lag splits the revenue transaction into two phases: (1) the physical phase, involving the transfer of assets or services from the seller to the buyer; and (2) the financial phase, involving the receipt of cash by the seller in payment of the account receivable. As a matter of processing convenience, most firms treat each phase as a separate transaction. Hence, the revenue cycle actually consists of two major subsystems: (1) the sales order processing subsystem and (2) the cash receipts subsystem.

This chapter is organized into two primary sections. The first section presents the conceptual revenue cycle. It provides an overview of key activities, the logical tasks, sources and uses of information, and the movement of accounting information through the organization. The second section examines physical revenue cycle systems. All physical systems are composed, to varying degrees, of technology and human activity. This section reviews system options that lie at different points on the technology/human continuum. Two objectives drive this discussion. The first is to illustrate system functionality, efficiency issues, and work flow characteristics of different technologies. The second is to demonstrate how internal control issues differ between systems at various points on the technology/human continuum. As part of this discussion we examine in detail basic technology systems, advanced integrated systems, and point-of-sale systems. We conclude this chapter with an introduction to electronic data interchange (EDI) and Internet sales systems.

Learning Objectives

After studying this chapter, you should:

- Understand the fundamental tasks performed in the revenue cycle, regardless of the technology in place.
- Be able to identify the functional departments involved in revenue cycle activities and trace the flow of revenue transactions through the organization.
- Be able to specify the documents, journals, and accounts that provide audit trails, promote the maintenance of historical records, support internal decision making, and sustain financial reporting.
- Understand the risks associated with the revenue cycle and recognize the controls that reduce those risks.
- Be aware of the operational and control implications of technology used to automate and reengineer the revenue cycle.

The Conceptual System

OVERVIEW OF REVENUE CYCLE ACTIVITIES

In this section, we examine the revenue cycle conceptually. Using data flow diagrams (DFDs) as a guide, we will trace the sequence of activities through three processes that constitute the revenue cycle for most retail, wholesale, and manufacturing organizations. These are sales order procedures, sales return procedures, and cash receipts procedures. Service companies such as hospitals, insurance companies, and banks would use different industry-specific methods.

This discussion is intended to be technology-neutral. In other words, the tasks described may be performed manually or by computer. At this point, our focus is on what (conceptually) needs to be done, not how (physically) it is accomplished. At various stages in the processes we will examine specific documents, journals, and ledgers as they are encountered. Again, this review is technology-neutral. These documents and files may be physical (hard copy) or digital (computer generated). In the next section, we examine examples of physical systems.

Sales Order Procedures

Sales order procedures include the tasks involved in receiving and processing a customer order, filling the order and shipping products to the customer, billing the customer at the proper time, and correctly accounting for the transaction. The relationships between these tasks are presented with the DFD in Figure 4-1 and described in the following section.

RECEIVE ORDER. The sales process begins with the receipt of a **customer order** indicating the type and quantity of merchandise desired. At this point, the customer order is not in a standard format and may or may not be a physical document. Orders may arrive by mail, by telephone, or from a field representative who visited the customer. When the customer is also a business entity, the order is often a copy of the customer's purchase order. A purchase order is an expenditure cycle document, which is discussed in Chapter 5.

Because the customer order is not in the standard format that the seller's order processing system needs, the first task is to transcribe it into a formal **sales order**, an example of which is presented in Figure 4-2.

The sales order captures vital information such as the customer's name, address, and account number; the name, number, and description of the items sold; and the quantities and unit prices of each item sold. At this point, financial information such as taxes, discounts, and freight charges may or may not be included. After creating the sales order, a copy of it is placed in the **customer order file** for future reference. The task of filling an order and getting the product to the customer may take days or even weeks. During this period, customers may contact their suppliers to check the status of their orders. The customer order file is updated each time the status of the order changes, such as credit approval, on back-order, and shipment. The customer order file thus enables customer service employees to respond promptly and accurately to customer questions.

CHECK CREDIT. Before processing the order further, the customer's creditworthiness needs to be established. The circumstances of the sale will determine the nature and degree of the credit check. For example, new customers may undergo a full financial investigation to establish a line of credit. Once a credit limit is set, however, credit checking on subsequent sales may be limited to ensuring that the customer has a history of paying his or her bills and that the current sale does not exceed the preestablished limit.

The credit approval process is an authorization control and should be performed as a function separate from the sales activity. In our conceptual system, the receive-order task sends the **sales order (credit copy)** to the check-credit task for approval. The returned **approved sales order** then triggers the continuation of the sales process by releasing sales order information simultaneously to various tasks. Several documents mentioned in the following sections, such as the stock release, packing slip, shipping notice, and sales invoice, are simply special-purpose copies of the sales order and are not illustrated separately.

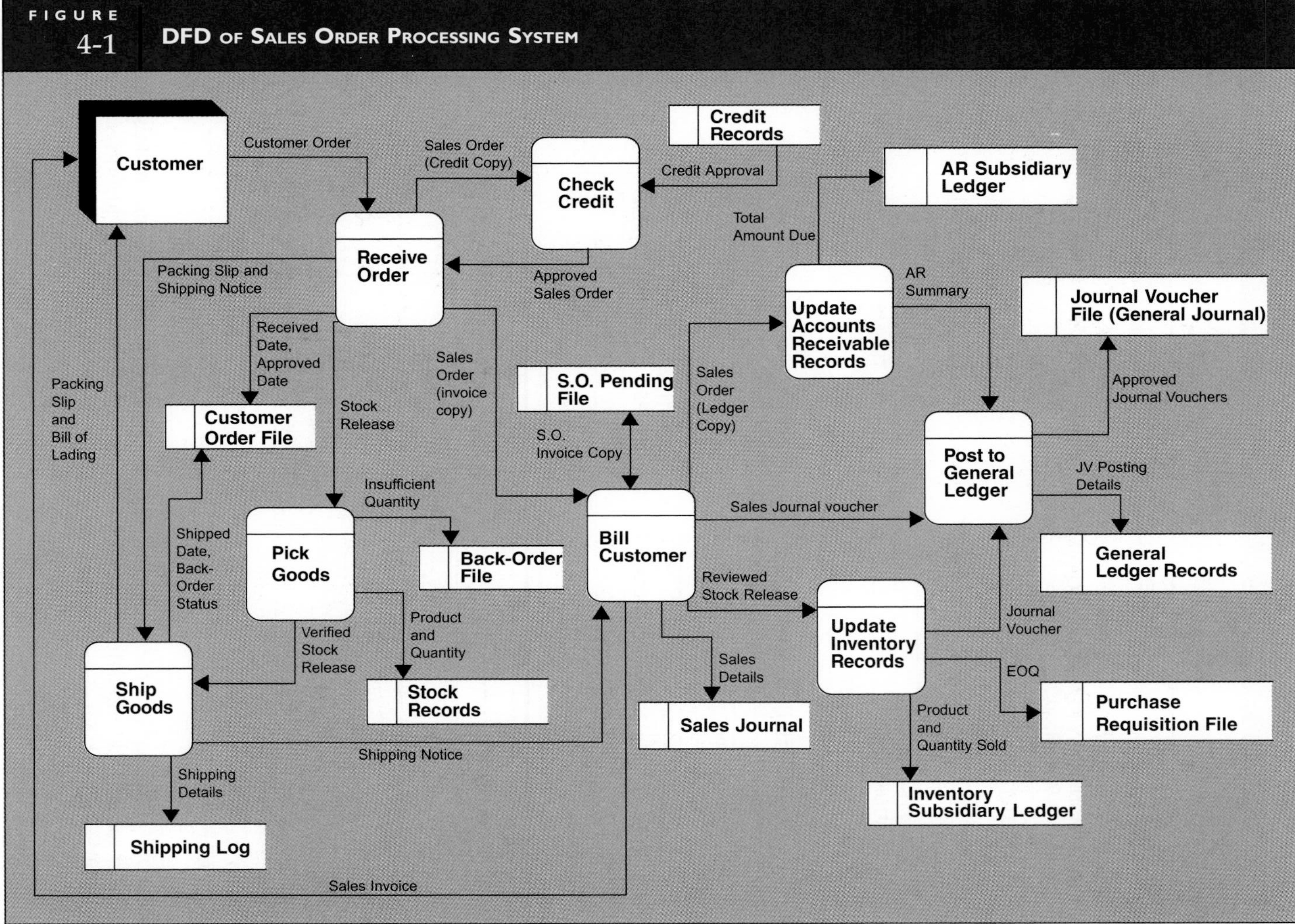

FIGURE 4-1 DFD OF SALES ORDER PROCESSING SYSTEM

FIGURE 4-2 SALES ORDER

CREDIT SALE INVOICE

MONTEREY PENINSULA CO-OP
527 River Road
Chicago, IL 60612
(312) 555-0407

INVOICE NUMBER ________

SOLD TO
FIRM NAME ____________
ATTENTION OF ____________
ADDRESS ____________
CITY ____________
STATE ____ ZIP ____________

INVOICE DATE ____________
PREPARED BY ____________
CREDIT TERMS ____________

CUSTOMER PURCHASE ORDER
NUMBER ____________
DATE ____________
SIGNED BY ____________

SHIPMENT DATE ____________
SHIPPED VIA ____________
BOL NO. ____________

QUANTITY ORDERED	PRODUCT NUMBER	DESCRIPTION	QUANTITY SHIPPED	UNIT PRICE	TOTAL
			TOTAL SALE		
			CUSTOMER ACCT. NO.		
			VERIFICATION		

PICK GOODS. The receive order activity forwards the **stock release** document (also called the picking ticket) to the pick goods function in the warehouse. This document identifies the items of inventory that must be located and picked from the warehouse shelves. It also provides formal authorization for warehouse personnel to release the specified items. After picking the stock, the order is verified for accuracy and the goods, along with the **verified stock release** document, are sent to the ship goods task. If inventory levels are insufficient to fill the order, a warehouse employee adjusts the verified stock release to reflect the amount actually going to the customer. The employee then prepares a **back-order** record, which stays on file until the inventories arrive from the supplier (not shown in Figure 4-1). Back-ordered items are shipped before new sales are processed.

Finally, the warehouse employee adjusts the **stock records** to reflect the reduction in inventory. These stock records are not the formal accounting records for controlling inventory assets. They are used for warehouse management purposes only. Assigning asset custody and record-keeping to the warehouse clerk would violate a key principle of internal control. The inventory control function, discussed later, maintains the formal accounting inventory records.

SHIP GOODS. Before the arrival of the goods and the verified stock release document, the shipping department receives the **packing slip** and **shipping notice** from the receive order function. The packing slip will ultimately travel with the goods to the customer to describe the contents of the order. The shipping notice will later be forwarded to the billing function as evidence that the customer's order was filled and shipped. This document conveys pertinent new facts such as the date of shipment, the items and quantities actually shipped, the name of the carrier, and the freight charges. In some systems, the shipping notice is a separate document prepared within the shipping function.

Upon receiving the goods from the warehouse, the shipping clerk reconciles the physical items with the stock release, the packing slip, and the shipping notice to verify that the order is correct. The ship goods function thus serves as an important independent verification control point and is the last opportunity to detect errors before shipment. The shipping clerk packages the goods, attaches the packing slip, completes the shipping notice, and prepares a **bill of lading**. The bill of lading, as shown in Figure 4-3, is a formal contract between the seller and the shipping company (carrier) to transport the goods to the customer. This document establishes legal ownership and responsibility for assets in transit. Once the goods are transferred to the carrier, the shipping clerk records the shipment in the **shipping log**, forwards the shipping notice and the stock release to the bill-customer function as proof of shipment, and updates the customer order file to reflect the "shipped" status of the transaction.

BILL CUSTOMER. The shipment of goods marks the completion of the economic event and the point at which the customer should be billed. Billing before shipment encourages inaccurate record keeping and inefficient operations. When the customer order is originally prepared, some details such as inventory availability, prices, and shipping charges may not be known with certainty. In the case of back-orders, for example, suppliers do not typically bill customers for out-of-stock items. Billing for goods not shipped causes confusion, damages relations with customers, and requires additional work to make adjustments to the accounting records.

To prevent such problems, the billing function awaits notification from shipping before it bills. Figure 4-1 shows that upon credit approval, the bill-customer function receives the **sales order (invoice copy)** from the receive order task. This document is placed in an **S.O. pending file** until receipt of the shipping notice, which describes the products that were actually shipped to the customer. Upon arrival, the items shipped are reconciled with those ordered, and unit prices, taxes, and freight charges are added to the invoice copy of the sales order. The completed **sales invoice** is the customer's bill, which formally depicts the charges to the customer. In addition, the billing function performs the following record-keeping tasks:

- Sends the stock release document to the update inventory records task.
- Forwards the ledger copy of the sales order to the update accounts receivable task.
- Records the sale in the sales journal.

The **sales journal** is a special journal used for recording completed sales transactions. The details of sales invoices are entered in the journal individually. At the end of the period, these entries are summarized in a sales **journal voucher**, which is sent to the general ledger task for posting to the following accounts:

	DR	**CR**
Accounts Receivable—Control	XXXX.XX	
Sales		XXXX.XX

Figure 4-4 illustrates a journal voucher. Each journal voucher represents a general journal entry and indicates the general ledger accounts affected. Summaries of transactions, adjusting entries, and closing entries are all entered into the general ledger via this method. When properly approved, journal vouchers are an effective control against unauthorized entries to the general ledger. The journal voucher system eliminates the need for a formal general journal, which is replaced by a **journal voucher file**.

FIGURE 4-3 **Bill of Lading**

UNIFORM STRAIGHT BILL OF LADING — Domestic

Monterey Peninsula Co-Op
527 River Road
Chicago, IL 60612
(312) 555-0407

Document No.__________

Shipper No.__________

Carrier No.__________

Date__________

TO:

Consignee __________

Street __________

City/State __________

Zip Code __________

____
(Name of Carrier)

Route:		Vehicle		
No. Shipping Units	Kind of packaging, description of articles, special marks and exceptions	Weight	Rate	Charges

TOTAL CHARGES $

The agreed or declared value of the property is hereby specifically stated by the shipper to be not exceeding: $ ________ per__________	IF WITHOUT RECOURSE: The carrier shall not make delivery of this shipment without payment of freight __________ (Signature of Consignor)
FREIGHT CHARGES Check appropriate box: [ ] Freight prepaid [ ] Collect [ ] Bill to shipper	Signature below signifies that the goods described above are in apparent good order, except as noted. Shipper hereby certifies that he is familiar with all the bill of lading terms and agrees with them.
SHIPPER Monterey Peninsula Co-op	CARRIER
PER	PER DATE

(This bill of lading is to be signed
by the shipper and agent of the
carrier issuing same.)
CONSIGNEE

FIGURE 4-4 JOURNAL VOUCHER

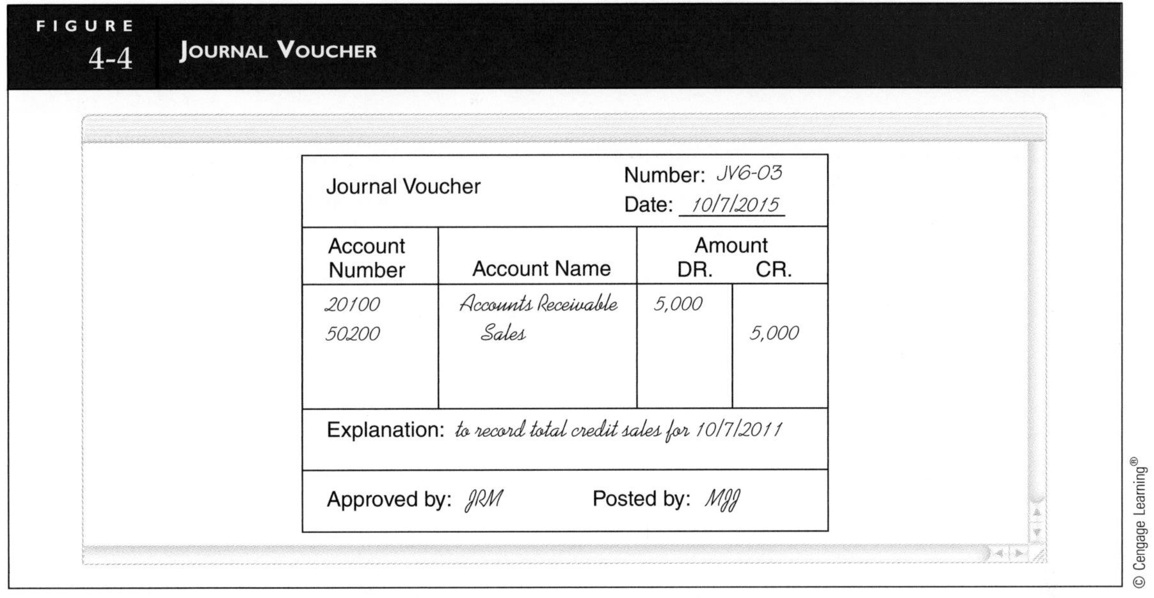

Journal Voucher

Number: JV6-03
Date: 10/7/2015

Account Number	Account Name	Amount DR.	CR.
20100	Accounts Receivable	5,000	
50200	Sales		5,000

Explanation: to record total credit sales for 10/7/2011

Approved by: JRM Posted by: MJJ

UPDATE INVENTORY RECORDS. The inventory control function updates **inventory subsidiary ledger** accounts from information contained in the stock release document. In a perpetual inventory system, every inventory item has its own record in the ledger containing, at a minimum, the data depicted in Figure 4-5. Each stock release document reduces the quantity on hand of one or more inventory accounts. When the quantity on hand falls below the reorder point, a record is added to the purchase requisition file, which will trigger the reordering process. Periodically, the financial value of the total reduction in inventory is summarized in a journal voucher and sent to the general ledger function for posting to the following accounts:

	DR	CR
Cost of Goods Sold	XXX.XX	
Inventory—Control		XXX.XX

UPDATE ACCOUNTS RECEIVABLE RECORDS. Customer records in the **accounts receivable (AR) subsidiary ledger** are updated from information provided by the sales order (**ledger copy**). Every

FIGURE 4-5 INVENTORY SUBSIDIARY LEDGER

Perpetual Inventory Record – Item # 86329

Item Description	Date	Units Received	Units Sold	Qnty on Hand	Reorder Point	EOQ	Qnty on Order	Purch Order #	Vendor Number	Standard Cost	Total Inven. Cost
3" Pulley	9/15		50	950	200	1,000	–	–	–	2	1,900
	9/18		300	650							1,300
	9/20		100	550							1,100
	9/27		300	250							500
	10/1		100	150	200	1,000	1,000	87310	851	2	300
	10/7	1,000		1,150			–				2,300

FIGURE 4-6 ACCOUNTS RECEIVABLE SUBSIDIARY LEDGER

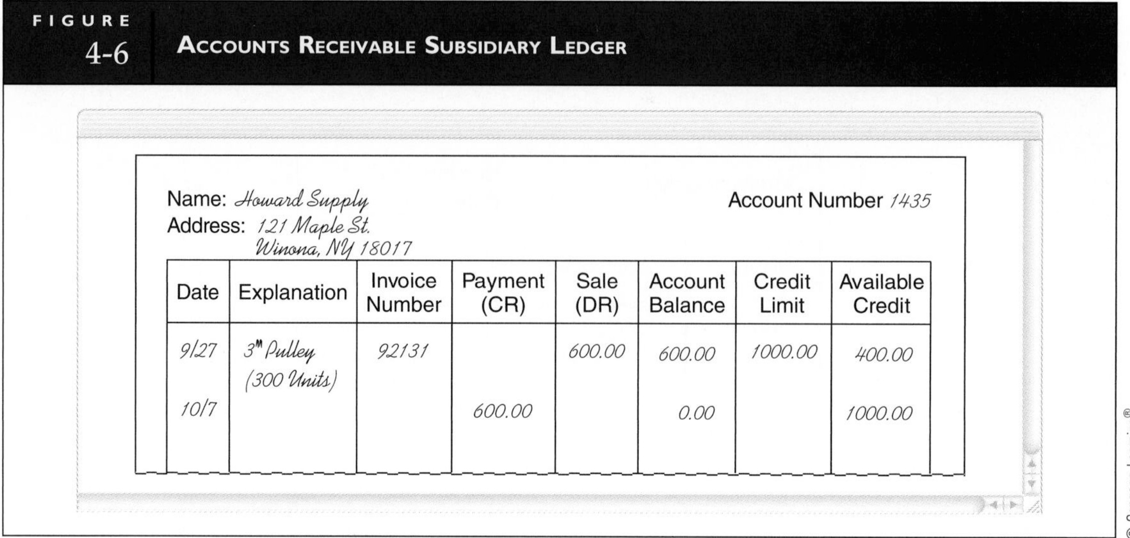

Name: Howard Supply	Account Number 1435
Address: 121 Maple St.
Winona, NY 18017

Date	Explanation	Invoice Number	Payment (CR)	Sale (DR)	Account Balance	Credit Limit	Available Credit
9/27	3" Pulley (300 Units)	92131		600.00	600.00	1000.00	400.00
10/7			600.00		0.00		1000.00

customer has an account record in the AR subsidiary ledger containing, at minimum, the following data: customer name; customer address; current balance; available credit; transaction dates; invoice numbers; and credits for payments, returns, and allowances. Figure 4-6 presents an example of an AR subsidiary ledger record. Periodically, the individual account balances are summarized in a report that is sent to the general ledger. The purpose for this is discussed next.

POST TO GENERAL LEDGER. By the close of the transaction processing period, the general ledger function has received journal vouchers from the billing and inventory control tasks and an account summary from the AR function. This information set serves two purposes. First, the general ledger uses the journal vouchers to post to the following control accounts:

	DR	CR
Accounts Receivable Control	XXXX.XX	
Cost of Goods Sold	XXX.XX	
Inventory Control		XXX.XX
Sales		XXXX.XX

Because general ledger accounts are used to prepare financial statements, they contain only summary figures (no supporting detail) and require only summary posting information. Second, this information supports an important independent verification control. The AR summary, which the AR function independently provides, is used to verify the accuracy of the journal vouchers from billing. The AR summary figures should equal the total debits to AR reflected in the journal vouchers for the transaction period. By reconciling these figures, the general ledger function can detect many types of errors. We examine this point more fully in a later section dealing with revenue cycle controls.

Sales Return Procedures

An organization can expect that a certain percentage of its sales will be returned. This occurs for a number of reasons, some of which are as follows:

- The company shipped the customer the wrong merchandise.
- The goods were defective.
- The product was damaged in shipment.
- The buyer refused delivery because the seller shipped the goods too late or they were delayed in transit.

When a return is necessary, the buyer requests credit for the unwanted products. This involves reversing the previous transaction in the sales order procedure. Using the DFD in Figure 4-7, let's now review the procedures for approving and processing returned items.

FIGURE 4-7 DFD OF SALES RETURN PROCEDURES

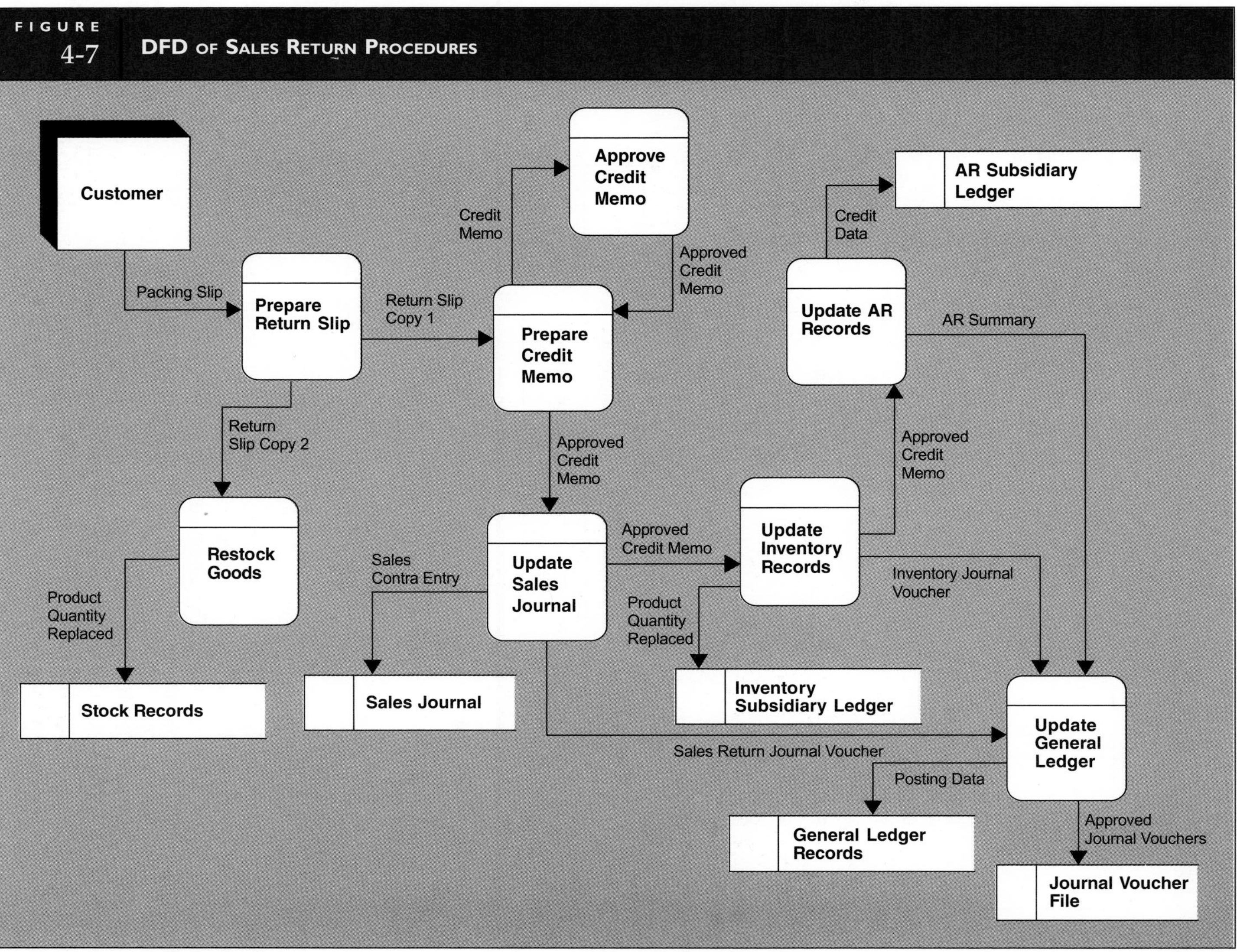

FIGURE 4-8 CREDIT MEMO

Credit Memo

Monterey Peninsula Co-Op
527 River Road
Chicago, IL 60612
(312) 555-0407

Customer
Invoice # ___________

Received from ______________
Address ______________
City ______________
State ________ Zip ________

Reason for Return
____
____
____

Product Number	Description	Quantity Returned	Unit Price	Total
Approved By:			Total Credit	

PREPARE RETURN SLIP. When items are returned, the receiving department employee counts, inspects, and prepares a **return slip** describing the items. The goods, along with a copy of the return slip, go to the warehouse to be restocked. The employee then sends the second copy of the return slip to the sales function to prepare a credit memo.

PREPARE CREDIT MEMO. Upon receipt of the return slip, the sales employee prepares a **credit memo**. This document is the authorization for the customer to receive credit for the merchandise returned. Note that the credit memo illustrated in Figure 4-8 is similar in appearance to a sales order. Some systems may actually use a copy of the sales order marked *credit memo.*

In cases in which specific authorization is required (i.e., if the amount of the return exceeds or the circumstances surrounding the return needs the sales employee's general authority to approve), the credit memo goes to the credit manager for approval. However, if the clerk has sufficient general authority to approve the return, the credit memo is sent directly to the billing function, where the customer sales transaction is reversed.

APPROVE CREDIT MEMO. The credit manager evaluates the circumstances of the return and makes a judgment to grant (or disapprove) credit. The manager then returns the **approved credit memo** to the sales department.

UPDATE SALES JOURNAL. Upon receipt of the approved credit memo, the transaction is recorded in the sales journal as a contra entry. The credit memo is then forwarded to the inventory control function for posting. At the end of the period, total sales returns are summarized in a journal voucher and sent to the general ledger department.

UPDATE INVENTORY AND AR RECORDS. The inventory control function adjusts the inventory records and forwards the credit memo to accounts receivable, where the customer's account is also adjusted. Periodically, inventory control sends a journal voucher summarizing the total value of inventory returns to the update general ledger task. Similarly, accounts receivable submits an AR account summary to the general ledger function.

UPDATE GENERAL LEDGER. Upon receipt of the journal voucher and account summary information, the general ledger function reconciles the figures and posts to the following control accounts:

	DR	CR
Inventory-Control	XXX.XX	
Sales Returns and Allowances	XXXX.XX	
Cost of Goods Sold		XXX.XX
Accounts Receivable-Control		XXXX.XX

Cash Receipts Procedures

The sales order procedure described a credit transaction that resulted in the establishment of an account receivable. Payment on the account is due at some future date, which the terms of trade determine. Cash receipts procedures apply to this future event. They involve receiving and securing the cash, depositing the cash in the bank, matching the payment with the customer and adjusting the correct account, and properly accounting for and reconciling the financial details of the transaction. The DFD in Figure 4-9 shows the relationship between these tasks. They are described in detail in the following section.

OPEN MAIL AND PREPARE REMITTANCE LIST. A mail room employee opens envelopes containing customers' payments and **remittance advices**. Remittance advices (see Figure 4-10) contain information needed to service individual customers' accounts. This includes payment date, account number, amount paid, and customer check number. In this example, only the portion above the perforated line is the remittance advice, which the customer removes and returns with the payment. The lower portion of the document in Figure 4-10 is the customer statement, which the billing department sends out periodically. In other cases, the customer invoice, which was described in the sales order procedures, serves as the remittance advice and statement.

The remittance advice is a form of a turnaround document, as described in Chapter 2. Its importance is most apparent in firms that process large volumes of cash receipts daily. For example, processing a check from John Smith with no supporting details would require a time-consuming and costly search through perhaps thousands of records to find the correct John Smith. This task is greatly simplified when the customer provides the necessary account number and posting information. Because of the possibility of transcription errors and omissions, however, sellers do not rely on their customers to provide this information directly on their checks. Errors are avoided and operational efficiency is greatly improved when using remittance advices.

Mail room personnel route the checks and remittance advices to an administrative clerk who endorses the checks "For Deposit Only" and reconciles the amount on each remittance advice with the corresponding check. The clerk then records each check on a form called a **remittance list** (or cash pre-list), where all cash received is logged. In this example, the clerk prepares three copies of the remittance list. The original copy is sent with the checks to the record and deposit checks function. The second copy goes with the remittance advices to the update AR function. The third goes to a reconciliation task.

RECORD AND DEPOSIT CHECKS. A cash receipts employee verifies the accuracy and completeness of the checks against the prelist. Any checks possibly lost or misdirected between the mail room and this function are thus identified. After reconciling the prelist to the checks, the

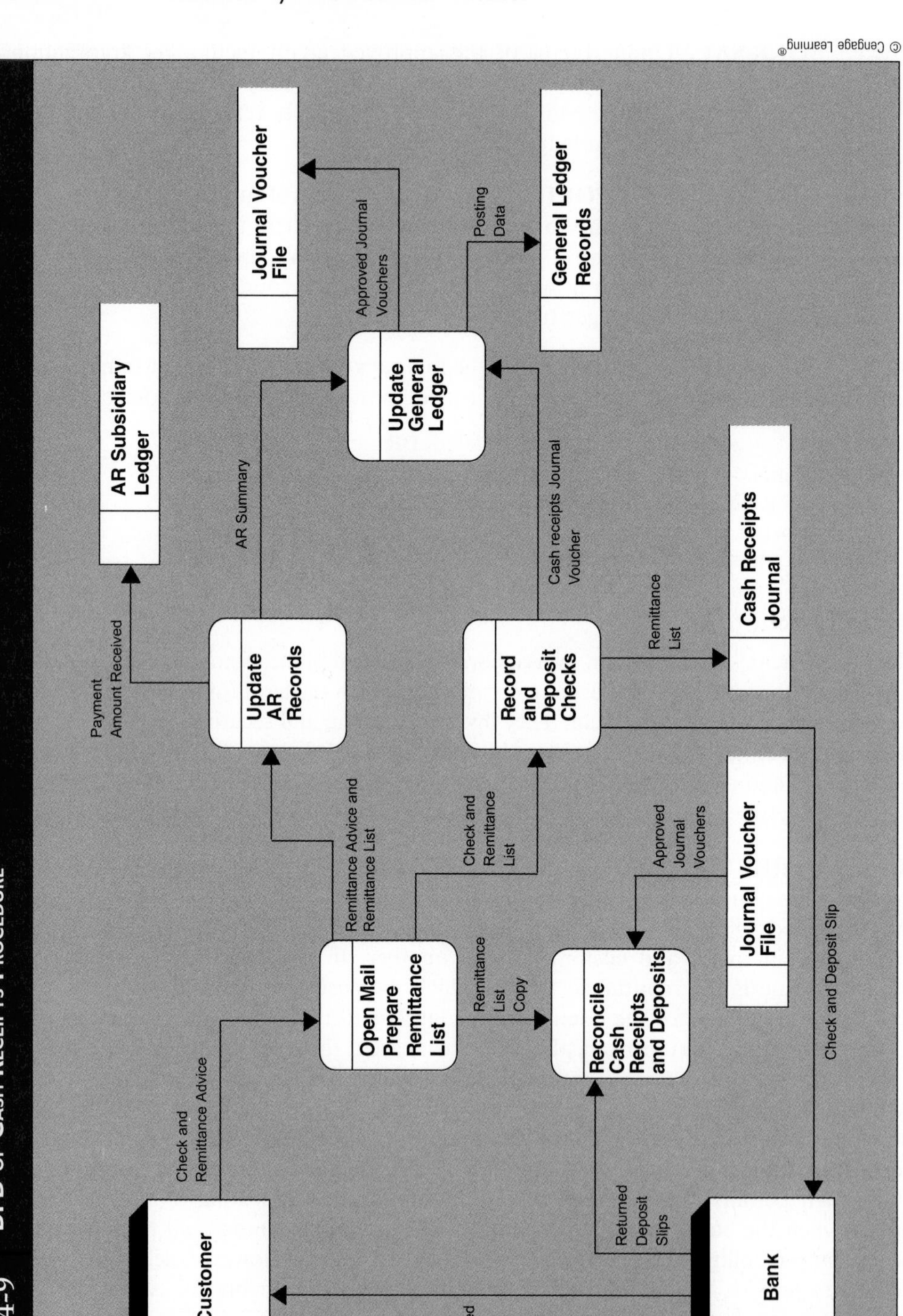

FIGURE 4-9 DFD OF CASH RECEIPTS PROCEDURE

FIGURE 4-10 **Remittance Advice**

Send To: MONTEREY PENINSULA CO-OP
527 River Road
Chicago, IL 60612
(312) 555-0407

Page: 1

Remittance Advice:

Date	Customer No.	Amount Pd.	Check No.
10/4/15	811901	125.00	2002

Please return the upper portion with your payment — Thank You

To: John Smith
R.D. #2, Box 312
Prunedale, CA 09278–5704

Due Date	Customer No.	Amount Due
10/10/15	811901	125.00

Date	Invoice Number	Description	Amount Due
9/28/15	6112115	Cleaning Supplies	125.00

Thank you for giving Monterey Peninsula the opportunity to serve you

Previous Bal.	300.00
Payments	300.00
Sales	125.00
Late Fees	—
Tax	—
Ending Bal.	125.00

FIGURE 4-11 CASH RECEIPTS JOURNAL

Cash Receipts Journal

Date	Account	Post Ref	Check #	Cash Acct. # 101 (Debit)	Sales Discounts Acct. # 430 (Debit)	Accounts Receivable Acct. # 102	Sales Acct. # 401 Credit	Sundry Accounts Debit (Credit)
9/3	Capital Stock	301	2150	14,000				14,000
9/5	Ogment Supply	✓	6712	2,970	30	3,000		
9/9	Marvin Co.		3491	1,000			1,000	

employee records the check in the **cash receipts journal**. All cash receipts transactions, including cash sales, miscellaneous cash receipts, and cash received on account, are recorded in the cash receipts journal. Figure 4-11 illustrates this with an example of each type of transaction. Notice that each check received from a customer is listed as a separate line item.

Next, the clerk prepares a bank **deposit slip** showing the amount of the day's receipts and forwards this along with the checks to the bank. Upon deposit of the funds, the bank teller validates the deposit slip and returns it to the company for reconciliation. At the end of the day, the cash receipts employee summarizes the journal entries and sends a journal voucher with the following entry to the general ledger function.

	DR	CR
Cash	XXXX.XX	
Accounts Receivable Control		XXXX.XX

UPDATE ACCOUNTS RECEIVABLE RECORDS. The remittance advices are used to post to the customers' accounts in the AR subsidiary ledger. Periodically, the changes in account balances are summarized and forwarded to the general ledger function.

UPDATE GENERAL LEDGER. Upon receipt of the journal voucher and the account summary, the general ledger function reconciles the figures, posts to the cash and AR control accounts, and files the journal voucher.

RECONCILE CASH RECEIPTS AND DEPOSITS. Periodically, a clerk from the **controller's** office (or an employee not involved with the cash receipts procedures) reconciles cash receipts by comparing the following documents: (1) a copy of the prelist, (2) deposit slips received from the bank, and (3) related journal vouchers.

Physical Systems

Physical accounting information systems are a combination of computer technology and human activity. This technology/human mix creates a continuum of alternative design options. At one end of the continuum are systems that employ minimal technology and rely heavily on human involvement and manual procedures. At the other end are advanced technology systems, which, to a great extent, replace human activity with automated processes. As a general rule, smaller businesses tend to rely less on technology and more on manual procedures, whereas larger companies tend to employ advanced technologies. The nature of the technology/human mix employed in a particular system has a direct bearing on the nature of internal controls needed to control the system.

The objectives of this section are to: 1) illustrate AIS functionality and work flow patterns under different levels of technology, and 2) demonstrate how the internal control profile changes as the technology/human mix changes. To accomplish this we review examples of systems at different points on the technology continuum. The first example is a basic technology system that employs independent PCs, which function primarily as record keeping devices. The second example is an advanced technology system that integrates all business functions through a centralized computer application. Next, we review the key features of **point-of-sale (POS) systems** that are commonly used in department stores and supermarkets. Finally, we examine electronic data interchange (EDI) and the Internet as alternative techniques for reengineering the revenue cycle. The appendix to this chapter presents an example of a sales return system and examples of batch processing technologies that are associated with older legacy systems, which, although rare, are still in operation.

BASIC TECHNOLOGY REVENUE CYCLE

This section presents examples of basic technology revenue cycle systems. The computers used in these systems are independent (non-networked) PCs. Therefore, information flows between departments are communicated via hard-copy documents. In addition, in such systems, maintaining physical files of source documents is critical to the audit trail. As we walk through the various flowcharts notice that in many departments, after an individual completes his or her assigned task, documents are filed as evidence that the tasks were performed.

BASIC TECHNOLOGY SALES ORDER PROCESSING SYSTEM

The system flowchart in Figure 4-12 shows the processes, documents, and data files of a basic technology sales order system. The following sections outline the key activities in this system.

Sales Department

The sales process begins with a customer contacting the sales department by telephone, mail, e-mail, fax, or in person. The sales department clerk manually records the essential details on a sales order. This multipart document will later trigger many tasks, but for the moment it is filed while one copy of it is sent to the credit department for approval.

Credit Department Approval

To provide independence to the credit authorization process, the credit department is organizationally and physically segregated from the sales department. The credit department clerk verifies the customer's credit worthiness by using the department computer to review the customer's credit history in the Customer Records file. Alternatively, for new customers the clerk may access an online credit bureau. When credit is approved, the sales department clerk pulls the various copies of the sales orders from the pending file and releases them to the billing, warehouse, and shipping departments. The customer order and credit approval are then placed in the customer order file.

Warehouse Procedures

The next step is to ship the merchandise. The warehouse clerk receives the stock release copy of the sales order and uses this to locate the inventory. The inventory items and stock release are then sent to the shipping department. Finally, the warehouse clerk uses the department PC to record the inventory reduction in the stock records file.

The Shipping Department

The shipping clerk reconciles the products received from the warehouse with the shipping notice copy of the sales order received earlier. As discussed previously, this reconciliation is an important

FIGURE 4-12 BASIC TECHNOLOGY SALES ORDER PROCESSING SYSTEM

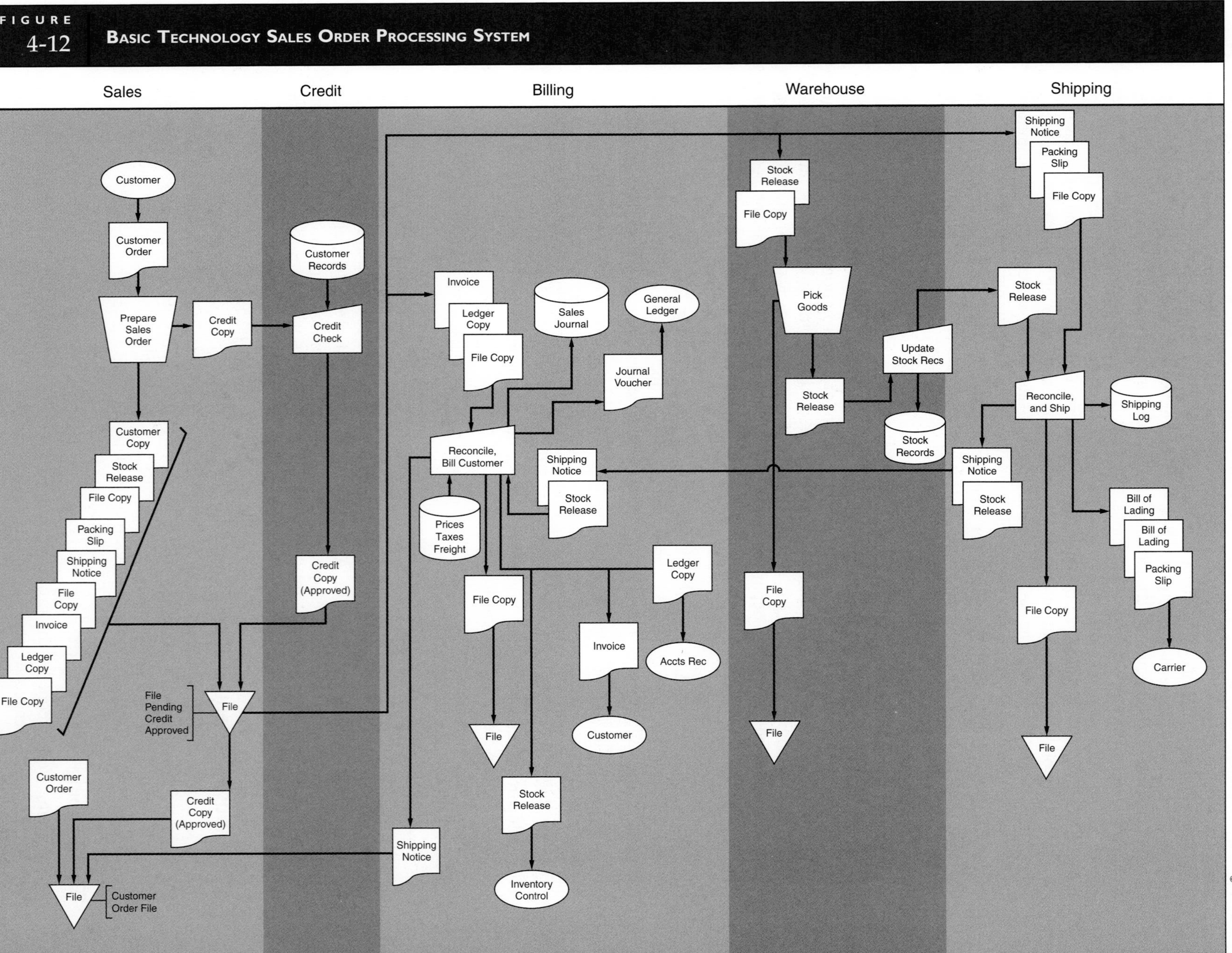

FIGURE 4-12 (CONTINUED)

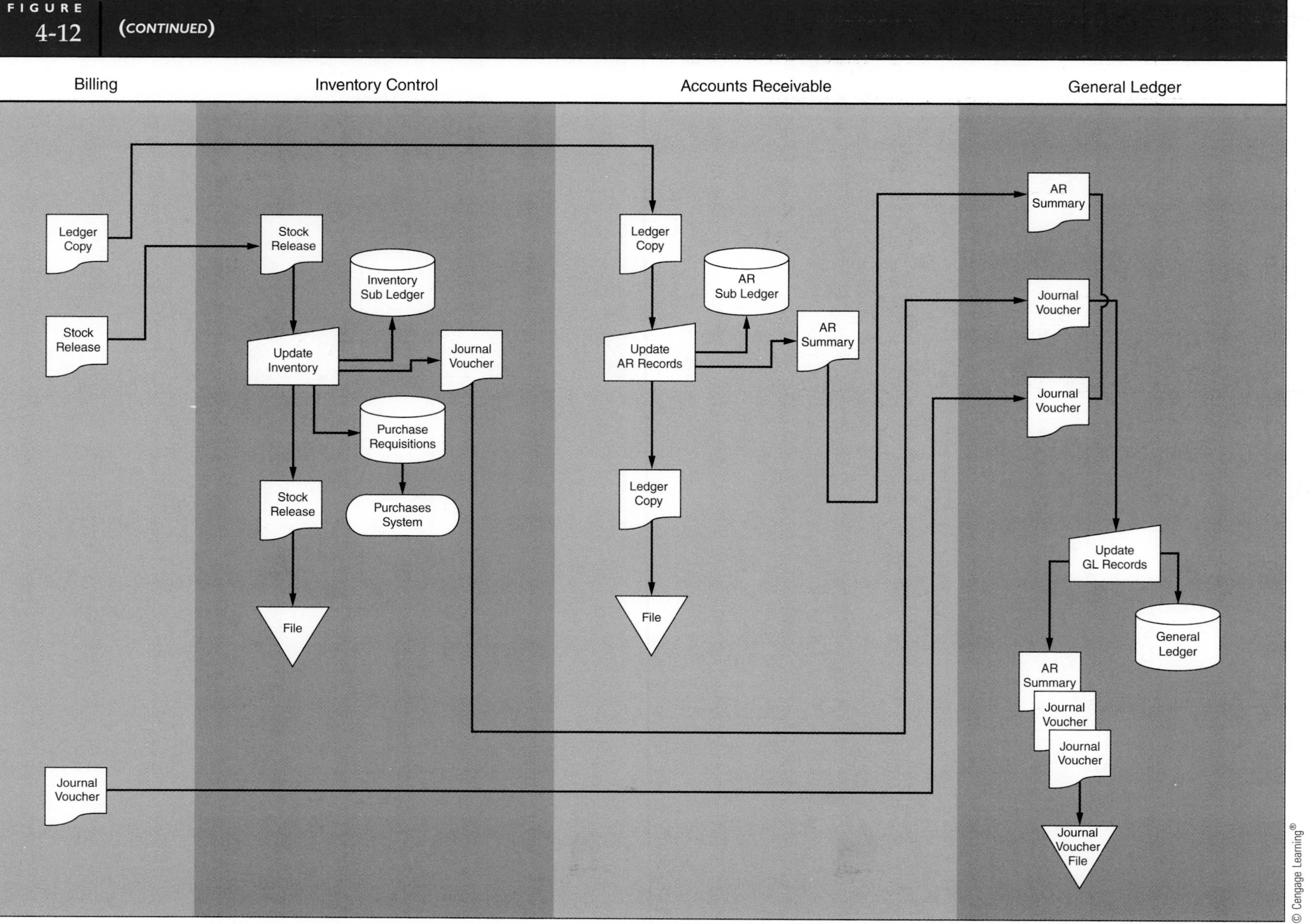

control point, which ensures that the firm sends the correct products and quantities to the customer. When the order is determined correct, a bill of lading is prepared, and the products are packaged and shipped via common carrier to the customer. The clerk then uses the department PC to record the transaction in the shipping log and sends the shipping notice and stock release document to the billing department.

The Billing Department

The shipping notice provides proof that the product has been shipped and is the trigger document that initiates the billing process. Upon receipt of the shipping notice and stock release, the billing clerk uses the department PC to compile the relevant facts about the transaction (product prices, handling charges, freight, taxes, and discount terms) and bills the customer. The billing clerk then enters the transaction into the sales journal file and distributes stock release and ledger copies of the sales order to the inventory control and AR departments, respectively. The shipping notice is sent to the sales department where it is filed in the customer order file to reflect the order's shipped status. Periodically, the clerk prints out a hard-copy journal voucher reflecting total sales and sends it to the general ledger department.

Accounts Receivable, Inventory Control, and General Ledger Departments

Upon receipt of the documents from the billing department, the AR and inventory control clerks update their respective subsidiary ledgers. Figure 4-13 shows the file structures of the AR Subsidiary and Inventory Subsidiary files in relation to the sales order document used to update them. The clerks search their respective files for the correct records by entering primary key data from the sales orders into their computer systems. The AR clerk enters the customer number, and the inventory control clerk enters the inventory number. The systems search their respective files and retrieve the matching records. The AR clerk updates the current balance field in the AR record by entering the sales order amount data into the system. Similarly, the inventory control clerk updates the quantity-on-hand field from the sales

FIGURE 4-13 STRUCTURES FOR AR AND INVENTORY SUBSIDIARY FILES

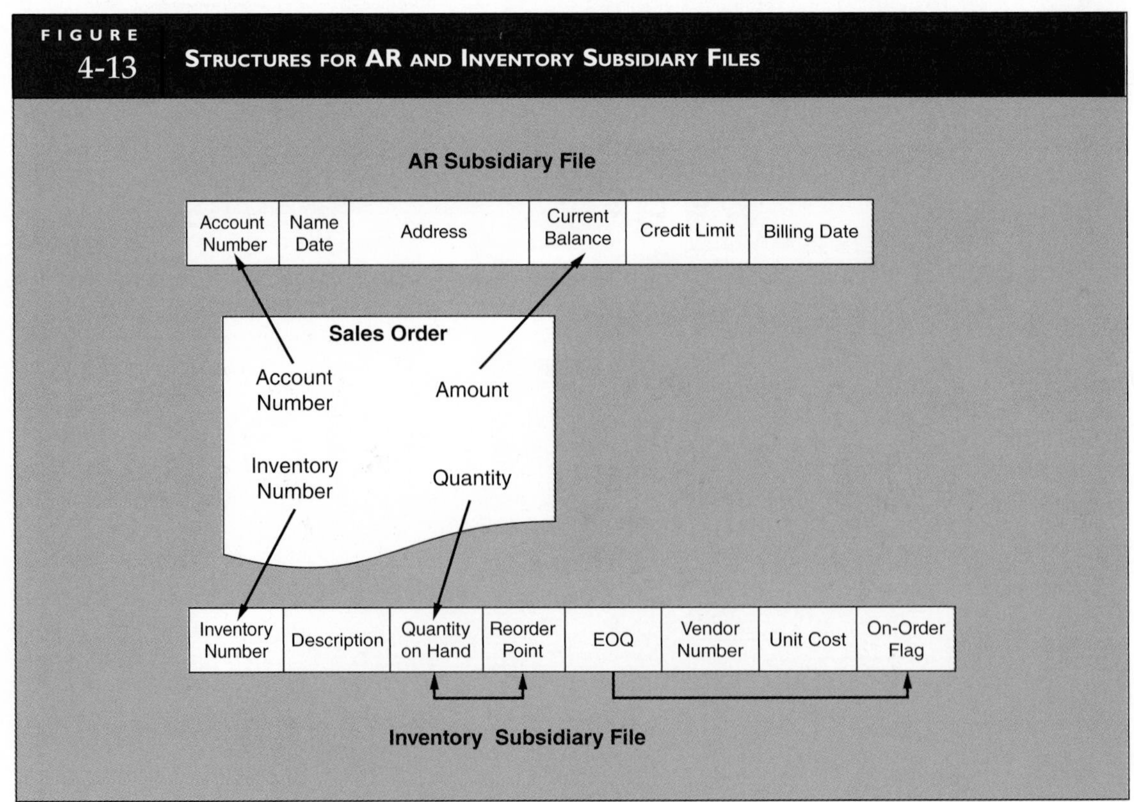

order quantity value. As each inventory item is updated, the inventory control clerk's system automatically checks to see if the quantity on hand has fallen below the reorder point. If this is the case, the inventory record is flagged "on order" to prevent it from being ordered again before the inventory is replaced through the purchases process. A flag can be set in a number of ways, in this example the quantity to be ordered (EOQ) is placed in the on-order flag field. Next, a record is added to the purchase requisition file, which triggers the purchases procedures (covered in Chapter 5). Periodically, the AR and inventory control clerks prepare hard-copy journal vouchers and account summaries, which they send to the general ledger department for reconciliation and posting to the GL accounts.

BASIC TECHNOLOGY CASH RECEIPTS SYSTEM

Figure 4-14 presents a system flowchart depicting the cash receipts procedures, which begin in the mail room.

Mail Room

Customer payments and remittance advices arrive at the mail room, where a clerk opens the envelopes, reconciles the checks and remittance advices, endorses the checks, gathers the remittance advices and checks into batches, and prepares a remittance list. Next the clerk sends the checks and a copy of the remittance list to the cashier in the cash receipts department. The remittance advices and a copy of the remittance list are sent to the AR department.

Cash Receipts

The cashier records the checks in the cash receipts journal and promptly sends them to the bank, accompanied by two copies of the deposit slip. Periodically, the employee prepares a journal voucher and sends it to the general ledger department.

Accounts Receivable

The AR department uses the remittance advices to reduce the customers' account balances consistent with the amount paid. The AR clerk prepares a summary of changes to account balances, which is sent to the general ledger department.

General Ledger Department

Upon receipt of the journal voucher and account summary from cash receipts and AR, respectively, the general ledger clerk reconciles the information and posts to the control accounts.

Controller's Office

Because cash is a liquid asset and subject to misappropriation, someone from the controller's office periodically performs a bank reconciliation by comparing deposit slips returned from the bank, account summaries used to post to the accounts, and journal vouchers.

ADVANCED TECHNOLOGY REVENUE CYCLE

Advanced technologies allow systems designers to integrate accounting and other business functions through a common information system. The objective of integration is to improve operational performance and reduce costs by identifying and eliminating nonvalue-added tasks. This involves replacing traditional procedures with procedures that are very different. In this section we see how advanced technologies can significantly alter and simplify the revenue cycle, compared to the basic technology system presented in the previous section. We begin by reviewing the operational features of an integrated sales order system and then we examine an integrated cash receipts system.

INTEGRATED SALES ORDER PROCESSING SYSTEM

The flowchart in Figure 4-15 illustrates an integrated sales order system. Compare this flowchart to the basic technology system presented in Figure 4-12. Notice that the functions of credit checking,

FIGURE 4-14 Basic Technology Cash Receipts System

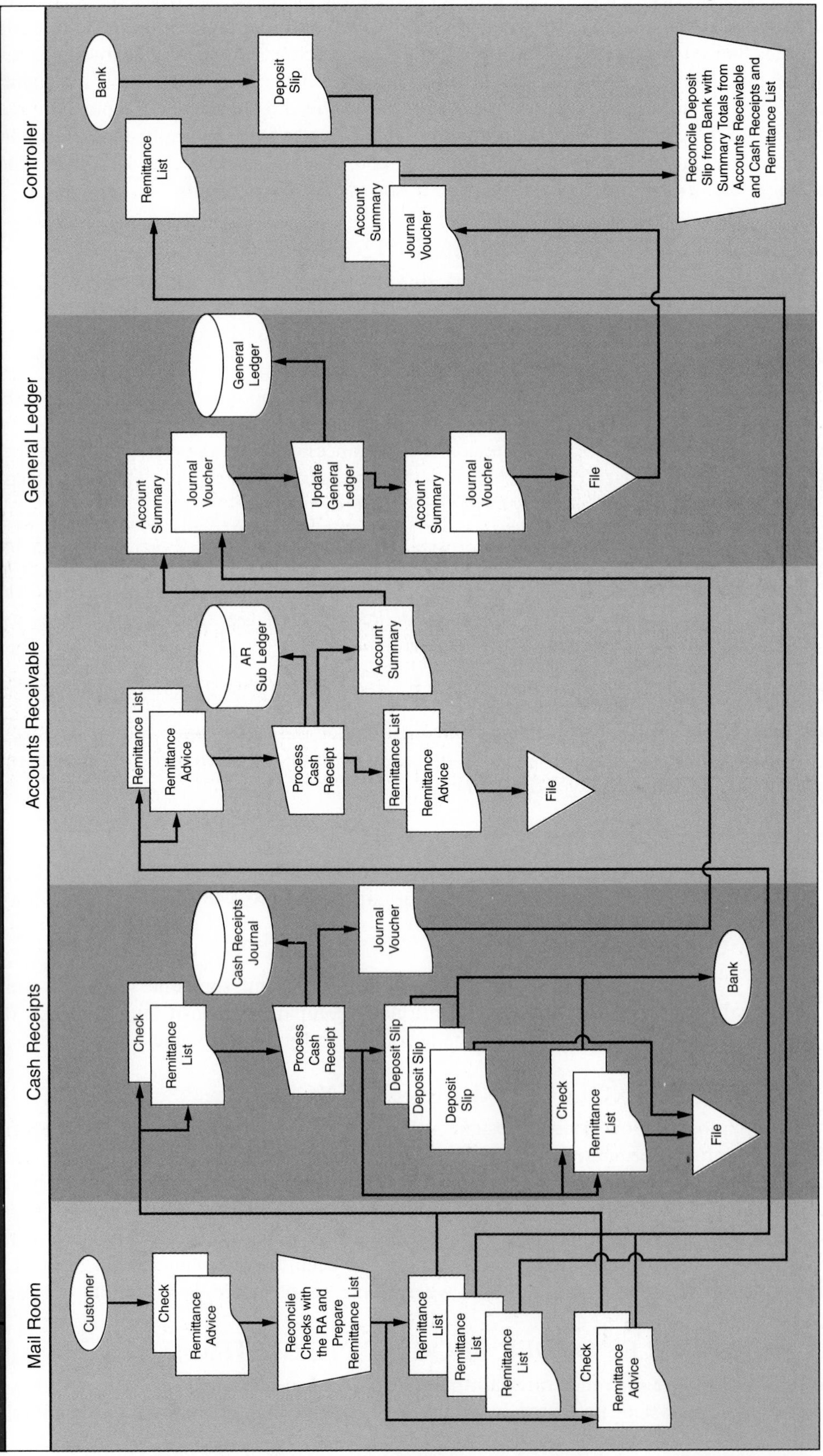

FIGURE 4-15 INTEGRATED SALES ORDER SYSTEM

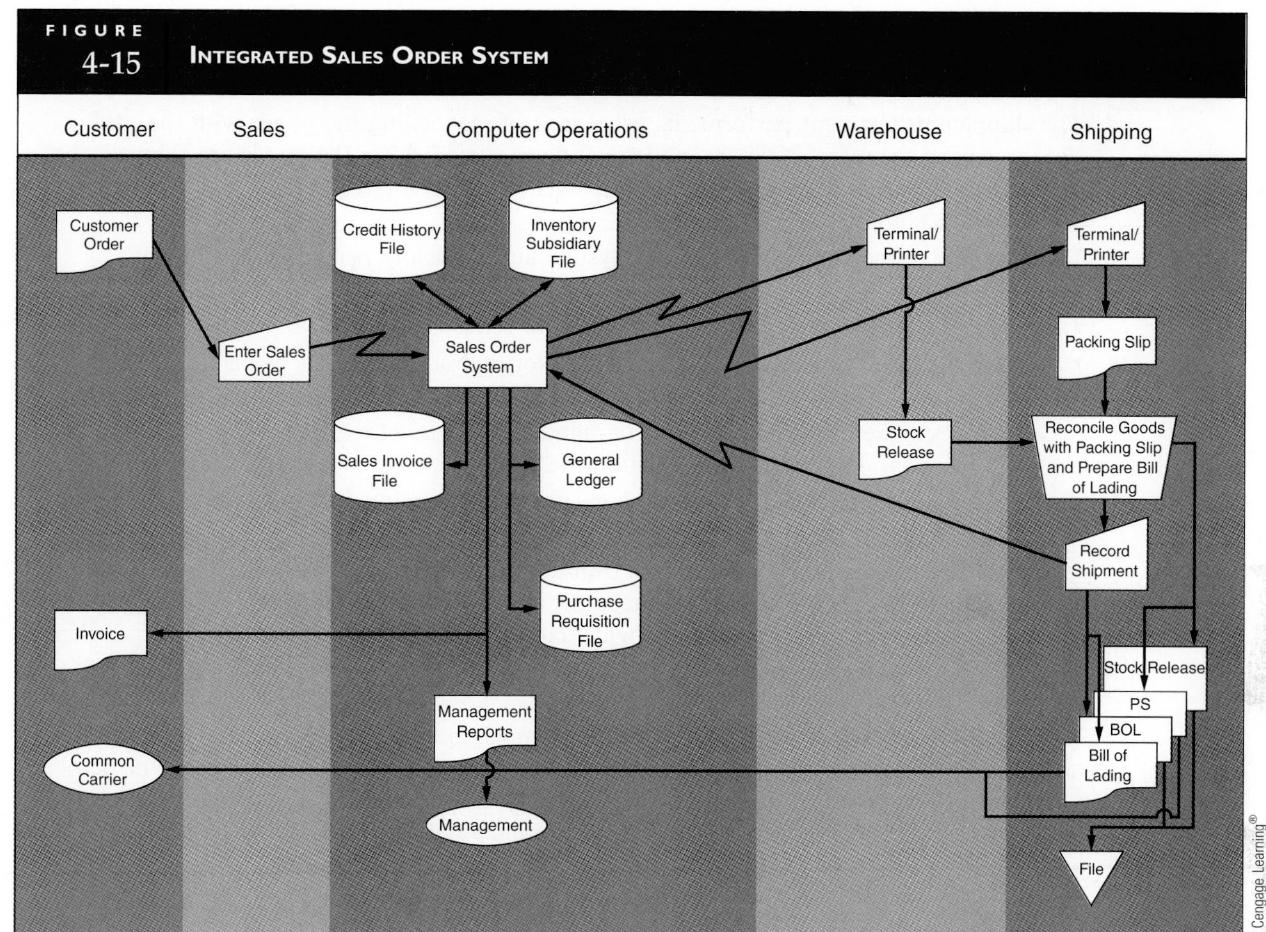

accounts receivable updating, customer billing, inventory updating, and posting to the general ledger are performed automatically by the central computer system illustrated in Figure 4-15. These labor-intensive activities add greatly to operating costs and contribute to human error. In the advanced technology system, computer programs perform these tasks, which is cheaper and far less prone to error. Although these traditional departments still exist in the advanced technology environment, their responsibilities are refocused on exception-based problem solving, rather than on day-to-day clerical tasks. As a result, these departments are smaller and more efficient than their basic technology counterparts. Each phase of this reengineered system is described next.

Sales Procedures

The process begins with sales clerks receiving customer orders, which may be hard-copy documents as illustrated in Figure 4-15 or may be received via e-mail, fax, or phone. Using a computer terminal connected to a central sales order system, the clerk enters the sales order and initiates the following tasks:

1. The system accesses the inventory subsidiary file and checks the availability of the inventory items requested. It then performs a credit check by reviewing the customer's credit record in the credit history file. This file contains information such as the customer's credit limit, current balance, date of last payment, and current credit status. Based on programmed criteria, the customer's request for credit is either approved or denied.
2. If credit is approved, the system adds a record to the sales invoice file, transmits a digital stock release document to the warehouse, and sends a digital copy of the packing slip to the shipping department.

3. The warehouse clerk's terminal immediately produces a hard-copy printout of the electronically transmitted stock release document. The clerk picks out the goods and sends them to the shipping department, accompanied by a copy of the stock release.
4. The shipping department performs its usual task of reconciling the goods with the packing slip, preparing them for shipment, and selecting a carrier. After the goods are shipped, the shipping clerk accesses the system and transmits a digital shipping notice to signal that the transaction is complete.
5. Upon receipt of the shipping notice, the system automatically performs the following accounting tasks:
   - Updates the customer's credit history record to reflect the sale.
   - Reduces the quantity-on-hand field in the inventory subsidiary records by the quantities of items sold to present an accurate and current picture of inventory on hand and available for sale.
   - Determines if the inventory quantity on-hand has fallen below the reorder point and, if so, adds a record to the purchase requisition file.
   - Places an "on-order" flag in the inventory record, as previously described.
   - Inserts a shipped date in sales invoice record to indicate the order's status. Many companies engaged in business-to-business (B2B) transactions use the sales invoice file as a substitute for the traditional sales journal and account receivable subsidiary ledger. The shipped sales invoices in the file provide a chronological record of total sales for the period (equivalent to the sales journal), and the unpaid shipped invoices at any point in time constitute the organization's accounts receivable.
   - Updates the general ledger accounts. In this example, the GL accounts are updated in real time. Depending upon an organization's transaction volume, however, this activity may be performed in batch mode. Recall from Chapter 2 that batch updating of general ledger records is done to achieve operational efficiency in high-volume transaction processing systems.
   - Finally, the system produces and distributes various management reports, such as sales summaries, inventory status reports, and general ledger change reports. Management reports are discussed in detail in Chapter 8.

INTEGRATED CASH RECEIPTS SYSTEM

Figure 4-16 illustrates an integrated cash receipts system. By comparison to the basic technology system presented in Figure 4-14, we again see a shift away from clerical activities through the use of automation.

The system presented here and the discussion below assumes an organization in which customers make payments on account with physical checks that are mailed to the company. Organizations that use electronic funds transfer (EFT) to receive customer payments employ different procedures that are described in Chapter 12.

Mail Room

The mail room clerk opens the envelopes containing the checks and remittance advices and endorses the checks for deposit only. The clerk then reconciles the checks and remittances advices and prepares a remittance list. The checks, remittance advices, and a copy of the remittance list are sent to the cash receipts department.

Cash Receipts Department

The cash receipts clerk reconciles the checks and the remittance advices with the remittance list and prepares deposit slips. Via terminal, the clerk accesses the cash receipts system and creates a record in the remittance file (cash receipts journal) for each remittance advice received. The clerk files the remittance list, remittance advices, and one copy of the deposit slip. At the end of the day, a member of the security group deposits the checks in the bank.

FIGURE 4-16 INTEGRATED CASH RECEIPTS SYSTEM

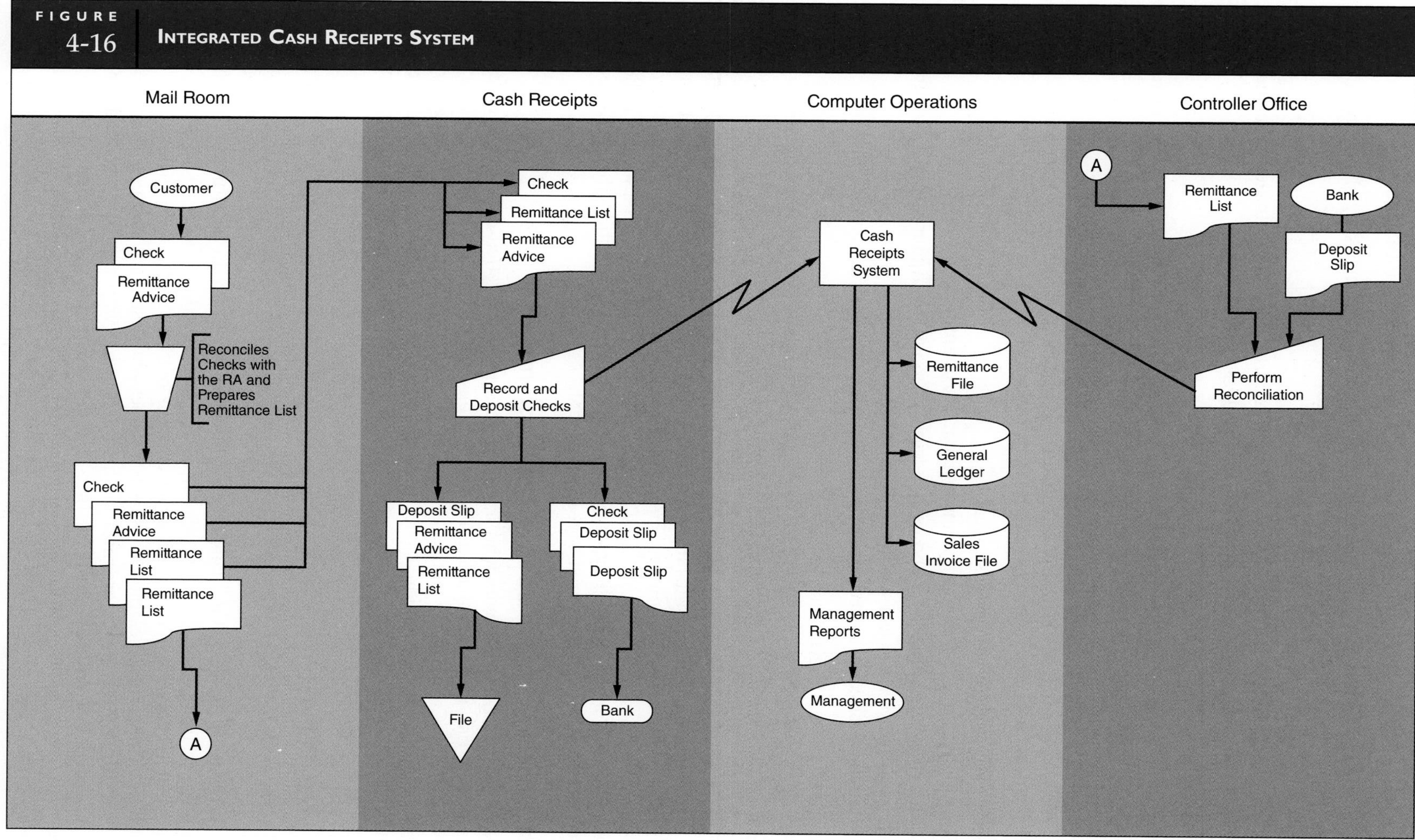

Automatic Data Processing Procedures

When the cash receipts data entry is complete, the system automatically performs the following tasks:

- Closes the sales invoices that are covered by the customer checks by placing the customer check number and payment date in the invoice record.
- Posts to the GL accounts.
- Prepares and distributes various management reports, including transaction listings, discrepancy (out of balance) reports, and general ledger change reports.

Controller's Office

Finally, a clerk in the controller's office periodically performs a reconciliation of remittance lists, bank deposit slips, cash receipts journal, and the GL cash account.

REVENUE CYCLE RISKS AND INTERNAL CONTROLS

An objective of internal control is to mitigate the risk from errors and fraud. The following are the primary risks associated with revenue cycle transactions:

- Selling to un-creditworthy customers
- Shipping customers the wrong items or incorrect quantities
- Inaccurately recording sales and cash receipts transactions in journals and accounts
- Misappropriation of cash receipts and inventory
- Unauthorized access to accounting records and confidential reports

Chapter 3 defined internal control activities as consisting of two major categories: 1) physical controls and 2) IT controls. The purpose of physical controls is to control the actions of people. These consist of six classes of internal control activities: transaction authorization, segregation of duties, supervision, accounting records, access control, and independent verification. IT controls are comprised of general controls and application controls. General controls are not specific to a particular cycle or subsystem and thus do not apply to revenue cycle risks directly. Computer application controls consist of: input controls, processing controls, and output controls. The discussion that follows, examines and compare show physical and IT control techniques apply in both basic technology and advanced technology systems to reduce the risks identified above. Table 4-1 at the end of the section provides a summary of this material.

Risk of Selling to Un-Creditworthy Customers

Selling on credit to customers who have not been properly vetted can lead to excessive bad debt losses. This risk is more apparent in organizations whose sales staff are compensated on a commission basis. Consider the potential conflict in objectives between the salesperson, whose compensation is based on individual sales performance, and the organization. In such cases, the sales staff have an incentive to maximize sales volume and thus may not adequately consider the creditworthiness of prospective customers.

Physical Controls

TRANSACTION AUTHORIZATION. The objective of transaction authorization is to ensure that only valid transactions are processed. The authorization process in the sales function is a credit check of the customer. This task is a function of the credit department, which has responsibility for ensuring the proper application of the firm's credit policies. Determining the creditworthiness of the customer is the principal concern of this function. In making this judgment, the credit department may employ various techniques and tests. The complexity of credit procedures will vary depending on the organization, its relationship with the customer, and the materiality of the transaction. Credit approval for first-time customers may take time and involve consultation with an outside credit bureau. In contrast, credit decisions about existing customers that involve ensuring only that the current transaction does not exceed the customer's credit limit may be dealt with very quickly. Whatever level of test is deemed necessary by company policy, the sales transaction should not proceed further until credit is approved.

SEGREGATION OF DUTIES. An objective of segregation of duties as stated in chapter 3 is to separate *Transaction authorization from transaction processing.*

To provide independence to the credit authorization process, the credit function should be organizationally and physically segregated from the sales function. This will help ensure that the task of reviewing prospective customers is objectively performed and that the credit function is unconstrained in detecting risky transactions and disallowing poor and irresponsible sales decisions.

IT Controls

AUTOMATED CREDIT CHECKING. Credit checking may be performed automatically by the system as a programmed process control. The system logic, not a human being, makes the decision to grant or deny credit based on the customer's credit history contained in the credit history file. If credit is denied, the sales clerk should not be able to force the transaction to continue. To allow for operational flexibility in unusual circumstances, however, systems will typically provide a management override option that may only be performed by a supervisor. Any such overrides should be fully documented in the credit history record and in management reports.

Risk of Shipping Customers Incorrect Items or Quantities

Shipping customers the wrong items or incorrect quantities may result in damaged customer relations, excessive sales returns, lost future sales, and accounting errors. These risks may be due to human errors in the process of picking up items from the inventory warehouse or because of unanticipated inventory shortages known as stock-outs.

Physical Controls

INDEPENDENT VERIFICATION. The shipping function verifies that the goods sent from the warehouse are correct in type and quantity. The stock release document and the packing slip should be reconciled before the goods are sent to the customer.

IT Controls

SCANNER TECHNOLOGY. Product code scanners in the warehouse and shipping department will reduce the risk of human error in picking and shipping incorrect products. When scanned by the warehouse and/or shipping clerk the system will verify that the items selected match those on the sales order.

AUTOMATED INVENTORY ORDERING. When an inventory record is updated to reflect a sale, the computer logic should check to determine if the reduction in inventory drops the inventory quantity on hand to a point below the inventory reorder point. When this is the case, the organization needs to reorder inventory to avoid a stock out. The system logic should create a purchase requisition record, which is added to the purchase requisition file. Once an item is on order, however, a control should be in place to ensure that it is not ordered again until the original order has been received from the supplier. One method of accomplishing this is to "flag" the inventory item "on order" by entering a value (e.g., the number of items ordered) in the on-order field of the inventory record. This field has a value of zero when the item in question is not on order. The following pseudo code illustrates how the computer logic should function to test for and control a low stock condition:

If Quantity-on-Hand < Reorder Point **AND** On-Order field = zero

Then create a purchase requisition record and place the quantity ordered in the inventory On-Order field

Else Do Nothing

Under this logic, the first time the low stock condition is detected, the on-order field is zero, and a purchase requisition will be created. The computer program then places a nonzero quantity value in the on-order field. As the inventory item in question continues to be sold, the system will continue to test for low stock and will determine with each subsequent sale that quantity on-hand is below the reorder point. However, since the on-order field contains a nonzero value the "AND" condition in the pseudo code above is not met, no additional purchase requisitions are created. In Chapter 5 we see that when the inventory is received from the supplier and the inventory record is updated, the on-order flag is reset to zero.

Without this flag control, or a variation of it, a purchase requisition will be created every time the low-stock condition is detected. This could result in significant financial losses for the organization as it unintentionally orders large quantities of unneeded and unwanted inventory.

Risk of Inaccurately Recording Transactions in Journals and Accounts

Inaccurate record keeping can take many forms.The following outlines some common revenue cycle errors but is not intended to be an exhaustive list:

- Sales to customers are incorrectly calculated.
- Sales are recorded in the wrong period.
- Customers are billed for items they did not receive (back ordered).
- Customer cash receipts are inaccurately posted to accounts or are posted to the wrong customer accounts.
- Summaries of sales, accounts receivable, cash receipts, and inventory levels are incorrectly posted to their respective general ledger accounts.

Physical Controls

TRANSACTION AUTHORIZATION. The remittance list or cash prelist provides a means for verifying that customer checks and remittance advices match in amount and represent valid transactions. Discrepancies between the check and remittance advice should be noted when the documents are logged in the remittance list.

ACCOUNTING RECORDS. Chapter 2 described how a firm's source documents, journals, and ledgers form an audit trail that allows independent auditors to trace transactions through various stages of processing. This control is also an important operational feature of well-designed accounting systems. Sometimes transactions get lost in the system. By following the audit trail, management can discover where an error occurred. Several specific control techniques contribute to the audit trail.

PRENUMBERED DOCUMENTS. **Prenumbered documents** (sales orders, shipping notices, remittance advices, and so on) are sequentially numbered by the printer and allow every transaction to be identified uniquely. This permits the isolation and tracking of a single event (among many thousands) through the accounting system. Without a unique tag, one transaction looks very much like another. Verifying financial data and tracing transactions would be difficult or even impossible without prenumbered source documents.

SPECIAL JOURNALS. By grouping similar transactions together into special journals, the system provides a concise record of an entire class of events. For this purpose, revenue cycle systems use the sales journal and the cash receipts journal.

SUBSIDIARY LEDGERS. Two subsidiary ledgers are used for capturing transaction event details in the revenue cycle: the inventory and AR subsidiary ledgers. The sale of products reduces quantities on hand in the inventory subsidiary records and increases the customers' balances in the AR subsidiary records. The receipt of cash reduces customers' balances in the AR subsidiary records. These subsidiary records provide links back to journal entries and to the source documents that captured the events.

GENERAL LEDGERS. The general ledger control accounts are the basis for financial statement preparation. Revenue cycle transactions affect the following general ledger accounts: sales, inventory, cost of goods sold, AR, and cash. Journal vouchers that summarize activity captured in journals and subsidiary ledgers flow into the general ledger to update these accounts. Thus we have a complete audit trail from the financial statements to the source documents via the general ledger, subsidiary ledgers, and special journals.

FILES. The revenue cycle employs several temporary and permanent files that contribute to the audit trail. The following are typical examples:

- Customer order file shows the status of customer orders.
- Shipping log specifies orders shipped during the period.
- Customer records file provides customer credit data.
- Back-order file contains customer orders for out-of-stock items.
- Journal voucher file is a compilation of all journal vouchers posted to the general ledger.

INDEPENDENT VERIFICATION. The objective of independent verification is to verify the accuracy and completeness of tasks performed by other functions in the process. To be effective, independent verifications must occur at key points in the process where errors can be detected quickly and corrected. Independent verification controls in the revenue cycle exist at the following points:

1. The shipping department reconciles the goods being shipped against the packing slip to ensure that the customer is receiving the correct items and quantities.
2. The billing function reconciles the original sales order with the shipping notice to ensure that customers are billed for only the quantities shipped and that sales are recorded in the sales journal only after the goods have been shipped and in the correct period.
3. Prior to posting to control accounts, the general ledger function reconciles journal vouchers and summary reports prepared independently in different functional areas. The billing function summarizes the sales journal, inventory control summarizes changes in the inventory subsidiary ledger, the cash receipts function summarizes the cash receipts journal, and accounts receivable summarizes the AR subsidiary ledger.

Discrepancies between the numbers supplied by these various sources will signal errors that need to be resolved before posting to the general ledger can take place. For example, the general ledger function would detect a sales transaction that had been entered in the sales journal but not posted to the customer's account in the AR subsidiary ledger. The journal voucher from billing, summarizing total credit sales, would not equal the total increases posted to the AR subsidiary ledger. The specific customer account causing the out-of-balance condition would not be determinable at this point, but the error would be noted. Finding it would involve tracing transactions described previously.

IT Controls

DATA INPUT EDITS. A basic assumption in transaction processing system design is that master files, such as inventory, accounts receivable, and the general ledger are "clean" and error free. Transaction data, in contrast, are assumed to be "dirty" and contain various errors such as transposed digits in account numbers, invalid part numbers of items sold, and clerical errors. If not detected before being processed, these errors will corrupt the master files of the system. The following input controls, or edits, are programed into the system to minimize the risk from data input errors:

1. Checks for missing data, numeric-alphabetic data, and valid data values, would reduce the risk of undetected data entry errors by clerks in the accounts receivable, inventory control, billing, and cash receipts departments.
2. Check digit edits provide control over accessing the wrong accounts when posting customer sales and cash receipts transactions. Long customer account numbers are susceptible to transcription and transposition errors during data entry. Check digit controls reduce the risk of such errors in both basic and advanced technology systems.

AUTOMATED POSTING TO SUBSIDIARY AND GL ACCOUNTS. The record keeping functions, which in the basic technology system were performed manually by accounting clerks, are automated in the advanced technology system. In a manual environment, segregation of duties between accounts receivable, billing, and the general ledger functions are important physical controls designed to prevent or detect human errors and fraud. In the advanced technology system, a computer application, which is not influenced by the situational pressures, opportunities, and ethical shortcomings discussed in Chapter 3, determines which accounts to update and by how much. By eliminating the human element from such accounting activities, the potential for errors and opportunity for fraud are significantly reduced. Also, since these are labor-intensive activities, automating them greatly improves efficiency of operations.

FILE BACKUP. The physical loss, destruction, or corruption of digital accounting records are serious concerns. To reduce the risk of data loss, backup procedures need to be in place. These techniques (discussed in Chapter 3) are behind-the-scenes activities that may not appear on the system flowchart. The accountant should verify that such procedures are, in fact, performed for all subsidiary and general ledger files.

Risk of Misappropriation of Cash Receipts and Inventory

Cash and inventory are the physical assets at risk in the revenue cycle. In the absence of proper controls, cash from customer payments is at risk of being "skimmed" before it is recorded or "embezzled" after it has been received and recorded. Inventory in the warehouse can be stolen and sold for cash.

Physical Controls

TRANSACTION AUTHORIZATION. The remittance list provides a control against the loss or theft of checksand remittance advices as they flow through the system. The presence of an extra remittance advice in the AR department or the absence of a customer's check in the cash receipts department would be detected when the batch is reconciled with the prelist.

SUPERVISION. The mail room is a point of risk in most cash receipts systems. The individual who opens the mail has access both to cash (the asset) and to the remittance advice (the record of the transaction). A dishonest employee could use this opportunity to steal the check, cash it, and destroy the remittance advice, thus leaving no evidence of the transaction. Ultimately, this sort of fraud will come to light when the customer complains after being billed again and produces the canceled check to prove that payment was made. By the time the firm gets to the bottom of this problem, however, the perpetrator may have committed the crime many times and left the organization. Detecting crimes after the fact accomplishes little; prevention is the best solution. The deterrent effect of supervision can provide an effective preventive control.

Also, some firms have too few employees to achieve an adequate separation of functions. These firms must rely on supervision as a form of compensating control. By closely supervising employees who perform potentially incompatible functions such as cash receipts and AR updating a firm can compensate for this control weakness.

ACCESS CONTROLS. The following physical access controls should be in place to help prevent and detect unauthorized access to the firm's assets:

- Warehouse security, such as fences, alarms, and guards.
- Depositing cash daily in the bank.
- Using a safe or night deposit box for cash.
- Locking cash drawers and safes in the cash receipts department.

SEGREGATION OF DUTIES. Segregating duties ensures that no single individual or department processes a transaction in its entirety. Recall from Chapter 3 that one objective behind segregating duties is to separate those with asset custody from the task of record keeping. Consistent with this objective the following segregations of duties should exist:

1. The cash receipts function, which has custody of the cash asset, should be separated from the accounts receivable function that records the payment in the customer records. An individual with responsibility for both tasks could perpetrate a lapping fraud or possibly steal the customer's check and write off the AR as a bad debt.
2. The individual performing the cash receipts function should not have access to the general ledger cash account. He or she could remove cash from the firm and adjust the cash account to cover the act.
3. Inventory warehouse personnel who have physical custody of inventory assets, should not also be responsible for the accounting task of updating the inventory records. To combine these tasks would open the door to fraud and material errors. A person with combined responsibility could steal or lose inventory and adjust the inventory records to conceal the event.

IT Controls

MULTILEVEL SECURITY. In a basic technology environment, segregation of duties is accomplished by physically separating individuals and the data over which they have custody. In an integrated data processing environment, however, computer processes and data are highly concentrated and accessible through a common central application. In this environment, the segregations of duties described above are accomplished through multilevel security procedures that limit an individual's access to authorized processes and data. This technique is discussed in more detail in the next section.

Risk of Unauthorized Access to Accounting Records and Reports

Accounting information is at risk to unauthorized access from outsiders as well employees of the organization. The motives for accessing accounting information include:

- Attempts to perpetrate a fraud such as creating a false sales order or wiping out an account receivable balance.
- Theft of data such as stealing a customer list for a competitor, or downloading customer credit card numbers and PINs to be sold over the Internet.
- Malicious acts such as corrupting or deleting financial data.

Physical Controls

ACCESS CONTROLS. Source documents and accounting records need to be physically protected. Hard copy accounting records and department PCs that contain accounting information on hard drives should be kept in secure areas and access to them should be restricted on a need-to-know basis.

SEGREGATION OF DUTIES. An objective of segregation of duties provided in chapter three states that:

> *The organization should be so structured that the perpetration of a fraud requires collusion between two or more individuals.*

Compliance with this objective requires that certain record-keeping tasks be separated. Specifically, the subsidiary ledgers (AR and inventory), the journals (sales and cash receipts), and the general ledger should be separately maintained. An individual with total record-keeping responsibility, in collusion with someone with asset custody, is in a position to perpetrate a fraud. By separating these tasks the risk of collusion is not eliminated, but it is reduced because the collusion will require the involvement of more people. More the number of people involved, the greater the risk of detection. This will have a deterrent effect on those contemplating fraud.

IT Controls

PASSWORDS. Digital accounting records are vulnerable to unauthorized and undetected access. This may take the form of an attempt at fraud, a destructive act by a disgruntled employee, or an honest mistake. Also at risk are the computer programs that make programmed decisions, manipulate accounting records, and permit access to assets.

To mitigate these risks, organization management should implement a robust password control policy to prevent unauthorized access to computer files and programs that reside in each of the departments. The application logic should require, and prompt, users to change passwords periodically and not allow simple and easy-to-guess passwords. One way of strengthening password control is to require that passwords be sufficiently long (six or eight characters) and consist of both alphabetic and numeric characters. A detailed discussion of password control issues is provided in Chapter 16 when we deal with the broader issue of system security.

MULTILEVEL SECURITY. Multilevel security employs programmed techniques that permit simultaneous access to a central system by many users with different access privileges, but prevents them from obtaining information for which they lack authorization. Two common methods for achieving multilevel security are the **access control list (ACL)** and **role-based access control (RBAC)**. The ACL method assigns privileges, such as the right to perform computer program procedures and access data files, directly to the individual. In large organizations with thousands of employees, this can become a considerable administrative burden as access needs constantly change with changes in job responsibilities. RBAC involves creating standard tasks (e.g., cash receipts processing) called roles. Each **role** is assigned access privileges to specific data and procedures, such as the right to add a record to the cash receipts journal. Once a role is created, individuals are assigned to it. Using this technique, individuals may be easily added or deleted from roles as their job responsibilities change. Individuals assigned to a particular role

TABLE 4-1 SUMMARY OF REVENUE CYCLE RISKS AND CONTROLS

Risk	Physical Control	IT Control
Sales to un-creditworthy customers	Transaction Authorization – credit check Segregation of duties – separate credit and sales functions	Automated credit check
Shipping wrong items/quantities	Independent verification – Shipping Department reconciles shipment with order	Scanner technology Automated inventory ordering
Inaccurate record keeping	Transaction authorization – remittance list Accounting records – audit trail documents, journals, accounts, and files Independent verification – shipping, billing, and GL	Input data edits Automated posting to accounts File backup
Misappropriation of assets	Transaction authorization -- remittance list Supervision – mail room Access control – warehouse security, daily deposits of cash, night deposit box, locked safes Segregation of duties – cash receipts, general ledger, AR function, warehouse, inventory records	Multilevel security to achieve segregation of duties
Unauthorized access to data	Access control – source documents, journals, ledgers Segregation of duties – sub legers, GL, asset custody	Password control Multilevel security to prevent unauthorized access to data

may not access program procedures and data that are not specified by that role. ACL and RBAC are discussed in greater detail in later chapters.

POINT-OF-SALE (POS) SYSTEMS

The revenue cycle systems that we have examined so far are used by organizations that extend credit to their customers. Obviously, this assumption is not valid for all types of business enterprises. For example, grocery stores do not usually function in this way. Such businesses exchange goods directly for cash in a transaction that is consummated at the point of sale.

POS systems, like the one shown in Figure 4-17, are used extensively in grocery stores, department stores, and other types of retail organizations. In this example, the organization maintains no customer accounts receivable; all transactions are for cash, checks, or bank credit/debit cards. Also, inventory is kept on the store's shelves, not in a separate warehouse. Customers personally pick the items they wish to buy and carry them to the checkout location where the transaction begins.

FIGURE 4-17 POINT OF SALE SYSTEM

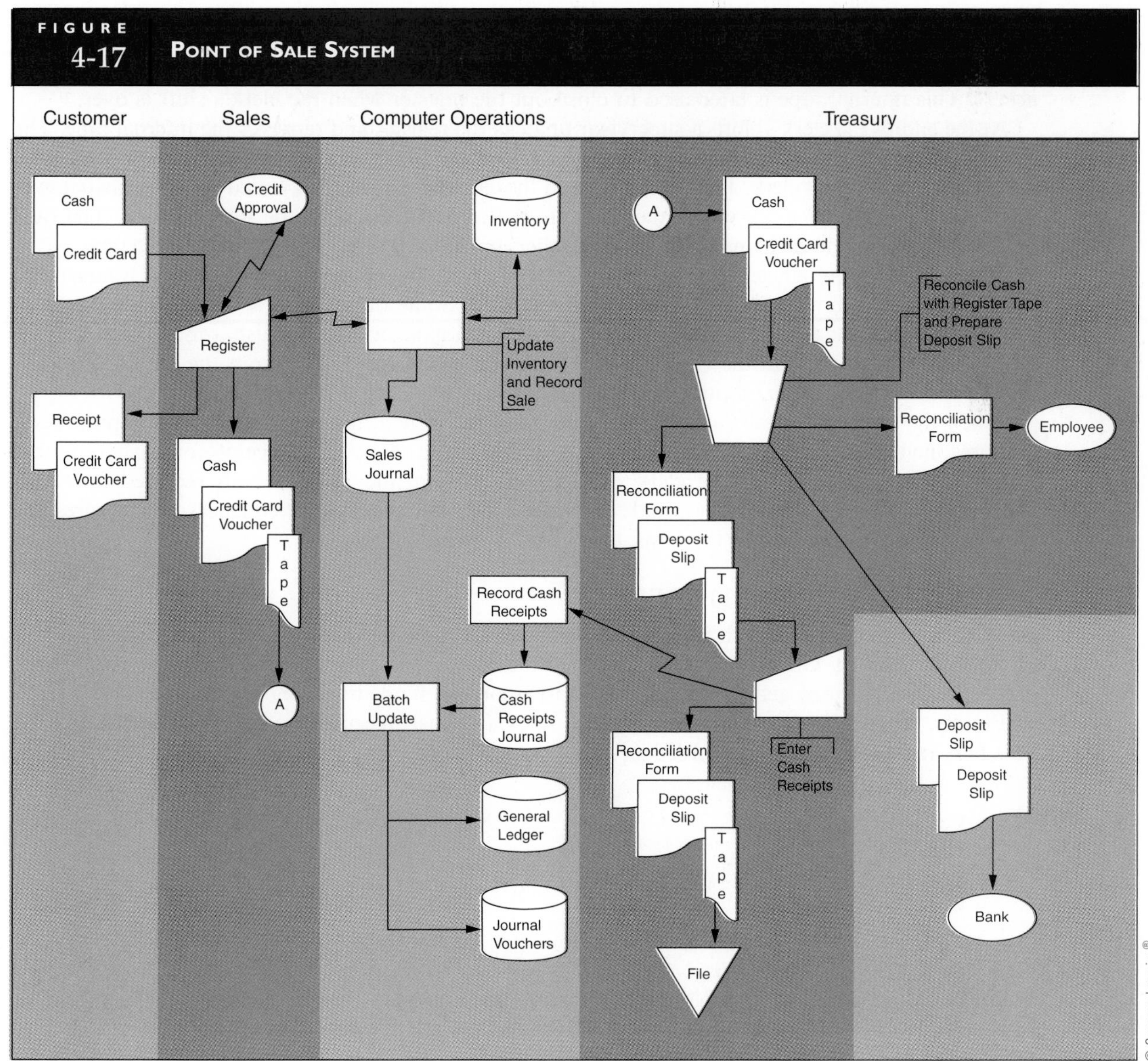

DAILY PROCEDURES

First, the checkout clerk scans the **Universal Product Code (UPC)** label on the items being purchased with a laser light scanner. The scanner, which is the primary input device in the POS system, may be handheld or mounted on the checkout counter. The POS system is connected online to the inventory file from which it retrieves product price data, and it displays the data on the clerk's terminal. The inventory quantity on hand is reduced in real-time to reflect the items sold. As items fall to minimum levels, they are automatically reordered.

When all the UPCs are scanned, the system automatically calculates taxes, discounts, and the total for the transaction. In the case of credit card transactions, the sales clerk obtains transaction approval from the credit card issuer via an online connection. When the approval is returned, the clerk prepares a credit card voucher for the amount of the sale, which the customer signs. The clerk gives the customer one copy of the voucher and secures a second copy in the cash drawer of the register. For cash sales, the customer renders cash for the full amount of the sale, which the clerk secures in the cash drawer.

The clerk enters the transaction into the POS system via the register's keypad, and a record of the sale is added to the sales journal in real time. The record contains the following key data: date, time, terminal number, total amount of sale, cash or credit card sale, cost of items sold, sales tax, and discounts taken. The sale is also recorded on a two-part paper tape. One copy is given to the customer as a receipt; the other is secured internally within the register, which the clerk cannot access. This internal tape is later used to close out the register when the clerk's shift is over.

At the end of the clerk's shift, a supervisor unlocks the register and retrieves the internal tape. The cash drawer is removed and replaced with a new cash drawer containing a known amount of start-up cash (float) for the next clerk. The supervisor and the clerk whose shift has ended take the cash drawer to the cash room (treasury), where the contents are reconciled against the internal tape. The cash drawer should contain cash and credit card vouchers equal to the amount recorded on the tape.

Often, small discrepancies exist because of errors in making change for customers. Organization policy will specify how cash discrepancies are handled. Some organizations require sales clerks to cover all cash shortages via payroll deductions. Other organizations establish a materiality threshold. Cash shortages within the threshold are recorded but not deducted from the employee's pay. Excess shortages, however, should be reviewed for possible disciplinary action.

When the contents of the cash drawer have been reconciled, the cash receipts clerk prepares a cash reconciliation form and gives one copy to the sales clerk as a receipt for cash remitted. From a computer terminal, the clerk accesses the system and records cash received and cash short/over in the cash receipts journal. The clerk files the credit card vouchers and secures the cash in the safe for deposit in the bank at the end of the day.

END-OF-DAY PROCEDURES

At the end of the day, the cash receipts clerk prepares a three-part deposit slip for the total amount of the cash received. One copy is filed and the other two accompany the cash to the bank. Because cash is involved, armed guards are often used to escort the funds to the bank repository.

Finally, a batch program summarizes the sales and cash receipts journals, prepares a journal voucher, and posts to the general ledger accounts as follows:

	DR	**CR**
Cash	XXXX.XX	
Cash Over/Short	XX.XX	
Accounts Receivable (credit card company)	XXX.XX	
Cost of Goods Sold	XXX.XX	
Sales		XXXX.XX
Inventory		XXX.XX

The accounting entry in the table may vary among businesses. Some companies will treat credit card sales as cash. Others will maintain an AR until the credit card issuer transfers the funds into their account.

POINT-OF-SALE CONTROL ISSUES

The IT control issues previously discussed apply also to POS transaction processing systems and are not revisited here. The POS environment, however, is associated with unique risks that give rise to the need for additional physical controls, which are discussed next.

Authorization

In POS systems, the authorization process involves validating credit card charges and establishing that the customer is the valid user of the card. After receiving online approval from the credit card company, the clerk should match the customer's signature on the sales voucher with the one on the credit card.

Supervision

The POS environment places both inventory and cash at risk. Customers have direct access to inventory, and the crime of shoplifting is of great concern to management. Similarly, cash can be removed from the cash drawer by a dishonest employee. Supervision using surveillance cameras and shop floor security personnel can reduce these risks.

Access Control

Because POS systems involve cash transactions, the organization must restrict access to cash assets. One method is to assign each sales clerk to a separate cash register for an entire shift. When the clerk leaves the register to take a break, the cash drawer should be locked to prevent unauthorized access. This can be accomplished with a physical lock and key or by password control. At the end of the clerk's shift, he or she should remove the cash drawer and immediately deposit the funds in the cash room. When clerks need to share registers, responsibility for asset custody is split among them and accountability is reduced.

Inventory in the POS system must also be protected from unauthorized access and theft. Both physical restraints and electronic devices are used to achieve this. For example, steel cables are often used in clothing stores to secure expensive leather coats to the clothing rack. Locked showcases are used to display jewelry and costly electronic equipment. Magnetic tags are attached to merchandise, which will sound an alarm when removed from the store.

Accounting Records

In addition to the usual revenue cycle records, the internal cash register's tape is an important accounting document. The tape is a record of all sales transactions processed at the register. Only the clerk's supervisor should have access to the tape, which is used at the end of the shift to balance the cash drawer.

Independent Verification

When the clerk whose shift has ended takes the cash drawer to the cash room, its contents are reconciled against the internal register tape. The cash drawer should contain cash and credit card vouchers equal to the amount recorded on the tape.

REENGINEERING USING EDI

Doing Business via EDI

Many organizations have reengineered their sales order process through **electronic data interchange (EDI)**. EDI technology was devised to expedite routine transactions between manufacturers and wholesalers, and between wholesalers and retailers. The customer's computer is connected to the seller's computer via a private network or the Internet. When the customer's computer system detects the need to order inventory, it automatically transmits a purchase order (customer order) to the seller. The seller's system receives the customer order and processes it automatically. This system employs little or no human involvement.

EDI is more than just a technology. It represents a strategic business arrangement between buyer and seller in which they agree, in advance, to the terms of their relationship. For example, they agree to the selling price, the quantities to be sold, guaranteed delivery times, payment terms, and methods of handling disputes. These terms are specified in a **trading partner agreement** and are legally binding. Once the agreement is in place, no individual in either the buying or the selling company actually authorizes or approves a particular EDI transaction. In its purest form, the exchange is completely automated.

EDI poses unique control problems for organizations. One problem is ensuring that, in the absence of explicit authorization, only valid transactions are processed. Another risk is that a trading partner, or someone masquerading as a trading partner, will access the firm's accounting records in a way that is unauthorized by the trading partner agreement. Chapter 12 presents the key features of EDI and its implications for business. EDI control issues are discussed in Chapter 16.

REENGINEERING USING THE INTERNET

Doing Business on the Internet

Thousands of organizations worldwide have home pages on the Internet to promote their products and solicit sales. By visiting the seller's home page, a potential customer can access the seller's product list, scan the product line, and place an order. Typically, Internet sales are credit card transactions that are sent to the seller's e-mail file.

At the seller's end, an employee reviews the order, verifies credit, and enters the transaction into the seller's system for processing in the normal way. Because of the need to review the e-mail file before processing, the turnaround time for processing Internet sales is sometimes longer than for telephone orders. To expedite processing, some organizations employ intelligent agents (software programs) that review and validate Internet orders automatically as they are received.

Unlike EDI, which is exclusively a business-to-business (B2B) arrangement between trading partners, Internet sales are both B2B and business-to-consumer (B2C) transactions. The Internet opens an organization's doors to thousands of potential business partners with whom it has no formal agreement. In addition to unprecedented business opportunities, risks for both the seller and the buyer accompany this technology. Connecting to the Internet exposes the organization to threats from computer hackers, viruses, and transaction fraud. Most organizations take these threats seriously and implement controls, including password techniques, message encryption, and firewalls, to minimize their risk. Internet technology and Internet commerce are topics of Chapter 12. In Chapter 16, we examine techniques for controlling the risks associated with these technologies and business models.

Summary

This chapter is organized into two primary sections. The first examined conceptually the revenue cycle of a typical merchandising firm and focused on: (1) the functional areas and the flow of transaction information that triggers key tasks; and (2) the documents, journals, and accounts that support audit trails, decision making, and financial reporting.

The second section examined physical revenue cycle systems that lie at different points on the technology/human continuum. The objectives of this section were to: (1) illustrate the system functionality, efficiency issues, and workflow characteristics of different technologies; and (2) demonstrate how internal control issues differ between systems at various points on the technology/human continuum. This section reviewed physical controls and computer controls associated with several system configurations, including basic technology systems, advanced integrated systems, and point-of-sale (POS) systems. The chapter concluded by outlining the key features and risks associated with electronic data interchange (EDI) and Internet sales systems. EDI and Internet systems are discussed in detail in later chapters.

Appendix

Sales Return System

Most organizations have specific rules for granting cash refunds and credits to customers based on the materiality of the transaction and the circumstances of the return. Depending on these factors, the return authorization may involve the credit department or management. The concepts of specific and general authority discussed in Chapter 3 influence this activity. Figure 4-18 illustrates the procedures and documents used for processing sales returns.

Receiving Department

The sales return process begins in the receiving department, where personnel receive, count, inspect for damage, and send returned products to the warehouse. The receiving clerk manually prepares a return slip, which is forwarded to the sales department for processing.

Sales Department

Upon receipt of the return slip, the clerk manually prepares a credit memo. Depending on the materiality and circumstance of the return, company policy will dictate whether credit department approval (not shown) is required.

Processing the Credit Memo

The objective of the sales return system is to reverse the effects of the original sales transaction. The billing department records an entry into the sales return and allowances journal (alternatively, a contra entry into the sales journal), and inventory control debits the inventory records to reflect the return of goods. The AR clerk credits the customer account in the AR subsidiary ledger. All departments periodically prepare hard-copy journal vouchers and account summaries, which they send to the general ledger department for reconciliation and posting to the GL accounts.

Legacy Systems

Legacy accounting systems often employ batch processing. This appendix examines two batch techniques: (1) batch with sequential files, and (2) batch with direct access files.

Batch Processing Using Sequential Files

Figure 4-19 illustrates a legacy sales order system that uses batch computer processing with sequential files. The system employs manual procedures in the sales, credit, warehouse, and shipping departments. The computer portion of the system is executed depending on transaction volume and the

FIGURE 4-18 BASIC TECHNOLOGY SALES RETURNS SYSTEM

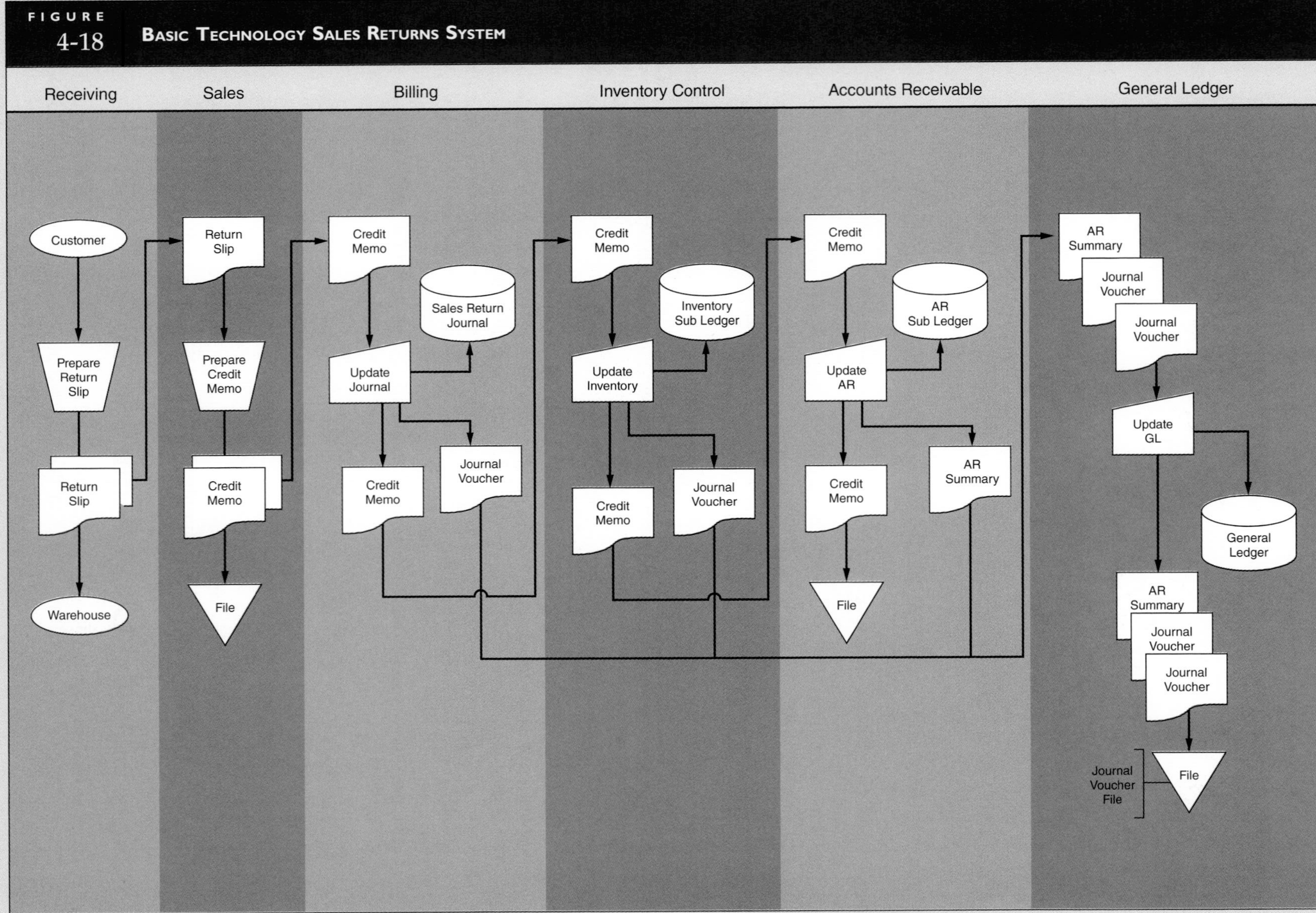

FIGURE 4-19 BATCH PROCESSING WITH SEQUENTIAL FILES

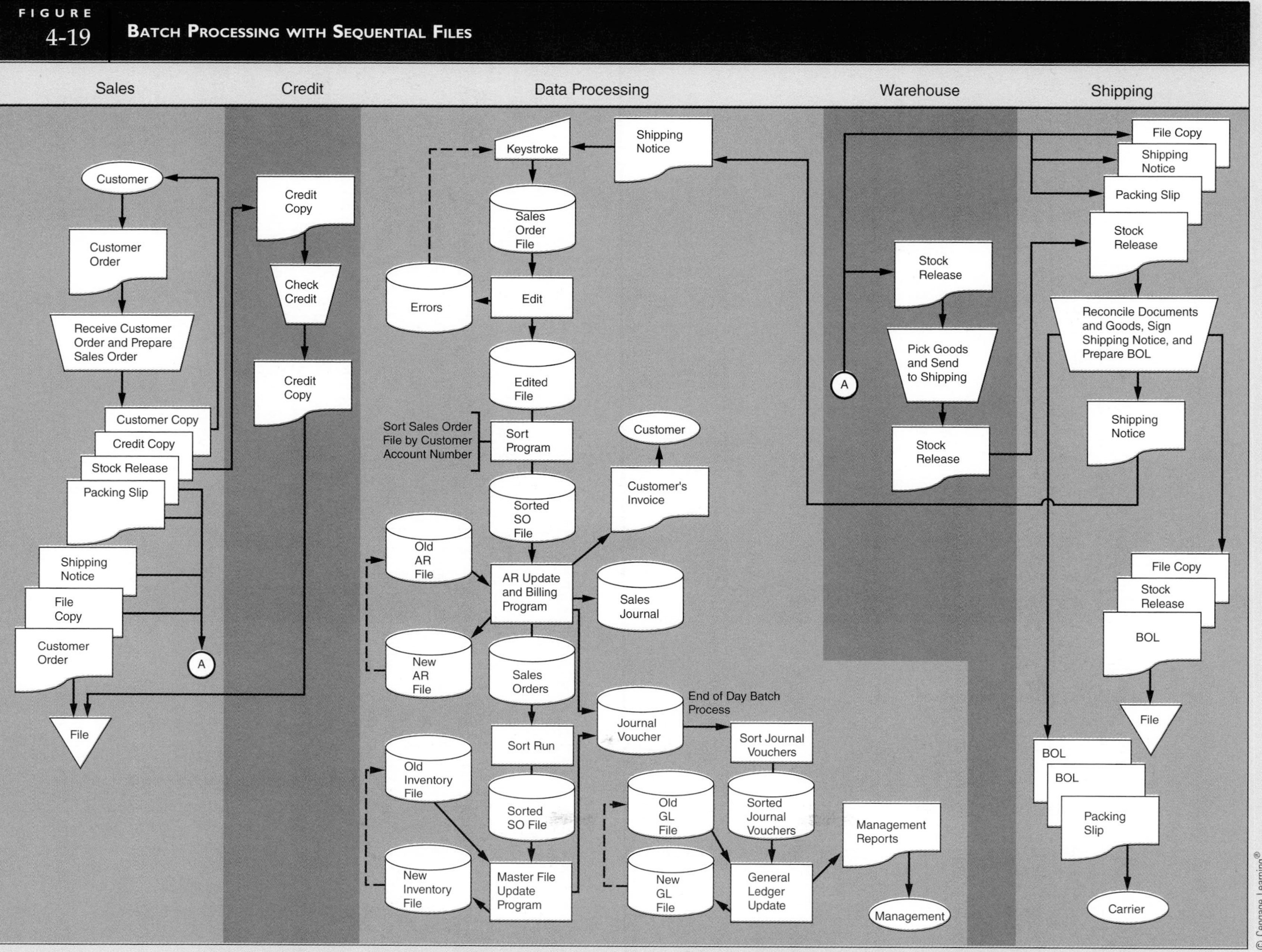

need for current information. This could be a single end-of-day task or performed several times per day. The main elements of the computer operations are reviewed in the following paragraphs.

DATA ENTRY

The process begins with the arrival of shipping notices from the shipping department. These documents are copies of the sales orders that contain accurate information about the number of units shipped and information about the carrier. The shipping notices are arranged in batches that the data entry clerk converts to digital media to produce a transaction file of sales orders. This transaction file will actually contain many separate batches of sales orders. Batch control totals are calculated for each batch on the file.[1]

EDIT RUN

A batch system is composed of a series of program runs. In this example, the edit program is the first run, which validates transactions by testing each record for the existence of clerical or logical errors. Typical tests include field checks, limit tests, range tests, and price-times-quantity extensions.[2] Any detected errors are removed from the batch and copied to a separate error file. Later, these are corrected by an authorized person and resubmitted for processing with the next day's business. The edit program recalculates the batch control totals to reflect changes due to the removal of error records. The edited transaction file is then passed to the next run in the process.

SORT RUN

At this point, the sales order transaction file is in no useful sequence. Recall from the Chapter 2 Appendix that a transaction file must be sorted in the same sequence as the master file it is updating. In this example the first master file to be updated is the accounts receivable file, whose primary key is ACCOUNT NUMBER. The first sort run in this system therefore rearranges the sales order file in order of customer ACCOUNT NUMBER, which is a secondary key in the transaction file.

AR UPDATE AND BILLING RUN

Now that the transaction file is sorted in the correct sequence, the AR master file can be updated. Figure 4-20 illustrates this process with some sample records. The AR update program sequentially matches the ACCOUNT NUMBER key in the first sales order transaction record with the corresponding record in the AR subsidiary master file. The program then recalculates the AR CURRENT BALANCE stored in the master file record by adding to it the INVOICE AMOUNT in the transaction record. This recalculated value, along with the other data fields in the master record, are written to a new master file. This process is repeated for the next sales order record and continues until all the transaction records are processed. Any master file records for which there is no corresponding sales order record is copied from the original file to the new master file. Thus, the update procedure actually creates a new AR subsidiary master file that incorporates all the changes to customer accounts affected by the transaction records as well as those records that were unaffected by transactions. Also, the process leaves the original AR subsidiary master file complete and unchanged. This automatic backup feature is an advantage of sequential file processing.

As part of the update process, each successfully processed (no errors) sales transaction is added to the sales journal file. At the end of the run, all the transactions are summarized, and an entry is made to the journal voucher file to reflect total sales and total increases to AR. Finally, the run prepares customer invoices, which are mailed to the customers.

---

1 Batch controls are designed to manage the flow of large numbers of records through the system. They consist of summary figures pertaining to the number of records in the batch, total dollar amount of the batch, and a hash total of a nonfinancial field. See Chapter 3 for a detailed discussion.

2 Chapter 3 provides a complete discussion of computer application controls.

FIGURE 4-20 UPDATE OF ACCOUNTS RECEIVABLE FROM SALES ORDERS

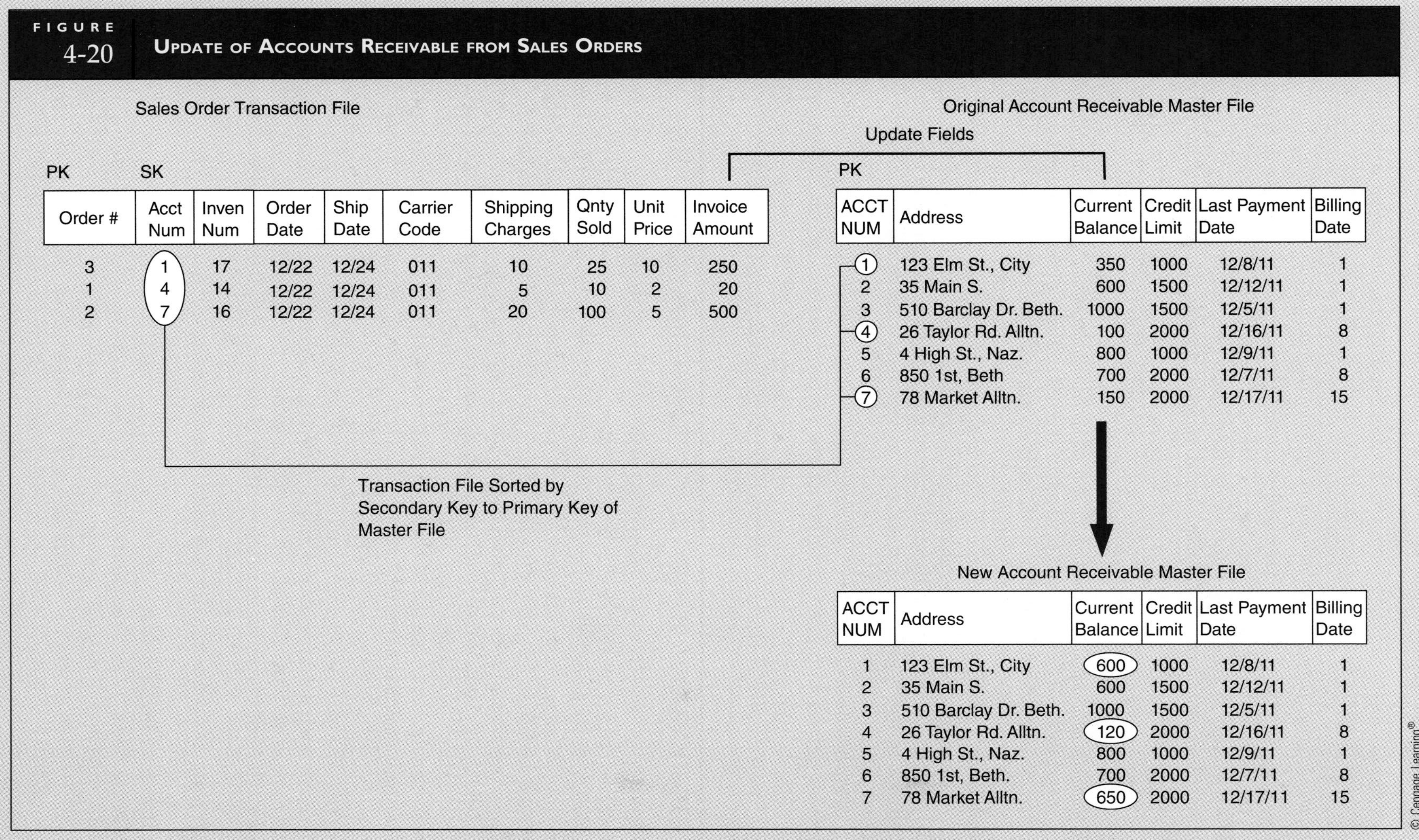

SORT AND INVENTORY UPDATE RUNS

The procedures for the second sort and inventory update runs are similar to those previously described. The sort program sorts the sales order transaction file on the secondary key—INVENTORY NUMBER. The inventory update program reduces the QUANTITY ON HAND field in the affected inventory records by the QUANTITY SOLD field in each sales order record. A new inventory master file is also created in the process. Figure 4-21 illustrates the process with some sample data.

In addition, the program compares values of the QUANTITY ON HAND and the REORDER POINT fields to identify inventory items that need to be replenished. This information is sent to the purchasing department. Finally, a journal voucher is prepared to reflect cost of goods sold and the reduction in inventory.

GENERAL LEDGER UPDATE RUN

Under the sequential file approach, the general ledger master file is not updated after each batch of transactions. To do so would result in the re-creation of the entire general ledger every time a batch of transactions (such as sales orders, cash receipts, purchases, cash disbursements, and so on) is processed. Firms using sequential files typically employ separate end-of-day procedures to update the general ledger accounts. This technique is depicted in Figure 4-19.

At the end of the day, the general ledger run accesses the journal voucher file. This file contains journal vouchers reflecting all of the transactions processed by the organization that day. The journal vouchers are sorted by general ledger account number and posted to the general ledger in a single run, and a new general ledger is created.

The end-of-day procedures will also generate a number of management reports. These may include sales summaries, inventory status reports, general ledger change reports, transaction listings, journal voucher listings, and budget and performance reports. Quality management reports play a key role in helping management monitor operations to ensure that controls are in place and functioning properly.

Batch Processing Using Direct Access Files

Figure 4-22 illustrates a batch sales order system that employs direct access files. As with the previous example, the system employs manual procedures in the sales, credit, warehouse, and shipping departments. The main elements of its computers operations are reviewed in the following paragraphs.

KEYSTROKE

The process begins with the arrival of batches of shipping notices from the shipping department. The data entry clerk converts the hard-copy shipping notices to digital form to produce a transaction file of sales orders. This process takes place several times throughout the day, resulting in a transaction file that contains many separate batches of records. For each batch stored on the file, the system automatically calculates batch control totals.

EDIT RUN

The edit program first validates all transaction records in the batch by performing clerical and logical tests on the data. Detected errors are removed from the batch and copied to a separate error file (not shown in Figure 4-22), which are later corrected and resubmitted for processing with the next day's business. The edit program recalculates the batch control totals to reflect any changes due to the removal of error records. The edited sales order file is then passed to the file update run.

FILE UPDATE RUN

Because direct access files are used in this system, the transaction file does not need to be sorted before the update process. Also, note that the update process does not recreate new master files. Figure 4-23 illustrates the direct access update process using sample data. Starting at the beginning of the edited sales order file, the update program posts the first transaction to the corresponding inventory and AR subsidiary records using the secondary keys (INVENTORY NUMBER and

FIGURE 4-21 **UPDATE OF INVENTORY FROM SALES ORDER**

Sales Order Transaction File

PK: Order #; SK: Inven Num

Order #	Acct Num	Inven Num	Order Date	Ship Date	Carrier Code	Shipping Charges	Qnty Sold	Unit Price	Invoice Amount
1	4	14	12/22	12/24	011	5	10	2	20
2	7	16	12/22	12/24	011	20	100	5	500
3	1	17	12/22	12/24	011	10	25	10	250

Update Fields

Transaction File Sorted by Secondary Key to Primary Key of Master File

Original Inventory Master File

PK: Inven Num

Inven Num	Description	Qnty on Hand	Reorder Point	Qnty on Order	EOQ	Vendor Number	Standard Cost	Total Inven Cost
11		300	100	0	500	25	1	300
12		100	20	0	200	25	2	200
13		200	150	0	500	18	3	600
14		800	100	0	1000	25	2	1600
15		250	300	800	800	18	3	750
16		700	60	0	500	18	4	2800
17		850	200	0	1000	25	1	850

New Inventory Master File

PK: Inven Num

Inven Num	Description	Qnty on Hand	Reorder Point	Qnty on Order	EOQ	Vendor Number	Standard Cost	Total Inven Cost
11		300	100	0	500	25	1	300
12		100	20	0	200	25	2	200
13		200	150	0	500	18	3	600
14		790	100	0	1000	25	2	1580
15		250	300	800	800	18	3	750
16		600	50	0	500	18	4	2400
17		825	200	0	1000	25	1	825

FIGURE 4-22 Batch Sales Order System

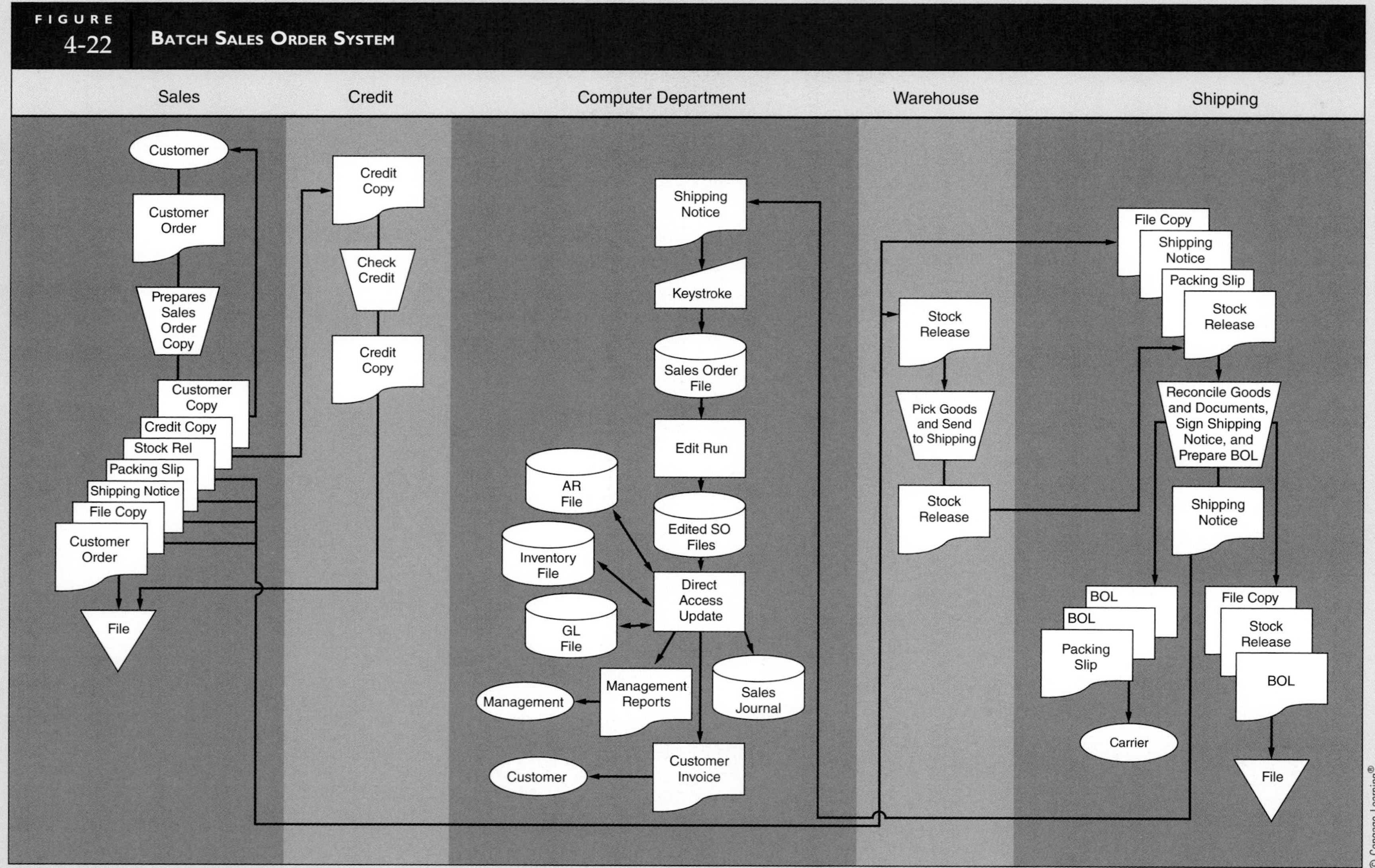

FIGURE 4-23 Direct Access Update of AR and Inventory Files Concurrently

Sales Order Transaction File

Order # (PK)	Acct Num (SK)	Inven Num (SK)	Qnty Sold	Unit Price	Invoice Amount
1	4	14	10	2	20
2	7	16	100	5	500
3	1	17	25	10	250

Inventory Master File

Inven Num (PK)	Units Received	Units Sold	Qnty on Hand	Reorder Point	Qnty on Order	EOQ	Vendor Number	Standard Cost	Total Inven Cost
11			300	100	0	500	25	1	300
12			100	20	0	200	25	2	400
13			200	150	0	500	18	3	600
14			790	100	0	1000	25	2	1590
15			250	300	800	800	18	3	750
16			600	60	0	500	18	4	2400
17			825	200	0	1000	25	1	825

Master file records are accessed directly and updated in place. This process does not create a new master file.

Accounts Receivable Master

Acct Num (PK)	Address	Current Balance	Credit Limit	Last Payment Date	Billing Date
1	123 Elm St., City	600	1000	12/8/11	1
2	35 Main S.	600	1500	12/12/11	1
3	510 Barclay Dr. Beth.	1000	1500	12/5/11	1
4	26 Taylo Rd. Alltn.	120	2000	12/16/11	8
5	4 High St., Naz.	800	1000	12/9/11	1
6	850 1st, Beth.	700	2000	12/7/11	8
7	78 Market Alltn.	650	2000	12/17/11	15

ACCOUNT NUMBER) to locate the records directly. The QUANTITY ON HAND and CURRENT BALANCE fields in the inventory and AR subsidiary records, respectively, are updated by the transaction record, and the transaction is recorded in the journal. The update program then moves to the next transaction record and repeats the process. This continues until all records in the transaction file have been posted. The general ledger accounts are typically updated after each batch. When the update program reaches the end of the transaction file, it terminates. Finally, the system generates a number of management reports, including sales summaries, inventory status reports, transaction listings, journal voucher listings, and budget and performance reports.

Key Terms

access control list (ACL) (176)
accounts receivable (AR) subsidiary ledger (153)
approved credit memo (156)
approved sales order (148)
back-order (150)
bill of lading (151)
cash receipts journal (160)
controller's (160)
credit memo (156)
customer order (148)
customer order file (148)
deposit slip (160)
electronic data interchange (EDI) (179)
inventory subsidiary ledger (153)
journal voucher (151)
journal voucher file (151)
ledger copy (153)
multilevel security (176)
packing slip (151)
point-of-sale (POS) systems (161)
prenumbered documents (172)
remittance advices (157)
remittance list (157)
return slip (156)
role (176)
role based access control (RBAC) (176)
sales invoice (151)
sales journal (151)
sales order (148)
sales order (credit copy) (148)
sales order (invoice copy) (151)
shipping log (151)
shipping notice (151)
S.O. pending file (151)
stock records (150)
stock release (150)
trading partner agreement (180)
Universal Product Code (UPC) (178)
verified stock release (150)

Review Questions

1. What document initiates the sales process?
2. Distinguish between a packing slip, a shipping notice, and a bill of lading.
3. What function does the receiving department serve in the revenue cycle?
4. The general ledger clerk receives summary data from which departments? What form of summary data?
5. What are the three authorization controls?
6. What are the three rules that ensure that no single employee or department processes a transaction in its entirety?
7. At which points in the revenue cycle are independent verification controls necessary?
8. What is the purpose of physical controls?
9. How can we prevent inventory from being reordered automatically each time the system detects a low inventory level?
10. Distinguish between an edit run, a sort run, and an update run.
11. What are the key features of a POS system?
12. How is a credit check in the advanced technology system fundamentally different from a credit check in the basic technology system?
13. What is multilevel security?
14. Why does billing receive a copy of the sales order when the order is approved but does not bill until the goods are shipped?
15. Why was EDI devised?
16. What assets are at greatest risk in a POS system?

17. In a manual system, after which event in the sales process should the customer be billed?
18. What is a bill of lading?
19. What document initiates the billing process?
20. Where in the cash receipts process does supervision play an important role?

Discussion Questions

1. Why do firms have separate departments for warehousing and shipping? What about warehousing and inventory control? Doesn't this just create more paperwork?
2. Distinguish between the sales order, billing, and AR departments. Why can't the sales order or AR departments prepare the bills?
3. Explain the purpose of having mail room procedures.
4. Explain how segregation of duties is accomplished in an integrated data processing environment.
5. How could an employee embezzle funds by issuing an unauthorized sales credit memo if the appropriate segregation of duties and authorization controls were not in place?
6. What task can the AR department engage in to verify that all customers' checks have been appropriately deposited and recorded?
7. Why is access control over revenue cycle documents just as important as the physical control devices over cash and inventory?
8. How can reengineering of the sales order processing subsystem be accomplished using the Internet?
9. What financial statement misrepresentations may result from an inconsistently applied credit policy? Be specific.
10. Give three examples of access control in a POS system.
11. Discuss the trade-off in choosing to update the general ledger accounts in real time versus batch.
12. If an automated credit checking function denies a customer credit, should the sales clerk ever be authorized to override the decision? If so when?
13. How can advanced technology transaction processing systems reduce fraud?
14. What makes POS systems different from revenue cycles of manufacturing firms?
15. Is a POS system that uses bar coding and a laser light scanner foolproof against inaccurate updates? Discuss.
16. How is EDI more than technology? What unique control problems may it pose?
17. Discuss the two common methods of achieving multilevel security in a system.

Multiple-Choice Questions

1. Which function or department records a sale in the sales journal?
   a. Warehouse
   b. Sales department
   c. Billing department
   d. Inventory control
2. Which functions should be segregated?
   a. Picking goods from the warehouse shelves and updating the inventory subsidiary ledger
   b. Authorizing credit and determining reorder quantities
   c. Billing customers and posting the bills to the sales journal
   d. Providing information on inventory levels and reconciling the bank statement
3. Which of the following are incompatible tasks?
   a. The AR clerk authorizes the write-off of bad debts.
   b. The record-keeping clerk maintains both AR and AP subsidiary ledgers.
   c. The inventory control clerk authorizes inventory purchases.
   d. The AR clerk prepares customer statements every month.
4. Which control helps to ensure that the inventory items shipped to the customer are the correct type and the correct amount?
   a. Reconciliation BOL and shipping notice
   b. Issuance of a blind copy of purchase order
   c. Reconcile stock release document and packing slip
   d. The way match

5. The bill of lading is prepared by the
   a. sales clerk
   b. shipping clerk
   c. warehouse clerk
   d. billing clerk
6. Which of the following is NOT an independent verification control?
   a. The shipping department verifies that the goods sent from the warehouse are correct in type and quantity.
   b. General ledger clerks reconcile journal vouchers that were independently prepared in various departments.
   c. The billing department reconciles the shipping notice with the sales invoice to ensure that customers are billed for only the quantities shipped.
   d. Cash receipts reconcile checks from customers and remittance advices to ensure that payments are correct in amount.
   e. All of the above are independent verification controls.
7. Which document defines terms for shipped goods ownership?
   a. Packing slip
   b. Shipping notice
   c. Bill of lading
   d. Customer invoice
8. Which of the following sets of tasks should not be separated?
   a. Processing customer sales orders and approving credit
   b. Receiving cash and updating the accounts receivable subsidiary ledger
   c. Storing inventory in the warehouse and updating the inventory subsidiary ledger
   d. Processing customer sales orders and posting to the sales journal
   e. All of the above tasks should be separated
9. Which of the following is often called a compensating control?
   a. Supervision
   b. Access control
   c. Segregation of duties
   d. Accounting records
10. Which document triggers the billing function?
   a. Bill of lading
   b. Customer order
   c. Sales order
   d. Shipping notice

Problems

1. SYSTEM DESCRIPTION AND INTERNAL CONTROLS

Customer checks and remittance advices are received in the mailroom each morning along with the general mail. Mail volume is typically high requiring a mailroom staff of 40 clerks and one supervisor. The clerks share equally in the task of sorting the mail and directing it to the appropriate recipient. In the case of cash receipts the clerks open the envelopes to verify that the checks are signed and are constant in amount with the remittance advice. The checks and remittance advices are collected into batches and sent to the Accounts receivable department where the AR clerk reviews them for correctness, posts to the AR-Sub ledger. The clerk then prepares two copies of a remittance list. One of these is filed in the department along with the remittance advice and the other is sent to the cash receipts department with the checks. Finally the clerk summarizes the batch of cash receipts transaction and post to the general ledger AR-Control account and the Cash account.

Upon receipt of the checks and remittance list, the Cash Receipts clerk reconciles the documents and post the checks to the Cash Receipts journal. At the end of the day the clerk prepares a deposit slip and sends it along with the checks to the bank.

Required

a. Prepare a flowchart of the cash receipts procedures described above
b. Describe the risks, if any, that are inherent in the current system configuration.
c. Describe the controls, if any, that are needed to reduce or eliminate the risks identified in (b) above.

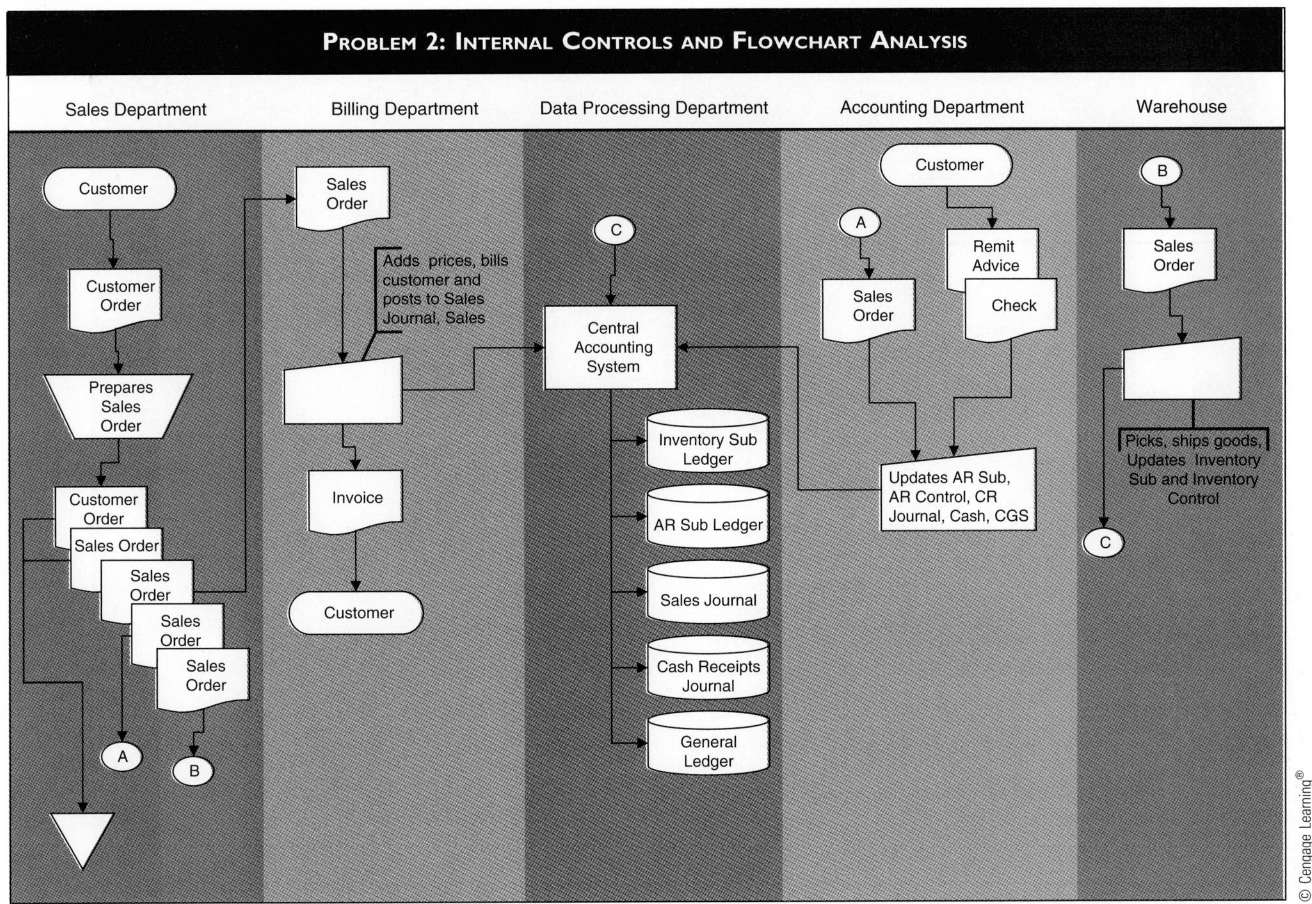

2. INTERNAL CONTROLS AND FLOWCHART ANALYSIS

a. Identify the physical control weaknesses depicted in the flowchart for Problem 2.
b. Describe the IT controls that should be in place in this system.

3. FLOWCHART ANALYSIS

Use the flowchart for Problem 3 to answer these questions:

a. What accounting document is represented by the symbol A?
b. What is an appropriate name for the department labeled B?
c. What would be an appropriate description for process C?
d. What is the location represented by the symbol D?
e. What accounting record is represented by the symbol E?
f. What is an appropriate name for the department labeled H?
g. What process is represented by the symbol F?
h. What accounting record is represented by the symbol G?
i. What accounting record is represented by symbol G?

4. SEGREGATION OF FUNCTIONS

Which, if any, of the following situations represent improper segregation of functions?

a. The billing department prepares the customers' invoices, and the accounts receivable department posts to the customers' accounts.
b. The sales department approves sales credit memos as the result of product returns, and subsequent adjustments to the customer accounts are per formed by the accounts receivable department.
c. The shipping department ships goods that have been retrieved from stock by warehouse personnel.
d. The general accounting department posts to the general ledger accounts after receiving journal vouchers that are prepared by the billing department.

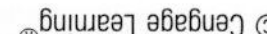

Problem 3: System Flowchart Analysis

Mail Room	B	H

Customer

Checks

Remittance Advice

Separate Checks and Remittance Advices

Remittance Advice

1

Checks

A

C

E

Checks

D

1

Remittance Advice

F

G

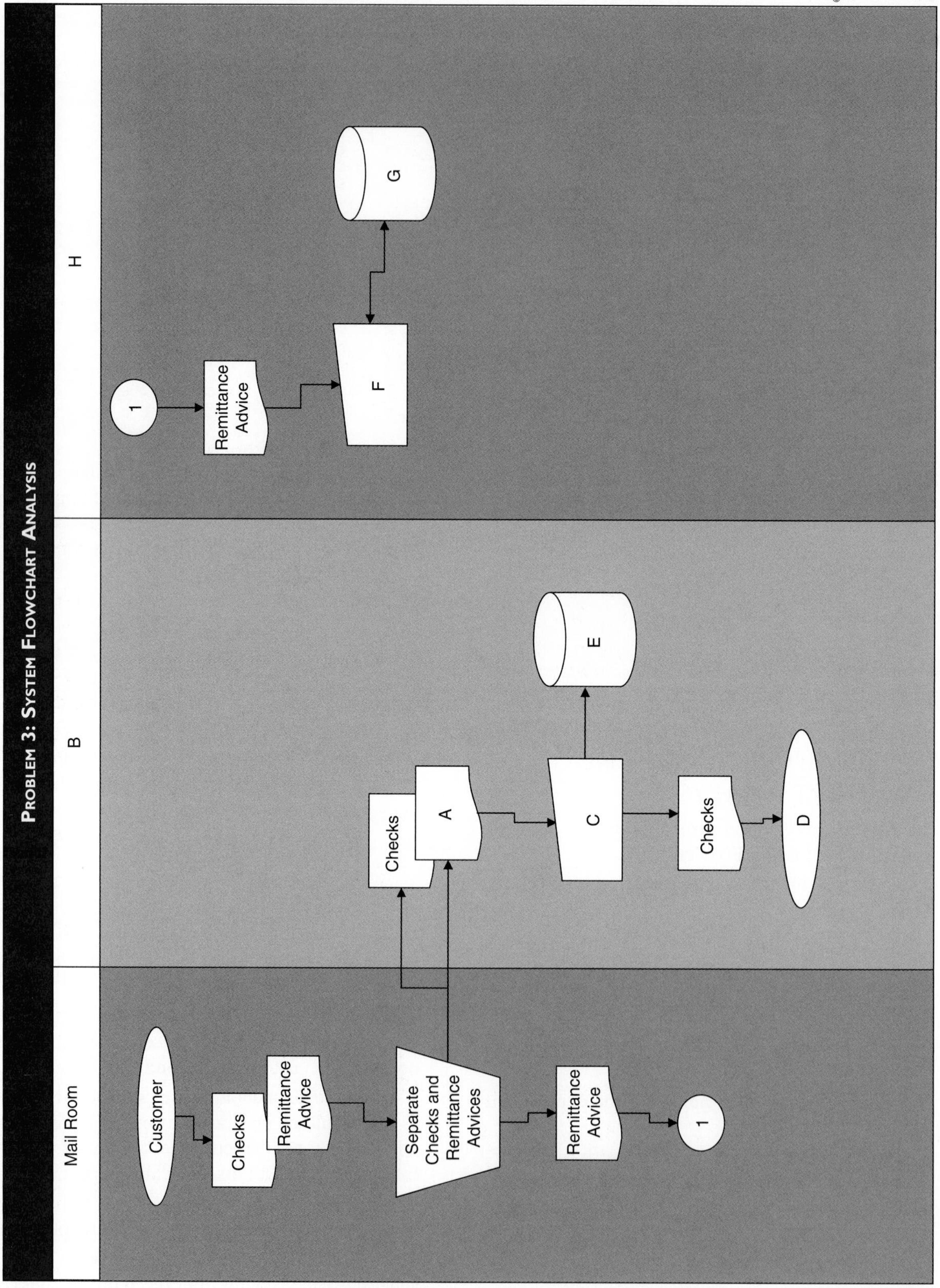

5. RISKS AND INTERNAL CONTROLS

Following describes the credit sales procedures for clothing wholesaler that sells name-brand clothing to department stores and boutique dress shops. The company sells to both one-time and recurring customers. A flowchart of the system is provided in the figure labeled Problem 5: Internal Control.

Customer orders are received by fax and e-mail in the sales department. The sales clerk, who works on commission, approves the credit sale, calculates commissions and discounts, and records the sale in the sales journal from the PC in the sales department. The clerk then prepares a sales order, a customer invoice, and a packing slip, which are sent to the accounting department for processing. The accounting clerk updates the AR Subsidiary ledger and sends an invoice to the customer. The clerk then forwards the sales order and packing slip to the Warehouse-Shipping Department. The warehouse-shipping clerk picks the items from inventory and sends them and the packing slip to the carrier for shipment to the customer. Finally the clerk updates the inventory subsidiary ledger and files the sales order in the department.

Cash receipts from customers go to the mailroom, which has one supervisor overseeing 32 employees performing similar tasks: a clerk opens the envelope containing the customer check and remittance advice, inspects the check for completeness, reconciles it with the remittance advice, and sends the remittance advice and check to the accounting department.

The accounting department clerk reviews the remittance advice and the checks, updates the AR subsidiary ledger and records the cash receipt in the cash receipts journal. At the end of the day, the clerk updates the AR Control, Cash, and Sales accounts in the general ledger to reflect the day's sales and cash receipts.

Required

a. Describe the uncontrolled risks associated with this system as it is currently designed.
b. For each risk describe the specific internal control weakness(s) in the system that causes or contributes to the risk

6. INTERNAL CONTROL EVALUATION

a. Identify the physical control weaknesses depicted in the flowchart for Problem 6.
b. Describe the IT controls that should be in place in this system.

7. STEWARDSHIP

Identify which department has stewardship over the following journals, ledgers, and files.

a. Customer open order file
b. Sales journal
c. Journal voucher file
d. Cash receipts journal
e. Inventory subsidiary ledger
f. Accounts receivable subsidiary ledger
g. Sales history file
h. Shipping report file
i. Credit memo file
j. Sales order file
k. Closed sales order file

8. CONTROL WEAKNESSES

For the past 11 years, Elaine Wright has been an employee of the Star-Bright Electrical Supply store. Elaine is a very diligent employee who rarely calls in sick and staggers her vacation days throughout the year so that no one else gets bogged down with her tasks for more than one day. Star-Bright is a small store that employs only four people other than the owner. The owner and one of the employees help customers with their electrical needs. One of the employees handles all receiving, stocking, and shipping of merchandise. Another employee handles the purchasing, payroll, general ledger, inventory, and AP functions. Elaine handles all of the point-of-sale cash receipts and prepares the daily deposits for the business. Furthermore, Elaine opens the mail and deposits all cash receipts (about 30 percent of the total daily cash receipts). Elaine also keeps the AR records and bills the customers who purchase on credit.

Required

Point out any control weaknesses you see in the scenario. List some recommendations to remedy any weaknesses you have found working under the constraint that no additional employees can be hired.

9. INTERNAL CONTROL

Iris Plant owns and operates three floral shops in Magnolia, Texas. The accounting functions are performed manually. Each of the shops has a manager who oversees the cash receipts and purchasing functions for the shop. A clerk at the central shop pays all the bills and also prepares payroll checks and maintains the general journal. Iris is seriously considering switching to a computerized system. With so many information system packages on the market, Iris is overwhelmed.

Problem 5: Internal Control

Sales Department

Customer

Customer Order

Approve credit, prepare Sales Order and Record Sale

Sales Journal

Sales Order

Sales Invoice

Packing slip

Accounting Department

Sales Order

Sales Invoice

Packing Slip

A

Check

Remittance advice

Bill Customer, record CR, Update Accounts

AR Sub Ledger

GL Accounts

CR Journal

Sales Invoice

Customer

Check

Deposit Slip

Bank

Sales Order

Packing Slip

Warehouse/Shipping

Sales Order

Packing Slip

Pick Goods, Update Inventory, send goods to Carrier

Inventory Sub ledger

Sales Order

Packing Slip

Carrier

Mailroom

Customer

Check

Remittance Advice

Open mail and reconcile RA and Check

Check

Remittance Advice

A

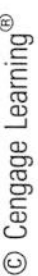

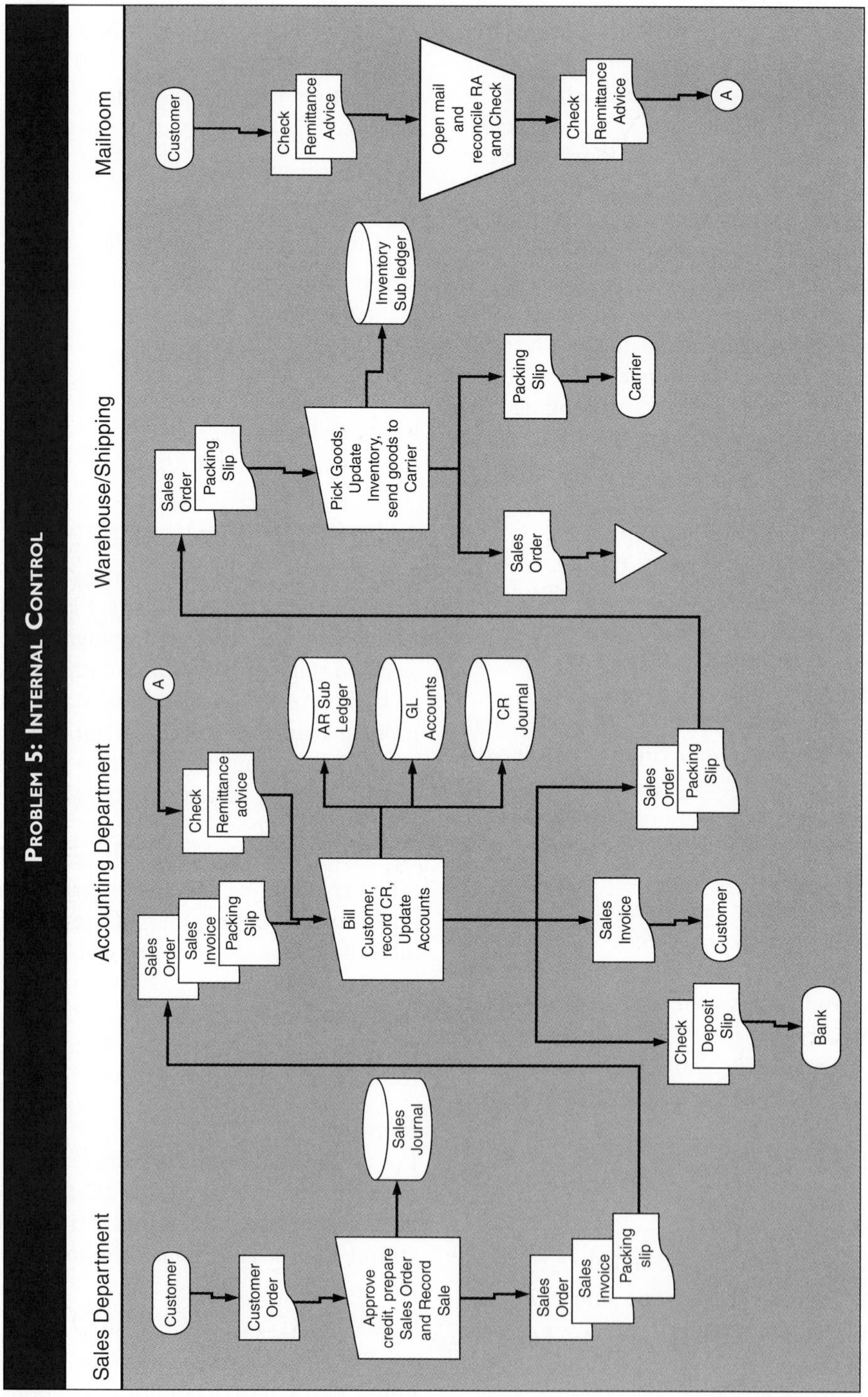

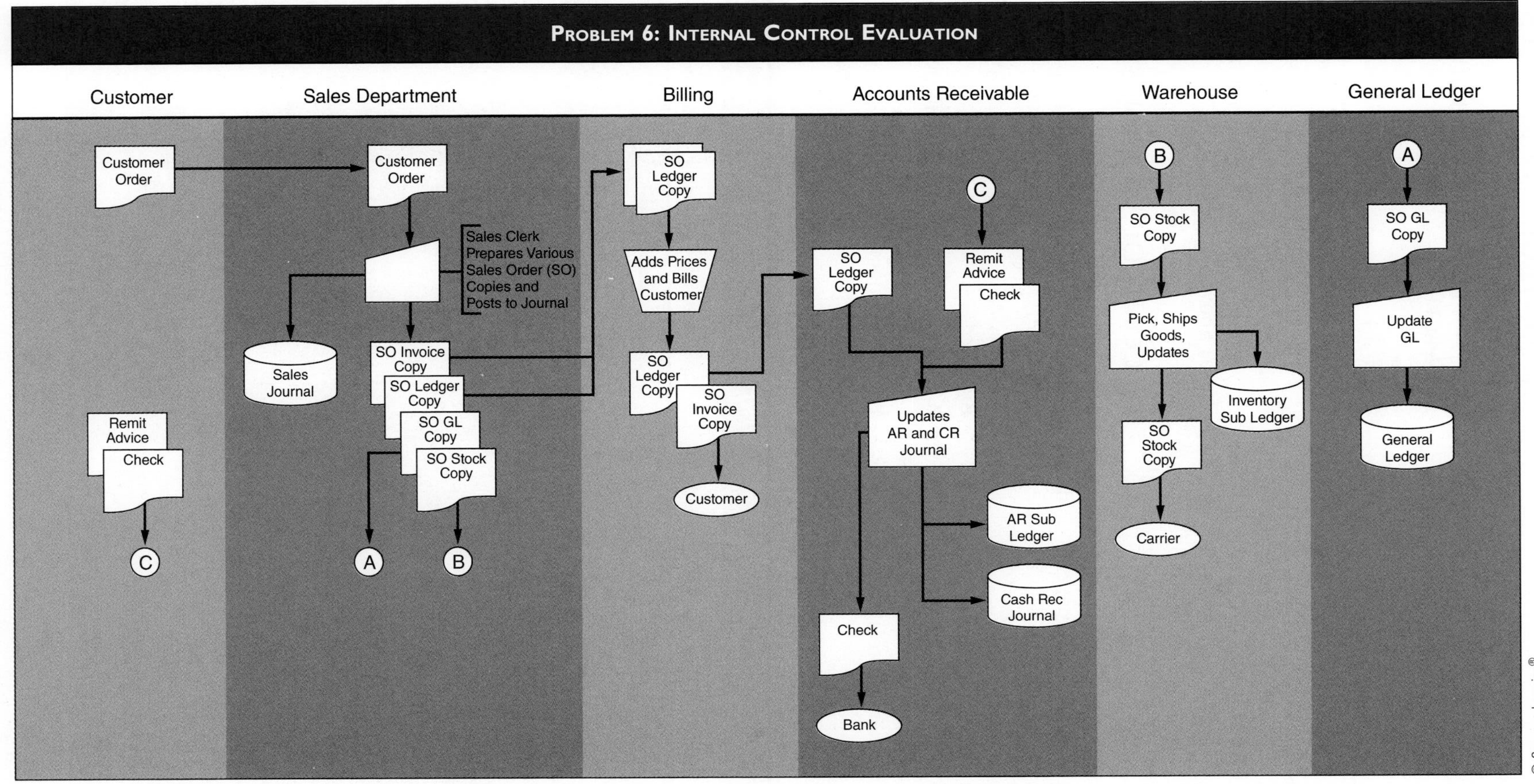
PROBLEM 6: INTERNAL CONTROL EVALUATION
Customer
Sales Department
Billing
Accounts Receivable
Warehouse
General Ledger
Customer Order
Remit Advice
Check
C
Customer Order
Sales Clerk Prepares Various Sales Order (SO) Copies and Posts to Journal
Sales Journal
SO Invoice Copy
SO Ledger Copy
SO GL Copy
SO Stock Copy
A
B
SO Ledger Copy
Adds Prices and Bills Customer
SO Ledger Copy
SO Invoice Copy
Customer
C
SO Ledger Copy
Remit Advice
Check
Updates AR and CR Journal
AR Sub Ledger
Cash Rec Journal
Check
Bank
B
SO Stock Copy
Pick, Ships Goods, Updates
Inventory Sub Ledger
SO Stock Copy
Carrier
A
SO GL Copy
Update GL
General Ledger

Required

Advise Iris as to which business modules you think her organization could find beneficial. Discuss advantages, disadvantages, and internal control issues.

10. INTERNAL CONTROL

You are a consultant who has been hired to design a point-of-sale (POS) system with appropriate controls for a restaurant that accepts cash and credit cards including Visa, MC, and AMEX. The restaurant also issues coupons through the mail and in local newspapers, which it accepts as cash from customers. The system will employ computer terminals with cash drawers that are connected to a central computer. Servers take orders and receive payments from customers. At the end of the shift, servers reconcile their cash drawers with the manager. The system automatically updates the journals and GL accounts.

Required

a. Prepare a flowchart for the new system.
b. Describe the risks inherent in the system and the physical and computer controls needed to mitigate the risks.

11. CONTROL WEAKNESSES AND RELATED RISKS

Refer to the system flowchart in the figure labeled Problem 11.

Required

a. Discuss the uncontrolled risks associated with the systems as currently configured.
b. Describe the controls that need to be implemented into the system to mitigate the risks in (a) above.

12. CONTROL WEAKNESSES AND RELATED RISKS

Refer to the system flowchart in the figure labeled Problem 12.

Required

a. Describe the control weaknesses depicted in the system flowchart.
b. Discuss the risks associated with the control weaknesses in identified (a) above.

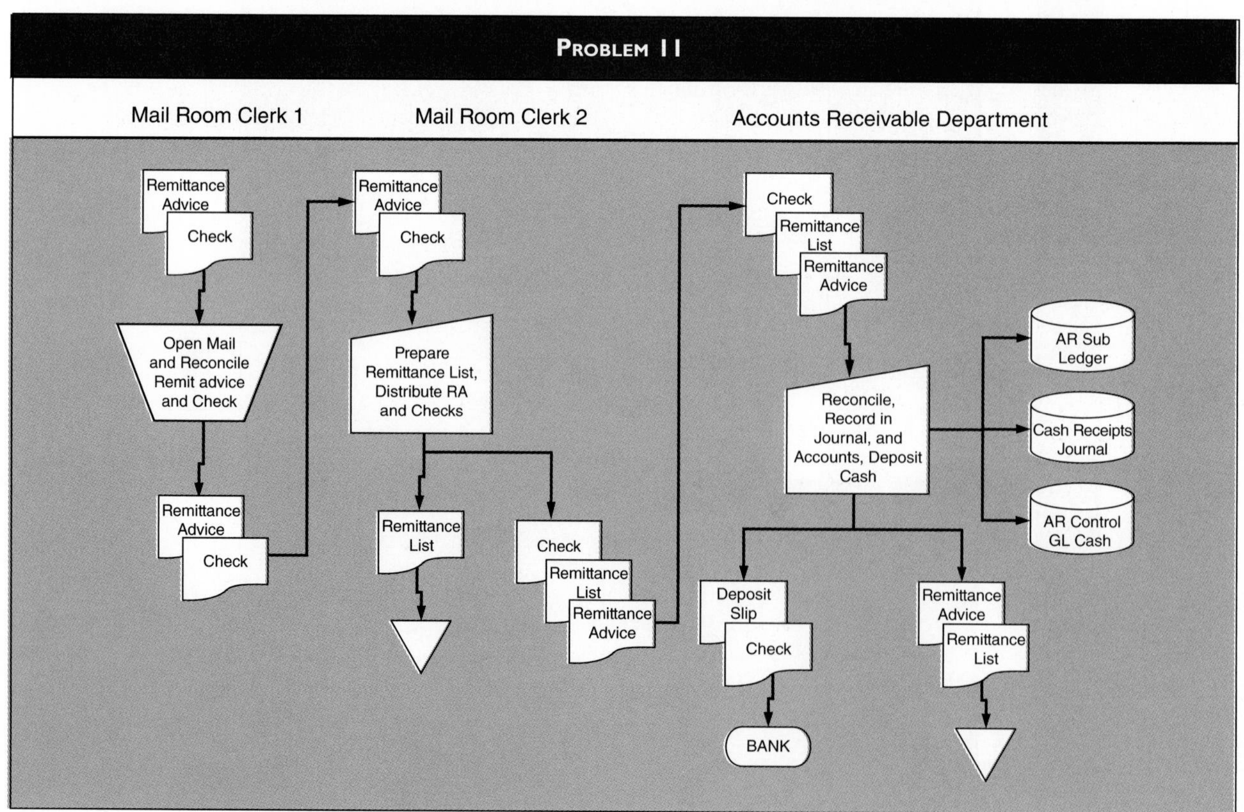

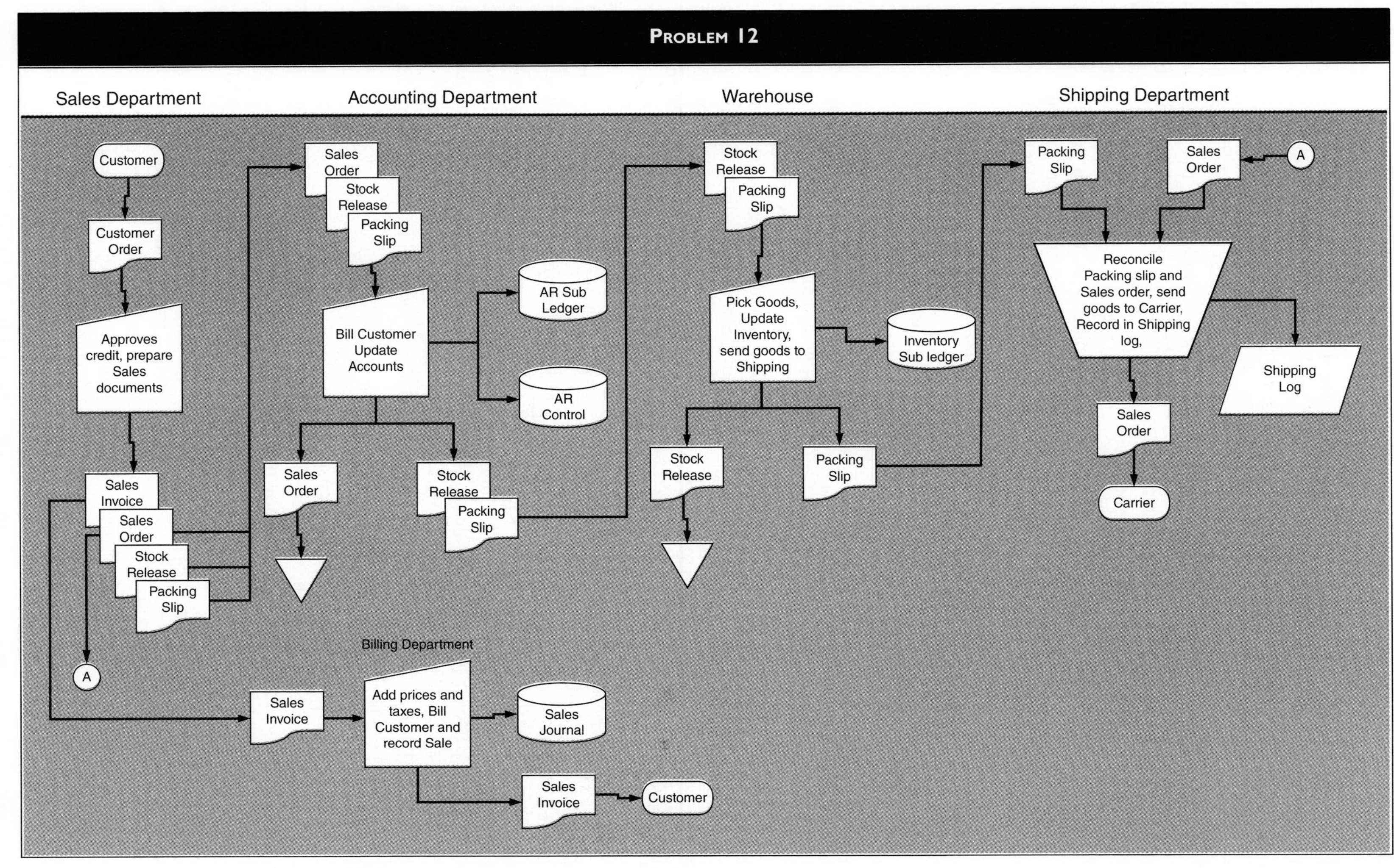
PROBLEM 12
Sales Department
Accounting Department
Warehouse
Shipping Department
Customer
Customer Order
Approves credit, prepare Sales documents
Sales Invoice
Sales Order
Stock Release
Packing Slip
A
Sales Order
Stock Release
Packing Slip
Bill Customer Update Accounts
AR Sub Ledger
AR Control
Sales Order
Stock Release
Packing Slip
Billing Department
Sales Invoice
Add prices and taxes, Bill Customer and record Sale
Sales Journal
Sales Invoice
Customer
Stock Release
Packing Slip
Pick Goods, Update Inventory, send goods to Shipping
Inventory Sub ledger
Stock Release
Packing Slip
Packing Slip
Sales Order
A
Reconcile Packing slip and Sales order, send goods to Carrier, Record in Shipping log,
Shipping Log
Sales Order
Carrier

Internal Control Cases

1. SMITH'S MARKET (SMALL BUSINESS POS ACCOUNTING SYSTEM)

In 1989, Robert Smith opened a small fruit and vegetable market in Bethlehem, Pennsylvania. Originally Smith sold only produce grown on his family farm and orchard. As the market's popularity grew, however, he added bread, canned goods, fresh meats, and a limited supply of frozen goods. Today Smith's market is a full range farmers' market with a strong local customer base. Indeed, the market's reputation for low prices and high quality draws customers from other Pennsylvania cities and even from the neighboring state of New Jersey. Currently Smith's market has 40 employees. These include sales staff, shelf stockers, farm laborers, shift supervisors, and clerical staff. Recently Smith has noticed a decline in profits and sales, while his purchases of products for resale have continued to rise. Although the company does not prepare audited financial statements, Robert Smith has commissioned your public accounting firm to assess his company's sales procedures and controls. Smith's market revenue cycle procedures are described in the following paragraphs:

Revenue Cycle

Customers push their shopping carts to the checkout register where a clerk processes the sale. The market has four registers, but they are not dedicated to specific sales clerks because the clerks play many roles in the day-to-day operations. In addition to checking out customers, sales clerks will stock shelves, unload delivery trucks, or perform other tasks as demand in various areas rises and falls throughout the day. This fluid-work demand makes the assignment of clerks to specific registers impractical.

At the beginning of the shift, the shift supervisor collects four cash register drawers from the treasury clerk in an office in the back of the market. The drawers contain $100 each in small bills (known as float) to enable the clerks to make change. The supervisor signs a log indicating that he has taken custody of the float and places the drawers into the respective cash registers.

Sales to customers are for cash, check, or credit card only. Credit card sales are performed in the usual way.

The clerk swipes the card and obtains online approval from the card issuer at the time of sale. The customer then signs the credit card voucher, which the clerk places in a special compartment of the cash register drawer. The customer receives a receipt for the purchase and a copy of the credit card voucher.

For payments by check, the clerk requires the customer to present a valid driver's license. The license number is added to the check and the check is matched against a "black" list of customers who have previously passed bad checks. If the customer is not on the list, the check is accepted for payment and placed in the cash register drawer. The clerk then gives the customer a receipt.

The majority of sales are for cash. The clerk receives the cash from the customer, makes change, and issues a receipt for the purchase.

At the end of the shift the supervisor returns the cash register drawers containing the cash, checks, and credit cards receipts to the treasury clerk and signs a log that he has handed in the cash drawers. The clerk later counts the cash and credit card sales. Using a standalone PC, he records the total sales amounts in the sales journal and the general Ledger Sales and Cash accounts. The Treasury clerk then prepares a deposit slip and delivers the cash, checks, and credit card vouchers to the local branch of the bank two blocks away from the market.

Required

a. Create a data flow diagram of the current system.
b. Create a system flowchart of the existing system.
c. Analyze the physical internal control weaknesses in the system. Model your response according to the six categories of physical control activities specified in the COSO internal control model.
d. Describe the IT controls that should be in place in this system.

2. TIGHT LINES FISHING AND CAMPING SUPPLIES (NETWORKED COMPUTER SYSTEM AND MANUAL PROCEDURES)

Tight Lines Fishing and Camping Supplies is a New York-based wholesaler of fishing and camping equipment that serves fishing and camping retailers throughout the north east. You have been hired by Tight Lines to evaluate their processes, risks, and internal controls. The following paragraphs describe Tight Lines revenue cycle procedures.

Revenue Cycle

SALES ORDER PROCESSING PROCEDURES. Wholesale customer orders are mailed, e-mailed or faxed to the sales department. When the order is received the sales clerk checks the customer's credit worthiness from a computer terminal. After the customer's credit is verified, the clerk then records the sales order through his computer terminal. A digital copy of the order is distributed to the warehouse and the shipping department terminals for further processing. The computer system automatically records the sale in the sales journal. Finally, the clerk files the hard copy of the customer order in the sales department.

The warehouse manager is prompted by receipt of the digital sales order on the warehouse terminal. The manager prints out two copies of order: the stock release and a shipping notice. Using the stock release copy, a warehouse clerk picks the selected items from the shelves and sends them to the shipping department along with stock release and the shipping notice. The warehouse manager then updates the inventory subsidiary ledger and the general ledger control account from his computer terminal.

When the shipping clerk receives the goods, the stock release, and the shipping notice, he matches them to the corresponding digital sales order displayed on his terminal. If everything matches, he prints out three hard copies of the bill of lading and a packing slip. Two copies of the bill of lading and the packing slip are sent, along with the goods, to the carrier. The stock release copy and the shipping notice are sent to the accounts receivable department. The third bill of lading copy is filed in the shipping department.

Upon receipt of the stock release and shipping notice, the accounts receivable clerk manually creates a hard-copy invoice, which is immediately mailed to the customer. After mailing the invoice, the clerk uses information on the stock release to update the accounts receivable subsidiary ledger and general ledger from his computer terminal. After the records are updated, the clerk files the stock release and shipping notice in the accounts receivable department.

Cash Receipts Procedures

Customer payments come directly to the general mail room along with other mail items. The mail clerk sorts the mail, opens the customer payment envelope, removes the customer's check and remittance advice, and reconciles the two documents. To control the checks and remittance advices, the clerk manually prepares two hard copies of a remittance list. He sends one copy to the accounts receivable department, along with the corresponding remittance advices. The other copy of the remittance list accompanies the checks to the cash receipts department.

Once the checks and remittance list arrive in the cash receipts department, the treasurer reconciles the documents, endorses the checks, and manually prepares three hard copies of a deposit slip. He then updates the cash receipts journal and the general ledger from his computer terminal. Next, the treasurer sends the checks and two copies of the deposit slip to the bank. Finally, he files the third copy of the deposit slip and the remittance in the department.

When the accounts receivable clerk receives the remittance list and remittance advices from the mail room, he reconciles the two documents. He then updates the accounts receivable subsidiary ledger and the general ledger. Finally, he files the two documents in the department.

Required

a. Create a data flow diagram of the current system.
b. Create a system flowchart of the existing system.
c. Describe internal control weaknesses in the system and discuss the risks associated with these weaknesses.
d. (Optional) Prepare a system flowchart of a redesigned computer-based system that resolves the control weaknesses that you identified. Explain your solution.

3. TVR CLASSICS (MANUAL AND STAND-ALONE COMPUTER PROCESSING)

TVR Classics specializes in the sale of original and reproduction restoration parts for classic sports cars and muscle cars of the 1960s and 1970s. The classic car industry has grown significantly in recent years as the baby boomers age, become wealthier, and want to relive fond memories. Classic car sales and restoration is a multibillion dollar industry that employs more than 30,000 people in the United States. It is, however, a highly fragmented industry comprised of many small businesses. TVR is headquartered in Los Angeles, California and currently employs 95 full-time employees, including sales staff, sales representatives, and general office staff. TVR's primary customer base consists of small restoration shops and classic car dealers on the west coast. They source many of their parts from abroad, but a growing percentage of these are now being manufactured in the United States.

TVR has a legacy accounting system that employs a combination of manual procedures supported by standalone PCs in various departments. Recently, they have experienced business inefficiencies that have been linked to their antiquated accounting system. You have been retained by TVR management to review their procedures for compliance with effective internal control standards. TVR's revenue cycle procedures are presented in the following paragraphs.

Sales Order Procedures

TVR has one sales department at its headquarters in Los Angeles. All customer orders go through sales representatives who visit current and prospective customers in their sales districts. The orders are faxed, mailed, or delivered in person to the sales department by the representative at the end of each day.

In the sales department a sales clerk receives the orders and manually prepares a three-part hard-copy sales order. The clerk sends one sales order copy to the billing department, the stock release copy to the warehouse, and the packing slip copy to the shipping department. The original customer order is filed in the sales department.

Upon receipt of the sales order, the billing clerk records the sale in the digital sales journal using the department PC. The clerk then prints a hard-copy invoice, which is sent to the customer. Next, the clerk sends the sales order to the accounts receivable department for further processing. At the end of the day the clerk prints a hard-copy sales journal voucher from the PC and sends it to the general ledger department.

The warehousing clerk uses the stock release copy to pick the goods from the shelves and then updates the digital inventory subsidiary ledger using the warehouse PC. Next, the clerk sends the goods and the stock release to the shipping department. At the end of the business day the clerk prints an inventory summary from the PC and sends it to the general ledger department.

The shipping clerk reconciles the packing slip sent from the sales department with the stock release and goods received from the warehouse. If all is correct, the clerk manually prepares a hard-copy bill of lading. He then attaches the packing slip and bill of lading to the goods, which go to the carrier for delivery to the customer. Finally, the clerk files the stock release in the department.

The accounts receivable clerk receives the sales order from the billing department and uses it to update the digital AR subledger from the department PC. The sales order is then filed in the department. At the end of the day the clerk prints an AR summary from the PC and sends it to the general ledger department.

CASH RECEIPTS PROCESS. Customer payments come into the mail room where mail clerks open the envelopes and send the checks and remittance advices to the accounts receivable department. The accounts receivable clerk reconciles the remittance advice with the check and updates the customer's account in the digital accounts receivable subsidiary ledger. The clerk then files the remittance advices in the department and sends the checks to the cash receipts department. As previously mentioned, at the end of the day the accounts receivable clerk prints a hard-copy accounts receivable summary from the department PC and sends it to the general ledger department.

The cash receipt clerk receives the checks and records the payments in the digital cash receipts journal. The clerk then manually prepares a hard-copy deposit slip and sends the checks and deposit slip to the bank. At the end of the day the clerk prints a cash receipt journal voucher from the department PC and sends it to the general ledger department.

The general ledger clerk receives the sales journal voucher, cash receipts journal voucher, accounts receivable summary, and inventory summary. The clerk reconciles these documents and posts them to the appropriate control accounts in the digital general ledger from the department PC. Finally, the general ledger clerk files the summaries and journal vouchers in the department.

Required

a. Create a data flow diagram of the current system.
b. Create a system flowchart of the existing system.
c. Analyze the physical internal control weaknesses in the system.
d. (Optional) Prepare a system flowchart of a redesigned computer-based system that resolves the control weaknesses that you identified. Explain your solution.

4. DISCOUNT TOOLS, INC. (NETWORKED COMPUTER SYSTEM WITH MANUAL PROCEDURES)

Discount tools is a rapidly growing online and catalogue-based retailer of low cost tools and equipment directed to the do-it-yourself consumers and to small service companies in the automotive repair and home improvement industries. Discount Tools offices and warehouse are located in Atlanta, Georgia. The firm purchases from a large number of manufacturers in China and India, and to a lesser extent from US-based suppliers.

The company employs a networked accounting system with distributed terminals in several departments, but some tasks are performed manually. Until recently the system has functions satisfactorily, but Discount Tools is now experiencing operational inefficiencies and accounting errors. Your firm has been hired to evaluate Discount Tools' business processes and internal controls. The revenue cycle is described in the following paragraphs.

Sales Order Procedures

Discount Tools' revenue process is initiated when a customer places an order either online, by mail, or through a telephone representative. Online orders are entered automatically by the system, mail and phone orders are manually entered. When the customer order is entered, the system automatically performs an online credit check. If credit is approved, the sales process continues. If credit is denied, the process ends, and the customer is notified of the automatic rejection.

For approved orders, the clerk manually prepares four hard copies of each sales order. The clerk then enters the sale into the digital sales journal from his terminal and files one copy of the sales order in the sales department. A second copy is sent to the billing department, where it is further processed. A third copy is sent to the warehouse. A final copy is sent to the customer as a receipt stating that the order has been received and processed.

The warehouse clerk uses the sales order as a stock release document to pick the requested items from the shelves. The clerk then manually prepares a bill of lading and packing slip, which accompany the goods to the carrier. The warehouse clerk then accesses the computer terminal and creates a digital shipping notice for the billing department. Finally, the clerk files the stock release hard copy in the warehouse.

The billing department clerk reconciles the hard-copy sales order and the digital shipping notice, which is displayed on her terminal. She then prints two hard copies of an invoice. One copy is sent to the customer as a bill and the other is sent to the accounts receivable department. The clerk then files the sales order copy in the department.

Upon receipt of the hard-copy invoice, the accounts receivable clerk creates a digital record in the accounts receivable subsidiary ledger from his terminal. The clerk then files the invoice copy in the department.

Cash Receipts Procedures

Customer payments and remittance advices come into the mail room. A clerk separates the documents and sends the remittance advices to accounts receivable and the checks to the cash receipts department.

Upon receipt of the remittance advices, the accounts receivable clerk accesses the customer's account in the accounts receivable subsidiary ledger from a terminal and adjusts the balance accordingly. The clerk files the remittance advices in the department.

The cash receipts clerk receives the checks and posts them to the cash receipts journal from her terminal. The clerk then manually prepares a hard-copy deposit slip and sends it with the cash to the bank.

Finally, at the end of each day the system prepares batch totals of all sales and cash receipts transactions and posts them automatically to the control accounts in the digital general ledger.

Required

a. Create a data flow diagram of the current system.

b. Create a system flowchart of the existing system.

c. Analyze the physical internal control weaknesses in the system.

d. Describe the IT controls that should be in place in this system.

e. (Optional) Prepare a system flowchart of a redesigned computer-based system that resolves the control weaknesses that you identified. Explain your solution.

5. ABE PLUMBING, INC. (CENTRALIZED SMALL BUSINESS ACCOUNTING SYSTEM)

ABE Plumbing, Inc., opened its doors in 1979 as a wholesale supplier of plumbing equipment, tools, and parts to hardware stores, home-improvement centers, and professional plumbers in the Allentown-Bethlehem-Easton metropolitan area. Over the years, they have expanded their operations to serve customers across the nation and now employ over 200 people as technical representatives, buyers, warehouse workers, and sales and office staff. Most recently, ABE has experienced fierce competition from the large online discount stores such as Harbor Freight and Northern Supply. In addition, the company is suffering from operational inefficiencies related to its archaic information system. ABE's revenue cycle procedures are described in the following paragraphs.

Revenue Cycle

ABE's sales department consists of 17 full-time and part-time employees. The company receives orders via traditional mail, e-mail, telephone, and the occasional walk-in customer. Because ABE is a wholesaler, the vast majority of its business is conducted on a credit basis. The process begins in the sales department, where the sales clerk enters the customer's order into the centralized computer sales order system. The computer and file server are housed in ABE's small data processing department.

If the customer has done business with ABE in the past, his or her data are already on file. If the customer is a first-time buyer, however, the clerk creates a new record in the customer file. The system then creates a record of the transaction in the open sales order file. When the order is entered, an electronic copy of it is sent to the customer's e-mail address as confirmation.

A clerk in the warehouse department periodically reviews the open sales order file from a terminal and prints two copies of a stock release document for each new sale, which he uses to pick the items sold from the shelves. The warehouse clerk sends one copy of the stock release to the sales department and the second copy, along with the goods, to the shipping department. The warehouse clerk then updates the inventory subsidiary file to reflect the items and quantities shipped. Upon receipt of the stock release document, the sales clerk accesses the open sales order file from a terminal, closes the sales order, and files the stock release document in the sales department. The sales order system automatically posts these transactions to the sales, inventory control, and cost-of-goods-sold accounts in the general ledger file.

Upon receipt of the goods and the stock release, the shipping department clerk prepares the goods for shipment to the customer. The clerk prepares three copies of the bill of lading. Two of these go with the goods to the carrier and the third, along with the stock release document, is filed in the shipping department.

The billing department clerk reviews the closed sales orders from a terminal and prepares two copies of the sales invoice. One copy is mailed to the customer and the other is filed in the billing department. The clerk then creates a new record in the account receivable subsidiary file. The sales order system automatically updates the account receivable control account in the general ledger file.

ABE has hired your public accounting firm to review its sales order procedures for internal control compliance and to make recommendations for changes.

Required

a. Create a data flow diagram of the current system.
b. Create a system flowchart of the existing system.
c. Analyze the physical internal control weaknesses in the system.
d. (Optional) Prepare a system flowchart of a redesigned computer-based system that resolves the control weaknesses that you identified. Explain your solution.

6. GREEN PRODUCTS GARDEN SUPPLY (STAND-ALONE PC-BASED ACCOUNTING SYSTEM)

Green Products Garden (GPG) Supply sells and distributes a wide range of garden products and equipment including organic fertilizers, premium flower and grass seeds, organic pesticides, and garden spreaders. GPG's headquarters and warehouse is located in Hopewell, Virginia. Their customers are primarily small garden centers and landscape companies in the Mid-Atlantic States. Sales are on credit.

GPG's current information system includes manual procedures supported by independent (non-networked) PCs in each department. Communications between departments is entirely through hard-copy documents. Recently, GPG has been receiving complaints from customers and suppliers about billing, shipping, and payment errors. Management believes that these complaints stem, in part, from their antiquated computer system. You have been hired to assess GPG's procedures and internal controls. The following is a description of GPG's revenue cycle.

Sales Procedures

The revenue cycle begins when a customer places an order with a sales representative by phone or fax. A sales department employee enters the customer order into a standard sales order format using a word processor installed on a PC to produce: three sales order copies, a stock release document, a shipping notice, and a packing slip. The accounting department receives a copy of the sales order, the warehouse receives the stock release and a copy of the sales order, and the shipping department receives a shipping notice and packing slip. The sales clerk files a copy of the sales order in the department.

Upon receipt of the sales order, the accounting department clerk manually prepares an invoice and sends it to the customer. Using data from the sales order, the clerk then enters the sale in the department PC and records the sale in the sales journal and in the AR subsidiary ledger. At the end of the day the clerk prepares a hard-copy sales journal voucher, which is sent to the general ledger department.

Upon receipt of the sales order and stock release the warehouse clerk picks the products and sends them to the shipping department, along with the stock release. The warehouse clerk then updates the inventory records on the warehouse PC and files the sales order in the warehouse. At the end of the day the clerk prepares a hard-copy inventory account summary and sends it to the general ledger department.

The shipping department clerk receives a shipping notice and packing slip from the sales department. The clerk files the shipping notice and holds open the packing slip until he receives the stock release and products from the warehouse. Upon receipt of the stock release, the shipping clerk prepares the two copies of a bill of lading using a word processor. The bills of lading and the packing slip are sent with the product to the carrier. The clerk then files the stock release in the department.

The general ledger clerk posts the journal voucher and inventory summary to the general ledger, which is stored on the department PC, and the clerk then files these documents in the general ledger department.

Cash Receipts Procedure

Mail room employees open cash receipts from customers and reconcile the amounts on the checks and remittance advices. The remittance advices are sent to the accounting department, where a clerk records each remittance advice on a remittance list. The remittance list is then sent to the cash receipts department. Using the remittance advices, the accounting clerk updates the customer accounts receivable on the department PC and files the advice in the department. At the end of the day the clerk prepares an AR summary on the PC. A hard copy of the summary is sent to the general ledger department.

The mail room clerk sends the checks to the cash receipts department, where a clerk endorses each check with the words "For Deposit Only." Next, the clerk reconciles the checks with the remittance list and records the cash receipts in the cash receipts journal on the department PC. Finally, the clerk prepares a deposit slip and sends it and the checks to the bank.

The general ledger clerk posts the accounts receivable summary to general ledger and files it in the general ledger department.

Required

a. Create a data flow diagram of the current system.
b. Create a system flowchart of the existing system.
c. Analyze the physical internal control weaknesses in the system.
d. (Optional) Prepare a system flowchart of a redesigned computer-based system that resolves the control weaknesses that you identified. Explain your solution.

7. CUSTOM FABRICATIONS (STAND ALONE PC BASED ACCOUNTING SYSTEM)

(Prepared by Will Richens and Michael Catchpole, Lehigh University)

CUSTOM FABRICATIONS Inc., is a bicycle manufacturing firm founded in 2000 that currently employs 126 people. The company produces custom bicycles in its factory located near Los Angeles, CA. Each bicycle is tailored to a rider based on a number of different measurements, including height, weight, inseam, and arm length. These measurements are taken at 30 professional bicycle shops around Southern California, which are certified to size CUSTOM FABRICATIONS cycles. By accepting orders only through licensed dealers, CUSTOM FABRICATIONS ensures that each bike matches its rider precisely. CUSTOM FABRICATIONS custom bikes are considered extremely high quality, and the company takes pride in using only the best components sourced from around the world. Accordingly, CUSTOM FABRICATIONS purchases from a cast of hundreds of suppliers, chosen for their commitment to quality and reliability.

Demand for CUSTOM FABRICATIONS' cycles has grown exponentially in recent years. The surge in demand was somewhat unexpected and the company's factory has been operating at capacity for over a year. As a result, current orders face a production backlog of approximately 5–6 weeks. The company's operations have been further hampered by severe inefficiencies and control weaknesses attributed to its legacy accounting system. Your firm has been hired as an outside consultant to suggest improvements in the company's accounting procedures. The following paragraphs describe the company's revenue cycle.

Revenue Cycle

SALES ORDER SYSTEM. The sales order process begins when a licensed CUSTOM FABRICATIONS dealer faxes a completed customer order and measurement form to the sales department. When the fax is received, a sales representative calls the dealer to confirm the order details and generates a quote based on the complexity of the order. The sales clerk then enters the measurements and quoted price into his PC terminal, which automatically generates a sales order form. The clerk prints three hard copies of the sales order form. The first copy is sent to the billing department and the second is sent to the factory. The clerk files the third copy, along with the customer order in the sales department's open customer order file.

The billing department clerk uses the first copy of the sales order to compute the final sales price and manually prepares two copies of the customer invoice. One copy of this invoice is sent to the customer, while the second is used by the billing clerk to update the sales order journal and accounts receivable subsidiary from his terminal. At the end of each day the clerk prints out a hard-copy summary of the AR ledger and the sales journal and forward them to the general ledger department.

When the second copy of the sales order is received in the factory, it is forwarded to the production planning clerk for scheduling. The clerk sets a production date and manually prepares one copy of the materials requisition form and two copies of the production order. The first copy of the production order is sent to the sales department and filed in the open customer order file to inform the customer of the intended date of production. The second copy of the production order form and the materials-requisition form are temporarily filed in the factory.

At the beginning of each day the factory production line manager accesses the temporary production file and pulls the production orders to be completed for the day. He then forwards the materials-requisition form to the warehouse to obtain the raw material and components needed for production. Once the materials have been forwarded to the production department, the warehouse clerk updates the digital inventory subsidiary account from his terminal. At the end of every day, the clerk prints a hard-copy journal voucher and sends it to the general ledger department.

When production of a cycle is completed, the bike and the second copy of the production order form are sent to the warehouse to await shipping. The warehouse clerk receives a bike and its accompanying production order, and he or she packs the bike for shipping. The clerk then manually prepares a stock release document from the production order document. Finally, the warehouse clerk forwards the packaged bike, along with the stock release document, to the shipping department.

On the date the bike is due to be shipped, the shipping clerk uses the stock release document to prepare three copies of the bill of lading and one copy of the packing slip from the department PC. From this PC he updates the company's shipping log. Two copies of the bill of lading and the packing slip are forwarded along with the packaged bike to the carrier. The third copy of the bill of lading is sent the sales department to close the open customer order file.

At the close of business each day when the general ledger department clerk receives journal vouchers and the AR summary, he updates the general ledger-accounts from the PC in the department. The AR summary and vouchers are filed in the department.

CASH RECEIPTS SYSTEM. Customer payments are processed in CUSTOM FABRICATIONS' mail room along with all other mail received by the organization. A mail room clerk selects and opens customer remittances envelopes and reviews the checks and remittance advice. Next, the clerk manually prepares three copies of a remittance list.

The first copy of the remittance list is sent, along with the checks, to the cash receipts department. Once the clerk there receives the remittance list, he reconciles the checks and remittance list and updates the cash receipts journal from his PC. He then prints two copies of the deposit slip, which are sent along with the checks to the bank.

The second copy of the remittance list, along with the remittance advice, is sent to the billing department. The clerk reconciles these documents and updates the accounts receivable subsidiary account to reflect the payment received.

The third remittance list is sent to the general ledger department, which uses it to update the accounts receivable control and cash accounts.

Required

a. Create a data flow diagram of the current system.
b. Create a system flowchart of the existing system.
c. Analyze the physical internal control weaknesses in the system.
d. Describe the risks associated with these control weaknesses
e. (Optional) Prepare a system flowchart of a redesigned computer-based system that resolves the control weaknesses that you identified. Explain your solution.

8. PERFORMANCE WATER PUMPS (CENTRALIZED SYSTEM WITH DISTRIBUTED TERMINALS)

Performance Water Pumps (PWP) is a leading manufacturer of water pumps with high capacity capability. These pumps are used in both civil and private disaster situations. PWP's primary market is disaster recovery companies that assist home owners following basement flooding. They also sell to building contractors, municipalities, and rental companies. The company publishes an industry catalog of pumps and other auxiliary equipment, which is distributes to customers and prospective customers. PWP's headquarters and manufacturing facilities are in Leesville, Louisiana where they employ 125 manufacturing and clerical staff.

PWP employs a centralized computer system with distributed terminals in the departments. Recently they have been having operational problems with it. PWP has hired your auditing firm to assess its operations and internal control procedures.

Sales Order Procedures

The revenue process begins in the sales department of the firm where customers submit orders by fax, e-mail, or phone. A clerk in the sales department creates a sales order that details the items needed. Next, the sales clerk performs a credit check on the customer. If it is a returning customer, then the sales clerk checks the customer's payment history from the centralized credit records. For new customers a full credit check is performed via an online credit bureau. Once the sales clerk approves the creditworthiness of the customer, he prints a sales order, a packing slip, and a stock release document from his terminal. The clerk adds a record to the digital open sales order file and sends the hard copy sales order, packing slip, and stock release documents to the billing department, shipping department, and warehouse, respectively.

When the warehouse receives the stock release, a warehouse clerk arranges for the merchandise to be sent to the shipping department, along with the stock release document. Finally, the warehouse clerk updates the inventory subsidiary ledger from the terminal in the warehouse.

When the shipping department receives clerk the stock release, he compares it to the packing slip previously received from the sales department. The clerk then prepares a bill of lading, which accompanies the goods to the carrier. Finally, the shipping clerk records the shipment in the digital shipping log.

Upon receipt of the sales order, the billing department clerk adds prices and freight charges to create a sales invoice, which is sent to the customer. From the department terminal, the clerk then updates the digital account receivable subsidiary ledger and records the sales details in the sales journal. At the end of the day the billing department clerk prints a hard-copy account receivable summary and sales journal voucher, which she sends to the general ledger department.

Upon receipt of the account receivable summary and the sales journal voucher, the general ledger department clerk updates the general ledger and posts the voucher details to the journal voucher file from the department terminal.

Cash Receipts Procedures

Mail room clerks open customer cash receipts, reviews the check and remittance advices for completeness, and prepares two copies of a remittance list. One copy is sent with the checks to the cash receipts department. The second copy the remittance advices are sent to the billing department.

When the cash receipts clerk receives the checks and remittance list, he verifies the checks received against those on the remittance list and signs the checks "For Deposit Only." Once the checks are endorsed, he records the receipts in the cash receipts journal from his terminal. The clerk then fills out a deposit slip and deposits the checks in the bank. At the end of the day, the clerk prints a hard-copy cash receipts journal voucher and sends it to the general ledger department.

Upon receipt of the remittances, the billing department clerk records the amounts in the account receivable subsidiary ledger from the department terminal. At day's end the clerk also prints a hard-copy AR summary and sends it to the general ledger department.

The general ledger department verifies the AR summary with the journal vouchers and then updates the journal voucher file and the general ledger with the verified transaction amounts.

Required

a. Create a data flow diagram of the current system.
b. Create a system flowchart of the existing system.
c. Analyze the physical internal control weaknesses in the system.
d. Describe the IT controls that should be in place in this system.
e. (Optional) Prepare a system flowchart of a redesigned computer-based system that resolves the control weaknesses that you identified. Explain your solution.

CHAPTER

5

The Expenditure Cycle Part I: Purchases and Cash Disbursements Procedures

Learning Objectives

After studying this chapter, you should:

- Recognize the fundamental tasks that constitute the purchases and cash disbursements process.
- Be able to identify the functional areas involved in purchases and cash disbursements activities, and trace the flow of these transactions through the organization.
- Be able to specify the documents, journals, and accounts that provide audit trails, promote the maintenance of historical records, and support internal decision making and financial reporting.
- Understand the risks associated with purchases and cash disbursements activities and be familiar with the controls that reduce these risks.
- Be aware of the operational features and the control implications of technologies used in purchases and cash disbursements systems.

The objective of the expenditure cycle is to convert the organization's cash into the physical materials and human resources it needs to conduct business. In this chapter, we concentrate on systems and procedures for acquiring raw materials and finished goods from suppliers. We examine payroll and fixed asset systems in Chapter 6.

Most business entities operate on a credit basis and do not pay for resources until after acquiring them. The time lag between these events splits the procurement process into two phases: (1) the physical phase, involving the acquisition of the resource and (2) the financial phase, involving the disbursement of cash. As a practical matter, these are treated as independent transactions that are processed through separate subsystems.

This chapter examines the principal features of the two major subsystems that constitute the expenditure cycle: (1) the purchases processing subsystem and (2) the cash disbursements subsystem. The chapter is organized into two main sections. The first section provides an overview of the conceptual system, including the logical tasks, the key entities, the sources and uses of information, and the flow of key documents through an organization. The second section deals with physical systems, which are composed, to varying degrees, of technology and human activity. This section reviews system options that lie at different points on the technology/human continuum. Two objectives drive this discussion. The first is to illustrate system functionality, efficiency issues, and work flow characteristics of different technologies. The second is to demonstrate how internal control issues differ between systems at various points on the technology/human continuum. As part of this discussion, we examine basic technology systems and advanced integrated systems. We conclude the chapter with an overview of electronic data interchange (EDI).

The Conceptual System

OVERVIEW OF PURCHASES AND CASH DISBURSEMENTS ACTIVITIES

In this section, we examine the expenditure cycle conceptually. Using data flow diagrams (DFDs) as a guide, we will trace the sequence of activities through the purchases processing and cash disbursements procedures. Payroll and fixed asset systems, which also support the expenditure cycle, are covered in Chapter 6.

As in Chapter 4, the conceptual system discussion is intended to be technology-neutral. The tasks described in this section may be performed manually or by computer. At this point, our focus is on what (conceptually) needs to be done, not how (physically) it is accomplished. At various stages in the processes, we will examine specific documents, journals, and ledgers as they are encountered. Again, this review is technology-neutral. These documents and files may be physical (hard copy) or digital (computer generated). Later in this chapter, we examine examples of physical systems.

Purchases Processing Procedures

Purchases procedures include the tasks involved in identifying inventory needs, placing the order, receiving the inventory, and recognizing the liability. The relationships between these tasks are presented with the DFD in Figure 5-1. In general, these procedures apply to both manufacturing and retailing firms. A major difference between the two business types lies in the way purchases are authorized. Manufacturing firms purchase raw materials for production, and their purchasing decisions are authorized by the production planning and control function. These procedures are described in Chapter 7. Merchandising firms purchase finished goods for resale. The inventory control function provides the purchase authorization for this type of firm.

MONITOR INVENTORY RECORDS. Firms deplete their inventories by transferring raw materials into the production process (the conversion cycle) and by selling finished goods to customers (revenue cycle). Our illustration assumes the latter case, in which inventory control monitors and records finished goods at inventory levels. When inventories drop to a predetermined reorder point, a **purchase requisition** is prepared and sent to the prepare purchase order function to initiate the purchase process. Recall that the task of identifying a low-level inventory condition and creating a purchase requisition is a revenue cycle activity that was described in detail in Chapter 4. Figure 5-2 presents an example of a purchase requisition.

For efficiency and control purposes, the purchase requisition contains routine ordering information taken from the inventory subsidiary ledger and **valid vendor file.** This includes the name and address of the primary supplier, the economic order quantity[1] of the item, and the standard or expected unit cost of the item. Providing this information to the purchasing agent allows him or her to deal with routine purchases as efficiently as good control permits and to devote his or her primary efforts to nonroutine problems such as sourcing scarce, expensive, or unusual inventory items. The valid vendor file provides an important control by listing only approved vendors. The purpose is to ensure that the organization purchases inventories only from authorized vendors. This helps to reduce certain vendor fraud schemes such as an agent buying from suppliers with whom he or she has a relationship (a relative or friend) or buying at excessive prices from vendors in exchange for a kickback or bribe.

Although procedures vary from firm to firm, typically a separate purchase requisition is prepared for each inventory item as the need is recognized. This often results in multiple purchase requisitions for a single vendor. The purchase requisitions therefore need to be combined into a

1 The economic order quantity model and other inventory models are covered in Chapter 7.

FIGURE 5-1 DFD FOR PURCHASE SYSTEM

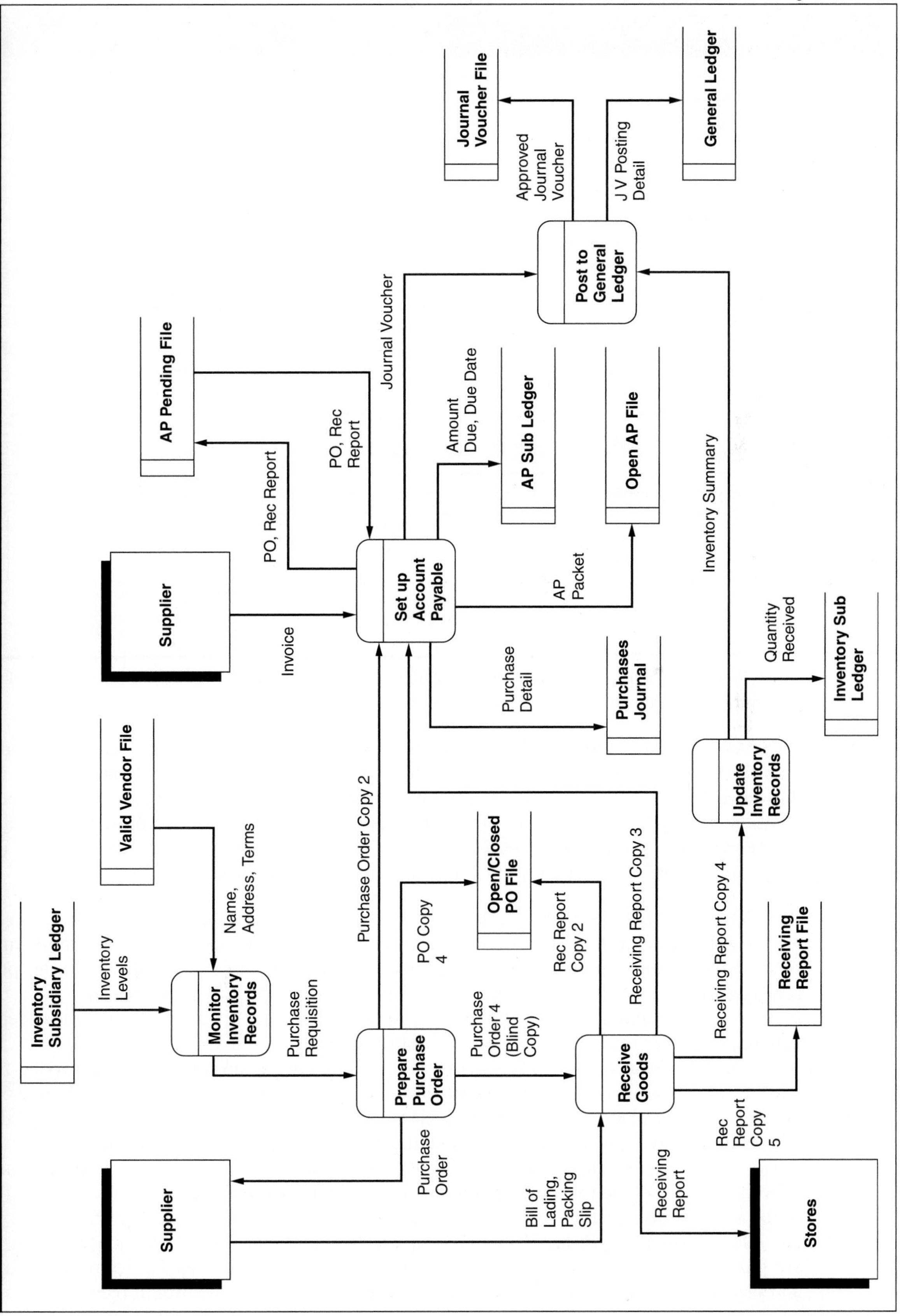

FIGURE 5-2 **PURCHASE REQUISITION**

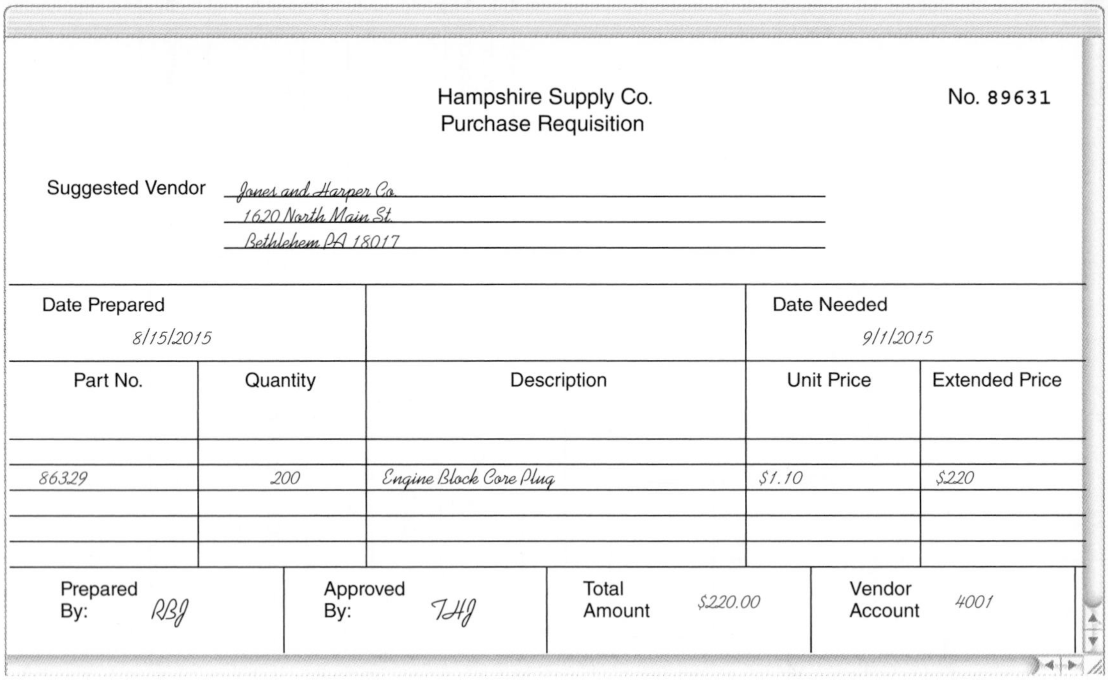

Hampshire Supply Co.
Purchase Requisition

No. 89631

Suggested Vendor Jones and Harper Co.
1620 North Main St.
Bethlehem PA 18017

Date Prepared		Date Needed	
8/15/2015		9/1/2015	

Part No.	Quantity	Description	Unit Price	Extended Price
86329	200	Engine Block Core Plug	$1.10	$220

Prepared By: RBJ	Approved By: THJ	Total Amount $220.00	Vendor Account 4001

single purchase order (discussed next), which is then sent to the vendor. In this type of system, each purchase order is associated with one or more purchase requisitions.

PREPARE PURCHASE ORDER. The prepare purchase order function receives the purchase requisitions, which are then sorted by vendor if necessary. Next a **purchase order** (PO), which is illustrated in Figure 5-3, is prepared for each vendor. A copy of the PO is sent to the vendor. In addition, a copy is sent to the set up accounts payable (AP) function for filing temporarily in the AP pending file, and a blind copy is sent to the receive goods function, where it is held until the inventories arrive. The last copy is filed in the **open/closed purchase order file.**

RECEIVE GOODS. Most firms encounter a time lag (sometimes a significant one) between placing the order and receiving the inventory. During this time, the copies of the PO reside in temporary files in various departments. Note that no economic event has yet occurred. At this point, the firm has received no inventories and incurred no financial obligation. Hence, there is no basis for making a formal entry into any accounting record. However, firms often make memo entries of pending inventory receipts and associated obligations.

The next event in the expenditure cycle is the receipt of the inventory. Goods arriving from the vendor are reconciled with the blind copy of the PO. The **blind copy**, illustrated in Figure 5-4, contains no quantity or price information about the products being received. The purpose of the blind copy is to force the receiving clerk to count and inspect inventories prior to completing the receiving report. At times, receiving docks are very busy, and receiving staff are under pressure to unload the delivery trucks and sign the bills of lading so the truck drivers can go on their way. If receiving clerks are provided quantity information, they may be tempted to accept deliveries on the basis of this information alone, rather than verify the quantity and condition of the goods. Shipments that are missing items or contain damaged or incorrect items must be detected before the firm accepts and places the goods in inventory. The blind copy is an important control in reducing this risk.

FIGURE 5-3 PURCHASE ORDER

Hampshire Supply Co.
Purchase Order

No. 23591

Please show the above number on all shipping documents and invoices.

To : Jones and Harper Co.
1620 North Main St.
Bethlehem PA 18017

Vendor Number	Date Ordered		Date Needed	Purchasing Agent	Terms
4001	8/15/15		9/1/15	J. Buell	2/10, n/30
Purchase Req. No.	Part No.	Quantity	Description	Unit Price	Extended Price
89631	86329	200	Engine Block Core Plug	$ 1.10	$220.00
89834	20671	100	Brake Shoes	9.50	950.00
89851	45218	10	Spring Compressors	33.00	330.00
Prepared By : BKG		Approved By : RMS		Total Amount	$1,500.00

FIGURE 5-4 BLIND COPY PURCHASE ORDER

Hampshire Supply Co.
Purchase Order

No. 23591

Please show the above number on all shipping documents and invoices.

To : Jones and Harper Co.
1620 North Main St.
Bethlehem PA 18017

Vendor Number	Date Ordered		Date Needed	Purchasing Agent	Terms
4001	8/15/15		9/1/15	J. Buell	2/10, n/30
Purchase Req. No.	Part No.	Quantity	Description	Unit Price	Extended Price
89631	86329		Engine Block Core Plug		
89834	20671		Brake Shoes		
89851	45218		Spring Compressors		
Prepared By : BKG		Approved By : RMS		Total Amount	

FIGURE 5-5 RECEIVING REPORT

Hampshire Supply Co.
Receiving Report

No. 62311

Vendor	Jones and Harper Co.	Shipped Via :	Vendor
Purchase Order No.	23591	Date Received	9/1/15

Part No.	Quantity	Description	Condition
86329	200	Engine Block Core Plug	Good
20671	100	Brake Shoes	Good
45218	10	Spring Compressors	Ear on one unit bent

Received By:	Inspected By:	Delivered To:
RTS	LEW	DYT

Upon completion of the physical count and inspection, the receiving clerk prepares a **receiving report** stating the quantity and condition of the inventories. Figure 5-5 presents an example of a receiving report. One copy of the receiving report accompanies the physical inventories to either the raw materials storeroom or finished goods warehouse for safekeeping. Another copy is filed in the open/closed PO file to close out the PO. A third copy of the receiving report is sent to the set up account payable function, where it is filed in the **AP pending file.** A fourth copy of the receiving report is sent to inventory control for updating the inventory records. Finally, a copy of the receiving report is placed in the **receiving report file.**

UPDATE INVENTORY RECORDS. Depending on the inventory valuation method in place, the inventory control procedures may vary somewhat among firms. Organizations that use a **standard cost system** carry their inventories at a predetermined standard value regardless of the price actually paid to the vendor. Figure 5-6 presents a copy of a standard cost inventory ledger.

Posting to a standard cost inventory ledger requires only information about the quantities received. Because the receiving report contains the quantity information, it serves this purpose. Updating an **actual cost inventory ledger** requires additional financial information, such as a copy of the supplier's invoice when it arrives.

SET UP ACCOUNTS PAYABLE. During the course of this transaction, the set up AP function has received and temporarily filed copies of the PO and receiving report. The organization has received inventories from the vendor and has incurred (realized) an obligation to pay for the goods.

At this point in the process, however, the firm has not received the **supplier's invoice**[2] containing the financial information needed to record the transaction. The firm will thus defer recording

2 Note that the supplier's invoice in the buyer's expenditure cycle is the sales invoice of the supplier's revenue cycle.

FIGURE 5-6 INVENTORY SUBSIDIARY LEDGER USING STANDARD COST

HAMPSHIRE MACHINE CO.									
Perpetual Inventory Record—Item #86329									
Item Description	Units Received	Units Sold	Qnty on Hand	Reorder Point	Qnty on Order	EOC	Vendor Number	Standard Cost	Total Inven. Cost
Engine Block Core Plug	200		200	30		200	4001	$1.10	$220
		30	170						$187
		20	150						$165

(recognizing) the liability until the invoice arrives. This common situation creates a slight lag (a few days) in the recording process, during which time the firm's liabilities are technically understated. As a practical matter, this misstatement is a problem only at period-end when the firm prepares financial statements. To close the books, the accountant will need to estimate the value of the obligation until the invoice arrives. If the estimate is materially incorrect, an adjusting entry must be made to correct the error. Because the receipt of the invoice typically triggers AP procedures, accountants need to be aware that unrecorded liabilities may exist at period-end closing.

When the invoice arrives, the AP clerk reconciles the financial information with the receiving report and PO in the AP pending file. This is called a three-way match, which verifies that what was ordered was received and is fairly priced. Once the reconciliation is complete, the AP clerk prepares an **AP packet**, which consists of the supporting documents (PO, receiving report, and invoice), and files the AP packet in the **open AP file.** Once reconciled, the AP packet is the formal authority to record the liability and subsequently make payment. Next, the transaction is recorded in the purchases journal and posted to the supplier's account in the **AP subsidiary ledger.** Figure 5-7 shows the relationship between these accounting records.

Recall that the inventory valuation method will determine how inventory control will have recorded the receipt of inventories. If the firm is using the actual cost method, the AP clerk will send a copy of the supplier's invoice to inventory control. If standard costing is used, this step is not necessary.

Finally, the AP clerk summarizes the entries in the purchases journal for the period (or batch) and prepares a journal voucher for the general ledger function (see Figure 5-7). Assuming the organization uses the perpetual inventory method, the journal entry will be:

	DR	CR
Inventory—Control	6,800.00	
Accounts Payable—Control		6,800.00

If the periodic inventory method is used, the entry will be:

	DR	CR
Purchases	6,800.00	6,800.00
Accounts Payable—Control		

Vouchers Payable System

As an alternative to the AP procedures described in the previous section, some firms use a **vouchers payable system.** Under this system, the AP department uses **cash disbursement vouchers** and maintains

FIGURE 5-7 RELATIONSHIP BETWEEN PURCHASE JOURNAL, AP SUBSIDIARY LEDGER, AND JOURNAL VOUCHER

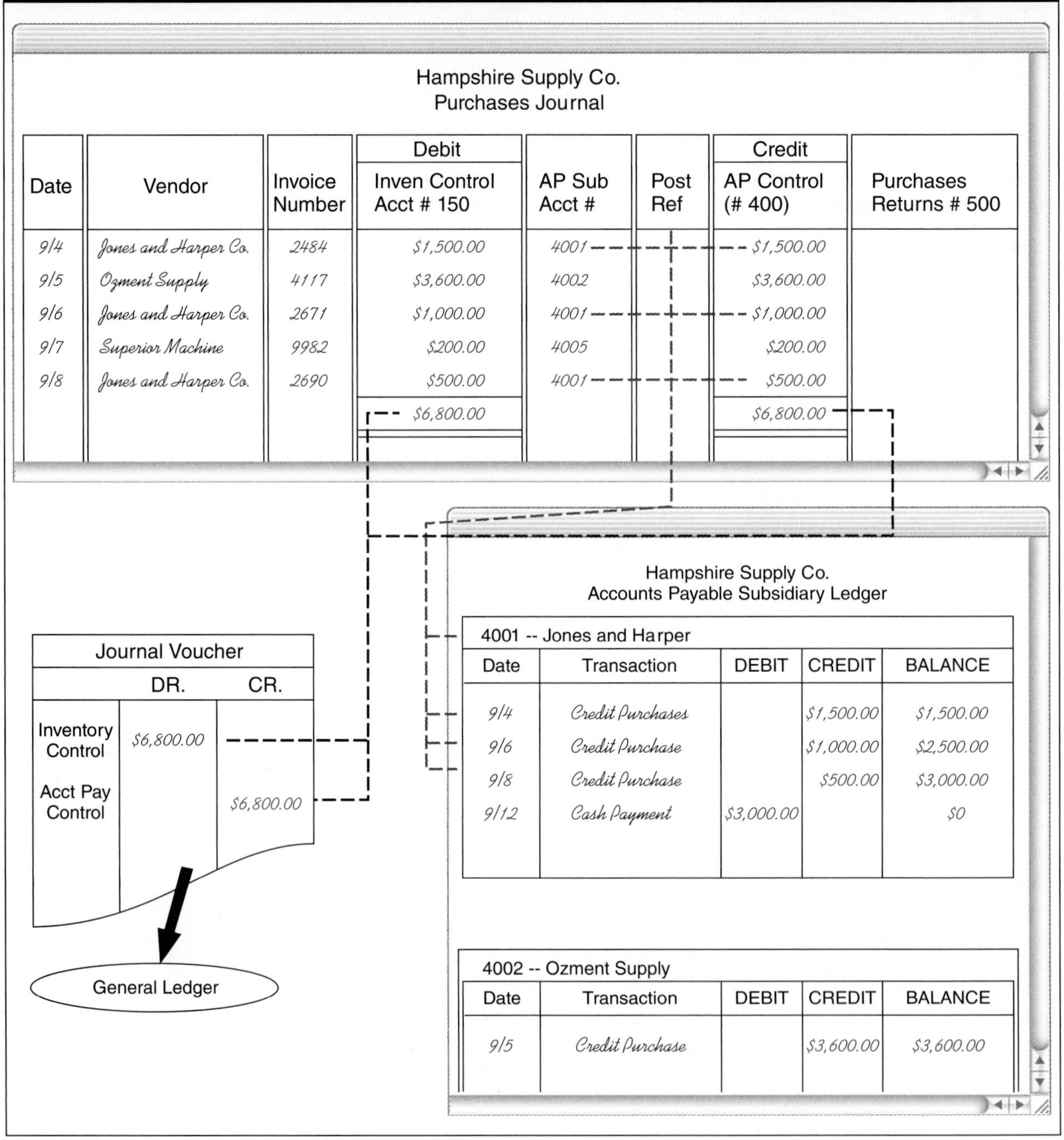

Hampshire Supply Co.
Purchases Journal

Date	Vendor	Invoice Number	Debit Inven Control Acct # 150	AP Sub Acct #	Post Ref	Credit AP Control (# 400)	Purchases Returns # 500
9/4	Jones and Harper Co.	2484	$1,500.00	4001		$1,500.00	
9/5	Ozment Supply	4117	$3,600.00	4002		$3,600.00	
9/6	Jones and Harper Co.	2671	$1,000.00	4001		$1,000.00	
9/7	Superior Machine	9982	$200.00	4005		$200.00	
9/8	Jones and Harper Co.	2690	$500.00	4001		$500.00	
			$6,800.00			$6,800.00	

Journal Voucher

	DR.	CR.
Inventory Control	$6,800.00	
Acct Pay Control		$6,800.00

General Ledger

Hampshire Supply Co.
Accounts Payable Subsidiary Ledger

4001 -- Jones and Harper

Date	Transaction	DEBIT	CREDIT	BALANCE
9/4	Credit Purchases		$1,500.00	$1,500.00
9/6	Credit Purchase		$1,000.00	$2,500.00
9/8	Credit Purchase		$500.00	$3,000.00
9/12	Cash Payment	$3,000.00		$0

4002 -- Ozment Supply

Date	Transaction	DEBIT	CREDIT	BALANCE
9/5	Credit Purchase		$3,600.00	$3,600.00

a voucher register. After the AP clerk performs the three-way match, he or she prepares a cash disbursement voucher to approve payment. Vouchers provide improved control over cash disbursements and allow firms to consolidate several payments to the same supplier on a single voucher, thus reducing the number of checks written. Figure 5-8 shows an example of a voucher.

Each voucher is recorded in the **voucher register,** as illustrated in Figure 5-9. The voucher register reflects the AP liability of the firm; the sum of the unpaid vouchers in the register (those with no check numbers and paid dates) is the firm's total AP balance. The AP clerk files the cash

FIGURE 5-8 CASH DISBURSEMENT VOUCHER

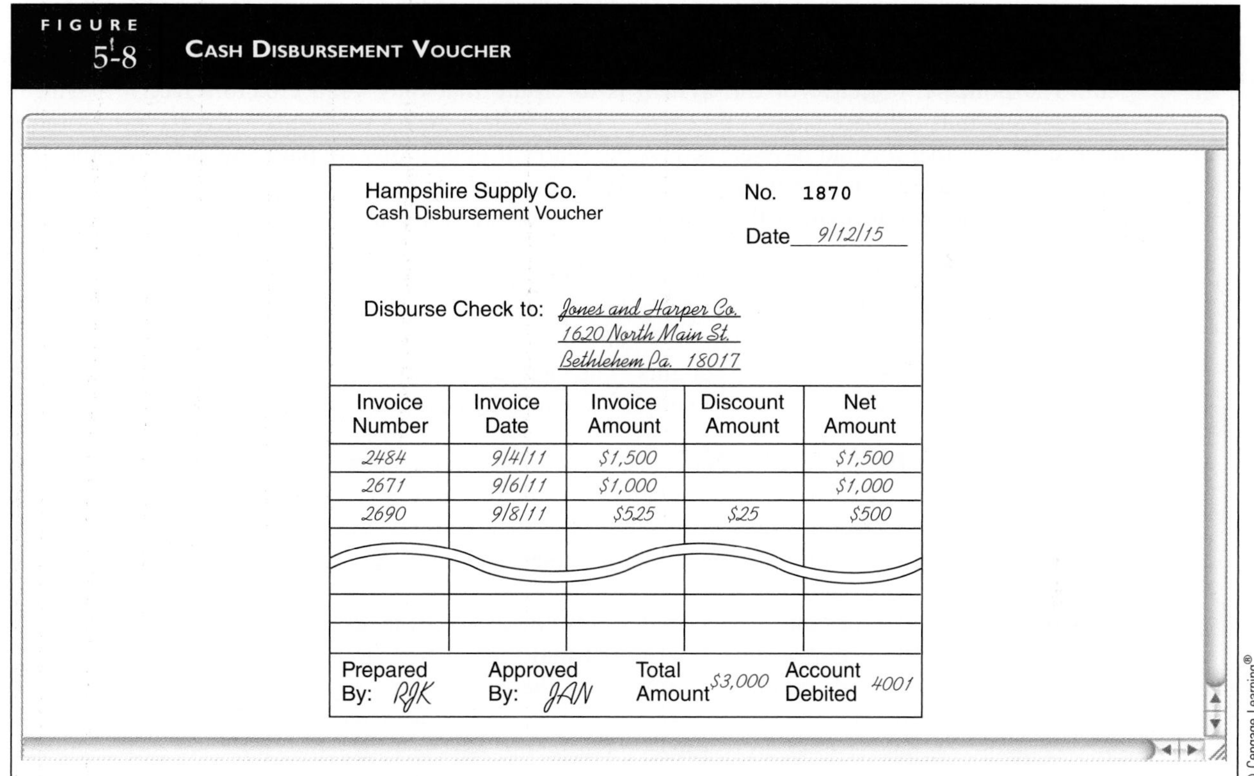

Hampshire Supply Co.
Cash Disbursement Voucher

No. 1870

Date 9/12/15

Disburse Check to: Jones and Harper Co.
1620 North Main St.
Bethlehem Pa. 18017

Invoice Number	Invoice Date	Invoice Amount	Discount Amount	Net Amount
2484	9/4/11	$1,500		$1,500
2671	9/6/11	$1,000		$1,000
2690	9/8/11	$525	$25	$500

Prepared By: RJK   Approved By: JAN   Total Amount $3,000   Account Debited 4001

disbursement voucher, along with supporting source documents, in the **vouchers payable file.** This file is equivalent to the open AP file discussed earlier.

POST TO GENERAL LEDGER. The general ledger function receives a journal voucher from the AP department and an account summary from inventory control. The general ledger function posts the data contained in the journal voucher to the inventory and AP control accounts and reconciles the inventory control account with the inventory subsidiary summary. The journal voucher is then filed in the approved journal voucher file. With this step, the purchases phase of the expenditure cycle is completed.

FIGURE 5-9 VOUCHER REGISTER

Hampshire Supply Co.
Voucher Register

Date	Voucher No.	Paid		Voucher Payable (Credit)	Merchandise Debit	Supplies Debit	Selling Expense Debit	Administrative Expense Debit	Fixed Assets Debit	Misc. Debits	
		Check No.	Date							Acct. No.	Amount
9/12/15	1870	104	9/14	$3,000	$3,000						
9/13/15	1871			$3,600		$3,600					
9/14/15	1872	105	9/15	$500			$500				

The Cash Disbursements System

The cash disbursements system processes the payment of obligations created in the purchases system. The principal objective of this system is to ensure that only valid creditors receive payment and that amounts paid are timely and correct. If the system makes payments early, the firm forgoes interest income that it could have earned on the funds. If obligations are paid late, however, the firm will lose purchase discounts or may damage its credit standing. Figure 5-10 presents a DFD conceptually depicting the information flows and key tasks of the cash disbursements system.

IDENTIFY LIABILITIES DUE. The cash disbursements process begins in the AP department, where each day the AP clerk reviews the open AP file for items due for payment. Typically, this file is organized by payment due date to ensure that debts are paid on the last possible date without missing due dates and losing discounts. The clerk sends payment approval in the form of the AP packet (PO, receiving report, and supplier's invoice) to the cash disbursements department.

PREPARE CASH DISBURSEMENT. The cash disbursements clerk receives the AP packet and reviews the documents for completeness and clerical accuracy. For each disbursement, the clerk prepares a check and records the check number, dollar amount, and other pertinent data in the **check register,** which is also called the **cash disbursements journal.** Figure 5-11 shows an example of a check register.

Depending on the organization's materiality threshold, the check may require additional approval by the cash disbursements department manager or treasurer (not shown in Figure 5-10). The negotiable portion of the check is mailed to the supplier; a copy of it is attached to the AP packet as proof of payment; and a check copy is filed in the department. The clerk marks the documents in the packet paid and returns them to the AP clerk. Finally, the cash disbursements clerk summarizes the entries made to the check register and sends a journal voucher with the following journal entry in to the general ledger function:

	DR	CR
Accounts Payable	XXXX.XX	
Cash		XXXX.XX

UPDATE AP RECORD. Upon receipt of the paid AP packet, the AP clerk removes the liability by debiting the vendor's AP subsidiary ledger account. The AP packet is then filed in the **closed AP file,** and an account summary is prepared and sent to the general ledger function.

POST TO GENERAL LEDGER. The general ledger function receives the journal voucher from cash disbursements and the AP account summary from accounts payable. The voucher shows the total reductions in the firm's obligations and cash account as a result of payments to suppliers. These numbers are reconciled with the AP summary, and the AP control and cash accounts in the general ledger are updated accordingly. The approved journal voucher is then filed. This concludes the cash disbursements procedures.

Physical Systems

We saw in Chapter 4 that physical accounting information systems are a combination of computer technology and human activity. The mix of possible technology/human options creates a continuum. At one end are minimal technology systems that rely heavily on human involvement and manual procedures. At the other end of the continuum are advanced technology systems, which replace human activity with automated processes.

Systems at different points on the continuum operate differently and present different internal control issues. The objectives of this section are to: (1) illustrate AIS functionality and work flow patterns under different levels of technology, and (2) demonstrate how the internal control profile changes as the technology/human mix changes. To accomplish this we review examples of systems at different

FIGURE 5-10 DFD FOR CASH DISBURSEMENTS SYSTEM

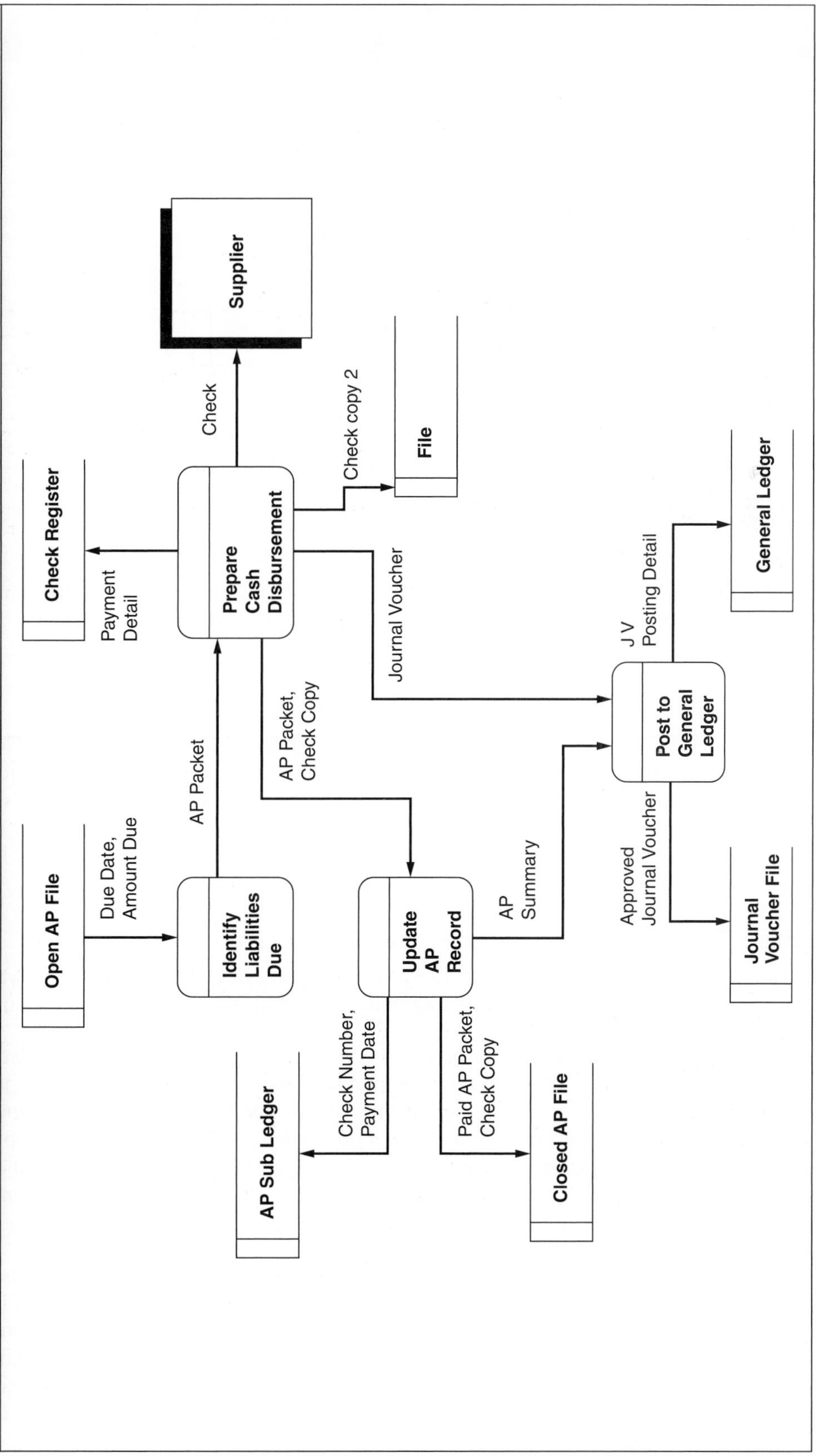

Open AP File
Due Date, Amount Due
Identify Liabilities Due
AP Packet
Prepare Cash Disbursement
Payment Detail
Check Register
Check
Supplier
Check copy 2
File
Journal Voucher
AP Packet, Check Copy
Update AP Record
Check Number, Payment Date
AP Sub Ledger
Paid AP Packet, Check Copy
Closed AP File
AP Summary
Post to General Ledger
J V Posting Detail
General Ledger
Approved Journal Voucher
Journal Voucher File

FIGURE 5-11 CASH DISBURSEMENTS JOURNAL (CHECK REGISTER)

Cash Disbursements Journal

Date	Check No.	Voucher No.	Description	Credit: Cash	Credit: Purch. Disc.	GL / Subsidiary Account Debited	Posted	AP 401	Freight-in 516	Op Expen 509	Other	Posted
9/4/15	101	1867	Martin Motors	$500		Auto					$500	✓
9/4/15	102	1868	Pen Power	$100		Utility	✓			$100		
9/12/15	103	1869	Acme Auto	$500		Purchases					$500	✓
9/14/15	104	1870	Jones and Harper	$3,000				$3,000				

points on the continuum. The first example is a basic technology system that employs independent PCs, which function primarily as record keeping devices. The second example is an advanced technology system that integrates all business functions through a centralized computer application.

BASIC TECHNOLOGY EXPENDITURE CYCLE

This section presents examples of basic technology expenditure cycle systems. The computers used in these systems are independent (non-networked) PCs. Therefore, information flows between departments are communicated via hard-copy documents. In addition, in such systems, maintaining physical files of source documents is critical to the audit trail. As we walk through the flowcharts, notice that in many departments, after an individual completes his or her assigned task, documents are filed as evidence that the tasks were performed.

Basic Technology Purchases Processing System

The system flowchart in Figure 5-12 shows the processes, documents, and data files of a basic technology sales order system. The following sections outline the key activities in this system.

INVENTORY CONTROL. The process begins when the inventory control clerk prints purchase requisitions from his PC by accessing the **purchase requisition file.** Recall that this file was created during the sales activity when the inventories dropped to their predetermined reorder point. One copy of the requisition is sent to the purchasing department, and one copy is placed in the hard-copy **open purchase requisition file.** Note that to provide proper authorization control, the inventory control department is segregated from the purchasing department, which executes the purchase transaction.

PURCHASING DEPARTMENT. The purchasing department receives the purchase requisitions, sorts them by vendor, and adds a record to the digital **open purchase order file.** The clerk then prints a multipart PO for each vendor. One copy of the PO is sent to the vendor. One copy is sent to inventory control, where the clerk files it with the open purchase requisition. One copy of the PO is sent to the AP for filing in the AP pending file. One copy (the blind copy) is sent to the receiving department, where it is filed until the inventories arrive. The clerk files the last copy along with the purchase requisition in the department.

FIGURE 5-12 BASIC TECHNOLOGY PURCHASES SYSTEM

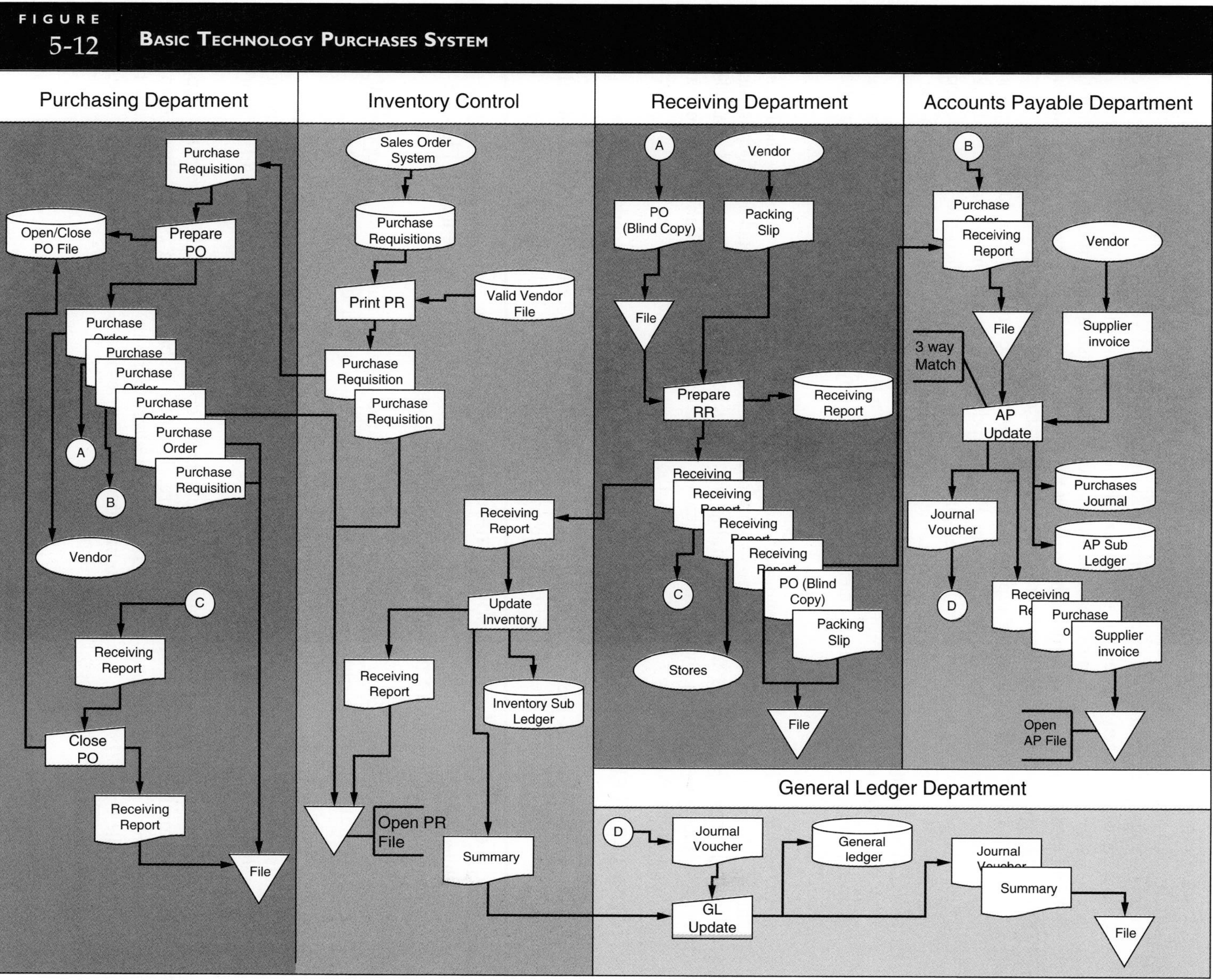

RECEIVING. The receiving department clerk receives the goods and the packing slip from the vendor and reconciles the goods with the blind copy of the PO. Upon completion of the physical count and inspection, the receiving clerk adds a digital record to the receiving report file and prints a multipart hard-copy receiving report stating the quantity and condition of the inventories. One copy of the receiving report accompanies the physical inventories to the storeroom. Another copy is sent to the purchasing department, where the purchasing clerk reconciles it with the open PO and closes the digital record in the open PO file. The purchasing clerk then files the hard-copy receiving report along with the previously filed purchase requisition and PO.

A third copy of the receiving report is sent to inventory control where (assuming a standard cost system) the clerk uses the department PC to update the digital inventory subsidiary ledger. The system automatically removes the "on-order" flag that was set when the purchase requisition was created. The inventory control clerk then files the hard-copy receiving report in the department, along with the PO and the purchase requisition.

A fourth copy of the receiving report is sent to the AP department, where it is filed in the AP pending file. Finally, the receiving clerk files the blind copy PO and the packing slip in the receiving department.

AP DEPARTMENT. When the supplier's invoice arrives, the AP clerk reconciles the invoice, purchase order, and receiving report (three-way match) and prepares an AP packet, which in this paper-oriented system is simply a folder containing the reconciled supporting documents. The clerk next records the transaction in the digital purchases journal, and posts the liability to the supplier's account in the AP subsidiary ledger. The clerk then files the AP packet in the open AP file.

GENERAL LEDGER DEPARTMENT. The general ledger department receives a journal voucher from the AP department and an account summary from inventory control. The general ledger clerk reconciles these and posts to the inventory and AP control accounts. With this step, the purchases phase of the expenditure cycle is completed.

Basic Technology Cash Disbursements System

A detailed system flowchart of a basic cash disbursements system is presented in Figure 5-13. The tasks performed in each of the key processes are discussed next.

AP DEPARTMENT. Each day, the AP clerk reviews the AP packets in the open AP file for items due, and sends the supporting documents to the cash disbursements department.

CASH DISBURSEMENTS DEPARTMENT. The cash disbursements clerk receives the AP packets and reviews the documents for completeness and clerical accuracy. For each disbursement, the clerk prepares a three-part check and records the check number, dollar amount, and other pertinent data in the check register.

The check, along with the supporting documents, goes to the cash disbursements department manager, or treasurer, for his or her signature. The negotiable portion of the check is mailed to the supplier. The clerk returns the AP packet and check copy to the AP department and files one copy of the check. Finally, the clerk summarizes the entries made to the check register and sends a journal voucher to the general ledger department.

AP DEPARTMENT. Upon receipt of the AP packet, the AP clerk removes the liability by debiting the vendor's digital AP subsidiary record. Next, the AP packet is filed in the closed AP file. Finally, the clerk sends an AP summary to the general ledger department.

GENERAL LEDGER DEPARTMENT. Based on the journal voucher from cash disbursements and the account summary from AP, the general ledger clerk uses the department PC to post to the general ledger control accounts and files the documents. This concludes the cash disbursements procedures.

FIGURE 5-13 Basic Technology Cash Disbursements System

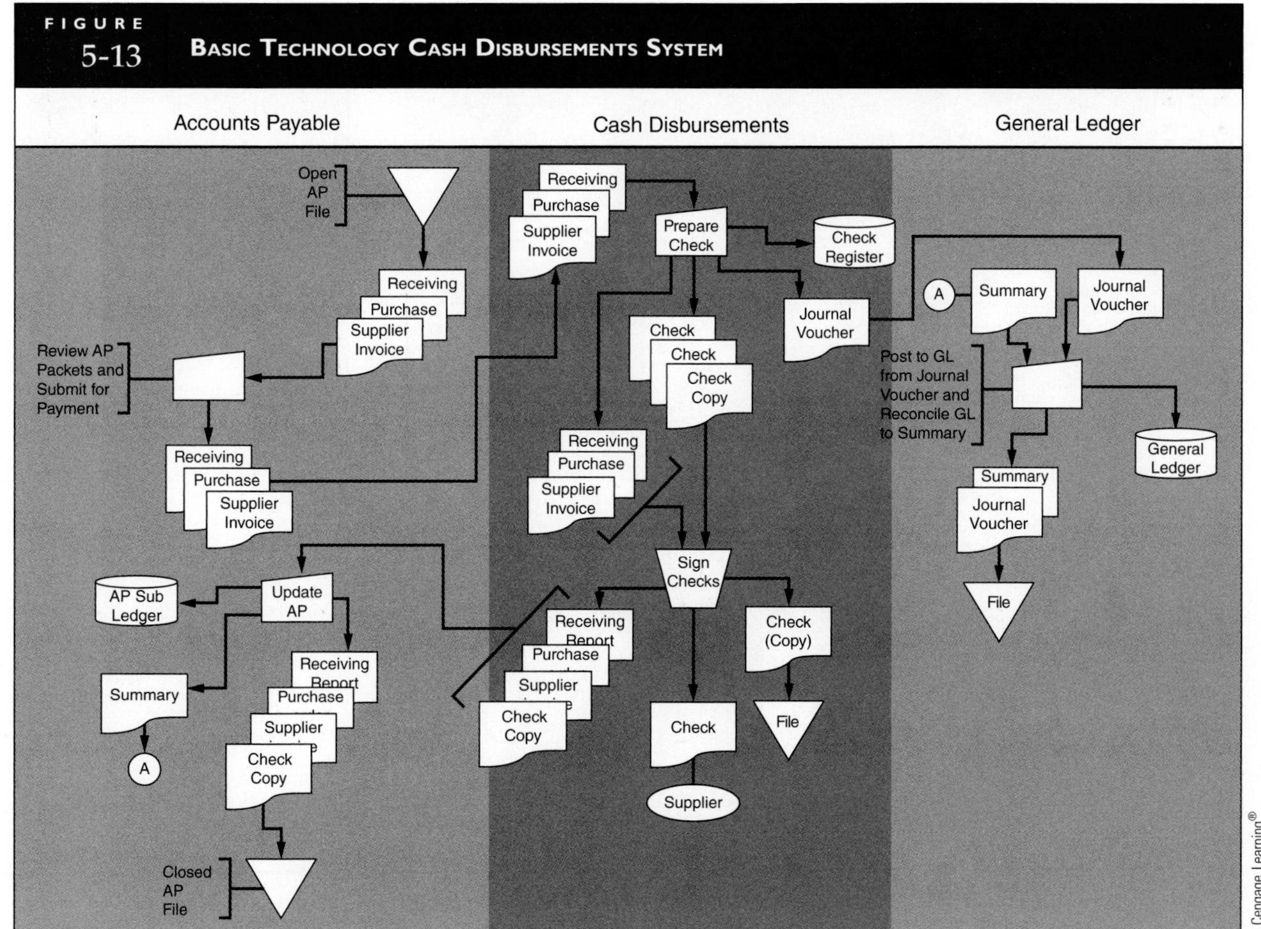

ADVANCED TECHNOLOGY EXPENDITURE CYCLE

Recall from Chapter 4 that the purpose of advanced technologies in AIS is to integrate accounting and other business functions through a common information system. Integration improves operational performance and reduces costs by eliminating nonvalue-added tasks. In this section, we see how advanced technologies can significantly alter and simplify the expenditure cycle, compared to the basic technology system presented in the previous section. We begin by reviewing the operational features of an integrated purchases system, and then we examine an integrated cash disbursements system.

INTEGRATED PURCHASES PROCESSING SYSTEM

The flowchart in Figure 5-14 illustrates an integrated purchase system. Notice that the level of departmental activity is significantly lower than that of the basic technology system presented in Figure 5-12. Labor-intensive activities that characterize the basic technology system add greatly to the cost of system operation and result in human error. In the advanced technology system, computer programs perform many clerical tasks, which is much cheaper and far less prone to error. Although the traditional department structure still exists in advanced technology environments, personnel responsibilities are refocused on financial analysis and exception-based problem solving, rather than on day-to-day clerical tasks. As a result, these departments are smaller and more efficient than their basic technology counterparts. Each phase of this reengineered system is described next.

FIGURE 5-14 INTEGRATED PURCHASES SYSTEM

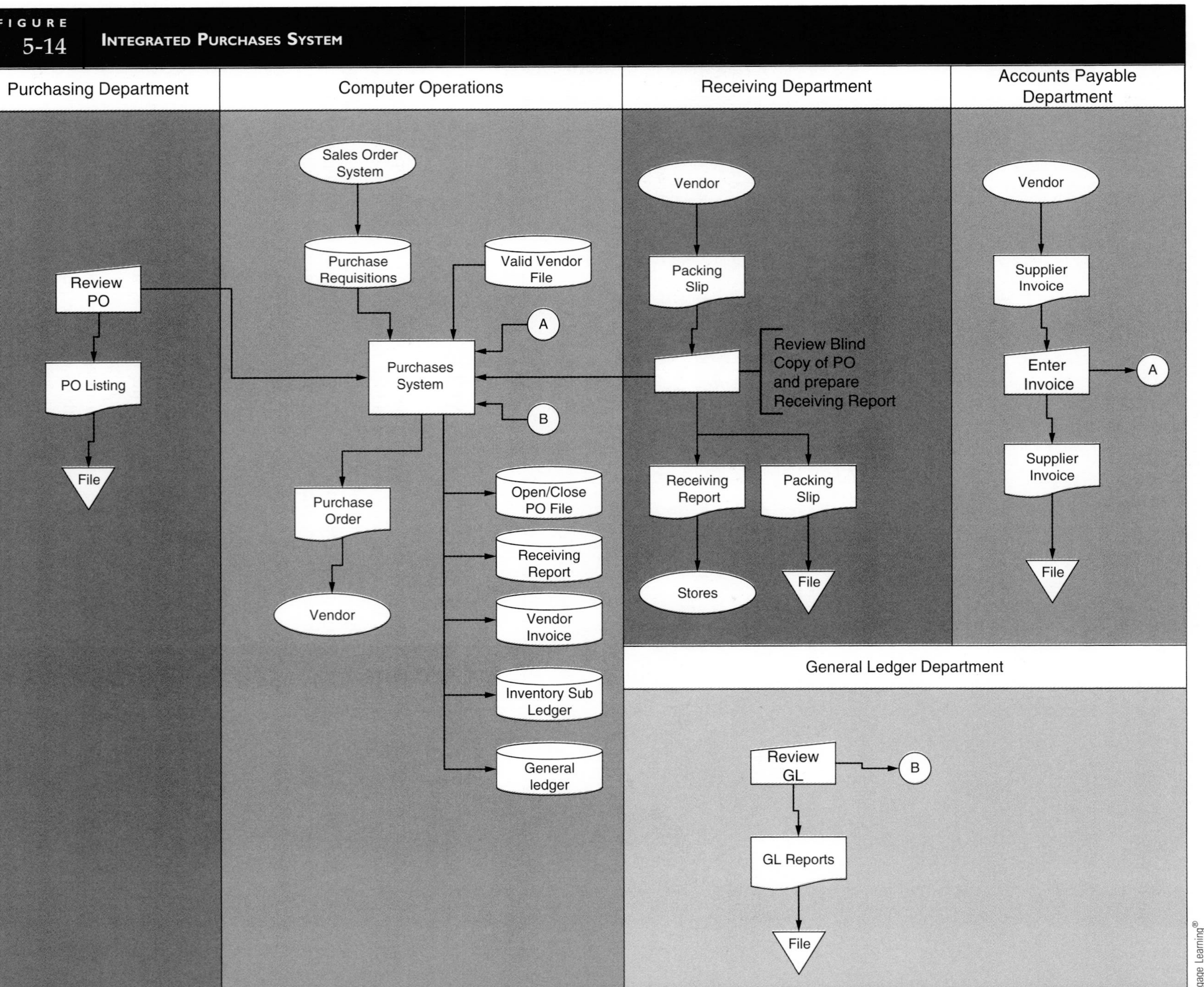

Computer Operations

The purchases computer application performs the following tasks automatically.

1. The system reads the purchases requisition file for items that need to be replenished. The requisitions are then sorted by the vendor and matched against the valid vendor file for vendor address and contact information.
2. Hard-copy purchase orders are prepared and sent to the vendor.
3. A record is added to the open PO file.
4. A digital transaction listing of POs is created, which is downloaded by the purchasing agent, reviewed, and filed in the department.

Receiving Department

When the goods arrive, the receiving clerk accesses a blind copy of the open PO file in real time by entering the PO number taken from the packing slip. The receiving screen, illustrated in Figure 5-15, then prompts the clerk to enter the quantities received for each item on the PO. The following tasks are performed automatically by the system.

1. A record is added to the receiving report file.
2. Quantities of items received are matched against the open PO record, and the PO is closed by placing the receiving report number in the PO closed flag. Figure 5-16 presents possible structures for the PO and receiving report files.
3. The inventory subsidiary records are updated to reflect the receipt of the inventory items.
4. The general ledger inventory control account is updated.

Accounts Payable Department

When the AP clerk receives the supplier's invoice, the clerk accesses the system and adds a record to the vendor invoice file. The clerk then files the hard-copy invoice in the department. The following tasks are performed automatically by the system.

1. Using the PO number as a common attribute, the system links the vendor invoice to the associated purchase order and receiving report records (see Figure 5-16).

FIGURE 5-15 RECEIVING SCREEN

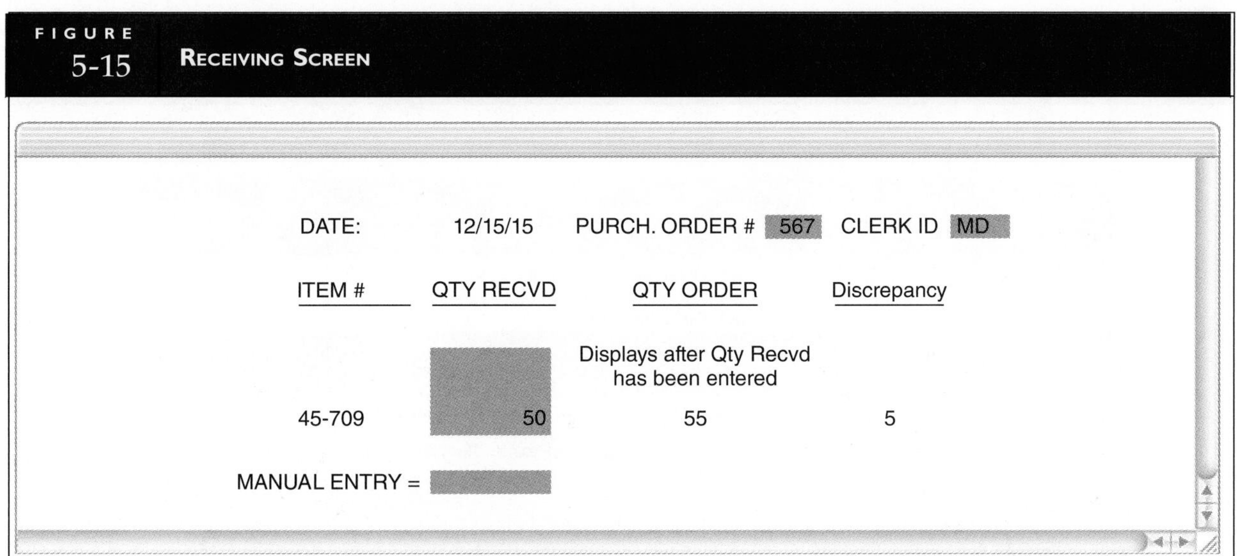

FIGURE 5-16 FILE STRUCTURE FOR AP SUPPORTING DOCUMENTS

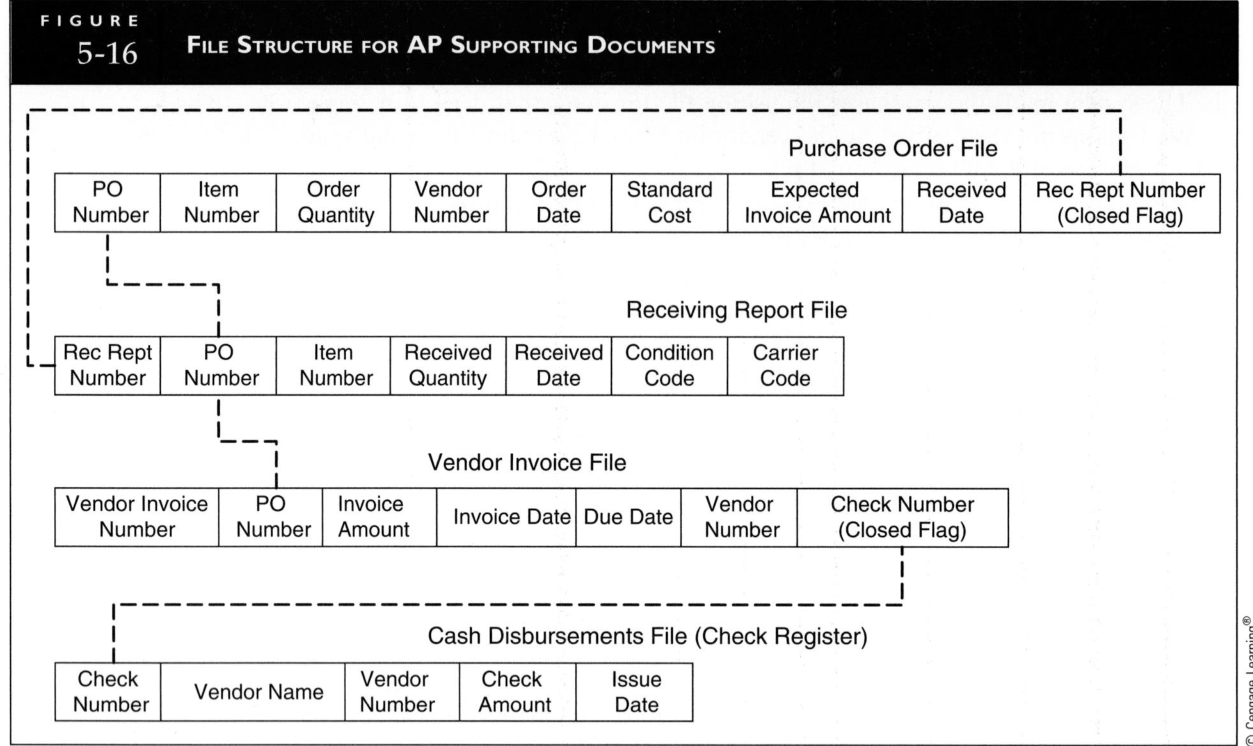

2. The system reconciles the supporting documents and creates a virtual AP packet to authorize payment.
3. The system displays the virtual AP packet on the AP clerk's computer screen for review. Figure 5-17 presents an example of an AP packet screen display. The virtual AP packet allows the AP clerk to browse the supporting documents and modify documents if necessary to reconcile quantity or price discrepancies that may exist.
4. Assuming no discrepancies that demand the AP clerk's intervention, the system automatically approves payment and sets a payment due date.

FIGURE 5-17 VIRTUAL AP PACKET

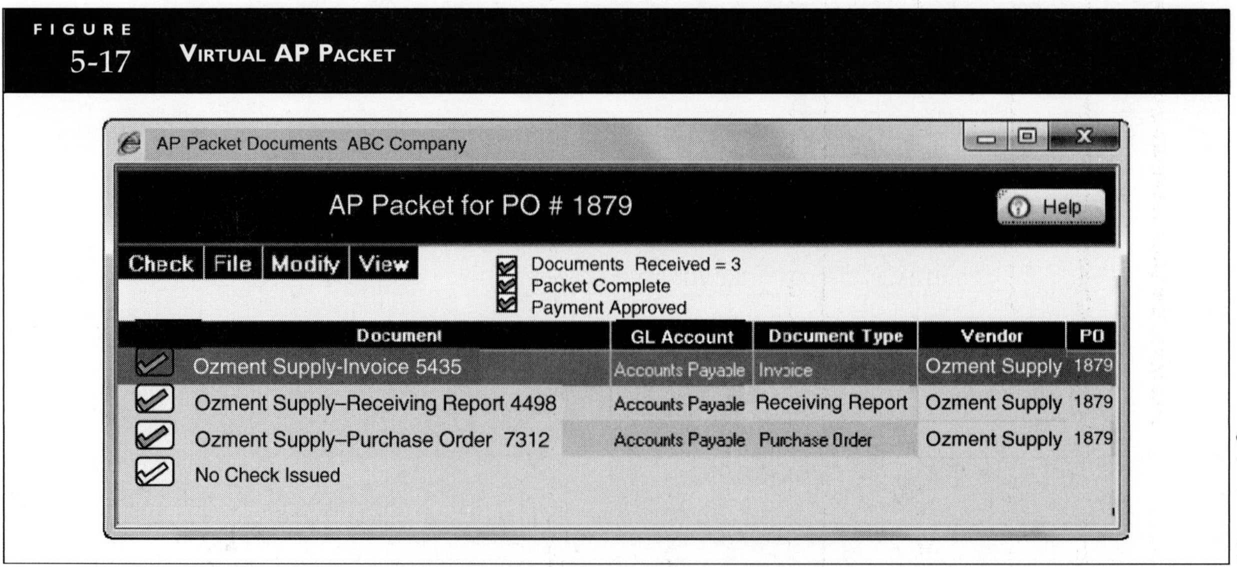

Many companies engaged in business-to-business (B2B) transactions use the vendor invoice file as a substitute for the traditional purchases journal and accounts payable subsidiary ledger. The invoices in the file provide a chronological record of total purchases for the period (equivalent to the purchases journal), and the unpaid invoices at any point in time constitute the organization's accounts payable.

INTEGRATED CASH DISBURSEMENTS SYSTEM

Figure 5-18 illustrates a cash disbursements system in which the organization makes vendor payments with hard-copy checks that are mailed to the vendor. Organizations that use electronic funds transfer (EFT) to transmit payments employ different procedures that are described in Chapter 12. Each day, the DUE DATE fields of the vendor invoice records are scanned for items due to be paid. The following procedures are performed on items that are due.

1. Checks are automatically printed, signed, and distributed to the mail room for mailing to vendors. Checks above a preset materiality threshold will receive additional signatures (not shown) prior to being mailed.
2. The payments are automatically recorded in the check register file.
3. Vendor invoices are closed by placing the check number in the closed flag field (see Figure 5-16).
4. The general ledger AP control and cash accounts are updated.
5. Reports detailing these transactions are transmitted via a terminal to the AP and cash disbursements departments for management review and filing.

FIGURE 5-18 INTEGRATED CASH DISBURSEMENTS SYSTEM

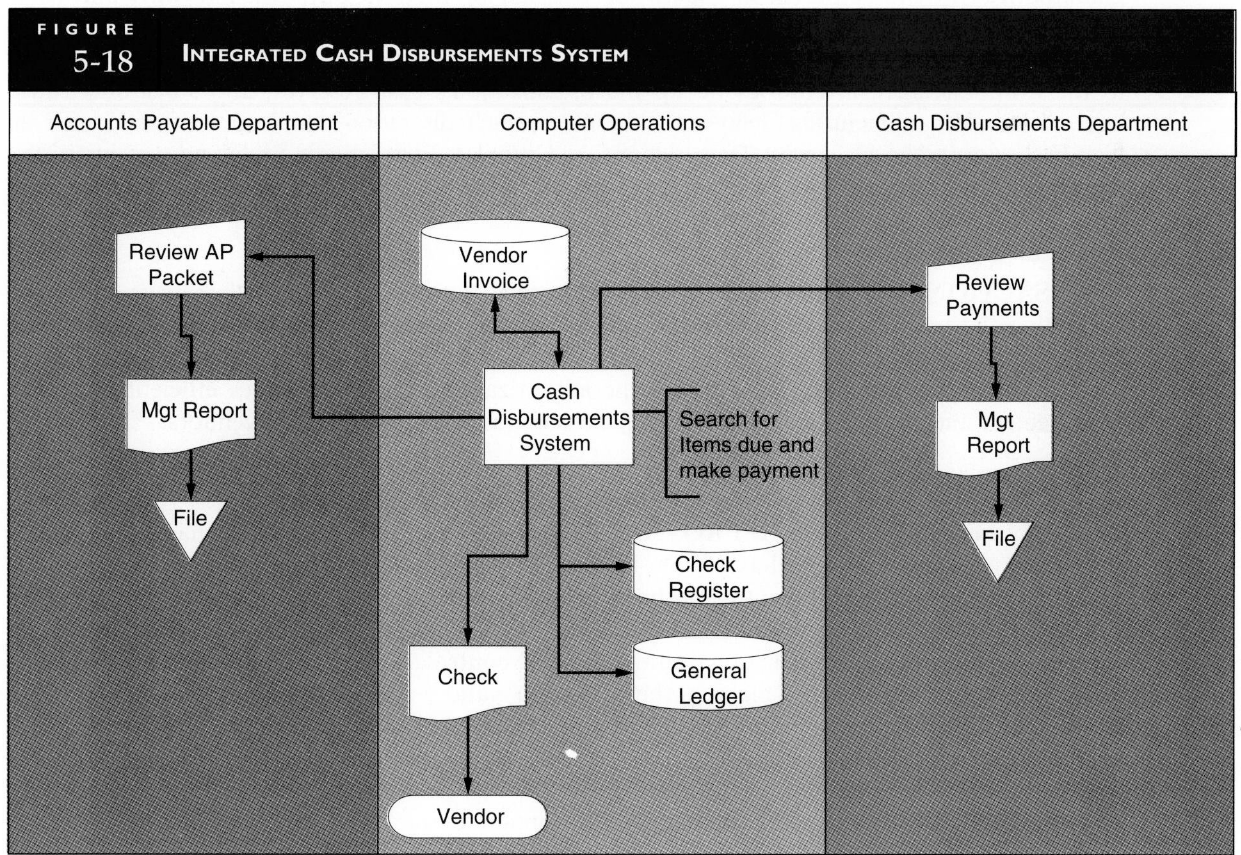

EXPENDITURE CYCLE RISKS AND INTERNAL CONTROLS

An objective of internal control is to mitigate the risk from errors and fraud. The following are the primary risks associated with expenditure cycle transactions:

- Unauthorized inventory purchases
- Receiving wrong items, incorrect quantities, or damaged goods
- Inaccurately recording purchases and cash disbursement transactions in journals and accounts
- Misappropriation of cash and inventory
- Unauthorized access to accounting records and confidential reports

To reiterate an important concept introduced in Chapter 3, internal control activities consist of: 1) physical controls, and 2) IT controls. The purpose of physical controls is to control the actions of people. These consist of six classes of internal control activities: transaction authorization, segregation of duties, supervision, accounting records, access control, and independent verification. IT controls are comprised of general controls and application controls. General controls are not specific to a particular cycle or subsystem and thus do not apply to expenditure cycle risks directly. Computer application controls consist of: input controls, processing controls, and output controls. The discussion that follows examines and compares how physical and IT control techniques apply in both basic technology and advanced technology systems to reduce the risks identified above. Table 5-1 at the end of the section provides a summary of this material.

Risk of Unauthorized Inventory Purchases

Unauthorized inventory purchases places the decision of what to buy, when to buy, and from whom to buy solely at the discretion of the purchasing agent. This can result in excessive inventory levels for some items, while others go out of stock. Either situation is potentially damaging to the firm. Excessive inventories tie up the organization's cash reserves, and stock-outs cause lost sales and manufacturing delays. Furthermore, such discretion can lead to frauds such as kick-backs to purchasing agents from unapproved suppliers who charge above-market prices for their inventory.

Physical Controls

TRANSACTION AUTHORIZATION. The objective of transaction authorization is to ensure that only valid transactions are processed. When inventory levels drop to their predetermined reorder points, inventory control formally authorizes replenishment with a purchase requisition to trigger the purchasing function. Formalizing the authorization process promotes efficient inventory management and ensures the legitimacy of purchase transactions with valid vendors.

IT Controls

AUTOMATED PURCHASE APPROVAL. The objective of automated purchase approval is to prevent unauthorized purchases from unapproved vendors. Therefore, computer logic, not a human being, decides when to purchase, what to purchase, and from which vendor. The key attributes needed to execute this logic come from the purchase requisition file and the valid vendor file. Proper functioning of this control depends on adequate procedures for identifying vendors and placing them on the valid vendor list. If access to the valid vendor file is not specifically controlled via password and/or encryption (discussed in Chapter 12), an unapproved vendor could be added to the file, and the control would be circumvented. To allow for operational flexibility in unusual circumstances, however, the system should provide a management override option to purchase from unapproved vendors, which may be performed only by a supervisor. Any such overrides should be fully documented in management reports.

Risk of Receiving Incorrect Items, Quantities, or Damaged Goods

The receiving department is responsible for inspecting and counting large quantities of valuable assets that arrive from vendors. Once inspected, a receiving report is prepared and the inventories are stored in the warehouse. Failure to perform the receiving task correctly places the firm at risk of accepting incorrect items, incomplete orders and damaged goods.

Physical Controls

INDEPENDENT VERIFICATION. When goods arrive from the supplier, receiving clerks verify that the items are correct in type and quantity and inspect them for condition (damage, spoilage, and so on). To perform this verification the clerk obtains a "blind copy" of the original PO from purchasing. A blind PO has all the relevant information about the goods being received except for the quantities and prices. To obtain quantity information, which is needed for the receiving report, the receiving personnel are forced to physically count and inspect the goods.

SUPERVISION. Supervision is critical at this point to ensure that the clerks properly carry out these important duties. Packing slips, which contain quantity information, and could be used to circumvent the inspection process, typically accompany the incoming goods. A supervisor should take custody of the packing slip while receiving clerks count and inspect the goods. If receiving clerks are provided with quantity information via an open PO or packing slip they may be tempted to transfer this information to the receiving report without performing a physical count and inspection.

IT Controls

SCANNER TECHNOLOGY. The basic concept of inspection can be enhanced through the use of IT controls. Product code scanners in the receiving department and warehouse will reduce the risk of human error in receiving and storing incorrect products. When scanned by the receiving clerk and the warehouse, the system will verify that the items received match those on the purchase order.

Risk of Inaccurately Recording Transactions in Journals and Ledgers

Inaccurate record keeping can take many forms. The following outlines some common expenditure cycle errors but is not intended to be an exhaustive list.

- Purchases from vendors are incorrectly calculated.
- Accounts Payable go unrecorded or are recorded in the wrong period.
- Vendor bills customers for items they did not receive (back ordered).
- Vendor cash payments are inaccurately posted to AP or are posted to the wrong vendor AP.
- Summaries of purchases, accounts payable, cash disbursements, and inventory levels are incorrectly posted to their respective general ledger accounts.

Physical Controls

TRANSACTION AUTHORIZATION. The AP function authorizes cash disbursements via the AP packet. To provide effective control over the flow of cash from the firm, the cash disbursement function should not write checks without this explicit authorization.

ACCOUNTING RECORDS. The control objective of accounting records is to maintain an audit trail adequate for tracing a transaction from its source document to the financial statements. The expenditure cycle employs the following accounting records: AP subsidiary ledger, check register, and general ledger. The auditor's concern in the expenditure cycle is that obligations may be materially understated on financial statements because of unrecorded transactions.

This is a normal occurrence at year-end closing simply because some supplier invoices do not arrive in time to record the liabilities. This also happens, however, in an attempt to intentionally underreport liabilities. Hence, in addition to the routine accounting records, expenditure cycle systems must be designed to provide supporting information, such as the purchase requisition file, the PO file, and the receiving report file. By reviewing these peripheral files, auditors may obtain evidence of inventory purchases that have not been recorded as liabilities.

INDEPENDENT VERIFICATION. The general ledger function provides an important independent verification in the system. It receives journal vouchers and summary reports from inventory control, AP, and cash disbursements. From these sources, the general ledger function verifies that the total obligations recorded equal the total inventories received and that the total reductions in AP equal the total disbursements of cash. Many transaction errors that might occur in the source subsystems will be flagged by discrepancies in the summary numbers that they submit.

IT Controls

INPUT DATA EDITS. Recall that a basic assumption in transaction processing system design is that master files, such as inventory, accounts payable, and the general ledger are "clean" and error free. Transaction data, in contrast, are assumed to be "dirty" and contain various errors such as transposed digits in account numbers, invalid inventory part numbers, and clerical errors. If not detected before being processed, these errors will corrupt the master files of the system.

Input controls are edits that focus on the integrity of transaction data being entered into the application. The following edits are programed into the system to minimize the risk from data input errors.

1. Controls, including checks for missing data, numeric-alphabetic data, and invalid data values, will reduce the risk of undetected data entry errors by clerks in the accounts payable, inventory control, receiving, and cash disbursements departments.
2. Check digit control will provide control over accessing the wrong accounts. Long vendor and inventory account numbers are susceptible to transcription and transposition errors during data entry. A check digit control will reduce the risk of such errors when department clerks enter account numbers into their systems.

ERROR MESSAGES. When posting to the inventory and AP subsidiary ledgers, the computer program logic must correctly identify the inventory and vendor records being updated by matching the inventory item numbers and the vendor account numbers in the receiving report and supplier's invoice to those in the inventory and AP subsidiary files, respectively. Any mismatch conditions should produce an error message to the computer operator.

AUTOMATED POSTINGS TO SUBSIDIARY AND GL ACCOUNTS. The record keeping functions, which in basic technology systems are performed manually by accounting clerks, are automated in the advanced technology system. In a manual environment, segregation of duties between inventory control, purchasing, accounts payable, cash disbursements, and the general ledger functions are important physical controls designed to prevent or detect human errors and fraud. In the advanced technology system, a computer application, which is not subject to human failings such as yielding to situational pressures and/or lacking ethical standards, decides which accounts to update and by how much. By eliminating the human element from accounting activities, the potential for errors and opportunities for fraud are significantly reduced. Also, since these are labor intensive activities, automating them greatly improves efficiency of operations.

These automation benefits depend upon the proper functioning of the computer applications that perform accounting tasks. An undetected program error may affect thousands or even millions of transactions with devastating consequences to the financial statements. An organization's systems development and program change process is therefore critical to ensuring that computer applications do what they are intended to do when they are placed into service and are protected from accidental, malicious, or fraudulent modifications over their service lifetime. In assessing application integrity, auditors seek answers to such questions as: Is the logic of the computer program correct? Has anyone tampered with the application since it was last tested? Have changes been made to the program that could have caused an undisclosed error? The general controls and audit tests that provide answers to these questions are discussed at length in Chapter 17.

FILE BACKUP. The physical loss, destruction, or corruption of digital accounting records are serious concerns that were discussed in Chapter 3. File backup procedures need to be in place as part of the daily processing of transaction data. The accountant should verify that such procedures are performed for all subsidiary and general ledger files.

Risk of Misappropriation of Cash and Inventory

The greatest risk of inventory theft occurs in the receiving department and the warehouse. Misappropriation of cash may take the form of fraudulent payments to individuals posing as vendors. It may also involve erroneous payments for items not ordered or not received. These risks can be reduced through controls such as supervision, independent verification, segregation of duties, and automated procedures.

Physical Controls

SUPERVISION. Receiving departments are sometimes hectic and cluttered during busy periods. In this environment, incoming inventories are exposed to theft until they are secured in the warehouse. Inadequate supervision can create an environment conducive to the theft of inventories in transit.

INDEPENDENT VERIFICATION. The AP function plays a vital role in the verification of the work others in this system have done. Copies of key source documents flow into this department for review and comparison. Each document contains unique facts about the purchase transaction, which the AP clerk must reconcile before the firm recognizes an obligation. This control is called a three-way match and involves the following three documents:

1. The PO, which shows that the purchasing agent ordered only the needed inventories from a valid vendor.
2. The receiving report, which is evidence of the physical receipt of the goods, their condition, and the quantities received. The reconciliation of this document with the PO signifies that the organization has a legitimate obligation to pay.
3. The supplier's invoice, which provides the financial information needed to record the obligation as an account payable. The AP clerk verifies that the prices on the invoice are reasonable compared with the expected prices on the PO.

SEGREGATION OF DUTIES—INVENTORY CONTROL FROM INVENTORY WAREHOUSE. This point was made in Chapter 4. Inventory control keeps the detailed records of the asset, while the warehouse (stores) has asset custody. These tasks should be kept separate. At any point, an auditor should be able to reconcile inventory records to the physical inventory.

SEGREGATION OF DUTIES—ACCOUNTS PAYABLE FROM CASH DISBURSEMENTS. An individual with combined responsibilities for establishing accounts payable and for writing checks to vendors in payment of accounts payable could perpetrate a fraud against the firm. For instance, he or she could establish fraudulent liabilities (to an associate posing as a vendor company) and then write checks to discharge the phony obligations. Segregating these functions greatly reduce the potential for this type of fraud.

IT Controls

Automated Three-Way Match and Payment Approval

An automated three-way match replicates the manual counterpart as follows: When the AP clerk receives the supplier's invoice, the clerk accesses the system and adds a record to the vendor invoice file. This act prompts the system to automatically create a virtual AP packet by linking the vendor invoice to the associated purchase order and receiving report records, using the PO number as a common attribute. The application then reconciles the supporting documents, using programmed criteria for assessing discrepancies. For example, the system may be programmed to approve payment of any invoice amount that does not exceed $100 and 1 percent of the estimated price on the purchase order. Items that fall within limits are automatically approved and paid on their due date. Discrepancies in excess of the threshold are submitted to management for review and manual approval. Through the virtual AP packet screen, management may view the supporting documents and exercise an override of the system controls to force payment. The override should be performed only by authorized management and should be fully documented in management reports.

MULTILEVEL SECURITY. Is a programmed technique that allows multiple individuals to simultaneously access a system, but provides segregation of duties to limit their access privileges and activities. This technique is discussed further in the next section.

Risk of Unauthorized Access to Accounting Records and Reports

Accounting information is at risk to unauthorized access from outsiders as well employees of the organization. The motives for accessing accounting information include:

- Attempts to perpetrate a vendor fraud.
- Theft of physical inventory. Access to inventory records allows the perpetrator to conceal the theft.
- Malicious acts such as corrupting or deleting financial data.

Physical Controls

ACCESS CONTROL. A firm must limit access to documents that control its physical assets. For example, an individual with access to purchase requisitions, purchase orders, and receiving reports has the ingredients to construct a fraudulent purchase transaction. With the proper supporting documents, a fraudulent transaction can be made to look legitimate to the system and could be paid.

SEGREGATION OF DUTIES. An objective of segregation of duties provided in Chapter 3 states that:

> *The organization should be so structured that the perpetration of a fraud requires collusion between two or more individuals.*

To achieve this objective, certain record-keeping tasks should be separated. Specifically, subsidiary ledgers (AP and inventory), journals (purchases and cash disbursements), and the general ledger should be separately maintained. An individual with total record-keeping responsibility, in collusion with someone with asset custody, is in a position to perpetrate a fraud. Although not entirely eliminated, the risk of collusion is reduced while segregating these tasks. The more people involved in a task the more difficult it is to collude and greater the risk of detection. This will have a deterrent effect on those contemplating fraud.

IT Controls

PASSWORD CONTROL. In Chapter 4, we discussed how digital accounting records are vulnerable to unauthorized access. To mitigate these risks, organization management should implement a robust password control policy to prevent unauthorized access to computer files and programs that reside in each of the departments. The application logic should require, and prompt, users to change passwords periodically. Corporate policy should require strong passwords of six or eight characters that consist of both alphabetic and numeric characters. We examine password control issues in detail in Chapter 16.

MULTILEVEL SECURITY. Chapter 4 introduced the concept of multilevel security, which employs programmed techniques that permit simultaneous access to a central system by many users with different access privileges, but prevents them from obtaining information for which they lack authorization. Two methods for achieving multilevel security are the access control list (ACL) and role-based access control (RBAC). Through these techniques, purchasing, receiving, accounts payable, cash disbursements, and general ledger personnel are limited in their access based on the privileges assigned to them. ACL and RBAC are discussed in greater detail in later chapters.

TABLE 5-1 SUMMARY OF EXPENDITURE CYCLE RISKS AND CONTROLS

Risk	Physical Control	IT Control
Unauthorized inventory purchases	Transaction Authorization—formal purchase requisition	Automated purchase approval
Receiving Incorrect Items	Independent verification—Receiving Department reconciles receipt with PO Supervision in Receiving Department	Scanner technology
Inaccurate record keeping	Transaction authorization—AP department authorizes cash disbursements to make payment Accounting records—audit trail documents, journals, accounts, and files Independent verification—inventory control, AP, cash disbursements, and GL	Input data edits Error Messages Automated posting to accounts File backup
Misappropriation of Cash and inventory	Supervision—receiving department Independent verification—three-way match Segregation of duties—cash disbursements, general ledger, AP function, warehouse, inventory records	Automated three-way match Multilevel Security to provide segregation of duties
Unauthorized access to data	Access control—source documents, journals, ledgers Segregation of duties—sub-ledgers, GL, asset custody	Password control Multilevel security to prevent unauthorized access to data

REENGINEERING USING EDI

We saw in Chapter 4 that EDI technology was devised to expedite routine transaction processing between manufacturers, wholesalers, and retailers by connecting buyer and seller computers via a private network or the Internet. When the buyer's computer system detects the need to order inventory, it automatically transmits a purchase order to the seller, which is approved and processed by the vendor system with little or no human involvement.

A key element of successful EDI is the implementation of a trading partner agreement to eliminate the discrepancies that require human involvement to resolve. In particular, the receiving function and the accounts payable task of reconciling purchase orders, receiving reports, and supplier invoices are labor-intensive and costly. The following examples show how reengineering these activities can produce considerable cost savings.

The Ford Motor Company employed more than 500 clerks in its North American AP department. Analysis of the function showed that a large part of the clerks' time was devoted to reconciling discrepancies among supplier invoices, receiving reports, and POs. These discrepancies were the result of too many vendors and unreliable vendors. The first step in solving the problem was to change the business environment; therefore, Ford initiated trading partner agreements with a reduced number of suppliers. The parties agreed in advance to terms of trade such as price, quality, quantities to be shipped, discounts, and lead times. Also, each item used by Ford would be supplied by a single vendor. With key sources of discrepancy eliminated, Ford reengineered their work flow to take advantage of the new environment. The key features of the system are as follows:

1. As inventory needs are detected, the system automatically sends a digital EDI purchase order to the vendor.
2. When the goods arrive, receiving personnel perform only cursory inspection since quality and quantity are guaranteed by the trading partner agreement.
3. Because the financial information about purchases is known in advance from the trading partner agreement, the **vendor's invoice** provides no critical information that cannot be derived from the receiving report. By eliminating this source of potential discrepancy, Ford was able to eliminate the three-way match for the majority of purchase transactions.
4. Payment is made automatically by electronic funds transfer (EFT) directly to the vendor's bank account.

As a result of its reengineering effort, Ford was able to simplify its workflow and reduce its AP staff from 500 to 125.

Some organizations have taken reengineering even further by eliminating the receiving function entirely. The objective of this is to send goods directly to the production department and thus bypass the receiving area and avoid production delays and the associated handling costs. An accounting and auditing problem that must be overcome is how to account for inventory receipts when there is no receiving function and no receiving report. One way of dealing with this is to calculate the number of parts received based on the products produced in which the parts are components. Supplier payments are distributed based on production (part usage), and by having only one supplier per part, the question of which supplier to pay is self-evident. An additional problem to deal with is accounting for scrap in the production process. Since scrap does not end up in finished production, it will not be counted, and vendors will not be paid for materials that were scrapped. Separate accounting procedures need to be implemented to record and monitor scrap. This issue is examined in Chapter 7.

EDI Control Issues

EDI poses unique risks for organizations that need to be recognized and controlled. One of them is ensuring that, in the absence of explicit authorization, only valid transactions are processed. Another risk is that a trading partner, or someone masquerading as a trading partner, will access the firm's accounting records in a way that is unauthorized by the trading partner agreement. Chapter 12 presents EDI in more detail and its implications for business. EDI control issues are discussed in Chapter 16.

Summary

This chapter is organized into two primary sections. The first examined conceptually the expenditure cycle of a typical merchandising firm and focused on (1) the functional areas and the flow of transaction information that triggers key tasks, and (2) the documents, journals, and accounts that support audit trails, decision making, and financial reporting.

The second section examined physical expenditure cycle systems that lie at different points on the technology/human continuum. The objectives of this section were to (1) illustrate system functionality, efficiency issues, and workflow characteristics of different technologies, and (2) demonstrate how internal control issues differ between systems at various points on the technology/human continuum. The section reviewed physical controls and computer controls associated with basic technology systems and advanced integrated systems. The chapter concluded by outlining the benefits, key features, and risks associated with electronic data interchange (EDI) systems. EDI systems are discussed in detail in later chapters.

Key Terms

actual cost inventory ledger (214)
AP packet (215)
AP pending file (214)
AP subsidiary ledger (215)
blind copy (212)
cash disbursement vouchers (215)
cash disbursements journal (218)
check register (218)
closed AP file (218)
open AP file (215)
open purchase order file (220)
open purchase requisition file (220)
open/closed purchase order file (212)
purchase order (212)
purchase requisition (210)
purchase requisition file (220)
receiving report (214)
receiving report file (214)
standard cost system (214)
supplier's invoice (214)
valid vendor file (210)
vendor's invoice (234)
voucher register (216)
vouchers payable file (217)
vouchers payable system (215)

Review Questions

1. Differentiate between a purchase requisition and a purchase order.
2. What purpose does a purchasing department serve?
3. Distinguish between an accounts payable file and a vouchers payable file.
4. What are the three logical steps of the cash disbursements system?
5. What general ledger journal entries does the purchases system trigger? From which departments do these journal entries arise?
6. What two types of risks can close supervision of the receiving department reduce?
7. What is a three-way match?
8. What steps of independent verification does the general ledger department perform?
9. What is (are) the purpose(s) of maintaining a valid vendor file?
10. Some organizations do not use an AP subsidiary ledger or a purchases journal. How is this possible?
11. What is the purpose of the blind copy of a purchase order?
12. Give one advantage of using a vouchers payable system.

Discussion Questions

1. What documents constitute the AP packet? What evidence does each document provide?
2. In the basic technology system, the inventory control clerk reviews the purchase requisition file to identify inventory needs. Explain how this file is created.
3. Discuss the importance of supervision controls in the receiving department and the reasons behind blind fields on the receiving report.
4. The level of day-to-day department activity in advanced technology systems is significantly lower than that of basic technology systems. Are these departments no longer necessary?
5. Discuss the following statement: even in advanced technology systems, the AP clerk must perform a three-way match to approve all vendor invoices for payment.
6. What is central to a successful EDI implementation?
7. Discuss the objective of eliminating the receiving function. What accounting/audit problems need to be resolved?
8. What purpose does multilevel security control play in an integrated purchases/cash disbursements system?
9. You are conducting an end-of-year audit. Assume that the terms of trade between a buyer and a seller are free on board (FOB) destination. What document provides evidence that a liability exists and may be unrecorded?
10. How does the general control area of systems development and program change impact day-to-day transaction processing?

Multiple-Choice Questions

1. Which of the following statements is correct?
   a. The cash disbursement function is part of accounts payable.
   b. Cash disbursement is an independent accounting function.
   c. Cash disbursement is a treasury function.
   d. The cash disbursement function is part of the general ledger department.
2. Which of the following represents incompatible tasks?
   a. Cash disbursement maintains the check register.
   b. Accounts payable maintains the accounts payable subsidiary ledger.
   c. Accounts payable is responsible for paying invoices.
   d. Accounts payable is responsible for authorizing payment of invoices
3. Which document typically triggers the three-way match?
   a. Purchase requisition
   b. Purchase order
   c. Receiving report
   d. Supplier's invoice
4. Which one of the following departments does not receive a copy of the purchase order?
   a. General ledger
   b. The receiving department
   c. Accounts payable
   d. The purchasing department
5. Which control helps to ensure that the inventory items received are the correct type and the correct amount, and are in good condition?
   a. Reconciliation with the packing slip
   b. Issuance of a blind copy of purchase order
   c. Preparation of a shipping notice
   d. The way match
6. Which of the following expenditure cycle tasks should not be separated?
   a. Purchasing inventory items and updating inventory subsidiary ledger
   b. Receiving inventory items and updating inventory subsidiary ledger
   c. Storing inventory in the warehouse and updating inventory subsidiary ledger
   d. Updating accounts payable records and posting to the cash disbursements journal
   e. All of the above should be separated

7. Which of the following describe incompatible duties?

a. Matching purchase requisitions, receiving reports and invoices, and authorizing payment

b. Authorizing payment and maintaining the check register

c. Writing checks and maintaining the check register

d. Authorizing payment and maintaining the accounts payable subsidiary ledger

8. Which of the following tasks should the cash disbursements clerk NOT perform?

a. Review the supporting documents for completeness and accuracy

b. Prepare checks

c. Approve the liability

d. Mark the supporting documents paid

9. Which ledger can be updated solely from the receiving report?

a. Standard cost inventory ledger

b. Actual cost inventory subsidiary ledger

c. General ledger

d. Accounts payable subsidiary ledger

10. Which of the following documents would most likely provide audit evidence of an unrecorded liability?

a. Invoices

b. Purchase orders

c. Purchase requisitions

d. Receiving reports

Problems

1. UNRECORDED LIABILITIES

You are auditing the financial statements of a New York City company that buys a product from a manufacturer in Los Angeles. The buyer closes its books on June 30. Assume the following details:

Terms of trade FOB shipping point
June 10, buyer sends purchase order to seller
June 15, seller ships goods
July 5, buyer receives goods
July 10, buyer receives seller's invoice

Required

a. Could this transaction have resulted in an unrecorded liability in the buyer's financial statements?

b. If yes, what documents provide audit trail evidence of the liability?

c. On what date did the buyer realize the liability?

d. On what date did the buyer recognize the liability?
- New assumption:
Terms of trade FOB destination.

e. Could this transaction have resulted in an unrecorded liability in the buyer's financial statements?

f. If yes, what documents provide audit trail evidence of the liability?

g. On what date did the buyer realize the liability?

h. On what date did the buyer recognize the liability?

2. INVENTORY ORDERING ALTERNATIVES

The flowchart for Problem 2 illustrates two alternative inventory ordering methods.

Required

a. Distinguish between a purchase requisition and a purchase order.

b. Discuss the primary advantage of alternative two over alternative one. Be specific.

c. Under what circumstances can you envision management using alternative one rather than alternative two?

3. SYSTEM FLOWCHART ANALYSIS

Using the Flowchart labeled Problem 3, answer the following questions:

a. What are the names of Departments X and Y?

b. What are the names of the documents that are identified by letters in the system? Use the following format:
Doc A = (Name of document here), for example.

c. What are the processes that are represented by letters in the system?

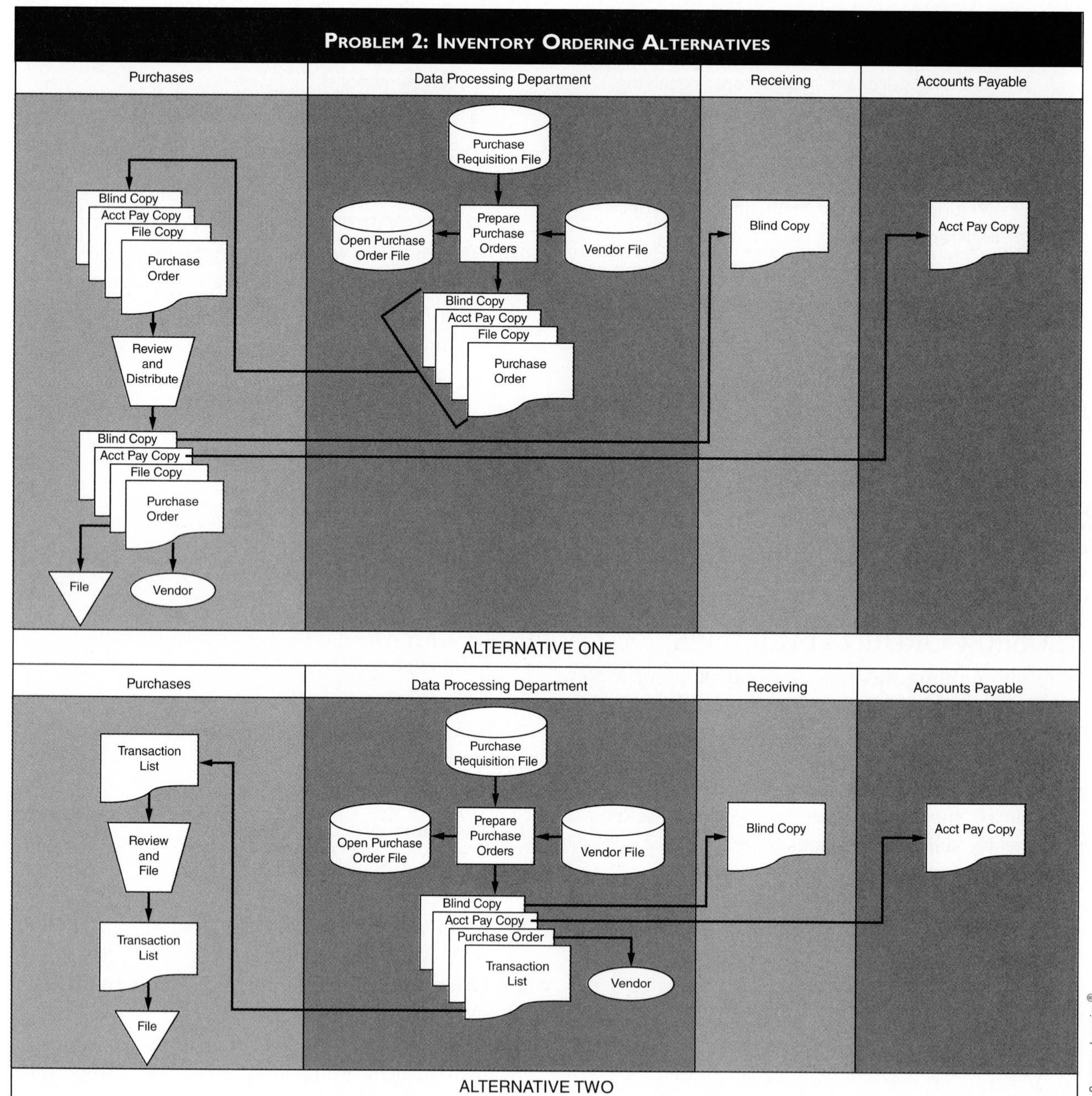

d. What are the files that are represented by letters in the system?
e. What is represented by the terminal labeled "Z"?

4. SYSTEM FLOWCHART ANALYSIS

Refer to the system flowchart labeled Problem 4.

Required

a. Discuss the uncontrolled risks associated with the systems as currently configured.
b. Describe the controls that need to be implemented into the system to mitigate the risks in the given scenario.

5. RISK ANALYSIS AND INTERNAL CONTROL

The following describes the purchases and cash disbursements procedures for a lawn and garden supply wholesaler that uses a central computer system with distributed terminals in departments.

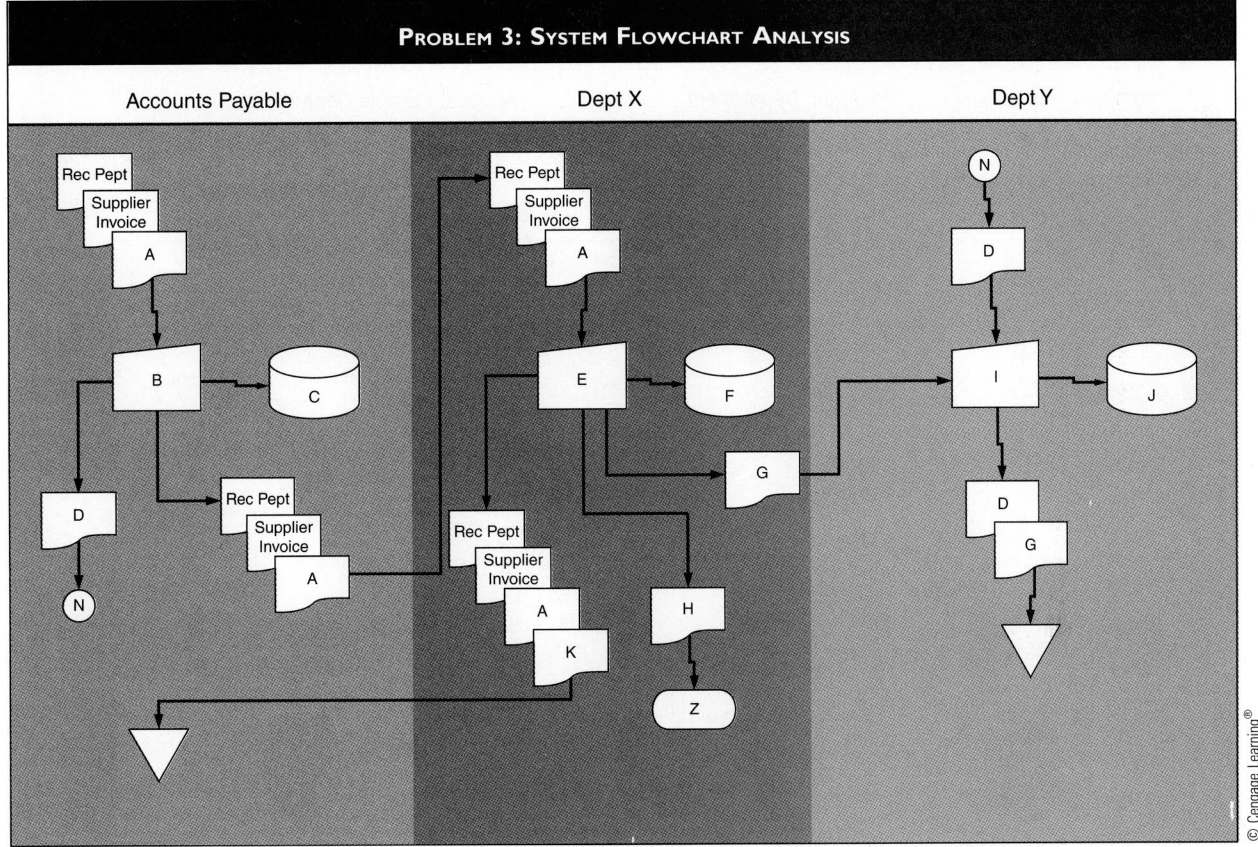

The inventory control clerk visually reviews inventory levels from his computer terminal to identify items that need to be ordered. He then prints and sends a hard copy purchase requisition for the needed items to the purchasing agent. Based on the requisition, the purchasing agent selects a vendor and adds a digital record to the purchase order file from his terminal in the purchasing department. The clerk then prints a hard copy of the purchase order and mails it to the vendor. Finally, the purchasing agent destroys the purchase requisition, which it is no longer needed since the relevant details are on the PO.

When the materials arrive at the receiving department a receiving clerk prints a copy of the purchase order from his terminal and reconciles it to the packing slip. The clerk then manually creates a two-part hard copy receiving report. One copy of the receiving report is sent to Inventory Control and the other is sent to the purchasing department. The packing slip is sent with inventory to the warehouse.

When the purchasing agent receives the receiving report, he closes the digital PO record and adds a record to the digital receiving report file. He then destroys the hard copy receiving report, which is no longer needed.

Upon receipt of receiving report copy, the inventory control clerk updates the inventory subsidiary ledger to record the receipt. The clerk then destroys the hard copy receiving report.

Vendors send hard copy invoices to the AP clerk for processing. When the clerk receives an invoice, she reconciles it with the digital purchase order and receiving report. She then selects a due date and adds a record to the Vendor Invoice file, which serves the AP Subsidiary ledger. The clerk then files the invoice in the department.

On the due date the computer system automatically prints a check, mails it to the vendor, closes the Vendor Invoice record to discharge the liability, and records the payment in the Cash Disbursement file.

Required

a. Create a system flowchart of the system.
b. Describe the uncontrolled risks in the system.

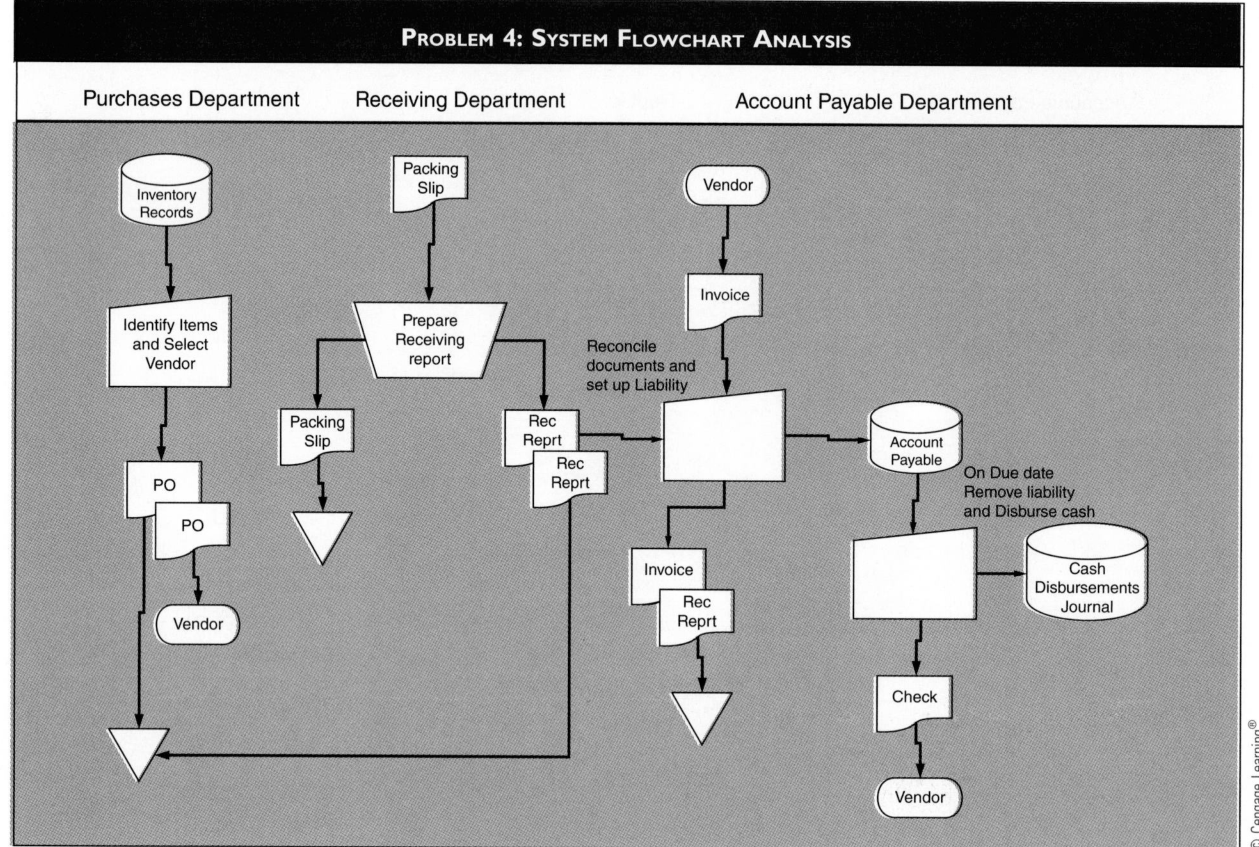

c. Describe the physical controls needed to reduce the risks identified in (b).
d. Describe the IT controls that are appropriate in this system.

6. RISK ANALYSIS AND INTERNAL CONTROL

Review the following description of a purchases system and answer the questions at the end.

The purchasing agent periodically checks inventory levels from a computer terminal, which is connected to a central accounting system. The agent searches the inventory file for items that need to be ordered. He then selects a supplier, prints a hard copy of the purchase order, and mails it to the vendor. The clerk files one copy of the PO in the department and sends a second copy to the AP Clerk.

When the inventories arrive at the receiving department, a receiving clerk reconciles the items with the packing slip, inspects them for condition, and manually prepares a three-part receiving report. The clerk sends one copy to the purchasing department to close out the open PO, files one copy along with the packing slip in the receiving department, and sends one copy with the inventory to the warehouse.

When the accounts payable clerk receives a hardcopy invoice from the vendor, she reconciles the invoice with the purchase order, records the liability in the AP Subsidiary Ledger from the terminal in her office, and assigns a due date for payment.

The warehouse clerk receives the inventory, reconciles it with the receiving report, and updates the inventory subsidiary ledger from a terminal in the warehouse.

Required

a. Create a system flowchart of the system.
b. Describe the uncontrolled risks in the system.
c. Describe the physical controls needed to reduce the risks identified in (b).

7. IT CONTROLS

Using the flowchart for Problem 7, describe the IT application controls that would apply to the system. Be specific as to the role each control plays.

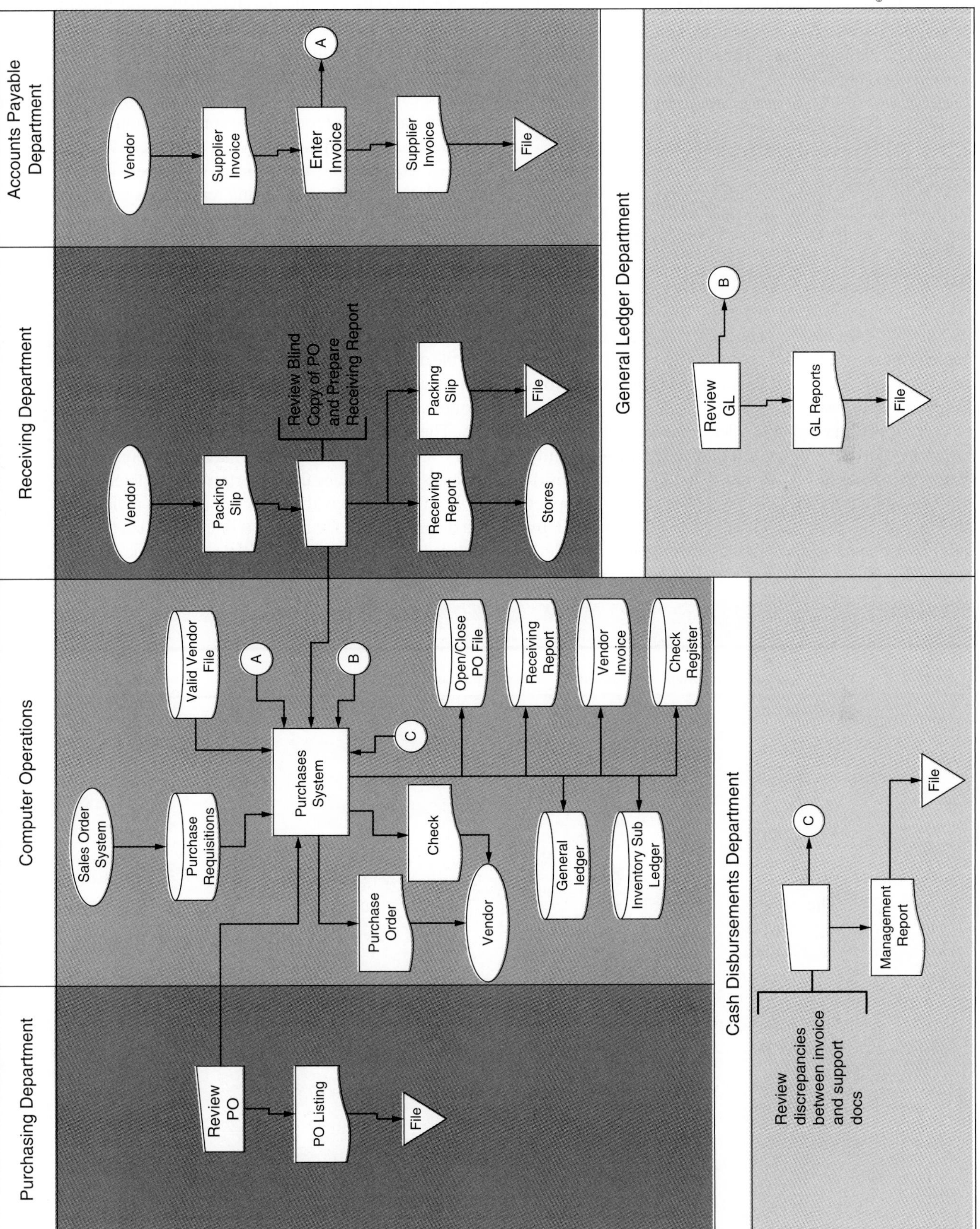
Purchasing Department
Computer Operations
Receiving Department
Accounts Payable Department
General Ledger Department
Cash Disbursements Department
Review PO
PO Listing
File
Sales Order System
Purchase Requisitions
Valid Vendor File
A
B
C
Purchases System
Purchase Order
Vendor
Check
General ledger
Inventory Sub Ledger
Open/Close PO File
Receiving Report
Vendor Invoice
Check Register
Vendor
Packing Slip
Review Blind Copy of PO and Prepare Receiving Report
Receiving Report
Packing Slip
Stores
File
Vendor
Supplier Invoice
Enter Invoice
Supplier Invoice
File
A
Review GL
B
GL Reports
File
Review discrepancies between invoice and support docs
C
Management Report
File

8. PHYSICAL CONTROLS

Using the flowchart of a purchases system for Problem 8, identify six major physical control weaknesses in the system. Discuss and classify each weakness in accordance with the COSO internal control framework.

9. IT CONTROLS

Using the flowchart for Problem 8, describe the IT application controls that would apply to the system. Be specific as to the role each control plays.

10. INTERNAL CONTROL

The following is a description of a manufacturing company's purchasing procedures. All computers in the company are networked to a centralized accounting system so that each terminal has full access to a common database.

The inventory control clerk periodically checks inventory levels from a computer terminal to identify items that need to be ordered. Once the clerk considers that inventory is too low, he chooses a supplier and creates a purchase order from the terminal by adding a record to the purchase order file. The clerk prints a hard copy of the purchase order and mails it to the vendor. An electronic notification is also sent to accounts payable and receiving, giving the clerks of each department access to the purchase order from their respective terminals.

When the raw materials arrive at the unloading dock, a receiving clerk prints a copy of the purchase order from his terminal and reconciles it to the packing slip. The clerk then creates a receiving report on a computer system. An electronic notification is sent to accounts payable and inventory control, giving the respective clerks access to the receiving report. The inventory control clerk then updates the inventory records.

When the accounts payable clerk receives a hard-copy invoice from the vendor, she reconciles the invoice with the digital purchase order and receiving report, and she prepares an AP packet and places it into the open accounts payable file in a filing cabinet until the due date. The clerk also updates the accounts payable subsidiary ledger and records the liability amount in the purchase journal from the department computer terminal. The accounts payable clerk periodically reviews the cash disbursements file for items due and, when they are identified, prepares a check for the amount due. Finally,

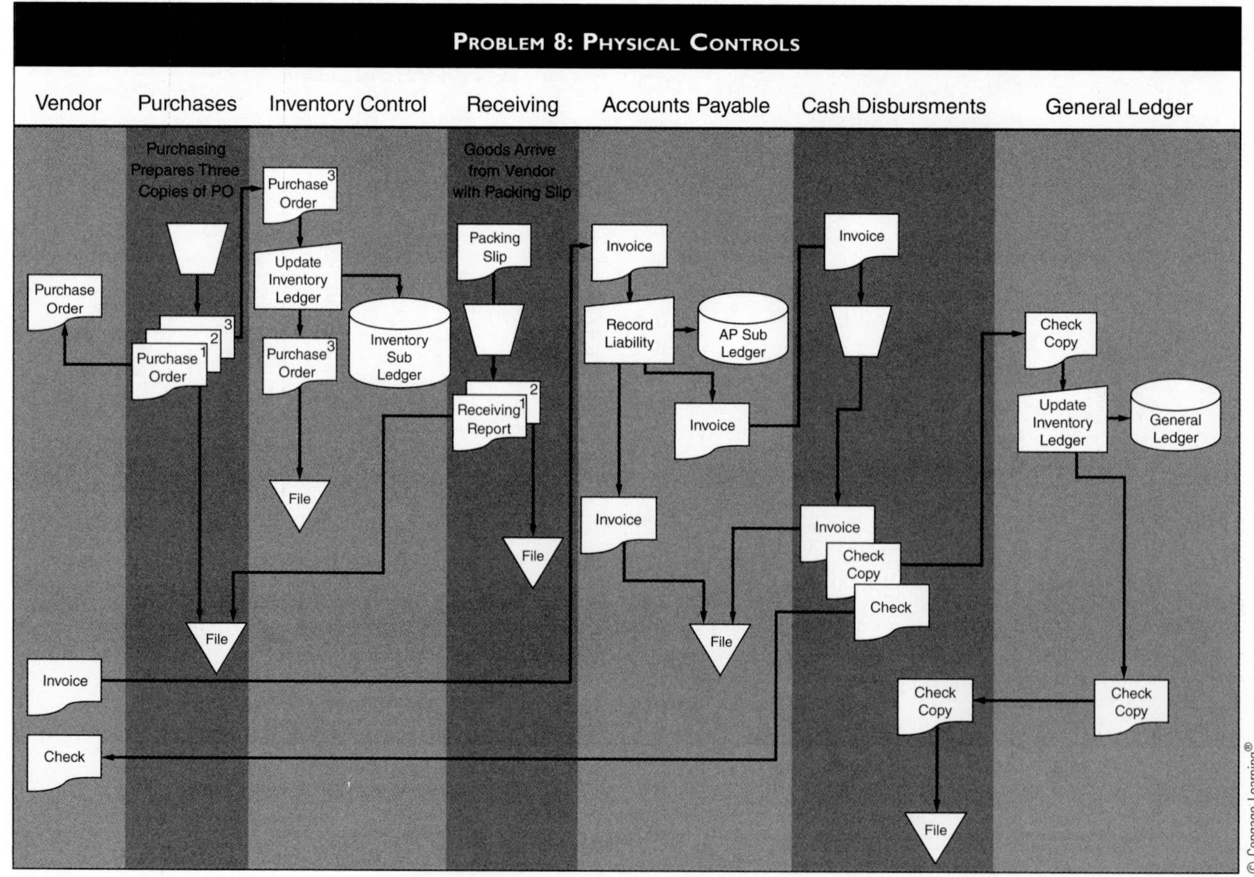

using the department terminal, the clerk removes the liability from the accounts payable subsidiary file and posts the disbursement to the cash account.

Required

a. Create a system flowchart of the system.
b. Analyze the physical internal control weaknesses in the system.
c. Describe the IT controls that should exist in the system. Be specific as to how the controls apply.

11. ACCOUNTING DOCUMENTS

Required

Answer the following questions.

a. Which department is responsible for initiating the purchase of materials?
b. What is the name of the document generated by the department identified in (a)?
c. Typically, multiple copies of a purchase order are prepared. One copy should go to the vendor, and one is retained in the purchasing department. To achieve proper control, which other departments should receive copies of the purchase order?
d. What documents does the accounts payable clerk review before setting up a liability?
e. Which document transfers responsibility for goods sold to a common carrier?

Internal Control Cases

I. SMITH'S MARKET (SMALL BUSINESS CASH SALES ACCOUNTING SYSTEM)

In 1989, Robert Smith opened a small fruit and vegetable market in Bethlehem, Pennsylvania. Originally, Smith sold only produce grown on his family farm and orchard. As the market's popularity grew, however, he added bread, canned goods, fresh meats, and a limited supply of frozen goods. Today Smith's Market is a full-range farmers' market with a strong local customer base. Indeed, the market's reputation for low prices and high quality draws customers from other Pennsylvania cities and even from the neighboring state of New Jersey. Currently Smith's has 40 employees. These include sales staff, shelf stockers, farm laborers, shift supervisors, and clerical staff. Recently, Smith has noticed a decline in profits and sales, while his purchases of products for resale have continued to rise. Although the company does not prepare audited financial statements, Robert Smith has commissioned your public accounting firm to assess his company's sales procedures and internal controls. Smith's Market expenditure cycle procedures are described below.

Expenditure Cycle

The expenditure cycle begins in the warehouse adjacent to the market where Smith's keeps its inventory of nonperishable goods such as canned goods and paper products. The company also maintains a one-day inventory of produce and other perishable products in the warehouse so clerks can quickly restock the shelves when necessary. At close of business each evening, the warehouse clerk reviews the market shelves for items that need to be replenished. The clerk restocks the shelves and adjusts the digital stock records accordingly from the warehouse PC. At this time, the clerk takes note of what needs to be reordered from the suppliers and prints purchase orders from the PC. Depending upon the nature of the product and urgency of the need, the clerk either mails the purchase order to the supplier or orders by phone. Phone orders are followed up by faxing the purchase order to the supplier. When the goods arrive from the vendor, the warehouse clerk reviews the packing slip, restocks the warehouse shelves, and updates the stock records from the PC. At the end of the day the clerk prepares a hard-copy purchases summary from the PC and sends it to the treasury clerk for posting to general ledger.

The vendor's invoice is sent to the accounting clerk. She examines it for correctness and files it in a temporary file until it is due to be paid. The clerk reviews the temporary file daily looking for invoices to be paid. Using the accounting department PC, the clerk prints a check and records it in the digital check register. She then files the invoice and mails the check to the supplier. At the end of the day she prints a hard-copy journal voucher from the PC, which summarizes the day's cash disbursements, and sends it to the treasury clerk for posting to the general ledger.

Using the department PC, the treasury clerk posts the journal voucher and purchases summary information to the appropriate general ledger accounts.

Required

a. Create a data flow diagram of the current system.
b. Create a system flowchart of the current system.
c. Analyze the physical internal control weaknesses in the system. Model your response according to the six categories of physical control activities specified in the COSO internal control model.
d. Describe the IT controls that should be in place in this system.

2. TIGHT LINES FISHING AND CAMPING SUPPLIES (NETWORKED COMPUTER SYSTEM AND MANUAL PROCEDURES)

Tight Lines Fishing and Camping Supplies is a New York-based wholesaler of fishing and camping equipment that serves fishing and camping retailers throughout the north east. Tight Lines obtains its inventories of fly rods, reels, tents, and other products from manufactures in the United States and from abroad. Tight Lines uses a centralized accounting system with networked terminals in the departments. You have been hired by Tight Lines to evaluate their processes, risks, and internal controls. The following paragraphs describe Tight Lines expenditure cycle procedures.

Expenditure Cycle

Purchases System

The process begins when the purchasing clerk checks the inventory subsidiary ledger on his computer terminal each morning. When an item is deemed to be too low, the clerk selects a vendor from the valid vendor file and prepares a digital purchase order. The clerk prints two hard copies: one copy is sent to the vendor, and the other is filed in the department. Digital purchase order record is added to the PO File.

When the goods arrive in the receiving department, the receiving clerk inspects them and reconciles the items against the information in the digital PO and the packing slip. The clerk then manually prepares two hard copies of the receiving report. One of these accompanies the goods to the inventory warehouse, where the clerk shelves the goods and updates the inventory subsidiary ledger from his terminal. The clerk then files the receiving report in the department. The other copy of the receiving report is sent to the accounts payable department, where the AP clerk files it until the supplier's invoice arrives. When the AP clerk receives the invoice he pulls the receiving report from the temporary file, prints a hard copy of the digital PO, and reconciles the three documents. At this time, the clerk updates the digital accounts payable subsidiary ledger, the AP control account and the inventory control account in the GL from his terminal. The clerk then sends the invoice, receiving report, and the purchase order copy to the cash disbursements department.

Cash Disbursements System

Upon receipt of the documents from the accounts payable department, the cash disbursements clerk files the documents until their payment due date. On the due date, the clerk prepares a check for the invoiced amount, which is sent to the treasurer who signs it and mails the check to the vendor.

The cash disbursement clerk then updates the check register, accounts payable subsidiary ledger, and the AP control account from his terminal. Finally, the clerk files the invoice, purchase order copy, receiving report, and check copy in the department.

Required

a. Create a data flow diagram of the current system.
b. Create a system flowchart of the existing system.
c. Describe internal control weaknesses in the system and discuss the risks associated with these weaknesses.
d. (Optional) Prepare a system flowchart of a redesigned computer-based system that resolves the control weaknesses that you identified. Explain your solution.

3. TVR CLASSICS (MANUAL AND STAND-ALONE COMPUTER PROCESSING)

TVR Classics specializes in the sale of original and reproduction restoration parts for classic sports cars and muscle cars of the 1960s and 1970s. The classic car industry has grown significantly in recent years as the baby boomers age, has become wealthier, and wants to relive fond memories. Classic car sales and restoration is a multibillion dollar industry that employs more than 30,000 people in the United States. It is, however, a highly fragmented industry comprised of many small businesses. TVR is headquartered in Los Angeles, California and currently employs 95 full-time employees, including a sales staff, sales representatives, and general office staff. TVR's primary customer base consists of small restoration shops and classic car dealers on the west coast. They source many of their parts from abroad, but a growing percentage of these are now being manufactured in the United States.

TVR has a legacy accounting system that employs a combination of manual procedures supported by standalone PCs in the various departments. Recently, they have experienced business inefficiencies that have been linked to their antiquated accounting system. You have been retained by TVR management to review their procedures for compliance with effective internal control standards. TVR's expenditure cycle procedures are presented in the following paragraphs.

Expenditure Cycle

When the quantity on hand of a particular product falls to a low level, the warehouse clerk selects a vendor and manually prepares two hard copies of a purchase order. The clerk sends one copy of the purchase order to the vendor and the other to the receiving department. When the goods arrive from the vendor, the receiving clerk matches the packing slip in the shipment to the purchase order that the warehouse clerk had previously sent. If everything is in order the receiving clerk signs the purchase order and sends it to the accounting department. The clerk then manually prepares a hard-copy receiving report, which he sends with the goods to the warehouse. From his department PC, the warehouse clerk uses the receiving report to update the inventory subsidiary ledger to reflect the receipt of the goods.

Subsequently, the accounting department's accounts payable clerk receives the supplier's invoice, which she matches and reconciles to the previously received purchase order from the receiving clerk. From her department PC, the accounts payable clerk then updates the digital accounts payable subsidiary ledger to reflect the new liability and records the event in the digital purchases journal.

Cash Disbursements Procedures

The accounts payable clerk in the accounting department reviews the liabilities that are due by searching the accounts payable subsidiary ledger from the department PC. The clerk then prints out a hard-copy cash disbursement voucher for each item due for payment. The clerk then sends a cash disbursement voucher to the cash disbursements department for payment. At the end of the day, the clerk prints a hard-copy accounts payable summary from the department PC and sends it to the general ledger department.

From his department PC, the cash disbursements clerk uses the cash disbursement voucher to record the payment in the digital check register and then prints a three-part check. The clerk signs the negotiable portion of the check and sends it to the vendor. One check copy is filed in the department, and the clerk sends the second check copy, along with the original cash disbursement voucher, to the accounting department accounts payable clerk. At the end of the day, the clerk prints a hard-copy summary of the check register and sends it to the general ledger department.

From the accounting department PC, the accounts payable clerk uses the check copy and cash disbursement voucher to record the payment in the voucher register and to close out the liability in the accounts payable subsidiary ledger. The clerk then files the hard-copy cash disbursement voucher and check copy in the department.

From the department PC, the general ledger clerk posts the summaries received from the accounting and cash disbursement departments to the appropriate general ledger accounts. The clerk files the hard-copy summaries in the general ledger department.

Required

a. Create a data flow diagram of the current system.
b. Create a system flowchart of the existing system.
c. Analyze the physical internal control weaknesses in the system.
d. (Optional) Prepare a system flowchart of a redesigned computer-based system that resolves the control weaknesses that you identified. Explain your solution.

4. DISCOUNT TOOLS INC. (NETWORKED COMPUTER SYSTEM WITH MANUAL PROCEDURES)

Discount tools is a rapidly growing online and catalogue-based retailer of low cost tools and equipment directed to the do-it-yourself consumers and to small service companies in the automotive repair and home improvement industries. Discount Tools offices and warehouse are located in Atlanta, Georgia. The firm purchases from a large number of manufacturers in China and India, and to a lesser extent from U.S.-based suppliers.

The company employs a networked accounting system with distributed terminals in several departments, but some tasks are performed manually.

Until recently the system had functioned satisfactorily, but Discount Tools is now experiencing operational inefficiencies and accounting errors. Your firm has been hired to evaluate Discount Tools' business processes and internal controls. The expenditure cycle is described in the following paragraphs.

Purchase System Procedures

Discount Tools' purchase transactions are initiated when the purchasing department clerk reviews the inventory file for items that need to be replenished. The clerk selects a vendor, adds a record to the digital PO File, and prints four hard copies of the purchase order. One copy is filed in the department; the second copy is sent to the receiving department; the third copy is sent to the accounts payable department; and the final copy is sent to the vendor.

When the goods and the packing slip arrive at the receiving department, the receiving clerk examines the items for condition and verifies the quantities received against the packing slip. Upon completion of the inspection, the clerk manually creates two hard copies of a receiving report. One copy is filed in the department and the second accompanies the goods to the warehouse.

In the warehouse, the clerk receives and shelves the goods. In addition, the clerk updates the inventory file by posting the amounts received to the various inventory records affected.

When the accounts payable department clerk receives the invoice from the supplier, he visually matches it to the hard copy purchase order on file. The clerk then adds a record to the vendor invoice file, which serves as the AP subsidiary ledger and sets a due date for payment.

Finally, at the end of each day, the warehouse clerk and the AP clerk create digital journal vouchers to reflect the day's transactions. The system automatically posts the journal vouchers to the relevant GL control accounts.

Required

a. Create a data flow diagram of the current system.
b. Create a system flowchart of the existing system.
c. Analyze the physical internal control weaknesses in the system.
d. Describe the IT controls that should be in place in this system.
e. (Optional) Prepare a system flowchart of a redesigned computer-based system that resolves the control weaknesses that you identified. Explain your solution.

5. ABE PLUMBING INC. (CENTRALIZED SMALL BUSINESS ACCOUNTING SYSTEM)

ABE Plumbing Inc. opened its doors in 1979 as a wholesale supplier of plumbing equipment, tools, and parts to hardware stores, home-improvement centers, and professional plumbers in the Allentown-Bethlehem-Easton metropolitan area. Over the years they have expanded their operations to serve customers across the nation, and now employ over 200 people as technical representatives, buyers, warehouse workers, and sales and office staff. Most recently, ABE has experienced fierce competition from the large online discount stores such as Harbor Freight and Northern Supply. In addition, the company is suffering from operational inefficiencies related to its archaic information system. ABE's expenditure cycle procedures are described in the following paragraphs.

Expenditure Cycle

ABE uses a centralized accounting system for managing inventory purchases and recording transactions. The system is almost entirely paperless. Each department has a computer terminal that is networked to the purchases/accounts payable system that is run from a small data processing department. All accounting records are maintained on centralized computer files that are stored on a file server in the data processing department.

Purchasing

The process begins in the purchasing department. Each morning the purchasing agent reviews the inventory levels from his department terminal and searches for items that have fallen to their reorder points and need to be replenished. The purchasing agent then selects the vendors and creates digital purchase orders in the purchase order file. He then prints two hard copies of each purchase order and sends them to the respective vendors.

Receiving

When the items are received, the receiving department clerk reconciles the goods with the attached packing slip and the digital purchase order, which he accesses from his computer terminal. The clerk then creates a digital receiving report, stating the condition of the materials received. The system automatically closes the purchase order previously created by the purchasing agent. In addition, the receiving clerk prints a hard copy of the receiving report, which he sends with the inventory to the warehouse where the items are stored.

Warehouse

Upon receipt of the inventory, the warehouse clerk reconciles the items with the receiving report and updates the inventory subsidiary ledger. The accounting system automatically and immediately updates the inventory control account in the general ledger.

Accounts Payable

Once the accounts payable clerk receives the vendor's invoice, she reconciles it with the purchase order and receiving report from her terminal. The clerk then creates a digital vendor invoice record and sets a due date for payment. The system automatically updates the AP control account in the general ledger. Daily, the accounts payable clerk reviews the open vendor invoice records from her terminal, looking for items that need to be paid. The clerk then records the payment in the digital check register and closes the open vendor invoice. Finally, the clerk prints a hard copy of the check and sends it to the vendor. The system automatically updates the accounts payable and cash general ledger accounts.

Required

a. Create a data flow diagram of the current system.
b. Create a system flowchart of the existing system.
c. Analyze the physical internal control weaknesses in the system.
d. (Optional) Prepare a system flowchart of a redesigned computer-based system that resolves the control weaknesses that you identified. Explain your solution.

6. GREEN PRODUCTS GARDEN SUPPLY (STAND-ALONE PC-BASED ACCOUNTING SYSTEM)

Green Products Garden (GPG) Supply sells and distributes a wide range of garden products and equipment including organic fertilizers, premium flower and grass seeds, organic pesticides, and garden spreaders. GPG's headquarters and warehouse is located in Hopewell, Virginia. Their customers are primarily small garden centers and landscape companies in the Mid-Atlantic States. Sales are on credit.

GPG's current information system includes manual procedures supported by independent (non-networked) PCs in each department. Communications between departments is entirely through hard-copy documents. Recently, GPG has been receiving complaints from customers and suppliers about billing, shipping, and payment errors. Management believes that these complaints stem, in part, from their antiquated computer system. You have been hired to assess GPG's procedures and internal controls. The following is a description of GPG's expenditure cycle.

Purchasing Process

The purchasing agent monitors the inventory levels by reviewing the inventory subsidiary ledger from his department computer. He decides which items need to be replenished and selects a supplier. He then enters this information into the computer terminal to create a digital purchase order and prints three hard copies of the purchase order. The purchasing agent sends one copy to the supplier; one copy to the accounts payable department, where it is filed temporarily, and files the third copy in the purchasing department.

When the goods are received, the receiving department inspects and verifies them using the packing slip, which is attached to the goods. The receiving clerk manually prepares two hard copies of a receiving report. One copy accompanies the goods to the warehouse for storage. The receiving clerk sends the second copy to the purchasing agent, who uses it to update the inventory subsidiary ledger and to close the open purchase order. The purchase agent then files the receiving report in the department.

Accounts Payable and Cash Disbursements Procedures

The accounts payable clerk receives the supplier's invoice and reconciles it with the purchase order in the temporary file. From her computer terminal, the clerk records the purchase in the purchases journal and records the liability by adding a record to the AP subsidiary ledger. The clerk then updates the inventory control and accounts payable control accounts in the general ledger. The purchases order and invoice are then filed in the department.

Each day, the clerk visually searches the AP subsidiary ledger from her terminal for invoices that are due to be paid. The clerk prepares the check and records it in the digital check register. The negotiable portion of the check is mailed to the vendor, and a check copy is filed. The clerk then closes the liability in the AP subsidiary ledger and updates the accounts payable control and cash accounts in the general ledger.

Required

a. Create a data flow diagram of the current system.
b. Create a system flowchart of the existing system.
c. Analyze the physical internal control weaknesses in the system.
d. (Optional) Prepare a system flowchart of a redesigned computer-based system that resolves the control weaknesses that you identified. Explain your solution.

7. CUSTOM FABRICATIONS INC. (STAND-ALONE PC-BASED ACCOUNTING SYSTEM)

(Prepared by Will Richens and Michael Catchpole, Lehigh University)

CUSTOM FABRICATIONS Inc. is a bicycle manufacturing firm founded in 2000 that currently employs 126 people. The company produces custom bicycles in its factory located near Los Angeles, CA. Each bicycle is tailored to a rider based on a number of different measurements, including height, weight, inseam, and arm length. These measurements are taken at 30 professional bicycle shops around Southern California, which are certified to size CUSTOM FABRICATIONS cycles. By accepting orders only through licensed dealers, CUSTOM FABRICATIONS ensures that each bike matches its rider precisely. CUSTOM FABRICATIONS' custom bikes are considered extremely high quality and the company takes pride in using only the best components sourced from around the world. Accordingly, CUSTOM FABRICATIONS purchases from a cast of hundreds of suppliers, chosen for their commitment to quality and reliability.

Demand for CUSTOM FABRICATIONS' cycles has grown exponentially in recent years. The surge in demand was somewhat unexpected and the company's factory has been operating at capacity for over a year. As a result, current orders face a production backlog of approximately 5–6 weeks. The company's operations have been further hampered by severe inefficiencies and control weaknesses attributed to its legacy accounting system. Your firm has been hired as an outside consultant to suggest improvements in the company's accounting procedures. The following paragraphs describe the company's expenditure cycle.

Purchases System

All purchases of raw materials are initiated in the CUSTOM FABRICATIONS' purchasing department. A clerk in the department monitors inventory levels from his PC, which is linked to the inventory subsidiary ledger. Once a part needs to be replenished, he creates a hard-copy purchase order. One copy is mailed to the vendor, a blind copy of the purchase order is sent to the warehouse, and the third copy is filed in the purchasing department.

Typically within 3–5 business days, the warehouse receives the ordered parts and the packing slip from the vendor, which the warehouse clerk reconciles with the blind copy of the purchase order. Once the reconciliation is complete, the warehouse clerk prepares a three-part hard-copy receiving report stating the quantity and condition of the items received. One copy of the receiving report is sent to the general ledger department to update the digital inventory control account. The second copy is sent to the accounts payable department, and the third is sent to the purchasing department to update the inventory subsidiary ledger.

Within a week, the mail room receives the supplier's invoice, which is immediately sent to the accounts payable department. The AP clerk reconciles the invoice with the receiving report and then records a liability in the AP subsidiary ledger from the department PC. Finally, the clerk prints an AP summary from the terminal and sends it to the general ledger clerk.

Cash Disbursements System

The accounts payable clerk regularly checks the accounts payable subsidiary account at his terminal to ensure timely payment to vendors. For those items due for payment, he sends approval in the form of a payment voucher to the cash disbursements department.

For control purposes, cash disbursements are processed manually. The details of the check are recorded in the hard-copy cash disbursements journal, and the check is mailed to the vendor. The clerk then prepares a journal voucher and sends it to the general ledger.

Once the general ledger clerk receives the journal voucher, the AP summary, and the receiving report, she updates the affected general ledger accounts from the department PC.

Required

a. Create a data flow diagram of the current system.
b. Create a system flowchart of the existing system.
c. Analyze the physical internal control weaknesses in the system.

d. Describe the risks associated with these control weaknesses.
e. (Optional) Prepare a system flowchart of a redesigned computer-based system that resolves the control weaknesses that you identified. Explain your solution.

8. PERFORMANCE WATER PUMPS (CENTRALIZED SYSTEM WITH DISTRIBUTED TERMINALS)

Performance Water Pumps (PWP) is a leading manufacturer of water pumps with high capacity capability. These pumps are used in both civil and private disaster situations. PWP's primary market is disaster recovery companies that assist home owners following basement flooding. They also sell to building contractors, municipalities, and rental companies. The company publishes an industry catalog of pumps and other auxiliary equipment, which it distributes to customers and prospective customers. PWP's headquarters and manufacturing facilities are in Leesville, Louisiana where they employ 125 manufacturing and clerical staff.

PWP employs a centralized computer system with distributed terminals in the departments. Recently they have been having operational problems with it. PWP has hired your auditing firm to assess its operations and internal control procedures.

Purchasing System

When an inventory item falls to the reorder point, a purchase requisition is automatically created and printed on the terminal in the purchasing department. The clerk in the department selects suppliers and prepares a purchase order. A copy of the PO is sent to the vendor, and a copy is sent to the receiving department. Then, the clerk adds a record to the open/closed purchase order file through an update program in the data processing department.

When the receiving clerk receives the inventories, he reconciles the goods with the packing slip and the purchase order. After the reconciliation, the receiving clerk prepares a hard-copy receiving report recording the quantity and quality of the goods received. A copy of the receiving report accompanies the goods to the warehouse, and a copy is filed in the receiving department. Using the department terminal, the receiving clerk adds a record to the digital receiving report file. The system then automatically closes the purchase order. Upon receiving the inventories, the warehouse clerk updates the inventory subsidiary ledger through the terminal in the warehouse.

When the supplier's invoice arrives, the accounts payable clerk adds a record to the supplier invoice file, which triggers the system to automatically set up a liability in the AP subsidiary ledger based on the financial information contained in the invoice. The system then automatically updates all affected general ledger accounts.

Cash Disbursements System

Each day the system scans the AP ledger for items due to be paid and prints the checks. The check is sent to the vendor, and a copy is sent to cash disbursements, where it is filed. Next, the system adds a record to the check register file and removes the liability in the AP subsidiary ledger. Finally, the system automatically updates the general ledger accounts.

Required

a. Create a data flow diagram of the current system.
b. Create a system flowchart of the existing system.
c. Analyze the physical internal control weaknesses in the system.
d. Describe the IT controls that should be in place in this system.
e. (Optional) Prepare a system flowchart of a redesigned computer-based system that resolves the control weaknesses that you identified. Explain your solution.

The Expenditure Cycle Part II: Payroll Processing and Fixed Asset Procedures

CHAPTER 6

Learning Objectives

After studying this chapter, you should:

- Recognize the fundamental tasks that constitute the payroll and fixed asset processes.
- Be able to identify the functional departments involved in payroll and fixed asset activities, and trace the flow of these transactions through the organization.
- Be able to specify the documents, journals, and accounts that provide audit trails, promote the maintenance of historical records, and support internal decision making and financial reporting.
- Understand the risks associated with payroll and fixed asset activities and recognize the controls that reduce these risks.
- Be aware of the operational features and the control implications of technology used in payroll and fixed asset systems.

This chapter is divided into two major sections. The first section begins with a conceptual overview of the payroll process emphasizing logical tasks, key entities, sources and uses of information, and the flow of key documents through an organization. It then examines the operational features, risks, and controls specific to physical payroll systems, including a basic technology system and an integrated system that employs advanced technologies. The section concludes with a review of payroll outsourcing, which is an option that many companies pursue.

The second section examines fixed asset systems. Fixed assets are the property, plant, and equipment used in the operation of a business. This discussion focuses on processes pertaining to the acquisition, maintenance, and disposal of fixed assets. Finally, we illustrate these concepts with a system that employs real-time processing.

The Conceptual Payroll System

Payroll processing is actually a special-case purchases system in which the organization purchases labor rather than raw materials or finished goods for resale. The nature of payroll processing, however, creates the need for specialized procedures for the following reasons:

1. A firm can design general purchasing and disbursement procedures that apply to all vendors and inventory items. Payroll procedures, however, differ greatly among classes of employees. For example, different procedures are needed for hourly employees, salaried employees, piece workers, and commissioned employees. Also, payroll processing requires special accounting procedures for employee deductions and withholdings for taxes that do not apply to trade accounts.
2. General expenditure activities constitute a relatively steady stream of purchasing and disbursing transactions. Business organizations thus design purchasing systems to deal with their normal level of activity. Payroll activities, on the other hand, are discrete events in which disbursements to employees occur weekly, biweekly, or monthly. The task of periodically preparing large numbers of payroll checks in addition to the normal trade account checks can overload the general purchasing and cash disbursements system.
3. Writing checks to employees requires special controls. Combining payroll and trade transactions can encourage payroll fraud.

Although specific payroll procedures vary among firms, Figure 6-1 presents a data flow diagram depicting the general tasks of the payroll system in a manufacturing firm. The key points of the process are described in the following paragraphs.

Personnel Department

The personnel department prepares and submits **personnel action forms** to the prepare payroll function. These documents identify employees authorized to receive a paycheck and are used to reflect changes in hourly pay rates, payroll deductions, and job classification. Figure 6-2 shows a personnel action form used to advise payroll of an increase in an employee's salary.

Production Department

Production employees prepare two types of time records: job tickets and time cards. **Job tickets** capture the time that individual workers spend on each production job. Cost accounting uses these documents to allocate direct labor charges to work-in-process (WIP) accounts. **Time cards** capture the time the employee is at work. These are sent to the prepare payroll function for calculating the amount of the employee's paycheck. Figure 6-3 illustrates a job ticket, and Figure 6-4 illustrates a time card.

Each day at the beginning of the shift, employees place their time cards in a special clock that records the time. Typically, they clock out for lunch and at the end of the shift. This time card is the formal record of daily attendance. At the end of the week, the supervisor reviews, signs, and sends the time cards to the payroll department.

Update WIP Account

After cost accounting allocates labor costs to the WIP accounts, the charges are summarized in a **labor distribution summary** and forwarded to the general ledger function.

Prepare Payroll

The payroll department receives pay rate and withholding data from the personnel department and hours-worked data from the production department. A clerk in the payroll department then performs the following tasks.

1. Prepares the payroll register (Figure 6-5) showing gross pay, deductions, overtime pay, and net pay.
2. Enters this information into the **employee payroll records** (Figure 6-6).
3. Prepares employee paychecks (Figure 6-7).
4. Sends the **paychecks** to the distribute paycheck function.
5. Files the time cards, personnel action form, and copy of the **payroll register** (not shown).

FIGURE 6-1 DATA FLOW DIAGRAM OF PAYROLL PROCEDURES

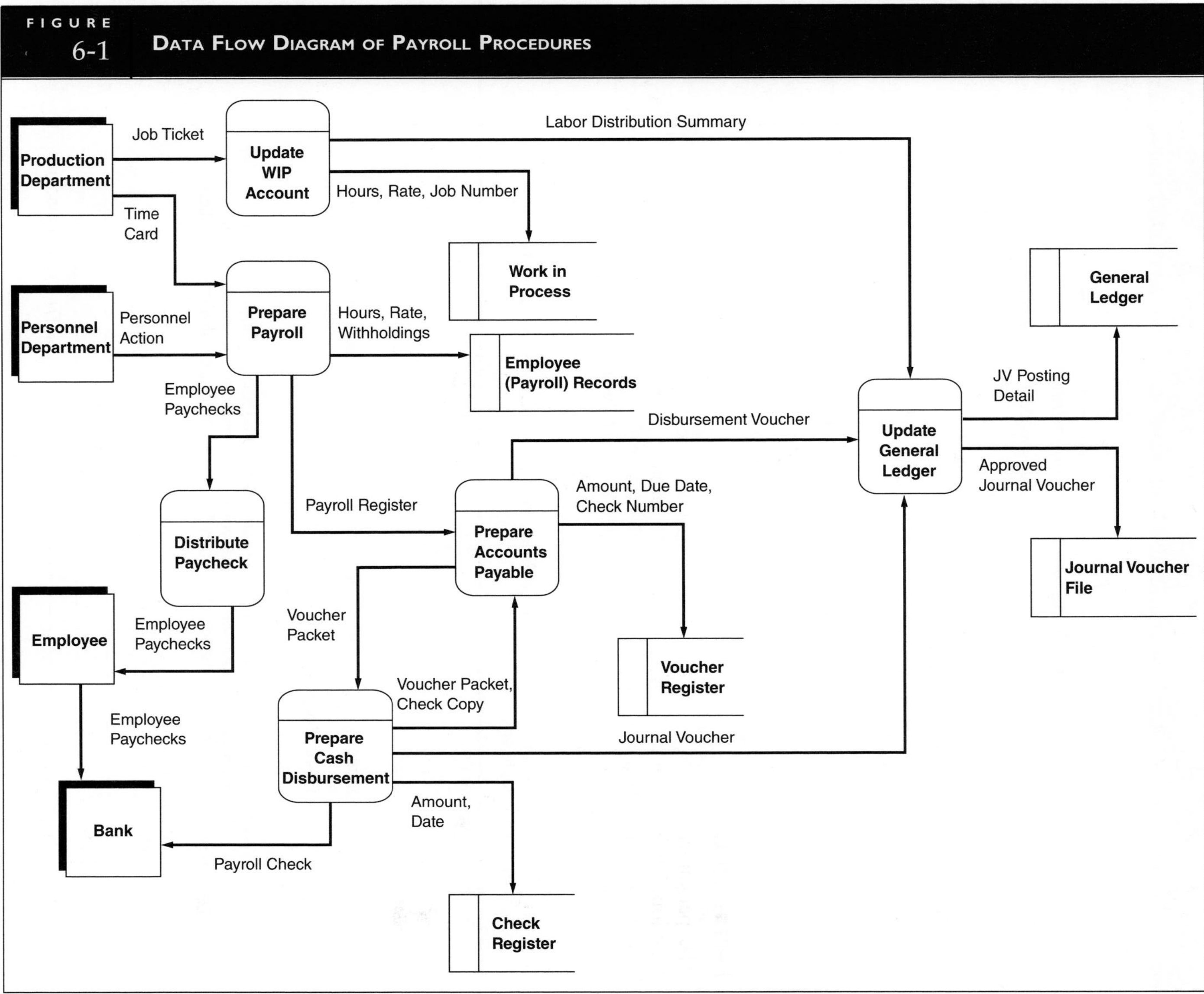

FIGURE 6-2 PERSONNEL ACTION FORM

Salary Increase Recommendation

Based on the attached appraisal form, the following recommendation is made for:

Name: Jane Doe
Position: Accounting Clerk
Social Security Number: 111 – 22 – 3333

Current Salary: 23,520.00
Current Bonus Level: 00%
Last Increase Date: 08/22/14
Next Increase Date: 08/22/15

Current Performance Rating:
(from attached appraisal) good

Salary Increase Guidelines:

Outstanding:	6–9%	9–12 months
Superior:	4–6%	12 months
Good:	3–4%	12–15 months
Provisional:	0%	Review again in 90 days.

In view of the Current Performance and the Salary Increase Guidelines, I recommend the following salary treatment:

Percentage Increase: 4 %
New Salary: $ 24,460
Effective Date: 8 / 22 / 15

Promotions:
In the case of a promotion, a standard 5% increase for the promotion and a prorated merit increase (based on time since last merit increase) are appropriate. The next increase will be considered from the date of promotion.

Other Considerations:
In some situations, it is possible to advance a salary beyond the above guidelines as an exception, with the president's approval. Some typical situations are, but are not limited to, equity adjustment and job reevaluation. If such is the case here, please provide justification below:

Approvals: J. R. Johnson Supervisor
H. M. Morris Director of Personnel

Exception approval if needed: N/A President

FIGURE 6-3 JOB TICKET

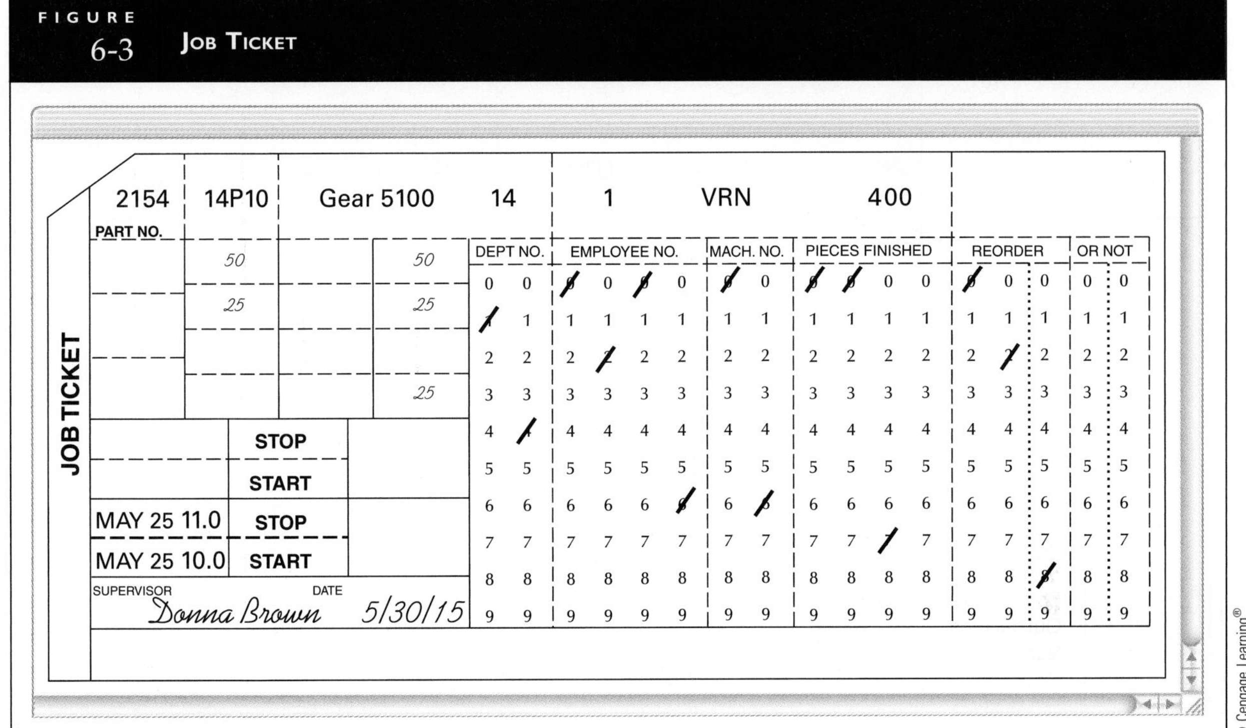

JOB TICKET

2154 | 14P10 | Gear 5100 | 14 | 1 | VRN | 400

PART NO.

50 | 50
25 | 25
25

STOP
START
MAY 25 11.0 STOP
MAY 25 10.0 START

SUPERVISOR Donna Brown DATE 5/30/15

DEPT NO.		EMPLOYEE NO.				MACH. NO.		PIECES FINISHED				REORDER			OR NOT	
0	0	0	0	0	0	0	0	0	0	0	0	0	0	0	0	0
1	1	1	1	1	1	1	1	1	1	1	1	1	1	1	1	1
2	2	2	2	2	2	2	2	2	2	2	2	2	2	2	2	2
3	3	3	3	3	3	3	3	3	3	3	3	3	3	3	3	3
4	4	4	4	4	4	4	4	4	4	4	4	4	4	4	4	4
5	5	5	5	5	5	5	5	5	5	5	5	5	5	5	5	5
6	6	6	6	6	6	6	6	6	6	6	6	6	6	6	6	6
7	7	7	7	7	7	7	7	7	7	7	7	7	7	7	7	7
8	8	8	8	8	8	8	8	8	8	8	8	8	8	8	8	8
9	9	9	9	9	9	9	9	9	9	9	9	9	9	9	9	9

Distribute Paycheck

A form of payroll fraud involves submitting time cards for nonexistent employees. The perpetrator of the fraud then collects the paycheck and cashes it. To prevent this, many companies use a paymaster to distribute the paychecks to employees. This individual is independent of the payroll process—not involved in payroll authorization or preparation tasks. If a valid employee does not claim a paycheck, the paymaster returns the check to payroll. The reason the check went unclaimed can then be investigated.

Prepare Accounts Payable

The accounts payable (AP) clerk reviews the payroll register for correctness and prepares copies of a cash disbursement voucher for the amount of the payroll. The clerk records the voucher in the voucher register and submits the voucher packet (voucher and payroll register) to cash disbursements. A copy of the disbursement voucher is sent to the general ledger function.

Prepare Cash Disbursement

Upon receipt of the voucher packet, the cash disbursement function prepares a single check for the entire amount of the payroll and deposits it in the **payroll imprest account.** The employee paychecks are drawn on this account, which is used only for payroll. Funds must be transferred from the general cash account to this imprest account before the paychecks can be cashed. The clerk sends a copy of the check along with the disbursement voucher and the payroll register to the AP department, where they are filed (not shown). Finally, a journal voucher is prepared and sent to the general ledger function.

FIGURE 6-4 Time Card

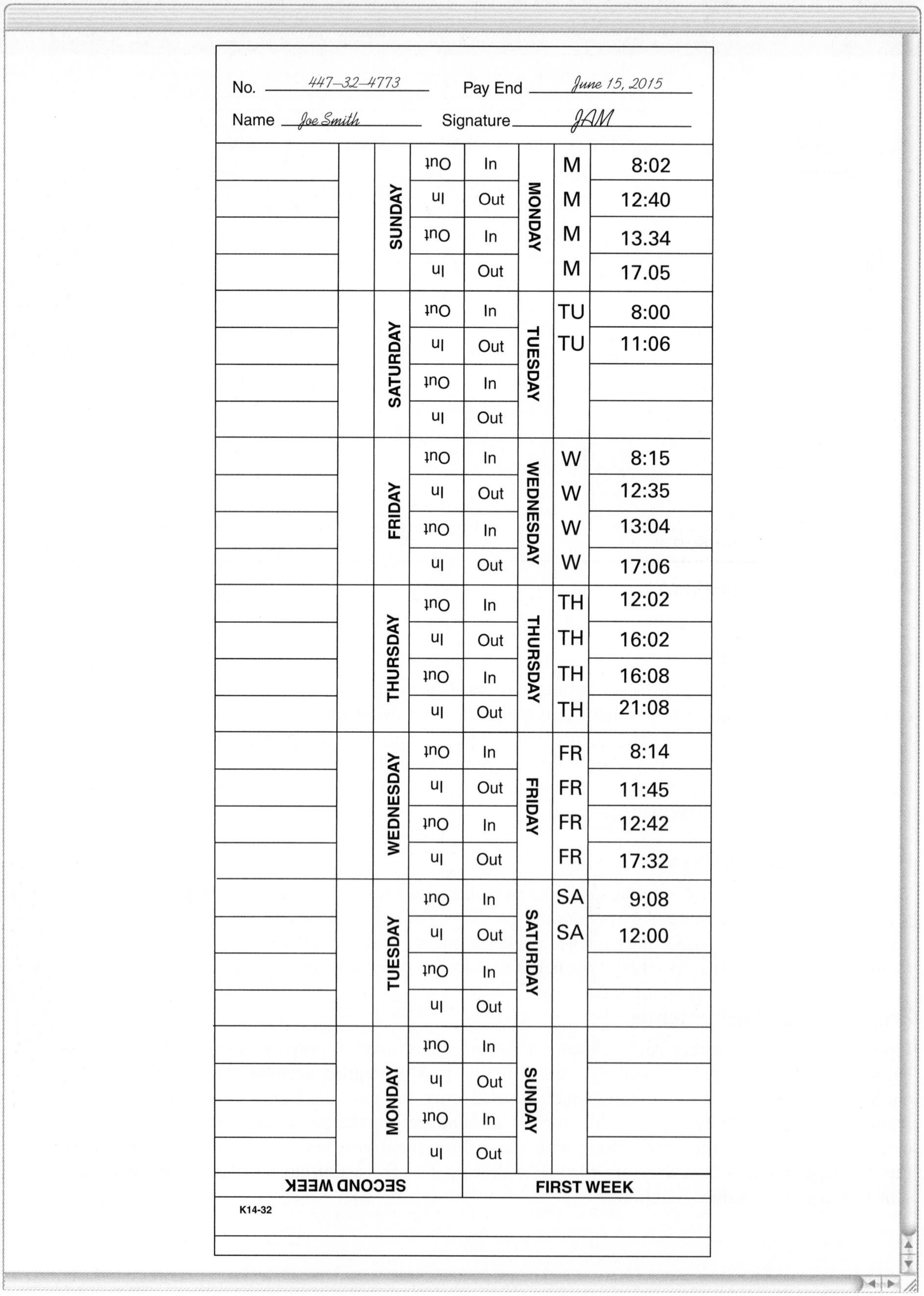

No. 447–32–4773 Pay End June 15, 2015

Name Joe Smith Signature JAM

Second Week		Second Week Day	Second Week In/Out	First Week In/Out	First Week Day	Day	Time
		SUNDAY	Out	In	MONDAY	M	8:02
			In	Out		M	12:40
			Out	In		M	13.34
			In	Out		M	17.05
		SATURDAY	Out	In	TUESDAY	TU	8:00
			In	Out		TU	11:06
			Out	In			
			In	Out			
		FRIDAY	Out	In	WEDNESDAY	W	8:15
			In	Out		W	12:35
			Out	In		W	13:04
			In	Out		W	17:06
		THURSDAY	Out	In	THURSDAY	TH	12:02
			In	Out		TH	16:02
			Out	In		TH	16:08
			In	Out		TH	21:08
		WEDNESDAY	Out	In	FRIDAY	FR	8:14
			In	Out		FR	11:45
			Out	In		FR	12:42
			In	Out		FR	17:32
		TUESDAY	Out	In	SATURDAY	SA	9:08
			In	Out		SA	12:00
			Out	In			
			In	Out			
		MONDAY	Out	In	SUNDAY		
			In	Out			
			Out	In			
			In	Out			
SECOND WEEK				FIRST WEEK			

K14-32

FIGURE 6-5 PAYROLL REGISTER

HAMPSHIRE SUPPLY COMPANY

Payroll register for period ending 10/31/15
Checks: All
Employee(s): All

Check# 5000 Paid to Emp# CAS : CASEY, SUE

PAY	Hours	Rate	Gross	DEDUCTIONS	
Regular	173.33		1,000.00	SD SDI	9.00
Overtime			0.00	HL INSUR	100.00
Sick			0.00	SV SAVINGS	100.00
Holiday			0.00		0.00
Vacation			0.00	Fed. withholding	16.25
			0.00	Addl. fed. withholding	0.00
				State withholding	21.77
Totals	173.33		1,000.00	Social Security	62.00
				Medicare	14.50
Days worked	21			NET PAY	676.48

Check# 5001 Paid to Emp# JON : JONES, JESSICA

PAY	Hours	Rate	Gross	DEDUCTIONS	
Regular	173.33	15.00	2,599.95	SD SDI	23.40
Overtime		30.00	0.00	HL INSUR	100.00
Sick		15.00	0.00	SV SAVINGS	260.00
Holiday		45.00	0.00		0.00
Vacation		15.00	0.00	Fed. withholding	256.24
			0.00	Addl. fed. withholding	0.00
				State withholding	116.98
Totals	173.33		2,599.95	Social Security	161.20
				Medicare	37.70
Days worked	21			NET PAY	1,644.43

Check# 5002 Paid to Emp # ROB : ROBERTS, WILLIAM

Regular	173.33	15.00	2,599.95	SD SDI	23.40
Overtime		30.00	0.00	HL INSUR	100.00
Sick		15.00	0.00	SV SAVINGS	260.00
Holiday		45.00	0.00		0.00
Vacation		15.00	0.00	Fed. withholding	396.07
			0.00	Addl. fed. withholding	0.00
				State withholding	208.04
Totals	173.33		2,599.95	Social Security	161.20
				Medicare	37.70
Days worked	21			NET PAY	1,413.54

FIGURE 6-6 EMPLOYEE PAYROLL RECORD

HSC HAMPSHIRE SUPPLY COMPANY

Employee pay and earnings information

Period Ending 10/31/15

Emp# : JON SS# : 682–63–0897 JESSICA JONES

Rate: 15.00/hour

Addl FITW/check: 0.00

Normal deduction(s)			Amount
Ded 1 SD	%	0.9000	0.00
Ded 2 HL	%	0.0000	100.00
Ded 3 SV	%	10.0000	0.00
Ded 4	%	0.0000	0.00

Earnings:	Quarter to date		Year to date	
	Hours	Amount	Hours	Amount
Regular	173.3	2,599.95	173.3	2,599.95
Overtime	0.0	0.00	0.0	0.00
Sick	0.0	0.00	0.0	0.00
Vacation	0.0	0.00	0.0	0.00
Holiday	0.0	0.00	0.0	0.00
	0.0	0.00	0.0	0.00
Withholding:				
FIT		256.24		256.24
SIT		116.98		116.98
Social Security		161.20		161.20
Medicare		37.70		37.70
Deductions:				
SDI		23.40		23.40
HEALTH INSUR		100.00		100.00
SAVINGS		260.00		260.00
		0.00		0.00

FIGURE 6-7 **EMPLOYEE PAYCHECK**

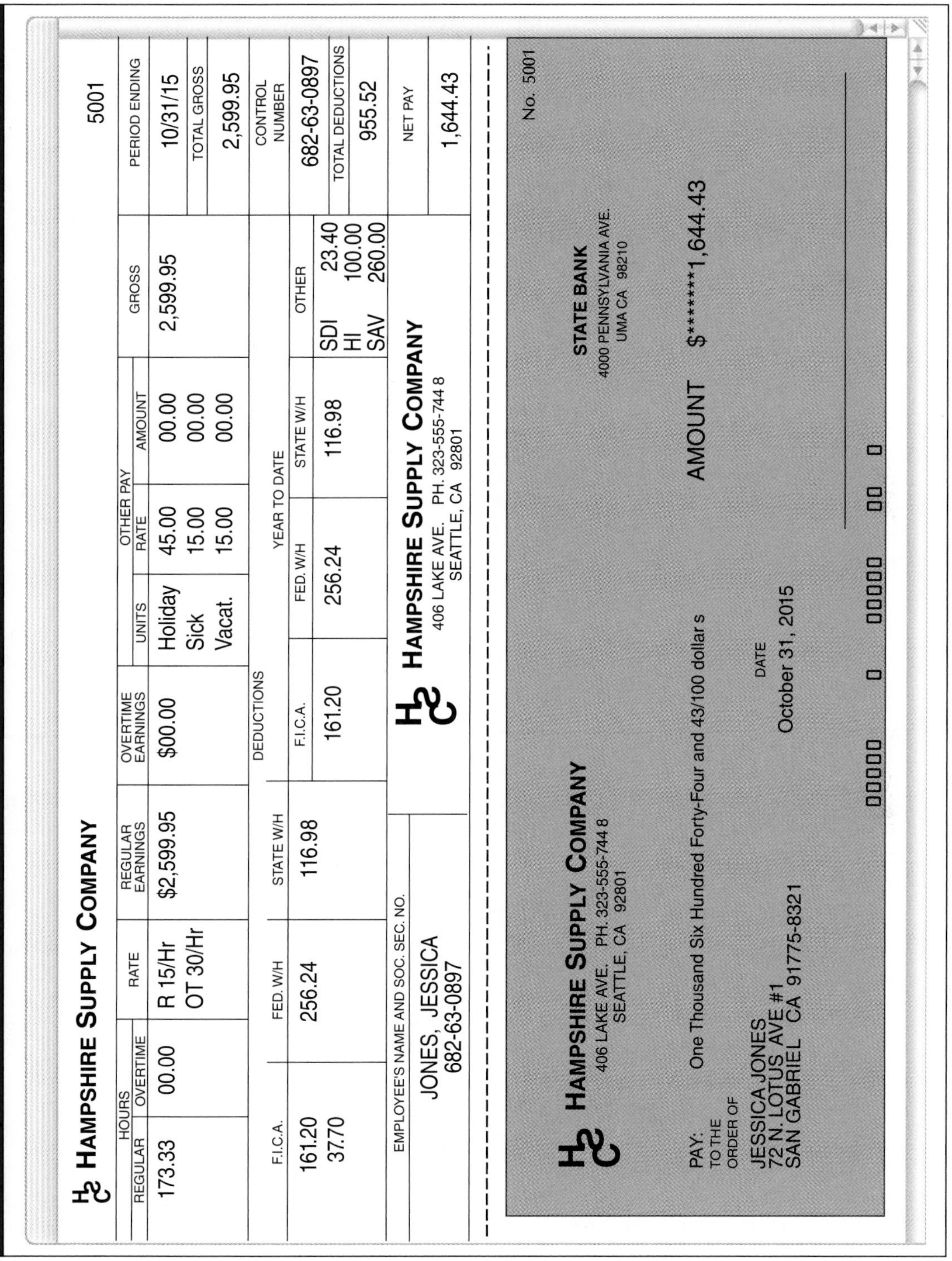

HAMPSHIRE SUPPLY COMPANY 5001

HOURS REGULAR	HOURS OVERTIME	RATE	REGULAR EARNINGS	OVERTIME EARNINGS	OTHER PAY UNITS	OTHER PAY RATE	OTHER PAY AMOUNT	GROSS	PERIOD ENDING
173.33	00.00	R 15/Hr OT 30/Hr	$2,599.95	$00.00	Holiday Sick Vacat.	45.00 15.00 15.00	00.00 00.00 00.00	2,599.95	10/31/15
									TOTAL GROSS
									2,599.95

DEDUCTIONS

F.I.C.A.	FED. W/H	STATE W/H	YEAR TO DATE F.I.C.A.	YEAR TO DATE FED. W/H	YEAR TO DATE STATE W/H	YEAR TO DATE OTHER	CONTROL NUMBER
161.20 37.70	256.24	116.98	161.20	256.24	116.98	SDI 23.40 HI 100.00 SAV 260.00	682-63-0897
							TOTAL DEDUCTIONS
							955.52

EMPLOYEE'S NAME AND SOC. SEC. NO.

JONES, JESSICA
682-63-0897

HAMPSHIRE SUPPLY COMPANY
406 LAKE AVE. PH. 323-555-744 8
SEATTLE, CA 92801

NET PAY
1,644.43

No. 5001

HAMPSHIRE SUPPLY COMPANY
406 LAKE AVE. PH. 323-555-744 8
SEATTLE, CA 92801

STATE BANK
4000 PENNSYLVANIA AVE.
UMA CA 98210

PAY: One Thousand Six Hundred Forty-Four and 43/100 dollar s AMOUNT $*******1,644.43

TO THE ORDER OF

JESSICA JONES
72 N. LOTUS AVE #1
SAN GABRIEL CA 91775-8321

DATE
October 31, 2015

00000 0 00000 00 0

UPDATE GENERAL LEDGER

The general ledger function receives the labor distribution summary from cost accounting, the disbursement voucher from AP, and the journal voucher from cash disbursements. With this information, the general ledger clerk makes the following accounting entries:

From the Labor Distribution Summary

	DR	CR
Work-in-Process (Direct labor)	XXX.XX	
Factory Overhead (Indirect labor)	XXX.XX	
Wages Payable		XXX.XX

From Disbursement Voucher

	DR	CR
Wages Payable	XXX.XX	
Cash		XXX.XX
Federal Income Tax Withholdings Payable		XXX.XX
State Income Tax Withholdings Payable		XXX.XX
FICA Income Tax Withholdings Payable		XXX.XX
Group Insurance Premiums Payable		XXX.XX
Pension Fund Withholdings Payable		XXX.XX
Union Dues Payable		XXX.XX

The debits and credits from these entries must be equal. If they are not, there is an error in the calculation of either labor distribution charges or payroll. When the equality has been verified, the clerk files the voucher and labor distribution summary.

The Physical Payroll System

In this section we examine the physical payroll system. This begins with a review of the operational features and control issues pertinent to a basic technology system. We then review the features and controls of an integrated system that uses advanced technologies.

BASIC TECHNOLOGY PAYROLL SYSTEM

Figure 6-8 presents a flowchart of a basic technology system. The following key tasks are represented in the flowchart.

1. Personnel action and time and attendance information from the personnel and production departments respectively, initiate the payroll process.
2. The payroll department reconciles this information, calculates the payroll, and sends the paychecks to the paymaster for distribution to employees.
3. Cost accounting receives information regarding the time spent on each job from production. This is used for posting to accounts in the WIP subsidiary ledger.
4. AP receives payroll summary information (payroll register) from the payroll department and authorizes the cash disbursements department to deposit a single check, in the amount of the total payroll, in a bank imprest account on which the payroll is drawn.
5. The general ledger department reconciles summary information from cost accounting and AP. GL accounts are updated to reflect these transactions.

ADVANCED TECHNOLOGY PAYROLL SYSTEM

For moderate-sized and large organizations, payroll processing is often integrated within the **human resource management (HRM) system.** The **HRM** system captures and processes a wide range of personnel-related data, including employee benefits, labor resource planning, employee relations, employee skills, internal training, personnel actions (pay rates, deductions, and so on), and payroll processing. HRM systems provide real-time access to personnel files for purposes of direct inquiries and making changes in employee status as they occur. Figure 6-9 illustrates an integrated payroll and HRM system. The key operating features of the payroll components of the system are presented next.

Human Resources

Human resources clerks enter data into the employee records file in real time from terminals. This includes additions of new employees, deletions of terminated employees, changes in work dependents, changes in withholdings, and changes in job status such as job title and pay rate.

Cost Accounting

The cost accounting department enters job cost data in real time to create the **labor usage file.**

Employee Timekeeping

Modern business is increasingly characterized by telecommuting employees working from multiple locations, both domestically and internationally. Capturing and maintaining accurate time and attendance data in this dynamic environment is a challenge that is addressed through advanced hardware and software technologies. Figure 6-9 illustrates how employees directly enter timekeeping data in real time to produce the **time and attendance file.** Several technologies developed for this task are outlined below.

Biometric time clocks verify employees' identities by using fingerprint or hand-vein scan technology. To protect employee privacy, these devices use a mathematical algorithm for verification rather than storing actual fingerprints in a database.

Magnetic swipe ID cards work like a credit card. Each employee is issued an ID card that has a magnetic strip containing employee information. The employee swipes the card through the time clock to record start and end time on the job. For additional verification, the employee may be asked to enter a password or PIN.

Proximity cards are similar to swipe cards but don't require the user to slide the card through a reader. Instead, the employee places the card in front of the reader to record attendance time. The advantage is that these cards can be read through wallets, purses, and card holders.

Mobile remote devices allow employees to clock in using handheld devices (PDA or cell phone) or web browsers from laptop computers. This option is popular among businesses with employees in the field who travel between clients and with companies engaged in global business with foreign-based employees.

Data Processing

At the end of the work period, the following tasks are performed in a batch process:

1. Labor costs are distributed to various WIP, overhead, and expense accounts.
2. An online labor distribution summary file is created. Copies of the file are accessible from terminals in the cost accounting and general ledger departments.
3. Payroll is calculated, and an online payroll register is created from the time and attendance file and the **employee records file.** The payroll register file is accessible from the AP and cash disbursements departments.
4. The employee records file is updated.
5. Paychecks are prepared, signed, and distributed to the employees.[2]
6. Funds sufficient to cover the full amount of the payroll are transferred to the payroll imprest account, and the transfer is recorded in the check register.
7. Digital journal vouchers are entered into the journal voucher file. The system automatically updates the general ledger from the journal voucher and labor distribution summary files.

FIGURE 6-8 Basic Technology Payroll System

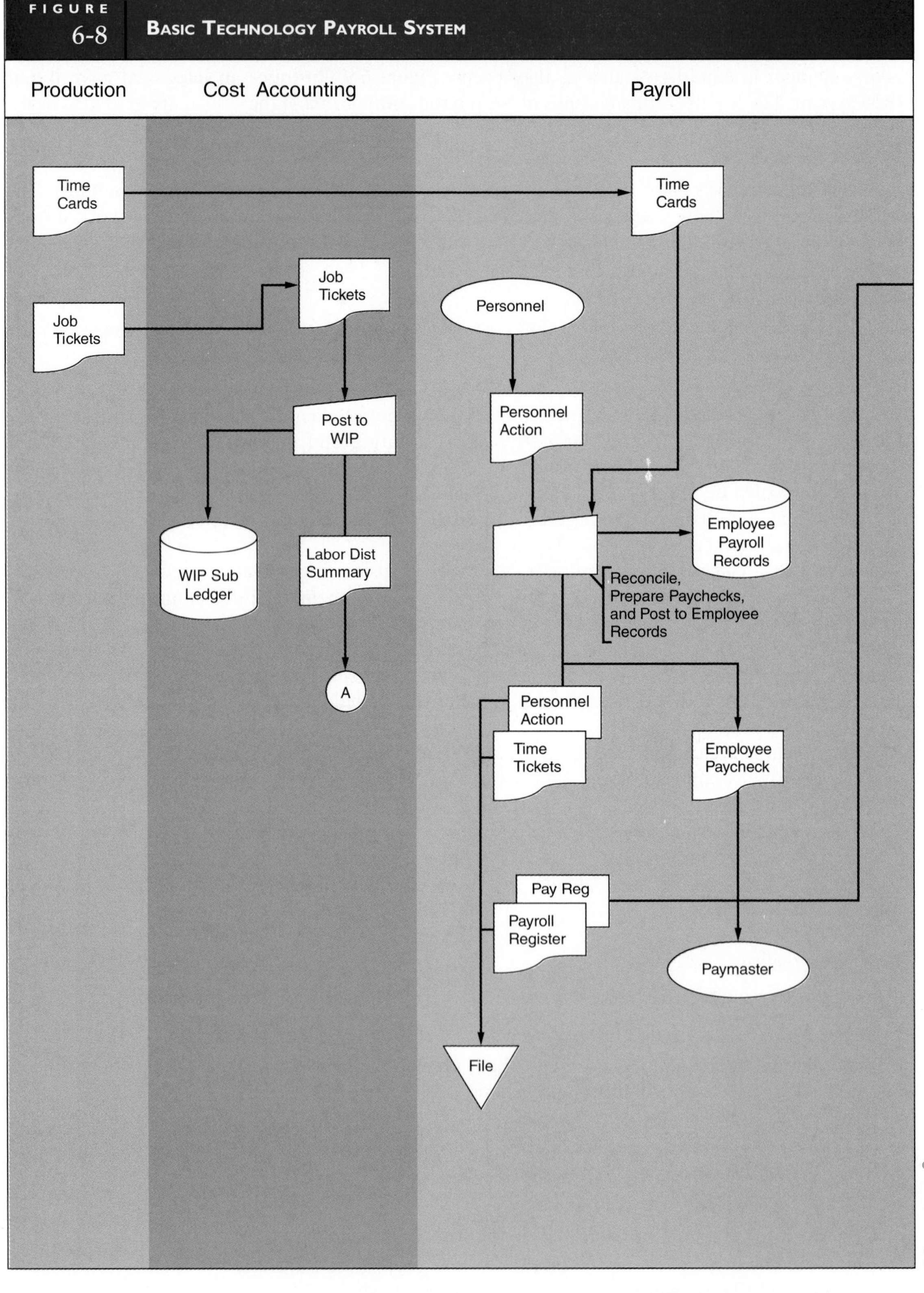

FIGURE 6-8 (CONTINUED)

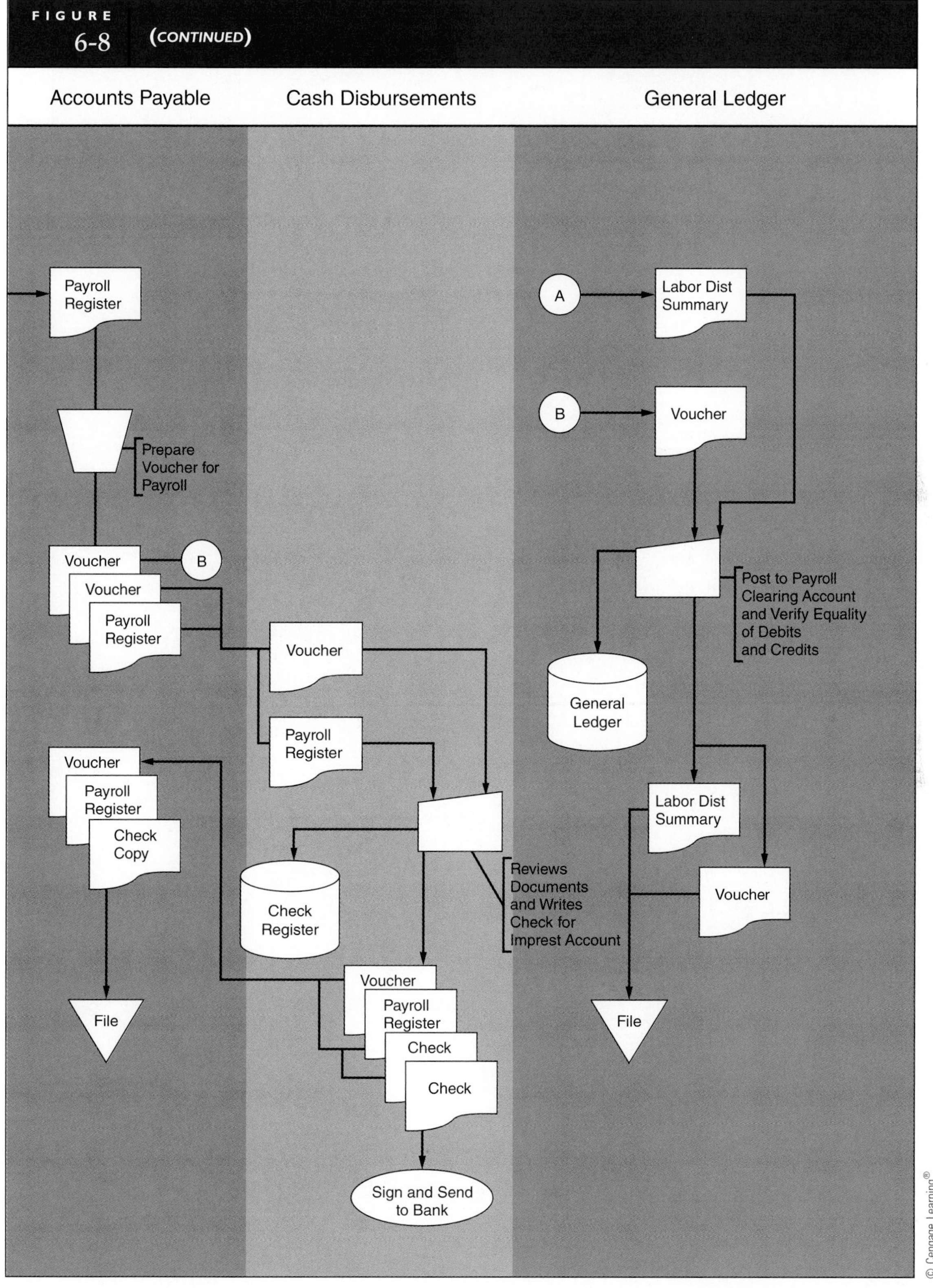

FIGURE 6-9 INTEGRATED PAYROLL AND HRM SYSTEM

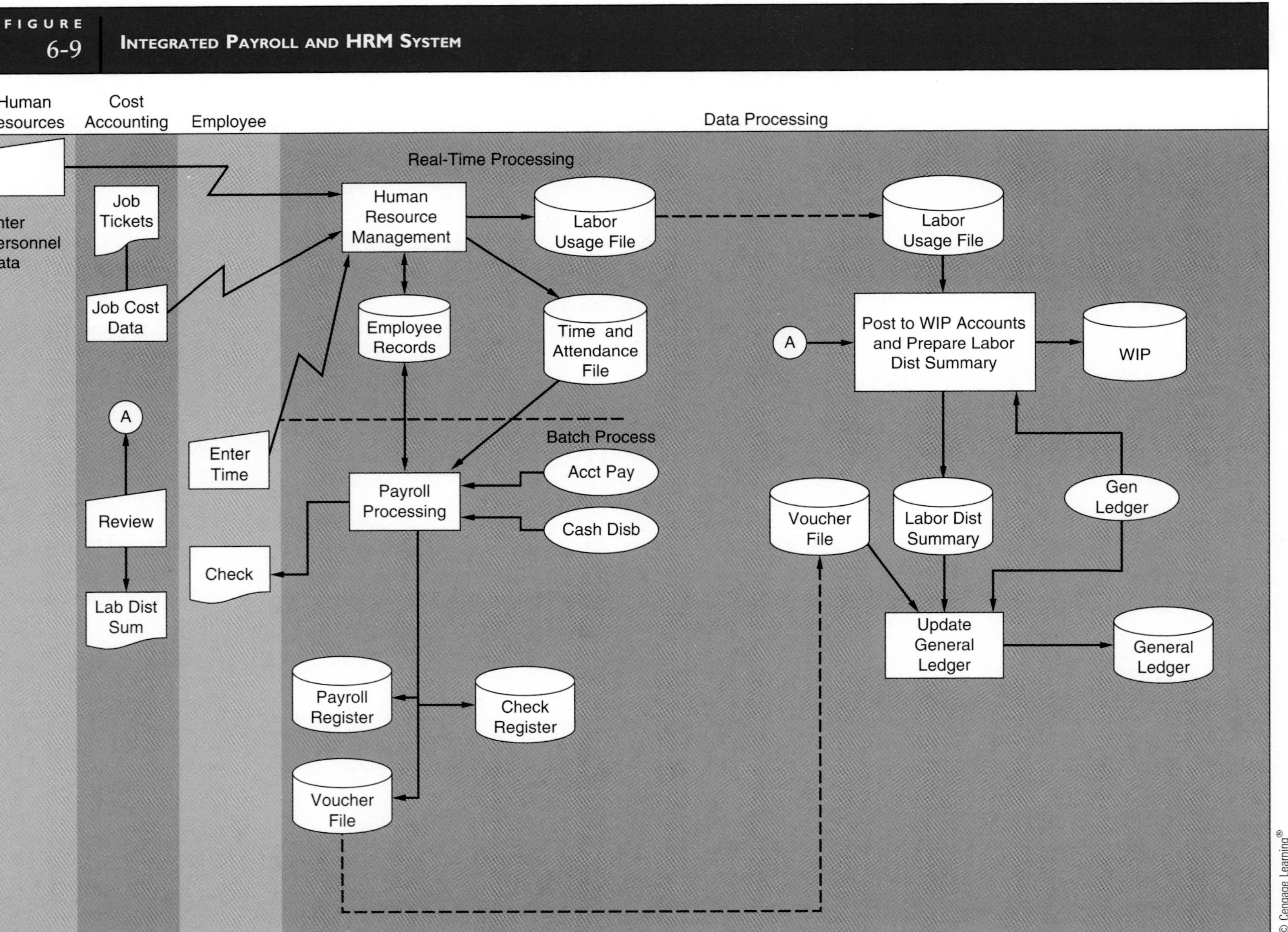

PAYROLL SYSTEM RISKS AND INTERNAL CONTROLS

As noted in previous chapters, an objective of internal control is to mitigate the risk from errors and fraud. The following are the primary risks associated with payroll system transactions:

- Inaccurately recording payroll transactions in accounts.
- Misappropriation of cash through payroll fraud.
- Unauthorized access to payroll records and confidential employee data.

Recall from previous discussion that internal control activities consist of: (1) physical controls, and (2) IT controls. The purpose of physical controls is to control the actions of people and consist of six classes of internal control activities: transaction authorization, segregation of duties, supervision, accounting records, access control, and independent verification. IT controls are comprised of general controls and application controls. General controls are not specific to a particular cycle or subsystem and thus do not apply to payroll system risks directly. Computer application controls consist of: input controls, processing controls, and output controls. The discussion that follows examines and compares how physical and IT control techniques apply in both basic technology and advanced technology systems to reduce the risks identified above. Table 6-1 at the end of the section provides a summary of this material.

Risk of Inaccurately Recording Transactions

Inaccurate record keeping can take many forms. The following outlines some possible payroll system errors.

- Time and attendance data are incorrectly calculated.
- Wages Payable go unrecorded or are recorded in the wrong period.
- Employee earnings and cash payments are inaccurately posted to employee records or are posted to the wrong employee.
- Payroll register, accounts payable, and cash disbursements amounts are incorrectly posted to their respective general ledger accounts.

Physical Controls

ACCOUNTING RECORDS. The control objective of accounting records is to maintain an audit trail adequate for tracing a transaction from its source document to the financial statements. The audit trail for payroll includes the following documents:

1. Time cards, job tickets, and disbursement vouchers.
2. Journal information, which comes from the labor distribution summary and the payroll register.
3. Subsidiary ledger accounts, which contain the employee records, WIP, and various expense accounts.
4. The general ledger accounts: payroll control, cash, and the payroll clearing (imprest) account.

The auditor's concern in the regarding payroll processing is that salary obligations are accurately and completely recorded and matched to the appropriate period.

INDEPENDENT VERIFICATION. The following are examples of independent verification controls in the payroll system:

1. **Time and Attendance**. Before submitting time cards to payroll, the supervisor must verify their accuracy and sign them.
2. **Accounts Payable**. The AP clerk verifies the accuracy of the payroll register before creating a disbursement voucher that transfers funds to the imprest account.
3. **General Ledger**. The general ledger department provides verification of the overall process by reconciling the labor distribution summary and the payroll disbursement voucher.

IT Controls

DATA INPUT EDITS. Recall that transaction data are assumed to be "dirty" and contain various errors. In the case of payroll processing, time and attendance and employee action data may contain transposed digits, invalid employee numbers, invalid pay rates, and other clerical errors. If not detected before being processed, these errors will corrupt the master files of the system.

Input controls verify the integrity of transaction data being entered into the application. Erroneous payroll data can corrupt WIP accounts, employee records, and the payroll register. Data entry errors are particularly problematic in mobile and/or distributed workforce environments in which employees directly enter time and attendance data into the system. Edits including checks for missing data, numeric-alphabetic data tests, tests for invalid data values, and check digits on employee account numbers will reduce the risk of data entry errors by clerks and remotely located employees.

The following processing controls pertain to payroll application logic:

ERROR MESSAGES. Any mismatch when posting time card or personnel action data to employee records should produce an error message to the computer operator.

FILE BACKUP. Backup procedures need to be in place to reduce the risk of data loss due to file destruction and/or corruption.

AUTOMATED POSTING TO ACCOUNTS. Record keeping functions, which in the basic technology system rely more heavily on human involvement, are automated in the advanced technology systems. In a manual environment, segregation of duties between timekeeping, personnel, accounts payable, cash disbursements, and the general ledger functions are important physical controls designed to prevent or detect human errors and fraud. In advanced technology systems, computer applications perform these tasks. Eliminating the human element reduces the potential for errors and significantly improves efficiency of operations. Again, we note that these benefits depend upon application integrity, which is the product of well-controlled systems development process.

Risk of Misappropriation of Cash through Payroll Fraud

Payroll frauds come in two general forms:

1. The first is the nonexistent employee who receives a paycheck. This fraud involves someone in the organization (a supervisor or above) creating a phantom employee, submitting time cards for the employee, and ultimately receiving the paycheck. The phantom employee may be a complete fabrication or, alternatively, may be a former employee who has left the organization, but remains on the employee file.
2. The second type of payroll fraud involves over payment of an employee. This is usually accomplished by inflating the hours worked on timecards and is particularly a problem where employees self-report and/or where supervisory control is inadequate.

The following controls reduce the risk of payroll fraud.

Physical Controls

TRANSACTION AUTHORIZATION. The personnel action form helps payroll keep current the employee records. This document describes additions, deletions, and other changes to the employee file and acts as an important authorization control to ensure that only the time cards of current and valid employees are processed.

SEGREGATION OF DUTIES. The following segregations of duties reduce the risk of various forms of payroll fraud:

1. The timekeeping function and the personnel function should be separated. The personnel function provides the payroll function with pay rate information for authorized hourly

employees. Typically, an organization will offer a range of valid pay rates based on experience, job classification, seniority, and merit. If the production (timekeeping) department were to provide this information, an employee may be able to submit a higher rate and perpetrate a fraud.

2. For purposes of operational efficiency, the payroll function performs certain tasks that are in contradiction with basic internal control objectives. Specifically, the payroll function has both asset custody (employee paychecks) and record-keeping responsibility (employee payroll records). This seemingly creates the opportunity for an individual to set up a false wages payable liability to himself (or a conspirator), approve payment, and write the check.

   To prevent this, control is returned to the system by assigning AP the responsibility of reviewing the work done by payroll (payroll register) and approving payment. Based on this approval the cash disbursements function then writes a single check to cover the entire payroll. The individual employee paychecks are not negotiable instruments until the payroll check is deposited into the imprest account at the bank.
3. The use of an independent paymaster to distribute checks (rather than the employee's supervisor) helps verify the existence of employees. Since the supervisor submits the timecards, he may be in a posi-tion to create nonexistent employees if he were also given responsibility for distributing the paychecks.

SUPERVISION. Sometimes, employees clock in for another worker who is late or absent. Supervisors should observe the timekeeping process and reconcile the time cards with actual attendance.

ACCESS CONTROL. The assets associated with the payroll system are labor and cash. Both can be misappropriated through improper access to accounting records. As we have already discussed, a dishonest individual can misrepresent the number of hours worked on the time cards and thus embezzle cash. Similarly, maintaining controls over access to all journals, ledgers, employee data, and source documents in the payroll system is important, as it is in all transaction processing systems.

IT Controls

In a mobile and/or distributed workforce environment in which employees self-report and directly enter time and attendance data into the system, the organization is at risk from payroll fraud. Input controls to reduce these risks include the following:

1. Limit tests to detect excessive hours reported per period.
2. Biometric scanners, swipe cards, and PINs reduce the risk of payroll fraud by ensuring that individuals clocking into the system are valid employees.
3. Automated tests to validate employee timecards against a valid and up-to-date employee file.
4. Paycheck direct deposit options for employees.

Risk of Unauthorized Access to Payroll Records and Confidential Employee Data

Payroll information is at risk to unauthorized access from outsiders as well employees of the organization. The motives for accessing accounting information include:

- Malicious acts such as corrupting or deleting payroll data.
- Theft of confidential employee information such as Social Security Numbers, pay rates, and other personal data.
- Attempts to perpetrate a payroll fraud.

IT Controls

PASSWORDS. Password control should be implemented on department computers to reduce the risk of unauthorized access to payroll files. The system logic should require, and prompt, users to change passwords periodically. Only strong passwords consisting of eight or more alphabetic and numeric characters should be accepted.

MULTILEVEL SECURITY. Previous chapters discussed multilevel security as a means of achieving segregation of duties in an integrated data processing environment where multiple users simultaneously access a common central application. Through this technique, HR, accounts payable, cash disbursements, cost accounting, and general ledger personnel are limited in their access based on the privileges assigned to them.

TABLE 6-1 SUMMARY OF PAYROLL SYSTEM RISKS AND CONTROLS

Risk	Physical Control	IT Control
Inaccurately recording transaction	Accounting records—audit trail documents, journals, accounts, and files	Input data edits Error Messages File backup Automated posting to accounts
Misappropriation of Cash through payroll fraud	Transaction authorization—personnel action form Segregation of duties—Time keeping, personnel, AP, cash disbursements, paymaster Supervision— time-keeping process Access control over source documents, journals, ledgers	Limit tests, biometric scanners, validation controls, direct deposit Multilevel Security to provide segregation of duties
Unauthorized access to Payroll data		Password control Multilevel security to prevent unauthorized access to data

Outsourcing the Payroll Function

Many organizations outsource their payroll function by transferring all payroll processing tasks to a third-party provider. The service provider collects time and personnel action data, calculates the payroll, withholds taxes, deposits funds to employee accounts, and provides W-2 forms at year end. In traditionally organized companies, the client firm submits employee time data to the service provider weekly or bi-weekly via web connection. Alternatively, distributed workforce employees may submit their time and attendance data directly to the service provider by laptop computers or handheld devices. Employees may also access their accounts online and make changes to withholdings, medical saving accounts, and retirement plans.

To accomplish this, the service provider needs access to sensitive internal information such as social security numbers, employment forms (W-4s and I-9s), and employee bank account information. The service provider also requires the client firm to set up a bank account and allow the payroll company to access it. The funds deposited into the bank account cover the total payroll, funds transfers to state and federal tax authorities, and the service provider's fees.

Advantages and Risks Associated with Payroll Outsourcing

The primary advantage of payroll outsourcing is cost savings. By transferring this function to a third party, the client organization avoids the salaries and benefit costs of running an in-house payroll department. Also, the cost of continuing education for payroll staff is a financial burden. An in-house payroll department needs to be up to date on an ever-changing array of legal and technical matters. Such training is disruptive, costly, and can be avoided by outsourcing the payroll function.

The risks associated with outsourcing are nontrivial. One is that an outside organization will have access to extremely confidential employee data and to the client firm's financial resources. Another risk is that the service provider may have poor internal controls and/or act incompetently in a way that allows material errors or fraud. A client organization may outsource any function it chooses, but it cannot outsource its responsibility for implementing adequate internal controls.

The Conceptual Fixed Asset System

Fixed assets are the property, plant, and equipment used in the operation of a business. These are relatively permanent items that often collectively represent the largest financial investment by the organization. Examples of fixed assets include land, buildings, furniture, machinery, and motor vehicles. A firm's fixed asset system processes transactions pertaining to the acquisition, maintenance, and disposal of its fixed assets. The specific objectives of the fixed asset system are to:

1. Process the acquisition of fixed assets as needed and in accordance with formal management approval and procedures.
2. Maintain adequate accounting records of asset acquisition, cost, description, and physical location in the organization.
3. Maintain accurate depreciation records for depreciable assets in accordance with acceptable methods.
4. Provide management with information to help plan for future fixed asset investments.
5. Properly record the retirement and disposal of fixed assets.

The fixed asset system shares some characteristics with the expenditure cycle presented in Chapter 5, but two important differences distinguish these systems. First, the expenditure cycle processes routine acquisitions of raw material and finished goods inventories. The fixed asset system processes nonroutine transactions for a wider group of users in the organization. Managers in virtually all functional areas of the organization make capital investments in fixed assets, but these transactions occur with less regularity than inventory acquisitions. Because fixed asset transactions are unique, they require specific management approval and explicit authorization procedures. In contrast, organizations often automate the authorization procedures for routine acquisitions of inventories.

The second difference between these systems is that organizations usually treat inventory acquisitions as an expense of the current period, while they capitalize fixed assets that yield benefits for multiple periods. Because the productive life of a fixed asset extends beyond one year, its acquisition cost is apportioned over its lifetime and depreciated in accordance with accounting conventions and statutory requirements. Therefore, fixed asset accounting systems include cost allocation and matching procedures that are not part of routine expenditure systems.

THE LOGIC OF A FIXED ASSET SYSTEM

Figure 6-10 presents the general logic of the fixed asset system. The process involves three categories of tasks: asset acquisition, asset maintenance, and asset disposal.

Asset Acquisition

Asset acquisition usually begins with the departmental manager (user) recognizing the need to obtain a new asset or replace an existing one. Authorization and approval procedures over the transaction will depend on the asset's value. Department managers typically have authority to approve purchases below a certain materiality limit. Capital expenditures above the limit will require approval from the higher management levels. This may involve a formal cost-benefit analysis and the formal solicitation of bids from suppliers.

Once the request is approved and a supplier is selected, the fixed asset acquisition task is similar to the expenditure cycle procedures described in Chapter 5, with two noteworthy differences. First, the receiving department delivers the asset into the custody of the user/manager rather than a central store or warehouse. Second, the fixed asset department, not inventory control, performs the record keeping function.

FIGURE 6-10 DATA FLOW DIAGRAM FOR FIXED ASSET SYSTEM

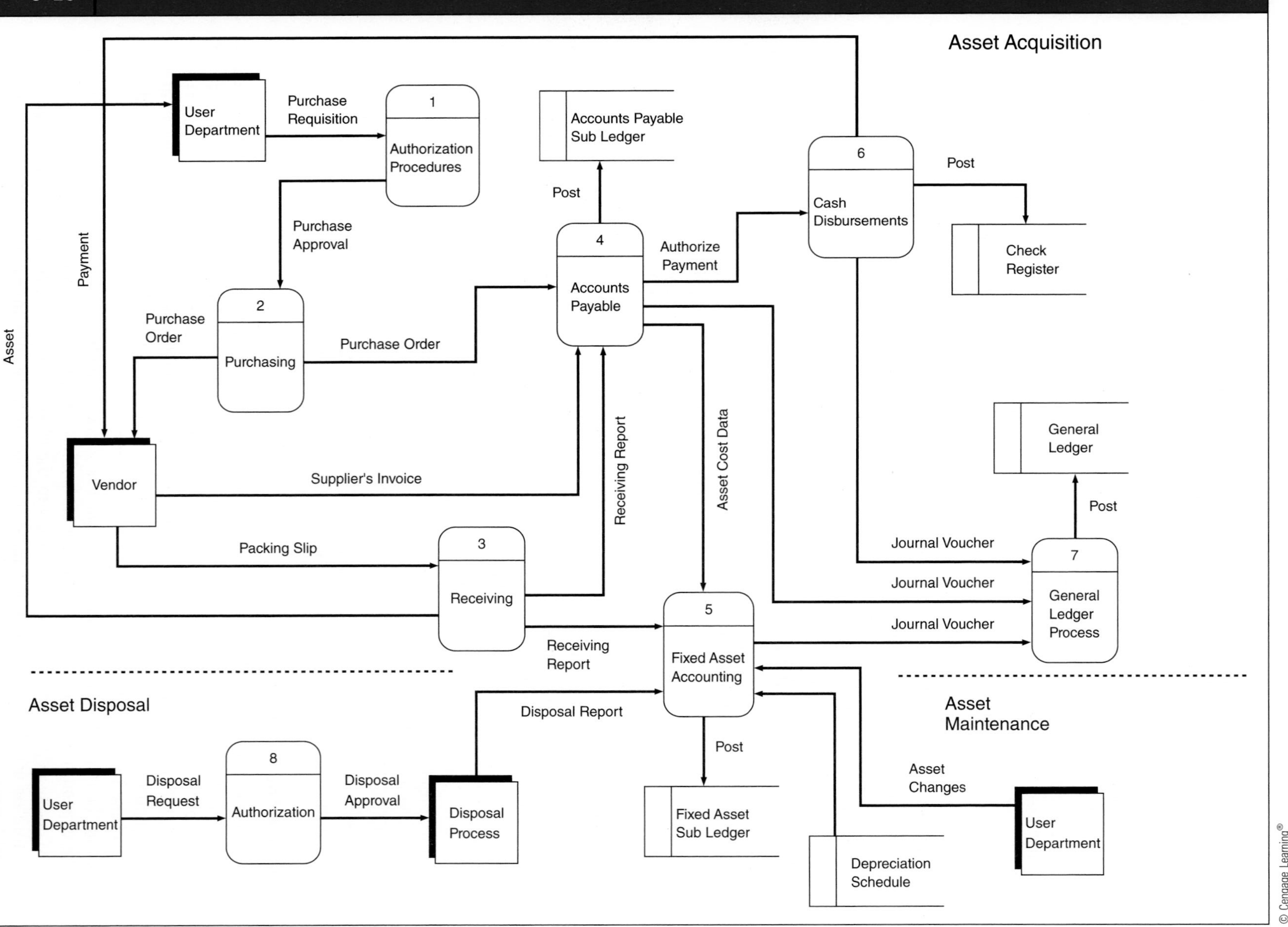

Asset Maintenance

Asset maintenance involves adjusting the fixed asset subsidiary account balances as the assets (excluding land) depreciate over time or with usage. Common depreciation methods in use are straight line, sum-of-the-years' digits, double-declining balance, and units of production. The method of depreciation and the period used should reflect, as closely as possible, the asset's actual decline in utility to the firm. Accounting conventions and Internal Revenue Service rules sometimes specify the depreciation method to be used. For example, businesses must depreciate new office buildings using the straight-line method and use a period of at least 40 years. The depreciation of fixed assets used to manufacture products is charged to manufacturing overhead and then allocated to WIP. Depreciation charges from assets not used in manufacturing are treated as expenses in the current period.

Depreciation calculations are transactions that the fixed asset system must be designed to anticipate internally when no external event (source document) triggers the action. An important record used to initiate this task is the **depreciation schedule.** A separate depreciation schedule, such as the one illustrated in Figure 6-11, will be prepared by the system for each fixed asset in the fixed asset subsidiary ledger.

A depreciation schedule shows when and how much depreciation to record. It also shows when to stop taking depreciation on fully depreciated assets. This information in a management report is also useful for planning asset retirement and replacement.

Asset maintenance also involves adjusting asset accounts to reflect the cost of physical improvements that increase the asset's value or extend its useful life. Such enhancements, which are themselves capital investments, are processed as new asset acquisitions.

Finally, the fixed asset system must promote accountability by keeping track of the physical location of each asset. Unlike inventories, which are usually consolidated in secure areas, fixed assets are distributed throughout the organization and are subject to risk from theft and misappropriation. When one department transfers custody of an asset to another department, information about the transfer should be recorded in the fixed asset subsidiary ledger. Each subsidiary record should indicate the current location of the asset. The ability to locate and verify the physical existence of fixed assets is an important component of the audit trail.

Asset Disposal

When an asset has reached the end of its useful life or when management decides to dispose of it, the asset must be removed from the fixed asset subsidiary ledger. The bottom left portion of Figure 6-10 illustrates the **asset disposal** process. It begins when the responsible manager issues a request to dispose of the asset. Like any other transaction, the disposal of an asset requires proper approval. The disposal options open to the firm are to sell, scrap, donate, or retire the asset in place. A disposal report describing the final disposition of the asset is sent to the fixed asset accounting department to authorize its removal from the ledger.

THE PHYSICAL FIXED ASSET SYSTEM

Because many of the tasks in the fixed asset system are similar in concept to the purchases system covered in Chapter 5, we will focus on the operational features and controls that are specific to the fixed asset processing. Figure 6-12 illustrates a fixed asset system with real-time processing. The top portion of the flowchart presents the fixed asset acquisition procedures, the center portion presents fixed asset maintenance procedures, and the bottom portion presents the asset disposal procedures. To simplify the flowchart and focus on the key features of the system, we have omitted the processing steps for AP and cash disbursements.

Acquisition Procedures

The process begins when the fixed asset accounting clerk receives a receiving report and a cash disbursement voucher. These documents provide evidence that the firm has physically received the asset and show its cost. From the computer terminal, a clerk creates a record of the asset in the fixed asset subsidiary ledger. Figure 6-13 presents a possible record structure for this file.

FIGURE 6-11 DEPRECIATION SCHEDULE

OZMENT'S INDUSTRIAL SUPPLY
ASSET LISTING WITH DEPRECIATION SCHEDULES
FROM 200 THROUGH 200

Code	Type	Description	Month#	Depn. exp.	Acc. depn.	Book value
200	OFF&F					
		OFFICE FURNITURE				
		Depn. method: SYD				
		Life in years: 5				
		Date acquired 2/01/15				
		Date retired				
		Cost 5,500.00				
		Residual 500.00				
		Acc. Depn. 2,222.23				
			1	138.89	138.89	5,361.11
			2	138.89	277.78	5,222.22
			3	138.89	416.67	5,083.33
			4	138.89	555.56	4,944.44
			5	138.89	694.45	4,805.55
			6	138.89	833.34	4,666.66
			7	138.89	972.23	4,527.77
			8	138.89	1,111.12	4,388.88
			9	138.89	1,250.01	4,249.99
			10	138.89	1,388.90	4,111.10
			•	•	•	•
			•	•	•	•
			•	•	•	•
			52	27.78	4,777.80	722.20
			53	27.78	4,805.58	694.42
			54	27.78	4,833.36	666.64
			55	27.78	4,861.14	638.86
			56	27.78	4,888.92	611.08
			57	27.78	4,916.70	583.30
			58	27.78	4,944.48	555.52
			59	27.78	4,972.26	527.74
			60	27.78	5,000.04	499.96

Assets listed: 1

Notice that in addition to the historic cost information, the record contains data specifying the asset's useful life, its salvage (residual) value, the depreciation method to be used, and the asset's location in the organization.

The fixed asset system automatically updates the fixed asset control account in the general ledger and prepares journal vouchers for the general ledger department as evidence of the entry. The system also produces reports for accounting management. Figure 6-14 illustrates

FIGURE 6-12 COMPUTER-BASED FIXED ASSET SYSTEM

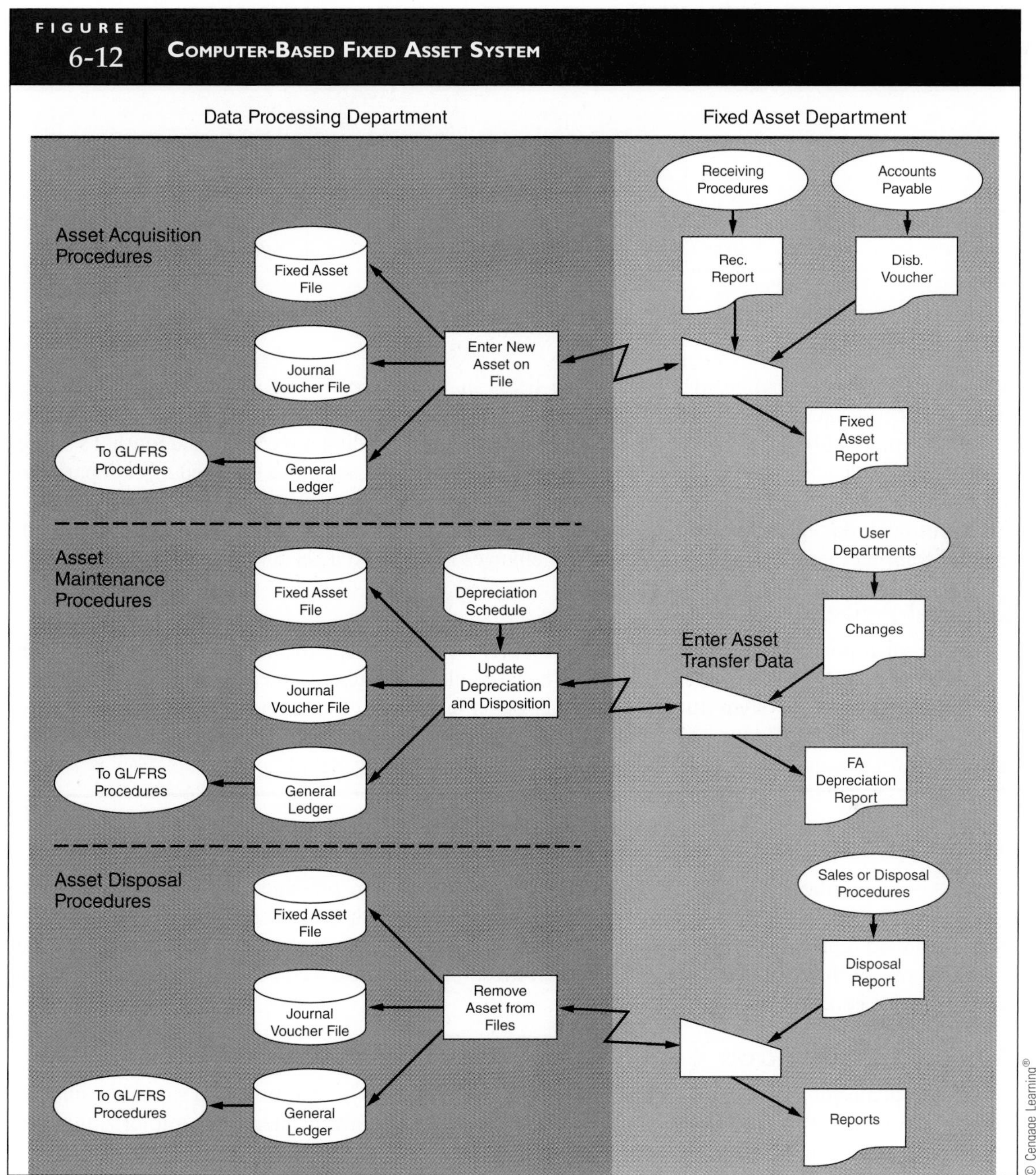

the fixed asset status report showing the cost, the accumulated depreciation (if any), and residual value for each of the firm's fixed assets.

Based on the depreciation parameters contained in the fixed asset records, the system prepares a depreciation schedule for each asset when its acquisition is originally recorded. The schedule is stored on computer disk to permit future depreciation calculations.

Asset Maintenance

The fixed asset system uses the depreciation schedules to record end-of-period depreciation transactions automatically. The specific tasks include (1) calculating the current period's depreciation, (2) updating

FIGURE 6-13 FIXED ASSET RECORD STRUCTURE

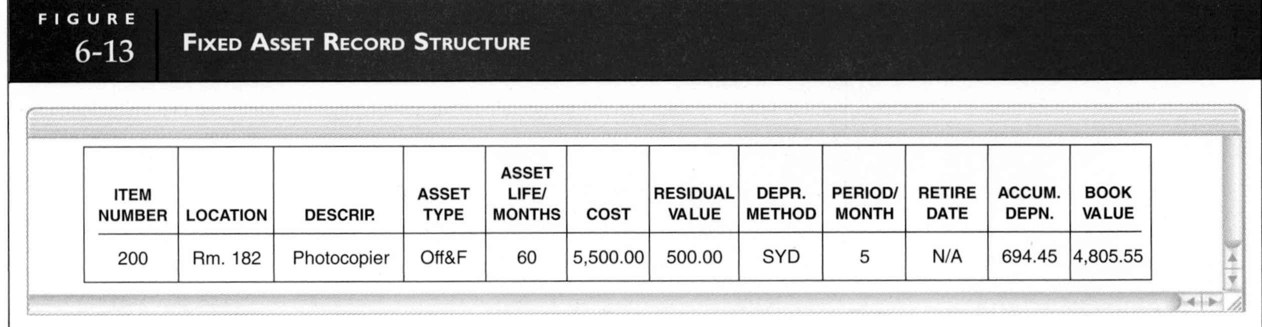

ITEM NUMBER	LOCATION	DESCRIP.	ASSET TYPE	ASSET LIFE/ MONTHS	COST	RESIDUAL VALUE	DEPR. METHOD	PERIOD/ MONTH	RETIRE DATE	ACCUM. DEPN.	BOOK VALUE
200	Rm. 182	Photocopier	Off&F	60	5,500.00	500.00	SYD	5	N/A	694.45	4,805.55

the accumulated depreciation and book value fields in the subsidiary records, (3) posting the total amount of depreciation to the affected general ledger accounts (depreciation expense and accumulated depreciation), and (4) recording the depreciation transaction by adding a record to the journal voucher file. Finally, a fixed asset depreciation report, shown in Figure 6-15, is sent to the fixed asset department for review.

Department managers report changes in the custody or status of assets to the fixed asset department. From a computer terminal, a clerk records such changes in the fixed asset subsidiary ledger.

Disposal Procedures

The disposal report formally authorizes the fixed asset department to remove from the ledger an asset disposed of by the user department. When the clerk deletes the record from the fixed asset subsidiary ledger, the system automatically (1) posts an adjusting entry to the fixed asset control account in the general ledger, (2) records loss or gain associated with the disposal, and (3) prepares a journal voucher. A fixed asset status report containing details of the deletion is sent to the fixed asset department for review.

FIXED ASSET SYSTEM RISKS AND CONTROLS

Because of similarities to the purchases/cash disbursements system presented in Chapter 5, the fixed asset system has many of the same risks and control issues, which have already been discussed. The physical distribution of fixed assets throughout the organization, however, makes them more susceptible to the risk of theft and misappropriation than inventories that are secured in a warehouse. The following control issues are specific to this risk.

Authorization Controls

Fixed asset acquisitions should be formal and explicitly authorized. Each transaction should be initiated by a written request from the user or department. In the case of high-value items, the authorization process should include an independent approval process that evaluates the merits of the request.

Supervision Controls

Management supervision is an important element in the physical security of fixed assets. Supervisors must ensure that fixed assets are being used in accordance with the organization's policies and business practices. For example, microcomputers purchased for individual employees should be secured in their proper location and should not be removed from the premises without explicit approval. Company vehicles should be secured in the organization's motor pool at the end of the shift and should not be taken home for personal use unless authorized by the appropriate supervisor.

Independent Verification Controls

Periodically, the internal auditor should review the asset acquisition and approval procedures to determine the reasonableness of factors used in such decisions. These include the useful life of the

FIGURE 6-14 ASSET STATUS REPORT

OZMENT'S INDUSTRIAL SUPPLY
ASSET LISTING

Code	Type		Description
100	OFF&F		
	COMPUTER SYSTEM		
	Depn. method:	SL	
	Life in years:	5	
	Date acquired	1/01/15	
	Date retired		
	Cost		40,000.00
	Residual		4,000.00
	Acc. Depn.		10,800.00
200	OFF&F		
	OFFICE FURNITURE		
	Depn. method:	SL	
	Life in years:	5	
	Date acquired	2/01/15	
	Date retired		
	Cost		5,500.00
	Residual		500.00
	Acc. Depn.		2,222.23
300	MACH		
	SNOWBLOWER		
	Depn. method:	DDB	
	Life in years:	5	
	Date acquired	2/01/15	
	Date retired		
	Cost		1,000.00
	Residual		0.00
	Acc. Depn.		499.96
400	MACH		
	TRUCK		
	Depn. method:	SL	
	Life in years:	3	
	Date acquired	12/01/15	
	Date retired		
	Cost		2,000.00
	Residual		0.00
	Acc. Depn.		2,333.31

asset, the original financial cost, the proposed cost savings as a result of acquiring the asset, the discount rate used, and the capital budgeting method used in the analysis.

The internal auditor should verify the location, condition, and fair value of the organization's fixed assets against the fixed asset records in the subsidiary ledger. In addition, depreciation charges calculated on fixed assets should be reviewed and verified for accuracy. Miscalculated depreciation can result in the material misstatement of operating expenses, reported earnings, asset values, and may result in premature disposal of otherwise serviceable assets.

FIGURE 6-15 FIXED ASSET DEPRECIATION REPORT

OZMENT'S INDUSTRIAL SUPPLY
DEPRECIATION CALCULATIONS LISTING THROUGH
6/30/07 POSTED AS BATCH #1327

Code	Method		Description	Depn. Expense
100	SL	5 yr	COMPUTER SYSTEM	3,600.00
200	SYD	5 yr	OFFICE FURNITURE	694.44
300	DDB	5 yr	SNOWBLOWER	133.33
400	SL	3 yr	DELIVERY TRUCK	0.00
500	SL	3 yr	DELIVERY TRUCK	0.00
600	SL	3 yr	TRUCK	2,333.31
Assets listed: 6			Total	6,761.08
GL summary:				
615	DEPRECIATION EXPENSE		6,761.08	
151	ACCUM DEPN. EQUIPMENT			6,761.08

Summary

This chapter began with an examination of payroll procedures. The discussion focused on fundamental tasks; the functional departments; and the documents, journals, and accounts that constitute the payroll system. Risks inherent in payroll activities and the controls that reduce risks were explained. The first section reviewed the operational features of both basic and advanced technology payroll systems. It concluded with a review of the payroll outsourcing option that many companies pursue.

The second section of this chapter presented the typical features of the fixed asset system. Fixed asset accounting involves three classes of procedures: asset acquisition, asset maintenance, and asset disposal. We examined the files, procedures, and reports that constitute the fixed asset system. We concluded our discussion by reviewing the principal risks and controls in the system.

Key Terms

asset acquisition (269)
asset disposal (271)
asset maintenance (271)
biometric time clocks (261)
depreciation schedule (271)
employee payroll records (252)
employee records file (261)
fixed assets (269)
human resource management (HRM) system (260)
job tickets (252)
labor distribution summary (252)
labor usage file (261)
magnetic swipe ID cards (261)
mobile remote devices (261)
paychecks (252)
payroll imprest account (255)
payroll register (252)
personnel action forms (252)
proximity cards (261)
time and attendance file (261)
time cards (252)

Review Questions

1. Which document is used by the cost accounting department to allocate direct labor charges to work in process?
2. Which department authorizes changes in employee pay rates?
3. Why should the employee's supervisor not distribute paychecks?
4. Why should employee paychecks be drawn against a special checking account?
5. Why should employees clocking on and off the job be supervised?
6. What is a personnel action form?
7. What tasks does a payroll clerk perform upon receipt of hours-worked data from the production department?
8. What documents are included in the audit trail for payroll?
9. What is a biometric time clock?
10. What is a proximity card?
11. What are the objectives of a fixed asset system?
12. How do fixed asset systems differ from purchases systems?
13. What are three tasks of the fixed asset system?
14. What information is found on the depreciation schedule? How can this information be verified?
15. Why is it crucial to the integrity of the financial statements that the fixed asset department be informed of asset improvements and disposals?
16. What is the auditor's role with respect to the fixed asset system?
17. Which department performs the formal record keeping function for fixed assets?
18. What document shows when fixed assets are fully depreciated?
19. Who should authorize disposal of fixed assets?
20. Assets used for production are secured in a warehouse. Who has custody of fixed assets?

Discussion Questions

1. What is the importance of the job ticket? Illustrate the flow of this document and its information from inception to impact on the financial statements.
2. Are any time lags in recording economic events typically experienced in payroll systems? If so, what are they? Discuss the accounting profession's view on this matter as it pertains to financial reporting.
3. The management of an organization with a remote workforce is concerned that employees are clocking on for others who are not actually at work. What controls would reduce this risk?
4. Discuss the main advantages of payroll outsourcing.
5. Discuss some specific examples in which information systems can reduce time lags and how the firm is positively affected by such time lags.
6. Discuss some service industries that may require their workers to use job tickets.
7. What are the risks associated with payroll outsourcing?
8. If an asset that is not fully depreciated is sold or disposed, but the fixed asset records are not adjusted, what effect will this have on the financial statements?
9. Discuss the fundamental risk and control issues associated with fixed assets that are different from raw materials and finished goods.
10. Describe an internal control that would prevent an employee from removing a computer and then reporting it as scrapped.
11. Describe an internal control that would prevent the payment of insurance premiums on an automobile the company no longer owns.
12. Describe an internal control that would prevent the charging of depreciation expense to the maintenance department for a sweeper that is now located in and used by the engineering department.
13. Describe an internal control that would prevent the acquisition of office equipment that the firm does not need.
14. What negative consequences result when fixed asset records include assets that the firm no longer owns?

Multiple-Choice Questions

1. Who below is most likely to distribute paychecks?
   a. Personnel clerk
   b. Timekeeping clerk
   c. Paymaster
   d. Supervisor
2. Which one of the following functions is responsible for submitting employee pay rate changes?
   a. Payroll
   b. Treasurer
   c. Personnel
   d. Cash disbursements
   e. None of the above
3. Which of the following is not a payroll system internal control?
   a. Supervisors verify the accuracy of employee time cards.
   b. The accounts payable department verifies the accuracy of the payroll register before transferring payroll funds to the general checking account.
   c. Paychecks are distributed by an independent paymaster.
   d. The general ledger department reconciles the labor distribution summary and the payroll disbursement voucher.
   e. All are payroll system controls.
4. An important reconciliation in the payroll system is when
   a. the general ledger department compares the labor distribution summary from cost accounting to the disbursement voucher from accounts payable.
   b. the personnel department compares the number of employees authorized to receive a paycheck to the number of paychecks prepared.
   c. the production department compares the number of hours reported on job tickets to the number of hours reported on time cards. The payroll department compares the labor distribution summary to the hours reported on time cards.
5. Which one of the following documents captures the total amount of time that individual workers spend on each production job?
   a. Time card
   b. Job ticket
   c. Personnel action form
   d. Labor distribution form
   e. None of the above
6. Which of the following are fixed asset system tasks?
   a. Authorizing the acquisition of fixed assets
   b. Recording depreciation expense
   c. Computing gain and/or loss on the disposal of fixed assets
   d. All of the above are tasks
   e. a and b are tasks but c is not
7. Which control is not a part of the fixed asset system?
   a. Formal analysis of the purchase request
   b. Review of the assumptions used in the capital budgeting model
   c. Development of an economic order quantity model
   d. Estimates of anticipated cost savings
8. Which of the following data items is not likely to be included in a fixed asset record?
   a. Residual value of the asset
   b. Book value of the asset
   c. Depreciation method being used
   d. Location of the asset
   e. All of the above would likely be included
9. Which of the following best describes depreciation?
   a. Is calculated by the department that uses the fixed asset
   b. Allocates the cost of the asset over its useful life
   c. Is recorded weekly
   d. Results in book value approximating fair market value
10. Which transaction is not processed in the fixed asset system?
    a. Purchase of building
    b. Repair of equipment
    c. Purchase of raw materials
    d. Sale of company van
    e. All are fixed asset transactions

Problems

1. PAYROLL FRAUD

John Smith worked in the stockyard of a large building supply company. One day he unexpectedly left for California, never to return. His foreman seized the opportunity to continue to submit time cards for John to the payroll department. Each week, as part of his normal duties, the foreman received the employee paychecks from payroll and distributed them to the workers on his shift. Because John was not present to collect his paycheck, the foreman forged John's name and cashed it.

Required
Describe two control techniques to prevent or detect this fraud scheme.

2. PAYROLL CONTROLS

Refer to the flowchart for Problem 2.

Required

a. What risks are associated with the payroll procedures depicted in the flowchart?
b. Discuss two control techniques that will reduce or eliminate the risks.

3. PAYROLL CONTROLS

Sherman Company employs 400 production, maintenance, and janitorial workers in eight separate departments. In addition to supervising operations, the supervisors of the departments are responsible for recruiting, hiring, and firing workers within their areas of responsibility. The organization attracts casual labor and experiences a 20 to 30 percent turnover rate in employees per year.

Employees clock on and off the job each day to record their attendance on time cards. Each department has its own clock machine located in an unattended room away from the main production area. Each week, the supervisors gather the time cards, review them for accuracy, and sign and submit them to the payroll department for processing. In addition, the supervisors submit personnel action forms to reflect newly hired and terminated employees. From these documents, the payroll clerk prepares payroll checks and updates the employee records. The supervisor of the payroll department signs the paychecks, which are drawn on the general cash account, and sends them to the department supervisors for distribution to the employees. A payroll register is sent to the cash disbursements department where it is filed.

Required

1. Prepare a flowchart of the Sherman's payroll system.
2. Discuss the risks for payroll fraud in the Sherman Company payroll system.
3. What controls would you implement to reduce the risks?

PROBLEM 2: PAYROLL CONTROLS

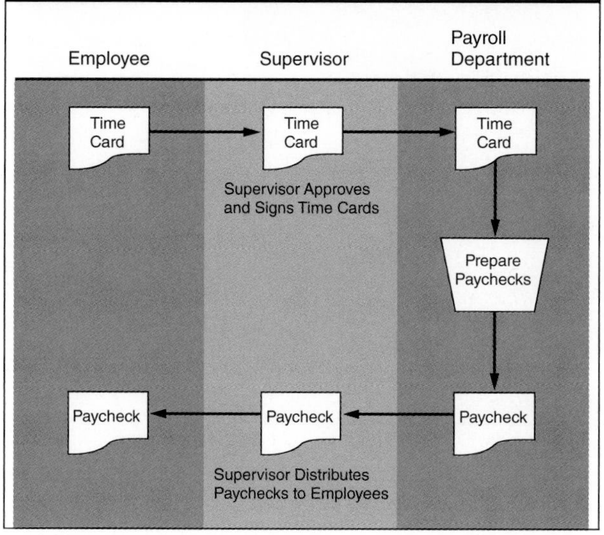

4. FLOWCHART ANALYSIS

Discuss any control weaknesses found in the flowchart for Problem 4. Recommend any necessary changes.

5. SEPARATION OF DUTIES

Human resource management systems necessitate that employees from both the payroll and personnel departments have access to confidential employee data.

1. List the tasks that personnel and payroll department employees respectively should and should not be able to perform.
2. Describe the data types in such a system that are sensitive and confidential.
3. What IT controls will provide the necessary separation of duties to limit access to functions and data?

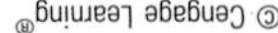

PROBLEM 4: FLOWCHART ANALYSIS

Personnel	Production	Payroll	Accounts Payable	Employees

New Employees

Terminated Employees

Time Cards

Prepare Payroll

Employee Records

Paychecks

A

Payroll Register

Review and File

Payroll Register

A

Paychecks

Bank

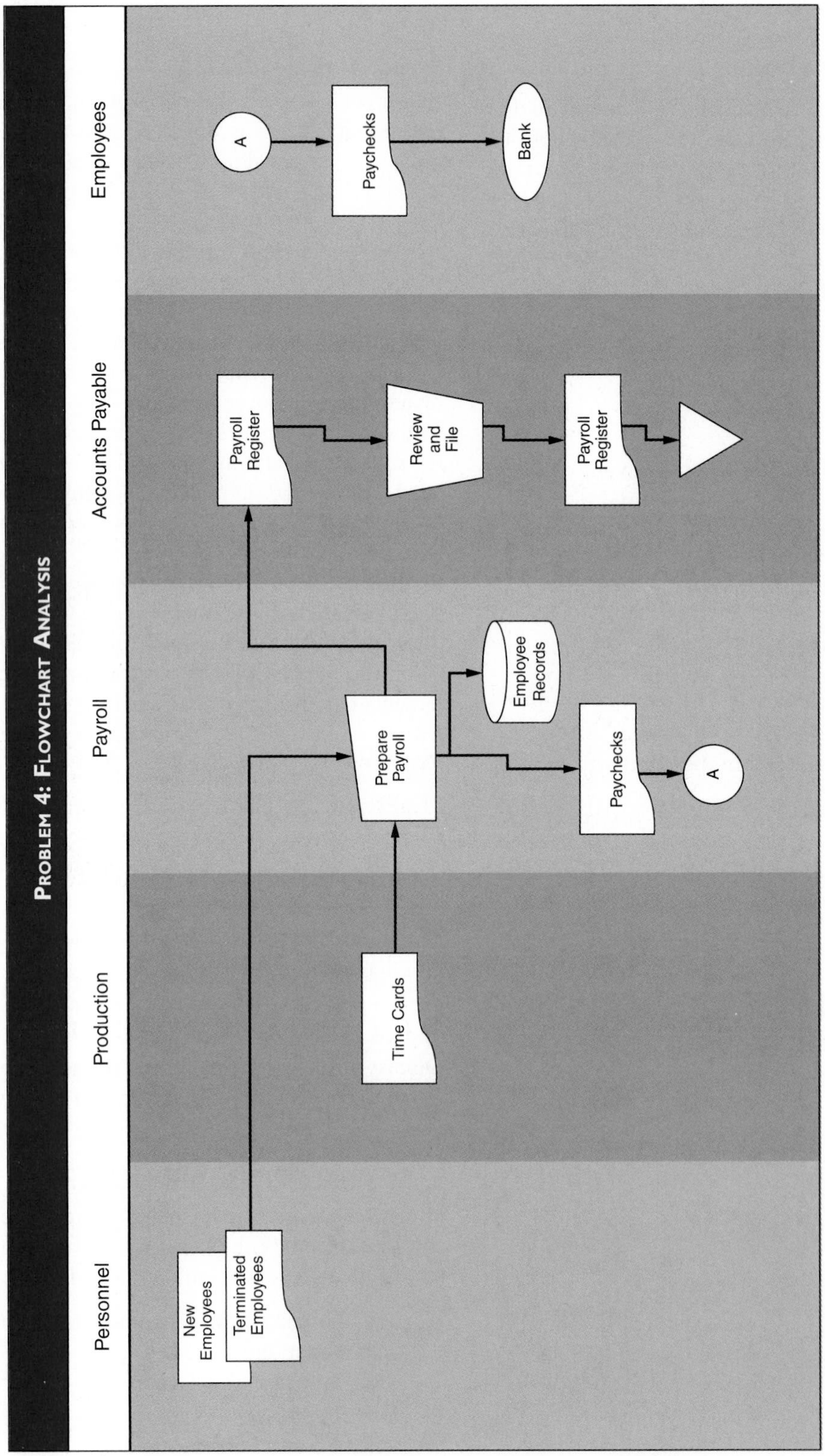

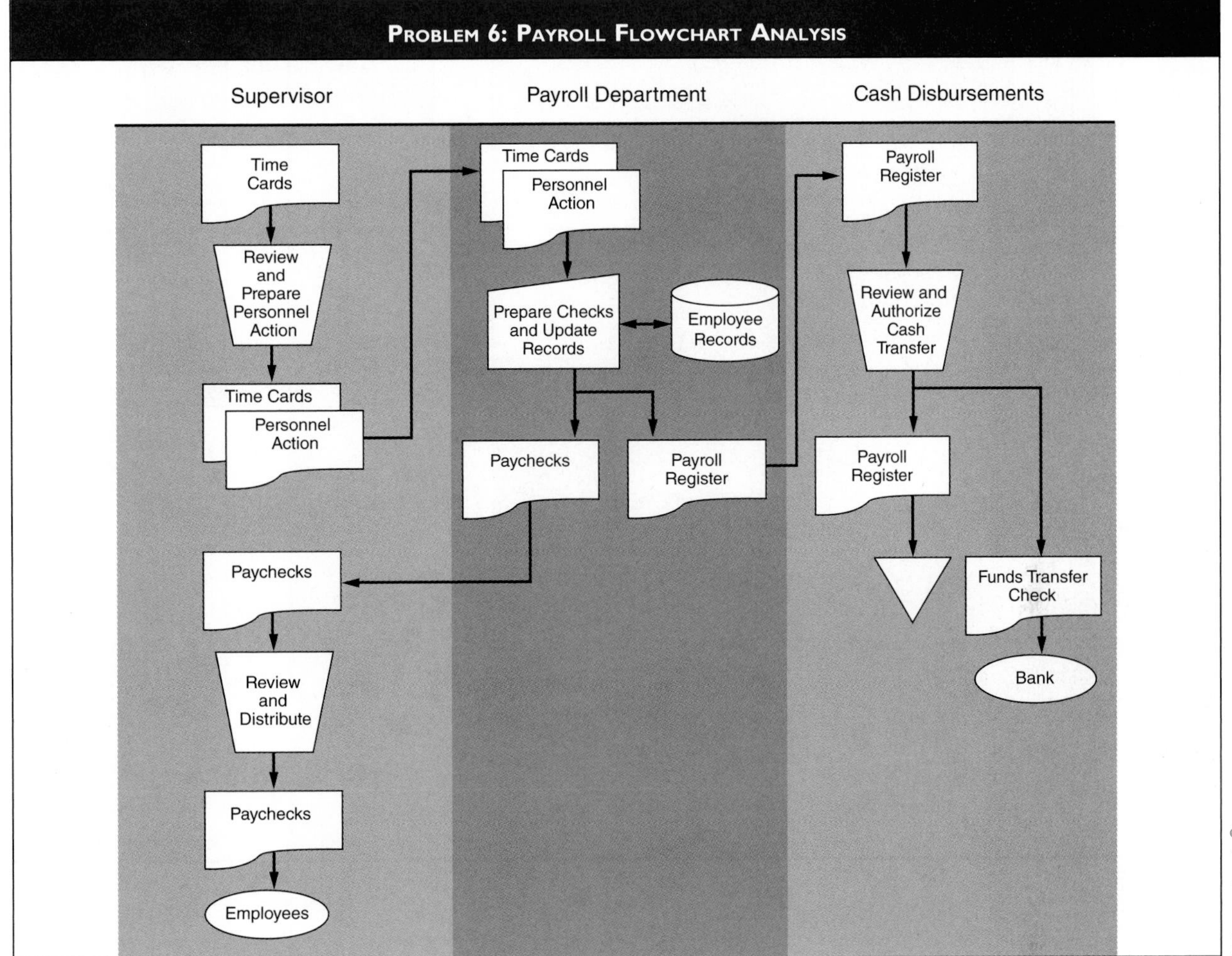

6. PAYROLL FLOWCHART ANALYSIS

Discuss the risks depicted by the payroll system flowchart for Problem 6. Describe the internal control improvements to the system that are needed to reduce these risks.

7. COMPREHENSIVE FLOWCHART ANALYSIS

Discuss the internal control weaknesses in the expenditure cycle flowchart for Problem 7. Structure your answer in terms of the control activities within the COSO control model.

8. FIXED ASSET SYSTEM

The fixed asset acquisition procedures for Turner Brothers, Inc., are as follows.

Supervisors in the user departments determine their fixed asset needs and submit bids or orders directly to contractors, vendors, or suppliers. In the case of competitive bidding, the user makes the final selection of the vendor and negotiates the prices paid. The assets are delivered directly to the user areas. The users inspect and formally receive the assets. They submit the invoice to the cash disbursements department for payment.

Required

Discuss the risks associated with this process. Describe the controls that should be implemented to reduce these risks.

9. FIXED ASSET SYSTEM

Holder Co. maintains a large fleet of automobiles, trucks, and vans for their service and sales force. Supervisors in the various departments maintain the fixed asset records for these vehicles, including routine maintenance, repairs, and mileage information. This information is periodically submitted to the fixed asset department, which uses it to calculate

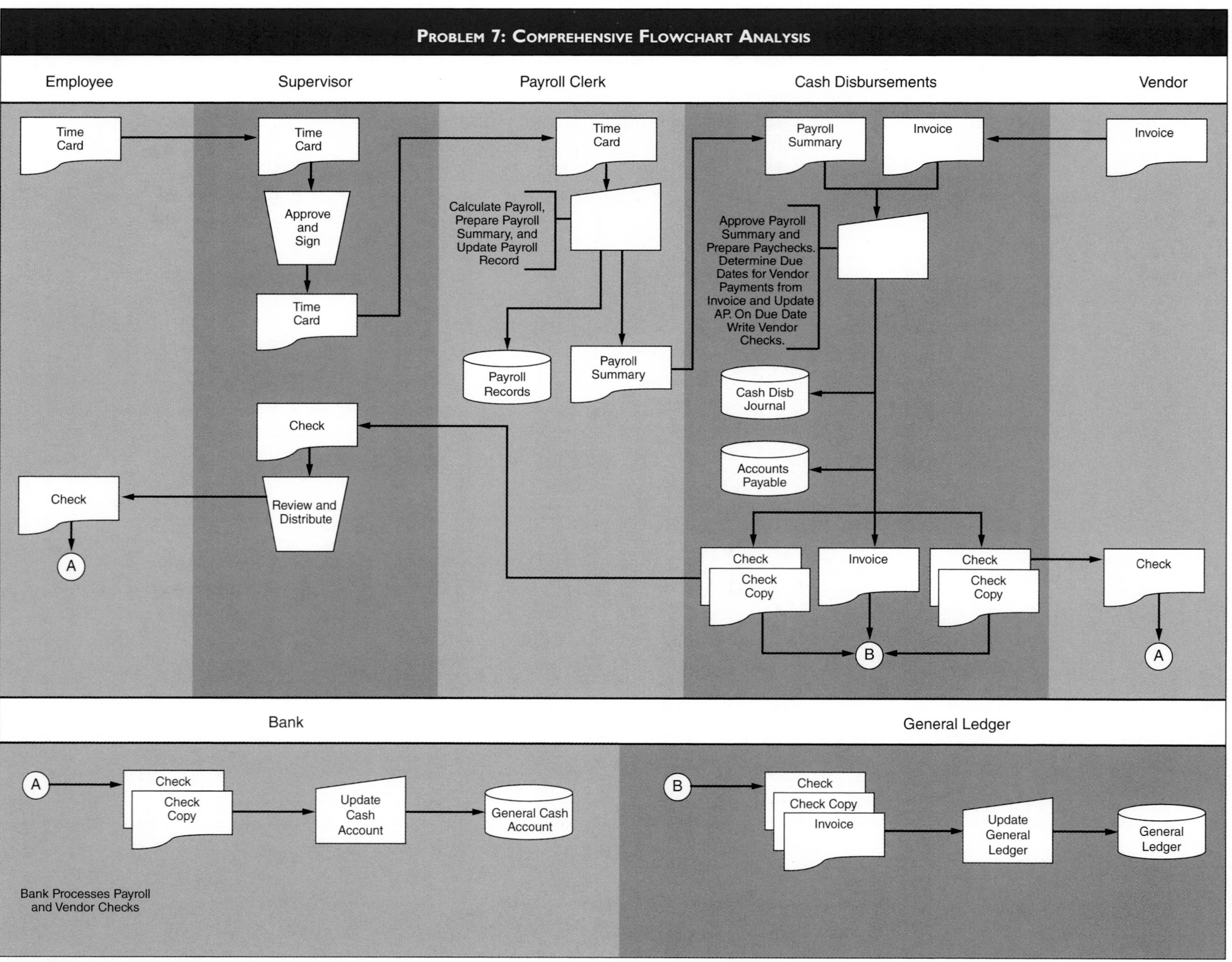
Problem 7: Comprehensive Flowchart Analysis
Employee
Supervisor
Payroll Clerk
Cash Disbursements
Vendor
Time Card
Time Card
Approve and Sign
Time Card
Time Card
Calculate Payroll, Prepare Payroll Summary, and Update Payroll Record
Payroll Records
Payroll Summary
Payroll Summary
Invoice
Invoice
Approve Payroll Summary and Prepare Paychecks. Determine Due Dates for Vendor Payments from Invoice and Update AP. On Due Date Write Vendor Checks.
Cash Disb Journal
Accounts Payable
Check
Review and Distribute
Check
A
Check
Check Copy
Invoice
Check
Check Copy
B
Check
A
Bank
General Ledger
A
Check
Check Copy
Update Cash Account
General Cash Account
Bank Processes Payroll and Vendor Checks
B
Check
Check Copy
Invoice
Update General Ledger
General Ledger

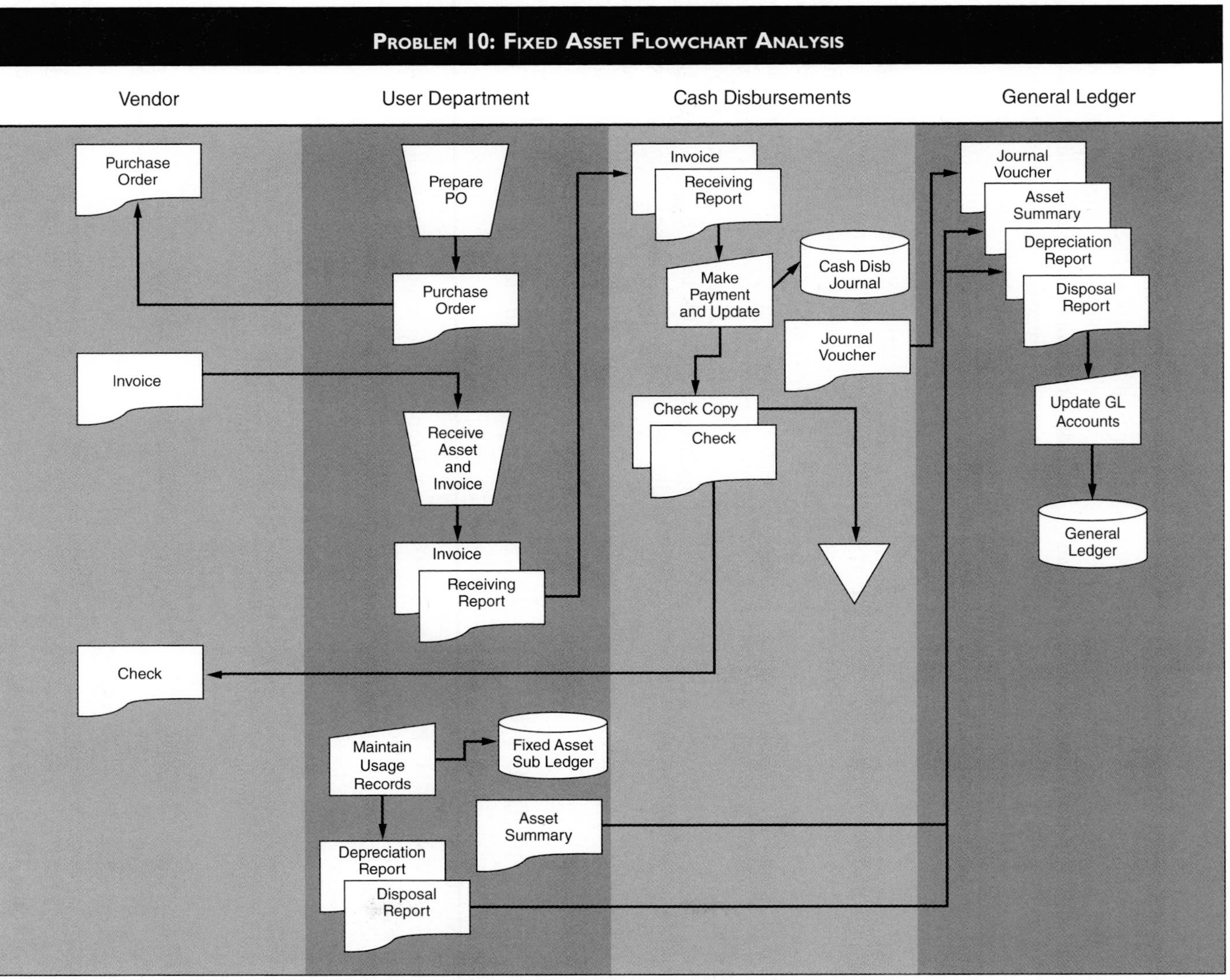
PROBLEM 10: FIXED ASSET FLOWCHART ANALYSIS
Vendor
User Department
Cash Disbursements
General Ledger
Purchase Order
Invoice
Check
Prepare PO
Purchase Order
Receive Asset and Invoice
Invoice
Receiving Report
Maintain Usage Records
Fixed Asset Sub Ledger
Asset Summary
Depreciation Report
Disposal Report
Invoice
Receiving Report
Make Payment and Update
Cash Disb Journal
Journal Voucher
Check Copy
Check
Journal Voucher
Asset Summary
Depreciation Report
Disposal Report
Update GL Accounts
General Ledger

depreciation on the vehicle. To ensure a reliable fleet, the company disposes of vehicles when they accumulate 80,000 miles of service. Depending on usage, some vehicles reach this point sooner than others. When a vehicle reaches 80,000 miles, the supervisor is authorized to use it in trade for a new replacement vehicle or to sell it privately. Employees of the company are given the first option to bid on the retired vehicles. Upon disposal of the vehicle, the supervisor submits a disposal report to the fixed asset department, which writes off the asset.

Required

Discuss the potential for abuse and fraud in this system. Describe the controls that should be implemented to reduce the risks.

10. FIXED ASSET FLOWCHART ANALYSIS

Discuss the risks depicted by the fixed asset system flowchart for Problem 10. Describe the internal control improvements to the system that are needed to reduce these risks.

11. PAYROLL PROCEDURES

The following describes the payroll procedures for the Albright Manufacturing company.

At the start and end of each shift, hourly employees register their time and attendance data on time cards at a time clock, which is located in a remote corner of the factory. This location was chosen so that the time-keeping activities would not interfere with the workflow on the shop floor of the small factory. Each Friday the time keeper, who is located in a separate administrative building, retrieves the time cards and submits them to the payroll department clerk.

The payroll clerk enters the time and attendance data into the centralized payroll system form the terminal in her office. The system calculates the payroll for each employee, updates the employee payroll records, prints the paychecks, and prints two copies of the payroll register. The clerk sends one copy of the payroll register to the accounts payable department and files the other in the payroll department. Finally, the clerk sends the paychecks to the cash disbursement department.

The AP clerk reviews the payroll register and prints a cash disbursement voucher, which he sends to the cash disbursement department. The CD voucher authorizes the cash disbursement clerk to sign the paychecks and send them to the supervisor for distribution to the employees. Using the terminal in the department, the CD clerk then updates the digital cash disbursement journal for the full amount of the payroll. Finally, both the accounts payable and cash disbursement clerks print and send a summary of transactions to the general ledger department where the GL clerk updates the relevant GL accounts using the terminal in the department.

Required

a. Prepare a flowchart of payroll procedures described above.
b. Using the control activities of the COSO internal control framework, analyze the internal control weaknesses in the system.
c. Make recommendations for improving the system.

Internal Control Cases

1. HOLLY COMPANY—PAYROLL SYSTEMS (SMALL COMPANY USES MANUAL PROCEDURES WITH PC SUPPORT)

Holly Company is a small family-run manufacturer of wooden garden furniture, sheds, and storage containers. The company is located outside Pittsburgh, Pennsylvania, and currently employs 185 workers. Much of the manufacturing work involves casual labor in the lumberyard and sawmill. The work is hard, and employees often move on after a few months. Although the company does not issue audited financial statements, its owner has retained your firm to conduct a review of its internal controls. The focus of your review at this time is the payroll process.

Payroll Processing System

Holly employees use a time clock in an unsupervised area to record their time on the job. The timekeeping clerk tries to monitor the process but is often distracted by other duties. Every Friday, the shop foremen collect the time cards for their subordinates, review and approve them, and deliver them to the payroll clerk.

The payroll clerk uses a stand-alone PC to record the employee earnings in the employee records and print a hard-copy payroll register. The payroll clerk sends one copy of the payroll register to the accounting department. The clerk then files the time cards and a copy of the payroll register in the payroll department.

The accounting department clerk receives the payroll register, reviews it for accuracy, and uses the department computer to record the transaction by posting to subsidiary and general ledger accounts, including wages expense, cash, and various withholding accounts. The clerk then prints the hard-copy checks, which are written on the general cash account. The clerk signs the paychecks and sends them to the foremen who distribute them to the employees. Finally, the clerk files the payroll register in the department.

Required

a. Prepare a data flow diagram of the current system.
b. Prepare a system flowchart of the existing system.
c. Describe the uncontrolled risks associated with this system as it is currently designed.
d. Describe the physical and IT controls needed to reduce the risks identified in "C" above.

2. TIGHT LINES FISHING AND CAMPING SUPPLIES (NETWORKED COMPUTER SYSTEM AND MANUAL PROCEDURES)

Tight Lines Fishing and Camping Supplies is a New York–based wholesaler of fishing and camping equipment that serves fishing and camping retailers throughout the north east. Tight Lines uses a centralized accounting system with networked terminals in the departments. You have been hired by Tight Lines to evaluate their processes, risks, and internal controls. The following paragraphs describe Tight Lines payroll and fixed asset systems.

Payroll System

Each day Tight Lines employees record their hours worked on time cards, which their supervisors review for correctness and submit to the payroll department at the end of the work week. Using a terminal connected to the central payroll system, which is located in the data processing department, the payroll clerk inputs the time-card data, prints hard copies of the paychecks, prints two copies of the payroll register, and posts to digital employee records. The payroll clerk files the time cards in the payroll department and sends the employee paychecks to the various supervisors for review and distribution to their respective department employees. The payroll clerk then sends one copy of the payroll register to the AP department, and files the other with the time cards in the payroll department.

The AP department clerk reviews the payroll register and manually prepares a disbursement voucher. The clerk sends the voucher and the payroll register to the general ledger department. The AP clerk then writes a check for the entire payroll and deposits it in the imprest account at the bank. Finally the clerk files a copy of the check in the AP department.

Once the general ledger clerk receives the voucher and payroll register, the clerk posts to the general ledger from the department terminal and files the voucher and payroll register in the department.

Fixed Asset System

Asset acquisition begins with the departmental manager recognizing the need to obtain a new asset or replace an existing one. The manager prepares two copies of a purchase requisition; one is filed within the department, and the other is sent to the purchasing department. The purchasing department clerk manually prepares three copies of a purchase order from the purchase requisition. One copy of the purchase order is sent to the supplier, another copy is sent to the AP department, and the third copy is filed within the purchasing department.

The AP clerk receives a packing slip and invoice from the vendor and visually reconciles them with the purchase order received from the purchasing department. The clerk enters the information into the department computer terminal and sets up an account payable liability. Using a computer terminal, the AP clerk then updates the purchases journal, prints a hard copy journal voucher and sends it to the general ledger department, and sends a cash disbursement voucher to the cash disbursements department with the supplier invoice. The clerk files the packing slip and purchase order in the AP department.

Using information from the supplier's invoice and the cash disbursement voucher the cash disbursements clerk prints a check from her terminal and records it in the digital check register. She sends the check to the vendor and the cash disbursement voucher to the general ledger department.

The user department manager handles both asset maintenance and asset disposal. The manager adjusts the fixed asset subsidiary account balances to match asset depreciation schedules over time. When an asset reaches the end of its useful life the manager issues a disposal report. The manager sends a fixed asset summary to the general ledger department.

The general ledger department clerk reconciles the cash disbursement voucher, journal voucher, and fixed asset summary, posts to the general ledger accounts from the department terminal, and files the remaining documents.

Required

a. Prepare a data flow diagram of the current payroll and fixed asset systems.
b. Prepare system flowcharts for the payroll and fixed asset systems.
c. Describe the uncontrolled risks associated with these systems as they are currently designed.
d. Describe the physical and IT controls needed to reduce the risks identified in "C" above.

3. TVR CLASSICS. (MANUAL AND STAND-ALONE COMPUTER PROCESSING)

TVR Classics specializes in the sale of original and reproduction restoration parts for classic sports cars and muscle cars of the 1960s and 1970s. The classic car industry has grown significantly in recent years as the baby boomers age, become wealthier, and want to relive fond memories. Classic car sales and restoration is a multibillion dollar industry that employs more than 30,000 people in the United States. It is, however, a highly fragmented industry comprised of many small businesses. TVR is headquartered in Los Angeles, California and currently employs 95 full-time employees, including a sales staff, sales representatives, and general office staff. TVR's primary customer base consists of small restoration shops and classic car dealers on the west coast. They source many of their parts from abroad, but a growing percentage of these are now being manufactured in the United States.

TVR has a legacy accounting system that employs a combination of manual procedures supported by stand-alone PCs in the various departments. The company's payroll and fixed asset systems are described in the following paragraphs.

Payroll Procedures

Employees manually register their hours worked on timesheets. Each Friday afternoon they submit to the time sheets to their department supervisor for approval. The supervisor then forwards the timesheets to the payroll clerk, who manually prepares checks for each employee's approved timesheet. The clerk, using a laptop computer, then posts to the digital employee records. The clerk then mails the check to the employee and files a copy of the check in the department. Finally the clerk prints two payroll summaries from his computer. One of these he sends to the accounts payable department, and the other to the general ledger department.

The accounts payable clerk receives the payroll summary, approves it, and writes a check to cover the entire payroll. The clerk then sends the check to the bank where it is deposited into the payroll imprest account.

The general ledger clerk receives the payroll summary and posts to the related accounts in the digital general ledger, using the department PC.

Fixed Asset Procedures

Users in individual departments verbally report their fixed asset requirements to their respective managers. If the request is approved, the manager manually prepares a fixed asset request form and submits it to the purchasing department. Upon receipt of the fixed asset request form, the purchasing department clerk manually prepares two copies of a purchase order. The clerk sends one copy to the supplier and files one in the purchasing department. Finally, the purchasing department clerk manually prepares a hard-copy fixed asset change report and sends it to the fixed asset department.

When fixed assets are received, the receiving clerk reconciles the goods with the packing slip and invoice and then manually prepares a receiving report. The clerk sends the goods to the user department and forwards the packing slip, invoice, and receiving report to the accounts payable department.

The accounts payable clerk reconciles the documents from receiving, manually writes a check to the supplier, and manually prepares a journal voucher, which she subsequently sends to the general ledger department. The general ledger clerk posts journal vouchers to the digital general ledger using the department PC.

Required

a. Prepare a data flow diagram of the current payroll and fixed asset systems.
b. Prepare system flowcharts for the payroll and fixed asset systems.
c. Describe the uncontrolled risks associated with these systems as they are currently designed.

d. Describe the physical and IT controls needed to reduce the risks identified in "C" above.

4. PATRIOT GENERATORS, INC.—PAYROLL AND FIXED ASSET SYSTEMS (MANUAL AND STAND-ALONE PC PROCEDURES)

Patriot Generators, Inc., was founded in 1991 in Maple View, New Hampshire. The company specializes in a range of gasoline-powered electric generators for home backup, recreation, and commercial use. They have seen rapid growth over the past few years and currently employ 150 production, sales, and administrative employees.

Patriot's current information system includes manual procedures supported by independent (non-networked) PCs in each department. Communications between departments is through hard-copy documents. You have been hired to assess Patriot's procedures and internal controls. The following is a description of their payroll and fixed asset systems.

Payroll System

In the Patriot production departments, each worker records the number of hours he or she has worked each day by clocking in and out on a time card machine. The supervisor, oversees this process and each week sends the hard-copy time cards to the payroll department. Using a stand-alone PC, the payroll department clerk enters time card data and prepares hard-copy paychecks. This process automatically updates the digital employee payroll records. The clerk files the time cards in the payroll department and sends the employee paychecks to the supervisor for review and distribution to the employees. The payroll clerk also prepares three copies of a payroll register. Copies one and two are sent to accounts payable and the general ledger departments, respectively. The clerk files copy three in the payroll department. Upon receipt of the payroll register, the accounts payable clerk manually prepares a check for the entire payroll, which she deposits in the payroll imprest account at the bank. A copy of the check is filed in the department, along with the payroll register. Using the payroll register and the department PC, the general ledger department clerk posts to the appropriate general ledger control accounts. The clerk then files the payroll register.

Fixed Asset System

Asset acquisition begins in the user department when the manager recognizes the need to obtain a new or replace an existing fixed asset. The user manually prepares two copies of a purchase requisition, filing one copy in the user department and sending one copy to the purchasing department. The purchasing department uses the purchase requisition to prepare three copies of a purchase order. One copy of the purchase order is sent to the supplier, one is sent to the accounts payable department, and the last copy is filed in purchasing with the purchase requisition.

The accounts payable clerk receives the purchase order from purchasing, the asset invoice from the vendor, and a packing slip from the receiving dock after the assets arrive. The accounts payable clerk reconciles the purchase order with the packing slip and invoice. Then, using a department PC, the clerk posts a liability to the accounts payable subsidiary ledger and records the asset in the fixed asset inventory subsidiary ledger. The purchase order and packing slip are filed in the accounts payable department. Next, the clerk prepares a cash disbursement voucher, which she sends along with the invoice to the cash disbursements clerk. At the end of the day, the clerk prints hard-copy summaries of the accounts payable and fixed asset inventory ledgers, which she sends to the general ledger department.

Upon receipt of the cash disbursement voucher and invoice, the cash disbursements clerk, using the department PC, prepares a check and posts the relevant data to the check register. The clerk then prints a hard copy of the check and sends it to vendor. The cash disbursement voucher and invoice are then sent to the general ledger department.

User department managers handle the asset maintenance and disposal. They calculate depreciation and approve asset disposal for retired assets. Related to these actions, the managers prepare depreciation and asset disposal reports, which they send to the accounts payable clerk, who updates the appropriate fixed asset inventory accounts. Finally, the general ledger department clerk receives and reconciles the vendor invoices, cash disbursement vouchers, and account summaries. Using the department PC, the clerk posts to the respective general ledger accounts and files the documents in the department.

Required

a. Prepare a data flow diagram of the current payroll and fixed asset systems.
b. Prepare system flowcharts for the payroll and fixed asset systems.
c. Describe the uncontrolled risks associated with these systems as they are currently designed.

d. Describe the physical and IT controls needed to reduce the risks identified in "C" above. Explain the control weaknesses that you identified. Explain your solution.

5. TURNER PATIO FURNITURE (MANUAL AND STAND-ALONE PC SYSTEM)

In 2002, Thomas Turner opened the doors of Turner Patio Furniture (TPF) in Maryville, PA. The company, which began with only 3 employees (Thomas and his two sons), has grown over a decade from a small business serving the local community into a privately held corporation that supports 156 manufacturing, sales, and administrative employees. TPF now supplies garden centers and home improvement companies throughout the northeast United States with high quality patio furniture.

TPF's success has, however, caused the company to outgrow its information system, which consists of manual procedures supported by independent (non-networked) PCs in each department. You have been hired to assess TPF's procedures and internal controls related to its payroll and fixed asset systems, which are described below.

Payroll System

Production

Each week the production department supervisor submits employee time cards to the payroll department for processing. The supervisor also sends the job tickets to the cost accounting department, which uses them to allocate labor and manufacturing overhead costs to the work-in-process account.

The payroll department clerk receives the time cards and uses the department PC to update the employee payroll records. The clerk also prints the employee paychecks and a payroll register. A copy of the payroll register is sent to the accounts payable department, and the paychecks are signed and sent to the supervisors for distribution to the employees. A copy of the payroll register and the time cards are filed in the department.

The accounts payable department uses the payroll register to manually prepare two copies of a cash disbursement voucher. One copy of the voucher and the payroll register are sent to the cash disbursements department. The second copy of the voucher is sent to the general ledger department.

The cash disbursements department uses the payroll register and the cash disbursement voucher to manually prepare a check for the total payroll. The payroll check is signed and sent to the bank for deposit into the payroll imprest account. The voucher, the payroll check copy, and payroll register are filed in the department.

The general ledger uses the cash disbursement voucher to update the digital general ledger payroll account from the department PC. The voucher is then filed in the department.

Fixed Asset System

Purchasing

Managers in the user areas submit requisitions for fixed assets to the purchasing department. When the purchasing department clerk receives the purchase requisition, she manually creates a purchase order and sends it to the vendor. The purchase requisition is filed in the purchasing department.

When the asset is shipped, the vendor sends the invoice to the accounts payable department and delivers the asset directly to the user department, where it is reconciled to the packing slip and placed into service. The user then sends the packing slip to the fixed asset department.

Upon receipt of the invoice from the vendor, the accounts payable clerk calculates a due date for payment and, using the department PC, records the liability in the accounts payable subsidiary ledger. The clerk then files the invoice in the open accounts payable file. Periodically, the clerk reviews the open accounts payable file for items to be paid. When an accounts payable is due, the clerk accesses the department PC, prints a hard-copy cash disbursement voucher, and sends it to the cash disbursements department. The clerk then removes the liability from the digital accounts payable subsidiary ledger. Finally, the clerk files the hard-copy invoice in the closed accounts payable file.

Upon receipt of the cash disbursement voucher, the cash disbursements clerk accesses the department PC, prints a vendor check, and records the check in the digital check register. Next, the clerk sends the check to the vendor and sends the hard-copy cash disbursement voucher to the general ledger department.

When the fixed asset department clerk receives the packing slip from the user department, he accesses the department computer and records the asset in the fixed asset subsidiary ledger. Periodically, the clerk prepares an account summary that he sends to the general ledger. *NOTE: The fixed asset department has additional procedures to manage the maintenance and disposal of fixed assets. These procedures are not part of this assignment.*

The general ledger clerk receives the cash disbursement voucher from the cash disbursements department and the account summary from the fixed assets department. The general ledger clerk then accesses the department PC and posts to the cash, accounts payable control, and fixed asset control accounts. Finally, the general ledger clerk files the voucher and account summary in the department.

Required

a. Prepare a data flow diagram of the current payroll and fixed asset systems.
b. Prepare system flowcharts for the payroll and fixed asset systems.
c. Describe the uncontrolled risks associated with these systems as they are currently designed.
d. Describe the physical and IT controls needed to reduce the risks identified in "C" above.

6. GREEN PRODUCTS GARDEN SUPPLY (STAND-ALONE PC-BASED ACCOUNTING SYSTEM)

Green Products Garden (GPG) Supply sells and distributes a wide range of garden products and equipment including organic fertilizers, premium flower and grass seeds, organic pesticides, and garden spreaders. GPG's headquarters and warehouse is located in Hopewell, Virginia.

GPG's current information system includes manual procedures supported by independent (non-networked) PCs in each department. Communications between departments is entirely through hard-copy documents. You have been hired to assess GPG's procedures and internal controls. The following is a description of GPG's payroll and fixed asset systems.

Payroll System

On Thursday, every two weeks, employees submit their hours-worked data from their personally maintained time cards to their department supervisors who review and send the time card to the payroll department. The supervisors also provide payroll with personnel action forms that record any employee changes in employee status such as new hires, terminated employees, or changes in pay rate.

Upon receipt of the time cards and personnel action forms, the payroll clerk updates the digital employee records from the department PC and prints the payroll register. A copy of the payroll register, along with the time cards, and the personnel action form are filed in the payroll department. A second copy of the payroll register is sent to general ledger clerk, who posts to the general cash account and wages expense for the full amount of the payroll. Next, the payroll clerk prepares the paychecks and sends them to the employee's respective supervisors, who distribute the checks to the employees.

Fixed Asset System

Asset acquisition begins when the user department manager recognizes the need to obtain new or replace an existing fixed asset. The manager manually prepares two copies of a purchase requisition; one copy is filed temporarily in the department, and one is sent to the purchasing department. From the purchase requisition, the purchasing department clerk manually prepares three copies of a purchase order. One copy is sent to the supplier, another copy is sent to the accounts payable department, and the third copy is filed in the purchasing department. When the asset arrives, the user department receives it along with the packing slip. The packing slip and goods are reconciled with the purchase requisition on file, and then the packing slip and requisition are filed permanently in the user department.

The accounts payable clerk receives the purchase order from the purchasing department and files it temporarily. Upon receipt of the invoice from the vendor, the accounts payable clerk reconciles it with the purchase order on file. Using the department PC, the accounts payable clerk then sets up an account payable and records the asset in the fixed asset inventory ledger. The clerk then prints a cash disbursement voucher and sends it to the cash disbursements department. At the end of the day, the clerk prints account summaries for accounts payable and fixed asset inventory, which she sends to the general ledger department. The purchase order and invoice are permanently filed in the department.

The cash disbursements clerk receives the cash disbursement voucher from accounts payable and posts the payment to the check register from the department PC. The clerk then prints a check, which he sends to the vendor. At the end of the day, the clerk prints a hard-copy journal voucher from the PC and sends it to the general ledger department.

When an asset has reached the end of its useful life, the user department manager prepares a disposal report and sends it to the accounts payable clerk, who adjusts the fixed asset inventory record.

The general ledger department clerk reconciles the journal voucher, the accounts payable summary, and the inventory summary received from accounts payable and cash disbursements. These figures are then posted to the general ledger from the department PC, and the account summaries and journal vouchers are filed in the department.

Required

a. Prepare a data flow diagram of the current payroll and fixed asset systems.
b. Prepare system flowcharts for the payroll and fixed asset systems.
c. Describe the uncontrolled risks associated with these systems as they are currently designed.
d. Describe the physical and IT controls needed to reduce the risks identified in "C" above.

CHAPTER

7

The Conversion Cycle

A company's conversion cycle transforms (converts) input resources, such as raw materials, labor, and overhead, into finished products or services for sale. The conversion cycle exists conceptually in all organizations, including those in service and retail industries. It is most formal and apparent, however, in manufacturing firms, which are the focus of this chapter. We begin with a review of the traditional batch production model, which consists of four basic processes: (1) plan and control production, (2) perform production operations, (3) maintain inventory control, and (4) perform cost accounting. The discussion focuses on the activities, documents, and controls pertaining to these traditional processes. This chapter then examines manufacturing techniques and technologies in world-class companies. Many firms pursuing world-class status follow a philosophy of lean manufacturing. This approach evolved from the Toyota Production System (TPS). The goal of lean manufacturing is to improve efficiency and effectiveness in product design, supplier interaction, factory operations, employee management, and customer relations. Key to successful lean manufacturing is achieving manufacturing flexibility, which involves the physical organization of production facilities and the employment of automated technologies, including computer numerical controlled (CNC) machines, computer-integrated manufacturing (CIM), automated storage and retrieval systems (AS/RS), robotics, computer-aided design (CAD), and computer-aided manufacturing (CAM).

This chapter then examines problems associated with applying standard cost accounting techniques in a highly automated environment. The key features of two alternative accounting models are discussed: (1) activity-based costing (ABC) and (2) value stream accounting. This chapter concludes with a discussion of the information systems commonly associated with lean manufacturing and world-class companies. Materials requirements planning (MRP) systems are used to determine how much raw materials are required to fulfill production orders. Manufacturing resources planning (MRP II) evolved

Learning Objectives

After studying this chapter, you should:

- Understand the basic elements and procedures encompassing a traditional production process.
- Understand the data flows and procedures in a traditional cost accounting system.
- Be familiar with the accounting controls found in a traditional environment.
- Understand the principles, operating features, and technologies that characterize lean manufacturing.
- Understand the shortcomings of traditional accounting methods in a world-class environment.
- Be familiar with the key features of activity-based costing and value stream accounting.
- Be familiar with the information systems commonly associated with lean manufacturing and world-class companies.

from MRP to integrate additional functionality into the manufacturing process, including sales, marketing, and accounting. Enterprise resource planning (ERP) systems take MRP II a step further by integrating all aspects of the business into a set of core applications that use a common database.

The Traditional Manufacturing Environment

The conversion cycle consists of both physical and information activities related to manufacturing products for sale. The context-level data flow diagram (DFD) in Figure 7-1 illustrates the central role of the conversion cycle and its interactions with other business cycles. Production is triggered by customer orders from the revenue cycle and/or by sales forecasts from marketing. These inputs are used to set a production target and prepare a production plan, which drives production activities. Purchase requisitions for the raw materials needed to meet production objectives are sent to the purchases procedures (expenditure cycle), which prepares purchase orders for vendors. Labor used in production is transmitted to the payroll system (expenditure cycle) for payroll processing. Manufacturing costs associated with intermediate work-in-process and finished goods (FG) are sent to the general ledger (GL) and financial reporting system.

Depending on the type of product being manufactured, a company will employ one of the following production methods:

1. Continuous processing creates a homogeneous product through a continuous series of standard procedures. Cement and petrochemicals are produced by this manufacturing method. Typically, under this approach firms attempt to maintain finished-goods inventory at levels needed to meet expected sales demand. The sales forecast, in conjunction with information on current inventory levels, triggers this process.

FIGURE 7-1 CONVERSION CYCLE IN RELATION TO OTHER CYCLES

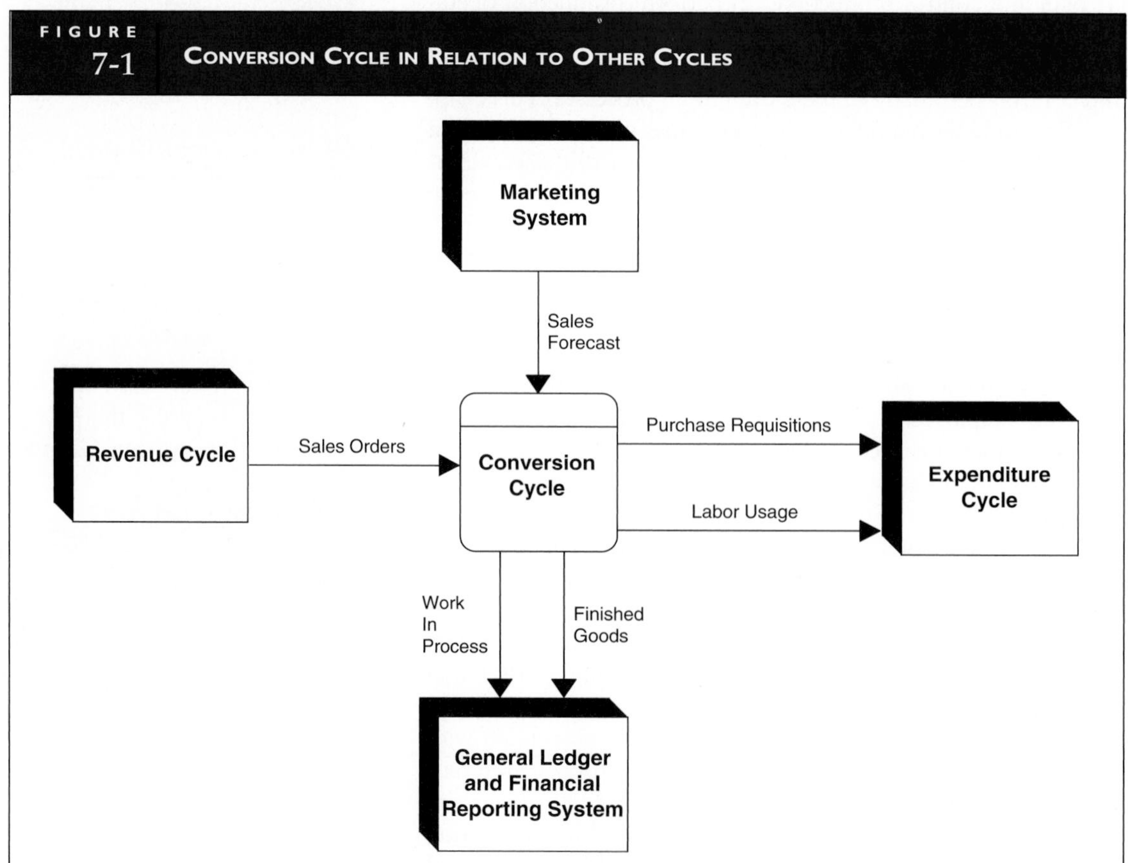

2. Make-to-order processing involves the fabrication of discrete products in accordance with customer specifications. This process is initiated by sales orders rather than depleted inventory levels.
3. Batch processing produces discrete groups (batches) of products. Each item in the batch is similar and requires the same raw materials and operations. To justify the cost of setting up and retooling for each batch run, the number of items in the batch tends to be large. This is the most common method of production and is used to manufacture products such as automobiles, household appliances, canned goods, automotive tires, and textbooks. The discussion in this chapter is based on a batch processing environment.

BATCH PROCESSING SYSTEM

The DFD in Figure 7-2 provides a conceptual overview of the batch processing system, which consists of four basic processes: plan and control production, perform production operations, maintain inventory control, and perform cost accounting. As in previous chapters, the conceptual system discussion is intended to be technology-neutral. The tasks described in this section may be performed manually or by computer. The figure also depicts the primary information flows (documents) that integrate these activities and link them to other cycles and systems. Again, system documents are technology-neutral and may be hard-copy or digital. We begin our study of batch processing with a review of the purpose and content of these documents.

Documents in the Batch Processing System

A manufacturing process such as that shown in Figure 7-2 could be triggered either by individual sales orders from the revenue cycle or by a sales forecast the marketing system provides. For discussion purposes, we will assume the latter. The sales forecast shows the expected demand for a firm's FG for a given period. For some firms, marketing may produce a forecast of annual demand by product. For firms with seasonal swings in sales, the forecast will be for a shorter period (quarterly or monthly) that can be revised in accordance with economic conditions.

- The **production schedule** is the formal plan and authorization to begin production. This document describes the specific products to be made, the quantities to be produced in each batch, and the manufacturing timetable for starting and completing production. Figure 7-3 contains an example of a production schedule.
- The **bill of materials (BOM)**, an example of which is illustrated in Figure 7-4, specifies the types and quantities of the raw material (RM) and subassemblies used in producing a single unit of finished product. The RM requirements for an entire batch are determined by multiplying the BOM by the number of items in the batch.
- A **route sheet**, illustrated in Figure 7-5, shows the production path that a particular batch of product follows during manufacturing. It is similar conceptually to a BOM. Whereas the BOM specifies material requirements, the route sheet specifies the sequence of operations (machining or assembly) and the standard time allocated to each task.
- The **work order** (or production order) draws from BOMs and route sheets to specify the materials and production (machining, assembly, and so on) for each batch. These, together with move tickets (described next), initiate the manufacturing process in the production departments. Figure 7-6 presents a work order.
- A **move ticket**, shown in Figure 7-7, records work done in each work center and authorizes the movement of the job or batch from one work center to the next.
- A **materials requisition** authorizes the storekeeper to release materials (and subassemblies) to individuals or work centers in the production process. This document usually specifies only standard quantities. Materials needed in excess of standard amounts require separate requisitions that may be identified explicitly as excess materials requisitions. This allows for closer control over the production process by highlighting excess material usage. In some cases, less than the standard amount of material is used in production. When this happens, the work

FIGURE 7-2 DFD of Batch Production Process

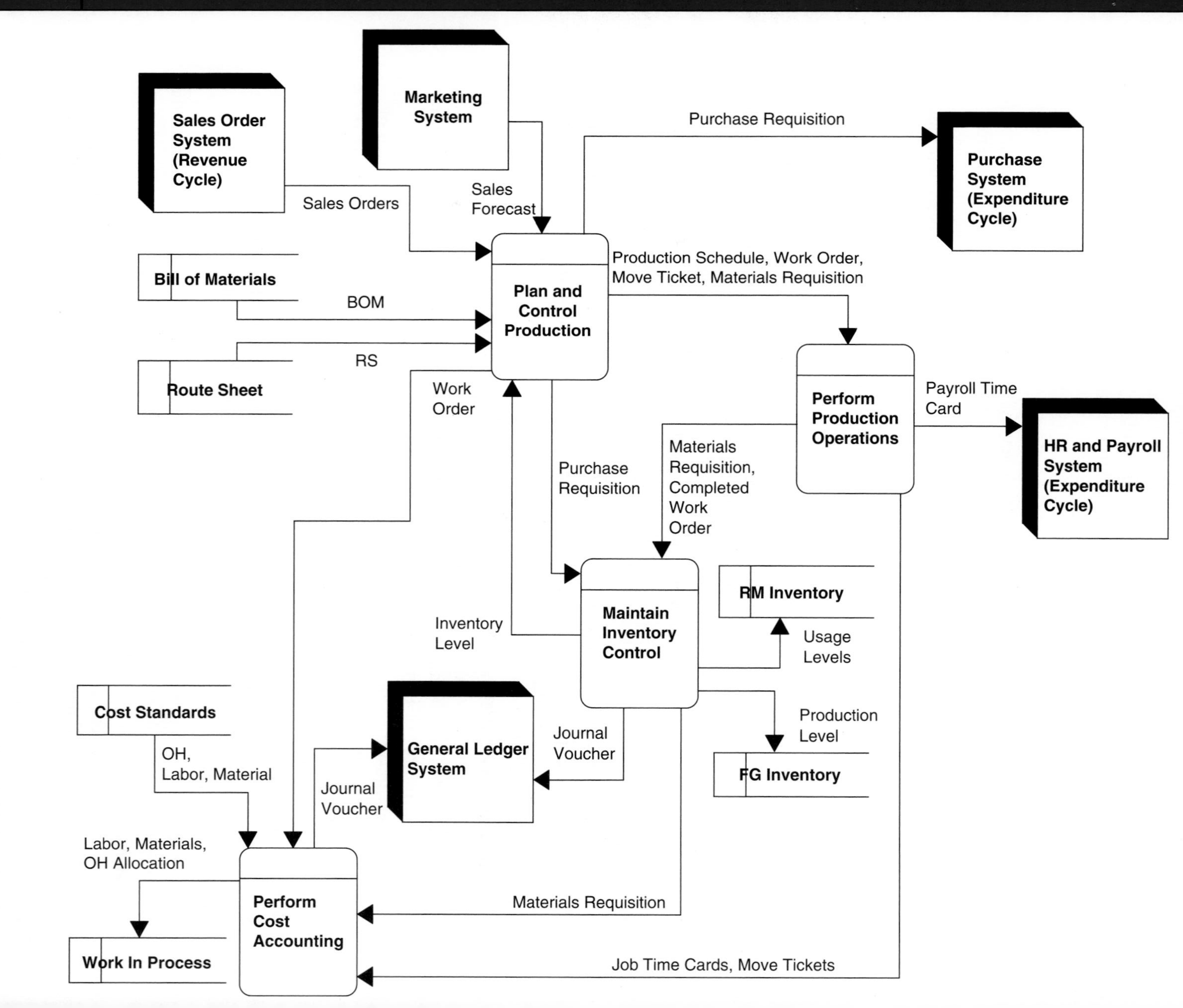

FIGURE 7-3 PRODUCTION SCHEDULE

ABC COMPANY	PRODUCTION SCHEDULE					JAN 2015	
		OPER #1		OPER #2		OPER #3	
Batch Num	Qnty Units	Start	Complete	Start	Complete	Start	Complete
1237	800	1/2/15	1/5/15			1/8/15	1/23/15
1567	560	1/3/15	1/8/15	1/9/15	1/15/15	1/16/15	1/18/15
1679	450			1/2/15	1/5/15	1/8/15	1/10/15
4567	650	1/5/15	1/10/15	1/11/15	1/15/15	1/16/15	1/23/15
5673	1000	•	•	•	•	•	•
•	•	•	•	•	•	•	•
•	•	•	•	•	•	•	•

centers return the unused materials to the storeroom accompanied by a materials return ticket. Figure 7-8 presents a format that could serve all three purposes.

Batch Production Activities

The flowchart in Figure 7-9 presents a physical batch processing system. The flowchart depicts the organization departments involved, the tasks performed in each department, and the documents that trigger or result from each task. To more clearly illustrate the information flows in the process, documents are represented in Figure 7-9 as hard copy. Many organizations, however, transmit data digitally and use bar code scanners to track the movement of production through the process. In this section, we examine three of the four conversion cycle processes depicted by the DFD in Figure 7-2. Cost accounting procedures are discussed later.

FIGURE 7-4 BILL OF MATERIALS

BILL OF MATERIALS

PRODUCT ENGINE TR6 2500 CC — NORMAL BATCH QNTY 100

Material Item Num	Description	Quantity Reg/Unit Product
28746	Crank shaft	1
387564	Main bearing set	4
735402	Piston	6
663554	Connecting rods	6
8847665	Rod bearing set	6
663345	Core plug 2"	6
663546	Core plug 1 1/2"	4

FIGURE 7-5 Route Sheet

ROUTE SHEET

PRODUCT
ENGINE TR6
2500 CC

Work Center	Operation	Description	Standard Time/Unit	
			Set Up	Process
101	1a	Mill block and fit studs	.6	1.6
153	4a	Clean block and fit crank	.3	1.5
154	1	Fit pistons and bearings	.1	.7
340	2	Fit water pump, fuel pump, oil pump, and cylinder head	.1	1.4

PRODUCTION PLANNING AND CONTROL. We first examine the production planning and control function. This consists of two main activities: (1) specifying materials and operations requirements, and (2) production scheduling.

MATERIALS AND OPERATIONS REQUIREMENTS. The RM requirement for a batch of any given product is the difference between what is needed and what is available in the RM inventory. This information comes from analysis of inventory on hand, the sales forecast, engineering specifications (if any), and the BOM. A product of this activity is the creation of purchase

FIGURE 7-6 Work Order

WORK ORDER #5681

PART NAME: ENGINE CRANK SHAFT — Drawing # CS-87622

MATERIAL:
CRANK CASTING

Work Center	Operation	Description	Standard Hrs		Actual Proc	Unit Compltd	Units Scrap	Insp #
			Set Up	Proc				
184	21	Draw castings from stores	—	2.2	2.5	100	0	
186	23	Turn journals and main bearings per specs	2.3	14.9	16.00	99	1	
156	01	Balance crank	4.0	21.5	32.00	99	0	
•	•	•	•	•	•	•	•	•
•	•	•	•	•	•	•	•	•

FIGURE 7-7 Move Ticket

MOVE TICKET

Batch Num: **1292**
Units: **100**

Move To: Work Center 153
Operation: 4a
Start Date: 1/8/15
Finish Date: 1/10/15
Qnty Received: 100
Received By:________________

requisitions for additional RMs. Procedures for preparing purchase orders and acquiring inventories are the same as those described in Chapter 5. The operations requirements for the batch involve the assembly and/or manufacturing activities that will be applied to the product. This is determined by assessing route sheet specifications.

PRODUCTION SCHEDULING. The second activity of the planning and control function is production scheduling. The master schedule for a production run coordinates the production of many different batches. The schedule is influenced by time constraints, batch size, and specifications derived from BOMs and route sheets. The scheduling task also produces work orders, move tickets, and materials requisitions for each batch in the production run. A copy of each work order is sent to cost accounting to set up a new work-in-process (WIP) account for the batch. The work orders, move tickets, and materials requisitions enter the production process and flow through the various work centers in accordance with the route sheet. To simplify the flowchart in Figure 7-9, only one work center is shown.

FIGURE 7-8 Materials Requisition, Excess Materials Requisition, and Materials Return Ticket

MATERIALS REQUISITION/RETURNS

Issued To: ________________ **Work Order Number**________________
Date: ________________

Material Item #	Description	Quantity Issued	Unit Cost	Extended Cost

Authorized By: ________________
Received By: ________________
Cost Accounting: ________________

FIGURE 7-9 BATCH PRODUCTION PROCESS

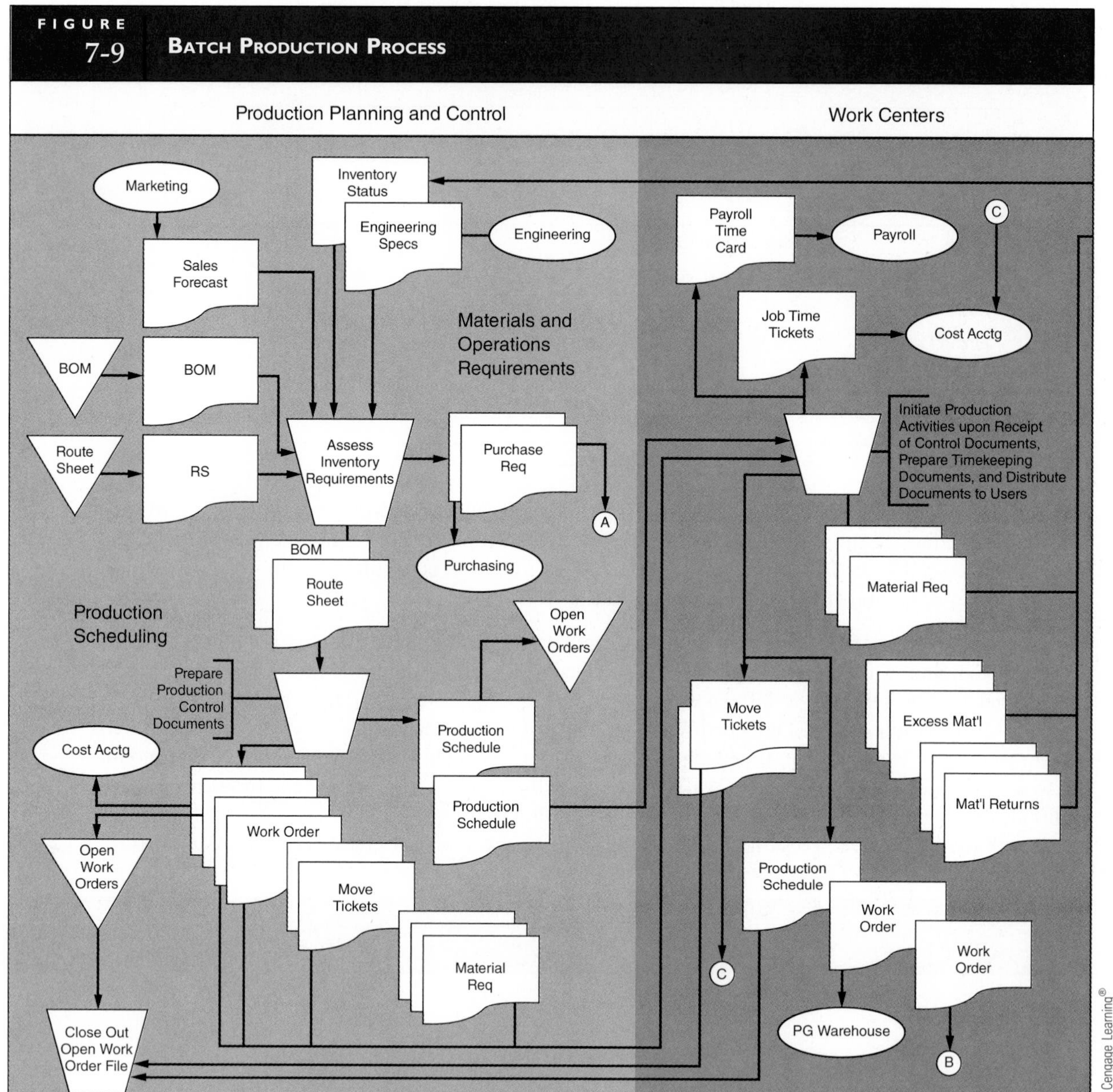

WORK CENTERS AND STOREKEEPING. The actual production operations begin when workers obtain raw materials from storekeeping in exchange for materials requisitions. These materials, as well as the machining and the labor required to manufacture the product, are applied in compliance with the work order. When the task is complete at a particular work center, the supervisor or other authorized person signs the move ticket, which authorizes the batch to proceed to the next work center. To evidence that a stage of production has been completed, a copy of the move ticket is sent back to production planning and control to update the open work order file. Upon receipt of the last move ticket, the open work order file is closed. The finished product, along with a copy of the work order, is sent to the finished goods (FG) warehouse. Also, a copy of the work order is sent to inventory control to update the FG inventory records.

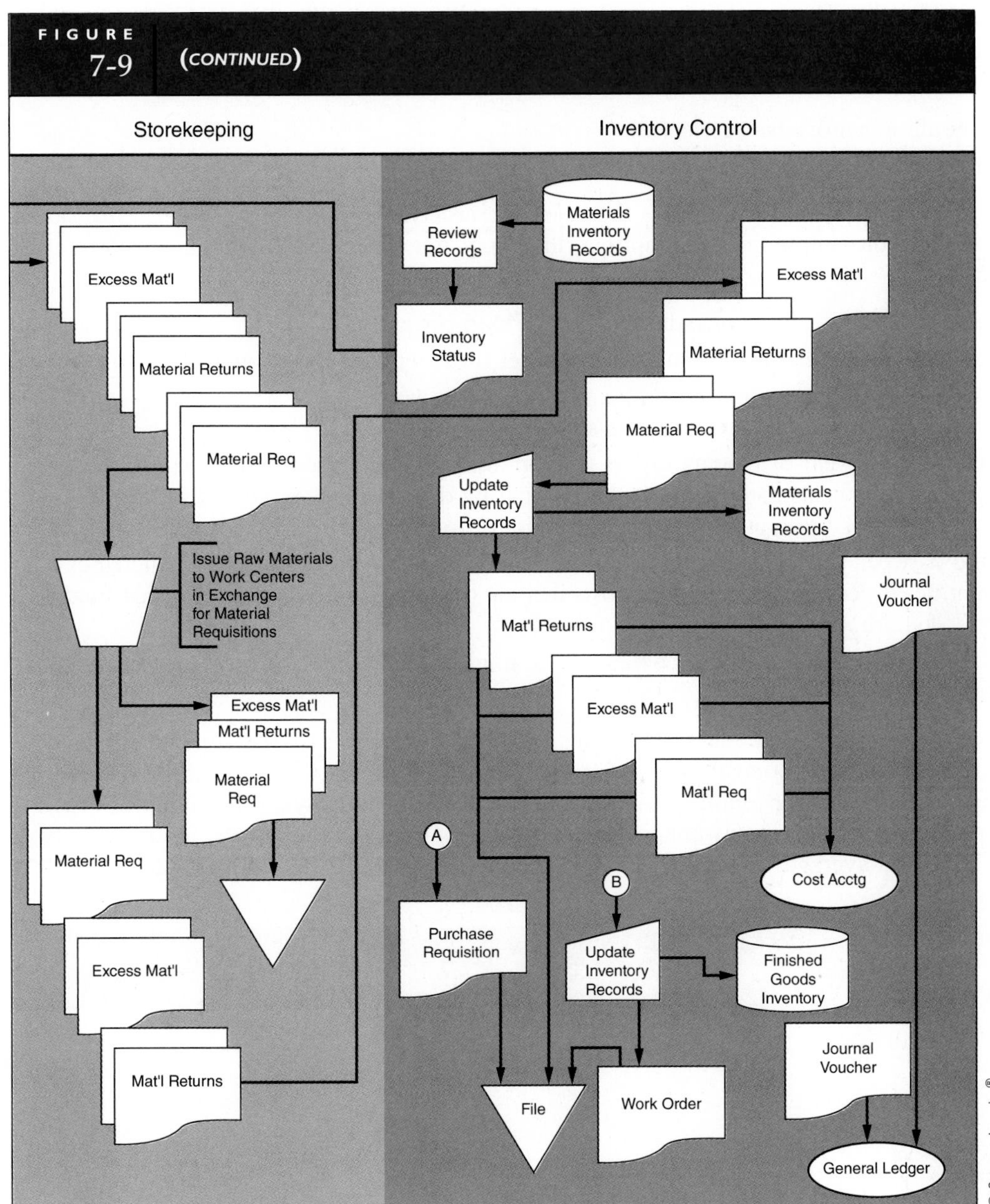

Work centers also fulfill an important role in recording labor time costs. This task is handled by work center supervisors who, at the end of each workweek, send employee time cards and job tickets to the payroll and cost accounting departments, respectively.

INVENTORY CONTROL. The inventory control function consists of three main activities. First, it provides production planning and control with status reports on finished goods and raw materials inventory. Second, the inventory control function is continually involved in updating the raw material inventory records from materials requisitions, excess materials requisitions, and materials return tickets. Finally, upon receipt of the work order from the last work center, inventory control records the completed production by updating the finished goods inventory records.

An objective of inventory control is to minimize total inventory cost while ensuring that adequate inventories exist to meet current demand. Inventory models used to achieve this objective help answer two fundamental questions:

1. When should inventory be purchased?
2. How much inventory should be purchased?

A commonly used inventory model is the **economic order quantity (EOQ) model**. This model, however, is based on simplifying assumptions that may not reflect the economic reality. These assumptions are:

1. Demand for the product is constant and known with certainty.
2. The lead time—the time between placing an order for inventory and its arrival—is known and constant.
3. All inventories in the order arrive at the same time.
4. The total cost per year of placing orders is a variable that decreases as the quantities ordered increase. Ordering costs include the cost of preparing documentation, contacting vendors, processing inventory receipts, maintaining vendor accounts, and writing checks.
5. The total cost per year of holding inventories (carrying costs) is a variable that increases as the quantities ordered increase. These costs include the opportunity cost of invested funds, storage costs, property taxes, and insurance.
6. There are no quantity discounts. Therefore, the total purchase price of inventory for the year is constant.

The objective of the EOQ model is to reduce total inventory costs. The significant parameters in this model are the carrying costs and the ordering costs. Figure 7-10 illustrates the relationship between these costs and order quantity. As the quantity ordered increases, the number of ordering events decreases, causing the total annual cost of ordering to decrease. As the quantity ordered increases, however, average inventory on hand increases, causing the total annual inventory

FIGURE 7-10 THE RELATIONSHIP OF TOTAL INVENTORY COST AND ORDER QUANTITY

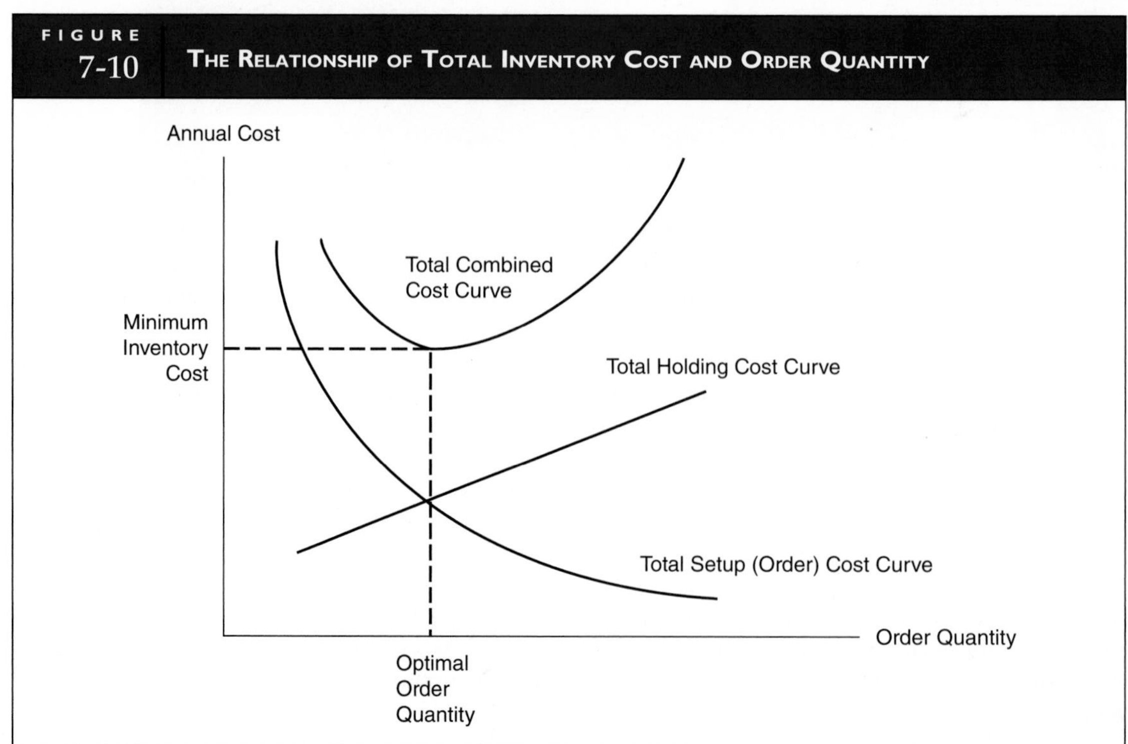

carrying cost to increase. Because the total purchase price of inventory is constant (assumption 6), we minimize total inventory costs by minimizing the total carrying cost and total ordering costs. The combined total cost curve is minimized at the intersection of the ordering-cost curve and the carrying-cost curve. This is the EOQ.

The following equation is used to determine the EOQ:

$$Q = \sqrt{\frac{2DS}{H}}$$

where Q = economic order quantity
D = annual demand in units
S = the fixed cost of placing each order
H = the holding or carrying cost per unit per year

To illustrate the use of this model, consider the following example:

A company has an annual demand of 2,000 units, a per-unit order cost of $12, and a carrying cost per unit of 40 cents. Using these values, we calculate the EOQ as follows:

$$Q = \sqrt{\frac{2DS}{H}}$$

$$Q = \sqrt{\frac{2(2{,}000)(12)}{0.40}}$$

$$Q = \sqrt{120.000}$$

$$Q = \sqrt{346}$$

Now that we know how much to purchase, let's consider the second question: When do we purchase? The **reorder point (ROP)** is usually expressed as follows:

$$ROP = I \times d$$

where I = lead time
d = daily demand (total demand/number of working days)

In simple models, both I and d are assumed to be known with certainty and are constant. For example, if:

d = 5 units, and
I = 8 days, then
ROP = 40 units.

The assumptions of the EOQ model produce the saw-toothed inventory usage pattern illustrated in Figure 7-11. Values for Q and ROP are calculated separately for each type of inventory item. Each time inventory is reduced by sales or used in production, its new quantity on hand (QOH) is compared to its ROP. When QOH = ROP, an order is placed for the amount of Q. In our example, when inventory drops to 40 units, the firm orders 346 units.

If the parameters d and I are stable, the organization should receive the ordered inventories just as the quantity on hand reaches zero. If either or both parameters are subject to variation, however, then additional inventories called **safety stock** must be added to the reorder point to avoid unanticipated stock-out events. Figure 7-12 shows an additional 10 units of safety stock to carry the firm through a lead time that could vary from 8 to 10 days. The new reorder point is 50 units. Stock-outs result in either lost sales or back-orders. A back-order is a customer order that cannot be filled because of a stock-out and will remain unfilled until the supplier receives replenishment stock.

When an organization's inventory usage and delivery patterns depart significantly from the assumptions of the EOQ model, more sophisticated models such as the back-order quantity model and the production order quantity model may be used. However, a discussion of these models is beyond the scope of this text.

FIGURE 7-11 INVENTORY USAGE

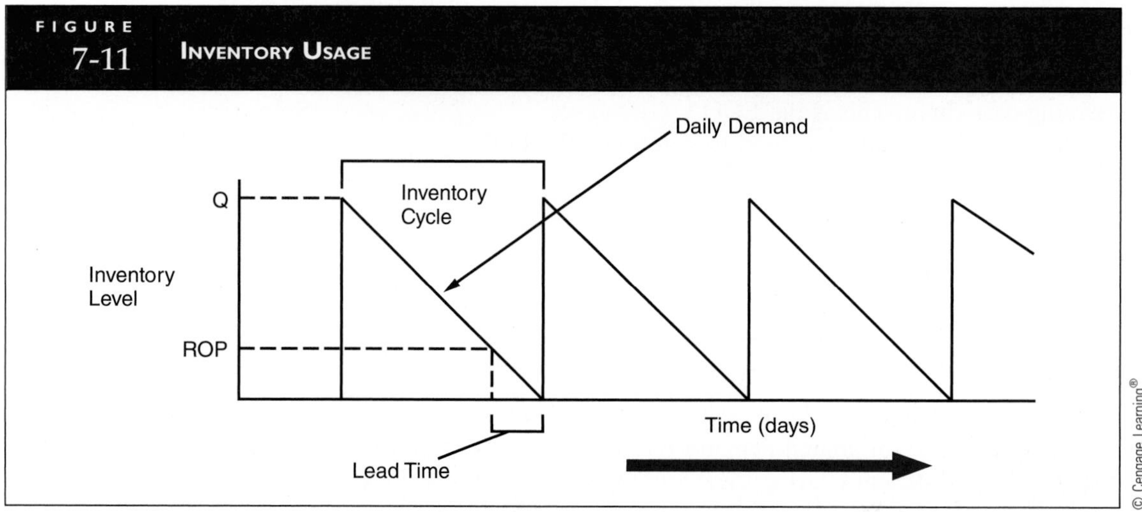

FIGURE 7-12 THE USE OF SAFETY STOCK TO PREVENT STOCK-OUTS

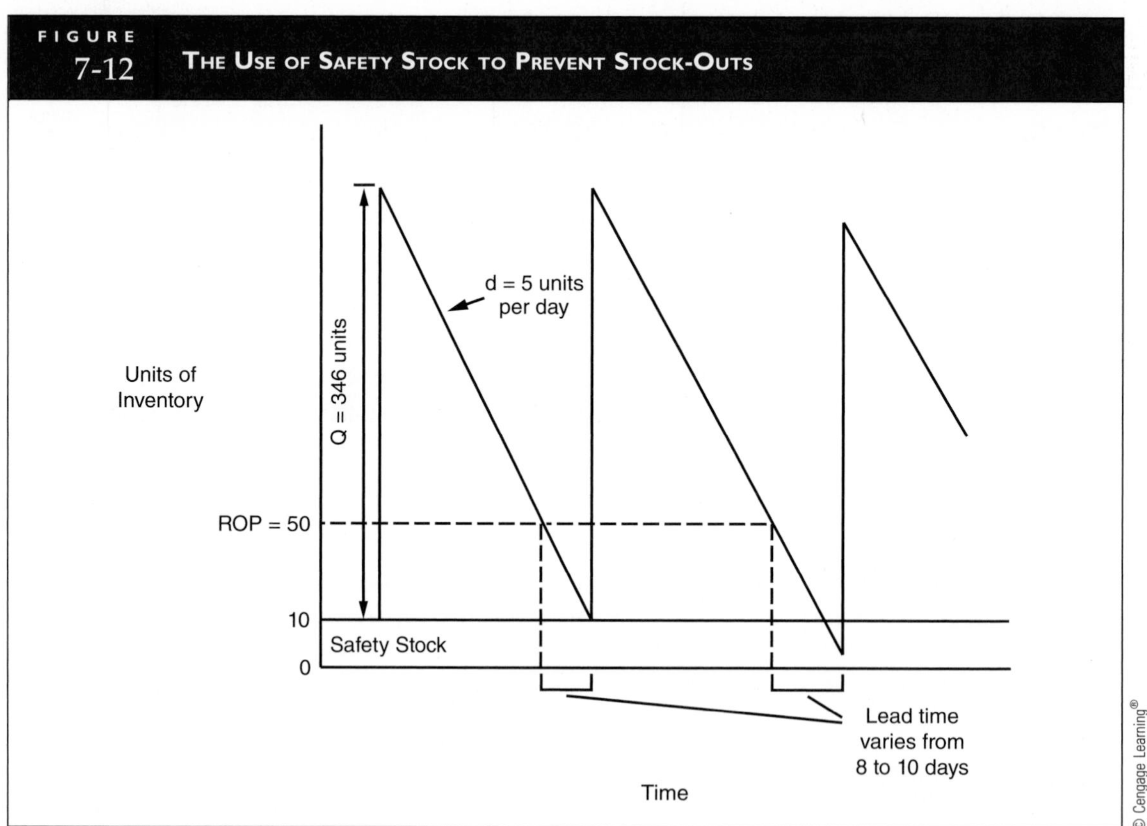

Cost Accounting Activities

Cost accounting activities of the conversion cycle record the financial effects of the physical events that are occurring in the production process. Figure 7-13 represents typical cost accounting information tasks and data flows. The cost accounting process for a given production run begins when the production planning and control department sends a copy of the original work order to the cost accounting department. This marks the beginning of the production event by causing a new record to be added to the WIP file, which is the subsidiary ledger for the WIP control account in the general ledger.

FIGURE 7-13 COST ACCOUNTING PROCEDURES

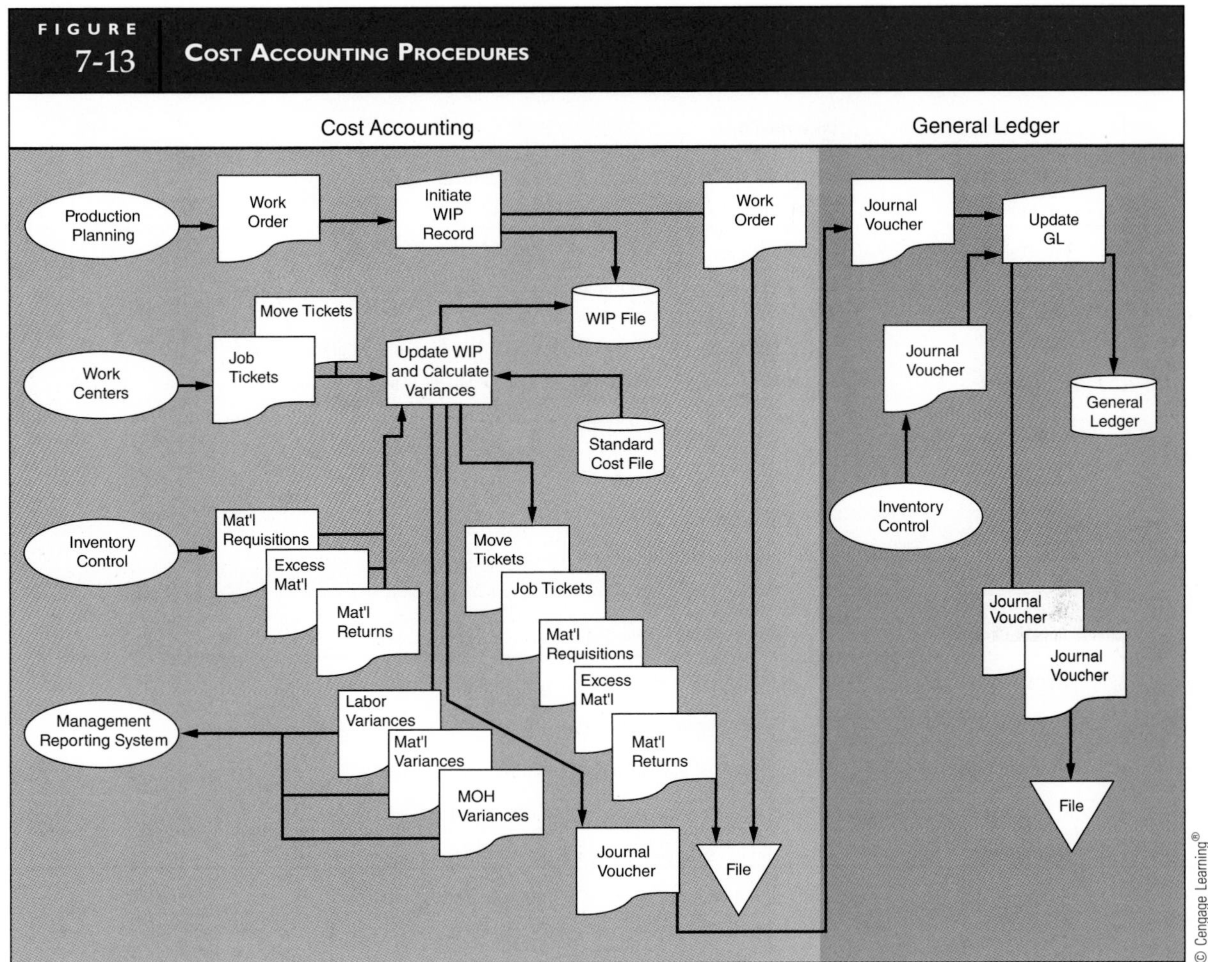

As materials and labor are added throughout the production process, documents reflecting these events flow to the cost accounting department. Inventory control sends copies of materials requisitions, excess materials requisitions, and materials returns. The various work centers send job tickets and completed move tickets. These documents, along with standards provided by the standard cost file, enable cost accounting to update the affected WIP accounts with the standard charges for direct labor, material, and manufacturing overhead (MOH). Deviations from standard usage are recorded to produce material usage, direct labor, and manufacturing overhead variances.

The receipt of the last move ticket for a particular batch signals the completion of the production process and the transfer of products from WIP to the FG inventory. At this point, cost accounting closes the WIP account. Periodically, summary information regarding charges (debits) to WIP, reductions (credits) to WIP, and variances are recorded on journal vouchers and sent to the GL department for posting to the control accounts.

CONTROLS IN THE TRADITIONAL ENVIRONMENT

The IT controls summarized in Table 7-1 apply in the batch production environment. These controls and the risks they address have been discussed in previous chapters and need no additional comment. Table 7-2 summarizes the physical controls specific to the conversion cycle and are further explained in the following section.

TABLE 7-1 SUMMARY OF IT APPLICATION CONTROLS

Control Category	Conversion Cycle
Input controls	Edit controls to detect clerical errors in input data Check digit for validating account numbers
Processing controls	Error messages to signify account mismatch Password control to prevent unauthorized access to the system Backup procedures to protect digital files Multilevel security (roles) to limit access to data files and program modules Automated posting to subsidiary and general ledger accounts
Output controls	Security over distribution of production documents and management reports

TABLE 7-2 SUMMARY OF CONVERSION CYCLE PHYSICAL CONTROLS

Control Category	Control Points in the System
Transaction authorization	Work orders, move tickets, and materials requisitions
Segregation of duties	1. Inventory control separate from RM and FG inventory custody 2. Cost accounting separate from work centers 3. GL separate from other accounting functions
Supervision	Supervisors oversee usage of RM and timekeeping
Access control	Limit physical access to FG, RM stocks, and production processes Use formal procedures and documents to release materials into production
Accounting records	Work orders, cost sheets, move tickets, job tickets, materials requisitions, WIP records, FG inventory file
Independent verification	Cost accounting function reconciles all cost of production GL reconciles overall system

Transaction Authorization

The following describes the transaction authorization procedure in the conversion cycle.

1. In the traditional manufacturing environment, production planning and control authorize the production activity via a formal work order. This document reflects production requirements, which are the difference between the expected demand for products (based on the sales forecast) and the FG inventory on hand.
2. Move tickets signed by the supervisor in each work center authorize activities for each batch and for the movement of products through the various work centers.
3. Materials requisitions and excess materials requisitions authorize the storekeeper to release materials to the work centers.

Segregation of Duties

One objective of this control procedure is to separate the tasks of transaction authorization and transaction processing. As a result, the production planning and control department is organizationally segregated from the work centers.

Another control objective is to segregate record keeping from asset custody. The following separations apply:

1. Inventory control maintains accounting records for RM and FG inventories. This activity is kept separate from the materials storeroom and from the FG warehouse functions, which have custody of these assets.
2. Similarly, the cost accounting function accounts for WIP and should be separate from the work centers in the production process.

Finally, to maintain the independence of the GL function as a verification step, the GL department must be separate from departments keeping subsidiary accounts. Therefore, the GL department is organizationally segregated from inventory control and cost accounting.

Supervision

The following supervision procedures apply to the conversion cycle:

1. The supervisors in the work centers oversee the usage of RM in the production process. This helps to ensure that all materials released from stores are used in production and that waste is minimized. Employee time cards and job tickets must also be checked for accuracy.
2. Supervisors also observe and review timekeeping activities. This promotes accurate employee time cards and job tickets.

Access Control

The conversion cycle allows both direct and indirect access to assets.

DIRECT ACCESS TO ASSETS. The nature of the physical product and the production process influences the type of access controls needed.

1. Firms often limit access to sensitive areas, such as storerooms, production work centers, and FG warehouses. Control methods used include identification badges, security guards, observation devices, and various electronic sensors and alarms.
2. The use of standard costs provides a type of access control. By specifying the quantities of material and labor authorized for each product, the firm limits unauthorized access to those resources. To obtain excess quantities requires special authorization and formal documentation.

INDIRECT ACCESS TO ASSETS. Assets, such as cash and inventories, can be manipulated through access to the source documents that control them. In the conversion cycle, critical documents include materials requisitions, excess materials requisitions, and employee time cards. A method of control that also supports an audit trail is the use of prenumbered documents.

Accounting Records

As we have seen in preceding chapters, the objective of this control technique is to establish an audit trail for each transaction. In the conversion cycle, this is accomplished through the use of work orders, cost sheets, move tickets, job tickets, materials requisitions, the WIP file, and the FG inventory file. By prenumbering source documents and referencing these in the WIP records, a company can trace every item of FG inventory back through the production process to its source. This is essential in detecting errors in production and record keeping, locating batches lost in production, and performing periodic audits.

Independent Verification

Verification steps in the conversion cycle are performed as follows:

1. Cost accounting reconciles the materials and labor usage taken from materials requisitions and job tickets with the prescribed standards. Cost accounting personnel may then identify departures from prescribed standards, which are formally reported as variances. In the

traditional manufacturing environment, calculated variances are an important source of data for the management reporting system.

2. The GL department also fulfills an important verification function by checking the total movement of products from WIP to FG. This is done by reconciling journal vouchers from cost accounting with summaries of the inventory subsidiary ledger from inventory control.
3. Finally, internal and external auditors periodically verify the RM and FG inventories on hand through a physical count. They compare actual quantities against the inventory records and make adjustments to the records when necessary.

World-Class Companies and Lean Manufacturing

The traditional conversion cycle described in the previous section represents how many manufacturing firms operate today. Over the past three decades, however, rapid swings in consumer demands, shorter product life cycles, and global competition have radically changed the rules of the marketplace. In an attempt to cope with these changes, manufacturers have begun to conduct business in a dramatically different way. The term *world-class* defines this modern era of business. The pursuit of world-class status is a journey without destination because it requires continuous innovation and continuous improvement. A recent survey of corporate executives revealed that 80 percent claim to be pursuing principles that will lead their companies to world-class status. Skeptics argue, however, that as few as 10 or 20 percent of these firms are truly on the right path.

WHAT IS A WORLD-CLASS COMPANY?

The following features characterize the world-class company:

- World-class companies must maintain strategic agility and be able to turn on a dime. Top management must be intimately aware of customer needs and not become rigid and resistant to paradigm change.
- World-class companies motivate and treat employees like appreciating assets. To activate the talents of everyone, decisions are pushed to the lowest level in the organization. The result is a flat and responsive organizational structure.
- A world-class company profitably meets the needs of its customers. Its goal is not simply to satisfy customers, but to positively delight them. This is not something that can be done once and then forgotten. With competitors aggressively seeking new ways to increase market share, a world-class firm must continue to delight its customers.
- The philosophy of customer satisfaction permeates the world-class firm. All of its activities, from the acquisition of raw materials to selling the finished product, form a chain of customers. Each activity is dedicated to serving its customer, which is the next activity in the process. The final paying customer is the last in the chain.
- Finally, manufacturing firms that achieve world-class status do so by following a philosophy of **lean manufacturing**. This involves doing more with less, eliminating waste, and reducing production cycle time.

The following section reviews the principles of lean manufacturing. The remainder of this chapter examines the techniques, technologies, accounting procedures, and information systems that enable it.

PRINCIPLES OF LEAN MANUFACTURING

Lean manufacturing evolved from the **Toyota Production System (TPS)**, which is based on the **just-in-time (JIT)** production model. This manufacturing approach is in direct opposition to traditional manufacturing, which is typified by high inventory levels, large production lot sizes, process inefficiencies, and waste. The goal of lean production is improved efficiency and effectiveness in every area, including product design, supplier interaction, factory operations, employee management, and customer relations. Lean manufacturing involves getting the right products to the right place, at the right time, in the right quantity while minimizing waste and remaining flexible.

Success depends, in great part, on employees understanding and embracing lean manufacturing principles. Indeed, the cultural aspects of this philosophy are as important as the machines and methodologies it employs. The following principles characterize lean manufacturing.

Pull Processing

As the name implies, **pull processing** involves pulling products from the consumer end (demand), rather than pushing them from the production end (supply). Under the lean approach, inventories arrive in small quantities from vendors several times per day, just in time to go into production. They are pulled into production as capacity downstream becomes available. Unlike the traditional push process, this approach avoids the creation of batches of semifinished inventories at bottlenecks.

Perfect Quality

Success of the pull processing model requires zero defects in RM, WIP, and FG inventory. Poor quality is very expensive to a firm. Consider the cost of scrap, reworking, scheduling delays, and extra inventories to compensate for defective parts, warranty claims, and field service. In the traditional manufacturing environment, these costs can represent between 25 and 35 percent of total product cost. Also, quality is a basis on which world-class manufacturers compete. Quality has ceased to be a trade-off against price. Consumers demand quality and seek the lowest-priced quality product.

Waste Minimization

All activities that do not add value and maximize the use of scarce resources must be eliminated. Waste involves financial, human, inventory, and fixed assets. The following are examples of waste in traditional environments, which lean manufacturing seeks to minimize.

- Overproduction of products, which includes making more than needed and/or producing earlier than needed.
- Transportation of products farther than is minimally necessary.
- Bottlenecks of products waiting to move to the next production step.
- Idle workers waiting for work to do as production bottlenecks clear.
- Inefficient motion of workers who must walk more than necessary in the completion of their assigned tasks.
- Islands of technology created by stand-alone processes that are not linked to upstream or downstream processes.
- Production defects that require unnecessary effort to inspect and/or correct.
- Safety hazards that cause injuries and lost work hours and associated expenses.

Inventory Reduction

The hallmark of lean manufacturing firms is their success in inventory reduction. Such firms often experience annual inventory turnovers of 100 times per year. While other firms carry weeks and even months of inventories, lean firms have only a few days or sometimes even a few hours of inventory on hand. The three common problems outlined below explain why inventory reduction is important.

1. Inventories cost money. They are an investment in materials, labor, and overhead that cannot be realized until sold. Inventories also contain hidden costs. They must be transported throughout the factory. They must be handled, stored, and counted. In addition, inventories lose value through obsolescence.
2. Inventories camouflage production problems. Bottlenecks and capacity imbalances in the manufacturing process cause WIP inventory to build up at the choke points. Inventories also build up when customer orders and production are out of sync.
3. Willingness to maintain inventories can precipitate overproduction. Because of setup cost constraints, firms tend to overproduce inventories in large batches to absorb the allocated costs and create the image of improved efficiency. The true cost of this dysfunctional activity is hidden in the excess inventories.

Production Flexibility

Long machine setup procedures cause delays in production and encourage overproduction. Lean companies strive to reduce setup time to a minimum, which allows them to produce a greater diversity of products quickly, without sacrificing efficiency at lower volumes of production.

Established Supplier Relations

A lean manufacturing firm must have established and cooperative relationships with vendors. Late deliveries, defective raw materials, or incorrect orders will shut down production immediately because this production model allows no inventory reserves to draw upon.

Team Attitude

Lean manufacturing relies heavily on the team attitude of all employees involved in the process. This includes those in purchasing, receiving, manufacturing, shipping—everyone. Each employee must be vigilant of problems that threaten the continuous flow operation of the production line.

Lean manufacturing requires a constant state of quality control along with the authority to take immediate action. When Toyota first introduced TPS, its production employees had the authority to shut down the line when defects were discovered. In the early days, the line was often shut down to bring attention to a problem. Whether caused by a defective part from a vendor or a faulty machine in a cell, the problem was properly addressed so that it did not recur. After an adjustment period, the process stabilized.

Techniques and Technologies That Promote Lean Manufacturing

Modern consumers want quality products, they want them quickly, and they want variety of choice. This demand profile imposes a fundamental conflict for traditional manufacturers, whose structured and inflexible orientation renders them ineffective in this environment. In contrast, lean companies meet the challenges of modern consumerism by achieving **manufacturing flexibility**. This section examines techniques and technologies that lean manufacturing firms employ to achieve manufacturing flexibility.

PHYSICAL REORGANIZATION OF THE PRODUCTION FACILITIES

Traditional manufacturing facilities tend to evolve in piecemeal fashion over years into snakelike sequences of activities. Products move back and forth across shop floors, and upstairs and downstairs through different departments. Figure 7-14 shows a traditional factory layout. The inefficiencies inherent in this layout add handling costs, conversion time, and even inventories to the manufacturing process. Furthermore, because production activities are usually organized along functional lines, this structure tends to create parochialism among employees, promoting an us-versus-them mentality, which is contrary to a team attitude.

A much simplified facility, which supports flexible manufacturing, is presented in Figure 7-15. The flexible production system is organized into a smooth-flowing stream of activities. Computer-controlled machines, robots, and manual tasks that comprise the stream are grouped physically into factory units called cells. This arrangement shortens the physical distances between the activities, which reduces setup and processing time, handling costs, and inventories flowing through the facility.

AUTOMATION OF THE MANUFACTURING PROCESS

Automation is at the heart of the lean manufacturing philosophy. By replacing labor with automation, a firm can reduce waste, improve efficiency, increase quality, and improve flexibility. The deployment of automation, however, varies considerably among manufacturing firms. Figure 7-16 portrays automation as a continuum with the traditional manufacturing model at one end and the CIM model at the other.

FIGURE 7-14 THE TRADITIONAL FACTORY LAYOUT

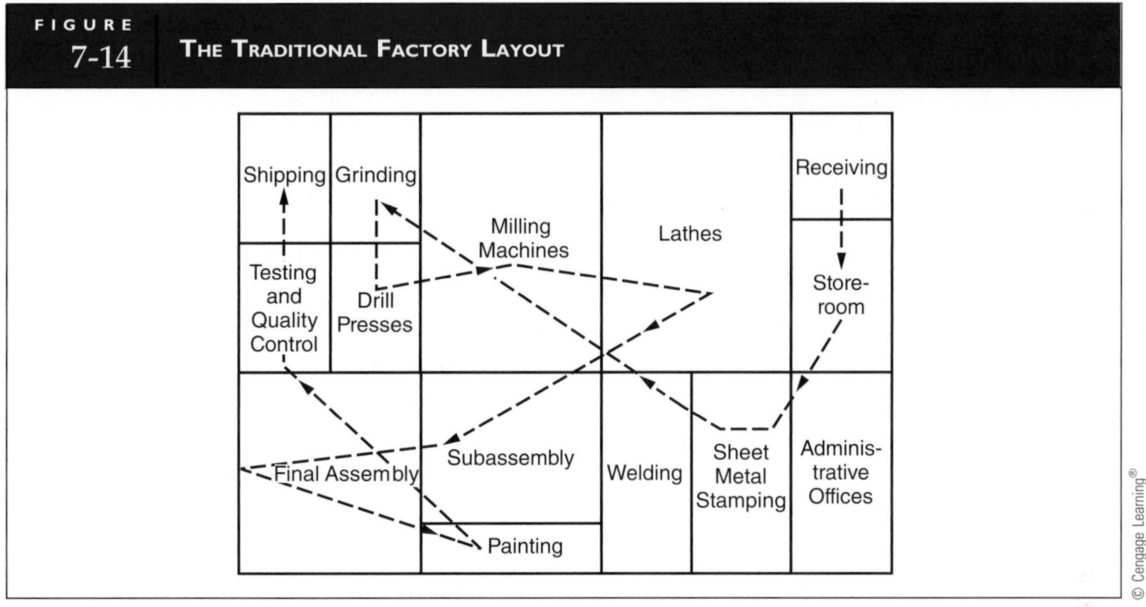

FIGURE 7-15 FLEXIBLE PRODUCTION SYSTEM

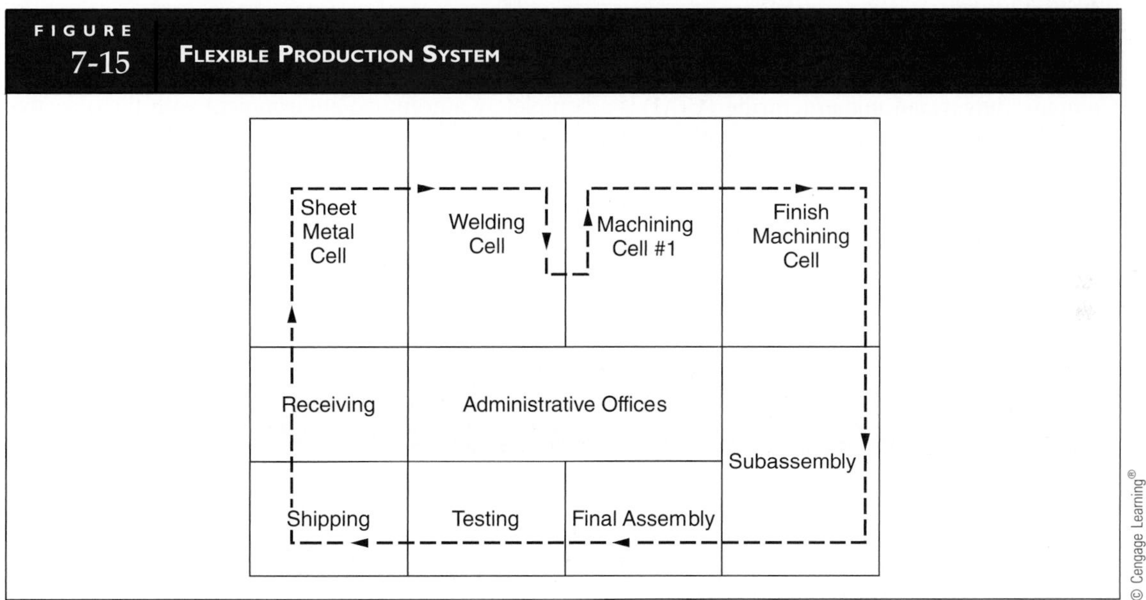

Traditional Manufacturing

The traditional manufacturing environment consists of a range of different types of machines, each controlled by a single operator. Because these machines require a great deal of setup time, the cost of setup must be absorbed by large production runs. The machines and their operators are organized into functional departments, such as milling, grinding, and welding. The WIP follows a circuitous route through the different operations across the factory floor.

Islands of Technology

Islands of technology describes an environment in which modern automation exists in the form of islands that stand alone within the traditional setting. The islands employ **computer numerical controlled (CNC)** machines that can perform multiple operations with little human involvement. CNC machines contain computer programs for all the parts that are manufactured by the machine.

FIGURE 7-16 THE AUTOMATION CONTINUUM

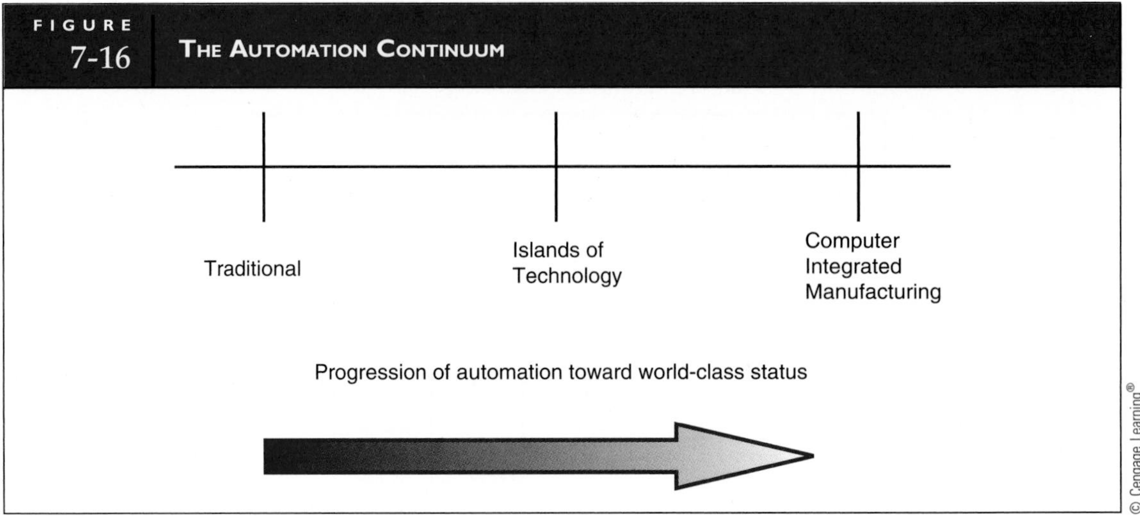

Under a CNC configuration, humans still set up the machines. A particularly important benefit of CNC technology is, however, that little setup time (and cost) is needed to change from one operation to another.

Computer-Integrated Manufacturing

Computer-integrated manufacturing (CIM) is a completely automated environment with the objective of eliminating non-value-added activities. A CIM facility makes use of group technology cells composed of various types of CNC machines to produce an entire part from start to finish in one location. In addition to CNC machines, the process employs automated storage and retrieval systems and robotics. CIM supports flexible manufacturing by allowing faster development of high-quality products, shorter production cycles, reduced production costs, and faster delivery times. Figure 7-17 depicts a CIM environment and shows the relationship between various technologies employed.

FIGURE 7-17 COMPUTER-INTEGRATED MANUFACTURING SYSTEM

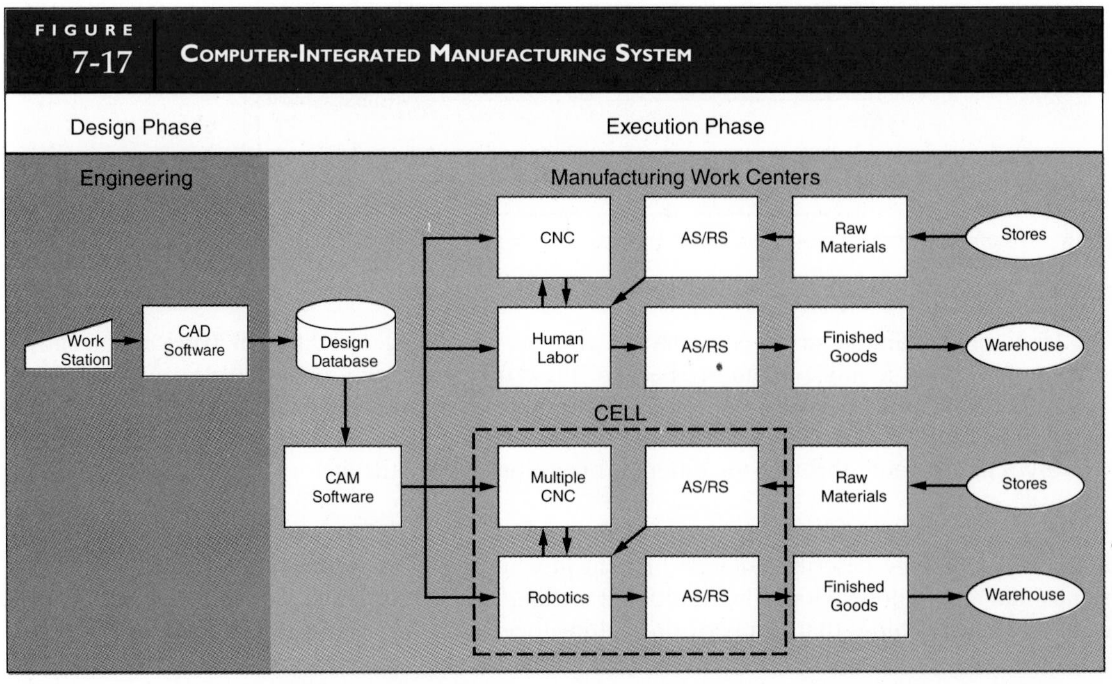

AUTOMATED STORAGE AND RETRIEVAL SYSTEMS (AS/RS). Many firms have increased productivity and profitability by replacing traditional forklifts and their human operators with **automated storage and retrieval systems (AS/RS)**. AS/RS are computer-controlled conveyor systems that carry raw materials from stores to the shop floor and finished products to the warehouse. The operational advantages of AS/RS technology over manual systems include reduced errors, improved inventory control, and lower storage costs.

ROBOTICS. Manufacturing robots are programmed to perform specific actions over and over with a high degree of precision and are widely used in factories to perform jobs such as welding and riveting. They are also useful in hazardous environments or for performing dangerous and monotonous tasks that are prone to causing accidents.

COMPUTER-AIDED DESIGN (CAD). Engineers use **computer-aided design (CAD)** to design better products faster. CAD systems increase engineers' productivity, improve accuracy by automating repetitive design tasks, and allow firms to be more responsive to market demands. Product design has been revolutionized through CAD technology, which was first applied to the aerospace industry in the early 1960s.

CAD technology greatly shortens the time frame between initial and final design. This allows firms to adjust their production quickly to changes in market demand. It also allows them to respond to customer requests for unique products. The CAD systems often have an interface to the external communication network to allow a manufacturer to share its product design specifications with its vendors and customers. This communications link also allows the manufacturer to receive product design specifications electronically from its customers and suppliers for its review. Advanced CAD systems can design both product and process simultaneously. Thus, aided by CAD, management can evaluate the technical feasibility of the product and determine its "manufacturability."

COMPUTER-AIDED MANUFACTURING (CAM). Computer-aided manufacturing (CAM) is the use of computers to assist the manufacturing process. CAM focuses on the shop floor and the control of the physical manufacturing process. The output of the CAD system (see Figure 7-17) is fed to the CAM system. The CAD design is thus converted by CAM into a sequence of processes such as drilling, turning, or milling by CNC machines. The CAM system monitors and controls the production process and routing of products through the cell. Benefits from deploying a CAM technology include improved process productivity, improved cost and time estimates, improved process monitoring, improved process quality, decreased setup times, and reduced labor costs.

Value Stream Mapping

The activities that constitute a firm's production process are either essential or they are not. Essential activities add value; nonessential activities do not, and should be eliminated. A company's **value stream** includes all the steps in the process that are essential to producing a product. These are the steps for which the customer is willing to pay. For example, balancing the wheels of each car off the production line is essential because the customer demands a car that rides smoothly and is willing to pay the price of the balancing.

Companies pursuing lean manufacturing often use a tool called a **value stream map (VSM)** to graphically represent their business processes to identify aspects of it that are wasteful and should be removed. A VSM identifies all of the actions required to complete processing on a product (batch or single item), along with key information about each action item. Specific information will vary according to the process under review but may include total hours worked, overtime hours, cycle time to complete a task, and error rates. Figure 7-18 presents a VSM of a production process from the point at which an order is received to the point of shipping the product to the customer. Under each processing step, the VSM itemizes the amount of overtime, staffing, work shifts, process uptime, and task error rate. The VSM shows the total time required for each processing step and the time required between steps. It also identifies the types of time spent between steps, such as the outbound batching time, transit time, and inbound queue time.

FIGURE 7-18 VALUE STREAM MAP

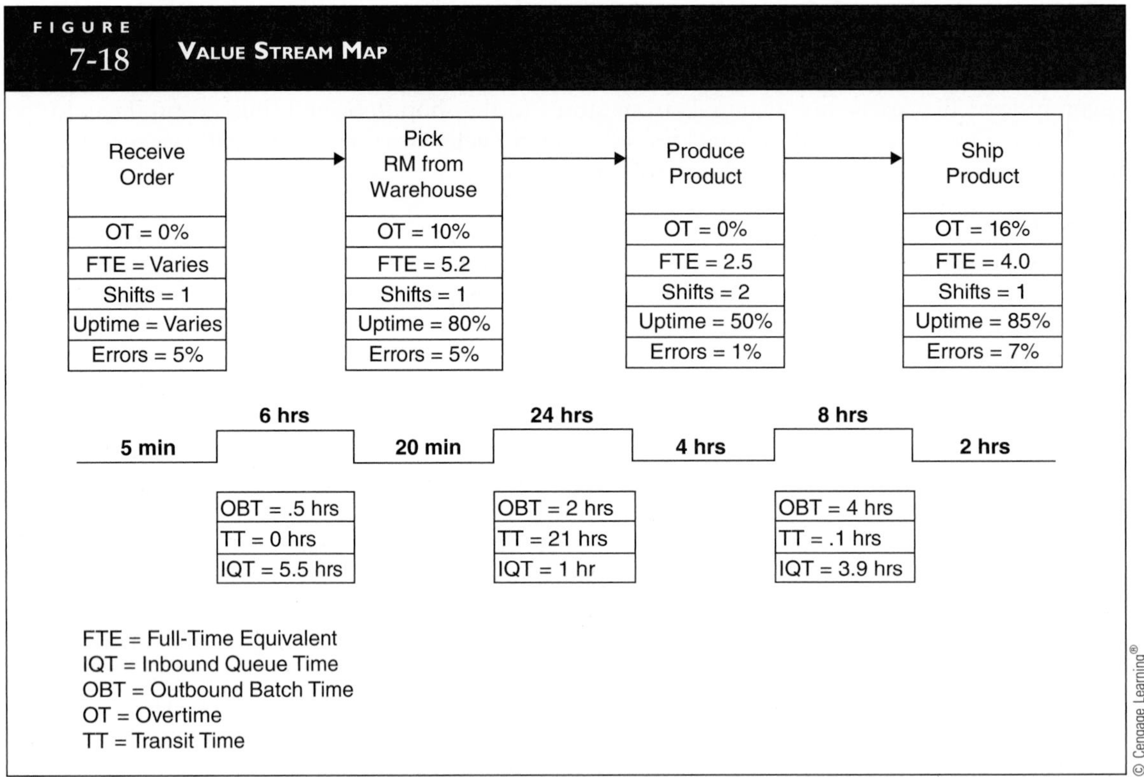

The VSM in Figure 7-18 reveals that considerable production time is wasted between processing steps. In particular, the transit time of raw materials from the warehouse to the production cell contributes significantly to the overall cycle time. Also, the shipping function appears to be inefficient and wasteful, with a 16 percent overtime rate and a 7 percent error rate. To reduce total cycle time, perhaps the distance between the warehouse and production cell should be shortened. The shipping function's overtime rate may be due to a bottleneck situation. The high error rate may actually be due to errors in the upstream order-taking function that are passed to downstream functions.

Some commercial VSM tools produce both a current-state map and a future-state map depicting a leaner process with most of the waste removed. From this future map, action steps can be identified to eliminate the non-value-added activities within the process. The future-state VSM thus is the basis of a lean implementation plan. VSM works best in highly focused, high-volume processes in which real benefit is derived from reducing repetitive processes by even small amounts of time. This technique is less effective at eliminating waste in low-volume processes in which the employees are frequently switched between multiple tasks.

Accounting in a Lean Manufacturing Environment

The lean manufacturing environment carries profound implications for accounting. Traditional information produced under conventional accounting techniques does not adequately support the needs of lean companies. They require new accounting methods and new information that:

1. Shows what matters to its customers (such as quality and service).
2. Identifies profitable products.
3. Identifies profitable customers.
4. Identifies opportunities for improvement in operations and products.

5. Encourages the adoption of value-added activities and processes within the organization and identifies those that do not add value.
6. Efficiently supports multiple users with both financial and nonfinancial information.

In this section, we examine the nature of the accounting changes under way. The discussion reviews the problems associated with standard cost accounting and outlines two alternative approaches: (1) activity-based costing and (2) value stream accounting.

WHAT'S WRONG WITH TRADITIONAL ACCOUNTING INFORMATION?

Traditional standard costing techniques emphasize financial performance rather than manufacturing performance. The techniques and conventions used in traditional manufacturing do not support the objectives of lean manufacturing firms. The following are the most commonly cited deficiencies of standard accounting systems.

INACCURATE COST ALLOCATIONS. An assumption of standard costing is that all overheads need to be allocated to the product and that these overheads directly relate to the amount of labor required to make the product. A consequence of automation is the restructuring of manufacturing cost patterns. Figure 7-19 shows the changing relationship between direct labor, direct materials, and overhead cost under different levels of automation. In the traditional manufacturing environment, direct labor is a much larger component of total manufacturing costs than in the CIM environment. Overhead, on the other hand, is a far more significant element of cost under automated manufacturing. Applying standard costing leads to product cost distortions in a lean environment, causing some products to appear to cost more and others to appear to cost less than they actually do. Poor decisions regarding pricing, valuation, and profitability may result.

FIGURE 7-19 CHANGES IN COST STRUCTURE BETWEEN DIFFERENT MANUFACTURING ENVIRONMENTS

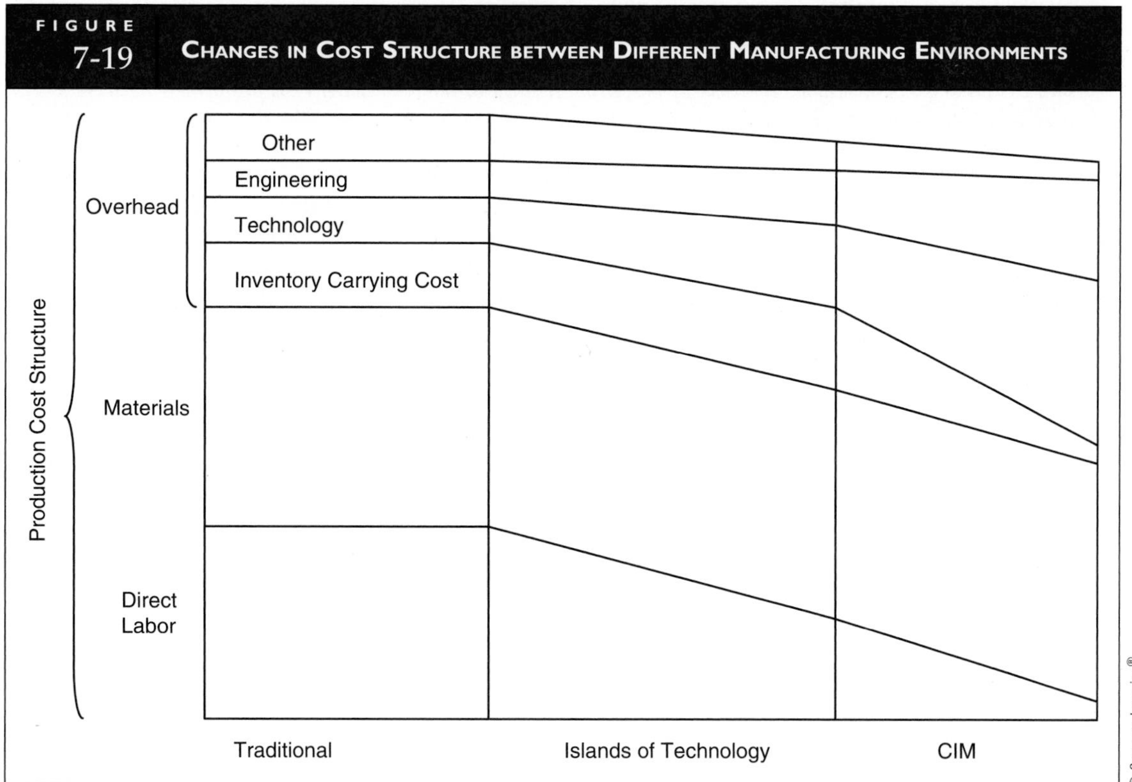

PROMOTES NONLEAN BEHAVIOR. Standard costing motivates nonlean behavior in operations. The primary performance measurements used in standard costing are personal efficiency of production workers, the effective utilization of manufacturing facilities, and the degree of overhead absorbed by production. In addition, standard costing conceals waste within the overhead allocations that is difficult to detect. To improve their personal performance measures, management and operations employees are inclined to produce large batches of products and build inventory. This built-in motivation is in conflict with lean manufacturing.

TIME LAG. Standard cost data for management reporting are historic in nature. Data lag behind the actual manufacturing activities on the assumption that control can be applied after the fact to correct errors. In a lean setting, however, shop floor managers need immediate information about abnormal deviations. They must know in real time about a machine breakdown or a robot out of control. After-the-fact information is too late to be useful.

FINANCIAL ORIENTATION. Accounting data use dollars as a standard unit of measure for comparing disparate items being evaluated. Decisions pertaining to the functionality of a product or process, improving product quality, and shortening delivery time, however, are not necessarily well served by financial information produced through standard cost techniques. Indeed, attempts to force such data into a common financial measure may distort the problem and promote bad decisions.

ACTIVITY-BASED COSTING (ABC)

Many lean manufacturing companies have sought solutions to these problems through an accounting model called **activity-based costing (ABC)**. ABC is a method of allocating costs to products and services to facilitate better planning and control. It accomplishes this by assigning cost to activities based on their use of resources and assigning cost to cost objects based on their use of activities. These terms are defined below:

> **Activities** *describe the work performed in a firm. Preparing a purchase order, readying a product for shipping, or operating a lathe are examples of activities.*
>
> **Cost objects** *are the reasons for performing activities. These include products, services, vendors, and customers. For example, the task of preparing a sales order (the activity) is performed because a customer (the cost object) wishes to place an order.*

The underlying assumptions of ABC contrast sharply with standard cost accounting assumptions. Traditional accounting assumes that products cause costs. ABC assumes that activities cause costs, and products (and other cost objects) create a demand for activities.

The first step in implementing the ABC approach is to determine the cost of the activity. The activity cost is then assigned to the relevant cost object by means of an **activity driver**. This factor measures the activity consumption by the cost object. For example, if drilling holes in a steel plate is the activity, the number of holes is the activity driver.

Traditional accounting systems often use only one activity driver. For instance, overhead costs, collected into a single cost pool, are allocated to products on the basis of direct labor hours. A company using ABC may have dozens of activity cost pools, each with a unique activity driver. Figure 7-20 illustrates the allocation of overhead costs to products under ABC.

Advantages of ABC

ABC allows managers to assign costs to activities and products more accurately than standard costing permits. Some advantages that this offers are:

- More accurate costing of products/services, customers, and distribution channels.
- Identifying the most and least profitable products and customers. Accurately tracking costs of activities and processes.
- Equipping managers with cost intelligence to drive continuous improvements.

FIGURE 7-20 ALLOCATION OF OVERHEAD COSTS TO PRODUCTS UNDER ABC

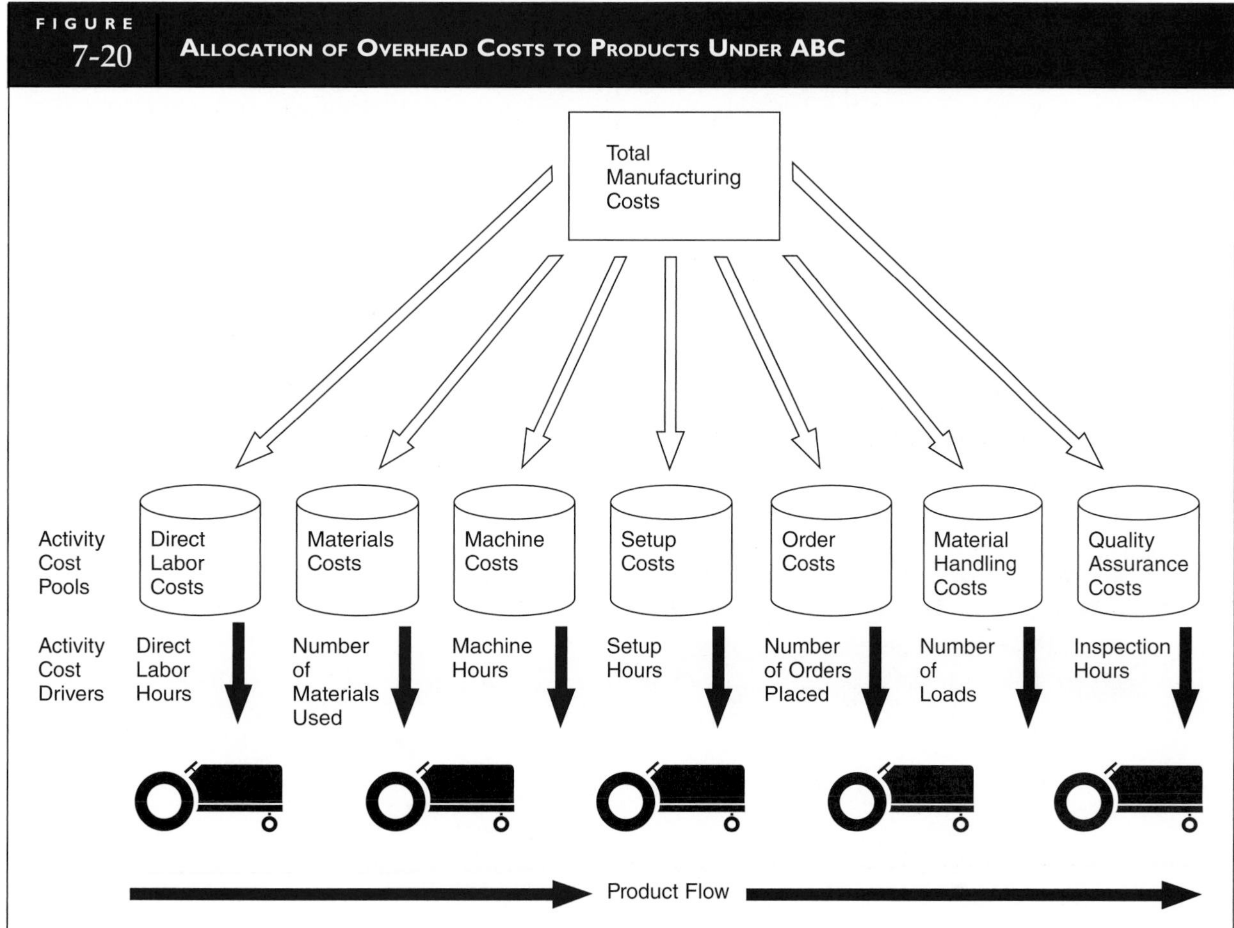

Source: Adapted from P. B. Turney, *Common Cents: The ABC Breakthrough* (Hillsboro, OR: Cost Technology, 1991), 96.

- Facilitating better marketing mix.
- Identifying waste and non-value-added activities.

Disadvantages of ABC

ABC has been criticized for being too time-consuming and complicated for practical applications over a sustained period. The task of identifying activity costs and cost drivers can be a significant undertaking that is not completed once and then forgotten. As products and processes change, so do the associated activity costs and drivers. Unless significant resources are committed to maintaining the accuracy of activity costs and the appropriateness of drivers, cost assignments become inaccurate. Critics charge that rather than promoting continuous improvement, ABC creates complex bureaucracies within organizations that are in conflict with the lean manufacturing philosophies of process simplification and waste elimination.

VALUE STREAM ACCOUNTING

The complexities of ABC have caused many firms to abandon this method in favor of a simpler accounting model called **value stream accounting**. Value stream accounting captures costs by value stream rather than by department or activity, as illustrated in Figure 7-21.

Notice that value streams cut across functional and departmental lines to include costs related to marketing, selling expenses, product design, engineering, materials purchasing, distribution, and more. An essential aspect in implementing value stream accounting is defining the **product family**.

FIGURE 7-21 COST ASSIGNMENT TO VALUE STREAM

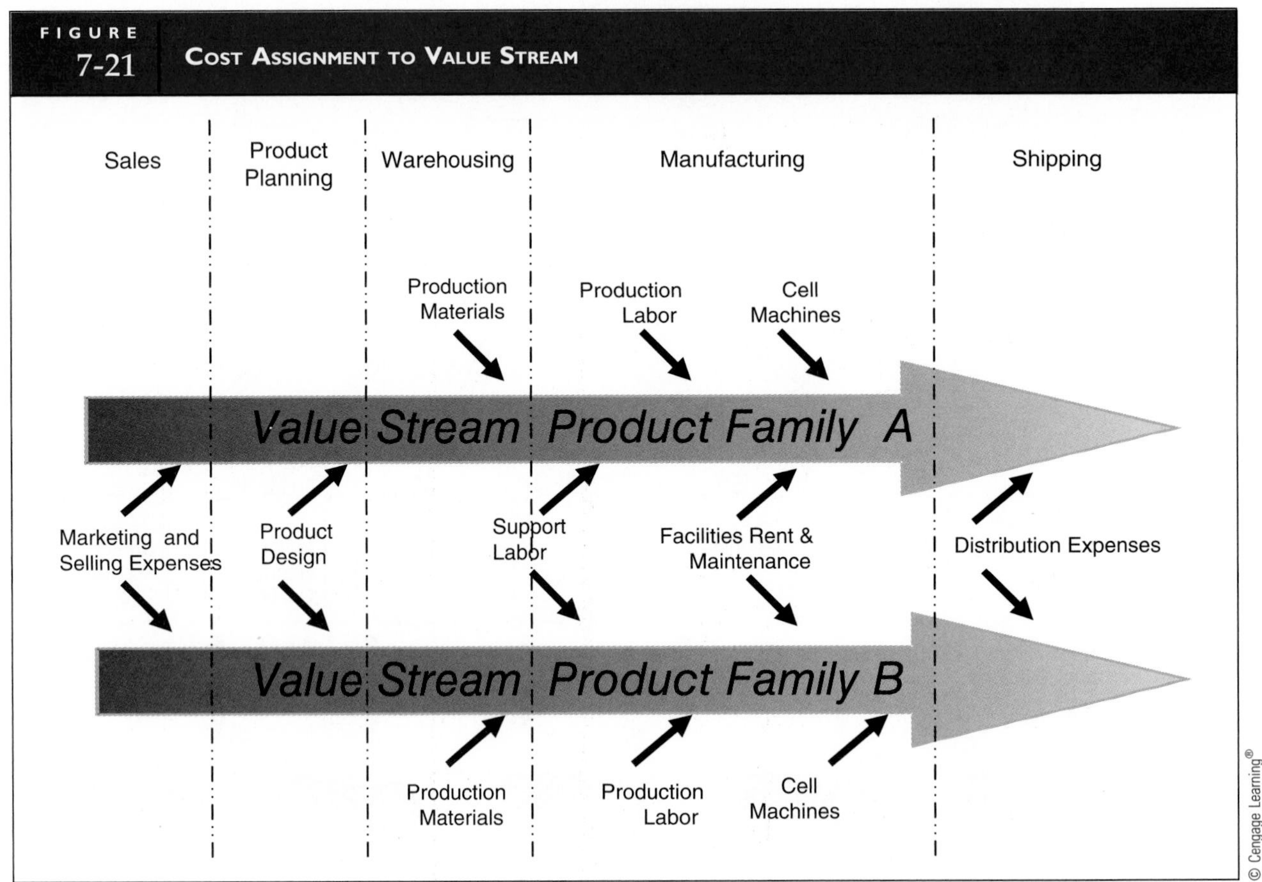

FIGURE 7-22 GROUPING PRODUCTS BY FAMILIES

Product	Product Family	Process: Pipe Bending – Machine	Process: Pipe Bending – Labor	Process: Welding Unit – Labor	Process: Assembly – Labor	Process: Packing and Shipping – Labor
QRM 180 V	A			X	X	X
QRM 192 V	A			X	X	X
RKX 45 F	B	X	X	X	X	X
LOC 67 Y	C		X	X	X	X
RKX 65 AF	B	X	X	X	X	X
RKX 95 XF	B	X	X	X	X	X

Most organizations produce more than one product, but these often fall into natural families of products. Product families share common processes from the point of placing the order to shipping the finished goods to the customer. Figure 7-22 illustrates how multiple products may be grouped into product families.

Value stream accounting includes all the costs associated with the product family but makes no distinction between direct costs and indirect costs. Raw material costs are calculated based on how much material has been purchased for the value stream, rather than tracking the input of the raw material to specific products. Thus, the total value stream material cost is the sum of everything purchased for the period. This simplified (lean) accounting approach works because RM and WIP inventories on hand are low, representing perhaps only one or two days of stock. This approach would not work well in a traditional manufacturing environment in which several months of inventory may carry over from period to period.

Labor costs of employees who work in the value stream are included whether they design, make, or simply transport the product from cell to cell. Labor costs are not allocated to individual products in the traditional way (time spent on a particular task). Instead, the sum of the wages and direct benefits paid to all individuals working in the value stream is charged to the stream. Support labor such as maintenance of machines, production planning, and selling are also included. Wherever possible, therefore, each employee should be assigned to a single value stream, rather than having their time split among several different streams.

Typically, the only allocated cost in the value stream is a charge per square foot for the value stream production facility. This allocation would include the cost of rent and building maintenance. The logic behind this is to promote efficiency by encouraging value stream team members to minimize the space used to operate the value stream. General overhead costs incurred outside the value stream, which cannot be controlled by the value stream team, are not attached to the product family. Thus, no attempt is made to fully absorb facilities costs. Although corporate overhead costs must be accounted for, they are not allocated to value streams.

Information Systems That Support Lean Manufacturing

In this section, we discuss the information systems commonly associated with lean manufacturing and world-class companies. It begins with a review of **materials requirements planning (MRP)**. As the name implies, MRP systems are limited in focus and geared toward determining how much raw materials are required to fulfill production orders. We then review **manufacturing resources planning (MRP II)**. These systems evolved from MRP to integrate additional functionality into the manufacturing process, including sales, marketing, and accounting. Finally, we examine some key features of **enterprise resource planning (ERP)** systems. ERP takes MRP II a step further by integrating all business functions into a core set of applications that use a common database.

MATERIALS REQUIREMENT PLANNING (MRP)

MRP is an automated production planning and control system used to support inventory management. Its operational objectives are to:

- Ensure that adequate raw materials are available to the production process.
- Maintain the lowest possible level of inventory on hand.
- Produce production and purchasing schedules and other information needed to control production.

Figure 7-23 illustrates the key features of an MRP system. Depending on the manufacturing process in place, inputs to the MRP system will include sales, sales forecasts, FG inventory on hand, RM inventory on hand, and the bill of materials. MRP is a calculation method geared toward determining how much of which raw materials are required and when they should be ordered to fill a production order. By comparing FG inventory on hand with the needed levels (based on the sales forecast), MRP calculates the total production requirements and the individual batch lot sizes needed. From this, the BOM is exploded to produce a list of raw materials needed for production, which is compared to the raw materials on hand. The difference is the amount that will be ordered from vendors. The primary outputs from the MRP system are RM purchase requisitions that are sent to the purchases system. In addition, the system output may include production schedules, management reports, and day-to-day production documents such as work orders and move tickets.

FIGURE 7-23 OVERVIEW OF MRP SYSTEM

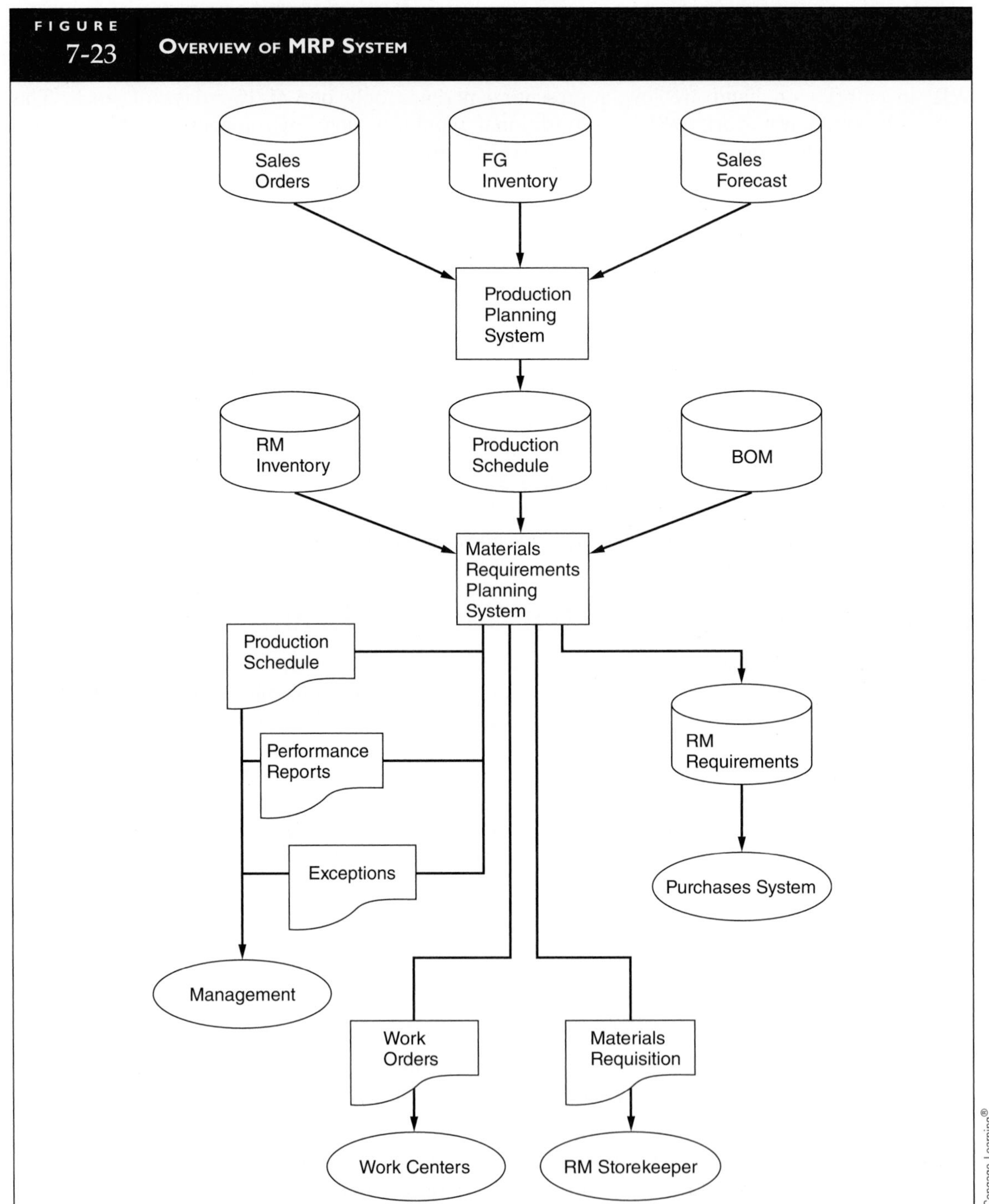

MANUFACTURING RESOURCE PLANNING (MRP II)

MRP II is an extension of MRP that has evolved beyond the confines of inventory management. It is both a system and a philosophy for coordinating a wide range of manufacturing activities. MRP II integrates product manufacturing, product engineering, sales order processing, customer billing, human resources, and related accounting functions. Figure 7-24 shows the functional integration under an MRP II environment.

FIGURE 7-24 THE INTEGRATION OF MANUFACTURING AND FINANCIAL SYSTEMS WITHIN THE MRP II ENVIRONMENT

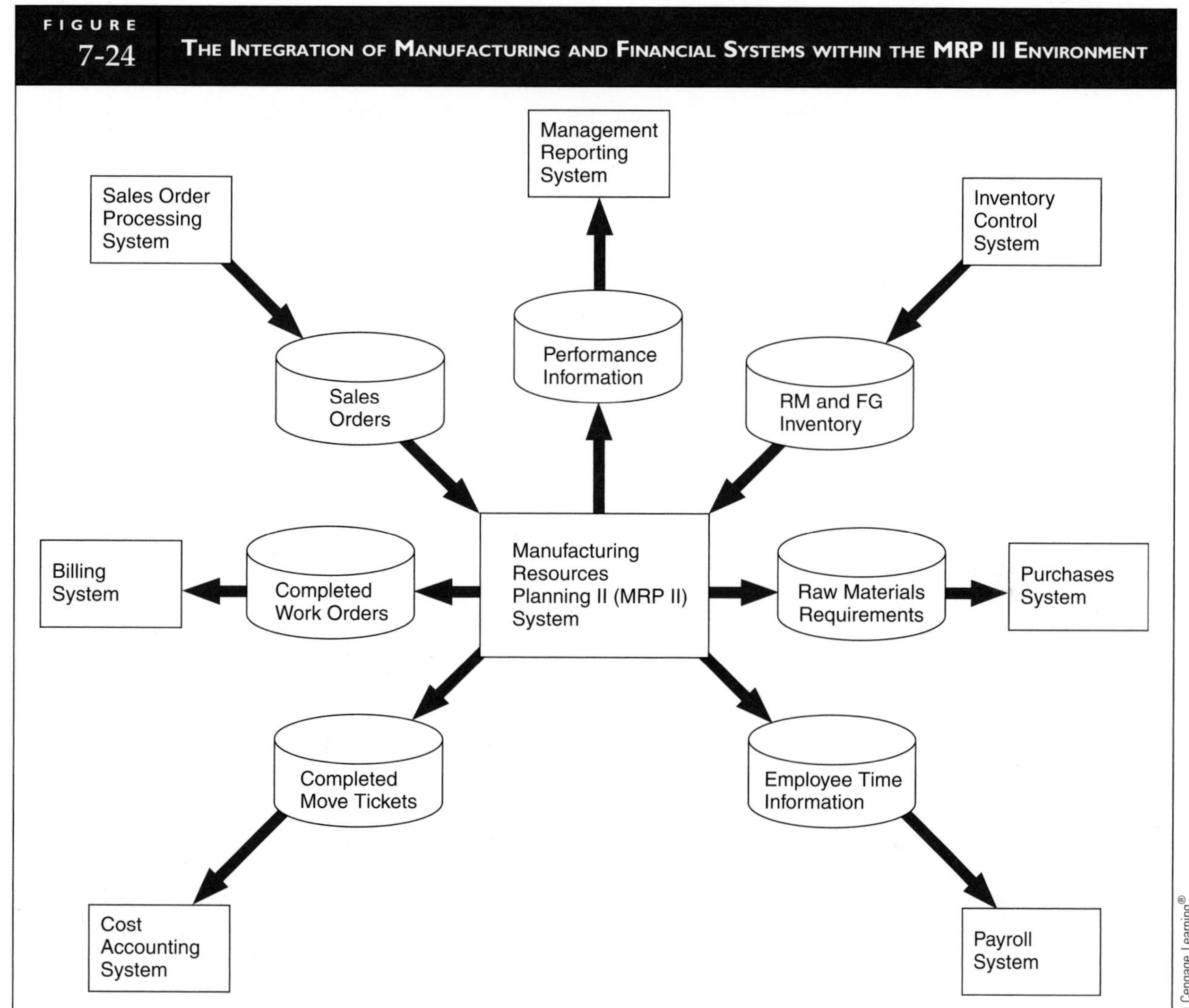

The MRP II system will produce a BOM for the product, fit the production of the product into the master production schedule, produce a rough-cut capacity plan based on machine and labor availability, design a final capacity plan for the factory, and manage the RM and FG inventories. In addition, MRP II will produce a materials requirements plan that will schedule the delivery of the raw materials on a JIT basis. The ordering of raw material must be coordinated with the manufacturing process to avoid waste (early arrival) while ensuring that stock-out situations do not disrupt the production processes. Manufacturing firms can realize considerable benefits from a highly integrated MRP II system. Among these are the following:

- Improved customer service
- Reduced inventory investment
- Increased productivity
- Improved cash flow
- Assistance in achieving long-term strategic goals
- Help in managing change (e.g., new product development or specialized product development for customers or by vendors)
- Flexibility in the production process

ENTERPRISE RESOURCE PLANNING (ERP) SYSTEMS

In recent years, **MRP** II has evolved into large suites of software called ERP systems. ERP integrates departments and functions across a company into one system of integrated applications that is connected to a single common database. This enables various departments to share information and communicate with each other. An ERP system is composed of function-specific modules that reflect industry best practices. Designed to interact with the other modules (e.g., accounts receivable, accounts payable, purchasing, and so on), these commercial packages support the information needs of the entire organization, not just the manufacturing functions. An ERP can calculate resource requirements, schedule production, manage changes to product configurations, allow for future planned changes in products, and monitor shop floor production. In addition, the ERP provides order entry, cash receipts, procurement, and cash disbursement functions along with full financial and managerial reporting capability.

A lean manufacturing company will have an ERP system that is capable of external communications with its customers and suppliers through **electronic data interchange (EDI)**. The EDI communications link (via Internet or direct connection) will allow the firm to electronically receive sales orders and cash receipts from customers, send invoices to customers, send purchase orders to vendors, and receive invoices from vendors and pay them, as well as send and receive shipping documents. EDI is a central element of many electronic commerce systems. We will revisit this important topic in Chapter 12.

Similarities in functionality between ERP and **MRP** II systems are quite apparent. Some argue that very little real functional difference exists between the two concepts. Indeed, the similarities are most noticeable when comparing top-end MRP II systems with low-end ERP packages. A primary distinction, however, is that the ERP has evolved beyond the manufacturing marketplace to become the system of choice among nonmanufacturing firms as well. On the other hand, cynics argue that changing the label from MRP II to ERP enabled software vendors to sell MRP II packages to nonmanufacturing companies.

The market for ERP systems was for many years limited by high cost and complexity to only the largest companies and was dominated by a few software vendors such as SAP, J.D. Edwards, Oracle, and PeopleSoft. In recent years, this market has expanded tremendously with the entry of many small vendors targeting small- and mid-sized customers with less expensive and more easily implemented ERP systems. The importance of the ERP phenomenon warrants separate treatment that goes beyond the scope of this chapter. In Chapter 11, therefore, we will examine ERP systems and related topics, including supply chain management (SCM) and data warehousing.

Summary

This chapter examined the conversion cycle, whereby a company transforms input resources (i.e., materials, labor, and capital) into marketable products and services. The principal aim was to highlight the changing manufacturing environment of the contemporary business world and to show how it calls for a shift away from traditional forms of business organization and activities toward a world-class way of doing business. We saw how companies that are attempting to achieve world-class status must pursue a lean manufacturing philosophy.

Key to successful lean manufacturing is achieving manufacturing flexibility, which involves the physical organization of production facilities and the employment of automated technologies. We also saw that achieving lean manufacturing requires significant departures from traditional standard costing techniques. In response to deficiencies in traditional accounting methods, lean manufacturing companies have adopted alternative accounting models including activity-based costing and value stream accounting. This chapter concluded with a discussion of three information systems commonly associated with lean manufacturing: (1) materials requirements planning (MRP), (2) manufacturing resources planning (MRP II), and enterprise resource planning (ERP).

Key Terms

activities (314)
activity-based costing (ABC) (314)
activity driver (314)
automated storage and retrieval systems (AS/RS) (311)
bill of materials (BOM) (293)
computer-aided design (CAD) (311)
Computer-aided manufacturing (CAM) (311)
Computer-integrated manufacturing (CIM) (310)
computer numerical controlled (CNC) (309)
Cost objects (314)
economic order quantity (EOQ) model (300)
electronic data interchange (EDI) (320)
enterprise resource planning (ERP) (317)
Islands of technology (309)
just-in-time (JIT) (306)
lean manufacturing (306)
manufacturing flexibility (308)
manufacturing resources planning (MRP II) (317)
materials requirements planning (MRP) (317)
materials requisition (293)
move ticket (293)
product family (315)
production schedule (293)
pull processing (307)
reorder point (ROP) (301)
route sheet (293)
safety stock (301)
Toyota Production System (TPS) (306)
value stream accounting (315)
value stream map (VSM) (311)
value stream (311)
work order (293)

Review Questions

1. Define the conversion cycle.
2. What activities are involved in the batch processing system?
3. Distinguish between continuous, batch, and made-to-order processing.
4. What documents trigger and support batch processing systems?
5. What are the primary determinants for both materials and operations requirements?
6. What are the objectives of inventory control in the production process?
7. What document triggers the beginning of the cost accounting process for a given production run?
8. What documents are needed for cost accounting clerks to update the work-in-process accounts with standard charges?
9. What types of management reports are prepared by the cost accounting system?
10. What document signals the completion of the production process?
11. What functions should be separated to segregate record keeping from asset custody?
12. Give an example for each of the following control activities in the conversion cycle: transaction authorization, segregation of duties, and access control.
13. Distinguish between computer-aided design and computer-aided manufacturing.
14. What is meant by the statement, "Inventories camouflage production problems and can cause overproduction"? What is wrong with overproduction if you already own the raw material?
15. What are the primary goals of lean manufacturing?
16. Distinguish between activities and cost objects in activity-based costing.
17. Differentiate between essential and nonessential activities.
18. What is meant by the term *islands of technology?*
19. Define *computer-integrated manufacturing.*
20. Define the term *value stream.*

Discussion Questions

1. Discuss the importance of the move ticket to the cost accounting department.
2. How realistic are the assumptions of the economic order quantity model? Discuss each assumption individually.
3. Explain why the economic order quantity is the intersection of the ordering-cost curve and the carrying-cost curve.
4. Supervisors in the work centers oversee the usage of raw material in production; explain why the work centers do not keep the records of the work-in-process.
5. Explain how prenumbered documents help to provide indirect access control over assets.
6. What role does the general ledger department play in the conversion cycle?
7. Describe the characteristics of a world-class company.
8. How does automation help achieve manufacturing flexibility?
9. Identify three areas where the consumer directly uses computer-aided design software applications to aid in designing the product.
10. How can poor quality be expensive to the firm, especially if low-cost raw materials are used to reduce cost of goods sold and raise net income?
11. Discuss how an emphasis on financial performance of cost centers, as measured by traditional cost accounting information, may lead to inefficient and ineffective production output.
12. How can activity-based costing be used to switch the management of business activities from a custodial task to a continuous improvement activity?
13. How are cost structures fundamentally different between the traditional and computer-integrated manufacturing environments?
14. How can a firm control against excessive quantities of raw materials being used in the manufacturing process?
15. What is a value stream map?
16. Discuss the advantages of activity-based costing.
17. Discuss the disadvantages of activity-based costing.
18. Explain why traditional cost allocation methods fail in a computer-integrated manufacturing environment.
19. Explain the concept of a product family and its relationship to value stream accounting.
20. Explain the relationship between MRP II and ERP.

Multiple-Choice Questions

1. Which statement describes the evolution of enterprise systems?
   a. MRP evolved directly from ERP.
   b. MRP II evolved from MRP and MRP II evolved into ERP.
   c. ERP evolved into MRP and MRP evolved into MRP II.
   d. None of the above is true.
2. Which of the following statements regarding traditional accounting are true?
   a. Traditional accounting does not provide managers in a JIT setting with timely information
   b. The measurement principle tends to ignore standards other than money
   c. Overhead allocations may lead to cost distortions
   d. All of the above are true statements
   e. A and B are true but C is not true
3. Refer to the equation for the EOQ in the text. Car Country, a local Ford dealer, sells 1,280 small SUVs each year. Keeping a car on the lot costs Car Country $200 per month, so the company prefers to order as few SUVs as is economically feasible. However, each time an order is placed, the company incurs total costs of $300. Of this $300, $240 is fixed and $60 is variable. Determine the company's economic order quantity.
   a. 8
   b. 16
   c. 18
   d. 56
   e. 62

Questions 4 through 6 are based on the diagram below, which represents the EOQ model.

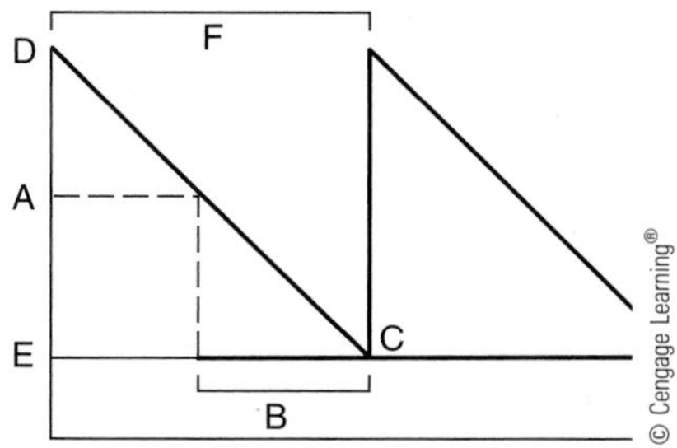

4. Which line segment represents the reorder lead time?
   a. DC
   b. AE
   c. F
   d. B
   e. AD
5. Which line segment identifies the quantity of safety stock maintained?
   a. DC
   b. AD
   c. AE
   d. EC
6. Which line segment represents the daily demand?
   a. DE
   b. DC
   c. AC
   d. AE
   e. B
7. Which of the following is NOT a problem associated with standard cost accounting?
   a. Standard costing motivates management to produce large batches of products and build inventory.
   b. Applying standard costing leads to product cost distortions in a lean environment.
   c. Standard costing data are associated with excessive time lags that reduce its usefulness.
   d. The financial orientation of standard costing may promote bad decisions.
   e. All of the above are problems with standard costing.
8. Which of the following is NOT a principle of lean manufacturing?
   a. Products are pushed from the production end to the customer.
   b. All activities that do not add value and maximize the use of scarce resources must be eliminated.
   c. Achieve high inventory turnover rate.
   d. A lean manufacturing firm must have established and cooperative relationships with vendors.
   e. All of the above are lean manufacturing principles.
9. The fundamental EOQ model
   a. provides for fluctuating lead times during reorder cycles
   b. is relatively insensitive to errors in demand, procurement costs, and carrying costs
   c. focuses on the trade-off between production costs and carrying costs
   d. is stochastic in nature
   e. is best used in conjunction with a periodic inventory system
10. Which of the following descriptions is not correct?
   a. The routing sheet shows the manufacturing path for a particular product.
   b. Bill of materials shows the cost of producing a single unit.
   c. Move ticket authorizes the movement of a batch from on department to another
   d. Materials requisition authorizes the storekeeper to release materials.

Problems

1. DOCUMENT FLOWCHART

Diagram the sequence in which the following source documents are prepared.

a. bill of materials
b. work order
c. sales forecast
d. materials requisition
e. move ticket
f. production schedule
g. route sheet

2. ECONOMIC ORDER QUANTITY

Out Camping is a manufacturer of supplies and has several divisions, one of which is the tent division that produces the deluxe tent Away From Home. Fourteen thousand of these tents are made each year. This model of tent incorporates two zipping doors in each model. Zippers for these doors are purchased from Zippy Zippers. Out Camping began this year with 500 zippers in inventory but is now adopting an economic order quantity approach to inventory. A review of last year's records reveals the following information concerning each order placed with Zippy Zippers: variable labor—\$12, variable supplies—\$1, fixed computer costs—\$4, fixed office expenses—\$2, fixed mailing expenses—\$2, and fixed supplies—\$1. No differences are expected this year. Last year, the cost of carrying one zipper in inventory for the entire year was \$1, but Out Camping has recently negotiated a new lease on its warehouse, and the cost of carrying each zipper is now expected to increase by 25 cents. Out Camping also found that it took 7 days from the time an order was sent to Zippy until the zippers were received.

Required

a. Compute the economic order quantity.
b. Compute the reorder point. Presume Out Camping has a desire to reduce its ending inventory to half of this year's beginning amount and that the company produces the Away From Home model 140 days each year.

3. WORLD-CLASS COMPANIES

'Conduct an online search using the keywords "world-class companies" and "manufacturing." Find five companies that claim to be world-class manufacturing companies and state the innovation(s) these companies have undertaken to become world-class.

4. INTERNAL CONTROL

Examine the flowchart for Problem 4 and determine any control threats. Specifically, discuss the control problems, the possible dangers, and any corrective procedures you would recommend.

5. DESIGN AND DOCUMENT MANUFACTURING PROCESSES

Design and document with a system flowchart a computer-based manufacturing process that possesses the information flows of the manual systems depicted in Figures 7-9 and 7-13. Assume that the manufacturing process is triggered by a monthly sales forecast, which is received periodically from the marketing department in digital form. Further assume that all functional areas (work centers, store-keeping, inventory control, and so on) employ terminals that are networked to a centralized data processing function. Your system design should minimize hard-copy documents.

6. ZERO DEFECTS PROCESS

Northern Tractor is a manufacturer of commercial and consumer garden tractors. In their 30 years of operation Northern has followed a traditional manufacturing process that included maintaining a significant raw material inventory. In an effort to streamline the manufacturing process and reduce inventory carrying costs, Northern's CEO wants to switch to a JIT manufacturing process. Production consultants have informed the CEO that moving to JIT will require a new philosophy; one aspect of this is moving toward zero defect manufacturing. Under this philosophy if a defective part from an out-of-control process is detected, no more units should be produced until the process is corrected. The consultants' estimate that the production process may occasionally be shut down anywhere from 30 minutes to several hours. Discuss the advantages and disadvantages of this new approach.

7. ACTIVITY DRIVERS

Cut It Up, Inc., is a manufacturer of wooden cutting boards that are sold through a chain of kitchen stores. For years, the company has allocated overhead based on total machine hours. A recent assessment of overhead costs has shown that these costs are now in excess of 40 percent of the company's total costs. As an attempt to better control overhead, Cut It Up is adopting an activity-based costing system. Each cutting board goes through the following processes:

a. Cutting—Boards are selected from inventory and are cut to the required width and length. Imperfections in boards (such as knots or cracks) are identified and removed.
b. Assembly—Cut wooden pieces are laid out on clamps, a layer of glue is applied to each piece, and the glued pieces are clamped together until the glue sets.

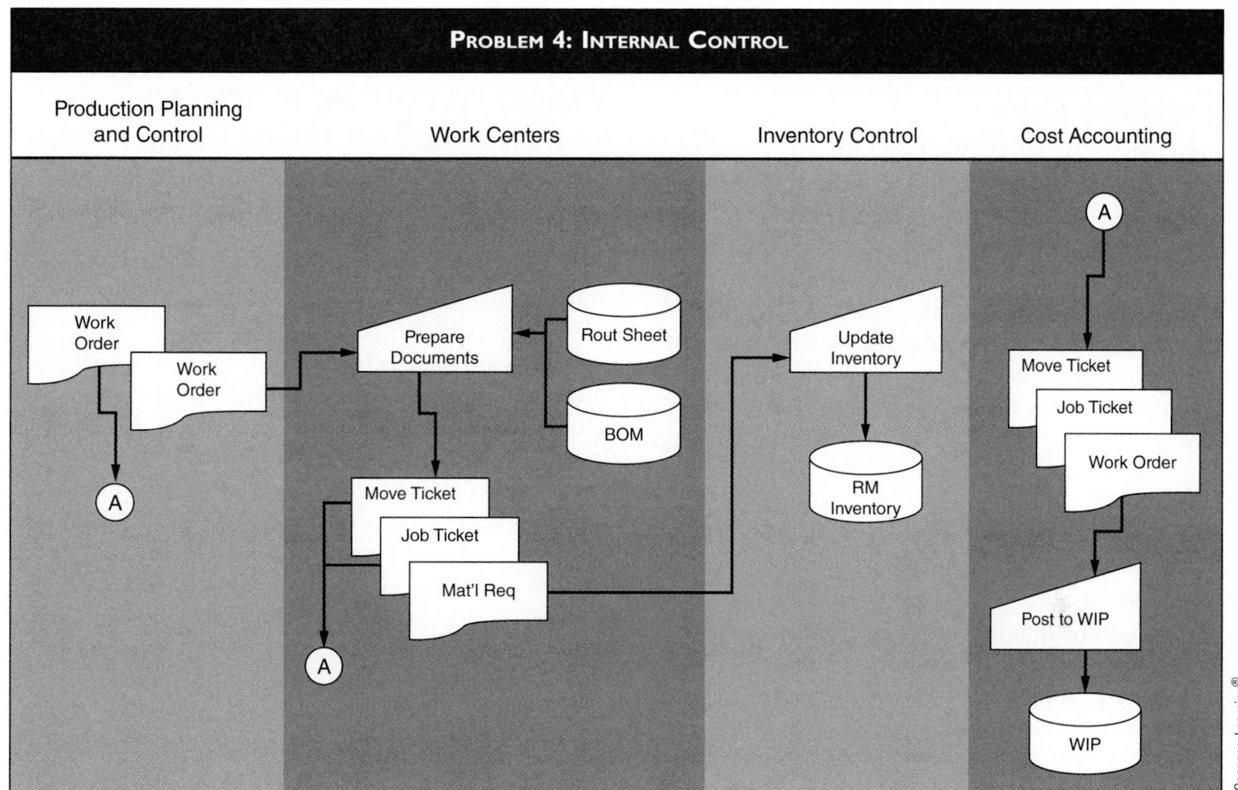

c. Shaping—Once the glue has set, the boards are sent to the shaping process, where they are cut into specific shapes.
d. Sanding—After being shaped, the cutting boards must be sanded smooth.
e. Finishing—Sanded cutting boards receive a coat of mineral oil to help preserve the wood.
f. Packing—Finished cutting boards are placed in boxes of 12. The boxes are sealed, addressed, and sent to one of the kitchen stores.

Required

What do you suppose are components of overhead for this company? Determine a logical cost driver for each process.

8. LEAN MANUFACTURING PRINCIPLES

Write an essay outlining the key principles of lean manufacturing.

Internal Control Cases

1. PERFORMANCE WATER PUMPS (CENTRALIZED SYSTEM WITH DISTRIBUTED TERMINALS)

Performance Water Pumps (PWP) is a leading manufacturer of water pumps with high capacity capability. These pumps are used in both civil and private disaster situations. PWP's primary market is disaster recovery companies that assist home owners following basement flooding. They also sell to building contractors, municipalities, and rental companies. The company publishes an industry catalog of pumps and other auxiliary equipment, which is distributed to customers and prospective customers. PWP's headquarters and manufacturing facilities are in Leesville, Louisiana where they employ 125 manufacturing and clerical staff.

PWP employs a centralized computer system with distributed terminals in the departments. Recently they have been experiencing manufacturing problems and cost overruns. PWP has hired your auditing firm to assess its operations and internal control procedures.

Conversion Cycle

'The current batch production process is initiated from a marketing forecast of expected sales for the quarter. The production planning and control clerk uses this to create a digital Production Schedule of the various batches to be produced during the quarter. From this schedule, the system automatically prepares weekly the digital work orders to be used by the production department.

The production department supervisor accesses the work orders from his terminal and prepares the necessary hard-copy move tickets and materials requisitions.

The move tickets and two copies of the purchase requisitions are distributed to each work center in the production process. Employees submit the two copies of the material requisitions to storekeeping in exchange for materials and sub-assemblies. If additional raw materials are needed beyond the standard quantity, the supervisor issues additional material requisitions. Work center employees record their labor time for each batch on hard-copy job cards, which they send to cost accounting. As the production is completed in each work center, the move ticket is submitted to cost accounting. Finally, upon completion of the batch, the supervisor closes the open work order file.

The storekeeping manager files one copy of the material requisition and updates the raw materials inventory file from the computer in his office. The manager then sends the second copy of the material requisition to cost accounting. At the end of the day, the manager prepares a digital journal voucher and posts it to the general ledger control accounts.

The cost accounting clerk accesses the digital work orders and sets up a WIP account for the batch. Throughout the production period, the clerk also receives move tickets, job tickets, and materials requisitions, which she uses to post to WIP. At the end of each day the cost accounting clerk prepares a digital journal voucher and posts to GL control accounts to reflect the status of WIP and to record transfers of WIP to finished good inventory.

Required

a. Create a data flow diagram of the current system.
b. Create a system flowchart of the existing system.
c. What risks exist in the system as it is currently designed?
d. Describe the changes needed to reduce the risks.

2. LITTLE TITAN ENGINES, INC. (MANUAL SYSTEM WITH STAND ALONE PC SUPPORT)

Little Titan Engines (LTE), Inc., is a manufacturer of a range of small high-quality gasoline engines that are installed in various types and brands of auxiliary equipment. LTE's primary market comprises the manufactures of small commercial tractors, commercial electric generators, and construction site water extraction pumps.

LTE's employs a batch production process whose inventory management, production planning, and accounting procedures consist of a combination of manual activities supported by standalone (non-networked) PC technology. The company is experiencing production delays and cost overruns. Its CEO has hired your firm to review its procedures and make recommendations for improving it.

The batch production process is initiated by e-mailed and hard-copy sales orders received from client companies. The production planning and control clerk enters the orders into the digital Production Schedule from his department PC and prints two hard-copy work orders. He sends one of these to cost accounting and the other to the production department.

The production department supervisor enters the work order into a PC application. The system automatically creates an open work order record and prints the hard copy move tickets, and materials requisitions.

The supervisor distributes the move tickets and two copies of the purchase requisitions to each work center involve in the production process. Work center employees exchange the two copies of the material requisitions for assembly parts and other materials needed to complete the batch. If additional parts or materials are needed beyond the standard quantity, the supervisor issues additional material requisitions. As the production is completed in each work center, employees record their labor time for each batch on hard copy job cards, which they send to cost accounting along with the move ticket. Finally, upon completion of the batch, the supervisor closes the open work order file.

The storekeeping clerk files one copy of the material requisition in the department and updates the raw materials inventory file from the computer in his office. The manager then sends the second copy of the material requisition to cost accounting. At the end of the day, the manager prepares a hard-copy journal voucher and sends it to the general ledger department.

The cost accounting clerk receives the work order and sets up a WIP account for the batch. Throughout the production period, the clerk also receives move tickets, job tickets, and materials requisitions, which she uses to post to WIP. At the end of each day, the cost accounting clerk prepares a hard copy journal voucher, which she sends to general ledger department. The journal voucher reflects the total value of WIP and transfers to finished good inventory.

The general ledger clerk receives the journal vouchers, posts to the appropriate GL accounts and files the journal vouchers in the department.

Required

a. Create a data flow diagram of the current system.
b. Create a system flowchart of the existing system.
c. What risks exist in the system as it is currently designed?
d. Describe the changes needed to reduce the risks.

3. GENERAL MANUFACTURING INC.—INTERNAL CONTROLS ASSESSMENT (MANUAL SYSTEM WITH STAND ALONE PC SUPPORT)

The production process at General Manufacturing, Inc., involves the planning, scheduling, and controlling of the physical products through the manufacturing process. General's manufacturing process begins in the production planning and control department, where the clerk determines the materials and operations requirements based on the marketing department sales forecast and the inventory status report from the storeroom. The clerk reviews this information and prepares a hard-copy purchase requisition, which she sends to the purchasing department. From her department PC the clerk then accesses the bill of materials and route sheets files and prints the following hard copy documents: work orders, move tickets, and materials requisitions. Three copies of each document are prepared. One copy of the work order, move ticket, and materials requisitions document are sent to cost accounting. The remaining copies are sent to the work center supervisor.

Upon receipt of the production control documents, the work center supervisor initiates the production process. The production employees submit a copy of the materials requisitions to the inventory storeroom in exchange for necessary raw material. When additional raw material is needed for a job in process, the storeroom clerk provides them on request. Materials in excess of those needed for production are kept in the work center and used for future production. When the job passes through all production stages and is complete, the work center supervisor sends the finished product to the finished goods warehouse. He files one copy each of the work order, move ticket, and materials requisition and sends the remaining copies of the work order and move ticket to the cost accounting department. The supervisor reviews the job tickets and the employee time cards, which he sends to cost accounting and payroll, respectively.

The inventory storeroom clerk accepts materials requisitions from the work center employees and releases the raw material to the work centers. He updates the raw material inventory records from the PC and files the materials requisitions in the storeroom. At the end of the day, he creates a journal voucher and sends it to the general ledger department.

The cost accounting clerk receives the following documents: work orders, move tickets, and materials requisitions from the production planning department; job tickets, work orders, and move tickets from the work center. The clerk uses these to initiate a WIP account and to update the WIP as work progresses. At the day's end, the cost accounting clerk prepares a journal voucher reflecting the WIP status and files all documents in the department.

The general ledger clerk receives the journal vouchers, posts to the appropriate GL accounts and files the journal vouchers in the department.

Required

a. Create a data flow diagram of the current system.
b. Create a system flowchart of the existing system.
c. Analyze the physical internal control weaknesses in the system. Model your response according to the six categories of physical control activities specified in the COSO internal control model.
d. (Optional) Prepare a system flowchart of a redesigned computer-based system that resolves the control weaknesses that you identified. Explain your solution.

4. HERCULES LADDERS (CENTRALIZED SYSTEM WITH DISTRIBUTED TERMINALS)

Hercules Ladders manufacturer of light-weight, industrial strength, extendible ladders and scaffolding that are used extensively by general contractors and many other industries. The company sells its products through its catalog and industry outlets. The company has its manufacturing facility, warehouse, and distribution center in Youngstown, Ohio where it employs 160 sales, clerical, and manufacturing staff.

Hercules employs batch processing and has a centralized computer system with distributed terminals in the departments. Recently, they have been having quality control and budgeting problems, so their CEO has hired you to review the company's operations and internal control procedures. The following describes their manufacturing process.

The production process is triggered by a three-month marketing forecast of expected sales, which goes to the production planning and control clerk. From her terminal, the clerk updates the digital Production Schedule to include the batches of ladders and scaffolding to be produced during the next quarter. Drawing upon data in the BOM and routing sheet files, the system automatically prepares weekly the digital work orders move tickets, and material requisitions, which it sends to the work center supervisor's terminal.

The work center supervisor accesses the digital documents and prints hard-copy work orders, move tickets, and materials requisitions. The supervisor distributes the move tickets and two copies of the purchase requisitions to each work center in the production process.

Employees submit the two copies of the material requisitions to storekeeping in exchange for raw materials such as aluminum stock and steel pipes. If additional raw materials are needed beyond the standard quantity, the supervisor issues additional material requisitions. As the production is completed in each work center, the employees send the move ticket to cost accounting to mark the completion of that phase of the batch. Employees also record labor time spent on each batch on hard-copy job cards, which they send to cost accounting. Finally, upon completion of the batch the supervisor closes the open work order file.

The storekeeping clerk files one copy of the material requisition and updates the raw materials inventory file from the terminal in his office. The clerk then sends the second copy of the material requisition to cost accounting. At the end of the day the clerk prepares a digital journal voucher and posts it to the general ledger control accounts.

The cost accounting clerk accesses the digital work orders and sets up a WIP account for the batch. The clerk also receives move tickets, job tickets, and materials requisitions throughout the production process, which she uses to post to WIP subsidiary ledger. At the end of each day, the cost accounting clerk prepares a digital journal voucher and posts to GL control accounts to reflect the status of WIP and to record transfers of WIP to finished good inventory.

Required

a. Create a data flow diagram of the current system.
b. Create a system flowchart of the existing system.
c. What risks exist in the system as it is currently designed?
d. Describe the changes needed to reduce the risks.

5. VOLTEC WELDING MACHINES, INC. (CENTRALIZED SYSTEM WITH DISTRIBUTED TERMINALS)

Voltec Welding Machines is a manufacturer of welding machines of various types including TIG, MIG, and ark welders and other electric tools. The company's primary markets are commercial and do-it-yourself enthusiasts. It reaches its customers through trade magazines and publishes an industry catalog of welders, plasma cutters, and electric generators. They sell direct to wholesalers and through supply houses and home improvement centers. Their manufacturing facility and distribution center are in Tulsa, Oklahoma, where they employ 120 manufacturing and clerical staff.

Voltec employs a centralized computer system with distributed terminals in the departments. Recently they have been having manufacturing problems and cost overruns. Voltec has hired your auditing firm to assess its operations and internal control procedures.

Voltec's conversion cycle is triggered by a report from the finished goods warehouse. The warehouse clerk periodically reviews the inventory records in a search for low stock items. When the quantity on hand of an inventory item in the finished goods warehouse falls below its pre-establish minimum, the warehouse clerk sends a digital inventory status report from the warehouse terminal to production planning and control advising them to schedule a production batch run for the item in question.

Upon receipt of the report, the production planning and control department clerk accesses the digital bill of materials and the route sheet files for that item to be produced and adds the production details to the digital production schedule. The system automatically adds a record to the open work order file and sends a digital work order to the work-center supervisor's terminal and to the cost accounting clerk's terminal.

The work-center supervisor accesses the work order from his terminal and prints hard-copy move tickets and material requisitions for each stage in the production process. Production employees take the materials requisitions to the store keeper and secure the components, subassemblies, and raw materials needed to perform their production tasks. If excess materials beyond the standard amount are needed, the supervisor prepares additional materials requisitions. The employees also complete job time tickets after each stage in the process to reflect the time spent on the job. When the employees complete their tasks they send the move tickets and time tickets to the cost accounting department.

The storekeeper receives the materials requisitions and releases the materials into production. He then updates the raw material inventory records and sends the requisition to cost accounting. When inventories of component parts and raw materials fall to their reorder points, the storekeeper prepares purchase orders and sends then to the respective vendors. Vendors deliver raw material inventories directly to the storeroom, at which time the storeroom clerk inspects them and updates the digital raw materials subsidiary ledger. Each day the storekeeper prepares a journal voucher and posts to the general ledger raw material control account.

The cost accounting clerk receives the digital work order and initiates a new WIP account for the batch. During the production process, the clerk receives hard-copy move tickets, materials requisitions, and job tickets from the work centers, which the clerk uses to update WIP account. When production is complete the clerk closes the WIP account for the batch and transfers it to the finished good inventory subsidiary ledger.

At the day's end, the cost accounting clerk prepares a digital journal voucher reflecting the WIP status and any transfers from WIP to finished goods inventory. The clerk then posts the journal voucher to the WIP and FG general ledger control accounts.

Required

a. Create a data flow diagram of the current system.
b. Create a system flowchart of the existing system.
c. What risks exist in the system as it is currently designed?
d. Describe the changes needed to reduce the risks.

CHAPTER

8

Financial Reporting and Management Reporting Systems

Learning Objectives

After studying this chapter, you should:

- Understand the operational features of the general ledger system (GLS), financial reporting system (FRS), and management reporting system (MRS).
- Be able to identify the principal operational controls governing the GLS and FRS.
- Understand the factors that influence the design of the MRS.
- Understand the elements of a responsibility accounting system.
- Be familiar with the financial reporting issues surrounding XBRL.

The chapter begins with a review of the objectives, operational features, and control issues of two related systems: the general ledger system (GLS) and the financial reporting system (FRS). The chapter illustrates the central role of the GLS as a hub system that is connected to transaction processing systems through formal information flows. Transaction cycles process individual events that are recorded in special journals and subsidiary accounts. Journal vouchers and account summaries of these transactions flow into the GLS, which provides input to the FRS. The financial reporting process is presented as a multistep activity that begins with the capture of the transaction and concludes with the preparation of financial statements. Significant changes to the traditional financial report process, in the form of XBRL (extendable business reporting language), are imminent. This chapter outlines the key features of XBRL and its implications for accountants. Finally, the management reporting system (MRS) is examined. The MRS is distinguishable from the FRS in one key respect: financial reporting is mandatory and management reporting is discretionary. Management reporting information is needed for planning and controlling business activities. Organization management implements MRS applications at their discretion, based on internal user needs. This chapter examines the factors that drive the design of such applications.

The General Ledger System

Figure 8-1 characterizes the general ledger system (GLS) as a hub connected to the other systems of the firm through spokes of information flows. Transaction cycles process individual events that are recorded in special journals and subsidiary accounts. Summaries of these transactions flow into the GLS and become sources of input for the management reporting system (MRS) and financial reporting system (FRS). The bulk of the flows into the GLS comes from the transaction processing subsystems. Note, however, that information also flows from the FRS as feedback into the GLS. We shall explore this point more thoroughly later. In this section we review key elements of the GLS.

THE JOURNAL VOUCHER

The source of input to the general ledger is the journal voucher, which is illustrated in Figure 8-2. A journal voucher, which can be used to represent summaries of similar transactions or a single unique transaction, identifies the financial amounts and affected general ledger (GL) accounts. Routine transactions, adjusting entries, and closing entries are all entered into the GL via journal vouchers. Because a responsible manager must approve journal vouchers, the manager offers a degree of control against unauthorized GL entries.

THE GLS DATABASE

The GLS database includes a variety of files. Whereas these will vary from firm to firm, the following examples are representative.

FIGURE 8-1 RELATIONSHIP OF GLS TO OTHER INFORMATION SUBSYSTEMS

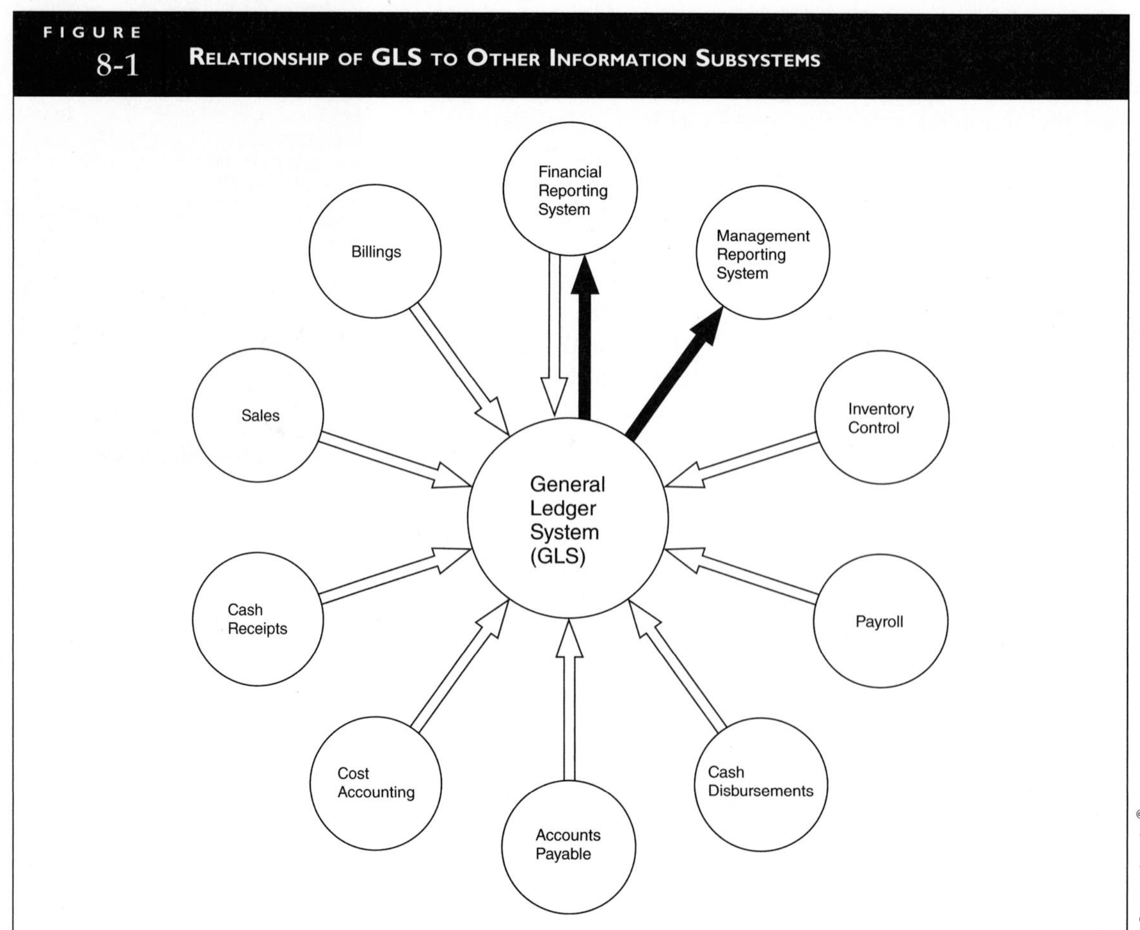

FIGURE 8-2 JOURNAL VOUCHER RECORD LAYOUT FOR A GENERAL LEDGER MASTER FILE

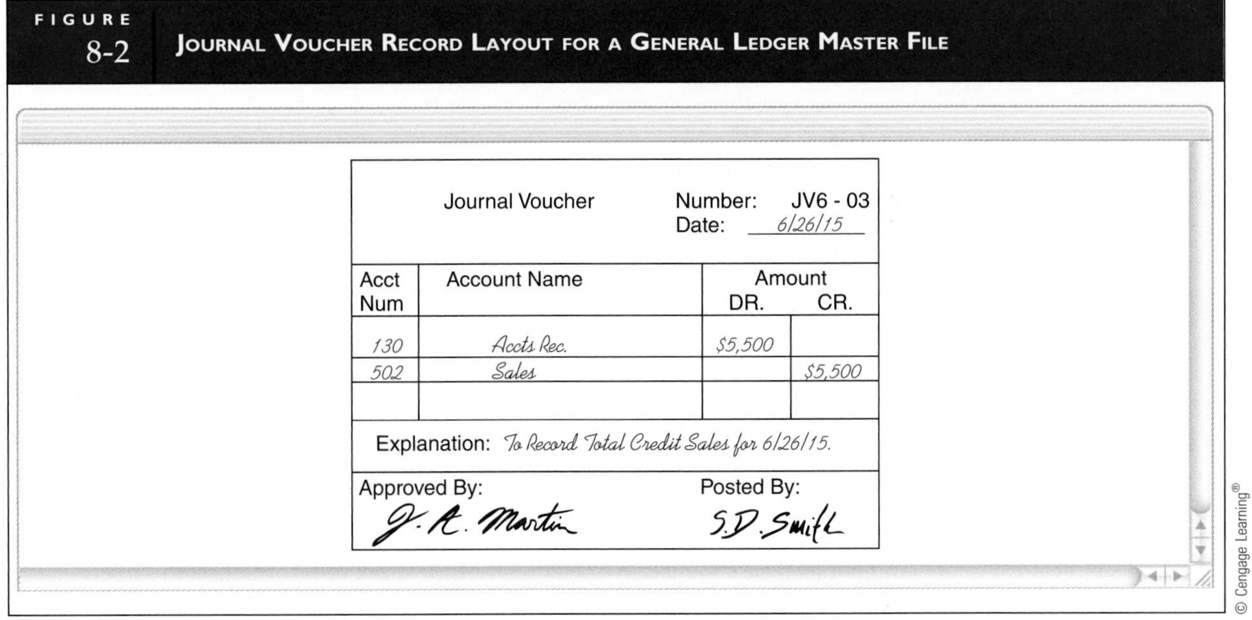
Journal Voucher
Number: JV6 - 03
Date: 6/26/15

Acct Num	Account Name	Amount DR.	Amount CR.
130	Accts Rec.	$5,500	
502	Sales		$5,500

Explanation: To Record Total Credit Sales for 6/26/15.

Approved By: J. A. Martin
Posted By: S.D. Smith

The ***general ledger master file*** *is the principal file in the GLS database. This file is based on the organization's published* ***chart of accounts****. Each record in the GL master is either a separate GL account (e.g., sales) or a control account (such as AR—control) for a corresponding subsidiary ledger in the transaction processing system. Figure 8-3 illustrates the structure of a typical GL master file. The FRS draws upon the GL master to produce the firm's financial statements. The MRS also uses this file to support internal information reporting.*

The ***general ledger history file*** *has the same format as the GL master. Its primary purpose is to provide historical financial data for comparative financial reports.*

The ***journal voucher file*** *is the total collection of the journal vouchers processed in the current period. This file provides a record of all general ledger transactions and replaces the traditional general journal.*

The ***journal voucher history file*** *contains journal vouchers for past periods. This historical information supports management's stewardship responsibility to account for resource utilization. Both the current and historical journal voucher files are important links in the firm's audit trail.*

The ***responsibility center file*** *contains the revenues, expenditures, and other resource utilization data for each responsibility center in the organization. The MRS draws upon these data for input in the preparation of responsibility reports for management.*

FIGURE 8-3 RECORD LAYOUT FOR A GENERAL LEDGER MASTER FILE

Account Number	Account Description	Acct Class A = Asset L = Liab R = Rev E = Expense OE = Equity	Normal Balance D = Debit C = Credit	Beginning Balance	Total Debits This Period	Total Credits This Period	Current Balance

*Finally, the **budget master file** contains budgeted amounts for revenues, expenditures, and other resources for responsibility centers. These data, in conjunction with the responsibility center file, are the basis for responsibility accounting, which is discussed later in the chapter.*

GLS PROCEDURES

As we have seen in previous chapters, certain aspects of GLS update procedures are performed as either a separate operation or an operation integrated within transaction processing systems. Our focus in the next section is on the interrelationship between the GLS and financial reporting. This involves additional updates in the form of reversing, adjusting, and closing entries. Let's now turn our attention to the financial reporting system.

The Financial Reporting System

The law dictates management's responsibility for providing stewardship information to external parties. This reporting obligation is met via the FRS. Much of the information provided takes the form of standard financial statements, tax returns, and documents required by regulatory agencies such as the Securities and Exchange Commission (SEC).

The primary recipients of financial statement information are external users, such as stockholders, creditors, and government agencies. Generally speaking, outside users of information are interested in the performance of the organization as a whole. Therefore, they require information that allows them to observe trends in performance over time and to make comparisons between different organizations. Given the nature of these needs, financial reporting information must be prepared and presented by all organizations in a manner that is generally accepted and understood by external users.

SOPHISTICATED USERS WITH HOMOGENEOUS INFORMATION NEEDS

Because the community of external users is vast and their individual information needs may vary, financial statements are targeted at a general audience. They are prepared on the proposition that the audience comprises **sophisticated users** with relatively homogeneous information needs. In other words, it is assumed that users of financial reports understand the conventions and accounting principles that are applied and that the statements have information content that is useful.

FINANCIAL REPORTING PROCEDURES

Financial reporting is the final step in the overall accounting process that begins in the transaction cycles. Figure 8-4 presents the FRS in relation to the other information subsystems. The steps illustrated and numbered in the figure are discussed briefly in the following section.

The process begins with a clean slate at the start of a new fiscal year. Only the balance sheet (permanent) accounts are carried forward from the previous year. From this point, the following steps occur:

1. *Capture the transaction.* Within each transaction cycle, transactions are recorded in the appropriate transaction file.
2. *Record in special journal.* Each transaction is entered into the journal. Recall that frequently occurring classes of transactions, such as sales, are captured in special journals. Those that occur infrequently are recorded in the general journal or directly on a journal voucher.
3. *Post to subsidiary ledger.* The details of each transaction are posted to the affected subsidiary accounts.
4. *Post to general ledger.* Periodically, journal vouchers, summarizing the entries made to the special journals and subsidiary ledgers, are prepared and posted to the GL accounts. The frequency of updates to the GL will be determined by the degree of system integration.
5. *Prepare the unadjusted trial balance.* At the end of the accounting period, the ending balance of each account in the GL is placed in a worksheet and evaluated in total for debit-credit equality.

FIGURE 8-4 FINANCIAL REPORTING PROCESS

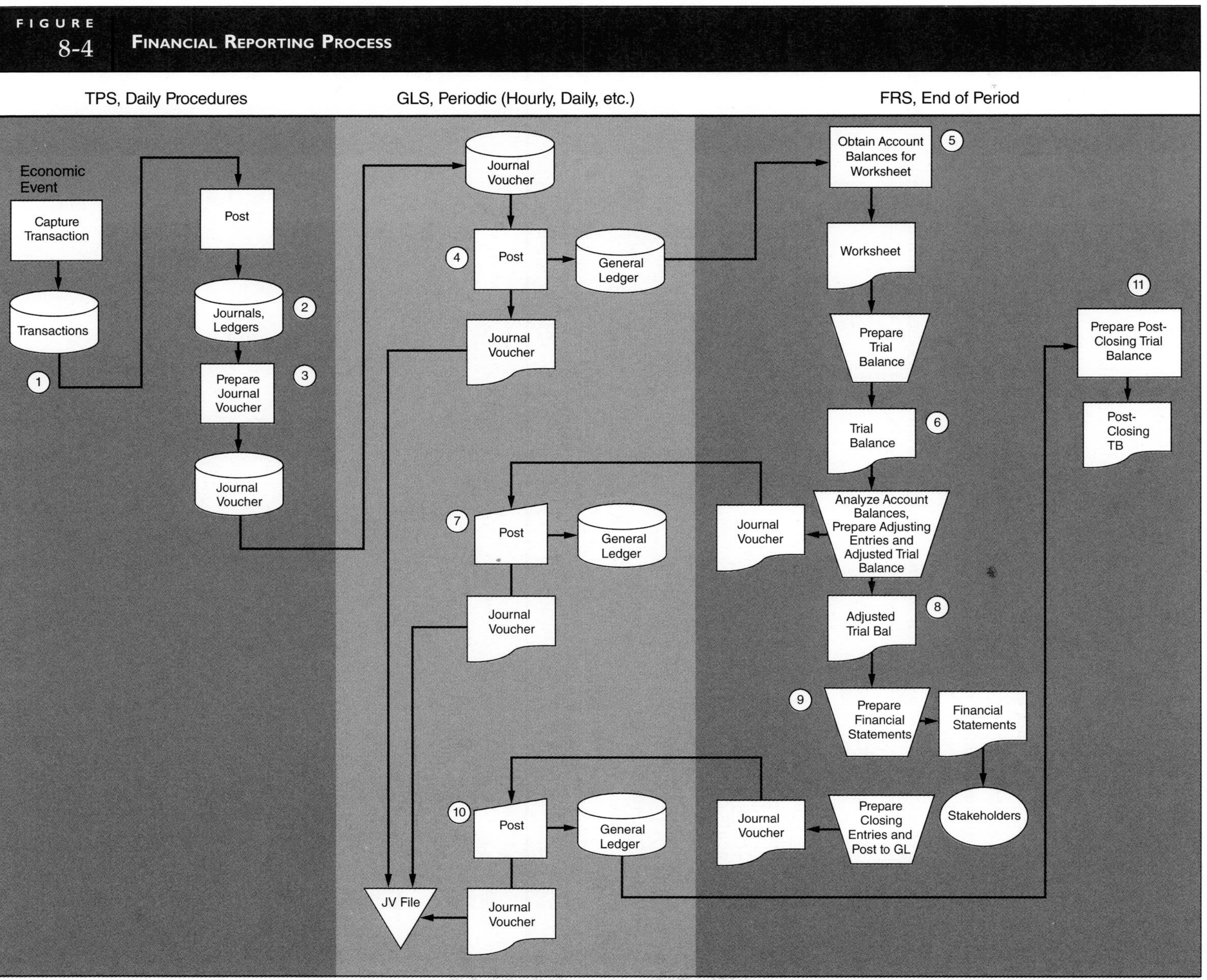

6. *Make adjusting entries.* Adjusting entries are made to the worksheet to correct errors and to reflect unrecorded transactions during the period, such as depreciation.
7. *Journalize and post adjusting entries.* Journal vouchers for the adjusting entries are prepared and posted to the appropriate accounts in the GL.
8. *Prepare the adjusted trial balance.* From the adjusted balances, a trial balance is prepared that contains all the entries that should be reflected in the financial statements.
9. *Prepare the financial statements.* The balance sheet, income statement, and statement of cash flows are prepared using the adjusted trial balance.
10. *Journalize and post the closing entries.* Journal vouchers are prepared for entries that close out the income statement (temporary) accounts and transfer the income or loss to retained earnings. Finally, these entries are posted to the GL.
11. *Prepare the post-closing trial balance.* A trial balance worksheet containing only the balance sheet accounts may now be prepared to indicate the balances being carried forward to the next accounting period.

The periodic nature of financial reporting in most organizations establishes it as a batch process, as illustrated in Figure 8-4. This often is the case for larger organizations with multiple streams of revenue and expense transactions that need to be reconciled before being posted to the GL. Many organizations, however, have moved to a real-time GL/FRS that produces financial statements on short notice. Figure 8-5 presents a flowchart of a real-time GL/FRS. A noteworthy

FIGURE 8-5 REAL-TIME GENERAL LEDGER AND FINANCIAL REPORTING SYSTEM

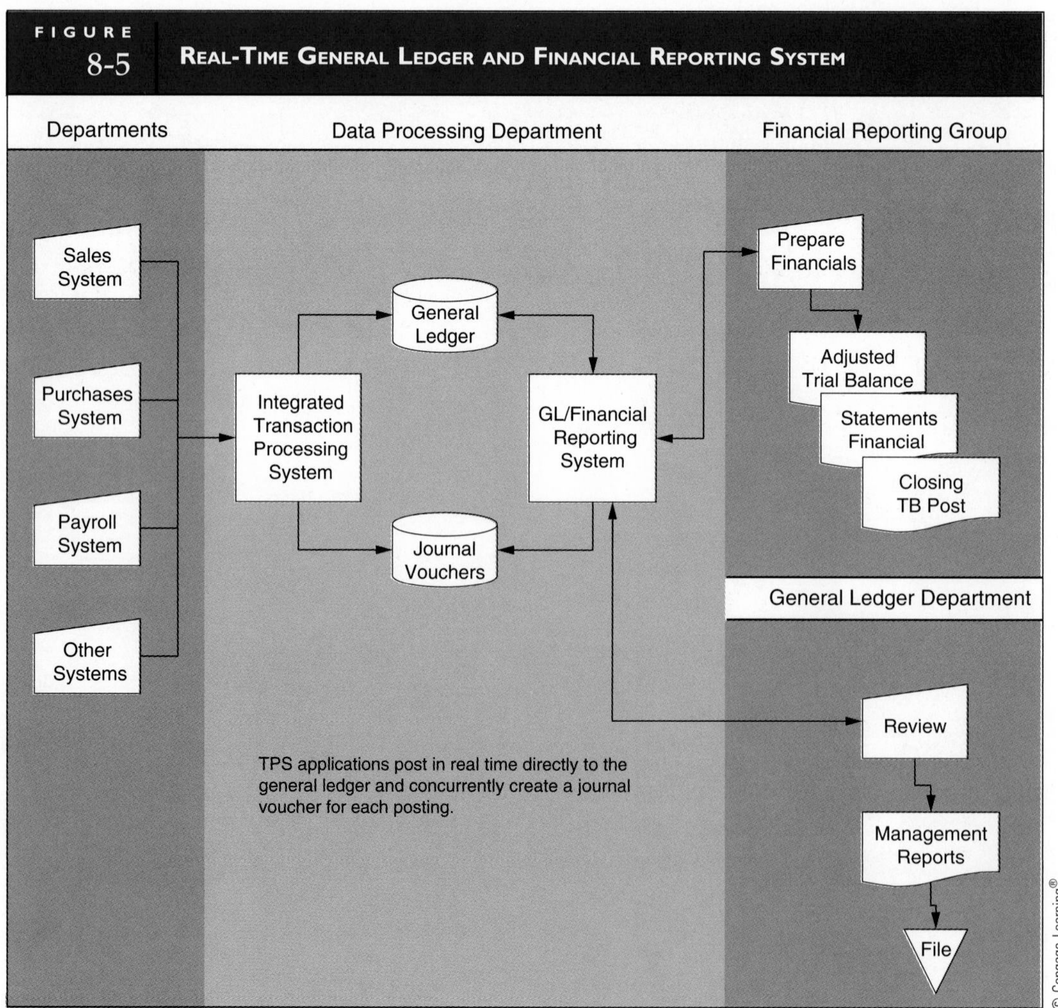

feature of this system is the changed role of the journal voucher. In batch GL systems, transaction processing applications summarize and capture transactions in journal vouchers where they are held, reviewed, and later posted to the GL. In such systems, journal vouchers are the authority and the source of all GL postings. In contrast, a real-time GL system posts each transaction directly to the general ledger and concurrently creates a journal voucher. The journal voucher in this system does not authorize a GL entry in the traditional sense. Rather, it provides a posting reference and audit trail, which links GL summary account balances to specific transactions.

XBRL—Reengineering Financial Reporting

Online reporting of financial data has become a competitive necessity for publicly traded organizations. Currently, most organizations accomplish this by placing their financial statements and other financial reports on their respective websites as HTML (Hyper Text Markup Language[1]) documents. These documents can then be downloaded by users such as the SEC, financial analysts, and other interested parties. The HTML reports, however, cannot be conveniently processed through IT automation. Performing any analysis on the data contained in the reports requires them to be manually entered into the user's information system.

The solution to this problem is **XBRL (extensible Business Reporting Language)**, which is the Internet standard specifically designed for business reporting and information exchange. The objective of XBRL is to facilitate the publication, exchange, and processing of financial and business information. XBRL is a derivative of another Internet standard called **XML (extensible Markup Language)**.

XML

XML is a metalanguage for describing markup languages. The term *extensible* means that any markup language can be created using XML. This includes the creation of markup languages capable of storing data in relational form in which tags (or formatting commands) are mapped to data values. Thus, XML can be used to model the data structure of an organization's internal database.

The examples illustrated in Figure 8-6 serve to distinguish HTML from XML, using a bookstore order formatted in both languages. Although essentially the same information is contained in both examples, and they look similar in structure, important differences exist between them. Although both examples use tags (words that are bracketed by the symbols < and >) and attributes such as

FIGURE 8-6 COMPARISON OF HTML AND XML DOCUMENTS

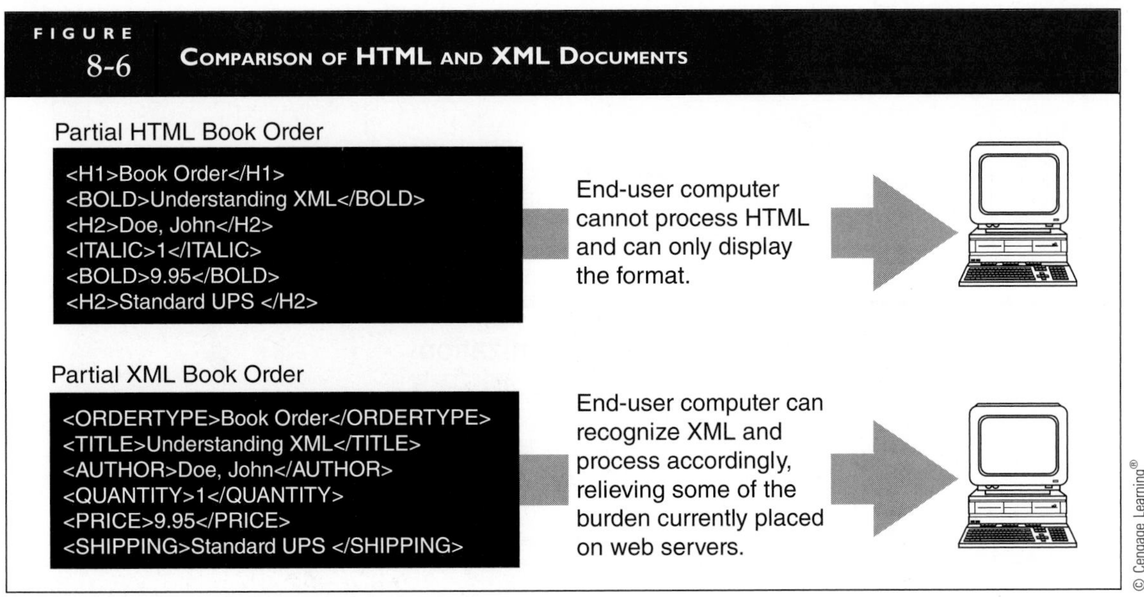

1 HTML is discussed in more detail in Chapter 12.

Doe, John, the way in which these tags and attributes are used differs. In the HTML example, the tags have predefined meaning that describes how the attributes will be presented in a document. The book order in this example can only be viewed visually (similar to a FAX) and must be manually entered into the bookstore's order entry system for processing. In the case of the XML order, the tags are customized to the user, and the user's application can read and interpret the tagged data. Thus, the bookstore order prepared in XML presents order attributes in a relational form that can be automatically imported into a bookseller's internal database.

XBRL

Recognizing the potential benefits of XML, the AICPA encouraged research into the creation of an accounting-specific markup language. XBRL is an XML-based language that was designed to provide the financial community with a standardized method for preparing, publishing, and automatically exchanging financial information, including financial statements of publicly held companies. XBRL is typically used for reporting aggregated financial data, but can also be applied to communicating information pertaining to individual transactions. Figure 8-7 presents an overview of the XBRL reporting process, the key elements of which are discussed in the following sections.

The first step in the process is to select an **XBRL taxonomy**. Taxonomies are classification schemes that are compliant with XBRL specifications to accomplish a specific information exchange or reporting objective such as filing with the SEC. In essence, the XBRL taxonomy specifies the data to be included in an exchange or report. The XBRL Standards Committee has created several taxonomies for widespread use. The illustrations in Figures 8-8 through 8-11 are based on XBRL Taxonomy for Financial Reporting for Commercial and Industrial Companies, referred to as CI taxonomy.[2]

FIGURE 8-7 OVERVIEW OF XBRL REPORTING PROCESS

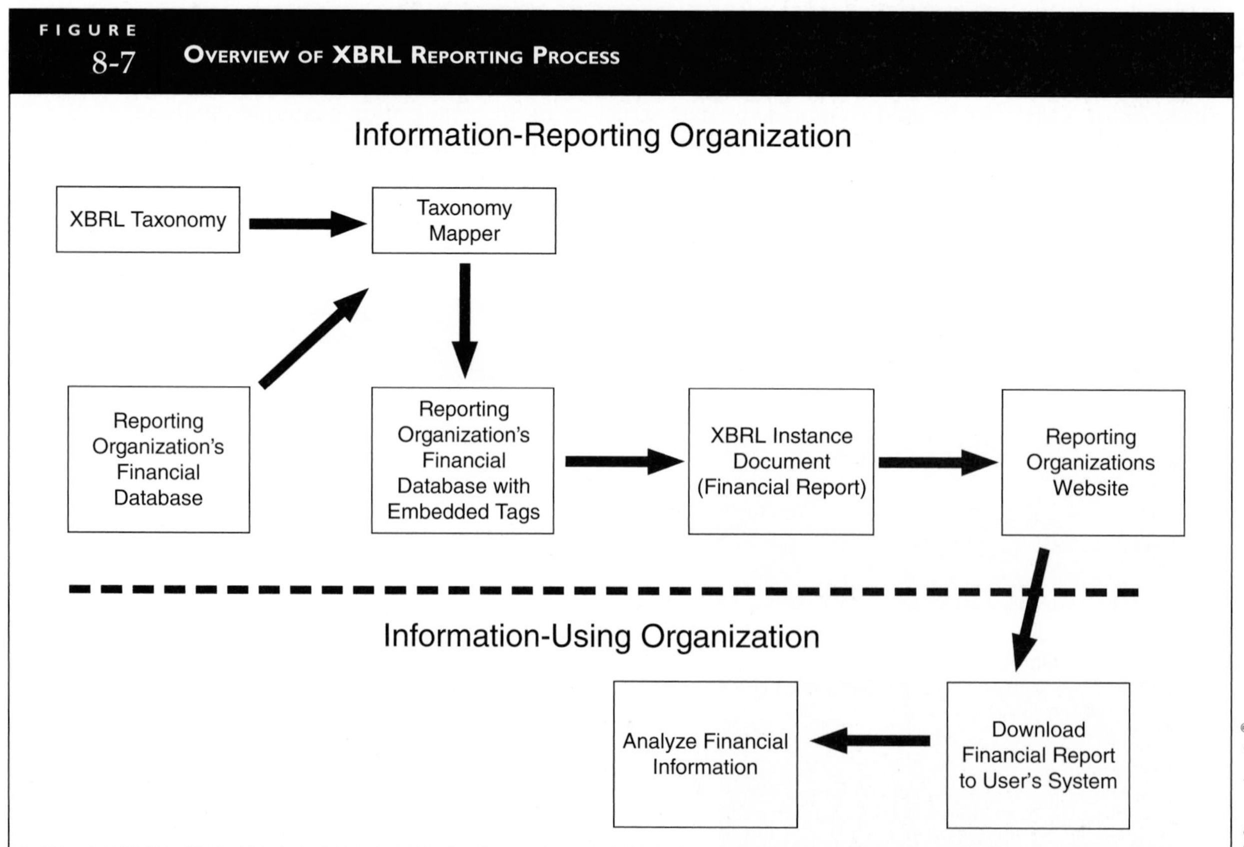

2 This illustration is based on an example prepared by Charles Hoffman, member of the XBRL Steering Committee Specification Working Group, with assistance from Neal Hannon, XBRL Steering Committee Education co-chair.

FIGURE 8-8 Internal Corporate Database

qryMappedTrialBalance : Select Query

FullAccount	TrialBalanceDate	Amount	AccountDescription
000-1100-00	5/31/2015	$608,637.31	Cash - Operating Account
000-1101-00	5/31/2015	$8,957.84	Cash in Bank - Canada
000-1102-00	5/31/2015	$18,302.17	Cash in Bank - Australia
000-1103-00	5/31/2015	$6,007.94	Cash in Bank - New Zealand
000-1104-00	5/31/2015	$7,909.80	Cash in Bank - Germany
000-1105-00	5/31/2015	$12,697.77	Cash in Bank - United Kingdom
000-1106-00	5/31/2015	$7,501.90	Cash in Bank - South Africa
000-1107-00	5/31/2015	$6,963.24	Cash in Bank - Singapore
000-1110-00	5/31/2015	$139,080.67	Cash - Payroll
000-1120-00	5/31/2015	$345.32	Cash - Flex Benefits Program
000-1130-00	5/31/2015	$319.54	Petty Cash
000-1140-00	5/31/2015	$16,316.12	Savings
000-1200-00	5/31/2015	$1,740,867.12	Accounts Receivable
000-1205-00	5/31/2015	$3,871.03	Sales Discounts Available
000-1210-00	5/31/2015	($45,963.30)	Allowance for Doubtful Accounts
000-1220-01	5/31/2015	$22,500.00	Credit Card Receivable-American Express
000-1230-00	5/31/2015	$250.00	Interest Receivable
000-1240-00	5/31/2015	$5,000.00	Notes Receivable
000-1260-00	5/31/2015	$250.00	Employee Advances
000-1271-00	5/31/2015	$26,757.58	Accounts Receivable - Canada
000-1272-00	5/31/2015	$11,164.46	Accounts Receivables - Australia
000-1273-00	5/31/2015	$9,381.79	Accounts Receivable - New Zealand
000-1274-00	5/31/2015	$2,716.40	Accounts Receivable - Germany

Record: 1 of 231

This illustration is based on an example prepared by Charles Hoffman, member of the XBRL Steering Committee Specification Working Group, with assistance from Neal Hannon, XBRL Steering Committee Education co-chair.

FIGURE 8-9 GL TO TAXONOMY MAPPER

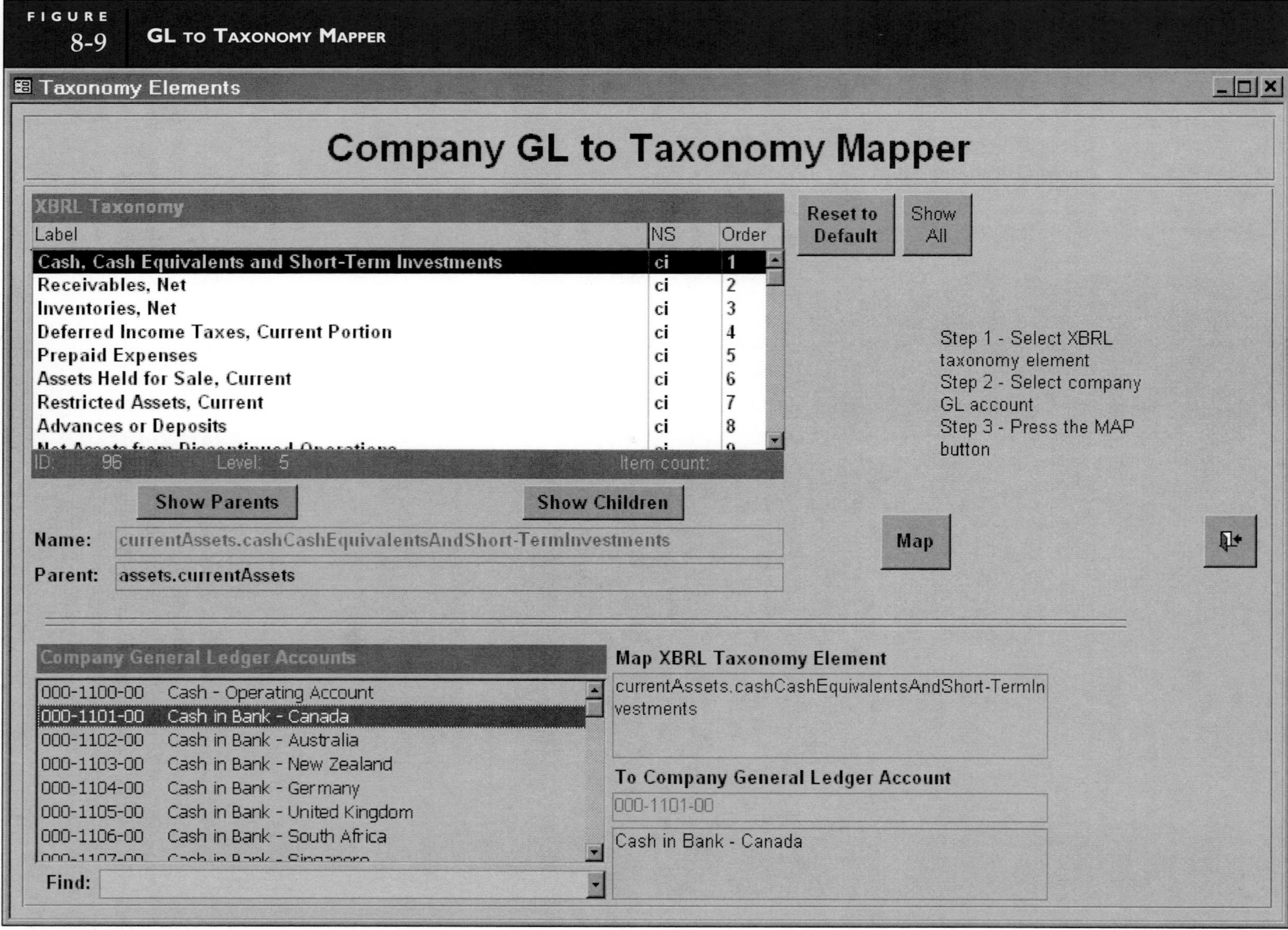

This illustration is based on an example prepared by Charles Hoffman, member of the XBRL Steering Committee Specification Working Group, with assistance from Neal Hannon, XBRL Steering Committee Education co-chair.

FIGURE 8-10 DATABASE STRUCTURE WITH XBRL TAG

qryMappedTrialBalance : Select Query

FullAccount	TrialBalanceDate	Amount	AccountDescription	TaxonomyElement
000-1100-00	5/31/2015	$608,637.31	Cash - Operating Account	cashAndCashEquivalents.cash
000-1101-00	5/31/2015	$8,957.84	Cash in Bank - Canada	currentAssets.cashCashEquivalentsAndShortTermInvestments
000-1102-00	5/31/2015	$18,302.17	Cash in Bank - Australia	currentAssets.cashCashEquivalentsAndShortTermInvestments
000-1103-00	5/31/2015	$6,007.94	Cash in Bank - New Zealand	currentAssets.cashCashEquivalentsAndShortTermInvestments
000-1104-00	5/31/2015	$7,909.80	Cash in Bank - Germany	currentAssets.cashCashEquivalentsAndShortTermInvestments
000-1105-00	5/31/2015	$12,697.77	Cash in Bank - United Kingdom	currentAssets.cashCashEquivalentsAndShortTermInvestments
000-1106-00	5/31/2015	$7,501.90	Cash in Bank - South Africa	currentAssets.cashCashEquivalentsAndShortTermInvestments
000-1107-00	5/31/2015	$6,963.24	Cash in Bank - Singapore	currentAssets.cashCashEquivalentsAndShortTermInvestments
000-1110-00	5/31/2015	$139,080.67	Cash - Payroll	currentAssets.cashCashEquivalentsAndShortTermInvestments
000-1120-00	5/31/2015	$345.32	Cash - Flex Benefits Program	currentAssets.cashCashEquivalentsAndShortTermInvestments
000-1130-00	5/31/2015	$319.54	Petty Cash	currentAssets.cashCashEquivalentsAndShortTermInvestments
000-1140-00	5/31/2015	$16,316.12	Savings	currentAssets.cashCashEquivalentsAndShortTermInvestments
000-1200-00	5/31/2015	$1,740,867.12	Accounts Receivable	accountsReceivableTradeNet.accountsReceivableTradeGross
000-1205-00	5/31/2015	$3,871.03	Sales Discounts Available	accountsReceivableTradeNet.allowanceForDoubtfulAccounts
000-1210-00	5/31/2015	($45,963.30)	Allowance for Doubtful Accounts	accountsReceivableTradeNet.allowanceForDoubtfulAccounts
000-1220-01	5/31/2015	$22,500.00	Credit Card Receivable-American Express	accountsReceivableTradeNet.allowanceForDoubtfulAccounts
000-1230-00	5/31/2015	$250.00	Interest Receivable	receivablesNet.otherReceivablesNet
000-1240-00	5/31/2015	$5,000.00	Notes Receivable	receivablesNet.notesReceivableNet
000-1260-00	5/31/2015	$250.00	Employee Advances	relatedPartyReceivablesNet.employeeReceivablesNet
000-1271-00	5/31/2015	$26,757.58	Accounts Receivable - Canada	currentAssets.receivablesNet
000-1272-00	5/31/2015	$11,164.46	Accounts Receivables - Australia	currentAssets.receivablesNet

Record: 1 of 231

This illustration is based on an example prepared by Charles Hoffman, member of the XBRL Steering Committee Specification Working Group, with assistance from Neal Hannon, XBRL Steering Committee Education co-chair.

FIGURE 8-11 XBRL INSTANCE DOCUMENT

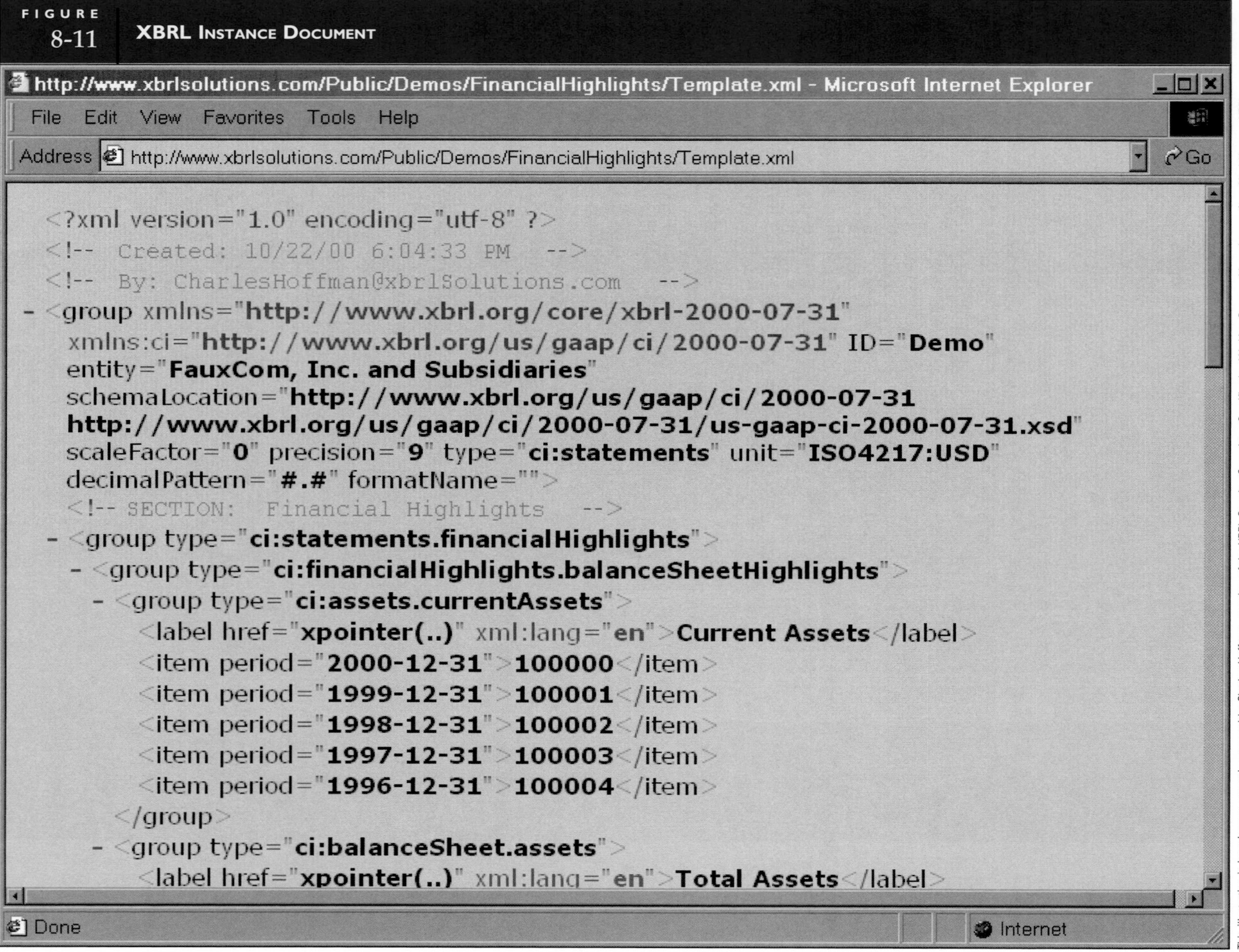

This illustration is based on an example prepared by Charles Hoffman, member of the XBRL Steering Committee Specification Working Group, with assistance from Neal Hannon, XBRL Steering Committee Education co-chair.

The next step is to cross-reference each account in the reporting organization's general ledger to an appropriate XBRL taxonomy element (tag). Figure 8-8 presents part of a hypothetical company's internal database.[3] This snapshot shows various GL accounts and their values. Currently, these data are organized and labeled according to the reporting company's internal needs and conventions. To make the data useful to outsiders and comparable with other firms, they need to be organized, labeled, and reported in a manner that all XBRL users generally accept. This involves mapping the organization's internal data to XBRL taxonomy elements.

The mapping process is accomplished using a simple tool such as Taxonomy Mapper, pictured in Figure 8-9.[4] Note how the XBRL tag labeled Cash, Cash Equivalents, and Short-Term Investments is mapped to the database account labeled Cash in Bank-Canada.

Once the mapping process is complete, each database record will contain a stored tag as depicted by the Taxonomy Element field in Figure 8-10.

Data mapping needs to be done only once, but the embedded tags are used whenever the data are placed in the XBRL format for dissemination to outsiders. This allows business entities to provide expanded financial information frequently and instantaneously to interested parties. Furthermore, companies that use native-XBRL database technology[5] internally as their primary information storage platform can further speed up the process of reporting. Users of such financial data (e.g., investors and analysts) can readily import XBRL documents into internal databases and analysis tools to greatly facilitate their decision-making processes.

From this new database structure, computer programs that recognize and interpret the tags associated with the data attributes can generate **XBRL instance documents** (the actual financial reports). Figure 8-11 presents an example of an instance document.[6]

The XBRL instance document can now be published and made available to users. The document can be placed on an intranet server for internal use, it can be placed on a private extranet for limited dissemination to customers or trading partners, or it can be placed on the Internet for public dissemination. In its current state, the instance document is computer-readable for analysis and processing. To make it more human-readable, HTML layout rules can be provided in a separate style sheet that web browsers use to present the XBRL information in a visually appealing manner.

THE CURRENT STATE OF XBRL REPORTING

All members of the financial reporting community should be aware of XBRL because it is an important information exchange technology. In the near future, XBRL will likely be the primary vehicle for delivering business reports to investors and regulators. Recent progress toward that end has been substantial both in the United States and internationally. Some of these developments are summarized here:

- Since October 2005, U.S. banking regulators have required quarterly "Call Reports" to be filed in XBRL. This requirement impacts more than 8,000 banks.
- In April 2005, the SEC began a voluntary financial reporting program that allows registrants to supplement their required filings with exhibits using XBRL.
- In September 2006, the SEC announced its new electronic reporting system to receive XBRL filings. The new system is called IDEA, short for Interactive Data Electronic Application.
- In May 2008, the SEC issued rules requiring large publicly held companies to adopt XBRL by December 15 to meet financial reporting requirements.
- Comparable developments to encourage or require XBRL have taken place internationally. Since early 2003, the Tokyo Stock Exchange has accepted XBRL information. In 2007,

3 http://www.xbrlsolutions.com.

4 Ibid.

5 As opposed to the use of standard databases such as Oracle or Sybase.

6 http://www.xbrlsolutions.com.

the Canadian Securities Administrators (CSA) established a voluntary program to help the Canadian marketplace gain practical knowledge in preparing, filing, and using XBRL information. Regulators in China, Spain, the Netherlands, and the United Kingdom are requiring certain companies to use XBRL.

In addition, the use of XBRL will facilitate fulfillment of legal requirements stipulated in the Sarbanes-Oxley Act, which was passed in response to widespread concern and skepticism about financial reporting standards. In particular, XBRL can play a role in facilitating earlier reporting of financial statements required under SOX legislation.

Controlling the GL/FRS

Sarbanes-Oxley legislation requires that management design and implement controls over the financial reporting process. This includes the transaction processing systems that feed data into the FRS. In previous chapters we studied control techniques necessary for the various transaction systems. Here we will examine only the controls that relate to the FRS. The potential risks to the FRS include:

1. A defective audit trail.
2. Unauthorized access to the general ledger.
3. GL accounts that are out of balance with subsidiary accounts.
4. Incorrect GL account balances because of unauthorized or incorrect journal vouchers.

If not controlled, these risks may result in misstated financial statements and other reports, thus misleading users of this information. The potential consequences are litigation, significant financial loss for the firm, and sanctions specified by SOX legislation.

COSO CONTROL ISSUES

This discussion of GL/FRS control activities follows the COSO framework, which by now is familiar to you. We begin with a review of the six categories of physical controls; this is followed by a brief examination of relevant IT application controls.

Transaction Authorization

The journal voucher is the document that authorizes an entry to the general ledger. Journal vouchers have numerous sources, such as the cash receipts processing, sales order processing, and the financial reporting group. It is vital to the integrity of the accounting records that the journal vouchers be properly authorized by a responsible manager at the source department.

Segregation of Duties

In previous chapters, we have seen how the general ledger provides verification control for the accounting process. To do so, the task of updating the general ledger must be separate from all accounting and asset custody responsibility within the organization. Therefore, individuals with access authority to GL accounts should not:

1. have record-keeping responsibility for special journals or subsidiary ledgers.
2. prepare journal vouchers.
3. have custody of physical assets.

Notice that in Figure 8-5, transactions are authorized, processed, and posted directly to the general ledger. To compensate for this potential risk, the system should provide end users and GL departments with detailed listings of journal voucher and account activity reports. These documents advise users of the automated actions taken by the system so that errors and unusual events, which warrant investigation, can be identified.

Access Controls

Unauthorized access to the GL accounts can result in errors, fraud, and misrepresentations in financial statements. SOX legislation explicitly addresses this area of risk by requiring organizations to implement controls that limit database access to authorized individuals only. A number of IT general controls designed to serve this purpose are presented in Chapter 16.

Accounting Records

The audit trail is a record of the path that a transaction takes through the input, processing, and output phases of transaction processing. This involves a network of documents, journals, and ledgers designed to ensure that a transaction can be accurately traced through the system from initiation to final disposition. An audit trail facilitates error prevention and correction when the data files are logically organized. Also, the general ledger and other files that constitute the audit trail should be detailed and rich enough to (1) provide the ability to answer inquiries, for example, from customers or vendors; (2) be able to reconstruct files if they are completely or partially destroyed; (3) provide historical data required by auditors; (4) fulfill government regulations; and (5) provide a means for preventing, detecting, and correcting errors.

Independent Verification

Previous chapters have portrayed the general ledger function as an independent verification step within the accounting information system. The FRS produces two operational reports—journal voucher listing and the GL change report—that provide proof of the accuracy of this process. The **journal voucher listing** provides relevant details about each journal voucher posted to the GL. The **general ledger change report** presents the effects of journal voucher postings to the GL accounts. Figures 8-12 and 8-13 present examples of these reports.

FIGURE 8-12 JOURNAL VOUCHER LISTING

Journal Voucher Listing

Date	JV Num	Description	Account Number	Debit	Credit
6/26/15	JV6 - 01	Cash receipts	10100	$109,000	
			20100		$50,000
			10600		$44,000
			10900		$15,000
6/26/15	JV6 - 02	Credit sales	20100	$505,000	
			50200		$505,000
6/26/15	JV6 - 03	Inventory usage	30300	$410,000	
			17100		$410,000
•	•	•	•	•	•
•	•	•	•	•	•
•	•	•	•	•	•
6/26/15	JV - 12	Cash disbursements	90310	$102,100	
			10100		$102,100
				$6,230,000	$6,230,000

FIGURE 8-13 GENERAL LEDGER CHANGE REPORT

General Ledger Change Report

Date	Acct	Description	JV Ref	Balance	Debits	Credits	Net Change	New Balance
6/26/15	10100	Cash receipts	JV6 - 01 JV6 - 12	$1,902,300	$109,000	$102,100	$6,900	$1,909,200
6/26/15	20100	Cash receipts Credit sales	JV6 - 01 JV6 - 02	$2,505,600	$505,000	$50,000	$455,000	$2,960,600
•	•	•	•	•	•	•	•	•
•	•	•	•	•	•	•	•	•
•	•	•	•	•	•	•	•	•
6/26/15	90310	Cash disburs.	JV6 - 12	$703,500	$102,100		$102,100	$805,600
6/26/15	17100	Inven. usage	JV6 - 03	$1,600,500		$410,000	$410,000	$2,010,500

Control Totals:

	Debits	Credits
Previous Balance	$23,789,300	$23,789,300
Total Net Change	$6,230,000	$6,230,000
Current Balance	$30,019,300	$30,019,300

IT Application Controls

The IT application controls presented in previous chapters apply also to the GL/FRS. Input controls in the form of edits and check digits ensure that data (journal vouchers) entering the GL are free from data entry errors that can corrupt general ledger accounts. Process controls, such as error messages, passwords, and multilevel security, serve the same objectives in the GLS as they do in transaction-processing applications. Likewise, output controls need to be in place to ensure that financial statements and other management reports produced by the FRS arrive at their intended destinations.

One process control issue, however, pertaining to automated direct postings to the GL, is specific to the GL/FRS and deserves additional comment. Real-time transaction posting to the GL bypasses the traditional human reconciliation and review of journal vouchers. This approach provides some benefits but also inserts risk into the financial reporting process. By eliminating the human element from GL posting activities, the potential for certain errors are reduced and efficiency of operations is improved. The risk lies in the potential for application logic errors that post transactions to the GL incorrectly with wrong amounts and/or to the wrong accounts. Such errors would be systematic (not isolated as human mistakes tend to be) and could have widespread and devastating implications for the FRS. Ensuring application integrity through effective systems development and program change procedures is essential to reducing this risk and is the topic of Chapter 17.

INTERNAL CONTROL IMPLICATIONS OF XBRL

Although the potential benefits of XBRL and associated web technologies have been extensively researched, less attention has been given to the potential control implications of using XBRL. Three specific areas of concern are discussed here.

TAXONOMY CREATION. Taxonomy may be generated incorrectly, which results in an incorrect mapping between data and taxonomy elements that could result in material misrepresentation of financial data. Controls must be designed and put in place to ensure the correct generation of XBRL taxonomies.

TAXONOMY MAPPING ERROR. The process of mapping the internal database accounts to the taxonomy tags needs to be controlled. Correctly generated XBRL tags may be incorrectly assigned to internal database accounts, resulting in material misrepresentation of financial data.

VALIDATION OF INSTANCE DOCUMENTS. As noted, once the mapping is complete and tags have been stored in the internal database, XBRL instance documents (reports) can be generated. Independent verification procedures need to be established to validate the instance documents to ensure that appropriate taxonomy and tags have been applied before posting to a web server.

The Management Reporting System

Management reporting is often called discretionary reporting because it is not mandated, as is financial reporting. One could take issue with the term *discretionary*, however, and argue that an effective management reporting system (MRS) is mandated by SOX legislation, which requires that all public companies monitor and report on the effectiveness of internal controls over financial reporting. Indeed, management reporting has long been recognized as a critical element of an organization's internal control structure. An MRS that directs management's attention to problems on a timely basis promotes effective management and thus supports the organization's business objectives.

Factors That Influence the MRS

Designing an effective MRS requires an understanding of the information that managers need to deal with the problems they face. This section examines several topics that provide insight into factors that influence management information needs. These are management principles; management function, level, and decision type; problem structure; types of management reports; responsibility accounting; and behavioral considerations.

MANAGEMENT PRINCIPLES

Management principles provide insight into management information needs. The principles that most directly influence the MRS are formalization of tasks, responsibility and authority, span of control, and management by exception.

Formalization of Tasks

The **formalization of tasks** principle suggests that management should structure the firm around the tasks it performs rather than around individuals with unique skills. Under this principle, organizational areas are subdivided into tasks that represent full-time job positions. Each position must have clearly defined limits of responsibility.

The purpose of formalization of tasks is to avoid an organizational structure in which the organization's performance, stability, and continued existence depend on specific individuals. The **organizational chart** in Figure 8-14 shows some typical job positions in a manufacturing firm.

Although a firm's most valuable resource is its employees, it does not own the resource. Sooner or later, key individuals leave and take their skills with them. By formalizing tasks, the firm can more easily recruit individuals to fill standard positions left open by those who leave. In addition, the formalization of tasks promotes internal control. With employee responsibilities formalized and clearly specified, management can construct an organization that avoids assigning incompatible tasks to an individual.

IMPLICATIONS FOR THE MRS. Formalizing the tasks of the firm allows formal specification of the information needed to support the tasks. Thus, when a personnel change occurs, the information the new employee will need is essentially the same as for his or her predecessor. The information system must focus on the task, not the individual performing the task. Otherwise, information

FIGURE 8-14 ORGANIZATIONAL CHART FOR A MANUFACTURING FIRM

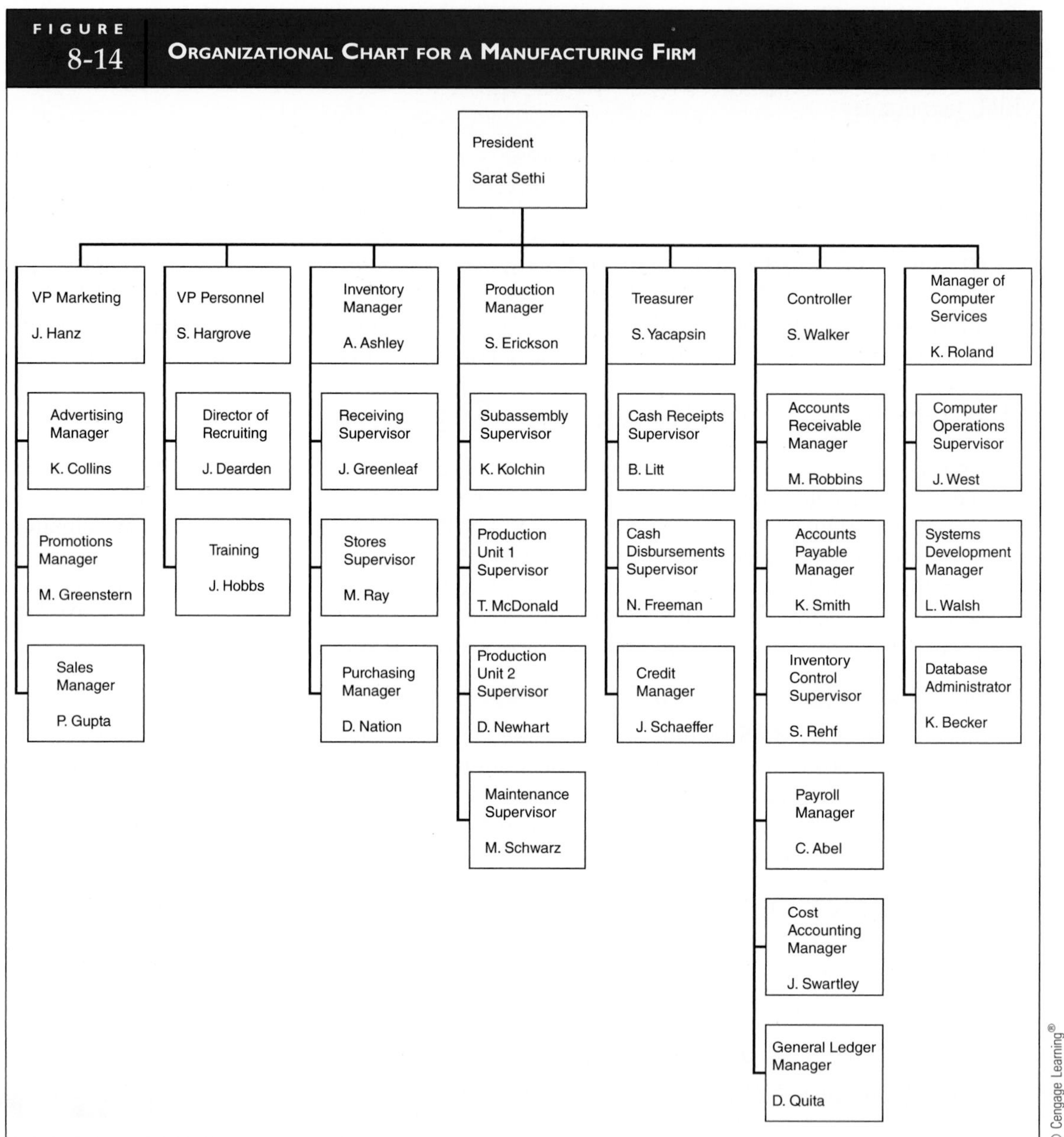

requirements would need to be reassessed with the appointment of each new individual to the position. Also, internal control is strengthened by restricting information based on need as defined by the task, rather than the whim or desire of the user.

Responsibility and Authority

The principle of **responsibility** refers to an individual's obligation to achieve desired results. Responsibility is closely related to the principle of authority. If a manager delegates responsibility to a subordinate, he or she must also grant the subordinate the **authority** to make decisions within the limits of that responsibility. In a business organization, managers delegate responsibility and authority downward through the organizational hierarchy from superior to subordinates.

IMPLICATIONS FOR THE MRS. The principles of responsibility and authority define the vertical reporting channels of the firm through which information flows. The manager's location in the reporting channel influences the scope and detail of the information reported. Managers at higher levels usually require more summarized information. Managers at lower levels receive information that is more detailed. In designing a reporting structure, the analyst must consider the manager's position in the reporting channel.

Span of Control

A manager's **span of control** refers to the number of subordinates directly under his or her control. The size of the span has an impact on the organization's physical structure. A firm with a narrow span of control has fewer subordinates reporting directly to managers. These firms tend to have tall, narrow structures with several layers of management. Firms with broad spans of control (more subordinates reporting to each manager) tend to have wide structures, with fewer levels of management. Figure 8-15 illustrates the relationship between span of control and organizational structure. Organizational behavior research suggests that wider spans of control are preferable because they allow more employee autonomy in decision making. This may translate into better employee morale and increased motivation. An important consideration in setting the span of control is the nature of the task. The more routine and structured the task, the more subordinates one manager can control. Therefore, routine tasks tend to be associated with a broad span of control. Less structured or highly technical tasks often require a good deal of management participation on task-related problems. This close interaction reduces the manager's span of control.

IMPLICATIONS FOR THE MRS. Managers with narrow spans of control are closely involved with the details of the operation and with specific decisions. Broad spans of control remove managers from these details. These managers delegate more of their decision-making authority to their subordinates. The different management approaches require different information. Managers with narrow spans of control require detailed reports. Managers with broad control responsibilities operate most effectively with summarized information.

Management by Exception

The principle of **management by exception** suggests that managers should limit their attention to potential problem areas (i.e., exceptions) rather than being involved with every activity or decision. Managers thus maintain control without being overwhelmed by the details.

IMPLICATIONS FOR THE MRS. Managers need information that identifies operations or resources at risk of going out of control. Reports should support management by exception by focusing

FIGURE 8-15 IMPACT OF SPAN OF CONTROL ON ORGANIZATIONAL STRUCTURE

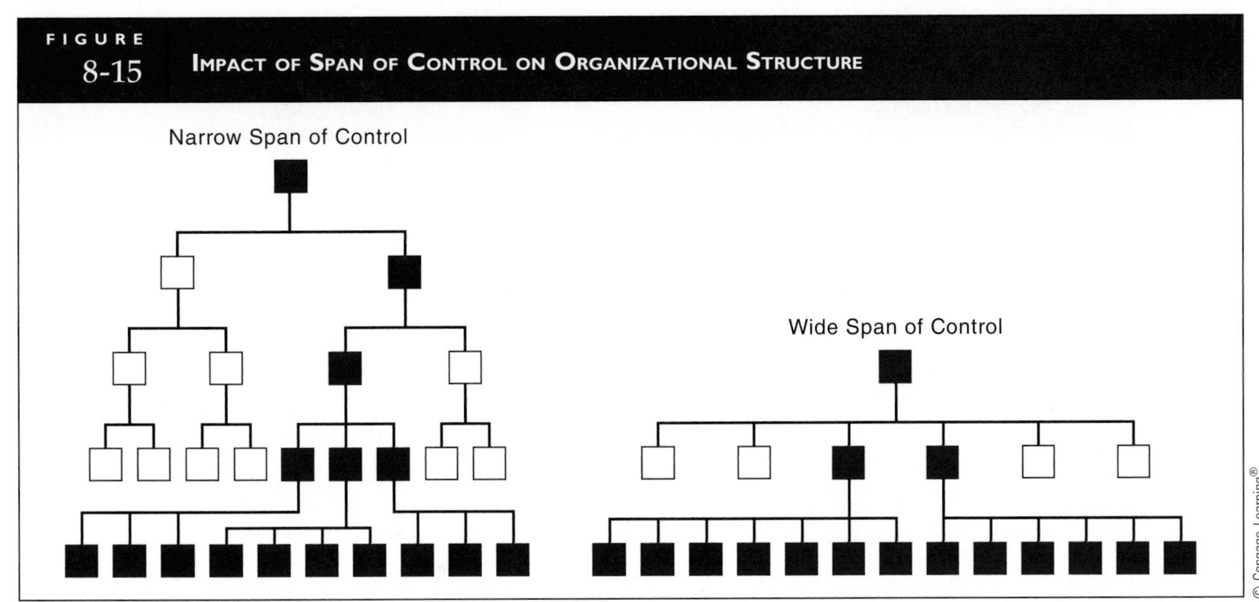

on changes in key factors that are symptomatic of potential problems. Unnecessary details that may draw attention away from important facts should be excluded from reports. For example, an inventory exception report may be used to identify items of inventory that turn over more slowly or go out of stock more frequently than normal. Management attention must be focused on these exceptions. The majority of inventory items that fluctuate within normal levels should not be included in the report.

MANAGEMENT FUNCTION, LEVEL, AND DECISION TYPE

The management functions of planning and control have a profound effect on the MRS. The planning function is concerned with making decisions about the future activities of the organization. Planning can be long range or short range. Long-range planning usually encompasses a period of between one and five years, but this varies among industries. For example, a public utility may plan 15 years ahead in the construction of a new power plant, while a computer manufacturer deals in a time frame of only one or two years in the planning of new products. Long-range planning involves a variety of tasks, including setting the goals and objectives of the firm, planning the growth and optimum size of the firm, and deciding on the degree of diversification among the firm's products.

Short-term planning involves the **implementation** of specific plans that are needed to achieve the objectives of the long-range plan. Examples include planning the marketing and promotion for a new product, preparing a production schedule for the month, and providing department heads with budgetary goals for the next three months.

The control function ensures that the activities of the firm conform to the plan. This entails evaluating the operational process (or individual) against a predetermined standard and, when necessary, taking corrective action. Effective control takes place in the present time frame and is triggered by feedback information that advises the manager about the status of the operation being controlled.

Planning and control decisions are frequently classified into four categories: strategic planning, tactical planning, managerial control, and operational control. Figure 8-16 relates these decisions to managerial levels.

STRATEGIC PLANNING DECISIONS

Figure 8-16 shows that top-level managers make **strategic planning decisions**, including:

- Setting the goals and objectives of the firm.
- Determining the scope of business activities, such as desired market share, markets the firm wishes to enter or abandon, the addition of new product lines and the termination of old ones, and merger and acquisition decisions.

FIGURE 8-16 MANAGEMENT LEVEL AND DECISION TYPE

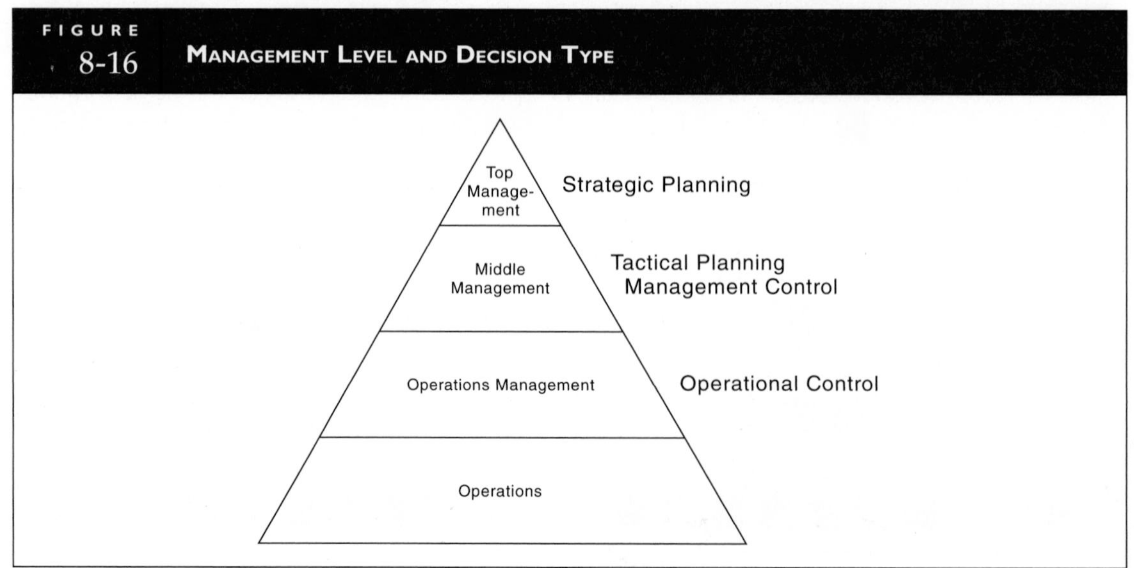

- Determining or modifying the organization's structure.
- Setting the management philosophy.

Strategic planning decisions have the following characteristics:

- They have long-term time frames. Because they deal with the future, managers making strategic decisions require information that supports forecasting.
- They require highly summarized information. Strategic decisions focus on general trends rather than detail-specific activities.
- They tend to be nonrecurring. Strategic decisions are usually one-time events. As a result, there is little historical information available to support the specific decision.
- Strategic decisions are associated with a high degree of uncertainty. The decision maker must rely on insight and intuition. Judgment is often central to the success of the decision.
- They are broad in scope and have a profound impact on the firm. Once made, strategic decisions permanently affect the organization at all levels.
- Strategic decisions require external as well as internal sources of information.

Tactical Planning Decisions

Tactical planning decisions are subordinate to strategic decisions and are made by middle management (see Figure 8-16). These decisions are of shorter term, are more specific, are recurring, have more certain outcomes, and have a lesser impact on the firm than strategic decisions. For example, assume that the president of a manufacturing firm makes the strategic decision to increase sales and production by 100,000 units over the prior year's level. One tactical decision that must result from this is setting the monthly production schedule to accomplish the strategic goal.

Management Control Decisions

Management control involves motivating managers in all functional areas to use resources, including materials, personnel, and financial assets, as productively as possible. The supervising manager compares the performance of his or her subordinate manager to pre-established standards. If the subordinate does not meet the standard, the supervisor takes corrective action. When the subordinate meets or exceeds expectations, he or she may be rewarded.

Uncertainty surrounds **management control decisions** because it is difficult to separate the manager's performance from that of his or her operational unit. We often lack both the criteria for specifying management control standards and the objective techniques for measuring performance. For example, assume that a firm's top management places its most effective and competent middle manager in charge of a business segment that is performing poorly. The manager's task is to revitalize the operations of the unit, and doing so requires a massive infusion of resources. The segment will operate in the red for some time until it establishes a foothold in the market. Measuring the performance of this manager in the short term may be difficult. Traditional measures of profit, such as return on investment (which measures the performance of the operational unit itself), would not really reflect the manager's performance. We shall examine this topic in more depth later in the chapter.

Operational Control Decisions

Operational control ensures that the firm operates in accordance with pre-established criteria. Figure 8-16 shows that operations managers exercise operational control. **Operational control decisions** are narrower and more focused than tactical decisions because they are concerned with the routine tasks of operations. Operational control decisions are more structured than management control decisions, more dependent on details than planning decisions, and have a shorter time frame than tactical or strategic decisions. These decisions are associated with a fairly high degree of certainty. In other words, identified symptoms tend to be good indicators of the root problem, and corrective actions tend to be obvious. This degree of certainty makes it easier to

TABLE 8-1 **Classification of Decision Types by Decision Characteristics**

	DECISION TYPE			
Decision Characteristic	**Strategic Planning**	**Tactical Planning**	**Management Control**	**Operational Control**
Time frame	Long term	Medium	Medium	Short
Scope	High impact	Medium impact	Lowest impact	Lowest impact
Level of details	Highly summarized	Detailed	Moderately summarized	Highly Detailed
Recurrence	Nonrecurring	Periodic recurring	Periodic recurring	Frequent recurring
Certainty	Uncertain	Highly certain	Uncertain	Highly certain

establish meaningful criteria for measuring performance. Operational control decisions have three basic elements: setting standards, evaluating performance, and taking corrective action.

STANDARDS. Standards are pre-established levels of performance that managers believe are attainable. Standards apply to all aspects of operations, such as sales volume, quality control, over production, costs for inventory items, material usage in the production of products, and labor costs in production. Once established, these standards become the basis for evaluating performance.

PERFORMANCE EVALUATION. The decision maker compares the performance of the operation in question against the standard. The difference between the two is the **variance**. For example, a price variance for an item of inventory is the difference between the expected price—the standard—and the price actually paid. If the actual price is greater than the standard, the variance is said to be unfavorable. If the actual price is less than the standard, the variance is favorable.

TAKING CORRECTIVE ACTION. After comparing the performance to the standard, the manager takes action to remedy any out-of-control condition. Recall from Chapter 3, however, that we must apply extreme caution when taking corrective action. An inappropriate response to performance measures may have undesirable results. For example, to achieve a favorable price variance, the purchasing agent may pursue the low-price vendors of raw materials and sacrifice quality. If the lower-quality raw materials result in excessive quantities being used in production because of higher-than-normal waste, the firm will experience an unfavorable material usage variance. The unfavorable usage variance may completely offset the favorable price variance to create an unfavorable total variance.

Table 8-1 classifies strategic planning, tactical planning, management control, and operational control decisions in terms of time frame, scope, level of details, recurrence, and certainty.

PROBLEM STRUCTURE

The structure of a problem reflects how well the decision maker understands the problem. Structure has three elements.[7]

1. Data—the values used to represent factors that are relevant to the problem.
2. Procedures—the sequence of steps or decision rules used in solving the problem.
3. Objectives—the results the decision maker desires to attain by solving the problem.

---

7 Adapted from F. L. Luconi, T. W. Malone, and M. S. Scott Morton, “Expert Systems: The Next Challenge for Managers,” *Sloan Management Review* (Summer 1986). Reprinted in P. Gray, W. R. King, E. R. McLean, and H. J. Watson, *MOIS: Management of Information Systems* (Chicago: Dryden Press, 1989), 69–84.

When all three elements are known with certainty, the problem is structured. Payroll calculation is an example of a **structured problem**:

1. We can identify the data for this calculation with certainty (hours worked, hourly rate, withholdings, tax rate, and so on).
2. Payroll procedures are known with certainty:

$$\text{Gross pay} = \text{Hours worked} \times \text{Pay rate}$$

$$\text{Net pay} = \text{Gross pay} - \text{Taxes} - \text{Withholdings}$$

3. The objective of payroll is to discharge the firm's financial obligation to its employees.

Structured problems do not present unique situations to the decision maker and, because their information requirements can be anticipated, they are well suited for traditional data processing techniques. In effect, the designer who specifies the procedures and codes the programs solves the problem.

Unstructured Problems

Problems are unstructured when any of the three characteristics identified previously are not known with certainty. In other words, an **unstructured problem** is one for which we have no precise solution techniques. Either the data requirements are uncertain, the procedures are not specified, or the solution objectives have not been fully developed. Such a problem is normally complex and engages the decision maker in a unique situation. In these situations, the systems analyst cannot fully anticipate user information needs, rendering traditional data processing techniques ineffective.

Figure 8-17 illustrates the relationship between problem structure and organizational level. We see from the figure that lower levels of management deal more with fully structured problems, whereas upper management deals with unstructured problems. Middle-level managers tend to work with partially structured problems. Keep in mind that these structural classifications are generalizations. Top managers also deal with some highly structured problems, and lower-level managers sometimes face problems that lack structure.

Figure 8-17 also shows the use of information systems by different levels of management. The traditional information system deals most effectively with fully structured problems. Therefore, operations management and tactical management receive the greatest benefit from these systems. Because management control and strategic planning decisions lack structure, the managers who make these decisions often do not receive adequate support from traditional systems alone.

FIGURE 8-17 PROBLEM STRUCTURE MANAGEMENT LEVEL AND INFORMATION SYSTEM USAGE

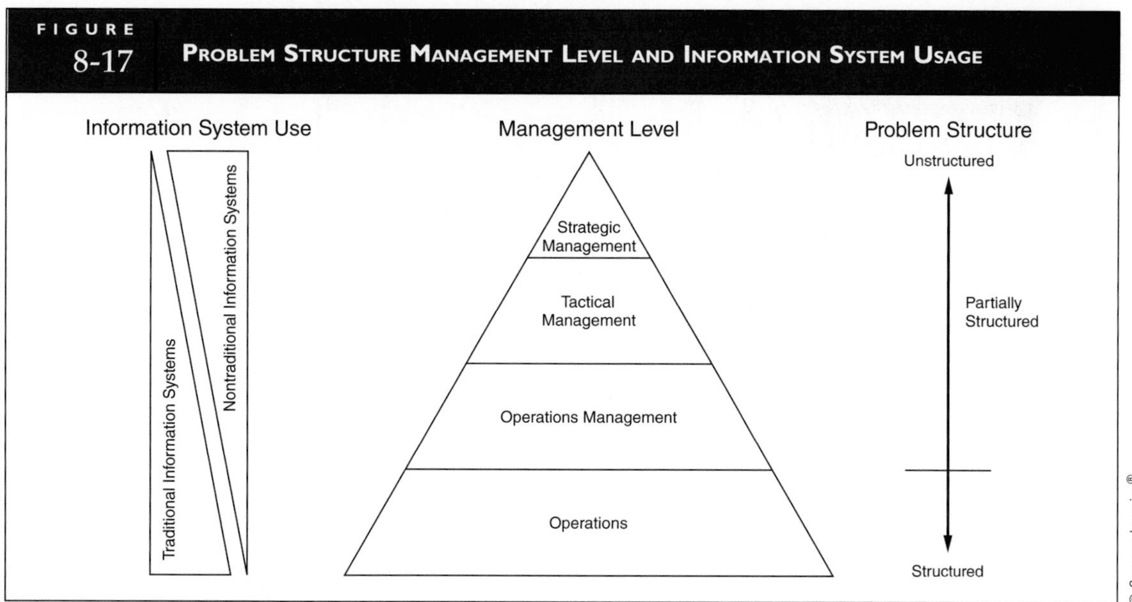

TYPES OF MANAGEMENT REPORTS

Reports are the formal vehicles for conveying information to managers. The term *report* tends to imply a written message presented on sheets of paper. In fact, a **management report** may be a paper document or a digital image displayed on a computer terminal. The report may express information in verbal, numeric, or graphic form, or any combination of these.

Report Objectives

Chapter 1 made the distinction between information and data. Recall that information leads the user to an action. Therefore, to be useful, reports must have **information content**. Their value is the effect they have on users. This is expressed in two general reporting objectives: (1) to reduce the level of uncertainty associated with a problem facing the decision maker and (2) to influence the decision maker's behavior in a positive way. Reports that fail to accomplish these objectives lack information content and have no value. In fact, reliance on such reports may lead to dysfunctional behavior (discussed later). Management reports fall into two broad classes: programmed reports and ad hoc reports.

Programmed Reporting

Programmed reports provide information to solve problems that users have anticipated. There are two subclasses of programmed reports: scheduled reports and on-demand reports. The MRS produces **scheduled reports** according to an established time frame. This could be daily, weekly, quarterly, and so on. Examples of such reports are a daily listing of sales, a weekly payroll action report, and annual financial statements. **On-demand reports** are triggered by events, not by the passage of time. For example, when inventories fall to their pre-established reorder points, the system sends an inventory reorder report to the purchasing agent. Another example is an accounts receivable manager responding to a customer problem over the telephone. The manager can, on demand, display the customer's account history on the computer screen. Note that this query capability is the product of an anticipated need. This is quite different from the ad hoc reports that we discuss later. Table 8-2 lists examples of typical programmed reports and identifies them as scheduled or on-demand.

TABLE 8-2 EXAMPLES OF PROGRAMMED REPORTS

Type of Report	Scheduled	On-Demand
Planning reports		
Financial budgets	X	
Materials requirements reports		X
Sales forecast reports	X	
Production schedules		X
Projected cash flows reports	X	
Control reports		
Cost center reports	X	
Profit center reports	X	
Profitability by line of product	X	
Quality control reports		X
Labor distribution reports	X	
Inventory exception reports		X
Equipment utilization reports	X	

Report Attributes

To be effective, a report must possess the following attributes: relevance, summarization, exception orientation, accuracy, completeness, timeliness, and conciseness. Each of these **report attributes** is discussed in the following section.

RELEVANCE. Each element of information in a report must support the manager's decision. Irrelevancies waste resources and may even be dysfunctional by distracting a manager's attention from the information content of the report.

SUMMARIZATION. Reports should be summarized according to the level of the manager within the organizational hierarchy. In general, the degree of summarization becomes greater as information flows from lower management upward to top management.

EXCEPTION ORIENTATION. Control reports should identify activities that are at risk of going out of control and should ignore activities that are under control. For example, consider a purchasing agent with ordering responsibility for an inventory of 10,000 different items. If the agent received a daily report containing the actual balances of every item, he or she would search through 10,000 items to identify a few that need reordering. An exception-oriented report would identify only those inventory items that have fallen to their reorder levels. From this report, the agent could easily prepare purchase orders.

ACCURACY. Information in reports must be free of material errors. A material error will cause the user to make the wrong decision (to or fail to make a required decision). We often sacrifice accuracy for timely information. In situations that require quick responses, the manager must factor this trade-off into the **decision-making process**.

COMPLETENESS. Information must be as complete as possible. Ideally, no piece of information that is essential to the decision should be missing from the report. Like the attribute of accuracy, we sometimes must sacrifice completeness in favor of timely information.

TIMELINESS. If managers always had time on their side, they may never make bad decisions. However, managers cannot always wait until they have all the facts before they act. Timely information that is sufficiently complete and accurate is more valuable than perfect information that comes too late to use. Therefore, the MRS must provide managers with timely information. Usually, information can be no older than the period to which it pertains. For example, if each week a manager decides on inventory acquisitions based on a weekly inventory status report, the information in the report should be no more than a week old.

CONCISENESS. Information in the report should be presented as concisely as possible. Reports should use coding schemes to represent complex data classifications and provide all the necessary calculations (such as extensions and variances) for the user. In addition, information should be clearly presented with titles for all values.

Ad Hoc Reporting

Managers cannot always anticipate their information needs. This is particularly true for top and middle management. In the dynamic business world, problems arise that require new information on short notice, and there may be insufficient time to write traditional computer programs to produce the required information. In the past, these needs often went unsatisfied. Now database technology provides direct inquiry and report generation capabilities. Managers with limited computer background can quickly produce **ad hoc reports** from a terminal or PC, without the assistance of data processing professionals.

Increases in computing power, point-of-transaction scanners, and continuous reductions in data storage costs have enabled organizations to accumulate massive quantities of raw data. This data resource is now being tapped to support ad hoc reporting needs through a concept known as data mining.

Data mining is the process of selecting, exploring, and modeling large amounts of data to uncover relationships and global patterns that exist in large databases but are hidden among the vast amount of facts. This involves sophisticated techniques such as database queries and artificial intelligence that model real-world phenomena from data collected from a variety of sources, including transaction processing systems, customer history databases, and demographics data from external sources such as credit bureaus. Managers employ two general approaches to data mining: verification and discovery.

The **verification model** uses a drill-down technique to either verify or reject a user's hypothesis. For example, assume a marketing manager needs to identify the best target market, as a subset of the organization's entire customer base, for an ad campaign for a new product. The data mining software will examine the firm's historical data about customer sales and demographic information to reveal comparable sales and the demographic characteristics shared by those purchasers. This subset of the customer base can then be used to focus the promotion campaign.

The **discovery model** uses data mining to discover previously unknown but important information that is hidden within the data. This model employs inductive learning to infer information from detailed data by searching for recurring patterns, trends, and generalizations. This approach is fundamentally different from the verification model in that the data are searched with no specific hypothesis driving the process. For example, a company may apply discovery techniques to identify customer buying patterns and gain a better understanding of customer motivations and behavior.

A central feature of a successful data mining initiative is a **data warehouse** of archived operational data. A data warehouse is a centralized relational database management system that has been designed specifically to meet the needs of data mining. The warehouse contains operational data about current events (within the past 24 hours) as well as events that have transpired over many years. Data are coded and stored in the warehouse in detail and at various degrees of aggregation to facilitate identification of recurring patterns and trends.

Management decision making can be greatly enhanced through data mining, but only if the appropriate data have been identified, collected, and stored in the data warehouse. Because many of the important issues related to data mining and warehousing require an understanding of relational database technology, these topics are examined further in Chapters 9 and 11.

RESPONSIBILITY ACCOUNTING

A large part of management reporting involves **responsibility accounting**. This concept implies that every economic event that affects the organization is the responsibility of and can be traced to an individual manager. The responsibility accounting system personalizes performance by saying to the manager, "This is your original budget, and this is how your performance for the period compares to your budget." Most organizations structure their responsibility reporting system around areas of responsibility in the firm. A fundamental principle of this concept is that responsibility area managers are accountable only for items (costs, revenues, and investments) that they control.

The flow of information in responsibility systems is both downward and upward through the information channels. Figure 8-18 illustrates this pattern. These top-down and bottom-up information flows represent the two phases of responsibility accounting: (1) creating a set of financial performance goals (budgets) pertinent to the manager's responsibilities and (2) reporting and measuring actual performance as compared to these goals.

Setting Financial Goals: The Budget Process

The **budget** process helps management achieve its financial objectives by establishing measurable goals for each organizational segment. This mechanism conveys to the segment managers the standards that senior managers will use for measuring their performance. Budget information flows downward and becomes increasingly detailed as it moves to lower levels of management. Figure 8-19 shows the distribution of budget information through three levels of management.

FIGURE 8-18 UPWARD AND DOWNWARD FLOW OF INFORMATION

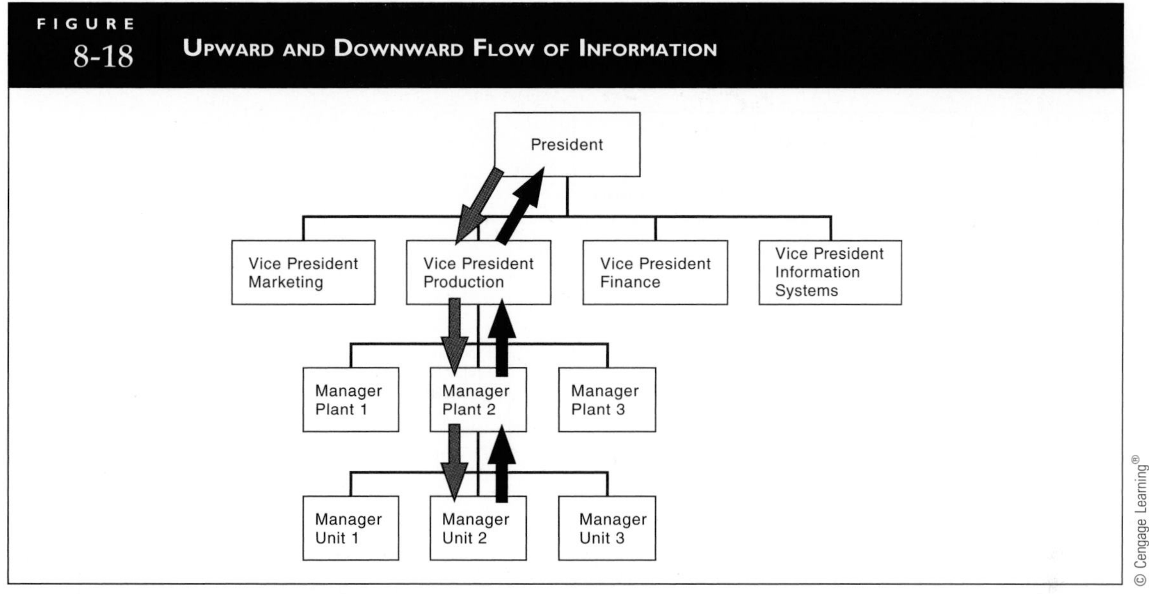

FIGURE 8-19 TOP-DOWN FLOW OF BUDGET INFORMATION

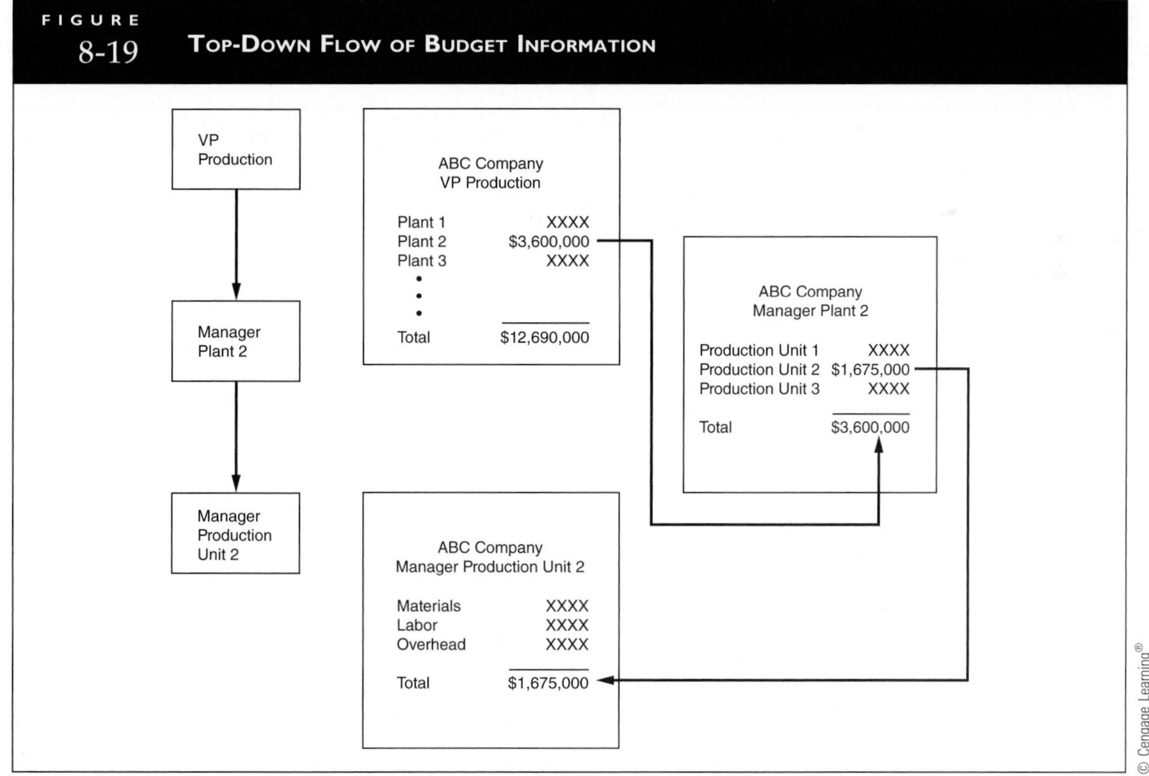

Measuring and Reporting Performance

Performance measurement and reporting take place at each operational segment in the firm. This information flows upward as **responsibility reports** to senior levels of management. Figure 8-20 shows the relationship between levels of responsibility reports. Notice how the information in the reports becomes increasingly summarized at each higher level of management.

FIGURE 8-20 THE BOTTOM-UP FLOW OF PERFORMANCE INFORMATION

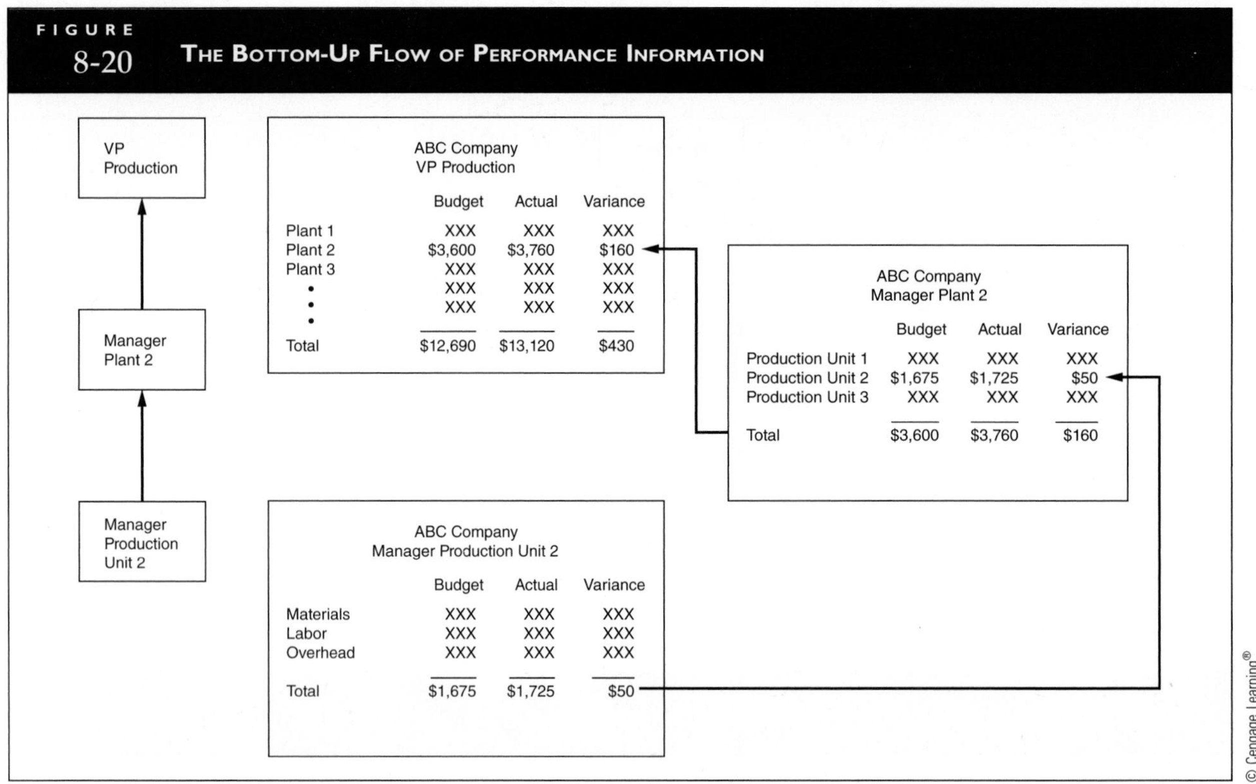

Responsibility Centers

To achieve accountability, business entities frequently organize their operations into units called **responsibility centers**. The most common forms of responsibility centers are cost centers, profit centers, and investment centers.

COST CENTERS. A cost center is an organizational unit with responsibility for cost management within budgetary limits. For example, a production department may be responsible for meeting its production obligation while keeping production costs (labor, materials, and overhead) within the budgeted amount. The performance report for the cost center manager reflects its controllable cost behavior by focusing on budgeted costs, actual costs, and variances from budget. Figure 8-21 shows an example of a cost center performance report. Performance measurements should not consider costs that are outside the manager's control, such as investments in plant equipment or depreciation on the building.

PROFIT CENTERS. A profit center manager has responsibility for both cost control and revenue generation. For example, the local manager of a national department store chain may be responsible for decisions about:

- The items of merchandise to stock in the store.
- The prices to charge.
- The kind of promotional activities for products.
- The level of advertising.
- The size of the staff and the hiring of employees.
- Building maintenance and limited capital improvements.

The performance report for the profit center manager is different from that for the cost center manager. Nevertheless, the reporting emphasis for both should be on controllable items. Figure 8-22 is an

FIGURE 8-21 COST CENTER PERFORMANCE REPORT

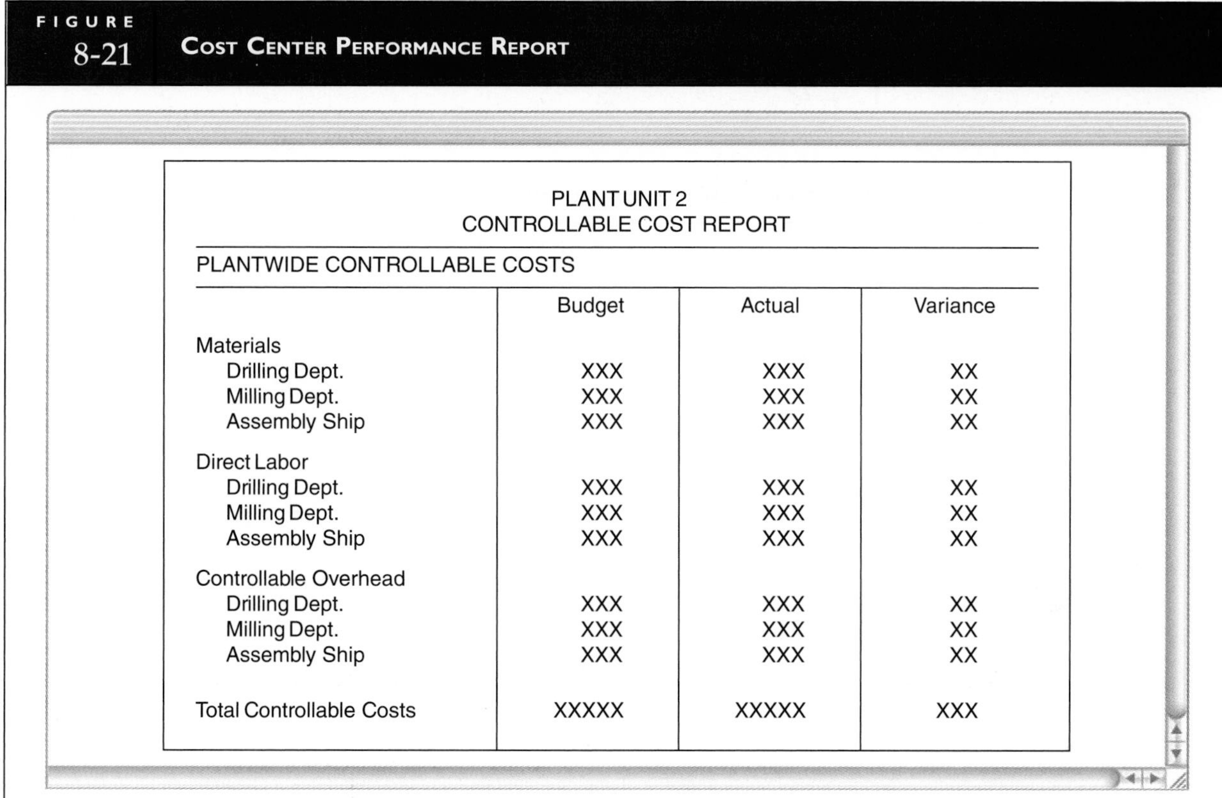

PLANT UNIT 2
CONTROLLABLE COST REPORT

PLANTWIDE CONTROLLABLE COSTS

	Budget	Actual	Variance
Materials			
Drilling Dept.	XXX	XXX	XX
Milling Dept.	XXX	XXX	XX
Assembly Ship	XXX	XXX	XX
Direct Labor			
Drilling Dept.	XXX	XXX	XX
Milling Dept.	XXX	XXX	XX
Assembly Ship	XXX	XXX	XX
Controllable Overhead			
Drilling Dept.	XXX	XXX	XX
Milling Dept.	XXX	XXX	XX
Assembly Ship	XXX	XXX	XX
Total Controllable Costs	XXXXX	XXXXX	XXX

FIGURE 8-22 PROFIT CENTER PERFORMANCE REPORT

XYZ COMPANY PROFIT STATEMENT

Sales		XXX	
Less:			
Cost of goods sold	XXX		
Gross profit		XXX	
Less controllable costs:		XXX	
Controllable overhead	XXX		
Controllable operating expenses	XXX		
Controllable operating profit		XXX	(Measure of management performance)
Depreciation on noncontrollable fixed assets	XXX		
Contribution after noncontrollable costs		XXX	(Measure of profit center performance)

FIGURE 8-23 Investment Center Performance Report

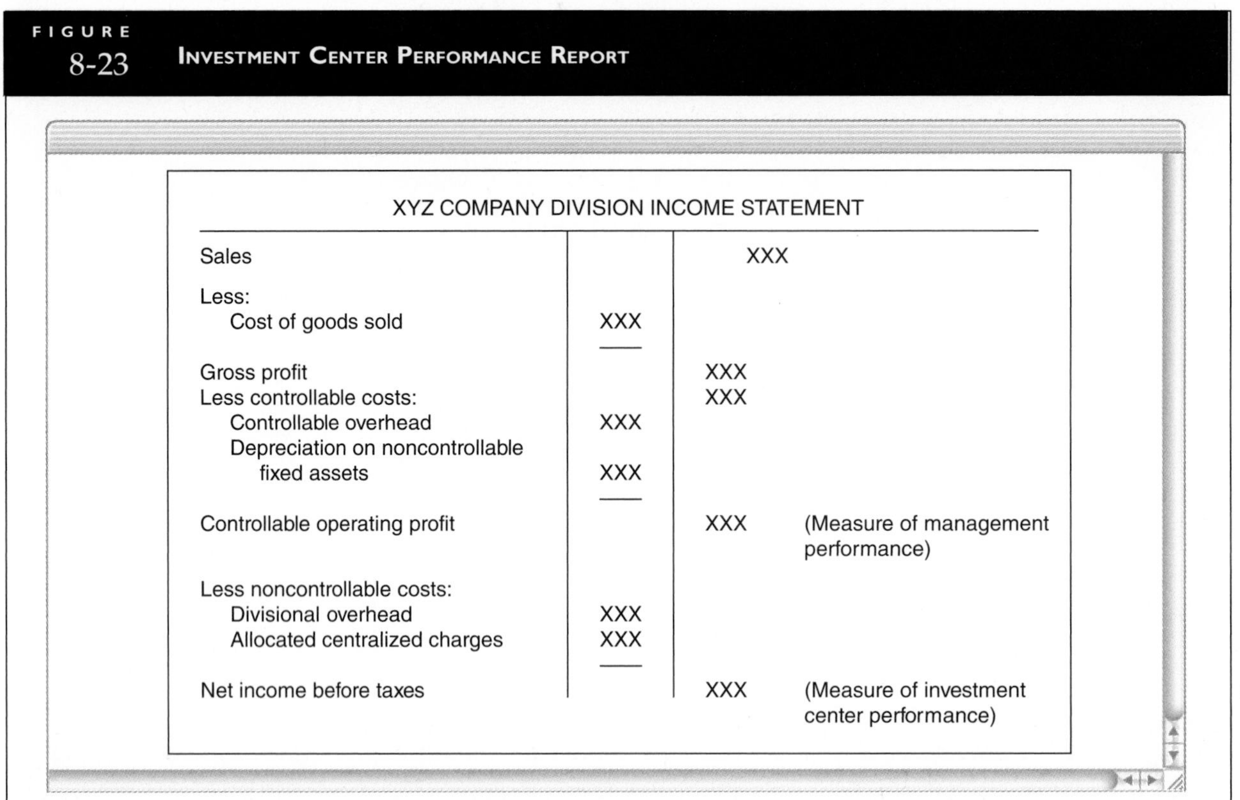

XYZ COMPANY DIVISION INCOME STATEMENT

Sales		XXX	
Less:			
Cost of goods sold	XXX		
Gross profit		XXX	
Less controllable costs:		XXX	
Controllable overhead	XXX		
Depreciation on noncontrollable fixed assets	XXX		
Controllable operating profit		XXX	(Measure of management performance)
Less noncontrollable costs:			
Divisional overhead	XXX		
Allocated centralized charges	XXX		
Net income before taxes		XXX	(Measure of investment center performance)

example of a profit center report. Whereas only controllable items are used to assess the manager's performance, the profit center itself is assessed by its contribution after noncontrollable costs.

INVESTMENT CENTERS. The manager of an **investment center** has the general authority to make decisions that profoundly affect the organization. Assume that a division of a corporation is an investment center with the objective of maximizing the return on its investment assets. The division manager's range of responsibilities includes cost management, product development, marketing, distribution, and capital disposition through investments of funds in projects and ventures that earn a desired rate of return. Figure 8-23 illustrates the performance report for an investment center.

BEHAVIORAL CONSIDERATIONS

Goal Congruence

Earlier in this chapter, we touched on the management principles of authority, responsibility, and the formalization of tasks. When properly applied within an organization, these principles promote **goal congruence**. Lower-level managers pursuing their own objectives contribute in a positive way to the objectives of their superiors. For example, by controlling costs, a production supervisor contributes to the division manager's goal of profitability. Thus, as individual managers serve their own best interests, they also serve the best interests of the organization.

A carefully structured MRS plays an important role in promoting and preserving goal congruence. On the other hand, a badly designed MRS can cause dysfunctional actions that are in opposition to the organization's objectives. Two pitfalls that cause managers to act dysfunctionally are information overload and inappropriate performance measures.

Information Overload

Information overload occurs when a manager receives more information than he or she can assimilate. This happens when designers of the reporting system do not properly consider the manager's organizational level and span of control. For example, consider the information volume that would flow to the president if the reports were not properly summarized (refer to Figure 8-18). The details required by lower-level managers would quickly overload the president's decision-making process. Although the report may have many of the information attributes discussed earlier (complete, accurate, timely, and concise), it may be useless if not properly summarized.

Information overload causes managers to disregard their formal information and rely on informal cues to help them make decisions. Thus, the formal information system is replaced by heuristics (rules of thumb), tips, hunches, and guesses. The resulting decisions run a high risk of being suboptimal and dysfunctional.

INAPPROPRIATE PERFORMANCE MEASURES

Recall that one purpose of a report is to stimulate behavior consistent with the objectives of the firm. When **inappropriate performance measures** are used, however, the report can have the opposite effect. Let's see how this can happen using a common performance measure—return on investment (ROI). Assume that the corporate management of an organization evaluates division management performance solely on the basis of ROI. Each manager's objective is to maximize ROI. Naturally, the organization wants this to happen through prudent cost management and increased profit margins. When ROI is used as the single criterion for measuring performance, however, the criterion itself becomes the focus of attention and object of manipulation. We illustrate this point with the multiperiod investment center report in Figure 8-24. Notice how actual

FIGURE 8-24 MULTIPERIOD INVESTMENT CENTER REPORT

	ACTUAL			BUDGET
YEAR	2012	2013	2014	2015
Sales	1,780.0	2,670.0	3,204.0	3,560.0
Less segment variable costs:				
Materials	445.0	667.5	801.0	890.0
Labor	89.0	133.5	89.0	178.0
Supplies	35.6	53.4	64.1	71.2
Less discretionary costs employee training	53.4	62.3	44.5	71.2
Maintenance	89.0	97.9	71.2	106.8
Less segment committed costs:				
Depreciation	213.6	284.8	284.8	356.0
Rent	142.4	178.0	195.8	249.2
Total cost	1,068.0	1,477.4	1,550.4	1,922.4
Contribution	712.0	1,192.6	1,653.6	1,637.6
Investment in assets				
Accounts receivable	178.0	267.0	320.4	356.0
Inventory	356.0	534.0	480.6	712.0
Fixed assets	2,830.2	4,565.7	4,984.0	6,016.4
Less accounts payable	(267.0)	(400.5)	(623.0)	(534.0)
Net investment	3,097.2	4,966.2	5,162.0	6,550.4
Return on investment	23%	24%	32%	25%

ROI went up in 2014 and exceeded the budgeted ROI in 2015. On the surface, this looks like favorable performance. A closer analysis of the cost and revenue figures, however, gives a different picture. Actual sales were below budgeted sales for 2015, but the shortfall in revenue was offset by reductions in discretionary operating expenditures (employee training and plant maintenance). The ROI figure is further improved by reducing investments in inventory and plant equipment (fixed assets) to lower the asset base.

The manager took actions that increased ROI, but were dysfunctional to the organization. Usually, such tactics can succeed in the short run only. As the plant equipment starts to wear out, customer dissatisfaction increases (because of stock-outs), and employee dissent becomes epidemic. The ROI figure will then begin to reflect the economic reality. By that time, however, the manager may have been promoted based on the perception of good performance, and his or her successor will inherit the problems left behind.

The use of any single-criterion performance measure can impose personal goals on managers that conflict with organizational goals and result in dysfunctional behavior.

Consider the following examples:

1. The use of price variance to evaluate a purchasing agent can affect the quality of the items purchased.
2. The use of quotas (such as units produced) to evaluate a supervisor can affect quality control, material usage efficiency, labor relations, and plant maintenance.
3. The use of profit measures such as ROI, net income, and contribution margin can affect plant investment, employee training, inventory reserve levels, customer satisfaction, and labor relations.

Performance measures should consider all relevant aspects of a manager's responsibility. In addition to measures of general performance (such as ROI), management should measure trends in key variables such as sales, cost of goods sold, operating expenses, and asset levels. Nonfinancial measures such as product leadership, personnel development, employee attitudes, and public responsibility may also be relevant in assessing management performance.

Summary

This chapter began by examining the GLS and the FRS, two operationally interdependent systems that are vital to the economic activities of the organization. We focused first on standard GLS procedures and on the files that constitute a GLS database. Then, turning to the FRS, we examined how financial information is provided to both external and internal users through a multistep reporting process. The emerging technology of XBRL is changing traditional financial reporting for many organizations. We reviewed the key features of XBRL and considered the internal control implications of this technology.

This chapter then looked at discretionary reporting systems that constitute the MRS. Discretionary reporting is not subject to the professional guidelines and legal statutes that govern nondiscretionary financial reporting. Rather, it is driven by several factors, including management principles; management function, level, decision type; problem structure; responsibility accounting; and behavioral considerations. The chapter investigated the impact of each factor on the design of the MRS.

Key Terms

ad hoc reports (355)
authority (348)
budget (356)
budget master file (334)
chart of accounts (333)
cost center (358)
data mining (356)
data warehouse (356)
decision-making process (355)
discovery model (356)

formalization of tasks (347)
general ledger change report (345)
general ledger history file (333)
general ledger master file (333)
goal congruence (360)
implementation (350)
inappropriate performance measures (361)
information content (354)
information overload (360)
investment center (360)
journal voucher file (333)
journal voucher history file (333)
journal voucher listing (345)
management by exception (349)
management control decisions (351)
management report (354)
on-demand reports (354)
operational control decisions (351)
organizational chart (347)
profit center (358)
programmed reports (354)
report attributes (355)
responsibility (348)
responsibility accounting (356)
responsibility center file (333)
responsibility centers (358)
responsibility reports (357)
scheduled reports (354)
sophisticated users (334)
span of control (349)
strategic planning decisions (350)
structured problem (353)
tactical planning decisions (351)
unstructured problem (353)
variance (352)
verification model (356)
XBRL (extensible Business Reporting Language) (337)
XBRL instance documents (343)
XBRL taxonomy (338)
XML (extensible Markup Language) (337)

Review Questions

1. What information is contained in a journal voucher?
2. How are journal vouchers used as a control mechanism?
3. What information is contained in the general ledger master file?
4. What is the purpose of the general ledger history file?
5. What is the purpose of a responsibility center file?
6. List the primary users of the FRS, and discuss their information needs.
7. Name, in order, the 11 steps of the financial reporting process.
8. What assumption is made regarding the external users of financial statements?
9. When are adjusting entries made, and what is their purpose? When are the corresponding voucher entries made?
10. What tasks should the general ledger clerk not be allowed to do?
11. What are the two operational reports produced by the FRS that provide proof of the accuracy of the process?
12. Explain which of the four potential risks to the FRS may be controlled better by a close examination of the journal voucher listing.
13. What does XML stand for?
14. What does XBRL stand for?
15. What is an XBRL taxonomy?
16. What is an XBRL instance document?
17. What is an XBRL tag?
18. Explain how the formalization of tasks promotes internal control.
19. Explain why it is important that both responsibility and authority are appropriately assigned to employees.
20. Distinguish between narrow and wide span of control. Give an example of tasks appropriate to each type.
21. How does management by exception help to alleviate information overload by a manager?
22. Identify instances for which feedback becomes useless in helping to control activities.
23. Contrast the four decision types—strategic planning, tactical planning, management control, and operational control—by the five decision characteristics—time frame, scope, level of details, recurrence, and certainty.
24. What are the three elements that distinguish structured and unstructured problems? Give an example of each type of problem. Which type of

problem is more suitable to a transaction processing system?

25. What management levels are more likely to deal with unstructured problems? With structured problems? Why?
26. What are the two objectives that enable reports to be considered useful?
27. List and define the seven report attributes.
28. What is responsibility accounting?
29. What are the two phases of responsibility accounting?
30. What are the three most common forms of responsibility centers?
31. What is goal congruence?
32. What is data mining?
33. What is a data warehouse?
34. What is information overload?
35. Explain some reporting techniques that may cause dysfunctional behavior by a manager.
36. Explain how ad hoc reports have allowed managers to make more timely and better-quality decisions. Give an example.
37. Explain how exception reporting would be invaluable to the manager of a credit department.
38. What types of variances are found on cost center reports? Explain what each variance is measuring and why this information is important.
39. Distinguish between a profit center and an investment center. Draw a diagram illustrating the relationship between cost, profit, and investment centers.

Discussion Questions

1. Discuss any separation of duties necessary to control against unauthorized entries to the general ledger. What other control procedures regarding the general ledger should be employed?
2. Discuss the various sources of data for the FRS output and how these data are processed into information (output) for the different external users.
3. Explain how erroneous journal vouchers may lead to litigation and significant financial losses for a firm.
4. Ultimately, is the purpose of an audit trail to follow a transaction from its input through its processing and finally to the financial statements, or vice versa? Explain your answer.
5. Describe the role of the journal voucher in both batch and real-time GL systems.
6. Controls are only as good as the predetermined standard on which they are based. Discuss the preceding comment and give an example.
7. Discuss three audit implications of XBRL.
8. Although HTML and XML documents look very similar, and both use tags, explain how they differ significantly as a financial reporting medium.
9. If management control and strategic planning decisions do not receive a high level of support from traditional information systems, then how do they get the support?
10. In terms of decision-making capabilities, which type of report do you think is generally more important—scheduled reports or on-demand reports? Explain your answer, and give an example of each type of report.
11. Scheduled reports may contain some information that is relevant to some decisions and irrelevant to other decisions. Why are some scheduled reports designed this way, rather than multiple reports being generated for various decision-making purposes?
12. Sometimes a trade-off must be made between information accuracy and timeliness. Give an example in which it is imperative to make an estimate now, rather than wait a couple of weeks for an exact number.
13. Figure 8-18 illustrates both upward and downward flows of information. What are the downward flows and their purpose? What about the upward flows? Are the downward and upward flows related?
14. Distinguish between the verification model and the discovery model approaches to data mining.

15. Explain how a data warehouse database is fundamentally different from a transaction processing database.
16. Why are cost centers considered to be more appropriate than profit centers for production departments?
17. Explain how a production quota used to evaluate a supervisor can adversely affect quality control, material usage efficiency, and labor relations.
18. Explain and give an example as to how a manager can manipulate the return on investment figures in the short run. Why are these manipulations bad for the company in the long run? Suggest some alternative performance evaluation and compensation schemes.
19. Comment on the following statement: "More information is always preferred to less; you can never have too much information."

Multiple-Choice Questions

1. Which statement below best describes an investment center?
   a. The authority to make decisions affecting the major determinants of profit, including the power to choose its markets and sources of supply.
   b. The authority to make decisions affecting the major determinants of profit, including the power to choose its markets and sources of supply, and significant control over the amount of invested capital
   c. The authority to make decisions over the most significant costs of operations, including the power to choose the sources of supply
   d. The authority to provide specialized support to other units within the organization
   e. The responsibility for developing markets for and selling of the output of the organization
2. Which statement below best describes a profit center?
   a. The authority to make decisions affecting the major determinants of profit, including the power to choose its markets and sources of supply
   b. The authority to make decisions affecting the major determinants of profit, including the power to choose its markets, sources of supply, and significant control over the amount of invested capital
   c. The authority to make decisions over the most significant costs of operations, including the power to choose the sources of supply
   d. The authority to provide specialized support to other units within the organization
   e. The responsibility for combining the raw materials, direct labor, and other factors of production into a final product
3. Which of the following is NOT an output report of the financial reporting system?
   a. Variance analysis report.
   b. Statement of cash flows.
   c. Tax return.
   d. Comparative balance sheet.
4. All of the following are characteristics of the strategic planning process except
   a. emphasis on both the short and long run
   b. analysis and review of departmental process
   c. review of the attributes and behavior of the organization's competition
   d. analysis of external economic factors
   e. analysis of consumer demand
5. An XBRL instance document is
   a. the document format used to produce web pages.
   b. the final product (report).
   c. a classification scheme.
   d. a tag stored in each database record.
6. Which task should the general ledger perform?
   a. Update the general ledger
   b. Prepare journal vouchers
   c. Have custody of physical assets
   d. Have record-keeping responsibility for special journals of subsidiary ledgers
   e. Both tasks A and B

7. Hercules Inc., uses a performance reporting system that shows data for each subordinate employee who reports to a supervisor, the actual costs incurred during the period, the budgeted costs, and all variances from budget for that subordinate's department. The name of this reporting system is
   a. contribution accounting.
   b. program budgeting.
   c. flexible budgeting.
   d. responsibility accounting.
   e. cost-benefit accounting.
8. An XBRL taxonomy is
   a. the document format used to produce web pages.
   b. the final product (report).
   c. a classification scheme.
   d. a tag stored in each database record.
9. Which of the following statements is true?
   a. Journal vouchers detailing transaction activity flow from various operational departments into the GLS, where they are independently reconciled and posted to the journal voucher history file.
   b. Journal vouchers summarizing transaction activity flow from the accounting department into the GLS, where they are independently reconciled and posted to the general ledger accounts.
   c. Journal vouchers summarizing transaction activity flow from various operational departments into the GLS, where they are independently reconciled and posted to the general ledger accounts.
   d. Journal vouchers summarizing transaction activity flow from operational departments into the GLS, are independently reconciled and posted to the journal voucher history file.
10. Which of the following budgeting processes is LEAST likely to motivate managers toward organizational goals?
    a. Setting budget targets at attainable levels
    b. Participation by subordinates in the budgetary process
    c. Use of management by exception
    d. Holding subordinates accountable for the items they control
    e. Having top management set budget levels
11. Which of the following would normally be considered in a strategic plan?
    a. Setting a target of 12 percent return on sales
    b. Maintaining the image of the company as the industry leader
    c. Setting a market price per share of stock outstanding
    d. Distributing monthly reports for departmental variance analysis
    e. Both a and c
12. At what level of management is the long-range planning function most important?
    a. At top-management levels
    b. At middle-management levels
    c. At lower-management levels
    d. For staff functions
    e. For line functions
13. Which is the fundamental purpose of responsibility accounting?
    a. Variance analysis
    b. Motivation
    c. Authority
    d. Budgeting
    e. Pricing
14. Which file below provides historical financial data for comparative financial reports?
    a. Journal voucher history file
    b. General ledger history file
    c. Responsibility file
    d. Budget master file
15. Which of the following statements is most true?
    a. Journal vouchers authorize all GL postings in a real-time GLS.
    b. Adjusting and reversing entries to the GL do not require journal vouchers because these entries are not transactions.
    c. Batch processing of journal vouchers is common for large organizations with multiple sources of transactions.
    d. Journal vouchers are used to capture summaries of multiple transactions but are not used to capture single transactions.

Problems

1. GENERAL LEDGER SYSTEM OVERVIEW

Draw a diagram depicting the relationship between the general ledger master file, control accounts, subsidiary files, and financial statements.

2. FINANCIAL REPORTING PROCESS

The following contains the various steps of the financial reporting process. Place these steps in the proper order, and indicate whether each step is a function of the TPS, GLS, or FRS.

- Record transaction in special journal
- Make adjusting entries
- Capture the transaction
- Prepare the post-closing trial balance
- Prepare the adjusted trial balance
- Prepare the financial statements
- Journalize and post the adjusting entries
- Post to the subsidiary ledger
- Post to the general ledger
- Journalize and post the closing entries
- Prepare the unadjusted trial balance

3. XBRL

John Ozment, director of special projects and analysis for Ozment's Corporation, is responsible for preparing corporate financial analyses and monthly statements, and for reviewing and presenting the financial impacts of proposed strategies to upper management. Data for such financial analyses are obtained from operations and financial databases through direct queries of Ozment's department staff. Reports and charts for presentations are then prepared by hand and typed. Multiple copies are prepared and distributed to various users. The pressure on Ozment's group has intensified as demand for more and more current information increases. A solution to this reporting problem must be found.

The systems department wants to develop a proprietary software package to produce the reports automatically. The project would require the company to make a considerable programming investment. Ozment is concerned about the accuracy, completeness, and currency of data in automatically produced reports. He has heard about a reporting system called XBRL and wonders whether a new system based on this technology would not be more effective and reliable.

Required

a. Research the current state of XBRL and deter mine if this technology is appropriate for internal reporting projects such as this.
b. Identify the enhancements to current information and reporting that the company could realize by using XBRL.
c. Discuss any data integrity, internal control, and reporting concerns associated with XBRL.

4. INTERNAL CONTROL

The accounting clerk for the Ram System company receives source documents such as purchase orders, sales invoices, and vendor invoices, which she uses to prepare journal vouchers for general ledger entries. Each day the clerk posts the journal vouchers to the general ledger and the related subsidiary ledgers. Each month the clerk reconciles the subsidiary accounts to their control accounts in the general ledger to ensure that they balance.

Required

Discuss any control weaknesses and risks associated with this scenario.

5. DATABASE GL SYSTEM

Crystal Corporation processes its journal vouchers using batch procedures similar to the process outlined in Figure 8-4 in the text. To improve customer satisfaction, the sales system is going to be converted to a real-time system. Redraw Figure 8-4 to reflect this change in the financial reporting process.

6. DATABASE GL SYSTEM

The top management team at Olympia, Inc., wishes to have real-time access to the general ledger. Currently, the general ledger is updated nightly via a batch processing system, similar to the one shown in Figure 8-4 in the text. Adjust Figure 8-4 to accommodate this request by top management, assuming that the nightly updates to the general ledger are sufficient.

7. INTERNAL CONTROL

Expand Figure 8-5 in the text to incorporate the journal voucher listing and general ledger change report as control mechanisms. Also discuss the specific controls they impose on the system.

8. ORGANIZATIONAL CHART

Prepare an organizational chart for your university. (Your campus phone directory catalog may be helpful.)

9. DECISION LEVEL

Classify the following decisions as being characteristic of strategic planning, tactical planning, managerial control, or operational control.

- Determining the mix of products to manufacture this year
- Examining whether the number of defective goods manufactured is within a certain range
- Expanding a product line overseas
- Determining the best distribution route
- Examining whether the cost of raw materials is within a certain range
- Examining whether personnel development cost is rising
- Employing more automated manufacturing this year
- Examining whether the amount of scrap material is acceptable
- Building a new plant facility
- Examining whether employees' attitudes are improving
- Examining whether production levels are within a predicted range
- Making purchasing arrangements with a new supplier
- Increasing production capabilities this year by purchasing a more efficient piece of machinery
- Closing a plant

10. REPORT CATEGORIZATION

Classify the following reports as being either scheduled or on-demand reports.

- Cash disbursements listing
- Overtime report
- Customer account history
- Inventory stock-out report
- Accounts receivable aging list
- Duplicate paycheck report
- Cash receipts listing
- Machine maintenance report
- Vendor delivery record report
- Journal voucher listing
- Investment center report
- Maintenance cost overrun report

11. ORGANIZATION STRUCTURE AND SPAN OF CONTROL

Refer to the organization charts labeled Structure A and Structure B in the figure for problem 11.

Required

a. For organizational structure A describe the
   1. advantages and disadvantages of this structure.
   2. impact of the resulting span of control.
   3. possible effect on employee behavior.

b. For organizational structure B describe the
   1. advantages and disadvantages of this structure.
   2. impact of the resulting span of control.
   3. effect on employee behavior.

c. When determining the appropriate span of control discuss the factors that should be considered.

12. ORGANIZATION STRUCTURE AND SPAN OF CONTROL

Refer to the organization charts labeled Structure A and Structure B in the figure for problem 12.

Required

a. For the organizational structure A describe the
   1. advantages and disadvantages of this structure.
   2. impact of the resulting span of control.
   3. effect of the organizational structure on employee behavior.

b. For the flat organizational structure B describe the
   1. advantages and disadvantages of that organizational structure.
   2. impact of the resulting span of control.
   3. effect of the organizational structure on employee behavior.

c. When determining the appropriate span of control for a company discuss the factors that should be considered.

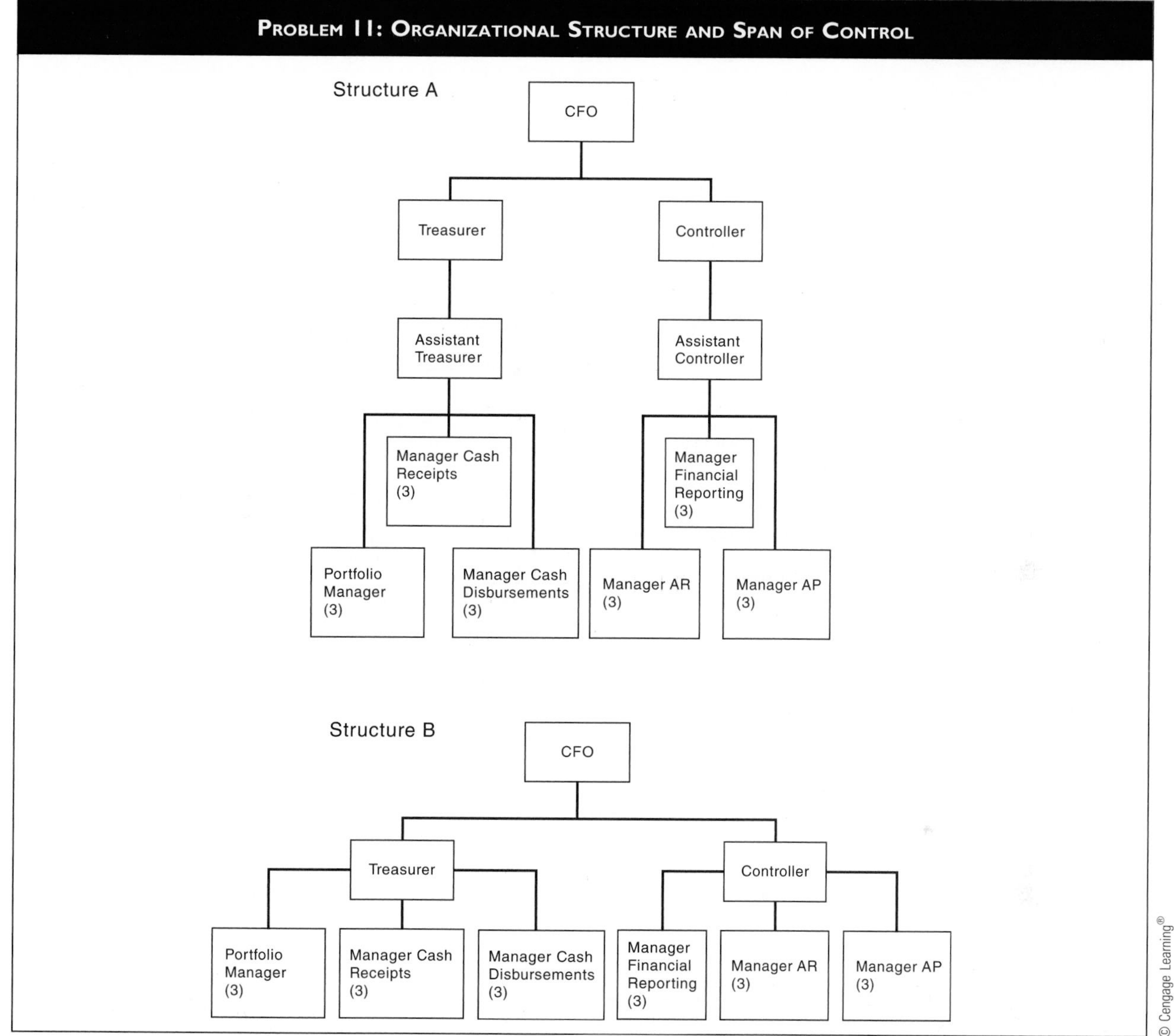

13. CMA ADAPTED—ORGANIZATIONAL STRUCTURE

While attending night school to earn a degree in computer engineering, Stan Wilson worked for Morlot Container Company (MCC) as an assembly line supervisor. MCC was located near Wilson's hometown and had been a prominent employer in the area for many years. MCC's main product was milk cartons that were distributed throughout the Midwest for milk processing plants. The technology at MCC was stable, and the assembly lines were monitored closely. MCC employed a standard cost system because cost control was considered important. The employees who manned the assembly lines were generally unskilled workers who had been with the company for many years; the majority of these workers belonged to the local union. Wilson was glad he was nearly finished with school because he found the work at MCC to be repetitive and boring, even as a supervisor. The supervisors were monitored almost as closely as the line workers, and standard policies and procedures existed that applied to most situations. Most of MCC's management had been with the company for several years and believed in clear lines of authority and well-defined responsibilities. Whereas he knew he had performed well against the company's standards, Wilson also knew that there probably would be little opportunity for advancement or significant compensation increases.

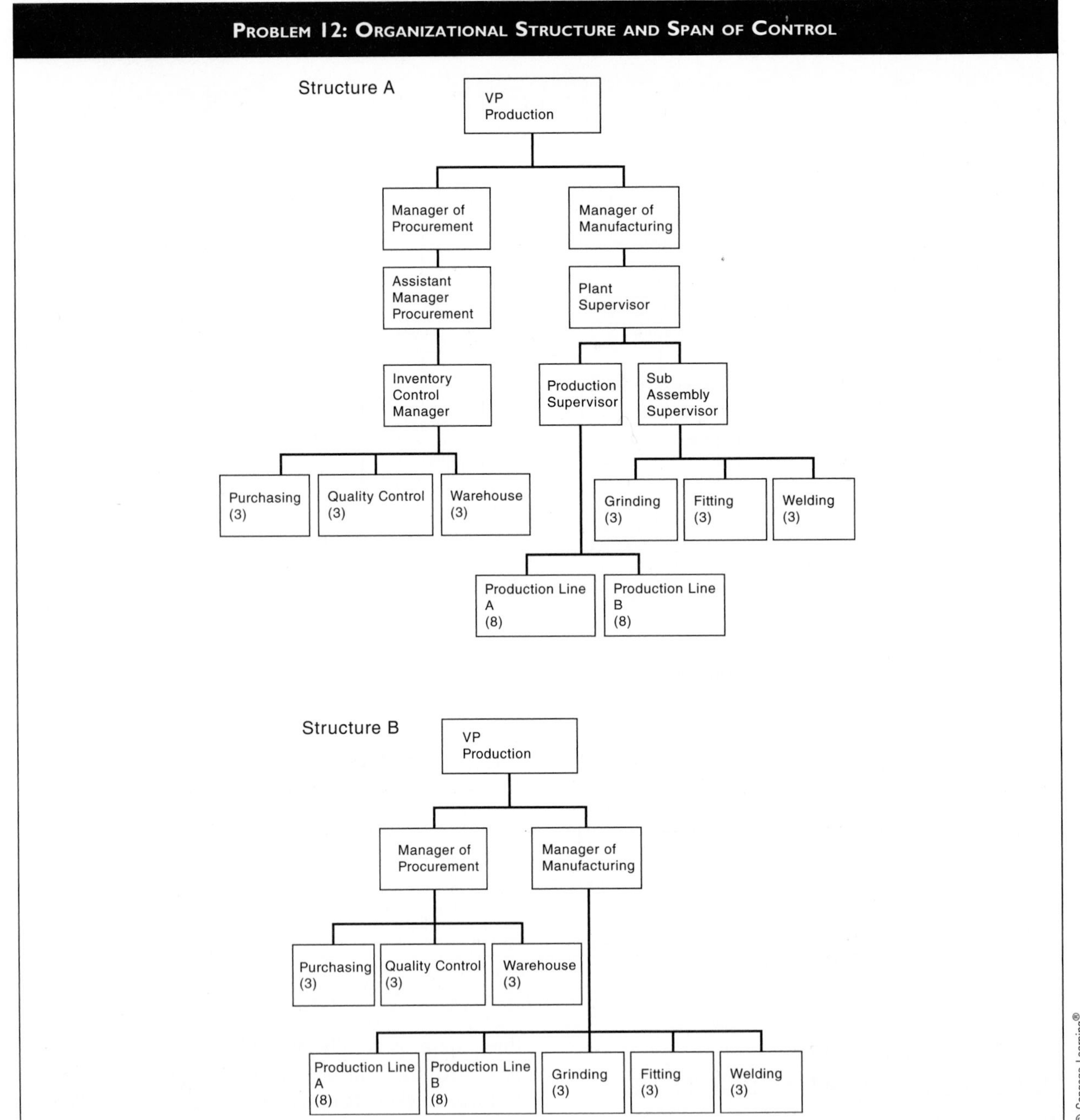

After receiving his degree, Wilson went to work in the research and development department of Alden Computers, a five-year-old company specializing in educational computer systems for elementary schools. The company was customer-oriented and willing to tailor its computer systems to the needs of the end users. The customization of its systems, combined with continual changes in technology, resulted in a job-shop orientation in the company's production facility. The employees who assembled Alden's systems were skilled technicians who worked closely with the engineering staff.

Wilson was gratified by the respect and authority his newly acquired knowledge and skills afforded him at Alden. If changes were required in his area of expertise, Wilson often made recommendations about how the work should proceed and was involved in decisions on new product development. The company's management team frequently "rolled up its sleeves" and worked alongside the technicians when production problems arose; the lines of authority were sometimes difficult to distinguish, and decisions were often made by the expert on the spot. Wilson believed that his skills were appreciated at Alden and he would be fairly compensated for his professional expertise.

Required

a. Morlot Container Company and Alden Computers represent two different types of organizational structures. In terms of each of the following points, explain how MCC differs from Alden Computers.
   1. General organizational structure and climate
   2. Bases of authority
   3. Evaluation criteria
   4. Bases of compensation

b. Both structures have potential benefits or can create problems. Discuss the features of the structure used by
   1. Alden Computers that might benefit MCC.
   2. Alden that might create problems for Alden.
   3. MCC that might benefit Alden Computers.

14. CMA-ADAPTED PERFORMANCE MEASURES

The Star Paper Division of Royal Industries is located near Los Angeles. A major expansion of the division's only plant was completed in April 2015. The expansion consisted of an addition to the existing building, additions to the production-line machinery, and the replacement of obsolete and fully depreciated equipment that was no longer efficient or cost-effective.

On May 1, 2015, George Harris became manager of Star. Harris had a meeting with Marie Fortner, vice president of operations for Royal, who explained to Harris that the company measured the performance of divisions and division managers on the basis of return on gross assets (ROA). When Harris asked if other measures were used in conjunction with ROA, Fortner replied, "Royal's top management prefers to use a single performance measure. Star should do well this year now that it has expanded and replaced all of that old equipment. You should have no problem exceeding the division's historical rate. I'll check with you at the end of each quarter to see how you are doing."

Fortner called Harris after the first quarter results were completed because Star's ROA was considerably below the historical rate for the division. Harris told Fortner that he did not believe that ROA was a valid performance measure for Star. Fortner indicated that she would discuss this with others at headquarters and get back to Harris. However, there was no further discussion of the use of ROA but only reports on divisional performance at the end of the second and third quarters. Now that the fiscal year has ended, Harris has received the memorandum in the figure designated Problem 14.

Harris is looking forward to meeting with Fortner as he plans to pursue the discussion about the appropriateness of ROA as a performance measure for Star. While the ROA for Star is below historical levels, the division's profits for the year are higher than at any previous time. Harris is going to recommend that ROA be replaced with multiple criteria for evaluating performance—namely, dollar profit, receivable turnover, and inventory turnover.

PROBLEM 14: PERFORMANCE MEASURES

TO: George Harris, Star Paper Division
FROM: Marie Fortner, Royal Industries
SUBJECT: Divisional Performance

The operating results for the fourth quarter and for our fiscal year ended on April 30 are now complete. Your fourth quarter return on gross assets was only 9 percent, resulting in a return for the year of slightly under 11 percent. I recall discussing your low return after the first quarter and reminding you after the second and third quarters that this level of return is not considered adequate for the Star Paper Division.

The return on gross assets at Star has ranged from 15 to 18 percent for the past five years. An 11 percent return may be acceptable at some of Royal's other divisions, but not at a proven winner like Star, especially in light of your recently improved facility. Please arrange to meet with me in the near future to discuss ways to restore Star's return on gross assets to its former level.

Required

a. Identify general criteria that should be used in selecting performance measures to evaluate operating managers.
b. Describe the probable cause of the decline in the Star Paper Division's return on gross assets during the fiscal year ended April 30, 2007.
c. On the basis of the relationship between Fortner and Harris, as well as the memorandum from Fortner, discuss apparent weaknesses in the performance evaluation process at Royal Industries.
d. Discuss whether the multiple performance evaluation criteria that Harris suggested would be appropriate for the evaluation of the Star Paper Division.

15. CMA-ADAPTED RESPONSIBILITY ACCOUNTING

Family Resorts, Inc., is a holding company for several vacation hotels in the northeastern and mid-Atlantic states. The firm originally purchased several old inns, restored the buildings, and upgraded the recreational facilities. Vacationing families have been well pleased with the inns because many services are provided that accommodate children and afford parents time for themselves. Since the completion of the restoration 10 years ago, the company has been profitable.

Family Resorts has just concluded its annual meeting of regional and district managers. This meeting is held each November to review the results of the previous season and to help the managers prepare for the upcoming year. Before the meeting, the managers submitted proposed budgets for their districts or regions, as appropriate. These budgets are reviewed and consolidated into an annual operating budget for the entire company. The 2015 budget has been presented at the meeting, and the managers accepted it.

To evaluate the performance of its managers, Family Resorts uses responsibility accounting. Therefore, the preparation of the budget is given close attention at headquarters. If major changes need to be made to the budgets that the managers submitted, all affected parties are consulted before the changes are incorporated. The two figures designated Problem 15 present two reports from the budget booklet that all managers received at the meeting.

Required

a. Responsibility accounting has been used effectively by many companies, both large and small.
   1. Define responsibility accounting.
   2. Discuss the benefits that accrue to a company using *responsibility accounting*.
   3. Describe the advantages of responsibility accounting for the managers of a firm.

PROBLEM 15: RESPONSIBILITY ACCOUNTING

FAMILY RESORTS, INC.
RESPONSIBILITY SUMMARY
($000 omitted)

Reporting Unit: Family Resorts	
Responsible Person: President	
Mid-Atlantic Region	$ 605
New England Region	365
Unallocated costs	(160)
Income before taxes	$ 810
Reporting Unit: New England Region	
Responsible Person: Regional Manager	
Vermont	$ 200
New Hampshire	140
Maine	105
Unallocated costs	(80)
Total contribution	$ 365

Reporting Unit: Maine District	
Responsible Person: District Manager	
Harbor Inn	$ 80
Camden Country Inn	60
Unallocated costs	(35)
Total contribution	$ 105
Reporting Unit: Harbor Inn	
Responsible Person: Innkeeper	
Revenue	$ 600
Controllable costs	(455)
Allocated costs	(65)
Total contribution	$ 80

Problem 15: Responsibility Accounting

FAMILY RESORTS, INC.
CONDENSED OPERATING BUDGET—MAINE DISTRICT
FOR THE YEAR ENDING DECEMBER 31, 2015
($000 OMITTED)

	Region			New England District				Maine District Inns		
	Family Resorts	Mid-Atlantic	New England	Not Allocated[1]	Vermont	New Hampshire	Maine	Not Allocated[2]	Harbor	Camden Country
Net sales	$7,900	$4,200	$3,700		$1,400	$1,200	$1,100		$600	$500
Cost of sales	4,530	2,310	2,220		840	720	660		360	300
Gross margin	$3,370	$1,890	$1,480		$ 560	$ 480	$ 440		$240	$200
Controllable expenses:										
Supervisory	$ 240	$ 130	$ 110		$ 35	$ 30	$ 45	$ 10	$20	$ 15
Training	160	80	80		30	25	25		15	10
Advertising	500	280	220	$ 50	55	60	55	15	20	20
Repairs and maintenance	480	225	255	—	90	85	80	—	40	40
Total controllable expenses	$1,380	$ 715	$ 665	$ 50	$ 210	$ 200	$ 205	$ 25	$ 95	$ 85
Controllable contribution	$1,990	$1,175	$ 815	$(50)	$ 350	$ 280	$ 235	$(25)	$145	$115
Expenses controlled by others:										
Depreciation	$ 520	$ 300	$ 220	$ 30	70	$ 60	$ 60	$ 10	$ 30	$ 20
Property taxes	200	120	80		30	30	20		10	10
Insurance	300	150	150	—	50	50	50	—	25	25
Total expenses controlled by others	$1,020	$ 570	$ 450	$ 30	$ 150	$ 140	$ 130	$ 10	$ 65	$ 55
Total contribution	$ 970	$ 605	$ 365	$(80)	$ 200	$ 140	$ 105	$(35)	$ 80	$ 60
Unallocated costs[3]	160									
Income before taxes	$ 810									

[1]Unallocated expenses include a regional advertising campaign and equipment used by the regional manager.
[2]Unallocated expenses include a portion of the district manager's salary, district promotion costs, and a district manager's car.
[3]Unallocated costs include taxes on undeveloped real estate, headquarters' expense, legal fees, and audit fees.

b. The regional and district managers accepted Family Resort's budget. Based on the facts presented, evaluate the budget process Family Resorts employs by addressing the following:
   1. What features of the budget presentation shown are likely to make the budget attractive to managers?
   2. What recommendations, if any, could be made to the budget preparers to improve the budget process? Explain your answer.

16. MANAGEMENT BY EXCEPTION

A variety of quantitative measures are used to evaluate employee performance, including standard costs, financial ratios, human resource forecasts, and operating budgets.

Required

a. Discuss the following aspects of a standard cost system.
   1. Discuss the characteristics that should be present to encourage positive employee motivation.
   2. Discuss how the system should be implemented to positively motivate employees.

b. The use of variance analysis often results in management by exception.
   1. Explain the meaning of *management by exception*.
   2. Discuss the behavioral implications of management by exception.

c. Explain how employee behavior could be adversely affected when actual-to-budget comparisons are used as the basis for performance evaluation.

17. CMA-ADAPTED VARIANCE ANALYSIS

Engineers Education Association (EEA) is a volunteer membership organization providing educational and professional services to its members. The professional staff is organized into four divisions with a total of 14 operating departments.

EEA adopted an annual budget program many years ago as a means for planning and controlling activities. Each department of EEA prepares an annual budget in consultation with its respective volunteer committee(s). After a series of reviews by both the professional staff and the volunteer structure, the budget is adopted. The professional staff is expected to comply with the budget in conducting its activities and operations.

The EEA's accounting department generates monthly income statements that present actual performance as compared to budget for each EEA department. The November 2015 statement for the publications department is shown in the first figure designated Problem 17. Accompanying the report this month was a memorandum from EEA's president, Daniel Riley, which is shown in the second figure designated as Problem 17.

Marie Paige, publications manager, was having lunch with Jon Franklin, continuing education manager, when the following conversation about Riley's memorandum took place.

PROBLEM 17: VARIANCE ANALYSIS

EEA—PUBLICATIONS DEPARTMENT
INCOME STATEMENT
FOR THE MONTH ENDED NOVEMBER 30, 2015
($000 OMITTED)

			Variance	
	Budget	**Actual**	**Dollar**	**Percent**
Revenues				
Subscriptions	$ 9.5	$ 8.4	$ (1.1)	(11.6)
Library subscriptions	3.4	3.3	(.1)	(2.9)
Research publications	13.6	15.2	1.6	11.8
Advertising	64.0	50.1	(13.9)	(21.7)
List rentals	15.2	13.9	(1.3)	(8.6)
Total revenue	$105.7	$90.9	$(14.8)	(14.0)
Operating expenses				
Salaries and wages	$ 24.0	$ 22.0	$ 2.0	8.3
Employee benefits	4.8	4.4	.4	8.3
Temporary help	0.0	1.5	(1.5)	(ERR)
Outside services	1.0	2.5	(1.5)	(150.0)
Education and training	0.5	0.0	.5	100.0
Promotion and advertising	7.5	4.0	3.5	46.6
Typesetting	8.0	12.0	(4.0)	(50.0)
Production printing	46.0	40.4	5.6	12.2
Postage, freight, and handling	12.0	11.0	1.0	8.3
Supplies	1.0	.8	.2	20.0
Total expenses	$104.8	$ 98.6	$ 6.2	5.9
Contribution	$ .9	$ (7.7)	$ (8.6)	(955.6)

PROBLEM 17: VARIANCE ANALYSIS

December 9, 2015

TO: Department Managers

FROM: Daniel Riley, President

SUBJECT: Performance Analysis

The November 2011 operating results for your department are attached. The results for the entire organization and most departments are unfavorable as compared to budget. In fact, our results for the first three months of this fiscal year are substantially below budget.

I want to determine our problems as quickly as possible. Prepare an explanation of all unfavorable (negative) variances by line item that exceed budget by 5 percent or more, and present a plan to eliminate such variances in the future. Remember that you played a key role in the development of the budget, and you have a responsibility to achieve the budget figures. These negative variances must be eliminated if we are to get back on steam.

Please submit your analysis to your divisional director and accounting by noon, Monday, December 14. Divisional directors will meet at 10 a.m. on Tuesday, December 15, to review these analyses.

Paige: The volunteers must be giving Riley some static—the memo doesn't sound like him.

Franklin: I think you're right. One of EEA's problems is that membership is down.

Paige: I heard that both growth and retention are bad. This is confirmed by my results. A set percentage of the membership dues of each member is assigned to us each month for the magazine subscription. This amount is down 12 percent. I have no control over this number because only members get the magazine.

Franklin: I wonder if the results are really as bad as they look. For instance, accounting has divided all of the annual budget figures by 12 to derive the monthly figures. This is okay for some things but not for most. What about you?

Paige: I agree. I don't know why they do that when we spend so much time up front developing the annual budget. I know what Riley is attempting, but I don't think he is going to get the results he wants. I know he wants to eliminate the negative variances, but some positive variances are really not favorable! We should be analyzing all significant variances—positive and negative.

Franklin: What are you going to do—analyze just the negatives? Should we do anything before we prepare our reports?

Required

a. The monthly income statements that EEA's accounting department prepares for each department of EEA are a form of communication.
   1. Explain why the departmental income statements are considered a form of communication.
   2. In terms of the format of the income statement presented for the publications department, evaluate EEA's departmental income statement as a communication device.

b. Paige stated that all significant variances should be analyzed because some positive variances are not favorable. Discuss why EEA's departments should be analyzing all significant variances, both positive (favorable) and negative (unfavourable). As support for your answer, identify a positive variance from the publications department's income statement that may not be favorable to EEA's operations, and explain why.

c. Recommend a course of action that Paige or Franklin could take to encourage Riley to have all significant variances reviewed.

PART

III

Advanced Technologies in Accounting Information

Database Management Systems

This chapter deals with the database approach to managing an organization's data resources. The database model is a particular philosophy whose objectives are supported by specific strategies, techniques, hardware, and software that are very different from those associated with flat-file environments.

Chapter 1 drew a distinction between two general data management approaches: the flat-file model and the database model. Because the best way to present the virtues of the database model is by contrast with the flat-file model, the first section of this chapter examines how traditional flat-file problems are resolved under the database approach. Important features of modern relational databases are covered later in the chapter. The second section describes in detail the functions and relationship between four primary elements of the database environment: the users, the database management system (DBMS), the database administrator (DBA), and the physical database. The third section focuses on key characteristics of the relational database model. The fourth section presents a number of database design topics including data modeling, deriving relational tables from entity relationship (ER) diagrams, the creation of user views, and data normalization techniques. The fifth section concludes the chapter with a discussion of distributed database issues. It examines three possible database configurations in a distributed environment: centralized, partitioned, and replicated databases.

Learning Objectives

After studying this chapter, you should:

- Understand the operational problems inherent in the flat-file approach to data management that gave rise to the database concept.
- Understand the relationships among the defining elements of the database environment.
- Understand the anomalies caused by unnormalized databases and the need for data normalization.
- Be familiar with the stages in database design, including entity identification, data modeling, constructing the physical database, and preparing user views.
- Be familiar with the operational features of distributed databases and recognize the issues that need to be considered in deciding on a particular database configuration.

Overview of the Flat-File versus Database Approach

Many so-called legacy systems are characterized by the **flat-file** approach to data management. In this environment, users own their data files. Exclusive ownership of data is a natural consequence of two problems associated with the legacy-system era. The first problem is a business culture that erects barriers between organizational units that inhibit entity-wide integration of data. The second problem stems from limitations in flat-file management technology that require data files to be structured to the unique needs of the primary user. Thus, the same data, used in slightly different ways by different users, may need to be restructured and reproduced in physically different files. Figure 9-1 illustrates this model.

In the figure, the file contents are represented conceptually with letters. Each letter could signify a single **data attribute** (field), a record, or an entire file. Note also that data element B is present in all user files. This is called **data redundancy** and is the cause of three types of data management problems: **data storage, data updating**, and **currency of information**. Each of these, as well as a fourth problem—**task-data dependency**, which is not directly related to data redundancy—will be examined next.

DATA STORAGE

Chapter 1 showed that an efficient information system captures and stores data only once and makes this single source available to all users who need it. This is not possible in the flat-file environment. To meet the private data needs of users, organizations must incur the costs of both multiple collection and multiple storage procedures. Indeed, some commonly used data may be duplicated dozens, hundreds, or even thousands of times, creating excessive storage costs.

DATA UPDATING

Organizations have a great deal of data stored on master files and reference files that require periodic updating to reflect operational and economic changes. For example, a change in a customer's

FIGURE 9-1 FLAT-FILE DATA MANAGEMENT

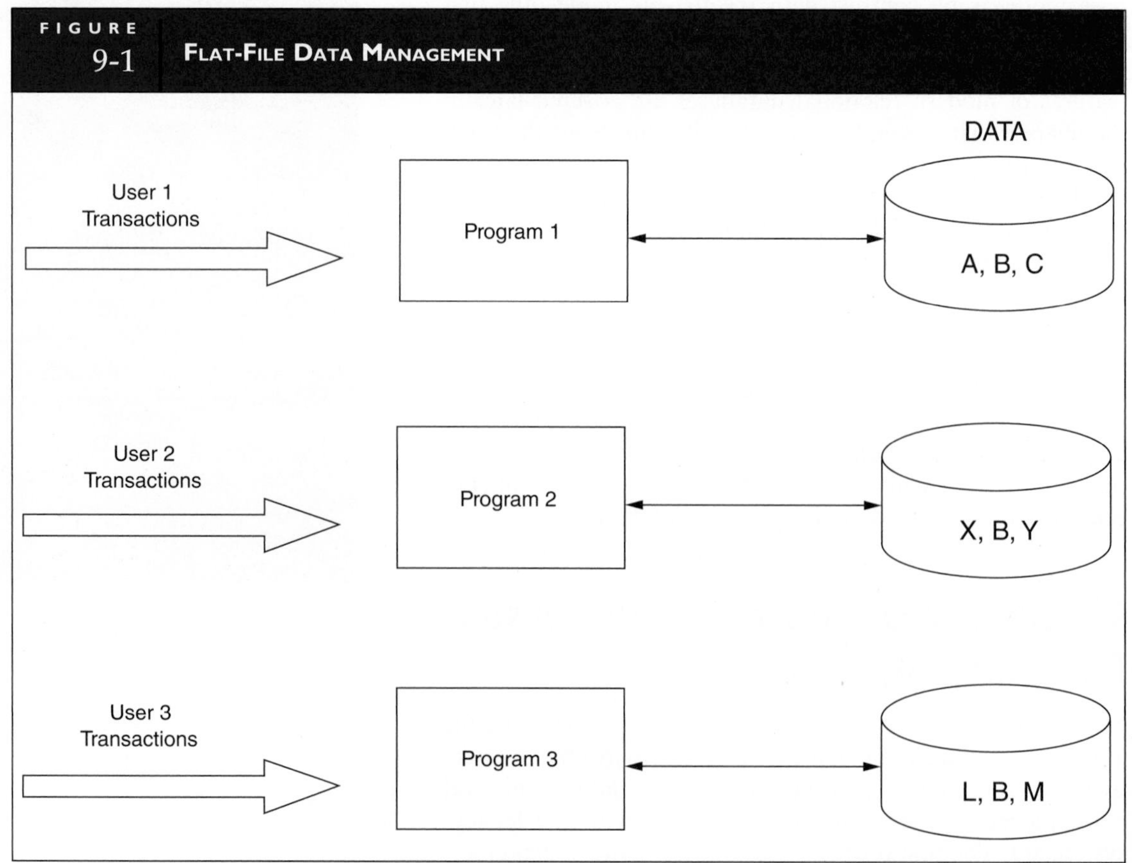

name or address must be reflected in the appropriate master files. This piece of information may be important to several user departments in the organization, such as sales, billing, credit, customer services, sales promotion, and catalog sales. When users maintain separate files, any such change must be made separately for each user. This adds significantly to the cost of data management.

CURRENCY OF INFORMATION

In contrast to the problem of performing multiple updates is the problem of failing to update the files of all users affected by a change. If update messages are not properly disseminated, then some users may not record the change and will perform their duties and make decisions based on outdated data.

TASK-DATA DEPENDENCY

Another problem with the flat-file approach is the user's inability to obtain additional information as his or her needs change. This problem is called task-data dependency. The user's information set is constrained by the data that he or she possesses and controls. For example, in Figure 9-1, if the information needs of User 1 change to include Data L, User 1's program would not have access to these data. Although Data L exists in the files of another user, keep in mind the culture of this environment. Users do not interact as members of a user community. They act independently. As such, User 1 may be unaware of the presence of Data L elsewhere in the organization. In this environment, it is difficult to establish a mechanism for the formal sharing of data. Therefore, Data L would need to be re-created from scratch. This will take time, inhibit User 1's performance, add to data redundancy, and drive data management costs even higher.

THE DATABASE APPROACH

Figure 9-2(a) presents a simple overview of the database approach with the same users and data requirements as in Figure 9-1. The most obvious change from the flat-file model is the pooling of data into a common database that is shared by all the users.

FIGURE 9-2(a) THE DATABASE CONCEPT

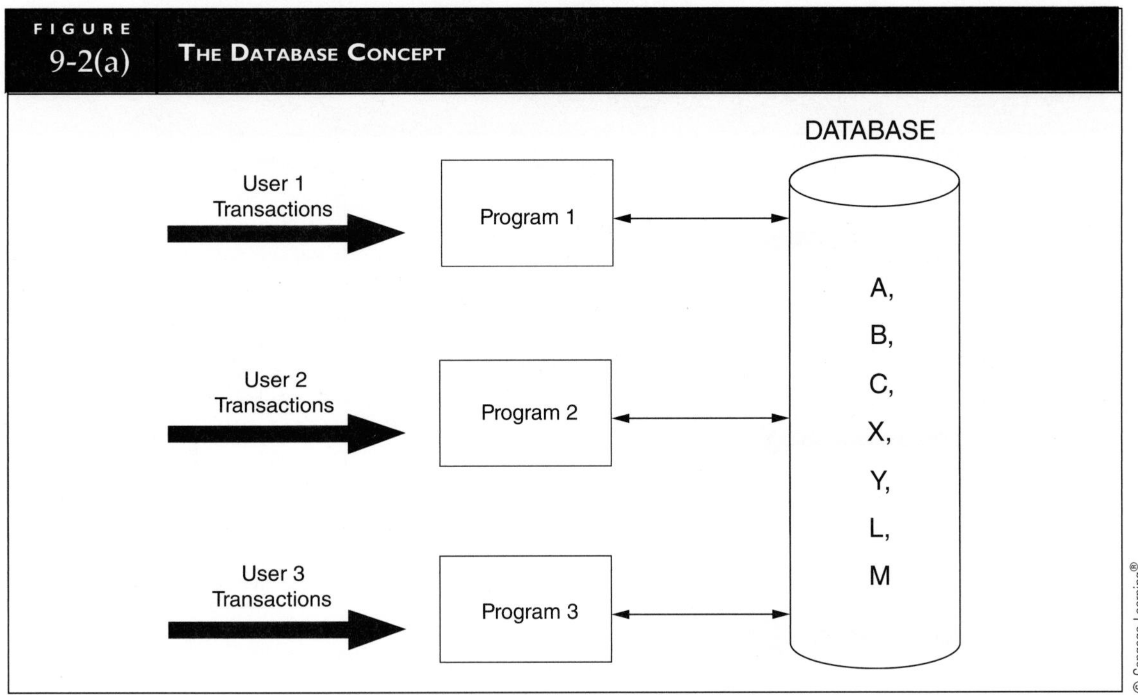

FLAT-FILE PROBLEMS SOLVED

Data sharing (the absence of ownership) is the central concept of the database approach. Let's see how this resolves the problems identified.

- *No data redundancy.* Each data element is stored only once, thereby eliminating data redundancy and reducing storage costs.
- *Single update.* Because each data element exists only in one place, it requires only a single update procedure. This reduces the time and cost of keeping the database current.
- *Current values.* A change any user makes to the database yields current data values for all other users. For example, when User 1 records a customer address change, User 3 has immediate access to this current information.
- *Task-data independence.* Users have access to the full domain of data available to the firm. As users' information needs expand beyond their immediate domain, the new needs can be more easily satisfied than under the flat-file approach. Only the limitations of the data available to the firm (the entire database), and the legitimacy of their need to access it, constrain users.

CONTROLLING ACCESS TO THE DATABASE

The database approach places all the firm's information eggs in one basket. It is essential, therefore, to take very good care of the basket. The example in Figure 9-2(a) has no provision for controlling access to the database. Assume Data X contain sensitive, confidential, or secret information that only User 3 is authorized to access. How can the organization prevent others from gaining unauthorized access to it?

THE DATABASE MANAGEMENT SYSTEM

Figure 9-2(b) adds a new element to Figure 9-2(a). Standing between the users' programs and the physical database is the **database management system (DBMS)**. The purpose of the DBMS is to provide controlled access to the database. The DBMS is a special software system that is programmed to know which data elements each user is authorized to access. The user's program sends requests for data to the DBMS, which validates and authorizes access to the database in

FIGURE 9-2(b) THE DATABASE CONCEPT

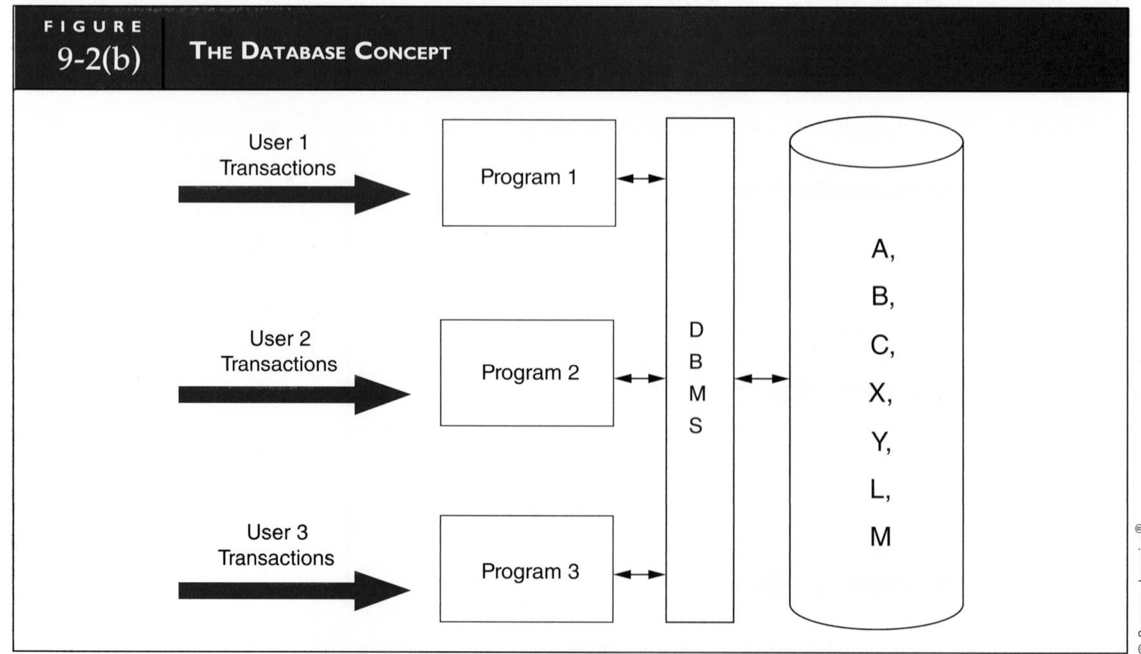

accordance with the user's level of authority. The DBMS will deny requests for data that the user is unauthorized to access. As one might imagine, the organization's criteria, rules, and procedures for assigning user authority are important control issues for accountants to consider.

THREE CONCEPTUAL MODELS

Over the years, several different architectures have represented the database approach. Early database models are as different from modern database models as they were from traditional flat files.

The most common database approaches used for business information systems are the **hierarchical model, network model**, and **relational model**. Because of certain conceptual similarities, the hierarchical and network databases are termed **navigational models** or **structured models**. The way that data are organized in these early database systems forces users to navigate between data elements using predefined structured paths. The relational model is far more flexible by allowing users to create new and unique paths through the database to solve a wider range of business problems.

Although their limitations are severe and their ultimate demise is inevitable, hierarchical and network models still exist as legacy systems that support mission-critical functions in some companies. Most modern systems, however, employ relational databases. The main text of the chapter focuses on the relational model. The key features of structured database models are outlined in the chapter appendix.

Elements of the Database Environment

Figure 9-3 presents a breakdown of the database environment into four primary elements: users, the DBMS, the database administrator, and the physical database. In this section, we examine each of these elements.

USERS

Figure 9-3 shows how **users** access the database in two ways. The first is via user application programs that systems professionals prepare. These programs send data access requests (calls) to the DBMS, which validates the requests and retrieves the data for processing. Under this mode of access, the presence of the DBMS is transparent to the users. Data-processing procedures (both batch and real-time) for transactions such as sales, cash receipts, and purchases are essentially the same as they would be in the flat-file environment.

The second method of database access is via direct query, which requires no formal user programs. The DBMS has a built-in query facility that allows authorized users to process data independent of professional programmers. The query facility provides a friendly environment for integrating and retrieving data to produce ad hoc management reports. This feature has been an attractive incentive for users to adopt the database approach.

THE DATABASE MANAGEMENT SYSTEM

The second element of the database approach depicted in Figure 9-3 is the database management system. The DBMS provides a controlled environment to assist (or prevent) user access to the database and to efficiently manage the data resource. Each DBMS model accomplishes these objectives differently, but some typical features include:

1. *Program development.* The DBMS contains application development software. Both programmers and end users may employ this feature to create applications to access the database.
2. *Backup and recovery.* During processing, the DBMS periodically makes backup copies of the physical database. In the event of a disaster (e.g., disk failure, program error, or malicious act) that renders the database unusable, the DBMS can recover an earlier version that is

FIGURE 9-3 ELEMENTS OF THE DATABASE CONCEPT

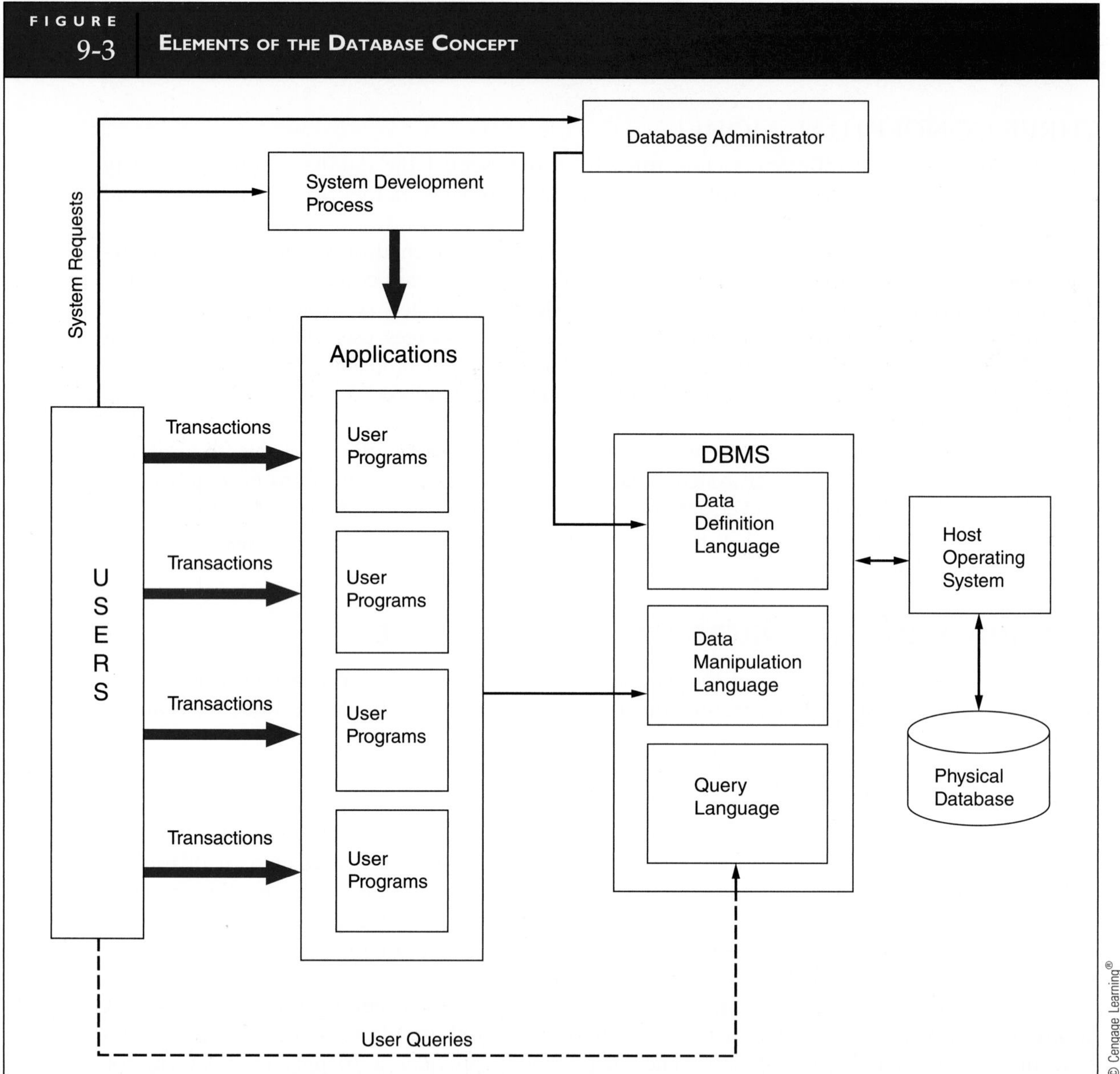

known to be correct. Although some data loss may occur, without the backup and recovery feature, the database would be vulnerable to total destruction.

3. *Database usage reporting.* This feature captures statistics on what data are being used, when they are used, and who uses them. The database administrator (DBA) uses this information to assign user authorization and to maintain the database. We discuss the role of the DBA later in this section.
4. *Database access.* The most important feature of a DBMS is to permit authorized user access to the database. Figure 9-3 shows the three software modules that facilitate this task. These are the data definition language, data manipulation language, and the query language.

Data Definition Language

Data definition language (DDL) is a programming language used to define the physical database to the DBMS. The definition includes the names and the relationship of all data elements, records, and files that constitute the database. The DDL defines the database on three levels called

FIGURE 9-4 OVERVIEW OF DBMS OPERATION

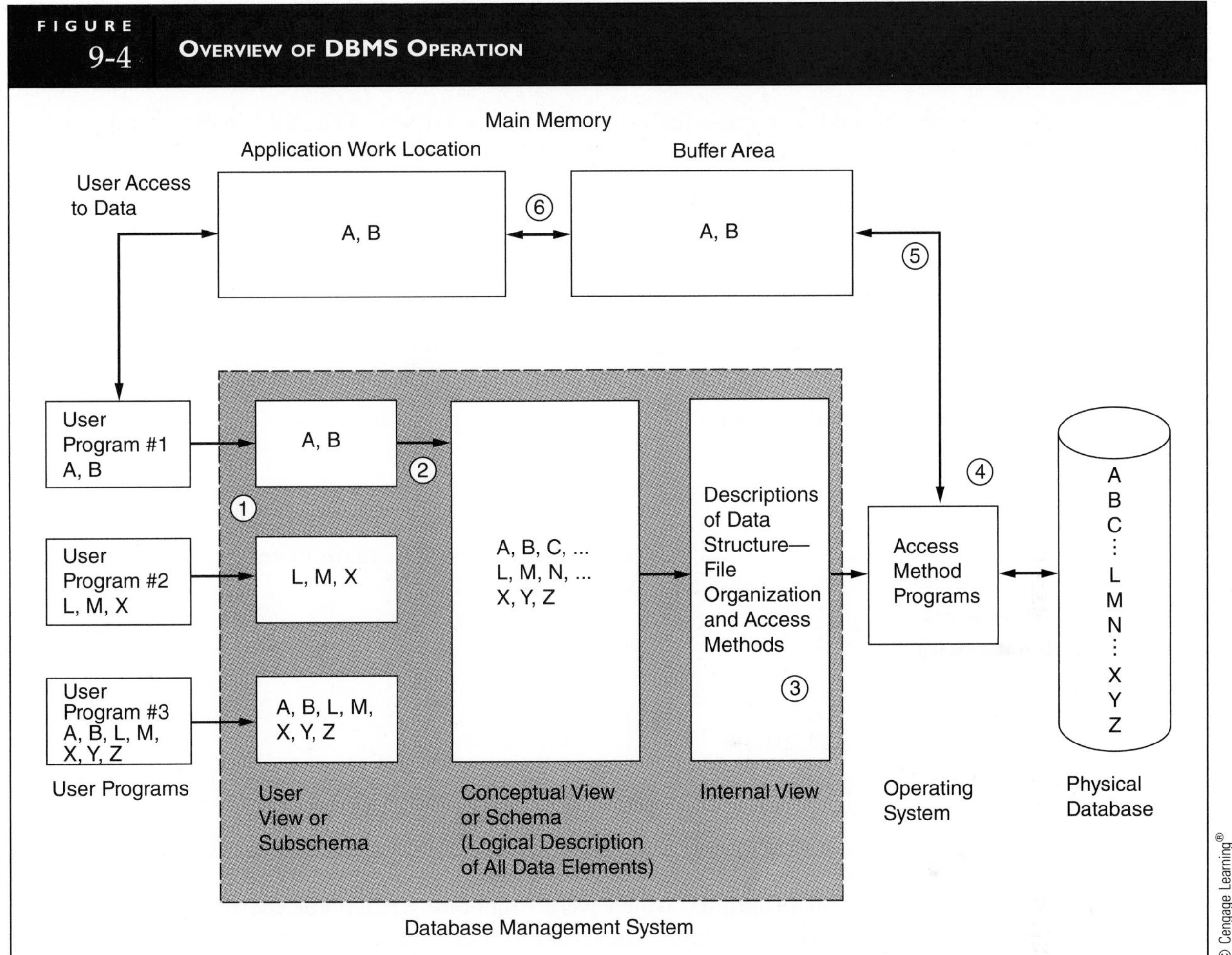

views: the internal view, the conceptual view (schema), and the user view (subschema). Figure 9-4 shows the relationship between these views.

INTERNAL VIEW. The **internal view** presents the physical arrangement of records in the database. This is the lowest level of representation, which is one step removed from the physical database. The internal view describes the structure of records, the linkages between them, and the physical arrangement and sequence of records in a file. There is only one internal view of the database.

CONCEPTUAL VIEW (SCHEMA). The conceptual view or **schema** represents the database logically and abstractly, rather than the way it is physically stored. This view allows users' programs to call for data without knowing or needing to specify how the data are arranged or where the data reside in the physical database. There is only one conceptual view for a database.

USER VIEW (SUBSCHEMA). The **user view** defines how a particular user sees the portion of the database that he or she is authorized to access. To the user, the user view is the database. Unlike the internal and conceptual views, many distinct user views exist. For example, a user in the personnel department may view the database as a collection of employee records and is unaware of the supplier and inventory records seen by the users in the inventory control department.

DBMS OPERATION. To illustrate the roles of these views, let's look at the typical sequence of events that occurs in accessing data through a DBMS. The following description is hypothetical, and certain technical details are omitted.

1. A user program sends a request (call) for data to the DBMS. The call is written in a special data manipulation language (discussed later) that is embedded in the user program.
2. The DBMS analyzes the request by matching the called data elements against the user view and the conceptual view. If the data request matches, it is authorized, and processing proceeds to Step 3. If it does not match the views, access is denied.
3. The DBMS determines the data structure parameters from the internal view and passes them to the operating system, which performs the actual data retrieval. Data structure parameters describe the organization and **access method** (an operating system utility program) for retrieving the requested data.
4. Using the appropriate access method, the operating system interacts with the disk storage device to retrieve the data from the physical database.
5. The operating system then stores the data in a main memory buffer area managed by the DBMS.
6. The DBMS transfers the data to the user's work location in main memory. At this point, the user's program is free to access and manipulate the data.
7. When processing is complete, Steps 4, 5, and 6 are reversed to restore the processed data to the database.

Data Manipulation Language

Data manipulation language (DML) is the proprietary programming language that a particular DBMS uses to retrieve, process, and store data. Entire user programs may be written in the DML, or alternatively, selected DML commands can be inserted into programs that are written in universal languages, such as PL/1, COBOL, and FORTRAN. Inserting DML commands enables legacy application programs, which were originally written for the flat-file environment or earlier types of DBMSs, to be easily converted to work in the current database environment. The use of standard language programs also provides the organization with a degree of independence from the DBMS vendor. If the organization decides to switch its vendors to one that uses a different DML, it will not be necessary to rewrite all the user programs. By replacing the old DML commands with the new commands, user programs can be modified to function in the new environment.

Query Language

The query capability of the DBMS permits end users and professional programmers to access data in the database directly without the need for conventional programs. IBM's **structured query language** (SQL, pronounced sequel) has emerged as the standard query language for both mainframe and microcomputer DBMSs. SQL is a fourth-generation, nonprocedural language with many commands that allow users to input, retrieve, and modify data easily. The SELECT command is a powerful tool for retrieving data. The example in Figure 9-5 illustrates the use of the SELECT command to produce a user report from a database called Inventory.

SQL is an efficient data processing tool. Although not a natural English language, SQL requires far less training in computer concepts and fewer programming skills than many languages. In fact, many database query systems require no SQL knowledge at all. Users select data visually by pointing and clicking at the desired attributes. The visual user interface then generates the necessary SQL commands automatically. This feature places ad hoc reporting and data processing capability in the hands of the user/manager. By reducing reliance on professional programmers, managers are better able to deal with problems that arise.

FIGURE 9-5 EXAMPLE OF SELECT COMMAND USED TO QUERY AN INVENTORY DATABASE

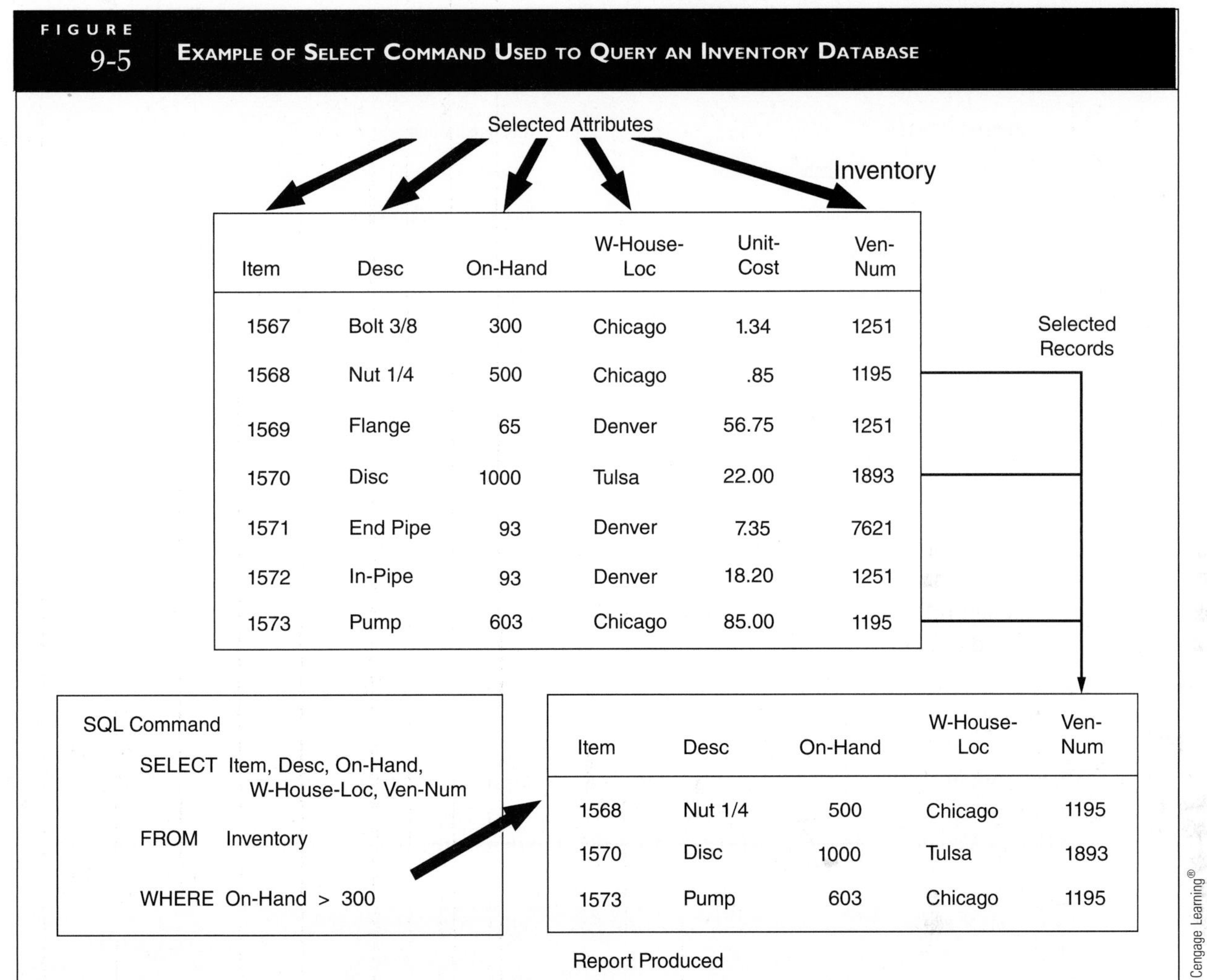

THE DATABASE ADMINISTRATOR

Refer to Figure 9-3 and note the administrative position of **database administrator (DBA)**. This position does not exist in the flat-file environment. The DBA is responsible for managing the database resource. Having multiple users share a common database requires organization, coordination, rules, and guidelines to protect the integrity of the database.

In large organizations, the DBA function may consist of an entire department of technical personnel under the database administrator. In smaller organizations, someone within the computer services group may assume DBA responsibility. The duties of the DBA fall into the following areas[1]: database planning, database design, database implementation, database operation and maintenance, and database change and growth. Table 9-1 presents a breakdown of specific tasks within these broad areas.

Organizational Interactions of the DBA

Figure 9-6 shows some of the organizational interactions of the DBA. Of particular importance is the relationship among the DBA, the end users, and the systems professionals of the organization. Refer again to Figure 9-3 during the examination of this relationship.

---

1 Adapted from F. R. McFadden and J. A. Hoffer, *Database Management,* 3rd ed. (Redwood City, CA: Benjamin/Cummings Publishing, 1991), 343.

TABLE 9-1 FUNCTIONS OF THE DATABASE ADMINISTRATOR

Database Planning	**Implementation**
Develop organization's database strategy	Determine access policy
Define database environment	Implement security controls
Define data requirements	Specify test procedures
Develop data dictionary	Establish programming standards
Design	**Operation and Maintenance**
Logical database (schema)	Evaluate database performance
External users' views (subschemas)	Reorganize database as user needs demand
Internal view of database	Review standards and procedures
Database controls	
	Change and Growth
	Plan for change and growth
	Evaluate new technology

As information needs arise, users send formal requests for computer applications to the systems professionals (programmers) of the organization. The requests are handled through formal systems development procedures, which produce the programmed applications. Figure 9-3 shows this relationship as the line from the user's block to the systems development process block. The user requests also go to the DBA, who evaluates these to determine the user's database needs. Once this is

FIGURE 9-6 ORGANIZATIONAL INTERACTIONS OF THE DATABASE ADMINISTRATOR

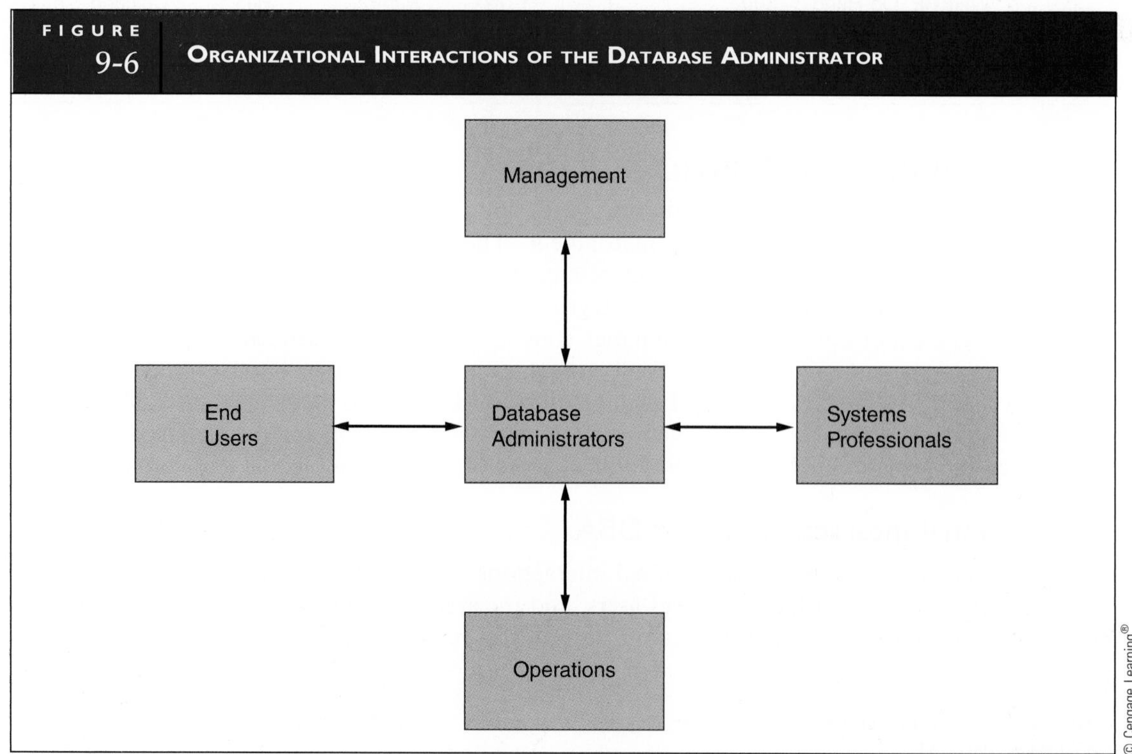

established, the DBA grants the user access authority by programming the user's view (subschema). This relationship is shown as the lines between the user and the DBA and between the DBA and DDL module in the DBMS.

By keeping access authority separate from systems development (application programming), the organization is better able to control and protect the database. Intentional and unintentional attempts at unauthorized access are more likely to be discovered when these two groups work independently. The rationale for this separation of duties is developed in Chapter 15.

The Data Dictionary

Another important function of the DBA is the creation and maintenance of the **data dictionary**. The data dictionary describes every data element in the database. This enables all users (and programmers) to share a common view of the data resource and greatly facilitates the analysis of user needs.

THE PHYSICAL DATABASE

The fourth major element of the database approach as presented in Figure 9-3 is the **physical database**. This is the lowest level of the database. The physical database consists of magnetic spots on magnetic disks. The other levels of the database (e.g., the user view, conceptual view, and internal view) are abstract representations of the physical level.

At the physical level, the database is a collection of records and files. Relational databases are based on the **indexed sequential file** structure. This structure, illustrated in Figure 9-7, uses an index in conjunction with a sequential file organization. It facilitates both direct access to individual records and batch processing of the entire file. Multiple indexes can be used to create a cross-reference, called an **inverted list**, which allows even more flexible access to data. Two indexes are shown in Figure 9-7. One contains the employee number (primary key) for uniquely locating records in the file. The second index contains record addresses arranged by year-to-date earnings. Using this nonunique field as a secondary key permits all employee records to be viewed in ascending or descending order according to earnings. Alternatively, individual records with selected earnings balances can be displayed. Indexes may be created for each attribute in the file, allowing data to be viewed from a multitude of perspectives.

The next section examines the principles that underlie the relational model and the techniques, rules, and procedures for creating relational tables from indexed sequential files. You will also see how tables are linked to other tables to permit complex data representations.

The Relational Database Model

E. F. Codd originally proposed the principles of the relational model in the late 1960s.[2] The formal model has its foundations in relational algebra and set theory, which provide the theoretical basis for most of the data manipulation operations used.

From a purist's point of view, a fully relational system is one that conforms to 12 stringent rules that Codd outlined.[3] As a practical matter, however, not all of Codd's rules are equally important. Other theorists have, therefore, proposed less rigid requirements for assessing the relational standing of a system.[4] Accordingly, a system is relational if it:

1. Represents data in the form of two-dimensional tables such as the database table, called Customer, shown in Figure 9-8.
2. Supports the relational algebra functions of restrict, project, and join:

   Restrict: *Extracts specified rows from a specified table. This operation, illustrated in Figure 9-9(a), creates a virtual table (one that does not physically exist) that is a subset of the original table.*

2 C. J. Date, *An Introduction to Database Systems,* Vol. 1, 4th ed. (Reading, MA: Addison-Wesley, 1986), 99.

3 For a complete discussion of these rules, see McFadden and Hoffer, *Database Management:* 698–703.

4 C. J. Date, *An Introduction to Database Systems:* 320–26.

FIGURE 9-7 **Indexed Sequential File**

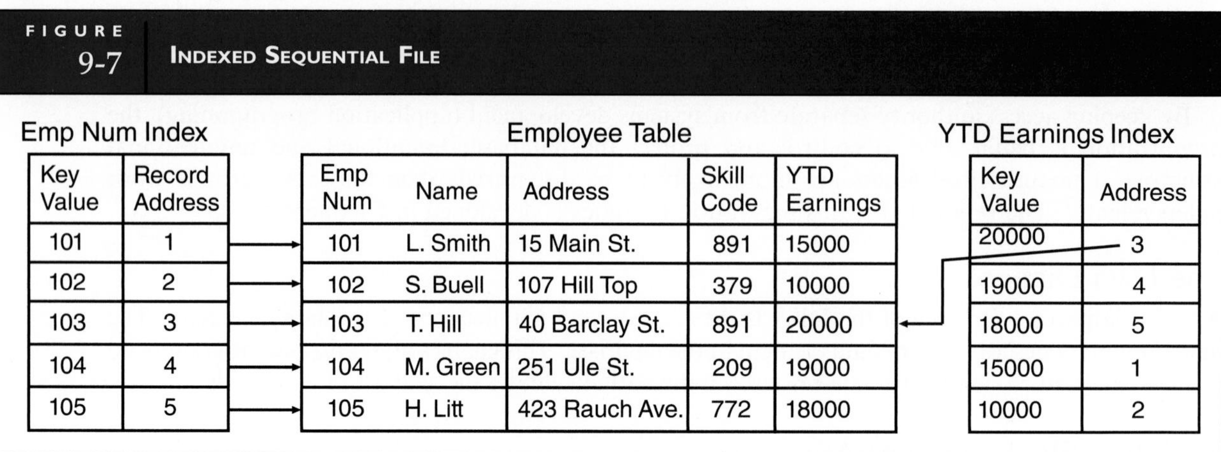

Emp Num Index

Key Value	Record Address
101	1
102	2
103	3
104	4
105	5

Employee Table

Emp Num	Name	Address	Skill Code	YTD Earnings
101	L. Smith	15 Main St.	891	15000
102	S. Buell	107 Hill Top	379	10000
103	T. Hill	40 Barclay St.	891	20000
104	M. Green	251 Ule St.	209	19000
105	H. Litt	423 Rauch Ave.	772	18000

YTD Earnings Index

Key Value	Address
20000	3
19000	4
18000	5
15000	1
10000	2

FIGURE 9-8 **A Relational Table Called Customer**

Attributes

Table Name = Customer

Tuples (Records)

Cust Num (Key)	Name	Address	Current Balance
1875	J. Smith	18 Elm St.	1820.00
1876	G. Adams	21 First St.	2400.00
1943	J. Hobbs	165 High St.	549.87
2345	Y. Martin	321 Barclay	5256.76
•	•	•	•
•	•	•	•
•	•	•	•
5678	T. Stem	432 Main St.	643.67

FIGURE 9-9 THE RELATIONAL ALGEBRA FUNCTIONS RESTRICT, PROJECT, AND JOIN

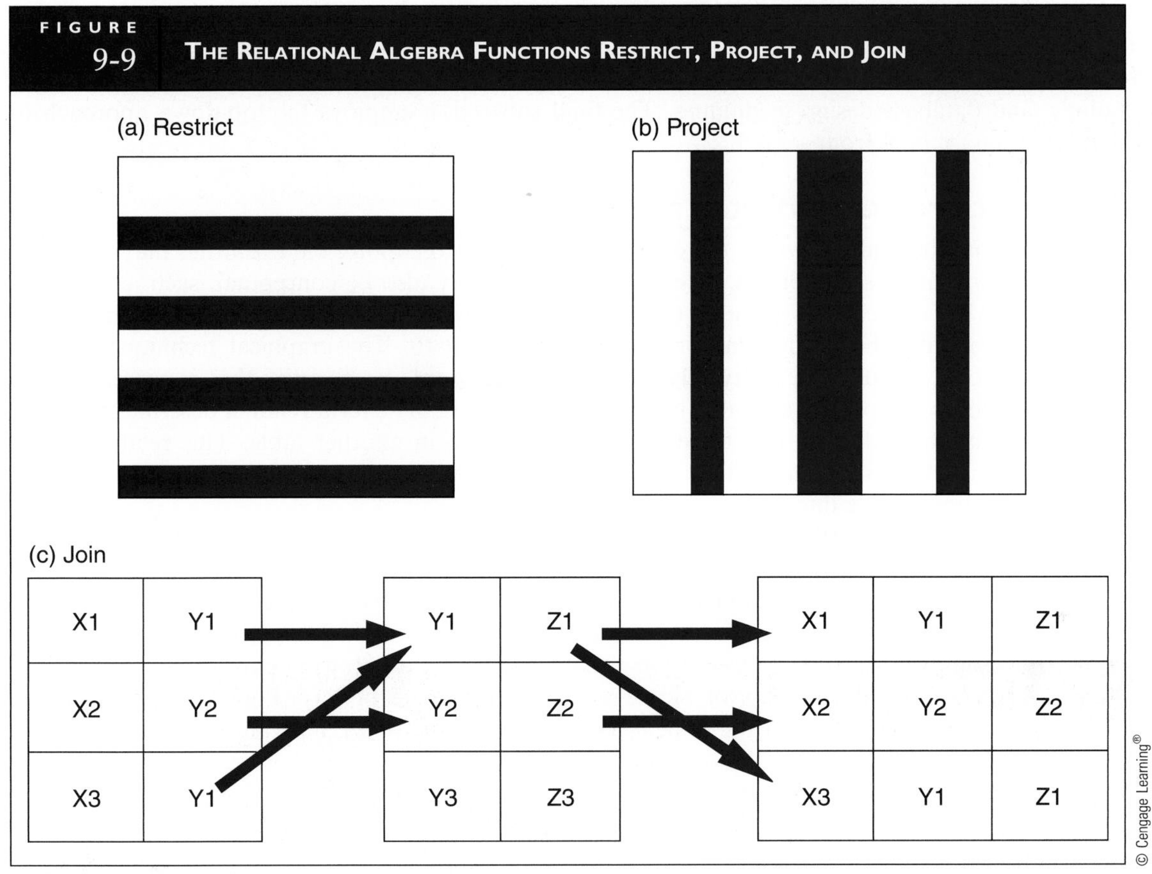

Project: *Extracts specified attributes (columns) from a table to create a virtual table. This is presented in Figure 9-9(b).*

Join: *Builds a new physical table from two tables consisting of all concatenated pairs of rows, from each table, as shown in Figure 9-9(c).*

Although not the complete set of relational functions, the subset of restrict, project, and join satisfies most business information needs.

DATA MODELING CONCEPTS

In this section, we review data modeling concepts. A **data model** is a visual representation of an organization's data. The model represents the nature of the data and the business rules that dictate how they are used. A data model is similar to a blueprint (plan) for a house. The blueprint is created by an architect based on the prospective owner's stated requirements. Once approved, the blueprint guides the physical building of the house. Similarly, database developers use the completed data model, often in the form of an ER diagram, to construct the physical database tables and the coding needed to make it function as prescribed. In theory, data models are designed in a **top-down approach**, which requires a detailed analysis of the organizations information needs. In practice, commercial database management systems typically provide a predefined data model and tables that are based on business best-practices. The client organization's database developers may then modify the model to suit the company's specific needs. This is often called the **bottom-up approach**.

Accountants and auditors work extensively with databases as part of their day-to-day activities. Whether preparing financial statements, tagging data attributes for XBRL reporting, or extracting financial data from tables during the conduct of audit tests, accountants and auditors need to understand how the data are structured. The purpose of this section, therefore, is to explain the basics of data modeling that will serve to guide the accountant when performing database-related tasks. Toward this end, the subsections that follow introduce relational concepts, database terminology, and database design techniques. The final subsection employs the top-down approach to develop a data model from scratch.

Entity, Occurrence, Attributes, and Relation

An **entity** is anything about which the organization wishes to capture data. Entities may be physical, such as inventories, customers, or employees. They may also be conceptual, such as accounts receivable (AR), or accounts payable (AP). Database developers identify entities and prepare a model of them like the partial one presented in Figure 9-10. The graphical technique used to depict the model is called an **entity relationship (ER) diagram**. Each entity that is represented in an ER diagram corresponds to a table in a physical database. The term **relation** describes the common situation where data in one table are related to data in another table. This relationship is represented in the ER diagram by the lines between the tables in Figure 9-10. We discuss the symbols and notation on the lines later.

As a matter of convention, entities are named in the singular noun form, such as Customer rather than Customers. The term **occurrence** (or instance) is used to describe the number of items associated with an entity. For example, if an organization has 100 employees, the Employee entity is said to consist of 100 occurrences or instances. **Attributes** are the data elements that define an entity. For example, an Employee entity may be defined by the following partial set of attributes: Name, Address, Job Skill, Years of Service, and Hourly Rate of Pay. Each occurrence in the Employee entity is defined by of the same types (classes) of attributes, but values for each attribute will vary among occurrences. For example, each employee is defined in part by an Address attribute, but the address values will differ with each employee.

Associations and Cardinality

The term **association** describes the nature of the functional connection between two entities in a relation. This association is represented in an ER diagram by a verb label on the connecting line such as ships, requests, receives, and so on. **Cardinality** is the degree of association between two entities. Simply stated, cardinality describes the number of possible occurrences in one table that is associated with a single occurrence in a related table. Four basic forms of cardinality are possible: zero or one (0,1), one and only one (1,1), zero or many (0,M), and one or many (1,M).

FIGURE 9-10 DATA MODEL USING AN ENTITY RELATIONSHIP DIAGRAM

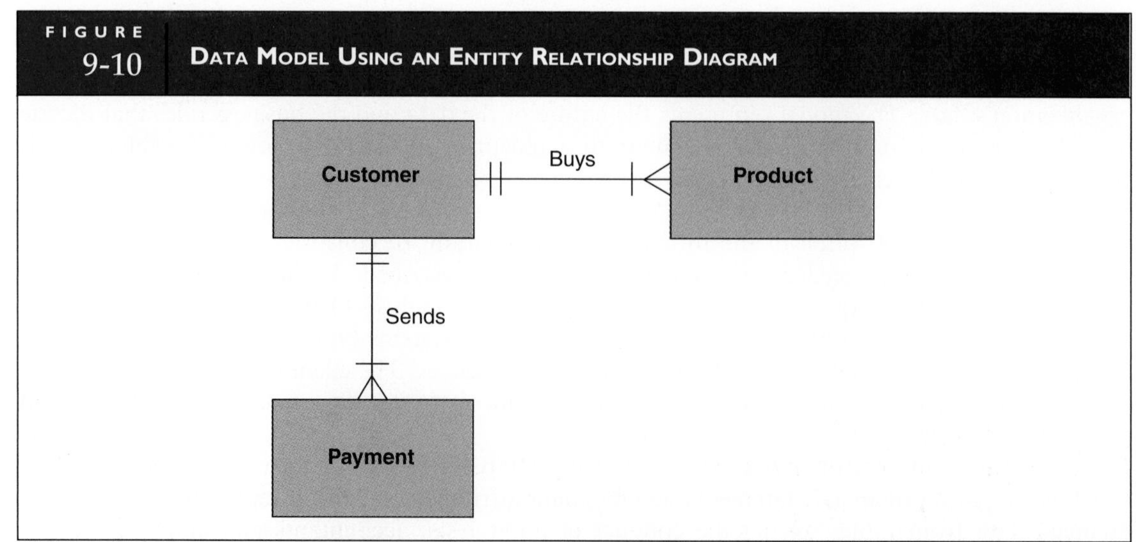

These are combined to describe the cardinality between entities in a relation. When determining the cardinality in a relation, consider a single occurrence on one side of the relation and answer the following question: What are the minimum and maximum number of occurrences in the related entity that may be associated with this single occurrence? Figure 9-11 presents several examples of entity cardinality and associations, which are discussed next.

EXAMPLE 1. Assume that a company has 1,000 employees but only 100 of them are sales staff. Assume also that each salesperson is assigned a company car, but nonsales staff are not.

Example 1 in Figure 9-11 shows that for each occurrence in the Employee entity, there is a possibility of zero or one occurrence in the Company Car entity.

To illustrate, select a single hypothetical occurrence in the Employee entity and look toward the Company Car entity. Only two cardinality values are possible. If the selected Employee record is that of a salesperson, then he or she is assigned one (and only one) company car. Thus the upper (highest) cardinality value is 1. If, however, the selected Employee record is that of a nonsalesperson, then the individual would be assigned no car and the lower cardinality value is zero. A circle

FIGURE 9-11 EXAMPLES OF ENTITY ASSOCIATIONS

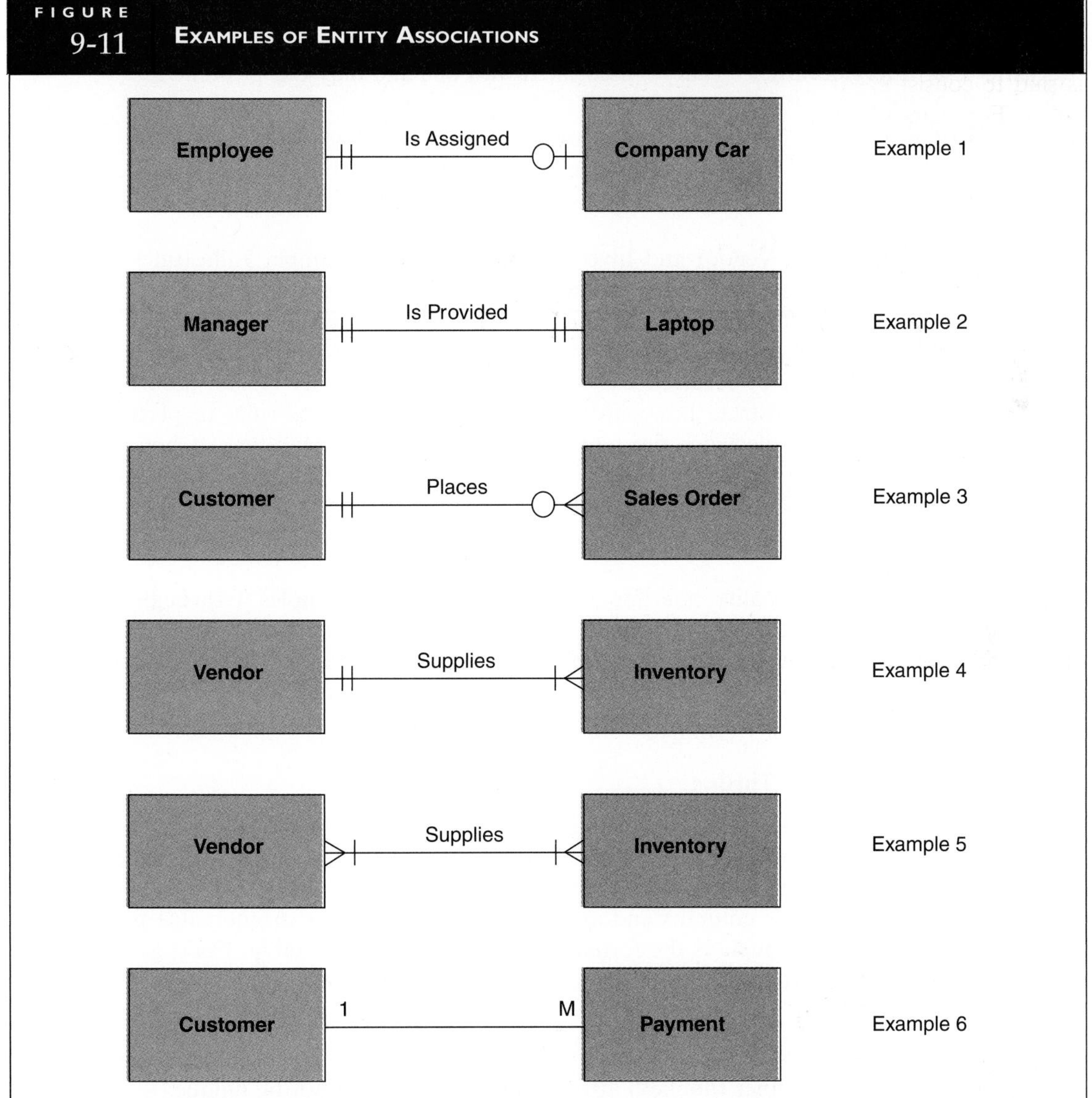

and a short line intersecting the association line at the Company Car entity side of the relation depicts this 0,1 degree of cardinality. Now, select a Company Car record and look back at the Employee entity. Because each company car is assigned to only one employee, both the minimum and maximum number of occurrences in the Employ entity is one. Two short intersecting lines at the Employee end of the association line signify this cardinality.

EXAMPLE 2. Example 2 illustrates a situation in which each occurrence in one entity is always associated with one (and only one) occurrence in the associated entity. In this case, each company Laptop computer is assigned to only one Manager, and every Manager is assigned only one computer. Two short lines intersecting the connecting line at both ends depict this cardinality.

EXAMPLE 3. Example 3 presents the relationship between Customer and Sales Order entities. Notice that the minimum number of Sales Order occurrences per Customer occurrence is zero, and the maximum is many. This cardinality exists because Customer is a physical entity that transcends the current accounting period. A customer may have been a customer for years. The Sales Order entity represents an event that takes place within a period. Therefore, it is possible for a particular customer to have purchased many times this period or not at all and, thus, the zero or many cardinality. The crow's foot symbol (which gives this form of notation its name) depicts the many (upper) cardinality at the Sales Order end of the association line. From the perspective of the Sales Order entity, however, every occurrence (sale) is associated with one and only one customer.

EXAMPLE 4. Example 4 represents a situation in which each specific item of inventory is supplied by one and only one Vendor, and each Vendor supplies one or many different inventory items to the company. Contrast this association with a similar situation in Example 5 below.

EXAMPLE 5. Using the Vendor and Inventory entities again, Example 5 illustrates a situation where company policy requires purchasing the same types of inventory from multiple suppliers. Management may do this to ensure that it gets the best prices or to avoid becoming dependent on a single supplier. Under such a policy, each Vendor occurrence is associated with one or many Inventory occurrences, and each Inventory occurrence is associated with one or many Vendor occurrences.

Examples 4 and 5 demonstrate how cardinality reflects the business rules in place within an organization. The database designer must obtain a thorough understanding of how the client-company and specific users conduct business to properly design the data model. If the data model is wrong, the resulting database tables will also be wrong. Examples 4 and 5 are both valid but different business options and, as we shall see, require different database designs.

EXAMPLE 6. The cardinality notation technique shown in Examples 1 through 5 is called crow's foot. Several alternative approaches are also used. One method is to explicitly write the upper and lower cardinality on the association line. Another is a shorthand version that notes only the upper cardinality such as 1:1, 1:M, and M:M, as illustrated in Example 6. For homework assignments, your instructor will advise you of the preferred method to use.

The Physical Database Tables

As mentioned previously, the data model is the blueprint for the physical database tables that constitute the database. The tables are constructed based on the entity specifications in the model. The attributes form columns with the attribute name at the top of each column. Occurrences form rows that cut across the columns and at their intersection is an attribute value that pertains to the occurrence. The term **tuple** is the formal name for a row in the table, Codd gave a precise definition when he first introduced this term. Accordingly, properly designed tables possess the following four characteristics:

1. The value of at least one attribute in each tuple must be unique. This attribute is the **primary key**. The values of the other (nonkey) attributes in the row need not be unique.

2. All attribute values in any column must be of the same class.
3. Each column in a given table must be uniquely named. However, different tables may contain columns with the same name.
4. Tables must conform to the rules of normalization. This means they must be free from structural dependencies, including repeating groups, partial dependencies, and transitive dependencies (see this chapter's appendix for a complete discussion).

Linkages between Relational Tables

Logically related tables need to be physically connected to achieve the associations described in the data model. This is accomplished by using **foreign keys**, as illustrated in Figure 9-12. In this example, the foreign keys are embedded in the related table. For instance, the primary key of the Customer table (CUST NUM) is embedded as a foreign key in both the Sales Invoice and Cash Receipts tables. Similarly, the primary key in the Sales Invoice table (INVOICE NUM) is an embedded foreign key in the Line Item table. Note that the Line Item table uses a composite

FIGURE 9-12 LINKAGES BETWEEN RELATIONAL TABLES

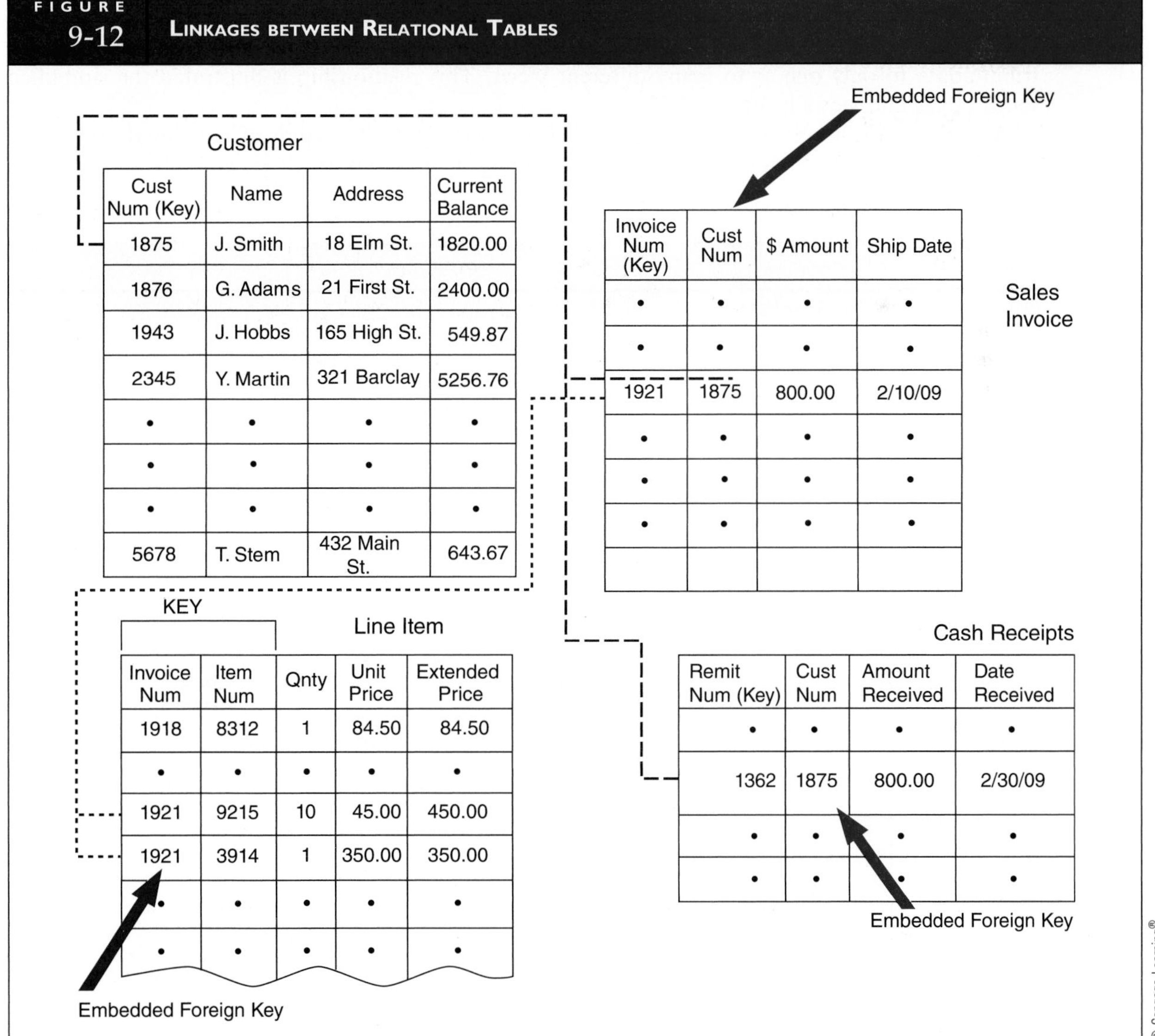

primary key composed of INVOICE NUM and ITEM NUM. Both fields are needed to identify each occurrence in the table uniquely, but only the invoice number portion of the key provides the logical link to the Sales Invoice table. Foreign keys are not always embedded like those in Figure 9-12. The degree of cardinality between the related tables determines the method used for assigning foreign keys. These methods are examined later.

With foreign keys in place, a computer program can be written to navigate among the tables of the database and provide users with the data they need to support their day-to-day tasks and decision-making responsibilities. For example, if a user wants all the invoices for Customer 1875, the program will search the Sales Invoice table for tuples with a foreign key value of 1875. We see from Figure 9-12 that there is only one such occurrence—invoice number 1921. To obtain the line-item details for this invoice, the program searches the Line Item table for occurrence with a foreign key value of 1921, and two tuples are retrieved.

User Views

A user view was defined earlier as the set of data that a particular user sees. Examples of user views are computer screens for entering or viewing data, management reports, or source documents such as an invoice or a purchase order. Views may be digital or hard copy, but in all cases, they derive from underlying database tables. Simple views may be constructed from a single table, while more complex views may require several tables. Furthermore, a single table may contribute data to only one or to many different views. This relationship is illustrated the simplified set of tables and views in Figure 9-13.

A large organization will have thousands of user views that thousands of individual tables support. The task of identifying all views and translating them into normalized tables is an important

FIGURE 9-13 RELATIONSHIP BETWEEN USER VIEWS AND ENTITIES

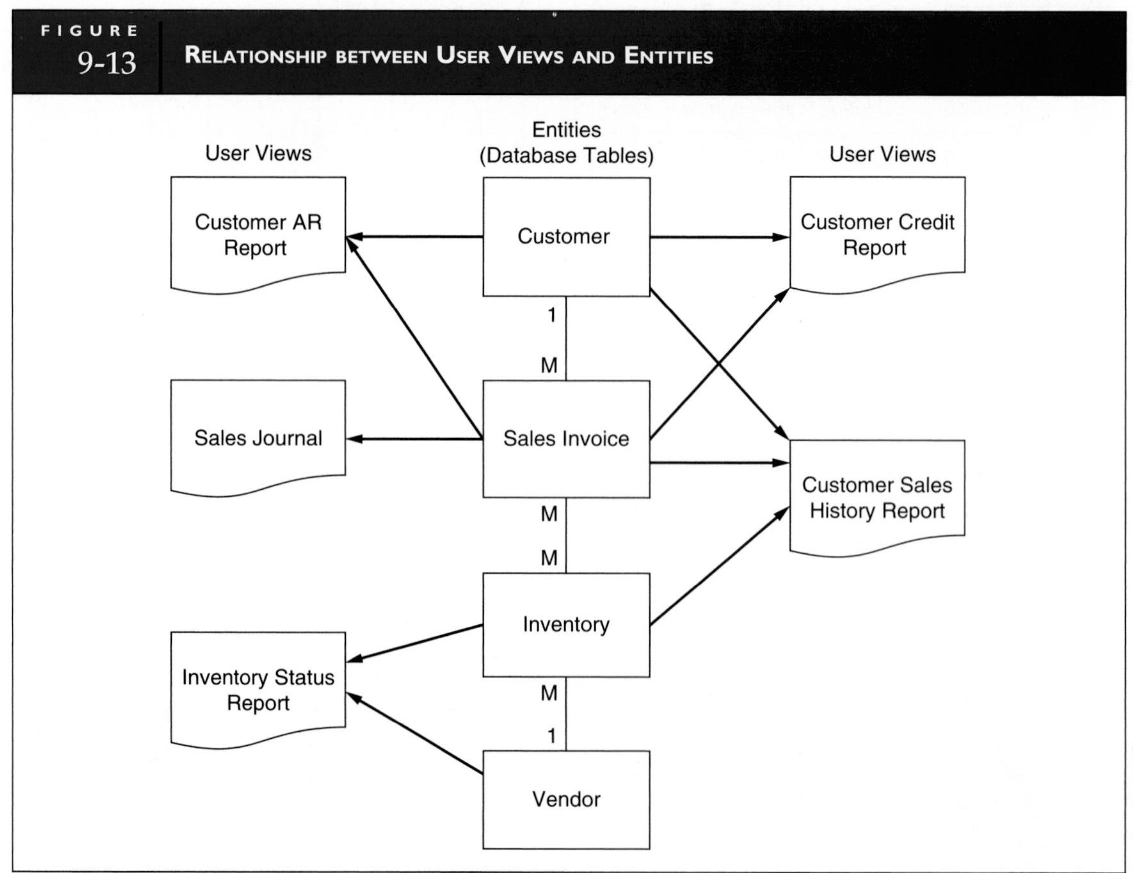

responsibility of database designers as it has internal control implications. The issues and techniques related to this task are examined next.

ANOMALIES, STRUCTURAL DEPENDENCIES, AND DATA NORMALIZATION

This section deals with why database tables need to be normalized. In other words, why is it necessary for the organization's database to form an elaborate network of normalized tables linked together like those illustrated in Figure 9-12? Why, instead, can we not simply consolidate the views of one user (or several) into a single common table from which all data needs may be met?

Database Anomalies

The answer to the above questions is that improperly normalized tables can cause DBMS processing problems that restrict, or even deny, users' access to the information they need. Such tables exhibit negative operational symptoms called **anomalies**. Specifically, these are the update anomaly, the insertion anomaly, and the deletion anomaly. One or more of these anomalies will exist in tables that are not normalized or are normalized at a low level, such as the **first normal form (lNF)** or **second normal form (2NF)**. To be free of anomalies, tables must be normalized to the **third normal form (3NF)** level.

We will demonstrate the negative impact of anomalies with the user view in Figure 9-14. This inventory status report would be used to provide a purchasing agent with information about inventory items to be ordered as well as the various suppliers (vendors) of those items. If this view were to be produced from a single table, it would look similar to the one presented in Figure 9-15. While such a table could indeed store the data to produce the view, it will exhibit the anomalies described next.

UPDATE ANOMALY. The **update anomaly** is the result of data redundancy in an unnormalized table. To illustrate, notice that Supplier Number 22 provides each of the three inventory items (Part Num 1, 2, and 3) shown in Figure 9-15. The data attributes pertaining to Supplier Number 22 (Name, Address, and Tele Num) are thus repeated in every record of every inventory item that Supplier Number 22 provides. Any change in the supplier's name, address, or telephone number

FIGURE 9-14 INVENTORY STATUS REPORT

Ajax Manufacturing Co.
Inventory Status Report

Part Number	Description	Quantity on Hand	Reorder Point	Supplier Number	Name	Address	Telephone
1	Bracket	100	150	22 24 27	Ozment Sup Buell Co. B&R Sup	123 Main St. 2 Broadhead Westgate Mall	555-7895 555-3436 555-7845
2	Gasket	440	450	22 24 28	Ozment Sup Buell Co. Harris Manuf	123 Main St. 2 Broadhead 24 Linden St.	555-7895 555-3436 555-3316
3	Brace	10	10	22 24 28	Ozment Sup Buell Co. Harris Manuf	123 Main St. 2 Broadhead 24 Linden St.	555-7895 555-3436 555-3316
⋮	⋮	⋮	⋮	⋮	⋮	⋮	⋮

FIGURE 9-15 UNNORMALIZED DATABASE TABLE

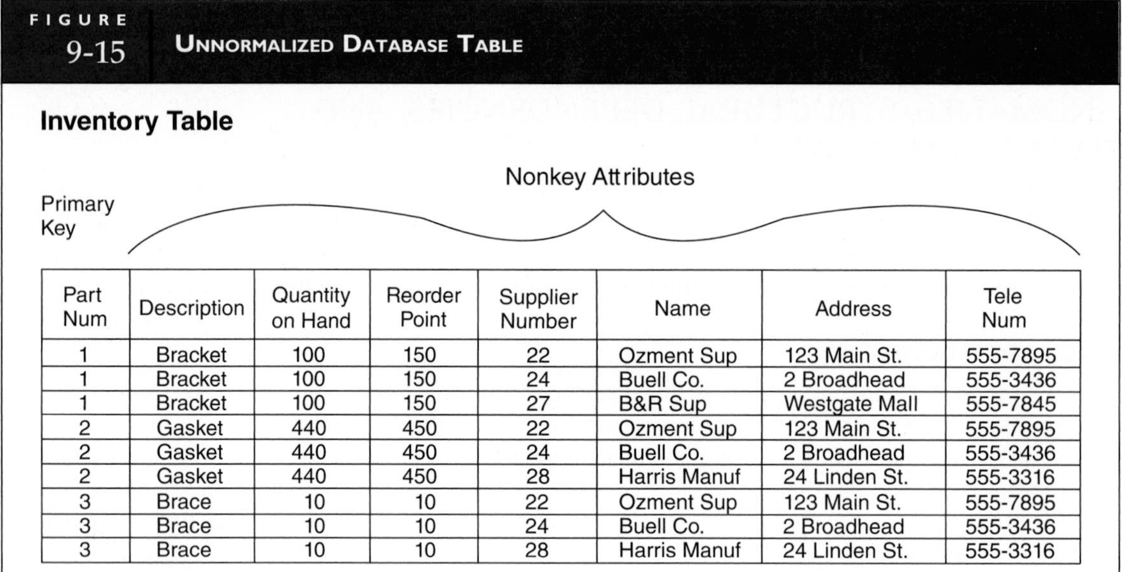

Part Num	Description	Quantity on Hand	Reorder Point	Supplier Number	Name	Address	Tele Num
1	Bracket	100	150	22	Ozment Sup	123 Main St.	555-7895
1	Bracket	100	150	24	Buell Co.	2 Broadhead	555-3436
1	Bracket	100	150	27	B&R Sup	Westgate Mall	555-7845
2	Gasket	440	450	22	Ozment Sup	123 Main St.	555-7895
2	Gasket	440	450	24	Buell Co.	2 Broadhead	555-3436
2	Gasket	440	450	28	Harris Manuf	24 Linden St.	555-3316
3	Brace	10	10	22	Ozment Sup	123 Main St.	555-7895
3	Brace	10	10	24	Buell Co.	2 Broadhead	555-3436
3	Brace	10	10	28	Harris Manuf	24 Linden St.	555-3316

must be made to each of these records in the table. In the example, this means three different updates. To better appreciate the implications of the update anomaly, consider a more realistic situation where the vendor supplies 10,000 different items of inventory. Any update to a vendor attribute must then be made 10,000 times.

INSERTION ANOMALY. To demonstrate the effects of the **insertion anomaly**, assume that a new vendor has entered the marketplace. The organization does not yet purchase from the vendor but may wish to do so in the future. In the meantime, the organization wants to add the vendor to the database. This is not possible, however, because the primary key for the Inventory table is PART NUM. Because the vendor does not supply the organization with any inventory items, the supplier data cannot be added to the table.

DELETION ANOMALY. The **deletion anomaly** involves the unintentional deletion of data from a table. To illustrate, assume that Supplier Number 27 provides the company with only one item: Part Number 1. If the organization discontinues this item of inventory and deletes it from the table, the data pertaining to Supplier Number 27 will also be deleted. Although the company may wish to retain the supplier's information for future use, the current table design prevents it from doing so.

The presence of the deletion anomaly is less conspicuous but potentially more serious than the update and insertion anomalies. A flawed database design that prevents the insertion of records or requires the user to perform excessive updates attracts attention quickly. The deletion anomaly, however, may go undetected, leaving the user unaware of the loss of important data until it is too late. This can result in the unintentional loss of critical accounting records and the destruction of audit trails. Proper table design, therefore, is not just an operational efficiency issue; it carries internal control significance that accountants need to recognize.

Normalizing Tables in a Relational Database

The database anomalies described above are symptoms of structural problems within tables called dependencies. Specifically, these are known as **repeating groups, partial dependencies**, and **transitive dependencies**. The normalization process involves identifying and removing structural dependencies from the table(s) being modeled such that the resulting 3NF table designs will meet two conditions:

1. All nonkey (data) attributes in the table are dependent on (defined by) the primary key.
2. All nonkey attributes are independent of the other nonkey attributes.

In other words, a 3NF table is one in which the primary key of a table wholly and uniquely defines each attribute in the table. Furthermore, none of the table attributes is defined by an attribute other than the primary key.

Figure 9-16 graphically illustrates the normalization process as an unnormalized table that progresses toward 3NF as each type of dependency issue is resolved. The process begins with a user view, such as an output report, a source document, or an input screen. Images of user views may be prepared using a word processor, graphics package, or simply pencil and paper. At this point, the view is merely a pictorial representation of a set of data the user will eventually have when the project is completed. To demonstrate the normalization process, we will use the customer sales invoice and sample data presented in Figure 9-17. The basic question here is: Can we store all the data needed for this view in a single table that also meets the two 3NF conditions?

REPRESENT THE VIEW AS A SINGLE TABLE

The next step is to represent the view as a single table that contains all of the view attributes. Figure 9-18 presents a single-table structure containing the sample data from Figure 9-17. Because the table contains customer invoices, the invoice number (INVOICE NUM) will serve as a logical primary key. Notice the attributes Ext Price and Total Due have been highlighted in Figure 9-18. The values for these attributes may be either stored or calculated. Because Ext Price is the product of two other attributes (Quantity and Unit Price), and Total Due is the sum of all Ext Price values, they both can be calculated from existing stored attributes rather than storing them

FIGURE 9-16 STEPS IN THE NORMALIZATION PROCESS

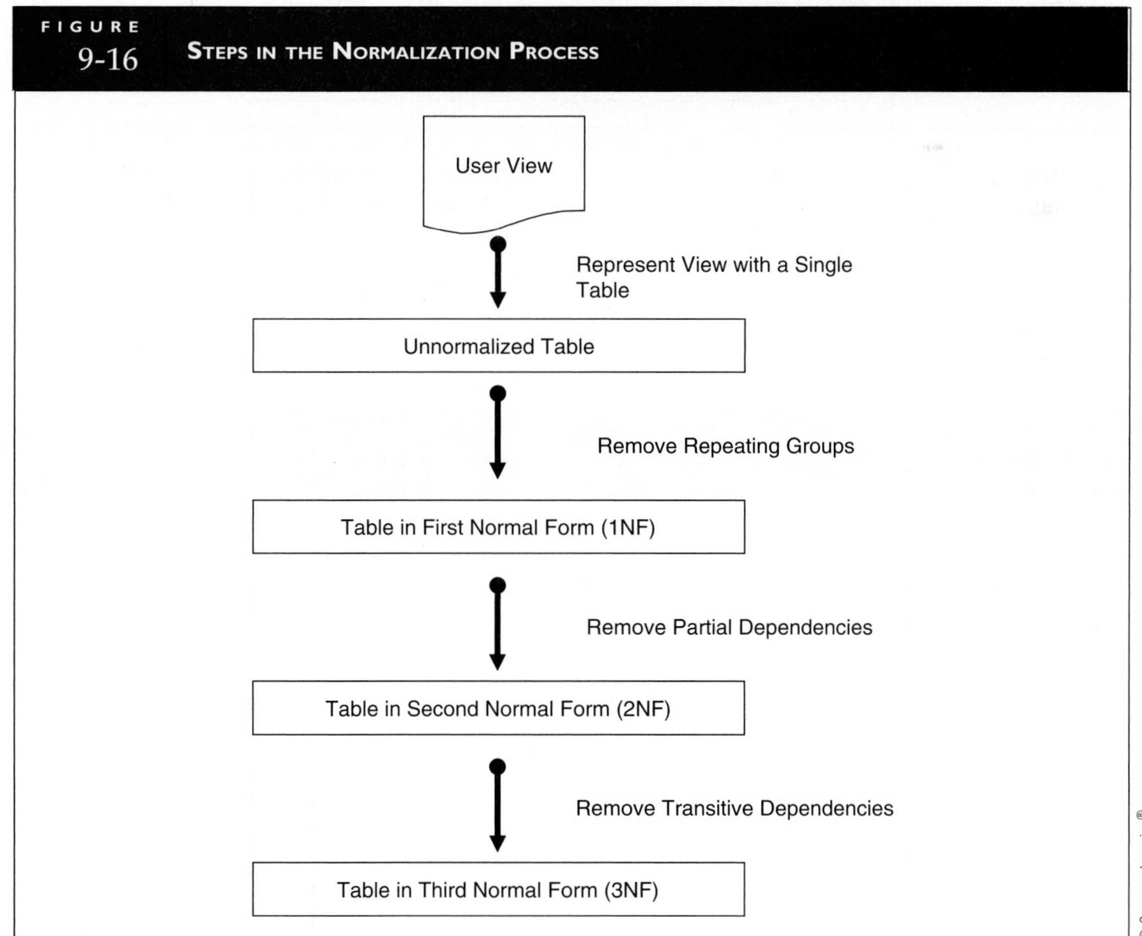

FIGURE 9-17 A User View

SALES INVOICE

Invoice Number: 16459
Order Date: 09/22/2009
Shipped Date: 09/27/2009
Shipped Via: UPS

Customer Number: **1765**
Customer Name: **ABC Associates**
Street Address: **132 Elm St.**
City: **Bethlehem**
State: **PA**
Telephone Number: **610-555-6721**

Prod Num	Description	Quantity	Unit Price	Ex Price
r234	Bolt cutter	2	$42.50	$85.00
m456	Gear puller	1	$16.50	$16.50
W62	Electric welder	1	$485.00	$485.00
			Total Due	**$586.50**

FIGURE 9-18 Unnormalized Table Supporting User View

PK Single-Table Structure for Sales Invoice

Invoice Num	Order Date	Shpd Date	Shpd Via	Total Due	Cust Num	Cust Name	Street Address	City	St	Tele Number	Prod Num	Description	Qunty	Unit Price	Ex Price
16459	09/22/09	09/27/09	UPS	586.50	1765	ABC Assoc	132 Elm St	Bethlehem	PA	**610-555-6721**	r234	Bolt cutter	2	42.50	85.00
16459	09/22/09	09/27/09	UPS	586.50	1765	ABC Assoc	132 Elm St	Bethlehem	PA	**610-555-6721**	m456	Gear puller	1	16.50	16.50
16459	09/22/09	09/27/09	UPS	586.50	1765	ABC Assoc	132 Elm St	Bethlehem	PA	**610-555-6721**	W62	Elec welder	1	485.00	485.00

Redundant Data (Invoice Num through Tele Number) — Repeating Group Data (Prod Num through Ex Price)

directly in the database table. To simplify this example, therefore, we will assume that the system will calculate these attributes and they will not be part of this analysis.

Now that we have a base table to work from, the next few steps in the normalization process involve identifying and eliminating any structural dependencies that exist. If dependencies exist, correcting them will involve splitting the original single-table structure into two or more smaller and independent 3NF tables. Each of the structural dependencies and the techniques for identifying and removing them is outlined in the following sections.

REMOVE REPEATING GROUP DATA

The first step in correcting structural dependencies is to determine if the table under review contains repeating groups. Repeating group data occur when multiple values for a particular attribute exist in a specific tuple. For example, the sales invoice in Figure 9-17 contains multiple values for the attributes PROD NUM, DESCRIPTION, QUANTITY, and UNIT PRICE (we ignore EXT PRICE). These repeating groups represent the transaction details of the invoice. We see repeating group data in many business user views, such as purchase orders, receiving reports, bills of lading, and so on. Relational database theory prohibits the construction of a table in which a single tuple (a row in the table) represents multiple values for an attribute (a column in the table). To represent repeating group values in a single table, therefore, will require multiple rows as illustrated in Figure 9-18. Notice that the invoice attributes, which are common to each occurrence of the repeating group data, will also be represented multiple times. For example, Order Date, Shipped Date, Customer Name, Customer Address, and so on, are stored along with each unique occurrence of Prod Num, Description, Quantity, and Unit Price. To avoid such data redundancy, the repeating group data need to be removed from the table and placed in a separate table. Figure 9-19 shows the resulting tables. One is called Sales Invoice Table, with INVOICE NUM as the primary key. The second table contains the transaction details for the invoice and is called Line Item Table.

Notice that the primary key of the Line Item Table is a **composite key** comprised of two attributes: INVOICE NUM and PROD NUM. Keep in mind that this table will contain the transaction details for our example invoice as well as the transaction details for the invoices of many thousands of customers. Relational database theory requires that a table's primary key uniquely identify each tuple stored in the table.

FIGURE 9-19 RESULTING TABLES AFTER REMOVING REPEATING GROUP DATA AND CALCULATED FIELDS

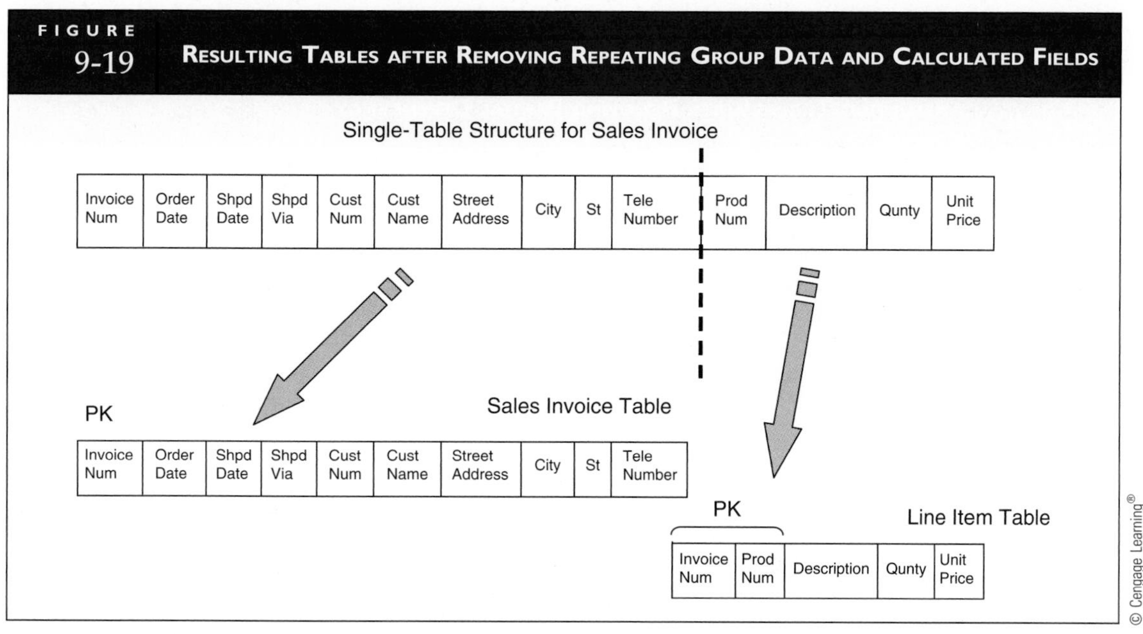

PROD NUM alone cannot do this since a particular product, such as r234 (bolt cutter), may well have been sold to many other customers whose transactions are also in the table. By combining PROD NUM with the INVOICE NUM, however, we can uniquely define each transaction because the table will never contain two occurrences with the same combined invoice number and product number.

REMOVE PARTIAL DEPENDENCIES

Next we check to see if the resulting tables contain partial dependencies. A partial dependency occurs when one or more nonkey attributes are dependent on (defined by) only part of the primary key, rather than the whole key. This can occur only in tables that have composite (two or more attributes) primary keys. Since the Sales Invoice Table has a single attribute primary key, we can ignore it in this step of the analysis. This table is already in 2NF. The Line Item Table, however, needs to be examined further. Figure 9-20 illustrates the partial dependencies in it.

In the Line Item Table, INVOICE NUM and PROD NUM together define the quantity sold attribute (Qunty). If we assume, however, that the price charged for r234 is the same for all customers, then the Unit Price attribute is common to all transactions involving product r234. Similarly, the attribute named Description is common to all such transactions. These two attributes are not dependent on the INVOICE NUM component of the composite key. Instead, they are defined by PROD NUM only and, therefore, are partially dependent rather than wholly dependent on the primary key.

We resolve this by splitting the table into two, as illustrated in Figure 9-20. The resulting Line Item Table is now left with the single nonkey attribute Qunty. Product description and unit price data are placed in a new table called Inventory. Notice that the Inventory Table will contain additional attributes that do not pertain to this user view. A typical inventory table may contain attributes such as reorder point, quantity on hand, supplier code, warehouse location, and more. This demonstrates how a single table may be used to support many different user views. We will return to this issue later.

At this point, both the tables in Figure 9-20 are in 3NF. The Line Item Table's primary key (INVOICE NUM, PROD NUM) wholly defines the attribute QUNTY. Similarly, in the Inventory Table, the Description and Unit Price attributes are wholly defined by the primary key PROD NUM.

FIGURE 9-20 RESULTING TABLES AFTER REMOVING PARTIAL DEPENDENCY

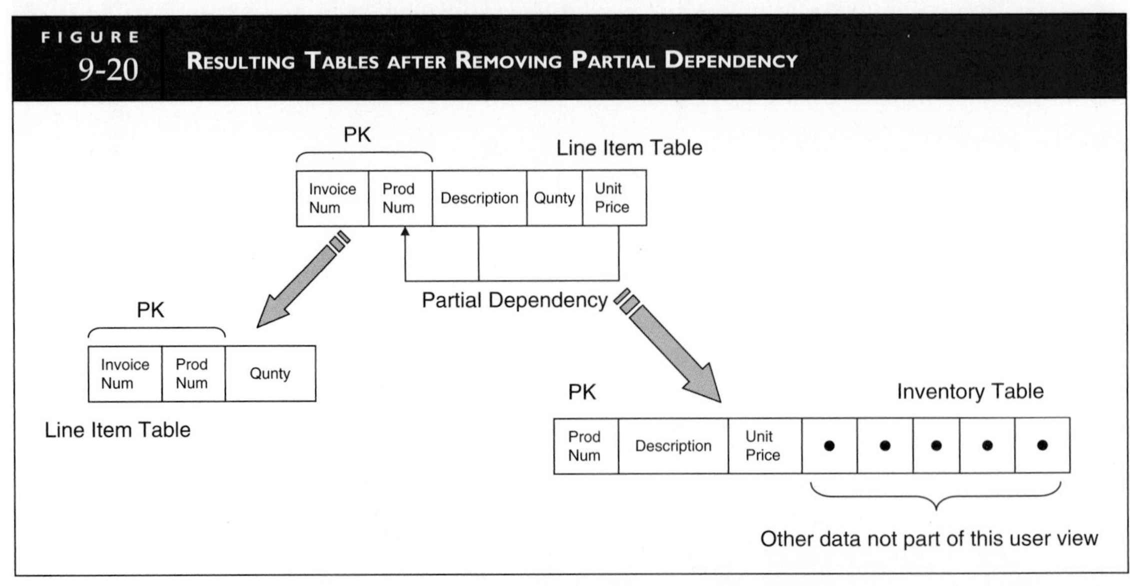

REMOVE TRANSITIVE DEPENDENCIES

The final step in resolving structural dependencies is to remove transitive dependencies. A transitive dependency occurs in a table where nonkey attributes are dependent on another nonkey attribute and independent of the table's primary key. An example of this is illustrated by the Sales Invoice Table in Figure 9-21. The primary key INVOICE NUM uniquely and wholly defines the economic event that the Order Date, Shpd Date, and Shpd Via attributes represent. The key does not, however, uniquely define the customer attributes. The attributes Cust Name, Street Address, and so on define an entity (Customer) that is independent of the specific transaction captured by a particular invoice record. For example, assume that during the period the firm had sold to a particular customer on 10 different occasions. This would result in 10 different invoice occurrences in the table. Using the current table structure, each of these occurrences would capture the data uniquely related to the respective transaction, along with customer data that are common to all 10 transactions. Therefore, the primary key does not uniquely define customer attributes in the table. Indeed, they are independent of the primary key.

We resolve this transitive dependency by splitting out the customer data and placing them in a new table called Customer. The logical key for this table is CUST NUM, which was the nonkey attribute in the former table on which the other nonkey customer attributes were dependent. With this dependency resolved, both the revised Sales Invoice Table and the new Customer Table are in 3NF.

LINKING THE NORMALIZED TABLES

At this point, the original single-table structure has been reduced to the four normalized but independent tables presented in Figure 9-22. The tables contain the sample data used in the original single-table structure presented in Figure 9-18. Notice how data redundancy in the original single-table structure has been eliminated from the more efficient structure represented here. To work together in the physical database, however, the tables in this data model need to be linked via foreign keys. This requires first determining the cardinality between the tables and then assigning foreign keys.

Determine Cardinality

In our example, the cardinality between the four tables is one-to-many (1:M), as explained below:

1. Each customer (Customer Table) may be associated with one or many sales events (Sales Invoice Table), but each invoice is for a single customer.
2. Each Sales Invoice record is associated with one or more Line-Item records, but each line item is associated with only one sales invoice.

FIGURE 9-21 RESULTING TABLES AFTER REMOVING TRANSITIVE DEPENDENCY

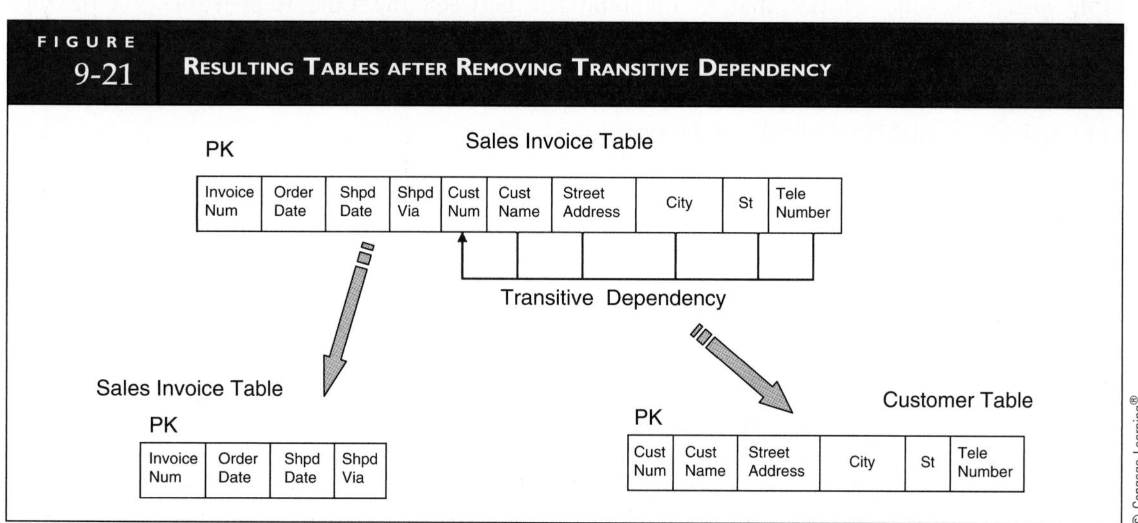

FIGURE 9-22 LINKAGES BETWEEN NORMALIZED TABLES

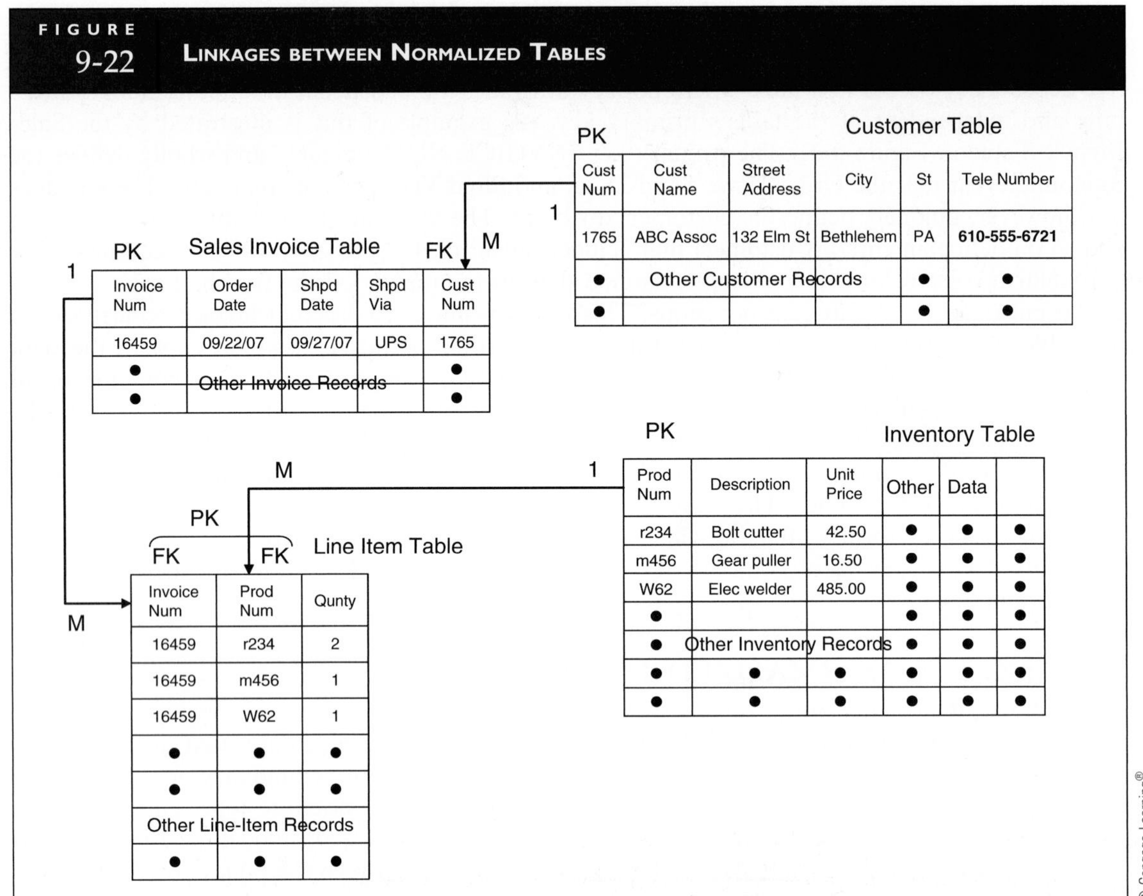

3. Each Inventory record is associated with one or more line items (a particular product has been sold many times to many customers), but each Line-Item record represents only one inventory item.

When linking in a 1:M relation as depicted in Figure 9-22, the database designer will use the primary key from the table on the 1 side of the relation and embed it as a foreign key in the table of the M side. Notice that in the relations between the Line Item Table, the Invoice Table, and the Inventory Table, this is already the case because of the Line Item Table's composite key. The Sales Invoice Table, however, needs to be modified to include CUST NUM as the foreign key, which links it to the Customer Table. The rules for linking normalized tables in (1:1, 1:M, or M:M) relations are discussed next.

KEYS IN 1:1 Cardinality. Where a true 1:1 cardinality exists between tables, either (or both) primary key(s) may be embedded as a foreign key in the related table. On the other hand, when the lower cardinality value on one side of the relation is zero (1,1:0,1), a more efficient table structure can be achieved by placing the one-one side (1,1:) table's primary key in the zero-or-one (:0,1) table as a foreign key. Using the Employee/Company Car example in Figure 9-11, we see the importance of this key-assignment rule. Imagine reversing the rule by placing the Company Car (0,1 side) table's primary key into the Employee (1,1 side) table. Since most employees are not assigned a company car, then most of the foreign keys in the Employee table will have null (blank) values. While this approach would work, it could cause technical problems during table searches. Correctly applying the key-assignment rule solves this problem because all Company Car occurrences will have an employee assigned, and no null values will occur in the foreign key.

KEYS IN 1:M Cardinality. Where a 1:M cardinality (both 1,1:0,M, and 1,1:1,M) exists, the primary key of the 1 side is embedded in the table of the M side. Figure 9-23 illustrates this with an example and some sample data based on Example 4 in Figure 9-11. In this example, a vendor supplies many different types of inventory, but each type of inventory is supplied only by one vendor. Thus, the 1-side primary key (Supplier Number) is embedded in the M-side Inventory Table as a foreign key.

KEYS IN M:M CARDINALITY. An M:M relation is presented in Figure 9-24, which is based on the inventory status report shown in Figure 9-14. In this situation the business rule specifies that each vendor supplies the firm with many inventory items and each item may be supplied by many different vendors. For example, Ozment Supply provides items 1, 2, and 3 and Harris Manufacturing also provides items 2 and 3. Since M:M relations have no 1-side, neither table in the relation can donate an embedded foreign key to the other. The solution, therefore, is to create a third **link table** containing the primary keys of the other two tables, which establishes two 1:M relations between the three tables. The Inventory and Supplier tables are the 1-side tables and the link table is the M-side.

Via the link table, each inventory item can be linked to the corresponding supplier of the item, and each supplier can be linked to the inventory items that it supplies. For example, by searching the Inventory table for PART NUM 1, we see that Suppliers 22, 24, and 27 provide this item. Searching in the opposite direction, SUPPLIER NUMBER 28 provides parts 2 and 3. The link table contains a tuple for each unique occurrence of the supplier/inventory association. For example, if Supplier 24 provides 500 different inventory items, then the link table will contain 500 tuples to depict these associations.

Accountants and Data Modeling

Although most accountants will not be directly responsible for normalizing an organization's databases, they should have an understanding of the process and be able to determine whether

FIGURE 9-23 APPLYING THE 1:M KEY-ASSIGNMENT RULE

(PK) Inventory Table (FK) — "Many" Side

Part Num	Description	Quant on Hand	Reorder Point	**Supplier Number**
1	Bracket	100	150	**22**
2	Gasket	440	450	**28**
3	Brace	10	10	**28**

(PK) Supplier Table — "1" Side

Supplier Number	Name	Address	Tele Num
22	Ozment Sup	123 Main St.	555-7895
24	Buell Co.	2 Broadhead	555-3436
28	Harris Manuf	24 Linden St.	555-3316

FIGURE 9-24 NORMALIZED DATABASE TABLES

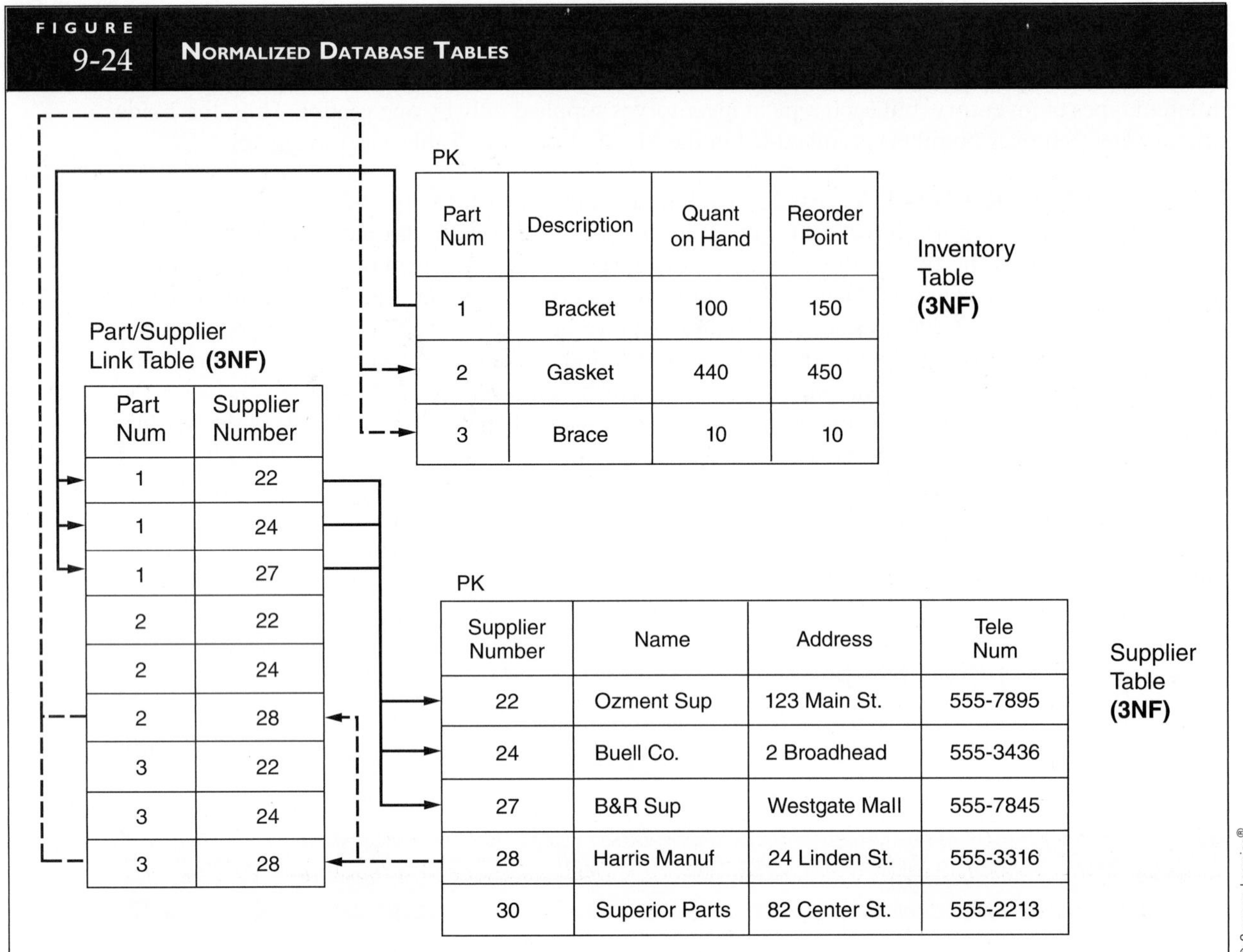

financial data are normalized properly to avoid anomalies. For example, the update anomaly can generate conflicting and/or obsolete database values in accounts, the insertion anomaly can result in unrecorded transactions and incomplete audit trails, and the deletion anomaly can cause the loss of accounting records and the destruction of audit trails. Also, the conduct of many financial audit procedures involves accessing data stored in normalized base tables similar to those in Figure 9-22. An organization's financial database may consist of thousands of normalized tables and navigating such a network requires an understanding of data structures.

Top-Down Approach to Designing Relational Databases

This section examines the steps involved in creating a relational database using a top-down approach. Keep in mind that database design is an element of a much larger systems development process that involves extensive analysis of user needs, which are not covered at this time. That body of material is the subject of Chapters 13 and 14. Thus, our starting point is one that normally follows considerable preliminary work to specify in detail the key elements of the system under development. With this caveat, the focus will be on the following phases of database design, which are known collectively as **view modeling:**

1. Identify the views to be modeled.
2. Normalize the data model and add primary keys.

3. Determine cardinalities and add foreign keys.
4. Construct the physical database.
5. Prepare the physical user views.

IDENTIFY THE VIEWS TO BE MODELED

View modeling begins by identifying the relevant views of the business function in question. This involves user interviews, and other techniques, to determine what users do and what information they need to support their tasks. To demonstrate view identification, we will analyze the following key features of a simplified purchasing function:

1. The purchasing agent reviews the inventory status report for items that need to be reordered.
2. The agent selects a supplier and prepares a digital purchase order from his terminal.
3. The agent prints a copy of the purchase order and sends it to the supplier.
4. The supplier ships the inventory to the company. Upon its arrival, the receiving clerk inspects the inventory and prepares the digital receiving report. The computer system automatically updates the inventory records.

This description identifies three views: (1) Inventory Status Report, (2) Purchase Order, and (3) Receiving Report. The data attributes to be used in the views are specified in Figures 9-14, 9-25a, and 9-25b respectively. Note that the Purchase Order attributes of Extended Cost and Total Cost can be calculated from other attributes and are not included in the model. Figure 9-26 presents the unnormalized entities that represent these views.

FIGURE 9-25 PURCHASE ORDER AND RECEIVING REPORT FOR PURCHASES SYSTEM

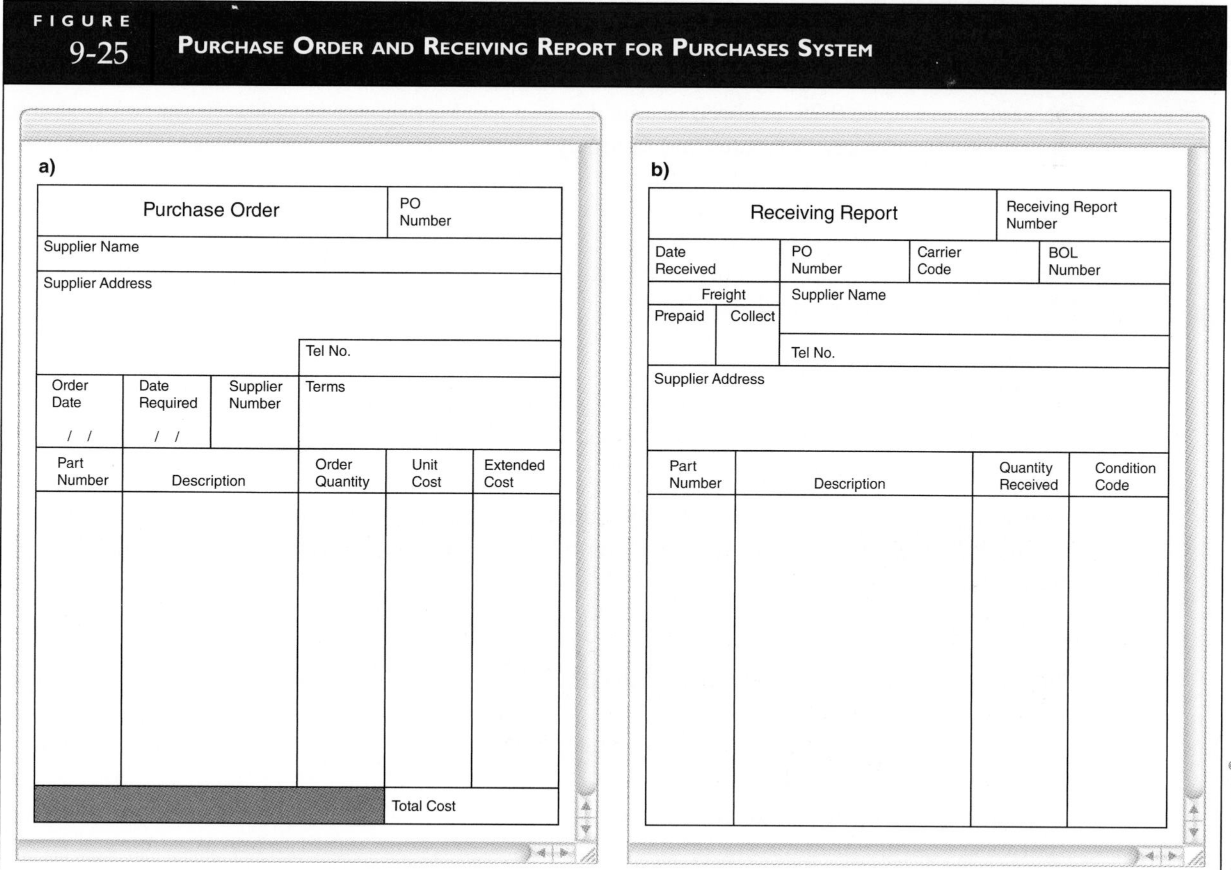

FIGURE 9-26 UNNORMALIZED DATA MODEL SHOWING PRIMARY KEYS AND ATTRIBUTES

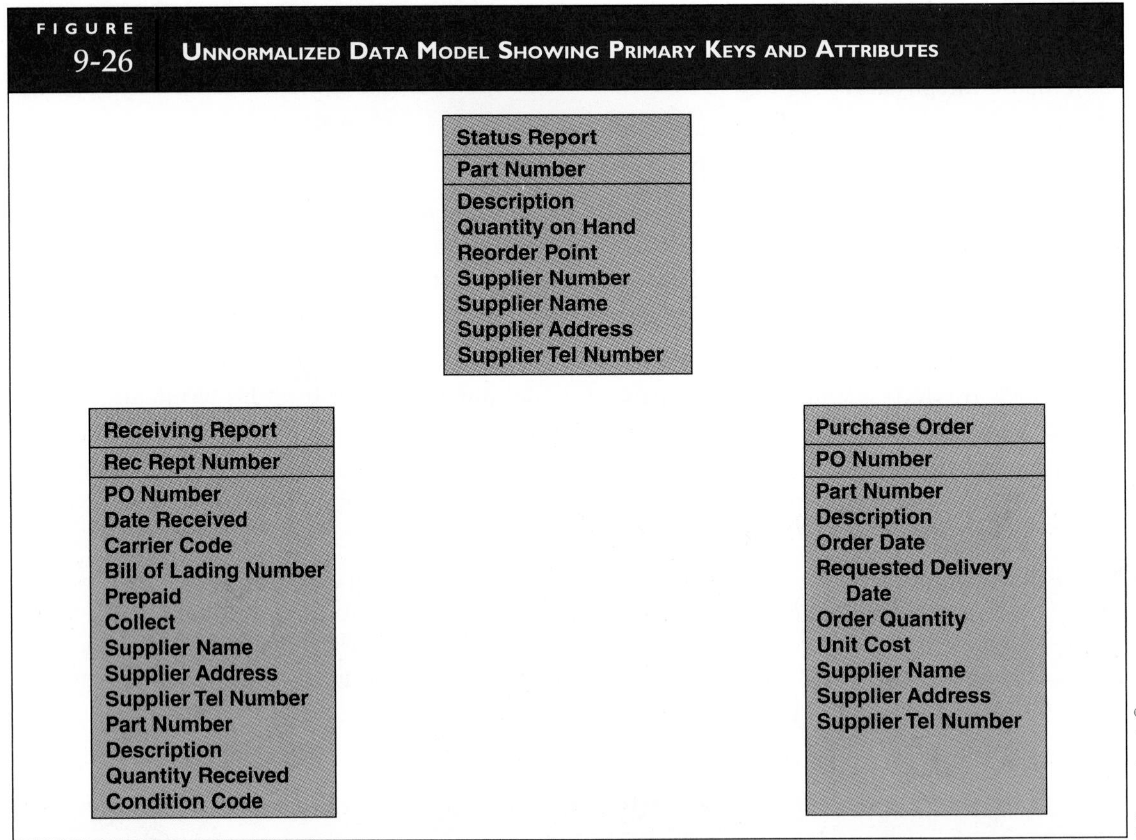

Each entity in Figure 9-26 has been assigned a name and a primary key. The primary key should logically define the nonkey attributes and uniquely identify each occurrence in the entity. Sometimes this is accomplished by using a simple sequential code such as an invoice number, check number, or purchase order number. Sequential codes, however, are not always appropriate keys. Block codes, group codes, alphabetic codes, and mnemonic codes, can also be assigned as primary keys. These techniques were discussed in detail in Chapter 2. The primary keys for the entities in our example are Part Number, PO Number, and Rec Rept Number.

NORMALIZE DATA MODEL AND ADD PRIMARY KEYS

Figure 9-27 presents a normalized data model. The following section describes the normalization procedures that produced this model:

1. **Repeating Group Data in Status Report Entity**. The non-key attributes of Supplier Number, Supplier Name, Supplier Address, and Supplier Tel Number are repeating group data in the Status Report. These data were removed and placed in a new table called Supplier and assigned a primary key of Supplier number. The remaining entity, which now contains only inventory attributes was renamed Inventory.
2. **Repeating Group Data in Purchase Order Entity**. The attributes of Part Number, Description, Order Quantity, and Unit Cost are repeating group data. To resolve this, these attributes data were removed to a new entity called PO Item Detail, which was assigned a primary key that is a composite of Part Number and PO Number.
3. **Partial Dependency in PO Item Detail Entity**. An analysis of the PO Item Detail entity reveals that its composite primary key uniquely defines only Order Quantity. The attributes of Description and Unit Cost are partially dependent on Part Number and therefore removed

FIGURE 9-27 NORMALIZED DATA MODEL

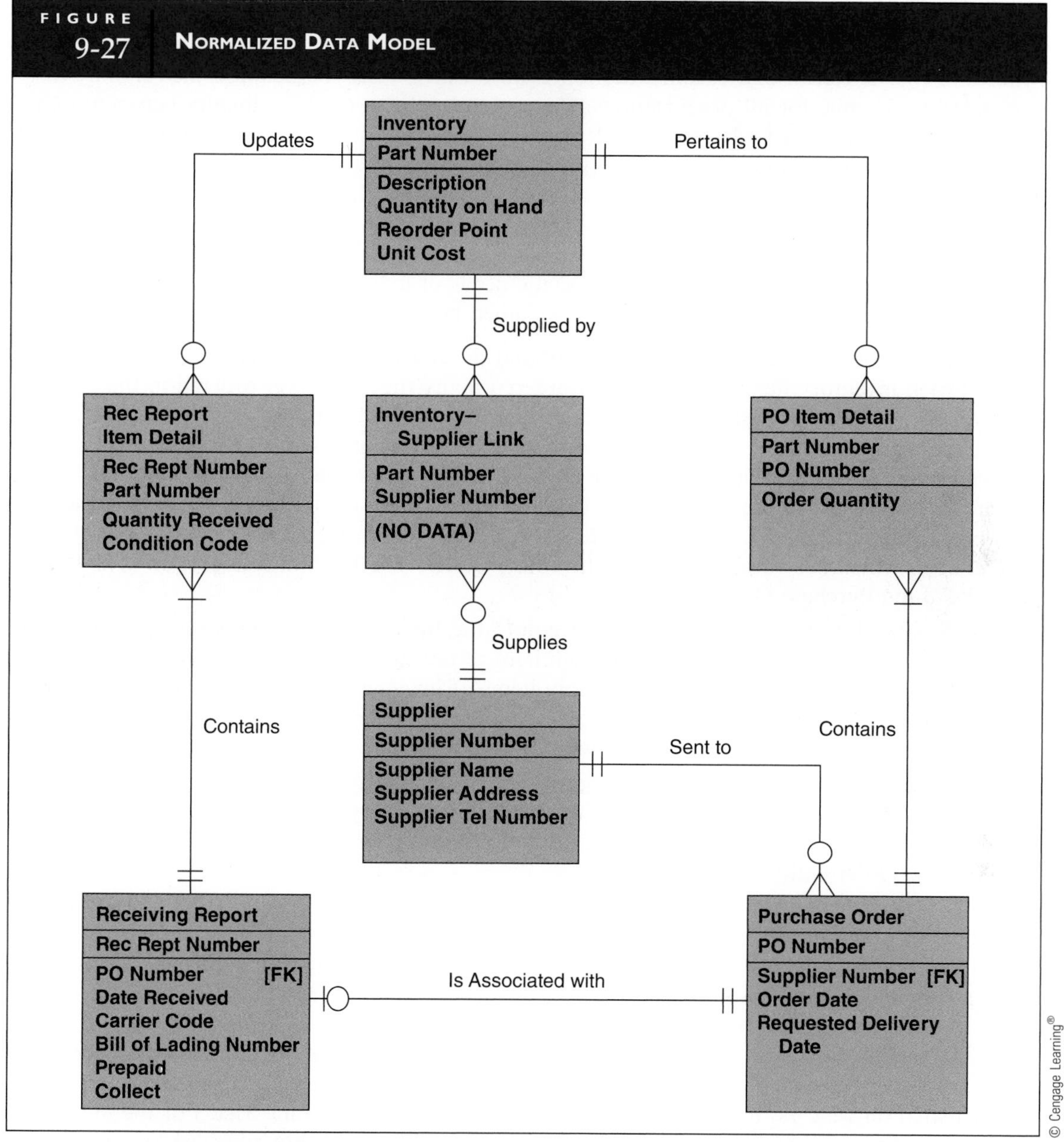

from the table leaving Order Quantity as the only non-key attribute. Unit Cost was added to the Inventory entity. Description was already a listed attribute of the Inventory entity.

4. **Transitive Dependency in Purchase Order Entity**. The attributes of Supplier Name, Supplier Address, and Supplier Tel Number are transitive dependencies, which are defined by Supplier Number. These attributes were therefore removed from the Purchase Order entity.
5. **Repeating Group Data in Receiving Report entity**. The attributes Part Number, Quantity Received, and Condition Code are repeating groups in the Receiving Report entity and were removed to a new entity called Rec Report Item Detail. A composite key composed of Part number and Rec Rept Number was assigned.
6. **Transitive Dependency in Receiving Report Entity**. The attributes Supplier Name, Supplier Address, and Supplier Tel Number are defined by Supplier Number and not defined by the primary key PO Number. They are Supplier entity attributes and therefore removed from the Purchase Order entity.

DETERMINE CARDINALITIES AND ADD FOREIGN KEYS

The next step in view modeling is to determine the cardinality between entities and link the entities with foreign keys. Recall that cardinalities represent business rules. Sometimes, the rules are obvious and are the same for all organizations. For example, the normal cardinality between a Customer entity and a Sales Order entity is 1:M. This signifies that one customer may place many orders during a sales period. The cardinality would never be 1:1. This would mean that the organization restricts each customer to a single sale, which is illogical.

Sometimes, the cardinality between entities is not apparent because different rules may apply in different organizations. If the database is to function properly, its designers need to understand the organization's business rules as well as the specific needs of individual users. The cardinalities and underlying business rules in our example are explained next.

1. The cardinality between the PO Item Detail and the Inventory entities is 1,1: 0,M. This means that each inventory item may have been ordered many times or never ordered in the current business period. Obviously, every inventory item must have been purchased at least once in the past, but to reiterate a point made earlier, transaction entities, such as Sales and Purchases, are associated with a particular time frame. If we assume that the PO Item Detail entity for this system represents only records of purchases made in the current period then the lower cardinality is zero. The composite key for the PO Item Detail entity includes Part Number, which provides a link to the Inventory entity. The PO Number portion of the key links to the Purchase Order entity.
2. Splitting the Inventory Status Report entity into the Inventory and Supplier entities created a 1,M:1,M cardinality. This means that each item of inventory is supplied by one or more vendors and each vendor supplies one or more items of inventory. This unworkable relation is resolved by creating the link entity called Inventory–Supplier Link, which contains the primary keys of both tables and creates two 1:M relations.
3. The Supplier and Purchase Order entities have a 1,1:0,M cardinality. This means that in the current period, each supplier may have received zero or many purchase orders, but each order was sent to only one supplier. This relation requires Supplier Number to be embedded in the Purchase Order entity as a foreign key.
4. Purchase Order and Receiving Report entities have a 0,1:1,1 cardinality. Let's first examine the upper cardinality value of "1" at the Receiving Report end of the association line. This implies that each purchase order will be received in its entirety and no back orders exist. This is a simplifying assumption for the purpose of this example. In reality, back orders do occur and require special procedures that are not covered here. The lower cardinality value of "0" at the Receiving Report end signifies that at any point in time there are purchase order occurrences that have not yet been received. For example, assume that a purchase order occurrence is created on June 1st but the items on order do not arrive until June 31st. For the month of June, an occurrence will exist in the Purchase Order table that is not associated with an occurrence in the Receiving Report table. The 1,1 cardinality at the Purchase Order end signifies that each receiving report is associated with a single purchase order and multiple purchase orders are not combined on a single receiving report. This relation requires that the primary key "Purchase Order" be embedded as a foreign key in the Receiving Report entity.
5. The cardinality between the Rec Report Item Detail and Inventory entities is 1,1: 0,M. This indicates that within a period an item of inventory may have been received many times or not at all. For example, a slow-moving or seasonal inventory item may not have been ordered during the period and thus not received. Each Rec Report Item Detail occurrence is associated with one and only one inventory occurrence. The Part Number component of the composite key links to the Inventory entity and the Rec Rept Number component links to the Receiving Report entity.

The view modeling process described above involved only one business function—the purchases system—and the example entities that resulted constitute only a small portion of that system. A modern company would employ thousands of views. Combining the data needs of all users into a single entity-wide schema is called **view integration**. This involves the consolidation of the attributes from all user views into a common set of normalized entities that meet the following conditions:

1. *An entity must consist of two or more occurrences.*
2. *No two entities may have the same primary key. The exceptions to this are entities with composite keys that are comprised of the primary keys of other entities.*
3. *No non-key attribute may be associated with more than one entity. For example, if Customer Address is an attribute of the Customer entity, it cannot also be an attribute of another entity. All views that use Customer Address will retrieve it from the Customer entity.*

CONSTRUCT THE PHYSICAL DATABASE

Figure 9-28 illustrates the 3NF table structures for the physical database. The dotted lines represent the primary and foreign keys linking the tables. The following points are worth further elaboration.

Each occurrence in the Rec Report Item Detail table represents an individual item on the receiving report. The table has a combined key comprised of REC REPT NUMBER and PART NUMBER. This composite key is needed to uniquely identify the Quantity Received and Condition attributes of each item-detail record. The REC REPT NUMBER portion of the key provides the link to the Receiving Report table that contains general data about the receiving event. The PART NUMBER portion of the key is used to access the Inventory table to facilitate updating the Quantity on Hand field from the Quantity Received field of the Rec Rept Item-Detail table.

The PO Item Detail table uses a composite primary key consisting of PO NUMBER and PART NUMBER to uniquely identify the Order Quantity attribute. The PO NUMBER component of the composite key provides a link to the Purchase Order table. The PART NUMBER element of the key is a link to the Inventory table where Description and Unit Cost data are stored.

The next step is to create the physical tables and populate them with data. This is an involved step that must be carefully planned and executed, and may take many months in a large installation. Programs will need to be written to transfer organization data currently stored in flat files or legacy databases to the new relational tables. Data currently stored on paper documents will be entered into database tables manually. Once this is done, the physical user views can be produced.

PREPARE THE PHYSICAL USER VIEWS

The normalized tables should be rich enough to support the views of all users of the system being modeled. For example, the Purchase Order in Figure 9-28, which could be the data entry screen for a purchasing clerk, has been constructed from attributes located in several tables. To illustrate the relationship, the fields in the user view are cross-referenced via circled numbers to the attributes in the supporting tables. Keep in mind that these tables may also provide data for many other views not shown here, such as the receiving report, purchase requisition listing, inventory status report, vendor purchases activity report, and many more.

Database developers use SQL to identify which tables to use and which attributes to select to create the user view. The Receiving Report, Purchase Order, and Inventory Status Report views in our example would all be created in this way. SQL commands needed to produce the inventory status report illustrated in Figure 9-14 are shown below:

```
SELECT inventory.part-num, description, quantity-on-hand, reorder-point, EOQ, inventory-supplier,
part-num, inventory-supplier.supplier-number, supplier.supplier-number, name, address, tele-num,
FROM inventory, part-supplier, supplier

WHERE inventory.part-num = inventory-supplier.part-num AND inventory-supplier.supplier-number
= supplier.supplier-number AND quantity-on hand < reorder-point.
```

- The SELECT command identifies all of the attributes to be contained in the view.
- The FROM command identifies the tables used in creating the view.

FIGURE 9-28 NORMALIZED TABLES

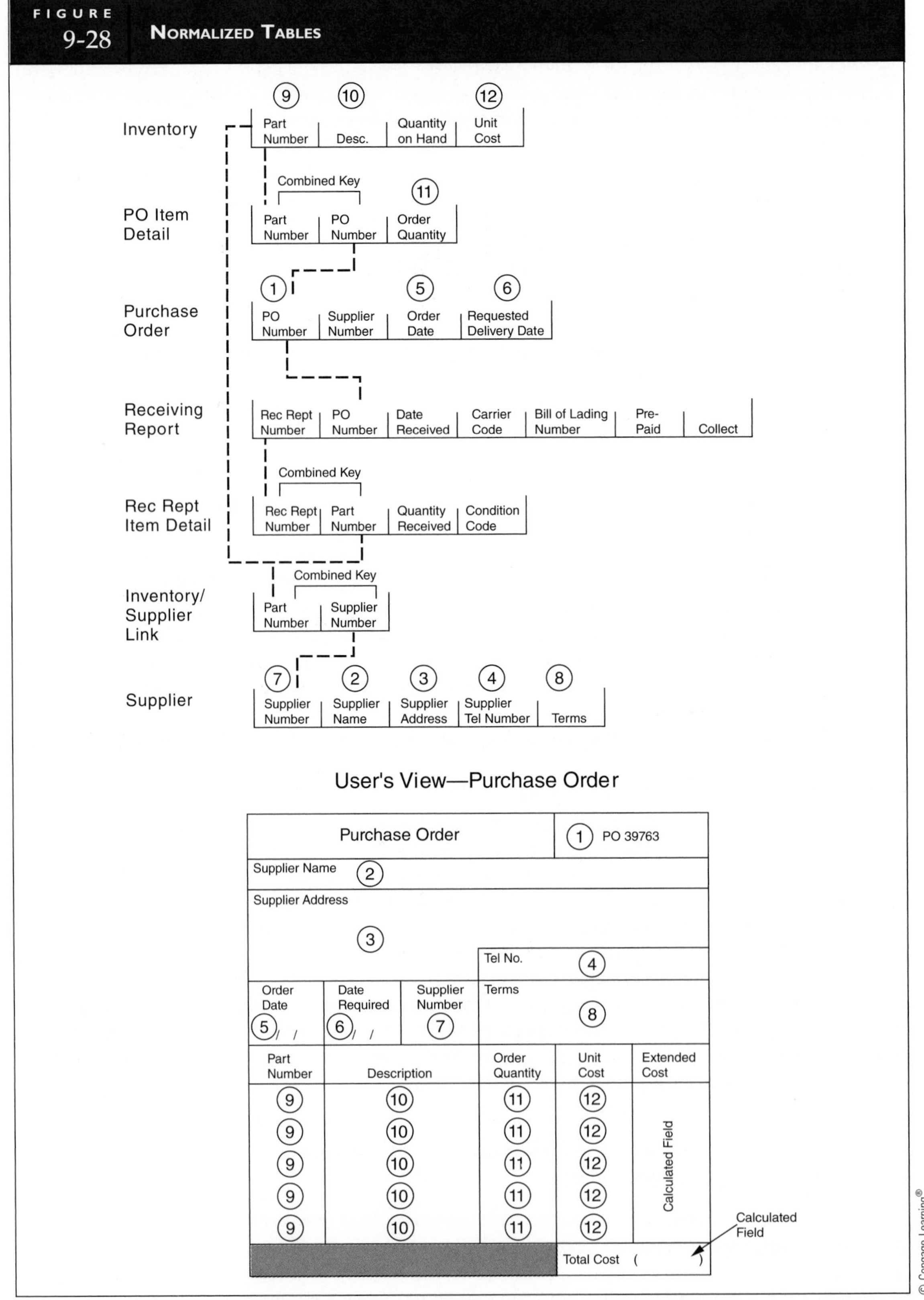

- The WHERE command specifies how rows in the Inventory, Part-Supplier, and Supplier tables are to be matched to create the view. In this case, the three tables are algebraically joined on the primary keys PART-NUM and SUPPLIER-NUMBER.
- Multiple expressions may be linked with the AND, OR, and NOT operators. In this example, the last expression uses AND to restrict the records to be selected with the logical expression quant-on-hand < reorder-point. Only records whose quantities on hand have fallen to or below their reorder points will be selected for the view and the user will not see the many thousands of other inventory items that have adequate quantities available.

These SQL commands will be saved in a user program called a query. To view the Inventory Status Report, the purchasing agent executes the query program. Each time this is done, the query builds a new view with current data from the Inventory and Vendor tables. By providing the user with his or her personal query, rather than permitting access to the underlying base tables, the user is limited only to authorized data.

A report program is used to make the view visually attractive and easy to read. Column headings can be added to produce a hard-copy or computer screen report that resembles the original user report in Figure 9-14. The report program will suppress unnecessary data from the view, such as duplicated fields and the key values in the Inventory/Vendor link table. These keys are necessary to build the view, but are not needed in the actual report.

COMMERCIAL DATABASE SYSTEM

Modeling the data needs of thousands of user views is a daunting undertaking when creating an entity-wide database from scratch. To facilitate this task, modern commercial database systems come equipped with a core schema, normalized tables, and templates for thousands of views. Commercial systems are designed to comply with proven industry best practices and to satisfy the most common needs of different client organizations. For example, all organizations that sell products to customers will need an Inventory table, a Customer table, a Supplier table, and so forth. Many of the attributes and keys in these tables are common to all organizations. Working from a commercial database package, developers can thus focus on configuring predefined views to accommodate specific user needs within their organizations rather than starting from scratch.

Database vendors cannot, however, anticipate the information needs of all users in advance. Therefore, new entities and new attributes may need to be added to the core schema. Although configuring the core database in this fashion is far more efficient than working from scratch, the objective is the same. The database designer must produce a set of integrated tables that are free of the update, insert, and deletion anomalies and sufficiently rich to serve the needs of all users.

Databases in a Distributed Environment

Chapter 1 introduced the concept of **distributed data processing (DDP)** as an alternative to the centralized approach. Most modern organizations use some form of distributed processing and networking to process their transactions. Some companies process all of their transactions in this way. An important consideration in planning a distributed system is the location of the organization's database. In addressing this issue, the planner has two basic options: databases can be centralized, or they can be distributed. Distributed databases fall into two categories: partitioned and replicated. This section examines issues, features, and trade-offs that should be carefully evaluated in deciding how databases should be distributed.

CENTRALIZED DATABASES

Under the **centralized database** approach, remote users send requests via terminals for data to the central site, which processes the requests and transmits the data back to the user. The central site performs the functions of a file manager that services the data needs of the remote users. The centralized database approach is illustrated in Figure 9-29.

FIGURE 9-29 CENTRALIZED DATABASE

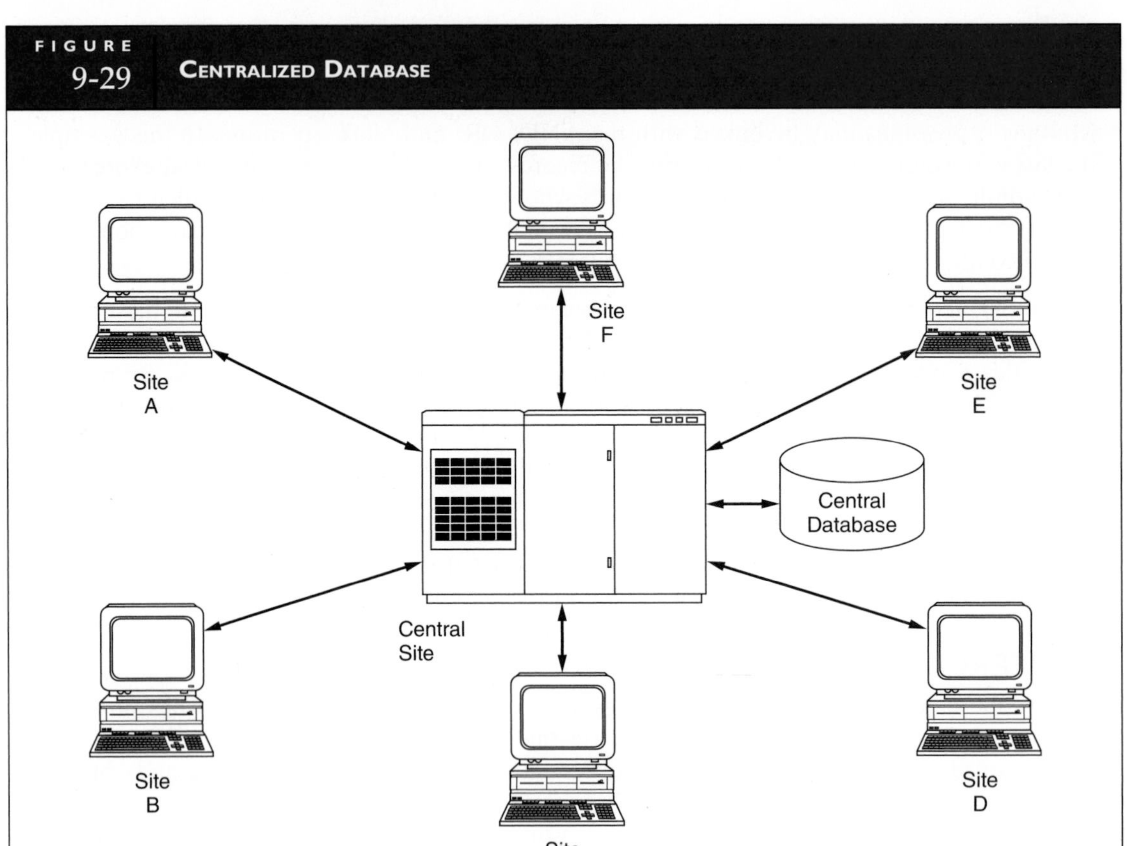

Earlier in the chapter, three primary advantages of the database approach were presented: the reduction of data storage costs, the elimination of multiple update procedures, and the establishment of **data currency** (i.e., the firm's data files reflect accurately the effects of its transactions). Achieving data currency is critical to database integrity and reliability. However, in the DDP environment, this can be a challenging task.

Data Currency in a DDP Environment

During data processing, account balances pass through a state of **temporary inconsistency** in which their values are incorrectly stated. This occurs during the execution of any accounting transaction. To illustrate, consider the computer logic for recording the credit sale of $2,000 to customer Jones.

	INSTRUCTION	DATABASE VALUES	
	START	AR-Jones	AR-Control
1.	Read AR-Sub account (Jones)	1500	
2.	Read AR-Control account		10000
3.	Write AR-Sub account (Jones) + $2000	3500	
4.	Write AR-Control account + $2000		12000
	END		

Immediately after the execution of Instruction Number 3, and before the execution of Instruction Number 4, the AR-Control account value is temporarily inconsistent by the sum of $2,000. This inconsistency is resolved only after the completion of the entire transaction. In a DDP environment, such temporary inconsistencies can result in the permanent corruption of the database. To illustrate the potential for damage, look at a slightly more complicated example. Using the same computer logic as before, consider the processing of two separate transactions from two remote sites: Transaction 1 (Tl) is the sale of $2,000 on account to customer Jones from Site A; Transaction 2 (T2) is the sale of $1,000 on account to customer Smith from Site B. The following logic shows the possible interweaving of the two processing tasks and the effect on data currency.

INSTRUCTION			**DATABASE VALUES**		
				Central Site	
SITE A	SITE B		AR-Jones	AR-Smith	AR-Control
Tl	T2	START			
1		Read AR-Sub account (Jones)	1500		
	1	Read AR-Sub account (Smith)		3000	
2		Read AR-Control account			10000
3		Write AR-Sub account (Jones) + $2000		3500	
	2	**Read AR-Control account**			10000
4		Write AR-Control account + $2000			12000
	3	Write AR-Sub account (Smith) + $1000		4000	
	4	Write AR-Control account + $1000			11000
		END			

Notice that Site B seized the AR-Control data value of $10,000 when it was in an inconsistent state. By using this value to process its transaction, Site B effectively destroyed the record of Transaction Tl that had been processed by Site A. Therefore, instead of $13,000, the new AR-Control balance is misstated at $11,000.

Database Lockout

To achieve data currency, simultaneous access to individual data elements by multiple sites needs to be prevented. The solution to this problem is to use a **database lockout**, which is a software control (usually a function of the DBMS) that prevents multiple simultaneous accesses to data. The previous example can be used to illustrate this technique: immediately upon receiving the access request from Site A for AR-Control (Tl, Instruction Number 2), the central site DBMS places a lock on AR-Control to prevent access from other sites until Transaction Tl is complete. Thus, when Site B requests AR-Control (T2, Instruction Number 2), it is placed on wait status until the lock is removed. Only then can Site B access AR-Control and complete Transaction T2.

DISTRIBUTED DATABASES

Distributed databases can be distributed using either the partitioned or replicated technique.

Partitioned Databases

The **partitioned database** approach splits the central database into segments or partitions that are distributed to their primary users. The advantages of this approach are:

- Storing data at local sites increases users' control.
- Permitting local access to data and reducing the volume of data that must be transmitted between sites improve transaction processing response time.
- Partitioned databases can reduce the potential for disaster. By having data located at several sites, the loss of a single site cannot terminate all data processing by the organization.

The partitioned approach, which is illustrated in Figure 9-30, works best for organizations that require minimal data sharing among users at remote sites. To the extent that remote users share data, the problems associated with the centralized approach still apply. The primary user must now manage requests for data from other sites. Selecting the optimum host location for the partitions will minimize data access problems. This requires an in-depth analysis of end-user data needs.

FIGURE 9-30 THE PARTITIONED DATABASE APPROACH

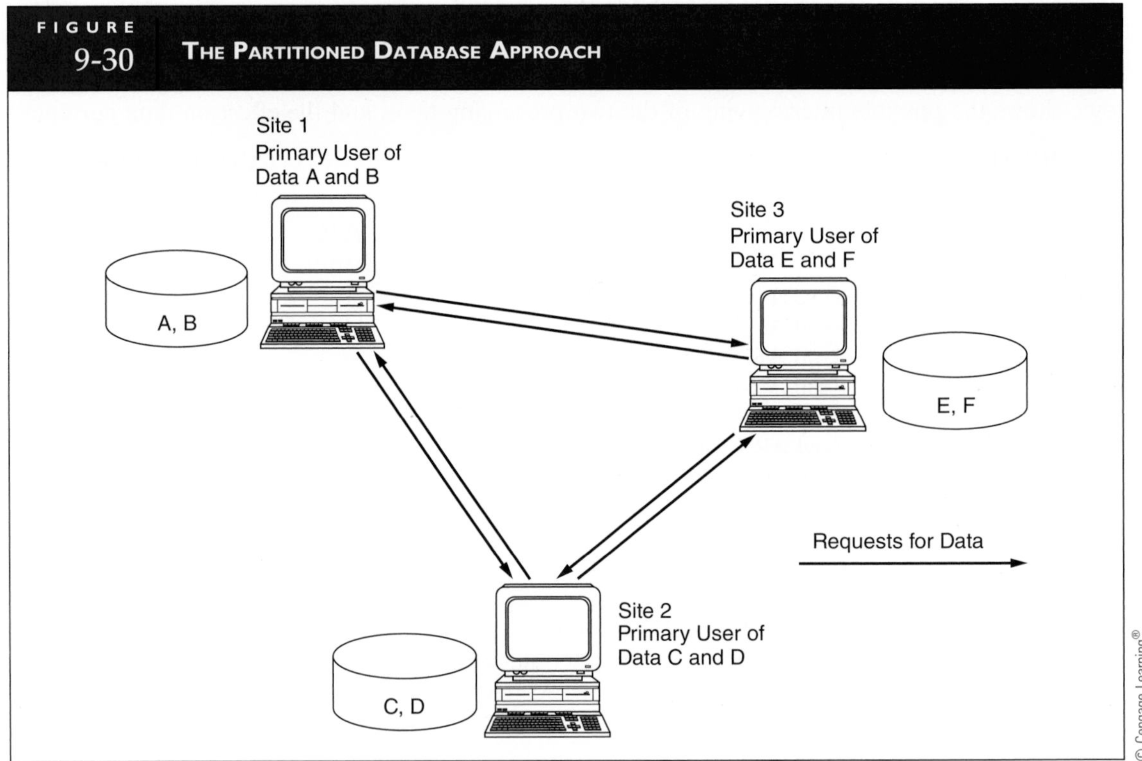

THE DEADLOCK PHENOMENON. In a distributed environment, it is possible that multiple sites will lock out each other, thus preventing each from processing its transactions. For example, Figure 9-31 illustrates three sites and their mutual data needs. Notice that Site 1 has requested (and locked) Data A and is waiting for the removal of the lock on Data C to complete its transaction. Site 2 has a lock on C and is waiting for E. Finally, Site 3 has a lock on E and is waiting for A. A **deadlock** occurs here because there is mutual exclusion to data, and the transactions are in a wait state until the locks are removed. This can result in transactions being incompletely processed and corruption of the database. A deadlock is a permanent condition that must be resolved by special software that analyzes each deadlock condition to determine the best solution. Because of the implications for transaction processing, accountants should be aware of the issues pertaining to deadlock resolutions.

DEADLOCK RESOLUTION. Resolving a deadlock usually involves sacrificing one or more transactions. These must be terminated to complete the processing of the other transactions in the deadlock. The preempted transactions must then be reinitiated. In preempting transactions, the deadlock resolution software attempts to minimize the total cost of breaking the deadlock. Although not an easy task to automate, some of the factors that influence this decision are as follows:

1. The resources currently invested in the transaction. This may be measured by the number of updates that the transaction has already performed and that must be repeated if the transaction is terminated.
2. The transaction's stage of completion. In general, deadlock resolution software will avoid terminating transactions that are close to completion.
3. The number of deadlocks associated with the transaction. Because terminating the transaction breaks all deadlock involvement, the software should attempt to terminate transactions that are part of more than one deadlock.

FIGURE 9-31 THE DEADLOCK CONDITION

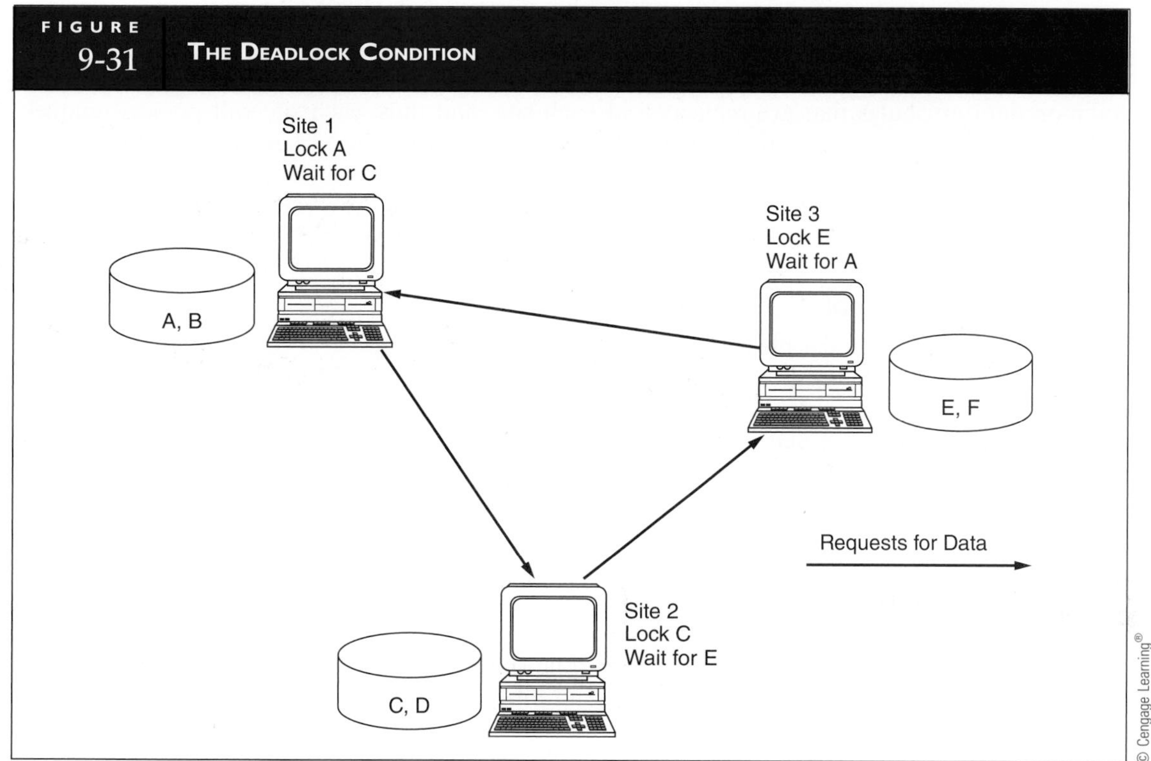

Replicated Databases

In some organizations, the entire database is replicated at each site. **Replicated databases** are effective in companies in which there exists a high degree of data sharing but no primary user. Because common data are replicated at each site, the data traffic between sites is reduced considerably. Figure 9-32 illustrates the replicated database model.

The primary justification for a replicated database is to support read-only queries. With data replicated at every site, data access for query purposes is ensured, and lockouts and delays because

FIGURE 9-32 REPLICATED DATABASE APPROACH

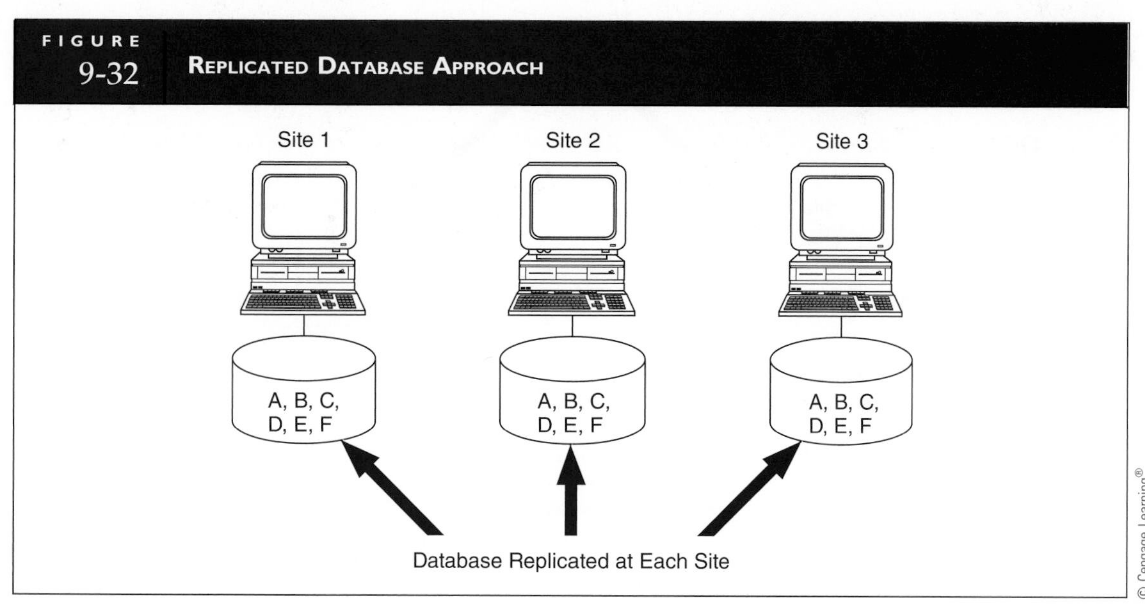

of network traffic are minimized. A problem arises, however, when local sites also need to update the replicated database with transactions.

Because each site processes only its local transactions, different transactions will update the common data attributes that are replicated at each site, and thus, each site will possess uniquely different values after the respective updates. Using the data from the earlier example, Figure 9-33 illustrates the effect of processing credit sales for Jones at Site A and Smith at Site B. After the transactions are processed, the value shown for the common AR-Control account is inconsistent ($12,000 at Site A and $11,000 at Site B) and incorrect at both sites.

Concurrency Control

Database concurrency is the presence of complete and accurate data at all remote sites. System designers need to employ methods to ensure that transactions processed at each site are accurately reflected in the databases at all other sites. This task, while problematic, has implications for accounting records and is a matter of concern for accountants.

A commonly used method for **concurrency control** is to serialize transactions. This involves labeling each transaction by two criteria. First, special software groups transactions into classes to identify potential conflicts. For example, read-only (query) transactions do not conflict with other classes of transactions. Similarly, AP and AR transactions are not likely to use the same data and do not conflict. However, multiple sales order transactions involving both read and write operations will potentially conflict.

The second part of the control process is to time stamp each transaction. A system-wide clock is used to keep all sites, some of which may be in different time zones, on the same logical time. Each time stamp is made unique by incorporating the site's identification number. When transactions are received at each site, they are examined first for potential conflicts. If conflicts exist, the transactions are entered into a serialization schedule. An algorithm is used to schedule updates to the database based on the transaction time stamp and class. This method permits multiple interleaved transactions to be processed at each site as if they were serial events.

FIGURE 9-33 REPLICATED DATABASES UPDATED INDEPENDENTLY

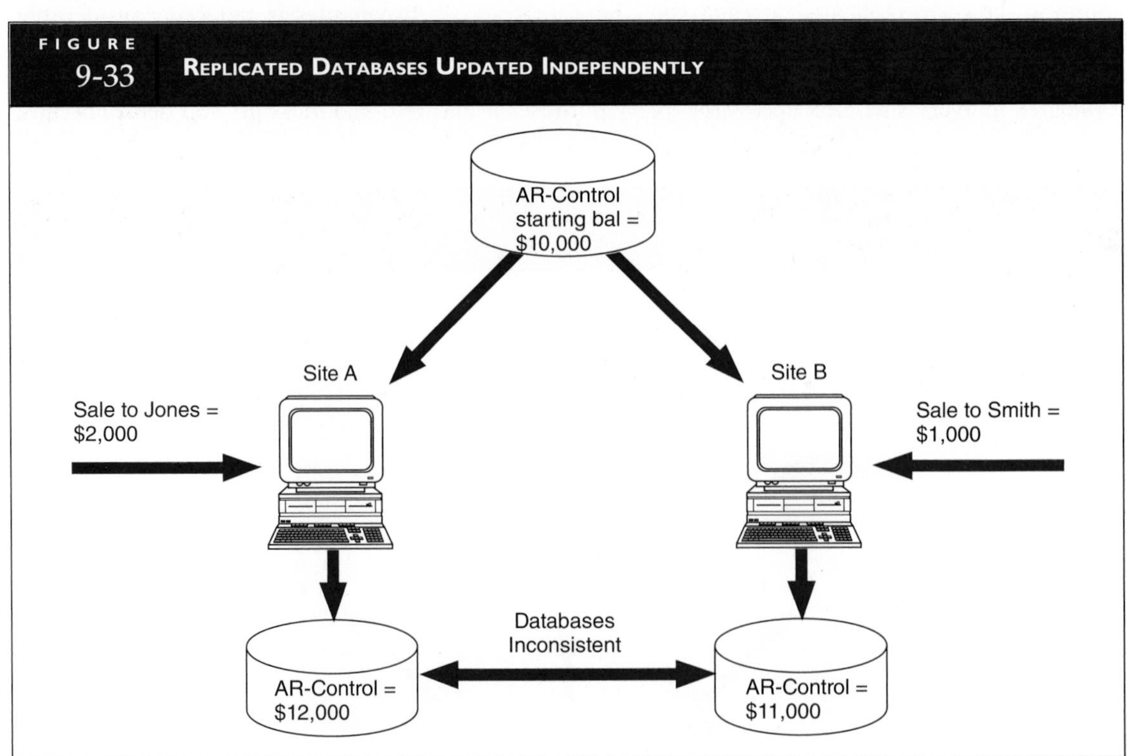

Distributed Databases and the Accountant

The decision to distribute databases is one that should be entered into thoughtfully. There are many issues and trade-offs to consider. Some of the most basic questions to be addressed are:

- Should the organization's data be centralized or distributed?
- If data distribution is desirable, should the databases be replicated or partitioned?
- If replicated, should the databases be totally replicated or partially replicated?
- If the database is to be partitioned, how should the data segments be allocated among the sites?

The choices involved in each of these questions impact the organization's ability to maintain database integrity. The preservation of audit trails and the accuracy of accounting records are key concerns. Clearly, these are decisions that the modern accountant should understand and influence intelligently.

Summary

This chapter examined the database approach to data management and showed how this approach enables business organizations to overcome data redundancy and the associated problems that plague the flat-file approach to data management. It showed that the database concept is composed of four dynamically interrelated components: users, the database management system, the database administrator, and the physical database. The DBMS stands between the physical database and the user community. Its principal function is to provide a controlled and secure environment for the database. This is achieved through software modules, such as a query language, a data definition language, and a data manipulation language. The DBMS also provides security against human error and natural disaster through various backup and recovery modules.

Database models are abstract representations of data about entities, events, and activities, and their relationships within an organization. The focus of attention was on the relational model. A number of database design topics were covered, including data modeling, data normalization, and the creation of user views from physical database tables. Finally, the chapter presented a number of issues associated with distributed databases. It examined three possible database configurations in a distributed environment: centralized, partitioned, and replicated databases.

Appendix

Distinguishing Features of Structured Databases

The Hierarchical Database Model

The earliest database management systems (DBMSs) were based on the hierarchical data model. This was a popular approach to data representation because it reflected, more or less faithfully, many aspects of an organization that are hierarchical in relationship. Also, it was an efficient data processing tool for highly structured problems. Figure 9-34 presents a data structure diagram showing a portion of a hierarchical database.

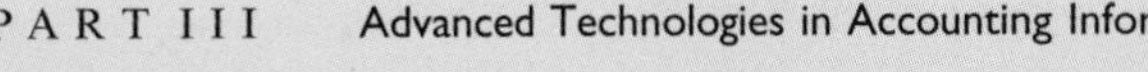

FIGURE 9-34 HIERARCHICAL DATA MODEL

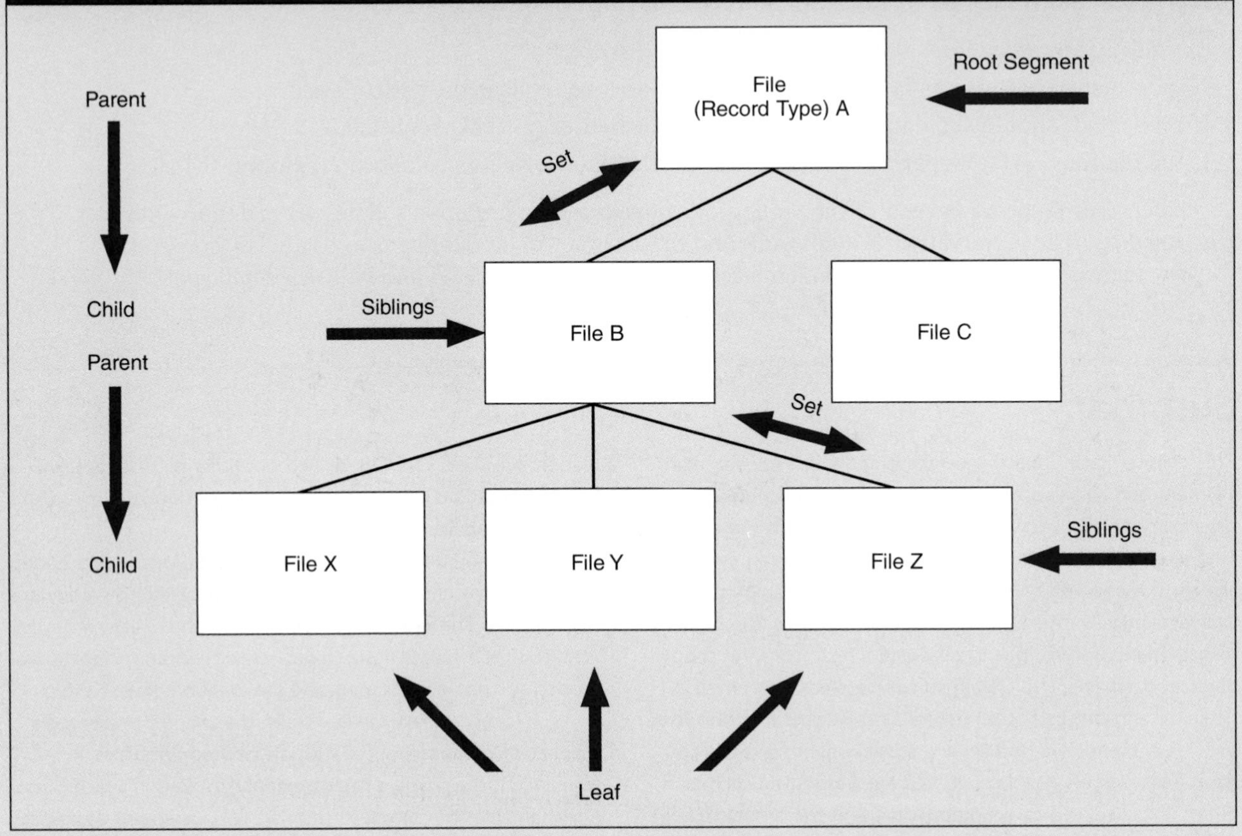

The hierarchical model is constructed of sets of files. Each set contains a parent and a child. Notice that File B, at the second level, is both the child in one set and the parent in another set. Files at the same level with the same parent are called siblings. This structure is also called a tree structure. The file at the most aggregated level in the tree is the root segment, and the file at the most detailed level in a particular branch is called a leaf.

A NAVIGATIONAL DATABASE

The hierarchical data model is called a navigational database because traversing it requires following a predefined path. This is established through pointers (discussed in the appendix to Chapter 2) that create explicit linkages between related records. The only way to access data at lower levels in the tree is from the root and via the pointers down the navigational path to the desired records. For example, consider the partial database in Figure 9-35. To retrieve an invoice line-item record, the DBMS must first access the customer record (the root). That record contains a pointer to the sales invoice record, which points to the invoice line-item record.

LIMITATIONS OF THE HIERARCHICAL MODEL

The hierarchical model presents a limited view of data relationships. Based on the proposition that all business relationships are hierarchical (or can be represented as such), this model does not always reflect reality. The following rules, which govern the hierarchical model, reveal its operating constraints:

1. A parent record may have one or more child records. For example, in Figure 9-30, the customer is the parent of both sales invoice and cash receipts.
2. No child record can have more than one parent.

FIGURE 9-35 PORTION OF A HIERARCHICAL DATABASE

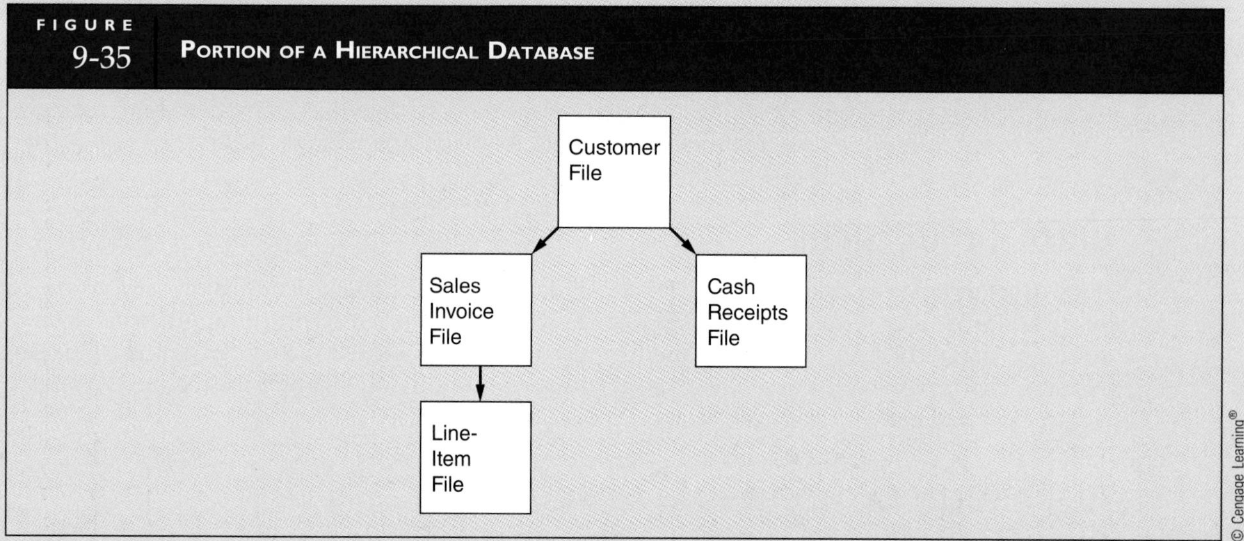

The second rule is often restrictive and limits the usefulness of the hierarchical model. Many firms need a view of data associations that permit multiple parents like that represented by Figure 9-36(a). In this example, the sales invoice file has two natural parents: the customer file and the salesperson file. A specific sales order is the product of both the customer's purchase activity and a salesperson's selling efforts. Management, wishing to keep track of sales orders by customer and by salesperson, will want to view sales order records as the logical child of both parents. This relationship, although logical, violates the single-parent rule of the hierarchical model. Figure 9-36(b) shows the most common way of resolving this problem. By duplicating the sales invoice file, two separate hierarchical representations are created. Unfortunately, this improved functionality is achieved at a cost—increased data redundancy. The network model, examined next, deals with this problem more efficiently.

The Network Database Model

The network model is a variation of the hierarchical model. The principal distinguishing feature between the two is that the network model allows a child record to have multiple parents. The multiple ownership

FIGURE 9-36 MULTIPLE PARENT ASSOCIATION

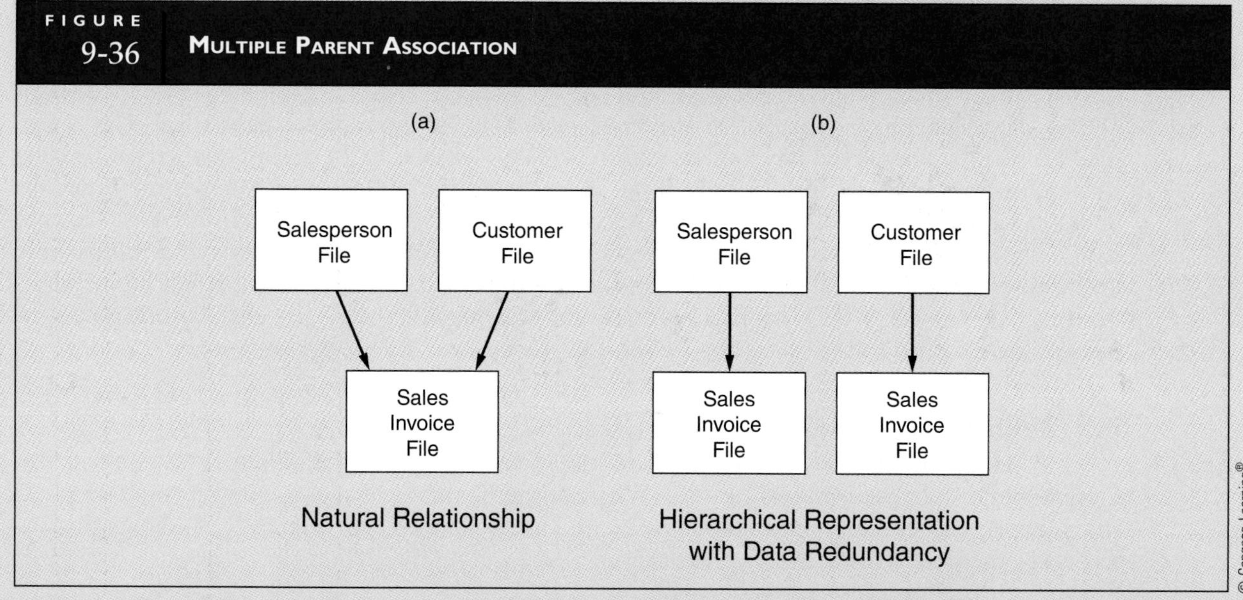

rule is flexible in allowing complex relationships to be represented. Figure 9-36(a) illustrates a simple network model in which the sales invoice file has two parent files—Customer and Salesperson. The navigational DBMS dominated the data-processing industry for many years, although the current trend is overwhelmingly toward the relational model. Many hierarchical and network systems still exist, and their manufacturers continue to maintain and upgrade them.

Data Structures

Data structures are the bricks and mortar of the database. The data structure allows records to be located, stored, and retrieved, and it enables movement from one record to another. Chapter 2 examined data structures commonly used by flat-file systems. These include sequential, indexed, hashing, and pointer structures. These basic structures form the foundation for the more complex hierarchical and network database structures discussed next.

HIERARCHICAL MODEL DATA STRUCTURE

Figure 9-37 shows the data structures and linkages between files for the partial database in Figure 9-35. Because the purpose is to illustrate the navigational nature of the data structure, the content of the records has been simplified.

Assume that a user of this system is using a query program to retrieve all the data pertinent to a particular sales invoice (Invoice Number 1921) for a customer John Smith (Account Number 1875). The access method used for this situation is the **hierarchical indexed direct access method**. Under this method, the root segment (customer file) of the database is organized as an indexed file. Lower-level records (e.g., sales invoice, invoice line item, and cash receipts records) use pointers in a linked-list arrangement. This allows both efficient processing of the root records for tasks, such as updating AR and billing customers, and direct access of detail records for inquiries.

The access method retrieves the primary key—CUST NUM 1875—entered by the user via the query program and compares this against the index for the root segment. Upon matching the key with the index, it directly accesses John Smith's customer record. Notice the customer record contains only summary information. The current balance figure represents the total dollar amount John Smith owes ($1,820). This is the difference between the sum of all sales to this customer and all cash received in payment on the account. The supporting details about these transactions are contained in the lower-level sales invoice and cash receipts records. In response to the user's inquiry for data pertaining to Invoice Number 1921, the access method follows the invoice record pointer to the sales invoice file.

The sales invoice file is a randomly organized file of invoices for all customers, arranged in a series of linked lists. The records in each linked list have a common property—they all relate to a specific customer. The first record in the list—the head record—has a pointer to the next in the list (if one exists), which points to the next, and so on. The pointer in the customer record (the level above) directs the access method to the head record in the appropriate linked list. The access method then compares the key value sought (Invoice Number 1921) against each record in the list until it finds a match. The records in the sales invoice file contain only summary information about sales transactions. Pointers in these records identify the supporting detail records (the specific items sold) in the invoice line-item file. The structure of the line-item file is also a linked-list arrangement. Starting with the head record, the access method retrieves the entire list of line items for Invoice Number 1921. In this list, there are two records. The sales invoice and line-item records are returned to the user's application for processing.

NETWORK MODEL DATA STRUCTURE

As with the hierarchical model, the network model is a navigational database with pointers creating explicit linkages between records. Whereas the hierarchical model allows only one path, the network model supports multiple paths to a particular record. Figure 9-38 shows the linkages for the data structure in Figure 9-36(a).

FIGURE 9-37 LINKAGES BETWEEN FILES IN A HIERARCHICAL DATABASE

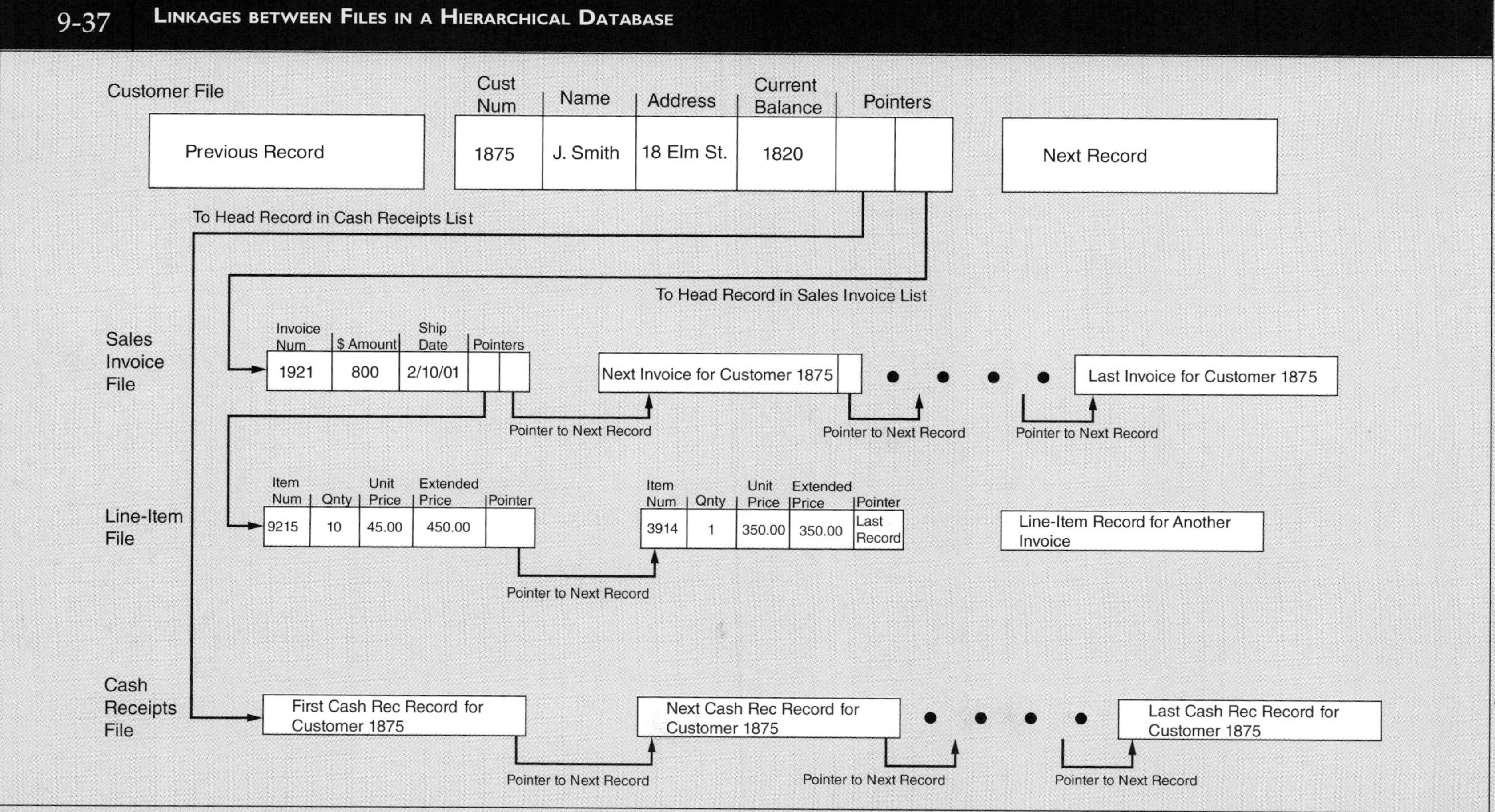

FIGURE 9-38 LINKAGES IN A NETWORK DATABASE

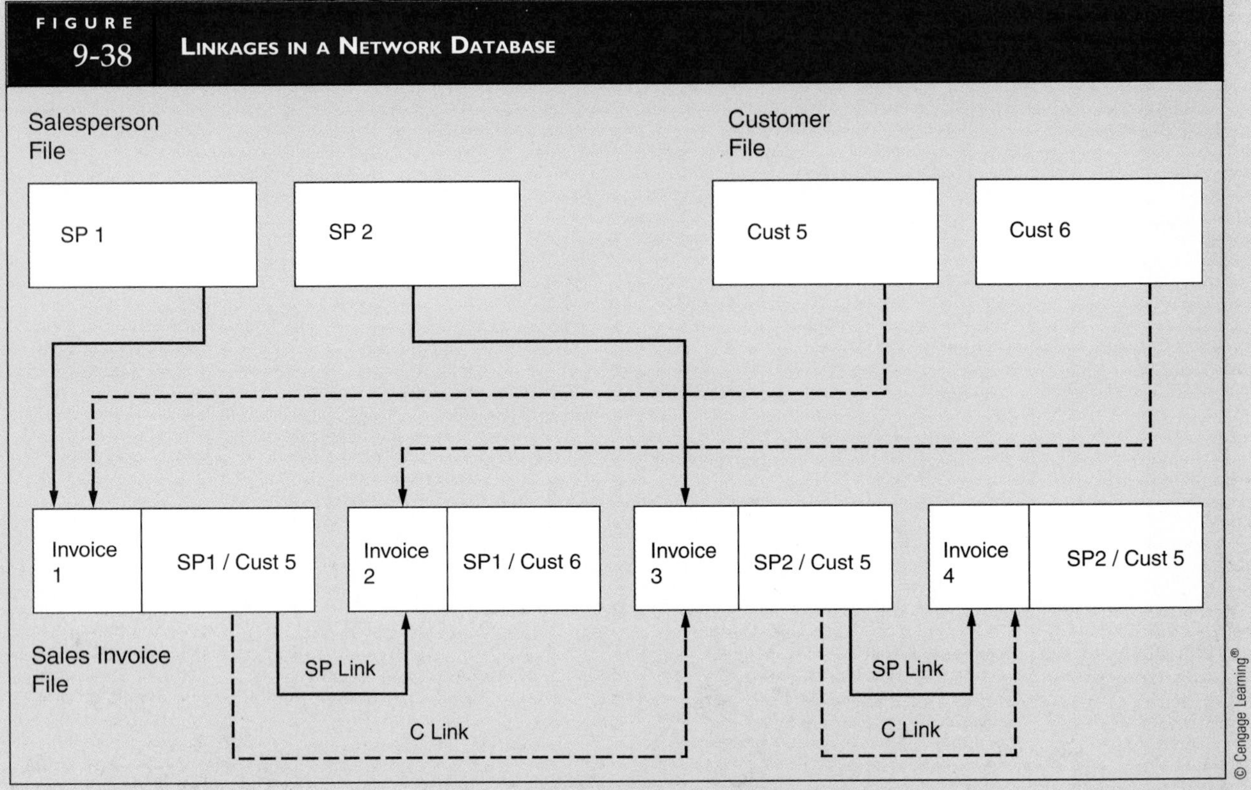

The structure can be accessed at either of the root-level records (salesperson or customer) by hashing their respective primary keys (SP NUM or CUST NUM) or by reading their addresses from an index.

A pointer field in the parent record explicitly defines the path to the child record, as discussed earlier. Notice the structure of the sales invoice file. In this example, each child now has two parents and contains explicit links to other records that form linked lists related to each parent. For example, Invoice Number 1 is the child of Salesperson Number 1 and Customer Number 5. This record structure has two links to related records. One of these is a salesperson (SP) link to Invoice Number 2. This represents a sale by Salesperson Number 1 to Customer Number 6. The second pointer is the customer (C) link to Invoice Number 3. This represents the second sale to Customer Number 5, which was processed this time by Salesperson Number 2. Under this data structure, management can track and report sales information pertaining to both customers and sales staff.

Key Terms

access method (386)
anomalies (397)
association (392)
attributes (392)
cardinality (392)
centralized database (413)
composite key (401)
concurrency control (418)
currency of information (380)
data attribute (380)
data currency (414)
data definition language (DDL) (384)
data dictionary (389)
data manipulation language (DML) (386)
data model (391)
data redundancy (380)
data storage (380)
data structures (422)

data updating (380)
database administrator (DBA) (387)
database lockout (415)
database management system (DBMS) (382)
deadlock (416)
deletion anomaly (398)
distributed data processing (DDP) (413)
distributed databases (415)
entity (392)
entity relationship (ER) diagram (392)
first normal form (INF) (397)
flat-file (379)
foreign keys (395)
hierarchical indexed direct access method (422)
hierarchical model (383)
indexed sequential file (389)
insertion anomaly (398)
internal view (385)
inverted list (389)
join (391)
navigational models (383)
network model (383)
occurrence (392)
partial dependencies (398)
partitioned database (415)
physical database (389)
primary key (394)
project (391)
relational model (383)
repeating groups (398)
replicated databases (417)
restrict (389)
schema (385)
second normal form (2NF) (397)
structured models (383)
structured query language (386)
task-data dependency (380)
temporary inconsistency (414)
third normal form (3NF) (397)
transitive dependencies (398)
update anomaly (397)
user view (385)
users (383)
view integration (411)
view modeling (406)

Review Questions

1. Give five general duties of the database administrator.
2. What are the four primary elements of the database environment?
3. How are the network and hierarchical models different?
4. What flat-file data management problems are solved as a result of using the database concept?
5. What are the four ways in which database management systems provide a controlled environment to manage user access and the data resources?
6. Explain the relationship between the three levels of the data definition language. As a user, which level would you be most interested in?
7. What is a primary key?
8. What is a foreign key?
9. What is a data dictionary, and what purpose does it serve?
10. Give an application for a partitioned database.
11. What is an entity?
12. Give an application for a replicated database.
13. Discuss and give an example of the following types of cardinality: (1:0,1), (1:1), (l:M), and (M:M).
14. Distinguish between association and cardinality.
15. Explain how a separate linking table works in a many-to-many cardinality.
16. What are the four characteristics of properly designed relational database tables?
17. What do the relational features *restrict*, *project*, and *join* mean?
18. What are the conditions for third normal form (3NF)?
19. Explain how the SELECT and WHERE commands help a user to view the necessary data from multiple database files (tables).
20. What is a data model?
21. How can a poorly designed database result in unintentional loss of critical records?
22. What is a user view?
23. Does a user view always require multiple tables to support it? Explain.
24. What three conditions must valid entities meet?
25. Can two different entities have the same defining attributes? Explain.

Discussion Questions

1. In the flat-file data management environment, users are said to own their data files. What is meant by the ownership concept?
2. Discuss the potential aggravations you might face as a student as a result of your university using a flat-file data management environment, that is, different files for the registrar, library, parking, and so on.
3. Discuss why control procedures over access to the data resource become more crucial under the database approach than in the flat-file environment. What role does the DBMS play in helping to control the database environment?
4. What is the relationship between a database table and a user view?
5. Explain how linkages between relational tables are accomplished.
6. Explain the purpose of an ER diagram in database design.
7. SQL has been said to place power in the hands of the user. What does this statement mean?
8. Discuss the importance of the role of the database administrator. In the flat-file environment, why is such a role not necessary? What tasks does the DBA perform?
9. As users determine new computer application needs, requests must be sent to both the system programmers and the DBA. Why is it important that these two groups perform separate functions, and what are these functions?
10. Why is a separate link table required when an M:M association exits between related tables?
11. As an accountant, why would you need to be familiar with data normalization techniques?
12. How does a database lockout contribute to financial data integrity?
13. How does concurrency control contribute to financial data integrity?
14. In a relational database environment, certain accounting records (e.g., journals, subsidiary ledgers, and event general ledger accounts) may not exist. How is this possible?
15. Explain how to link tables in a 1:1 cardinality. Why may this be different in a 1:0,1 cardinality?
16. Discuss the accounting implications of the update, insertion, and deletion anomalies associated with improperly normalized tables.
17. Give three examples that illustrate how cardinality reflects an organization's underlying business rules.
18. Discuss the key factors to consider in determining how to partition a corporate database.
19. Distinguish between a database lockout and a deadlock.
20. Replicated databases create considerable data redundancy, which is in conflict with the database concept. Explain the justification of this approach.

Multiple-Choice Questions

1. Of the following, select the attribute that would be the best primary key in an inventory table.
   a. ITEM NAME
   b. ITEM NUMBER
   c. ITEM COST
   d. ITEM LOCATION
   e. ITEM SUPPLIER
2. The advantages to using a partitioned database approach include all of the following EXCEPT that
   a. the possibility for the deadlock phenomenon is reduced.
   b. user control is increased.
   c. transaction processing time is decreased.
   d. the potential for wide-scale disaster is reduced.
   e. these are all advantages of partitioned databases.
3. A partial dependency
   a. is the result of simultaneous user requests for the same data in a partitioned database environment.
   b. is a name given to one of the three anomalies that result from unnormalized database tables.

c. can exist only in a table with a composite primary key.
d. may exist in tables that are normalized at the 2NF level.
e. is none of the above.

4. Repeating group data
   a. occur as a form of data redundancy common to replicated databases in a distributed database environment.
   b. refer to one of the three anomalies that result from unnormalized database tables.
   c. can exist only in a table with a composite primary key.
   d. cannot exist in tables that are normalized at the 2NF level.
   e. are none of the above.
5. What term describes the following data items: part number, description, quantity on hand, and reorder point?
   a. Attributes
   b. Relations
   c. Entities
   d. Occurrences
6. One of the first steps in the creation of a relational database is to
   a. perform view integration.
   b. normalize the tables.
   c. create a data model of the entities in the system.
   d. identify attributes and add foreign keys.
   e. construct the physical user view using SQL.
7. Entities in a data model
   a. may contain zero or many occurrences.
   b. are represented as verbs in an ER diagram.
   c. may represent both physical assets and intangible phenomena.
   d. are often defined by common attributes that also define other entities.
   e. are unique to a specific user view.
8. Which of the following is least likely to be an attribute of an employee table in a normalized database?
   a. Employee name
   b. Employee address
   c. Employee number
   d. Employee supervisor's name
   e. All of these would be attributes of the employee table in a normalized database.
9. Partitioned databases are most effective when
   a. users in the system need to share common data.
   b. read-only access is needed at each site.
   c. primary users of the data are clearly identifiable.
   d. all of the above.
10. Which of the following is true about a transitive dependency?
    a. Is a database condition that is resolved through special monitoring software.
    b. Is a name given to one of the three anomalies that result from unnormalized database tables.
    c. Can exist only in a table with a composite primary key.
    d. Cannot exist in tables that are normalized at the 2NF level.
    e. None of the above is true.
11. The installation of a database management system is likely to have the least impact on
    a. data redundancy.
    b. entity-wide sharing of common data.
    c. exclusive ownership of data.
    d. the logic needed to solve a problem in an application program.
    e. the internal controls over data access.
12. Which of the following describe best the functions of a database administrator?
    a. Database planning, data input preparation, and database design.
    b. Database design, database implementation, and database planning.
    c. Database design, database operation, and equipment operations.
    d. Data input preparation, database design, and database operation.
    e. Database operations, database maintenance, and data input preparation.
13. Database currency is achieved by
    a. implementing partitioned databases at remote sites.
    b. a database lockout that prevents multiple simultaneous access.

c. ensuring that the database is secure from accidental entry.

d. an external auditor's reconciliation of reports from multiple sites.

e. employing data-cleansing techniques.

14. Which of the following is true?

a. Each view requires at least one table that is unique to it.

b. Removing repeating groups places the table in 1NF.

c. Database anomalies cause structural dependencies.

d. Transitive dependencies can exist only in tables with composite primary keys.

e. All of the above are true.

15. Which of the following is true?

a. Linking 1:M relations requires placing the primary key of the M side into the table on the 1 side.

b. Linking tables contain keys but no data.

c. A table may have one or more occurrences.

d. Cardinality in an ER diagram describes the nature of the relation.

e. None of the above are true.

16. Which of the following is true?

a. User views limit access to the database.

b. Relational databases employ explicit links that are contained within the tables.

c. All data within a relational database system are shared by all users.

d. All the above are true.

17. Which of the following statements is not true.

a. Database systems have data independence; that is, the data and the programs are maintained separately except during processing.

b. Database systems contain a data definition language that helps describe each schema and subschema.

c. The database administrator is a software package that retrieves data by interacting with the operating system.

d. A primary goal of database systems is to minimize data redundancy.

e. Database systems provide increased accessibility to data and flexibility in its usage.

18. The data attributes that a particular user has permission to access are defined by the

a. user view.

b. systems design view.

c. database schema.

d. operating system view.

e. application program.

Problems

1. DISTRIBUTED DATABASES

The Mega Supply Corporation has three divisions: Commercial Products, Consumer Products, and Corporate Offices, which are located in Hatfield, SC; Palo Alto, CA; and Tulsa OK, respectively. The Commercial Products division deals exclusively in sales of industrial products and supplies to business organizations. The Consumer Products division sells nonindustrial products to private consumers. Both divisions have dedicated inventory warehouses at their respective locations in Hatfield and Palo Alto. Because of the dissimilar nature of the commercial and consumer division product lines, they do not share customers or vendors.

Currently Mega Supply uses a centralized database, which is located at their Corporate Division in Tulsa. Some relevant database tables and attributes are presented in the figure designated Problem 1.

When customers contact their respective sales division, the sales clerk logs into the corporate data base, checks credit, determines product availability, and creates a sales invoice. The corporate office typically bills the customer within 3 or 4 days and extends terms of net 30. Inventory control, AR processing, cash receipts, purchases from vendors and AP processing, and cash disbursements are performed by the corporate office.

Due to Mega's rapid growth, the company has seen a significant increase in sales and purchase transactions, which has resulted in excessive delays in processing transactions from the central database. Since customer service, including rapid response to customer inquiries and sales order processing, is a cornerstone of Mega's business model, these delays are unacceptable.

Required

Mega wants to improve response time by distributing some parts of the corporate database while keeping other parts of it centralized.

A) Develop a schema for distributing Mega Supply Corporation's database. Add new tables and attributes as needed but limit the schema to the tables needed to support sales, cash receipts, purchases/AP, and cash disbursements. In your schema, indicate whether tables are centralized, replicated, or partitioned.

B) Explain how the new system will operate.

2. DBMS VERSUS FLAT-FILE PROCESSING

Werner Manufacturing Corporation has a flat-file processing system. The information-processing facility is very large. Different applications, such as order processing, production planning, inventory management, accounting systems, payroll, and marketing systems, use separate tape and disk files. The corporation has recently hired a consulting firm to investigate the possibility of switching to a database management system. Prepare a memo to the top management team at Werner explaining the advantages of a DBMS. Also, discuss the necessity of a database administrator and the job functions this person would perform.

3. DATABASE DESIGN

Lester's Rentals is located in Cincinnati Ohio. The company rents party equipment such as tents, tables, chairs, linens, and china for small occasions and large weddings. They also rent a variety of home-improvement tools and contractor equipment including generators, grinders, power hammers, and drills. The company serves approximately 5,000 repeat customers and has more than 1,200 different inventory items for rent in stock. Lester's purchases replacement stock from 45 different vendors. Each vendor supplies different items, but Lestor's may purchase the same item from different vendors. Other business rules include: (1) each inventory type has multiple quantities on hand (2) customers use their telephone numbers to uniquely identify themselves for rentals; (3) customers may rent more than one item of the same type.

PROBLEM I

Customer Table

Customer Number	Customer Class	Billing Address	Shipping Address	Line of Credit

Sales Invoice (AR)

Sales Invoice Num	Customer Number	Product Number	Invoice Amount	Invoice Date

Inventory Table

Product Num	Inventory Class	Quantity on Hand	Unit Cost	Vendor Number

Vendor Invoice (AP)

Vendor Invoice Num	Vendor Number	Product Number	Invoice Amount	Invoice Date

Vendor Table

Vendor Num	Vendor Address	Tel Number

Note: Customer Class: Value 1 = Commercial, Value 2 = Consumer
Inventory Class: Value 1 = Industrial product, Value 2 = Consumer product

Required

Create a normalized data model for Lester's Rentals. Include the primary keys, data attributes, and foreign keys.

4. DATA NORMALIZATION

Using the view for a veterinarian practice designated problem 4, normalize the data into the required third normal form tables. Present the record structure for each normalized table and indicate the primary keys and embedded foreign keys. Note that an owner may own more than one animal.

5. DATABASE DEADLOCK

How is a lockout different from a deadlock? Give an accounting example to illustrate why a database lockout is necessary and how a deadlock can occur. Provide meaningful table names in your example.

6. DATABASE DESIGN

Premium Garden Products (PGP) supplies gardening enthusiasts and commercial garden centers throughout the northeast with a wide range of gardening equipment and products. Their wide range of inventory includes such items as tank sprayers, wheel barrows, fertilizers, plants, insecticides, and so on. Sales to commercial customers (garden centers) are on credit, whereas consumer sales are cash transactions (bank credit/debit cards). Sales orders are received via e-mail or phone at the Scranton PA home office. In the case of commercial customers' sales, the PGP sales clerk verifies customer credit worthiness by checking their available credit in the Customer table. The clerk then checks the availability of the product from the Inventory table and creates a record in the Sales Invoice table to record the sale. The clerk then sends a stock release notice to the distribution center nearest to the customer's location, from where the product is shipped. Shipments are made from two distribution centers: one in Scranton and one in Maryland. Commercial customers are given net 30 terms. They make payment by check, and the open Sales Invoice is then marked paid by placing the customers check number in the "payment" field of the invoice. Sales to consumer customers are processed similarly except no credit check is performed and the Sales Invoice record is marked paid at the time of sale by placing the last four digits of the customer's credit card number in the payment field.

PGP obtains its inventories from over 100 nurseries and producers of garden products throughout the United States. When inventory levels fall to their predetermined reorder points, the computer system automatically creates a record in the Purchase Order table and sends a hard copy PO to the supplier. When products arrive at the distribution centers, the receiving clerks log onto the main office computer and create a record in the Receiving Report table. Suppliers send their invoices to the AP clerk who adds a record to the Supplier Invoice table. On the due date the cash disbursement clerk writes a check in payment of the AP, marks the supplier invoice paid by placing the check number in the "paid" field.

Required

Design a partial relational database needed to support those aspects of PGP's process that are outlined above. Label the database tables and assign meaningful attributes to each. Assign primary keys and foreign keys as needed. Assume that invoices, purchase orders, and receiving reports may contain many items.

PROBLEM 4

Patient ID Number	Patient Name	Owner ID Number	Owner Last Name	Owner First Name	Address1	Address2	Date	Animal Code	Animal Description	Service Code	Service Description	Charge
417	Beau	Magel	Magee	Elaine	23 Elm St	Houston, TX	1/4/05	GR	Golden Retriever	238	Rabies Shot	15.00
417	Beau	Magel	Magee	Elaine	23 Elm St	Houston, TX	1/4/05	GR	Golden Retriever	148	Flea Dip	25.00
417	Beau	Magel	Magee	Elaine	23 Elm St	Houston, TX	1/4/05	GR	Golden Retriever	337	Bloodwork	20.00
632	Luigi	Cocil	Cociolo	Tony	8 Oak St	Houston, TX	1/9/05	DN	Dalmatian	238	Rabies Shot	15.00
632	Luigi	Cocil	Cociolo	Tony	8 Oak St	Houston, TX	1/9/05	DN	Dalmatian	500	Kennel–Medium	9.00
632	Luigi	Cocil	Cociolo	Tony	8 Oak St	Houston, TX	1/24/05	DN	Dalmatian	500	Kennel–Medium	9.00
632	Luigi	Cocil	Cociolo	Tony	8 Oak St	Houston, TX	2/1/05	DN	Dalmatian	148	Flea Dip	25.00
168	Astro	Jetsl	Jetson	George	3 Air Rd	Sprockley, TX	2/2/05	MX	Canine Mixed	368	Ear Cleaning	17.00

7. DISTRIBUTED DATABASES

The XYZ Company is a geographically distributed organization with several sites around the country. Users at these sites need rapid access to common data for read-only purposes. Which distributed database method is best under these circumstances? Explain your reasoning.

8. DISTRIBUTED DATABASES

The ABC Company is a geographically distributed organization with several sites around the country. Users at these sites need rapid access to data for transaction processing purposes. The sites are autonomous; they do not share the same customers, products, or suppliers. Which distributed database method is best under these circumstances? Explain your reasoning.

9. NORMALIZATION OF DATA

A table of data for a library is shown in the table for Problem 9. Normalize these data into the third normal form, preparing them for use in a relational database environment. The library's computer is programmed to compute the due date to be 14 days after the checkout date. Document the steps necessary to normalize the data similar to the procedures found in the chapter and show the linkages between the related tables (primary keys and foreign keys). Make the following assumptions: The call number is unique to the book, and not to the event of borrowing the book. Also assume that more than one copy of the book may exist in the library and that all copies have the same call number.

10. NORMALIZATION OF DATA

A college bookstore maintains all of its records on index cards. This has proven to be a very tedious chore, and the manager has asked you to design a database that will simplify this task. The index cards are preprinted and contain the following labels:

Title:
Author(s):
Edition:
Publisher:
Publisher Address:
Publisher Phone #:
Cost of Text:
Selling Price:
Number on Hand:
Professor:
Class:
Semester:
Year:
Professor Phone #:

Using your understanding of the business rules that exist in most colleges and for most college bookstores, prepare the base tables (in third normal form) that will be required to translate the index card information into a working database for the bookstore.

11. NORMALIZATION OF DATA

Prepare the base tables, in third normal form, needed to produce the user view in the table for Problem 11.

PROBLEM 9: NORMALIZATION OF DATA

STUDENT ID NUMBER	STUDENT FIRST NAME	STUDENT LAST NAME	NUMBER OF BOOKS OUT	BOOK CALL NO	BOOK TITLE	DATE OUT	DUE DATE
678-98-4567	Amy	Baker	4	hf351.j6	Avalanches	09-02-09	09-16-09
678-98-4567	Amy	Baker	4	hf878.k3	Tornadoes	09-02-09	09-16-09
244-23-2348	Ramesh	Sunder	1	i835.123	Politics	09-02-09	09-16-09
398-34-8793	James	Talley	3	k987.d98	Sports	09-02-09	09-16-09
398-34-8793	James	Talley	3	d879.39	Legal Rights	09-02-09	09-16-09
678-98-4567	Amy	Baker	4	p987.t87	Earthquakes	09-03-09	09-17-09
244-23-2348	Ramesh	Sunder	1	q875.i76	Past Heroes	09-03-09	09-17-09

PROBLEM 11: NORMALIZATION OF DATA

USER VIEW

Part Num	Description	QOH	Reorder Point	EOQ	Unit Cost	Ven Num	Ven Name	Ven Address	Tel
132	Bolt	100	50	1000	1.50	987	ABC Co.	654 Elm St	555 5498
143	Screw	59	10	100	1.75	987	ABC Co.	654 Elm St	555 5498
760	Nut	80	20	500	2.00	742	XYZ Co.	510 Smit	555 8921
982	Nail	100	50	800	1.00	987	ABC Co.	654 Elm St	555 5498

12. NORMALIZATION OF DATA

Prepare the base tables, in third normal form, needed to produce the user view in the table for Problem 12.

13. NORMALIZATION OF DATA

Prepare the 3NF base tables needed to produce the sales report view shown in the diagram for Problem 13.

14. NORMALIZATION OF DATA-PURCHASE ORDER

Acme Plywood Company uses the purchase order shown in the diagram for Problem 14. Acme business rules:

1. Each vendor may supply many items; an item is supplied by only one vendor.
2. A purchase order may list many items; an item may be listed on many purchase orders.
3. An employee may complete several purchase orders, but only one employee may fill out an individual PO.

Prepare the 3NF base tables needed to produce this purchase order.

15. TABLE LINKING

Solve this problem per the text in the diagram for Problem 15.

16. ENTITY RELATIONSHIP DIAGRAM

The diagram labeled problem 16 presents a partial entity relationship diagram of a purchase system. Describe the business rules represented by the cardinalities in the diagram.

17. ENTITY RELATIONSHIP DIAGRAM

Refer to the entity relationship diagram in Problem 16. Modify the diagram to deal with the payments of merchandise purchased. Explain the business rules represented by the cardinalities in the diagram.

PROBLEM 12: NORMALIZATION OF DATA

USER VIEW

Part Num	Description	QOH	Reorder Point	EOQ	Unit Cost	Ven Num	Ven Name	Ven Address	Tel
132	BOLT	100	50	1000	1.50	987	ABC Co.	654 Elm St	555 5498
					1.55	750	RST Co.	3415 8th St	555 3421
					1.45	742	XYZ Co.	510 Smit	555 8921
982	NAIL	100	50	800	1.00	987	ABC Co.	654 Elm St	555 5498
					1.10	742	XYZ Co.	510 Smit	555 8921
					1.00	549	LMN Co.	18 Oak St	555 9987

PROBLEM 13: NORMALIZATION OF DATA

Sales Report

Customer Number: 19321
Customer Name : Jon Smith
Address : 520 Main St., City

Invoice Num	Date	Invoice Total	Part Num	Quantity	Unit Price	Ext'd Price
12390	11/11/09	$850	2	5	$20	$100
			1	10	50	500
			3	25	10	250
12912	11/21/09	$300	4	10	$30	$300

Customer Total: $1,150

** * *** * *** * *** * *** * *** * ** *

Customer Number: 19322
Customer Name : Mary Smith
Address : 2289 Elm St., City

Invoice Num	Date	Invoice Total	Part Num	Quantity	Unit Price	Ext'd Price
12421	11/13/09	$1,000	6	10	$20	$200
			1	2	50	100
			5	7	100	700
12901	11/20/09	$500	4	10	$30	$300
			2	10	20	200

Customer Total: $1,500

** * *** * *** * *** * *** * *** * ** *

Next Customer

•
•
•

Next Customer

18. ENTITY RELATIONSHIP DIAGRAM

Prepare a entity relationship diagram for the revenue cycle that includes entities, cardinalities, and reflects the following business rules:

- Customers place many orders during the period
- Each sales order consists of one or more line items of inventory.
- Customers are billed twice a month for the purchases that they made during the period.
- Customers make payments once a month to settle their accounts.

19. DEFINING ENTITIES AND DATA MODELING—PAYROLL

Employees at the Sagerod Manufacturing Company record their hours worked on paper time cards that are inserted into a time clock machine at the beginning and end of each shift. On Fridays, the supervisor collects the time cards, reviews and signs them, and sends them to the payroll clerk. The clerk calculates the pay for each employee and updates the employee earnings file. This involves adding a new record for each employee in the pay period that reflects the employee's gross pay, tax

PROBLEM 14: NORMALIZATION OF DATA

Purchase Order

Acme Plywood Co.
1234 West Ave.
Somewhere, OH 00000

P.O. #
Date: __/__/__

Vendor: ______________________

Ship Via: ____________ Please refer to this P.O. number on all correspondence.

Prepared by: ______________________

Item #	Description	Quantity	Cost	Extension

deductions, and other withholdings for the period. The clerk then prepares a paycheck for each employee and records it in the check register. The check register and corresponding paychecks reflect each employee's net earnings for the period. Based on these records, the clerk prepares a payroll summary, which is sent with the paychecks to the cash disbursements clerk. The clerk reviews the payroll summary, updates the cash disbursements journal to record the total payroll, and prepares a check for the total payroll, which is deposited into the payroll imprest account. The clerk then signs the paychecks and distributes them to the employees.

Required
Assume that the manual system described is to be automated using a relational database system. Create a data model for the system including the entities and cardinalities between them that will support the tasks and user views depicted in the description. You may need to make assumptions about how certain automated activities will be performed. Normalize the model.

20. DEFINING ENTITIES AND DATA MODELING—PURCHASES PROCEDURES

The business rules that constitute the purchases system for the Safe Buy Grocery Stores chain are similar at all the store locations. The purchase manager at each location is responsible for selecting his or her local suppliers. If the manager needs a product, he or she chooses a supplier. Each store follows the steps described here.

1. The purchasing function begins with sales representatives from suppliers periodically observing the shelves and displays at each location and recognizing the need to restock inventory. Inventory declines by direct sales to the customers or by spoilage of perishable goods. In addition, the supplier's sales representatives review obsolescence reports that the purchase manager prepares. These reports identify slow-moving and dated products that are deemed unsalable at a particular location. These products are returned to the supplier and replaced with more successful products. The sales representatives prepare a hard-copy purchase requisition and meet with the purchase managers of the individual store locations. Together, the sales representative and the purchase manager create a purchase order defining the products, the quantity, and the delivery date.
2. At the intended delivery date, Safe Buy Grocery Stores receive the goods from the suppliers. Goods received are unloaded from the delivery

Problem 15: Table Linking

Several related tables with their primary keys (PK) are shown below. Place the foreign key(s) in the tables to link them according to the associations shown (e.g., 1:M and M:M). Create any new table(s) that may be needed.

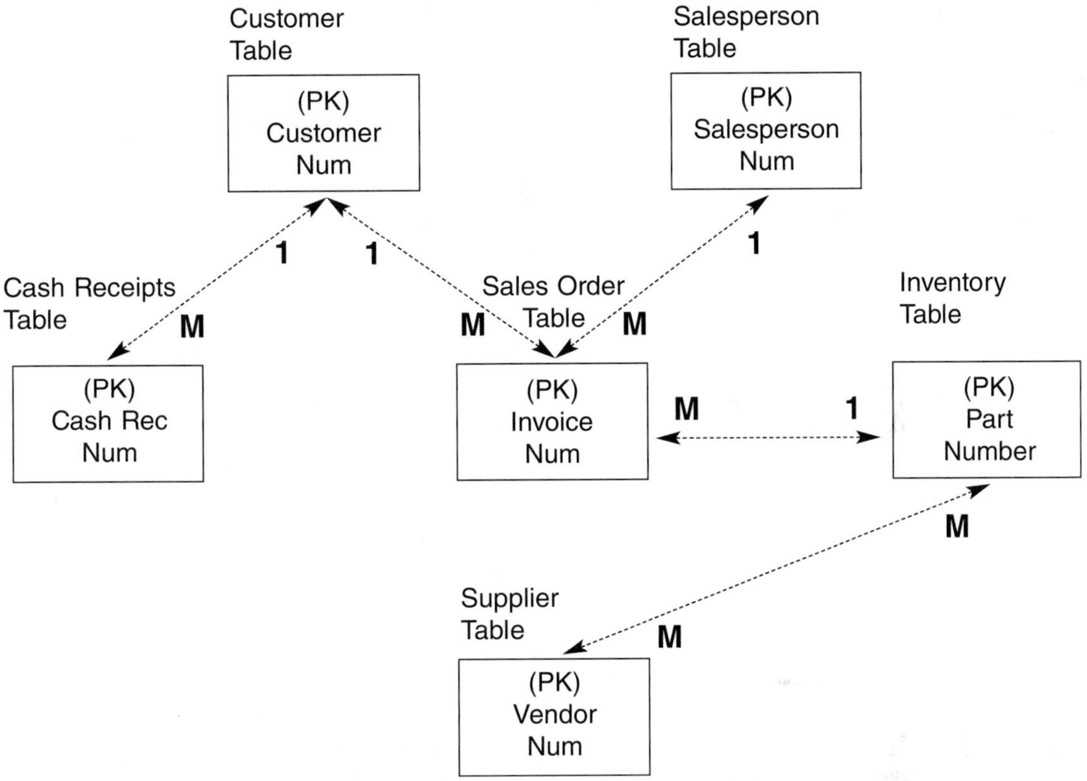

Customer Table: (PK) Customer Num

Salesperson Table: (PK) Salesperson Num

Cash Receipts Table: (PK) Cash Rec Num

Sales Order Table: (PK) Invoice Num

Inventory Table: (PK) Part Number

Supplier Table: (PK) Vendor Num

Customer (1) — (M) Cash Receipts

Customer (1) — (M) Sales Order

Salesperson (1) — (M) Sales Order

Sales Order (M) — (1) Inventory

Inventory (M) — (M) Supplier

Problem 16: Entity Relationship Diagram

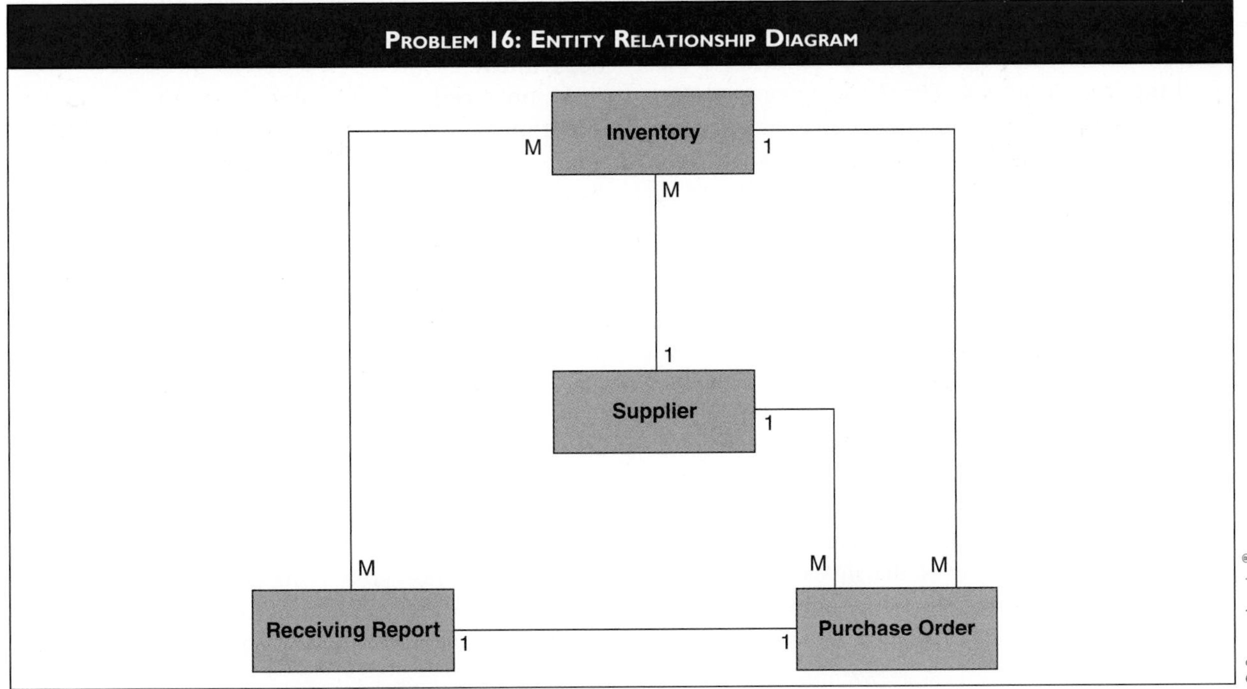

trucks and stocked on the shelves and displays by part-time employees.

3. The unloading personnel create a receiving report. Each day, a receiving report summary is prepared and sent to the purchase managers for review.
4. The supplier subsequently submits an invoice to the AP department clerk, who creates an invoice record. The clerk reconciles the invoice against the receiving report and purchase order and then creates a payment obligation to be paid at a future date, depending on the terms of trade.
5. On the due date, a check is automatically prepared and sent to the supplier, and the payment is recorded in the check register. At the end of each day, a payment summary is sent to the purchase managers for review.

Required

Assume that the manual system described is to be automated using a relational database system. Create a data model for the system including primary keys, foreign keys, and data attributes that will support the tasks and user views. You may need to make assumptions about how certain automated activities will be performed. Normalize the model.

21. DEFINING ENTITIES AND DATA MODELING—FIXED ASSET PROCEDURES

The business rules that constitute the fixed asset procedures for the Safe Buy Grocery Stores chain are similar at all the store locations. The store manager at each location is responsible for identifying needed fixed assets and for selecting the vendor. Freezers, refrigerators, delivery vans, and store shelving are examples of fixed asset purchases. Once the need has been identified, each store follows the following procedures.

The manager creates a purchase order, which is sent to the supplier. The supplier delivers the asset to the receiving clerk, who prepares a receiving report. Each week, the fixed asset department clerk reviews the fixed asset receiving report summary and creates a fixed asset inventory record for each receipt. The fixed asset clerk maintains the inventory records and depreciation schedules. The vendor subsequently submits an invoice to the AP department clerk, who creates an invoice record. The clerk reconciles the invoice against the receiving report and purchase order and then creates a payment obligation to be paid at a future date, depending on the terms of trade. On the due date, a check is automatically prepared and sent to the vendor, and the payment is recorded in the check register. At the end of each day, a payment summary is sent to the AP manager for review.

Required

Assume that the manual system described is to be automated using a relational database system. Create a normalized data model for the system including primary keys, foreign keys, and data attributes that will support the tasks and user views. You may need to make assumptions about how certain automated activities will be performed.

22. DEFINING ENTITIES AND DATA MODELING—SALES ORDER PROCEDURES

Sales Procedures

A customer of the Lotus Tea Importer Company places an order with a sales representative by phone or fax. The sales department employee then transcribes the customer order into a standard sales order format and produces the following documents: three copies of sales orders, a stock release document, a shipping notice, and a packing slip. The accounting department receives a copy of the sales order, the warehouse receives the stock release and a copy of the sales order, and the shipping department receives a shipping notice and packing slip. The sales clerk files a copy of the sales order in the department.

Upon receipt of the sales order, the accounting department clerk prepares a customer invoice by adding prices to the sales order, which she obtains from the official price list. She then sends the invoice to the customer. Using data from the sales order, the clerk then records the sale in the sales journal and in the AR subsidiary ledger. At the end of the day, the clerk prepares a sales journal voucher, which he or she sends to the general ledger department for posting to the sales and AR control accounts.

The warehouse receives a copy of the sales order and stock release document. A warehouse employee picks the product and sends it to the shipping department, along with the stock release document. A warehouse clerk then updates the inventory records to reflect the reduction of inventory on hand. At the end of the day, the clerk prepares a hard-copy inventory account summary and sends it to the general ledger department for posting to the inventory control and cost of goods sold accounts.

Upon receipt of the stock release document from the warehouse, the shipping clerk prepares the two copies of a bill of lading. The BOLs and the packing slip are sent with the product to the carrier. The clerk then files the stock release in the department.

Cash Receipts Procedure

The mail room has five employees who open mail and sort the checks from the remittance advices. The remittance advices are sent to the accounting department, where the accounting clerk updates the customer AR subsidiary ledger to reflect the reduction in accounts receivable. At the end of the day, the clerk prepares an account summary and sends it to the general ledger department for posting.

The mail room clerk sends the checks to the cash receipts department, where a clerk endorses each check with the words "For Deposit Only." Next, the clerk records the cash receipts in the cash receipts journal. Finally, the clerk prepares a deposit slip and sends it and the checks to the bank.

Required

Assume that the manual system described is to be automated using a relational database system. Create a normalized data model for the system including primary keys, foreign keys, and data attributes that will support the tasks and user views. You may need to make assumptions about how certain automated activities will be performed.

23. DEFINING ENTITIES AND DATA MODELING—BUSINESS RULES

Given the following business rules, construct an ER diagram so each rule is captured for the database. Presume each rule is to be treated individually. Construct an ER diagram for each rule.

a. A retail sales company prepares sales orders for its customers' purchases. A customer can make many purchases, but a sales order is written for a single customer.
b. A retail sales company orders inventory using a purchase order. An inventory item may be ordered many times, and a purchase order may be created for more than one inventory item.
c. A company that sells antique cars prepares a sales order for each car sold. The inventory for this company consists of unique automobiles, and only one of these automobiles may be listed on a sales order.
d. A grocery store identifies returning customers via a plastic card that the clerk scans at the time of each purchase. The purpose of this card is to track inventory and to maintain a database of customers and their purchases. Obviously, a customer may purchase an unlimited number of items from the grocery store. Items are unique only by a UPC code, and each UPC code may be associated with many different customers.
e. A video rental store uniquely identifies each of its inventory items so customers can rent a movie and return the movie via a drop box, and the store can identify which copy of the movie was rented and returned. A customer is allowed to rent up to six movies at a time, but a copy of a movie can be rented only by one customer at a time.

24. DEFINING ENTITIES AND DATA-MODELING—GENERAL LEDGER

Required

Prepare an ER diagram that illustrates a normalized data model for a general ledger update process. Base the model on a sales order system that updates sales transactions to the GL in real time from sales invoices. The model should allow an audit trail that links the summary accounts in the GL to specific transaction records. Show all attributes, primary keys, and secondary keys.

25. COMPREHENSIVE CASE

(Prepared by Katie Daley and Gail Freeston, Lehigh University)

D&F is a distributor of CDs that offers benefits such as discount prices and an introductory offer of 10 CDs for a penny (not including the shipping and handling costs). Its primary target customers are college students; its main marketing strategy is constant deals to club members. The company's main competitors in the industry are BMG and Columbia House; both offer similar promotions.

D&F started in 1993 with an office in Harrisburg, Pennsylvania, initially targeting college students in the surrounding area. The company realized there was a high demand for discounted music merchandise and the convenience of mail delivery within universities. After its second year, with a constant increase in customer orders, D&F relocated to Philadelphia, where it was located near more colleges and universities. The move has had a positive effect on net profits and demand, supporting the decision to continue the growth of the company. D&F recently expanded its facility to be able to fulfill a higher demand for its services. Its customer base ranges from areas as close as Villanova University to as far as Boston College. As of 2011, there were 103 employees. Their prior year's gross sales were $125 million.

D&F's market share is on the rise but is not yet comparable to the magnitude of BMG and Columbia House. However, the corporation's goals for the upcoming years include establishing itself as an industry player through increased customer satisfaction and loyalty. D&F is also considering the installation of a new information-processing system. This system will reengineer the company's current business functions by reducing loopholes in its internal control problems.

D&F receives CDs from various wholesale suppliers and music store chains, totaling 32 suppliers nationwide. The office has its own warehouse, stores its own merchandise, and is responsible for replenishing the inventory. D&F has had no substantial problems in the past with their suppliers. On the other hand, it has encountered problems with excess inventory, stock-outs, and discrepancies with inventory records.

Revenue Cycle

Becoming a member of D&F Music Club involves calling the toll-free number and speaking with a sales representative, who establishes a new customer account. A customer's account record contains his or her name, address, phone number, previous orders he or she made with the company, and a sequentially assigned unique customer account number.

Customers place orders using the Internet. A sales representative then prepares a sales order record. John, in the billing department, reviews the sales orders, adds prices and shipping charges, and prints a copy (invoice) that is sent to the customer. John then adds a record to the sales journal to record the sale.

Chris, a warehouse employee, verifies the information on the sales order, picks the goods, prints the packing slip, and updates the inventory subsidiary ledger. Chris then prepares the bill of lading for the carrier. The goods are then shipped.

Sandy in AR updates the customer accounts and general ledger control accounts. When customers make a payment on account, they send both the remittance advice (that was attached to the invoice) and a check with the account number on it. Scott, a mail room clerk, opens all the cash receipts. He separates the checks and remittance advices and prepares a remittance list, which, along with the checks, is sent to the cash receipts department.

Laura, the cash receipts clerk, reconciles the checks with the remittance list, updates the customer's account and the general ledger, and then deposits the checks in the bank. She sends the deposit slip to Sandy in the accounting department.

Upon receiving the bank receipt, Sandy files it and updates the cash receipts journal to record the amount deposited. Upon the receipt of the CDs ordered, the customer has a 15-day trial period. If, at the end of that period, he or she sends a payment, it is understood that the goods have been accepted. If, on the other hand, the customer is dissatisfied with the product for any reason, he or she can return it to D&F Music Club at no charge. However, to return the CD, the customer must call the company to obtain an authorization number. When the goods arrive, Chris prepares the return record and updates the inventory subsidiary ledger. Printed copies of the return record are sent to John and Sandy. John reviews the return record and updates the sales journal. Sandy credits the customer's account and updates the general ledger to reverse the transaction.

Expenditure Cycle

The purchases system and the cash disbursements system compose D&F Music Club's expenditure cycle. The three departments within the purchasing system are warehouse, purchasing, and accounting. The purchasing function begins in the warehouse, which stores the inventory of CDs. Jim, the warehouse manager, compares inventory records with the various demand forecasts of each week, which the market research analyst teams provide, to determine the necessary orders to make. At the end of the week, Jim prepares the purchase requisition record.

Sara, the purchasing clerk, reviews the purchase requisitions, selects the suppliers, and prepares the purchase orders. Copies of the purchase orders are sent to the supplier and to accounting.

When the shipment arrives, Chris, the warehouse clerk, working from a blind copy of the purchase order, counts and inspects the goods for damage. He then prepares a receiving report and updates the inventory records.

Upon receipt of the supplier's invoice, Diana, the accounting clerk, compares it to the respective purchase order and receiving report. If the invoice is accurate, Diana creates an AP record, sets a due date for payment, and updates general ledger accounts.

On the due date, Evan, the cash disbursements clerk, closes the AP record, cuts a check, and sends it to the supplier. He then updates the check register and the general ledger.

Required

Assume that the manual system described is to be automated using a relational database system. Perform the following tasks. You may need to make assumptions about how certain automated activities will be performed.

a. Create a data model of the processes showing entity associations.

b. Create a fully attributed model by adding primary keys, foreign keys, and data attributes. Normalize the model.

c. Prepare a data flow diagram of the system showing the data stores.

CHAPTER 10

The REA Approach to Database Modeling

Learning Objectives

After studying this chapter, you should:

- Recognize the economic foundations of the resources, events, and agents (REA) model.
- Understand the key differences between traditional entity relationship modeling and REA modeling.
- Understand the structure of an REA diagram.
- Be able to create an REA diagram by applying the view modeling steps to a business case.
- Be able to create an entity-wide REA diagram by applying the view integration steps to a business case.

This chapter examines the resources, events, and agents (REA) model as a means of specifying and designing accounting information systems that serve the needs of all of the users in an organization. The chapter is composed of three major sections. The first introduces the REA approach and comments on the general problems associated with traditional accounting practice that can be resolved through an REA approach. This section presents the REA model and describes the structure of an REA diagram.

The basic REA model consists of three entity types (resources, events, and agents) and a set of associations linking them. Resources are things of economic value to the organization and are the objects of economic exchanges with trading partners. REA events fall into two general groups: economic events and support events. Economic events are phenomena that effect changes (increases or decreases) in resources. Support events include control, planning, and management activities that are related to economic events but do not directly effect a change in resources. Agents are individuals inside and outside the organization who participate in an economic event. A key feature of REA is the concept of economic duality. Each economic event is mirrored by another event in the opposite direction. These dual events constitute the give event and receive event of an economic exchange.

The second section presents the multistep process of view modeling to create an REA model. The focus here is on modeling a single view of the entire database. The steps involved are as follows: (1) identify the event entities to be modeled, (2) identify the resource entities changed by events, (3) identify the agent entities participating in events, and (4) determine associations and cardinalities between entities.

The third and final section presents the task of view integration, in which several individual REA diagrams are integrated into a single enterprise-wide model. The steps involved in view integration are: (1) consolidate the individual models; (2) define primary keys, foreign keys, and attributes, and (3) construct physical database and produce user views. The section concludes with a discussion of the advantages of REA in achieving competitive advantage.

The REA Approach

Central to the database philosophy is the recognition that corporate data should support the information needs of all users in the organization. An important aspect of data modeling, therefore, is creating a model that faithfully reflects the organization's physical reality. This is not easily accomplished when different people within the organization see and use the same data differently.

You will recall from Chapter 9 that a **user view** is the set of data that a particular user needs to achieve his or her assigned tasks. For example, a general ledger clerk's user view will include the organization's chart of accounts but not detailed transaction data. A sales manager's view may include detailed customer sales data organized by product, region, and salesperson. A production manager's view may include finished goods inventory on hand, available manufacturing capacity, and vendor lead times.

A problem arises in meeting these diverse needs when a single view that is inappropriate for entity-wide purposes dominates the collection, summarization, storage, and reporting of transaction and resource data. The accounting profession has long been criticized for focusing too narrowly on the role of accounting information. Many researchers today encourage the profession to shift its emphasis away from debits, credits, double-entry accounting, and GAAP, and move toward providing useful information for decision making and helping organizations identify and control business risk.

Modern managers need both financial and nonfinancial information in formats, and at levels of aggregation, that the traditional GAAP-based accounting systems generally fail to provide. The response within many organizations to the dominant single view of accounting information has been to create separate information systems to support each user's view. This has resulted in organizations with multiple information systems that are functionally disconnected. Often, data entered in one system need to be re-entered in the others. With such widespread duplication of data, accuracy and data currency issues pose serious problems.

Such concerns have led a number of database researchers to develop **semantic models** or frameworks for designing accounting information systems that support multiple user views. A semantic model captures the operational meaning of the user's data and provides a concise description of it. One such example, of great importance to accounting, is the REA model. In 1982, REA was originally proposed as a theoretical framework for accounting.[1] Since that time, however, it has gained considerable attention as a practical alternative to traditional accounting systems.

THE REA MODEL

The **REA model** is an accounting framework for modeling an organization's critical resources, events, and agents and the relationships between them. Unlike some traditional accounting systems, REA systems permit both accounting and nonaccounting data to be identified, captured, and stored in a centralized database. From this repository, user views that meet the needs of all users in the organization can be constructed. REA models may be implemented within either relational or object-oriented database architectures. For purposes of discussion in this chapter, we will assume a relational database because this is the more common architecture for business applications.

Figure 10-1 illustrates the basic REA model, which is a unique version of an entity relationship (ER) diagram consisting of three entity types (resources, events, and agents) and a set of associations linking them. From this point, we will refer to this documentation technique as an **REA diagram**.

1 W. E. McCarthy, "The REA Accounting Model: A Generalized Framework for Accounting Systems in a Shared Data Environment," *The Accounting Review* (July 1982), 554–77.

FIGURE 10-1 BASIC REA MODEL

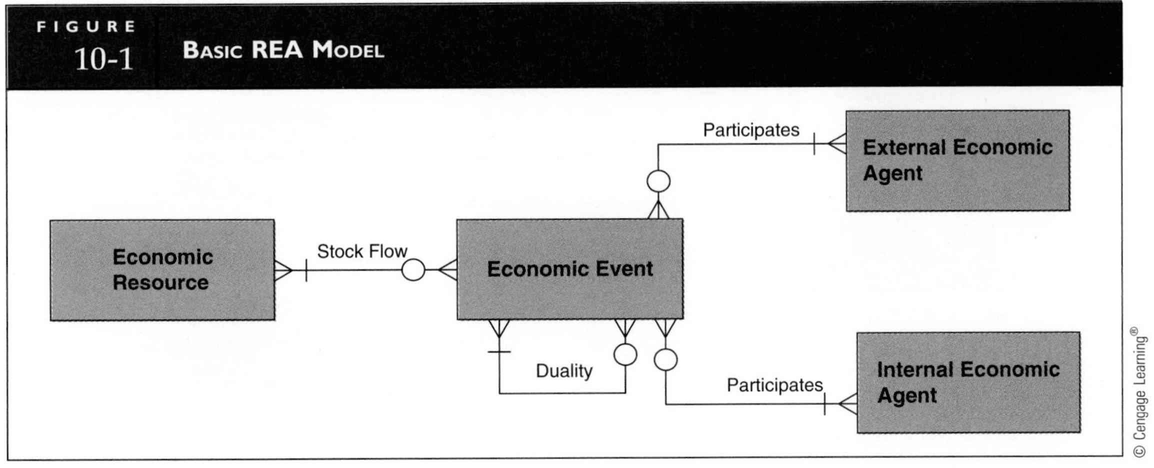

The conventions for describing associations, assigning cardinality, and normalizing tables as discussed in Chapter 9 for traditional ER diagrams also apply to REA diagrams.

Elements of an REA Model

RESOURCES. Economic **resources** are things of economic value to the organization. They are defined as objects that are both scarce and under the control of the enterprise. Resources are used in economic exchanges with trading partners and are either increased or decreased by the exchange.

EVENTS. REA modeling embraces two classes of events: economic events and support events. **Economic events** are phenomena that effect changes (increases or decreases) in resources as represented by the **stock flow** relation in Figure 10-1. They result from activities such as sales of products to customers, receipt of cash from customers, and purchases of raw material from vendors. Economic events are the critical information elements of the accounting system and must be captured in as disaggregated (highly detailed) form as possible to provide a rich database.

Support events (not shown in Figure 10-1) include control, planning, and management activities that are related to economic events but do not directly effect a change in resources. Examples of support events are (1) determining inventory availability for a customer prior to making a sale, (2) verifying supporting information (performing a three-way match) prior to disbursing cash to a vendor, and (3) checking customer credit before processing a sale.

AGENTS. Economic **agents** are individuals and departments that participate in economic and support events. They are parties either inside or outside the organization with discretionary power to use or dispose of economic resources. Each economic event is associated with at least one **internal agent** and one **external agent** who participate in the exchange. The respective roles of internal and external agents in transactions with outsiders are usually apparent. For example, in a sales transaction, the internal agents are various employees of the company, and the external agent is the customer. For purely internal transactions, however, the roles of internal and external agents may not be so obvious. The convention in REA modeling is to treat such transactions as if they were sales. For example, in the transfer of products from work-in-process to finished goods inventory, the work-in-process clerk is viewed as selling the product to the finished goods clerk. Therefore, the clerk giving up control and reducing the resource (work-in-process clerk) is the internal agent, and the clerk assuming control and increasing the resource (finished goods clerk) is the external agent.

Internal and external agents are also involved in support events, but the exchange involves information rather than economic resources. For example, a customer (external agent) checking on product prices receives information from the sales clerk (internal agent), who gives the information. Linking internal agents to events in this way promotes control and permits organizations to assess the actions taken by their employees.

FIGURE 10-2 REA MODEL SHOWING DUALITY OF A GIVE AND RECEIVE EXCHANGE

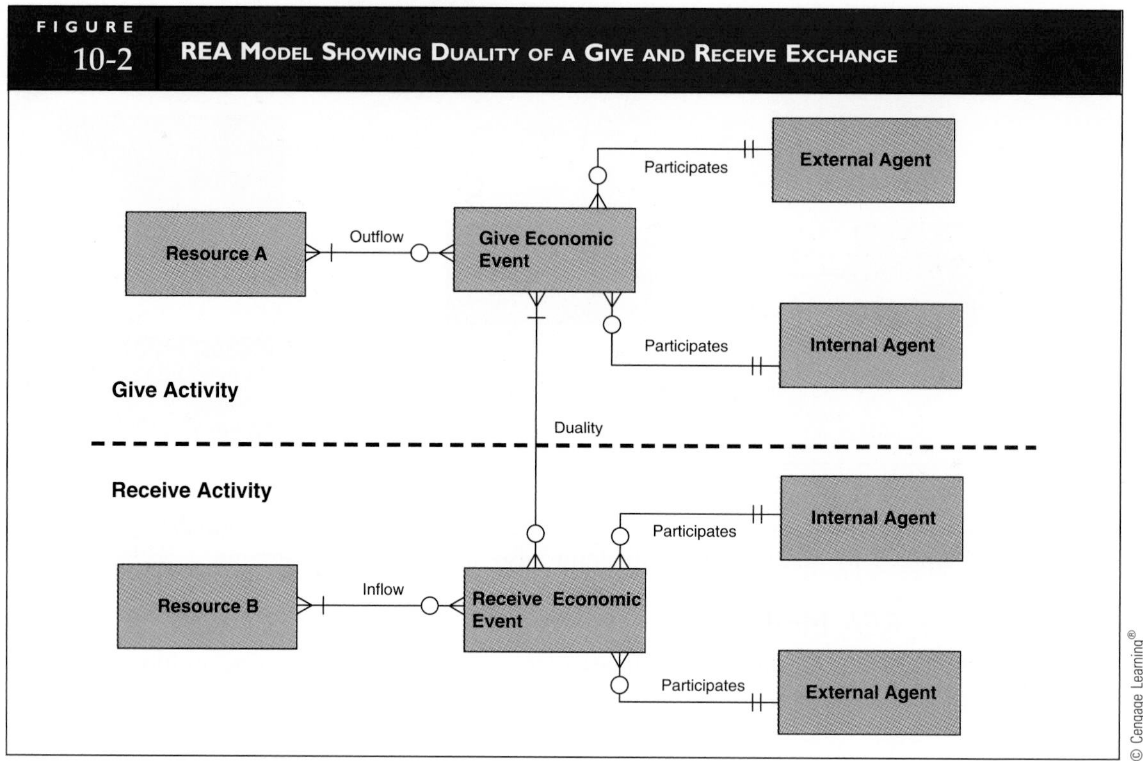

DUALITY. REA's semantic features are derived from the elements of an economic transaction. The rationale behind an economic transaction is that two agents each give the other a resource in exchange for another resource. In actuality, the exchange is a pair of economic events, which is expressed via the **duality** association shown in Figure 10-1. In other words, each economic event is mirrored by an associated economic event in the opposite direction. Figure 10-2 expands the basic REA model to illustrate the connection between these dual events: the **give event** and **receive event**. From the perspective of the organization function being modeled, the give half of the exchange decreases the economic resource, as represented by the outflow association. The receive half of the exchange increases the economic resources, represented by an inflow association. Figure 10-3 presents several examples of the give and receive events as they relate to the revenue, expenditure, and conversion cycles.

Note that an economic exchange does not require duality events to occur simultaneously. For example, inventory is reduced immediately by the sale to a customer, but cash may not be increased by the customer's remittance for several weeks. The REA model accommodates credit-based transactions and the associated time lags but does not employ traditional mechanisms such as AR or AP ledgers in accounting for these events. In fact, REA rejects the need for any accounting artifacts, including journals, ledgers, and double-entry bookkeeping. As mentioned previously, economic phenomena should be captured in a disaggregated form that is consistent with the needs of multiple users. Therefore, to reflect all relevant aspects of economic events, business data must not be preformatted or artificially constrained. Journals, ledgers, and double-entry bookkeeping are the traditional mechanisms for formatting and transmitting accounting data, but they are not essential elements of an accounting database. REA systems capture the essence of what accountants account for by modeling the underlying economic phenomena directly. Organizations employing REA can thus produce financial statements, journals, ledgers, and double-entry accounting reports directly from event database tables via user views. We demonstrate how this is done later in the chapter.

FIGURE 10-3 EXAMPLES OF GIVE AND RECEIVE EVENTS

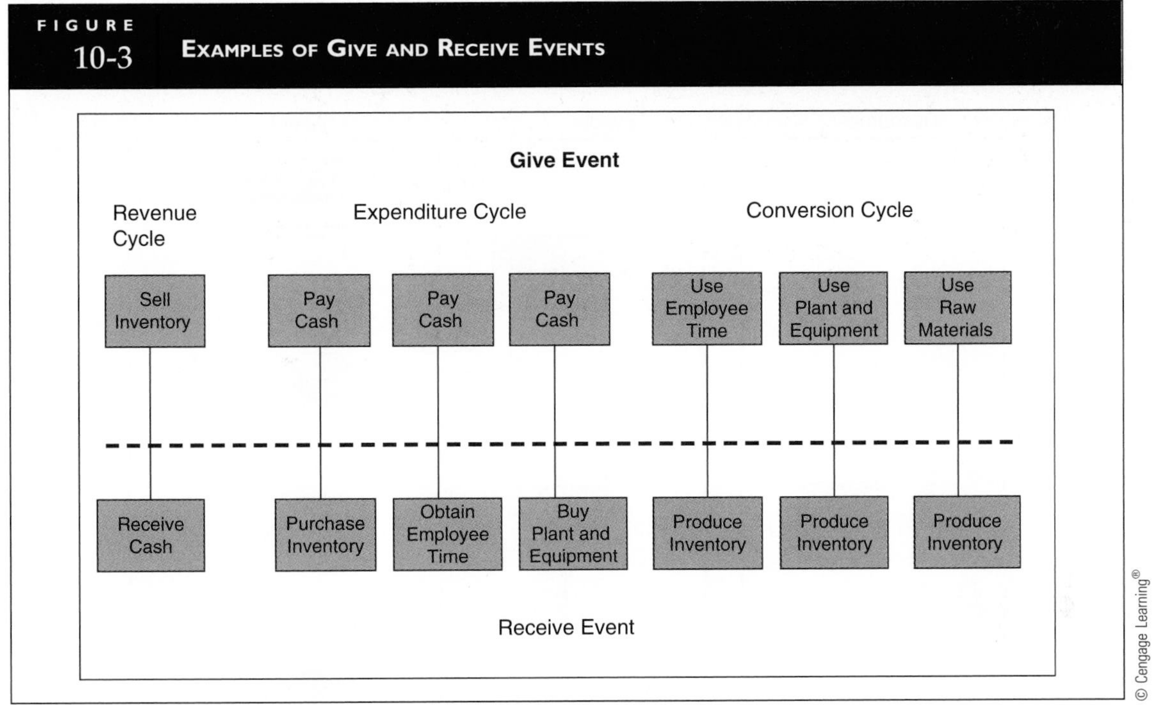

Developing an REA Model

In the previous chapter, we described the process of **view modeling**, in which the database designer identifies and models the set of data that individual users need to make a decision or to perform a task. The result of this process is an ER diagram depicting the user's data model. The REA approach uses semantic modeling to construct an REA diagram, which in some ways is similar to an ER diagram, but in other respects is quite different. Before we describe REA view modeling, we need to examine these differences.

DIFFERENCES BETWEEN ER AND REA DIAGRAMS

ER and REA diagrams differ visually in a significant way. Entities in ER diagrams are of one class, and their proximity to other entities is determined by their cardinality and by what is visually pleasing to keep the diagrams readable. Entities in an REA diagram, however, are divided into three classes (resources, events, and agents) and organized into constellations by class on the diagram. This arrangement is illustrated in Figure 10-4. Note that during view integration (discussed later) when several individual REA diagrams are merged to form a single global model, the constellations of entities may necessarily be altered. As a design tool during the view modeling phase, however, the constellation convention is typically followed.

A second difference between ER and REA diagrams involves the sequencing of events. ER diagrams present a static picture of the underlying business phenomena. Relationships between data are shown through cardinality and associations, but the sequence of activities that determine the cardinality and associations is not clearly represented. REA diagrams, however, are typically organized from top to bottom within the constellations to focus on the sequence of events. An advantage of this is that during systems development, management and nontechnical users better understand REA diagrams.

The third difference between ER and REA diagrams pertains to naming conventions for entities. In ER diagrams, entity names are always represented in the singular noun form. REA modeling applies this rule when assigning names to resource and agent entities. Event entities, however, are given verb (action) names such as Sell Inventory, Take Order, or Receive Cash. The reader

FIGURE 10-4 ARRANGEMENT OF ENTITIES IN AN REA DIAGRAM

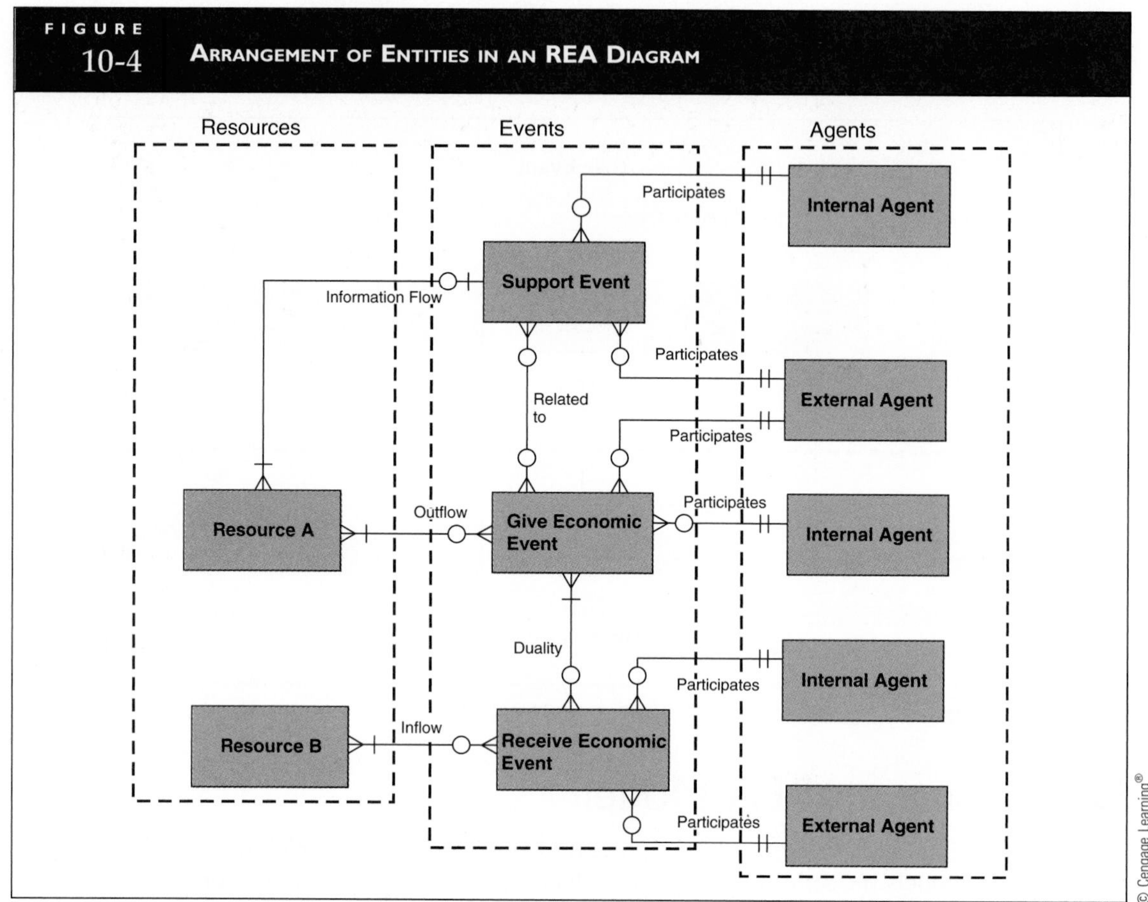

should, therefore, be careful to not confuse an event entity with a process. While event entities on an REA diagram represent and describe database tables that will store data about processes, they will not represent or describe the processes themselves.

VIEW MODELING: CREATING AN INDIVIDUAL REA DIAGRAM

This section describes the view modeling process as applied to creating an REA diagram. The process involves the following steps:

1. Identify the event entities.
2. Identify the resource entities.
3. Identify the agent entities.
4. Determine associations and cardinalities between entities.

These procedures are performed for each organizational function being modeled. The result is several individual REA diagrams. The modeling process is completed during the view integrating phase (described later), in which the individual models are consolidated into a single global model. To illustrate REA view modeling, we will use a simplified description of a revenue cycle process. The following are its key features:

Apex Supply Company is a downtown Philadelphia wholesaler of electrical products that sells to electrical retailers. It carries an inventory of approximately 10,000 items. Customers place orders by phone and buy on credit through a line-of-credit arrangement with Apex. A typical transaction involves the customer first contacting the customer services department to verify availability and to check the price of the item or items being sought. If the customer decides to buy, he or she is transferred to a sales agent, who takes the order. The shipping clerk sends the products to the customer by a common carrier. The billing clerk records the sale in the sales journal, prepares an invoice, and sends it to the customer, who is given 30 days to make payment. The AR clerk also receives a copy of the invoice and records it in the AR ledger. Subsequently (within 30 days), the customer sends a check and the remittance advice to Apex. The cash receipts clerk receives the check, records it in the cash receipts journal, and updates the cash account. The remittance advice goes to the AR clerk, who updates (reduces) the customer's account receivable.

Step I. Identify the Event Entities

The first step in developing an REA model is to identify the event entities in the function being modeled. The events in this revenue cycle example can be identified as the value-added actions that Apex employees take. These entities include Verify Availability, Take Order, Ship Product, and Receive Cash. An REA model must, at a minimum, include the two economic events that constitute the give and receive activities that reduce and increase economic resources in the exchange. In addition, it may include support events, which do not change resources directly. We will next examine each identified event to determine whether it should be classified as an economic event or a support event.

VERIFY AVAILABILITY. The Verify Availability event is a support event because it does not directly increase or decrease a resource. The decision to add this entity to the model will depend on management's need for information regarding customer inquiries. Such information could help the company determine which inventory items customers most frequently demand. This may be different from what Apex is actually selling to customers. For example, an analysis of inquiries that do not lead to placed orders may indicate that customers are shopping around for, and getting, better deals from Apex competitors. We will assume, therefore, that Verify Availability is a value-added activity that should be modeled in the REA diagram.

TAKE ORDER. Depending on the circumstances, Take Order could be either an economic or a support event. Taking an order typically involves only a commitment on the part of the seller to sell goods to the customer. It may even involve adjusting (decreasing) the inventory available for sale to prevent it from being sold or promised to other customers. This commitment, however, does not cause a real decrease in inventory and is not an economic exchange. Furthermore, if the client subsequently cancels the order before it is shipped, no economic exchange will occur. On the other hand, if taking an order causes the buyer to expend resources to obtain or manufacture the product on behalf of the customer, then an economic event will have occurred. For the purposes of this example, we will assume that no economic consequences derive directly from the Take Order event and it is, therefore, a support event.

SHIP PRODUCT. Ship Product is an economic event. This is the give half of an economic exchange and reduces the inventory resource directly.

RECEIVE CASH. Similarly, the Receive Cash event is an economic event. This is the receive half of the exchange that increases the cash resource.

INVALID ENTITY TYPES. REA modeling focuses on **value chain** events. These are the activities that use cash to obtain resources, including equipment, materials, and labor, and then employ those resources to earn new revenues. Bookkeeping tasks, such as recording a sale in the journal and setting up an account receivable, are not value chain activities. These are invalid entity types and should not be included in an REA diagram.

A fundamental precept of REA is the rejection of accounting artifacts, including journals, ledgers, and double-entry bookkeeping. Capturing transaction data in sufficient detail adequately serves traditional accounting requirements. For example, an account receivable is the difference between a sale to a customer and cash received in payment of the sale. Therefore, analyzing data pertaining to the Ship Product (sales) and Receive Cash events can satisfy the information needs related to the accounts receivable and billing functions described in the Apex case previously presented.

FIGURE 10-5 ARRANGEMENT OF EVENTS ENTITIES IN ORDER OF OCCURRENCE

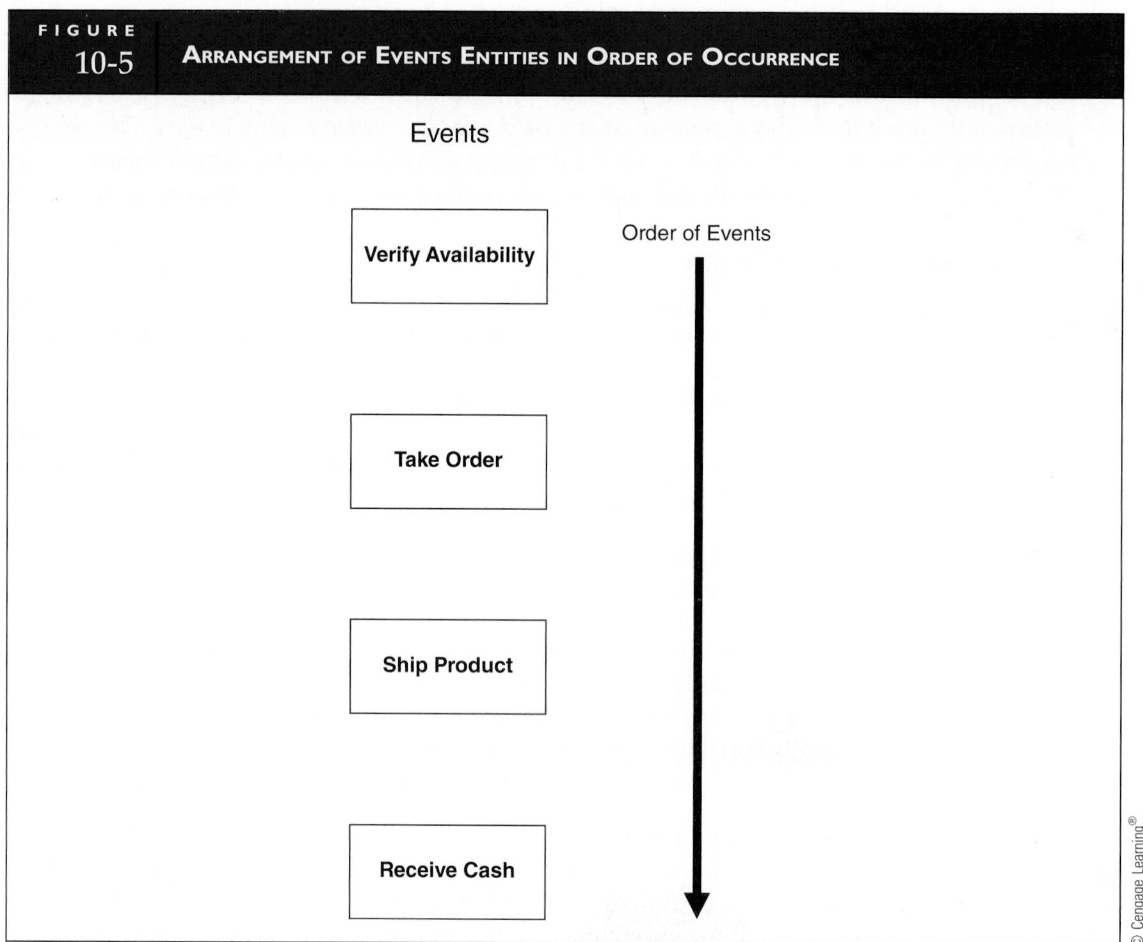

After the valid event entities are identified and classified as either economic or support events, they are placed on the REA diagram. REA convention is to arrange these entities in their sequence of occurrence from top to bottom on the diagram. Figure 10-5 presents the four events previously described in sequence of occurrence.

Step 2. Identify the Resource Entities

The next step in creating the REA diagram is identifying the resources that are impacted by the events selected to be modeled. Each economic event in an REA model must be linked to at least one resource entity whose economic value will be either reduced or increased by the event. Support events are also related to resources but do not effect a change in the resource value.

One could make the theoretical argument that all employee actions, including support events such as Verify Availability or Take Order, consume a resource called Employee Service. In fact, this resource is increased as employees render their services to the organization and is simultaneously decreased as those services are employed in the performance of a task. In situations in which employee services are tracked to specific projects or products, this entity would provide meaningful data and should be included in the REA model. Because we can presume that this is not the case for Apex Supply, Employee Services will not be modeled.

In the Apex revenue cycle, economic events change only two resources. The Ship Product event reduces the inventory resource and the Receive Cash event increases the cash resource. The Verify Availability and the Take Order support events are also associated with inventory, but they do not change it. The resource and associated event entities are presented in Figure 10-6.

FIGURE 10-6 REA MODEL SHOWING EVENTS AND RELATED RESOURCES AND AGENTS

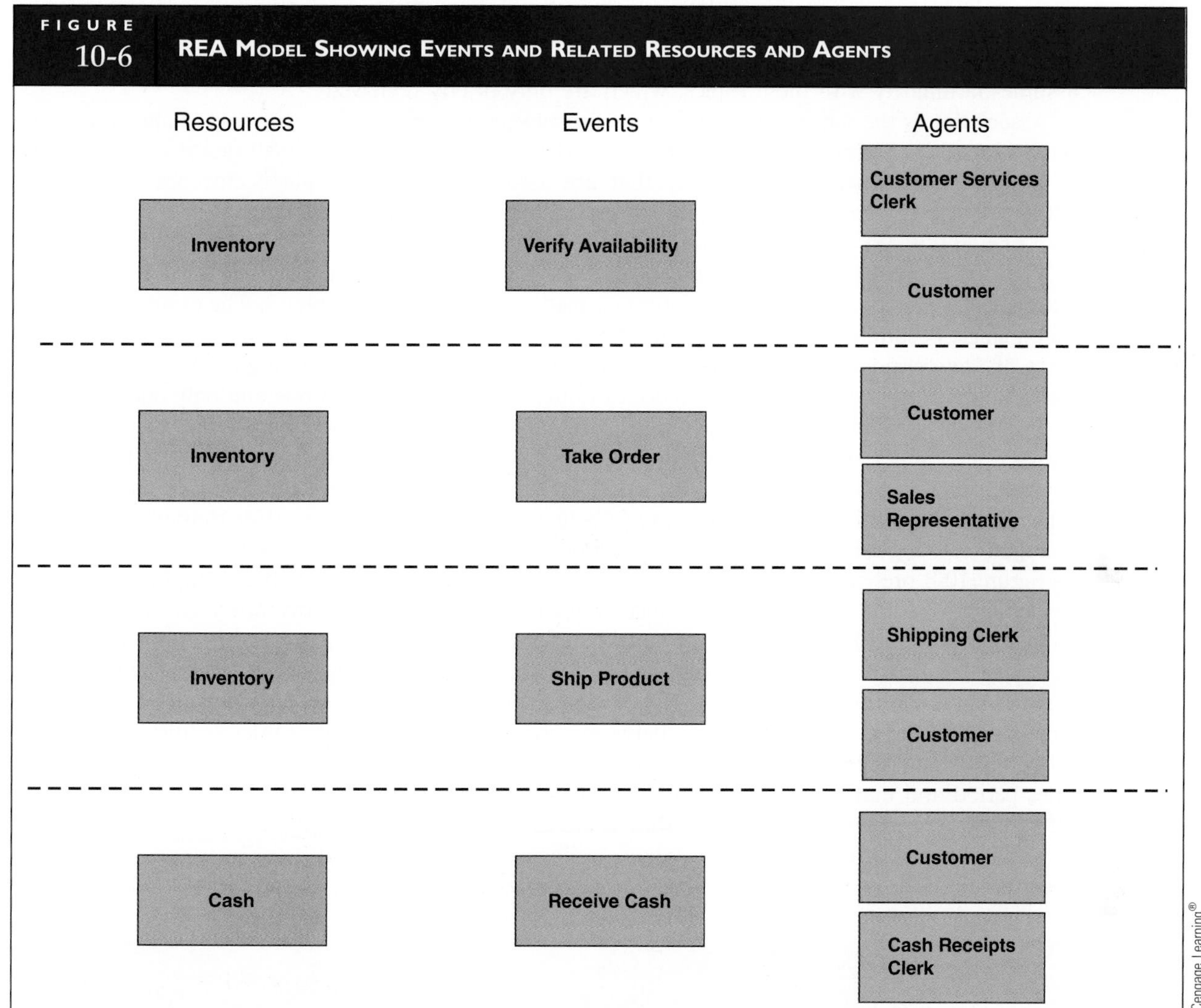

Step 3. Identify the Agent Entities

Each economic event entity in an REA diagram is associated with at least two agent entities. One of these is an internal agent and the other is an external agent. The external agent associated with all four events in the Apex case is Customer. In addition, four internal agents are associated with the four events:

1. The customer services clerk, who participates in the Verify Availability event.
2. The sales representative, who participates in the Take Order event.
3. The shipping clerk, who participates in the Ship Product event.
4. The cash receipts clerk, who participates in the Receive Cash event.

Note that each of these internal agents is in fact an instance of the Employee entity type. For illustration purposes on the REA diagram, we identify each instance of Employee (e.g., Sales Representative or Shipping Clerk) as a separate entity. The database that ultimately emerges from this model, however, will employ a single Employee table, and each instance shown in the model will be a row in that table. Figure 10-6 illustrates the relationship between the events and associated external and internal agents in the Apex case.

Step 4. Determine Associations and Cardinalities between Entities

We discussed in detail in Chapter 9 the topics of entity association and cardinality. This section assumes familiarity with these topics, which are only briefly reviewed.

Association is the nature of the relationship between two entities, as the labeled line connecting them represents. **Cardinality** (the degree of association between the entities) describes the number of possible occurrences in one entity that are associated with a single occurrence in a related entity. Four basic forms of cardinality are possible: zero or one (0, 1), one and only one (1,1), zero or many (0,M), and one or many (1,M).

Figure 10-7 presents three alternative methods for presenting cardinalities in an REA diagram. Alternative 1 presents the crow's foot notation method discussed in Chapter 9. The example illustrates that a single occurrence (record) in Entity A is associated with zero or many occurrences in Entity B. Thus, the lowest possible cardinality is zero, and the highest is many. Looking in the other direction, the notation states that a single occurrence in Entity B is associated with one and only one occurrence in Entity A. Sometimes, lower and upper cardinality are explicitly written on the association line between the entities, as shown in Alternative 2 in the figure. A shorthand version of this is presented as Alternative 3, which shows only the upper cardinality and presumes the lower cardinality to be zero. The upper cardinalities for each entity define the overall association. For example, the entities in Figure 10-7 are said to have a 1:M association. Other possible associations are 1:1 and M:M.

Figure 10-8 presents a revised data model for Apex. Notice that it has been simplified for better readability by eliminating redundant instances of the Customer and Inventory entities that were depicted in Figure 10-6. In addition, Figure 10-8 shows the association and cardinality between entities using the crow's foot notation method. Cardinality reflects the business rules that are in play for a particular organization. Sometimes the rules are obvious and are the same for all organizations. For example, the normal cardinality between the Customer and Take Order entities are 1,1 and 0,M. This signifies that a particular customer may have placed zero or many orders during the sales period and that each order is for only one customer. The association between these entities is 1:M and would never be 1:1 because this would mean that the organization restricts each customer to an upper limit of only one order, which is illogical. The association between internal agents and event entities follows this same pattern. An organization would expect its employees to participate in

FIGURE 10-7 ALTERNATIVE TECHNIQUES FOR REPRESENTING CARDINALITY

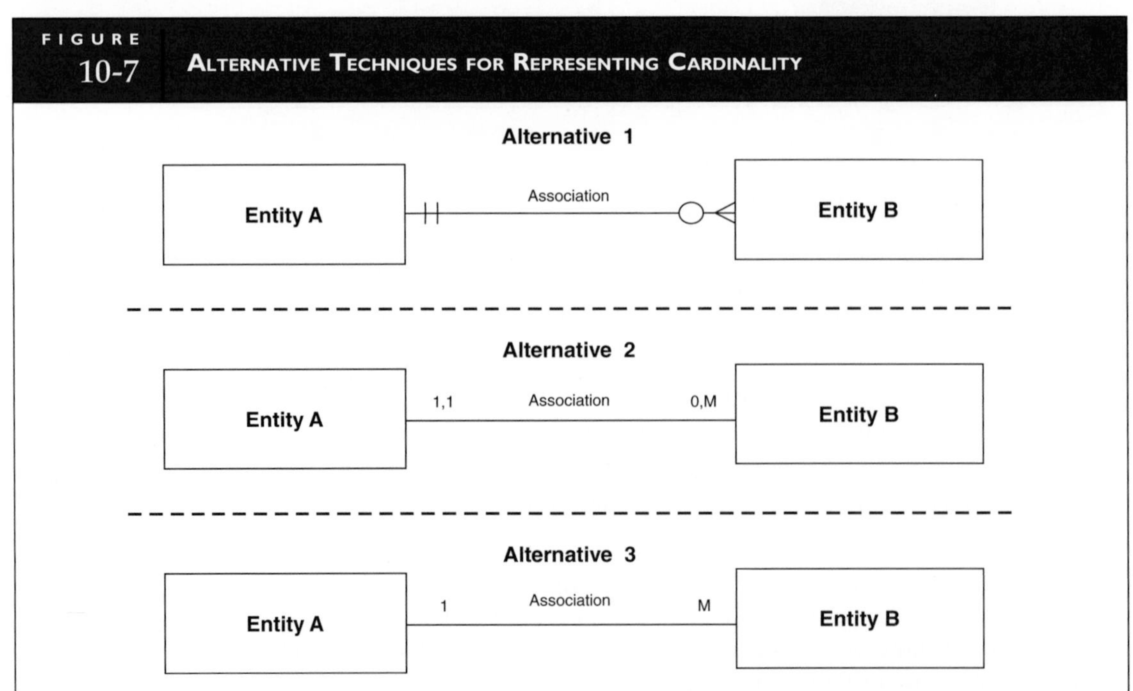

FIGURE 10-8 ASSOCIATIONS AND CARDINALITY IN AN REA DIAGRAM

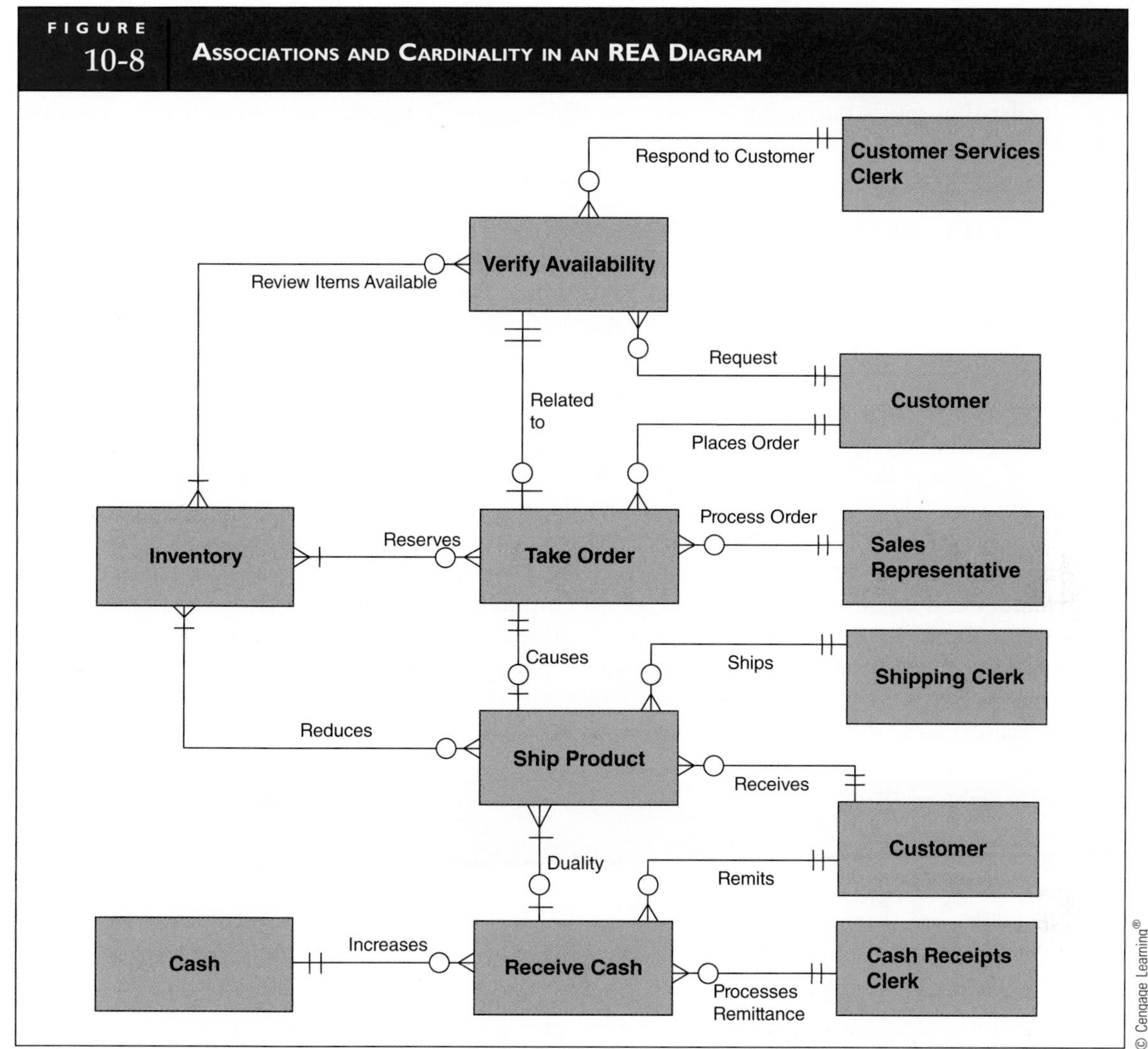

many events over time, not just one. Most of the cardinalities in Figure 10-8 reflect rules that are self-explanatory. A few points that need further explanation are presented next.

CARDINALITY BETWEEN THE VERIFY AVAILABILITY AND TAKE ORDER ENTITIES. Each occurrence of the Verify Availability entity is the result of a customer inquiry. We know from the case description, however, that not all inquiries result in a customer order. On the other hand, we will make the simplifying assumption that each Take Order occurrence is the result of an inquiry. Therefore, the cardinality on the Take Order side of the relation is 0,1 and on the Verify Availability side it is 1,1.

CARDINALITY BETWEEN THE TAKE ORDER AND SHIP PRODUCT ENTITIES. The 0,1 cardinality on the Ship Product side of the relation reflects the timing difference between orders taken and shipped. Because sales are not processed instantly, we can assume that an order will exist (occurrence of Take Order) that has not yet been shipped (no occurrence of Ship Product). Furthermore, an order that is canceled before being shipped would also result in no Ship Product record being created.

CARDINALITY BETWEEN THE SHIP PRODUCT AND RECEIVE CASH ENTITIES. Business terms of trade and payment policies vary greatly. Companies that make credit sales to consumers often accept partial payments over time. This would result in many cash receipts occurrences for a single shipment occurrence. On the other hand, companies whose customers are other businesses typically expect payment in full when due. Business customers, however, may consolidate several invoices on a single cash payment to reduce check writing. Because the Apex Company is a wholesaler that serves business customers, we will assume that debts are paid in full (no multiple partial payments) and that Apex customers may pay for multiple shipments with a single cash receipt. The cardinality in Figure 10-8 reflects this business rule.

CARDINALITY BETWEEN THE CASH AND RECEIVE CASH ENTITIES. The cash resource of an organization is composed of several different accounts, such as the general operating account, payroll imprest account, petty cash, and so on. These are consolidated for financial reporting into a single account but are used and tracked separately. The cardinality depicted in this relationship implies that cash is received from many customers and is deposited into one account.

MANY-TO-MANY ASSOCIATIONS. The model in Figure 10-8 depicts three examples of M:M associations. The first of these is between the Verify Availability and Inventory entities. A 1,M cardinality exists at the Inventory end of the association, and a 0,M cardinality lies at the Verify Availability end. This suggests that a particular customer query could involve one or many items of inventory, and each item may have been queried zero or many times in the period. The second M:M association exists between the Take Order and Inventory entities. A 1,M cardinality exists at the Inventory end of the association, and a 0,M cardinality is at the Take Order end. This means that a particular order may contain one or many different items of inventory and that a particular item may have never been ordered (perhaps a new product) or may have been ordered many times during the period. A similar situation exists between the Ship Goods and Inventory entities. In each of these cases, the upper cardinalities of M create an M:M association, which we know

FIGURE 10-9 Link Tables in an REA Diagram

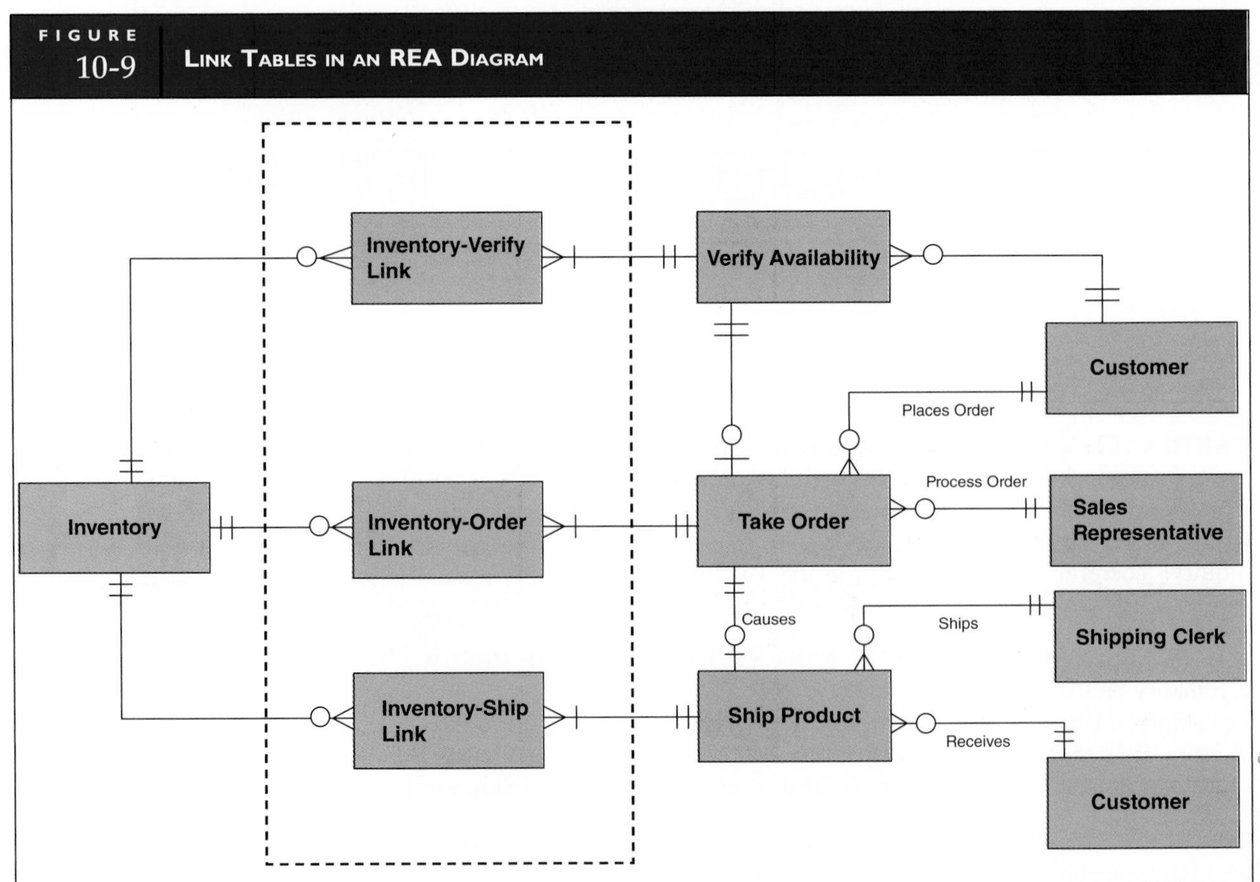

from Chapter 9 must be reconciled. These situations are the result of repeating group data that need to be normalized before implementing the model in a relational database.[2] The solution is to create three link tables that contain the primary keys of the associated tables. The link tables will also contain details pertaining to items queried, orders taken, and products shipped.

When modeling traditional ER diagrams, it is often convenient to include the link tables in the model (as in Chapter 9) so that it reflects closely the actual database. The inclusion of link tables in an REA diagram, however, creates a conflict with the rule that an event entity should be connected to at least one resource and at least two agent entities. Figure 10-9 shows how a portion of the Apex REA diagram would appear when link tables are inserted. Although link tables are a technical requirement for implementing an M:M association in a relational database, they are not a technical requirement for modeling the database. Including the link table in an REA diagram disrupts its visual integrity and adds little to one's understanding of the conceptual model. Ultimately, during implementation, the database designer will create the link tables. Indeed, the database cannot function without them. For REA diagramming purposes, however, the link tables need only be implied via the M:M associations.

View Integration: Creating an Enterprise-Wide REA Model

The view modeling process described in the previous section produced an individual REA model of the revenue cycle for Apex Supply. This section explains how multiple REA diagrams, each created in its own view modeling process, are integrated into a single global or enterprise model. The section then explains how the enterprise model is implemented into a relational database and user views are constructed. The **view integration** process involves three basic steps:

1. Consolidate the individual models.
2. Define primary keys, foreign keys, and attributes.
3. Construct the physical database and produce user views.

STEP 1. CONSOLIDATE THE INDIVIDUAL MODELS

Because Apex is a wholesale supply company with no production facilities, model consolidation for the company will include the previously developed revenue cycle model (Figure 10-8) and the expenditure cycle models for purchases/cash disbursements and payroll illustrated in Figures 10-10 and 10-11, respectively.

A brief explanation of the resources, events, agents, and cardinalities for two expenditure cycle models is provided next.

Purchases and Cash Disbursements Procedures

Figure 10-10 shows three event entities in Apex's purchases and cash disbursements system. The first of these, the Order Product entity, is a support event that does not directly increase the Inventory (resource) entity. Upon recognizing the need for inventory, which sales to customers (revenue cycle) depleted, the purchasing clerk (internal agent) selects a supplier (external agent) and places the order. This act does not constitute an economic event but is a commitment to buy. The link from the event entity to the Inventory entity indicates that the records will be adjusted to show that the items in question are on order. The quantity on hand, however, will not be increased at this time. The on-order information will prevent items from being accidentally reordered, and will assist customer service clerks in advising customers the status of inventory and expected due dates for out-of-stock items. The 1:M association between Supplier and Order Product indicates that each order goes to only one supplier and that a particular supplier may have received zero or many orders during the period.

2 See Chapter 9 and its appendix for a complete discussion about normalizing repeating group data.

FIGURE 10-10 REA DIAGRAM OF PURCHASES AND CASH DISBURSEMENTS PROCEDURES

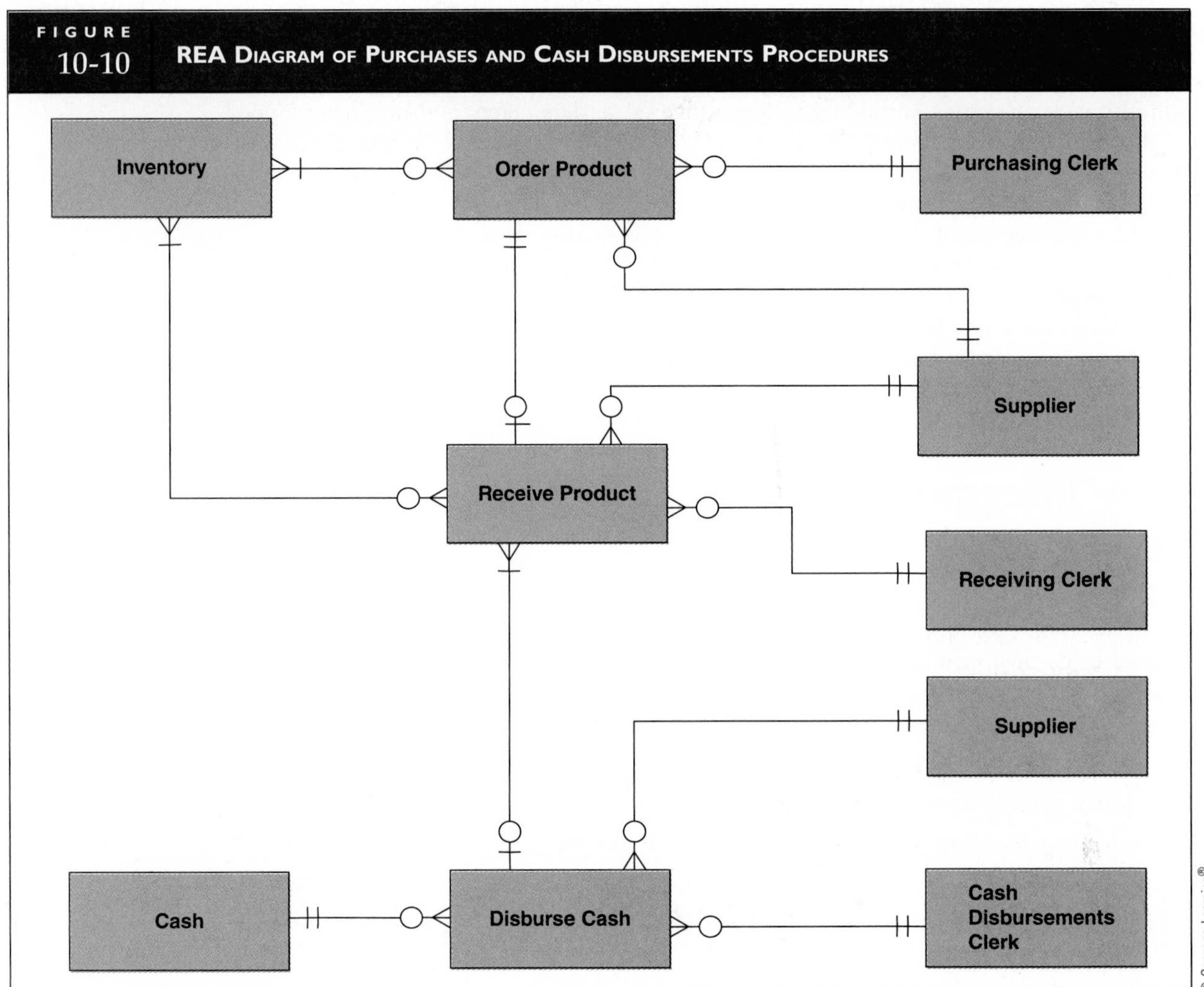

The second event entity is Receive Product, which is an economic event that causes a change in an economic resource. This is the receive half of the exchange, and it increases inventory. Goods are received from the supplier, and the receiving clerk processes them. This involves counting, inspecting, transporting the products into the warehouse, transferring title to Apex, and updating the inventory records. The 0,1 cardinality in the association between the Order Product and Receive Product entities implies that at any point in time, an order may exist (occurrence of Order Product) that has not yet been received (no occurrence of Receive Product).

The third event represented in the diagram is Disburse Cash. This is the economic event that constitutes the give half of an economic exchange. In this case, it causes the Cash resource to be decreased. The 1:M association with the Supplier entity implies that each disbursement is made to only one supplier, but each supplier may receive zero or many disbursements during the period. The 1:M association between Disburse Cash and Receive Product implies that each product receipt is paid in full (no multiple partial payments), but many receipts may be combined and paid with a single disbursement to reduce check writing.

Notice that M:M associations exist between the Order Product and Inventory entities, and between the Receive Product and Inventory entities. These illustrate that orders placed with suppliers and received from them may contain one or many items. From the opposite side, these associations signify that each item of inventory may have been ordered and received zero or many times in the period. As previously discussed, each M:M association needs to be resolved by adding

FIGURE 10-11 REA DIAGRAM OF PAYROLL PROCEDURES

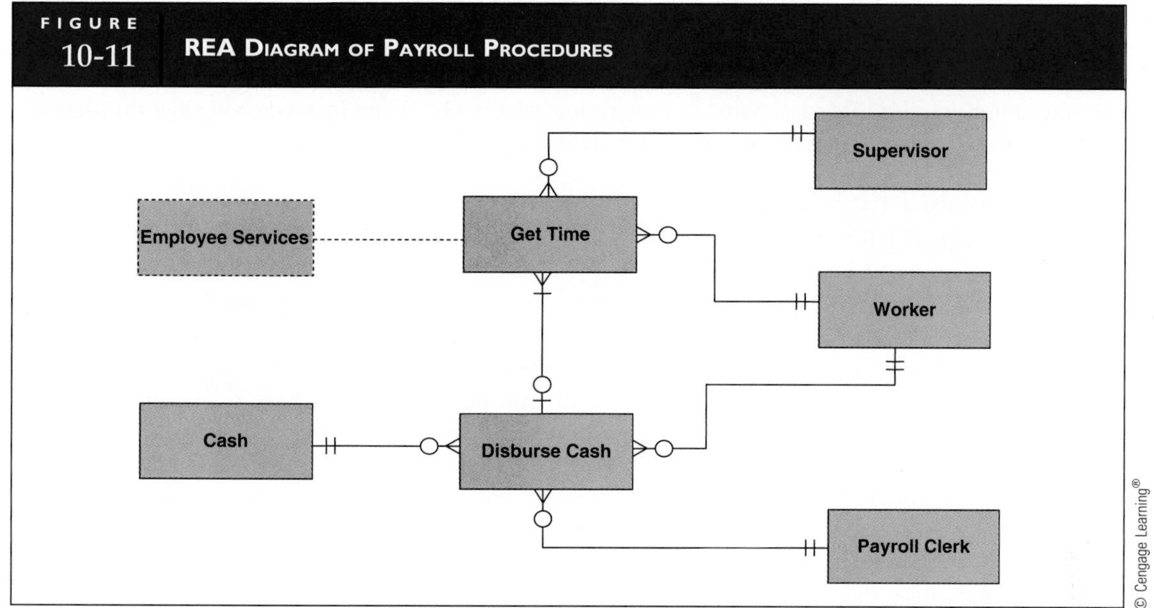

a linking entity. Tables for the linking entities will ultimately be created in the database, but the entities will not be included in the REA diagram. Keep in mind also that the internal agents are represented in the REA diagram as separate entities. This is done to illustrate more clearly their respective roles. In reality, these agents are instances of the Employee entity and will be collapsed into a single Employee table in the final database.

Payroll Procedures

The REA diagram in Figure 10-11 describes the data model for Apex Supply's payroll procedures. The model consists of only two economic events: Get Time and Disburse Cash. The Get Time event is the receive half of the economic exchange. This involves a worker (internal agent) giving up his or her time, which is represented by the Employee Services resource. The supervisor (external agent) assumes control of the resource. Unlike the tangible economic resources of cash and inventory, time does not have a stock flow element and cannot be stored. The Get Time event increases time, and various task performance events simultaneously decrease time. Earlier in the chapter, the Employee Services resource was discussed as a possible resource to be modeled in the Apex Supply database. In situations in which employee services are directly tracked to products produced or services rendered to clients (that is, consulting, legal services, or public accounting), it makes sense to model this resource. Because Apex does not track employee time to such activities as individual customers served or orders taken, transforming this entity into a physical database table serves no purpose. To maintain consistency with the REA modeling convention that each event must be linked to a resource, however, Employee Services is included in Figure 10-11 as a shadow resource (dotted lines) only. It will not be modeled in the final enterprise-wide REA diagram.

The Get Time event captures the daily time-giving instances of employees through a timekeeping mechanism, such as an electronic time clock. For salaried employees, the time-capturing process may simply involve the passage of time. The zero cardinality in the associations between the Get Time and the Worker and Supervisor entities reflects the possibility that some employees may not have contributed time during the period. This would include, for example, new employees or employees on sick leave.

The Disburse Cash event is the give half of the economic exchange. This involves distributing cash to an employee (now the external agent) for services rendered. The payroll clerk (internal agent) participates in this event, which reduces the cash resource. The association between the Disburse Cash and Get Time events reflects the timing differences between employees giving up their time and receiving payment for it, because they are usually not paid daily. Typically, employees work for a week, two weeks, or even a month before getting paid. Therefore, the 1,M cardinality on the Get Time side of the association implies that at least one and possibly many instances of Get Time will exist for each instance of Disburse Cash. The 0,1 cardinality on the Disburse Cash side of the association implies that at a point in time (midweek), a Get Time instance will exist that has not yet been paid. Each Get Time instance, however, is paid only once.

Merge Individual REA Diagrams

With the individual REA diagrams created and explained, we are now ready to consolidate them into a single enterprise-wide diagram (see Figure 10-12). By flipping the expenditure cycle diagrams to create a mirror image effect, the common resources of Inventory and Cash are centered in the diagram. These are flanked by two constellations of events, which increase and decrease them. The agents form periphery constellations in the diagram.

To simplify the diagram, redundant event, agent, and resource entities have been collapsed into a single entity where possible. For example, the Disburse Cash event, which is an element of both the Payroll and Purchase/Cash Disbursements procedures for Apex Supply, is represented only once in the consolidated model. Also, the Cash and Inventory entities are present only once on the consolidated diagram. To maintain perspective as to the roles played by internal agents, they are depicted as individual entities rather than collectively as Employee. Finally, to avoid crossing association lines between entities, the Supplier and Customer agents appear more than once in the diagram.

STEP 2. DEFINE PRIMARY KEYS, FOREIGN KEYS, AND ATTRIBUTES

With the data model constructed, we are now ready to design the relational database tables. This involves determining primary keys, assigning foreign keys, and defining the attributes of the tables. A separate table will be constructed for each valid entity in the REA integrated diagram in Figure 10-12. This will require 18 tables, which are explained in the following paragraphs:

- The ten internal agents represented in Figure 10-12 will be collapsed into a single Employee table.
- The two external agents (Customer and Supplier) will each require a separate table.
- The two resources Inventory and Cash will each require a table.
- The eight events will require a table each.
- The five M:M relations represented in the diagram will each require a linking table.

RULES FOR PRIMARY KEYS AND ATTRIBUTES. Table 10-1 presents the 18 tables in Apex's database, along with their primary keys, foreign keys, and attributes. The determination of primary keys and attributes comes from an understanding of each table's purpose, which results from a detailed analysis of user needs. The database designer should select a primary key that logically and uniquely defines the nonkey attributes in the table. In some cases, this is accomplished with a simple sequential code, such as an Invoice Number, Check Number, or Purchase Order number. In other situations, block codes, group codes, alphabetic codes, and mnemonic codes are better choices. We discussed the advantages and disadvantages of various coding techniques in detail in Chapter 2.

Some table attributes are common to all organizations and can be derived from common sense and adherence to best practices. Other attributes are unique to specific applications and can be derived only from thorough and detailed analyses of individual user views. Each attribute assigned to a table should, however, appear directly or indirectly (a calculated value) in one or more user views. If data stored in a table are not used in a document, report, or calculation that is reported in some way, then they serve no purpose and should not be part of the database.

RULES FOR FOREIGN KEYS. The degree of association between tables (i.e., 1:1, 1:M, or M:M) determines how foreign keys are assigned. We discussed the key-assignment rules for linking tables in Chapter 9, and they are briefly reviewed in this section.

KEYS IN 1:1 ASSOCIATIONS. In 1:1 associations, one side of the association will typically have a minimum cardinality of zero. When this is the case, the primary key of the table with the

FIGURE 10-12 INTEGRATED REA DIAGRAM

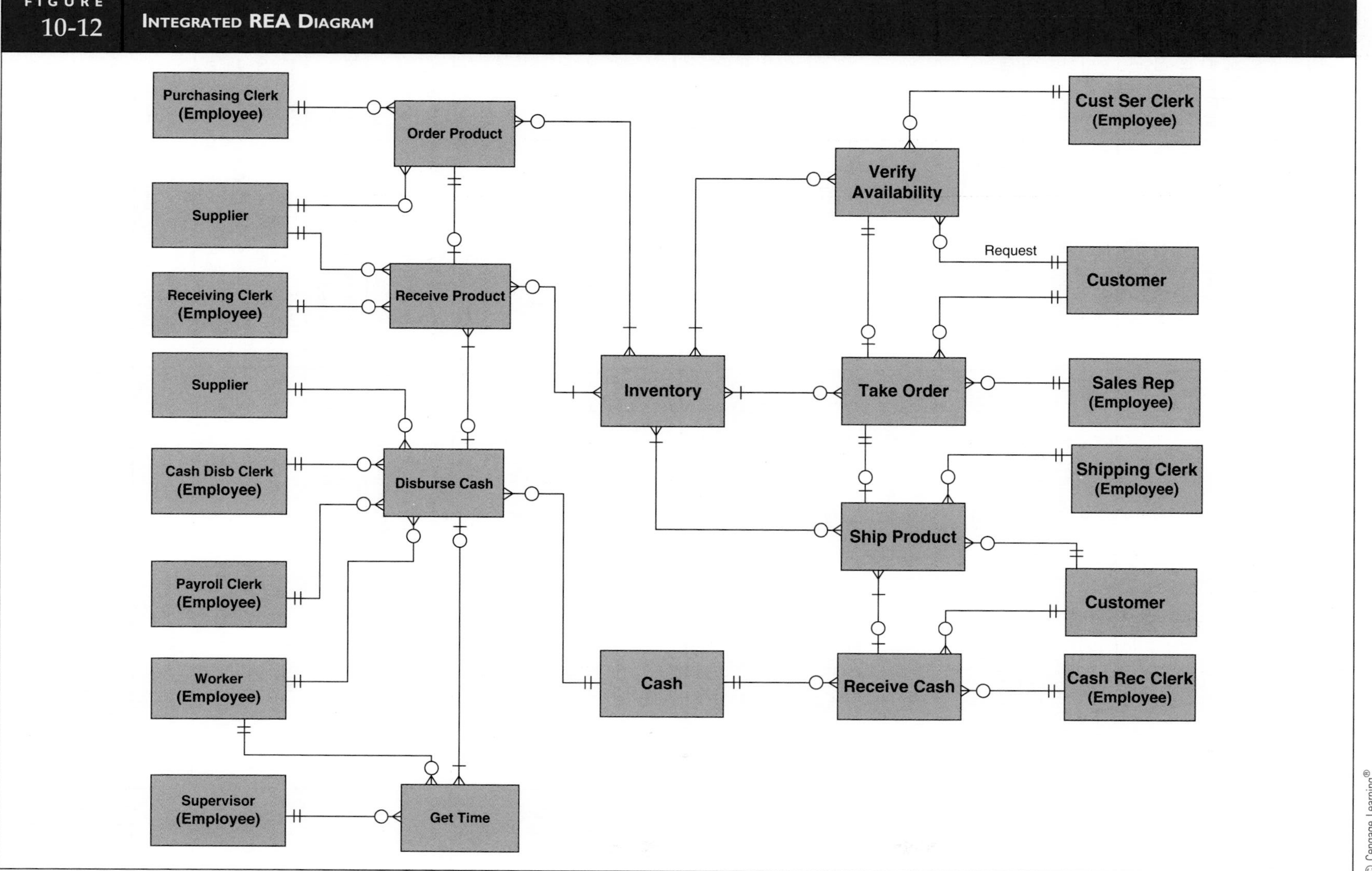

TABLE 10-1 **Tables, Keys, and Attributes in Apex Database**

Table Name	Primary Key	Foreign Key(s)	Attributes
Inventory	Item Number		Description, Warehouse Location, Quantity on Hand, Reorder Point, On-Order Quantity, Available for Sale, Supplier Number, Unit Cost, Retail Price, Turnover Rate, Lead Time, Usage Rate, Economic Order Quantity, Stock-Out History, Scrap History
Cash	Account Number		Balance
Verify Availability	Inquiry Number	Customer Number Employee Number	Date, Start Time, End Time
Take Order	Order Number	Inquiry Number Customer Number Employee Number	Order Date, Promised Date, Terms of Trade
Ship Product	Invoice Number	Order Number Customer Number Employee Number	Invoice Amount, Shipped Date, Due Date, Close Date
Receive Cash	Remittance Number	Customer Number Employee Number Account Number	Customer Check Number, Date, Amount
Order Product	Purchase Order Number	Supplier Number Employee Number	Order Date, Expected Delivery Date, Expected Total Price
Receive Product	Receiving Report Number	Supplier Number Employee Number Purchase Order Number Check Number	Date Received, Carrier, Total Amount Due, Due Date
Disburse Cash	Check Number	Supplier Number Cash Disb Clerk (EMPL) Worker (EMPL) Payroll Clerk (EMPL) Account Number	Amount, Date
Get Time	Time Card Number	Check Number Supervisor (EMPL) Worker (EMPL)	Pay Period, Day1 -in, Day1 -out, Day2-in, Day2-out, Day7-in, Day7-out
Customer	Customer Number		Name, Address, Line of Credit, Available Credit, Current Balance, Last Payment Date
Supplier	Supplier Number		Name, Address, Terms of Trade, Vendor Lead Time, Carrier Used, On-Time Delivery Record, Incomplete Shipments Record, Damaged Shipments Record, Price Disputes Record
Employee	Employee Number		SSN, Name, Address, Date of Birth, Job Title, Date Hired, Pay Rate, Vacation Time Accrued
Inventory-Verify Link	Item Number Inquiry Number		Quantity Requested, Quantity on Hand, Sale, Comments

TABLE 10-1 (CONTINUED)

Table Name	Primary Key	Foreign Key(s)	Attributes
Inventory-Order Link	Item Number Order Number		Quantity Ordered
Inventory-Ship Link	Item Number Invoice Number		Quantity Shipped, Actual Price
Ord-Prod-Inven Link	Item Number Purchase Order Number		Order Quantity
Rec-Prod-Inven Link	Item Number Receiving Report Number		Quantity Received, Actual Unit Cost, Condition

1,1 cardinality should be embedded as a foreign key in the table with the 0,1 cardinality. Reversing this rule will create a table structure in which the 1,1 cardinality table contains instances of foreign keys with a null (blank) value. Although such a link will work, it is a poor table design that can lead to inefficiencies and possible processing errors. By following the rule, however, all foreign key values in the table on the 0,1 cardinality side of the association will be non-null. For example, we can see from Table 10-1 that the primary key for the Verify Availability table (Inquiry Number) is assigned as a foreign key to the Take Order table.

KEYS IN 1:M ASSOCIATIONS. When a 1:M association exists between tables, the primary key of the 1 side is embedded in the table of the M side. For example, the primary key of the Employee table (EMPLOYEE NUMBER) has been assigned as a foreign key to the Verify Availability, Take Order, and Ship Product tables.

KEYS IN M:M ASSOCIATIONS. Tables in an M:M association cannot accept an embedded foreign key from the related table. Instead, the database designer must create a separate link table to contain the foreign keys. By inserting a link table between the original tables, the M:M association is transformed into two 1:M associations (see Figure 10-9). The link table can now accept the primary keys of the tables on the 1 side of the two new associations. This process results in a combined (composite) key that serves as a primary key for defining the attributes (if any) in the link table. Each component of the composite key also serves as a foreign key for locating related records in the associated tables. Five link tables are presented in Table 10-1: Inventory-Verify Link, Inventory-Order Link, Inventory-Ship Link, Ord-Prod-lnven Link, and Rec-Prod-lnven Link.

NORMALIZED TABLES. The assignment of primary keys and attributes to relational tables must always comply with the rules of normalization discussed in Chapter 9. Recall that improperly normalized tables exhibit negative operational symptoms called anomalies, including the update anomaly, the insertion anomaly, and the deletion anomaly. One or more of these anomalies will exist in tables that are not normalized to the **third normal form (3NF)** level. These anomalies are caused by structural problems within tables known as repeating groups, partial dependencies, and transitive dependencies. Normalization involves systematically identifying and removing these dependencies from the table(s) under review. Tables in 3NF will be free of anomalies and will meet two conditions:

1. All nonkey attributes will be wholly and uniquely dependent on (defined by) the primary key.
2. None of the nonkey attributes will be dependent on (defined by) other nonkey attributes.

The database tables in Table 10-1 are in 3NF, but contain only minimal attributes. Keep in mind that databases are not static. As user needs change and additional user views are developed, additional attributes, and perhaps additional tables, may need to be included in the database. These additions must comply with normalization rules to preserve the structural integrity of tables and avoid anomalies. For a complete discussion of anomalies, dependencies, and normalization techniques, please review the appropriate sections of Chapter 9 and its appendix.

STEP 3. CONSTRUCT THE PHYSICAL DATABASE AND PRODUCE USER VIEWS

At this point, the database designer is ready to create physical relational tables based on the descriptions in Table 10-1. After the tables have been constructed, some of them must be populated with data. Resource and agent tables must be initialized with data values, such as inventory quantities on hand, customer names and addresses, and employee data. The new system will start operations with beginning values for the attributes of these tables. In contrast, event tables start out empty and will be populated through actual transaction processing activities.

The resulting database should be rich enough to support the information needs of all users of the system being modeled. This includes the needs of accountants, operations personnel, and management. The reports, computer screens, and documents that constitute these views are derived from structured query language commands and computer programs that access the normalized tables in the database and navigate between them using the foreign keys as links. In this section, we present some examples of the reports that can be produced from event tables.

PRODUCING FINANCIAL STATEMENTS AND OTHER ACCOUNTING REPORTS. In a traditional system, financial statements are typically prepared from general ledger accounts, whose values are derived from journal voucher postings. Accounting artifacts, including journals, ledgers, and double-entry accounting, however, are not entities in an REA model. Instead, these traditional accounting mechanisms are reproduced from the event tables. To illustrate, Figure 10-13 presents the structures for several relational tables in the Apex database. These table structures correspond to the tables listed in Table 10-1, but some of the attributes have been omitted to simplify the figure. The figure demonstrates how financial statement accounting figures can be constructed from underlying event data. The calculations are as follows:

Total Sales = *The sum of the Invoice Amount attribute in the Ship Product table for all items shipped on or before the year-end closing date.*

Accounts Receivable = *Total Sales minus the sum of the Receive Cash table's Amount attribute for all remittances received on or before the year-end closing date.*

Cost of Goods Sold = *Sum of Quantity sold in the Inventory-Ship Link table multiplied by the Unit Cost attribute in the Inventory table.*

Inventory = *Quantity on Hand attribute multiplied by Unit Cost attribute in the Inventory table.*

Accounting figures extracted in this way from REA tables can be used to prepare income statements, balance sheets, and even journal entries, as illustrated with the journal voucher report in Figure 10-14.

PRODUCING MANAGEMENT REPORTS FROM REA TABLES. A key objective of REA is to create a database capable of supporting multiple user views. This section illustrates examples of nonaccounting user reports that Apex Supply could produce from its database. Figure 10-15 depicts an inventory status report that the company's purchasing agent would use. This report identifies items to be ordered and the respective suppliers. The data for this report come from the Inventory and Supplier tables in Table 10-1. Figure 10-16 is a sales activity report organized by customer and product, which the sales manager will use. The report is constructed from data in the Customer, Ship Product, Inventory-Ship Link, and Inventory tables. Figure 10-17 is a customer inquiry report. The purpose of this report is to track customer inquires against actual sales. The report indicates how much time is spent on each customer inquiry and whether it led

FIGURE 10-13 CALCULATING ACCOUNTING NUMBERS FROM REA TABLES

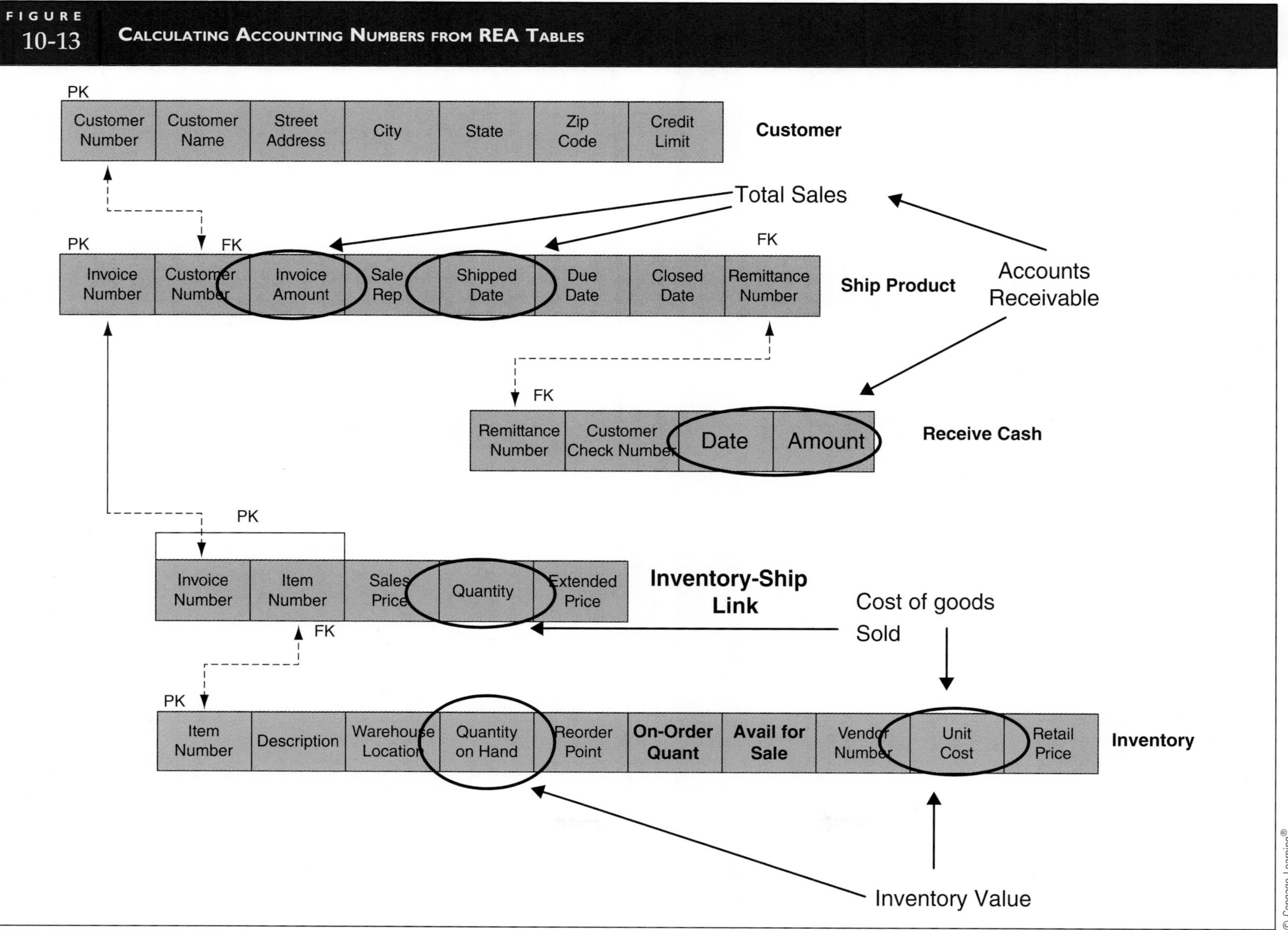

FIGURE 10-14 REPRODUCING JOURNAL ENTRIES FROM REA TABLES

Journal Voucher Report

JV Num	Date	Title	Acct Num	Debit	Credit
1	2/14/11	Cash Acct Rec Sales	101 103 401	1000 2000	 3000
2	2/14/11	Cost of Goods Sold Inventory	501 108	2500	 2500
⋮	⋮	⋮	⋮	⋮	⋮

FIGURE 10-15 INVENTORY STATUS REPORT

Item Number	Description	Quantity on Hand	Reorder Point	Supplier Number	Name	Address	Tele Num
At78	Bracket	100	150	22	Ozment Sup	123 Main St.	555–7895
Y24	3 Way Sw	95	150	24	Buell Co.	2 Broadhead	555–3436
TW23	120 V outlet	100	150	27	B&R Sup	Westgate Mall	555–7845
RT12	Toggle switch	440	450	22	Ozment Sup	123 Main St.	555–7895
Pp56	Gasket	400	450	24	Buell Co.	2 Broadhead	555–3436
qr2	Meter	442	450	28	Harris Manuf	24 Linden St.	555–3316
yu88	Brace	10	10	22	Ozment Sup	123 Main St.	555–7895

to a sale. The Customer, Verify Availability, Inventory-Verify Link, Inventory, and Take Order tables provide the data for the report.

REA AND VALUE CHAIN ANALYSIS

The competitive advantages to organizations that adopt the REA approach are most clearly seen from the perspective of the value chain. These are the activities that add value or usefulness to an organization's products and services. To remain competitive, organizations must differentiate between their various business activities, prioritizing them on the basis of their value in achieving organizational objectives. This means being adaptable and responsive to changes in the environment, including their relationships with suppliers, customers, and other external entities that influence performance. Modern decision makers need information systems that help them look beyond their internal operations to those of their trading partners.

One approach adopted for this purpose is known as **value chain analysis**. This analysis distinguishes between primary activities and support activities: primary activities create value; support

FIGURE 10-16 CONSTRUCTING A MANAGEMENT SALES REPORT FROM REA TABLES

Apex Sales Report

Customer Number : 19321
Customer Name : ABE Electric
Address : 520 Main St., City

Invoice #	Date	Invoice Total	Part Num	Quantity	Unit Price	Ext'd Price
12390	11/11/15	$850	Y24	5	$20	$100
			T W23	10	50	500
			Ey43	25	10	250
12912	11/11/15	$300	rw34	10	$30	$300

Customer Total: $1,150

* *

Customer Number : 19322
Customer Name : ARK Electronics
Address : 2289 Elm St., City

Invoice #	Date	Invoice Total	Part Num	Quantity	Unit Price	Ext'd Price
12421	11/13/15	$1,000	TW23	10	$20	$200
			Fr23	2	50	100
			LI45	7	100	700
12901	11/20/15	$500	TE67	10	$30	$300
			Ht12	10	20	200

Customer Total: $1,500

* *

Next Customer

•

•

Next Customer

activities assist in the achievement of the primary activities. By applying value chain analysis, an organization can look beyond itself and maximize its ability to create value, for example, by incorporating the needs of its customers in its products or accommodating the flexibility of its suppliers in scheduling its production.

Traditional information systems are not well suited to supporting value chain activities. Organizations that have applied value chain analysis have generally done so outside the traditional accounting information system by providing such information separately to the decision makers. Frequently, this involved the creation of separate information systems, which results in data redundancy, data concurrency, and system integration problems. As a single information system framework capable of capturing generic and fine-grained data, REA can overcome these problems and is capable of providing the following advantages.

1. The REA approach to modeling business processes helps managers focus on the key elements of economic events and identify the nonvalue-added activities that can be eliminated from

FIGURE 10-17 CUSTOMER INQUIRY REPORT

Customer Inquiry Report 2/14/15 – 7/14/15										
Inq Num	Date	Cust Num	Start Time	End Time	Product	Quantity Requested	Quantity on Hand	Sale	Emp Num	Comments
483	2/14	19334	9:22	9:30	TW23	5	61	yes	5	None
					TW67	18	4	no	7	Look elsewhere
					RB14	20	80	no	3	Too expensive
484	2/14	18325	9:38	9:42	HT12	8	22	yes	7	None
485	2/14	12325	10:03	10:20	NW34	1	6	no	7	Look elsewhere

operations. Improving the operational efficiency of individual departments thus generates excess capacity that can be redirected to increase the overall productivity of the firm.

2. The storage of both financial and nonfinancial data in a common database reduces the need for multiple data collection, storage, and maintenance procedures.
3. Storing financial and nonfinancial data about business events in detailed form permits a wider range of management decisions by supporting multiple user views.
4. The REA model provides managers with more relevant, timely, and accurate information. This will translate into better customer service, high-quality products, and flexible production processes.

REA COMPROMISES IN PRACTICE

The advantages to operational efficiency, systems integration, and value chain analysis have drawn great attention to REA as a theoretical model for system and database design. As a practical matter, however, larger organizations often compromise the REA model for financial statement reporting purposes. Although it is possible to extract traditional financial information from event data (as illustrated in Figure 10-13), doing so from millions of individual event records can be problematic. Instead, most companies implementing an REA model create an event database for operations, planning, and control purposes, and maintain a traditional general ledger system separately in the background for financial reporting. Enterprise resource planning systems, which are discussed in the next chapter, exemplify the successful integration of event-based plans and traditional database designs within a single system.

Summary

This chapter examined the REA model as a means of specifying and designing accounting information systems that serve the needs of all users in an organization. It began by defining the key elements of REA. The basic model employs a unique form of an ER diagram called an REA diagram, which consists of three entity types (resources, events, and agents) and a set of associations linking them. The rules for developing an REA diagram were then explained and illustrated in detail.

Each event in an REA diagram is linked to at least one resource and to at least two agents. An important aspect of the model is the concept of economic duality, which specifies that each economic event must be mirrored by an associated economic event in the opposite direction. These dual events constitute the give and receive activities in an economic exchange.

The chapter went on to illustrate the development of an REA database for a hypothetical firm following a multistep process called view modeling. The steps involved are: (1) identify the event to be modeled, (2) identify the resource changed by events, (3) identify the agents participating in events, and (4) determine associations and cardinalities between entities. The result of this process is an REA diagram for a single organizational function. This next section in the chapter explained how multiple REA diagrams (revenue cycle, purchases, cash disbursements, and payroll) are integrated into a global or an enterprise-wide model. The enterprise-wide model was then implemented into a relational database structure, and user views were constructed. The view integration process involved three steps: (1) consolidate the individual models; (2) define primary keys, foreign keys, and attributes; and (3) construct the physical database and produce the user views.

The chapter concluded with a discussion of how REA modeling can improve competitive advantage by allowing management to focus on the value-added activities of the company's operations. For financial statement reporting purposes, however, many companies compromise the pure REA model by maintaining a traditional general ledger system.

Key Terms

agents (443)
association (450)
cardinality (450)
duality (444)
economic events (443)
external agent (443)
give event (444)
internal agent (443)
REA diagram (442)
REA model (442)
receive event (444)
resources (443)
semantic models (442)
stock flow (443)
support events (443)
third normal form (3NF) (459)
user view (442)
value chain (447)
value chain analysis (462)
view integration (453)
view modeling (445)

Review Questions

1. What is a user view?
2. What is a semantic data model?
3. What is an REA diagram?
4. What are economic resources?
5. What are economic events?
6. What are support events?
7. What are economic agents?
8. Define *duality*.
9. What is view modeling?
10. What is represented by the labeled lines connecting entities in an REA diagram?
11. Why are journals and ledgers not modeled in an REA diagram?
12. Define *association*.
13. Define *cardinality*.
14. Name the four basic forms of cardinality.
15. What is view integration?
16. List the steps involved in view integration.
17. What is the rule for assigning foreign keys in a 1:1 association?
18. What is the rule for assigning foreign keys in a 1:M association?
19. What is the rule for assigning foreign keys in an M:M association?
20. Define *value chain*.

Discussion Questions

1. From the perspective of an organization, explain duality as it relates to the give and receive events of an economic exchange.
2. Explain the relationship between cardinality and association.
3. Discuss the rules for assigning primary keys to database tables.
4. Discuss the rules for linking events to resources and agents in an REA diagram.
5. How are external and internal agents modeled in REA diagrams for transactions that involve purely internal exchanges, such as raw material moving into production?
6. Explain how REA databases are able to support financial statement reporting when they do not employ journals and ledgers.
7. Distinguish between economic events and support events, and provide examples of each.
8. Describe the minimum number and types of events that an REA diagram must include.
9. Why are traditional accounting events, such as recording a transaction in a journal or posting to ledgers, not modeled in REA diagrams?
10. ER diagrams usually include the link tables in the model to resolve M:M associations, REA diagrams typically do not show link tables. Explain.
11. Employee time is a resource that is always used but is not always modeled in an REA diagram. Explain and give examples.
12. When are data in 3NF?

Multiple-Choice Questions

1. The concept of duality means that an REA diagram must consist of
   a. two events—one of them economic and the other, support.
   b. two agents—one of them internal and the other, external.
   c. two resources—one increased and the other decreased by the same event.
   d. all of the above.
   e. none of the above.
2. Each economic event in an REA diagram is always
   a. linked to at least two resource entities.
   b. linked to two external agents.
   c. linked to two internal agents.
   d. linked to another economic event.
   e. linked to a support event.
3. Which of the following are characteristics of economic agents?
   a. They participate in economic events but do not assume control of the resources.
   b. They participate in economic events but not in support events.
   c. Internal agents are employees of the company whose system is being modeled.
   d. External agents are not employees of the company whose system is being modeled.
   e. All of the above describe agents.
4. Which of the following is true?
   a. REA diagram entities are arranged in constellations by entity class.
   b. ER diagrams present a static picture of the underlying business phenomena.
   c. Entity names in ER diagrams are always in the noun form.
   d. Event entity names in REA diagrams are in the verb form.
   e. All of the above are true statements.
5. Which of the following events would be LEAST likely to be modeled in an REA diagram?
   a. customer inquiries
   b. sales to a customer
   c. accounts payable
   d. cash
   e. all of these events would be modeled

6. Which of the following associations would most likely describe the relationship between an internal agent and an economic event?
   a. I:M
   b. 1:1
   c. M:M
   d. 0:M
   e. none of the above
7. Which of the following tables would most likely have a composite key?
   a. Take Order
   b. Ship Goods
   c. Inventory-Ship Link
   d. Cash
   e. none of the above
8. Which of the following associations requires a separate table in the database?
   a. 1:1
   b. I:M
   c. M:M
   d. all of the above
9. When assigning foreign keys in a 1:1 association,
   a. the primary key of each table should be embedded as a foreign key in the related table.
   b. the primary key on the 0,1 side of the relation should be embedded as the foreign key on the 1,1 side.
   c. the primary key on the I,I side of the relation should be embedded as the foreign key on the 0,1 side.
   d. a link table must be created to accept the foreign keys of both tables.
   e. none of the above is true.
10. When assigning foreign keys in a I:M association,
   a. the primary key of each table should be embedded as a foreign key in the related table.
   b. the primary key on the 0,M side of the relation should be embedded as the foreign key on the 1,1 side.
   c. the primary key on the I,I side of the relation should be embedded as the foreign key on the 0,M side.
   d. a link table must be created to accept the foreign keys of both tables.
   e. none of the above is true.

Problems

1. REA DIAGRAMS

Describe the three differences between REA diagrams and ER diagrams.

2. REA ASSOCIATIONS

Bentley Restorations Company restores and sells top-end classic and antique automobiles. Most of its customers are private collectors, but some are investors who buy multiple cars and hold them for resale. Bentley extends no credit terms. All sales are for cash.

Required

Which of the relationships in the diagram for Problem 2 properly models the entity associations for Bentley Restorations? Explain your answer.

3. REA ASSOCIATIONS

Based on the data in Problem 2, which of the following relationships in the diagram for Problem 3 properly models the entity associations for Bentley Restorations? Explain your answer.

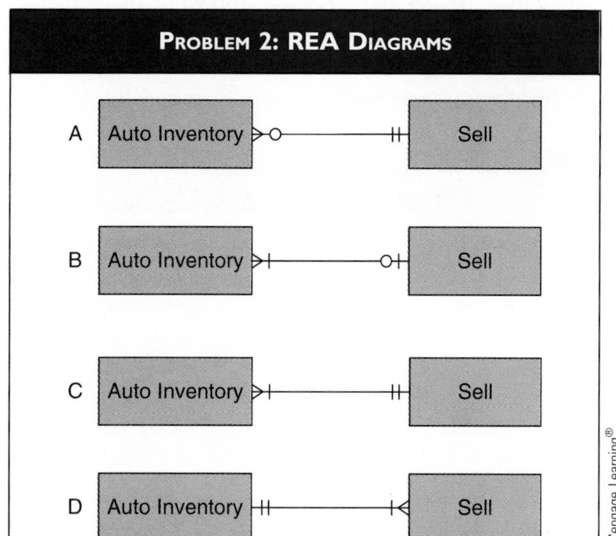

4. REA ASSOCIATIONS

Based on the data in Problem 2, which of the relationships in the diagram for Problem 4 properly

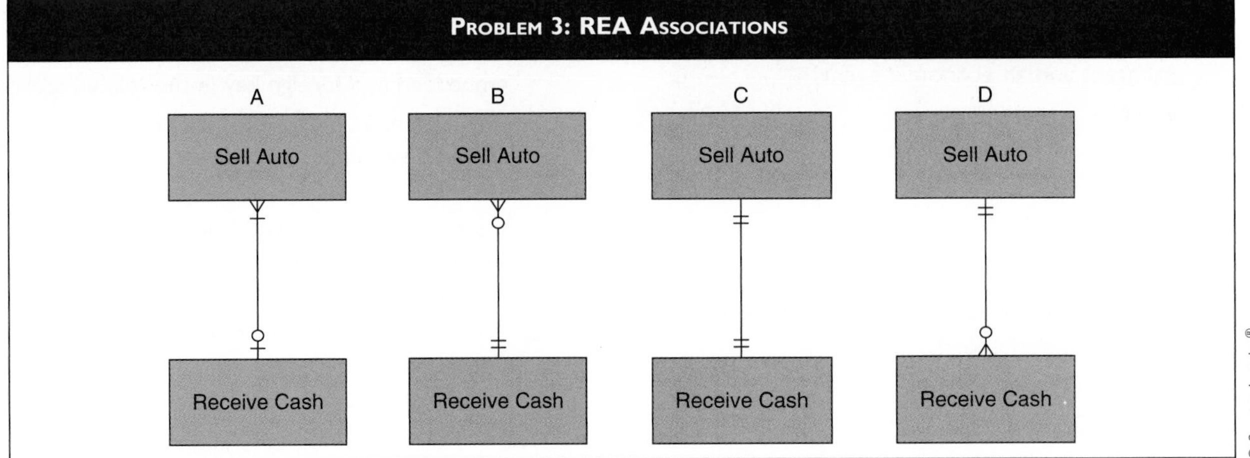

models the entity associations for this situation? Explain your answer.

5. REA MODEL EXTRACT

Prepare an REA model depicting the issuance of raw materials into the manufacturing process. Identify the resource, event, and agent entities. Show the cardinalities in the associations between entities.

6. REA MODEL—HORIZON BOOKS

Horizon Books is a bookstore in downtown Philadelphia. It carries an inventory of approximately 5,000 books. Customers come in and browse the shelves, select their books, and take them to the cashier. At the cashier's desk, they can also discover whether a particular book is in stock, place orders for books not currently available in the bookstore, and collect and pay for books previously ordered. There are no credit sales. All customers pay for their purchases at the time of purchase.

Required
Prepare an REA model for Horizon's database. Show all cardinalities in the associations.

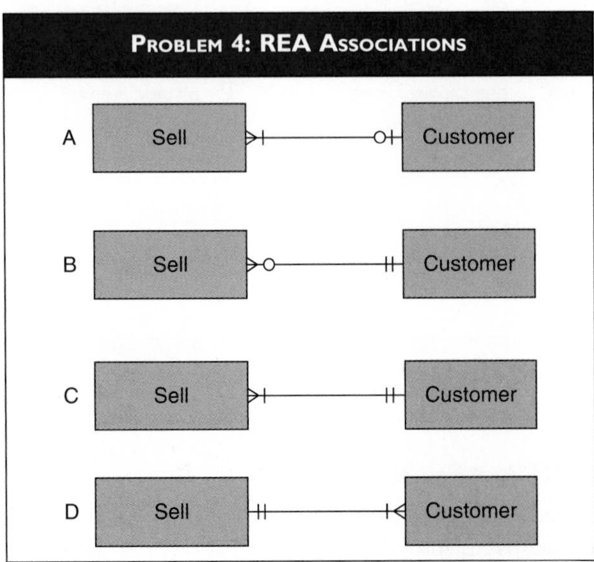

7. REA MODEL—FEINMAN COMPUTERS

Feinman Computers sells desktop computer systems that it manufactures from parts and software that third-party vendors provide. Customers are both private consumers and small businesses. Consumers pay cash or by credit card, but business customers buy on credit. A credit check is made of all new business customers before approving a line of credit. Sales are made online or by a hard-copy order document that customers mail or fax to the company.

When a credit order is received, the sales clerk verifies inventory availability, prepares a sales order, and sends the stock release copy to Willy, a warehouse employee who picks the goods and arranges shipment. Willy then prepares the bills of lading and shipping notices. Barb in the billing department receives the shipping notice from Willy and updates the inventory subsidiary ledger to account for the reduction in inventory. Barb files the stock release, prepares the invoice, and mails a copy of it to the customer. Barb then updates the sales journal and then sends the invoice, sales order, stock release, and shipping notice to the AR department.

Adam in the AR department files the documents that Barb sends him and updates the AR subsidiary ledger. Mickey in the mail room receives remittance advices and customer checks sent in payment of accounts. He sends the remittance advice to Adam for posting to the AR ledger and sends the checks to Carol, the cash receipts clerk. At the end of the day, Carol prepares a deposit slip and deposits the checks into the company's bank account, files the bank receipt, and updates the cash receipts journal.

Cash sales to consumer customers are handled in a manner similar to the process described here except that checks or credit card account numbers are submitted with the original order.

At the end of each week, John, an accounting clerk, reconciles all transactions and posts them to the general ledger.

Required

a. Prepare the REA model of the sales/collection process.
b. Show the cardinalities for all associations.
c. List the tables, keys, and attributes needed to implement this model in a relational database.

8. REA MODEL—K CANNON, INC.

K Cannon, Inc., is a manufacturer of portable MP3 players. The company purchases raw materials such as plastics and computer chips for its conversion cycle. The following describes K Cannon's purchases and payment procedures.

John, the purchasing department clerk, monitors raw material inventory levels and prepares a purchase requisition when purchases are necessary. These are sent to the purchasing agent, who prepares six copies of a purchase order. Two copies are sent directly to the vendor. One is placed in an open purchase order file in the purchasing department, and one is used to post to the purchases journal. Each week, the purchasing department clerk prepares a journal voucher from the purchases journal and sends it to the general ledger department for posting. The AP and the receiving departments also each receive a copy of the purchase order, which they file temporarily.

Upon receiving the raw materials, the receiving department clerk creates five copies of the receiving report. One copy is sent to the raw materials warehouse, and one copy is sent to the AP department. Two copies are sent to the purchasing department, where one is filed and one is used to update the inventory records. The final copy is filed in the receiving department with the purchase order and packing slip. Vendors send their invoices to the AP department, where they are used to update the AP subsidiary ledger.

In the cash disbursements department, Larry receives the information from the AP department, such as the purchase requisition, purchase order, receiving report, and invoice. He then prepares and signs the checks for the suppliers. After preparation of the checks, the supporting documents are sent back to the AP department. Each week, Larry prepares a journal voucher and sends it to the general ledger department for posting.

Required

a. Prepare the REA model of the purchase cash payments process.
b. Show the cardinalities for all associations.
c. List the tables, keys, and attributes needed to implement this model in a relational database.

9. REA MODEL—PAYROLL SYSTEM

Every two weeks, employees of a manufacturing firm submit their time cards to the supervisor, who reviews and approves them. They are the submitted to the payroll department. At that time, the human resources clerk also submits a personnel action to the payroll clerk. The payroll clerk enters the information from these source documents into the employee records and then adds the employee hours to a payroll register reflecting employee pay rates, deductions, and job classification. One copy of the payroll register, along with the time cards, is filed in the payroll department, and one copy is sent to the AP department.

Next, the payroll clerk sends the employee paychecks to the cash disbursements department. The checks are signed and distributed to the employees by the paymaster. The AP department prepares a cash disbursements voucher. A copy of the voucher and a copy of the payroll register are sent to the cash disbursements department and are then posted to the general ledger. The cash disbursements clerk writes a check for the entire payroll and deposits it in the payroll imprest cash account. A copy of the check, the disbursement voucher, and the payroll register are sent back to the AP department, where they are filed.

Required

a. Prepare the REA model of the payroll process.
b. Show the cardinalities for all associations.
c. List the tables, keys, and attributes needed to implement this model in a relational database.

10. REA MODEL—FIXED ASSET SYSTEM

Asset acquisition begins when the department manager recognizes the need to obtain or replace an existing fixed asset. The manager prepares two copies of a purchase requisition; one is filed in the department, and one is sent to the purchasing department. The purchasing department uses the purchase requisition to prepare three copies of a purchase order. One copy of the purchase order is sent to the supplier, another copy is sent to the AP department, and the third copy is filed in the purchasing department. The receiving department receives the assets and packing slip from the vendor and prepares a receiving report. One copy of the receiving report is sent to AP, one is sent to the department manager, and one is sent to the inventory department clerk who uses it to update the inventory records.

The AP clerk receives the invoice, which she compares to the purchase order and receiving report. The AP clerk inputs the information into the computer terminal, posts the liability, updates the purchase journal, and prints out hard copies of a journal voucher and cash disbursement voucher. The journal voucher is sent to the general ledger department, and the cash disbursement voucher and the supplier's invoice are sent to the cash disbursements department. The purchase order and the receiving report are filed in AP. The cash disbursements clerk prepares and posts a check to the check register using the information from the supplier's invoice and the cash disbursement voucher, and prints a hard copy of the check, which is sent to the vendor. The cash disbursement voucher is sent on to the general ledger department.

The department manager also handles asset maintenance and asset disposal. The manager adjusts the fixed asset inventory subsidiary account balances as the assets depreciate over time. When an asset has reached the end of its useful life, a disposal report is prepared. The department manager sends an asset status summary to the general ledger. The general ledger department clerk reconciles the cash disbursements voucher, the journal voucher, and the asset status summary, and posts to the general ledger accounts.

Required

a. Prepare the REA model of the fixed asset procedures.
b. Show the cardinalities for all associations.
c. List the tables, keys, and attributes needed to implement this model in a relational database.

CHAPTER 11

Enterprise Resource Planning Systems

Learning Objectives

After studying this chapter, you should:

- Understand the general functionality and key elements of ERP systems.
- Understand the various aspects of ERP configuration, including servers, databases, and the use of bolt-on software.
- Understand the purpose of data warehousing as a strategic tool and recognize the issues related to the design, maintenance, and operation of a data warehouse.
- Recognize the risks associated with ERP implementation.
- Be aware of the key considerations related to ERP implementation.
- Understand the internal control and auditing implications associated with ERPs.

Until recently, most large and midsized organizations designed and programmed custom information systems in-house. This resulted in an array of standalone systems that were designed to the unique needs of the users. Although these systems dealt efficiently with their designated tasks, they did not provide strategic decision support at the enterprise level because they lacked the integration needed for information transfer across organization boundaries. Today the trend in information systems is toward implementing highly integrated, enterprise-oriented systems. These are not custom packages designed for a specific organization. Instead, they are generalized systems that incorporate the best business practices in use. Organizations mix and match precoded software components to assemble an **enterprise resource planning (ERP)** system that best meets their business requirements. This means that an organization may need to change the way it conducts business to take full advantage of the ERP.

This chapter is composed of five major sections. The first section outlines the key features of a generic ERP system by comparing the function and data-storage techniques of a traditional flat file or database system to that of an ERP. The second section describes various ERP configurations related to servers, databases, and bolt-on software. The topic of the third section is data warehousing. A data warehouse is a relational or multidimensional database that supports online analytical processing (OLAP). The fourth section examines key risks associated with ERP implementation. The fifth section reviews the internal control and auditing issues related to ERPs, and the discussion follows the COSO framework.

What Is an ERP?

ERP systems are multiple module software packages that evolved primarily from traditional manufacturing resource planning (MRP II) systems. The Gartner Group coined the term *ERP*, which has become widely used in recent years. The objective of ERP is to integrate key processes of the organization, such as order entry, manufacturing, procurement and accounts payable, payroll, and human resources. By doing so, a single computer system can serve the unique needs of each functional area. Designing one system that serves everyone is an undertaking of massive proportions. Under the traditional model, each functional area or department has its own computer system optimized to the way it does its daily business. ERP combines all of these into a single, integrated system that accesses a single database to facilitate the sharing of information and to improve communications across the organization.

To illustrate, consider the traditional model for a manufacturing firm illustrated in Figure 11-1. This company employs **closed database architecture**, which is similar in concept to the basic flat-file model. Under this approach, a database management system is used to provide minimal technological advantage over flat-file systems. The database management system is little more than a private but powerful file system. As with the flat-file approach, the data remain the property of the application. Thus, distinct, separate, and independent databases exist. As is true with the flat-file architecture, there is a high degree of data redundancy in a closed database environment.

When a customer places an order, the order begins a paper-based journey around the company, where it is keyed and rekeyed into the systems of several different departments. These redundant tasks cause delays and lost orders, and promote data entry errors. During transit through various systems, the status of the order may be unknown at any point in time. For example, when responding to a customer query, the marketing department may be unable to look into the production database to determine whether an order has been manufactured and shipped. Instead, the frustrated customer is told to call the manufacturing department. Similarly, the procurement of raw materials from suppliers is not linked to customer orders until they reach the manufacturing stage. This results either in delays because manufacturing awaits the arrival of needed materials, or in excessive investment in inventories to avoid stock-outs.

The lack of effective communication between systems in the traditional model is often the consequence of a fragmented systems design process. Each system tends to be designed as a solution to a specific operational problem rather than as a part of an overall strategy. Furthermore,

FIGURE 11-1 TRADITIONAL INFORMATION SYSTEM

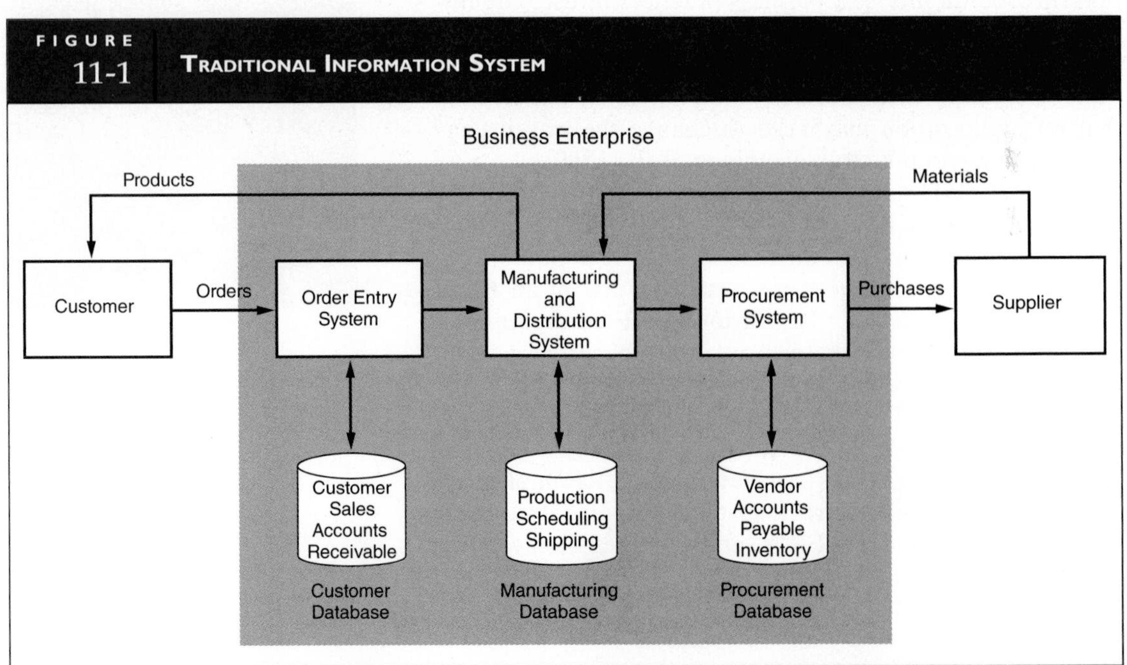

because systems designed in-house emerge independently and over time, they are often constructed on different and incompatible technology platforms. Thus, special procedures and programs need to be created so that older mainframe systems using flat files can communicate with newer distributed systems that use relational databases. Special software patches are also needed to enable commercial systems from different vendors to communicate with each other as well as with custom systems that were developed in-house. Although communications among such a hodgepodge of systems is possible, it is highly fragmented and not conducive to efficient operations.

ERP systems support a smooth and seamless flow of information across the organization by providing a standardized environment for a firm's business processes and a common operational database that supports communications. An overview of ERP is presented in Figure 11-2. Data in the operational database are modeled, structured, and stored in accordance with the internal attributes of the data. They remain independent of any specific application. Extensive data sharing among users occurs through application-sensitive views that present the data in a way that meets all user needs.

ERP CORE APPLICATIONS

ERP functionality falls into two general groups of applications: core applications and business analysis applications. **Core applications** are those applications that operationally support the day-to-day activities of the business. If these applications fail, so does the business. Typical core applications include, but are not limited to, sales and distribution, business planning, production planning, shop floor control, and logistics. Core applications are also called **online transaction processing (OLTP)** applications. Figure 11-2 illustrates these functions applied to a manufacturing firm.

Sales and distribution functions handle order entry and delivery scheduling. This includes checking on product availability to ensure timely delivery and verifying customer credit limits.

FIGURE 11-2 ERP SYSTEM

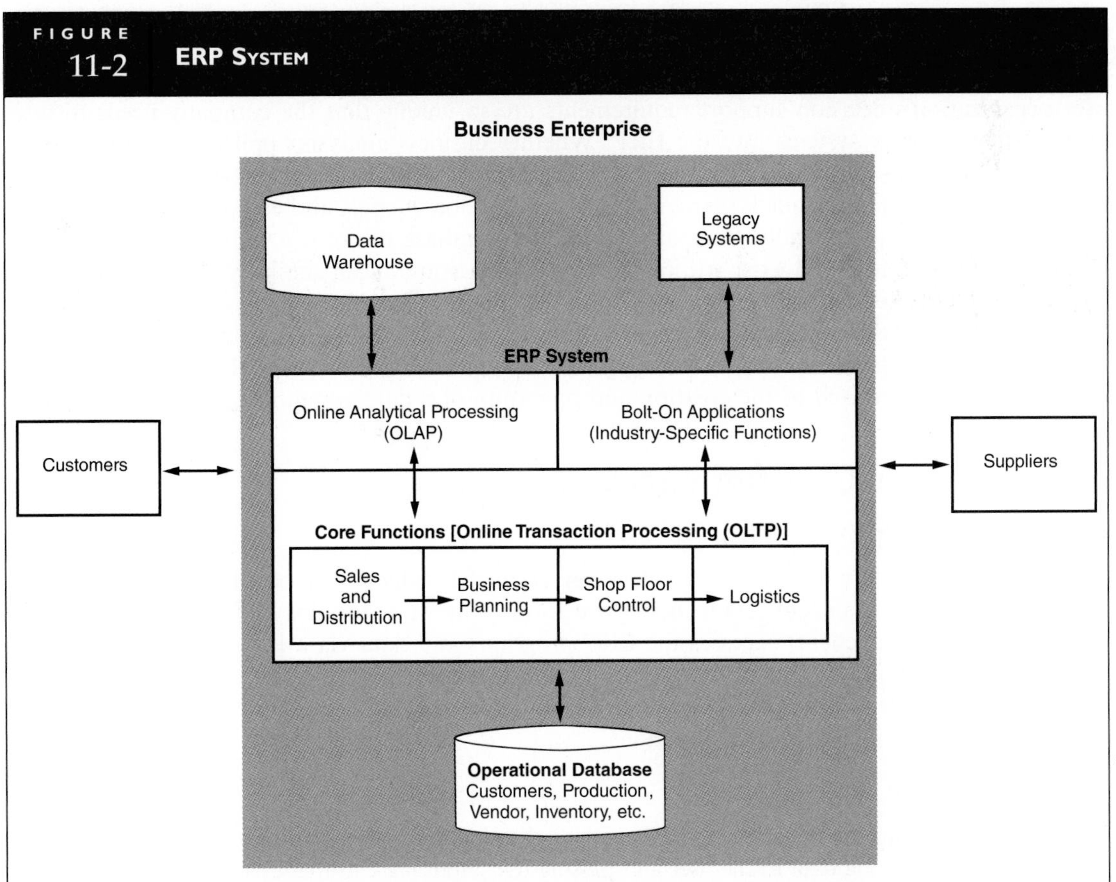

Unlike the previous example, customer orders are entered into the ERP only once. Because all users access a common database, the status of an order can be determined at any point. In fact, the customer will be able to check the order directly via an Internet connection. Such integration reduces manual activities, saves time, and decreases human error.

Business planning consists of forecasting demand, planning product production, and detailing routing information that describes the sequence and the stages of the actual production process. Capacity planning and production planning can be very complex; therefore, some ERPs provide simulation tools to help managers decide how to avoid shortages in materials, labor, or plant facilities. When the master production schedule is complete, the data are entered into the materials requirements planning (MRP) module, which provides three key pieces of information: an exception report, a materials requirements list, and inventory requisitions. The exception report identifies potential situations that will result in rescheduling production, such as late delivery of materials. The materials requirements list shows the details of vendor shipments and expected receipts of products and components needed for the order. Inventory requisitions are used to trigger material purchase orders to vendors for items not in stock.

Shop floor control involves the detailed production scheduling, dispatching, and job costing activities associated with the actual production process. Finally, the logistics application is responsible for ensuring timely delivery to the customer. This consists of inventory and warehouse management, as well as shipping. Most ERPs also include their procurement activities within the logistics function.

ONLINE ANALYTICAL PROCESSING

An ERP is more than simply an elaborate transaction processing system. It is a decision support tool that supplies management with real-time information and permits timely decisions that are needed to improve performance and achieve competitive advantage. **Online analytical processing (OLAP)** includes decision support, modeling, information retrieval, ad hoc reporting/analysis, and what-if analysis. Some ERPs support these functions with their own industry-specific modules that can be added to the core system. Other ERP vendors have designed their systems to accept and communicate with specialized bolt-on packages that third-party vendors produce. Sometimes, the user organization's decision support requirements are so unique that the company needs to integrate in-house legacy systems into the ERP. Whether business analysis applications are obtained or derived, they are central to their successful function as a data warehouse. A **data warehouse** is a database constructed for quick searching, retrieval, ad hoc queries, and ease of use. The data are normally extracted periodically from an operational database or from a public information service. An ERP system could exist without having a data warehouse; similarly, organizations that have not implemented an ERP may deploy data warehouses. The trend, however, is that organizations that are serious about competitive advantage deploy both. The recommended data architecture for an ERP implementation includes separate operational and data warehouse databases. We will examine issues related to the creation and operation of a data warehouse later in the chapter.

ERP System Configurations

SERVER CONFIGURATIONS

Most ERP systems are based on the **client-server model**, which will be discussed in detail in Chapter 12. Briefly, the client-server model is a form of network topology in which a user's computer or terminal (the client) accesses the ERP programs and data via a host computer called the server. The servers may be centralized, but the clients are usually located at multiple locations throughout the enterprise. Two basic architectures are the two-tier model and the three-tier model, as described in the following sections.

Two-Tier Model

In a typical **two-tier model**, the server handles both application and database duties. Client computers are responsible for presenting data to the user and passing user input back to the server. Some ERP vendors

FIGURE 11-3 TWO-TIER CLIENT SERVER

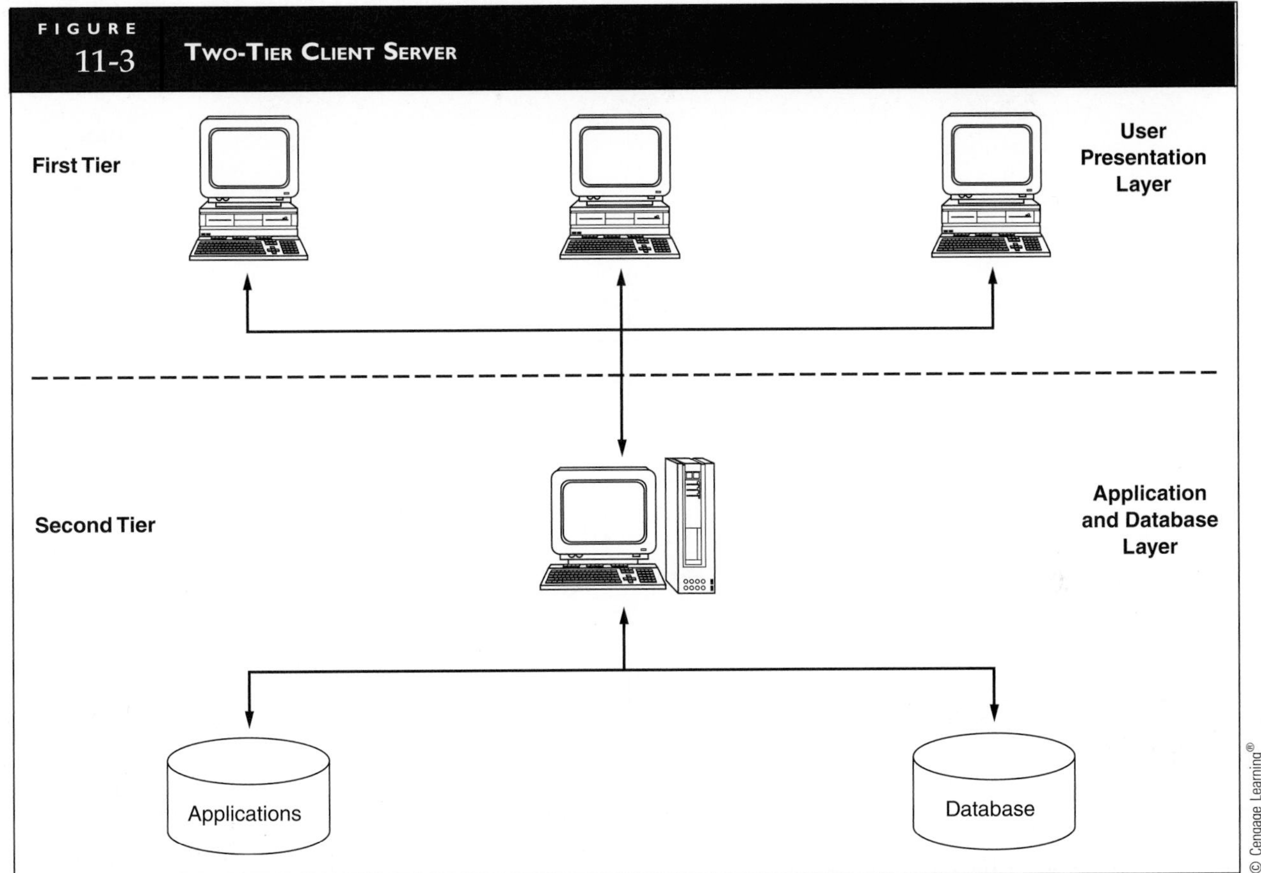

use this approach for local area network (LAN) applications for which the demand on the server is restricted to a relatively small population of users. This configuration is illustrated in Figure 11-3.

Three-Tier Model

The database and application functions are separated in the **three-tier model**. This architecture is typical of large ERP systems that use wide area networks (WANs) for connectivity among the users. Satisfying client requests requires two or more network connections. Initially, the client establishes communications with the application server. The application server then initiates a second connection to the database server. Figure 11-4 presents the three-tier model.

OLTP VERSUS OLAP SERVERS

When implementing an ERP system that will include a data warehouse, a clear distinction needs to be made between the competing types of data processing: OLTP and OLAP. OLTP events consist of large numbers of relatively simple transactions, such as updating accounting records that are stored in several related tables. For example, an order entry system retrieves all of the data relating to a specific customer to process a sales transaction. Relevant data are selected from the Customer table, Invoice table, and a detailed Line Item table. Each table contains an embedded key (i.e., CUSTOMER NUMBER), which is used to relate rows between different tables. The transaction processing activity involves updating the customer's current balance and inserting new records into the Invoice and Line Item tables. The relationships between records in such OLTP transactions are generally simple, and only a few records are actually retrieved or updated in a single transaction.

FIGURE 11-4 THREE-TIER CLIENT SERVER

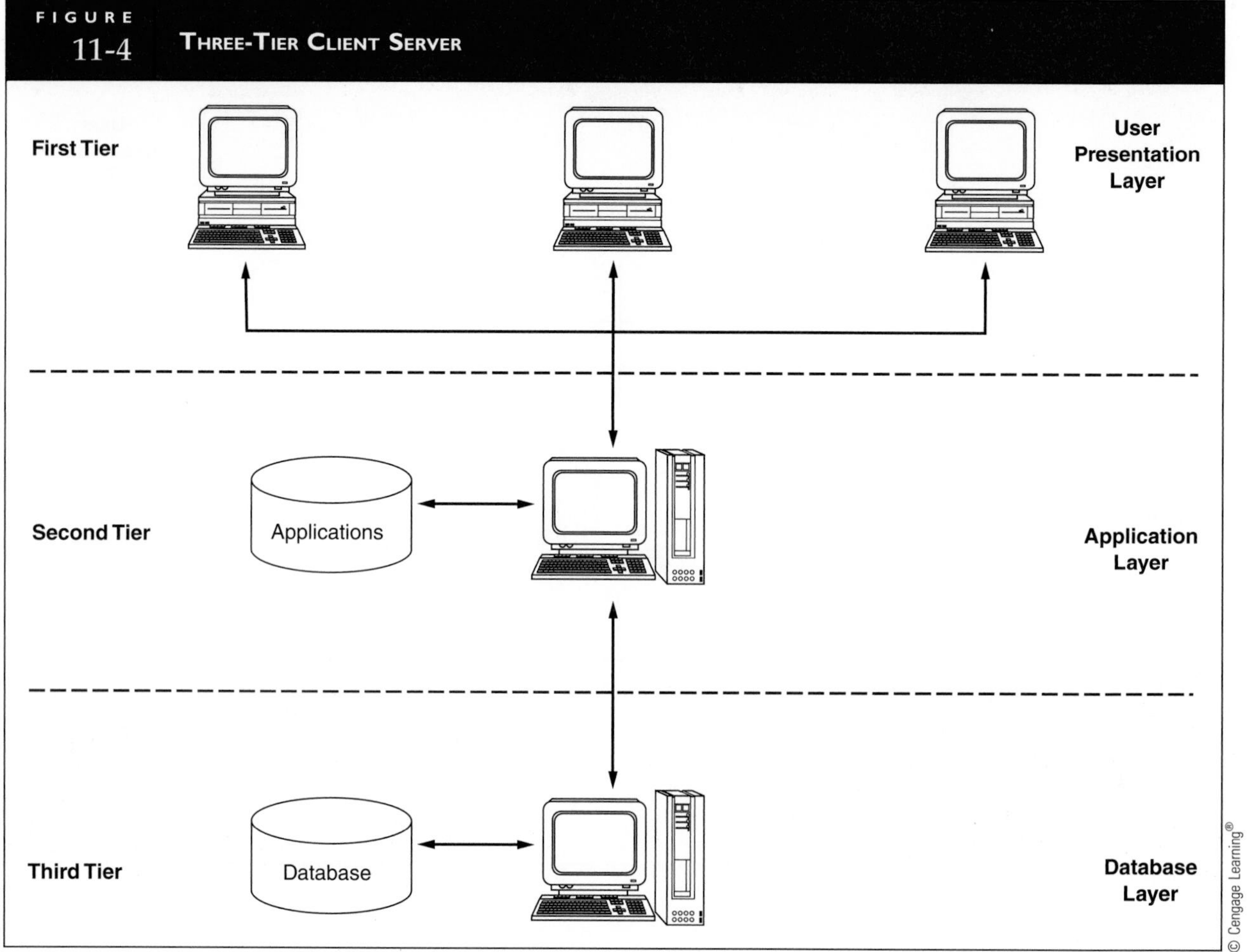

OLAP can be characterized as online transactions that:[1]

- Access very large amounts of data (e.g., several years of sales data).
- Analyze the relationships among many types of business elements, such as sales, products, geographic regions, and marketing channels.
- Involve aggregated data, such as sales volumes, budgeted dollars, and dollars spent.
- Compare aggregated data over hierarchical time periods (e.g., monthly, quarterly, yearly).
- Present data in different perspectives, such as sales by region, by distribution channel, or by product.
- Involve complex calculations among data elements, such as expected profit as a function of sales revenue for each type of sales channel in a particular region.
- Respond quickly to user requests so they can pursue an analytical thought process without being stymied by system delays.

An example of an OLAP transaction is the aggregation of sales data by region, product type, and sales channel. The OLAP query may need to access vast amounts of sales data over a multi-year period to find sales for each product type within each region. The user can further refine the query to identify sales volume by product for each sales channel within a given region. Finally,

1 © Cengage Learning 2015.

FIGURE 11-5 OLTP AND OLAP CLIENT SERVER

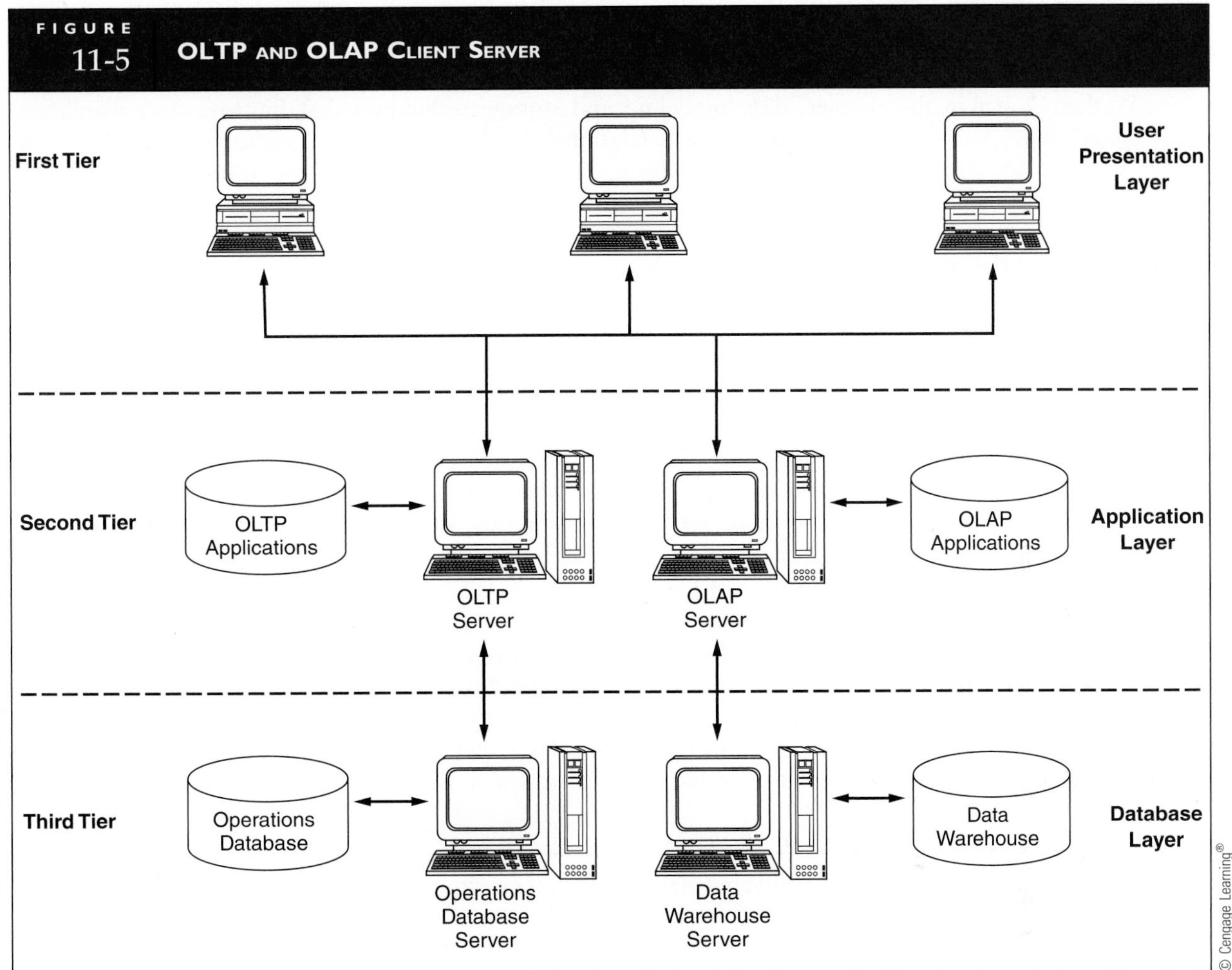

the user may decide to perform year-to-year or quarter-to-quarter comparisons for each sales channel. An OLAP application must be able to support this analysis online with rapid response.

The difference between OLAP and OLTP can be summarized as follows. OLTP applications support mission-critical tasks through simple queries of operational databases. OLAP applications support management-critical tasks through analytical investigation of complex data associations that are captured in data warehouses. OLAP and OLTP have specialized requirements that are in direct conflict. Figure 11-5 shows how the client-server architecture enables organizations to deploy separate and specialized application and database servers to resolve these conflicting data management needs. OLAP servers support common analytical operations, including consolidation, drill-down, and slicing and dicing.

> **Consolidation** *is the aggregation or roll-up of data. For example, sales offices data can be rolled up to districts, and districts can be rolled up to regions.*
>
> **Drill-down** *permits disaggregating data to reveal the underlying details that explain certain phenomena. For example, the user can drill down from total sales returns for a period to identify the actual products returned and the reasons for their return.*
>
> **Slicing and dicing** *enables the user to examine data from different viewpoints. One slice of data might show sales within each region. Another slice might present sales by product across regions. Slicing and dicing is often performed along a time axis to depict trends and patterns.*

OLAP servers allow users to analyze complex data relationships. The physical database itself is organized in such a way that related data may be rapidly retrieved across multiple dimensions. Thus, OLAP database servers need to be efficient when storing and processing multidimensional data. Later in the chapter, data modeling and storage techniques that improve data warehouse efficiency will be examined. In contrast, relational databases for operations are modeled and optimized to handle OLTP applications. They concentrate on reliability and transaction processing speed instead of decision support need.

DATABASE CONFIGURATION

ERP systems are composed of thousands of database tables. Each table is associated with business processes that are coded into the ERP. The ERP implementation team, which includes key users and information technology (IT) professionals, selects specific database tables and processes by setting switches in the system. Determining how all the switches need to be set for a given configuration requires a deep understanding of the existing processes used in operating the business. Often, however, choosing table settings involves decisions to reengineer the company's processes so that they comply with the best business practices in use. In other words, the company typically changes its processes to accommodate the ERP rather than modifying the ERP to accommodate the company.

BOLT-ON SOFTWARE

Many organizations have ascertained that ERP software alone cannot drive all the processes of the company. These firms use a variety of **bolt-on software** that third-party vendors provide. The decision to use bolt-on software requires careful consideration. Most of the leading ERP vendors have entered into partnership arrangements with third-party vendors that provide specialized functionality. The least risky approach is to choose a bolt-on that is endorsed by the ERP vendor. Some organizations, however, take a more independent approach. Domino's Pizza is a case in point.

Domino's Pizza

Domino's US distribution delivered 338 million pizzas in 1998.[2] The Company manufactures an average of 4.2 million pounds of dough per week in its 18 US distribution centers. A fleet of 160 trucks carries the dough, along with other food and paper products, to the 4,500 US Domino's franchises. Domino's has no cutoff time for ordering supplies. Therefore, a franchise can call and adjust its order even after the truck has rolled away from the distribution center. To help anticipate demand, Domino's uses forecasting software from Prescient Systems, Inc., which bolts on to its PeopleSoft ERP system. In addition, it uses a system from Manugistics, Inc., to schedule and route the delivery trucks. Each truck has an onboard computer system that feeds data into a time-and-attendance system from Kronos, Inc., which connects to the PeopleSoft human resources module. Domino's also has an extensive data warehouse. To anticipate its market, Domino's performs data mining with software from Cognos, Inc., and Hyperion Solutions Corp.

Domino's had been using these and other applications before it implemented an ERP. The company did not want to retire its existing applications but discovered that the legacy system required data fields that the ERP did not provide. For instance, the routing system tells the truck drivers which stores to visit and in what order. The ERP system did not have a data field for specifying the delivery stop sequence. The warehousing system needs this information, however, to tell loaders what to put in the trucks and in what order. Having confidence in its in-house IT staff, Domino's management decided to take the relatively drastic step of modifying the ERP software to include these fields.

Supply Chain Management

Another development regarding the bolt-on software issue is the rapid convergence between ERP and bolt-on software functionality. **Supply chain management (SCM)** software is a case in point. The supply chain is the set of activities associated with moving goods from the raw materials

2 Slater, D. "The Ties That Bolt," Enterprise Resource Planning, *CIO Magazine* (April 15, 1999), 4–9.

stage to the consumer. This includes procurement, production scheduling, order processing, inventory management, transportation, warehousing, customer service, and forecasting the demand for goods. SCM systems are a class of application software that supports this task. Successful SCM systems coordinate and integrate these activities into a seamless process. In addition to the key functional areas within the organization, SCM links all of the partners in the chain, including vendors, carriers, third-party logistics companies, and information systems providers. An organization can achieve competitive advantage by linking the activities in its supply chain more efficiently and effectively than its competitors.

ERP systems and SCM systems are now on converging paths. Many ERP vendors have moved decisively to add SCM functionality to their ERP products. On the other hand, SCM software vendors are expanding their functionality to appear more like ERP systems. As larger ERP vendors move into the midsize company market, the smaller SCM and ERP vendors will likely be pushed out of business.

Data Warehousing

Data warehousing is one of the fastest growing IT issues for businesses today. Not surprisingly, data warehousing functionality is being incorporated into all leading ERP systems. A data warehouse is a relational or multidimensional database that may consume hundreds of gigabytes or even terabytes of disk storage. When the data warehouse is organized for a single department or function, it is often called a **data mart**. Rather than containing hundreds of gigabytes of data for the entire enterprise, a data mart may have only tens of gigabytes of data. Other than size, we make no distinction between a data mart and a data warehouse. The issues discussed in this section apply to both.

The process of data warehousing involves extracting, converting, and standardizing an organization's operational data from ERP and legacy systems and loading them into a central archive—the data warehouse. Once loaded into the warehouse, data are accessible via various query and analysis tools that are used for data mining. Data mining, which was introduced in Chapter 8, is the process of selecting, exploring, and modeling large amounts of data to uncover relationships and global patterns that exist in large databases but are hidden among the vast number of facts. This involves sophisticated techniques that use database queries and artificial intelligence to model real-world phenomena from data collected from the warehouse.

Most organizations implement a data warehouse as part of a strategic IT initiative that involves an ERP system. Implementing a successful data warehouse involves installing a process for gathering data on an ongoing basis, organizing it into meaningful information, and delivering it for evaluation. The data warehousing process has the following essential stages:[3]

- Modeling data for the data warehouse
- Extracting data from operational databases
- Cleansing extracted data
- Transforming data into the warehouse model
- Loading data into the data warehouse database

MODELING DATA FOR THE DATA WAREHOUSE

Chapters 9 and 10 stressed the importance of data normalization to eliminate three serious anomalies: update, insertion, and deletion anomalies. Normalizing data in an operational database is necessary to reflect accurately the dynamic interactions among entities. Data attributes are constantly updated, new attributes are added, and obsolete attributes are deleted on a regular basis. Even though a fully normalized database will yield the flexible model needed for supporting multiple users in this dynamic operational environment, it also adds to complexity that is translated into performance inefficiency.

3 P. Fiore, "Everyone Is Talking about Data Warehousing," *Evolving Enterprise* (Spring 1998), 2.

Denormalized Data Warehouse

Because of the vast size of a data warehouse, performance inefficiency can be devastating. A three-way join between many thousands of tables in a large data warehouse may take an unacceptably long time to complete, and may be unnecessary. In the data warehouse model, the relationship among attributes does not change. Because historical data are static in nature, nothing is gained by constructing normalized tables with dynamic links.

For example, in an operational database system, Product X may be an element of work-in-process (WIP) in Department A this month and part of Department B's WIP next month. In a properly normalized data model, it would be incorrect to include Department A's WIP data as part of a Sales Order table that records an order for Product X. Only the product item number would be included in the Sales Order table as a foreign key linking it to the Product table. Relational theory would call for a join (link) between the Sales Order table and Product table to determine the production status (i.e., which department the product is currently in) and other attributes of the product. From an operational perspective, complying with relational theory is important because the relation changes as the product moves through different departments over time. Relational theory does not apply to a data warehousing system because the Sales Order/Product relation is stable.

Wherever possible, therefore, normalized tables pertaining to selected events may be consolidated into denormalized tables. Figure 11-6 illustrates how sales order data are reduced to a single denormalized Sales Order table for storage in a data warehouse system.

EXTRACTING DATA FROM OPERATIONAL DATABASES

Data extraction is the process of collecting data from operational databases, flat files, archives, and external data sources. Operational databases typically need to be out of service when data extraction occurs to avoid data inconsistencies. Because of their large size and the need for a speedy transfer to minimize the downtime, little or no conversion of data occurs at this point. A technique called **changed data capture** can dramatically reduce the extraction time by capturing only newly modified data. The extraction software compares the current operational database with an image of the data taken at the last transfer of data to the warehouse. Only data that have changed in the interim are captured.

Extracting Snapshots versus Stabilized Data

Transaction data stored in the operational database go through several stages as economic events unfold. For example, a sales transaction first undergoes credit approval, then the product is shipped, then billing occurs, and finally payment is received. Each of these events changes the state of the transaction and associated accounts, such as inventory, accounts receivable, and cash. A key feature of a data warehouse is that the data contained in it are in a nonvolatile, stable state. Typically, transaction data are loaded into the warehouse only when the activity on them has been completed. Potentially important relationships between entities may, however, be absent from data that are captured in this stable state. For example, information about canceled sales orders will probably not be reflected among the sales orders that have been shipped and paid for before they are placed in the warehouse. One way to reflect these dynamics is to extract the operations data in slices of time. These slices provide snapshots of business activity. For example, decision makers may want to observe sales transactions approved, shipped, billed, and paid at various points in time, along with snapshots of inventory levels at each state. Such data may be useful in depicting trends in the average time taken to approve credit or ship goods that might help explain lost sales.

CLEANSING EXTRACTED DATA

Data cleansing involves filtering out or repairing invalid data prior to being stored in the warehouse. Operational data are dirty for many reasons. Clerical, data entry, and computer program errors can create illogical data, such as negative inventory quantities, misspelled names, and blank fields. Data cleansing also involves transforming data into standard business terms with standard data values. Data are often combined from multiple systems that use slightly different spellings to represent common terms, such as cust, cust_id, or cust_no. Some operational systems may use entirely different

FIGURE 11-6 DENORMALIZED DATA

A. Normalized Representation for an Operational Database System

Customer Table

Customer Number	Name	Street	City	State
34675	John Smith	10 Elm	Bath	PA

Invoice Table

Invoice Number	Invoice Date	Shipped Date	Invoice Amount	Customer Number
8866376	06/12/09	06/23/09	600	34675

Line Item Table

Invoice Number	Item Number	Quantity	Price	Extended Price
8866376	j683	2	200	400
8866376	r223	5	40	200

B. Denormalized Representation for Data Warehouse System

Sales Order Table

Customer Number	Name	Street	City	State	Invoice Number	Invoice Date	Shipped Date	Invoice Amount	Item Number	Quantity	Price	Extended Price
34675	John Smith	10 Elm	Bath	PA	8866376	06/12/09	06/23/09	600	j683	2	200	400
34675	John Smith	10 Elm	Bath	PA	8866376	06/12/09	06/23/09	600	r223	5	40	200

FIGURE 11-7 DATA WAREHOUSE SYSTEM

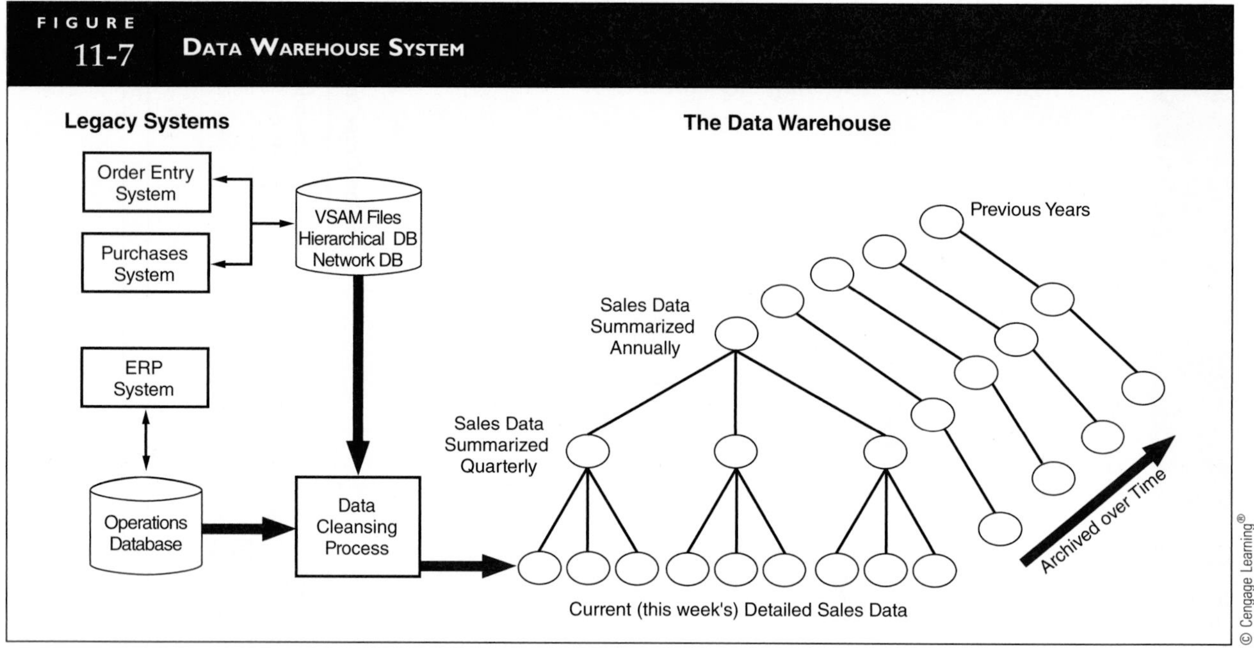

terms to refer to the same entity. For example, a bank customer with a certificate of deposit and an outstanding loan may be called a lender by one system and a borrower by another. The source application may use cryptic or difficult-to-understand terms for a number of reasons. For example, some older legacy systems were designed at a time when programming rules placed severe restrictions on naming and formatting data attributes. Also, a commercial application may assign attribute names that are too generic for the needs of the data warehouse user. Businesses that purchase commercial data, such as competitive performance information or market surveys, need to extract data from whatever format the external source provides and reorganize them according to the conventions used in the data warehouse. During the cleansing process, therefore, the attributes taken from multiple systems need to be transformed into uniform, standard business terms. This tends to be an expensive and labor-intensive activity, but one that is critical in establishing data integrity in the warehouse. Figure 11-7 illustrates the role of data cleansing in building and maintaining a data warehouse.

TRANSFORMING DATA INTO THE WAREHOUSE MODEL

A data warehouse is composed of both detail and summary data. To improve efficiency, data can be transformed into summary views before they are loaded into the warehouse. For example, many decision makers may need to see product sales figures summarized weekly, monthly, quarterly, or annually. It may not be practical to summarize information from detail data every time the user needs it. A data warehouse that contains the most frequently requested summary views of data can reduce the amount of processing time during analysis. Referring again to Figure 11-7, we see the creation of summary views over time. These are typically created around business entities such as customers, products, and suppliers. Unlike operational views, which are virtual in nature with underlying base tables, data warehouse views are physical tables. Most OLAP software will, however, permit the user to construct virtual views from detail data when one does not already exist.

A data warehouse will often provide multiple summary views based on the same detailed data such as customers or products. For example, several different summary views may be generated from sales order detail data; these may include summaries by product, customer, and region. From such views, an analyst can drill down into the underlying detail data. Many business problems require a review of detail data to fully evaluate a trend, a pattern, or an anomaly exhibited in the summarized reports. Also, a single anomaly in detail data may manifest itself differently in different summary views.

LOADING THE DATA INTO THE DATA WAREHOUSE DATABASE

Most organizations have found that data warehousing success requires that the data warehouse be created and maintained separately from the operational (transaction processing) databases. This point is developed further in the next sections.

Internal Efficiency

One reason for a separate data warehouse is that the structural and operational requirements of transaction processing and data mining systems are fundamentally different, making it impractical to keep both operational (current) and archive data in the same database. Transaction processing systems need a data structure that supports performance, while data mining systems need data organized in a manner that permits broad examination and the detection of underlying trends.

Integration of Legacy Systems

The continued influence of legacy systems is another reason that the data warehouse needs to be independent of operations. A remarkably large number of business applications continue to run in the mainframe environment of the 1970s. By some estimates, more than 70 percent of business data for large corporations still resides in the mainframe environment. The data structures these systems employ are often incompatible with the architectures of modern data mining tools. Hence, transaction data that are stored in navigational databases and Virtual Storage Access Method systems often end up in large tape libraries that are isolated from the decision process. A separate data warehouse provides a venue for integrating the data from legacy and contemporary systems into a common structure that supports entity-wide analysis.

Consolidation of Global Data

Finally, the emergence of the global economy has brought about fundamental changes in business organizational structure and has profoundly changed the information requirements of business entities. Unique business complexities challenge decision makers in the global corporation. For example, they need to assess the profitability of products built and sold in multiple countries with volatile currencies. Such challenges add complexity to data mining. A separate centralized data warehouse is an effective means of collecting, standardizing, and assimilating data from diverse sources.

In conclusion, the creation of a data warehouse separate from operational systems is a fundamental data warehousing concept. Many organizations now consider data warehouse systems to be key components of their information systems strategy. As such, they allocate considerable resources to build data warehouses concurrently with the operational systems being implemented.

DECISIONS SUPPORTED BY THE DATA WAREHOUSE

By making the data warehouse as flexible and friendly as possible, it becomes accessible to many end users. Some decisions that a data warehouse supports are not fundamentally different from those that traditional databases support. Other information uses, such as multidimensional analysis and information visualization, are not possible with traditional systems. Some users of the data warehouse need routine reports based on traditional queries. When standard reports can be anticipated in advance, they can be provided automatically as a periodic product. Automatic generation of standard information reduces access activity against the data warehouse and will improve its efficiency in dealing with more esoteric needs.

Drill-down capability is a useful data analysis technique associated with data mining. Drill-down analysis begins with the summary views of data described previously. When anomalies or interesting trends are observed, the user drills down to lower-level views and ultimately into the underlying detail data.

Obviously, such analysis cannot be anticipated like a standard report. Drill-down capability is an OLAP feature of data mining tools available to the user. Tools for data mining are evolving rapidly to satisfy the decision maker's need to understand the business unit's behavior in relation to key entities,

TABLE 11-1 APPLICATIONS OF DATA MINING

Business Field	Application
Banking/Investments	Detect patterns of fraudulent credit card use.
	Identify loyal customers and predict those likely to change their credit card affiliation.
	Examine historical market data to determine investors' stock trading rules.
	Predict credit card spending of key customer groups.
	Identify correlations between different financial indicators.
Health Care and Medical Insurance	Predict office visits from historical analysis of historical patient behavior.
	Identify successful and economic medical therapies for different illnesses.
	Identify which medical procedures tend to be claimed together.
	Predict which customers will buy new policies.
	Identify behavior patterns associated with high-risk customers.
	Identify indicators of fraudulent behavior.
Marketing	Identify buying patterns based on historical customer data.
	Identify relationships among customer demographic data.
	Predict response to various forms of marketing and promotion campaigns.

including customers, suppliers, employees, and products. Standard reports and queries produced from summary views can answer many *what* questions, but drill-down capability answers the *why* and *how* questions. Table 11-1 summarizes some of the applications of data mining in decision support.

SUPPORTING SUPPLY CHAIN DECISIONS FROM THE DATA WAREHOUSE

The primary reason for data warehousing is to optimize business performance. Many organizations believe that more strategic benefit can be gained by sharing data externally. By providing customers and suppliers with the information they need when they need it, the company can improve its relationships and provide better service. The potential gain to the giving organization is seen in a more responsive and efficient supply chain. Using Internet technologies and OLAP applications, an organization can share its data warehouse with its trading partners and, in effect, treat them like divisions of the firm. A few examples of this approach are outlined in the following extract.[4]

> *Western Digital Corporation, a leading manufacturer of bard drives, plans to grant certain suppliers access to its data warehouse so suppliers can view performance data on their parts. Because Western Digital maintains a limited engineering staff, the company relies on its suppliers to act as strategic partners in product development. Providing suppliers with performance data allows them to make improvements and participate in the engineering process. The suppliers improve their parts, which in turn improves Western Digital's products.*

The company's data warehouse holds more than 600 gigabytes of raw data collected from more than 100,000 drives that it manufactures each day. Approximately 800 attributes are collected on each drive, which can be analyzed using OLAP software. The systems feeding the warehouse include ERP applications, data from trouble-call centers, data from failure-analysis systems, and field test data from customer sites and service centers. The company routinely searches the data warehouse for failure information on every drive that it manufactures. All failures and their causes can be linked back to the supplier.

4 Davis, "Data Warehouses Open Up," *Information Week Online News in Review* (June 28, 1999).

The General Motors (GM) supply-chain data warehouse is available via the web to more than 5,000 suppliers worldwide. Suppliers can log on to a secure website and query information on the quantities of supplies shipped, delivery times, and prices. This information will help GM suppliers optimize their product planning, ability to source materials, and shipping-fulfillment processes.

MIM Health Plans, Inc., an independent pharmacy benefits management company, lets its customers view warehouse data to promote better buying decisions. For instance, benefits managers can view reports and drill down into the warehouse to see claims costs, overall costs, the number of prescriptions ordered in a given time period, the number of brand versus generic drugs, and other decision metrics.

Risks Associated with ERP Implementation

The benefits from ERP can be significant, but they do not come risk-free to the organization. An ERP system is not a silver bullet that will, by its mere existence, solve an organization's problems. If that were the case, there would never be ERP failures, but there have been many. This section examines some of the risk issues that need to be considered.

BIG BANG VERSUS PHASED-IN IMPLEMENTATION

Implementing an ERP system has more to do with changing the way an organization does business than it does with technology. As a result, most ERP implementation failures are the result of cultural problems within the firm that stand in opposition to the objective of process reengineering. Strategies for implementing ERP systems to achieve this objective follow two general approaches: the big bang approach and the phased-in approach.

The **big bang** method is the more ambitious and risky of the two. Organizations taking this approach attempt to switch operations from their old legacy systems to the new system in a single event that implements the ERP across the entire company. Although this method has certain advantages, it has been associated with numerous system failures. Because the new ERP system means new ways of conducting business, getting the entire organization on board and in sync can be a daunting task. On day 1 of the implementation, no one within the organization will have had any experience with the new system, that is, everyone in the company is a trainee learning a new job.

The new ERP system will initially meet with opposition because using it involves compromise. The legacy systems, which everyone in the organization was familiar with, had been honed over the years to meet exact needs. In most cases, ERP systems have neither the range of functionality nor the familiarity of the legacy systems that they replace. Also, because a single system is now serving the entire organization, individuals at data input points often find themselves entering considerably more data than they did previously with the more narrowly focused legacy system.

As a result, the speed of the new system often suffers and causes disruptions to daily operations. These problems are typically experienced whenever any new system is implemented. The magnitude of the problem is the issue under the big bang approach, in which everyone in the company is affected. Once the initial adjustment period has passed and the new culture emerges, however, the ERP becomes an effective operational and strategic tool that provides competitive advantage to the firm.

Because of the disruptions associated with the big bang, the **phased-in** approach has emerged as a popular alternative. It is particularly suited to diversified organizations whose units do not share common processes and data. In these types of companies, independent ERP systems can be installed in each business unit over time to accommodate the adjustment periods needed for assimilation. Common processes and data, such as the general ledger function, can be integrated across the organization without disrupting operations throughout the firm.

Organizations that are not diversified can also employ the phased-in approach. The implementation usually begins with one or more key processes, such as order entry. The goal is to get ERP up and running concurrently with legacy systems. As more of the organization's functions are converted to ERP, legacy systems are systematically retired. In the interim, the ERP is interfaced to legacy systems. During this period, the objectives of system integration and process reengineering, which are fundamental to the ERP model, are not achievable. To take full advantage of the ERP, process reengineering will still need to occur. Otherwise, the organization will have simply replaced its old legacy system with a very expensive new one.

OPPOSITION TO CHANGES IN THE BUSINESS'S CULTURE

To be successful, all functional areas of the organization need be involved in determining the culture of the firm and in defining the new system's requirements. The firm's willingness and ability to undertake a change of the magnitude of an ERP implementation is an important consideration. If the corporate culture is such that change is not tolerated or desired, then an ERP implementation will not be successful.

The technological culture must also be assessed. Organizations that lack technical support staff for the new system or have a user base that is unfamiliar with computer technology face a steeper learning curve and a potentially greater barrier to acceptance of the system by their employees.

CHOOSING THE WRONG ERP

Because ERP systems are prefabricated systems, users need to determine whether a particular ERP fits their organization's culture and its business processes. A common reason for system failure is when the ERP does not support one or more important business processes. In one example, a textile manufacturer in India implemented an ERP only to discover afterward that it did not accommodate a basic need.

The textile company had a policy of maintaining two prices for each item of inventory that it sold. One price was used for the domestic market, and a second price, which was four times higher, was for export sales. The ERP that the user implemented was not designed to allow two different prices for the same inventory item. The changes needed to make the ERP work were both extensive and expensive. Serious system disruptions resulted from this oversight. Furthermore, modifying an ERP program and database can introduce potential processing errors and can make updating the system to later versions difficult.

Goodness of Fit

Management needs to make sure that the ERP it chooses is right for the company. No single ERP system is capable of solving all the problems of all organizations. For example, SAP's R/3 was designed primarily for manufacturing firms with highly predictable processes that are relatively similar to those of other manufacturers. It may not be the best solution for a service-oriented organization that has a great need for customer-related activities conducted over the Internet.

Finding a good functionality fit requires a software selection process that resembles a funnel, which starts broad and systematically becomes more focused. It begins with a large number of software vendors that are potential candidates. Evaluation questions are asked of vendors in iterative rounds. Starting with a large population of vendors and a small number of high-level qualifier questions, the number of vendors is reduced to a manageable few. With proper questioning, more than half the vendors are removed from contention with as few as 10 to 20 questions. In each succeeding round, the questions asked become more detailed, and the population of vendors decreases.

When a business's processes are truly unique, the ERP system must be modified to accommodate industry-specific (bolt-on) software or to work with custom-built legacy systems. Some organizations, such as telecommunications service providers, have unique billing operations that off-the-shelf ERP systems cannot satisfy. Before embarking on the ERP journey, the organization's management needs to assess whether it can and should reengineer its business practices around a standardized model.

System Scalability Issues

If an organization's management expects business volumes to increase substantially during the life of the ERP system, then there is a scalability issue that needs to be addressed. **Scalability** is the system's ability to grow smoothly and economically as user requirements increase. The term *system* in this context refers to the technology platform, application software, network configuration, or database. Smooth and economic growth is the ability to increase system capacity at an acceptable incremental cost per unit of capacity without encountering limits that would demand a system upgrade or replacement. User requirements pertain to volume-related activities, such as transaction processing volume, data entry volume, data output volume, data storage volume, or increases in the user population.

To illustrate scalability, four dimensions of scalability are important: size, speed, workload, and transaction cost. In assessing scalability needs for an organization, each of these dimensions in terms of the ideal of linear scaling must be considered.[5]

Size. *With no other changes to the system, if database size increases by a factor of X, then query response time will increase by no more than a factor of X in a scalable system. For example, if business growth causes the database to increase from 100 to 500 gigabytes, then transactions and queries that previously took 1 second will now take no more than 5 seconds.*

Speed. *An increase in hardware capacity by a factor of X will decrease query response time by no less than a factor of X in a scalable system. For example, increasing the number of input terminals (nodes) from 1 to 20 will increase transaction processing time proportionately. Transactions that previously took 20 seconds will now take no more than 1 second in a system with linear scaling.*

Workload. *If workload in a scalable system is increased by a factor of X, then response time, or throughput, can be maintained by increasing hardware capacity by a factor of no more than x. For example, if transaction volume increased from 400 per hour to 4,000 per hour, the previous response time can be achieved by increasing the number of processors by a factor of 10 in a system that is linearly scalable.*

Transaction Cost. *In a scalable system, increases in workload do not increase transaction cost. Therefore, an organization should not need to increase system capacity faster than demand. For example, if the cost of processing a transaction in a system with one processor is 10 cents, then it should still cost no more than 10 cents when the number of processors is increased to handle larger volumes of transactions.*

Vendors of ERP systems sometimes advertise scalability as if it were a single-dimension factor. In fact, it is a multifaceted issue. Some systems accommodate growth in user populations better than others. Some systems can be scaled to provide more efficient access to large databases when business growth demands it. All systems, however, have their scaling limits. Because infinite scalability is impossible, prospective users need to assess their needs and determine how much scalability they want to purchase up front, and what form it should take. The key is to anticipate specific scalability issues before making an ERP investment and before the issues become reality.

CHOOSING THE WRONG CONSULTANT

Implementing an ERP system is an event that most organizations will undergo only once. Success of the projects rests on skills and experience that typically do not exist in-house. Because of this, virtually all ERP implementations involve an outside consulting firm, which coordinates the project, helps the organization to identify its needs, develops a requirements specification for the ERP, selects the ERP package, and manages the cutover. ERP consulting has grown into a $20 billion-per-year market. The fee for a typical implementation is normally between three and five times the cost of the ERP software license.

Consulting firms with large ERP practices at times have been desperately short of human resources. This was especially true in the mid- to late 1990s, when thousands of clients were rushing to implement ERP systems before the new millennium to avoid Y2K (year-2000) problems. As demand for ERP implementations grew beyond the supply of qualified consultants, more and more stories of botched projects materialized.

A frequent complaint is that consulting firms promise experienced professionals but deliver incompetent trainees. They have been accused of employing a bait-and-switch maneuver to get contracts. At the initial engagement interview, the consulting firm introduces their top consultants, who are sophisticated,

---

5 Winter, "Scalable Systems: Lexicology of Scale," *Intelligent Enterprise Magazine* (March 2000), 68–74.

talented, and persuasive. The client agrees to the deal with the firm, but incorrectly assumes that these individuals, or others with similar qualifications, will actually implement the system.

The problem has been equated to the airline industry's common practice of overbooking flights. Some suggest that consulting firms, not wanting to turn away business, are guilty of overbooking their consulting staff. The consequences, however, are far graver than the inconvenience of missing a flight—a free hotel room and meal cannot compensate for the damages done. Therefore, before engaging an outside consultant, management should:

- Interview the staff proposed for the project and draft a detailed contract specifying which members of the consulting team will be assigned to which tasks.
- Establish in writing how staff changes will be handled.
- Conduct reference checks of the proposed staff members.
- Align the consultants' interests with those of the organization by negotiating a pay-for-performance scheme based on achieving certain milestones in the project. For example, the actual amount paid to the consultant may be between 85 and 115 percent of the contracted fee, based on whether a successful project implementation comes in under or over schedule.
- Set a firm termination date for the consultant to avoid consulting arrangements becoming interminable, resulting in dependency and an endless stream of fees.

HIGH COST AND COST OVERRUNS

Total cost of ownership (TCO) for ERP systems varies greatly from company to company. For medium- to large-sized systems implementations, costs range from hundreds of thousands to hundreds of millions of dollars. TCO includes hardware, software, consulting services, internal personnel costs, installation, and upgrades and maintenance to the system for the first two years after implementation. The risk comes in the form of underestimated and unanticipated costs. Some of the more commonly experienced problems occur in the following areas.

Training. *Training costs are invariably higher than estimated because management focuses primarily on the cost of teaching employees the new software. This is only part of the needed training. Employees also need to learn new procedures, which is often overlooked during the budgeting process.*

System Testing and Integration. *In theory, ERP is a holistic model in which one system drives the entire organization. The reality, however, is that many organizations use their ERP as a backbone system that is attached to legacy systems and other bolt-on systems, which support the unique needs of the firm. Integrating these disparate systems with the ERP may involve writing special conversion programs or even modifying the internal code of the ERP. Integration and testing are done on a case-by-case basis; thus, the cost is extremely difficult to estimate in advance.*

Database Conversion. *A new ERP system usually means a new database. Data conversion is the process of transferring data from the legacy system's flat files to the ERP's relational database. When the legacy system's data are reliable, the conversion process may be accomplished through automated procedures. Even under ideal circumstances, a high degree of testing and manual reconciliation is necessary to ensure that the transfer was complete and accurate. More often, the data in the legacy system are not reliable (sometimes called dirty). Empty fields and corrupted data values cause conversion problems that demand human intervention and data rekeying Also, and more importantly, the structure of the legacy data is likely to be incompatible with the reengineered processes of the new system. Depending on the extent of the process reengineering involved, the entire database may need to be converted through manual data entry procedures.*

Develop Performance Measures

Because ERPs are extremely expensive to implement, many managers are often dismayed at the apparent lack of cost savings that they achieve in the short term. In fact, a great deal of criticism about the relative success of ERPs relates to whether they provide benefits that outweigh their cost.

To assess benefits, management first needs to know what it wants and needs from the ERP. It should then establish key performance measures such as reductions in inventory levels, inventory turnover, stock-outs, and average order fulfillment time that reflect its expectations. To monitor performance in such key areas, some organizations establish an independent value assessment group that reports to top management. Although financial breakeven on an ERP will take years, by developing focused and measurable performance indicators, an operational perspective on its success can be developed.

DISRUPTIONS TO OPERATIONS

ERP systems can wreak havoc in the companies that install them. In a Deloitte Consulting survey of 64 Fortune 500 companies, 25 percent of the firms surveyed admitted that they experienced a drop in performance in the period immediately following implementation. The reengineering of business processes that often accompanies ERP implementation is the most commonly attributed cause of performance problems. Operationally speaking, when business begins under the ERP system, everything looks and works differently from the way it did with the legacy system. An adjustment period is needed for everyone to reach a comfortable point on the learning curve. Depending on the culture of the organization and attitudes toward change within the firm, adjustment may take longer in some firms than in others. The list of major organizations that have experienced serious disruptions includes Dow Chemical, Boeing, Dell Computer, Apple Computer, Whirlpool Corporation, and Waste Management.

The most notorious case in the press was Hershey Foods Corporation, which had trouble processing orders through its new ERP system and was unable to ship products. As a result of these disruptions, Hershey's 1999 third-quarter sales dropped by 12.4 percent compared to the previous year's sales, and earnings were down by 18.6 percent. Hershey's problem has been attributed to two strategic errors related to system implementation. First, because of schedule overruns, it decided to switch to the new system during its busy season. The inevitable snags that arise from implementations of complex systems like SAP's R/3 are easier to deal with during slack business periods. Secondly, many experts believe that Hershey attempted to do too much in a single implementation. In addition to the R/3 system, it implemented a customer relations management system and logistics software from two different vendors, which had to interface with R/3. The ERP and these bolt-on components were all implemented using the big bang approach.

Implications for Internal Control and Auditing

As with any system, the internal control and audit of ERP systems are issues. Key concerns are examined next within the COSO framework.

TRANSACTION AUTHORIZATION

A key benefit of an ERP system is its tightly integrated architecture of modules. This structure, however, also poses potential problems for transaction authorization. For example, the bill of materials drives many manufacturing systems. If the procedures for the creation of the bill of materials are not configured correctly, every component that uses the bill of materials could be affected. Controls need to be built into the system to validate transactions before other modules accept and act upon them. Because of ERP's real-time orientation, systems are more dependent on programmed controls than on human intervention, as was the case with legacy systems. The challenge for auditors in verifying transaction authorization is to gain a detailed knowledge of the ERP system configuration, as well as a thorough understanding of the business processes and the flow of information between system components.

SEGREGATION OF DUTIES

Operational decisions in ERP-based organizations are pushed down to a point as close as possible to the source of the event. Manual processes that normally require segregation of duties are, therefore, often eliminated in an ERP environment. For example, shop supervisors may order inventories from suppliers, and receiving dock personnel may post inventory receipts to the inventory records in real time. Furthermore, ERP forces together many different business functions, such as order entry, billing, and accounts payable, under a single integrated system. Organizations using ERP systems must establish new security, audit, and control tools to ensure duties are properly segregated. An important aspect of such control is the assignment of *roles*, which is discussed in a later section.

SUPERVISION

An often-cited pitfall of an ERP implementation is that management does not fully understand its impact on business. Too often, after the ERP is up and running, only the implementation team understands how it works. Because their traditional responsibilities will be changed, supervisors need to acquire an extensive technical and operational understanding of the new system. Typically, when an organization implements an ERP, many decision-making responsibilities are pushed down to the shop floor level. The employee-empowered philosophy of ERP should not eliminate supervision as an internal control. Instead, it should provide substantial efficiency benefits. Supervisors should have more time to manage the shop floor and, through improved monitoring capability, increase their span of control.

ACCOUNTING RECORDS

ERP systems have the ability to streamline the entire financial reporting process. In fact, many organizations can and do close their books daily. OLTP data can be manipulated quickly to produce ledger entries, accounts receivable and payable summaries, and financial consolidation for both internal and external users. Traditional batch controls and audit trails are no longer needed in many cases. The risk of financial statement misrepresentations is mitigated by improved data entry accuracy through the use of default values, cross checking, and specified user views of data. In spite of ERP technology, some risk to accounting record accuracy may still exist. Because of the close interfaces with customers and suppliers, some organizations run the risk that corrupted or inaccurate data may be passed from these external sources and corrupt the ERP accounting database. Additionally, many organizations need to import data from legacy systems into their ERP systems. These data may be laden with problems, such as duplicate records, inaccurate values, or incomplete fields. Consequently, strict data cleansing is an important control. Special scrubber programs are used as interfaces between the ERP and the exporting systems to reduce these risks and ensure that the most accurate and current data are being received.

INDEPENDENT VERIFICATION

Because ERP systems employ OLTP, traditional, independent verification controls such as reconciling batch control numbers (discussed in Chapter 3) serve little purpose. Similarly, process reengineering to improve efficiency also changes the nature of independent verification. For example, the traditional three-way match of the purchase order, receiving report, and invoice, and the subsequent writing of a check, may be completely automated in an ERP environment. The focus of independent verification thus needs to be redirected from the individual transaction level to one that views overall performance. ERP systems come with canned controls and can be configured to produce performance reports that should be used as assessment tools. Internal auditors also play an important role in this environment and need to acquire a thorough technical background and comprehensive understanding of the ERP system. Ongoing independent verification efforts can be conducted only by a team well versed in ERP technology.

ACCESS CONTROLS

Access security is one of the most critical control issues in an ERP environment. The goal of ERP access control is to maintain data confidentiality, integrity, and availability. Security weaknesses can result in transaction errors, irregularities, data corruption, and financial statement misrepresentations. Also, uncontrolled access exposes organizations to cyber criminals who steal and subsequently sell critical data to competitors. Security administrators therefore need to control access to the tasks and operations that process or otherwise manipulate sensitive corporate data.

Traditional Access Control Models

Traditionally, the owner of system resources (data, functions, and processes) grants access privileges individually to users based on the individual's trust level and job description. Access control is typically achieved via an **access control list** (or access token) within the user's application.[6] The access control list specifies the user ID, the resources available to the user, and the level of permission granted, such as read only, edit, or create. Although this model allows for the assignment of specific access privileges to individuals, it is quite inflexible. The sheer volume and variety of access privilege needs in modern ERP environments present a significant administrative burden. Any access-granting model must efficiently keep up with new hires, changes to existing privileges brought about by promotions and individuals transferring from one department to another, and personnel terminations. To meet these demands, modern ERP systems employ **role-based access control (RBAC)**, which is discussed next.

Role-Based Access Control (RBAC)

A **role** is a formal technique for grouping together users according to the system resources they need to perform their assigned tasks. For example, a system administrator could create a Sales Role for the sales department personnel that permits access only to the ERP's Sales Module and certain documents such as customer orders, sales orders, and customer records. When an employee joins the sales department (a new hire or transfer from another department), he or she will be assigned to the Sales Role and, through it, can access its prespecified resources. Figure 11-8 illustrates the difference between RBAC and the traditional access control list approach.

FIGURE 11-8 ACCESS CONTROL LIST VERSUS RBAC

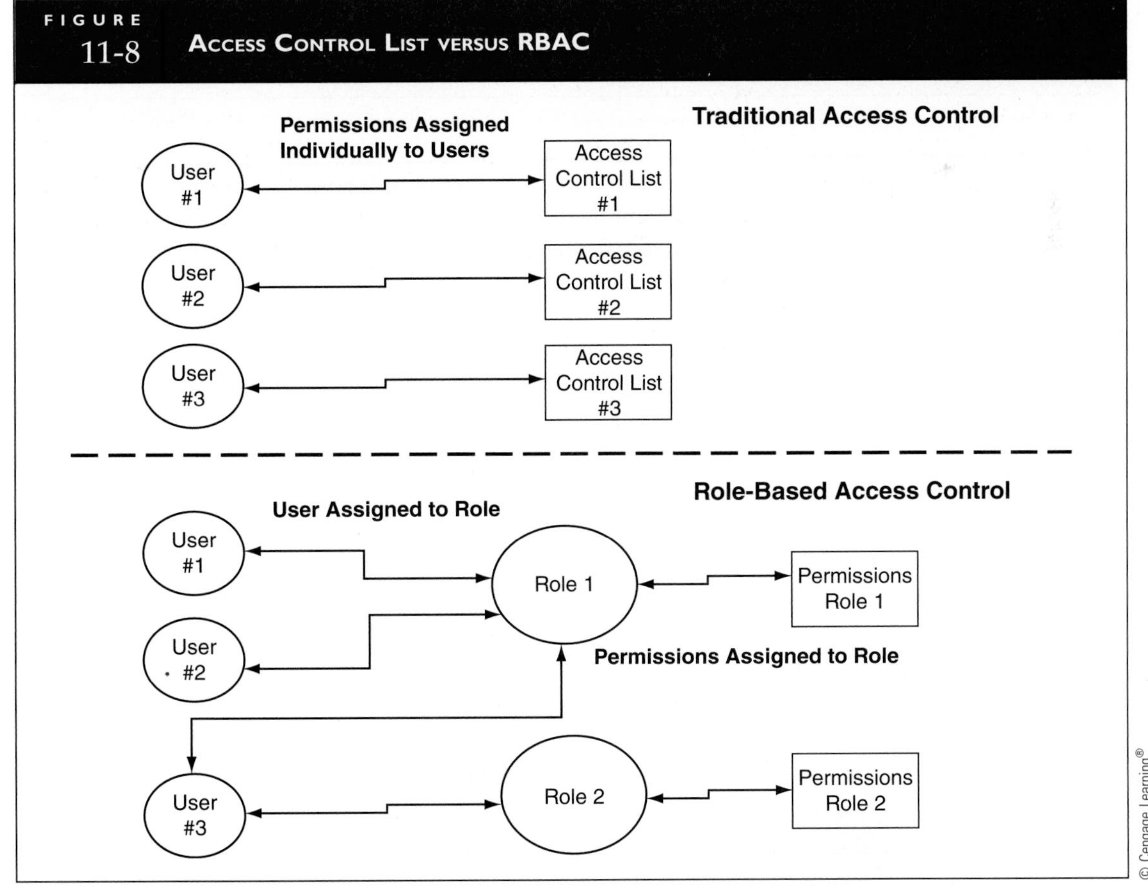

6 Access control list and access tokens are discussed in more detail in Chapter 16 within the broader context of general controls.

FIGURE 11-9 SAP ROLE DEFINITION

ERP Role Name: AP Processing **Location: AP Department**

Role Goal: Data Entry of Vendor Invoices and Check Requests

Knowledge, Skills: Knowledge of invoice processing from receipt to payment and relevant finance and procurement SAP modules, Vendor Master Data, P-card processes. Understanding of IRS 1099 reporting & processing requirements.

Responsibilities/Tasks:

--Review and verify parked invoices and submit to Accounts Payable
--Park non-P.O. invoices (check request)
--Enter invoices for goods received into SAP; code invoices for payment (park)

SAP Security Considerations:

AP	Transaction Type		
FB03	Display Document	FB04	Display Changes
FBD3	Display Recurring Entry	FBL1	
FBL1N	Display Vendor Line Item	FBL3N	Account Line Item Display
FBV2	Change Parked Document	FBV3	Display Parked Documents
FCH1	Display Check Information	FCH2	Display Payment Document checks
FCHN	Check Register	FK10N	Vendor Balance Display
FV60	Park/Edit Invoice	PV65	Park/Edit Credit Memo
MIR4	Display Invoice Document	MIR5	Display List of Invoice

Notice from the figure how this technique assigns access permissions to the role an individual plays in the organization rather than directly to the individual. Therefore, more than one individual can be assigned to a role and a predefined set of access permissions. Also, an individual may be assigned more than one role but can log into the system only under one role at a time. Thus, RBAC conveniently handles many-to-many relationships between users and permissions and facilitates dealing efficiently with vast numbers of employees.

ERPs come with predefined roles with preassigned permissions. Administrators and line managers may also create new roles, modify existing roles, and delete roles that are no longer needed. Creating a role involves defining the following role attributes:

1. A stated set of business responsibilities to be performed within the role
2. The technical competencies needed to perform the role
3. The specific transactions (permissions) required to carry out the stated responsibilities

Figure 11-9 presents a SAP role definition for an accounts payable role in a hypothetical organization. The individual(s) assigned this role is governed in his or her access to specific SAP program modules (in this case AP) and to specific activities within the module by the transaction code list in the *SAP Security Considerations* section of the role definition.

INTERNAL CONTROL ISSUES RELATED TO ERP ROLES

Although RBAC is an excellent mechanism for efficiently managing access control, the process of creating, modifying, and deleting roles is an internal control issue of concern for management and auditors alike. The following points highlight the key concerns:

1. The creation of unnecessary roles
2. The rule of least access should apply to permission assignments
3. Monitor role creation and permission-granting activities

The Creation of Unnecessary Roles

The fundamental objective of RBAC is to provide access in accordance with an organization's needs, which derive from defined tasks rather than an individual's wants. Managers in ERP environments, however, have significant discretion in creating new roles for individuals. This may be done for employees who need access to resources for special and/or one-time projects. Such access-granting authority needs to be tempered with judgment to prevent the number of roles from multiplying to the point of becoming dysfunctional and thus creating a control risk. Indeed, an oft-cited problem in ERP environments is that roles tend to proliferate to a point at which their numbers actually exceed the number of employees in the organization. Policies need to be in place to prevent the creation of unnecessary new roles and to ensure that temporary role assignments are deleted when the reason for them terminates.

The Rule of Least Access

Access privileges (permissions) should be granted on a need-to-know basis only. Nevertheless, ERP users tend to accumulate unneeded permissions over time. This is often due to two problems:

1. Managers fail to exercise adequate care in assigning permissions as part of their role-granting authority. Because managers are not always experts in internal controls, they may not recognize when excessive permissions are awarded to an individual.
2. Managers tend to be better at issuing privileges than removing them. As a result, an individual may retain unneeded access privileges from a previous job assignment that creates a segregation-of-duties violation when combined with a newly assigned role.

Policies should be in place to require managers to apply due diligence in assigning permissions to roles to avoid the granting of excessive access. They should assign privileges based on the task at hand and be aware of the individual's existing permissions that may pose a control violation.

Monitor Role Creation and Permission-Granting Activities

Effective RBAC management demands procedures that monitor role creation and permission granting to ensure compliance with internal control objectives. Verifying role compliance across all applications and users in an ERP environment, however, poses a highly complex and technical problem that does not lend itself to manual techniques. **Role-based governance** systems are available for this purpose. These systems allow managers to:

- View the current and historical inventory of roles, permissions granted, and the individuals assigned to roles.
- Identify unnecessary or inappropriate access entitlements and segregation-of-duties violations.
- Verify that changes to roles and entitlements have been successfully implemented.

These systems can continually monitor for risk and issue alerts when violations are detected so that remedial action can be taken. In addition, role-based governance can maintain an audit trail to provide a record of violations and evidence of compliance.

CONTINGENCY PLANNING

The implementation of an ERP creates an environment with a single point of failure, which places the organization at risk from equipment failure, sabotage, or natural disaster. To control this risk, an organization needs an effective contingency plan that can be invoked quickly in the event of a disaster. Two general approaches are outlined next, but a more extensive discussion is presented in Chapter 15 within the broader context of IT governance.

Centralized organizations with highly integrated business units may need a single global ERP system that is accessed via the Internet or private lines from around the world to consolidate data from subsidiary systems. A server failure under this model could leave the entire organization unable to process transactions. To control this, two linked servers may be connected in redundant backup mode. All production processing is done on one server. If it fails, processing is automatically transferred to the other server. Organizations that want more security and resilience may arrange servers in a cluster of three or more that dynamically share the workload. Processing can be redistributed if one or more of the servers in the cluster fail.

Companies whose organizational units are autonomous and do not share common customers, suppliers, or product lines often choose to install regional servers. This approach permits independent processing and spreads the risk associated with server failure. For example, BP Amoco implemented SAP's R/3 into 17 separate business groups.

Summary

This chapter opened by comparing the function and data storage techniques of a traditional flat file or database system with that of an ERP. An important distinction was drawn between OLTP and OLAP applications. Similarly, the differences between the ERP's operational database and the data warehouse were discussed. Next, ERP configurations were examined relating to servers, databases, and bolt-on software. We discussed SCM as an area of contention. ERP vendors are moving quickly to provide SCM functionality. Simultaneously, SCM vendors are encroaching on traditional ERP territory. Data warehousing was the topic of the third section. A data warehouse is a relational or multidimensional database that supports OLAP. A number of data warehouse issues were discussed, including data modeling, data extraction from operational databases, data cleansing, data transformation, and data loading into the warehouse.

The fourth section examined common risks associated with ERP implementation. Among these are the risks associated with the big bang approach, internal opposition to changing the way a company does its business, choosing the wrong ERP model, choosing the wrong consultant, cost overrun issues, and disruptions to operations. Also presented were a number of issues to consider when implementing an ERP. These include selecting a system that is a good fit for the organization, understanding that the term *scalability* can mean different things to different people, potential problems associated with customizing the software, the need for assigning performance measures, and the need to control outside consultants. The chapter concluded with a review of the internal control and auditing issues related to ERPs.

Key Terms

access control list (491)
big bang (485)
bolt-on software (478)
changed data capture (480)
client-server model (474)
closed database architecture (472)
consolidation (477)
core applications (473)
data mart (479)
data warehouse (474)
drill-down (477)
enterprise resource planning (ERP) (471)
online analytical processing (OLAP) (474)
online transaction processing (OLTP) (473)
phased-in (485)
role (491)
role-based access control (RBAC) (491)
role-based governance (493)
scalability (486)
slicing and dicing (477)
supply chain management (SCM) (478)
three-tier model (475)
two-tier model (474)

Review Questions

1. Define ERP.
2. What is closed database architecture?
3. Define *core applications*, and give some examples.
4. Define OLAP, and give some examples.

5. What is the client-server model?
6. Describe the two-tier client-server model.
7. Describe the three-tier client-server model.
8. What is bolt-on software?
9. What is SCM software?
10. What is changed data capture?
11. What is a data warehouse?
12. What is data mining?
13. What does *data cleansing* mean?
14. Why are denormalized tables used in data warehouses?
15. What is the drill-down approach?
16. What is the big bang approach?
17. What is scalability?
18. What is a role?
19. What is an access control list?
20. How is the access control list approach different from RBAC?
21. What is the OLAP operation of consolidation?
22. What is the OLAP operation of drill-down?
23. What is meant by the term *slicing and dicing?*

Discussion Questions

1. How are OLTP and OLAP different? Provide some examples to explain.
2. Distinguish between the two-tier and three-tier client-server models. Describe when each would be used.
3. Why do ERP systems need bolt-on software? Give an example of bolt-on software.
4. Your organization is considering acquiring bolt-on software for your ERP system. What approaches are open to you?
5. Explain why the data warehouse needs to be separate from the operational database.
6. Data in a data warehouse are in a stable state. Explain how this can hamper data mining analysis. What can an organization do to alleviate this problem?
7. This chapter stressed the importance of data normalization when constructing a relational database. Why, then, is it important to denormalize data in a data warehouse?
8. What problems does the data cleansing step attempt to resolve?
9. How are the summary views in a data warehouse different from views in an operational database?
10. Would drill-down be an effective audit tool for identifying an unusual business relationship between a purchasing agent and suppliers in a large organization with several hundred suppliers? Explain.
11. Disruptions to operations are a common side effect of implementing an ERP. Explain the primary reason for this.
12. ERP systems use the best-practices approach in designing their applications, yet goodness of fit is considered to be an important issue when selecting an ERP. Shouldn't the client just be able to use whatever applications the ERP system provides?
13. Explain the issues of size, speed, workload, and transaction as they relate to scalability.
14. Explain how SAP uses roles as a way to improve internal control.
15. How would you deal with the problem of file-server backup in a highly centralized organization?
16. How would you deal with the problem of file-server backup in a decentralized organization with autonomous divisions that do not share common operational data?
17. Distinguish between the OLAP operations of consolidation and drill-down.
18. When would slicing and dicing be an appropriate OLAP tool? Give an example.
19. Explain the risks associated with the creation of unnecessary roles and why it can happen.
20. What is the fundamental concept behind the rule of least access? Explain why this is a potential problem in an ERP environment.
21. What is the purpose of role-based governance software?

Multiple-Choice Questions

1. Closed database architecture is
   a. a control technique intended to prevent unauthorized access by trading partners.
   b. a limitation inherent in traditional information systems that prevents data sharing.
   c. a data warehouse control that prevents unclean data from entering the warehouse.
   d. a technique used to restrict access to data marts.
   e. a database structure that many of the leading ERPs use to support OLTP applications.
2. Each of the following is a necessary element for the successful warehousing of data EXCEPT
   a. cleansing extracted data.
   b. transforming data.
   c. modeling data.
   d. loading data.
   e. all of the above are necessary.
3. Which of the following is typically NOT part of an ERP's OLAP applications?
   a. decision support systems
   b. information retrieval
   c. ad hoc reporting/analysis
   d. logistics
   e. what-if analysis
4. There are a number of risks that may be associated with ERP implementation. Which of the following was NOT stated as a risk in the chapter?
   a. A drop in firm performance after implementation because the firm looks and works differently than it did while using a legacy system.
   b. Implementing companies have found that staff members, employed by ERP consulting firms, do not have sufficient experience in implementing new systems.
   c. Implementing firms fail to select systems that properly support their business activities.
   d. The selected system does not adequately meet the adopting firm's economic growth.
   e. ERPs are too large, complex, and generic for them to be well integrated into most company cultures.
5. Which statement is NOT true?
   a. In a typical two-tier, client-server architecture, the server handles both application and database duties.
   b. Client computers are responsible for presenting data to the user and passing user input back to the server.
   c. Two-tier architecture is for local area network applications where the demand on the server is restricted to a relatively small population of users.
   d. The database and application functions are separated in the three-tier model.
   e. In three-tier client-server architectures, one tier is for user presentation, one is for database and applications access, and the third is for Internet access.
6. Which statement is NOT true?
   a. Drill-down capability is an OLAP feature of data mining tools available to the user.
   b. The data warehouse should be separate from operational systems.
   c. Denormalization of data involves dividing the data into very small tables that support detailed analysis.
   d. Some decisions supported by a data warehouse are not fundamentally different from those that are supported by traditional databases.
   e. Data cleansing involves transforming data into standard business terms with standard data values.
7. Which statement is LEAST accurate?
   a. Implementing an ERP system has more to do with changing the way an organization does business than it does with technology.
   b. The phased-in approach to ERP implementation is particularly suited to diversified organizations whose units do not share common processes and data.
   c. Because the primary reason for implementing an ERP is to standardize and integrate operations, diversified organizations whose units do not share common processes and data do not benefit and tend not to implement ERPs.
   d. To take full advantage of the ERP process, reengineering will need to occur.
   e. A common reason for ERP failure is that the ERP does not support one or more important business processes of the organization.
8. Which of the following is not a typical core application in an ERP system?
   a. Sales and distribution
   b. business planning

c. production planning
d. On-line analytical processing (OLAP)
e. Logistics

9. Auditors of ERP systems
   a. need not be concerned about segregation of duties because these systems possess strong computer controls.
   b. focus on output controls such as independent verification to reconcile batch totals.
   c. are concerned that managers fail to exercise adequate care in assigning permissions.
   d. do not see the data warehouse as an audit or control issue at all because financial records are not stored there.
   e. need not review access levels granted to users because these are determined when the system is configured and never change.

10. Which statement below is correct?
   a. Only one individual can be assigned to a role.
   b. A role is a formal technique for grouping together users according to the system resources they need to perform their assigned tasks.
   c. RBAC assigns specific access privileges to individuals.
   d. Because of the use of roles, access security concerns are essentially eliminated in ERP environments.
   e. None of the above is correct.

Problems

1. DATA WAREHOUSE ACCESS CONTROL

You are the CEO of a large organization that implemented a data warehouse for internal analysis of corporate data. The operations manager has written you a memo advocating opening the data warehouse to your suppliers and customers. Explain any merit to this proposal. What are the control issues, if any?

2. PROJECT IMPLEMENTATION

Your organization is planning to implement an ERP system. Some managers in the organization favor the big bang approach. Others are advocating a phased-in approach. The CEO has asked you, as project leader, to write a memo summarizing the advantages and disadvantages of each approach and to make a recommendation. This is a traditional organization with a strong internal hierarchy. The company was acquired in a merger two years ago, and the ERP project is an effort on the part of the parent company to standardize business processes and reporting across the organization. Prior to this, the organization had been using a general ledger package that it acquired in 1979. Most of the transaction processing is a combination of manual and batch processing. Most employees think that the legacy system works well. At this point, the implementation project is behind schedule.

3. OLTP VERSUS OLAP SERVERS

For each of the following processes, state whether OLTP or OLAP is appropriate, and why.

a. An order entry system that retrieves customer information, invoice information, and inventory information for local sales.
b. An order entry system that retrieves customer information, invoice information, inventory information, and several years of sales information about both the customer and the inventory items.
c. An order entry system that retrieves customer information, invoice information, inventory information, and information to compare the current sale to sales across several geographic regions.
d. An order entry system that retrieves customer information, invoice information, inventory information, and accounts receivable information for sales within one marketing region.
e. An insurance company requires a system that will allow it to determine total claims by region, whether a relationship exists between claims and meteorological phenomena, and why one region seems to be more profitable than another.
f. A manufacturing company has only one factory, but that factory employs several thousand people and has nearly $1 billion in revenue each year. The company has seen no reason to make comparisons about its operations from year to year or from process to process. Its information needs

focus primarily on operations, but it has maintained backup of prior-year operations activities. Examination of prior-year financial reports has shown that the company, while profitable, is not growing, and return on investment is decreasing. The owners are not satisfied with this situation.

4. SELECTING A CONSULTANT

You are the chief information officer for a midsized organization that has decided to implement an ERP system. The CEO has met with a consulting ERP firm based on a recommendation from a personal friend at his club. At the interview, the president of the consulting firm introduced the chief consultant, who was charming, was personable, and seemed very knowledgeable. The CEO's first instinct was to sign a contract with the consultant, but he decided to hold off until he had received your input.

Required

Write a memo to the CEO presenting the issues and the risks associated with consultants. Also, outline a set of procedures that could be used as a guide in selecting a consultant.

5. AUDITING ERP DATABASES

You are an independent auditor attending an engagement interview with the client. The client's organization has recently implemented a data warehouse. Management is concerned that the audit tests that you perform will disrupt operations and suggests that instead of running tests against the live operational database, you draw the data for your analytical reviews and substantive tests of details from the data warehouse. Management points out that operational data are copied weekly into the warehouse and everything you need is contained there. This will enable you to perform your tests without disrupting routine operations. You agree to give this some thought and get back to the client with your answer.

Required

Draft a memo to the client outlining your response to the client's proposal. Mention any concerns you might have.

6. BIG BANG VERSUS PHASED-IN APPROACH

The Nevada Department of Motor Vehicles (DMV) is the agency responsible for licensing both drivers and vehicles in the state of Nevada. Until recently, legacy systems were used for both licensing needs. The legacy system for drivers' licenses maintained the following information about each licensed driver: name, age, address, violation, license classification, organ donation, and restrictions. The vehicle licensing system maintained information about each vehicle, including cost, taxes, vehicle identification number (VIN), weight, insurance, and ownership. In the summer of 1999, over a three-day weekend, information from the two legacy systems was transferred to a new ERP. The ERP and all new hardware were installed in every DMV across the state, and when employees returned from their long weekend, an entirely new system was in place.

The DMV employees were not well trained on the new system, and the system itself presented a few bugs. As a result of these obstacles, customers at the DMV faced excessively long lines and extended waiting times, and several of the employees simply quit their jobs because of frustrations with the system and difficulty dealing with irate customers. Knowing that the waiting times were so long, many drivers simply refused to renew licenses or obtain new licenses.

Assume that the ERP the DMV management selected was correctly configured and was capable of meeting all requirements of the DMV; consider data warehousing implications, business culture implications, and disruption to operations; and discuss the advantages and disadvantages associated with the decision to implement the new system using the big bang approach versus the phased-in approach.

7. ERP FAILURE

When an ERP implementation fails, who is to blame? Is it the software manufacturer, the client firm, or the implementation strategy?

Required

Research this issue and write a brief paper outlining the key issues.

8. ERP MARKET GROWTH

Because many large corporations implemented ERP systems prior to 2000, what direction will growth of the ERP market take?

Required

Research this issue and write a brief paper outlining the key issues.

9. ERP CONSULTANTS

Do an Internet search of complaints about ERP consultants. Write a report about the most common complaints, and cite examples.

10. ERP BOLT-ON SOFTWARE

Go to 10 websites of companies that supply bolt-on software. Write a report containing URLs that briefly describe the software features and its compatibility with specific ERP systems.

Electronic Commerce Systems

CHAPTER 12

Learning Objectives

After studying this chapter, you should:

- Be acquainted with the topologies that are employed to achieve connectivity across the Internet.
- Possess a conceptual appreciation of protocols and understand the specific purposes that several Internet protocols serve.
- Understand the business benefits associated with Internet commerce and be aware of several Internet business models.
- Be familiar with the risks associated with intranet and Internet electronic commerce.
- Understand issues of security, assurance, and trust pertaining to electronic commerce.
- Be familiar with the electronic commerce implications for the accounting profession.

Upon hearing the term *electronic commerce*, many people think of browsing an electronic catalog on the web or going Internet shopping at a virtual mall. This may be the predominant component of electronic commerce, but it is not the entire story.

Electronic commerce involves the electronic processing and transmission of data. This broad definition encompasses many diverse activities, including the electronic buying and selling of goods and services, online delivery of digital products, electronic funds transfer (EFT), electronic trading of stocks, and direct consumer marketing. Electronic commerce is not an entirely new phenomenon; many companies have engaged in electronic data interchange (EDI) over private networks for decades.

Driven by the Internet revolution, however, electronic commerce has dramatically expanded and undergone radical changes in recent years. This fast-moving environment has engendered an array of innovative markets and trading communities. While electronic commerce promises enormous opportunities for consumers and businesses, its effective implementation and control are urgent challenges facing organization management and accountants.

To properly evaluate the potential exposures and risks in this environment, the modern accountant must be familiar with the technologies and techniques that underlie electronic commerce. Hardware failures, software errors, and unauthorized access from remote locations can expose the organization's accounting system to specific threats. For example, transactions can be lost in transit and never processed, digitally altered to change their financial effect, corrupted by transient signals on transmission lines, and diverted to or initiated by the perpetrator of a fraud.

In this chapter and its appendix, we consider five aspects of electronic commerce: (1) Intra-organizational Networks and EDI, (2) Internet Commerce, (3) Risks Associated with

Electronic Commerce, (4) Security, Assurance, and Trust, and (5) Implications for the Accounting Profession. We examine the technologies, topologies, and applications of electronic commerce in each of these areas.

Intra-organizational Networks and EDI

Local area networks (LANs), wide area networks (WANs), and EDI are electronic commerce technologies that have been with us for decades. As such, these topics are frequently found among the subject matter of introductory information technology courses. Because many accounting and information systems students become familiar with these topics before taking an AIS course, this material is covered in the chapter's appendix. The body of the chapter focuses on the salient issues pertaining to Internet-based electronic commerce. Students who have not been exposed to network and EDI topologies and technologies, however, should review the appendix before proceeding, because the treatment in the chapter presumes this background.

Internet Commerce

Internet commerce has enabled thousands of business enterprises of all sizes, as well as millions of consumers, to congregate and interact in a worldwide virtual shopping mall. Along with enormous opportunities, however, the electronic marketplace has engendered unique risks. This section of the chapter examines the technologies, benefits, risks, and security issues associated with Internet commerce.

INTERNET TECHNOLOGIES

The Internet was originally developed for the U.S. military and later became used widely for academic and government research. Over recent years, it has evolved into a worldwide information highway. This growth is attributed to three factors. First, in 1995, national commercial telecommunications companies, such as MCI, Sprint, and UUNET, took control of the backbone elements of the Internet, and they have continued to enhance their infrastructures. Large Internet service providers (ISPs) can link into these backbones to connect their subscribers, and smaller ISPs can connect directly to the national backbones or into one of the larger ISPs. Second, online services like CompuServe and America Online connect to the Internet for e-mail, which enables users of different services to communicate with each other. Third, the development of graphics-based web browsers, such as Microsoft's Internet Explorer, has made accessing the Internet a simple task. The Internet thus became the domain of everyday people with personal computers rather than just scientists and computer hackers. As a result, the web has grown exponentially and continues to grow daily.

Packet Switching

The Internet employs communications technologies based on **packet switching.** Figure 12-1 illustrates this technique, whereby messages are divided into small packets for transmission. Individual packets of the same message may take different routes to their destinations. Each packet contains address and sequencing codes so they can be reassembled into the original complete message at the receiving end. The choice of transmission path is determined according to criteria that achieve optimum utilization of the long-distance lines, including the degree of traffic congestion on the line, the shortest path between the end points, and the line status of the path (that is, working, failed, or experiencing errors). Network switches provide a physical connection for the addressed packets only for the duration of the message; the line then becomes available to other users. The first international standard for wide area packet switching networks was X.25, which was defined when all circuits were analog and very susceptible to noise. Subsequent packet technologies, such as frame relay and SMDS (switched multimegabit data service), were designed for today's almost error-free digital lines.

FIGURE 12-1 MESSAGE PACKET SWITCHING

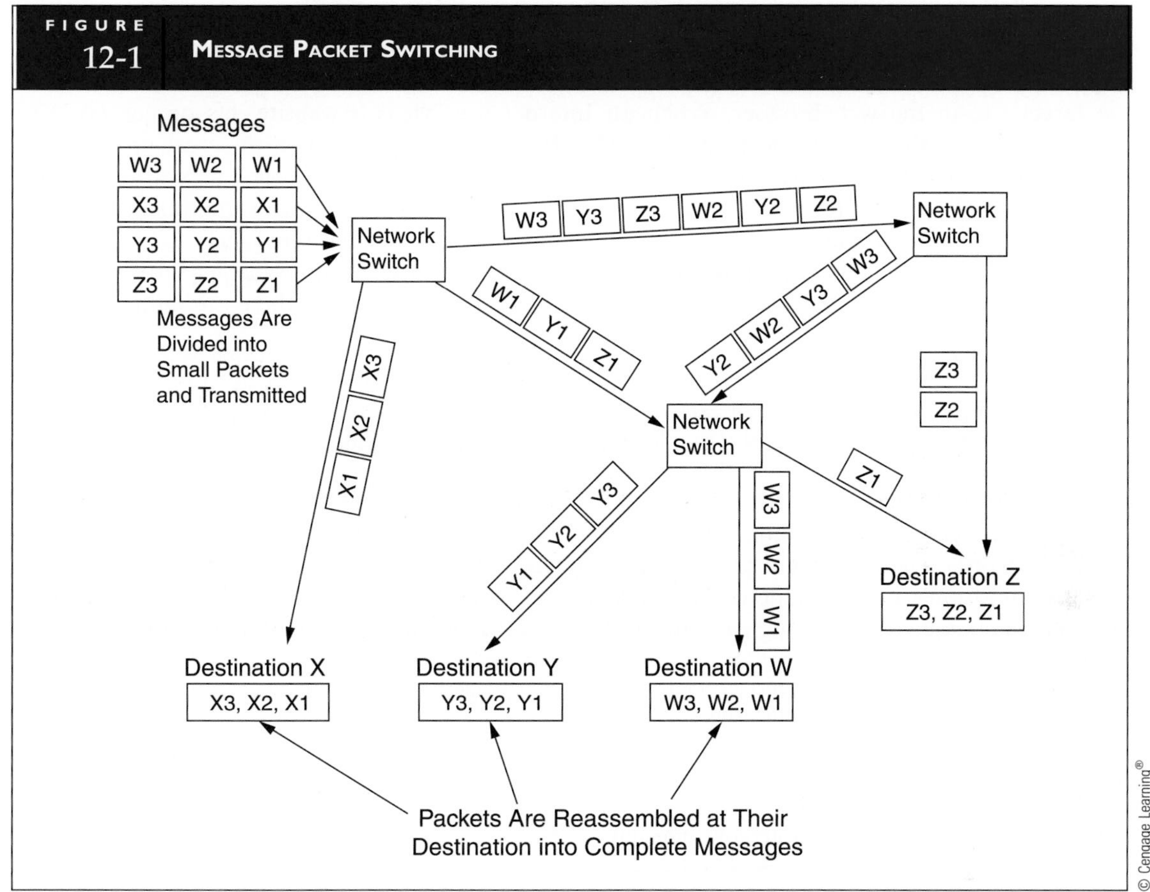

Virtual Private Networks

A **virtual private network (VPN)** is a private network within a public network. For years, common carriers have built VPNs, which are private from the client's perspective, but physically share backbone trunks with other users. VPNs have been built on X.25 and frame-relay technologies. Today, Internet-based VPNs are of great interest. Maintaining security and privacy in this setting, however, requires encryption and authentication controls discussed later in the chapter.

Extranets

Another variant on Internet technology is the **extranet.** This is a password-controlled network for private users rather than the general public. Extranets are used to provide access between trading partner internal databases. Internet sites containing information intended for private consumption frequently use an extranet configuration.

World Wide Web

The World Wide Web (web) is an Internet facility that links user sites locally and around the world. In 1989, Tim Berners-Lee of the European Center for Nuclear Research in Geneva developed the web as a means of sharing nuclear research information over the Internet. The fundamental format for the web is a text document called a **web page** that has embedded **Hyper Text Markup Language (HTML)** codes that provide the formatting for the page as well as hypertext links to other pages. The linked pages may be stored on the same server or anywhere in the world. HTML codes are simple alphanumeric characters that can be typed with a text editor or word processor. Most word processors support web publishing features that allow text documents to be converted to HTML format.

Web pages are maintained at **websites**, which are computer servers that support **Hyper Text Transfer Protocol (HTTP).** The pages are accessed and read via a web browser such as Internet Explorer. To access a website, the user enters the **Uniform Resource Locator (URL)** address of the target site in the web browser. When an Internet user visits a website, his or her point of entry is typically the site's **home page.** This HTML document serves as a directory to the site's contents and other pages. Through browsers, the web provides point-and-click access to the largest collection of online information in the world. The web has also become a multimedia delivery system that supports audio, video, videoconferencing, and three-dimensional animation. The ease of web page creation and navigation via browsers has driven the unprecedented growth of the web. In 1994, there were approximately 500 websites in the world; today there are millions.

Internet Addresses

The Internet uses three types of addresses for communications: (1) e-mail addresses, (2) website URL addresses, and (3) Internet protocol (IP) addresses of individual computers attached to a network.

E-MAIL ADDRESS. The format for an e-mail address is USER NAME@DOMAIN NAME. For example, the address of the author of this textbook isjahO@lehigh.edu. There are no spaces between any of the words. The user name (or in this case, the user identification [ID]) is jahO. A domain name is an organization's unique name combined with a top-level domain (TLD) name. In the previous example, the unique name is lehigh and the TLD is edu. Following are examples of TLD names:

.net	network provider
.org	nonprofit organization
.edu	education and research
.gov	government
.mil	military agency
.int	international/intergovernmental

Outside the United States, the TLD names consist of the country code, such as .uk for the United Kingdom and .es for Spain. The Internet Ad Hoc Committee has introduced a category called a generic top-level domain, which includes the following:

.firm	a business
.store	goods for sale
.web	WWW activities
.arts	culture/entertainment
.rec	recreation/entertainment
.info	information service
.nom	individual/personal

The Internet e-mail addressing system allows the user to send e-mail directly to the mailboxes of users of all major online services.

URL ADDRESS. The URL is the address that defines the path to a facility or file on the Web. URLs are typed into the browser to access website home pages and individual web pages, and they can be embedded in web pages to provide hypertext links to other pages. The general format for a URL is **protocol prefix, domain name, subdirectory name**, and **document name.** The entire URL is not always needed. For example, to access the South-Western Publishing home page, only the following protocol and domain name are required:

http://www.cengage.com/accounting/hall

The protocol prefix is http:// and the domain name is www.cengage.com/accounting/hall. From this home page, the user can activate hyperlinks to other pages as desired. The user can go directly to a linked page by providing the complete address and separating the address components with slashes. For example,

http://www.cengage.com/accounting/hall

Subdirectories can be several levels deep. To reference them, each must be separated with a slash. For example, the elements of the following URL for a hypothetical sporting goods company are described next.

http://www.flyfish.com/equipment/rods/brand_name.html

http://	protocol prefix (most browsers default to HTTP if a prefix is not typed)
www.flyfish.com/	domain name
equipment/	subdirectory name
rods/	subdirectory name
brand_name.html	document name (web page)

IP ADDRESS. Every computer node and host attached to the Internet must have a unique Internet Protocol (IP) address. For a message to be sent, the IP addresses of both the sending and the recipient nodes must be provided. Currently, IP addresses are represented by a 32-bit data packet. The general format is four sets of numbers separated by periods. The decomposition of the code into its component parts varies depending on the class to which it is assigned. Class A, class B, and class C coding schemes are used for large, medium, and small networks, respectively. To illustrate the coding technique, the IP address 128.180.94.109 translates into:

128.180	Lehigh University
94	Business Department faculty server
109	A faculty member's office computer (node)

PROTOCOLS

The word **protocol** has been used several times in this section. Let's now take a closer look at the meaning of this term. Protocols are the rules and standards governing the design of hardware and software that permit users of networks, which different vendors have manufactured, to communicate and share data. The general acceptance of protocols within the network community provides both standards and economic incentives for the manufacturers of hardware and software. Products that do not comply with prevailing protocols will have little value to prospective customers.

The data communications industry borrowed the term *protocol* from the diplomatic community. Diplomatic protocols define the rules by which the representatives of nations communicate and collaborate during social and official functions. These formal rules of conduct are intended to avoid international problems that could arise through the misinterpretation of ambiguous signals passed between diplomatic counterparts. The greatest potential for error naturally exists between nations with vastly dissimilar cultures and conventions for behavior. Establishing a standard of conduct through protocols, which all members of the diplomatic community understand and practice, minimizes the risk of miscommunications between nations of different cultures.

An analogy may be drawn to data communications. A communications network is a community of computer users who also must establish and maintain unambiguous lines of communication. If all network members had homogeneous needs and operated identical systems, this would not be much of a problem; however, networks are characterized by heterogeneous systems components. Typically, network users employ hardware devices (PC, printers, monitors, data storage devices, modems, and so on) and software (user applications, network control programs, and operating systems) that a variety of vendors produce. Passing messages effectively from device to device in such a multivendor environment requires ground rules or protocols.

What Functions Do Protocols Perform?

Protocols serve several network functions. First, they facilitate the physical connection between the network devices. Through protocols, devices are able to identify themselves to other devices as legitimate network entities and initiate (or terminate) a communications session.

Second, protocols synchronize the transfer of data between physical devices. This involves defining the rules for initiating a message, determining the data transfer rate between devices, and acknowledging message receipt.

Third, protocols provide a basis for error checking and measuring network performance. This is done by comparing measured results against expectations. For example, performance measures pertaining to storage device access times, data transmission rates, and modulation frequencies are critical to controlling the network's function. Thus, the identification and correction of errors depend on protocol standards that define acceptable performance.

Fourth, protocols promote compatibility among network devices. To transmit and receive data successfully, the various devices involved in a particular session must conform to a mutually acceptable mode of operation, such as synchronous, asynchronous and duplex, or half-duplex. Without protocols to provide such conformity, messages sent between devices would be distorted and garbled.

Finally, protocols promote network designs that are flexible, expandable, and cost effective. Users are free to change and enhance their systems by selecting from the best offerings of a variety of vendors. Manufacturers must, of course, construct these products in accordance with established protocols.

The Layered Approach to Network Protocol

The first networks used several different protocols that emerged in a rather haphazard manner. These protocols often provided poor interfaces between devices that actually resulted in incompatibilities. Also, early protocols were structured and inflexible, thus limiting network growth by making system changes difficult. A change in the architecture at a node on the network could have an unpredictable effect on an unrelated device at another node. Technical problems such as these can translate into unrecorded transactions, destroyed audit trails, and corrupted databases. Out of this situation emerged the contemporary model of layered protocols. The purpose of a layered-protocol model is to create a modular environment that reduces complexity and permits changes to one layer without adversely affecting another.

The data communication community, through the **International Standards Organization**,[1] has developed a layered set of protocols called the **Open System Interface (OSI).** The OSI model provides standards by which the products of different manufacturers can interface with one another in a seamless interconnection at the user level. This seven-layer protocol model is discussed in detail in the appendix.

INTERNET PROTOCOLS

Transfer Control Protocol/Internet Protocol (TCP/IP) is the basic protocol that permits communication between Internet sites. It was invented by Vinton Cerf and Bob Kah under contract from the U.S. Department of Defense to network dissimilar systems. This protocol controls how individual packets of data are formatted, transmitted, and received. This is known as a reliable protocol because delivery of all the packets to a destination is guaranteed. If delivery is interrupted by hardware or software failure, the packets are automatically retransmitted.

The TCP portion of the protocol ensures that the total number of data bytes transmitted was received. The IP component provides the routing mechanism. Every server and computer in a TCP/IP network requires an IP address, which is either permanently assigned or dynamically assigned at start-up. The IP part of the TCP/IP protocol contains a network address that is used to route messages to different networks.

Although TCP/IP is the fundamental communications protocol for the Internet, the following are some of the more common protocols that are used for specific tasks.

File Transfer Protocols

File Transfer Protocol (FTP) is used to transfer text files, programs, spreadsheets, and databases across the Internet. **TELNET** is a terminal emulation protocol used on TCP/IP-based networks.

---

1 The International Standards Organization (ISO) is a voluntary group comprising representatives from the national standards organizations of its member countries. The ISO works toward the establishment of international standards for data encryption, data communication, and protocols.

It allows users to run programs and review data from a remote terminal or computer. TELNET is an inherent part of the TCP/IP communications protocol. While both protocols deal with data transfer, FTP is useful for downloading entire files from the Internet; TELNET is useful for perusing a file of data as if the user were actually at the remote site.

Mail Protocols

Simple Network Mail Protocol (SNMP) is the most popular protocol for transmitting e-mail messages. Other e-mail protocols are **Post Office Protocol** and **Internet Message Access Protocol.**

Security Protocols

Secure Sockets Layer (SSL) is a low-level encryption scheme used to secure transmissions in higher-level HTTP format. **Private Communications Technology (PCT)** is a security protocol that provides secure transactions over the web. PCT encrypts and decrypts a message for transmission. Most web browsers and servers support PCT and other popular security protocols, such as SSL. **Secure Electronic Transmission** is an encryption scheme developed by a consortium of technology firms and banks (Netscape, Microsoft, IBM, Visa, MasterCard, and so on) to secure credit card transactions. Customers making credit card purchases over the Internet transmit their encrypted credit card number to the merchant, who then transmits the number to the bank. The bank returns an encrypted acknowledgment to the merchant. The customer need not worry about an unscrupulous merchant decrypting the customer's credit card number and misusing the information. **Privacy Enhanced Mail (PEM)** is a standard for secure e-mail on the Internet. It supports encryption, digital signatures, and digital certificates as well as both private and public key methods (which will be discussed later).

Network News Transfer Protocol

Network News Transfer Protocol (NNTP) is used to connect to Usenet groups on the Internet. Usenet newsreader software supports the NNTP protocol.

HTTP and HTTP-NG

HTTP controls web browsers that access the web. When the user clicks on a link to a web page, a connection is established and the web page is displayed, and then the connection is broken. **HyperText Transport Protocol-Next Generation (HTTP-NG)** is an enhanced version of the HTTP protocol that maintains the simplicity of HTTP while adding important features such as security and authentication.

HTML

HyperText Markup Language (HTML) is the document format used to produce web pages. HTML defines the page layout, fonts, and graphic elements as well as hypertext links to other documents on the web. HTML is used to lay out information for display in an appealing manner, such as one sees in magazines and newspapers. The ability to lay out text and graphics (including pictures) is important in terms of appeal to users in general. Even more pertinent is HTML's support for hypertext links in text and graphics that enable the reader to virtually jump to another document located anywhere on the World Wide Web.

Advances in Internet technology and connectivity have moved corporations toward disclosure of corporate financial information in a form compatible with standard web-browsing tools. In this way, investors and analysts may have access to current corporate information. Dissemination of HTML-based financial reports, however, is limited to presentation only. If the receiving organization wishes to perform computer analysis on this information, such as comparing performance of several corporations within an industry, it must manually enter the financial data into its system for processing. Unlike XML and XBRL (discussed in Chapter 8), HTML does not support the exchange of information in a relational form that can be automatically imported into the receiving organization's internal database and analyzed.

INTERNET BUSINESS MODELS

Virtually all businesses engage in some form of Internet commerce to achieve one or more of the following benefits:

- Access to a worldwide customer and/or supplier base.
- Reductions in inventory investment and carrying costs.
- The rapid creation of business partnerships to fill market niches as they emerge.
- Reductions in retail prices through lower marketing costs.
- Reductions in procurement costs.
- Better customer service.

The actual benefits attained depend upon the degree of organizational commitment to an Internet business strategy. The following section describes three levels of Internet activity.

INFORMATION LEVEL. At the **information level** of activity, an organization uses the Internet to display information about the company, its products, services, and business policies. This level involves little more than creating a website, and it is the first step taken by most firms entering the Internet marketplace. When customers access the website, they generally first visit the home page. This is an index to the site's contents through other web pages. Large organizations often create and manage their websites internally. Smaller companies have their sites hosted on servers maintained by an ISP.

TRANSACTION LEVEL. Organizations involved at the **transaction level** use the Internet to accept orders from customers and/or to place them with their suppliers. This involves engaging in business activities with total strangers from remote parts of the world. These may be customers, suppliers, or potential trading partners. Many of the risks that are discussed later in the chapter relate to this (and to the next) level of electronic commerce. Success in this domain involves creating an environment of trust by resolving the key concerns listed below:

- Ensure that data used in the transaction are protected from misuse.
- Verify the accuracy and integrity of business processes used by the potential customer, partner, or supplier.
- Verify the identity and physical existence of the potential customer, partner, or supplier.
- Ascertain the reputation of the potential customer, partner, or supplier.

DISTRIBUTION LEVEL. Organizations operating on the **distribution level** use the Internet to sell and deliver digital products to customers. These include subscriptions to online news services, software products and upgrades, and music and video products. In addition to these traditional consumer products, recent years have seen rapid growth in the sale and distribution of an array of computing services to business entities that are collectively referred to as **cloud computing.** Key elements of this concept are presented in the next section.

CLOUD COMPUTING

A number of definitions exist for cloud computing. This section is based on the following one:

> *Cloud computing is a model for enabling convenient, on-demand network access to a shared pool of configurable computing resources (e.g., networks, servers, storage, applications, and services) that can be rapidly provisioned and released with minimal management effort or service provider interaction.*[2]

---

2 The NIST Definition of Cloud Computing, Peter Mell and Tim Grance, 10-7-09, http://csrc.nist.gov/groups/SNS/cloud-computing/index.html

The key features of cloud computing implied by this definition are:

- Client firms can acquire IT resources from vendors on demand and as needed. This is in contrast to the traditional IT outsourcing model (see Chapter 15) in which resources are provided to client firms in strict accordance with long-term contracts that stipulate services and time frames.
- Resources are provided over a network (private or Internet) and accessed through network terminals at the client location.
- Acquisition of resources is rapid and infinitely scalable. A client can expand and contract the service demanded almost instantly and often automatically.
- Computing resources are pooled to meet the needs of multiple client firms. A consequence of this, however, is that an individual client has no control over, or knowledge of, the physical location of the service being provided.

Cloud computing offers three primary classes of computing services. These are: *Software-as-a-Service (SaaS), Infrastructure-as-a-Service (IaaS)*, and *Platform-as-a-Service (PaaS)*.

Software-as-a-Service (SaaS)is a software distribution model in which service providers host applications for client organizations over a private network or the Internet. The 1990s saw the emergence of business software hosting organizations called Application Service Providers (ASP). SaaS is an extension of this concept. A key difference is the nature of the software product being hosted. ASPs typically host the software of third-party software vendors, which is configured to the unique needs of the client organization and requires installation of software on the client's in-house computers. SaaS vendors typically develop and manage their own web-based software, which is general purpose, designed to serve multiple businesses and users, and requires only an Internet connection to access.

Another difference between ASP and SaaS is the licensing and payment model used. ASP contracts are typically fixed-period or one-time licensing agreements. SaaS vendors often employ a subscription model in which clients pay as they go based on usage. SaaS applications may be acquired directly from the vendors or from third-party consolidators who bundle various SaaS products and offer them as a suite of resources.

Infrastructure-as-a-Service (IaaS) is the provision of computing power and disk space to client firms who access it from desktop PCs. The client firm can configure the infrastructure for storage, networks, and other computing needs, including running operating systems and data processing applications. The advantage to the client is that the IaaS provider owns, houses, and maintains the equipment, and the client pays for it on a per-use basis. Another advantage is scalability, which is the ability to rapidly respond to usage changes. IaaS providers, such as Amazon Web Services (AWS), offer infrastructure capacity that can grow and contract almost instantly with an organization's shifts in demand.

Platform-as-a-Service (PaaS) enables client firms to develop and deploy onto the cloud infrastructure consumer-generated applications using facilities provided by the PaaS vendor. PaaS tools include facilities for application development, program testing, program implementation, system documentation, and security. The advantage to the client organization is that it can, with limited internal expertise, rapidly build and deploy web applications.

Virtualization

The technology that has unleashed cloud computing is **virtualization.** In the traditional (nonvirtual) computing environment, a single computer runs a single operating system and a single real-time application. This results in considerable unused physical hardware capacity. Virtualization multiplies the effectiveness of the physical system by creating virtual (software) versions of the computer with separate operating systems that reside in the same physical equipment. In other words, virtualization is the concept of running more than one "virtual computer" on a single physical computer. Since each virtual system runs its own application, total computing power is multiplied with no additional hardware investment.

In addition to virtual computers, virtualization has exploded into two other areas of IT that have enabled the concept of cloud computing to gain traction in recent years: *network virtualization* and *storage virtualization*.

Network virtualization increases effective network bandwidth by dividing it into independent channels, which are then assigned to separate virtual computers. Network virtualization optimizes network speed, flexibility, and reliability; most importantly, it improves network scalability. Network virtualization is especially effective in networks that experience sudden, large, and unforeseen surges in usage.

Storage virtualization is the pooling of physical storage from multiple network storage devices into what appears to be a single virtual storage device. This pool is then managed from a central server. Storage virtualization increases storage capacity utilization by allowing multiple servers to consolidate their private data onto an array of disks. Storage virtualization accelerates data access and dynamically expands storage capacity as demand increases.

Cloud Computing Implementation Issues

In spite of its convenience and potential for cost savings, cloud computing is not a realistic option for all companies. For smaller businesses, startup companies, and some new applications, the cloud concept is a promising alternative to in-house computing. The information needs of large companies, however, are often in conflict with the cloud solution for the following three reasons.

- First, large firms have typically already incurred massive investments in equipment, proprietary software, and human resources. These organizations are not inclined to walk away from their investments and turn over their entire IT operations to a cloud vendor.
- Second, many large enterprises have mission-critical functions running on legacy systems that are many decades old. These systems continue to exist because they continue to add value. The task of migrating legacy systems to the cloud would require new architectures and considerable reprogramming. Given their typically high utilization, performance, and throughput, the cost/benefit of the cloud alternative is debatable.
- Third, a central tenant of cloud computing is the philosophy that IT is a one-size-fits-all commodity asset. Indeed, the economies of scale that cloud vendors achieve depend upon standardization of solutions across all clients. Cloud vendors treat all workloads and all clients as commodities and do not provide the special treatment required by some organizations. Larger companies are more likely to have esoteric information needs and pursue strategic advantage through IT systems. A commodity provision approach is incompatible with the need for unique strategic information.

Finally, internal control and security issues are concerns for companies of all sizes that outsource their IT to the cloud. When an organization's critical data reside outside its corporate walls, it is at risk. The client firm has little option but to trust to the ethics, competence, and internal controls of the vendor. The relevant risk issues include an extensive set of topics, such as technology failures in the cloud, distributed denial of service attacks, hacking, vendor exploitation, vendor failure to perform, and the loss of strategic advantage. Internet risks are examined later in this chapter, and the security and controls that mitigate such risks are presented in Chapter 16. Outsourcing (both traditional and cloud) risks and controls are covered in Chapter 15.

Dynamic Virtual Organizations

Perhaps the greatest potential benefit to be derived from electronic commerce is the firm's ability to forge dynamic business alliances with other organizations to fill unique market niches as opportunities arise. These may be long-lasting partnerships or one-time ventures. Electronic partnering of business enterprises forms a **dynamic virtual organization** that benefits all parties involved.

For example, consider a company that markets millions of different products, including books, music, software, and toys, over the Internet. If this were a traditional organization created to serve walk-in customers, it would need a massive warehouse to store the extensive range of physical products that it sells. It must also make significant financial investments in inventory and personnel to maintain stock, fill customer orders, and control the environment. A virtual organization does not need this physical infrastructure. Figure 12-2 illustrates the partnering relationship possible in a virtual organization.

FIGURE 12-2 DYNAMIC VIRTUAL ORGANIZATION

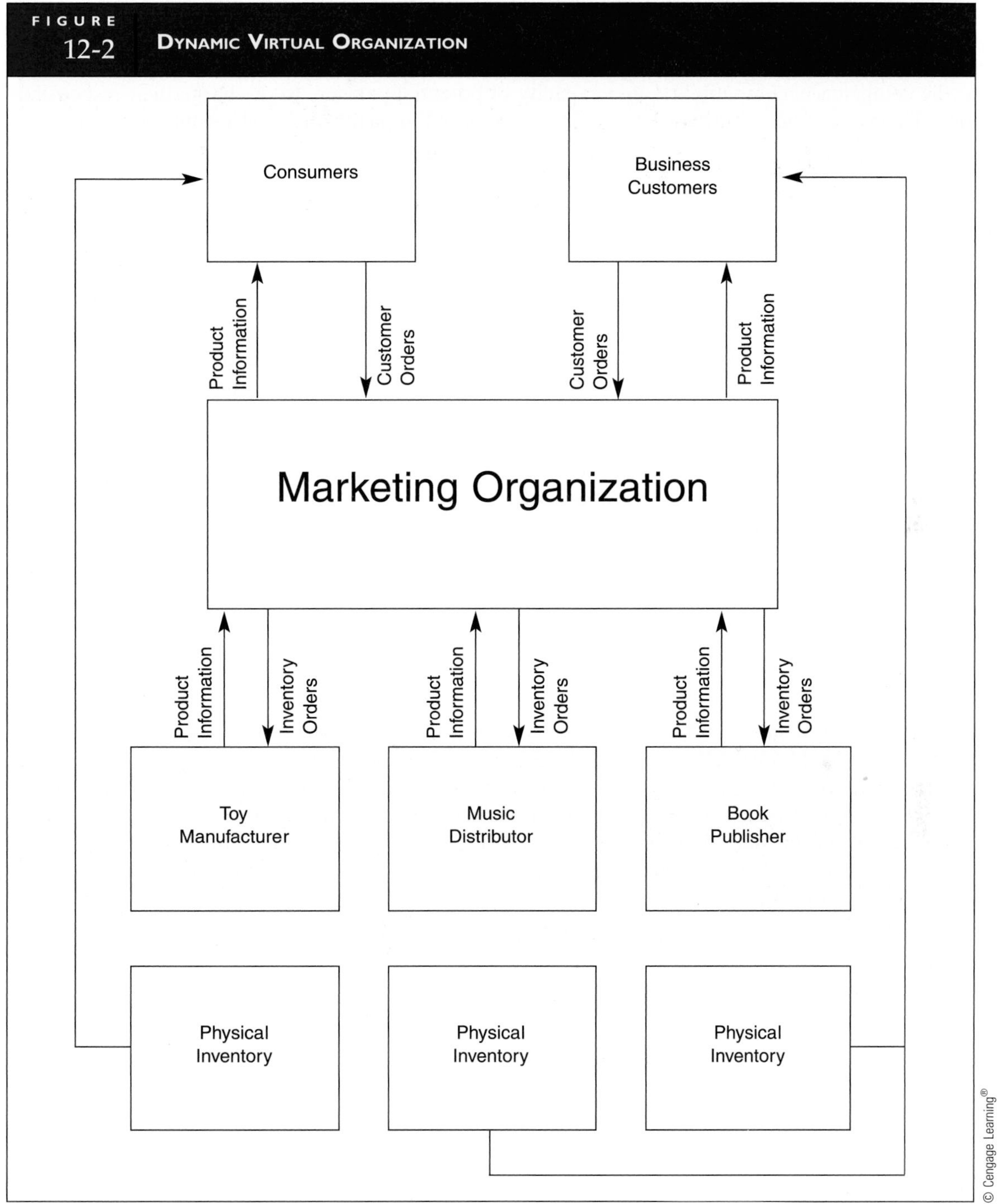

The selling organization maintains a website for advertising product offerings. The products themselves are not physically in the custody of the seller but are stored at the facilities of the trading partner (e.g., manufacturer, publisher, or distributor). The seller provides customers with product descriptions, consumer reports, prices, availability, and expected delivery times. This information comes from trading partners through an Internet connection. The seller validates customer orders placed through the website and automatically dispatches these to the trading partner firm, which actually ships the product.

The virtual organization can expand, contract, or shift its product line and services by simply adding or eliminating trading partners. To fully exploit this flexibility, organizations often forge relationships with total strangers. Managers in both firms need to make quick determinations as to the competence, compatibility, and capacity of potential partners to discharge their responsibilities. These and other security-related risks are potential impediments to electronic commerce.

Risks Associated with Electronic Commerce

Reliance on electronic commerce poses concern about unauthorized access to confidential information. As LANs become the platform for mission-critical applications and data, proprietary information, customer data, and financial records are at risk. Organizations connected to their customers and business partners via the Internet are particularly exposed. Without adequate protection, firms open their doors to computer hackers, vandals, thieves, and industrial spies, both internally and from around the world.

The paradox of networking is that networks exist to provide user access to shared resources, yet the most important objective of any network is to control such access. Hence, for every productivity argument in favor of remote access, there is a security argument against it. Organization management constantly seeks balance between increased access and the associated business risks.

In general, business **risk** is the possibility of loss or injury that can reduce or eliminate an organization's ability to achieve its objectives. In terms of electronic commerce, risk relates to the loss, theft, or destruction of data as well as the use of computer programs that financially or physically harm an organization. The following sections deal with various forms of risk. This includes intranet risks posed by dishonest employees who have the technical knowledge and the position to perpetrate frauds, and Internet risks that threaten both consumers and business entities.

INTRANET RISKS

Intranets consist of small LANs and large WANs that may contain thousands of individual nodes.[3] Intranets are used to connect employees within a single building, between buildings on the same physical campus, and between geographically dispersed locations. Typical intranet activities include e-mail routing, transaction processing between business units, and linking to the outside Internet.

Unauthorized and illegal employee activities internally spawn intranet threats. Their motives for doing harm may be vengeance against the company, the challenge of breaking into unauthorized files, or to profit from selling trade secrets or embezzling assets. The threat from employees (both current and former) is significant because of their intimate knowledge of system controls and/or the lack of controls. Discharged employees, or those who leave under contentious circumstances, raise particular concerns. Trade secrets, operations data, accounting data, and confidential information to which the employee has access are at greatest risk.

Interception of Network Messages

The individual nodes on most intranets are connected to a shared channel across which travel user IDs, passwords, confidential e-mails, and financial data files. The unauthorized interception of this information by a node on the network is called sniffing. The exposure is even greater when the intranet is connected to the Internet. Network administrators routinely use commercially available sniffer software to analyze network traffic and to detect bottlenecks. Sniffer software, however, can also be downloaded from the Internet. In the hands of a computer criminal, sniffer software can be used to intercept and view data sent across a shared intranet channel.

Privileged Employees with Access to Corporate Databases

Intranets connected to central corporate databases increase the risk that an employee will view, corrupt, change, or copy data. Outsiders may bribe employees who have access privileges to digital financial accounts to write-off an account receivable or sell sensitive information such as social security

3 See the chapter appendix for a complete discussion of LANs and WANs.

numbers, customer listings, credit card information, recipes, formulas, and design specifications. In 2010 the FBI charged two GM employees with downloading and stealing thousands of GM documents regarding the company's hybrid technology worth an estimated 40 million dollars. The employees offered this information to an automotive manufacturer based in China and a competitor of GM.

Reluctance to Prosecute

A factor that contributes to computer crime is the reluctance on the part of many victim organizations to prosecute the criminals because of fear of negative publicity. By pursuing prosecution in public court, a victim organization will necessarily expose its weaknesses in policy, procedures, and internal control to its customers, suppliers, and other business partners. Apart from the public criticism that such disclosures will likely provoke, customers may abandon the firm, and trading partners may impose greatly restrictive business practices on it.

Many computer criminals are repeat offenders, and performing background checks on prospective employees can significantly reduce an organization's hiring risk and avoid criminal acts. In the past, employee background checking was difficult to achieve because former employers, fearing legal action, were reluctant to disclose negative information to prospective employers. A "no comment" policy prevailed.

The legal doctrine of negligent hiring liability is changing this. This doctrine effectively requires employers to check into an employee's background. Increasingly, courts are holding employers responsible for criminal acts that employees, both on and off the job, perpetrated if a background check could have prevented crimes. Many states have passed laws that protect a former employer from legal action when providing work-related performance information about a former employee when (1) the inquiry comes from a prospective employer, (2) the information is based on credible facts, and (3) the information is given without malice.

INTERNET RISKS

This section looks at some of the more significant risks associated with Internet commerce. First, the risks related to consumer privacy and transaction security are examined. The risks to business entities from fraud and malicious acts are then reviewed.

RISKS TO CONSUMERS

As more and more people connect to the web, Internet fraud increases. Because of this, many consumers view the Internet as an unsafe place to do business. In particular, they worry about the security of credit card information left on websites and the confidentiality of their transactions. Some of the more common threats to consumers from cyber criminals are discussed here.

THEFT OF CREDIT CARD NUMBERS. The perception that the Internet is not secure for credit card purchases is considered to be the biggest barrier to electronic commerce. Some Internet companies are negligent or even fraudulent in the way they collect, use, and store credit card information. One hacker successfully stole 100,000 credit card numbers with a combined credit limit of $1 billion from an Internet service provider's customer files. He was arrested when he tried to sell the information to an undercover FBI agent.

Another fraud scheme involves establishing a fraudulent business operation that captures credit card information. For example, the company may take orders to deliver flowers on Mother's Day. When the day arrives, the company goes out of business and disappears from the web. Of course, the flowers are never delivered, and the perpetrator either sells or uses the credit card information.

THEFT OF PASSWORDS. One form of Internet fraud involves establishing a website to steal a visitor's password. To access the web page, the visitor is asked to register and provide an e-mail address and password. Many people use the same password for different applications such as ATM services, e-mail, and employer-network access. In the hopes that the website visitor falls into this pattern of behavior, the cyber criminal uses the captured password to break into the victim's accounts.

CONSUMER PRIVACY. Concerns about the lack of privacy discourage many consumers from engaging in Internet commerce. One aspect of privacy involves the way in which websites capture and use cookies.

Cookies are files containing user information that are created by the web server of the site being visited. The cookies are then stored on the visitor's computer hard drive. They contain the URLs of visited sites. When the site is revisited, the user's browser sends the specific cookies to the web server. The original intent behind the cookie was to improve efficiency in processing return visits to sites where users are required to register for services. For example, on the user's first visit to a particular website, the URL and user ID may be stored as a cookie. On subsequent visits, the website retrieves the user ID, thus saving the visitor from rekeying the information.

Cookies allow websites to off-load the storage of routine information about vast numbers of visitors. It is far more efficient for a web server to retrieve this information from a cookie file stored on the user's computer than to search through millions of such records stored at the website. Most browsers have preference options to disable cookies or to warn the user before accepting one.

The privacy controversy over cookies relates to what information is captured and how it is used. For example, the cookie may be used to create a profile of user preferences for marketing purposes. The profile could be based on the pages accessed or the options selected during the site visit, the time of day or night of the visit, and the length of time spent at the site. The profile could also include the user's e-mail address, zip code, home phone number, and any other information the user is willing to provide to the website.

This type of information is useful to online marketing firms that sell advertising for thousands of Internet firms. The user profile enables the marketing firm to customize ads and to target them to Internet consumers. To illustrate, let's assume a user visiting an online bookstore browses sports car and automobile racing listings. This information is stored in a cookie and transmitted to the online marketing firm, which then sends JavaScript ads for general automotive products to the bookstore's web page to entice the visitor to click on the ads. Each time the consumer visits the site, the contents of the cookie will be used to trigger the appropriate ads. User profile information can also be compiled into a mailing list, which is sold and used in the traditional way for solicitation.

Risks to Businesses

Business entities are also at risk from Internet commerce. IP spoofing, denial of service attacks, and malicious programs are three significant concerns.

IP SPOOFING. IP spoofing is a form of masquerading to gain unauthorized access to a web server and/or to perpetrate an unlawful act without revealing one's identity. To accomplish this, a perpetrator modifies the IP address of the originating computer to disguise his or her identity. A criminal may use IP spoofing to make a message appear to be coming from a trusted or authorized source and thus slip through control systems designed to accept transmissions from certain (trusted) host computers and block out others. This technique could be used to crack into corporate networks to perpetrate frauds, conduct acts of espionage, or destroy data. For example, a hacker may spoof a manufacturing firm with a false sales order that appears to come from a legitimate customer. If the spoof goes undetected, the manufacturer will incur the costs of producing and delivering a product that was never ordered.

DENIAL OF SERVICE ATTACK. A **denial of service attack (DoS)** is an assault on a web server to prevent it from servicing its legitimate users. Although such attacks can be aimed at any type of website, they are particularly devastating to business entities that are prevented from receiving and processing business transactions from their customers. Three common types of DoS attacks are: SYN flood, smurf, and distributed denial of service (DDoS).

SYN FLOOD ATTACK. When a user establishes a connection on the Internet through TCP/IP, a three-way handshake takes place. The connecting server sends an initiation code called a SYN (SYNchronize) packet to the receiving server. The receiving server then acknowledges the request by returning a **SYNchronize-ACKnowledge (SYN-ACK)** packet. Finally, the initiating host machine responds with an ACK packet code. The **SYN flood attack** is accomplished by not sending the final acknowledgment to the server's SYN-ACK response, which causes the server to keep signaling for acknowledgement until the server times out.

The individual or organization perpetrating the SYN flood attack transmits hundreds of SYN packets to the targeted receiver, but never responds with an ACK to complete the connection. As a result, the ports of the receiver's server are clogged with incomplete communication requests that prevent legitimate transactions from being received and processed. Organizations under attack thus may be prevented from receiving Internet messages for days at a time.

If the target organization could identify the server that is launching the attack, a firewall (discussed later) could be programmed to ignore all communication from that site. Such attacks, however, are difficult to prevent because they use IP spoofing to disguise the source of the messages. IP spoofing programs that randomize the source address of the attacker have been written and publicly distributed over the Internet. Therefore, to the receiving site, it appears that the transmissions are coming from all over the Internet.

SMURF ATTACK. A **smurf attack** involves three parties: the perpetrator, the intermediary, and the victim. It is accomplished by exploiting an Internet maintenance tool called a **ping**, which is used to test the state of network congestion and determine whether a particular host computer is connected and available on the network. The ping works by sending an echo request message (like a sonar ping) to the host computer and listening for a response message (echo reply). The ping signal is encapsulated in a message packet that also contains the return IP address of the sender. A functioning and available host must return an echo reply message that contains the exact data received in the echo request message packet.

The perpetrator of a smurf attack uses a program to create a ping message packet that contains the forged IP address of the victim's computer (IP spoofing) rather than that of the actual source computer. The ping message is then sent to the intermediary, which is actually an entire subnetwork of computers. By sending the ping to the network's **IP broadcast address**, the perpetrator ensures that each node on the intermediary network receives the echo request automatically. Consequently, each intermediary node sends echo responses to the ping message, which are returned to the victim's IP address, not that of the source computer. The resulting flood echoes can overwhelm the victim's computer and cause network congestion that makes it unusable for legitimate traffic. Figure 12-3 illustrates a smurf attack.

The intermediary in a smurf attack is an unwilling and unaware party. Indeed, the intermediary is also a victim and to some extent suffers the same type of network congestion problems the target victim suffers. One method of defeating smurf attacks is to disable the IP broadcast addressing option at each network firewall and thus eliminate the intermediary's role. In response to this move, however, attackers have developed tools to search for networks that do not disable broadcast addressing. These networks may subsequently be used as intermediaries in smurf attacks. Also, perpetrators have developed tools that enable them to launch smurf attacks simultaneously from multiple intermediary networks for maximum effect on the victim.

DISTRIBUTED DENIAL OF SERVICE. A **distributed denial of service (DDoS)** attack may take the form of a SYN flood or smurf attack. The distinguishing feature of the DDoS is the sheer scope of the event. The perpetrator of a DDoS attack may employ a virtual army of so-called **zombie** or bot (robot) computers to launch the attack. Because vast numbers of unsuspecting intermediaries are needed, the attack often involves one or more **Internet Relay Chat (IRC)** networks as a source of zombies. IRC is a popular interactive service on the Internet that lets thousands of people from around the world engage in real-time communications via their computers.

The problem with IRC networks is that they tend to have poor security. The perpetrator can thus easily access the IRC and upload a malicious program, such as a Trojan horse (see the appendix in Chapter 16 for a definition), which contains DDoS attack script. This program is subsequently downloaded to the PCs of the many thousands of people who visit the IRC site. The attack program runs in the background on the new zombie computers, which are now under the control of the perpetrator. These collections of compromised computers are known as **botnets.** Figure 12-4 illustrates this technique.

FIGURE 12-3 Smurf Attack

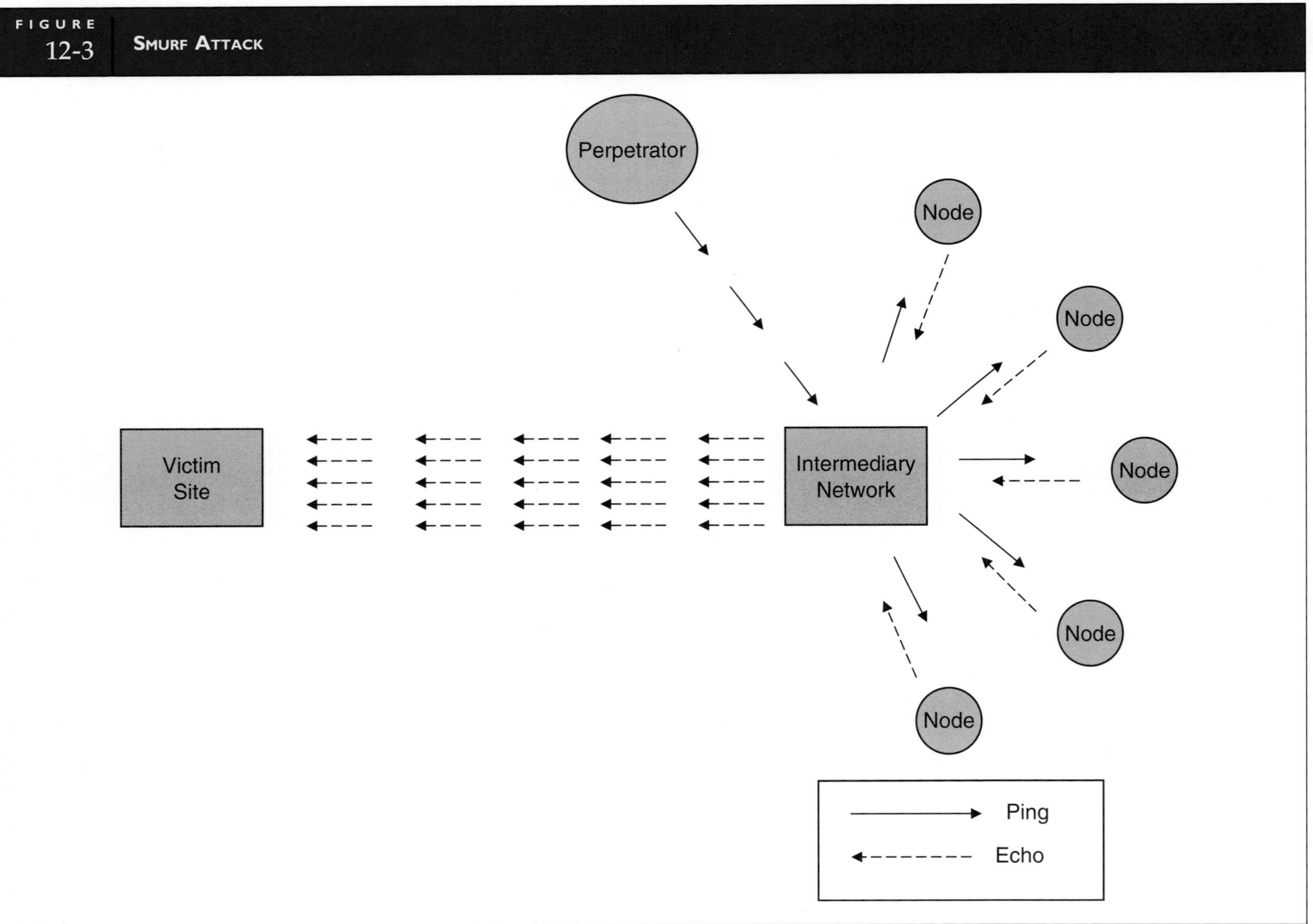

FIGURE 12-4 DISTRIBUTED DENIAL OF SERVICE ATTACK

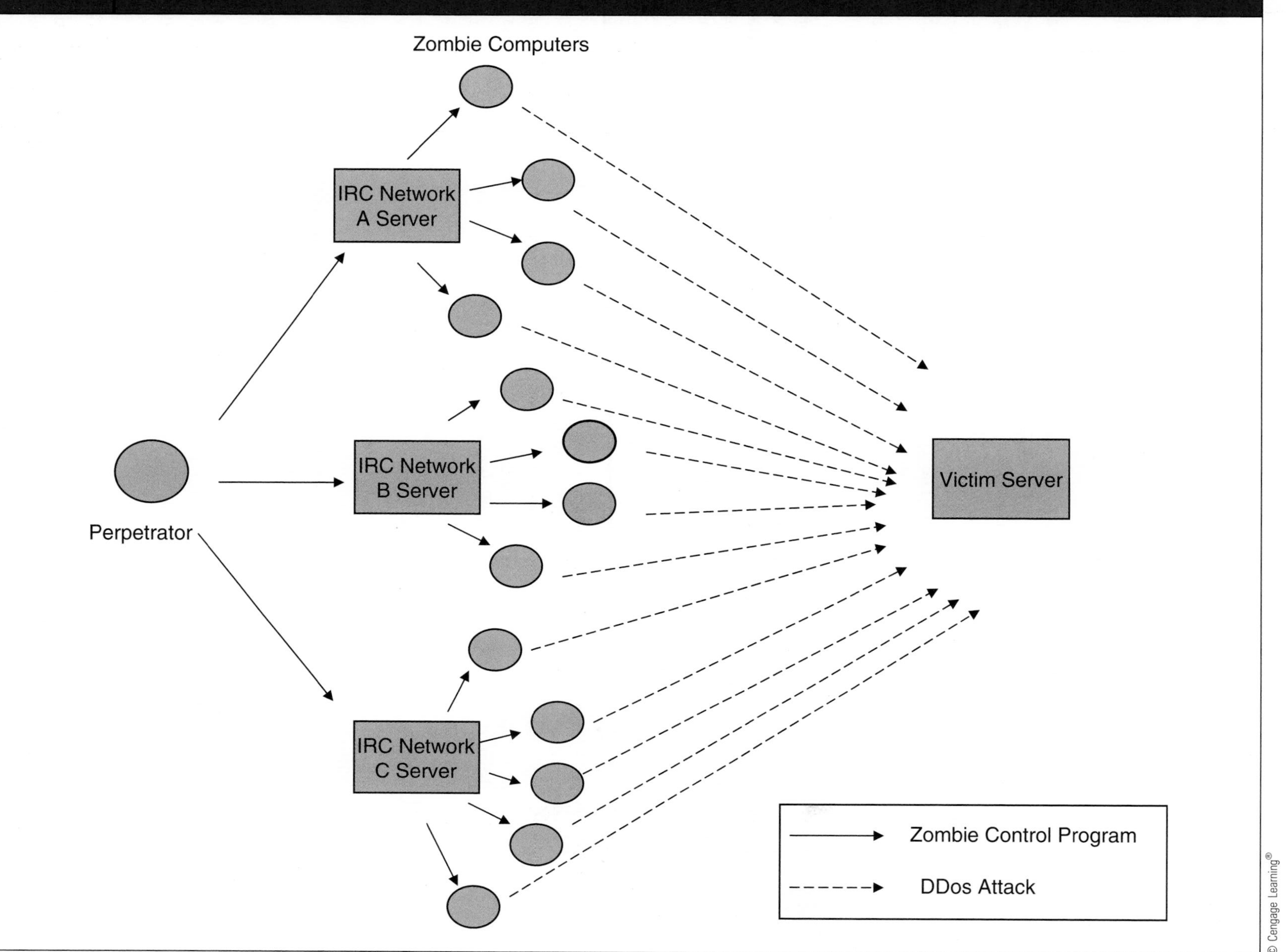

Via the zombie control program, the perpetrator has the power to direct the DDoS to specific victims and turn on or off the attack at will. The DDoS attack poses a far greater threat to the victim than a traditional SYN flood or smurf attack. For instance, a SYN flood coming from thousands of distributed computers can do far more damage than one from a single computer. Also, a smurf attack coming from a subnetwork of intermediary computers all emanate from the same server. In time, the server can be located and isolated by programming the victim's firewall to ignore transmissions from the attacking site. The DDoS attack, on the other hand, literally comes from sites all across the Internet. Thousands of individual attack-computers are harder to track down and turn off.

MOTIVATION BEHIND DOS ATTACKS. The motivation behind DoS attacks may originally have been to punish an organization with which the perpetrator had a grievance or simply to gain bragging rights for being able to do it. Today, DoS attacks are also perpetrated for financial gain. Financial institutions, which are particularly dependent on Internet access, have been prime targets. Organized criminals threatening a devastating attack have extorted several institutions, including the Royal Bank of Scotland. The typical scenario is for the perpetrator to launch a short DDoS attack (a day or so) to demonstrate what life would be like if the organization were isolated from the Internet. During this time, legitimate customers are unable to access their online accounts and the institution is unable to process many financial transactions. After the attack, the CEO of the organization receives a phone call demanding that a sum of money be deposited in an offshore account, or the attack will resume. Compared to the potential loss in customer confidence, damaged reputation, and lost revenues, the ransom may appear to be a small price to pay. DDoS attacks are relatively easy to execute and can have a devastating effect on the victim. Many experts believe that the best defense against DDoS attacks is to implement a layered security program with multiple detection point capability. We revisit this issue in Chapter 16 to examine methods for dealing with DDoS attacks.

OTHER MALICIOUS PROGRAMS. Viruses and other forms of malicious programs, such as worms, logic bombs, and Trojan horses, pose a threat to both Internet and intranet users. These may be used to bring down a computer network by corrupting its operating systems, destroying or corrupting corporate databases, or capturing passwords that enable hackers to break in to the system. Malicious programs, however, are not exclusively an electronic commerce issue; database management, operating systems security, and application integrity are also threatened. Because of the broad-based implications, this class of risk is examined at length in Chapter 16.

Security, Assurance, and Trust

Trust is the catalyst for sustaining electronic commerce. Both consumers and businesses are drawn to organizations that are perceived to have integrity. Organizations must convey a sense that they are competent and conduct business fairly with their customers, trading partners, and employees. This is a two-pronged problem. First, the company must implement the technological infrastructure and controls needed to provide for adequate security. Second, the company must assure potential customers and trading partners that adequate safeguards are in place and working. A large part of data security involves data encryption, digital authentication, and firewalls. These security techniques are outlined in the following section but are presented in more detail in Chapter 16. This section concludes with a review of seals of assurance techniques that promote trust in electronic commerce.

ENCRYPTION

Encryption is the conversion of data into a secret code for storage in databases and transmission over networks. The sender uses an encryption algorithm to convert the original message (called cleartext) into a coded equivalent (called ciphertext). At the receiving end, the ciphertext is decoded (decrypted) back into cleartext.

The earliest encryption method is called the **Caesar cipher**, which Julius Caesar is said to have used to send coded messages to his generals in the field. Like modern-day encryption, the Caesar cipher has two fundamental components: a key and an algorithm.

The **key** is a mathematical value that the sender selects. The **algorithm** is the procedure of shifting each letter in the cleartext message the number of positions that the key value indicates. Thus, a key value of +3 would shift each letter three places to the right. For example, the letter A in cleartext would be represented as the letter D in the ciphertext message. The receiver of the ciphertext message reverses the process to decode it and recreates the cleartext, in this case shifting each ciphertext letter three places to the left. Obviously, both the sender and receiver of the message must know the key.

Modern-day encryption algorithms, however, are far more complex, and encryption keys may be up to 128 bits in length. The more bits in the key, the stronger the encryption method. Today, nothing less than 128-bit algorithms are considered truly secure. Two commonly used methods of encryption are private key and public key encryption.

Advanced encryption standard (AES), also known as Rijndael, is a **private key** (or **symmetric key**) encryption technique. The U.S. government has adopted it as an encryption standard. To encode a message, the sender provides the encryption algorithm with the key, which produces the ciphertext message. This is transmitted to the receiver's location, where it is decoded using the same key to produce a cleartext message. Because the same key is used for coding and decoding, control over the key becomes an important security issue. The more individuals that need to exchange encrypted data, the greater the chance that the key will become known to an intruder who could intercept a message and read it, change it, delay it, or destroy it.

To overcome this problem, **public key encryption** was devised. This approach uses two different keys: one for encoding messages and the other for decoding them. The recipient has a private key used for decoding, which is kept secret. The encoding key is public and published for everyone to use. This approach is illustrated in Figure 12-5.

Receivers never need to share private keys with senders, which reduces the likelihood that they fall into the hands of an intruder. One of the most trusted public key encryption methods is **Rivest-Shamir-Adleman (RSA).** This method is, however, computationally intensive and much slower than private key encryption. Sometimes, both private key and public key encryption are used together in what is called a **digital envelope.**

DIGITAL AUTHENTICATION

Encryption alone cannot resolve all security concerns. For example, how does the supplier (receiver) know for sure that a hacker did not intercept and alter a customer's (sender) purchase order (message) for 1,000 units of product to read 100,000? If such an alteration went undetected, the supplier would incur the labor, material, manufacturing, and distribution costs for the order. Litigation between the innocent parties may ensue.

A **digital signature** is an electronic authentication technique that ensures the transmitted message originated with the authorized sender and that it was not tampered with after the signature was applied. The digital signature is derived from a mathematically computed digest of the document that has been encrypted with the sender's private key. Both the digital signature and the text message are encrypted using the receiver's public key and transmitted to the receiver. At the receiving end, the message is decrypted using the receiver's private key to produce the digital signature (encrypted digest) and the cleartext version of the message. Finally, the receiver uses the sender's public key to decrypt the digital signal to produce the digest. The receiver recalculates the digest from the cleartext using the original hashing algorithm and compares this to the transmitted digest. If the message is authentic, the two digest values will match. If even a single character of the message was changed in transmission, the digest figures will not be equal.

Another concern facing the receiver is determining if the expected sender actually initiated a message. For example, suppose that the supplier receives a purchase order addressed from Customer A for 100,000 units of product, which was actually sent from an unknown computer criminal. Once again, significant costs would accrue to the supplier if it acts on this fraudulent order.

FIGURE 12-5 PUBLIC KEY ENCRYPTION

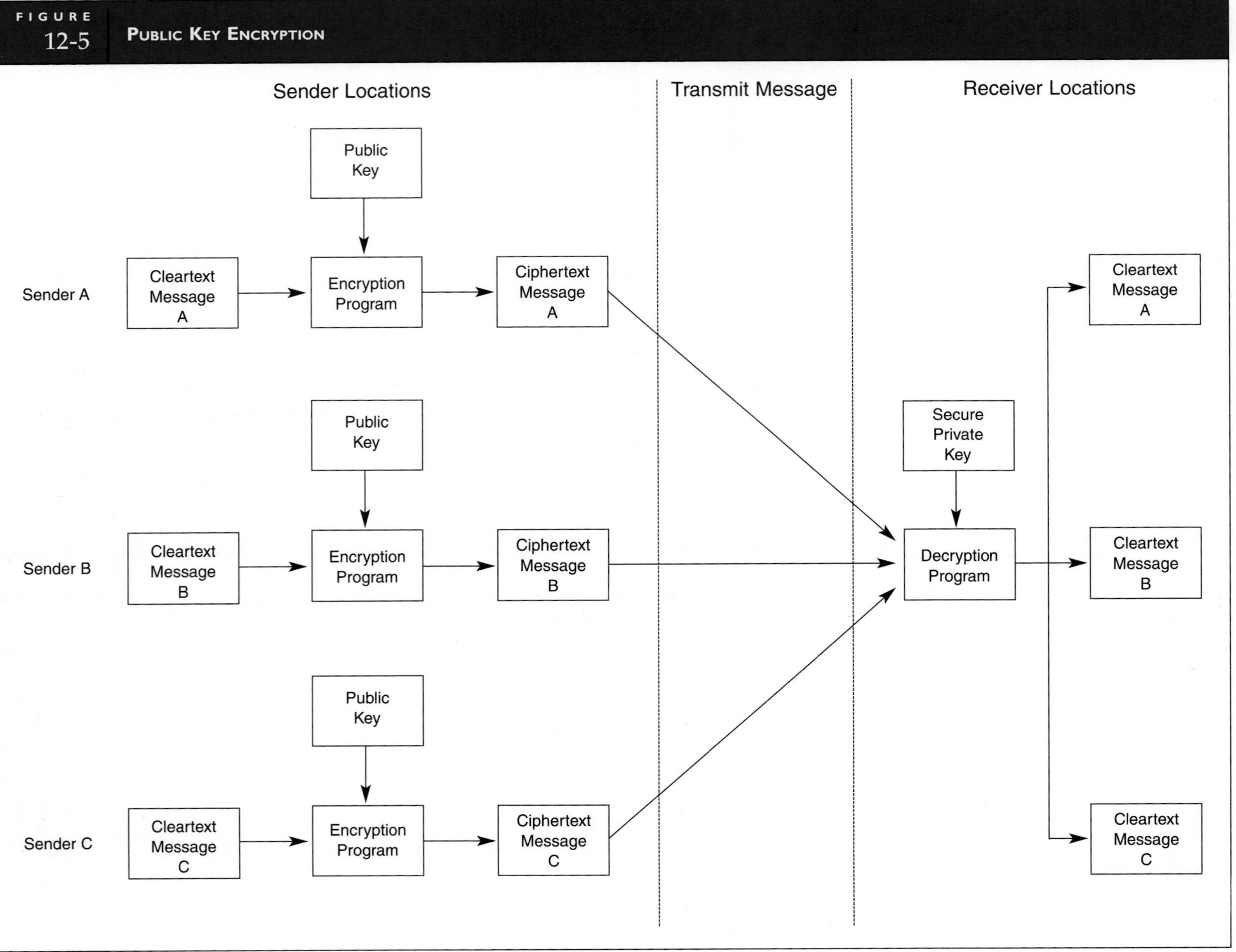

A digital certificate is like an electronic identification card that is used in conjunction with a public key encryption system to verify the authenticity of the message sender. Trusted third parties known as **certification authorities** (CAs) (e.g., Veri-Sign, Inc.) issue digital certificates, also called digital IDs. The digital certificate is actually the sender's public key that the CA has digitally signed. The digital certificate is transmitted with the encrypted message to authenticate the sender. The receiver uses the CA's public key to decrypt the sender's public key, which is attached to the message, and then uses the sender's public key to decrypt the actual message.

Because public key encryption is central to digital authentication, public key management becomes an important internal control issue. **Public key infrastructure (PKI)** constitutes the policies and procedures for administering this activity. A PKI system consists of:

1. A certification authority that issues and revokes digital certificates.
2. A registration authority that verifies the identity of certificate applicants. The process varies depending on the level of certification desired. It involves establishing one's identity with formal documents, such as a driver's license, notarization, fingerprints, and proving one's ownership of the public key.
3. A certification repository, which is a publicly accessible database that contains current information about current certificates and a certification revocation list of certificates that have been revoked and the reasons for revocation.

FIREWALLS

A **firewall** is a system used to insulate an organization's intranet from the Internet. It can be used to authenticate an outside user of the network, verify his or her level of access authority, and then direct the user to the program, data, or service requested. In addition to insulating the organization's network from external networks, firewalls can also be used to protect LANs from unauthorized internal access.

A common configuration employs two firewalls: a network-level firewall and an application-level firewall. The **network-level firewall** provides basic screening of low-security messages (for example, e-mail) and routes them to their destinations based on the source and destination addresses attached. The **application-level firewall** provides high-level network security. These firewalls are configured to run security applications called proxies that perform sophisticated functions, such as verifying user authentication.

SEALS OF ASSURANCE

In response to consumer demand for evidence that a web-based business is trustworthy, a number of trusted third-party organizations are offering seals of assurance that businesses can display on their website home pages. To legitimately bear the seal, the company must show that it complies with certain business practices, capabilities, and controls. This section reviews six seal-granting organizations: Better Business Bureau (BBB), TRUSTe, Veri-Sign, Inc., International Computer Security Association (ICSA), AICPA/CICA WebTrust, and AICPA/CICA SysTrust.

Better Business Bureau

The BBB is a nonprofit organization that has been promoting ethical business practices through self-regulation since 1912. The BBB has extended its mission to the Internet through a wholly owned subsidiary called BBBOnline, Inc. To qualify for the BBBOnline seal, an organization must:

- Become a member of the BBB.
- Provide information about the company's ownership, management, address, and phone number. This is verified by a physical visit to the company's premises.
- Be in business for at least one year.
- Promptly respond to customer complaints.
- Agree to binding arbitration for unresolved disputes with customers.

The assurance BBBOnline provides relates primarily to concern about business policies, ethical advertising, and consumer privacy. BBBOnline does not verify controls over transaction processing integrity and data security issues.

TRUSTe

Founded in 1996, TRUSTe is a nonprofit organization dedicated to improving consumer privacy practices among Internet businesses and websites. To qualify for the TRUSTe seal, the organization must:

- Agree to follow TRUSTe privacy policies and disclosure standards.
- Post a privacy statement on the website disclosing the type of information being collected, the purpose for collecting information, and with whom it is shared.
- Promptly respond to customer complaints.
- Agree to site compliance reviews by TRUSTe or an independent third party.

TRUSTe addresses consumer privacy concerns exclusively and provides a mechanism for posting consumer complaints against its members. If a member organization is found to be out of compliance with TRUSTe standards, its right to display the trust seal may be revoked.

Veri-Sign, Inc.

Veri-Sign, Inc., was established as a for-profit organization in 1995. It provides assurance regarding the security of transmitted data. The organization does not verify security of stored data or address concerns related to business policies, business processes, or privacy. Its mission is to provide digital certificate solutions that enable trusted commerce and communications. Their products allow customers to transmit encrypted data and verify the source and destination of transmissions. Veri-Sign, Inc., issues three classes of certificates to individuals, businesses, and organizations. To qualify for class three certification, the individual, business, or organization must provide a third-party confirmation of name, address, telephone number, and website domain name.

International Computer Security Association

The ICSA established its web certification program in 1996. ICSA certification addresses data security and privacy concerns. It does not deal with concerns about business policy and business processes. Organizations that qualify to display the ICSA seal have undergone an extensive review of firewall security from outside hackers. Organizations must be recertified annually and undergo at least two surprise checks each year.

AICPA/CICA WebTrust

The AICPA and CICA established the WebTrust program in 1997. To display the AICPA/CICA Web-Trust seal, the organization undergoes an examination according to the AICPA's Standards for Attestation Engagements, No. 1, by a specially web-certified CPA or CA. The examination focuses on the areas of business practices (policies), transaction integrity (business process), and information protection (data security). The seal must be renewed every 90 days.

AICPA/CICA SysTrust

In July 1999, the AICPA/CICA introduced an exposure draft describing a new assurance service called SysTrust. It is designed to increase management, customer, and trading partner confidence in systems that support entire businesses or specific processes. The assurance service involves the public accountant evaluating the system's reliability against four essential criteria: availability, security, integrity, and maintainability.

The potential users of SysTrust are trading partners, creditors, shareholders, and others who rely on the integrity and capability of the system. For example, Virtual Company is considering outsourcing some of its vital functions to third-party organizations. Virtual needs assurance that the third-party systems are reliable and adequate to provide the contracted services. As part of the outsourcing contract, Virtual requires the servicing organizations to produce a clean SysTrust report every three months.

In theory, the SysTrust service will enable organizations to differentiate themselves from their competitors. Those organizations that undergo a SysTrust engagement will be perceived as competent service providers and trustworthy. They will be more attuned to the risks in their environment and equipped with the necessary controls to deal with the risks.[4]

Implications for the Accounting Profession

The issues discussed in this chapter carry many implications for auditors and the public accounting profession. As mission-critical functions, such as inventory procurement, sales processing, shipping notification, and cash disbursements, are performed automatically, digitally, and in real time, auditors are faced with the challenge of developing new techniques for assessing control adequacy and verifying the occurrence and accuracy of economic events. The following describes issues of increasing importance to auditors in the electronic commerce age.

PRIVACY VIOLATION

Privacy pertains to the level of confidentiality that an organization employs in managing customer and trading partner data. Privacy applies also to data that web sites collect from visitors who are not customers. Specific concerns include:

- Does the organization have a stated privacy policy?
- What mechanisms are in place to ensure the consistent application of stated privacy policies?
- What information on customers, trading partners, and visitors does the company capture?
- Does the organization share or sell its customer, trading partner, or visitor information?
- Can individuals and business entities verify and update the information captured about them?

The **Safe Harbor Agreement** implemented in 1995 addresses the importance of privacy. The two-way agreement between the United States and the European Union establishes standards for information transmittal. Approved by the European Commission in July 2000, the Safe Harbor principles essentially enable U.S. companies to do business in the European Union by establishing what is deemed to be an adequate level of privacy protection. Although the document is still evolving, it establishes that companies need to enter the Safe Harbor Agreement or provide evidence that they are abiding by the privacy regulations set forth in it. Noncompliant organizations may be effectively banned from doing business in the European Union. Compliance with the Safe Harbor Agreement requires that a company meet six conditions that are described next.[5]

NOTICE. Organizations must provide individuals with clear notice of "the purposes for which it collects and uses information about them, the types of third parties to which it discloses the information, and how to contact the company with inquiries or complaints."

CHOICE. Before any data are collected, an organization must give its customers the opportunity to choose whether to share their sensitive information (e.g., data related to factors such as health, race, or religion).

ONWARD TRANSFER. Unless they have the individual's permission to do otherwise, organizations may share information only with those third parties that belong to the Safe Harbor Agreement or follow its principles.

---

4 American Institute of Certified Public Accountants, Inc., and Canadian Institute of Chartered Accountants, AICPA/CICA SysTrust Principle and Criteria for Systems Reliability (1999), 3.

5 "A New Covenant with Stakeholders: Managing Privacy as a Competitive Advantage, Privacy Risk Management," KPMG LLP, the U.S. member firm of KPMG International, a Swiss association (2001), 22–23.

SECURITY AND DATA INTEGRITY. Organizations need to ensure that the data they maintain are accurate, complete, and current, and thus reliable for use. They must also ensure the security of the information by protecting it against loss, misuse, unauthorized access, disclosure, alteration, and destruction.

ACCESS. Unless they would be unduly burdened or violate the rights of others, organizations must give individuals "access to personal data about themselves and provide an opportunity to correct, amend, or delete such data."

ENFORCEMENT. Organizations must "enforce compliance, provide recourse for individuals who believe their privacy rights have been violated, and impose sanctions on their employees and agents for non-compliance."

CONTINUOUS AUDITING

Continuous auditing techniques need to be developed that will enable the auditor to review transactions at frequent intervals or as they occur. To be effective, such an approach will need to employ **intelligent control agents** (computer programs) that embody auditor-defined heuristics that search electronic transactions for anomalies. Upon finding unusual events, the control agent will first search for similar events to identify a pattern. If the anomaly cannot be explained, the agent alerts the auditor with an alarm or exception report.

ELECTRONIC AUDIT TRAILS

In an EDI environment, a client's trading partner's computer automatically generates electronic transactions, which are relayed across a **value-added network** (VAN),[6] and the client's computer processes the transactions without human intervention. In such a setting, audits may need to be extended to critical systems of all parties involved in the transactions. Validating EDI transactions may involve the client, its trading partners, and the VAN that connects them. This could take the form of direct review of these systems or collaboration between the auditors of the trading partners and VANs.

CONFIDENTIALITY OF DATA

As system designs become increasingly open to accommodate trading partner transactions, mission-critical information is at risk of being exposed to intruders both from inside and outside the organization. Accountants need to understand the cryptographic techniques used to protect the confidentiality of stored and transmitted data. They need to assess the quality of encryption tools used and the effectiveness of key management procedures that CAs use. Furthermore, the term *mission-critical* defines a set of information that extends beyond the traditional financial concerns of accountants. This broader set demands a more holistic approach to assessing internal controls that ensure the confidentiality of data.

AUTHENTICATION

In traditional systems, the business paper on which it was written determines the authenticity of a sales order from a trading partner or customer. In electronic commerce systems, determining the identity of the customer is not as simple a task. With no physical forms to review and approve, authentication is accomplished through digital signatures and digital certificates. To perform their assurance function, accountants must develop the skill set needed to understand these technologies and their application.

NONREPUDIATION

Accountants are responsible for assessing the accuracy, completeness, and validity of transactions that constitute client sales, accounts receivable, purchases, and liabilities. Transactions that a trading

6 See the appendix for discussion of VANs.

partner can unilaterally repudiate can lead to uncollected revenues or legal action. In traditional systems, signed invoices, sales agreements, and other physical documents provide proof that a transaction occurred. As with the problem of authentication, electronic commerce systems can also use digital signatures and digital certificates to promote nonrepudiation.

DATA INTEGRITY

A nonrepudiated transaction from an authentic trading partner may still be intercepted and rendered inaccurate in a material way. In a paper-based environment, such alterations are easy to detect. Digital transmissions, however, pose much more of a problem. To assess data integrity, accountants must become familiar with the concept of computing a digest of a document and the role of digital signatures in data transmissions.

ACCESS CONTROLS

Controls need to be in place that prevent or detect unauthorized access to an organization's information system. Organizations whose systems are connected to the Internet are at greatest risk from outside intruders. Accounting firms need to be expert in assessing their clients' access controls. Many firms are now performing penetration tests, designed to assess the adequacy of their clients' access control by imitating known techniques that hackers and crackers use.

A CHANGING LEGAL ENVIRONMENT

Accountants have traditionally served their clients by assessing risk (both business and legal) and devising techniques to mitigate and control risk. This risk-assessment role is greatly expanded by Internet commerce, whose legal framework is still evolving in a business environment fraught with new and unforeseen risks. To estimate a client's exposure to legal liability in this setting, the public accountant must understand the potential legal implications (both domestic and international) of transactions that the client's electronic commerce system processes. For example, a web page from which customers order goods opens the organization to national and international business communities and exposes it to multiple and possibly conflicting legal statutes. Legal issues relating to taxes, privacy, security, intellectual property rights, and libel create new challenges for the accounting profession, which must provide its clients with rapid and accurate advice on a wide range of legal questions.

Summary

This chapter focused on Internet commerce, including business-to-consumer and business-to-business relationships. Internet commerce has been the source of intense interest because it enables thousands of business enterprises of all sizes and millions of consumers to congregate and participate in worldwide commerce. The chapter examined Internet technologies, including packet switching, the World Wide Web, Internet addressing, and protocols. Several advantages of Internet commerce were reviewed, including access to worldwide markets, reductions in inventory, creation of business partnerships, reductions in prices, and better customer service.

Electronic commerce is also associated with unique risks. The primary concerns intranets pose (discussed in the appendix) come from employees. Internet risks were characterized as a number of specific fraud schemes that threaten consumer privacy and the security of transmitted and stored data. Several measures were examined that can reduce risks and promote an environment of security and trust. These include data encryption, digital certificates, firewalls, and third-party trust seals for websites.

The chapter concluded with a review of implications for accountants and the profession. The issues covered included privacy issues, continuous process auditing, electronic audit trails, and the auditors' need for new skill sets to deal with highly technical, evidential matter that redefine traditional auditing concerns.

Appendix

Intra-organizational Electronic Commerce

Distributed data processing was introduced in Chapter 1 as an alternative to the centralized model. Most modern organizations use some form of distributed processing to process their transactions; some companies process all of their transactions in this way. Organizations that own or lease networks for internal business use intranets. The following section examines several intranet topologies and techniques for network control.

Network Topologies

A network topology is the physical arrangement of the components (e.g., nodes, servers, communications links) of the network. In this section, we examine the features of five basic network topologies: star, hierarchical, ring, bus, and client-server. Most networks are a variation on, or combination of, these basic models. However, before proceeding, working definitions are presented for some of the terms that will be used in the following sections.

LOCAL AREA NETWORKS AND WIDE AREA NETWORKS

One way of distinguishing between networks is the geographic area that their distributed sites cover. Networks are usually classified as either local area networks (LANs) or wide area networks (WANs). LANs are often confined to a single room in a building, or they may link several buildings within a close geographic area. However, a LAN can cover distances of several miles and connect hundreds of users. The computers connected to a LAN are called nodes.

When networks exceed the geographic limitations of the LAN, they are called WANs. Because of the distances involved and the high cost of telecommunication infrastructure (telephone lines and microwave channels), WANs are often commercial networks (at least in part) that the organization leases. The nodes of a WAN may include microcomputer workstations, minicomputers, mainframes, and LANs. The WAN may be used to link geographically dispersed segments of a single organization or connect multiple organizations in a trading partner arrangement.

NETWORK INTERFACE CARDS

The physical connection of workstations to the LAN is achieved through a network interface card (NIC), which fits into one of the expansion slots in the microcomputer. This device provides the electronic circuitry needed for internode communications. The NIC works with the network control program to send and receive messages, programs, and files across the network.

SERVERS

LAN nodes often share common resources such as programs, data, and printers, which are managed through special-purpose computers called servers, as depicted in Figure 12-6. When the server receives requests for resources, the requests are placed in a queue and are processed in sequence.

FIGURE 12-6 LAN WITH FILE AND PRINT SERVERS

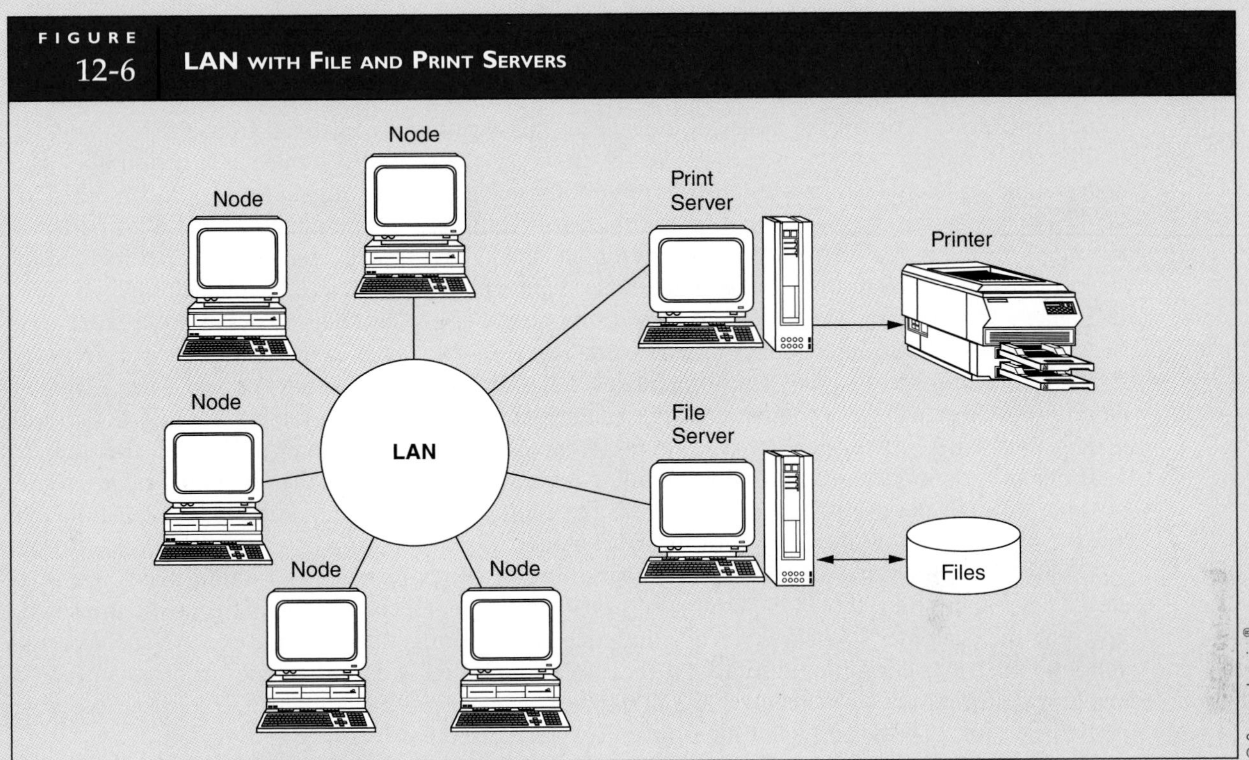

In a distributed environment, there is often a need to link networks. For example, users of one LAN may share data with users on a different LAN. Networks are linked via combinations of hardware and software devices called bridges and gateways. Figure 12-7 illustrates this technique. Bridges provide a means for linking LANs of the same type, for example, an IBM token ring to another IBM token ring. Gateways connect LANs of different types and are also used to link LANs to WANs. With these definitions in mind, we now turn our attention to the five basic network topologies.

FIGURE 12-7 BRIDGES AND GATEWAYS LINKING LANs AND WANs

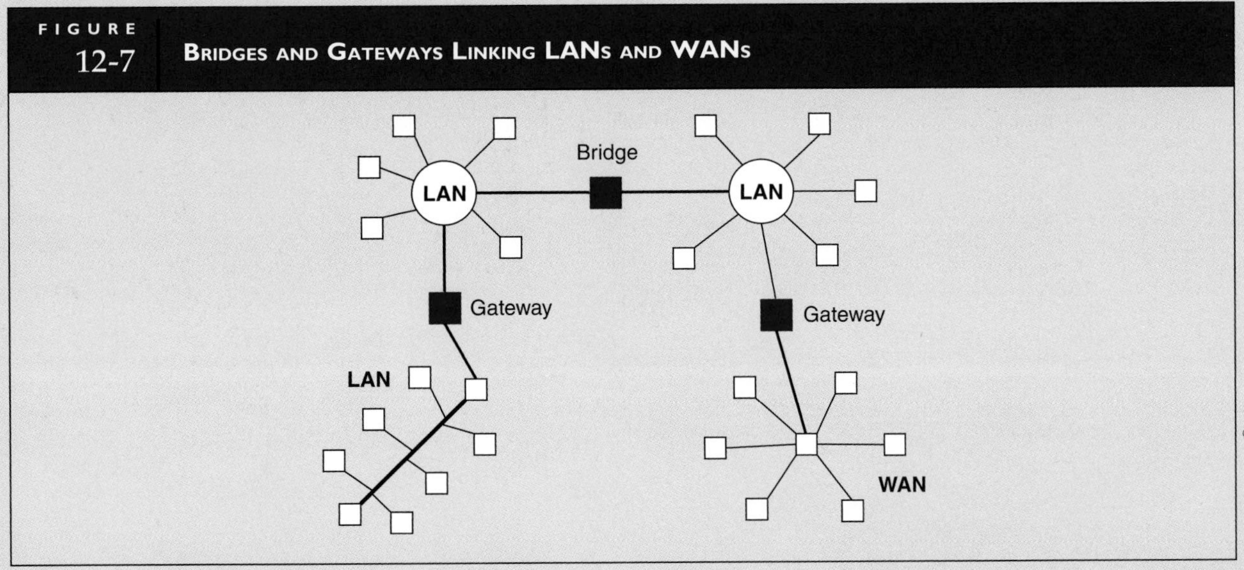

STAR TOPOLOGY

The star topology shown in Figure 12-8 describes a network of computers with a large central computer (the host) at the hub that has direct connections to a periphery of smaller computers. Communications between the nodes in the star are managed and controlled from the host site.

The star topology is often used for a WAN, in which the central computer is a mainframe. The nodes of the star may be microcomputer workstations, minicomputers, mainframes, or a combination. Databases under this approach may be distributed or centralized. A common model is to partition local data to the nodes and centralize the common data. For example, consider a department store chain that issues its own credit cards. Each node represents a store in a different metropolitan area. In Figure 12-8, these are Dallas, St. Louis, Topeka, and Tulsa. The nodes maintain local databases, such as records for customers holding credit cards issued in their areas and records of local inventory levels. The central site—Kansas City—maintains data common to the entire regional area, including data for customer billing, accounts receivable maintenance, and overall inventory control. Each local node is itself a LAN, with point-of-sales (POS) terminals connected to a minicomputer at the store.

If one or more nodes in a star network fail, communication between the remaining nodes is still possible through the central site. However, if the central site fails, individual nodes can function locally, but cannot communicate with the other nodes.

Transaction processing in this type of configuration could proceed as follows. Sales are processed in real time at the POS terminals. Local processing includes obtaining credit approval, updating the customer's available credit, updating the inventory records, and recording the transaction in the transaction file (journal). At the end of the business day, the nodes transmit sales and inventory information to the central site in batches. The central site updates the control accounts, prepares customer bills, and determines inventory replenishment for the entire region.

The assumption underlying the star topology is that primary communication will be between the central site and the nodes. However, limited communication between the nodes is possible. For example, assume a customer from Dallas was in Tulsa and made a purchase from the Tulsa store on credit. The Tulsa database would not contain the customer's record, so Tulsa would send the transaction for

FIGURE 12-8 STAR NETWORK

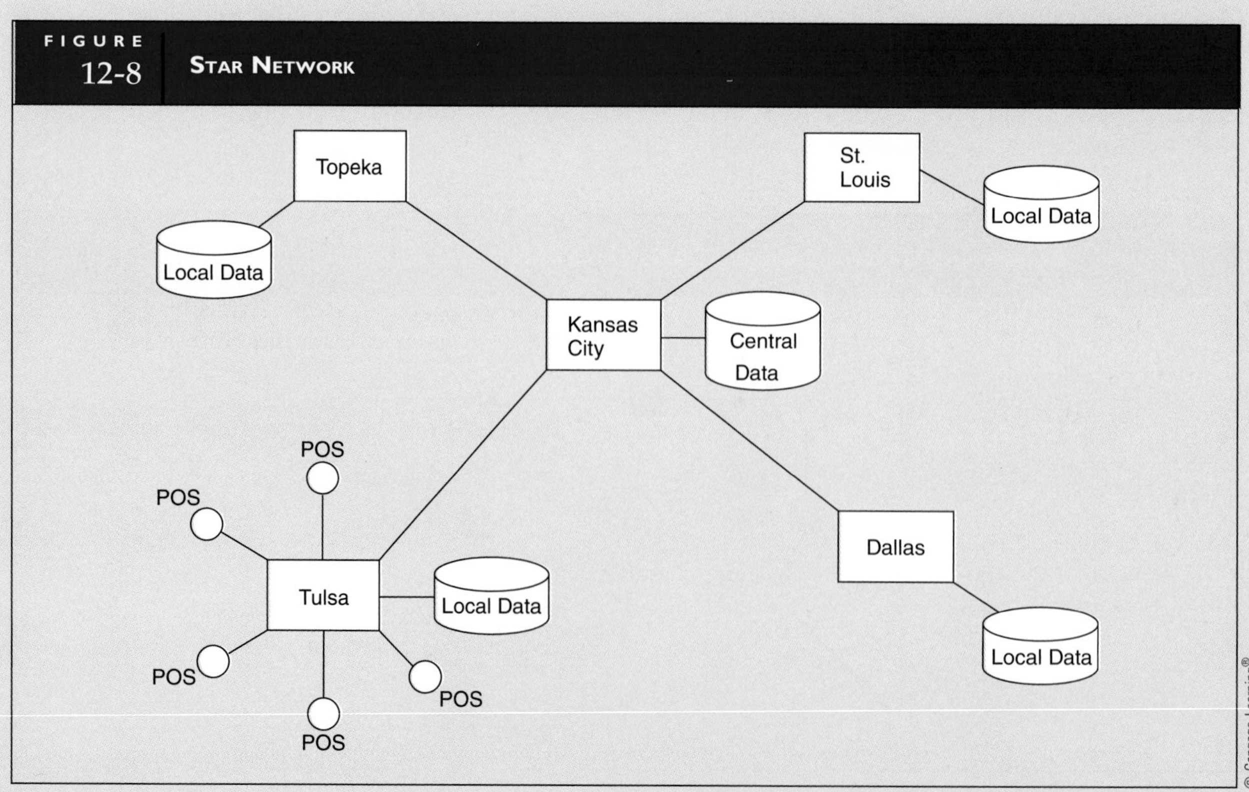

FIGURE 12-9 HIERARCHICAL TOPOLOGY

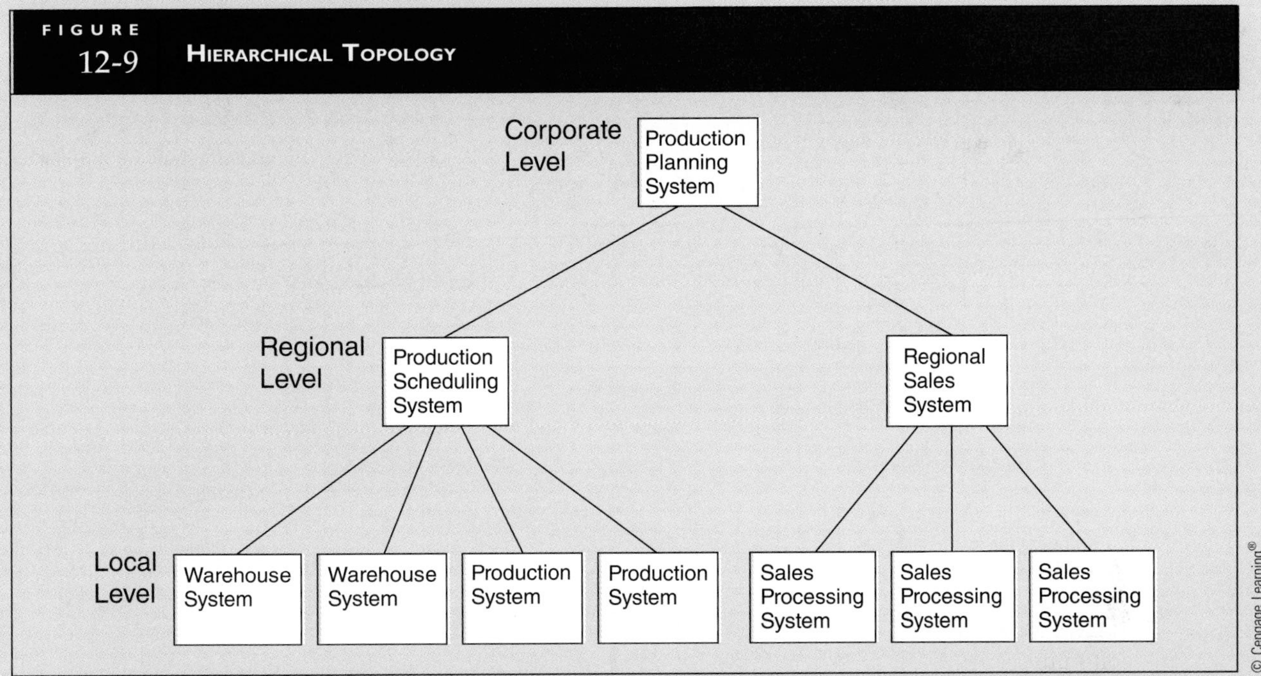

credit approval to Dallas via Kansas City. Dallas would then return the approved transaction to Tulsa via Kansas City. Inventory and sales journal updates would be performed at Tulsa.

This transaction-processing procedure would differ somewhat depending on the database configuration. For example, if local databases are partial replicas of the central database, credit queries could be made directly from Kansas City. However, this would require keeping the central database current with all the nodes.

HIERARCHICAL TOPOLOGY

A hierarchical topology is one in which a host computer is connected to several levels of subordinate, smaller computers in a master-slave relationship. This structure is applicable to firms with many organizational levels that must be controlled from a central location. For example, consider a manufacturing firm with remote plants, warehouses, and sales offices like the one illustrated in Figure 12-9. Sales orders from the local sales departments are transmitted to the regional level, where they are summarized and uploaded to the corporate level. Sales data, combined with inventory and plant capacity data from manufacturing, are used to compute production requirements for the period, which are downloaded to the regional production scheduling system. At this level, production schedules are prepared and distributed to the local production departments. Information about completed production is uploaded from the production departments to the regional level, where production summaries are prepared and transmitted to the corporate level.

RING TOPOLOGY

The ring topology illustrated in Figure 12-10 eliminates the central site. This is a peer-to-peer arrangement in which all nodes are of equal status; thus, responsibility for managing communications is distributed among the nodes. Every node on the ring has a unique electronic address, which is attached to messages such as an address on an envelope. If Node A wishes to send a message to Node D, then Nodes B and C receive, regenerate, and pass on the message until it arrives at its destination. This is a popular topology for LANs. The peer nodes manage private programs and databases locally. However, a file server that is also a node on the network ring can centralize and manage common resources that all nodes share.

The ring topology may also be used for a WAN, in which case the databases may be partitioned rather than centralized. For example, consider a company with widely separated warehouses, each with

FIGURE 12-10 RING TOPOLOGY

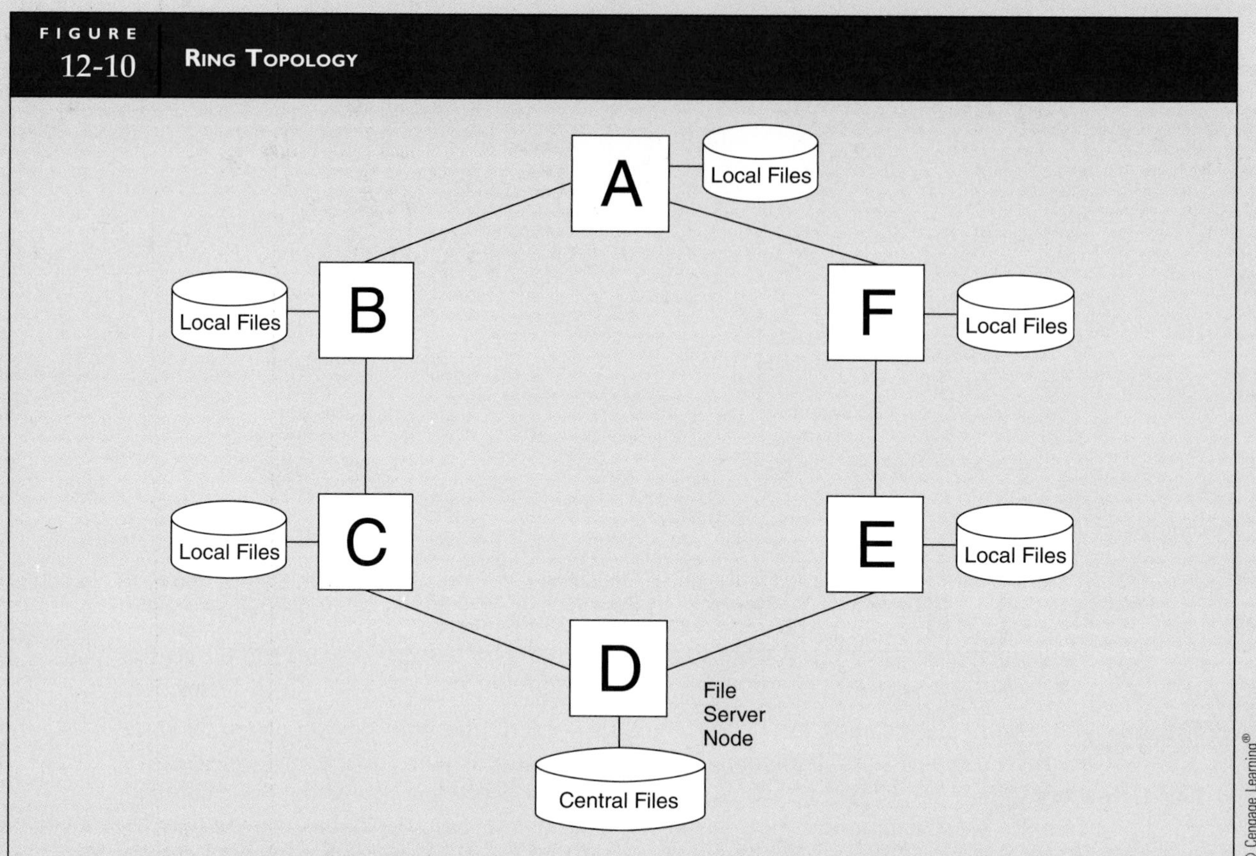

different suppliers and customers, and each processing its own shipping and receiving transactions. In this case, where there are few common data, it is more efficient to distribute the database than to manage it centrally. However, when one warehouse has insufficient stock to fill an order, it can communicate through the network to locate the items at another warehouse.

BUS TOPOLOGY

The bus topology illustrated in Figure 12-11 is the most popular LAN topology. It is so named because the nodes are all connected to a common cable—the bus. One or more servers centrally control communications and file transfers between workstations. As with the ring topology, each node on the bus has a unique address, and only one node may transmit at a time. The technique, which has been used for over two decades, is simple, reliable, and generally less costly to install than the ring topology.

CLIENT-SERVER TOPOLOGY

The term *client-server* is often misused to describe any type of network arrangement. In fact, the client-server topology has specific characteristics that distinguish it from the other topologies. Figure 12-12 illustrates the approach.

To explain the client-server difference, let's review the features of a traditional distributed data processing (DDP) system. DDP can result in considerable data traffic jams. Users competing for access to shared data files experience queues, delays, and lockouts. A factor influencing the severity of this problem is the structure of the database in use. For example, assume that User A requests a single record from a database table located at a central site. To meet this request, the file server at the central site must lock and transmit the entire table to User A. The user's application performs the search for the specific record at the remote site. When the record is updated, the entire file is then transmitted back to the central site.

FIGURE 12-11 **Bus Topology**

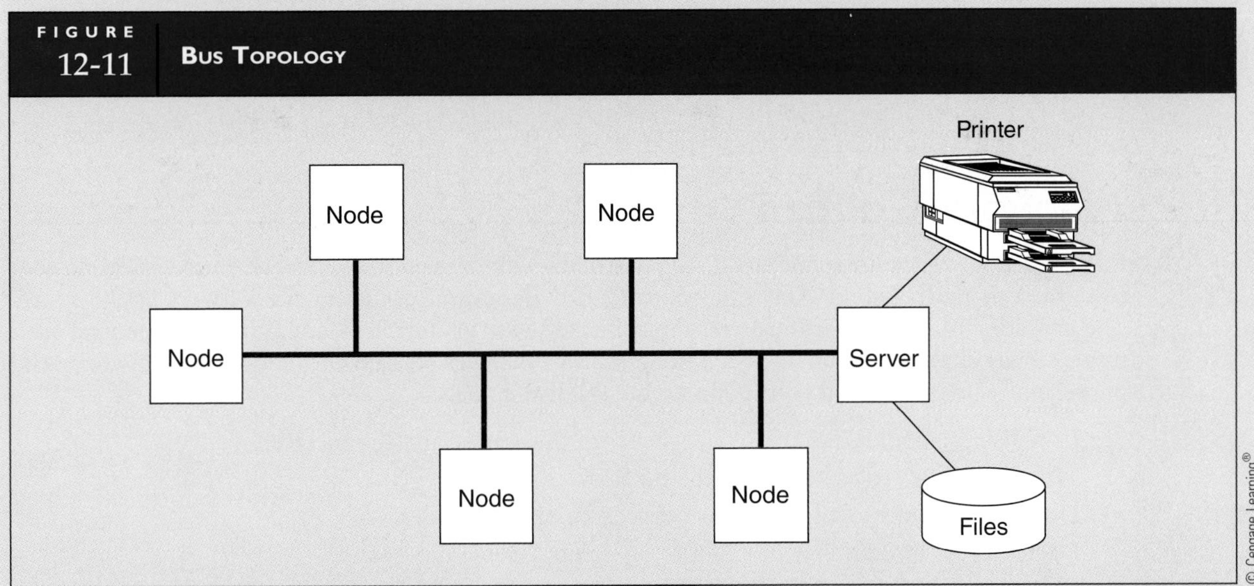

The client-server model distributes the processing between User A's (client) computer and the central file server. Both computers are part of the network, but each is assigned functions that it performs best. For example, the record-searching portion of an application is placed at the server, and the data-manipulation portion is on the client computer. Thus, only a single record, rather than the entire file, must be locked and sent to the client for processing. After processing, the record is returned to the

FIGURE 12-12 **Client-Server Topology**

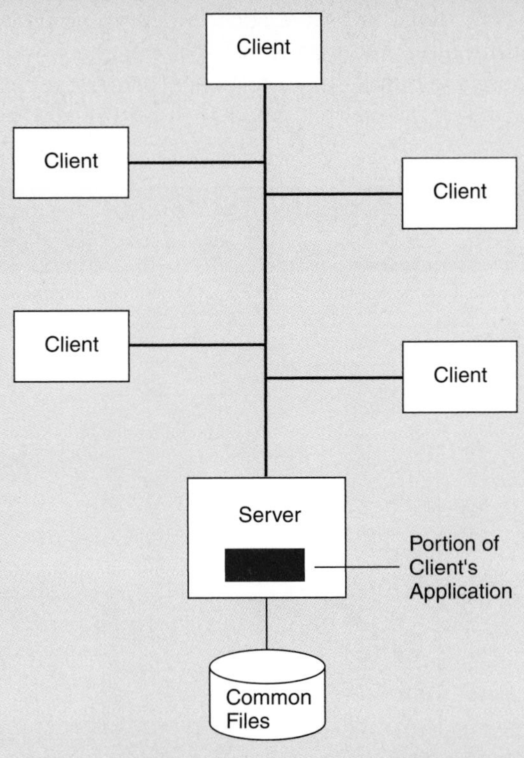

server, which restores it to the table and removes the lock. This approach reduces traffic and allows more efficient use of shared data. Distributing the record-searching logic of the client's application to the server permits other clients to access different records in the same file simultaneously. The client-server approach can be applied to any topology (e.g., ring, star, or bus). Figure 12-12 illustrates the client-server model applied to a bus topology.

Network Control

In this section, we examine methods for controlling communications between the physical devices connected to the network. Network control exists at several points in the network architecture. The majority of network control resides with software in the host computer, but control also resides in servers and terminals at the nodes and in switches located throughout the network. The purpose of network control is to perform the following tasks:

1. Establish a communications session between the sender and the receiver.
2. Manage the flow of data across the network.
3. Detect and resolve data collisions between competing nodes.
4. Detect errors in data that line failure or signal degeneration cause.

DATA COLLISION

To achieve effective network control, there must be an exclusive link or session established between a transmitting and a receiving node. Only one node at a time can transmit a message on a single line. Two or more signals transmitted simultaneously will result in a **data collision**, which destroys both messages. When this happens, the messages must be retransmitted. There are several techniques for managing sessions and controlling data collisions, but most of them are variants of three basic methods: polling, token passing, and carrier sensing.

Polling

Polling is the most popular technique for establishing a communications session in WANs. One site, designated the master, polls the slave sites to determine if they have data to transmit. If a slave responds in the affirmative, the master site locks the network while the data are transmitted. The remaining sites must wait until they are polled before they can transmit. The polling technique illustrated in Figure 12-13 is well suited to both the star and the hierarchical topologies.

FIGURE 12-13 POLLING METHOD OF CONTROLLING DATA COLLISIONS

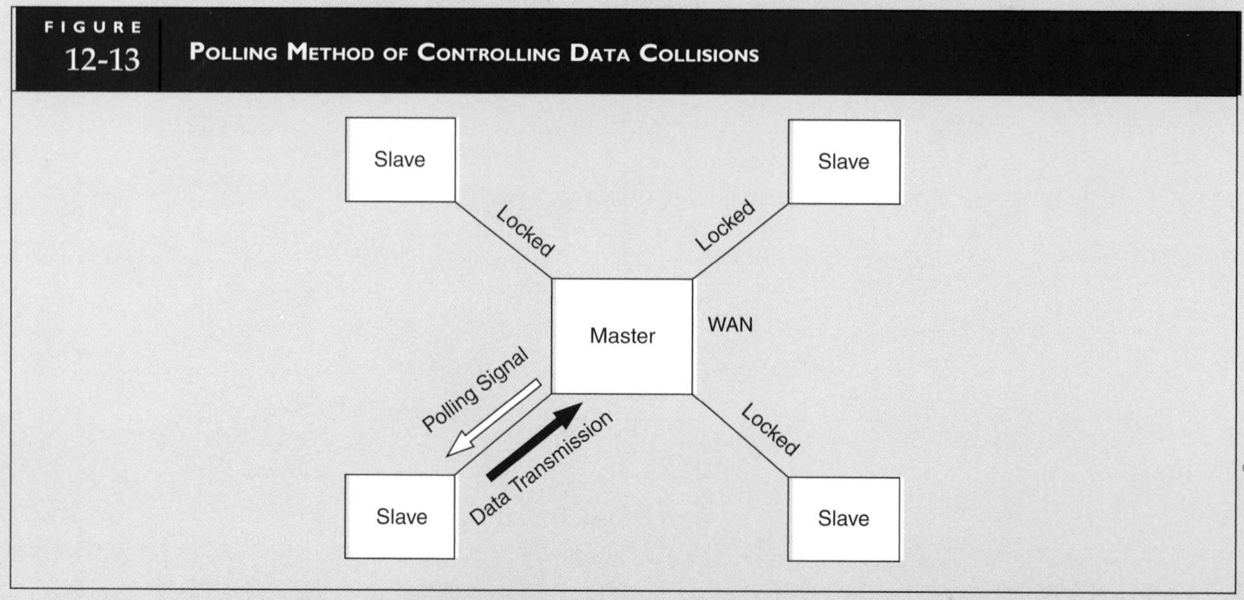

There are two primary advantages to polling. First, polling is noncontentious. Because nodes can send data only when the master node requests, two nodes can never access the network at the same time. Data collisions are, therefore, prevented. Second, an organization can set priorities for data communications across the network. Important nodes can be polled more often than less important nodes.

Token Passing

Token passing involves transmitting a special signal—the token—around the network from node to node in a specific sequence. Each node on the network receives the token, regenerates it, and passes it to the next node. Only the node possessing the token is allowed to transmit data.

Token passing can be used with either ring or bus topologies. On a ring topology, the order in which the nodes are physically connected determines the token-passing sequence. With a bus, the sequence is logical, not physical. The token is passed from node to node in a predetermined order to form a logical ring. Token bus and token ring configurations are illustrated in Figure 12-14.

FIGURE 12-14 TOKEN-PASSING APPROACH TO CONTROLLING DATA COLLISION

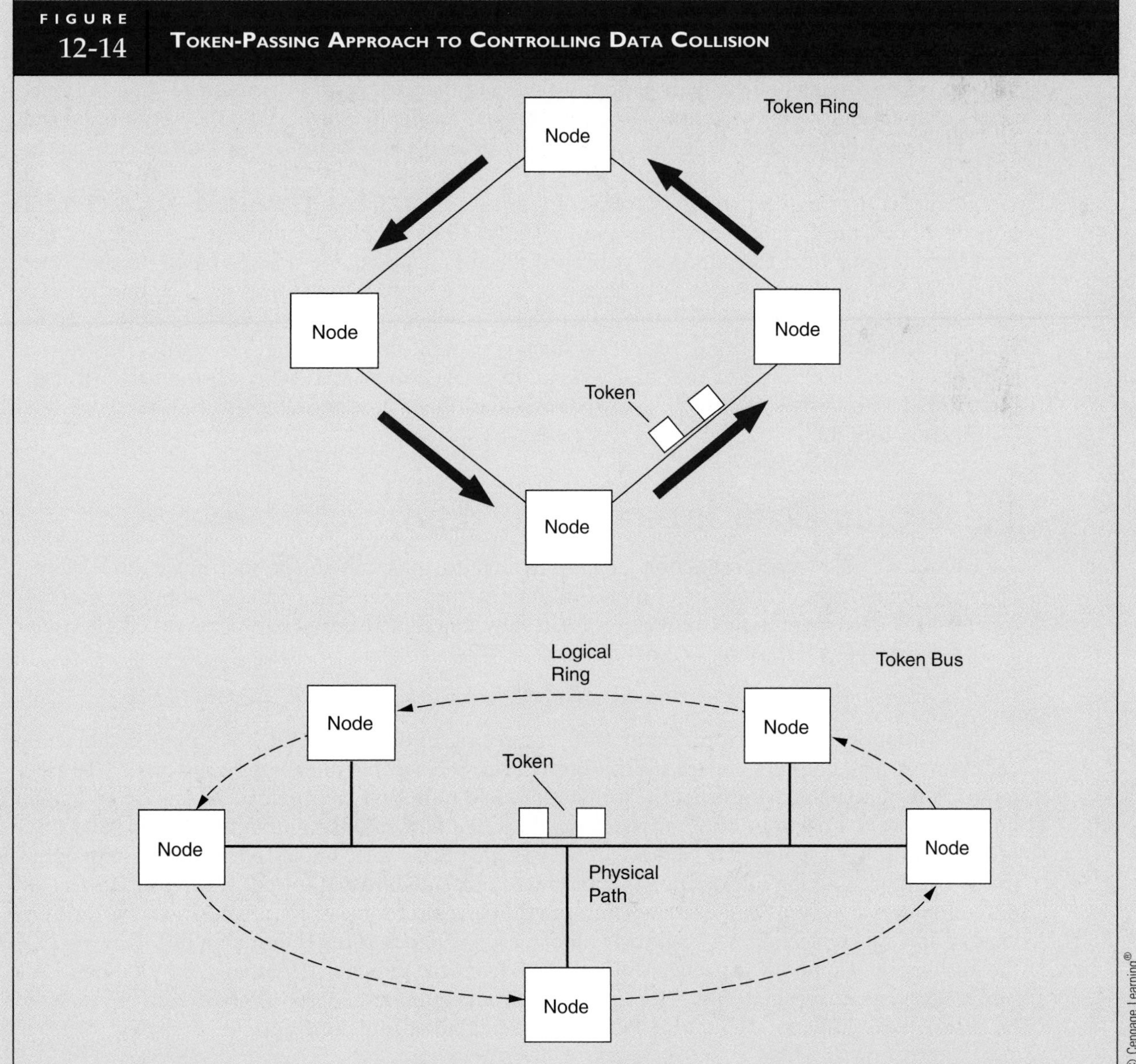

Because nodes are permitted to transmit only when they possess the token, the node wishing to send data across the network seizes the token upon receiving it. Holding the token blocks other nodes from transmitting and ensures that no data collisions will occur. After the transmitting node sends its message and receives an acknowledgment signal from the receiving node, it releases the token. The next node in sequence then has the option of either seizing the token and transmitting data or passing the token to the next node in the circuit.

A major advantage of token passing is its deterministic access method, which avoids data collisions. This is in contrast with the random access approach of carrier sensing (discussed in the following paragraphs). IBM's version of a token ring is emerging as an industry standard.

Carrier Sensing

Carrier sensing is a random access technique that detects collisions when they occur. This technique, which is formally labeled carrier-sensed multiple access with collision detection (CSMA7 CD), is used with the bus topology. The node wishing to transmit listens to the bus to determine if it is in use. If it senses no transmission in progress (no carrier), the node transmits its message to the receiving node. This approach is not as fail-safe as token passing. Collisions can occur when two or more nodes, unaware of each other's intent to transmit, do so simultaneously when they independently perceive the line to be clear. When this happens, the network server directs each node to wait a unique and random period of time and then retransmit the message. In a busy network, data collisions are more likely to occur; thus, it results in delays while the nodes retransmit their messages. Proponents of the token-passing approach point to its collision-avoidance characteristic as a major advantage over the CSMA/CD model.

Ethernet is the best-known LAN software that uses the CSMA/CD standard. Xerox Corporation developed the Ethernet model in the 1970s. In 1980, Digital Equipment Corporation, in a joint venture with Intel Corporation, published the specifications for a LAN based on the Ethernet model. The greatest advantage of Ethernet is that it is established and reliable, and network specialists understand it well. Ethernet also has a number of economic advantages over token ring: (1) the technology, being relatively simple, is well suited to the less costly twisted-pair cabling, whereas token ring works best with more expensive coaxial cable; (2) the network interface cards Ethernet uses are much less expensive than those used in the token ring topology; and (3) Ethernet uses a bus topology, which is easier to expand.

Electronic Data Interchange (EDI)

To coordinate sales and production operations and to maintain an uninterrupted flow of raw materials, many organizations enter into a trading partner agreement with their suppliers and customers. This agreement is the foundation for a fully automated business process called **Electronic Data Interchange (EDI).** A general definition of EDI is:

The intercompany exchange of computer-processible business information in standard format.

The definition reveals several important features of EDI. First, EDI is an inter-organization endeavor. A firm does not engage in EDI on its own. Second, the information systems of the trading partners automatically process the transaction. In a pure EDI environment, there are no human intermediaries to approve or authorize transactions. Authorizations, mutual obligations, and business practices that apply to transactions are all specified in advance under the trading partner agreement. Third, transaction information is transmitted in a standardized format. Therefore, firms with different internal systems can exchange information and do business. Figure 12-15 shows an overview of an EDI connection between two companies. Assume that the transaction in Figure 12-15 is the customer's (Company A) inventory purchase from the supplier (Company B). Company A's purchases system automatically creates an electronic purchase order (PO), which it sends to its translation software. Here, the PO is converted to a standard format electronic message

FIGURE 12-15 OVERVIEW OF EDI

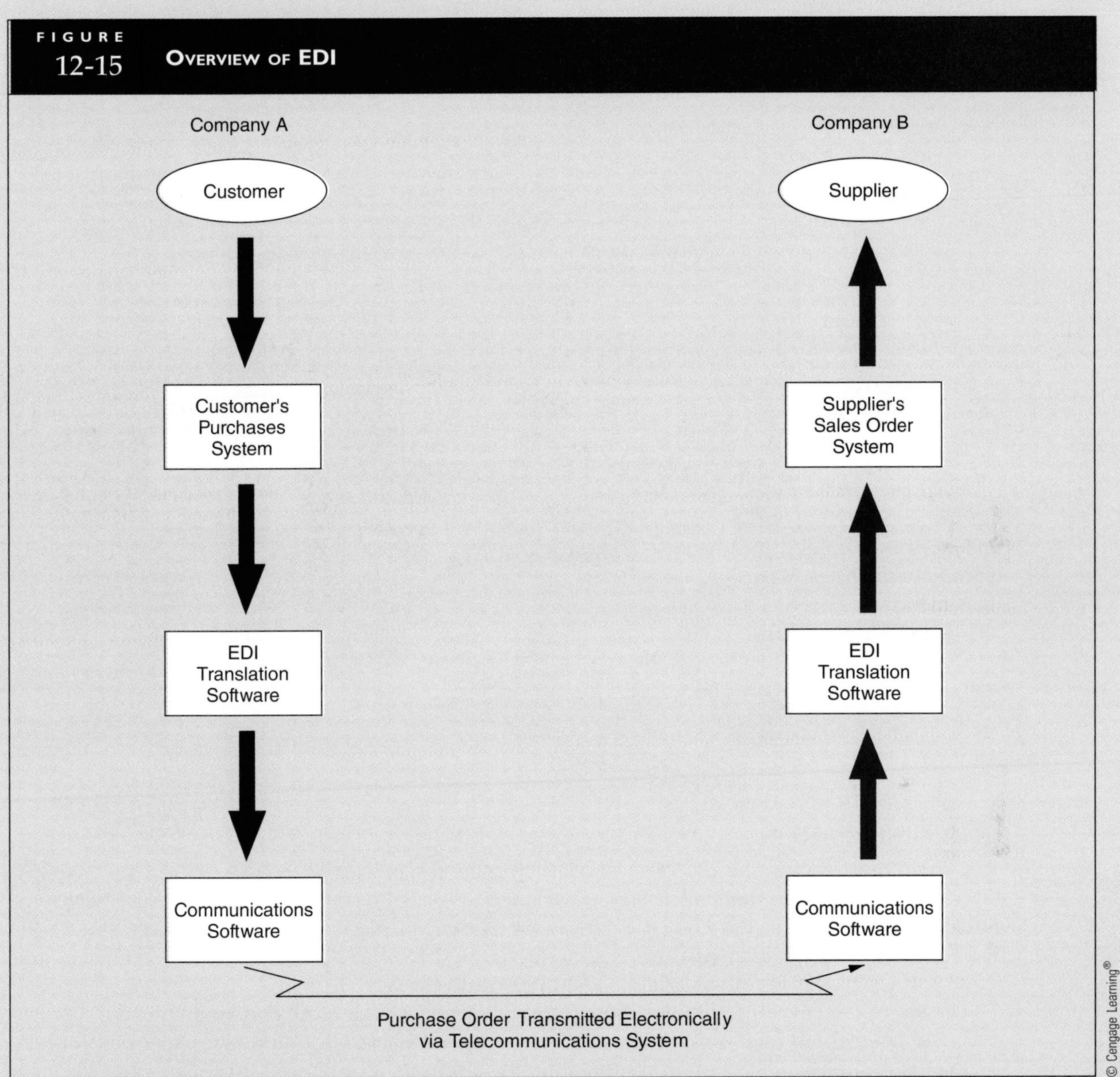

ready for transmission. The message is transmitted to Company B's translation software, where it is converted to the supplier's internal format. Company B's sales order processing system receives the customer order, which it processes automatically.

Figure 12-15 shows a direct communications link between companies. But many companies choose to use a third-party VAN to connect to their trading partners. Figure 12-16 illustrates this arrangement. The originating company transmits its EDI messages to the network rather than directly to the trading partner's computer. The network directs each EDI transmission to its destination and deposits the message in the appropriate electronic mailbox. The messages stay in the mailboxes until the receiving companies' systems retrieve them. The network is a VAN because it provides service by managing the distribution of the messages between trading partners. VANs can also provide an important degree of control over EDI transactions. We examine EDI control issues in Chapter 16.

FIGURE 12-16 VALUE-ADDED NETWORK AND EDI

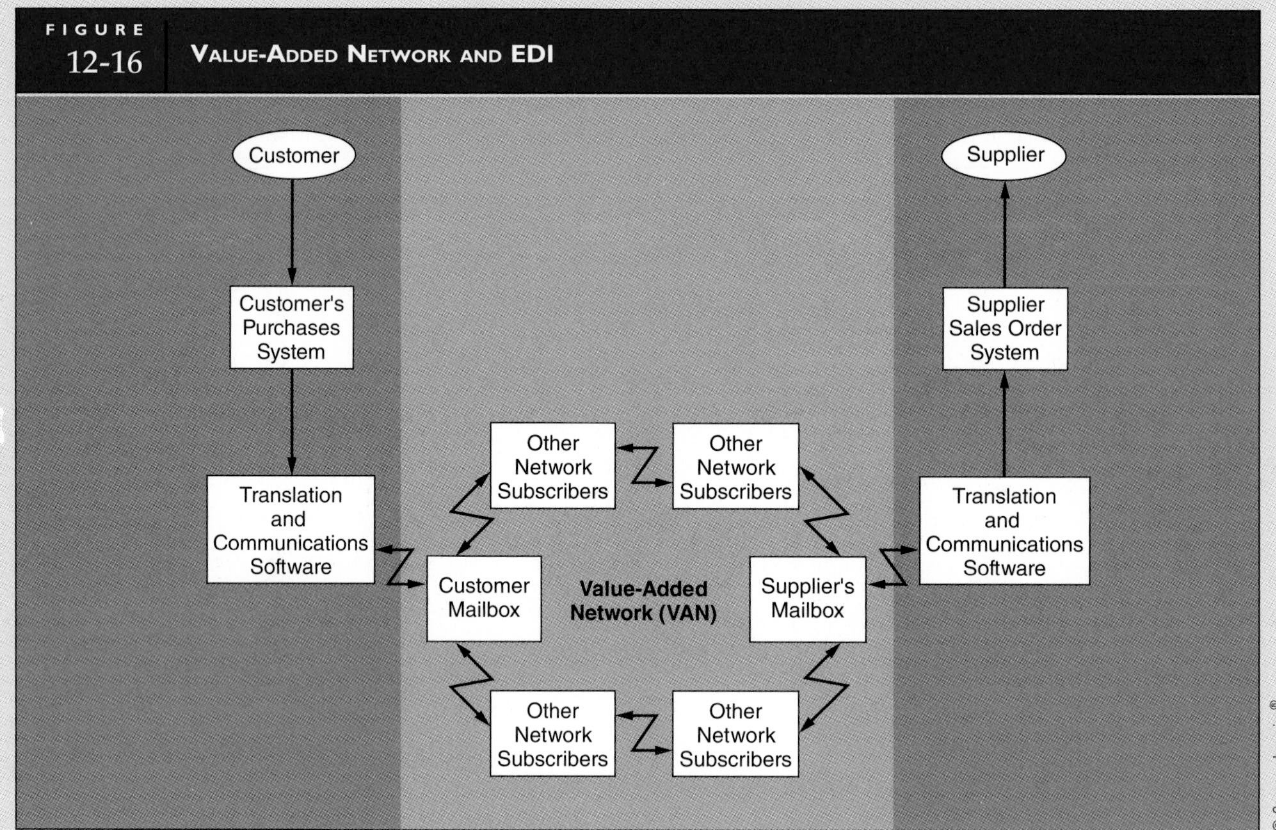

EDI STANDARDS

Key to EDI success is the use of a standard format for messaging between dissimilar systems. Over the years, both in the United States and internationally, a number of formats have been proposed. The standard in the United States is the American National Standards Institute (ANSI) X.12 format. The standard used internationally is the EDI For Administration, Commerce, and Transport (EDIFACT) format. Figure 12-17 illustrates the X.12 format.

The electronic envelope contains the electronic address of the receiver, communications protocols, and control information. This is the electronic equivalent of a traditional paper envelope. A functional group is a collection of transaction sets (electronic documents) for a particular business application, such as a group of sales invoices or purchase orders. The transaction set is the electronic document and is composed of data segments and data elements. Figure 12-18 relates these terms to a conventional document.

Each data segment is an information category on the document, such as part number, unit price, or vendor name. The data elements are specific items of data related to a segment. In the example in Figure 12-18, these include such items as REX-446, $127.86, and Ozment Supply.

BENEFITS OF EDI

EDI has made considerable inroads in a number of industries, including automotive, groceries, retail, health care, and electronics. The following are some common EDI cost savings that justify the approach.

- *Data keying*. EDI reduces or even eliminates the need for data entry.
- *Error reduction*. Firms using EDI see reductions in data keying errors, human interpretation and classification errors, and filing (lost document) errors.

FIGURE 12-17 THE X.12 FORMAT

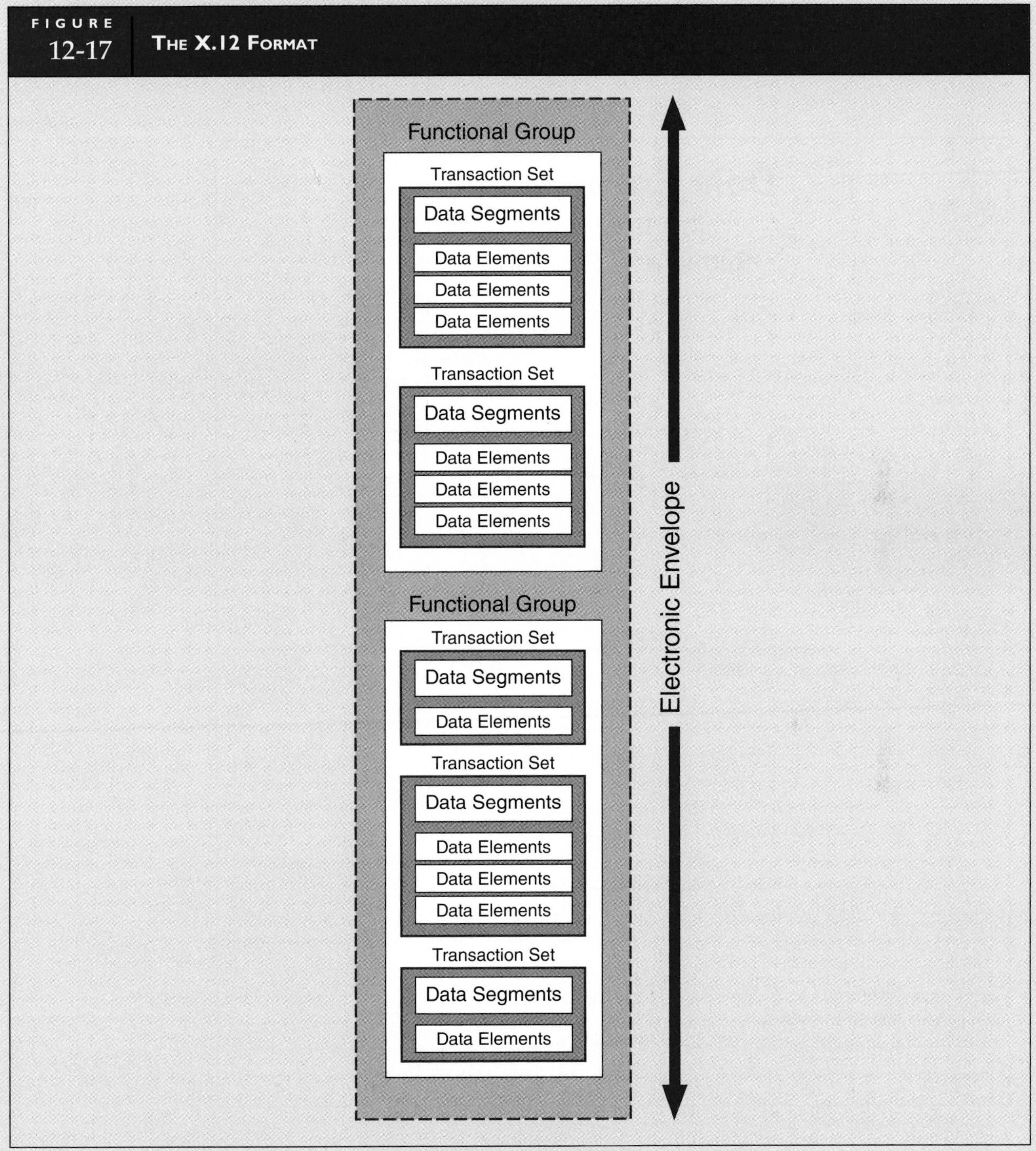

Source: *B. K. Stone, One to Get Ready: How to Prepare Your Company for EDI* (CoreStates, 1988): 1212.

- *Reduction of paper*. The use of electronic envelopes and documents reduces drastically the paper forms in the system.
- *Postage*. Mailed documents are replaced with much cheaper data transmissions.
- *Automated procedures*. EDI automates manual activities associated with purchasing, sales order processing, cash disbursements, and cash receipts.
- *Inventory reduction*. By ordering directly as needed from vendors, EDI reduces the lag time that promotes inventory accumulation.

FIGURE 12-18 RELATIONSHIP BETWEEN X.12 FORMAT AND A CONVENTIONAL SOURCE DOCUMENT

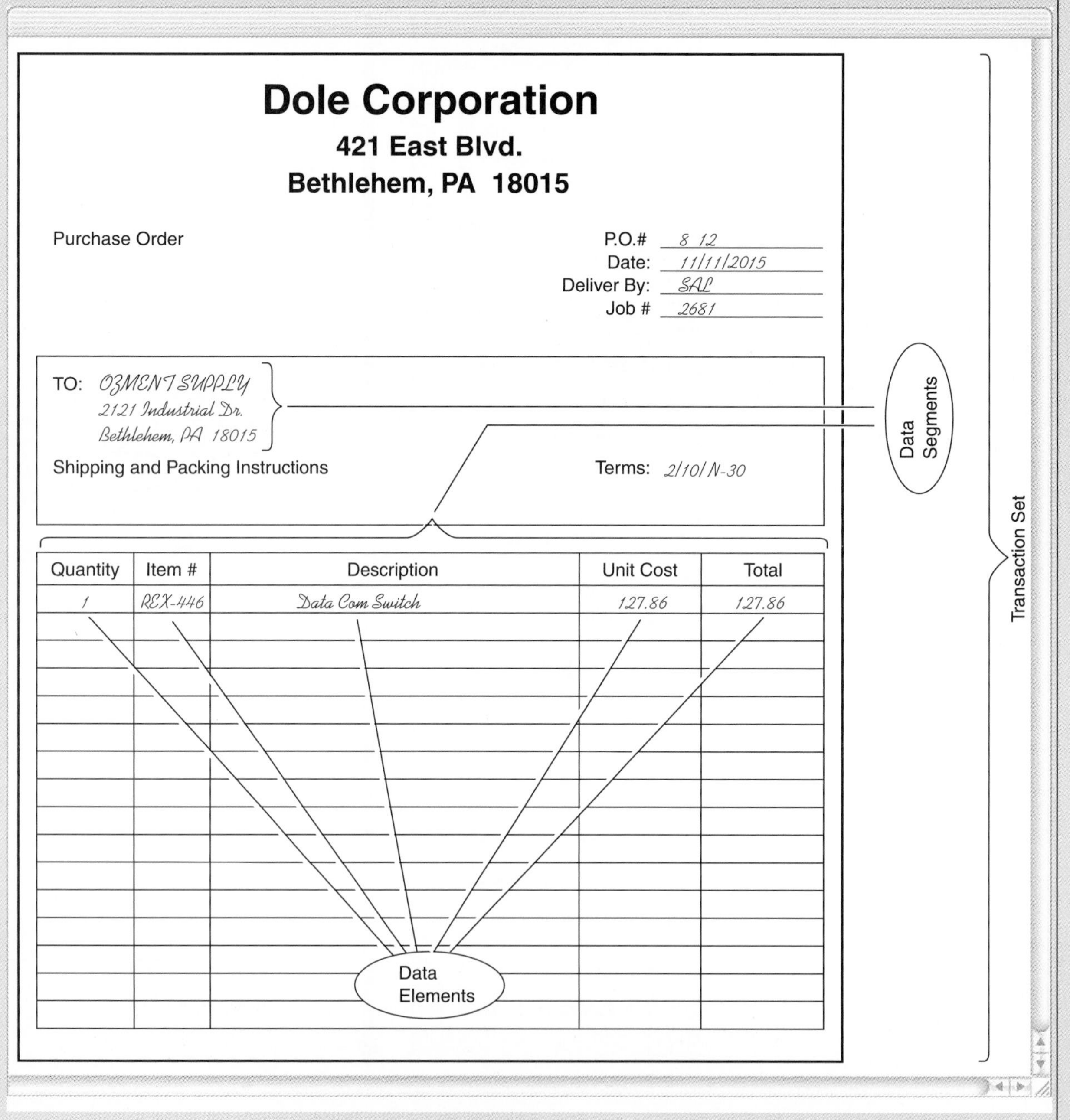

Source: J. M. Cathey, "Electronic Data Interchange: What the Controller Should Know," *Management Accounting* (November 1991): 4.

FINANCIAL EDI

Using electronic funds transfer (EFT) for cash disbursement and cash receipts processing is more complicated than using EDI for purchasing and selling activities. EFT requires intermediary banks between trading partners. This arrangement is shown in Figure 12-19. The buyer's EDI system receives the purchase invoices and automatically approves them for payment. On the payment date, the buyer's system automatically makes an EFT to its originating bank (OBK). The OBK

FIGURE 12-19 EFT TRANSACTIONS BETWEEN TRADING PARTNERS

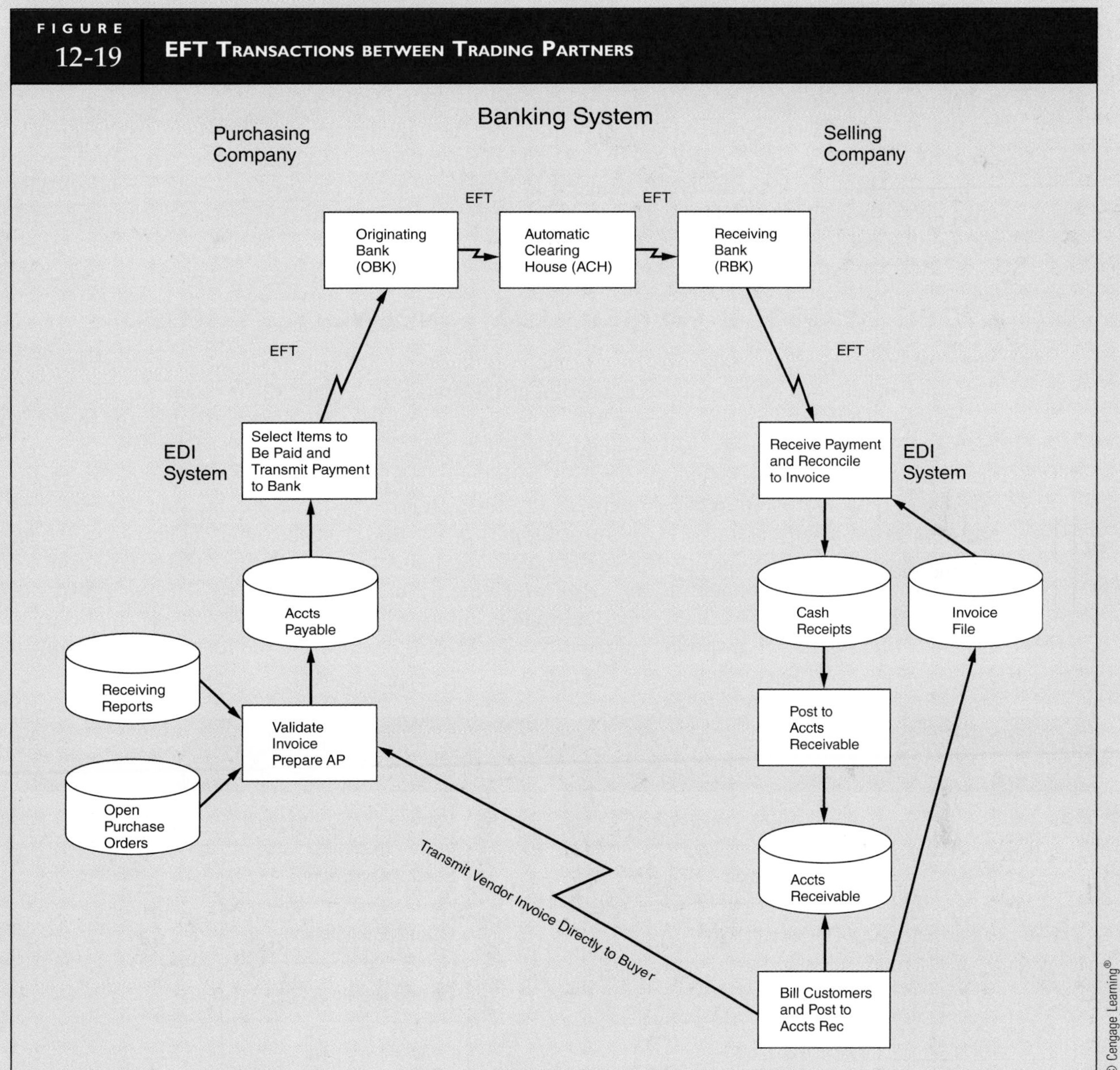

removes funds from the buyer's account and transmits them electronically to the automatic clearing house (ACH) bank. The ACH is a central bank that carries accounts for its member banks. The ACH transfers the funds from the OBK to the receiving bank (RBK), which in turn applies the funds to the seller's account.

Transferring funds by EFT poses no special problem. A check can easily be represented within the X.12 format. The problem arises with the remittance advice information that accompanies the check. Remittance advice information is often quite extensive because of complexities in the transaction. The check may be in payment of multiple invoices or only a partial invoice. There may be disputed amounts because of price disagreements, damaged goods, or incomplete deliveries. In traditional systems, modifying the remittance advice and/or attaching a letter explaining the payment resolves these disputes.

Converting remittance information to electronic form can result in very large records. Members of the ACH system are required to accept and process only EFT formats limited to 94 characters of data—a record size sufficient for only very basic messages. Not all banks in the ACH system support the ANSI standard format for remittances, ANSI 820. In such cases, remittance information must be sent to the seller by separate EDI transmission or conventional mail. The seller must then implement separate procedures to match bank and customer EDI transmissions in applying payments to customer accounts.

Recognizing the void between services demanded and those the ACH system supplies, many banks have established themselves as value-added banks (VABs) to compete for this market. A VAB can accept electronic disbursements and remittance advices from its clients in any format. It converts EDI transactions to the ANSI X.12 and 820 formats for electronic processing. In the case of non-EDI transactions, the VAB writes traditional checks to the creditor. The services VABs offer allow their clients to employ a single cash disbursement system that can accommodate both EDI and non-EDI customers.

Open System Interface (OSI) Network Protocol

The OSI model provides standards by which the products of different manufacturers can interface with one another in a seamless interconnection at the user level. Figure 12-20 shows the seven-layer OSI model. The OSI standard has the following general features. First, each layer in the model is independent, which allows the development of separate protocols specifically for each layer. Second, the layers at each node communicate logically with their counterpart layers across nodes. The physical flow of data and parameters pass between layers. Each layer performs specific subtasks that support the layer above it and are in turn supported by the layer below it. Third, the model distinguishes between the tasks of data communications and data manipulation. The first four layers are dedicated to data communications tasks, which are a function of hardware devices and special software. The last three layers support data manipulation, which is a function of user applications and operating systems. The specific function of each layer is described in the following paragraphs.

FIGURE 12-20 THE OSI PROTOCOL

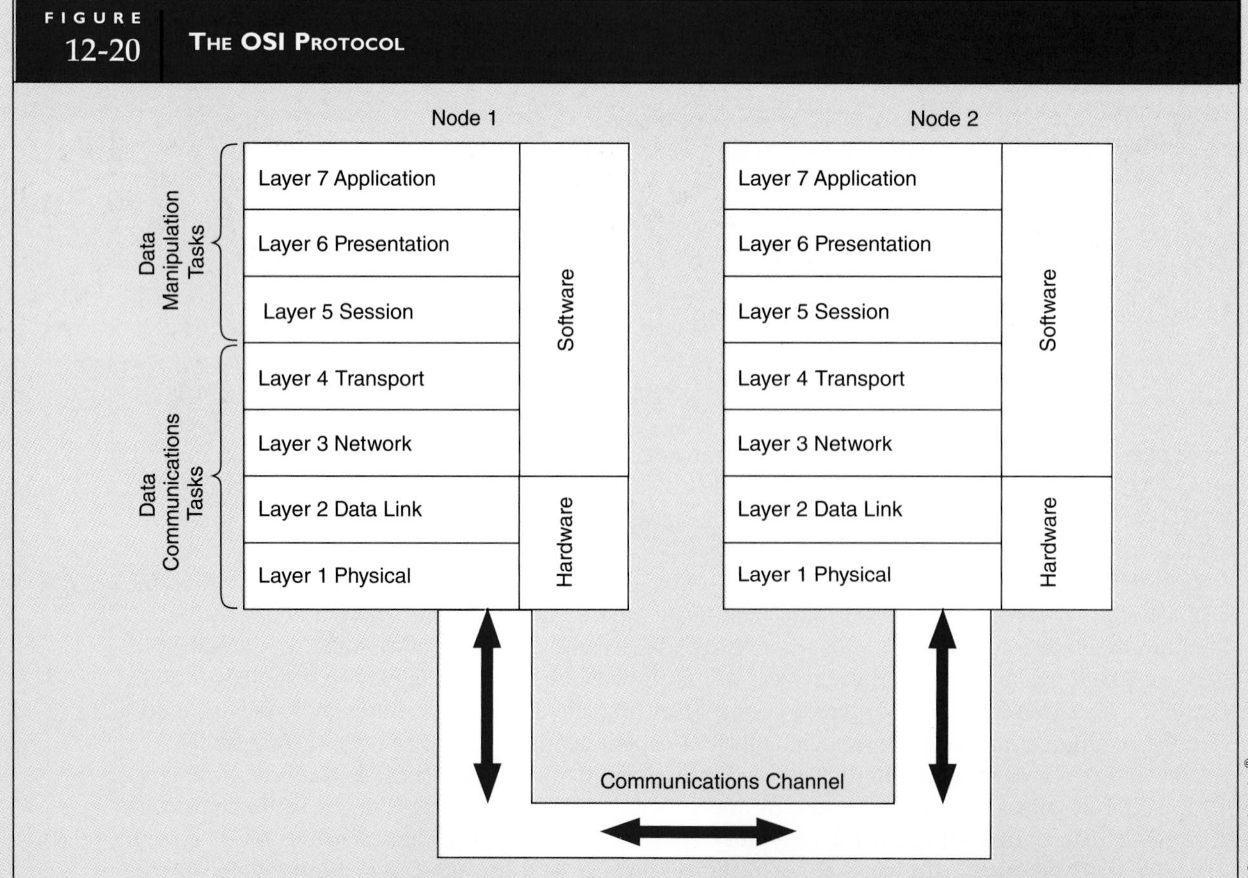

LAYER FUNCTIONS

Physical Layer

The physical layer, the first and lowest level in the protocol, defines standards for the physical interconnection of devices to the electronic circuit. This level is concerned with pin connections to devices, the wiring of workstations, and cabling standards. An example of a standard at this layer is the RS-232 connector cable that virtually all microcomputer manufacturers use.

Data Link Layer

Data link layer protocols are concerned with the transmission of packets of data from node to node based on the workstation address. This includes message origination, acknowledgment of message receipt, and error detection and retransmission.

Network Layer

Network layer protocols deal with the routing and relaying of data to different LANs and WANs based on the network address. They specify how to identify nodes on a network and regulate the sequencing of messages to the nodes. In addition, this third layer describes how packet data are transferred between networks with different architectures, which permits the synchronization of data.

Transport Layer

The purpose of the transport layer is to ensure delivery of the entire file or message across individual networks and multiple networks, regardless of the number and type of dissimilar devices involved. If a transmission error is detected, this layer defines the retransmission methods to ensure the complete and accurate delivery of the message.

In addition, the transport layer seeks the connection between users that best meets the users' needs for message packeting and multiplexing messages. These protocols provide the logic for segmenting long messages into smaller units and, at the receiving end, reassembling the packets into the original message.

Session Layer

A session layer is a specific connection between two users or entities on the network. The purpose of this layer is to guarantee a correct and synchronized connection. At this level, the protocols for starting a session may require a user password to establish the legitimacy of the connection. Protocols may also determine priorities of sessions and rules for interrupting and reestablishing the session. For example, a transmission of higher priority may interrupt the transmission of a large document. Session protocols define the rules for such interruptions and the procedures for resuming the original transmission.

Presentation Layer

In the presentation layer, data in transit are often in a format that is very different from what the user's application requires. During transmission, data may be compressed to increase transfer speeds, blocked for efficiency, and encrypted for security. Presentation protocols provide the rules for editing, formatting, converting, and displaying data to the user's system.

Application Layer

The application layer provides the overall environment for the user or the user's application to access the network. This layer provides what are called common application services. These services—common to all communicating applications—include protocols for network management, file transfer, and e-mail. The uniqueness of user applications makes this layer the least amenable to general standards. By their very nature, protocols at this level impinge upon application structure and function. Consequently, these are the least rigorously defined rules. Most of the protocols here tend to be vendor defined. For example, an individual vendor's database management system may provide the application layer protocols for managing file transfers.

Key Terms

Advanced encryption standard (AES) (519)
algorithm (519)
application-level firewall (521)
botnets (515)
caesar cipher (519)
certification authorities (521)
cloud computing (508)
cookies (514)
data collision (532)
denial of service attack (DoS) (514)
digital certificate (521)
digital envelope (519)
digital signature (519)
distributed denial of service (DDoS) (515)
distribution level (508)
document name (504)
domain name (504)
dynamic virtual organization (510)
Electronic Data Interchange (EDI) (534)
extranet (503)
File Transfer Protocol (FTP) (506)
firewall (521)
home page (504)
HyperText Markup Language (HTML) (503)
HyperText Transfer Protocol (HTTP) (504)
HyperText Transport Protocol-Next Generation (HTTP-NG) (507)
information level (508)
Infrastructure-as-a-Service (IaaS) (509)
intelligent control agents (524)
International Standards Organization (506)
Internet Message Access Protocol (507)
Internet Relay Chat (IRC) (515)
IP broadcast address (515)
IP spoofing (514)
key (519)
Network News Transfer Protocol (NNTP) (507)
network virtualization (510)
network-level firewall (521)
Open System Interface (OSI) (506)
packet switching (502)
ping (515)
platform-as-a-Service (PaaS) (509)
polling (532)
Post Office Protocol (507)
privacy (523)
Privacy Enhanced Mail (PEM) (507)
Private Communications Technology (PCT) (507)
private key (519)
protocol (505)
protocol prefix (504)
public key encryption (519)
public key infrastructure (PKI) (521)
risk (512)
Rivest-Shamir-Adleman (RSA) (519)
Safe Harbor Agreement (523)
Secure Electronic Transmission (507)
Secure Sockets Layer (SSL) (507)
Simple Network Mail Protocol (SNMP) (507)
Smurf attack (515)
Software-as-a-Service (SaaS) (509)
storage virtualization (510)
Subdirectory name (504)
symmetric key (519)
SYN flood attack (515)
SYNchronize-ACKnowledge (SYN-ACK) (514)
TELNET (506)
transaction level (508)
Transfer Control Protocol/Internet Protocol (TCP/IP) (506)
Uniform Resource Locator (URL) (504)
value-added network (VAN) (524)
virtualization (509)
virtual private network (VPN) (503)
web page (503)
websites (504)
zombie (515)

Review Questions

1. What is packet switching?
2. What is a VPN?
3. Name the three types of addresses used on the Internet.
4. Describe the elements of an e-mail address.
5. Networks would be inoperable without protocols. Explain their importance and the functions they perform.
6. What is the purpose of the TCP portion of TCP/IP?
7. What does the HTTP do?
8. How do HTTP and HTTP-NG differ?
9. What is virtualization?
10. Define *IP spoofing*.
11. What is a cookie?
12. What is network virtualization?
13. Who are the three parties in a smurf attack?
14. What is a ping, and how does it work?
15. What is a seal of assurance?
16. What is a VAN?
17. What is a LAN?
18. What is a WAN?
19. What is a NIC?
20. What is a server?
21. What are the three classes of cloud computing services?
22. What is Software as a Service (SaaS)?
23. Give two advantages of Infrastructure as a Service (IaaS).
24. What is OSI?

Discussion Questions

1. What purpose do protocols serve?
2. Explain the purpose of the two elements of TCP/IP.
3. Distinguish between the FTP and TELNET protocols.
4. Discuss the three levels of Internet business models.
5. What is a dynamic virtual organization?
6. Give two differences between ASP and SaaS.
7. Why is cloud computing not the best option for all companies?
8. What are cookies, and why are they used?
9. What security concerns pertain to cookies?
10. How does IP spoofing support Internet crime?
11. Describe a distributed denial of service (DDoS) attack
12. What is a digital envelope?
13. What is a digital signature?
14. What is a digital certificate? How is it different from a digital signature?
15. Distinguish between a network-level firewall and an application-level firewall.
16. What is a certification authority, and what are the implications for the accounting profession?
17. Discuss the key aspects of the following five seal-granting organizations: BBB, TRUSTe, Veri-Sign, Inc., ICSA, and AICPA/CICA WebTrust.
18. Differentiate between a LAN and a WAN. Do you have either or both at your university or college?
19. Explain the purpose of each of the layers in the OSI protocol model.

Multiple-Choice Questions

1. A DDoS attack
   a. is more intensive than a DoS attack because it emanates from a single source.
   b. may take the form of either a SYN flood or smurf attack.
   c. is so named because it affects many victims simultaneously, which are distributed across the Internet.
   d. turns the target victim's computers into zombies that are unable to access the Internet.
   e. none of the above is correct.

2. A digital signature
   a. is the encrypted mathematical value of the message sender's name.
   b. is derived from the digest of a document that has been encrypted with the sender's private key.
   c. is derived from the digest of a document that has been encrypted with the sender's public key.
   d. is the computed digest of the sender's digital certificate.
   e. allows digital messages to be sent over an analog telephone line.
3. Which of the following statements is correct?
   a. Cloud computing allows client firms to acquire IT resources from vendors in strict accordance with long-term contracts that stipulate services.
   b. A packet combines the messages of multiple users into a unit for transmission. At the receiving end, the packet is disassembled into individual messages and distributed to the user.
   c. A virtual private network (VPN) is a private network within a public network.
   d. Infrastructure-as-a-Service (IaaS) is a software distribution model in which service providers host applications for client organizations over a private network or the Internet.
   e. An advantage of cloud computing over traditional outsourcing is that internal control and security issues are not concerns for the client firm, but are the responsibility of the cloud service provider'
4. Which of the following statements about cookies is true?
   a. Cookies were originally intended to facilitate advertising on the web.
   b. Cookies always contain encrypted data.
   c. Cookies are text files and never contain encrypted data.
   d. Cookies allow websites to off-load the storage of information about visitors.
   e. Web browsers cannot function without cookies.
5. A message that is contrived to appear to be coming from a trusted or authorized source is called
   a. a DDoS attack.
   b. digital signature forging.
   c. a SYN-ACK packet
   d. URL masquerading.
   e. Internet protocol spoofing..
6. Which of the following statements is correct?
   a. TCP/IP is the basic protocol that permits communication between Internet sites.
   b. TCP/IP controls web browsers that access the web.
   c. TCP/IP is the document format used to produce web pages.
   d. TCP/IP is used to transfer text files, programs, spreadsheets, and databases across the Internet. TCP/IP is a low-level encryption scheme used to secure transmissions in higher-level (HTTP) format.
7. A ping signal is
   a. used to perpetrate URL masquerading.
   b. an Internet maintenance tool.
   c. use for Internet protocol spoofing.
   d. an Internet protocol
   e. a SYN-ACK packet.
8. A system of computers that connects the internal users of an organization distributed over a wide geographic area is a(n)
   a. LAN
   b. Internet
   c. decentralized network
   d. intranet
   e. multidrop network
9. The client-server model
   a. is best suited to the token ring topology because the random-access method this topology uses detects data collisions.
   b. is most effective when used as a bus topology because its deterministic access method avoids collisions and prevents data loss during transmissions.
   c. distributes both data and processing tasks to the server node. The client-server model can use the bus or ring topology.
   d. is more efficient than the bus or ring topologies because it transmits an entire file of records to the requesting node rather than only a single record.
   e. is not used in conjunction with either the bus or ring topology.

10. Which statement about Sniffer software is true?

a. It used by malicious websites to sniff data from cookies stored on the user's hard drive.

b. illegal software for decoding encrypted messages transmitted over a shared intranet channel.

c. It used by bus topology intranets to sniff for carriers before transmitting a message to avoid data collisions.

d. It an illegal program downloaded from the web to decode encrypted data of Internet customers. And sniff passwords their passwords.

e. It is used by network administrators to analyze network traffic.

Problems

1. ENCRYPTION

The coded message that follows is an encrypted message from Brutus to the Roman Senate. It was produced using the Caesar cipher method, in which each letter is shifted by a fixed number of places (determined by the key value).

OHWV GR MXOLXV RQ PRQGDB PDUFK
48 GUHW: WRJD FDVXDO (EBRG)

Required

Determine the key used to produce the coded message and decode it.

2. ENCRYPTION

a. Develop a Caesar cipher-type encryption algorithm with a little more complexity in it. For example, the algorithm could alternatively shift the cleartext letters positive and negative by the amount of the key value. Variations on this are limitless.

b. Select a single-digit key.

c. Code a short message using the algorithm and key.

d. Give your instructor the algorithm, key, cleartext, and ciphertext.

e. Optional: Your instructor will randomly redistribute to the class the ciphertext messages completed in part d above. You are to decode the message you receive as an additional assignment.

3. SEALS OF ASSURANCE

Visit 10 websites that sell products or services, and record the following for each:

a. The URL.

b. Did the site issue you a cookie?

c. Did the site have a published privacy policy?

d. Does the site reserve the right to distribute or sell customer data?

e. Does the site use encryption for transmission of personal/financial data?

4. CERTIFICATION AUTHORITY LICENSING

Research the current state of certification authority licensing in the United States and Europe. Write a brief report of your findings.

5. CLOUD COMPUTING.

Write an essay on the relative benefits of cloud computing for large and small companies.

6. ELECTRONIC DATA INTERCHANGE

The purchase order for one firm is the source document for the sales order of another firm. Consider the following purchase order and sales order data elements stored for two firms. Discuss any differences that may be problematic in transferring information between the two firms.

Purchasing Firm:

GH BETTIS

A Division of Galveston-Houston Corp.

1200 Post Oak Blvd.

P.O. Box 4768

Houston, TX 77637-9877

Data Elements

Vendor Number

Vendor Name

Vendor Address

Vendor City

Vendor State
Vendor Country
Vendor Zip Code
Purchase Order No.
Date
Shipment Destination Code
Vendor Part No.
Item Description
Quantity Ordered
Unit Price
Total
Selling Firm:
Oakland Steel Company
469 Lakeland Blvd.
Chicago, IL 60613-8888
Data Elements
Customer Number
Customer Name
Customer Address
Customer City
Customer State
Customer Country
Customer Zip Code
Purchase Order No.
Sales Order No.
Date
Shipping Company
Vendor Part No.
Item Description
Quantity Ordered
Unit Price
Total
Discount Offered
Tax
Freight Charges

7. VITUALIZATION

Virtualization technology is credited with unleashing cloud computing. Write an essay explaining virtualization and its impact on cloud computing.

8. DIGITAL FRAUD

In a financial fraud case, city employees in Brooklyn, New York, accessed digital databases to defraud the city of $20 million. Several employees, in collusion with the former deputy tax collector, completely erased or reduced $13 million in property taxes and $7 million in accrued interest that taxpayers owed. In exchange for this service, the taxpayers paid the employees involved bribes of 10 to 30 percent of their bills.

Required

Discuss the control techniques that could prevent or detect this fraud.

PART IV

Systems Development Activities

CHAPTER

13

Managing the Systems Development Life Cycle*

A responsive, user-oriented information system is a valuable asset of the modern business organization. Well-designed systems can increase business performance by reducing inventories, eliminating nonvalue-added activities, improving customer service, and coordinating supply chain activities.

This chapter examines several topics related to the process by which organizations acquire information systems. It begins with an overview of the **systems development life cycle (SDLC).** This multistage process guides organization management through the development and/or purchase of information systems. Next, the chapter presents the key issues pertaining to developing a systems strategy, including its relationship to the strategic business plan, the current legacy situation, and feedback from the user community. The chapter provides a methodology for assessing the feasibility of proposed projects and for selecting individual projects to go forward for construction and delivery to their users. The chapter concludes by reviewing the role of accountants in managing the SDLC.

Learning Objectives

After studying this chapter, you should:

- Be able to identify the key stages in the SDLC.
- Recognize how a firm's business strategy will shape its information system.
- Understand the relationship between strategic systems planning and legacy systems.
- Understand what transpires during systems analysis.
- Understand the TELOS model for assessing project feasibility.
- Be familiar with cost-benefit analysis issues related to information systems projects.
- Understand the role of accountants in the SDLC.

The Systems Development Life Cycle

Moderate and large firms with unique information needs often develop information systems in-house. That is to say that the information technology (IT) professionals within the firm design and program the systems. A greater number of smaller companies and large firms with relatively standardized information needs opt to purchase information systems from software vendors. Both approaches represent significant financial

*This chapter was co-authored by Jiri Polak, PhD, Deloitte & Touche, and Vojtech Merunka, PhD, Deloitte & Touche.

FIGURE 13-1 SYSTEMS DEVELOPMENT LIFE CYCLE

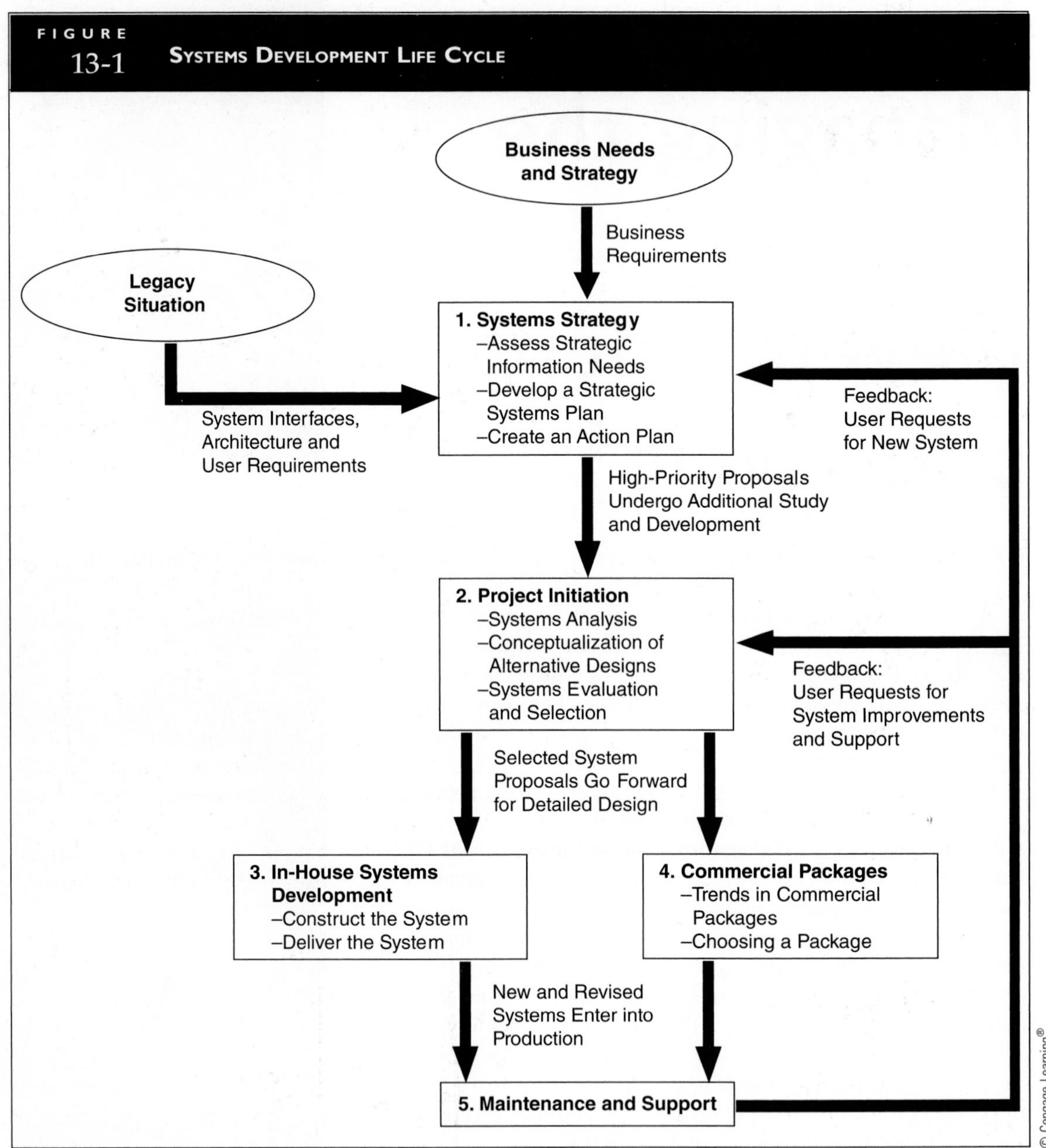

and operational risks. The SDLC shown in Figure 13-1 is a model for reducing this risk through careful planning, execution, control, and documentation of key activities. The five phases of this model are outlined in the following paragraphs. Systems strategy and project initiation are discussed in this chapter. The remaining phases are the topics of Chapter 14.

SYSTEMS STRATEGY. The first step in the SDLC is to develop a systems strategy, which requires understanding the strategic business needs of the organization. This may be derived from the organization's mission statement, an analysis of competitive pressures on the firm, and the nature of current and anticipated market conditions. These needs reflect the organization's current position relative to where it needs to be in the long term to maintain strategic advantage. In addition, project management must consider the information systems' implications pertaining to legacy systems and concerns registered through user feedback. A strategic plan for meeting these various and complex needs, along with a timetable for implementation of selected systems, is produced.

PROJECT INITIATION. Project initiation is the process by which systems proposals are assessed for consistency with the strategic systems plan and evaluated in terms of their feasibility and cost-benefit characteristics. Alternative conceptual designs are considered and those selected, enter the construct phase of the SDLC. Depending upon the nature of the project and the needs of the organization, the proposal will require in-house development, a commercial package, or both.

IN-HOUSE DEVELOPMENT. As mentioned earlier, some organizations have unique information needs that can be adequately met only through internal development. The in-house development step includes analyzing user needs, designing processes and databases, creating user views, programming the applications, and testing and implementing the completed system.

COMMERCIAL PACKAGES. When the nature of the project and the needs of the user permit, most organizations will seek a precoded commercial software package rather than develop a new system from scratch. The organizations that can implement commercial software accrue a number of advantages. These include lower initial cost, shorter implementation time, better controls, and rigorous vendor testing. All of these benefits translate into cost savings for the user. This process, however, is not without risk. Formal procedures need to be followed to ensure that the user gets a package that adequately meets his or her needs and is compatible with existing systems.

MAINTENANCE AND SUPPORT. Maintenance involves both acquiring and implementing the latest software versions of commercial packages as well as making in-house modifications to existing systems to accommodate changing user needs. Maintenance may be relatively trivial, such as modifying an application to produce a new report, or more extensive, such as programming new functionality into a system. The feedback loops from maintenance to the project initiation and systems strategy steps, respectively, despite these relationships.

Traditionally, systems maintenance was viewed as a separate and distinct stage of the SDLC that could last 5 to 10 years. Modern businesses in highly competitive industries, however, see frequent changes in technology and much shorter system life spans. Indeed, this is becoming the norm for many organizations. Many complex systems today are developed and implemented using an incremental approach that integrates maintenance and new development. Systems maintenance is often viewed as the first phase of a new development cycle. Existing (maintained) applications are the prototypes for their new versions. Thus, instead of implementing an application in a single big-bang release, modern systems are delivered in parts continuously and quickly as smaller releases that can more accurately reflect changing business needs. Another aspect of modern maintenance includes establishing a user support infrastructure. This could include helpdesk services, providing user training and education classes, and documenting user feedback pertaining to problems and system errors.

PARTICIPANTS IN SYSTEMS DEVELOPMENT

The participants in systems development can be classified into three broad groups: systems professionals, end users, and stakeholders.

Systems professionals are systems analysts, systems designers, and programmers. These individuals actually build the system. They gather facts about problems with the current system, analyze these facts, and formulate a solution to solve the problems. The product of their efforts is a new system.

End users are those for whom the system is built. Many users exist at all levels in an organization. These include managers, operations personnel, accountants, and internal auditors. In some organizations, it is difficult to find someone who is not a user. During systems development, systems professionals work with the primary users to obtain an understanding of the users' problems and a clear statement of their needs.

As defined in Chapter 1, **stakeholders** are individuals either within or outside the organization who have an interest in the system but are not end users. These include accountants, internal auditors, external auditors, and the internal steering committee that oversees systems development.[1]

1 Accountants and auditors are end users of some systems, but are the stakeholders in all accounting information systems.

Systems Strategy

The objective of **systems strategy** is to link individual system projects to the strategic objectives of the firm. Firms that take systems strategy seriously establish a steering committee to provide guidance and oversight for systems projects. The composition of the **steering committee** may include the chief executive officer (CEO), the chief financial officer, the chief information officer, senior management from user areas, the internal auditor, and senior management from computer services. External parties, such as management consultants and the firm's external auditors, may also supplement the committee. This committee is involved not only in developing system strategy but also in every major phase of the SDLC.

The strategy stage in the SDLC consists of three fundamental tasks: assessing the organization's strategic information needs, developing a strategic systems plan, and creating action plans. The inputs to the systems strategy phase are the business plan, the legacy system situation, and feedback from the user community. In this section, we see how these pieces come together to form a comprehensive strategic plan that will generate action plans for selecting and developing individual systems projects.

ASSESS STRATEGIC INFORMATION NEEDS

Strategic systems planning involves the allocation of systems resources at the macro level, which usually involves a time frame of three to five years. This process is similar to budgeting resources for other strategic activities, such as product development, plant expansions, market research, and manufacturing technology. For most companies, the key inputs in developing a sound systems strategy include the strategic business needs of the organization, the legacy system situation, and user feedback. These are discussed in the following sections.

STRATEGIC BUSINESS NEEDS

All functional areas should support the business strategy of the organization. Because this is most certainly true for the information systems function, we begin with an overview of business strategy. We will briefly review some common aspects of business strategy that bear directly on developing a sound systems strategy.

Vision and Mission

Developing a systems strategy requires an understanding of top management's vision, which has shaped the organization's business strategy. Many CEOs communicate their strategic vision through a formal mission statement. In some cases, however, top management's strategic view for the company is not fully articulated or formulated. Organizations without a well-considered mission statement might have individuals who lack a clear vision for the future. Not surprisingly, companies in this situation often lack a viable systems strategy. Consequently, their management is prone to making knee-jerk responses to information systems needs that emerge out of crisis rather than planning.

Industry and Competency Analysis

In addition to needing a durable vision component, the strategic planning process has many dynamic business factors that drive it, including consolidations, competition, rapidly evolving technology, changes in the regulatory landscape, and increasing demands from stakeholders. Industry analysis and competency analysis are two strategic planning methodologies used to capture information on these factors.

Industry analysis provides management with an analysis of the driving forces that affect its industry and its organization's performance. Such analysis offers a fact-based perspective on the industry's important trends, significant risks, and potential opportunities that may impact the business's performance.

Competency analysis provides a complete picture of the organization's effectiveness as seen via four strategic filters: resources, infrastructure, products/services, and customers. By assessing these factors, an organization can develop an accurate view of its relative strengths, weaknesses, and core competencies. The analysis helps in developing strategic options, which are based on an understanding of the future environment and the firm's core competencies. Strategic opportunities may include market-entry options or new product development options.

In developing a business strategy, many organizations perform competency analyses on their key competitors as well as potential business partners. By knowing the strengths and weaknesses of competitors, management can identify imminent threats and spot new business opportunities for growth. Similarly, by examining the competencies of potential trading partners, strategic gaps and/or synergies from the partnership may materialize.

LEGACY SYSTEMS

Applications, databases, and business processes that are currently in full operation constitute a firm's legacy systems. Often, these are complicated systems to maintain and enhance. Even in modern companies, the information system is usually a mixture of old and modern technologies, which are critical to the organization's business success.

Legacy components need to be mapped to current business processes to determine the extent to which they support the mission of the company. This evaluation, together with an assessment of future strategic business needs, will enable management to develop the migration strategy needed to move from legacy systems to future systems with minimum disruption to business operations.

Developing an Architecture Description

System architecture is the structure of components, their interrelationships, and the principles and guidelines governing their design and evolution over time. An **architecture description** is a formal description of an information system, organized in a way that identifies the structural properties of the system and defines the components or building blocks that make up the overall information system. This description provides the elements for a plan from which new systems can be developed and commercial packages procured that will work together as harmonious components of the overall system. It also provides the technical foundation for a legacy migration strategy. Finally, the technical advantages that result from an architecture description translate into important business benefits, which are presented in Table 13-1.

TABLE 13-1 Business Benefits from Architecture Description

Efficient IT operation

- Lower software development, support, and maintenance costs
- Increased portability of applications
- Improved interoperability and easier system and network management

Ability to address critical enterprise-wide issues

- Easier upgrade and exchange of system components
- Better return on existing investment and reduced risk on future investment
- Reduced complexity in IT infrastructure
- Maximum return on investment in existing IT infrastructure
- The flexibility to make, buy, or outsource IT solutions
- Reduced risk overall in the new investment and the costs of IT ownership

Improved procurement

- Buying decisions are simpler because the information governing procurement is readily available in a coherent plan.
- The procurement process is faster, maximizing procurement speed and flexibility without sacrificing architectural coherence.

USER FEEDBACK

Assessing user feedback involves identifying areas of user needs, preparing written proposals, evaluating each proposal's feasibility and contribution to the business plan, and prioritizing individual projects. User feedback at this point pertains to substantial perceived problems rather than minor systems modifications, which are dealt with at a later point in the SDLC. Next, we examine the following key phases of this activity:

1. Recognizing the problem
2. Defining the problem
3. Specifying system objectives
4. Determining project feasibility
5. Preparing a formal project proposal

Recognizing the Problem

The need for a new, improved information system may be manifested through various symptoms. In the early stages of a problem, these symptoms may seem vague and innocuous or may go unrecognized.

However, as the underlying source of the problem grows in severity, so does its symptoms, until they are alarmingly apparent. At this point, operations may have reached a state of crisis. Therefore, the point at which the problem is recognized is important. This is often a function of the philosophy of a firm's management. The reactive management philosophy characterizes an extreme position; in contrast with this is the philosophy of proactive management.

Reactive management responds to problems only when they reach a crisis state and can no longer be ignored. This approach creates a great deal of pressure to solve the problem quickly once it has been recognized. Too often, this results in hurried analysis, incomplete problem identification, shortcuts in design, poor user participation, and a final product that is generally suboptimal.

Proactive management stays alert to the subtle signs of problems and aggressively looks for ways to improve the organization's systems. This management style is more likely to recognize symptoms early and, therefore, implement better solutions. Early problem detection avoids the crisis stage and provides the necessary time for a complete and thorough study.

Who reports problem symptoms? Typically, lower-level managers and operations personnel first report symptoms. Being in continuous contact with day-to-day operations, these individuals are quick to notice operational difficulties with customers, suppliers, and the financial community. As a result, most systems requests originate with lower-level management.

Defining the Problem

The manager must avoid the temptation to take a leap in logic from symptom recognition to problem definition. One must keep an open mind and avoid drawing conclusions about the nature of the problem that may channel attention and resources in the wrong direction. For example, increased product returns, excessive delays in product shipments to customers, excessive overtime for operations personnel, and slow inventory turnover rates are all problem symptoms. These are evidence of underlying problems, but they do not, in themselves, define the problems. The manager must learn enough about the problem to pursue a solution intelligently. The manager cannot, however, collect all the information needed to define the problem accurately and specify a solution. This would require a detailed system evaluation. The manager must specify the nature of the problem as he or she sees it based on the nature of the difficulties identified.

The manager reports this problem definition to the computer systems professionals within the firm. This begins an interactive process between the systems professionals and the user, which results in a formal project proposal that will go before the steering committee for approval. The following three stages in the planning phase—specifying system objectives, determining project feasibility, and preparing a formal project proposal—represent the cooperative efforts of the manager and the systems professional.

Specifying System Objectives

User information requirements need to be specified in terms of operational objectives for the new information system. For example, the user may need an order entry system that can handle 5,000 transactions per hour, maintain up-to-the-minute inventory status, and allow all orders received by 2 PM to be shipped to the customer by the end of the day. At this point, we need only define the objectives in general terms. More precise system requirements will be developed later in the SDLC.

Preliminary Project Feasibility

A preliminary **project feasibility** study is conducted at this early stage to determine how best to proceed with the project. By assessing the major constraints on the proposed system, management can evaluate the project's feasibility, or likelihood for success, before committing large amounts of financial and human resources. The acronym **TELOS** provides guidance for assessing project feasibility. The term stands for technical, economic, legal, operational, and schedule feasibility.

Technical feasibility is concerned with whether the system can be developed under existing technology or whether new technology is needed. As a general proposition, the technology in the marketplace is far ahead of most firms' ability to apply it. Therefore, from an availability viewpoint, technical feasibility is not usually an issue. For most firms, the real issue is their desire and ability to apply available technology. Given that technology is the physical basis for most of the system's design features, this aspect bears heavily on the overall feasibility of the proposed system.

Economic feasibility pertains to the availability of funds to complete the project. At this point, we are concerned with management's financial commitment to this project in view of other competing capital projects under consideration. The level of available economic support directly impacts the operational nature and scope of the proposed system. Later, in the system justification and selection step, cost-benefit analysis is used to identify the best system design for the cost.

Legal feasibility involves ensuring that the proposed system does not conflict with the company's ability to discharge its legal responsibilities. In previous chapters, we have studied the need to comply with the control requirement laid down in the Foreign Corrupt Practices Act of 1977, SAS 109, the COSO framework, and Sarbanes-Oxley legislation. In addition, many regulations and statutes deal with invasion of privacy and the confidentiality of stored information. We must be certain the proposed system does not breach any legal boundaries.

Operational feasibility pertains to the degree of compatibility between the firm's existing procedures and personnel skills and the operational requirements of the new system. Implementing the new system may require adopting new procedures and retraining operations personnel. The question that must be answered is: Can enough procedural changes be made, personnel retrained, and new skills obtained to make the system operationally feasible?

Schedule feasibility relates to the firm's ability to implement the project within an acceptable time. This feasibility factor impacts both the scope of the project and whether it will be developed in-house or purchased from a software vendor. If the project, as originally envisioned, cannot be produced internally by the target date, then its design, its acquisition method, or the target date must be changed.

Preparing a Formal Project Proposal

The **systems project proposal** provides management with a basis for deciding whether to proceed with the project. The formal proposal serves two purposes. First, it summarizes the findings of the study conducted to this point into a general recommendation for a new or modified system. This enables management to evaluate the perceived problem along with the proposed system as a feasible solution. Second, the proposal outlines the linkage between the objectives of the proposed system and the business objectives of the firm. It shows that the proposed new system complements the strategic direction of the firm. Figure 13-2 shows an example of a project proposal.

FIGURE 13-2 SYSTEMS PROJECT PROPOSAL

Project Proposal

Requested by: *J.J. Johnson* Date: *11/13/15*

Nature of System Requested: *Inventory Control System*

Reason for New System: *Better manage inventory, reduce obsolescence, increase turnover, and reduce inventory carrying costs*

Resource Requirements of New System:

	High	Moderate	Low
Personnel	☐	☐	☑
Hardware	☐	☑	☐
Software	☐	☑	☐

Rate project's feasibility factors on a scale of 1 to 10 where 10 is most feasible:

Technical Feasibility *9*
Economic Feasibility *8*
Legal Feasibility *10*
Operational Feasibility *10*
Schedule Feasibility *8*

Project Priority: High ✓ Moderate ___ Low ___

DEVELOP A STRATEGIC SYSTEMS PLAN

After collecting and documenting input from the business plan, legacy issues, and user feedback, members of the steering committee and systems professionals evaluate the pros and cons of each proposal. This involves assessing each potential project's benefits, costs, and strategic implications to the organization. Development will proceed on proposals that show the greatest potential for supporting the organization's business objectives at the lowest cost. Figure 13-3 shows how the merits of competing projects may be presented to provide a sense of relative scale. The vertical dimension shows project priority in terms of organizational need. The horizontal plane shows the expected costs of each project, and the size of the circle reflects the projects' strategic impact. For example, an enterprise resource planning (ERP) system is a high-priority project of great strategic importance. Such a project would, however, be extremely costly. On the other hand, the human resources project is of strategic importance also, but at a much lower cost.

CREATE AN ACTION PLAN

An important skill for top management is the ability to translate strategy into action. Although most US-based companies are taking measures to decrease the distance between those who formulate the strategy and those who carry it out, translating vision into work is difficult. If organizations want to be successful, however, they must learn to implement strategy and beat the high failure rates often experienced by their peers.

The **balanced scorecard (BSC)** is a management system that enables organizations to clarify their vision and strategy and translate them into action. It provides feedback both from internal business

FIGURE 13-3 RELATIONSHIP BETWEEN PRIORITY, COST, AND STRATEGIC IMPACT

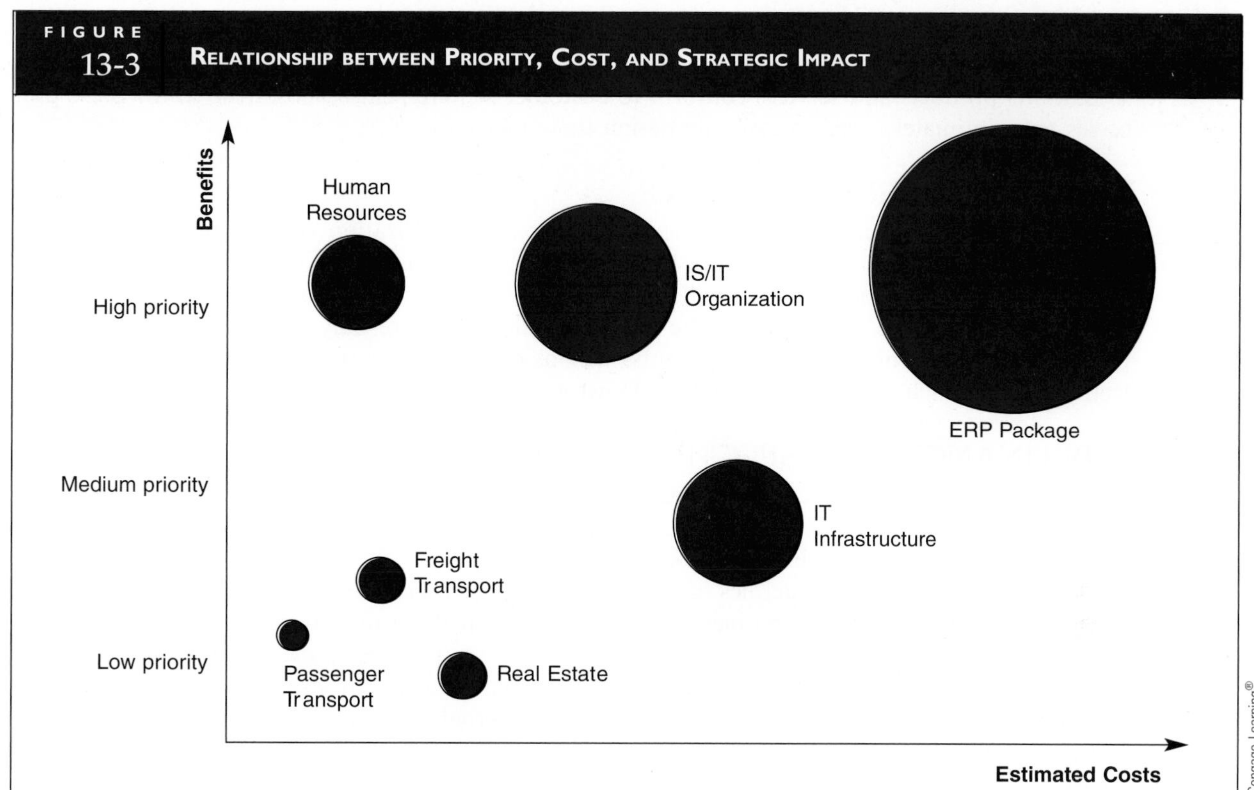

processes and external outcomes to continuously improve strategic performance. When fully deployed, the balanced scorecard transforms strategic planning from an academic exercise into operational tasks.

Today, the BSC enjoys increasing attention and is likely to become ubiquitous in senior management circles. Much of the BSC's appeal stems from its ability to integrate financial and operational measures into a single comprehensive framework that can translate a company's strategic objectives into a coherent set of performance measures.

The BSC approach lends itself especially well to one of the fundamental challenges facing CEOs and IT executives, namely, how to measure, improve, and understand the value that IT delivers to the business. The BSC can help managers identify opportunities for improvement in IT and track the impact of improvement initiatives through a wide range of performance indicators.

The BSC suggests that we view the organization from four perspectives. We develop metrics, collect data, and analyze it relative to each of the following perspectives:

1. The learning and growth perspective
2. The internal business process perspective
3. The customer perspective
4. The financial perspective

THE LEARNING AND GROWTH PERSPECTIVE

Learning and growth constitute the essential foundation for the success of any organization. This perspective includes employee training and corporate cultural attitudes related to both individual and corporate self-improvement. In our current climate of rapid technological change, workers need to be in a continuous learning mode. Government agencies often find themselves unable to hire new technical workers and at the same time are showing a decline in training existing employees. Metrics can be developed to guide managers in channeling training funds where they can be of greatest benefit.

THE INTERNAL BUSINESS PROCESS PERSPECTIVE

Metrics based on this perspective allow managers to know how well their business is running and whether its products and services conform to customer requirements. Those who know these processes most intimately need to carefully design these metrics.

THE CUSTOMER PERSPECTIVE

Recent management philosophy has shown an increasing realization of the importance of customer focus in any business. These are leading indicators: if customers are not satisfied, they will eventually find other suppliers that will meet their needs. Poor performance from this perspective predicts future decline, even though the current financial picture may look good. The customer perspective includes objective measurements, such as customer retention rate, as well as more subjective criteria, such as market research and customer satisfaction surveys.

THE FINANCIAL PERSPECTIVE

The financial perspective includes traditional measurements, such as profitability, revenues, and sales. An overemphasis on financial performance, however, may stimulate short-run decisions that create an imbalance with other perspectives.

The power of the BSC model lies in the linkages between these four core measurement perspectives. Consider, for example, a business experiencing poor performance from a financial perspective, as measured by low sales growth, and from a customer perspective, as measured by low customer retention and satisfaction. Using the BSC approach, management can examine measures from the learning and innovation perspective, and from the internal process perspective, to identify root causes as well as potential solutions to the problem. By identifying imbalances that exist in these measurement areas, the scorecard can be used to take corrective action.

BALANCED SCORECARD APPLIED TO IT PROJECTS

Figure 13-4 illustrates a BSC that measures the business benefits of a hypothetical online banking proposal. The bank's retail customers are producing low profit margins because of the high overhead and service costs of managing their accounts. Electronic banking is seen as a way to address this problem.

FIGURE 13-4 BALANCED SCORECARD FOR ONLINE BANKING SYSTEM

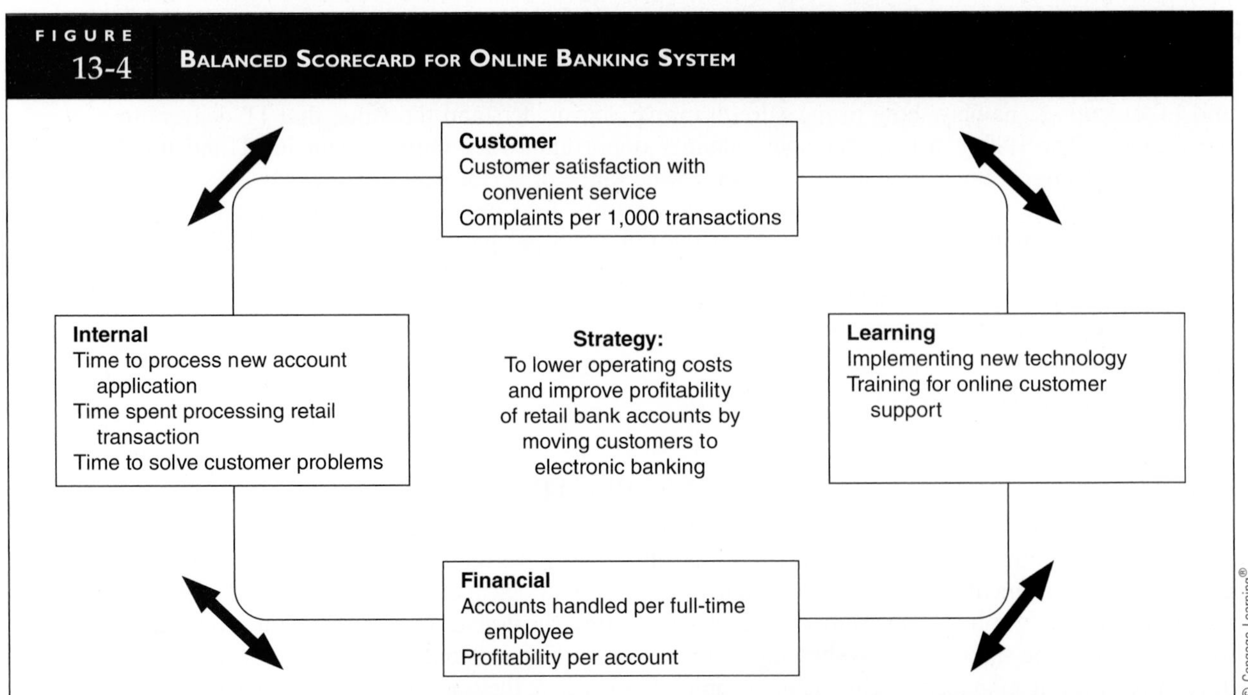

If a strategic goal is to increase account profitability, performance indicators, such as number of accounts managed per full-time employee and cost per transaction, are relevant measures. Relationships can be drawn between these measures. For example, hours spent training support staff can have an impact on reducing customer complaints.

Through analysis of BSC indicators, the steering committee can establish priorities to competing proposals based on their strategic impact as viewed from multiple perspectives. The committee will use these metrics to identify the proposals that go forward to the project initiation phase of the SDLC. This is the first major decision point in a project's life cycle. If the committee approves a proposal, then the proposal will undergo further detailed study and development. If a proposal is rejected, it will not be considered further within the current budget period.

Project Initiation

Project initiation involves obtaining a detailed understanding of the user problem and proposing multiple alternative solutions. Each of these proposals is assessed in terms of its feasibility and cost-benefit characteristics. The option selected at this step then proceeds to the construct phase of the SDLC. Depending upon the nature of the project and the needs of the organization, a system will require in-house development, a commercial package, or a combination of both.

SYSTEMS ANALYSIS

The systems analyst must fully understand a business problem before he or she can formulate a solution. An incomplete or defective analysis will lead to an incomplete or defective solution. Therefore, systems analysis is the foundation for the rest of the SDLC. **Systems analysis** is actually a two-step process involving an initial survey of the current system and then an analysis of the user's needs.

THE SURVEY STEP

Most systems are not developed from scratch. Usually, some form of information system and related procedures are currently in place. The analyst often begins the analysis by determining what elements, if any, of the current system should be preserved as part of the new system. This involves a rather detailed **system survey**. Facts pertaining to preliminary questions about the system are gathered and analyzed. As the analyst obtains a greater depth of understanding of the problem, he or she develops more specific questions for which more facts must be gathered. This process may go on through several iterations. When all the relevant facts have been gathered and analyzed, the analyst arrives at an assessment of the current system. Surveying the current system has both disadvantages and advantages.

Disadvantages of Surveying the Current System

Perhaps the most compelling argument against a current system survey centers on a phenomenon known as the current physical tar pit.[2] This is the tendency on the part of the analyst to be sucked in and then bogged down by the task of surveying the current dinosaur system.

Some argue that current system surveys stifle new ideas. By studying and modeling the old system, the analyst may develop a constrained notion about how the new system should function. The result is an improved old system rather than a radically new approach. An example is the implementation of an ERP system. The task of reviewing current organizational procedures may serve no purpose because the successful implementation of an ERP depends on reengineering these processes to employ the best business practices of the industry.

Advantages of Surveying the Current System

There are three advantages to studying the current system. First, it is a way to identify what aspects of the old system should be kept. Some elements of the system may be functionally sound

---

2 W. Keuffel, "House of Structure," *Unix Review* 9 (February 1991), 36.

and can provide the foundation for the new system. By fully understanding the current system, the analyst can identify those aspects worth preserving or modifying for use in the new system.

Second, when the new system is implemented, the users must go through a conversion process in which they formally break away from the old system and move to the new one. The analyst must determine what tasks, procedures, and data will be phased out with the old system and which will continue. To specify these conversion procedures, the analyst must know not only what is to be done by the new system but also what was done by the old one. This requires a thorough understanding of the current system.

Finally, by surveying the current system, the analyst may determine conclusively the cause of the reported problem symptoms. Perhaps the root problem is not the information system at all; it may be a management or employee problem that can be resolved without redesigning the information system. We may not be able to identify the root cause of the problem if we discard the existing system without any investigation into the symptoms.

Gathering Facts

The survey of the current system is essentially a fact-gathering activity. The facts the analyst gathers are pieces of data that describe key features, situations, and relationships of the system. System facts fall into the following broad classes:

DATA SOURCES. These include external entities, such as customers or vendors, as well as internal sources from other departments.

USERS. These include both managers and operations users.

DATA STORES. Data stores are the files, databases, accounts, and source documents used in the system.

PROCESSES. Processing tasks are manual or computer operations that represent a decision or an action that information triggers.

DATA FLOWS. The movement of documents and reports between data sources, data stores, processing tasks, and users represent data flows.

CONTROLS. These include both accounting and operational controls and may be manual procedures or computer controls.

TRANSACTION VOLUMES. The analyst must obtain a measure of the transaction volumes for a specified period of time. Many systems are replaced because they have reached their capacity. Understanding the characteristics of a system's transaction volume and its rate of growth are important elements in assessing capacity requirements for the new system.

ERROR RATES. Transaction errors are closely related to transaction volume. As a system reaches capacity, error rates increase to an intolerable level. Although no system is perfect, the analyst must determine the acceptable error tolerances for the new system.

RESOURCE COSTS. The resources the current system uses include the costs of labor, computer time, materials (for example, invoices), and direct overhead. Any resource costs that disappear when the current system is eliminated are called escapable costs. Later, when we perform a cost-benefit analysis, escapable costs will be treated as benefits of the new system.

BOTTLENECKS AND REDUNDANT OPERATIONS. The analyst should note points where data flows come together to form a bottleneck. At peak-load periods, these can result in delays and promote processing errors. Likewise, delays may be caused by redundant operations, such as unnecessary approvals or sign-offs. By identifying these problem areas during the survey phase, the analyst can avoid making the same mistakes in the design of the new system.

Fact-Gathering Techniques

Systems analysts use several techniques to gather the previously cited facts. These include observation, task participation, personal interviews, and reviewing key documents.

OBSERVATION. Observation involves passively watching the physical procedures of the system. This allows the analyst to determine what gets done, who performs the task, when they do it, how they do it, why they do it, and how long it takes.

TASK PARTICIPATION. Participation is an extension of observation, where the analyst takes an active role in performing the user's work. This allows the analyst to experience firsthand the problems involved in the operation of the current system. For example, the analyst may work on the sales desk, taking orders from customers and preparing sales orders. The analyst can determine that documents are improperly designed, that insufficient time exists to perform the required procedures, or that peak-load problems cause bottlenecks and processing errors. With hands-on experience, the analyst can often envision better ways to perform the task.

PERSONAL INTERVIEWS. Interviewing is a method of extracting facts about the current system and user perceptions about the requirements for the new system. The instruments used to gather these facts may be open-ended questions or formal questionnaires.

Open-ended questions allow users to elaborate on the problem as they see it and offer suggestions and recommendations. Answers to these questions tend to be difficult to analyze, but they give the analyst a feel for the scope of the problem. The analyst in this type of interview must be a good listener and able to focus on the important facts. Examples of open-ended questions are: "What do you think is the main problem with our sales order system?" and "How could the system be improved?"

Questionnaires are used to ask more specific, detailed questions and to restrict the user's responses. This is a good technique for gathering objective facts about the nature of specific procedures, volumes of transactions processed, sources of data, users of reports, and control issues.

REVIEWING KEY DOCUMENTS. The organization's documents are another source of facts about the system being surveyed. Examples of these include:

- Organizational charts
- Job descriptions
- Accounting records
- Charts of accounts
- Policy statements
- Descriptions of procedures
- Financial statements
- Performance reports
- System flowcharts
- Source documents
- Transaction listings
- Budgets
- Forecasts
- Mission statements

Following the fact-gathering phase, the analyst formally documents his or her impressions and understanding about the system. This will take the form of notes, system flowcharts, and various levels of data flow diagrams.

THE ANALYSIS STEP

Systems analysis is an intellectual process that is commingled with fact gathering. The analyst is simultaneously analyzing as he or she gathers facts. The mere recognition of a problem presumes some understanding of the norm or desired state. It is therefore difficult to identify where the survey ends and the analysis begins.

System Analysis Report

The event that marks the conclusion of the systems analysis phase is the preparation of a formal **systems analysis report**. This report presents management or the steering committee with the survey findings, the problems identified with the current system, the user's needs, and the requirements of the new system. Figure 13-5 contains a possible format for this report.

The primary purpose for conducting systems analysis is to identify user needs and specify requirements for the new system. The report should set out in detail what the system must do rather than how to do it.

The requirements statement within the report establishes an understanding between systems professionals, management, users, and other stakeholders. This document constitutes a formal contract that specifies the objectives and goals of the system. The systems analysis report should establish in clear terms the data sources, users, data files, general processes, data flows, controls, and transaction volume capacity.

The systems analysis report does not specify the detailed design of the proposed system. For example, it does not specify processing methods, storage media, record structures, and

FIGURE 13-5 OUTLINE OF MAIN TOPICS IN A SYSTEMS ANALYSIS REPORT

Systems Analysis Report

I. Reasons for System Analysis
   A. Reasons specified in the system project proposal
   B. Changes in reasons since analysis began
   C. Additional reasons

II. Scope of Study
   A. Scope as specified by the project proposal
   B. Changes in scope

III. Problems Identified with Current System
   A. Techniques used for gathering facts
   B. Problems encountered in the fact-gathering process
   C. Analysis of facts

IV. Statement of User Requirements
   A. Specific user needs in key areas, such as:
      1. Output requirements
      2. Transaction volumes
      3. Response time
   B. Nontechnical terms for a broad-based audience, including:
      1. End users
      2. User management
      3. Systems management
      4. Steering committee

V. Resource Implications
   A. Preliminary assessment of economic effect
   B. Is economic feasibility as stated in proposal reasonable?

VI. Recommendations
   A. Should the project continue?
   B. Has analysis changed feasibility, strategic impact, or priority of the project?

other details needed to design the physical system. Rather, the report remains at the objectives level to avoid placing artificial constraints on the conceptual design phase. Several possible designs may serve the user's needs, and the development process must be free to explore all of these.

CONCEPTUALIZATION OF ALTERNATIVE DESIGNS

The purpose of the conceptualization phase is to produce several alternative conceptual solutions that satisfy the system requirements identified during systems analysis. By presenting users with a number of plausible alternatives, the project team avoids imposing preconceived constraints onto the new system. These alternative designs then go to the systems selection stage, where their respective costs and benefits are compared, and a single optimum design is chosen for construction.

HOW MUCH DESIGN DETAIL IS NEEDED?

The conceptual design phase should highlight the differences between critical features of competing systems rather than their similarities. Therefore, system designs at this point should be general. The designs should identify all the inputs, outputs, processes, and special features necessary to distinguish one alternative from another. In some cases, this may be accomplished at the context diagram level. In situations in which the important distinctions between systems are subtle, designs may need to be represented by lower-level data flow diagrams (DFDs) and even with structure diagrams. However, detailed DFDs and structure diagrams are more commonly used at the detailed design phase of the SDLC. We shall discuss the transition from detailed DFD to structure diagram in Chapter 14.

Figure 13-6 presents two alternative conceptual designs for a purchasing system. These designs lack the details needed to implement the system. For instance, they do not include such necessary components as:

- Database record structures
- Processing details
- Specific control techniques
- Formats for input screens and source documents
- Output report formats

The designs do, however, possess sufficient detail to demonstrate how the two systems are conceptually different in their functions. To illustrate, let's examine the general features of each system.

Option A is a traditional batch purchasing system. The initial input for the process is the purchase requisition from inventory control. When inventories reach their predetermined reorder points, new inventories are ordered according to their economic order quantity. Transmittal of purchase orders to suppliers takes place once a day via the United States mail. In contrast, Option B employs electronic data interchange (EDI) technology. The trigger to this system is a purchase requisition from production planning. The purchases system determines the quantity and the vendor and then transmits the order online via EDI software to the vendor.

Both alternatives have pros and cons. The benefits of Option A is its simplicity of design, ease of implementation, and lower demand for systems resources than Option B. A negative aspect of Option A is that it requires the firm to carry inventories. On the other hand, Option B may allow the firm to reduce or even eliminate inventories. This benefit comes at the cost of more expensive and sophisticated system resources. It is premature, at this point, to attempt to evaluate the relative merits of these alternatives. This is done formally in the next phase of the SDLC. At this point, system designers are concerned only with identifying plausible alternative designs.

FIGURE 13-6 ALTERNATIVE CONCEPTUAL DESIGNS FOR A PURCHASING SYSTEM

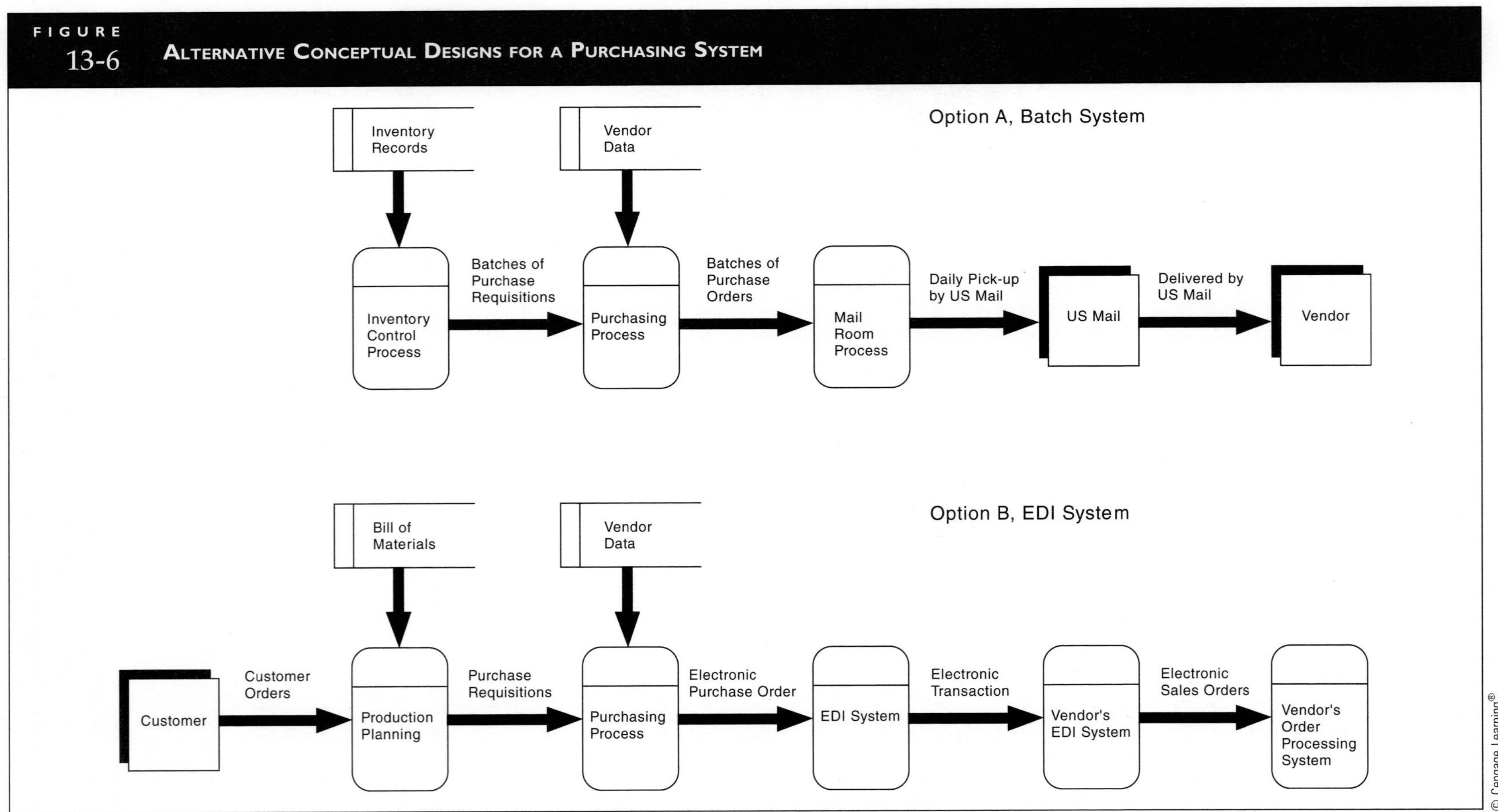

Systems Evaluation and Selection

This phase in the SDLC is a formal mechanism for selecting the one system from the set of alternative conceptual designs that will go forward for construction. The **systems evaluation and selection** phase is an optimization process that seeks to identify the best system. This decision represents a critical juncture in the SDLC. At this point, there is a great deal of uncertainty about the system, and a poor decision can be disastrous. The purpose of a formal evaluation and selection procedure is to structure this decision-making process and thereby reduce both uncertainty and the risk of making a poor decision.

There is no magic formula to ensure a good decision. Ultimately, the decision comes down to management judgment. The objective is to provide a means by which management can make an informed judgment. This selection process involves two steps:

1. Perform a detailed feasibility study.
2. Perform a cost-benefit analysis.

The results of these evaluations are then reported formally to the steering committee for final system selection.

PERFORM A DETAILED FEASIBILITY STUDY

We begin the system selection process by reexamining the feasibility factors that were evaluated on a preliminary basis as part of the systems proposal. Originally, the scores assigned to these factors were based largely on the judgment and intuition of the systems professional. Now that specific system features have been conceptualized, the designer has a clearer picture of these factors. Also, at the proposal stage, these factors were evaluated for the entire project. Now they are evaluated for each alternative conceptual design. Informed evaluators should perform the **detailed feasibility study**. Objectivity is essential to a fair assessment of each design. This group should consist of the project manager, a user representative, and systems professionals who have expertise in the specific areas that the feasibility study covers. Also, for operational audit reasons, the group should contain a member of the internal audit staff. The feasibility factors that were introduced in the previous section provide a framework for identifying the key issues that evaluators should consider.

Technical Feasibility

In evaluating technical feasibility, a well-established and understood technology represents less risk than an unfamiliar one. If the systems design calls for established technology, the feasibility score will be high, say 9 or 10. The use of technology that is new (first release) and unfamiliar to systems professionals who must install and maintain it, or that is a hybrid of several vendors' products, is a more risky option. Depending on the number and combination of risk factors, the feasibility score for such technology will be lower.

Legal Feasibility

In financial transaction processing systems, the legality of the system is always an issue. However, legality is also an issue for nonfinancial systems that process sensitive data, such as hospital patient records or personal credit ratings. Different systems designs may represent different levels of risk when dealing with such data. The evaluator should be concerned that the conceptual design recognizes critical control, security, and audit trail issues, and that the system does not violate laws pertaining to rights of privacy and/or the use and distribution of information.

Operational Feasibility

The availability of well-trained, motivated, and experienced users is the key issue in evaluating the operational feasibility of a design. If users lack these attributes, the move to a highly technical environment may be risky and will require extensive retraining. This may also affect the economic feasibility of the system. On the other hand, a user community that is comfortable with technology is more likely to make a smooth transition to an advanced technology system. The operational feasibility score of each alternative design should reflect the expected ease of this transition.

Schedule Feasibility

At this point in the design, the system evaluator is in a better position to assess the likelihood that the system will be completed on schedule. The technology platform, the systems design, and the need for user training may influence the original schedule. The systems development technology being used is another influence. The use of computer-aided software engineering (CASE) and prototyping tools (discussed in Chapter 14) can significantly reduce the development time of any systems design option.

Economic Feasibility

The preliminary economic feasibility study was confined to assessing management's financial commitment to the overall project. This is still a relevant issue. Whether the economic climate has changed since the preliminary study or whether one or more of the competing designs does not have management's support should now be determined.

The original feasibility study could specify the project's costs only in general terms. Now that each competing design has been conceptualized and expressed in terms of its unique features and processes, designers can be more precise in their estimates of the costs of each alternative. The economic feasibility study can now be taken a step further by performing a cost-benefit analysis.

PERFORM COST-BENEFIT ANALYSIS

Cost-benefit analysis helps management determine whether (and by how much) the benefits received from a proposed system will outweigh its costs. This technique is frequently used for estimating the expected financial value of business investments. In this case, however, the investment is an information system, and the costs and benefits are more difficult to identify and quantify than those of other types of capital projects. Although imperfect in this setting, cost-benefit analysis is employed because of its simplicity and the absence of a clearly better alternative. In spite of its limitations, cost-benefit analysis, combined with feasibility factors, is a useful tool for comparing competing systems designs.

There are three steps in the application of cost-benefit analysis: identifying costs, identifying benefits, and comparing costs and benefits.

Identify Costs

One method of identifying costs is to divide them into two categories: one-time costs and recurring costs. One-time costs include the initial investment to develop and implement the system. Recurring costs include operating and maintenance costs that recur over the life of the system. Table 13-2 shows a breakdown of typical one-time and recurring costs.

One-Time Costs

HARDWARE ACQUISITION. This includes the cost of mainframe servers, PCs, and peripheral equipment, such as networks and disk packs. The cost figures for items can be obtained from the vendor.

SITE PREPARATION. This involves such frequently overlooked costs as building modifications, for example, adding air-conditioning or making structural changes; equipment installation, which may include the use of heavy equipment; and freight charges. Estimates of these costs can be obtained from the vendor and the subcontractors who do the installation.

SOFTWARE ACQUISITION. These costs apply to all software purchased for the proposed system, including operating system software, if not bundled with the hardware; network control software; and

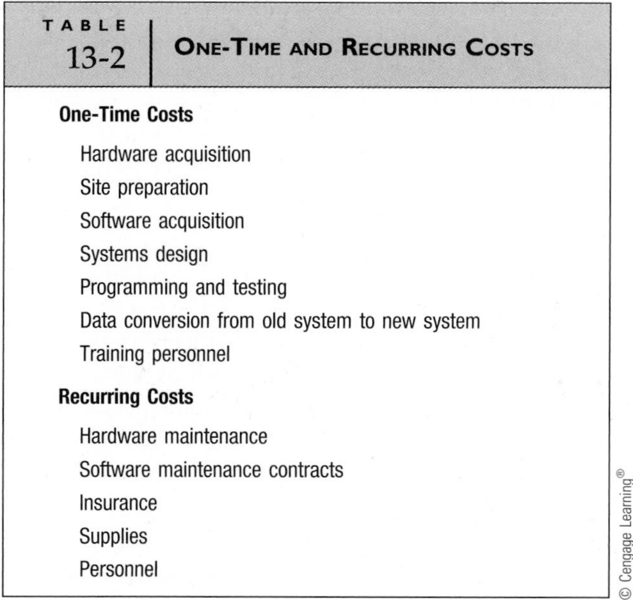

TABLE 13-2 ONE-TIME AND RECURRING COSTS

One-Time Costs
Hardware acquisition
Site preparation
Software acquisition
Systems design
Programming and testing
Data conversion from old system to new system
Training personnel
Recurring Costs
Hardware maintenance
Software maintenance contracts
Insurance
Supplies
Personnel

commercial applications, such as accounting packages. Estimates of these costs can be obtained from vendors.

SYSTEMS DESIGN. These are the costs that systems professionals incur performing the planning, analysis, and design functions. Technically, such costs incurred up to this point are sunk and irrelevant to the decision. The analyst should estimate only the costs needed to complete the detailed design.

PROGRAMMING AND TESTING. Programming costs are based on estimates of the personnel hours required to write new programs and modify existing programs for the proposed system. System testing costs involve bringing together all the individual program modules for testing as an entire system. This must be a rigorous exercise if it is to be meaningful. The planning, testing, and analysis of the results may demand many days of involvement from systems professionals, users, and other stakeholders of the system. The experience of the firm in the past is the best basis for estimating these costs.

DATA CONVERSION. These costs arise in the transfer of data from one storage medium or structure to another. For example, the accounting records of a manual system must be converted to digital form when the system becomes computer-based. This can represent a significant task. The basis for estimating conversion costs is the number and size of the files to be converted.

TRAINING. These costs involve educating users to operate the new system. This could be done in an extensive training program that an outside organization provides at a remote site or through on-the-job training by in-house personnel. The cost of formal training can be easily obtained. The cost of an in-house training program includes instruction time, classroom facilities, and lost productivity.

Recurring Costs

HARDWARE MAINTENANCE. This involves the cost of upgrading the computer (e.g., increasing the memory), as well as preventive maintenance and repairs to the computer and peripheral equipment. The organization may enter into a maintenance contract with the vendor to minimize and budget these costs. Estimates for these costs can be obtained from vendors and existing contracts.

SOFTWARE MAINTENANCE. These costs include upgrading and debugging operating systems, purchased applications, and applications developed in-house. Maintenance contracts with software vendors can be used to specify these costs fairly accurately. Estimates of in-house maintenance can be derived from historical data.

INSURANCE. This covers such hazards and disasters as fire, hardware failure, vandalism, and destruction by disgruntled employees.

SUPPLIES. These costs are incurred through routine consumption of such items as printer cartridges and paper, magnetic disks, magnetic tapes, and general office supplies.

PERSONNEL. These costs include salaries of individuals who are part of the information system. Some employee costs are direct and easily identifiable, such as the salaries of operations personnel exclusively employed as part of the system under analysis. Some personnel involvement, for example, the database administrator and computer room personnel, is common to many systems. Such personnel costs must be allocated on the basis of expected incremental involvement with the system.

Identify Benefits

The next step in the cost-benefit analysis is to identify the benefits of the system. These may be both tangible and intangible.

TANGIBLE BENEFITS. Tangible benefits are benefits that can be measured and expressed in financial terms. Table 13-3 lists several types of tangible benefits.

Tangible benefits fall into two categories: those that increase revenue and those that reduce costs. For example, a proposed EDI system will allow the organization to reduce inventories and at the same time improve customer service by reducing stock-outs. The reduction of inventories is a cost-reducing benefit. The proposed system will use fewer resources (inventories) than the current system. The value of this benefit is the dollar amount of the carrying costs that the annual reduction in inventory saves. The estimated increase in sales because of better customer service is a revenue-increasing benefit.

When measuring cost savings, only escapable costs should be included in the analysis. Escapable costs are directly related to the system and cease to exist when the system ceases to exist. Some costs that appear to be escapable to the user are not truly escapable and, if included, can lead to a flawed analysis. For example, data processing centers often charge back their operating costs to their user constituency through cost allocations. The charge-back rate they use for this includes both fixed costs (allocated to users) and direct costs that the activities of individual users create. Figure 13-7 illustrates this technique.

Assume the management in User Area B proposes to acquire a computer system and perform its own data processing locally. One benefit of the proposal is the cost savings derived by escaping the charge-back from the current data processing center. Although the user may see this as a

TABLE 13-3 TANGIBLE BENEFITS

Increased Revenues
- Increased sales within existing markets
- Expansion into other markets

Cost Reduction
- Labor reduction
- Operating cost reduction (such as supplies and overhead)
- Reduced inventories
- Less-expensive equipment
- Reduced equipment maintenance

FIGURE 13-7 DP CENTER COST CHARGE-BACK TO USER AREAS

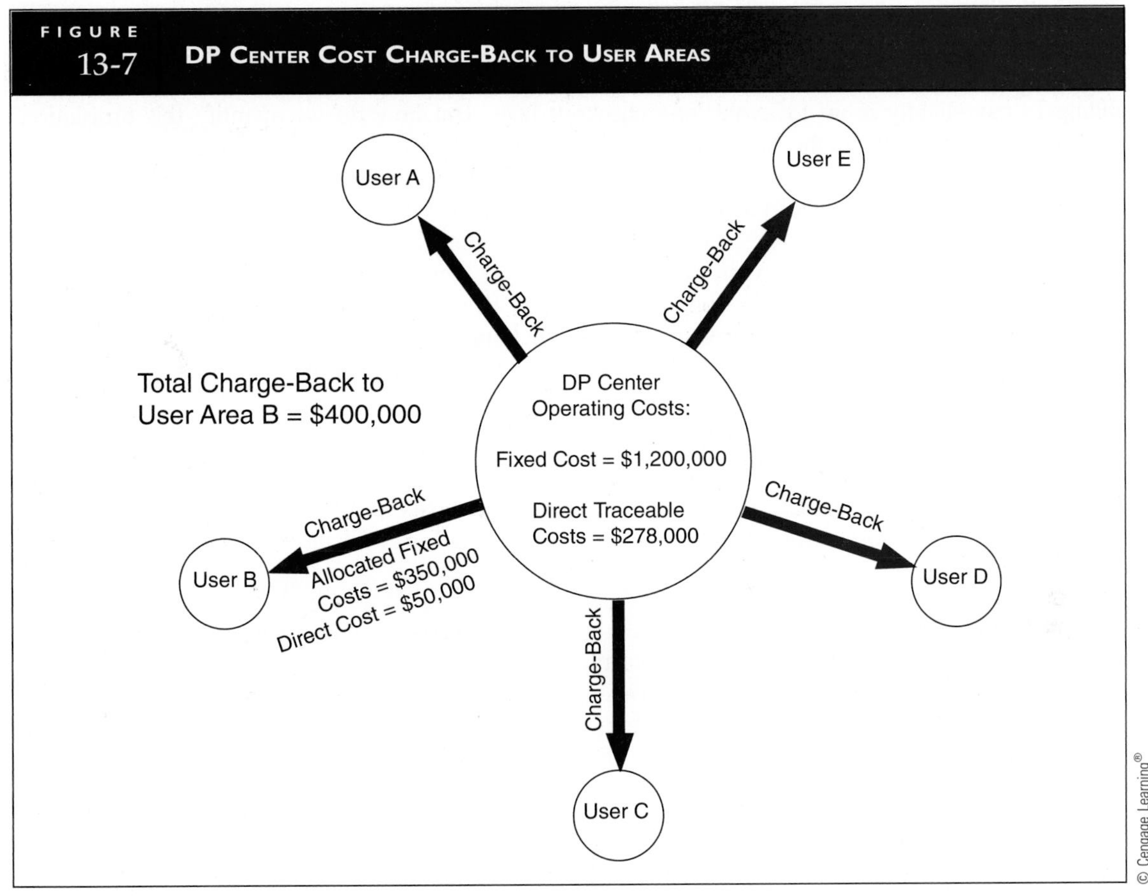

$400,000 annual charge, the organization as a whole can only escape the direct cost portion ($50,000). Should the proposal be approved, the remaining $350,000 of the charge-back does not go away. The remaining users of the current system must now absorb this cost.

INTANGIBLE BENEFITS. Table 13-4 lists some common categories of intangible benefits. Although intangible benefits are often of overriding importance in information system decisions, they cannot be easily measured and quantified. For example, assume that a proposed point-of-sale system for a department store will reduce the average time to process a customer sales transaction from 11 minutes to 3 minutes. The time saved can be quantified and produces a tangible benefit in the form of an operating

TABLE 13-4 INTANGIBLE BENEFITS
Increased customer satisfaction
Improved employee satisfaction
More current information
Improved decision making
Faster response to competitor actions
More efficient operations
Better internal and external communications
Improved planning
Operational flexibility
Improved control environment

cost savings. An intangible benefit is improved customer satisfaction; no one likes to stand in long lines to pay for purchases. But what is the true value of this intangible benefit to the organization? Increased customer satisfaction may translate into increased sales. More customers will buy at the store—and may be willing to pay slightly more to avoid long checkout lines. But how do we quantify this translation? Assigning a value is often highly subjective.

Systems professionals draw upon many sources in attempting to quantify intangible benefits and manipulate them into financial terms. Some common techniques include customer (and employee) opinion surveys, statistical analysis, expected value techniques, and simulation models. Even though systems professionals may succeed in quantifying some of these intangible benefits, more often they must be content to simply state the benefits as precisely as good judgment permits.

Because they defy precise measurement, intangible benefits are sometimes exploited for political reasons. By overstating or understating these benefits, a system's proponents may push it forward or its opponents may kill it.

Compare Costs and Benefits

The last step in the cost-benefit analysis is to compare the costs and benefits identified in the first two steps. The two most common methods used for evaluating information systems are net present value and payback.

THE NET PRESENT VALUE METHOD. Under the **net present value method**, the present value of the costs is deducted from the present value of the benefits over the life of the system. Projects with a positive net present value are economically feasible. When comparing competing projects, the optimal choice is the project with the greatest net present value. Figure 13-8 illustrates the net present value method by comparing two competing designs. The example is based on the following data:

	Design A	Design B
Project completion time	1 year	1 year
Expected useful life of system	5 years	5 years
One-time costs (thousands)	$300	$140
Recurring costs (thousands) incurred at beginning of Years 1 through 5	$ 45	$ 55
Annual tangible benefits (thousands) incurred at end of Years 1 through 5	$170	$135

If costs and tangible benefits alone were being considered, then Design A would be selected over Design B. However, the value of intangible benefits, along with the design feasibility scores, must also be factored into the final analysis.

FIGURE 13-8 NET PRESENT VALUE METHOD OF COST-BENEFIT ANALYSIS

Beginning Year Time	End Year Outflows	Inflows	Beginning Year Time	End Year Outflows	Inflows
0	$(300,000)		0	$(140,000)	
1	(45,000)	170,000	1	(55,000)	135,000
2	(45,000)	170,000	2	(55,000)	135,000
3	(45,000)	170,000	3	(55,000)	135,000
4	(45,000)	170,000	4	(55,000)	135,000
5	(45,000)	170,000	5	(55,000)	135,000
PV Out	$(479,672)		PV Out	$(359,599)	
PV In	$628,482		PV In	$499,089	
NPV	$148,810		NPV	$139,490	
Interest Rate	8.00%				

THE PAYBACK METHOD. The **payback method** is a variation of break-even analysis. The break-even point is reached when total costs equal total benefits. Figures 13-9(a) and 13-9(b) illustrate this approach, using the data from the previous example.

The total cost curve consists of the one-time costs plus the present value of the recurring costs over the life of the project. The total benefits curve is the present value of the tangible benefits. The intersection of these lines represents the number of years into the future when the project breaks even, or pays for itself. The shaded area between the benefit curve and the total cost curve represents the present value of future profits that the system earned.

In choosing an information system, payback speed is often a decisive factor. With brief product life cycles and rapid advances in technology, the effective lives of information systems tend to be short. Using this criterion, Design B, with a payback period of four years, would be selected over Design A, whose payback will take more than four years. The length of the payback period often takes precedence over other considerations represented by intangible benefits.

PREPARE SYSTEMS SELECTION REPORT

The deliverable portion of the systems selection process is the **systems selection report**. This formal document consists of a revised feasibility study, a cost-benefit analysis, and a list and explanation of intangible benefits for each alternative design. On the basis of this report, the steering committee will select a single system that will go forward to the construct phase of the SDLC.

In-House Development or Purchase Commercial Software

Two general options are open to the organization in the construct phase: develop the system in-house or purchase commercial software. At this juncture, management should have a good sense

FIGURE 13-9(a) DISCOUNTED PAYBACK METHOD OF COST-BENEFIT ANALYSIS

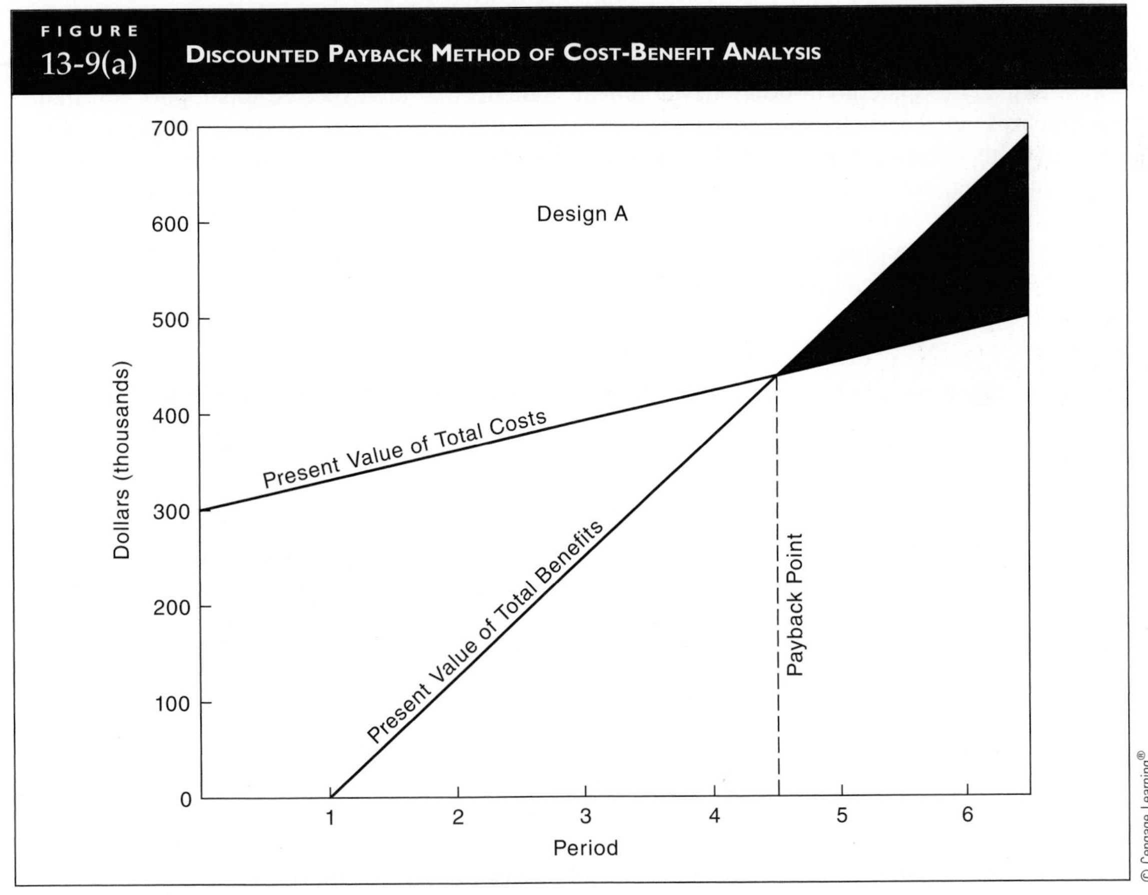

FIGURE 13-9(b) DISCOUNTED PAYBACK METHOD OF COST-BENEFIT ANALYSIS (CONTINUED)

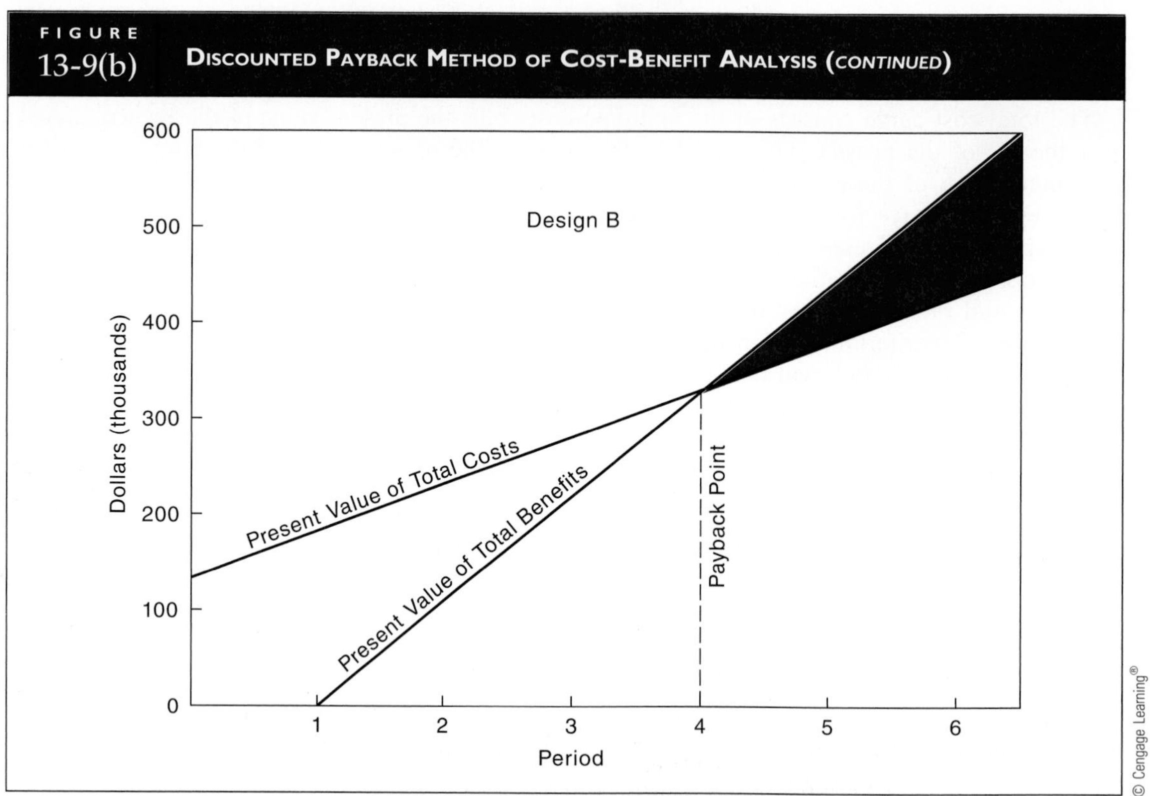

as to which option it will follow. Systems that need to meet unique and proprietary business needs are more likely to undergo in-house development. Systems that are expected to support best industry practices may be better suited to the purchased software option. A third approach, which involves both options, is to tailor the commercial system to meet the organization's needs. This may require making extensive in-house modifications to the package. The previous analysis of system architecture, TELOS factors, system survey results, and preliminary cost-benefit issues will have revealed to decision makers the suitability of one approach over the other. Both the in-house and the commercial package options are examined in detail in Chapter 14.

ANNOUNCING THE NEW SYSTEM PROJECT

Management's formal announcement of the new system to the rest of the organization is the last and most delicate step in the project initiation phase of the SDLC. This exceedingly important communique, if successful, will pave the way for the new system and help ensure its acceptance among the user community.

A new system can sometimes generate considerable political backlash that may threaten its success. For example, not all users may understand the objectives of the new system. In fact, the uncertainty surrounding the system may cause some users to feel threatened. As we have seen, new systems must improve the productivity and efficiency of operations. These objectives sometimes translate into organizational restructuring that erodes the personal powerbase of some users. Because a new system brings about operational changes, some employees may be displaced or may be required to undergo re-training to function in the new workplace.

The fears that take root and grow in this environment of uncertainty are often revealed in acts of opposition, both overt and covert, to the new system. To minimize opposition, top management must quell unnecessary fears and fully explain the business rationale for the new system before formal construction begins. If lower-level management and operating staff are assured that the system will be beneficial, the project's chances for success are vastly improved.

USER FEEDBACK

The preceding discussion was based on the assumption that the project under development passed through the strategic planning phase presented in the previous section. Not all systems projects should be, or can be, initiated in this manner. Systems maintenance is an integral component of the modern SDLC environment. This function needs to be receptive to user feedback and responsive to their legitimate needs. Therefore, user requests are also directed to the project initiation phase (refer to Figure 13-1). At this point in the SDLC, user requests involve relatively small enhancements to existing systems rather than major retrofits or entirely new systems. The IT budget must, therefore, be flexible enough to accommodate short-term quick hit projects that emerge on a daily basis.

The Accountant's Role in Managing the SDLC

The SDLC process is of interest to accountants for two reasons. First, the creation of an information system represents a significant financial transaction that consumes both financial and human resources. Systems development is like any manufacturing process that produces a complex product through a series of stages. Such transactions must be planned, authorized, scheduled, accounted for, and controlled. Accountants are as concerned with the integrity of this process as they are with any manufacturing process that has financial resource implications.

The second, and more pressing, concern for accountants is with the products that emerge from the SDLC. The quality of accounting information systems rests directly on the SDLC activities that produce them. These systems are used to deliver accounting information to internal and external users. The accountant's responsibility is to ensure that the systems apply proper accounting conventions and rules and possess adequate controls. Therefore, accountants are concerned with the quality of the process that produces accounting information systems. For example, a sales order system produced by a defective SDLC may suffer from serious control weaknesses that introduce errors into databases and, ultimately, the financial statements.

HOW ARE ACCOUNTANTS INVOLVED WITH SDLC?

Accountants are involved in systems development in three ways. First, accountants are users. All systems that process financial transactions impact the accounting function in some way. Like all users, accountants must provide a clear picture of their problems and needs to the systems professional. For example, accountants must specify accounting techniques to be used; internal control requirements, such as audit trails; and special algorithms, such as depreciation models.

Second, accountants participate in systems development as members of the development team. Their involvement often extends beyond the development of strictly accounting information systems applications. Systems that do not process financial transactions may still draw on accounting data. The accountant may be consulted to provide advice or to determine if the proposed system constitutes an internal control risk.

Third, accountants are involved in systems development as auditors. Accounting information systems must be auditable. Some computer audit techniques require special features that must be designed into the system. The auditor/accountant has a stake in such systems and must be involved early in their design.

THE ACCOUNTANT'S ROLE IN SYSTEMS STRATEGY

Auditors routinely review the organization's systems strategy. History has shown that careful systems planning is a cost-effective activity in reducing the risk of creating unneeded, unwanted, inefficient, and ineffective systems. Both internal and external auditors have vested interests in this outcome.

THE ACCOUNTANT'S ROLE IN CONCEPTUAL DESIGN

The accountant plays an important role in the conceptual design of the system. He or she must recognize control implications of each alternative design and ensure that accounting conventions and legal requirements are understood. These issues need not be specified in detail at this point, but they should be recognized as items to be addressed during the construct phase of the system. Furthermore, the auditability of a system depends in part on its design characteristics. Some computer auditing techniques require systems to be designed with built-in audit features. Such features require resources and need to be considered at conceptual design.

THE ACCOUNTANT'S ROLE IN SYSTEMS SELECTION

The economic feasibility of proposed systems is of primary concern to accountants. Specifically, the accountant should ensure that:

- Only escapable costs are used in calculations of cost-savings benefits.
- Reasonable interest rates are used in measuring present values of cash flows.
- One-time and recurring costs are completely and accurately reported.
- Realistic useful lives are used in comparing competing projects.
- Intangible benefits are assigned reasonable financial values.

Errors, omissions, and misrepresentations in the accounting for such items can distort the analysis and result in a suboptimal decision.

Summary

This chapter dealt with managing the SDLC. It began with a review of the key phases of a modern SDLC. The first of these involves strategic systems planning, which derives input from the strategic business plan, the diverse needs and concerns of the user community, and the organization's existing legacy system.

The chapter then reviewed the project initiation phase of the SDLC. This includes systems analysis and conceptualization of alternative designs. To ensure a correct systems solution, management must gather and weigh relevant information regarding the various systems alternatives under consideration. Systems evaluation and final selection are accomplished through a detailed feasibility study and careful cost-benefit analysis of these alternative solutions. Because success at this stage depends, in large part, on an accurate identification of prospective costs and benefits, we devoted special attention to the principle of one-time and recurring costs associated with systems and to the various tangible and intangible benefits they can be expected to yield. The chapter concluded with a review of the accountant's role in managing the SDLC.

Key Terms

Review Questions

1. What are the five stages of the systems development life cycle?
2. What is the balanced scorecard?
3. What is the role of the accountant in the SDLC? Why might accountants be called on for input into the development of a nonaccounting information system?
4. What is the learning and growth perspective?
5. Why is it often difficult to obtain competent and meaningful user involvement in the SDLC?
6. Is the SDLC a step-by-step procedure that must be followed precisely, or is it more interactive and recursive? Explain your answer.
7. Explain why a survey of the current system may serve no purpose when an organization is planning to implement an ERP.
8. Why is it crucial that the strategic objectives of the firm be considered when conducting the systems planning phase?
9. Who should sit on the systems steering committee? What are the committee members' typical responsibilities?
10. Explain the internal business process perspective.
11. Contrast proactive and reactive management styles. Which style would you prefer for your organization? Why?
12. What purposes do system objectives serve? Should they be broadly or narrowly defined? Why?
13. Why can the formal announcement of a new system technique be crucial?
14. Discuss the various feasibility measures that should be considered. Give an example of each.
15. What are the broad classes of facts that need to be gathered in the system survey?
16. What are the primary fact-gathering techniques?
17. What are the relative merits and disadvantages of a current system survey?
18. What is the primary objective of conceptual design?
19. How much design detail is needed in the conceptual design phase?
20. What is the accountant's primary role in conceptual design?
21. Who should be included in the group of evaluators performing the detailed feasibility study?
22. What makes the cost-benefit analysis more difficult for information systems than most other investments an organization may make?
23. Classify each of the following as either one-time or recurring costs:
    a. Training personnel
    b. Initial programming and testing
    c. Systems design
    d. Hardware costs
    e. Software maintenance costs
    f. Site preparation
    g. Rent for facilities
    h. Data conversion from old system to new system
    i. Insurance costs
    j. Installation of original equipment
    k. Hardware upgrades
24. Distinguish between escapable and inescapable costs. Give an example of each.
25. Distinguish between tangible and intangible benefits.
26. What is a systems selection report?
27. Explain the net present value and the payback methods. Which method do you prefer? Why?
28. What is the role of the accountant in evaluation and selection?

Discussion Questions

1. Accounting educators are discussing ways to incorporate communication skills, both oral and written, into accounting information systems courses. Why do you think these skills are deemed crucial for proper execution of the SDLC?

2. Comment on the following statement: "The maintenance stage of the SDLC involves making trivial changes to accommodate changes in user needs."
3. Discuss how rushing the system's requirements stage may delay or even result in the failure of a systems development process. Conversely, discuss how spending too long in this stage may result in analysis paralysis.
4. Discuss the independence issue when audit firms also provide consulting input into the development and selection of new systems.
5. Should system users perform the systems development tasks, or should these tasks be left to systems professionals who are trained specifically in systems development techniques? Why?
6. Why are customer-perspective measures important when a company is doing well financially?
7. Some may argue that a company's financial bottom line is all important. Comment on this from the financial perspective of the BSC approach.
8. Is a good strategic plan detail-oriented?
9. Distinguish between a problem and a symptom. Give an example. Are these usually noticed by upper-, middle-, or lower-level managers?
10. What purposes do the systems project proposal serve? How are these evaluated and prioritized? Is the prioritizing process objective or subjective?
11. Most firms underestimate the cost and time requirements of the SDLC by as much as 50%. Why do you think this occurs? In what stages do you think the underestimates are most dramatic?
12. A lack of top management support has led to the downfall of many new systems projects during the implementation phase. Why is this support so important?
13. Many new systems projects grossly underestimate transaction volumes because they do not take into account how the new, improved system can actually increase demand. Explain how this can happen, and give an example.
14. Do you think legal feasibility is an issue for a system that incorporates the use of machines to sell lottery tickets?

Multiple-Choice Questions

1. Which of the following cost-benefit factors is least likely to be measured precisely?
   a. one-time costs
   b. recurring costs
   c. tangible benefits
   d. intangible benefits
   e. none of the above because they must all be measured precisely
2. Which of the following is not a one-time cost of system development?
   a. site preparation
   b. hardware maintenance
   c. programming
   d. hardware acquisition
   e. data conversion
3. Which of the following tasks are least likely to be part of the accountant's role in the SDLC?
   a. user
   b. consultant on accounting rules
   c. auditor
   d. consult on internal control
   e. all of these are likely roles
4. Which of the following is the most important factor in planning for a system change?
   a. having an auditor as a member of the design team
   b. using state-of-the-art techniques
   c. concentrating on software rather than hardware
   d. involving top management and end users
   e. selecting a user to lead the design team
5. What name is given to the time value of money technique that discounts the after-tax cash flows for a project over its life to time period zero using the company's minimum desired rate of return?
   a. net present value method
   b. capital rationing method
   c. payback method
   d. average rate of return method
   e. accounting rate of return method

6. Which of the following steps is NOT considered to be part of this systems survey?

a. Interviews are conducted with operations personnel and managers.

b. The complete documentation of the system is obtained and reviewed.

c. Measures of processing volume are obtained for each operation.

d. Work measurement studies are conducted to determine the time required to complete various tasks or jobs.

e. All of the above are part of a system survey.

7. A systems development approach that starts with broad organizational goals and the types of decisions organizational executives make is called

a. bottom-up

b. network

c. top-down

d. strategic

e. sequential

8. Within the context of the TELOS acronym, the "S" refers to whether

a. The proposed system can be completed in an acceptable time frame.

b. The proposed system is in conflict with legal obligations.

c. Management is financially committed to the proposed system.

d. The company's current employees are adequately trained to operate the proposed system.

e. None of the above is true.

9. A feasibility study for a new computer system should

a. consider costs, savings, controls, profit improvement, and other benefits analyzed by application area

b. provide the preliminary plan for converting existing manual systems and clerical operations

c. provide management with assurance from qualified, independent consultants that the use of a computer system appeared justified

d. include a report by the internal audit department that evaluated internal control features for each planned application

10. The TELOS acronym is often used for determining the need for system changes. Which of the following types of feasibility studies are elements of TELOS?

a. legal, environmental, and economic

b. environmental, operational, and economic

c. technical, economic, legal, and practical

d. practical, technical, and operational

e. technical, operational, and economic

11. Within the context of the TELOS acronym, the "T" refers to whether

a. The system can be developed given the existing technology.

b. The proposed system will require users to undergo technical training.

c. An adequate computer site exists for the pro posed system.

d. The proposed system will produce technical benefits that exceed the current system.

e. The proposed technical system will be effective and efficient

12. Which of the following represents the correct order in problem resolution?

a. define the problem, recognize the problem, perform feasibility studies, specify system objectives, and prepare a project proposal

b. recognize the problem, define the problem, perform feasibility studies, specify system objectives, and prepare a project proposal

c. define the problem, recognize the problem, specify system objectives, perform feasibility studies, and prepare a project proposal.

d. recognize the problem, define the problem, specify system objectives, perform feasibility studies, and prepare a project proposal.

13. Which of the following individuals would not likely be participating in the SDLC?

a. auditors

b. end users

c. management

d. programmers

e. all of the above would likely participate

Problems

1. SYSTEMS PLANNING

Announcing a New Information System

The AJAX Company is considering implementing a new accounting system, which will automate sales processing, cash receipts, accounts payable, and cash disbursement procedures. Roger Moore, AJAX's CIO sent an announcement letter to the AJAX community. In the letter, Moore said: "I have contracted with Spartan Consulting Group to do the needs analysis, system selection, and design work. The programming and implementation will be performed in-house using existing IT department staff. The development process will be unobtrusive to user departments because Spartan knows what needs to be done. They will work independently, in the background, and will not disrupt departmental and internal audit work flow with time consuming interviews, surveys, and questionnaires. This promises to be an efficient process that will produce a system that will be appreciated by all users."

Required

a. Draft a memo from George Jones, director of internal audits in response to Moore's letter.

2. PROBLEM IDENTIFICATION

Classify each of the following as a problem or a symptom. If it is a symptom, give two examples of a possible underlying problem. If it is a problem, give two examples of a possible symptom that may be detected.

a. Declining profits
b. Defective production process
c. Low-quality raw materials
d. Shortfall in cash balance
e. Declining market share
f. Shortage of employees in the accounts payable department
g. Shortage of raw material due to a drought in the Midwest
h. Inadequately trained workers
i. Decreasing customer satisfaction

3. SYSTEMS DEVELOPMENT AND USER INVOLVEMENT

Kruger Designs hired a consulting firm three months ago to redesign the information system that the architects use. The architects will be able to use state-of-the-art computer-aided design (CAD) programs to help in designing the products. Further, they will be able to store these designs on a network server from which they and other architects may be able to call them back for future designs with similar components. The consulting firm has been instructed to develop the system without disrupting the architects. In fact, top management believes that the best route is to develop the system and then to introduce it to the architects during a training session. Management does not want the architects to spend precious billable hours guessing about the new system or putting work off until the new system is working. Thus, the consultants are operating in a back room under a shroud of secrecy.

Required

a. Do you think that management is taking the best course of action for the announcement of the new system? Why?
b. Do you approve of the development process? Why?

4. SYSTEMS ANALYSIS

Consider the following dialogue between a systems professional, Joe Pugh, and a manager of a department targeted for a new information system, Lars Meyer:

Pugh: The way to go about the analysis is to first examine the old system, such as reviewing key documents and observing the workers performing their tasks. Then we can determine which aspects are working well and which should be preserved.

Meyer: We have been through these types of projects before, and what always ends up happening is that we do not get the new system we are promised; we get a modified version of the old system.

Pugh: Well, I can assure you that will not happen this time. We just want a thorough understanding of what is working well and what is not.

Meyer: I would feel much more comfortable if we first started with a list of our requirements. We should spend some time up front determining exactly what we want the system to do for my department. Then, you systems people can come in and determine what portions to salvage if you wish. Just don't constrain us to the old system!

Required

a. Obviously these two workers have different views on how the systems analysis phase should be con ducted. Comment on whose position you sympathize with the most.
b. What method would you propose they take? Why?

PROBLEM 7: COST–BENEFIT ANALYSIS

COST OF CAPITAL = .14

	A		B	
	Probability	**Amount**	**Probability**	**Amount**
Project completion time	0.5	12 months	0.6	12 months
	0.3	18 months	0.2	18 months
	0.2	24 months	0.1	24 months
Expected useful life	0.6	4 years	0.5	4 years
	0.25	5 years	0.3	5 years
	0.15	6 years	0.2	6 years
One-time costs	0.35	$200,000	0.2	$210,000
	0.4	250,000	0.55	250,000
	0.25	300,000	0.25	260,000
Recurring costs	0.1	$ 75,000	0.4	$ 85,000
	0.55	95,000	0.4	100,000
	0.35	105,000	0.2	110,000
Annual tangible benefits starting with weighted average completion date	0.3	$220,000	0.25	$215,000
	0.5	233,000	0.5	225,000
	0.2	240,000	0.25	235,000

5. FACT-GATHERING TECHNIQUES

Your company, Tractors Inc., is employing the SDLC for its new information system. You have been chosen as a member of the development team because of your strong accounting background. This background includes a good understanding of both financial and managerial accounting concepts and required data. You also possess a great understanding of internal control activities. You do not, however, fully understand exactly what the internal auditors will need from the system in order to comply with Section 404 of the Sarbanes-Oxley Act. Lay out the fact-gathering techniques you might employ to increase your understanding of this important component of your new system.

6. SYSTEMS SELECTION

Your company, Kitchen Works, is employing the SDLC for its new information system. The company is currently performing a number of feasibility studies, including the economic feasibility study. A draft of the economic feasibility study has been presented to you for your review. You have been charged with determining whether only escapable costs have been used, the present value of cash flows is accurate, the one-time and recurring costs are correct, realistic useful lives have been used, and the intangible benefits listed in the study are reasonable. Although you are a member of the development team because of your strong accounting background, you have questions about whether some costs are escapable, for example, the interest rates used to perform present value analysis, and the estimated useful lives that have been used. How might you resolve your questions?

7. COST-BENEFIT ANALYSIS

Listed in the diagram for Problem 7 are some probability estimates of the costs and benefits associated with two competing projects.

a. Compute the net present value of each alter native. Round off the cost projections to the nearest month. Explain what happens to the answer if the probabilities of the recurring costs are in correct, and a more accurate estimate is as follows:

A		B	
0.10	$ 75.000	0.4	$ 85,000
0.55	95,000	0.4	100,000
0.35	105,000	0.2	110,000

b. Repeat step (a) for the payback method.
c. Which method do you think provides the best source of information? Why?

8. BALANCED SCORECARD

An organization's IT function has the following goals:

- Improve the quality of IT solutions and services to its internal users.
- Increase the ratio of planned benefits to realized benefits from systems solutions.
- Fully match IT strategy with enterprise strategies.
- Integrate information systems architectures to minimize database redundancy and increase systems reusability across the user community.

Required
Develop a BSC depicting specific measures for each of the four BSC perspectives.

Systems Development Cases

Several systems development cases that draw upon the material in this chapter and Chapter 14 are available online at www.cengage.com/accounting/hall.

CHAPTER

14

Construct, Deliver, and Maintain Systems Project*

Learning Objectives

After studying this chapter, you should:

- Be able to identify the sequence of events that constitute the in-house development phase of the SDLC.
- Be familiar with the tools used to improve the success of system construction and delivery activities, including prototyping, CASE tools, and the use of PERT and Gantt charts.
- Understand the distinction between the structured and object-oriented design approaches.
- Understand the use of multilevel DFDs in the design of business processes.
- Be familiar with the different types of system documentation and the purposes they serve.
- Recognize the role of accountants in the construct and delivery of systems.
- Understand the advantages and disadvantages of the commercial software option and be able to discuss the decision-making process used to select commercial software.

This chapter covers the final three phases of the systems development life cycle (SDLC). The chapter first examines the many activities associated with in-house development. These activities fall conceptually into two categories: (1) construct the system and (2) deliver the system. Through these activities, systems selected in the project initiation phase (discussed in Chapter 13) are designed in detail and implemented. This involves creating input screen formats, output report layouts, database structures, and application logic. Finally, the completed system is tested, documented, and rolled out to the user.

The chapter then examines the increasingly important option of using commercial software packages. The majority of companies today, particularly smaller firms and large firms with standardized information needs, employ prewritten software systems rather than develop in-house systems from scratch. Conceptually, the commercial software approach also consists of construct and delivery activities. In this section, we examine the pros, cons, and issues involved in selecting off-the-shelf systems.

Finally, the chapter addresses the important activities associated with systems maintenance. This stage in the SDLC carries significant financial and operational risks that are of particular importance to management, accountants, and auditors. A trend in systems development, maintenance, and operation within organizations is to outsource part of or all system activities. The SDLC does not change in such a case, but its component parts are provided by an outsourcing provider. Therefore, special controls should be introduced to prevent increasing costs, decreasing functionality of systems, and loss of strategic advantage.

*This chapter was co-authored by Jiri Polak, PhD, Deloitte & Touche, and Vojtech Merunka, PhD, Deloitte & Touche.

In-House Systems Development

Organizations usually acquire information systems in two ways: (1) they develop customized systems in-house through formal systems development activities, and/or (2) they purchase commercial systems from software vendors. Numerous commercial vendors offer high-quality, general-purpose information systems. These vendors primarily serve organizations with generic information needs. Typically, their client firms have business practices so standardized that they can purchase predesigned information systems and employ them with little or no modifications. However, many organizations require systems that are highly tuned to their unique operations. These firms design their own information systems through in-house systems development activities.

Although each approach has advantages and disadvantages, they are not mutually exclusive options. A firm may satisfy some of its information systems needs by purchasing commercial software and developing other systems in-house. This section is concerned with the in-house systems development component of Figure 14-1.

TOOLS FOR IMPROVING SYSTEMS DEVELOPMENT

Systems development projects are not always success stories. In fact, by the time they are implemented, some systems are obsolete or defective and must be replaced. Estimates hold that up to 25 percent of all systems projects fail. That is, they are terminated prematurely and never implemented, or they must be redesigned within six months of implementation. Historically, three problems that account for most systems failures have plagued the SDLC.

1. *Poorly specified systems requirements.* Systems development is not a precise science. The process involves human communications and the sharing of ideas between users and systems professionals. This information exchange is often imperfect. Mistakes are made in identifying problems and needs, new ideas emerge as the true nature of the problem unfolds, and people simply change their minds about what they really want and need from the system.

   Because of this uncertainty, the SDLC tends not to be a smooth, linear process, where one stage is completed before the next one begins. In reality, the process is iterative or cyclical. For example, it is not uncommon for a systems designer to return to the analysis stage from the construct stage to gather additional information as his or her perception of the problem changes.

   The cyclical nature of this process results in time-consuming false starts, much repeated work, and pressure from all fronts to get the job done. Too often, the result is a system that is poorly designed, over budget, and behind schedule.
2. *Ineffective development techniques.* The problems cited above are amplified by ineffective techniques for presenting, documenting, and modifying systems specifications. In the worst-case scenario, systems development tools are simply paper, pencils, rulers, templates, and erasers. The use of computer-based graphics software that permits original designs and changes to be made electronically considerably improves the situation. Nevertheless, days or even weeks of work may need to be redone because of a change in a system's specifications.
3. *Lack of user involvement in systems development.* The major cause of systems failure is the lack of end-user involvement during critical development stages. At one time, computer systems development was thought to be the exclusive domain of the systems professionals. During this period, users (including accountants) abdicated their traditional responsibility for systems design. Too often, this led to business problems because system designs reflected the analyst's perception of information needs rather than the perception of accountants and other users. Systems often lacked adequate controls and audit trails.

Today, we recognize that user involvement in a system's development is the key to its ultimate success. However, achieving competent user involvement is still difficult to accomplish. There are two reasons for this: (1) users tend to become discouraged when they discover the amount of time they must actually invest, and (2) communication between end users and systems professionals is generally not fluent. It is often said that these groups speak different languages. Each tends to

FIGURE 14-1 SYSTEMS DEVELOPMENT LIFE CYCLE

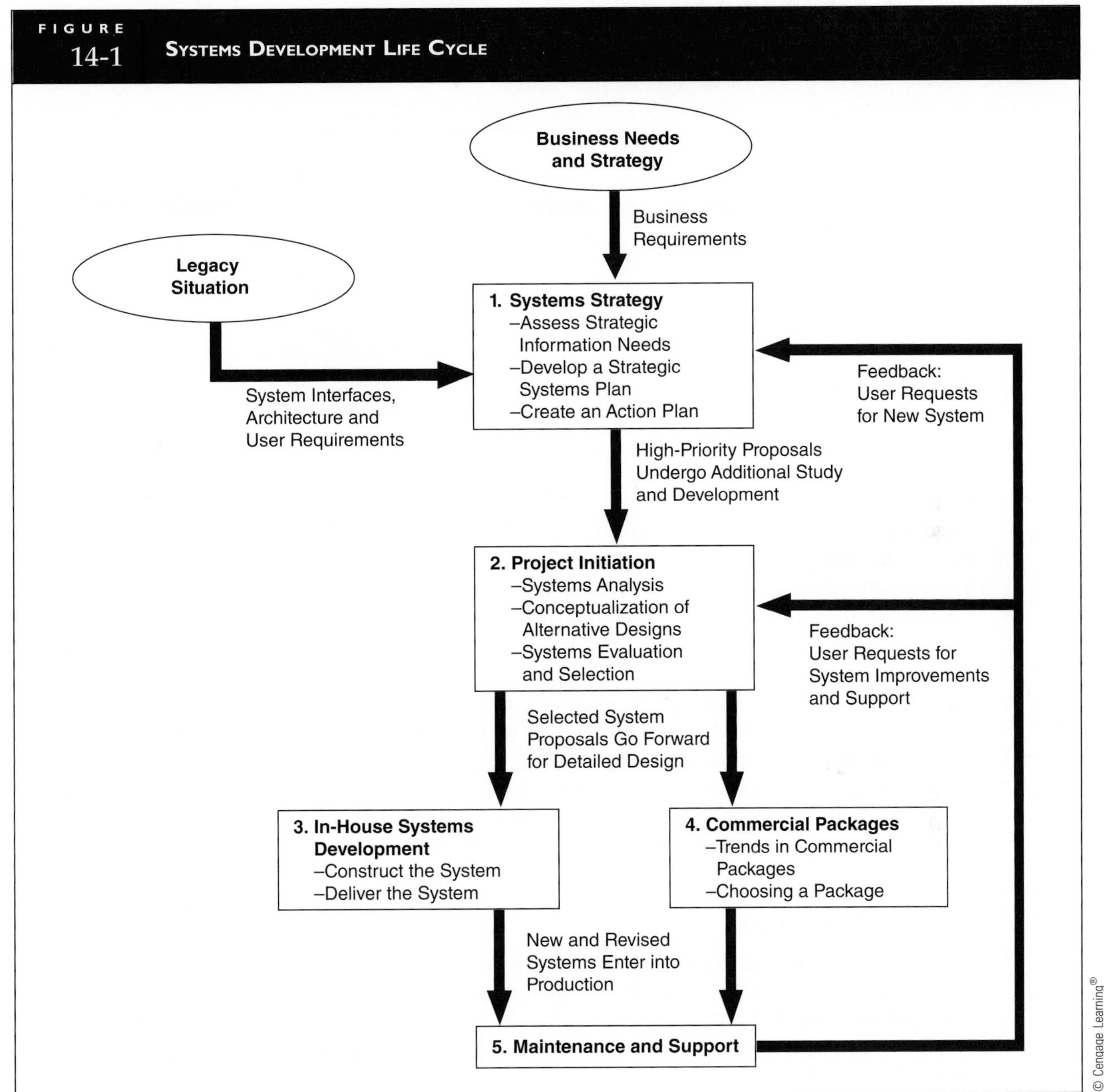

resort to its own jargon when communicating with the other. Therefore, much time is spent identifying user problems and needs and formulating acceptable solutions. Miscommunications between users and systems professionals lead to mistakes that, sometimes, are discovered too late.

These problems have led researchers to seek ways to improve the development process. The focus of this effort has been on techniques to reduce development time, facilitate better information transfer, encourage user involvement, and improve overall systems quality. Several widely used techniques for improving systems development are reviewed in the following section.

Prototyping

Prototyping is a technique for providing users a preliminary working version of the system. The prototype is built quickly and inexpensively, with the intention that it will be modified. The objective of this technique is for the prototype to represent "an unambiguous functional specification,

FIGURE 14-2 PROTOTYPING TECHNIQUES

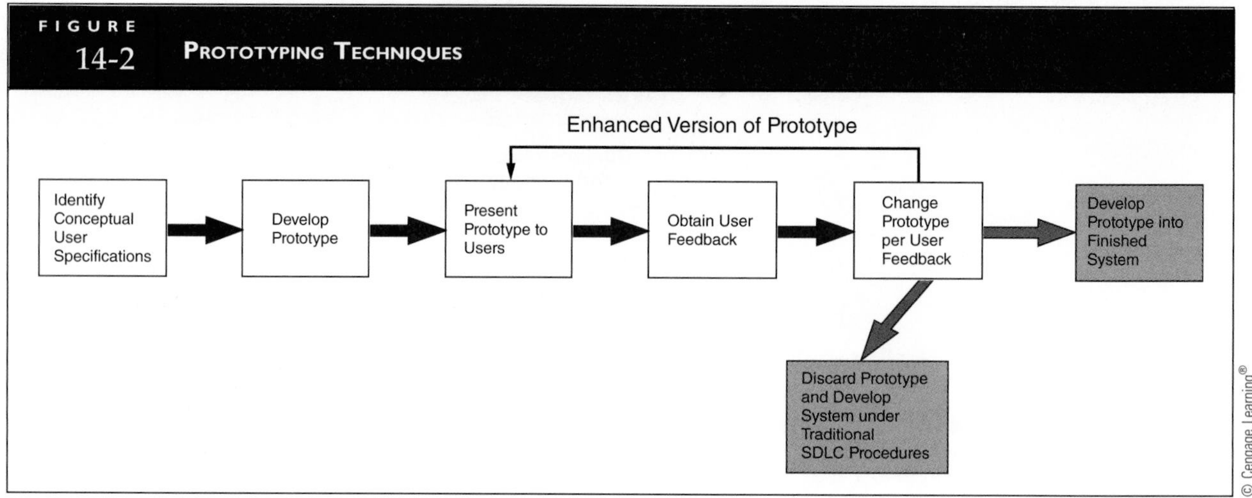

serve as a vehicle for organizing and learning, and evolve ultimately into a fully implemented" system.[1] As the users work with the prototype and make suggestions for changes, both they and the systems professional develop a better understanding of the true requirements of the system.

Reducing its features to the essential elements keeps the costs of a prototype model low. For example, the prototype system will not contain the complex code necessary to perform transaction validation, exception-handling capabilities, and internal controls. Typically, prototypes are limited to user input screens, output reports, and some principal functions.

When incorporated in the front-end stages of the SDLC, prototyping is an effective tool for establishing user requirements. Once these are obtained, the prototype is discarded. This throw-away prototyping is used for developing structured applications, such as accounting systems.[2] An alternative technique continues the prototyping process until the system is completed. This approach is used for developing decision support systems and expert systems. Figure 14-2 illustrates the prototyping model.

The CASE Approach

Computer-aided software engineering (CASE) technology involves the use of computer systems to build computer systems. CASE tools are commercial software products consisting of highly integrated applications that support a wide range of SDLC activities. This methodology was developed to increase the productivity of systems professionals, improve systems design quality, and expedite the SDLC.

Most CASE products comprise both upper and lower tools or applications. Upper CASE tools support the conceptual activities of analysis and design. Lower CASE tools support the physical activities associated with application programming and system maintenance. CASE tools are used to define user requirements, create physical databases from conceptual entity relationship (ER) diagrams, produce system design specifications, automatically generate computer program code, and facilitate the maintenance of programs that both CASE and non-CASE techniques create. Figure 14-3 illustrates the CASE spectrum of tools as they apply to various stages in the SDLC. The appendix to this chapter presents more detailed discussion of CASE features.

1. J. C. Emery, *Management Information Systems: The Critical Strategic Resource* (New York: Oxford University Press, 1987), 325.

2. V. Zwass, *Management Information Systems* (Dubuque, Iowa: Wm. C. Brown, 1992), 740.

FIGURE 14-3 CASE SPECTRUM OF SUPPORT TOOLS FOR THE SDLC

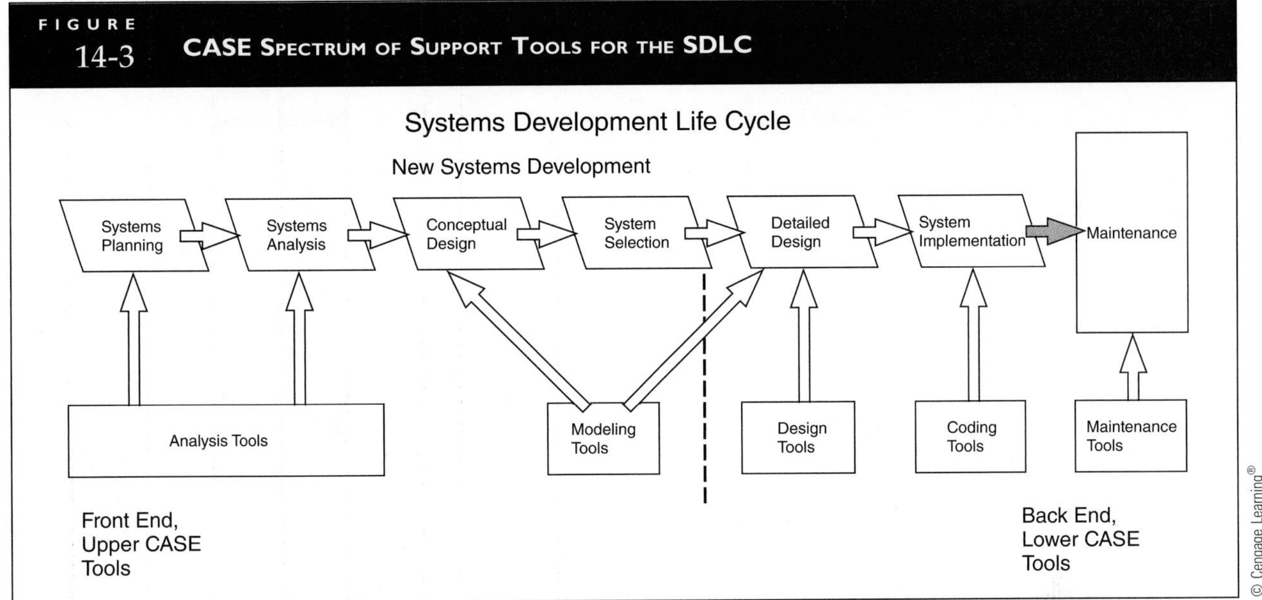

PERT Chart

The project evaluation and review technique (PERT) is a tool for showing the relationship among key activities that constitute the construct and delivery process. Figure 14-4 presents a **PERT chart** for a hypothetical project. The principal features of this diagram are:

1. *Activities*—the tasks to be completed in the project. These are labeled (and lettered A through L) on the lines, along with the time estimate for their completion. For example, the process design activity (C) is estimated to take 4 weeks.
2. *Events*—mark the completion of one activity and the beginning of the next. The events in this diagram are numbered 1 through 9.
3. *Paths*—routes through the diagram that connect the events from the first to the last.
4. *Critical path*—the path with the greatest overall time. The critical path in this project is C-F-G-J-L, with a total time of 20 (4+5+3+4+4) weeks. Any time delays in the activities along this path will extend the overall project time, which is why this path is critical.

Gantt Chart

The **Gantt chart** is a horizontal bar chart that presents time on a horizontal plane and activities on a vertical plane. Figure 14-5 illustrates a Gantt chart for the same project that the PERT chart represents in Figure 14-4. A bar marking its starting and ending dates represents the time associated with each activity. The Gantt chart is popular because it can show the current status of the project at a glance. By comparing projected time and work completed to date, we can see which projects are on, ahead of, or behind schedule.

CONSTRUCT THE SYSTEM

The main goal of the **construct** phase is to design and build working software that is ready to be tested and delivered to its user community. This phase involves modeling the system, programming the applications, and application testing. The design and programming of modern systems follow one of two basic approaches: the structured approach and the object-oriented approach. We begin this section with a review of these competing methodologies. We then examine construct issues related to system design, programming, and testing.

FIGURE 14-4 PERT CHART FOR IN-HOUSE DEVELOPMENT PROJECT

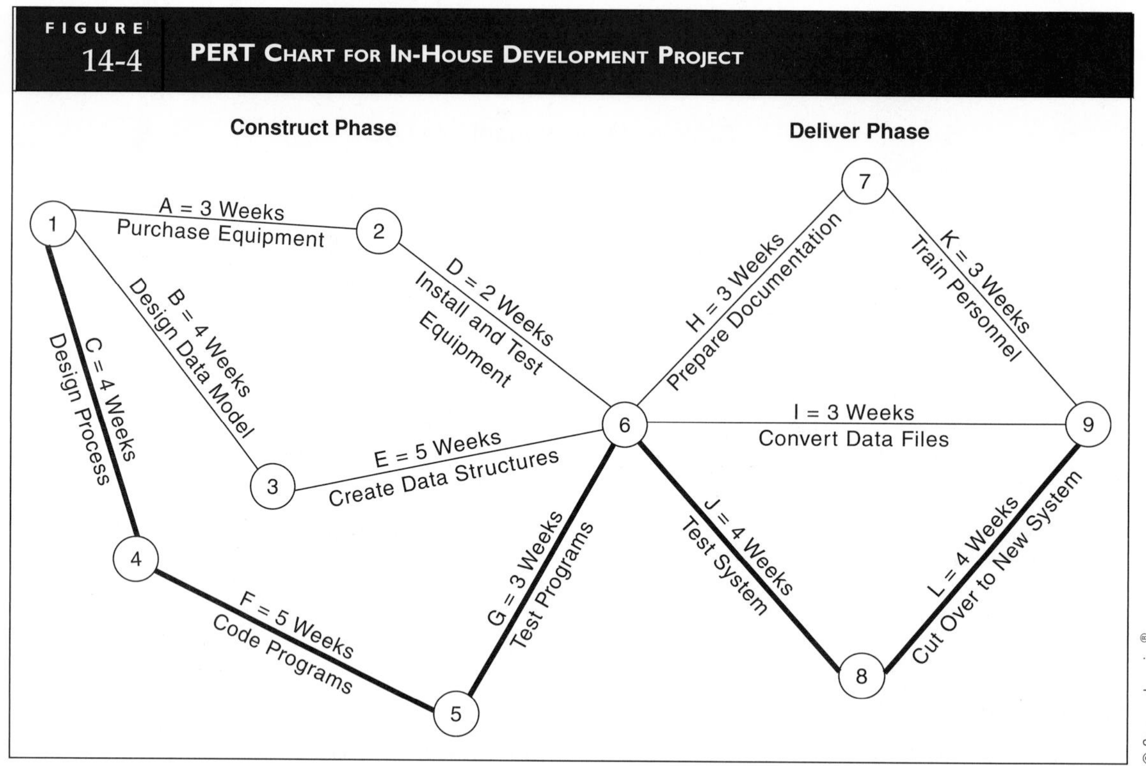

THE STRUCTURED DESIGN APPROACH

The **structured design** approach is a disciplined way of designing systems from the top down. It consists of starting with the big picture of the proposed system that is gradually decomposed into more and more detail until it is fully understood. Under this approach, the business process under design is usually documented by data flow and structure diagrams. Figure 14-6 shows the use of these techniques to depict the top-down decomposition of a hypothetical business process.

We can see from these diagrams how the systems designer follows a top-down approach. The designer starts with an abstract description of the system and, through successive steps, redefines this view to produce a more detailed description. In our example, Process 2.0 in the context diagram is decomposed into an intermediate-level data flow diagram (DFD). Process 2.3 in the intermediate DFD is further decomposed into an elementary DFD. This decomposition could involve several levels to obtain sufficient details. Let's assume that three levels are sufficient in this case. The final step transforms Process 2.3.3 into a structure diagram that defines the program modules that will constitute the process.

THE OBJECT-ORIENTED DESIGN APPROACH

The **object-oriented design** approach is to build information systems from reusable standard components or objects. This approach may be equated to the process of building an automobile. Car manufacturers do not create each new model from scratch. New models are actually built from standard components that also go into other models. For example, each model of car that a particular manufacturer produces may use the same type of engine, gearbox, alternator, rear axle, radio, and so on. Some of the car's components will be industry-standard products that other manufacturers use. Such things as wheels, tires, spark plugs, and headlights fall into this category. In fact, it may be that the only component actually created from scratch for a new car model is the body.

The automobile industry operates in this fashion to stay competitive. By using standard components, car manufacturers minimize production and maintenance costs. At the same time, they can remain responsive to consumer demands for new products and preserve manufacturing flexibility by mixing and matching components according to the customer's specification.

FIGURE 14-5 GANTT CHART

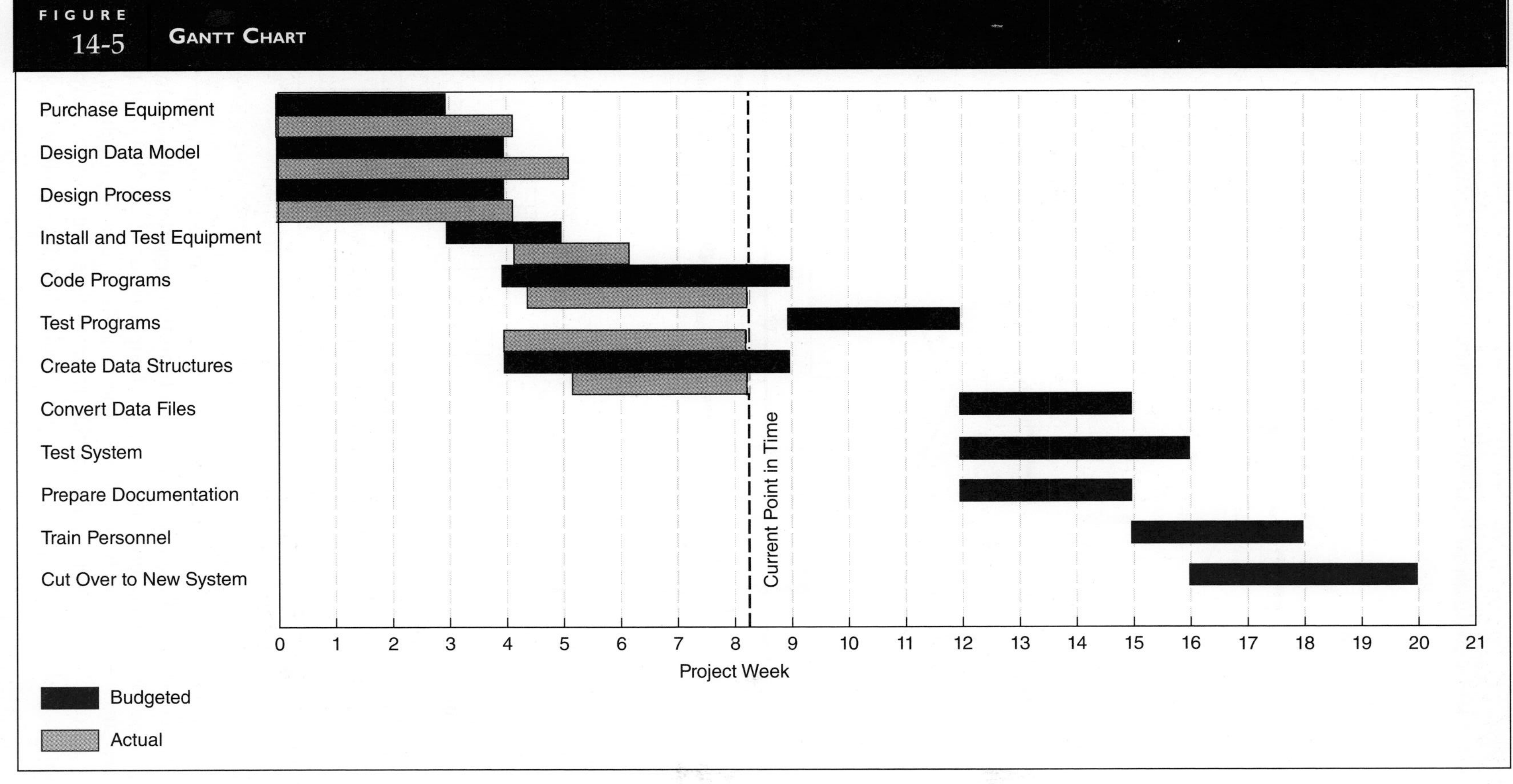

FIGURE 14-6 TOP-DOWN DECOMPOSITION OF THE STRUCTURED DESIGN APPROACH

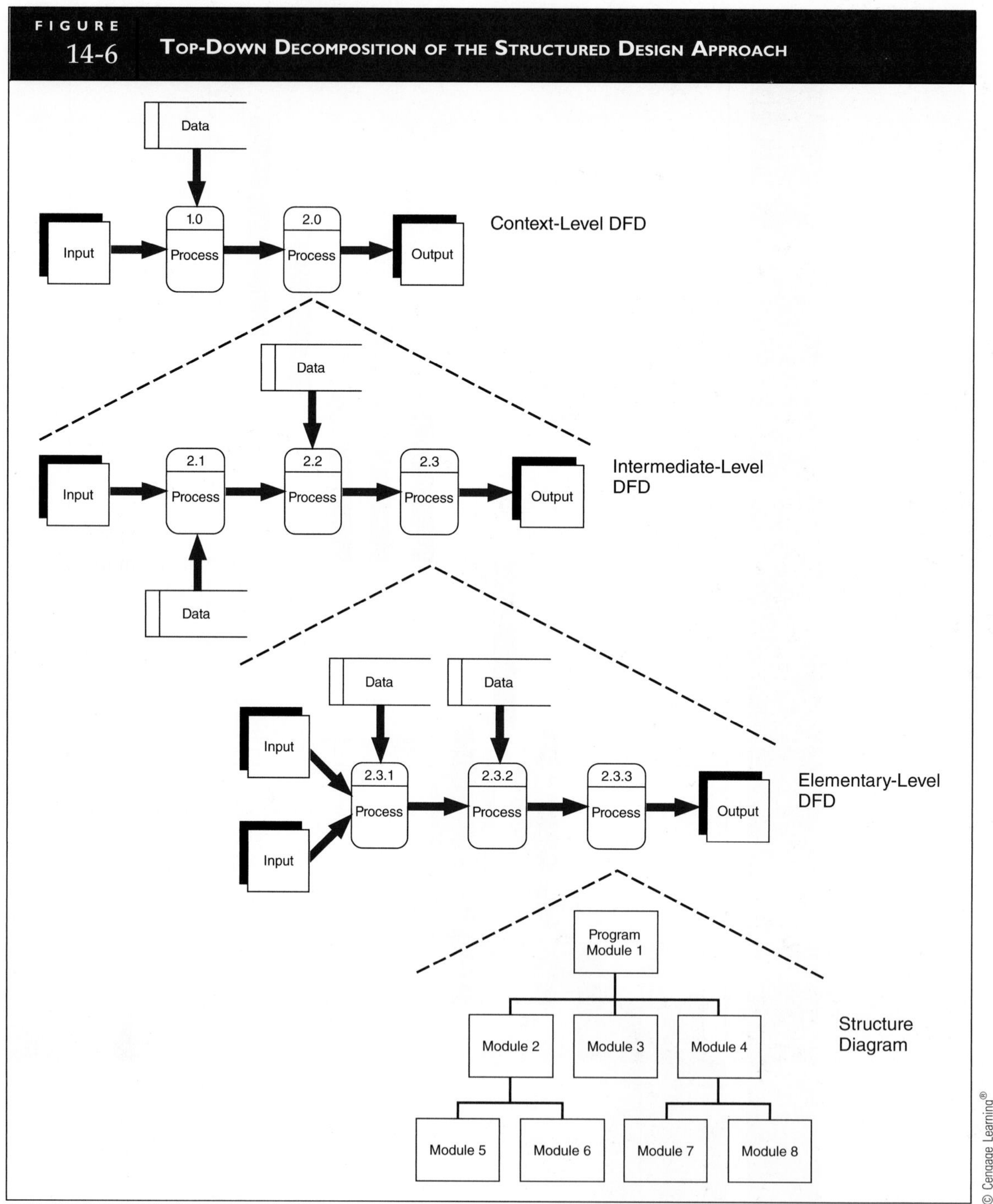

The concept of reusability is central to the object-oriented design approach to systems design. Once created, standard modules can be used in other systems with similar needs. Ideally, the systems professionals of the organization will create a library (inventory) of modules that other systems designers within the firm can use. The benefits of this approach are similar to those stated for the automobile example. They include reduced time and cost for development, maintenance, and testing, and improved user support and flexibility in the development process.

FIGURE 14-7 CHARACTERISTICS OF OBJECTS

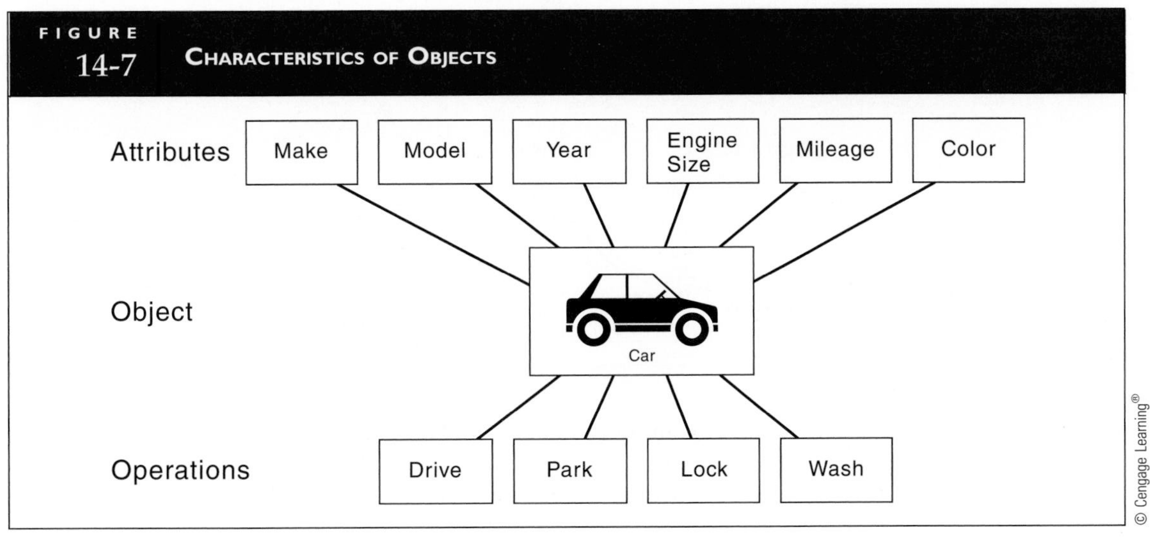

Elements of the Object-Oriented Design Approach

A distinctive characteristic of the object-oriented design approach is that both data and programming logic, such as integrity tests, accounting rules, and updating procedures, are encapsulated in modules to represent objects. The following discussion deals with the principal elements of the object-oriented approach.

OBJECTS. **Objects** are equivalent to nouns in the English language. For example, vendors, customers, inventory, and accounts are all objects. These objects possess two characteristics: attributes and methods.

Attributes are the data that describe the objects. **Methods** are the actions that are performed on or by objects that may change their attributes. Figure 14-7 illustrates these characteristics with a nonfinancial example. The object in this example is an automobile whose attributes are its make, model, year, engine size, mileage, and color. Methods that may be performed on this object include drive, park, lock, and wash. Note that if we perform a drive method on the object, the mileage attribute will be changed.

Figure 14-8 illustrates these points with an inventory accounting example. In this example, the object is inventory, and its attributes are part number, description, quantity on hand, reorder point, order quantity, and supplier number. The methods that may be performed on inventory are reduce inventory

FIGURE 14-8 CHARACTERISTICS OF AN INVENTORY OBJECT

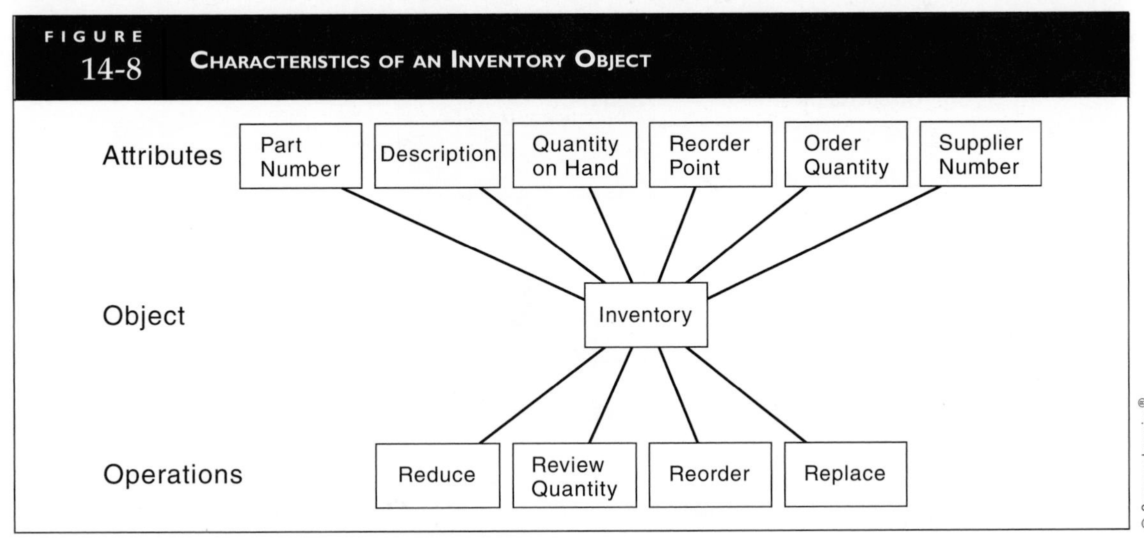

FIGURE 14-9 RELATIONSHIP BETWEEN OBJECT CLASS AND INSTANCE

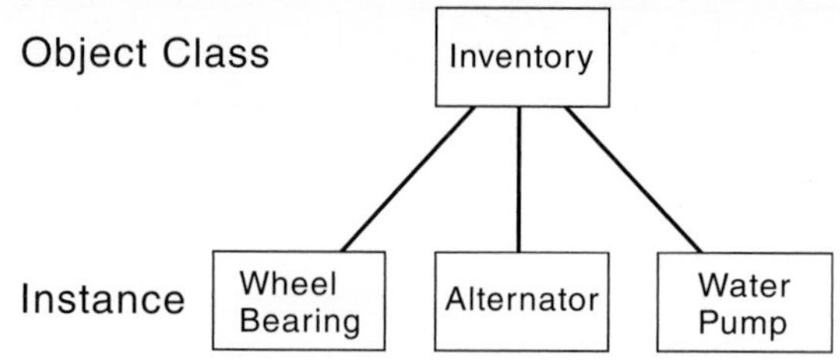

Object Class — Inventory

Instance — Wheel Bearing | Alternator | Water Pump

(from product sales), review available quantity on hand, reorder inventory (when quantity on hand is less than the reorder point), and replace inventory (from inventory receipts). Again, note that performing any of the methods will change the attribute quantity on hand.

CLASSES AND INSTANCES. An **object class** is a logical grouping of individual objects that share the same attributes and methods. An **instance** is a single occurrence of an object within a class. For example, Figure 14-9 shows the inventory class consisting of several instances or specific inventory types.

INHERITANCE. Inheritance means that each object instance inherits the attributes and methods of the class to which it belongs. For example, all instances within the inventory class hierarchy share the attributes of part number, description, and quantity on hand. These attributes would be defined once and only once for the inventory object. Thus, the object instances of wheel bearing, water pump, and alternator will inherit these attributes. Likewise, these instances will inherit the methods (reduce, review, reorder, and replace) defined for the class.

Object classes can also inherit from other object classes. For example, Figure 14-10 shows an object hierarchy made up of an object class called control and three subclasses called accounts payable, accounts receivable, and inventory. This diagramming technique is an example of unified modeling language (UML). The object is represented as a rectangle with three levels: name, attributes, and methods.

The three object subclasses have certain control methods in common. For example, no account should be updated without first verifying the values Vendor Number, Customer Number, or Part

FIGURE 14-10 OBJECTS, CLASSES, AND INHERITANCE

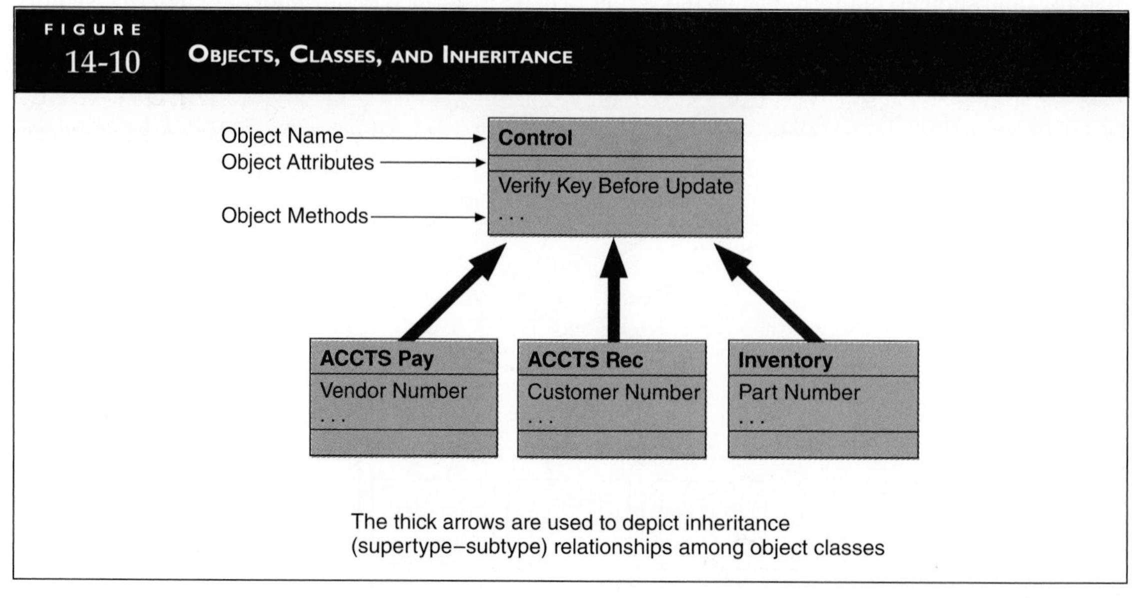

The thick arrows are used to depict inheritance (supertype–subtype) relationships among object classes

Number. This method (and others) may be specified for the control object (once and only once), and then all the subclass objects to which this method applies inherit it.

Because object-oriented designs support the objective of reusability, portions of systems, or entire systems, can be created from modules that already exist. For example, any future system that requires the attributes and methods that the existing control module specifies can inherit them by being designated a subclass object.

Finally, the object-oriented approach offers the potential of increased security over the structured model. Each object's collection of methods, which creates an impenetrable **wall of code** around the data, determines its functionality (behavior). This means that the internal data of the object can be manipulated only by its methods. Direct access to the object's internal structure is not permitted.

SYSTEM DESIGN

The purpose of the **design phase** is to produce a detailed description of the proposed system that both satisfies the system requirements identified during systems analysis and is in accordance with the conceptual design. In this phase, all system components—user views, database tables, processes, and controls—are meticulously specified. At the end of this phase, these components are presented formally in a detailed design report. This report constitutes a set of blueprints that specify input screen formats, output report layouts, database structures, and process logic. These completed plans then proceed to the final phase in the SDLC—system implementation—in which the system is physically constructed.

The Design Sequence

The **systems design** phase of the SDLC follows a logical sequence of events: create a data model of the business process, define conceptual user views, design the normalized database tables, design the physical user views (output and input views), develop the process modules, specify the system controls, and perform a system walk-through. In this section, each of the design steps is examined in detail.

An Iterative Approach

Typically, the design sequence listed in the previous section is not a purely linear process. Inevitably, system requirements change during the detailed design phase, causing the designer to revisit previous steps. For example, a last-minute change in the process design may influence data collection requirements that, in turn, changes the user view and requires alterations to the database tables.

To deal with this material as concisely and clearly as possible, the detailed design phase is presented here as a neat linear process. However, the reader should recognize its circular nature. This characteristic has control implications for both accountants and management. For example, a control issue that was previously resolved may need to be revisited as a result of modifications to the design.

DATA MODELING, CONCEPTUAL VIEWS, AND NORMALIZED TABLES

Data modeling is the task of formalizing the data requirements of the business process as a conceptual model. The primary documentation instrument used for data modeling is the entity relationship (ER) diagram. This technique is used to depict the entities or data objects in the system. Once the entities have been represented in the data model, the data attributes that define each entity can then be described. They should be determined by careful analysis of user needs and may include both financial and nonfinancial data. These attributes represent the **conceptual user views** that must be supported by normalized database tables. To the extent that the data requirements of all users have been properly specified in the data model, the resulting databases will support multiple user views. We described data modeling, defining user views, and designing normalized base tables in Chapter 9 and its appendix.

DESIGN PHYSICAL USER VIEWS

The physical views are the media for conveying and presenting data. These include output reports, documents, and input screens. The remainder of this section deals with a number of issues related to the design of physical user views. The discussion examines output and input views separately.

Design Output Views

Output is the information the system produces to support user tasks and decisions. Table 14-1 presents examples of output that several AIS subsystems produce. At the transaction processing level, output tends to be extremely detailed. Revenue and expenditure cycle systems produce control reports for lower-level management and operational documents to support daily activities. Conversion cycle systems produce reports for scheduling production, managing inventory, and cost management. These systems also produce documents for controlling the manufacturing process.

The general ledger/financial reporting system (GL/FRS) and the management reporting system (MRS) produce output that is more summarized. The intended users of these systems are management, stockholders, and other interested parties outside the firm. The GL/FRS is a nondiscretionary reporting system that produces formal reports required by law. These include financial

TABLE 14-1 EXAMPLES OF SYSTEM OUTPUTS

System	Output
Expenditure cycle	Purchase orders Cash disbursement voucher Payment check Purchases summary report Cash disbursements summary
Revenue cycle	Sales invoice Remittance advice Bill of lading Packing slip Customer statements Deposit slips Cash receipts prelist Sales summary Cash receipts summary
Conversion cycle	Purchase requisitions Work orders Move tickets Materials requisitions Production schedules Job tickets Employee time cards Work-in-process status reports Summary of changes to finish goods
General ledger and financial reporting system	Financial statements Comparative financial statements Tax returns Reports to regulatory agencies
Management reporting system	Various status and analysis reports such as: Inventory turnover reports Inventory status reports Vendor analysis reports Budget and performance reports

statements, tax returns, and other reports that regulatory agencies demand. The output requirements of the GL/FRS tend to be predictable and stable over time and between organizations.

The management reporting system (MRS) serves the needs of internal management users. MRS applications may be stand-alone systems, or they may be integrated in the revenue, conversion, and expenditure cycles to produce output that contains both financial and nonfinancial information. The MRS produces problem-specific reports that vary considerably between business entities.

OUTPUT ATTRIBUTES. Regardless of their physical form, whether operational documents, financial statements, or discretionary reports, output views should possess the following attributes: relevance, summarization, exceptions orientation, timeliness, accuracy, completeness, and conciseness.

RELEVANCE. Each element of information output must support the user' decision or task. Irrelevant facts waste resources and detract attention from the information content of the output. Output documents that contain unnecessary facts tend to be cluttered, take time to process, cause bottlenecks, and promote errors.

SUMMARIZATION. Reports should be summarized according to the level of the user in the organization. The degree of summarization increases as information flows upward from lower-level managers to top management. We see this characteristic clearly in the responsibility reports represented in Figure 14-11.

EXCEPTION ORIENTATION. Operations control reports should identify activities that are about to go out of control and ignore those that are functioning within normal limits. This allows managers to focus their attention on areas of greatest need. An example of this is illustrated with the inventory reorder report presented in Figure 14-12. Only the items that need to be ordered are listed on the report.

TIMELINESS. Timely information that is reasonably accurate and complete is more valuable than perfect information that comes too late to be useful. Therefore, the system must provide the user with information that is timely enough to support the desired action.

FIGURE 14-11 RESPONSIBILITY REPORTS SHOWING CONSOLIDATION OF INFORMATION

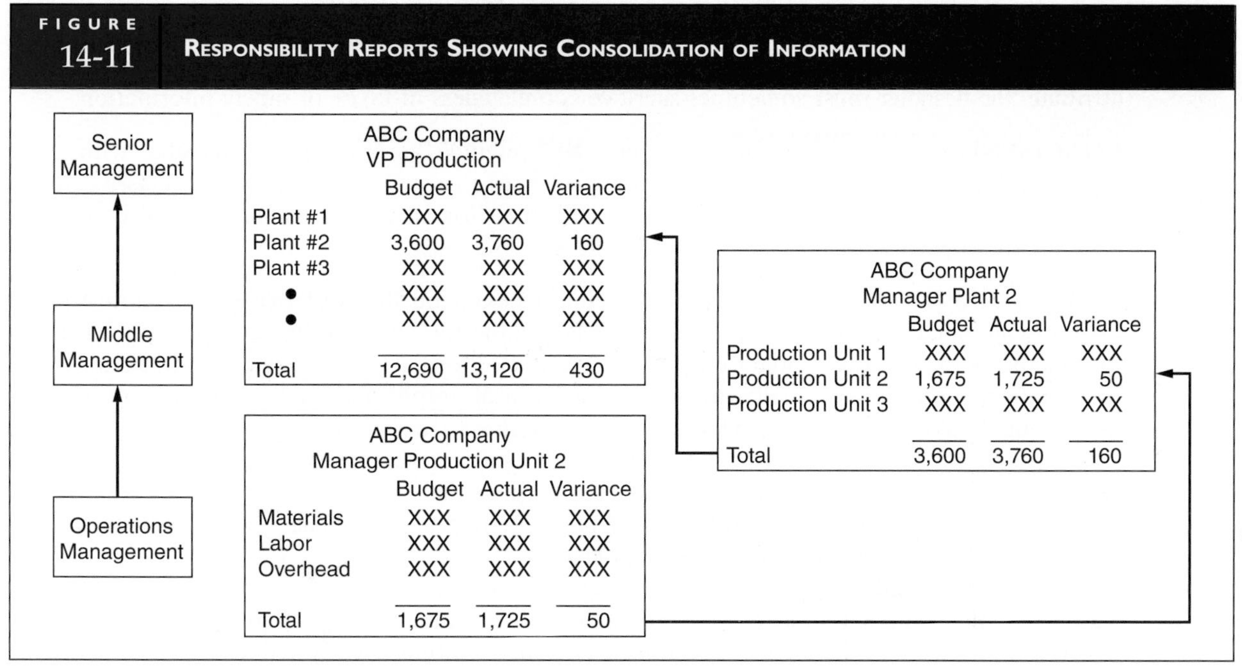

FIGURE 14-12 INVENTORY REORDER REPORT

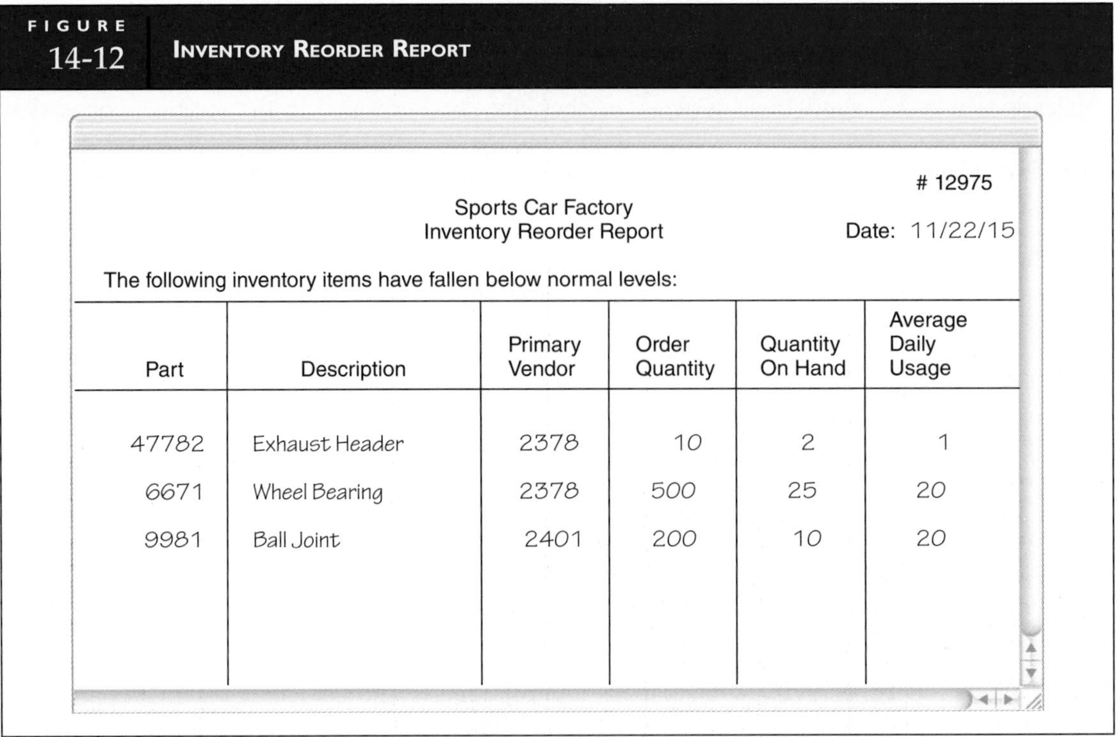

\# 12975

Sports Car Factory
Inventory Reorder Report

Date: 11/22/15

The following inventory items have fallen below normal levels:

Part	Description	Primary Vendor	Order Quantity	Quantity On Hand	Average Daily Usage
47782	Exhaust Header	2378	10	2	1
6671	Wheel Bearing	2378	500	25	20
9981	Ball Joint	2401	200	10	20

ACCURACY. Information output must be free of material errors. A material error is one that causes the user to take an incorrect action or to fail to take the correct action. Operational documents and low-level control reports usually require a high degree of accuracy. However, for certain planning reports and reports that support rapid decision making, the system designer may need to sacrifice accuracy to produce information that is timely. Managers cannot always wait until they have all the facts before they must act. The designer must seek a balance between the competing needs for accuracy and timeliness when designing output reports.

COMPLETENESS. Information must be as complete as possible. Ideally, no piece of information essential to the task or decision should be missing from the output. As with the accuracy attribute, the designer must sometimes sacrifice completeness in favor of timely information.

CONCISENESS. Information output should be presented as concisely as possible within the report or document. Output should use coding schemes to represent complex data classifications. Also, information should be clearly presented with titles for all values. Reports should be visually pleasing and logically organized.

OUTPUT REPORTING TECHNIQUES. While recognizing that differences in cognitive styles exist among managers, systems designers must determine the output type and format most useful to the user. Some managers prefer output that presents information in tables and matrices. Others prefer information that is visually oriented in the form of graphs and charts. The issue of whether the output should be hard copy (paper) or electronic must also be addressed.

Despite predictions for two decades or more, we have not yet achieved a paperless society. On the contrary, trees continue to be harvested, and paper mills continue to be productive. In some firms, top management receives hundreds of pages of paper output each day. Paper documents also continue to flow at lower organizational levels.

On the other hand, many firms are moving to paperless audit trails and support daily tasks with electronic documents. Insurance companies, law firms, and mortgage companies make extensive use of electronic documents. The use of electronic output greatly reduces or eliminates the problems associated with paper documents (purchasing, handling, storage, and disposal). However, the use of electronic output has obvious implications for accounting and auditing.

The query and report-generating features of modern database management systems permit the manager to quickly create standard and customized output reports. Custom reports can present information in different formats, including text, matrices, tables, and graphs. Section 1 in the chapter appendix examines these formats and provides some examples.

Design Input Views

Data input views are used to capture the relevant facts about the resources, events, and agents involved in business process transactions. In this section, we divide input into two classes: hard-copy input and electronic input.

DESIGN HARD-COPY INPUT. Businesses today still make extensive use of paper input documents. In designing **hard-copy** documents, the system designer must keep in mind several aspects of the physical business process.

HANDLING. How will the document be handled? Will it be on the shop floor around grease and oil? How many hands must it go through? Is it likely to get folded, creased, or torn? Input forms are part of the audit trail and must be preserved in legible form. If they are to be subjected to physical abuse, they must be made of high-quality paper.

STORAGE. How long will the form be stored? What is the storage environment? Length of storage time and environmental conditions will influence the appearance of the form. Data entered onto poor-quality paper may fade under extreme conditions. Again, this may have audit trail implications. A related consideration is the need to protect the form against erasures.

NUMBER OF COPIES. Source documents are often created in multiple copies to trigger multiple activities simultaneously and provide a basis for reconciliation. For example, the system may require that individual copies of sales orders go to the warehouse, the shipping department, billing, and accounts receivable. Manifold forms are often used in such cases. A manifold form produces several carbon copies from a single writing. The copies are normally color-coded to facilitate distribution to the correct users.

FORM SIZE. The average number of facts captured for each transaction affects the size of the form. For example, if the average number of items received from the supplier for each purchase is 20, the receiving report should be long enough to record them all. Otherwise, additional copies will be needed, which will add to the clerical work, clog the system, and promote processing errors.

Standard forms sizes are full-size, 8½ by 11 inches; and half-size, 8½ by 5½ inches. Card form standards are 8 by 10 inches and 8 by 5 inches. The use of nonstandard forms can cause handling and storage problems and should be avoided.

FORM DESIGN. Clerical errors and omissions can cause serious processing problems. Input forms must be designed to be easy to use and collect the data as efficiently and effectively as possible. This requires that forms be logically organized and visually comfortable to the user. Two techniques used in well-designed forms are zones and embedded instructions.

ZONES. **Zones** are areas on the form that contain related data. Figure 14-13 provides an example of a form divided into zones. Each zone should be constructed of lines, captions, or boxes that guide the user's eye to avoid errors and omissions.

EMBEDDED INSTRUCTIONS. **Embedded instructions** are contained within the body of the form itself rather than on a separate sheet. It is important to place instructions directly in the zone to which they pertain. If an instruction pertains to the entire form, it should be placed at the top of the form. Instructions should be brief and unambiguous. As an instructive technique, active voice is

FIGURE 14-13 ZONES OF A FORM

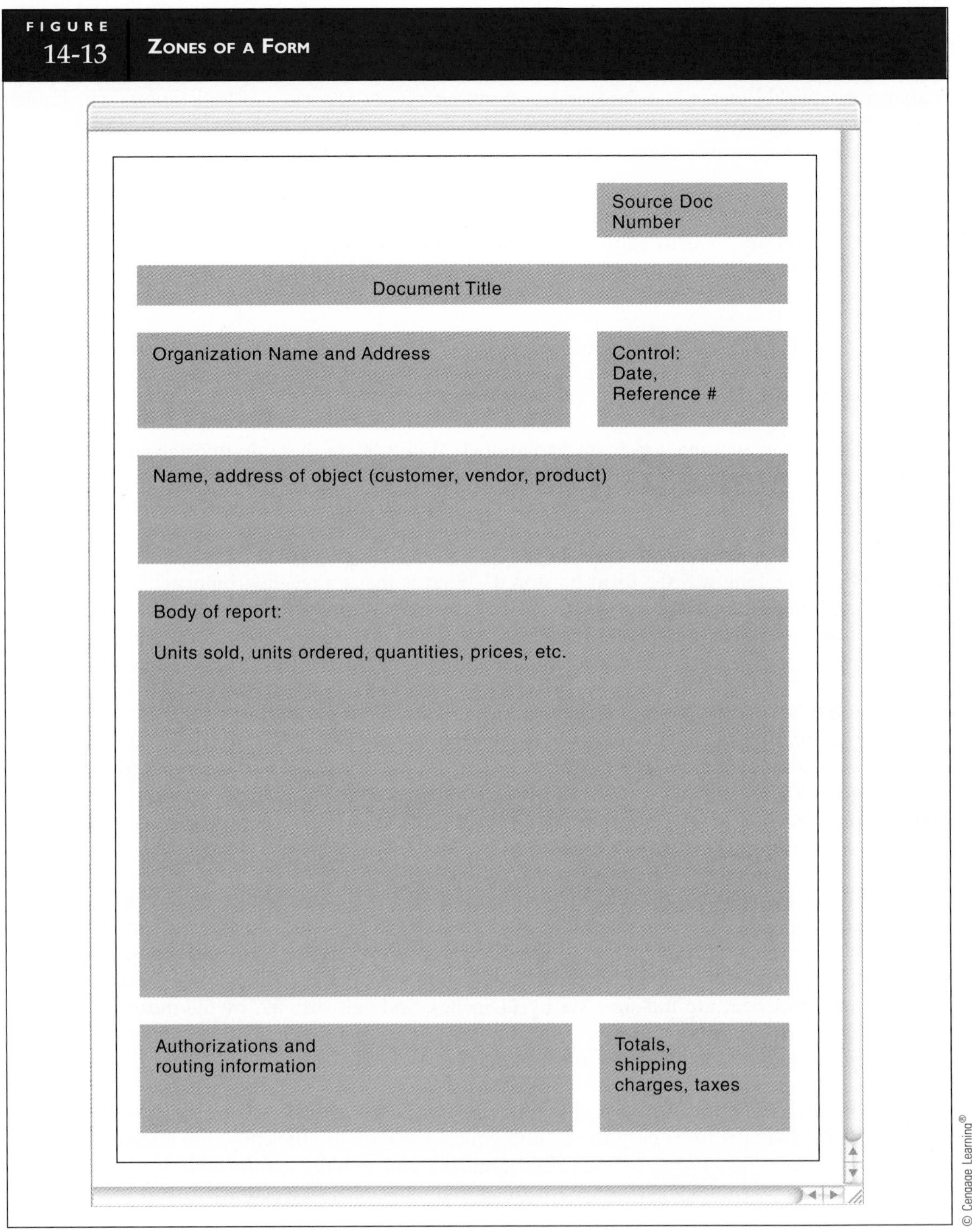

stronger, more efficient (needing fewer words), and less ambiguous than passive voice. For example, the first instruction that follows is written in passive voice. The second is in active voice.

1. This form should be completed in ink.
2. Complete this form in ink.

Notice the difference: the second sentence is stronger, shorter, and clearer than the first; it is an instruction rather than a suggestion.

FIGURE 14-14 INPUT FROM SOURCE DOCUMENT AND DIRECT INPUT

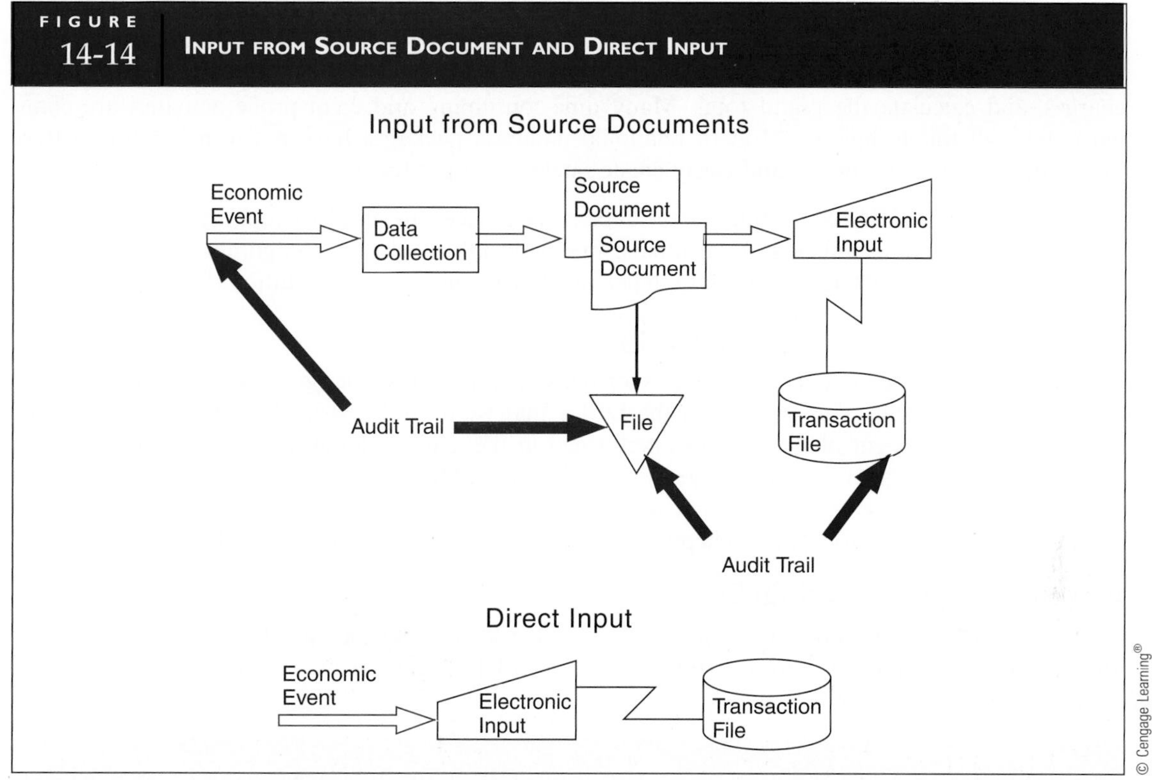

DESIGN ELECTRONIC INPUT. Electronic input techniques fall into two basic types: input from source documents and direct input. Figure 14-14 illustrates the difference in these techniques. Input from source documents involves the collection of data on paper forms that are then transcribed to electronic forms in a separate operation. Direct input procedures capture data directly in electronic form, via terminals at the source of the transaction.

INPUT FROM SOURCE DOCUMENTS. Firms use paper source documents for a number of reasons. Some firms prefer to maintain a paper audit trail that goes back to the source of an economic event. Some companies capture data onto paper documents because direct input procedures may be inconvenient or impossible. Other firms achieve economies of scale by centralizing electronic data collection from paper documents.

An important aspect of this approach is to design input screens that visually reflect the source document. The captions and data fields should be arranged on the electronic form exactly as they are on the source document. This minimizes eye movement between the source and the screen and maximizes throughput of work.

DIRECT INPUT. Direct data input requires that data collection technology be distributed to the source of the transaction. A very common example of this is the point-of-sale terminal in a department store.

An advantage of direct input is the reduction of input errors that plague downstream processing. By collecting data once, at the source, clerical errors are reduced because the subsequent transcription step associated with paper documents is eliminated. The more times a transaction is manually transcribed, the greater the potential for error.

Direct data collection uses **intelligent forms** for online editing that help the user complete the form and make calculations automatically. The input screen is attached to a computer that performs logical checks on the data being entered. This reduces input errors and improves the efficiency of the data collection procedures. During data entry, the intelligent form will detect transcription errors, such as illegal characters in a field, incorrect amounts, and invalid item numbers. A beep can be used to draw attention to an error, an illegal action, or a screen message. Thus, corrections to input can be made on the spot.

Given minimal input, an intelligent form can complete the input process automatically. For example, a sales clerk need enter in the terminal only the item numbers and quantities of products sold. The system will automatically provide the descriptions, prices, price extensions, taxes, and freight charges, and calculate the grand total. Many time-consuming and error-prone activities are eliminated through this technique. Modern relational database packages have a screen painting feature that allows the user to quickly and easily create intelligent input forms.

DATA ENTRY DEVICES. A number of data entry devices are used to support direct electronic input. These include point-of-sale terminals, magnetic ink character recognition devices, optical character recognition devices, automatic teller machines, and voice recognition devices.

DESIGN THE SYSTEM PROCESS

Now that the database tables and user views for the system have been designed, we are ready to design the process component. This starts with the DFDs that were produced in the general design phase. Depending on the extent of the activities performed in the general design phase, the system may be specified at the context level or may be refined in lower-level DFDs. The first task is to decompose the existing DFDs to a degree of detail that will serve as the basis for creating structure diagrams. The structure diagrams will provide the blueprints for writing the actual program modules.

Decompose High-Level DFDs

To demonstrate the decomposition process, we will use the intermediate DFD of the purchases and cash disbursements system illustrated in Figure 14-15. This DFD was decomposed from the

FIGURE 14-15 DFD FOR PURCHASES AND CASH DISBURSEMENTS SYSTEM

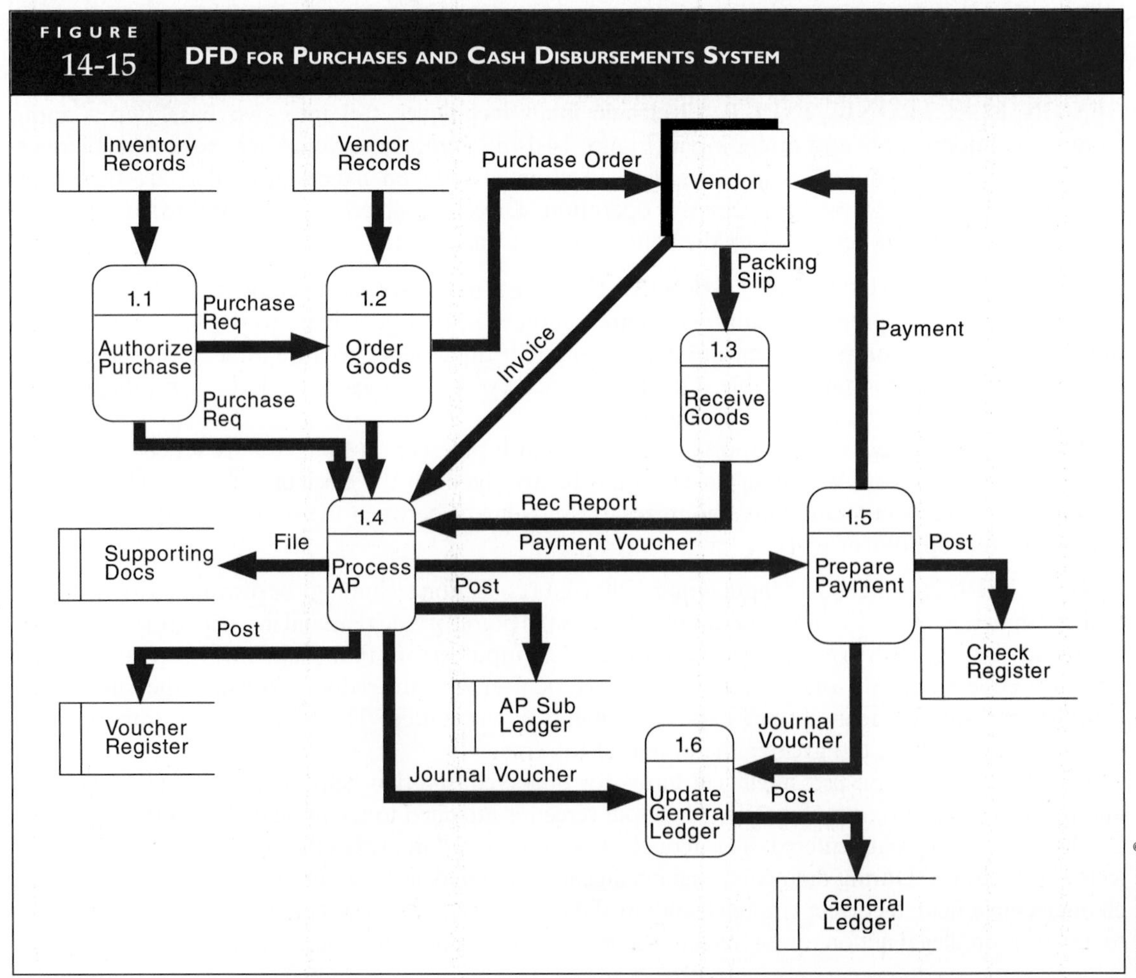

FIGURE 14-16 LOWER-LEVEL DFD FOR AP PROCESS 1.4

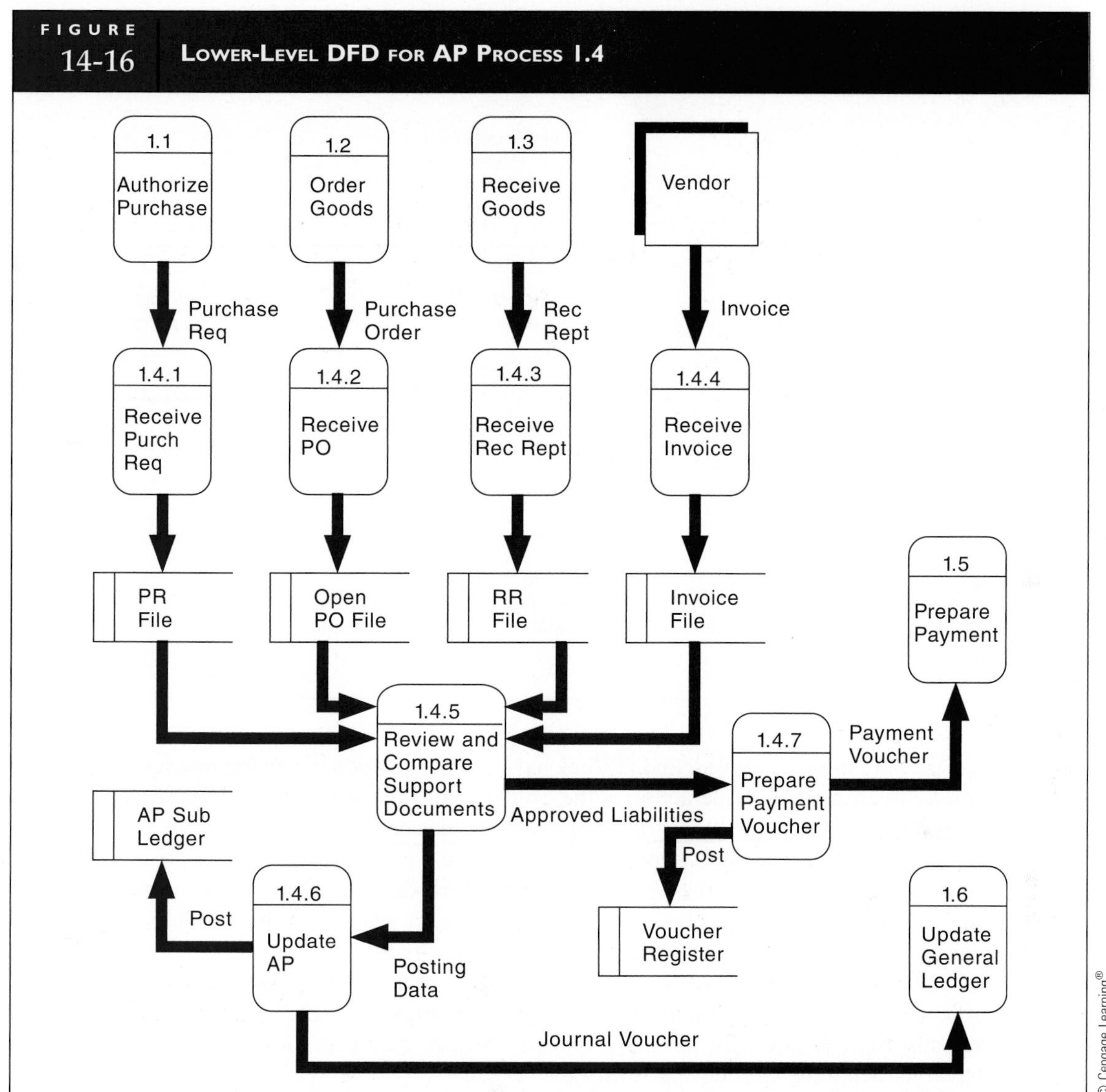

context-level DFD (Figure 13-6, Option A) originally prepared in the conceptual design phase. We will concentrate on the accounts payable process numbered 1.4 in the diagram. This process is not yet sufficiently detailed to produce program modules.

Figure 14-16 shows Process 1.4 decomposed into the next level of detail. Each of the resulting subprocesses is numbered with a third-level designator, such as 1.4.1, 1.4.2, 1.4.3, and so on. We will assume that this level of DFD provides sufficient detail to prepare a structure diagram of program modules. Many CASE tools will automatically convert DFDs to structure diagrams. However, to illustrate the concept, we will go through the process manually.

Design Structure Diagrams

The creation of the **structure diagram** requires analysis of the DFD to divide its processes into input, process, and output functions. Figure 14-17 presents a structure diagram showing the program modules based on the DFD in Figure 14-16.

The Modular Approach

The modular approach presented in Figure 14-17 involves arranging the system in a hierarchy of small, discrete modules, each of which performs a single task. Correctly designed modules possess two

FIGURE 14-17 **STRUCTURE DIAGRAM FOR AP PROCESS**

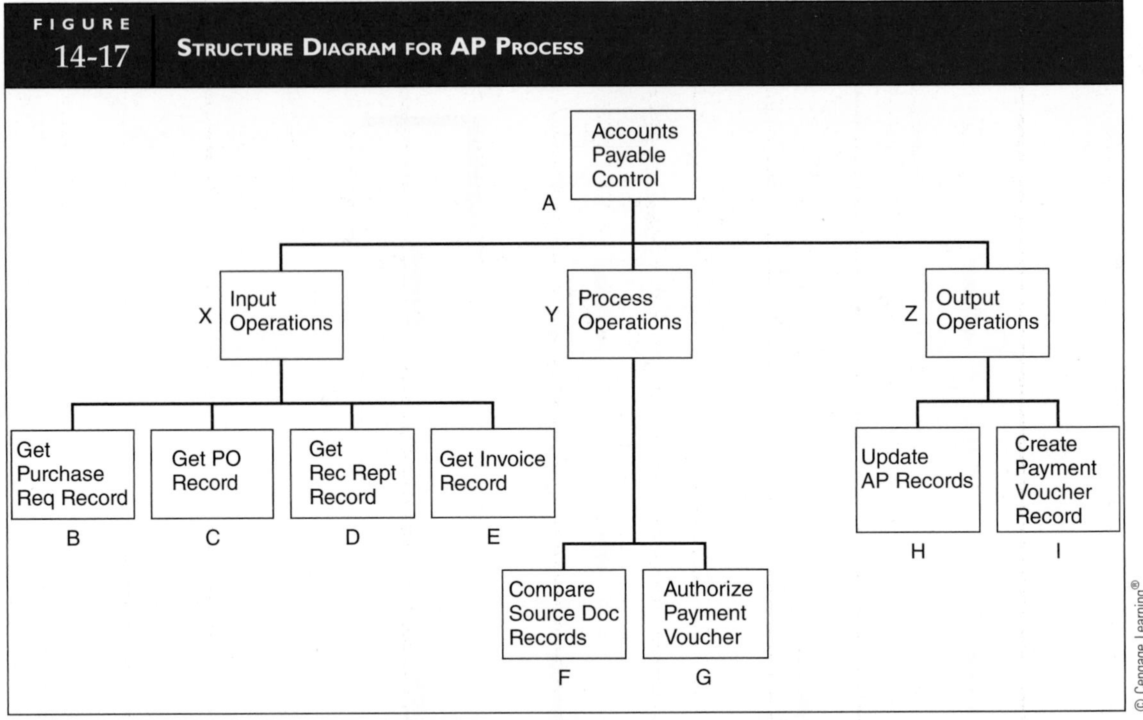

attributes: (1) they are loosely coupled, and (2) they have strong cohesion. **Coupling** measures the degree of interaction between modules. Interaction is the exchange of data between modules. A loosely coupled module is independent of the others. Modules with a great deal of interaction are tightly coupled. Figure 14-18 shows the relationship between modules in loosely coupled and tightly coupled designs.

In the loosely coupled system, the process starts with Module A. This module controls all the data flowing through the system. The other modules interact only with this module to send and receive data. Module A then redirects the data to other modules.

Cohesion refers to the number of tasks a module performs. Strong cohesion means that each module performs a single, well-defined task. Returning to Figure 14-17, Module D gets receiving reports and only that. It does not compare reports to open purchase orders, nor does it update accounts payable. Separate modules perform these tasks.

Modules that are loosely coupled and strongly cohesive are much easier to understand and easier to maintain. Maintenance is an error-prone process, and it is not uncommon for errors to be accidentally inserted into a module during maintenance. Thus, changing a single module within a

FIGURE 14-18 **LOOSELY AND TLGHTLY COUPLED MODULES**

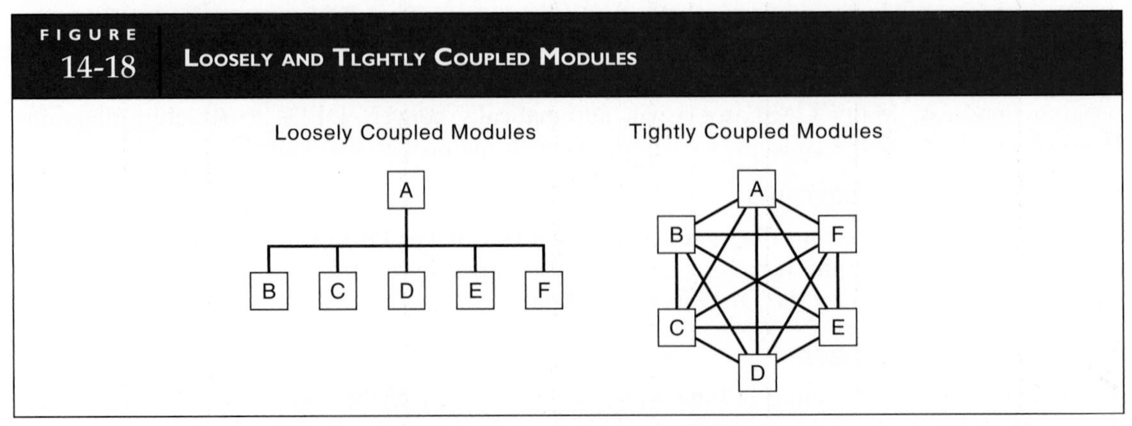

tightly coupled structure can have an impact on the other modules with which it interacts. Look again at the tightly coupled structure in Figure 14-18. These interactions complicate maintenance by extending the process to the other modules. Similarly, modules with weak cohesion—those that perform several tasks—are more complex and difficult to maintain.

Pseudocode the System Modules

Each module in Figure 14-17 represents a separate computer program. The higher-level programs will communicate with lower-level programs through call commands. System modules are coded in the implementation phase. When we get to that phase, we will examine programming language options. At this point, the designer must specify the functional characteristics of the modules through other techniques.

Next, we illustrate how **pseudocode** may be used to describe the function of Module F in Figure 14-17. This module authorizes payment of accounts payable by validating the supporting documents.

```
COMPARE-DOCS (Module F)
READ PR-RECORD FROM PR-FILE
READ PO-RECORD FROM PO-FILE
READ RR-RECORD FROM RR-FILE
READ INVOICE-RECORD FROM INVOICE-FILE
IF ITEM-NUM, QUANNTY-RECEIVED, TOTAL AMOUNT IS EQUAL FOR ALL
RECORDS
THEN PLACE "Y" IN AUTHORIZED FIELD OF PO-RECORD
ELSE READ ANOTHER RECORD
```

The use of pseudocode for specifying module functions has two advantages. First, the designer can express the detailed logic of the module, regardless of the programming language to be used. Second, although the end user may lack programming skills, he or she can be actively involved in this technical but crucial step.

DESIGN SYSTEM CONTROLS

The last step in the design phase is the design of system controls. This includes computer processing controls, database controls, and manual controls over input to and output from the system, as well as controls over the operational environment (e.g., distributed data processing controls). In practice, many controls that are specific to a type of technology or technique will, at this point, have already been designed, along with the modules to which they relate. This step in the design phase allows the design team to review, modify, and evaluate controls with a system-wide perspective that did not exist when each module was being designed independently. Because of the extensive nature of computer-based system controls, treatment of this aspect of the systems design is deferred to Chapters 15, 16, and 17, where they can be covered in depth.

PERFORM A SYSTEM DESIGN WALK-THROUGH

After completing the detailed design, the development team usually performs a system design **walk-through** to ensure the design is free from conceptual errors that could become programmed into the final system. Many firms have formal, structured walk-throughs that a **quality assurance group** conducts. This is an independent group of programmers, analysts, users, and internal auditors. The job of this group is to simulate the operation of the system to uncover errors, omissions, and ambiguities in the design. Most system errors emanate from poor designs rather than programming mistakes. Detecting and correcting errors in the design thus reduce costly reprogramming later.

Review System Documentation

The **detailed design report** documents and describes the system to this point. This report includes:

- Designs of all screen outputs, reports, and operational documents.
- ER diagrams describing the data relations in the system.

- Third normal form designs for database tables specifying all data elements.
- An updated **data dictionary** describing each data element in the database.
- Designs for all screen inputs and source documents for the system.
- Context diagrams for the overall system.
- Low-level data flow diagrams of specific system processes.
- Structure diagrams for the program modules in the system, including a pseudocode description of each module.

The quality control group scrutinizes these documents, and any errors are recorded in a walkthrough report. Depending on the extent of the system errors, the quality assurance group will make a recommendation. The system design will be accepted without modification, accepted subject to modification of minor errors, or rejected because of material errors.

At this point, a decision is made either to return the system for additional design or to proceed to the next phase—systems implementation. Assuming the design goes forward, the documents just mentioned constitute the blueprints that guide programmers and system designers in constructing the physical system.

PROGRAM APPLICATION SOFTWARE

The next stage of the in-house development is to select a programming language from among the various languages available and suitable to the application. These include procedural languages such as COBOL, event-driven languages such as Visual Basic, or object-oriented programming (OOP) languages such as Java or C++. This section presents a brief overview of various programming approaches. Systems professionals will make their decision based on the in-house standards, architecture, and user needs.

Procedural Languages

A **procedural language** requires the programmer to specify the precise order in which the program logic is executed. Procedural languages are often called **third-generation languages** (3GLs). Examples of 3GLs include COBOL, FORTRAN, C, and PL1. In business (particularly in accounting) applications, COBOL was the dominant language for years. COBOL has great capability for performing highly detailed operations on individual data records and handles large files efficiently. On the other hand, it is an extremely wordy language that makes programming a time-consuming task. COBOL has survived as a viable language because many of the legacy systems written in the 1970s and 1980s, which were coded in COBOL, are still in operation today. Major retrofits and routine maintenance to these systems need to be coded in COBOL. More than 12 billion lines of COBOL code are executed daily in the United States.

Event-Driven Languages

Event-driven languages are not procedural. Under this model, the program's code is not executed in a predefined sequence. Instead, external actions or events that the user initiates dictate the control flow of the program. For example, when the user presses a key or clicks on a computer icon on the screen, the program automatically executes code associated with that event. This is a fundamental shift from the 3GL era. Now, instead of designing applications that execute sequentially from top to bottom in accordance with the way the programmer thinks they should function, the user is in control. Microsoft's Visual Basic is the most popular example of an event-driven language. The syntax of the language is simple yet powerful. Visual Basic is used to create real-time and batch applications that can manipulate flat files or relational databases. It has a screen-painting feature that greatly facilitates the creation of sophisticated graphical user interfaces.

Object-Oriented Languages

Central to achieving the benefits of this approach is developing software in an **object-oriented programming (OOP) language**. The most popular true OOP languages are Java and Smalltalk.

However, the learning curve of **OOP** languages is steep. The time and cost of retooling for OOP are the greatest impediments to the transition process. Most firms are not prepared to discard millions of lines of traditional COBOL code and retrain their programming staffs to implement object-oriented systems. Therefore, a compromise, intended to ease this transition, has been the development of hybrid languages, such as Object COBOL, Object Pascal, and C++.

Programming the System

Regardless of the programming language used, modern programs should follow a modular approach. This technique produces small programs that perform narrowly defined tasks. The following three benefits are associated with modular programming.

PROGRAMMING EFFICIENCY. Modules can be coded and tested independently, which vastly reduces programming time. A firm can assign several programmers to a single system. Working in parallel, the programmers each design a few modules. These are then assembled into the completed system.

MAINTENANCE EFFICIENCY. Small modules are easier to analyze and change, which reduces the start-up time during program maintenance. Extensive changes can be parceled out to several programmers simultaneously to shorten maintenance time.

CONTROL. By keeping modules small, they are less likely to contain material errors of fraudulent logic. Because each module is independent of the others, errors are contained within the module.

SOFTWARE TESTING

Programs must be thoroughly tested before they are implemented. Program testing issues of direct concern to accountants are discussed in this section.

Testing Individual Modules

Programmers should test completed modules independently before implementing them. This usually involves the creation of test data. Depending on the nature of the application, this could include test transaction files, test master files, or both. Figure 14-19 illustrates the test data approach. We examine this and several other testing techniques in detail in Chapter 17.

FIGURE 14-19 THE TEST DATA TECHNIQUE

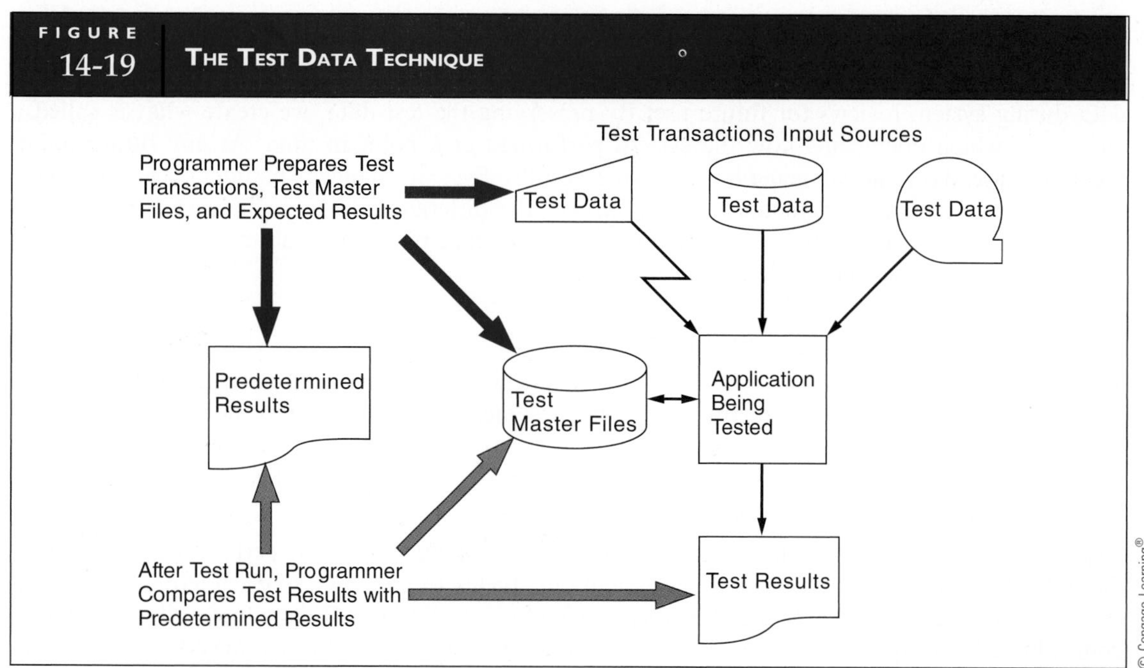

Assume the module under test is the Update AP Records program (Module H) represented in Figure 14-17. The approach taken is to test the application thoroughly within its range of functions. To do this, the programmer must create some test accounts payable master file records and test transactions. The transactions should contain a range of data values adequate to test the logic of the application, including both good and bad data. For example, the programmer may create a transaction with an incorrect account number to see how the application handles such errors. The programmer will then compare the amounts posted to accounts payable records to see if they tally with precalculated results. Tests of all aspects of the logic are performed in this way, and the test results are used to identify and correct errors in the logic of the module.

DELIVER THE SYSTEM

The system is now ready to be implemented. In this phase, database structures are populated with data, equipment is purchased and installed, employees are trained, and the system is documented. This phase concludes with the roll-out of the new system and the termination of the old system.

The implementation process engages the efforts of designers, programmers, database administrators, users, and accountants. All the steps in this stage warrant careful management. Nevertheless, not all steps are part of every system's implementation, and not all are of direct concern to accountants. For example, the implementation activities of ordering equipment from vendors, preparing the site, installing equipment, and training employees are not performed with each new system. Moreover, these are technical tasks that do not usually involve the accounting function. This section focuses on those activities that have the greatest direct implications for accountants and auditors.

TESTING THE ENTIRE SYSTEM

When all modules have been coded and tested, they must be brought together and tested as a whole. User personnel should direct system-wide testing as a prelude to the formal system cutover. The procedure involves using the system to process hypothetical data. The outputs of the system are then reconciled with predetermined results, and the test is documented to provide evidence of the system's performance. Finally, when those conducting the tests are satisfied with the results, a formal acceptance document should be completed. This is an explicit acknowledgment by the user that the system in question meets stated requirements. The user acceptance document becomes important in reconciling differences and assigning responsibilities during the post-implementation review of the system.

Saving Test Data

The preparation of test data is a tedious, time-consuming activity. The auditor should save these data during system reviews for future use. By preserving the test data, we create what is called a base case, which documents how the system performed at a point in time. At any future point, the base case data should generate the same results. System changes (maintenance) that have occurred since system implementation will explain the differences between base case results and current test results. Hence, the base case provides a reference point for analyzing the effects of system changes and eases the burden of creating test data.

DOCUMENTING THE SYSTEM

The system's **documentation** describes how the system works. In this section, we consider the documentation requirements of four groups: systems designers and programmers, computer operators, end users, and accountants.

Designer and Programmer Documentation

Systems designers and programmers need documentation to debug errors and perform maintenance on the system. This group is involved with the system on a highly technical level, which requires both general and detailed information. Some of this is provided through DFDs, ER diagrams, and structure diagrams. In addition, system flowcharts, program flowcharts, and listings of program code are important forms of documentation. The system flowchart shows the relationship of input files, programs, and output files. However, it does not reveal the logic of individual programs that constitute the system. The program flowchart provides a detailed description of the sequential and logical operation of the program. A separate program flowchart represents each program in the system's flowchart. From these, the programmer can visually review and evaluate the program's logic. The program code should itself be documented with comments that describe each major program segment.

Operator Documentation

Computer operators use documentation describing how to run the system, called a **run manual**. The typical contents of a run manual include:

- The name of the system, such as Purchases System.
- The run schedule (daily, weekly, time of day, etc.).
- Required hardware devices (tapes, disks, printers, or special hardware).
- File requirements specifying all the transaction (input) files, master files, and output files used in the system.
- Run-time instructions describing the error messages that may appear, actions to be taken, and the name and telephone number of the programmer on call, should the system fail.
- A list of users who receive the output from the run.

For security and control reasons, system flowcharts, logic flowcharts, and program code listings are not part of the operator documentation. Operators should not have access to the details of a system's internal logic. We will discuss this point more fully in Chapter 15.

User Documentation

Users need documentation describing how to use the system. User tasks include such things as entering input for transactions, making inquiries of account balances, updating accounts, and generating output reports. The nature of user documentation will depend on the user's degree of sophistication with computers and technology. Thus, before designing user documentation, the systems professional must assess and classify the user's skill level. The following is one classification scheme:

- Novices
- Occasional users
- Frequent light users
- Frequent power users

Novices have little or no experience with computers and may be embarrassed to ask questions. Novices also know little about their assigned tasks. User training and documentation for novices must be extensive and detailed.

Occasional users once understood the system but have forgotten some essential commands and procedures. They require less training and documentation than novices.

Frequent light users are familiar with limited aspects of the system. Although they understand the basic functions, they tend not to explore beneath the surface and lack depth of knowledge. This group knows only what it needs to know and requires training and documentation for unfamiliar areas.

Frequent power users understand the existing system and will readily adapt to new systems. They are intolerant of detailed instructions that waste their time. They like to find shortcuts and use macro commands to improve performance. This group requires only abbreviated documentation.

With these classes in mind, user documentation often takes the form of a user handbook, as well as online documentation. The typical **user handbook** will contain the following items:

- An overview of the system and its major functions
- Instructions for getting started
- Descriptions of procedures with step-by-step visual references

- Examples of input screens and instructions for entering data
- A complete list of error message codes and descriptions
- A reference manual of commands to run the system
- A glossary of key terms
- Service and support information

Online documentation will guide the user interactively in the use of the system. Some commonly found online features include tutorials and help features.

TUTORIALS. Online tutorials can be used to train the novice or the occasional user. The success of this technique is based on the tutorial's degree of realism. Tutorials should not restrict the user from access to legitimate functions.

HELP FEATURES. Online help features range from simple to sophisticated. A simple help feature may be nothing more than an error message displayed on the screen. The user must walk through the screens in search of the solution to the problem. More sophisticated help is context related. When the user makes an error, the system will send the message, "Do you need help?" The help feature analyzes the context of what the user is doing at the time of the error and provides help with that specific function (or command).

Accountant (Auditor) Documentation

With responsibility for the design of certain security procedures, accounting controls, and audit trails, accountants are stakeholders in all AIS applications. For these tasks, accountants may draw upon all of the documentation described previously. As internal and external auditors, accountants also require document flowcharts of manual procedures. We have encountered numerous examples of document flowcharts in the chapters dealing with the revenue, expenditure, and conversion cycles. Document flowcharts differ from DFDs in an important way. DFDs describe the overall logic of the system. Document flowcharts show explicitly the flow of information between departments, the departments in which tasks are actually performed, and the specific types and number of documents that carry information. A physical view such as this is needed to understand the segregation of duties, the adequacy of source documents, and the location of files that support the audit trail. Document flowcharts are not always included as part of the system's documentation. When not provided, auditors must create their own during the audit process.

CONVERTING THE DATABASES

Database conversion is a critical step in the implementation phase. This is the transfer of data from its current form to the format or medium the new system requires. The degree of conversion depends on the technology leap from the old system to the new one. Some conversion activities are very labor-intensive, requiring data to be entered into new databases manually. For example, the move from a manual system to a computer system will require converting files from paper to magnetic disk or tape. In other situations, writing special conversion programs may accomplish data transfer. A case in point is changing the file structure of the databases from sequential direct access files. In any case, data conversion is risky and must be carefully controlled. The following precautions should be taken:

1. *Validation.* The old database must be validated before conversion. This requires analyzing each class of data to determine whether it should be reproduced in the new database.
2. *Reconciliation.* After the conversion action, the new database must be reconciled against the original. Sometimes this must be done manually, record by record and field by field. In many instances, writing a program that will compare the two sets of data can automate this process.
3. *Backup.* Copies of the original files must be kept as backup against discrepancies in the converted data. If the current files are already in magnetic form, a backup of these files can be

conveniently made and stored. However, paper documents can create storage problems. When the user feels confident about the accuracy and completeness of the new databases, the paper documents may be destroyed.

CONVERTING TO THE NEW SYSTEM

The process of converting from the old system to the new one is called the **cutover**. A system cut-over will usually follow one of three approaches: cold turkey, phased, or parallel operation.

Cold Turkey Cutover

Under the **cold turkey cutover** approach (also called the big bang approach), the firm switches to the new system and simultaneously terminates the old system. When implementing simple systems, this is often the easiest and least costly approach. With more complex systems, it is the riskiest. Cold turkey cutover is akin to skydiving without a reserve parachute. As long as the main parachute functions properly, there is no problem. But things don't always work the way they are supposed to. System errors that were not detected during the walk-through and testing steps may materialize unexpectedly. Without a backup system, an organization can find itself in serious trouble.

Phased Cutover

Sometimes an entire system cannot, or need not, be cut over at once. The **phased cutover** begins operating the new system in modules. For example, Figure 14-20 shows how we might implement a system, starting with the sales subsystem, followed by the inventory control subsystem, and finally the purchases subsystem. By phasing in the new system in modules, we reduce the risk of a devastating system failure. However, the phased approach can create incompatibilities between new subsystems and yet-to-be-replaced old subsystems. Implementing special conversion systems that provide temporary interfaces during the cutover period may alleviate this problem.

Parallel Operation Cutover

Parallel operation cutover involves running the old system and the new system simultaneously for a period of time. Figure 14-21 illustrates this approach, which is the most time-consuming and costly of the three. Running two systems in parallel essentially doubles resource consumption. During the cutover period, the two systems require twice the source documents, twice the processing time, twice the databases, and twice the output production.

The advantage of parallel cutover is the reduction in risk. By running two systems, the user can reconcile outputs to identify and debug errors before running the new system solo. Parallel

FIGURE 14-20 PHASED CUTOVER

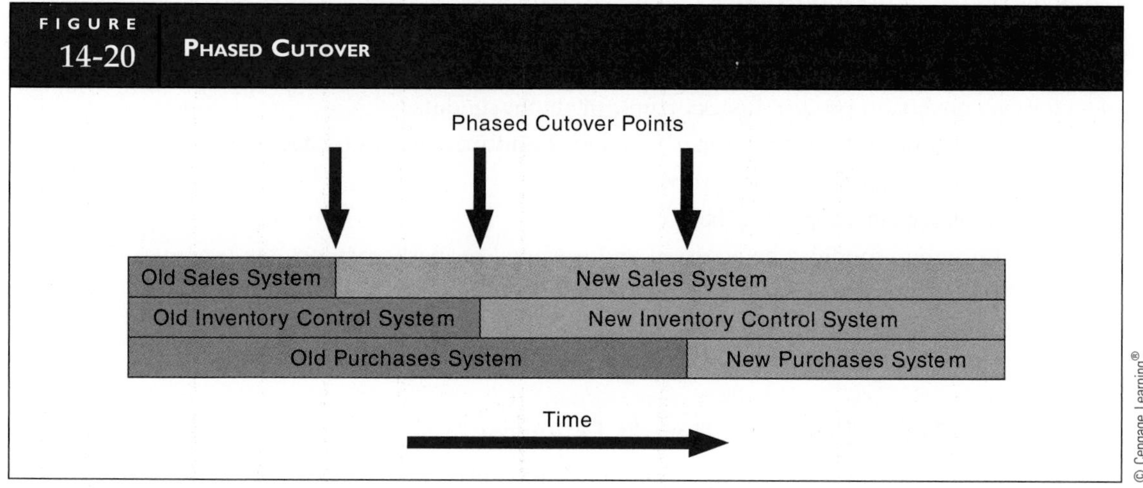

FIGURE 14-21 PARALLEL OPERATION CUTOVER

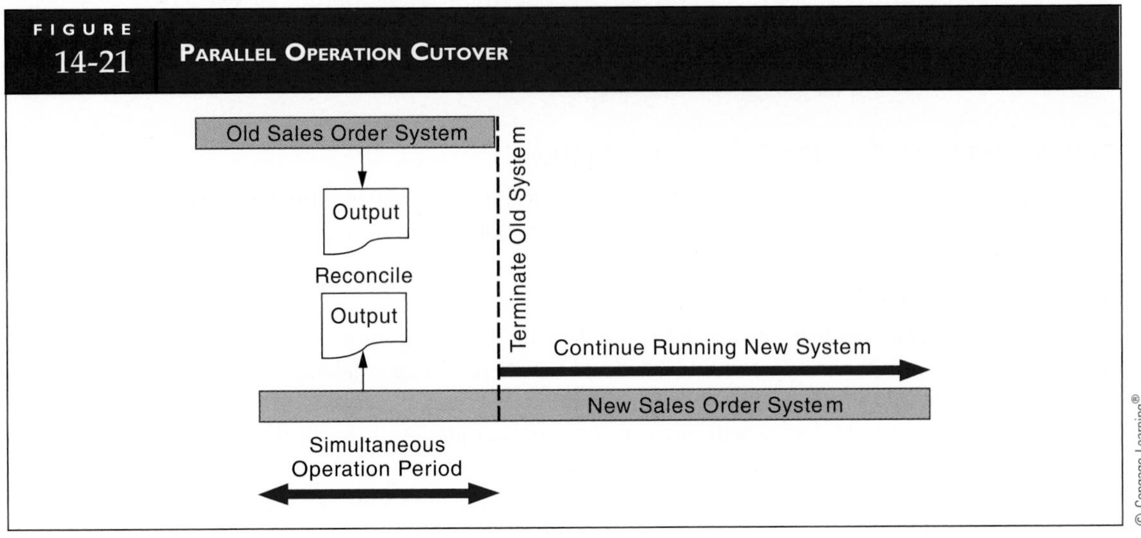

operation should usually extend for one business cycle, such as one month. This allows the user to reconcile the two outputs at the end of the cycle as a final test of the system's functionality.

POST-IMPLEMENTATION REVIEW

The final step in the implementation phase actually takes place some months later in a post-implementation review. The objective is to measure the success of the system and of the process after the dust has settled. Although systems professionals strive to produce systems that are on budget, on time, and meet user needs, this does not always happen. The post-implementation review of the newly installed system can provide insight into ways to improve the process for future systems. The areas discussed in the following section are of particular concern.

System Design Adequacy

The physical features of the system should be reviewed to see if they meet user needs. The reviewer should seek answers to the following types of questions:

1. Does the output from the system possess such characteristics of information as relevance, timeliness, completeness, accuracy, and so on?
2. Is the output in the format most useful and desired by the user (such as tables, graphs, electronic, hard copy, etc.)?
3. Are the databases accurate, complete, and accessible?
4. Did the conversion process lose, corrupt, or duplicate data?
5. Are input forms and screens properly designed and meeting users' needs?
6. Are the users using the system properly?
7. Does the processing appear to be correct?
8. Can all program modules be accessed and executed properly, or does the user ever get stuck in a loop?
9. Is user documentation accurate, complete, and easy to follow?
10. Does the system provide the user adequate help and tutorials?

Accuracy of Time, Cost, and Benefit Estimates

Uncertainty complicates the task of estimating time, costs, and benefits for a proposed system. This is particularly true for large projects involving many activities and long time frames.

The more variables in the process, the greater the likelihood for material error in the estimates. History is often the best teacher for decisions of this sort. Therefore, a review of actual performance compared to budgeted amounts provides critical input for future budgeting decisions. From such information, we can learn where mistakes were made and how to avoid them the next time. The following questions provide some insight:

1. Were PERT and Gantt chart estimates accurate to within 10 percent?
2. What were the areas of significant departures from budget?
3. Were departures from the budget controllable (internal) in the short run or noncontrollable (e.g., supplier problems)?
4. Were estimates of the number of lines of program code accurate?
5. Was the degree of rework due to design and coding errors acceptable?
6. Were actual costs in line with budgeted costs?
7. Are users receiving the expected benefits from the system?
8. Do the benefits seem to have been fairly valued?

THE ROLE OF ACCOUNTANTS

The role of accountants in the construct and deliver phases of the SDLC should be significant. Most system failures are due to poor designs and improper implementation. Being a major stakeholder in all financial systems, accountants must apply their expertise in this process to guide and shape the finished system. Specifically, accountants should get involved in the following ways.

Provide Technical Expertise

The detailed design phase involves precise specifications of procedures, rules, and conventions to be used in the system. In the case of an AIS, these specifications must comply with GAAP, GAAS, SEC regulations, and IRS codes. Failure to so comply can lead to legal exposure for the firm. For example, choosing the correct depreciation method or asset valuation technique requires a technical background that systems professionals don't necessarily possess. The accountant must provide this expertise to the systems design process.

Specify Documentation Standards

In the implementation phase, the accountant plays a role in specifying system documentation. Because financial systems must periodically be audited, they must be adequately documented. The accountant must actively encourage adherence to effective documentation standards.

Verify Control Adequacy

The applications that emerge from the SDLC must possess controls that are in accordance with the provisions of Statement on Auditing Standards No. 78. This requires the accountant's involvement at both the detailed design and implementation phases. Controls may be programmed or manual procedures. Some controls are part of the daily operation of the system, while others are special actions that precede, follow, or oversee routine processing. The extent of control techniques makes it impossible to treat them within this chapter. Instead, we have devoted the next two chapters to the study of control concepts and design.

Commercial Packages

Thus far we have examined system construction and delivery activities pertaining to in-house development. Not all systems are acquired in this fashion; the trend today is toward purchased software. Faced with many competing packages, each with unique features and attributes, management must choose the system and the vendor that best serves the needs of the organization. Making the optimal choice requires that this be an informed decision.

Before moving on to the next phase of the SDLC, we will examine the issues surrounding the purchase of commercial software. Our discussion will focus primarily on a technique that can help structure and evaluate the many intangible factors that complicate the process of selecting commercial software.

TRENDS IN COMMERCIAL PACKAGES

Four factors have stimulated the growth of the commercial software market: (1) the relatively low cost of general commercial software as compared to customized software, (2) the emergence of industry-specific vendors who target their software to the needs of particular types of businesses, (3) a growing demand from businesses that are too small to afford an in-house systems development staff, and (4) the trend toward downsizing of organizational units and the resulting move toward the distributed data processing environment, which has made the commercial software option more appealing to larger organizations.

Indeed, organizations that maintain their own in-house systems development staff will purchase commercial software when the nature of their need permits. Commercial software can be divided into a number of general groups, which are discussed in the following section.

Turnkey Systems

Turnkey systems are completely finished and tested systems that are ready for implementation. Often these are general-purpose systems or systems customized to a specific industry. Turnkey systems are usually sold only as compiled program modules, and users have limited ability to customize such systems to their specific needs. Some turnkey systems have software options that allow the user to customize input, output, and some processing through menu choices. Other turnkey system vendors will sell their customers the source code if program changes are desired. For a fee, the user or the vendor can then reprogram the original source code to customize the system. Some examples of turnkey systems are described in the following section.

GENERAL ACCOUNTING SYSTEMS. General accounting systems are designed to serve a wide variety of user needs. By mass producing a standard system, the vendor is able to reduce the unit cost of these systems to a fraction of in-house development costs. Powerful systems of this sort can be obtained for under $2,000.

To provide as much flexibility as possible, general accounting systems are designed in modules. This allows users to purchase the modules that meet their specific needs. Typical modules include accounts payable, accounts receivable, payroll processing, inventory control, general ledger, financial reporting, and fixed asset.

SPECIAL-PURPOSE SYSTEMS. Some software vendors have targeted their systems to selected segments of the economy. For example, the medical field, the banking industry, and government agencies have unique accounting procedures, rules, and conventions that general-purpose accounting systems do not always accommodate. Software vendors have thus developed standardized systems to deal with industry-specific procedures.

OFFICE AUTOMATION SYSTEMS. Office automation is the use of computer systems to improve the productivity of office workers. Examples of office automation systems include word processing packages, database management systems, spreadsheet programs, and desktop publishing systems.

Backbone Systems

As we learned in Chapter 1, **backbone systems** provide a basic system structure on which to build. Backbone systems come with all the primary processing modules programmed. The vendor designs and programs the user interface to suit the client's needs. This approach can produce highly customized systems. But customizing a system is expensive and time-consuming. Many vendors thus employ object-oriented systems design, which takes advantage of reusable modules and thereby reduces the costs of tailoring the system to the user.

Vendor-Supported Systems

Vendor-supported systems are hybrids of custom systems and commercial software. Under this approach, the vendor develops (and maintains) custom systems for its clients. The systems themselves are custom products, but the systems development service is commercially provided. This option is popular in the health care and legal services industries. Because the vendor serves as the organization's in-house systems development staff, the client organization must rely on the vendor to provide custom programming and on-site maintenance of systems. Much of each client's system may be developed from scratch, but by using an object-oriented approach, vendors can produce common modules that can be reused in other client systems. This approach helps to reduce development costs charged to the client firms.

ERP Systems

Enterprise resource planning (ERP) systems are difficult to classify into a single category because they have characteristics of all of the previously discussed systems. They are prewritten systems, which in some cases are implemented as turnkey applications. On the other hand, they can be modified to meet user needs. An ERP may be installed as a backbone system that interfaces with other legacy systems, or it may constitute an entirely new system. Because of their complexity, ERP systems are most often vendor-supported packages that an outside service provider installs.

ADVANTAGES OF COMMERCIAL PACKAGES

Implementation Time

Custom systems often take a long time to develop. Months or even years may pass before a custom system can be developed through in-house procedures. Unless the organization successfully anticipates future information needs and schedules application development accordingly, it may experience long periods of unsatisfied need. On the other hand, small commercial software systems can be implemented almost immediately upon recognizing a need. The user does not need to wait. The implementation of a single module of larger systems such as PeopleSoft, SAP, or ORACLE-FIN, however, could take from several weeks to a few months. An entire ERP could take years, but this is still much quicker than in-house or outsourced development would take.

Cost

A single user must wholly absorb in-house development costs. However, because the cost of commercial software is spread across many users, the unit cost is reduced to a fraction of the cost of a system developed in-house.

Reliability

Most reputable commercial software packages are thoroughly tested before their release to the consumer market. Any system errors that were not discovered during testing that organizations likely uncover shortly after release are corrected. Although no system is certified as being free from errors, commercial software is less likely to have errors than an equivalent in-house system.

DISADVANTAGES OF COMMERCIAL PACKAGES

Independence

Purchasing a vendor-supported system makes the firm dependent on the vendor for maintenance. The user runs the risk that the vendor will cease to support the system or even go out of business. This is perhaps the greatest disadvantage of vendor-supported systems.

The Need for Customized Systems

The prime advantage of in-house development is the ability to produce applications to exact specifications. This advantage also describes a disadvantage of commercial software. Sometimes, the user's needs are unique and complex, and commercially available software is either too general or too inflexible.

Maintenance

Business information systems undergo frequent changes. If the user's needs change, it may be difficult or even impossible to modify commercial software. On the other hand, in-house development provides users with proprietary applications that can be maintained.

CHOOSING A PACKAGE

Having made the decision to purchase commercial software, the systems development team is now faced with the task of choosing the package that best satisfies the organization's needs. On the surface, there may appear to be no clear-cut best choice from the many options available. The following four-step procedure can help structure this decision-making process by establishing decision criteria and identifying key differences between options.

Step 1: Needs Analysis

As with in-house development, the commercial option begins with an analysis of user needs. These are formally presented in a statement of systems requirements that provides a basis for choosing between competing alternatives. For example, the stated requirement of the new system may be to:

1. Support the accounting and reporting requirements of federal, state, and local agencies.
2. Provide access to information in a timely and efficient manner.
3. Simultaneously support both accrual accounting and fund accounting systems.
4. Increase transaction processing capacity.
5. Reduce the cost of current operations.
6. Improve user productivity.
7. Reduce processing errors.
8. Support batch and real-time processing.
9. Provide automatic general ledger reconciliations.
10. Be expandable and flexible to accommodate growth and changes in future needs.

The systems requirements should be as detailed as the user's technical background permits. Detailed specifications enable users to narrow the search to only those packages most likely to satisfy their needs. Although computer literacy is a distinct advantage in this step, the technically inexperienced user can still compile a meaningful list of desirable features that the system should possess. For example, the user should address such items of importance as compliance with accounting conventions, special control and transaction volume requirements, and so on.

Step 2: Send Out the Request for Proposals

Systems requirements are summarized in a document called a **request for proposal (RFP)**, which is sent to each prospective vendor. A letter of transmittal accompanies the RFP to explain to the vendor the nature of the problem, the objectives of the system, and the deadline for proposal submission.

The RFP provides a format for vendor responses and thus a comparative basis for initial screening. Some vendors will choose not to respond to the RFP, while others will propose packages that clearly do not meet the stated requirements. The reviewer should attempt to select from these responses those proposals that are feasible alternatives.

Step 3: Gather Facts

In this next step in the selection process, the objective is to identify and capture relevant facts about each vendor's system. The following describes techniques for fact gathering.

VENDOR PRESENTATIONS. At some point during the review, vendors should be invited to make formal presentations of their systems at the user's premises. This provides the principal decision makers and users with an opportunity to observe the product firsthand.

Technical demonstrations are usually given at these presentations using modified versions of the packages that run on microcomputers. This provides an opportunity to obtain answers to detailed questions. Sufficient time should therefore be allotted for an in-depth demonstration followed by a question-and-answer period. If vendor representatives are unable or unwilling to demonstrate the full range of system capabilities or to deal with specific questions from the audience, this may indicate a functional deficiency of the system.

Failure to gain satisfactory responses from vendor representatives may also be a sign of their technical incompetence. The representatives either do not understand the user's problem or their own system and how it relates to the user's situation. In either case, the user has cause to question the vendor's ability to deliver a quality product and to provide adequate support.

BENCHMARK PROBLEMS. One often-used technique for measuring the relative performance of competing systems is to establish a benchmark problem for them to solve. The benchmark problem could consist of important transactions or tasks that key components of the system perform. In the benchmark example illustrated in Figure 14-22, both systems are given the same data and processing task. The results of processing are compared on criteria such as speed, accuracy, and efficiency in performing the task.

VENDOR SUPPORT. For some organizations, vendor support is an important criterion in systems selection. The desired level of support should be carefully considered. Organizations with competent in-house systems professionals may need less vendor support than firms without such internal resources. Support can vary greatly from vendor to vendor. Some vendors provide full-service support, including:

- Client training
- User and technical documentation
- Warranties

FIGURE 14-22 BENCHMARK APPROACH TO TESTING COMPETING SOFTWARE

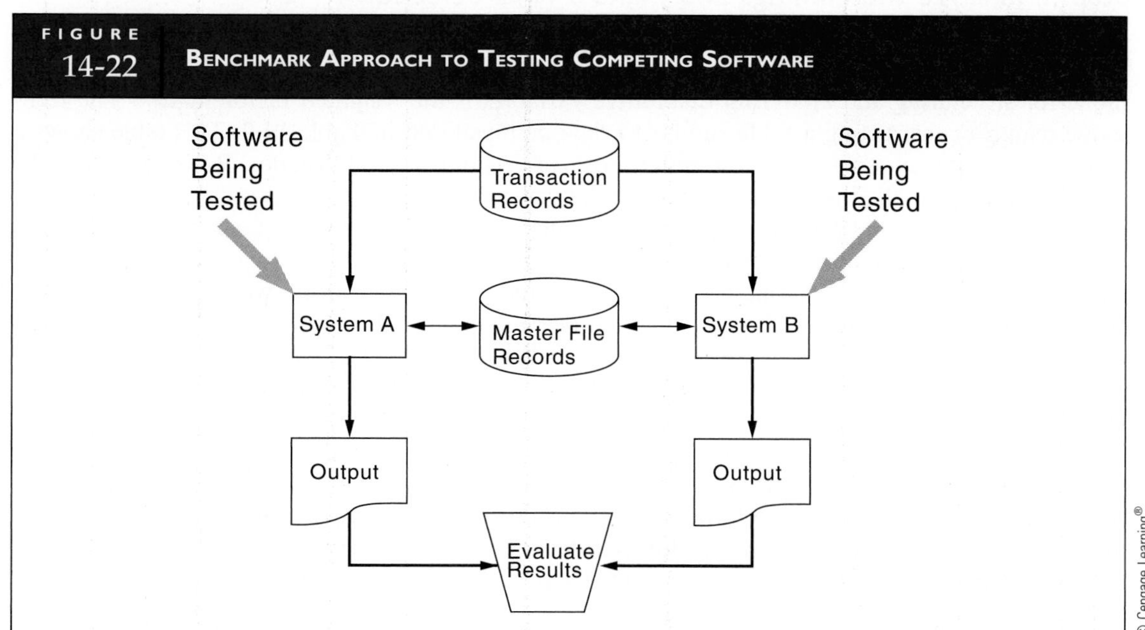

- Maintenance programs to implement system enhancements
- Toll-free help numbers
- Annual seminars to obtain input from users and apprise them of the latest developments

At the other extreme, some vendors provide virtually no support. The buyer should be wary of a promise of support that seems too good to be true, because it probably is. The level of support the vendor provides can account for a large portion of its product's price. To avoid dump-and-run vendors, the buyer must be prepared to pay for support.

CONTACT USER GROUPS. A vendor's current user list is an important source of information. The prospective user, not the vendor, should select a representative sample of users with the latest version of the package and with similar computer configurations. A standard set of questions directed to these users will provide information for comparing packages. The following list provides examples of the types of questions to ask:

- When did you purchase the package?
- Which other vendors did you review?
- Why did you select this package?
- Are you satisfied with the package?
- Are you satisfied with the vendor support?
- Does the system perform as advertised?
- Were modifications required?
- What type of training did the vendor provide?
- What is the quality of the documentation?
- Have any major problems been encountered?
- Do you subscribe to the vendor's maintenance program?
- If so, do you receive enhancements?

To reiterate an important point, the prospective user, not the vendor, should select the user references. This provides for a more objective appraisal and reduces the possibility of receiving biased information from showcase installations.

Step 4: Analyze the Findings and Make a Final Selection

The final step in the selection process is to analyze the facts and choose the best package. The principal problem is dealing with the many qualitative aspects of this decision. A popular technique for structuring and analyzing qualitative variables is the weighted factor matrix. The technique requires constructing a table similar to the one illustrated in Table 14-2. This table shows a comparison between only two proposals, those of Vendor A and Vendor B. In practice, the approach can be applied to all the vendors under consideration.

The table presents the relevant decision criteria under the heading *Factor*. Each decision factor is assigned a weight that implies its relative importance to the user. Two steps are critical to this analysis technique: (1) identify all relevant decision factors, and (2) assign realistic weights to each factor. Because these factors represent all of the relevant decision criteria, their weights should total 100 percent. These weights will likely vary among decision makers. One reviewer may consider vendor support an important factor and thus assign a high numeric value to its weight. Another decision maker may give this a low weight because support is not important in his or her firm, relative to other factors.

After assigning weights, each vendor package is evaluated according to its performance in each factor category. Based upon the facts gathered in the previous steps, each individual factor is scored on a scale of 1 to 5, where 1 is poor performance and 5 is excellent. The weighted scores are computed by multiplying the raw score by the weight for each factor. Using the previous example, a weight of 15 for vendor support is multiplied by a score of 4 for Vendor A and 3 for Vendor B, yielding the weighted scores of 60 and 45, respectively.

TABLE 14-2 WEIGHTED FACTOR MATRIX

		PROPOSAL A		PROPOSAL B	
Factor	Weight	Raw Score	Weighted Score	Raw Score	Weighted Score
Response time	10	5	50	4	40
Compatibility	9	3	27	5	45
Reputation and experience	5	3	15	5	25
Ability to deliver on schedule	7	4	28	5	35
Range of capabilities	15	4	60	4	60
Modularity	12	4	48	3	36
User friendliness	15	4	60	3	45
Supports database	9	2	18	5	45
Supports networking	3	2	6	5	15
Vendor support	15	4	60	3	45
Total	100		372		391

The weighted scores are then totaled, and each vendor is assigned a composite score. This is the vendor's overall performance index. Table 14-2 shows a score of 391 for Vendor B and 372 for Vendor A. This composite score suggests that Vendor B's product is rated slightly higher than Vendor A's.

This analysis must be taken a step further to include financial considerations. For example, assume Proposal A costs $150,000 and Proposal B costs $190,000. An overall performance/cost index is computed as follows.

$$\text{Proposal A}: \frac{372}{\$150{,}000} = 2.48 \text{ per } \$1{,}000$$

$$\text{Proposal B}: \frac{391}{\$190{,}000} = 2.06 \text{ per } \$1{,}000$$

This means that Proposal A provides 2.48 units of performance per $1,000 versus only 2.06 units per $1,000 from Proposal B. Therefore, Proposal A provides the greater value for the cost.

The option with the highest performance/cost ratio is the more economically feasible choice. Of course, this analysis rests on the user's ability to identify all relevant decision factors and assign to them weights that reflect their relative importance to the decision. If any relevant factors are omitted or if their weights are misstated, the results of the analysis will be misleading.

Maintenance and Support

Maintenance involves both implementing the latest software versions of commercial packages and making in-house modifications to existing systems to accommodate changing user needs. Maintenance may be relatively trivial, such as modifying an application to produce a new report, or more extensive, such as programming new functionality into a system.

Some organizations view systems maintenance services as commodity activities that should be outsourced to third-party vendors on a low-cost bidder basis. The underlying justification for this is short-term economic benefit. By outsourcing maintenance and support, management can channel financial resources into the organization's core competencies. Unfortunately, isolating maintenance activities from the organization also disrupts the flow of system-related knowledge that may be of strategic importance to the organization.

Some organizations take a strategic view of maintenance. Maintenance is an integral part of the SDLC. Rather than representing the end of the line, it can be an incubator for new ideas. If management captures the appropriate data, each currently running system can be the prototype for the next version. To ensure success, the organization needs to collect all relevant data from comments, requests, observed symptoms, and ideas for improvement from the user community.

USER SUPPORT

Typically, the first point of contact for such data transfer is through the user support function. This includes help desk services, user training and education classes, and formally documented user feedback pertaining to problems and system errors. To facilitate data gathering and analysis, **knowledge management** systems are effective maintenance tools.

KNOWLEDGE MANAGEMENT AND GROUP MEMORY

Knowledge management is a concept consisting of four basic processes: gathering, organizing, refining, and disseminating. **Gathering** brings data into the system. **Organizing** associates data items with subjects, giving them context. **Refining** adds value by discovering relationships between data, performing synthesis, and abstracting. **Disseminating** gets knowledge to the recipients in a usable form. The most difficult of these processes to automate is refining.

A knowledge management system can be used to create a **group memory**, which makes an organization more effective, just as human beings become more effective and mature with the accumulation of thoughts and memories. From a technology viewpoint, a knowledge management system is a database-oriented software tool that allows users, developers, and the operations community to contribute to the group memory. Contributors add their comments, suggestions, or complaints about a system or process into forms from their desktop PCs. The knowledge management software uses a parsing utility that takes incoming strings of data and infers relationships from them. A notable strength of the system is that it can deal with both historical and emerging data. The goal of the system is not simply to store information in a central repository for record keeping or archival recall. Rather, it analyzes the heterogeneous data and disseminates information to users and systems management. Group memory is thus a potentially valuable input to the organization's evolving systems strategy.

Summary

The chapter dealt with the construction and delivery of information systems. The first section presented topics and issues related to in-house development. This began with a review of techniques used for improving systems construction, including prototyping, CASE technology, PERT charts, and Gantt charts. Next, we discussed two design approaches: the structured approach and the object-oriented approach. The discussion followed a design sequence that dealt with system components in the following order: create a data model of the business process, define conceptual user views, design the normalized database tables, design the physical user views (output and input views), develop the process modules, specify the system controls, and perform a system walkthrough. The delivery stage involves populating database structures, purchasing and installing equipment, employee training, and system documentation. This phase concludes with the roll-out of the new system and the termination of the old system. The section concluded with a discussion of the accountant's role in in-house development.

We next examined issues related to commercial software, an option that businesses are increasingly using. After briefly identifying the pros and cons of commercial software, we examined a four-step procedure that can be employed in the selection of commercial software packages. The chapter concluded with a brief discussion of the strategic role of system maintenance and the importance of group memory as a key input to systems strategy.

Appendix

Section A: Case Tools

Figure 14-23 (first seen as Figure 14-3) presents the CASE spectrum of support in relation to the relevant stages of the SDLC. CASE tools are used to define user requirements, create physical databases from conceptual user views, produce systems design specifications, automatically generate computer program code, and facilitate the maintenance of programs that both CASE and non-CASE tools create. Figure 14-24 presents an overview diagram of a comprehensive CASE system. The sections below follow the main points of this diagram.

Central Repository

The heart of the CASE system is the central repository. Essentially, this is a database of attributes, relations, and elements that describe all the applications created under the CASE system. These items include:

1. Definition of all databases.
2. Systems documentation, such as context diagrams, data flow diagrams, and structure charts.
3. The program code.
4. Reusable program modules.
5. User prototype screens.

FIGURE 14-23 **CASE Spectrum of Support Tools for the SDLC**

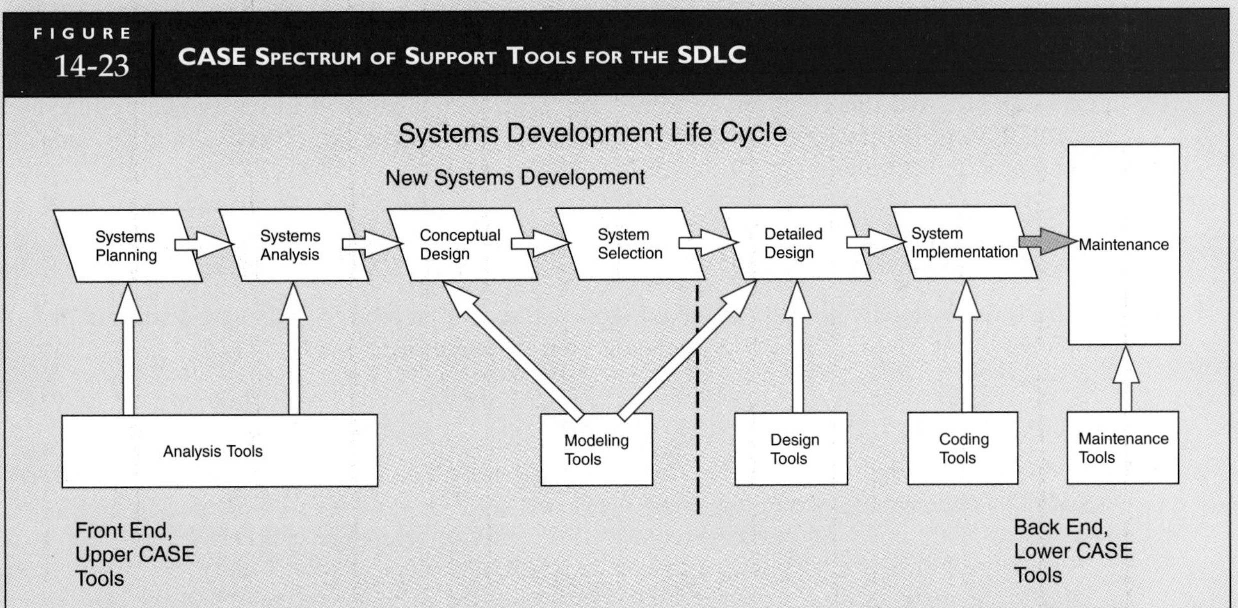

FIGURE 14-24 OVERVIEW OF CASE SYSTEM

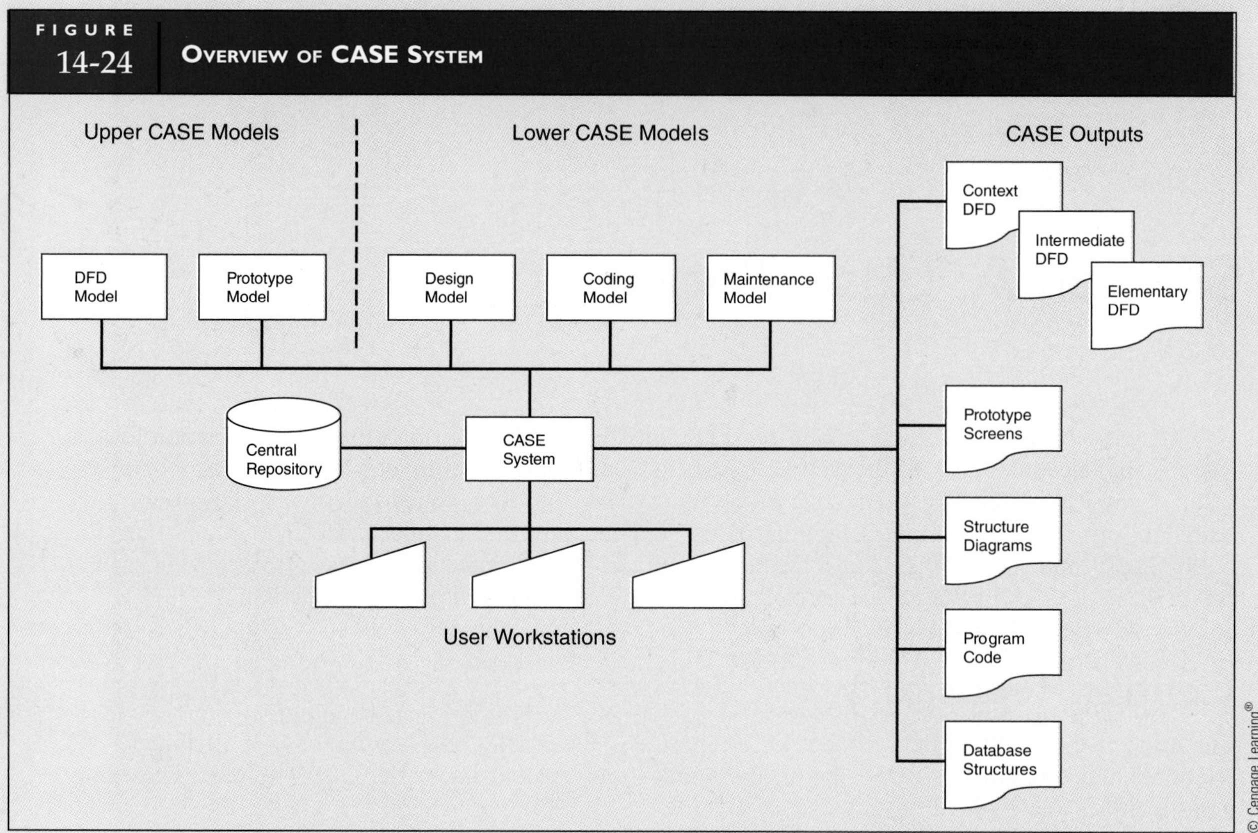

The central repository system helps to integrate the activities of system designers working on the same project or on separate but related projects. For example, if the size or the name of a data attribute must be changed, then all the applications that use that attribute must also be changed. In a moderate-sized firm, this could involve hundreds of programs. Normally, this would require many days of manual searching to identify the affected programs. However, the central repository system can quickly identify and list the applications that use the attribute being changed. Another example of the integration of activities is the ability to reuse program code. Different applications may use the same routines. These routines can be created, tested, and then used many times. The central repository stores reusable modules for immediate implementation in other systems. This reduces the overall development time of subsequent applications.

CASE Models

CASE products employ several functional models that can be used to support activities in different phases of the SDLC. The following models are representative.

THE DATA FLOW DIAGRAM MODEL

We introduced the data flow diagram (DFD) in Chapter 2. This section presents a more extensive use of this documentation technique. The DFD uses a set of symbols to represent the processes, data sources, data flows, and process sequences of a current or proposed system.

As a systems design tool, DFDs are used to represent multiple levels of detail. From the most general to the most detailed, these are the context level, the intermediate level, and the elementary level.

FIGURE 14-25 CONTEXT-LEVEL DATA FLOW DIAGRAM FOR THE REVENUE CYCLE

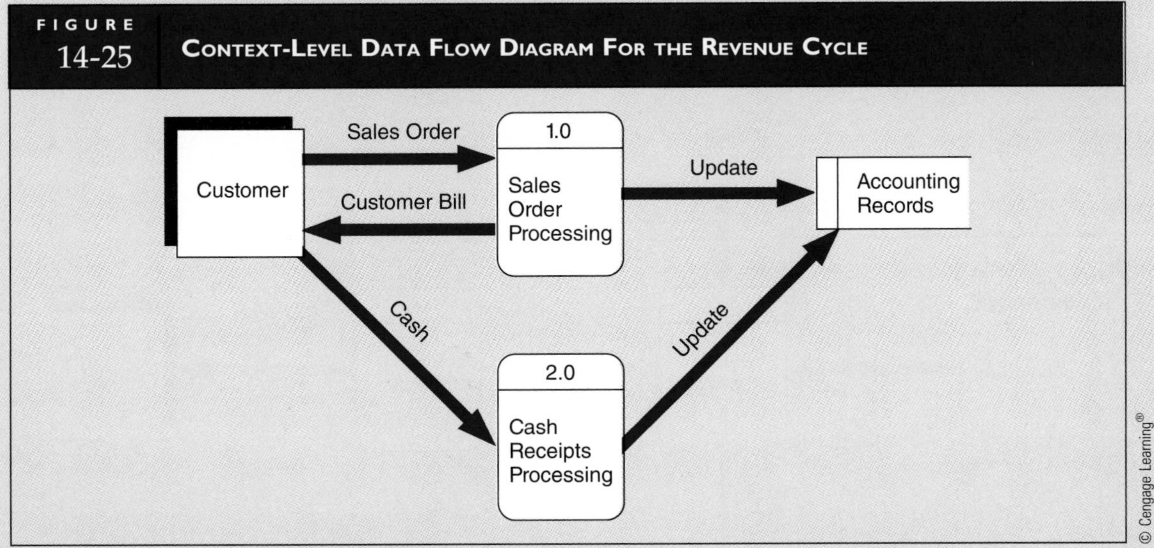

The Context-Level DFD

The analyst can use the context-level DFD to present an overview model of the business activities and the primary transactions that the system processes. Figure 14-25 presents an example of a context diagram of the revenue cycle for a company. The context diagram is a very high-level representation of the system. It does not include a detailed definition of data files and specific procedures. The focus is on the overall relationship between the entities (data, sources of data, and processes) in the system. This relationship is represented by symbols, lines, and arrows that show the direction of the data flows.

The Intermediate-Level DFD

The next step is to explode the context-level DFD into one or more intermediate-level DFDs, as illustrated in Figure 14-26. Notice how Process 1.0 in Figure 14-25 is decomposed into the following subprocesses.

1. Sales Approval
2. Ship Goods
3. Bill Customer
4. Update Accounts Receivable

Several levels of intermediate DFDs may be needed to present enough detail for the systems professional and user to fully understand the system. In this example, we show only one intermediate level.

The Elementary-Level DFD

Figure 14-27 presents the elementary-level DFD for Process 1.3 in Figure 14-26. An elementary-level DFD provides a clear and precise definition of all elements of a portion of the system. In this example, Process 1.3 (bill customer) is explained in detail. Other elementary-level DFDs will be required for Processes 1.1, 1.2, and 1.4.

The preparation of DFDs in a non-CASE environment can be time-consuming for the analyst. Because of inevitable changes in specifications during the system's development, the analyst may produce many versions of the DFD documents before arriving at the final product. The graphics capability of CASE tools greatly expedites this task by providing functions for labeling, modifying, and rearranging the DFD. However, the CASE DFD is more than simply a graphic representation of the system. The elementary-level DFD is the physical input to lower CASE models that automatically produce program code and database tables. Any and all changes to the system during its development and maintenance are thus made directly through the DFD.

FIGURE 14-26 INTERMEDIATE-LEVEL DATA FLOW DIAGRAM FOR SALES ORDER PROCESSING SYSTEM

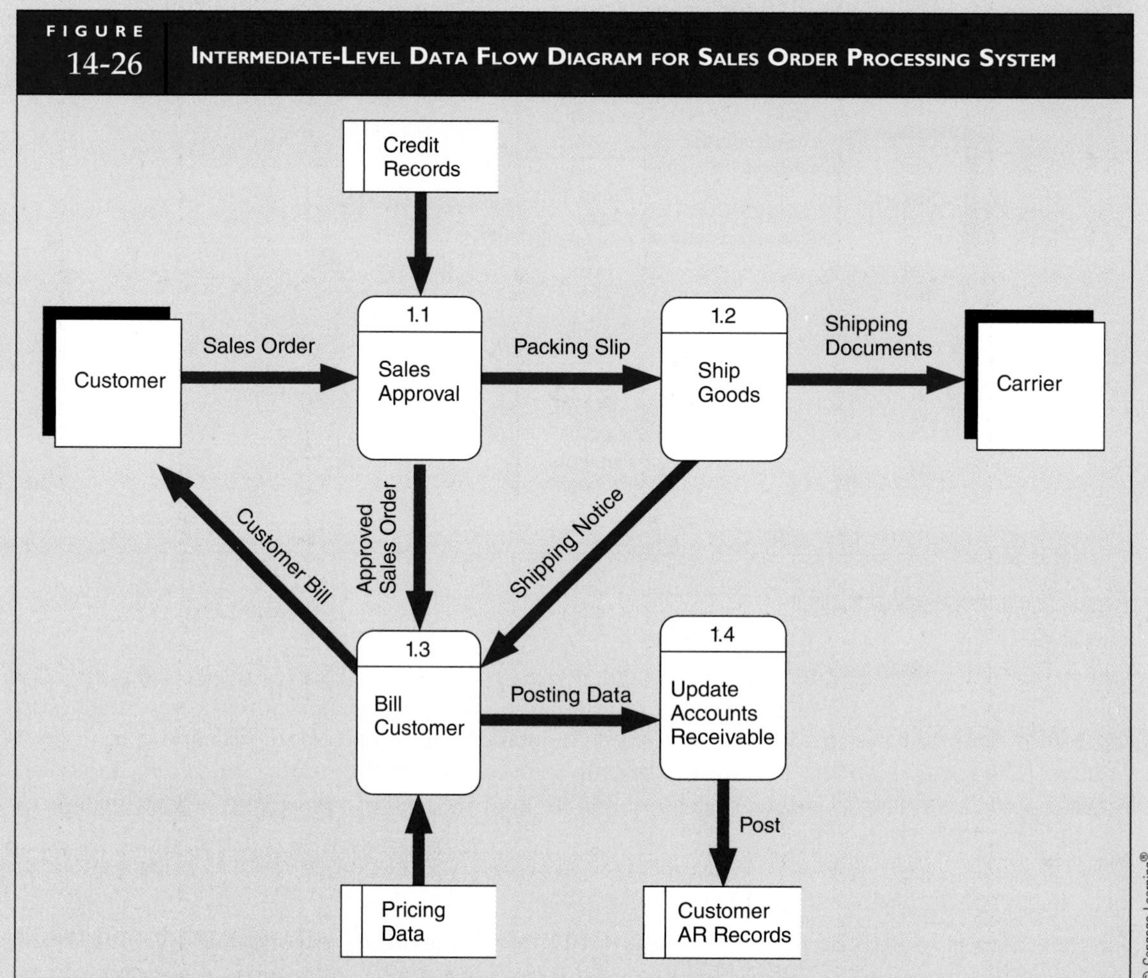

THE PROTOTYPE MODEL

The prototype model supports the prototyping concept presented earlier. This is a powerful feature that helps ensure that user requirements are being met. Systems professionals can immediately provide users with input screens and report formats. The user can thus visualize certain features of the system before it is actually designed and evaluate the proposed system. Any changes can be implemented before the system is designed and at virtually no cost to the project schedule.

THE DESIGN MODEL

The logic of the design model is based on the concept of system decomposition, which was introduced in Chapter 1. Recall that any system can be decomposed from the top down into smaller and smaller subsystems, each with a specific function. The design model takes the elementary-level DFD as input and produces from this a structure diagram. The DFD is a model of the conceptual system, and the structure diagram is a model of the program code that constitutes the physical system. Figure 14-28 shows a structure diagram for the elementary-level DFD in Figure 14-27. The structure diagram shows the overall relationship between the modules that constitute the system. Each of these modules represents a separate program that must be coded, unless it already exists as a reusable program module. We examine the issue of reusable modules later in the chapter.

FIGURE 14-27 ELEMENTARY-LEVEL DATA FLOW DIAGRAM FOR THE BILLING PROCESS

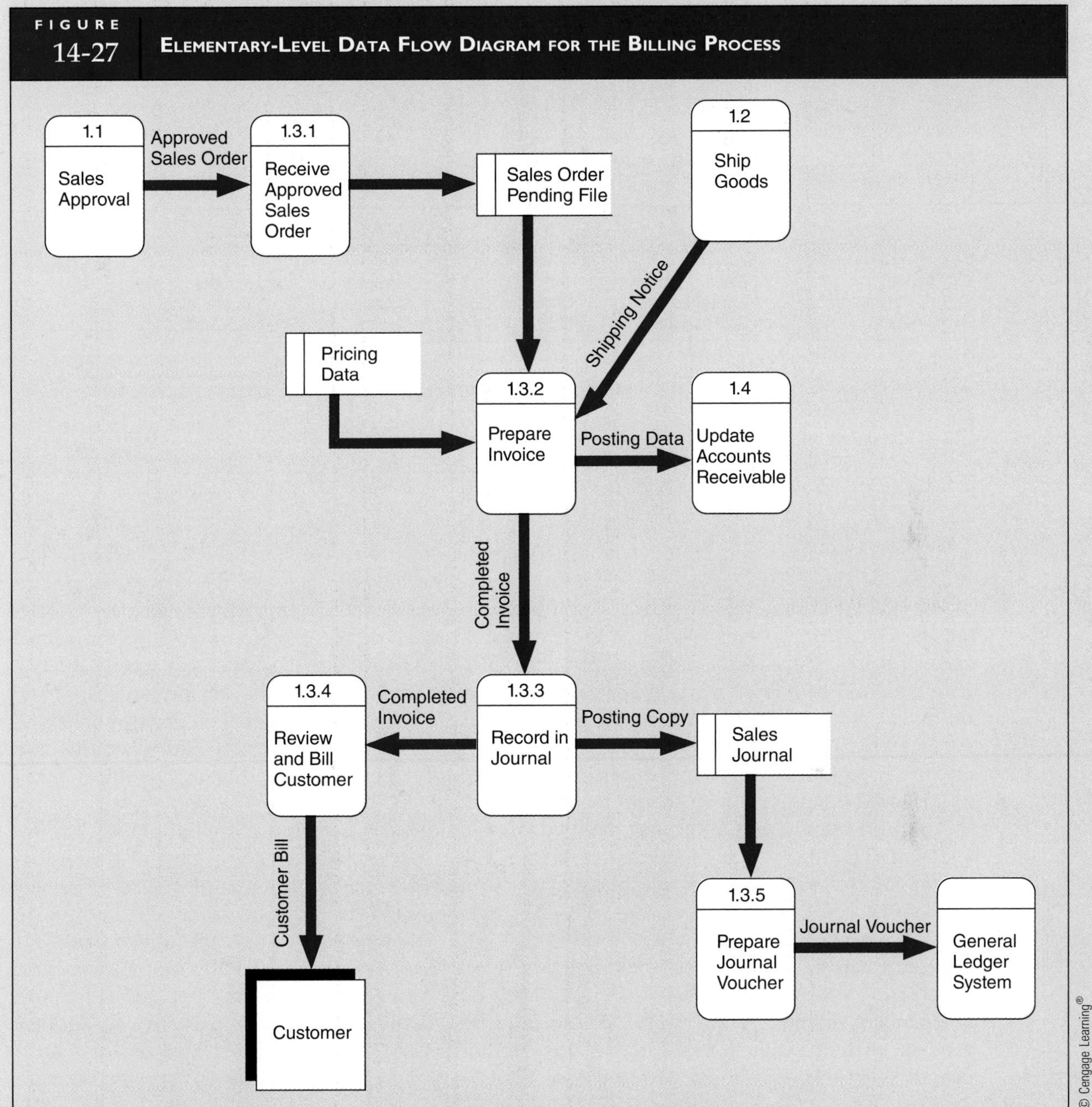

Many CASE tools document the details of each module in the form of pseudocode or structured English. Pseudocode explains what the module is supposed to do, regardless of the programming language used.

THE CODING MODEL

One of the great labor-saving advantages of CASE is its facility for transforming the structure diagram into computer modules. Many top-end CASE tools produce program source code, such as COBOL, C, and C++. These source programs must then be compiled (translated) into executable machine code modules.

FIGURE 14-28 STRUCTURE DIAGRAM FOR ELEMENTARY-LEVEL DFD OF THE BILLING PROCESS IN FIGURE 14-27

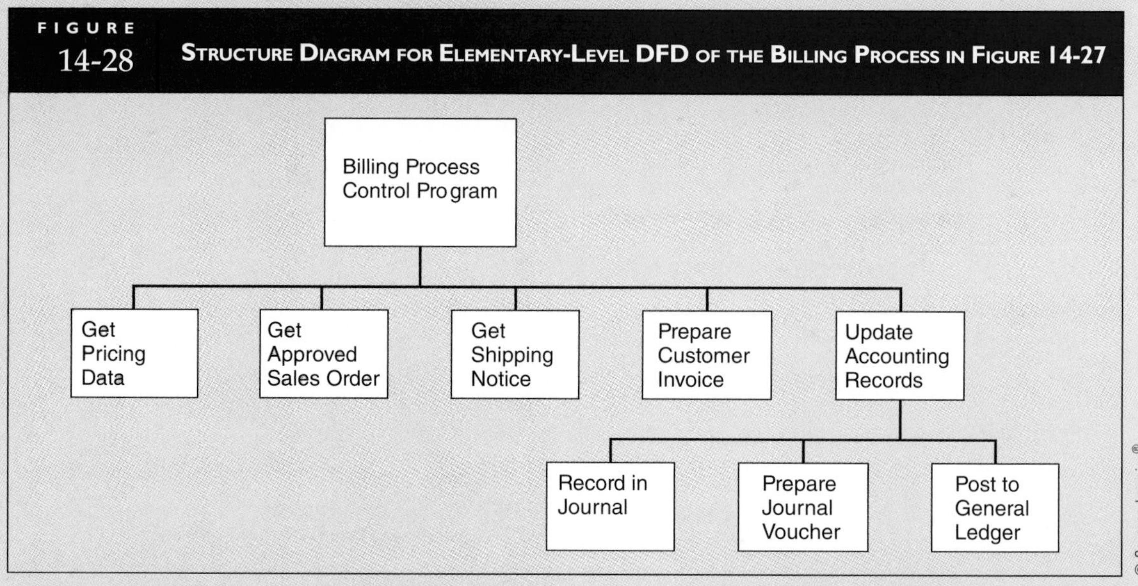

Some CASE tools convert the structure diagrams directly to machine code and eliminate the source-code stage. The reason for this is to preserve the integrity between the conceptual system model (the DFD) and the physical system (the program). Sometimes, during maintenance or original development, systems specialists are tempted to make design changes directly to the source code. If these changes are not also made to the DFDs and structure diagrams that specify the system, there will be a discrepancy between documentation that describes what the program does and the actual program. By eliminating the source code, the systems professional is forced to make all systems changes via the DFDs. The CASE tool will then modify the structure diagrams and rewrite the computer (machine-level) code automatically. This ensures that the system's description is always consistent with the program code.

The nonsource code approach has two implications for accountants, auditors, and management. The first is a potential control issue. The program source code is part of the system documentation. To properly design their test procedures, auditors sometimes need to review the source code. If it is not available, this may hamper testing and force the auditor to employ alternative, less efficient, and more costly procedures. Second, the nonsource code approach can have the effect of committing the firm to a particular CASE tool and vendor. By creating source code as a by-product of the development process, the application remains independent of the CASE system. Should the firm's management decide to switch to another vendor, current applications can still be maintained. Most CASE tools will accept source programs written in standard source code.

THE MAINTENANCE MODEL

Of the total cost of a system, 80 to 90 percent is expended during the maintenance phase of the SDLC. This is often referred to as the iceberg effect. Figure 14-29 illustrates this phenomenon. All systems must be maintained throughout their lives, and some iceberg effect is inevitable. However, poorly designed systems can significantly contribute to the problem. To make a change to a computer program in a non-CASE environment, the maintenance programmer must first thoroughly review the program code in an attempt to understand the original programmer's logic. This review often requires a great deal of time and is protracted by awkward, inefficient, and redundant program logic. Even companies that use CASE tools will have some badly designed systems. Often these systems are old and precede CASE usage.

The CASE maintenance model facilitates program maintenance and greatly reduces the iceberg effect. Applications originally developed under CASE are relatively easy to maintain.

FIGURE 14-29 THE ICEBERG EFFECT

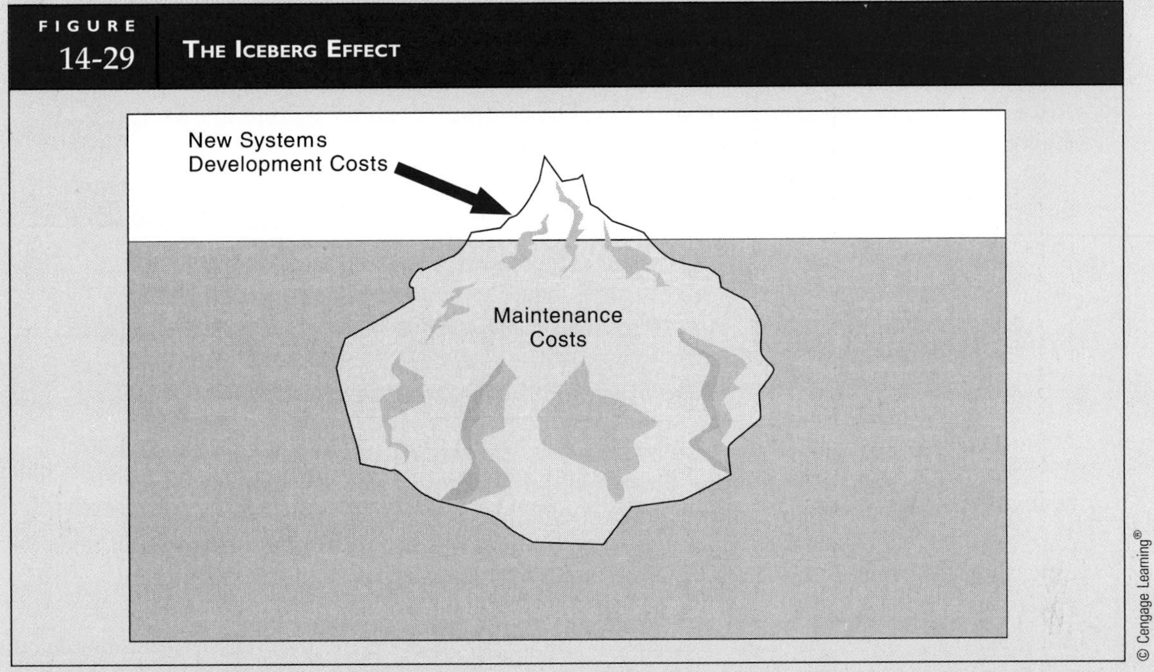

The maintenance programmer reviews the documentation for the application and makes the required changes, at the conceptual level, to the DFDs. The CASE system then makes the changes to the structure diagrams and program code automatically. Finally, the programmer thoroughly tests and installs the modified application.

CASE tools can also be used to maintain applications that were not originally developed under the CASE system. The CASE maintenance model provides two such tools for this purpose: reverse engineering and reengineering. Reverse engineering extracts from the source code meaningful design specifications that the maintenance programmer can use to understand the application logic. Reengineering restructures and documents the old source code logic to conform to CASE standards. This includes preparing DFDs and structure diagrams. Thus, future maintenance of the system can proceed as if the application were originally created under CASE.

Advantages of CASE

The following is a list of the commonly cited advantages of the CASE approach.

1. *Reduced system complexity.* CASE systems are more easily comprehended than traditional methods and support structured logic concepts.
2. *Increased flexibility.* The systems development process does not usually proceed in a purely linear fashion in which each stage is totally complete before the next one begins. Rather, it tends to be a cyclical process. It will be necessary to return to a previous stage if proceeding to the next stage will result in a flawed design or an improper implementation. As the details of the problem unfold in the downstream stages, it may be necessary to reconsider and revise upstream models. Compared to manual techniques, CASE provides a great deal of flexibility to the analyst in making such revisions.
3. *Capacity to review alternative designs.* Because CASE systems can be rapidly produced and changed, users and systems specialists can review prototypes of many alternative designs before committing to a particular system.
4. *Quicker development process.* The development process under CASE is three to six times faster than traditional methods, depending on the complexity of the system and the degree of CASE expertise within the firm.

5. *Promotion of user involvement.* Through its prototyping features, CASE has great potential for improving user involvement in the development process. We discuss this point in more detail in the following section.
6. *Reusable program code and documentation.* The central repository feature allows CASE systems to share common program modules and documentation.
7. *Reduced maintenance cost.* By maintaining the system at the conceptual level, maintenance time and programming errors are reduced. This translates into a more efficient process that responds more quickly to user needs. The iceberg effect is reduced by as much as 50 percent.

Disadvantages of CASE

In spite of these many virtues, CASE is not without its disadvantages, including:

1. *Product cost.* The cost of a CASE system is proportional to its features and sophistication. Microcomputer CASE tools with limited features may be obtained for hundreds of dollars. Fully equipped CASE tools for a mainframe environment can cost hundreds of thousands of dollars.
2. *Start-up time and cost.* Developing a pool of CASE expertise within the organization takes time. Systems professionals must be trained, and the learning curve for sophisticated CASE systems is steep.
3. *Incompatible CASE tools.* The hundreds of CASE products on the market are often incompatible with one another. This limits a firm's choices when selecting CASE tools and tends to tie the firm to a single product and vendor.
4. *Program inefficiency.* The source code that CASE tools produce is not as efficient as code written by a skilled programmer. To improve program efficiency, programmers often modify the CASE-generated modules. This practice can produce discrepancies between the DFD system logic and the program logic.

Section B: Output Reporting Alternatives

This section presents various output design alternatives, along with a number of example output reports.

Tables and Matrices

Tables and matrices can be used to summarize large amounts of information. A table is a report arranged in columns and rows, such as the supplier analysis report in Figure 14-30. This table shows columns of evaluation data for suppliers with whom the firm does business. This is an effective means for comparing and contrasting relevant facts.

A matrix is a rectangular arrangement of data into rows and columns. Each element (the intersection of a row and a column) is a data value. This form of report is particularly useful for presenting binary state relations—the presence or absence of a state—among elements. Figure 14-31 is a matrix report showing which vendors supply which major inventory items.

FIGURE 14-30 SUPPLIER ANALYSIS REPORT

Attribute	Acme Motors	Morgan Supply	Norton Co.	The Roadster Factory
	VENDOR			
Yrs in Business	$1^1/_2$	4	9	3
Terms of Trade	2/10, n/30 offers quantity discounts	40% off retail, no quantity discounts	2/10, n/30, offers quantity discounts	Wholesale price list, no quantity discounts
Price Structure	Competitive	Lowest-priced supplier	Competitive	
Lead Time	5–7 days	7–10 days	7–10 days for most Items	3 days guaranteed
Rush Service	1 day delivery at 3% charge	None	None	Overnight—2% charge
Delivery Reliability	Good	Good	Poor	Good

Graphs and Charts

Graphs and charts present numeric data as geometric shapes. This visual approach to reporting presumes that a picture is worth a thousand words. Certainly this is true when conveying such summarized messages as the big picture and trends over time and comparing the performance of multiple products. For these purposes, visual reports are far more effective than numeric reports alone. In this section, we examine five visual reporting techniques: line graph, scatter graph, bar graph, pie chart, and layer chart.

LINE GRAPH

The simple line graph is used to show the fluctuations in an item of interest over time. Figure 14-32 illustrates this approach. We can use different colors and different-shaped lines to track multiple items. In Figure 14-32, the solid line is projected sales, and the dashed line is actual sales. The increments of the scale (sales dollars) should be small enough to detect material fluctuations. However, in using line graphs, we must guard against using a scale that is too small, because it might portray an exaggerated picture to the user.

SCATTER GRAPH

The purpose of a scatter graph is to reveal relationships among underlying data. To illustrate, Figure 14-33 superimposes a line graph and scatter graph. The line graph shows only the movement from Point A to Point B in the form of a trend line that takes the average path through the data. In some instances, this could result in the loss of important information to the user. The points in the scatter graph show the degree of dispersion associated with the underlying activity.

FIGURE 14-31 **Matrix Report Showing Vendors (Columns) and Inventory (Rows) Provided**

Inventory Item Supplied	Vendor: Acme Motors	Morgan Supply	Norton Co.	The Roadster Factory
109873 k	X	X	X	X
109873 q	X		X	X
1098745		X		X
1098746	X		X	
•		X		
•				X
•	X		X	
•		X		
•		X		
•	X	X		
•		X		
•			X	
•	X			X
•			X	X
7893279				X
8237419	X			X
9495581	X	X	X	
				X

FIGURE 14-32 **Line Graph Showing Fluctuations in Sales over Time at One-Month Intervals**

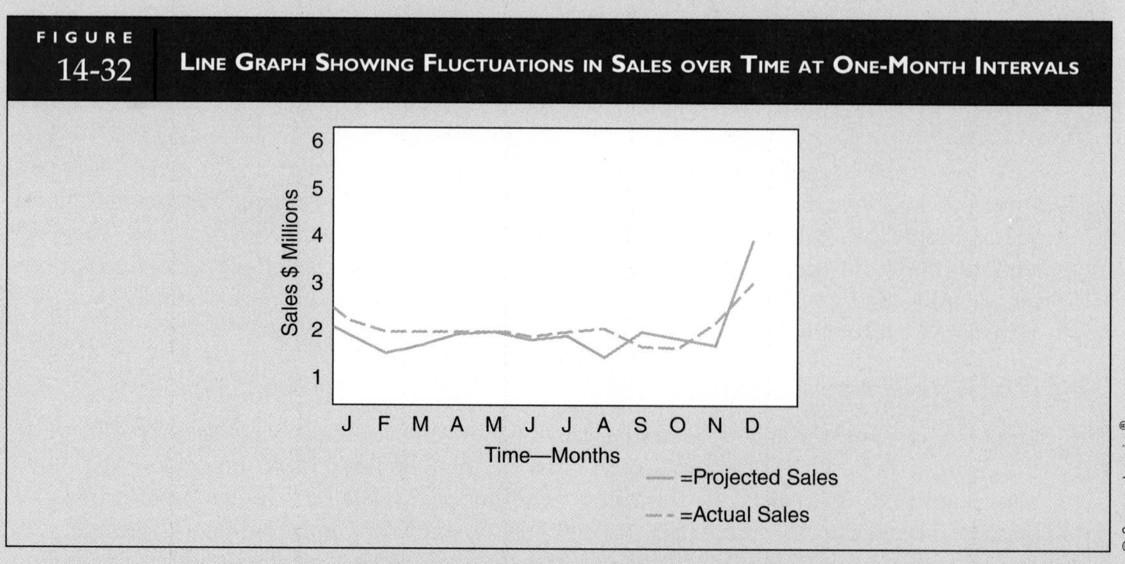

FIGURE 14-33 SCATTER GRAPH SUPERIMPOSED ON LINE GRAPH

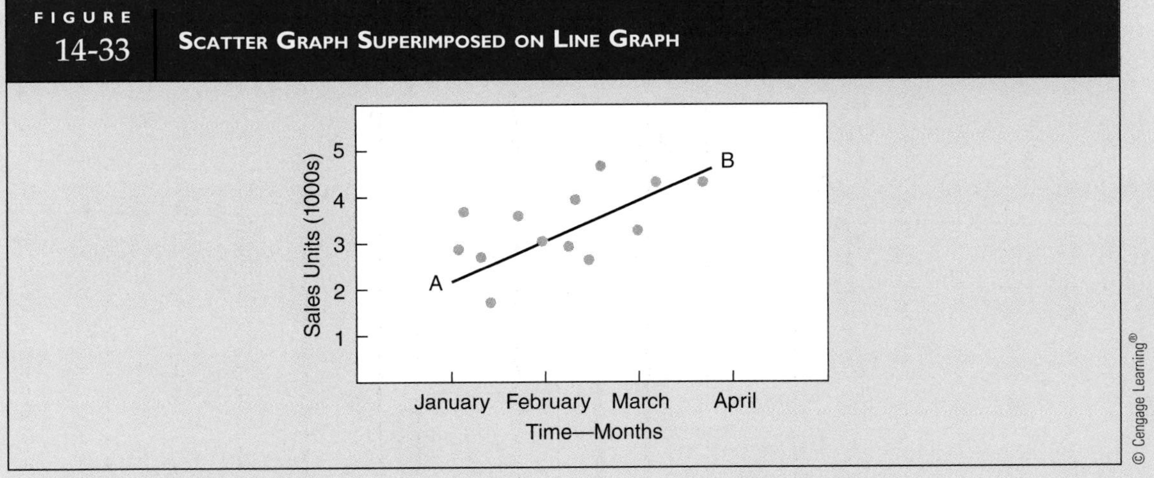

BAR GRAPH

The purpose of a bar graph is to show the relationship of total quantities or proportions. Figure 14-34 uses a vertical bar graph to show the relationship over time between actual computer usage for a firm and budgeted usage.

The height of the bars represents the total amount of computer usage. If we were to plot the top points of each bar, we could construct a line graph showing the trend in usage and the relationship between actual and budgeted usage. However, the emphasis of a bar graph is on total amounts at specific points rather than on trends.

The horizontal bar graph is used to compare multiple items in the same time frame. For example, Figure 14-35 compares output from four production plants for the month of January.

PIE CHART

A pie chart presents the proportional relationship of different items to the whole. For example, Figure 14-36 shows the proportions of several items that together constitute total manufacturing cost. We can differentiate the segments by using color or by exploding them slightly from the rest

FIGURE 14-34 BAR GRAPH SHOWING ACTUAL COMPUTER USAGE TO BUDGETED USAGE—SHOWS CPU HOURS PER MONTH

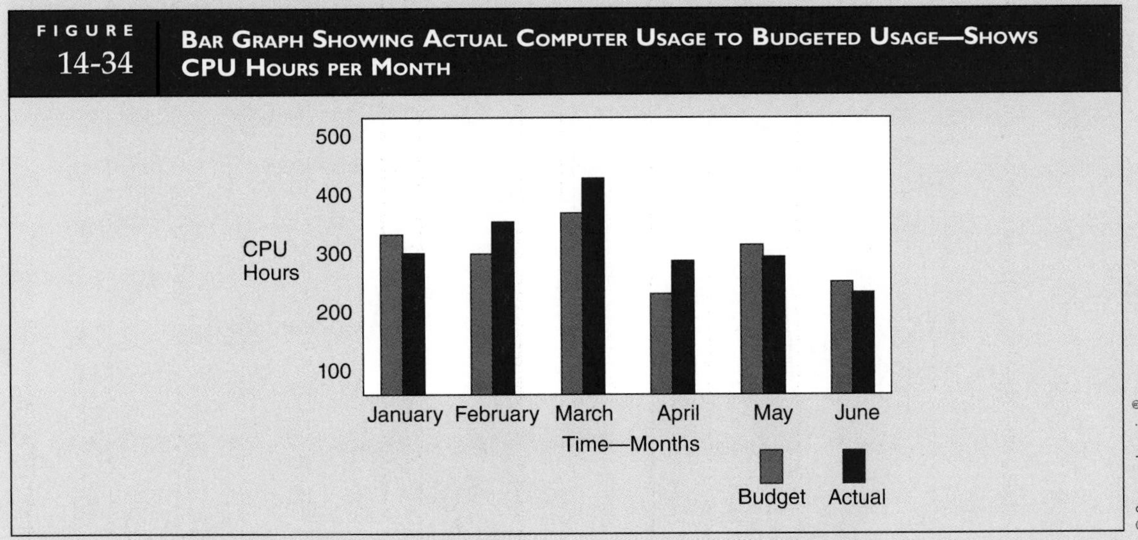

FIGURE 14-35 HORIZONTAL BAR GRAPH COMPARING PRODUCTION OF MULTIPLE PLANTS

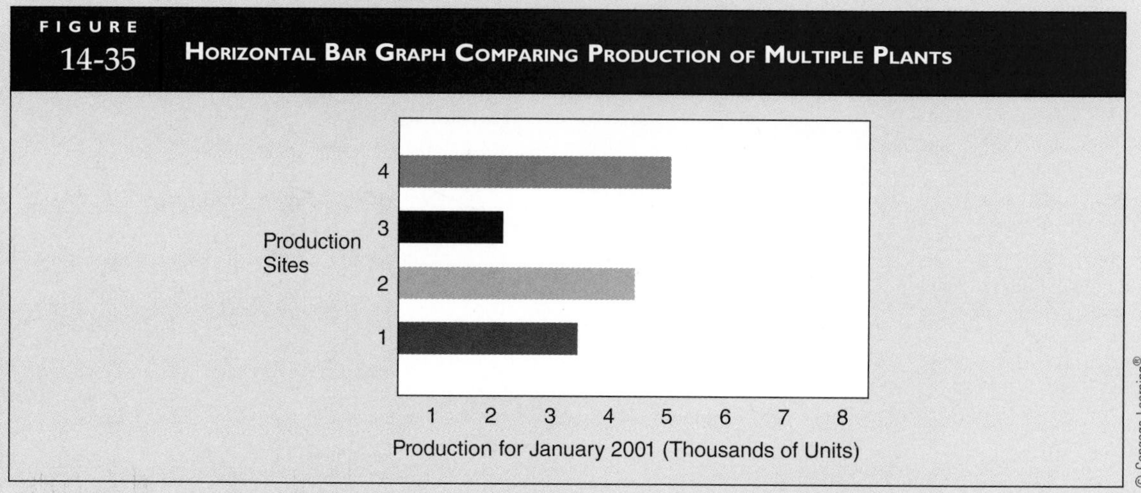

of the pie. To maintain the visual power of the message, however, the designer should attempt to restrict the number of segments. Too many pie wedges make differentiation difficult and complicate the chart.

LAYER CHART

A layer chart also shows proportional relationships but allows the addition of another dimension, such as time or condition. Figure 14-37 illustrates this by showing the change in the proportion of individual item costs to total manufacturing cost under different technology bases.

Colors

Colors can greatly enhance the usefulness of a report. Choosing colors that are widely spaced on the color spectrum—such as red, green, and blue—provides for the greatest visual

FIGURE 14-36 PIE CHART FOR MANUFACTURING COSTS

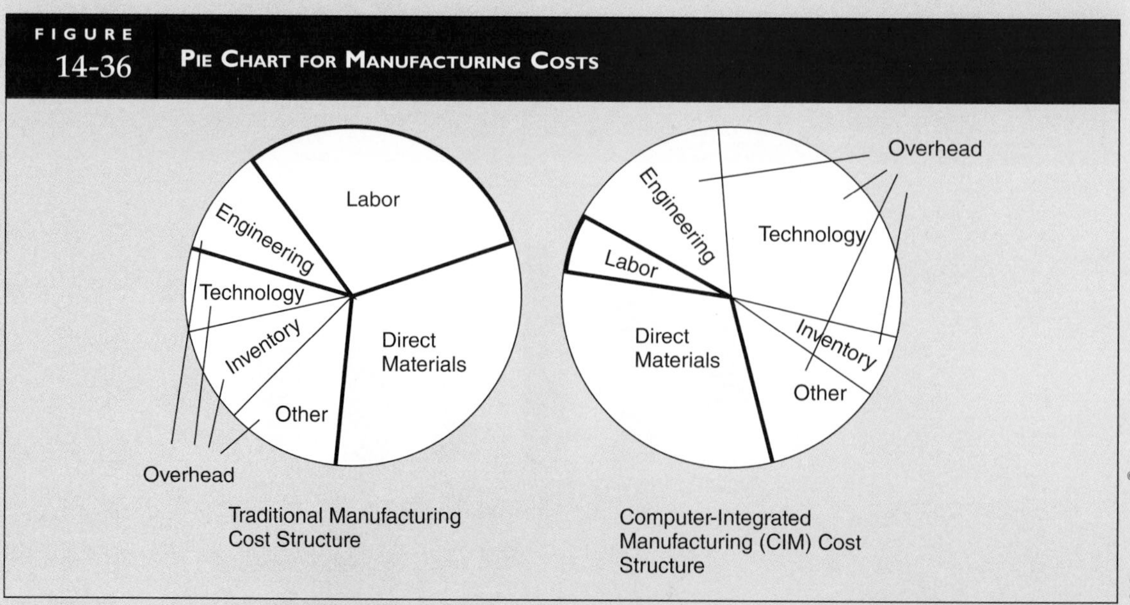

FIGURE 14-37 LAYER CHART OF COST PROPORTION CHANGES UNDER DIFFERENT TECHNOLOGY BASES

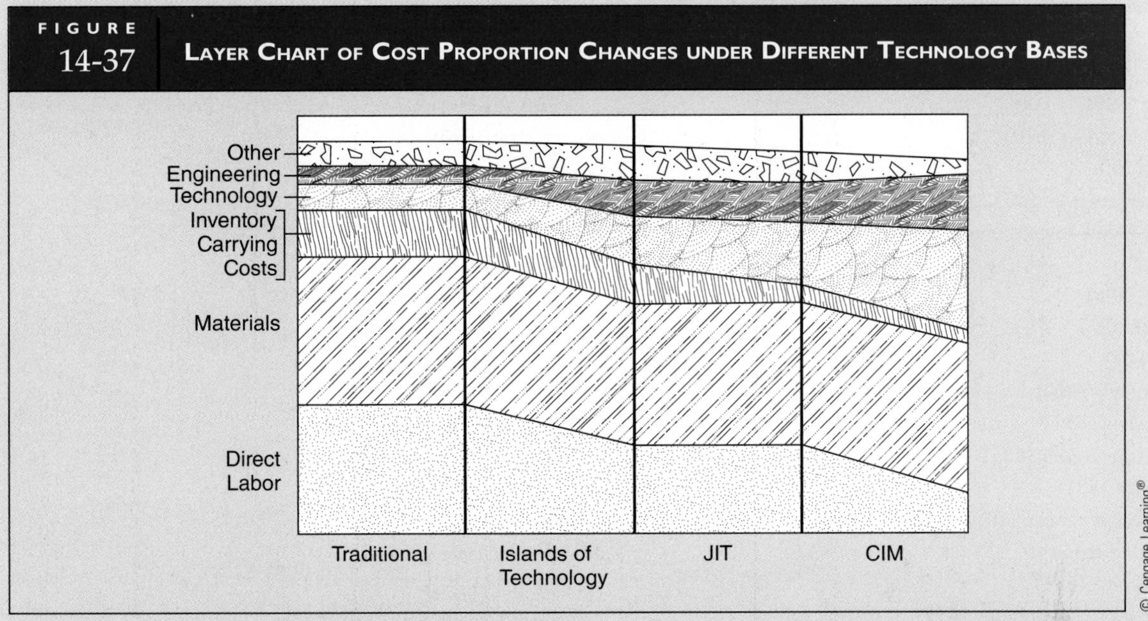

discrimination. This approach can be used to present data that are being compared or contrasted within a report. The level of color intensity can be used to emphasize material items or to de-emphasize normal (or less important) data. For example, the variance report in Figure 14-38 shows budgeted amounts, actual amounts, and the variance from budget for each line item.

High-intensity color is used here to draw attention to line items with a material variance (e.g., a variance greater than 10 percent). Line items whose variance is under this materiality threshold are deemed under control and are de-emphasized by the use of low-intensity color.

FIGURE 14-38 VARIANCE REPORT USING INTENSITY TO HIGHLIGHT MATERIAL VARIANCES

Date 11/20/15

Sports Car Factory
Cost Variance Report for Production Dept. 6 ***CVAR 1***

Item	Budget	Actual	(Over) Under Budget
Direct labor	36,000	36,800	<800>
Direct materials	122,000	141,600	<19,600>
Job setup	4,000	3,600	400
Supplies	2,200	2,330	<130>
Scheduled maintenance	1,200	1,200	0

Key Terms

attributes (589)
backbone systems (610)
cohesion (600)
cold turkey cutover (607)
computer-aided software engineering (CASE) (584)
conceptual user views (591)
construct (585)
coupling (600)
cutover (607)
data dictionary (602)
data modeling (591)
database conversion (606)
design phase (591)
detailed design report (601)
disseminating (616)
documentation (604)
electronic input techniques (597)
embedded instructions (595)
event-driven languages (602)
Gantt chart (585)
gathering (616)
group memory (616)
hard-copy (595)
inheritance (590)
instance (590)
intelligent forms (597)
knowledge management (616)
methods (589)
object class (590)
object-oriented design (586)
object-oriented programming (OOP) language (602)
objects (589)
online documentation (606)
operations control reports (593)
organizing (616)
parallel operation cutover (607)
PERT chart (585)
phased cutover (607)
procedural language (602)
prototyping (583)
pseudocode (601)
quality assurance group (601)
refining (616)
request for proposal (RFP) (612)
run manual (605)
structure diagram (599)
structured design (586)
systems design (591)
third-generation languages (602)
turnkey systems (610)
user handbook (605)
walk-through (601)
wall of code (591)
zones (595)

Review Questions

1. How does a prototype differ from the final product? Why discard the prototype? What role does the end user play in prototyping?
2. What functions do CASE tools serve?
3. Distinguish between upper and lower CASE tools.
4. What is a central repository in a CASE system?
5. How can program code be reused?
6. What is a data flow diagram? What are the different levels from most general to most detailed? Draw the common symbols used.
7. What is the relationship between an elementary-level DFD and a structure diagram? Which must be prepared first?
8. Is pseudocode programming language-specific? How about the coding model?
9. What is the difference between source code and machine code? Why is it preferable to have the CASE tools convert the structure diagrams into machine code rather than source code?
10. What is the iceberg effect? How can CASE tools help to minimize this phenomenon?
11. Distinguish between reverse engineering and reengineering.
12. Contrast the advantages and disadvantages of CASE tools. What should determine whether CASE is used?
13. What is an object, and what are its characteristics in the object-oriented approach? Give two examples.
14. Distinguish between object classes and instances.
15. What is meant by inheritance? Give an example.
16. Why is the object-oriented approach particularly suited to ERP system design?

17. What are the four factors that have stimulated the growth of commercial software?
18. Distinguish between turnkey and backbone systems. Which is more flexible?
19. What are the four steps involved in choosing a package?
20. What is an RFP?
21. Discuss the relative merits of in-house programs versus commercially developed software.
22. List, in sequential order, the system components that are designed in the detailed design phase.
23. What is data modeling? What is its primary tool?
24. What are the three basic symbols in an ER diagram?
25. Distinguish between primary and foreign keys.
26. What is a data dictionary?
27. What document is used to determine which tables of data are necessary?
28. Once the conceptual links between tables have been determined, how are the physical links incorporated?
29. What attributes should output views possess?
30. Why is the quality of the paper a major consideration in the design of a hard-copy input?
31. What are the two classes of design input views?
32. What are zones?
33. In what form should embedded instructions be written—active or passive voice? Why?
34. What are the relative merits of input from source documents and direct input?
35. What is pseudocode? Are end users or systems designers involved in this process?
36. What are the controls designated in the systems controls stage?
37. Typically, which is more difficult to detect and more costly to fix—a design flaw in the processes or a programming error?
38. Who is included in the quality assurance group? What are their tasks? What documents do they need to perform their tasks?
39. Which activities during the systems implementation phase have the greatest implications for accountants and auditors?
40. Which chart, a PERT or a Gantt, shows the project status at a glance for a given point in time? Which method illustrates the critical path at a glance?
41. Discuss the relative merits and drawbacks to 3GL How might changing technology affect some of these issues in the future?
42. What is a hybrid language?
43. What are the advantages to the modular programming approach?
44. Why should test data be saved after it has been used?
45. Explain the importance of documentation by the systems programmers.
46. What documents do accountants and auditors need for the new system that other stakeholders typically do not?
47. What very important precautions must be taken during the data conversion procedures?

Discussion Questions

1. Data flow diagrams are often described as exploding from one level to the next. What is meant by "exploding"? Also, data flow diagrams must reconcile from the general level to the next level of detail. What is meant by "reconcile"? How do you think CASE tools help in this procedure?
2. What issues are accountants concerned with when determining their preference for CASE tools that convert structure diagrams into machine code or source code? What are the costs associated with each?
3. What documentation techniques are used in the structured design approach to conceptual design? What is the purpose of each of these documentation techniques, and how do they vary from each other? How much detail is provided?
4. Compare and contrast the structured design approach and the object-oriented design approach. Which do you feel is most beneficial? Why?
5. If a firm decides early to go with a special-purpose system, such as SAP, based upon the

recommendations of the external audit firm, should the SDLC be bypassed?

6. Explain how benchmarking works. Should this be conducted on the vendor's computer or the customer's computer? What about technical presentations by the vendor? Why?
7. Discuss the importance of the weights assigned to factors in the final selection process. What method might you suggest be used to investigate the appropriateness of the weights?
8. Who should select the contact user group—the vendor or the prospective user? Why?
9. What processes should be used to develop useful and meaningful output? Who should be involved in the development process?
10. Are input requirements or output requirements examined to determine the attributes of tables? Should all of these attributes physically be in the data file? Why or why not?
11. Are direct input systems (i.e., point-of-sale using bar codes) error free? Why or why not?
12. Why is it necessary to decompose the DFD to a level of high detail before preparing the structure diagram? How do you know when to stop this process?
13. A good structure diagram should be loosely coupled yet strongly cohesive. How can you achieve both characteristics simultaneously? What implications do these characteristics have on error-prone problems during maintenance?
14. Why bother with pseudocode? Why not spend the time developing actual source code?
15. During a test data procedure, why should the developers bother testing bad data?
16. During implementation, if the system is behind schedule and if each program module is tested and no problems are found, is it necessary to test all modules in conjunction with one another? Why or why not?
17. Run manuals for computer operators are similar in theory to the checklists that airplane pilots use for takeoffs and landings. Explain why these are important.
18. How might the decision to use CASE tools affect the choice of a programming language?
19. What are the three implementation (cutover) methods? Which appears to be the most costly up front? Which could very likely end up being the most costly in the long run?
20. Who conducts the post-implementation review? When should it be conducted? If an outside consulting firm were hired to design and implement the new system, or a canned software package were purchased, would a post-implementation review still be useful?
21. Discuss the importance of involving accountants in the detailed design and implementation phases. What tasks should they perform?

Multiple-Choice Questions

1. Which sequence of events bests describes the activities in the systems development life cycle?
   a. design, analysis, implementation, and operation
   b. design, implementation, analysis, and operation
   c. analysis, design, implementation, and operation
   d. programming, analysis, implementation, and operation
2. Which of the following sets of application characteristics of an accounting application might influence the selection of data entry devices and media for a computerized accounting system?
   a. timing of feedback needs relative to input, need for documentation of an activity, and the necessity for reliability and accuracy
   b. cost considerations, volume of input, complexity of activity, and liquidity of assets involved
   c. need for documentation, necessity for accuracy and reliability, volume of output, and cost considerations
   d. relevancy of data, volume of input, cost considerations, volume of output, and timing of feedback needs relative to input
   e. type of file used, reliability of manufacturer's service, volume of output, and cost considerations

3. The following are principle features of a PERT chart except
   a. paths
   b. events
   c. starting and ending dates
   d. activities
4. Many firms have formal, structured walk-throughs by an independent quality control group. Who is least likely to be a member of the group?
   a. application programmers
   b. systems analysts
   c. end users
   d. external auditors
   e. all would be members of the group
5. Which of the following is NOT part of the systems implementation process?
   a. converting databases
   b. documentation
   c. systems design
   d. testing and correction
6. What is the critical path in the PERT method for network analysis?
   a. shortest path through the network
   b. longest path through the network
   c. path with the most slack
   d. path with the most variability in estimated times
   e. least cost path
7. Which of the following is NOT an advantage of commercial software?
   a. lower overall cost compared to in-house development
   b. thoroughly tested and reliable
   c. rapid implementation
   d. ease of modification to meet specific needs
   e. all of the above are advantages
8. Which of the following is NOT an output attribute?
   a. relevance
   b. exception orientation
   c. zones
   d. accuracy
9. What is the name given to the systems development approach used to quickly produce a model of user interfaces, user interactions with the system, and process logic?
   a. neural networking
   b. prototyping
   c. reengineering
   d. application generation
10. Which of the following is the most risky strategy for converting from a legacy system to a new system?
    a. phased cutover
    b. parallel operation
    c. pilot conversion
    d. cold turkey cutover
    e. none of the above
11. Which of the following is the least risky strategy for converting from a legacy system to a new system?
    a. file conversion
    b. parallel conversion
    c. pilot conversion
    d. big bang conversion
    e. direct conversion
12. At which stage are errors most costly to correct?
    a. programming
    b. conceptual design
    c. analysis
    d. detailed design
    e. implementation

Problems

1. CASE TOOLS

Reeve Lumber Company has a small information systems department consisting of five people. A backlog of approximately 15 months exists for requests for new systems applications to even be considered. Both information users and systems personnel are unhappy with this state of affairs. The users feel that the systems department is not responsive enough to their needs, while the systems personnel feel overworked, frustrated, and unappreciated.

Janet Hubert, the manager of the systems department, has decided that she needs to take a proactive measure. She is requesting the funds to purchase a CASE system for approximately $75,000 that requires about two months to install and train workers to use it. The president of the company, Mike Cassidy, initially responded by questioning the wisdom of taking the systems personnel away from their duties when they are backlogged so they can learn a system. Prepare a memo from Hubert to Cassidy. In the memo, outline the expected benefits of purchasing and using a CASE system, and address Cassidy's concern regarding the two-month training and implementation period.

2. DATA FLOW DIAGRAMS

Sawicki Music Supply is a mail-order business that accepts merchandise orders by telephone and mail. All payments must be prepaid with a major credit card. Once an order is received, either the item is found in inventory and shipped immediately, the item is not found in inventory and is ordered from the manufacturer, or a notice is sent to the customer indicating that the item is no longer stocked.

Required

Prepare a context-, intermediate-, and elementary-level data flow diagram for Sawicki Music Supply. For the elementary-level diagram, explode the inventory function.

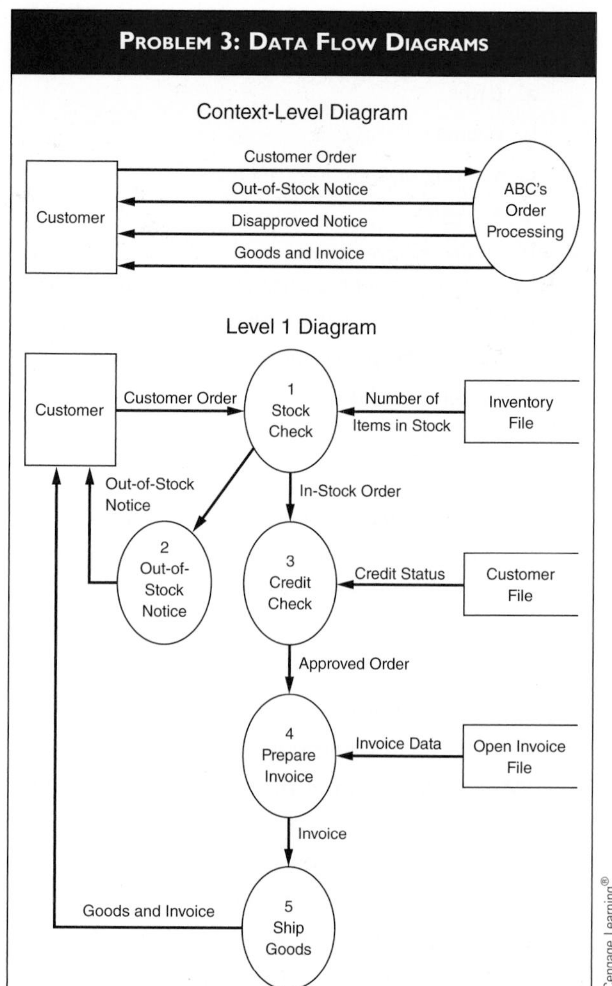

3. DATA FLOW DIAGRAMS

Examine the context and intermediate (Level 1) data flow diagrams in the diagram for Problem 3 and indicate what is incorrect about them.

4. DESIGN INPUT VIEW

During the system design phase of the SDLC, input interfaces or input views must be sketched out so programmers can specify the necessary elements when they program the user interfaces for the system. Figure 14-12 presents an interface for a Reorder Report. Sketch a similar interface that could be used to program a sales invoice interface. Include areas for a document heading, customer information, shipping information, sales employee information, and items sold.

5. SYSTEMS DESIGN

Robin Alper, a manager of the credit collections department for ACME Building Supplies, is extremely unhappy with a new system that was installed three months ago. Her complaint is that the data flows from the billing and accounts receivable departments are not occurring in the manner originally requested. Further, the updates to the database files are not occurring as frequently as she had envisioned. Thus, the hope that the new system would provide more current and timely information has not materialized. She claims that the systems analysts spent three days interviewing her and other workers. During that time, she and the other workers thought they had clearly conveyed their needs. She feels as if their needs were ignored and their time was wasted.

Required
What went wrong during the systems design process? What suggestions would you make for future projects?

6. ATTRIBUTES AND OPERATIONS

Prepare a list of attributes and operations for the following items:

a. general ledger
b. accounts payable ledger
c. accounts receivable ledger
d. fixed assets ledger
e. inventory ledger

7. COMMERCIAL SOFTWARE

Robert Hamilton was hired six months ago as the controller of a small oil and gas exploration and development company, Gusher Inc., headquartered in Beaumont, Texas. Before working at Gusher, Hamilton was the controller of a larger petroleum company, Eureka Oil Company, based in Dallas.

The joint interest billing and fixed asset accounting systems of Gusher are outdated, and frequent processing problems and errors have been occurring. Hamilton immediately recognized these problems and informed the president, Mr. Barton, that it was crucial to install a new system. Barton concurred and met with Hamilton and Sally Jeffries, the information systems senior manager. Barton instructed Jeffries to make the new system a top priority. Basically, he told Jeffries to deliver the system to meet Hamilton's needs as soon as possible.

Jeffries left the meeting feeling overwhelmed because the IT department is currently working on two other very big projects, one for the production department and the other for the geological department. The next day, Hamilton sent a memo to Jeffries indicating the name of a system he had 100 percent confidence in—Amarillo Software—and he also indicated that he would very much like this system to be purchased as soon as possible. He stated that the system had been used with much success during the past four years in his previous job.

When commercial software is purchased, Jeffries typically sends out requests for proposals to at least six different vendors after conducting a careful analysis of the needed requirements. However, due to the air of urgency demonstrated in the meeting with the president and the overworked systems staff, she decided to go along with Hamilton's wishes and sent only one RFP, which went to Amarillo Software. Amarillo promptly returned the completed questionnaire. The purchase price ($75,000) was within the budgeted amount. Jeffries contacted the four references provided and was satisfied with their comments. Further, she felt comfortable because the system was for Hamilton, and he had used the system for four years.

The plan was to install the system during the month of July and try it for the August transaction cycle. Problems were encountered, however, during the installation phase. The system processed extremely slowly on Gusher's hardware platform. When Jeffries asked Hamilton how the problem had been dealt with at Eureka, he replied that he did not remember having such a problem. He called the systems manager from Eureka and discovered that Eureka has a much more powerful mainframe than Gusher. Further investigation revealed that Gusher has more applications running on its mainframe than Eureka does, because Eureka uses a two-mainframe distributed processing platform.

Also, the data transfer did not go smoothly. A few data elements being stored in the system were not available as an option in the Amarillo system. Jeffries found that the staff at Amarillo was very friendly when she called, but they could not always identify the problem over the phone. They needed to come out to the site and investigate. Hamilton was surprised at the delays between requesting an Amarillo consultant to come out and the time in which he or she actually arrived. Amarillo explained that it had to fly a staff member from Dallas to Beaumont for each trip.

The system finally began to work somewhat smoothly in January, after a grueling fiscal year-end close in October. Hamilton's staff views the project as an unnecessary inconvenience. At one point, two staff accountants threatened to quit. The extra consulting fees amounted to $35,000. Further, the systems department at Gusher spent 500 more hours during the implementation process than it had expected. These additional hours caused other projects to fall behind schedule.

Required
Discuss what could have been done differently during the design phase. Why were most of the problems encountered? How might a detailed feasibility study have helped?

8. DATA FLOW DIAGRAM

The detailed data flow diagram in Figure 14-16 decomposes the DFD for the expenditure cycle in Figure 14-15. Further decompose the process numbered 1.4.4, Receive Invoice, in detail.

9. PERT CHART

The Peabody Coal Corporation recently completed the final feasibility report for a new general ledger accounting system. It has hired a consulting firm to program and install the new system. The consulting firm is charging $350,000 for the remaining tasks to be performed. These tasks are to be performed over the next 10 months, as detailed in the Gantt chart in the diagram for Problem 9. The consulting firm is extremely concerned with the project staying on schedule because it is receiving a flat fee. The release of the final payment is contingent upon the system performing as stated in the contract and upon Pea-body receiving appropriate documentation of the system.

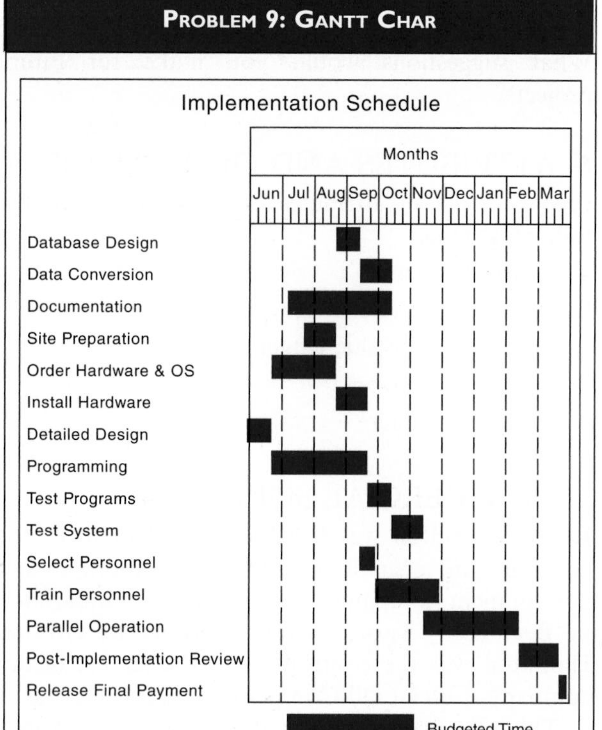

Required

a. Prepare a PERT diagram and indicate the critical path.

b. What happens to the time frame of the implementation of the project if the manufacturer is four weeks late shipping the hardware?

c. What happens if the data conversion does not go smoothly and takes an additional three weeks?

d. Who should conduct the post-implementation review? What activities should be conducted during this review? Do you think enough time has been allotted for this activity?

10. PERT AND GANTT CHARTS

The lottery commission of a state with about $500 million a year in revenue has looked to modern technology for increasing lottery sales. The strategy is to place self-service sales machines around the state. Customers simply fill out the bubbles on the form and insert the form into the computer. If they wish, they may enter their numbers directly in the computer and skip the form altogether. The machine accepts cash and automatic teller machine cards. The lottery commission is very excited about this project because it thinks it could boost lottery ticket sales by as much as 30 percent.

The systems department has finished the final feasibility report and has determined the following estimates for implementing the system. It plans on purchasing a larger, more powerful mainframe computer to handle the processing of the transactions. The manufacturer has promised a delivery date of three months from the time the order is placed. The lottery sales machines must be special ordered and require a lead time of five months. The plan is to initially order 15 machines and test them for 12 weeks. If all goes well, the lottery commission will order a total of 500 machines, with 20 delivered and installed each month. This order will not be placed until the results of the pilot test have been analyzed.

The writing of the programs is expected to take six weeks. The testing of the programs on the mainframe is expected to take four weeks, with an additional three weeks once the sales machines have been received. The state gaming commission is expected to test for another two weeks. The design of the databases is expected to take only two weeks. Not much data transfer is expected to be necessary, so only three weeks is budgeted for this task.

An estimated 20 employees need to be hired and trained to install and maintain these machines around the state. The hiring process is expected to take six weeks, and the training should take an additional six weeks. The documentation should take about three months and should be completed before the training of the new employees. As soon as the gaming commission signs off on the programs, the 15 machines are to be installed at test sites around the state. Four weeks are allotted for this installation procedure. A one-week testing period is planned, with commission employees going to the sites and using the machines. An additional week is planned to review the results of these tests. The pilot test then begins and runs for eight weeks. The data will be analyzed for four weeks after the pilot test. The final order for the additional machines will be placed after the data analysis is conducted, and the demand for the number of machines is more accurately determined.

Required

a. Prepare a PERT chart for the process described. Identify the critical path.
b. Prepare a Gantt chart for the process described.

11. PREPARE PSEUDOCODE

Accountants understand their jobs very well. Programmers also understand their jobs. Unfortunately, accountants are rarely programmers, and programmers are rarely accountants. Although an accountant does not need to program, the accountant must be able to communicate his requirement to the programmer, an individual who may not understand the intricate needs of the accountants. To bridge this knowledge gap, the accountant may be called on to produce pseudocode—a set of detailed instructions written in English without syntax rules. Suppose you need a programmer to prepare code that will read sales information from an input screen, compute extensions for items sold, compute a total of these extensions, and update inventory balances, the sales ledger account, and accounts receivable as well as any subsidiary accounts. Prepare pseudocode for the programmer.

12. CMA 786 5-Y6

PERT Chart

Silver Aviation assembles small aircraft for commercial use. The majority of Silver's business is with small freight airlines serving areas where the airport does not accommodate larger planes. The remainder of Silver's customers are commuter airlines and individuals who use planes in their businesses. Silver recently expanded into Central and South America and expects to double its sales over the next three years.

To schedule work and keep track of all projects, Silver uses the PERT. The PERT diagram for the construction of a single cargo plane is shown in the diagram for Problem 12. The PERT diagram shows that there are four alternative paths, with the critical path being ABGEFJK.

Bob Peterson, president of Coastal Airlines, has recently placed an order with Silver Aviation for five cargo planes. At the time of contract negotiations, Peterson agreed to a delivery time of 13 weeks (5 working days per week) for the first plane, with the balance of the planes being delivered at the rate of one every 4 weeks. Because of problems with some of the aircraft Coastal is using, Peterson has contacted Grace Vander, sales manager for Silver Aviation, to ask about improving the delivery date of the first cargo plane. Vander replied that she believed the schedule could be shortened by as much as 10 working days, or 2 weeks, but the cost of construction would increase as a result. Peterson said he would be willing to consider the increased costs, and they agreed to meet the following day to review a revised schedule that Vander would prepare.

Because Silver Aviation has assembled aircraft on an accelerated basis before, the company has compiled a list of crash costs for this purpose. Vander used the data shown in the Crash Cost Listing table at the middle of the diagram for Problem 12 to develop a plan to cut 10 working days from the schedule at a minimal increase in cost to Coastal Airlines.

Upon completing her plan, Vander was pleased that she could report to Peterson that Silver would be able to cut 10 working days from the schedule. The associated increase in cost would be $6,600. Presented at the bottom of the diagram for Problem 12 is Vander's plan for the accelerated delivery of the cargo plane, starting from the regularly scheduled days and costs.

Required

a. PERT is a form of network analysis.
   1. Explain how the expected regular times for each activity are derived in using PERT.
   2. Define the term *critical path* and explain why path ABGEFJK is the critical path in this situation.

Problem 12: PERT Chart

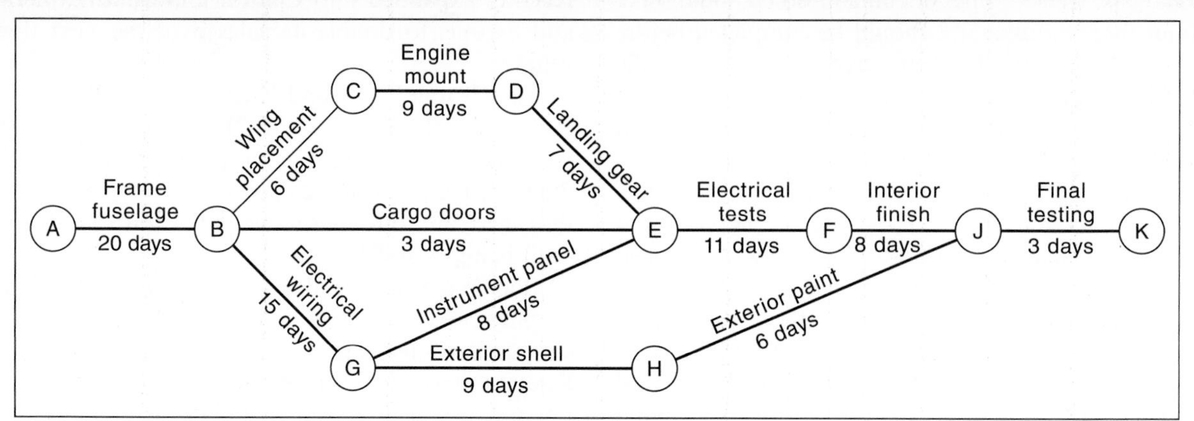

Crash Cost Listing

Activity		Expected Activity Times: Regular	Expected Activity Times: Crash	Direct Cost: Regular	Direct Cost: Crash	Added Crash Cost per Reduced Day
AB	Frame fuselage	20 days	16 days	$12,000	$16,800	$1,200
BC	Wing placement	6	5	3,600	5,000	1,400
CD	Engine mount	9	7	6,600	8,000	700
DE	Landing gear	7	5	5,100	6,700	800
BE	Cargo doors	3	3	1,400	1,400	—
BG	Electrical wiring	15	13	9,000	11,000	1,000
GE	Instrument panel	8	6	5,700	8,300	1,300
EF	Electrical tests	11	10	6,800	7,600	800
GH	Exterior shell	9	7	4,200	5,200	500
FJ	Interior finish	8	7	3,600	4,000	400
HJ	Exterior paint	6	5	3,600	4,000	400
JK	Final testing	3	2	3,500	4,400	900
				$65,100	$82,400	

Vander's plan for accelerated delivery

Completion Time	Activity Crashed	Additional Cost per Day	Total Direct Cost
65 days			$65,100
64	HJ by 1 day	$ 400	65,500
63	FJ by 1 day	400	65,900
61	GH by 2 days	500	66,900
59	CD by 2 days	700	68,300
58	EF by 1 day	800	69,100
56	DE by 2 days	800	70,700
55	BG by 1 day	1,000	71,700

b. Evaluate the accelerated delivery schedule that Grace Vander prepared.

1. Explain why Vander's plan as presented is unsatisfactory.
2. Revise the accelerated delivery schedule so that Coastal Airlines will take delivery of the first plane 2 weeks (10 working days) ahead of schedule at the least incremental cost to Coastal.
3. Calculate the incremental costs Bob Peterson will have to pay for this revised accelerated delivery.

13. DETAILED SYSTEMS DESIGN

Refer to the diagram for Problem 13 for the expenditure cycle.

Required

a. List the entity database tables, and describe which entities need representing from an AIS perspective.
b. For each item identified as relevant to AIS, prepare a list of database tables along with primary and embedded foreign keys.
c. Prepare database tables showing attributes in normalized form.

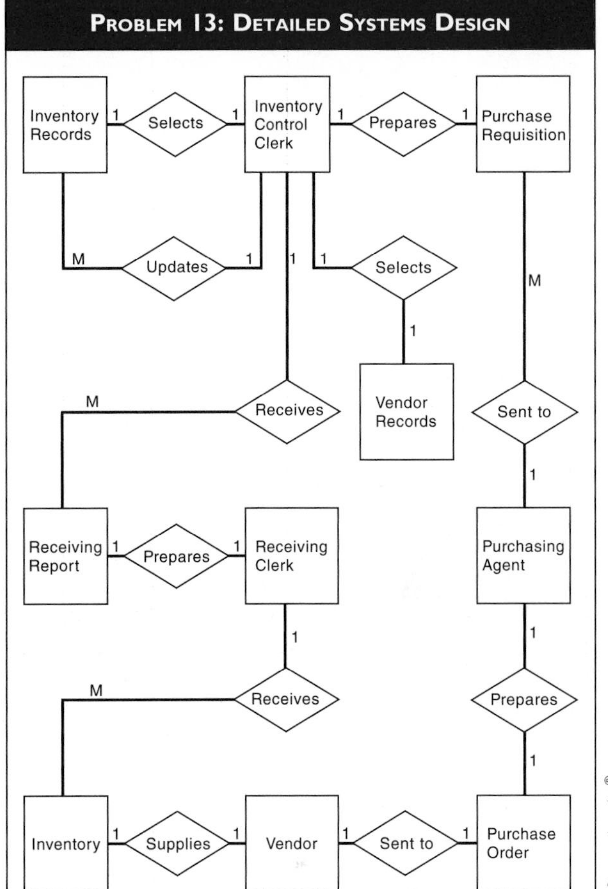

14. CONCEPTUAL DESIGN

Vince Malloy and Katy Smith, both systems personnel at Shamrock Steelworks, are designing a new expenditure cycle system. Vince has worked for Shamrock for 12 years and has been involved in many systems development projects. Katy recently began working for Shamrock. She has four years of experience in systems development with another comparably sized organization. Yesterday, Vince and Katy met to determine their plan for approaching the conceptual system design.

Following is an excerpt of some dialogue that occurred in that meeting.

Katy: I really think that the new system can be designed more efficiently if we use an object-oriented design approach. Further, future enhancements and maintenance will be easier if we use an object approach.

Vince: The method you are suggesting is a creation of modules. I do not have a problem with that concept in general. I just prefer using a top-down approach to design the system. We have been using that system for the past 12 years, and it has worked out OK.

Katy: Sure, your systems have worked for you, but perhaps they can be developed more efficiently, not to mention maintaining them. Further, we have approximately a two-year backlog of projects. Changing to a more efficient design system may help us to reduce that wait.

Vince: We may not end up with the system we want if we do not consider the big picture. I am afraid if we get too tied to using existing modules for future projects, we may design suboptimal systems that will require more maintenance and have shorter lives in the long run. What good will the more efficient system do us then?

Required

Prepare Katy's response and develop a strategy for systems design that will address both of their concerns.

Systems Development Cases

Several systems development cases that draw upon the material in this and the previous chapter are available online at www.cengage.com/accounting/hall.

PART

V

Computer Controls and IT Auditing

CHAPTER

15

Auditing IT Controls Part I: Sarbanes-Oxley and IT Governance

Learning Objectives

After studying this chapter, you should:

- Be familiar with the structure of a financial audit and the role of the IT audit component.
- Understand the key features of Sections 302 and 404 of the Sarbanes-Oxley Act.
- Understand management and auditor responsibilities under Sections 302 and 404.
- Understand the risks of incompatible functions and how to structure the IT function.
- Be familiar with the controls and precautions required to ensure the security of an organization's computer facilities.
- Understand the key elements of a disaster recovery plan.
- Be familiar with the benefits, risks, and audit issues related to IT outsourcing.

This chapter introduces the topic of IT auditing. It begins with an overview of the key components of an audit. Next, the chapter turns to internal control and audit issues related to Sections 302 and 404 of SOX. This section reviews the Management and auditor responsibilities under SOX. The section concludes with a discussion of computer fraud issues. The next section of the chapter presents risks and controls related to IT governance. The structure of the IT function within an organization and the risks that can arise from inappropriate structuring are issues of concern. The chapter then moves on to a review of computer center threats and controls, which include protecting against natural disasters, fire, temperature, and humidity. The chapter discusses important issues related to disaster recovery including provision for second-site backup, identifying critical applications, performing backup and off-site storage procedures and preparing a disaster recovery plan. The final section of the chapter examines issues surrounding the growing trend toward IT outsourcing. This popular practice is associated with both significant benefits and risks, which are addressed. The chapter concludes with a discussion of audit issues related to outsourcing including the SSAE 16 reporting standard.

Overview of Auditing

An external audit is an independent attestation performed by an expert—the auditor—who expresses an opinion regarding the presentation of financial statements. This attest service is performed by Certified Public Accountants (CPA) who work for public accounting firms that are independent of the client organization being audited. The audit objective is always associated with assuring the fair presentation of financial statements. These audits are, therefore, often referred to as *financial audits.* The Securities and Exchange Commission (SEC) requires that all publicly traded companies be subject to a financial audit annually. CPAs conducting such audits represent the interests of outsiders: stockholders, creditors, government agencies, and the general public.

The CPA's role is to collect and evaluate **evidence** and thus render an opinion. A key concept in this process is *independence.* The judge must remain independent in his or her deliberations and cannot be an advocate of either party in a trial. The judge must apply the law impartially based on the evidence presented. Likewise, the independent auditor collects and evaluates evidence, and renders an opinion based on the evidence. Throughout the audit process, the auditor must maintain independence from the client organization. Public confidence in the reliability of the company's internally produced financial statements rests directly on an evaluation of them by an independent auditor.

External auditors follow strict rules in conducting financial audits. These authoritative rules have been defined by the SEC, the Financial Accounting Standards Board (FASB), the American Institute of Certified Public Accountants (AICPA), and by federal law (Sarbanes-Oxley Act of 2002). With the passage of SOX, Congress established the Public Company Accounting Oversight Board (PCAOB), which has to a great extent replaced the function served by the FASB, and some of the functions of the AICPA (e.g., setting standards and issuing reprimands and penalties for CPAs who are convicted of certain crimes or found guilty of certain infractions). Regardless, under federal law the SEC has final authority over financial auditing.

Financial Audit Components

The product of the attestation function is a formal written report that expresses an opinion as to whether the financial statements are in conformity with *generally accepted accounting principles (GAAP).* External users of financial statements are presumed to rely on the auditor's opinion about the reliability of financial statements in making decisions. To do so, users must be able to place their trust in the auditor's competence, professionalism, integrity, and independence. Auditors are guided in their professional responsibility by the 10 *generally accepted auditing standards (GAAS)* presented in Table 15-1.

TABLE 15-1 GENERALLY ACCEPTED AUDITING STANDARDS

General Standards	Standards of Field Work	Reporting Standards
1. The auditor must have adequate technical training and proficiency.	1. Audit work must be adequately planned.	1. The auditor must state in the report whether financial statements were prepared in accordance with generally accepted accounting principles.
2. The auditor must have independence of mental attitude.	2. The auditor must gain a sufficient understanding of the internal control structure.	2. The report must identify those circumstances in which generally accepted accounting principles were not applied.
3. The auditor must exercise due professional care in the performance of the audit and the preparation of the report.	3. The auditor must obtain sufficient, competent evidence.	3. The report must identify any items that do not have adequate informative disclosures. 4. The report shall contain an expression of the auditor's opinion on the financial statements as a whole.

AUDITING STANDARDS

Auditing standards are divided into three classes: general qualification standards, field work standards, and reporting standards. Although GAAS establishes the framework for prescribing auditor performance, it is not sufficiently detailed to provide meaningful guidance in specific circumstances. To provide specific guidance, the AICPA issues *Statements on Auditing Standards (SASs)* as authoritative interpretations of GAAS.

The first SAS (SAS 1) was issued by the AICPA in 1972. Since then, many SASs have been issued to provide auditors with guidance on a spectrum of topics, including methods of investigating new clients, procedures for collecting information from attorneys regarding contingent liability claims against clients, and techniques for obtaining background information on the client's industry.

Statements on Auditing Standards are regarded as authoritative pronouncements because every member of the profession must follow their recommendations or be able to show why a SAS does not apply in a given situation. The burden of justifying departures from the SASs falls upon the individual auditor.

Structure of an Audit

Conducting an audit is a systematic and logical process that consists of three conceptual phases: audit planning, tests of controls, and substantive testing. Figure 15-1 illustrates the steps involved in these phases. An **IT audit** involves specialized procedures that are directed to those aspects of the client's system where technology plays a material role and thus injects an added degree of complexity into the audit. For example, transaction processing in an IT environment involves automated procedures performed by computer programs and digital source documents, journals, and ledgers that are stored in relational databases. Since modern accounting information systems employ significant levels of technology, IT auditing often constitutes a substantial component of the overall financial audit.

AUDIT PLANNING

The first phase of the audit is **audit planning**. Before the auditor can determine the nature and extent of the tests to be performed, he or she must gain a thorough understanding of the client's business. The auditor's objective at this point is to obtain sufficient information about the firm to

FIGURE 15-1 PHASES OF AN AUDIT

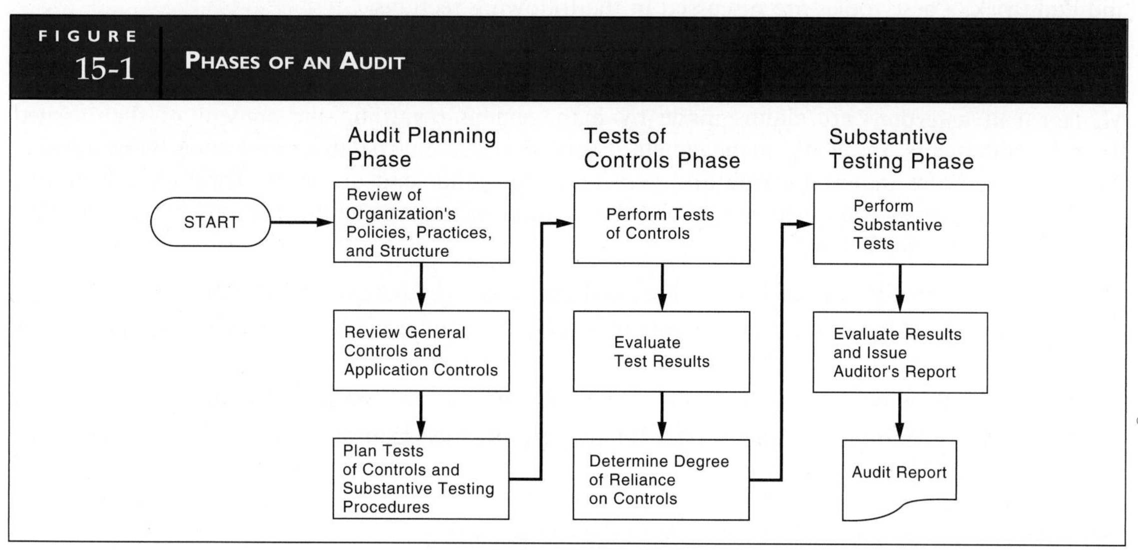

plan the other phases of the audit. During this phase the auditor attempts to understand the organization's policies, practices, and structure. The auditor also identifies the financially significant applications and attempts to identify and understand the controls over the transactions that are processed by these applications.

The techniques for gathering evidence at this phase include administering questionnaires, interviewing management, reviewing systems documentation, and observing day-to-day activities. The audit then proceeds to the next phase, where the auditor tests the controls for compliance with preestablished standards.

Tests of Controls

The objective of the **tests of controls** phase is to determine whether adequate internal controls are in place and functioning properly. The evidence-gathering techniques used in this phase include both manual techniques and specialized computer audit techniques known as **computer-aided audit tools and techniques (CAATTs)**. These techniques are discussed in detail in Chapter 17. At the conclusion of the tests-of-controls phase, the auditor assesses the quality of the internal controls by assigning a level for **control risk**. The level of risk ascribed to internal controls will affect the nature and extent of substantive testing that needs to be performed in the third phase. Control risk is discussed later in this section.

Substantive Testing

The third phase of the audit process focuses on gathering evidence pertaining to financial data. This phase involves a detailed investigation of specific account balances and transactions through what are called **substantive tests**. For example, a customer confirmation is a substantive test used to verify account receivable balances. The auditor selects a sample of customer accounts and contacts these customers directly to determine if the amount stated in the AR is correct and is owed by a bona fide customer. By so doing, the auditor determines the accuracy of sample and draws a conclusion about the fair value of the entire accounts receivable account as presented in the financial statements.

Substantive tests tend to be physical, labor-intensive activities such as counting cash, counting inventories in a warehouse, and verifying the existence of stock certificates in a safe. Much of the data needed to perform substantive tests (such as account balances and customer names and addresses) are stored in digital form in data files and must be extracted using CAATTs software.[1] The nature (what to examine), timing (when to examine), and extent (how many items to examine) of substantive tests are audit decisions that are driven by the concepts of management assertions and audit risk. These topics are discussed in the following sections.

MANAGEMENT ASSERTIONS

Management assertions are claims made by management regarding the content of their issued financial statements. Implicitly management asserts that account balances and underlying transactions are free from material errors and are complete, valid, and accurate. Through substantive procedures auditors gather evidence to test the validity of management assertions, which fall into the general categories below:[2]

1. Assertions about classes of transactions and events for the period under audit:
    - Occurrence. Transactions and events that have been recorded have occurred and pertain to the entity.
    - Completeness. All transactions and events that should have been recorded have been recorded.
    - Accuracy. Amounts and other data relating to recorded transactions and events have been recorded appropriately.

---

1 Chapter 17 describes the use of CAATTs in performing substantive tests.

2 Source: SAS No. 106.

- Cutoff. Transactions and events have been recorded in the correct accounting period.
- Classification. Transactions and events have been recorded in the proper accounts.

2. Assertions about account balances at the period end:
   - Existence. Assets, liabilities, and equity interests exist.
   - Rights and obligations. The entity holds or controls the rights to assets, and liabilities are the obligations of the entity.
   - Completeness. All assets, liabilities, and equity interests that should have been recorded have been recorded.
   - Valuation and allocation. Assets, liabilities, and equity interests are included in the financial statements at appropriate amounts and any resulting valuation or allocation adjustments are appropriately recorded.
3. Assertions about presentation and disclosure:
   - Occurrence and rights and obligations. Disclosed events and transactions have occurred and pertain to the entity.
   - Completeness. All disclosures that should have been included in the financial statements have been included.
   - Classification and understandability. Financial information is appropriately presented and described and disclosures are clearly expressed.
   - Accuracy and valuation. Financial and other information are disclosed fairly and at appropriate amounts.

The auditors develop **audit objectives** and design **audit procedures** to gather evidence that corroborates or refutes management's assertions. Table 15-2 provides some examples to illustrate the relationship between management assertions, audit objectives, and audit procedures.

TABLE 15-2 AUDIT OBJECTIVES AND AUDIT PROCEDURES BASED ON MANAGEMENT ASSERTIONS

Management Assertion	Audit Objective	Audit Procedure
Existence	Inventories listed on the balance sheet exist.	Observe the counting of physical inventory.
Completeness	Accounts payable include all obligations to vendors for the period.	Compare receiving reports, supplier invoices, purchase orders, and journal entries for the period and the beginning of the next period.
Rights and Obligations	Plant and equipment listed in the balance sheet are owned by the entity.	Review purchase agreements, insurance policies, and related documents.
Valuation or Allocation	Accounts receivable are stated at net realizable value.	Review entity's aging of accounts and evaluate the adequacy of the allowance for uncorrectable accounts.
Classification and Understandability	Contingencies not reported in financial accounts are properly disclosed in footnotes.	Obtain information from entity lawyers about the status of litigation and estimates of potential loss.

AUDIT RISK

Audit risk is the probability that the auditor will render an unqualified (clean) opinion on financial statements that are, in fact, materially misstated because of undetected errors or irregularities or both. Errors are unintentional mistakes. Irregularities are intentional misrepresentations associated with the commission of a fraud, such as misappropriation of physical assets or attempts to deceive financial statement users.

Audit Risk Components

The auditor's objective is to achieve a level of audit risk that is acceptable to the auditor. The auditor estimates acceptable audit risk (AR) based on the *ex ante* value of the components of the audit risk model—inherent risk, control risk, and detection risk.

Inherent Risk

Inherent risk (IR) is associated with the unique characteristics of the business or industry of the client.[3] Firms in declining industries have greater inherent risk than firms in stable or thriving industries. Likewise, industries that have a heavy volume of cash transactions have a higher level of inherent risk than those that do not. Furthermore, valuating inventory when the type of inventory is difficult to value due to its nature is associated with higher inherent risk than in situations where inventory values are more objective. For example, the valuation of diamonds is inherently more risky than assessing the value of automobile tires. Auditors cannot reduce the level of inherent risk. Even in a system protected by excellent controls, financial data and, consequently, financial statements can be materially misstated.

Control Risk

Control risk (CR) is the likelihood that the control structure is flawed because controls are either absent or inadequate to prevent or detect errors in the accounts.[4] To illustrate control risk, consider the following partial customer sales record, which is processed by the sales order system.

Quantity	Unit Price	Total
10 Units	$20	$2,000

Assuming the Quantity and Unit Price fields in the record are correctly presented, the extended amount (Total) value of $2,000 is in error. An accounting information system (AIS) with adequate controls should prevent or detect such an error. If, however, controls are lacking, and the value of Total in each record is not validated before processing, then the risk of undetected errors entering the data files increases.

Auditors assess the level of control risk by performing tests of internal controls. In the preceding example, the auditor could create test transactions, including some with incorrect Total values, which are processed by the application in a test run. The results of the test will indicate that price extension errors are not detected and are being incorrectly posted to the accounts receivable file.

Detection Risk

Detection risk (DR) is the risk that auditors are willing to take that errors not detected or prevented by the control structure will also go undetected by the auditor as he or she performs substantive tests. Auditors predetermine an acceptable level of detection risk (called planned detection risk), which influences the level of substantive tests that they must perform. For example, a planned detection risk of 10 percent requires more substantive testing that a detection is set at 20 percent. As we shall see next, the more reliable the internal controls, the more planned detection risk the auditor can assume, and less substantive testing is required.

3 Auditing Standards Board, *AICPA Professional Standards* (New York: AICPA, 1994), AU Sec. 312.20

4 Ibid.

Audit Risk Model

Auditors use the audit risk components in the model below to determine the scope, nature, and timing of substantive tests.

$$AR = IR \times CR \times DR$$

Assume that acceptable audit risk is assessed at a value of 5 percent, consistent with the 95 percent confidence interval associated with statistics. Further assume that IR is assessed at 40 percent, and CR is assessed at 60 percent. What level of planned detection risk (DR) is needed to achieve the acceptable audit risk (AR) of 5%?

$$5\% = 40\% \times 60\% \times DR$$
$$DR = .05/.24$$
$$DR = .20$$

Let's now reduce the control risk (CR) value to 40% and recalculate DR.

$$5\% = 40\% \times 40\% \times DR$$
$$DR = .31$$

Notice that to achieve an acceptable level of audit risk in the first example, the auditor must set planned detection risk lower (20%) than in the second example (31%). This is because the internal control structure in the first example is more risky (60%) than it is in the second case (40%). This greater risk necessitates more substantive testing to ensure that no material errors go undetected by the auditor.

In summary, the stronger the internal control structure, as determined through tests of controls, the lower the control risk, and the less substantive testing the auditor must do. This relationship is true because the likelihood of errors in the accounting records is reduced when controls are strong. Therefore, when controls are in place and effective, the auditor may limit substantive testing. In contrast, the weaker the internal control structure, the greater the control risk, and the more substantive testing the auditor must perform to reduce total audit risk. Evidence of weak controls thus forces the auditor to extend substantive testing to search for misstatements.

Audit Report

Upon completion of the audit the auditor submits an **audit report** to the audit committee of the board of directors. The audit report includes an opinion on the fair presentation of the financial statements and an opinion on the quality of internal controls over financial reporting. A single material weakness in the internal controls requires the auditor to issue a qualified opinion regarding internal controls over financial reporting. This does not mean, however, that the auditor's opinion on the financial statements must also be qualified. If the auditor can conclude through additional tests that the internal control weakness did not result in material misstatement of the financials, the auditor may issue an unqualified (clean) opinion on the financial statements while simultaneously issuing a qualified opinion on the internal controls.

Overview of SOX Sections 302 and 404

SOX of 2002 established corporate governance regulations and standards for public companies registered with the Securities and Exchange Commission (SEC). Although the act contains many sections, this chapter and the two following chapters concentrate on internal control and audit responsibilities pursuant to Sections 302 and 404.

Section 302 requires corporate management, including the chief executive officer (CEO), to certify financial and other information contained in the organization's quarterly and annual reports. The rule also requires corporate management to certify the internal controls over financial reporting. The certifying officers are required to have designed internal controls, or to have caused such controls to be designed, and to provide reasonable assurance as to the reliability of the financial reporting process. Furthermore, they must disclose any material changes in the company's internal controls that have occurred during the most recent fiscal quarter.

Section 404 requires the management of public companies to assess the effectiveness of their organization's internal controls over financial reporting. Under this section of the act, management is required to provide an annual report addressing the following points:

1. Describe the flow of transactions, including IT aspects, in sufficient detail to identify points at which a misstatement could arise.
2. Using a risk-based approach, assess both the design and operating effectiveness of selected internal controls related to material accounts.[5]
3. Assess the potential for fraud in the system and evaluate the controls designed to prevent or detect fraud.
4. Evaluate and conclude on the adequacy of controls over the financial statement reporting process.
5. Evaluate entity-wide (general) controls that correspond to COSO internal control framework.

Regarding the final point, the SEC has made specific reference to COSO as a recommended control framework. Furthermore, the Public Company Accounting Oversight Board (PCAOB) Auditing Standard No. 5 endorses the use of COSO as the framework for control assessment. Although other suitable frameworks have been published, any framework used should encompass all of COSO's general themes.[6]

RELATIONSHIP BETWEEN IT CONTROLS AND FINANCIAL REPORTING

Information technology drives the financial reporting processes of modern organizations. Automated systems initiate, authorize, record, and report the effects of financial transactions. As such, they are inextricable elements of the financial reporting processes that SOX considers, and must be controlled. The COSO model identifies two broad groupings of IT controls: application controls and general controls. As we saw in previous chapters, **application controls** ensure the validity, completeness, and accuracy of financial transactions. These controls are designed to be application-specific. Examples include:

- A cash disbursements batch balancing routine that verifies that the total payments to vendors reconciles with the total postings to the accounts payable subsidiary ledger.
- An accounts receivable check digit procedure that validates customer account numbers on sales transactions.
- A payroll system limit check that identifies employee time card records with reported hours worked in excess of the predetermined normal limit.

These examples illustrate how application controls have a direct impact on the integrity of data that make their way through various transaction processing systems and into the financial reporting process. IT **general controls** are so named because they are not application-specific, but rather apply to all systems. General controls have other names in other frameworks, including **general computer controls** and **information technology controls**. Whatever name is used, they include controls over IT governance, IT infrastructure, network and operating system security, databases access, application acquisition and development, and program changes.

Although general controls do not control specific transactions, they have an effect on transaction integrity. For example, consider an organization with poor database security controls. In such a situation, even data processed by systems with adequate built-in application controls may be at risk from an individual who circumvents database security (either directly or via a malicious

5 Management should design their assessment based on risks specific to the organization rather than follow a one-size-fits-all checklist.

6 A popular competing control framework is Control Objectives for Information and Related Technology (COBIT), published by the IT Governance Institute (ITGI). This framework maps into COSO's general themes.

program) and changes, steals, or corrupts stored transaction data. Thus, general controls are needed to support the environment in which application controls function, and both are needed to ensure accurate financial reporting.

AUDIT IMPLICATIONS OF SECTIONS 302 AND 404

Prior to SOX, external auditors were not required to test internal controls as part of their attest function. They were required to be familiar with the client organization's internal controls but had the option of not relying on them and thus not performing tests of controls. The audit could, and often did, therefore consist primarily of substantive tests.

SOX legislation dramatically expands the role of external auditors by mandating that they attest to the quality of internal controls. This constitutes the issuance of a separate audit opinion in addition to the opinion on the fairness of the financial statements. The standard for this additional audit opinion is high. Indeed, the auditor is precluded from issuing an unqualified opinion if only one material weakness in internal control is detected. As explained in the previous section, a qualified opinion on internal controls does not necessarily mean a qualified opinion on the financial statements. Auditors are permitted to simultaneously render a qualified opinion on controls and an unqualified opinion on the financial statements when they conclude through substantive tests that the control weakness(es) did not cause the financial statements to be materially misrepresented.

As part of the attestation responsibility, PCAOB Standard No. 5 specifically requires auditors to understand transaction flows, including the controls pertaining to how transactions are initiated, authorized, recorded, and reported. This involves first selecting the financial accounts that have material implications for financial reporting and identifying the application controls related to those accounts. As previously noted, the reliability of application controls rests on the IT general controls that support them. These include controls over access to databases, operating systems, and networks. The sum of these controls, both application and general, constitute the relevant internal controls over financial reporting that need to be reviewed. Figure 15-2 illustrates this IT control relationship.

FIGURE 15-2 INFORMATION TECHNOLOGY CONTROL RELATIONSHIP

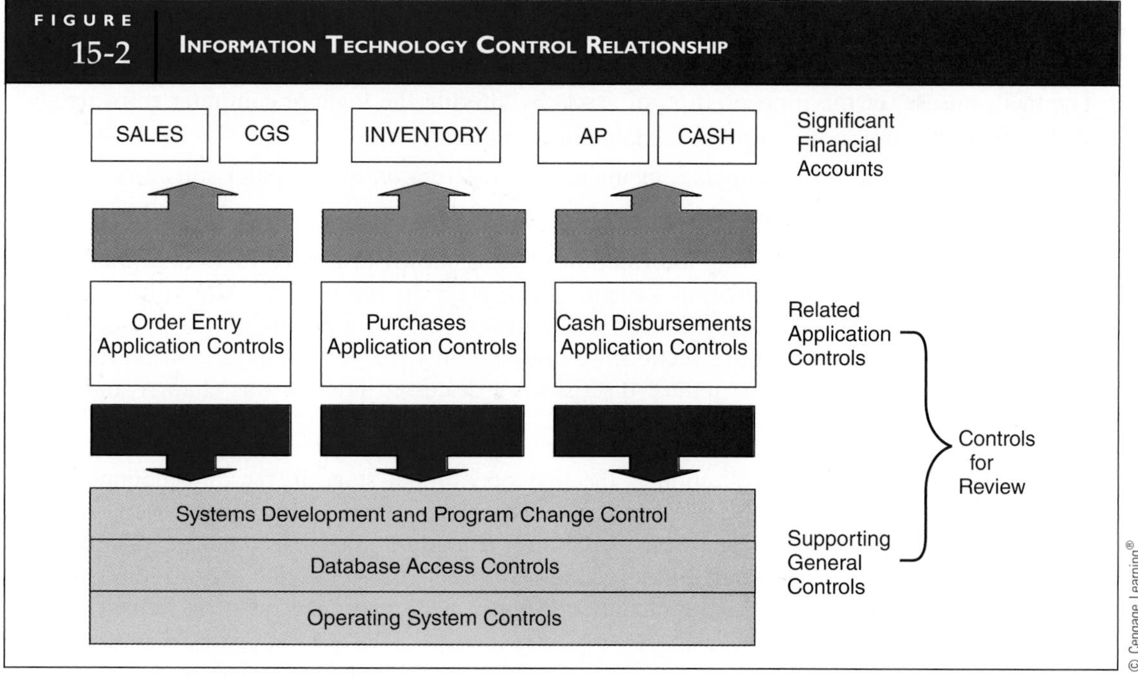

Compliance with Section 404 requires management to provide the external auditors with documented evidence of functioning controls related to selected material accounts in its report on control effectiveness. The organization's internal audit function, or a specialized SOX group, would likely perform these tests.

Section 302 also carries significant auditor implications. In addition to expressing an opinion on the effectiveness of internal control, auditors have responsibility regarding management's quarterly certifications of internal controls. Specifically, auditors must perform the following procedures quarterly to identify any material modifications in controls over financial reporting:

- Interview management regarding any significant changes in the design or operation of internal control that occurred subsequent to the preceding annual audit or prior review of interim financial information.
- Evaluate the implications of misstatements identified by the auditor as part of the interim review that relate to effective internal controls.
- Determine whether changes in internal controls are likely to materially affect internal control over financial reporting.

Finally, SOX places responsibility on auditors to detect fraudulent activity and emphasizes the importance of controls designed to prevent or detect fraud that could lead to material misstatement of the financial statements. Management is responsible for implementing such controls, and auditors are specifically required to test them. Because computers lie at the heart of the modern organizations' accounting and financial reporting systems, the topic of **computer fraud** falls within the management and audit responsibilities specified by SOX. The following section deals with several computer fraud issues.

Computer Fraud

We saw in Chapter 3 that fraud loss estimates for 2012 are $3.5 trillion. How much of this can be traced to computer fraud is difficult to say. One reason for uncertainty is that computer fraud is not well defined. For example, we saw in the ethics section of Chapter 3 that some people consider copying commercial computer software to be neither unethical nor illegal. On the other side of this issue, software vendors consider such acts to be criminal. Regardless of how narrowly or broadly computer fraud is defined, it is a rapidly growing phenomenon. For purposes of our discussion, computer fraud includes:

- The theft, misuse, or misappropriation of assets by altering computer-readable records and files.
- The theft, misuse, or misappropriation of assets by altering the logic of computer software.
- The theft or illegal use of computer-readable information.
- The theft, corruption, illegal copying, or intentional destruction of computer software.
- The theft, misuse, or misappropriation of computer hardware.

The general model for accounting information systems shown in Figure 15-3 conceptually portrays the key stages of an information system.[7] Each stage in the model—data collection, data processing, database management, and information generation—is a potential area of risk for certain types of computer fraud. In this section, we examine only the general nature of the risks; specific control techniques needed to reduce the risks are discussed later in this chapter and in the remaining two chapters.

DATA COLLECTION. Data collection is the first operational stage in the information system. The control objective is to ensure that event data entering the system are valid, complete, and free from material errors. In many respects, this is the most important stage in the system. Should erroneous or fraudulent transactions pass through data collection undetected, the organization runs the risk that the system will process the transaction and that it will impact the financial statements.

7 This model was introduced in Chapter 1.

FIGURE 15-3 THE GENERAL MODEL FOR ACCOUNTING INFORMATION SYSTEMS

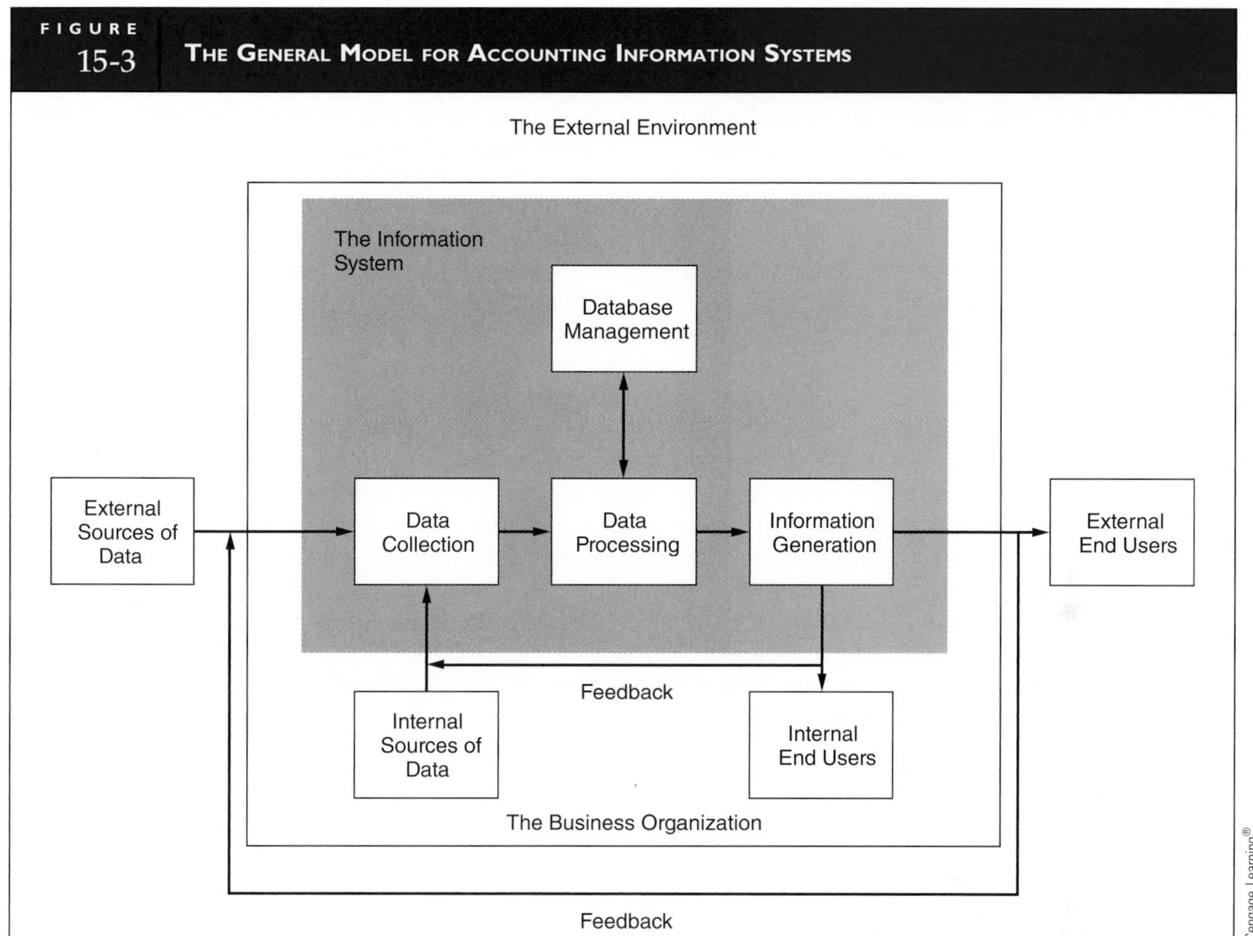

The most common access point for perpetrating computer fraud is at the data collection stage. Frauds of this type require little or no computer skills on the part of the fraudster, but they do require poorly designed controls. The perpetrator need only understand how the system works and the control weaknesses of the system. The fraudulent act involves entering falsified data into the system. This may involve deleting, altering, or creating a transaction. For example, to commit payroll fraud, the perpetrator may insert a fraudulent payroll transaction along with legitimate transactions. Unless internal controls are in place to detect the insertion, the system will generate an additional paycheck for the perpetrator. A variation on this type of fraud is to change the Hours Worked field in an otherwise legitimate payroll transaction to increase the amount of the paycheck.

Still another variant of this fraud is to disburse cash in payment of a false account payable. By entering fraudulent supporting documents (purchase order, receiving report, and supplier invoice) at the data collection stage of the accounts payable system, a perpetrator can fool the system into creating an accounts payable record for a nonexistent purchase. Once the record is created, the system will presume it is legitimate and, on the due date, disperse funds to the perpetrator in payment of a bogus liability.

Networked systems expose organizations to transaction frauds from remote locations. Masquerading, piggybacking, and hacking are examples of such fraud techniques. Masquerading involves a perpetrator gaining access to the system from a remote site by pretending to be an authorized user. This usually requires first gaining authorized access to a password. Piggybacking is a technique in which the perpetrator at a remote site taps in to the telecommunications lines and latches on to an authorized user who is logging in to the system. Once in the system, the perpetrator can masquerade as the authorized user. Hacking may involve piggybacking or masquerading techniques. Hackers are distinguished from other computer criminals because their motives are not usually to defraud for financial gain. More often, they are motivated by the challenge of breaking into the system rather than the theft of assets. Nevertheless, hackers have caused extensive damage and loss to organizations by destroying and corrupting corporate data.

DATA PROCESSING. Once collected, data usually require processing to produce information. Tasks in data processing include mathematical algorithms (such as linear programming models) used for production scheduling applications, statistical techniques for sales forecasting, and posting and summarizing procedures used for accounting applications. Data processing frauds fall into two classes: program fraud and operations fraud.

Program fraud includes the following techniques: (1) creating illegal programs that can access data files to alter, delete, or insert values into accounting records; (2) destroying or corrupting a program's logic using a computer virus; or (3) altering program logic to cause the application to process data incorrectly. For example, the program a bank uses to calculate interest on its customers' accounts typically will produce rounding errors because the precision of the interest calculation is greater than the reporting precision. Therefore, interest figures that are calculated to several decimal places produce values to a fraction of one cent and must be rounded to whole numbers for reporting purposes. Interest calculation programs typically have a standard rounding routine to keep track of the rounding errors so that the total interest charge to the bank equals the sum of the individual credits. This involves temporarily placing fractional amounts left over from each calculation in an internal memory accumulator. When the amount in the accumulator totals one cent (plus or minus), the penny is added to the specific customer's account that is being processed at that time. In other words, one cent is added to (or deducted from) customer accounts randomly. A form of program fraud called the salami fraud involves modifying the rounding logic of the program so it no longer adds the one cent randomly. Instead, the modified program always adds the plus cent to the perpetrator's account, but it still adds the minus cent randomly. This can divert a considerable amount of cash to the perpetrator, but the accounting records stay in balance to conceal the crime.

Operations fraud is the misuse or theft of the firm's computer resources. This often involves using the computer to conduct personal business. For example, a programmer may use the firm's computer time to write software that he sells commercially. A CPA in the controller's office may use the company's computer to prepare tax returns and financial statements for her private clients. Similarly, a corporate lawyer with a private practice on the side may use the firm's computer to search for court cases and decisions in commercial databases. The cost of accessing the database is charged to the organization and hidden among legitimate charges.

DATABASE MANAGEMENT. The organization's database is its physical repository for financial and nonfinancial data. **Database management fraud** includes altering, deleting, corrupting, destroying, or stealing an organization's data. Because access to database files is an essential element of this fraud, it is often associated with transaction or program fraud. A common fraud technique is to access the database from a remote site and browse the files for useful information that can be copied and sold to competitors.

Disgruntled employees have been known to destroy company data files simply to harm the organization. One method is to insert a destructive routine called a logic bomb into a program. At a specified time, or when certain conditions are met, the logic bomb erases the data files that the program accesses. For example, a disgruntled programmer who is contemplating leaving an organization inserts a logic bomb into the payroll system. Weeks later, when the system detects that the programmer's name has been removed from the payroll file, the logic bomb is activated and erases the entire payroll file.

INFORMATION GENERATION. Information generation is the process of compiling, arranging, formatting, and presenting information to users. Information can be an operational document such as a sales order, a report sent to a computer screen, or published financial statements.

A common form of computer fraud at the information generation stage is to steal, misdirect, or misuse computer output. One low-tech but effective technique called **scavenging** involves searching through the trash of the computer center for discarded output. Sometimes, output reports that are misaligned on the paper or slightly garbled during printing are discarded into the trash. A perpetrator may obtain useful information from hard-copy reports that were rejected during processing.

Another form of fraud called **eavesdropping** involves listening to output transmissions over telecommunication lines. Technologies are readily available that enable perpetrators to intercept messages being sent over unprotected telephone lines and microwave channels. Most experts agree that it is practically impossible to prevent a determined perpetrator from accessing data communication channels. Data encryption, however, can render useless any data captured in this way.

With this backdrop in place, the scene is set for viewing control techniques and tests of controls that might be required under SOX. PCAOB Auditing Standard No. 5 emphasizes that management and auditors use a risk-based approach rather than a one-size-fits-all approach to the design and assessment of controls. In other words, the size and complexity of the organization needs to be considered in determining the nature and extent of controls that are necessary. The reader should recognize, therefore, that the controls presented in the remainder of this chapter and in the following two chapters describe the needs of a generic organization and may not apply in specific situations.

IT Governance Controls

IT governance is a broad concept relating to the decision rights and accountability for encouraging desirable behavior in the use of IT. Although important, not all elements of IT governance relate specifically to control issues that SOX addresses and that are outlined in the COSO framework. In this chapter, we consider three governance issues that do organizational structure of the IT function, computer operations, and disaster recovery planning.

The discussion of each of these governance issues begins with an explanation of the nature of risk and a description of the controls needed to mitigate the risk. Then, the audit objective is presented. This establishes what needs to be verified regarding the function of the control in place. Finally, example tests of controls are offered that describe how auditors might gather evidence to satisfy the audit objective. These control objectives and associated tests may be performed by internal auditors providing evidence of management's compliance with SOX or by external auditors as part of their attest function. In this regard, we make no distinction between the two roles.

Organizational Structure Controls

Previous chapters have stressed the importance of segregating incompatible duties within manual activities. Specifically, operational tasks should be separated to:

1. Segregate the task of transaction authorization from transaction processing.
2. Segregate record keeping from asset custody.
3. Divide transaction-processing tasks among individuals so that fraud will require collusion between two or more individuals.

The tendency in an IT environment is to consolidate activities. A single application may authorize, process, and record all aspects of a transaction. Thus, the focus of segregation control shifts from the operational level (transaction processing tasks that computer programs now perform) to higher-level organizational relationships within the IT function. The interrelationships among systems development, application maintenance, database administration, and computer operations activities are of particular concern.

The following section examines organizational control issues within the context of two generic models—the centralized model and the distributed model. For discussion purposes, these are presented as alternative structures; in practice, the IT environments of most firms possess elements of both.

SEGREGATION OF DUTIES WITHIN THE CENTRALIZED FIRM

Figure 15-4 presents an organizational chart of a centralized IT function. A similar organizational chart was presented in Chapter 1 to provide the basis for discussing IT tasks. It is reexamined here to study the control objectives behind separating these tasks. If the positions represented in this chart are unfamiliar, you should review the relevant sections in Chapter 1 before continuing.

Separating Systems Development from Computer Operations

The segregation of systems development (both new systems development and maintenance) and operations activities is of great importance. The responsibilities of these groups should not be commingled. Systems development and maintenance professionals acquire (by in-house development and purchase) and maintain systems for users. Operations staff should run these systems and have no involvement in their design and implementation. Consolidating these functions invites fraud. With detailed knowledge of an application's logic and control parameters along with access to the computer operations, an individual could make unauthorized changes to application logic during program execution. Such changes may be temporary (on the fly) and will disappear with little or no trace when the application terminates.

Separating the Database Administrator from Other Functions

Another important organizational control is the segregation of the database administrator (DBA) function from other IT functions. The DBA is responsible for a number of critical tasks pertaining to database security, including creating the database schema, creating **user views** (subschemas), assigning access authority to users, monitoring database usage, and planning for future expansion. Delegating these responsibilities to others who perform incompatible tasks threatens database integrity. Figure 15-4 shows how the DBA function is organizationally independent.

SEPARATING THE DBA FROM SYSTEMS DEVELOPMENT. Programmers create applications that access, update, and retrieve data from the database. Chapter 9 illustrated how database

FIGURE 15-4 ORGANIZATIONAL CHART OF A CENTRALIZED INFORMATION TECHNOLOGY FUNCTION

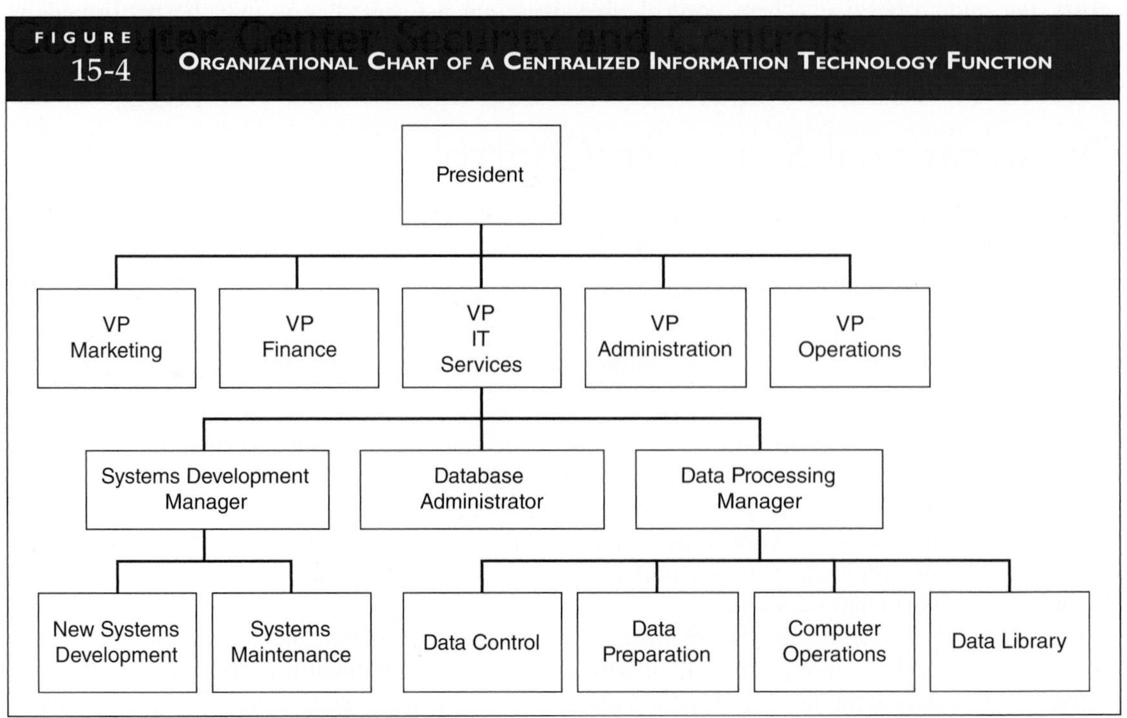

access control is achieved through the creation of user views, which is a DBA responsibility. To achieve database access, therefore, both the programmer and the DBA need to agree as to the attributes and tables (the user view) to make available to the application (or user) in question. If done properly, this permits and requires a formal review of the user data needs and security issues surrounding the request. Assigning responsibility for user view definition to individuals with programming responsibility removes this need to seek agreement and thus effectively erodes **access controls** to the DBMS.

Separating New Systems Development from Maintenance

Some companies organize their systems development function into two groups: systems analysis and programming. This organizational alternative is presented in Figure 15-5. The systems analysis group works with the user to produce a detailed design of the new system. The programming group codes the programs according to these design specifications. Under this approach, the programmer who codes the original programs also maintains them during the maintenance phase of the systems development life cycle. Although a popular arrangement, this approach promotes two potential problems: inadequate documentation and fraud.

INADEQUATE DOCUMENTATION. Poor-quality systems documentation is a chronic IT problem and a significant challenge for many organizations seeking SOX compliance. There are at least two explanations for this phenomenon. First, documenting systems is not as interesting as designing, testing, and implementing them. Systems professionals much prefer to move on to an exciting new project rather than document one just completed.

The second possible reason for poor documentation is job security. When a system is poorly documented, it is difficult to interpret, test, and debug. Therefore, the programmer who understands the system (the one who coded it) maintains bargaining power and becomes relatively indispensable. When the programmer leaves the firm, however, a new programmer inherits maintenance responsibility for the undocumented system. Depending on its complexity, the transition period may be long and costly.

PROGRAM FRAUD. When the original programmer of a system is also assigned maintenance responsibility, the potential for fraud is increased. Program fraud involves making unauthorized changes to program modules for the purpose of committing an illegal act. The original programmer may have successfully concealed fraudulent code among the thousands of lines of legitimate code and the hundreds of modules that constitute a system. For the fraud to work successfully,

FIGURE 15-5 ALTERNATIVE ORGANIZATION OF SYSTEMS DEVELOPMENT

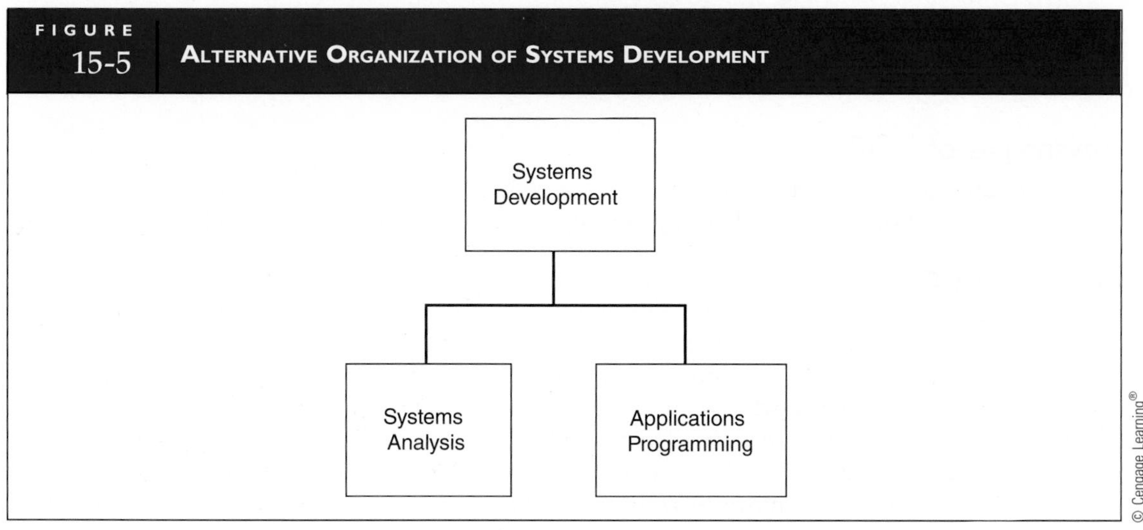

however, the programmer must be able to control the situation through exclusive and unrestricted access to the application's programs. The programmer needs to protect the fraudulent code from accidental detection by another programmer performing maintenance or by auditors testing application controls. Therefore, having sole responsibility for maintenance is an important element in the duplicitous programmer's scheme. Through this maintenance authority, the programmer may freely access the system, disabling fraudulent code during audits and then restoring the code when the coast is clear. Frauds of this sort may continue for years without detection.

A Superior Structure for Systems Development

Figure 15-4 presents a superior organizational structure in which the systems development function is separated into two independent groups: new systems development and systems maintenance. The new systems development group is responsible for designing, programming, and implementing new systems projects. Upon successful implementation, responsibility for the system's ongoing maintenance falls to the systems maintenance group. This structure helps resolve the two control problems described previously.

First, documentation standards are improved because the maintenance group will require adequate documentation to perform their maintenance duties. Without complete documentation, the formal transfer of system responsibility from new systems development to systems maintenance cannot occur.

Second, denying the original programmer future access to the application code deters program fraud. Fraudulent code within an application, which is out of the perpetrator's control, increases the risk that the fraud will be discovered. The success of this control depends on the existence of other controls that limit, prevent, and detect unauthorized access to programs. These controls are discussed in Chapter 17. Although organizational separations alone cannot guarantee that computer frauds will not occur, they are critical to creating the control environment needed to reduce the risk.

THE DISTRIBUTED MODEL

An alternative to the centralized model is the concept of **distributed data processing (DDP)**. The topic of DDP is quite broad, touching on such related topics as end-user computing, commercial software, networking, and office automation. Simply stated, DDP involves reorganizing the IT function into small units that are distributed to end users and placed under their control. Any or all of the IT activities represented in Figure 15-4 may be distributed. Figure 15-6 shows a possible new organizational structure following the distribution of all data processing tasks to the end-user areas.

Notice that the central IT function has been eliminated from the organizational structure. Individual IT units now perform this role. In recent years, **DDP** has become an economic and operational feasibility that has revolutionized business operations. However, DDP is a mixed bag of advantages and disadvantages.

Advantages of DDP

The most commonly cited advantages of DDP are related to cost savings, increased user satisfaction, and improved operational efficiency. Specific issues are discussed in the following section.

COST REDUCTIONS. Achieving economies of scale is the principal justification for the centralized approach. The economics of data processing favored large, expensive, powerful computers. The wide variety of needs that such centralized systems had to satisfy called for computers that were highly generalized and that employed complex operating systems. Powerful yet inexpensive small-scale computer systems, which can cost-effectively perform specialized functions, have changed the economics of data processing dramatically. In addition, the unit cost of data storage, which was once the justification for consolidating data in a central location, is no longer a prime consideration. Moreover, the move to **DDP** can reduce costs in two other areas: (1) data can be entered and edited locally, thus eliminating the centralized tasks of data conversion and data

FIGURE 15-6 ORGANIZATIONAL STRUCTURE FOR A DISTRIBUTED SYSTEM

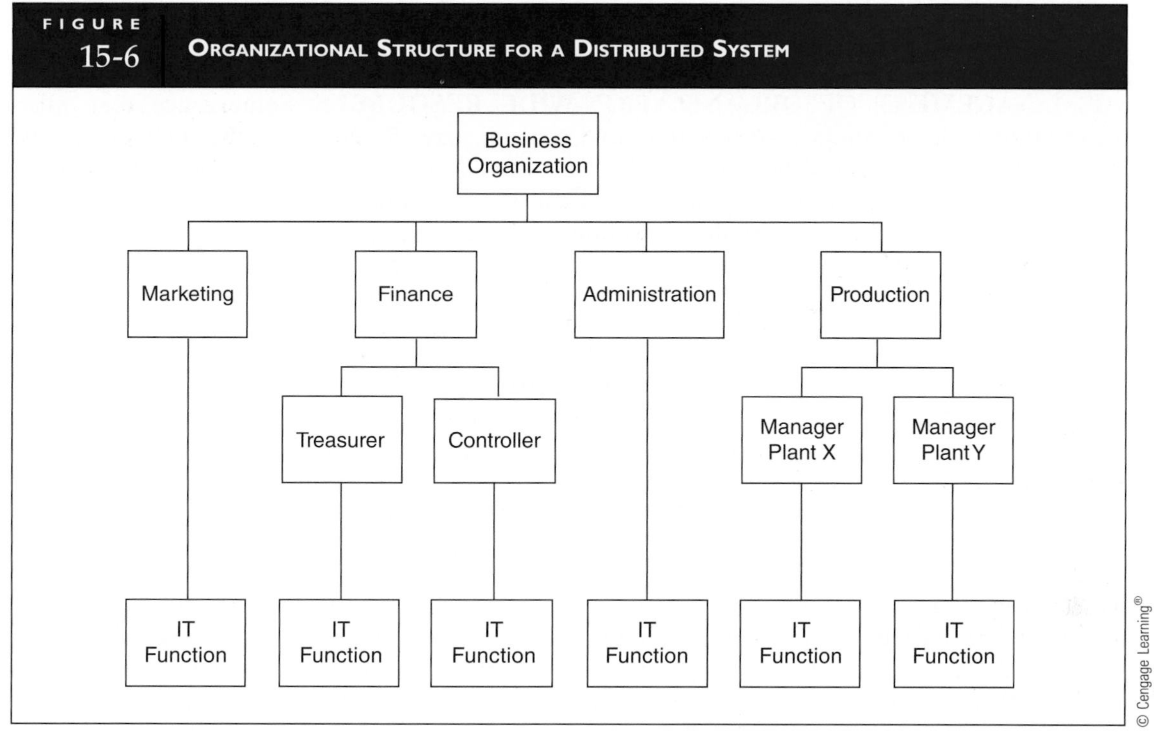

control, and (2) application complexity can be reduced, which in turn reduces development and maintenance costs.

IMPROVED COST CONTROL RESPONSIBILITY. Managers assume responsibility for the financial success of their operations. This requires that they be properly empowered with the authority to make decisions about resources that influence their overall success. Therefore, if information-processing capability is critical to the success of a business operation, then should management not be given control over these resources?

IMPROVED USER SATISFACTION. Perhaps the most often cited benefit of DDP is improved user satisfaction. This derives from three areas of need that too often go unsatisfied in the centralized approach: (1) as previously stated, users desire to control the resources that influence their profitability, (2) users want systems professionals (analysts, programmers, and computer operators) who are responsive to their specific situation, and (3) users want to become more actively involved in developing and implementing their own systems. Proponents of DDP argue that providing more customized support—feasible only in a distributed environment—has direct benefits for user morale and productivity.

BACKUP. The final argument in favor of DDP is the ability to back up computing facilities to protect against potential disasters such as fires, floods, sabotage, and earthquakes. One solution is to build excess capacity into each IT unit. If a disaster destroys a single site, its transactions can be processed by the other sites. This requires close coordination between decision makers to ensure that they do not implement incompatible hardware and software at their sites.

Disadvantages of DDP

This discussion focuses on important issues that carry control implications that accountants should recognize. The loss of control is one of the most serious disadvantages of DDP. Other potential problems include the inefficient use of resources, the destruction of audit trails, inadequate segregation of duties, an increased potential for programming errors and systems failures, and the lack of standards. Specific problems are examined in the following section.

MISMANAGEMENT OF ORGANIZATION-WIDE RESOURCES. Some argue that when organization-wide resources exceed a threshold amount, say, 5 percent of the total operations budget, the resources should be controlled and monitored centrally. This argument counters the argument presented earlier favoring the distribution of organization-wide resources. Information-processing services (such as computer operations, programming, data conversion, and database management) represent a significant expenditure for many organizations. Those opposed to DDP argue that distributing responsibility for these resources will inevitably lead to their mismanagement and suboptimal utilization.

HARDWARE AND SOFTWARE INCOMPATIBILITY. Distributing the responsibility for hardware and software purchases to user management can result in uncoordinated and poorly conceived decisions. Working independently, decision makers may settle on dissimilar and incompatible operating systems, technology platforms, spreadsheet programs, word processors, and database packages. Such hardware and software incompatibilities can degrade and disrupt communications between organizational units.

REDUNDANT TASKS. Autonomous systems development activities distributed throughout the firm can result in each user area reinventing the wheel. For example, application programs created by one user, which could be used with little or no change by others, will be redesigned from scratch rather than shared. Likewise, data common to many users may be recreated for each of them, resulting in a high level of data redundancy.

CONSOLIDATING INCOMPATIBLE ACTIVITIES. The distribution of the IT function to individual user areas results in the creation of many very small units that may not permit the necessary separation of incompatible functions. For example, within a single IT unit, the same person may program applications, perform program maintenance, enter transaction data into the computer, and operate the computer equipment. This situation represents a fundamental violation of internal control.

HIRING QUALIFIED PROFESSIONALS. End-user managers may lack the knowledge to evaluate the technical credentials and relevant experience of candidates applying for a position as a computer professional. Also, if the organizational unit into which a new employee is entering is small, the opportunity for personal growth, continuing education, and promotion may be limited. For these reasons, end-user managers sometimes experience difficulty attracting highly qualified personnel, which increases the risk of programming errors and systems failures.

LACK OF STANDARDS. Because of the distribution of responsibility in the DDP environment, standards for developing and documenting systems, choosing programming languages, acquiring hardware and software, and evaluating performance may be unevenly applied or nonexistent. Opponents of DDP argue that the risks associated with the design and operation of a data processing system is made tolerable only if such standards are consistently applied. This requires that standards be imposed centrally.

CREATING A CORPORATE IT FUNCTION

The completely centralized and the fully distributed models represent extreme positions on a continuum of structural alternatives. The needs of most firms fall somewhere between these end points. For these firms, the control problems associated with DDP can, to some extent, be overcome by implementing a **corporate IT function**. Figure 15-7 illustrates this organizational approach.

The corporate IT function is a leaner unit with a mission different from that of the centralized IT function shown in Figure 15-4. This group provides technical advice and expertise to the

FIGURE 15-7 DISTRIBUTED ORGANIZATION WITH CORPORATE IT FUNCTION

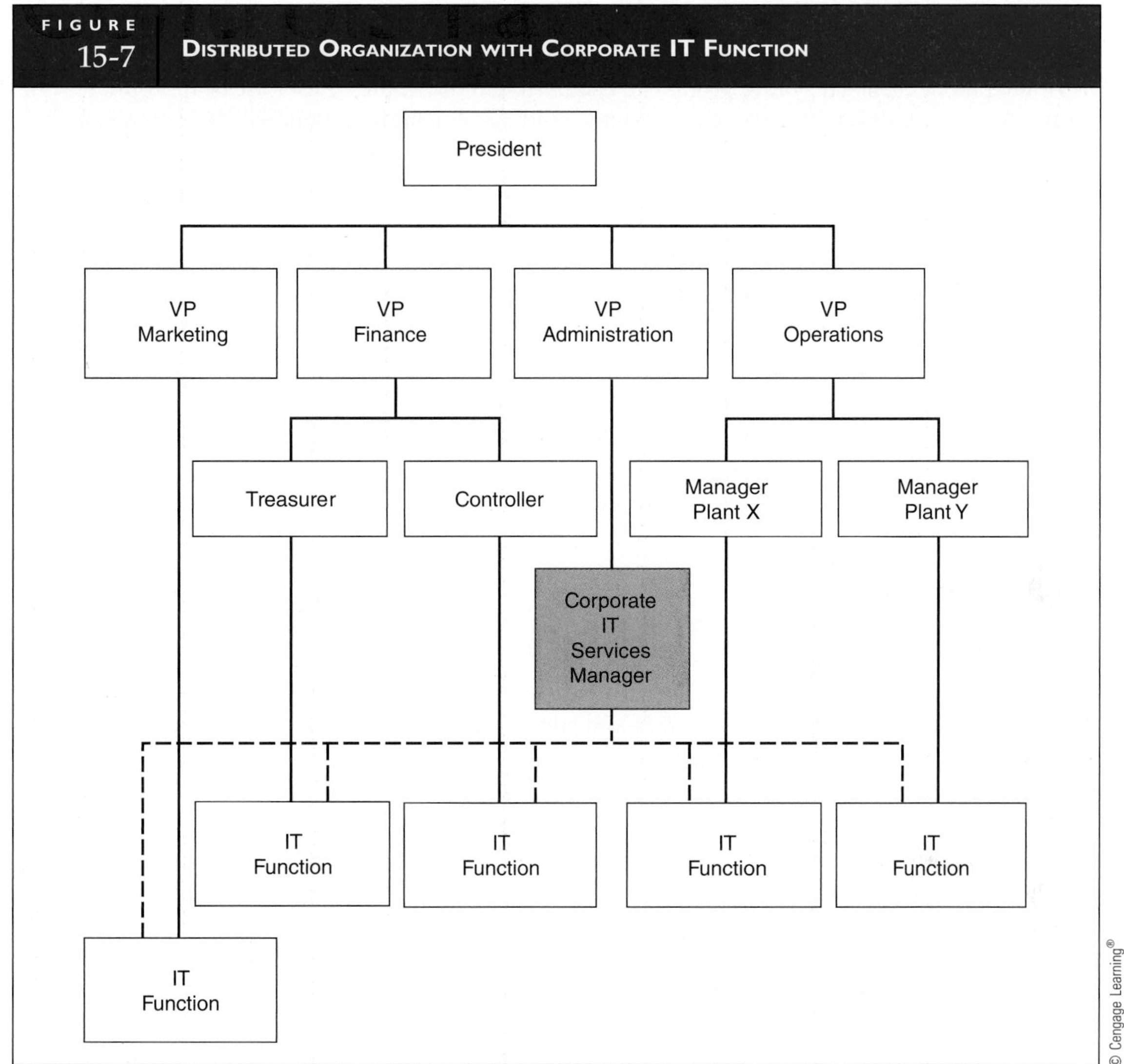

various distributed IT functions, as the dotted lines represent in Figure 15-7. Some of the support services provided are described in the following section.

Central Testing of Commercial Software and Hardware

The corporate IT group is better able to evaluate the merits of competing vendor software and hardware. A central, technically astute group such as this can evaluate systems features, controls, and compatibility with industry and organizational standards most efficiently. After testing, they can make recommendations to user areas for guiding acquisition decisions.

User Services

A valuable feature of the corporate group is its user services function. This activity provides technical help to users during the installation of new software and in troubleshooting hardware and software problems. The creation of an electronic bulletin board for users is an excellent way to distribute information about common problems and allows the sharing of user-developed programs with others in the organization. User services staff often teach technical courses for end users, which raises the level of user awareness and promotes the continued education of technical personnel.

Standard-Setting Body

Establishing central guidance can improve the relatively poor control environment common to the distributed model. The corporate group can establish and distribute to user areas appropriate standards for systems development, programming, and documentation that will be compliant with SOX requirements.

Personnel Review

The corporate group is better equipped than users to evaluate the technical credentials of prospective systems professionals. Although the prospective IT hires will work for the distributed user groups, the involvement of the corporate group in hiring decisions can render a valuable service to the organization.

AUDIT OBJECTIVES RELATING TO ORGANIZATIONAL STRUCTURE

The auditor's objective is to ascertain whether individuals serving in incompatible areas are segregated in accordance with an acceptable level of risk and in a manner that promotes an effective working environment.

AUDIT PROCEDURES RELATING TO ORGANIZATIONAL STRUCTURE

The following audit tests would provide evidence to achieve the audit objective.

- Obtain and review the corporate policy on computer security. Verify that the security policy is communicated to responsible employees and supervisors.
- Review relevant documentation, including the current organizational chart, mission statement, and job descriptions for key functions, to determine if individuals or groups are performing incompatible functions.
- Review systems documentation and maintenance records for a sample of applications. Verify that maintenance programmers assigned to specific projects are not also the original design programmers.
- Through observation, determine that the segregation policy is being followed in practice. Review operations room access logs to determine whether programmers enter the facility for reasons other than system failures.
- Review user roles to verify that programmers have access privileges consistent with their job descriptions.

Computer Center Security and Controls

Fires, floods, wind, sabotage, earthquakes, or even power outages can deprive an organization of its data processing facilities and bring to a halt those functions that are performed or aided by computer. Although the likelihood of such a disastrous event is remote, the consequences to the organization could be serious. If a disaster occurs, the organization not only loses its investment in data processing facilities, but more importantly, it also loses its ability to do business.

The objective of this section is to present computer center controls that help create a secure environment. We will begin with a look at controls designed to prevent and detect threats to the computer center. However, no matter how much is invested in control, some disasters simply cannot be anticipated and prevented. What does a company do to prepare itself for such an event? How will it recover? These questions are at the heart of the organization's disaster recovery plan. The next section deals specifically with issues pertaining to the development of a disaster recovery plan.

COMPUTER CENTER CONTROLS

Weaknesses in computer center security have a potential impact on the function of application controls related to the financial reporting process. Therefore, this physical environment is a control issue for SOX compliance. The following are some of the control features that contribute directly to computer center security.

Physical Location

The physical location selected for a computer center can influence the risk of disaster. To the extent possible, the computer center should be located away from human-made and natural hazards, such as processing plants, gas and water mains, airports, high-crime areas, flood plains, and geological faults.

Construction

Ideally, a computer center should be located in a single-story building of solid construction with controlled access (discussed in the following section). Utility (power and telephone) and communications lines should be underground. The building windows should not open. An air filtration system should be in place that is capable of excluding pollens, dust, and dust mites.

Access

Access to the computer center should be limited to the operators and other employees who work there. Programmers and analysts who occasionally need to correct program errors should be required to sign in and out. The computer center should maintain accurate records of all such events to verify the function of access control. The main entrance to the computer center should be through a single door, although fire exits with alarms are necessary. To achieve a higher level of security, closed-circuit cameras and video recording systems should monitor access.

Air Conditioning

Computers function best in an air-conditioned environment. For mainframe computers, providing adequate air conditioning is often a requirement of the vendor's warranty. Computers operate best in a temperature range of 70 to 75 degrees Fahrenheit and a relative humidity of 50 percent. Logic errors can occur in computer hardware when temperatures depart significantly from this range. Also, the risk of circuit damage from static electricity is increased when humidity drops. High humidity, on the other hand, can cause molds to grow and paper products (such as source documents) to swell and jam equipment.

Fire Suppression

The most common threat to a firm's computer equipment is fire. Half of the companies that suffer fires go out of business because of the loss of critical records, such as accounts receivable. The implementation of an effective fire-suppression system requires consultation with specialists. Some of the major features of such a system are listed in the following section.

1. Automatic and manual alarms should be placed in strategic locations around the installation. These alarms should be connected to a permanently staffed firefighting station.
2. There must be an automatic fire-extinguishing system that dispenses the appropriate type of suppressant (carbon dioxide or halon) for the location. For example, spraying water and certain chemicals on a computer can do as much damage as the fire.
3. Manual fire extinguishers should be placed at strategic locations.
4. The building should be of sound construction to withstand water damage that fire-suppression equipment causes.
5. Fire exits should be clearly marked and illuminated during a fire.

Fault Tolerance Controls

Fault tolerance is the ability of the system to continue operation when part of the system fails because of hardware failure, application program error, or operator error. Implementing redundant system components can achieve various levels of fault tolerance. Redundant disks and power supplies are two common examples.

> **Redundant arrays of independent disks (RAID)** *involves using parallel disks that contain redundant elements of data and applications. If one disk fails, the lost data are automatically reconstructed from the redundant components stored on the other disks.*
>
> **Uninterruptible power supplies** *help prevent data loss and system corruption. In the event of a power supply failure, short-term backup power is provided to allow the system to shut down in a controlled manner. Implementing fault tolerance control ensures that there is no single point of potential system failure. Total failure can occur only in the event of the failure of multiple components.*

Audit Objectives Relating to Computer Center Security

The audit objectives are to determine whether: (1) controls governing computer center security are adequate to reasonably protect the organization from physical damage or losses; (2) insurance coverage on equipment is adequate to compensate the organization for the destruction of, or damage to, its computer center; and (3) operator documentation is adequate to deal with system failures as well as routine operations.

Audit Procedures for Assessing Physical Security Controls

The following are tests of physical security controls.

TESTS OF PHYSICAL CONSTRUCTION. The auditor should obtain architectural plans to determine that the computer center is solidly built of fireproof material. There should be adequate drainage under the raised floor to allow water to flow away in the event of water damage from a fire in an upper floor or from some other source. In addition, the auditor should assess the physical location of the computer center. The facility should be located in an area that minimizes its exposure to fire, civil unrest, and other hazards.

TESTS OF THE FIRE DETECTION SYSTEM. The auditor should establish that fire detection and suppression equipment, both manual and automatic, are in place and are tested regularly. The fire detection system should detect smoke, heat, and combustible fumes. The evidence may be obtained by reviewing official fire marshal records of tests, which are stored at the computer center.

TESTS OF ACCESS CONTROL. The auditor must establish that routine access to the computer center is restricted to authorized employees. Details about visitor access (by programmers and others), such as arrival and departure times, purpose, and frequency of access, can be obtained by reviewing the access log. To establish the veracity of this document, the auditor may covertly observe the process by which access is permitted.

Tests of Fault Tolerance Controls

RAID. Many RAID configurations provide a graphical mapping of their redundant disk storage. From this mapping, the auditor should determine if the level of RAID in place is adequate for the organization, given the level of business risk associated with disk failure. If the organization is not employing RAID, the potential for a single point of system failure exists. The auditor should review with the system administrator alternative procedures for recovering from a disk failure.

POWER SUPPLIES BACKUP. The auditor should verify from test records that computer center personnel perform periodic tests of the backup power supply to ensure that it has sufficient capacity to run the computer and air conditioning. These important tests and their results should be formally recorded.

Audit Procedures for Verifying Insurance Coverage

The auditor should annually review the organization's insurance coverage on its computer hardware, software, and physical facility. The auditor should verify that all new acquisitions are listed on the policy and that obsolete equipment and software have been deleted. The insurance policy should reflect management's needs in terms of extent of coverage. For example, the firm may wish to be partially self-insured and require minimum coverage. On the other hand, the firm may seek complete replacement-cost coverage.

Audit Procedures for Verifying Adequacy of Operator Documentation

Computer operators use documentation called a run manual to run certain aspects of the system. In particular, large batch systems often require special attention from operators. During the course of the day, computer operators may execute dozens of computer programs, each of which might process multiple files and produce multiple reports. To achieve effective data processing operations, the run manual must be sufficiently detailed to guide operators in their tasks. The auditor should review the run manual for completeness and accuracy. The typical contents of a run manual include:

- The name of the system, such as "Purchases System"
- The run schedule (daily, weekly, time of day)
- Required hardware devices (tapes, disks, printers, or special hardware)
- File requirements specifying all the transaction (input) files, master files, and output files used in the system
- Run-time instructions describing the error messages that may appear, actions to be taken, and the name and telephone number of the programmer on call, should the system fail
- A list of users who receive the output from the run

Also, the auditor should verify that certain systems documentation, such as systems flowcharts, logic flowcharts, and program code listings, are not part of the operator's documentation. For reasons previously discussed, operators should not have access to the operational details of a system's internal logic.

Disaster Recovery Planning

Some disasters cannot be prevented or evaded. Recent events include hurricanes, widespread flooding, earthquakes, and the events of September 11, 2001. The survival of a firm affected by a disaster depends on how it reacts. With careful contingency planning, the full impact of a disaster can be absorbed, and the organization can still recover.

A **disaster recovery plan (DRP)** is a comprehensive statement of all actions to be taken before, during, and after a disaster, along with documented, tested procedures that will ensure the continuity of operations. Although the details of each plan are unique to the needs of the organization, all workable plans possess common features. The remainder of this section is devoted to a discussion of the following control issues: providing second-site backup, identifying critical applications, performing backup and **off-site storage** procedures, creating a disaster recovery team, and testing the DRP.

PROVIDING SECOND-SITE BACKUP

A necessary ingredient in a DRP is that it provides for duplicate data processing facilities following a disaster. The viable options available include the empty shell, recovery operations center, and internally provided backup.

The Empty Shell

The **empty shell** or cold site plan is an arrangement wherein the company buys or leases a building that will serve as a data center. In the event of a disaster, the shell is available and ready to receive whatever hardware the temporary user needs to run essential systems. This approach, however, has a fundamental weakness. Recovery depends on the timely availability of the necessary computer hardware to restore the data processing function. Management must obtain assurances (contracts) from hardware vendors that in the event of a disaster, the vendor will give priority to the company's computing needs. An unanticipated hardware supply problem at this critical juncture could be a fatal blow.

The Recovery Operations Center

A **recovery operations center (ROC)** or hot site is a fully equipped backup data center that many companies share. In addition to hardware and backup facilities, ROC service providers offer a range of technical services to their clients, who pay an annual fee for access rights. In the event of a major disaster, a subscriber can occupy the premises and, within a few hours, resume processing critical applications.

September 11, 2001, was a true test of the reliability and effectiveness of the ROC approach. Comdisco, a major ROC provider, had 47 clients who declared 93 separate disasters on the day of the attack. All 47 companies relocated and worked out of Comdisco's recovery centers. At one point, 3,000 client employees were working out of the centers. Thousands of computers were configured for clients' needs within the first 24 hours, and systems recovery teams were on-site wherever police permitted access. By September 25, nearly half of the clients were able to return to their facilities with a fully functional system.

A problem with this approach is the potential for competition among users for the ROC resources. A widespread natural disaster, such as a flood or an earthquake, may destroy the data processing capabilities of several ROC members located in the same geographic area. All the victims will find themselves vying for access to the same limited facilities. Because some ROC service providers oversell their capacity by a ratio of 20:1, the situation is analogous to a sinking ship that has an inadequate number of lifeboats.

The period of confusion following a disaster is not an ideal time to negotiate property rights. Therefore, before entering into an ROC arrangement, management should consider the potential problems of overcrowding and geographic clustering of the current membership.

Internally Provided Backup

Larger organizations with multiple data processing centers often prefer the self-reliance that creating internal excess capacity provides. This permits firms to develop standardized hardware and software configurations, which ensure functional compatibility among their data processing centers and minimize cutover problems in the event of a disaster.

Pershing, a division of Donaldson, Lufkin & Jenrette Securities Corporation, processes more than 36 million transactions per day, about 2,000 per second. Pershing management recognized that an ROC vendor could not provide the recovery time they wanted and needed. The company, therefore, built its own remote **mirrored data center**. The facility is equipped with high-capacity storage devices capable of storing more than 20 terabytes of data and two IBM mainframes running high-speed copy software. All transactions that the main system processes are transmitted in real time along fiber-optic cables to the remote backup facility. At any point in time, the mirrored data center reflects current economic events of the firm. The mirrored system has reduced Pershing's data recovery time from 24 hours to 1 hour.

IDENTIFYING CRITICAL APPLICATIONS

Another essential element of a DRP involves procedures to identify the critical applications and data files of the firm to be restored. Eventually, all applications and data must be restored to pre-disaster business activity levels. Immediate recovery efforts, however, should focus on restoring those applications and data that are critical to the organization's short-term survival. In any disaster scenario, it is short-term survivability that determines long-term survival.

For most organizations, short-term survival requires the restoration of those functions that generate cash flows sufficient to satisfy short-term obligations. For example, assume that the following functions affect the cash flow position of a particular firm:

- Customer sales and service
- Fulfillment of legal obligations
- Accounts receivable maintenance and collection
- Production and distribution
- Purchasing
- Communications between branches or agencies
- Public relations

The computer applications that support these functions directly are critical. Hence, these applications should be so identified and prioritized in the restoration plan.

Application priorities may change over time, and these decisions must be reassessed regularly. Systems are constantly revised and expanded to reflect changes in user requirements. Similarly, the DRP must be updated to reflect new developments and identify critical applications. Up-to-date priorities are important because they affect other aspects of the strategic plan. For example, changes in application priorities may cause changes in the nature and extent of second-site backup requirements and specific backup procedures.

The task of identifying and prioritizing critical applications requires active participation of management, user departments, and internal auditors. Too often, this task is incorrectly perceived to be an IT issue and delegated to IT professionals. Although the technical assistance of systems personnel is required, this is primarily a business decision and those best equipped to understand the business problem should make it.

PERFORMING BACKUP AND OFF-SITE STORAGE PROCEDURES

All data files, application documentation, and supplies needed to perform critical functions should be specified in the DRP. Data processing personnel should routinely perform backup and storage procedures to safeguard these critical resources.

Backup Data Files

The state-of-the-art in database backup is the remote mirrored site, described previously, which provides complete data currency. Not all organizations are willing or able to invest in such backup resources. As a minimum, however, databases should be copied daily to tape or disks and secured off-site. In the event of a disruption, reconstruction of the database is achieved by updating the most current backup version with subsequent transaction data. Likewise, master files and transaction files should be protected.

Backup Documentation

The system documentation for critical applications should be backed up and stored off-site in much the same manner as data files. The large volumes of material involved and constant application revisions complicate the task. The process can be made more efficient through the use of computer-aided software engineering (CASE) documentation tools.

Backup Supplies and Source Documents

The firm should maintain backup inventories of supplies and source documents used in critical applications. Examples of critical supplies are check stocks, invoices, purchase orders, and any other special-purpose forms that cannot be obtained immediately.

CREATING A DISASTER RECOVERY TEAM

Recovering from a disaster depends on timely corrective action. Failure to perform essential tasks (such as obtaining backup files for critical applications) prolongs the recovery period and diminishes the prospects for a successful recovery. To avoid serious omissions or duplication of efforts during implementation of the contingency plan, individual task responsibility must be clearly defined and communicated to the personnel involved.

Figure 15-8 presents an organizational chart depicting the possible composition of a disaster recovery team. The team members should be experts in their areas and have assigned tasks. Following a disaster, team members will delegate subtasks to their subordinates. It should be noted that traditional control concerns do not apply in this setting. The environment the disaster creates may necessitate the breaching of normal controls such as segregation of duties, access controls, and supervision. At this point, business continuity is the primary consideration.

FIGURE 15-8 DISASTER RECOVERY TEAM

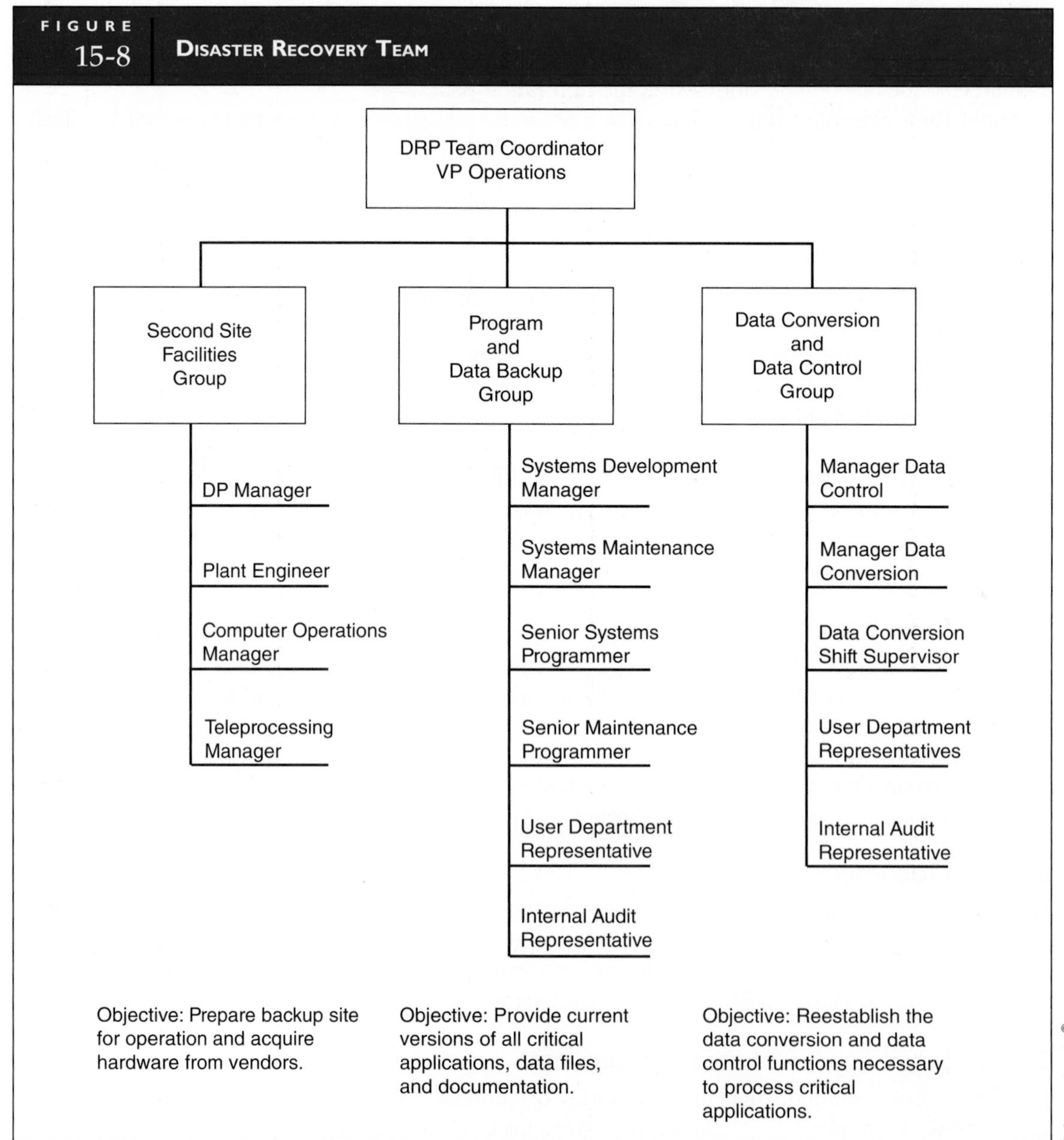

TESTING THE DRP

The most neglected aspect of contingency planning is testing of the plans. Nevertheless, DRP tests are important and should be performed periodically. Tests provide measures of the preparedness of personnel and identify omissions or bottlenecks in the plan.

A test is most useful in the form of a surprise simulation of a disruption. When the mock disaster is announced, the status of all processing that it affects should be documented. This provides a benchmark for subsequent performance assessments. The plan should be carried as far as is economically feasible. Ideally, this will include the use of backup facilities and supplies.

AUDIT OBJECTIVE: ASSESSING DISASTER RECOVERY PLANNING

The auditor should verify that management's disaster recovery plan is adequate and feasible for dealing with a catastrophe that could deprive the organization of its computing resources. The following tests focus on the areas of greatest concern.

AUDIT PROCEDURES FOR ASSESSING DISASTER RECOVERY PLANNING

Second-Site Backup

The auditor should evaluate the adequacy of the backup site arrangement. The client should possess vendor contracts guaranteeing timely equipment delivery to the cold site. In the case of ROC membership, the auditor should obtain information as to the total number of members and their geographic dispersion. A widespread disaster may create a demand that the backup facility cannot satisfy.

Critical Application List

The auditor should review the list of critical applications and ensure that it is up-to-date and complete. Missing applications may result in failure to recover. On the other hand, restoring noncritical applications diverts scarce resources to nonproductive tasks.

Backup Critical Applications and Critical Data Files

The auditor should verify that the organization has procedures in place to back up stored off-site copies of critical applications and data. Evidence of this can be obtained by selecting a sample of data files and programs and determining if they are being backed up as required.

Backup Supplies, Source Documents, and Documentation

The system documentation, supplies, and source documents needed to restore and run critical applications should be backed up and stored off-site. The auditor should verify that the types and quantities of items specified in the DRP exist in a secure location.

The Disaster Recovery Team

The DRP should clearly list the names, addresses, and emergency telephone numbers of the disaster recovery team members. The auditor should verify that members of the team are current employees and are aware of their assigned responsibilities. On one occasion, while reviewing a firm's DRP, the author discovered that a team leader listed in the plan had been deceased for nine months.

Outsourcing the IT Function

The costs, risks, and responsibilities associated with maintaining an effective corporate IT function are significant. Many executives have therefore opted to outsource their IT functions to third-party vendors who take over responsibility for the management of IT assets and staff and for delivery of IT services, such as data entry, data center operations, applications development, applications maintenance, and network management. Often-cited benefits of **IT outsourcing** include improved core business performance, improved IT performance (because of the vendor's expertise), and reduced IT costs. By moving IT facilities offshore to low labor-cost areas and/or through economies of scale (by combining the work of several clients), the vendor can perform the outsourced function more cheaply than the client firm could have otherwise. The resulting cost savings are then passed to the client organization. Furthermore, many IT outsourcing arrangements involve the sale of the client firm's IT assets, both human and machine, to the vendor, which the client firm then leases back. This transaction results in a significant one-time cash infusion into the firm.

The logic underlying IT outsourcing follows from **core competency** theory, which argues that an organization should focus exclusively on its core business competencies, while allowing outsourcing vendors to efficiently manage the noncore areas such as the IT functions. This premise, however, ignores an important distinction between commodity and specific IT assets.

Commodity IT assets are not unique to a particular organization and are thus easily acquired in the marketplace. These include such things as network management, systems operations, server maintenance, and help-desk functions. As we saw in Chapter 12, even IT infrastructure and application software are provided as commodities through the cloud computing options of IaaS and SaaS, respectively. **Specific IT assets**, in contrast, are unique to the organization and support its strategic objectives. Because of their idiosyncratic nature, specific assets have little value outside their current use. Such assets may be tangible (computer equipment), intellectual (computer programs), or human. Examples of specific assets include systems development, application maintenance, data warehousing, and highly skilled employees trained to use organization-specific software.

Transaction Cost Economics (TCE) theory is in conflict with the core competency school by suggesting that firms should retain certain specific noncore IT assets in-house. Because of their esoteric nature, specific assets cannot be easily replaced once they are given up in an outsourcing arrangement. Therefore, if the organization should decide to cancel its outsourcing contract with the vendor, it may not be able to return to its pre-outsource state. On the other hand, TCE theory supports the outsourcing of commodity assets, which are easily replaced or obtained from alternative vendors.

Naturally, a CEO's perception of what constitutes a commodity IT asset plays an important role in IT outsourcing decisions. Often, this comes down to a matter of definition and interpretation. For example, most CEOs would define their IT function as a noncore commodity, unless they are in the business of developing and selling IT applications. Consequently, a belief that *all* IT can, and should, be managed by large service organizations tends to prevail. Such misperception reflects, in part, both lack of executive education and the dissemination of faulty information regarding the virtues and limitations of IT outsourcing.[8]

RISKS INHERENT TO IT OUTSOURCING

Large-scale IT outsourcing events are risky endeavors, partly because of the sheer size of these financial deals, and also because of their nature. The level of risk is related to the degree of asset specificity of the outsourced function. The following sections outline some well-documented issues.

Failure to Perform

Once a client firm has outsourced specific IT assets, its performance becomes linked to the vendor's performance. The negative implications of such dependency are illustrated in the financial problems that have plagued the huge outsourcing vendor Electronic Data Systems Corp. (EDS). In a cost-cutting effort, EDS terminated 7000 employees, which impacted its ability to serve other clients. Following an 11-year low in share prices, EDS stockholders filed a class-action

8 This knowledge disconnect is not unique to IT outsourcing; it has been observed by Ramiller and Swanson in their research on how executives respond to what is termed *organizing visions* for IT.

lawsuit against the company. Clearly, vendors experiencing such serious financial and legal problems threaten the viability of their clients also.

Vendor Exploitation of Clients

Large-scale IT outsourcing involves transferring to a vendor "specific assets," such as the design, development, and maintenance of unique business applications that are critical to an organization's survival. Specific assets, while valuable to the client, are of little value to the vendor beyond the immediate contract with the client. Indeed, they may well be valueless should the client organization go out of business. Because the vendor assumes risk by acquiring the assets and can achieve no economies of scale by employing them elsewhere, the client organization will pay a premium to transfer such functions to a third party. Further, once the client firm has divested itself of such specific assets, it becomes dependent on the vendor. The vendor may exploit this dependency by raising service rates to an exorbitant level. As the client's IT needs develop over time beyond the original contract terms, it runs the risk that new or incremental services will be negotiated at a premium. This dependency may threaten the client's long-term flexibility, agility, and competitiveness, and result in even greater vendor dependency.

Outsourcing Costs Exceed Benefits

IT outsourcing has been criticized on the grounds that unexpected costs arise and that the full extent of expected benefits are not realized. One survey revealed that 47 percent of 66 firms surveyed reported that the costs of IT outsourcing exceeded outsourcing benefits. One reason for this is that outsourcing clients often fail to anticipate the costs of vendor selection, contracting, and the transitioning of IT operations to the vendors.

Reduced Security

Information outsourced to offshore IT vendors raises unique and serious questions regarding internal control and the protection of sensitive personal data. When corporate financial systems are developed and hosted overseas, and program code is developed through interfaces with the host company's network, US corporations are at risk of losing control of their information. To a large degree, US firms are reliant on the outsourcing vendor's security measures, data-access policies, and the privacy laws of the host country. For example, a woman in Pakistan obtained patient-sensitive medical data from the University of California Medical Center in San Francisco. She gained access to the data from a medical transcription vendor for whom she worked. The woman threatened to publish the records on the Internet if she did not get a raise in pay. Terrorism in Asia and the Middle East raises additional security concerns for companies outsourcing technology offshore. For example, on March 5, 2005, police in Delhi, India, arrested a cell of suspected terrorists who were planning to attack outsourcing firms in Bangalore, India.

LOSS OF STRATEGIC ADVANTAGE

IT outsourcing may cause incongruence between a firm's IT strategic planning and its business planning functions. Organizations that use IT strategically must align business strategy and IT strategy or run the risk of decreased business performance. To promote such alignment, firms need IT managers and chief information officers (CIOs) who have a strong working knowledge of the organization's business. A survey of 213 IT managers in the financial services industry confirmed that a firm's IT leadership needs to be closely aligned with the firm's competitive strategy. Indeed, some argue that the business competence of CIOs is more important than their IT competence in facilitating strategic congruence.

To accomplish such alignment necessitates a close working relationship between corporate management and IT management in the concurrent development of business and IT strategies. This, however, is difficult to accomplish when IT planning is geographically redeployed offshore or even domestically. Further, because the financial justification for IT outsourcing depends upon the vendor achieving economies of scale, the vendor is naturally driven toward seeking common solutions that may be used by many clients rather than creating unique solutions for each of them. This fundamental underpinning of IT outsourcing is inconsistent with the client's pursuit of strategic advantage in the marketplace.

AUDIT IMPLICATIONS OF IT OUTSOURCING

Management may outsource its organization's IT functions, but cannot outsource its management responsibilities under SOX for ensuring adequate IT internal controls. The PCAOB specifically states in its Auditing Standard No. 2, that the use of a service organization does not reduce management's responsibility to maintain effective internal control over financial reporting. Therefore, if an audit client firm outsources its IT function to a vendor that processes its transactions, hosts key data, or performs other significant services, the auditor will need to conduct an evaluation of the vendor organization's controls, or alternatively obtain an SSAE 16 auditor's report from the vendor organization.

Statement on Standards for Attestation Engagements No. 16 (SSAE 16) is an internationally recognized third-party attestation report designed for service organizations such as IT outsourcing vendors. SSAE 16 was promulgated by the Auditing Standards Board (ASB) of the AICPA and replaced Statement on Auditing Standards No. 70 (SAS 70) on June 15, 2011. Its purpose was to update the outdated SAS 70, which had been in service since 1992. More importantly, its objective was to keep pace with move toward globally accepted international accounting standards.

SSAE 16 is the definitive standard by which client organizations' auditors can determine whether processes and controls at the third-party vendor are adequate to prevent or detect material errors that could impact the client's financial statements. The SSAE 16 report, which is prepared by the service provider's auditor, attests to the functionality of the vendor's system and the adequacy of its internal controls. This is the means by which an outsourcing vendor can obtain a single attest report that may be used by its clients' auditors and thus preclude the need for each client firm auditor to conduct its own audit of the vendor organization's facilities and internal controls.

Figure 15-9 illustrates how an SSAE 16 report works in relation to the vendor, the client firms, and their respective auditors. The outsourcing vendor serves clients 1, 2, 3, and 4 with various IT services. The system processes and internal controls over the outsourced services reside at the vendor location. They are audited by the vendor's auditor, who expresses an opinion and issues an SSAE 16 report. Each of the client firms is audited by different auditors A, B, C, and D, respectively, who as part of their respective audits, rely on the vendor's SSAE 16 report and are thus not compelled to individually test the vendor's controls. Given that a vendor may have hundreds or even thousands of clients, individual testing under SOX would be highly disruptive to the vendor's operations, costly to the client, and impractical.

Service provider auditors issue two types of SSAE 16 reports, Type 1 and Type 2:

The Type 1 report attests to the vendor management's description of their system and the suitability of the design of controls.

The Type 2 report attests to management's description of their system, the suitability of the design of controls, and the operating effectiveness of controls.

The Type 1 report is the less rigorous of the two and comments only on the suitability of the controls' design. The Type 2 report goes further and assesses whether the controls are operating effectively based on tests conducted by the vendor organization's auditor. Because SOX Section 404 requires the explicit testing of controls, SSAE 16 Type 2 reports are necessary for client firms undergoing a financial statement audit.

SSAE 16 REPORT CONTENTS

The SSAE 16 attest report provides a description of the service provider's system including details of how transactions are processed and results are communicated to their client organizations. The

FIGURE 15-9 SSAE 16 REPORTING

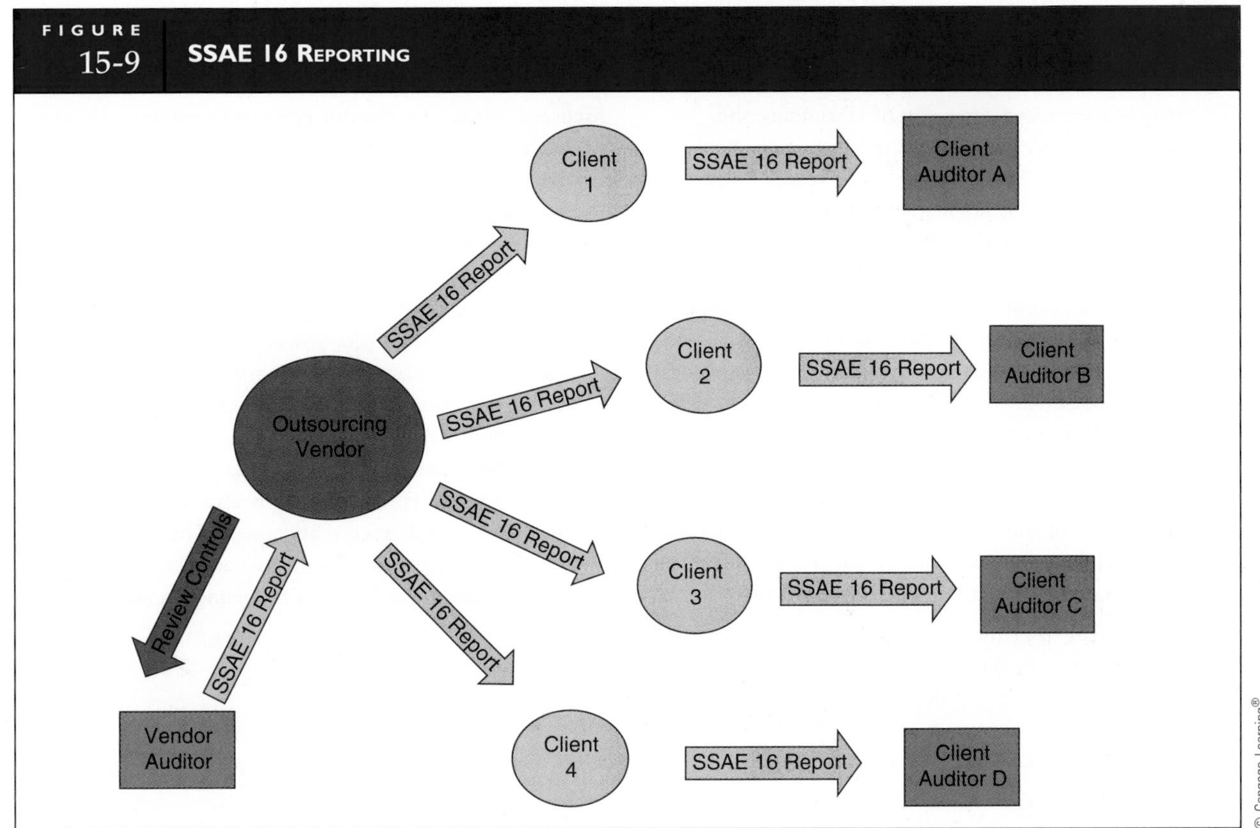

report also describes relevant internal control issues consistent with the COSO control model including the control environment, risk assessment, information and communication systems, control activities and control monitoring. In addition, the report specifies control objectives and the controls designed to achieve those objectives.

In the case of both Type 1 and Type 2 reports, the service provider's auditor will assess whether vendor management used appropriate criteria in evaluating the suitability of the control designs to achieve the control objectives. In the case of Type 2 reports, the auditor will also attest to whether the controls operated effectively throughout the specified period.

Service providers, particularly those in the cloud, may outsource their workload to other service providers. For example, assume Company A, a retailing firm outsources its accounts payable function to Company B who outsources the actual check printing and mailing to Company C. In this situation, Company A is the client firm, Company B is the service provider, and company C is a subservice organization. The importance of company C's system and controls in this relationship is obvious. The SSAE 16 standard was designed to address the subservice organization issue. Two reporting techniques are outlined next.

Carve-out Method: When using the carve-out method, service provider management would exclude the subservice organization's relevant control objectives and related controls from the description of its system. The description would, however, include the nature of the services performed by the subservice organization. Typically the service provider would obtain an SSAE 16 from the subservice organization, and must have controls in place to monitor the effectiveness of the controls at the subservice organization.

Inclusive Method: When using the inclusive method of subservice organization reporting the service provider's description of its system will include the services performed by the subservice organization. In addition, the report will include the relevant control objectives and related controls of the subservice organization.

Summary

This chapter introduced the topic of IT auditing and opened with an overview of auditing in which the key components of an audit were discussed. Topics in this section included auditing standards, the structure of an audit, management assertions, and the audit risk model. Next, the chapter turned to internal control and audit issues related to Sections 302 and 404 of SOX. It began with a review of management and auditor responsibilities under SOX. Then it examined the IT control relationship. This section concluded with a discussion of computer fraud issues. The next section of the chapter presented risks and controls related to IT governance. It began with a brief definition of IT governance and identified its implications for internal control and financial reporting. The structure of the IT function within an organization and the risks that can arise from inappropriate structuring were then discussed. Next, the chapter reviewed computer center threats and controls, which include protecting against damage and destruction from natural disasters, fire, temperature, and humidity. The chapter then presented the key elements of a disaster recovery plan. Several factors need to be considered in such a plan, including providing second-site backup, identifying critical applications, performing backup and off-site storage procedures, creating a disaster recovery team, and testing the DRP. The final section of the chapter examined issues surrounding the growing trend toward IT outsourcing. In particular, it reviewed the theories underlying outsourcing and the expected benefits. IT outsourcing is also associated with significant risks, which were addressed. The chapter concluded with a discussion of audit issues related to outsourcing including the SSAE 16 reporting standard.

Key Terms

access controls (657)
application controls (650)
audit objectives (647)
audit planning (645)
Audit risk (647)
Carve-out Method (673)
Commodity IT assets (670)
computer fraud (652)
computer-aided audit tools and techniques (CAATTs) (646)
control risk (646)
core competency (670)
corporate IT function (660)
Database management fraud (654)
Detection risk (648)
disaster recovery plan (DRP) (665)
distributed data processing (DDP) (658)
eavesdropping (655)
empty shell (666)
Fault tolerance (664)
general computer controls (650)
general controls (650)
Inclusive Method (673)
information technology controls (650)
Inherent risk (648)
IT outsourcing (670)
Management assertions (646)
mirrored data center (666)
off-site storage (665)
Operations fraud (654)
Program fraud (654)
recovery operations center (ROC) (666)
Redundant arrays of independent disks (RAID) (664)
scavenging (655)
Specific IT assets (670)
Statement on Standards for Attestation Engagements No. 16 (SSAE 16) (672)
substantive tests (646)
tests of controls (646)
Transaction Cost Economics (TCE) (670)
Uninterruptible power supplies (664)
user views (656)

Review Questions

1. SOX contains many sections. Which sections are the focus of this chapter?
2. Define audit risk.
3. Distinguish between errors and irregularities.
4. Distinguish between inherent risk and control risk. How do internal controls affect inherent risk and control risk, if at all? What is the role of detection risk?
5. What is the relationship between tests of controls and substantive tests?
6. Define general controls.
7. What is computer fraud, and what types of activities does it include?
8. At which stage of the general accounting model is it easiest to commit computer fraud?
9. How do automated authorization procedures differ from manual authorization procedures?
10. Explain why certain duties that are deemed incompatible in a manual system may be combined in a computer-based information system environment. Give an example.
11. What are the three primary IT functions that must be separated?
12. What exposures does data consolidation in a IT environment pose?
13. Differentiate between general and application controls. Give two examples of each.
14. What are the primary reasons for separating operational tasks?
15. What problems may occur as a result of combining applications programming and maintenance tasks into one position?
16. Why is poor-quality systems documentation a prevalent problem?
17. What is the role of a corporate computer services department? How does this differ from other configurations?
18. What are the five control implications of distributed data processing?
19. List the control features that directly contribute to the security of the computer center environment.
20. What is fault tolerance?
21. What is RAID?
22. What is the purpose of an audit?
23. Discuss the concept of independence within the context of an audit.
24. What is the meaning of the term *attest service?*
25. What are assurance services?
26. What are the conceptual phases of an audit? How do they differ between general auditing and IT auditing?
27. Distinguish between internal and external auditors.
28. What are the four primary elements described in the definition of auditing?
29. Explain the concept of materiality.
30. What tasks do auditors perform during audit planning, and what techniques are used?
31. Distinguish between tests of controls and substantive testing.
32. What is audit risk?
33. Distinguish between errors and irregularities. Which do you think concerns auditors the most?
34. Distinguish between inherent risk and control risk. How do internal controls affect inherent risk and control risk, if at all? What is the role of detection risk?
35. What is the relationship between tests of controls and substantive tests?
36. List the four general control areas.
37. What types of documents would an auditor review in testing organizational structure controls? Why is it also important to observe actual behavior?
38. What are some tests of physical security controls?
39. What are the often-cited benefits of IT outsourcing?
40. Define commodity IT asset.
41. Define *specific asset.*
42. List five risks associated with IT outsourcing.

Discussion Questions

1. Discuss the key features of Section 302 of SOX.
2. Discuss the key features of Section 404 of SOX.
3. 404 requires management to make a statement identifying the control framework used to conduct the assessment of internal controls. Discuss the options in selecting a control framework.
4. Explain how general controls impact transaction integrity and the financial reporting process.
5. Prior to SOX, external auditors were required to be familiar with the client organization's internal controls, but not to test them. Explain why.
6. Does a qualified opinion on internal controls over the financial reporting system necessitate a qualified opinion on the financial statements? Explain why or why not.
7. The PCAOB Standard No. 5 specifically requires auditors to understand transaction flows in designing their tests of controls. What steps does this entail?
8. What fraud detection responsibilities (if any) does SOX impose on auditors?
9. Explain at least three forms of computer fraud.
10. A bank in California has 13 branches spread throughout northern California, each with its own minicomputer where its data are stored. Another bank has 10 branches spread throughout California, with the data being stored on a mainframe in San Francisco. Which system do you think is more vulnerable to unauthorized access? Excessive losses from disaster?
11. Compare and contrast the following disaster recovery options: empty shell, recovery operations center, and internally provided backup. Rank them from most risky to least risky, as well as from most costly to least costly.
12. Who should determine and prioritize the critical applications? How is this done? How frequently is it done?
13. Discuss the differences between the attest function and assurance services.
14. Define the management assertions of existence or occurrence, completeness, rights and obligations, valuation or allocation, and presentation and disclosure.
15. An organization's internal audit department is usually considered an effective control mechanism for evaluating the organization's internal control structure. Birch Company's internal auditing function reports directly to the controller. Comment on the effectiveness of this organizational structure.
16. Discuss why any distinction between IT auditing and financial auditing is not meaningful.
17. Discuss how the process of obtaining audit evidence in a IT environment is inherently different from obtaining it in a manual system.
18. Some internal controls can be tested objectively. Discuss some internal controls that you think are relatively more subjective to assess in terms of adequacy than others.
19. Give a specific example, other than the one in the chapter, to illustrate the relationship between risk, control, audit objective, and tests of control.
20. Discuss the subjective nature of auditing computer center security.
21. Explain the outsourcing risk of failure to perform.
22. Explain vendor exploitation.
23. Explain why reduced security is an outsourcing risk.
24. Explain how IT outsourcing can lead to loss of strategic advantage.
25. Explain the role of Statement on Standards for Attestation Engagements No. 16 (SSAE 16) report in the review of internal controls.
26. How do SSAE 16 Type 1 and Type 2 differ?
27. How are the carve-out and inclusive methods of reporting on subservice organizations different?

Multiple-Choice Questions

1. Which of the following is NOT a task performed in the audit planning phase?
   a. Reviewing an organization's policies and practices
   b. Planning substantive testing procedures
   c. Reviewing general controls
   d. Determining the degree of reliance on controls
2. 2 Which of the following is the best example of an application control objective?
   a. Ensure that the computer operating system functions efficiently.
   b. Provide backup facilities in the event of a disaster.
   c. Prevent unauthorized access to corporate databases.
   d. Ensure the validity, completeness, and accuracy of sales transactions.
3. Which of the following statements is true?
   a. Both the SEC and the PCAOB require the use of the COSO framework.
   b. Any framework can be used that encompasses all of COSO's general themes.
   c. The SEC recommends COBIT and the PCAOB recommends COSO.
   d. Both the SEC and the PCAOB require the COBIT framework.
   e. None of the above are true.
4. Which of the following is NOT a control concern in a distributed data processing environment?
   a. Redundancy
   b. Hiring qualified professionals
   c. Incompatibility
   d. Lack of standards
   e. All of the above are control concerns
5. Which of the following disaster recovery techniques may be least optimal in the case of a widespread natural disaster?
   a. Empty shell
   b. Internally provided backup
   c. ROC
   d. They are all equally beneficial
6. Which of the following is NOT a potential threat to computer hardware and peripherals?
   a. Low humidity
   b. High humidity
   c. Carbon dioxide fire extinguishers
   d. Water sprinkler fire extinguishers
7. Which of the following is NOT requirement of Section 302 of SOX?
   a. Corporate management (including the CEO) must certify monthly and annually their organization's internal controls over financial reporting.
   b. Auditors must interview management regarding significant changes in the design or operation of internal control that occurred since the last audit.
   c. Auditors must determine whether changes in internal control have materially affected, or are likely to materially affect, internal control over financial reporting.
   d. Management must disclose any material changes in the company's internal controls that have occurred during the most recent fiscal quarter.
   e. All of the above are requirements.
8. Which of the following is NOT a requirement in management's report on the effectiveness of internal controls over financial reporting?
   a. Describe the flow of transactions in sufficient detail to points at which misstatement could arise.
   b. An evaluation of entity-wide controls that correspond to the COSO framework.
   c. A statement that the organization's internal auditors have issued an attestation report on management's assessment of the company's internal controls.
   d. An explicit written conclusion as to the effectiveness of internal control over financial reporting.
   e. All of the above are requirements.

9. Which of the following is associated with the unique characteristics of an industry?
   a. Inherent risk
   b. Detection risk
   c. Control risk
   d. None of the above
10. Which of the following is not true about the SSAE 16 report?
    a. It is a third-party attestation report.
    b. It replaced Statement on Auditing Standards No. 70 (SAS 70).
    c. The service provider prepares a separate SSAE 16 report tailored to the needs of each of its client firms, which the client auditors rely upon.
    d. When using the carve-out method, service provider management would exclude the subservice organization's relevant controls.
    e. All of the above are true.

Problems

1. SERVICE PROVIDER AUDIT

The Harvey Manufacturing Company is undergoing its annual financial statement audit. Last year the company purchased an SaaS application from Excel Systems (a cloud service provider) to run mission critical financial transactions. The SaaS application runs on an IaaS server, which Excel Systems outsourced to another service provider.

Required

Explain how the Harvey Manufacturing auditors will assess the relevant internal controls related to these mission critical transactions.

2. INTERNAL CONTROL

During the past year, Howard Industries has experienced excessive employee turnover in their IT function. Exit interviews with employees revealed that they were dissatisfied with the working environment. Howard employed the services of a management consulting firm that had expertise in employee relationship management. The consulting firm made recommendation to restructure IT operations to create a greater sense of "ownership" among the IT staff. After three months, under the new operation a survey indicated a marked increase in the level of job satisfaction among the IT group.

During the conduct of the audit planning phase of the annual financial audit, the auditor observed the following practices: Individual IT professionals are assigned exclusively to support specific business functions such as sales processing, billing, customer account maintenance, etc. Each professional provides a range of IT services for their respective users including computer operations, program changes, and documenting the system through record layouts, system flowcharts, and program listings. They also reconcile computer output reports and logs of transactions errors.

Required

a. Identify and explain any control concerns you have with the new operations.
b. What potential computer fraud might this operational approach permit?

3. DISTRIBUTED PROCESSING SYSTEM

The internal audit department of a manufacturing company conducted a routine examination of the company's distributed computer facilities. The auditor's report was critical of the lack of coordination in the purchase of PC systems and software that individual departments use. Several different hardware platforms, operating systems, spreadsheet packages, database systems, and networking applications were in use.

In response to the internal audit report, and without consulting with department users regarding their current and future systems needs, Mr. Marten, the vice president of Information Services, issued a memorandum to all employees stating the following new policies:

1. The Micromanager Spreadsheet package has been selected to be the standard for the company, and all employees must switch to it within the month.
2. All future PC purchases must be Megasoft compatible.
3. All departments must convert to the Megasoft Entree database package.
4. The office of the vice president of Information Services must approve all new hardware and software purchases.

Several managers of other operating departments have complained about Marten's memorandum.

Required

a. Regarding setting systems standards in a distributed processing environment, discuss factors pertinent to:
    1. Computer hardware and software considerations
    2. Controls considerations
b. Discuss the benefits of having standardized hardware and software distributed across departments in the firm.
c. Discuss the concerns that the memorandum is likely to create for distributed users in the company.

4. INTERNAL CONTROL

Gustave, CPA, during its preliminary review of the financial statements of Comet, Inc., found a lack of proper segregation of duties between the programming and operating functions. Comet owns its own computing facilities. Gustave diligently intensified the internal control study and assessment tasks relating to the computer facilities. Gustave concluded in its final report that sufficient compensating general controls provided reasonable assurance that the internal control objectives were being met.

Required

What compensating controls are most likely in place?

5. DISASTER RECOVERY PLANNING CONTROVERSY

The relevance of a disaster recovery plan (DRP) to a financial statement audit is a matter of debate. Some argue that the existence of a DRP is irrelevant to the audit. Others argue that it is an important control that needs to be considered in the assessment of internal control.

Required

Address both sides of this debate.

a. Provide a logical argument why a DRP should not be considered in the audit.
b. Argue why a DRP is an important control and should be reviewed within the conduct of a financial audit.

6. SEPARATION OF DUTIES

Transferring people from job to job within the organization is the philosophy at Arcadia Plastics. Management believes that job rotation deters employees from feeling that they are stagnating in their jobs and promotes a better understanding of the company. The computer services personnel typically work for six months as an operator, one year as a systems developer, six months as a database administrator, and one year in systems maintenance. At that point, they are assigned to a permanent position.

Required

Discuss the importance of separation of duties within the information systems department. How can Arcadia Plastics have both job rotation and well-separated duties?

7. DISASTER RECOVERY SERVICE PROVIDERS

Visit SunGard's website, http://www.sungard.com, and research its recovery services offered for the following classes: High Availability, System Recovery, and End-User Recovery. Write a report of your findings.

8. PHYSICAL SECURITY OF DATA CENTER

Big Apple Financials, Inc., is a financial services firm located in New York City. The company keeps client investment and account information on a server at its Brooklyn data center. This information includes the total value of the portfolio, type of investments made, the income structure of each client, and associated tax liabilities. The company has recently upgraded its Web site to allow clients to access their investment information.

The company's data center is in the basement of a rented building. Company management believes that the location is secure enough to protect their data from physical threats. The servers are housed in a room that has smoke detectors and associated sprinklers. It is enclosed, with no windows, and has temperature-controlled air conditioning. The company's auditors, however, have expressed concern that some of the measures at the current location are inadequate and that newer alternatives should be explored. Management has expressed counter concerns about the high cost of purchasing new equipment and relocating its data center.

Required

a. Why are Big Apple's auditors stressing the need to have a better physical environment for the server?
b. Describe six control features that contribute to the physical security of the computer center.
c. Big Apple management is concerned about the cost of relocating the data center. Discuss some options open to them that could reduce their operating costs and provide the security the auditors seek.

9. DISASTER RECOVERY PLAN

Hexagon is an online retailer of exotic foods including spices from around the world, canned sauces, and prepackaged breads such as tortillas and naan. The company does 100% of its business over the Internet to consumers and through private networks with retail trading partners. Recently, Hexagon moved its sales and business headquarters functions into a warehouse on the outskirts of San Francisco. Prior to the move, the company engaged the services of an architect to redesign the facility to be modern yet in keeping with the original character of the building. While remodeling the warehouse, the architects retained the wooden-shingled exterior and the exposed wooden beams throughout the interior. The data processing center, which contained the servers and networked terminals were situated in a large open area with high ceilings and skylights. The center was made accessible to the rest of the staff to be consistent with the firm's philosophy of removing barriers and encouraging a team approach to problem solving. Before occupying the new facility, city inspectors declared the building to be compliant with all relevant building codes.

In a recent compliance audit, Hexagon's auditors advised the company's management to develop a disaster recovery plan. Toward this end, the company entered into a mutual aid agreement with several other firms in the area that had similar technology systems. These firms all agreed verbally to provide emergency assistance to each other in the event of disasters or emergencies. In addition, Hexagon implemented a data backup system in which all files are copied daily to tapes and disks and each week the backup storage devices are taken to an offsite facility where they are secured.

The operator's manual with instructions on how to restore the system is stored in the main data processing area along with a list of names and phone numbers of key IT professionals to contact in case of an emergency.

Required

a. Describe the internal control weaknesses present at Hexagon.
b. List the components that should be included in a disaster recovery plan for a company like Hexagon.
c. What factors, other than those included in the plan itself, should a company consider when formulating a disaster recovery plan?

10. INTERNAL CONTROL AND DISTRIBUTED SYSTEM

Until a year ago, Dagwood Printing Company had always operated in a centralized computer environment. Now, 75 percent of the office employees have a PC. Users have been able to choose their own software packages, and no documentation of end-user-developed applications has been required. Next month, each PC will be linked into a local area network and to the company's mainframe.

Required

a. Outline a plan of action for Dagwood Printing Company to ensure that the proper controls over hardware, software, data, people, procedures, and documentation are in place.
b. Discuss any risks the company may face if the devised plan is not implemented.

11. INTERNAL CONTROL RESPONSIBILITY FOR OUTSOURCED IT

Explain why managers who outsource their IT function may or may not also outsource responsibility for IT controls. What options are open to auditors regarding expressing an opinion on the adequacy of internal controls?

12. COMPETING SCHOOLS OF THOUGHT REGARDING OUTSOURCING

Explain the *core competency* argument for outsourcing and compare/contrast it with *TCE theory*. Why does one theory tend to prevail over the other in making outsourcing decisions?

13. DISTRIBUTED DATA PROCESSING

Explain why an organization would choose to install a distributed instead of a centralized computer system.

CHAPTER

16

Auditing IT Controls Part II: Security and Access

This chapter continues the treatment of general IT controls as the COSO control framework describes. The focus of the chapter is on Sarbanes-Oxley (SOX) compliance regarding the security and control of operating systems, database management systems, and communication networks. This chapter examines the risks, controls, audit objectives, and tests of controls that may be performed to satisfy either compliance or attest responsibilities.

Learning Objectives

After studying this chapter, you should:

- Be able to identify the principal threats to the operating system and the control techniques used to minimize the possibility of actual exposures.
- Be familiar with the principal risks associated with electronic commerce conducted over intranets and the Internet and understand the control techniques used to reduce these risks.
- Be familiar with the risks to database integrity and the controls used to mitigate them.
- Recognize the unique exposures that arise in connection with electronic data interchange (EDI) and understand how these exposures can be reduced.

Controlling the Operating System

The **operating system** is the computer's control program. It allows users and their applications to share and access common computer resources, such as processors, main memory, databases, and printers. If operating system integrity is compromised, controls within individual accounting applications may also be circumvented or neutralized. Because the operating system is common to all users, the larger the computer facility, the greater the scale of potential damage. Thus, with an ever-expanding user community sharing more and more computer resources, operating system security becomes an important control issue.

OPERATING SYSTEM OBJECTIVES

The operating system performs three main tasks. First, it translates high-level languages, such as COBOL, C++, BASIC, and SQL, into the machine-level language that the computer can execute. The language translator modules of the operating system are called **compilers** and **interpreters**. The control implications of language translators are examined in Chapter 17.

Second, the operating system allocates computer resources to users, workgroups, and applications. This includes assigning memory work space (partitions) to applications and authorizing access to terminals, telecommunications links, databases, and printers.

Third, the operating system manages the tasks of job scheduling and multiprogramming. At any point, numerous user applications (jobs) are seeking access to the computer resources under the control of the operating system. Jobs are submitted to the system in three ways: (1) directly by the system operator, (2) from various batch-job queues, and (3) through telecommunications links from remote workstations. To achieve efficient and effective use of finite computer resources, the operating system must schedule job processing according to established priorities and balance the use of resources among the competing applications.

To perform these tasks consistently and reliably, the operating system must achieve five fundamental control objectives.[1]

1. The operating system must protect itself from users. User applications must not be able to gain control of, or damage in any way, the operating system, thus causing it to cease running or to destroy data.
2. The operating system must protect users from each other. One user must not be able to access, destroy, or corrupt the data or programs of another user.
3. The operating system must protect users from themselves. A user's application may consist of several modules stored in separate memory locations, each with its own data. One module must not be allowed to destroy or corrupt another module.
4. The operating system must be protected from itself. The operating system is also made up of individual modules. No module should be allowed to destroy or corrupt another module.
5. The operating system must be protected from its environment. In the event of a power failure or other disaster, the operating system should be able to achieve a controlled termination of activities from which it can later recover.

OPERATING SYSTEM SECURITY

Operating system security involves policies, procedures, and controls that determine who can access the operating system, which resources (files, programs, printers) they can access, and what actions they can take. The following security components are found in secure operating systems: log-on procedure, access token, access control list, and discretionary access privileges.

Log-On Procedure

A formal **log-on procedure** is the operating system's first line of defense against unauthorized access. When the user initiates the process, he or she is presented with a dialog box requesting the user's ID and password. The system compares the ID and password to a database of valid users. If the system finds a match, then the log-on attempt is authenticated. If, however, the password or ID is entered incorrectly, the log-on attempt fails, and a message is returned to the user. The message should not reveal whether the password or the ID caused the failure. The system should allow the user to reenter the log-on information. After a specified number of attempts (usually no more than five), the system should lock out the user from the system.

Access Token

If the log-on attempt is successful, the operating system creates an **access token** that contains key information about the user, including user ID, password, user group, and privileges granted to the user. The information in the access token is used to approve all actions the user attempts during the session.

---

1 F. M. Stepczyk, "Requirements for Secure Operating Systems," Data Security and Data Processing, vol. 5; Study Results: TRW Systems, Inc. (New York: IBM Corporation, 1974), 25–73.

Access Control List

An **access control list** assigned to each resource controls access to system resources, such as directories, files, programs, and printers. These lists contain information that defines the access privileges for all valid users of the resource. When a user attempts to access a resource, the system compares his or her ID and privileges contained in the access token with those contained in the access control list. If there is a match, the user is granted access.

Discretionary Access Privileges

The central system administrator usually determines who is granted access to specific resources and maintains the access control list. In distributed systems, however, end users may control (own) resources. Resource owners in this setting may be granted **discretionary access privileges**, which allow them to grant access privileges to other users. For example, the controller, who is the owner of the general ledger, may grant read-only privileges to a manager in the budgeting department. The accounts payable manager, however, may be granted both read and write permissions to the ledger. Any attempt the budgeting manager makes to add, delete, or change the general ledger will be denied. The use of discretionary access control needs to be closely supervised to prevent security breaches because of its liberal use.

THREATS TO OPERATING SYSTEM INTEGRITY

Operating system control objectives may not be achieved because of flaws in the operating system that are exploited either accidentally or intentionally. Accidental threats include hardware failures that cause the operating system to crash. Errors in user application programs, which the operating system cannot interpret, also cause operating system failures. Accidental system failures may cause whole segments of memory to be dumped to disks and printers, resulting in the unintentional disclosure of confidential information.

Intentional threats to the operating system are most commonly attempts to illegally access data or violate user privacy for financial gain. However, a growing threat is destructive programs from which there is no apparent gain. These exposures come from three sources:

1. Privileged personnel who abuse their authority. Systems administrators and systems programmers require unlimited access to the operating system to perform maintenance and to recover from system failures. Such individuals may use this authority to access users' programs and data files.
2. Individuals, both internal and external to the organization, who browse the operating system to identify and exploit security flaws.
3. Individuals who intentionally (or accidentally) insert computer viruses or other forms of destructive programs into the operating system.

OPERATING SYSTEM CONTROLS AND TESTS OF CONTROLS

This section describes a variety of control techniques for preserving operating system integrity. If operating system integrity is compromised, controls within individual accounting applications that impact financial reporting may also be compromised. For this reason, the design and assessment of these controls are SOX compliance issues. In this section, controls and associated tests over the following areas are examined: access privileges, password control, virus control, and audit trail control.

Controlling Access Privileges

User access privileges are assigned to individuals and to entire workgroups authorized to use the system. Privileges determine which directories, files, applications, and other resources an individual or group may access. They also determine the types of actions that can be taken. Recall that the systems administrator or the owner of the resource may assign privileges. Management should be concerned that individuals are not granted privileges that are incompatible with their assigned duties. Consider, for example, a cash receipts clerk who is granted the right to access and make changes to the accounts receivable file.

Overall, the way access privileges are assigned influences system security. Privileges should, therefore, be carefully administered and closely monitored for compliance with organizational policy and principles of internal control.

Audit Objectives Relating to Access Privileges

The objective of the auditor is to verify that access privileges are granted in a manner that is consistent with the need to separate incompatible functions and is in accordance with the organization's policy.

Audit Procedures Relating to Access Privileges

- Review the organization's policies for separating incompatible functions and ensure that they promote reasonable security.
- Review the privileges of a selection of user groups and individuals to determine if their access rights are appropriate for their job descriptions and positions. The auditor should verify that individuals are granted access to data and programs based on their need to know.
- Review personnel records to determine whether privileged employees undergo an adequately intensive security clearance check in compliance with company policy.
- Review employee records to determine whether users have formally acknowledged their responsibility to maintain the confidentiality of company data.
- Review the users' permitted log-on times. Permission should be commensurate with the tasks being performed.

Password Control

A **password** is a secret code the user enters to gain access to systems, applications, data files, or a network server. If the user cannot provide the correct password, the operating system should deny access. Although passwords can provide a degree of security, when imposed on nonsecurity-minded users, password procedures can result in end-user behavior that actually circumvents security. The most common forms of contra-security behavior include:

- Forgetting passwords and being locked out of the system.
- Failing to change passwords on a frequent basis.
- The Post-it syndrome, whereby passwords are written down and displayed for others to see.
- Simplistic passwords that a computer criminal easily anticipates.

REUSABLE PASSWORDS. The most common method of password control is the **reusable password**. The user defines the password to the system once and then reuses it to gain future access. The quality of the security a reusable password provides depends on the quality of the password itself. If the password pertains to something personal about the user, such as a child's name, pet's name, birth date, or hair color, a computer criminal can often deduce it. Even if the password is derived from nonpersonal data, it may be weak. For example, a string of keystrokes (such as A-S-D-F) or the same letter used multiple times can easily be cracked. Passwords that contain random letters and digits are more difficult to crack but are also more difficult for the user to remember.

To improve access control, management should require that passwords be changed regularly and disallow weak passwords. Software is available that automatically scans password files and notifies users that their passwords have expired and need to be changed. These systems also use extensive databases of known weak passwords to validate the new password and disallow weak ones. An alternative to the standard reusable password is the one-time password.

ONE-TIME PASSWORDS. The **one-time password** was designed to overcome the aforementioned problems. Under this approach, the user's password changes continuously. This technology employs a credit card-sized smart card that contains a microprocessor programmed with an algorithm that generates, and electronically displays, a new and unique password every 60 seconds. The card works in conjunction with special authentication software located on a mainframe or network server computer. Each user's card is synchronized to the authentication software so that at any point in time both the smart card and the network software are generating the same password for the same user.

To access the network, the user enters the PIN followed by the current password displayed on the card. The password can be used one time only. If, for example, a computer hacker intercepts the password and PIN during transmission and attempts to use them within the one-minute time frame, access will be denied. Also, if the smart card should fall into the hands of a computer criminal, access cannot be achieved without the PIN.

Another one-time password technique uses a challenge/response approach to achieve the same end. When the user attempts to log on, the network authentication software issues a six-character code (the challenge) that the card can either scan optically, or the code can be entered into the card via its built-in keypad. The card's internal algorithm then generates a one-time password (the response) that the user enters through the keyboard of the remote terminal. If the firewall recognizes the current password, access is permitted.

Audit Objectives Relating to Passwords

The auditor's objective here is to ensure that the organization has an adequate and effective password policy for controlling access to the operating system.

Audit Procedures Relating to Passwords

The auditor may achieve this objective by performing the following tests:

- Verify that all users are required to have passwords.
- Verify that new users are instructed in the use of passwords and the importance of password control.
- Review password control procedures to ensure that passwords are changed regularly.
- Review the password file to determine that weak passwords are identified and disallowed. This may involve using software to scan password files for known weak passwords.
- Verify that the password file is encrypted and that the encryption key is properly secured.
- Assess the adequacy of password standards, such as length and expiration interval. Review the account lockout policy and procedures. Most operating systems allow the system administrator to define the action to be taken after a certain number of failed log-on attempts. The auditor should determine how many failed log-on attempts are allowed before the account is locked. The duration of the lockout also needs to be determined. This could range from a few minutes to a permanent lockout that requires formal reactivation of the account.

Controlling against Malicious and Destructive Programs

Malicious and destructive programs are responsible for millions of dollars of corporate losses annually. The losses are measured in terms of data corruption and destruction, degraded computer performance, hardware destruction, violations of privacy, and the personnel time devoted to repairing the damage. This class of programs includes viruses, worms, logic bombs, back doors, and Trojan horses. Because these have become popular press terms in recent years, we will not devote space at this point to define them. The appendix to this chapter, however, contains a detailed discussion of this material. Threats from destructive programs can be substantially reduced through a combination of technology controls and administrative procedures. The following examples are relevant to most operating systems.

- Purchase software only from reputable vendors, and accept only those products that are in their original, factory-sealed packages.
- Issue an entity-wide policy pertaining to the use of unauthorized software or illegal (bootleg) copies of copyrighted software.
- Examine all upgrades to vendor software for viruses before they are implemented.
- Inspect all public-domain software for virus infection before using.
- Establish entity-wide procedures for making changes to production programs.
- Establish an educational program to raise user awareness regarding threats from viruses and malicious programs.
- Install all new applications on a stand-alone computer, and thoroughly test them with antiviral software prior to implementing them on the mainframe or local area network (LAN) server.
- Routinely make backup copies of key files stored on mainframes, servers, and workstations.
- Wherever possible, limit users to read and execute rights only. This allows users to extract data and run authorized applications, but it denies them the ability to write directly to mainframe and server directories.
- Require protocols that explicitly invoke the operating system's log-on procedures to bypass Trojan horses. A typical scenario is one in which a user sits down at a terminal that is already displaying the log-on screen and proceeds to enter his or her ID and password. This, however, may be a Trojan horse rather than the legitimate procedure. Some operating systems allow the user to directly invoke the operating system log-on procedure by entering a key sequence, such as CTRL + ALT + DEL. The user then knows that the log-on procedure on the screen is legitimate.
- Use antiviral software (also called vaccines) to examine application and operating system programs for the presence of a virus and remove it from the affected program. Antiviral programs are used to safeguard mainframes, network servers, and personal computers. Most antiviral programs run in the background on the host computer and automatically test all files that are uploaded to the host. The software, however, works only on known viruses. If a virus has been modified slightly (mutated), there is no guarantee that the vaccine will work. Therefore, maintaining a current version of the vaccine is critical.

Audit Objective Relating to Viruses and Other Destructive Programs

The key to computer virus control is prevention through strict adherence to organizational policies and procedures that guard against virus infection. The auditor's objective is to verify that effective management policies and procedures are in place to prevent the introduction and spread of destructive programs, including viruses, worms, back doors, logic bombs, and Trojan horses.

Audit Procedures Relating to Viruses and Other Destructive Programs

- Through interviews, determine that operations personnel have been educated about computer viruses and are aware of the risky computing practices that can introduce and spread viruses and other malicious programs.
- Verify that new software is tested on stand-alone workstations prior to being implemented on the host or network server.
- Verify that the current version of antiviral software is installed on the server and that upgrades are regularly downloaded to workstations.

System Audit Trail Controls

System audit trails are logs that record activity at the system, application, and user level. Operating systems allow management to select the level of auditing to be recorded in the log. They need to decide on their threshold between information and irrelevant facts. An effective audit policy will capture all significant events without cluttering the log with trivial activity. Audit trails typically consist of two types of audit logs: (1) detailed logs of individual keystrokes and (2) event-oriented logs.

KEYSTROKE MONITORING. Keystroke monitoring involves recording both the user's keystrokes and the system's responses. This form of log may be used after the fact to reconstruct the details of an event or as a real-time control to prevent unauthorized intrusion. Keystroke monitoring is the computer equivalent of a telephone wiretap. While some situations may justify this level of surveillance, keystroke monitoring may also be regarded as a violation of privacy. Before implementing this type of control, management and auditors should consider the possible legal, ethical, and behavioral implications.

EVENT MONITORING. Event monitoring summarizes key activities related to system resources. Event logs typically record the IDs of all users accessing the system; the time and duration of a user's session; programs that were executed during a session; and the files, databases, printers, and other resources accessed.

Setting Audit Trail Objectives

Audit trails can be used to support security objectives in three ways: (1) detecting unauthorized access to the system, (2) facilitating the reconstruction of events, and (3) promoting personal accountability.

DETECTING UNAUTHORIZED ACCESS. Detecting unauthorized access can occur in real time or after the fact. The primary objective of real-time detection is to protect the system from outsiders attempting to breach system controls. A real-time audit trail can also be used to report changes in system performance that may indicate infestation by a virus or worm. Depending on how much activity is being logged for review, real-time detection can add significantly to operational overhead and degrade performance. After-the-fact detection logs can be stored electronically and reviewed periodically or as needed. When properly designed, they can be used to determine if unauthorized access was accomplished, or attempted and failed.

RECONSTRUCTING EVENTS. Audit trail analysis can be used to reconstruct the steps that led to events such as system failures or security violations by individuals. Knowledge of the conditions that existed at the time of a system failure can be used to assign responsibility and to avoid similar situations in the future.

PERSONAL ACCOUNTABILITY. Audit trails can be used to monitor user activity at the lowest level of detail. This capability is a preventive control that can influence behavior. Individuals are less likely to violate an organization's security policy when they know that their actions are recorded in an audit log. A system audit log can also serve as a detective control to assign personal accountability for actions taken, such as abuse of authority. For example, consider an accounts receivable clerk with authority to access customer records. The audit log may disclose that the clerk has been printing an inordinate number of records, which may indicate that the clerk is selling customer information in violation of the company's privacy policy.

Implementing a System Audit Trail

The information contained in audit logs is useful to accountants in measuring the potential damage and financial loss associated with application errors, abuse of authority, or unauthorized access by outside intruders. Audit logs, however, can generate data in overwhelming detail. Important information can easily get lost among the superfluous details of daily operation. Thus, poorly designed logs can actually be dysfunctional. Protecting exposures with the potential for material financial loss should drive management's decision as to which users, applications, or operations to monitor, and how much detail to log. As with all controls, the benefits of audit logs must be balanced against the costs of implementing them.

Audit Objectives Relating to System Audit Trails

The auditor's objective is to ensure that the established system audit trail is adequate for preventing and detecting abuses, reconstructing key events that precede systems failures, and planning resource allocation.

Audit Procedures Relating to System Audit Trails

- Most operating systems provide some form of audit manager function to specify the events that are to be audited. The auditor should verify that the audit trail has been activated according to organization policy.
- Many operating systems provide an audit log viewer that allows the auditor to scan the log for unusual activity. These can be reviewed on screen or by archiving the file for subsequent review. The auditor can use general-purpose data extraction tools for accessing archived log files to search for defined conditions such as:
  - Unauthorized or terminated user
  - Periods of inactivity
  - Activity by user, workgroup, or department
  - Log-on and log-off times
  - Failed log-on attempts
  - Access to specific files or applications
- The organization's security group has responsibility for monitoring and reporting security violations. The auditor should select a sample of security violation cases and evaluate their disposition to assess the effectiveness of the security group.

Controlling Database Management Systems

Controls over database management fall into two general categories: access controls and backup controls. **Access controls** are designed to prevent unauthorized individuals from viewing, retrieving, corrupting, or destroying the entity's data. **Backup controls** ensure that in the event of data loss due to unauthorized access, equipment failure, or physical disaster, the organization can recover its files and databases.

ACCESS CONTROLS

Risks to corporate databases include corruption, theft, misuse, and destruction of data. These threats originate from both unauthorized intruders and authorized users who exceed their access privileges. Several database control features that reduce these risks are reviewed in the following sections.

User Views

The **user view** or subschema is a subset of the total database that defines the user's data domain and restricts his or her access to the database accordingly. Figure 16-1 illustrates the role of the user view. The database administrator typically is responsible for defining user views. The auditor is concerned that such access privileges are commensurate with the users' legitimate needs.

Although user views can restrict user access to a limited set of data, they do not define task privileges, such as read, delete, or write. Often, several users may share a single user view but have different authority levels. For example, users Smith, Jones, and Adams in Figure 16-1 all may have access to the same set of data: account number, customer name, account balance, and credit

FIGURE 16-1 SUBSCHEMA RESTRICTING ACCESS TO DATABASE

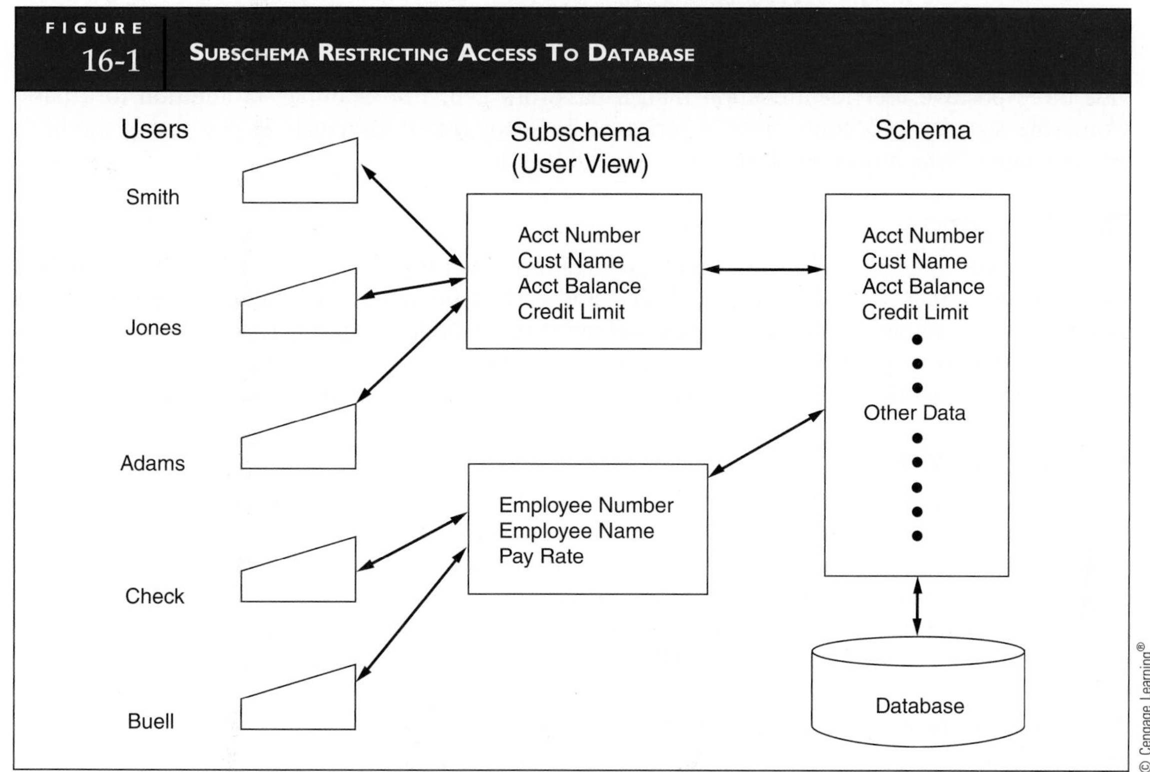

limit. Let's assume that all have read authority, but only Jones has authority to modify and delete the data. To achieve this level of restriction requires additional security measures, discussed next.

Database Authorization Table

The **database authorization table** contains rules that limit the actions a user can take. Each user is granted certain privileges that are coded in the authority table, which is used to verify the user's action requests. For example, the authorization table in Figure 16-2 shows that of the three users, only Jones has the authority to modify and delete the data.

FIGURE 16-2 DATABASE AUTHORIZATION TABLE

Dept	Accounts Rec			Billings	
User	Jones	Smith	Adams	Check	Buell
Password	Bugs	Dog	Katie	Lucky	Star
Authority:					
Read	Y	Y	Y	Y	Y
Insert	Y	N	Y	Y	N
Modify	Y	N	N	Y	N
Delete	Y	N	N	N	N

User-Defined Procedures

A **user-defined procedure** allows the user to create a personal security program or routine to provide more positive user identification than a password can. For example, in addition to a password, the security procedure asks a series of personal questions (such as the user's mother's maiden name), which only the legitimate user is likely to know.

Data Encryption

Many database systems use encryption procedures to protect highly sensitive data, such as product formulas, personnel pay rates, password files, and certain financial data. **Data encryption** uses an algorithm to scramble selected data, thus making it unreadable to an intruder browsing the database. In addition to protecting stored data, encryption is used for protecting data that are transmitted across networks. We discuss various encryption techniques later in this chapter.

Biometric Devices

The ultimate in user authentication procedures is the use of **biometric devices**, which measure various personal characteristics, such as fingerprints, voiceprints, retina prints, or signature characteristics. These user characteristics are digitized and stored permanently in a database security file or on an identification card that the user carries. When an individual attempts to access the database, a special scanning device captures his or her biometric characteristics, which it compares with the profile data stored internally or on the ID card. If the data do not match, access is denied.

Audit Objectives Relating to Database Access

The auditor's objectives are to verify (1) that individuals who are authorized to use the database are limited to accessing only the data needed to perform their duties, and (2) that unauthorized individuals are denied access to the database.

Audit Procedures for Testing Access Controls

RESPONSIBILITY FOR AUTHORITY TABLES AND SUBSCHEMAS. The auditor should verify that database administration personnel retain sole responsibility for creating authority tables and designing user views. Evidence of compliance can come from three sources: (1) by reviewing company policy and job descriptions, which specify these technical responsibilities; (2) by examining programmer authority tables for access privileges to data definition language **(DDL)** commands; and (3) through personal interviews with programmers and database administration personnel.

APPROPRIATE ACCESS AUTHORITY. The auditor can select a sample of users and verify that their access privileges stored in the authority table are consistent with their organizational functions.

BIOMETRIC CONTROLS. The auditor should evaluate the costs and benefits of biometric controls. Generally, these would be most appropriate when a very limited number of users may access highly sensitive data.

ENCRYPTION CONTROLS. The auditor should verify that sensitive data, such as passwords, are properly encrypted. This can be done by printing the file contents to hard copy.

BACKUP CONTROLS

Malicious acts from external hackers, disgruntled employees, disk failure, program errors, fires, floods, and earthquakes can corrupt and destroy data. To recover from such disasters, the organization needs to reconstruct the database to prefailure status. This can be done only if the database was properly backed up in the first place. Organizations must, therefore, implement policies,

FIGURE 16-3 DATABASE BACKUP AND RECOVERY

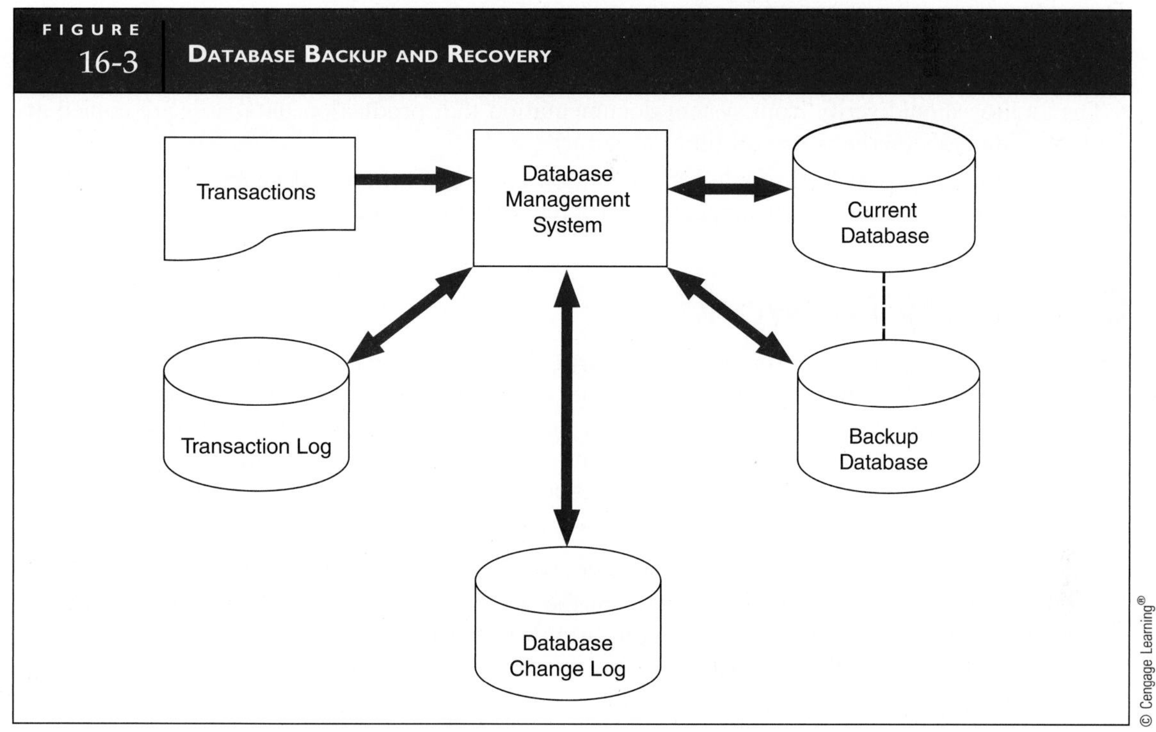

procedures, and techniques that systematically and routinely provide backup copies of critical data. This section examines backup controls used in the database environment. Legacy systems that use a flat-file structure present a different set of issues that were discussed in Chapter 3.

Large-scale database management systems employ a backup and recovery procedure similar to that illustrated in Figure 16-3. This system provides four backup and recovery features: database backup, a transaction log, checkpoints, and a recovery module. Each of these is described in the following section.

DATABASE BACKUP. The backup feature makes a periodic backup of the entire database. This is an automatic procedure that should be performed at least once a day. The backup copy should then be stored in a secure remote area.

TRANSACTION LOG (JOURNAL). The **transaction log** feature provides an audit trail of all processed transactions. It lists transactions in a transaction log file and records the resulting changes to the database in a separate database change log.

CHECKPOINT FEATURE. The **checkpoint feature** suspends all data processing while the system reconciles the transaction log and the database change log against the database. At this point, the system is in a quiet state. Checkpoints occur automatically several times an hour. If a failure occurs, it is usually possible to restart the processing from the last checkpoint. Thus, only a few minutes of transaction processing must be repeated.

RECOVERY MODULE. The **recovery module** uses the logs and backup files to restart the system after a failure.

Audit Objectives Relating to Database Backup

The auditor's objective is to verify that database backup controls are adequate to facilitate the recovery of lost, destroyed, or corrupted data.

Audit Procedures for Testing Backup Controls

Database backup should be a routine activity.

- The auditor should verify from system documentation that production databases are copied at regular intervals (perhaps several times an hour).
- The auditor should verify through documentation and observation that backup copies of the database are stored off-site to support disaster recovery procedures.

Controlling Networks

Chapter 12 examined the operational characteristics of several network topologies used in Internet and intranet communications. Network topologies consist of various configurations of (1) communications lines (twisted-pair wires, coaxial cable, microwaves, and fiber optics), (2) hardware components (modems, multiplexers, servers, and front-end processors), and (3) software (protocols and network control systems). The technology of network communications are subject to two general forms of risk:

1. Risks from subversive threats. These include, but are not limited to, a computer criminal intercepting a message transmitted between the sender and the receiver, a computer hacker gaining unauthorized access to the organization's network, and a denial of service attack from a remote location of the Internet.
2. Risks from equipment failure. For example, equipment failures in the communications system can disrupt, destroy, or corrupt transmissions between senders and receivers. Equipment failure can also result in the loss of databases and programs stored on network servers.

CONTROLLING RISKS FROM SUBVERSIVE THREATS

Firewalls

Organizations connected to the Internet or other public networks often implement an electronic firewall to insulate their intranet from outside intruders. A **firewall** is a system that enforces access control between two networks. To accomplish this:

- All traffic between the outside network and the organization's intranet must pass through the firewall.
- Only authorized traffic between the organization and the outside, as formal security policy specifies, is allowed to pass through the firewall.
- The firewall must be immune to penetration from both outside and inside the organization.

Firewalls can be used to authenticate an outside user of the network, verify his or her level of access authority, and then direct the user to the program, data, or service requested. In addition to insulating the organization's network from external networks, firewalls can also be used to insulate portions of the organization's intranet from internal access. For example, a LAN controlling access to financial data can be insulated from other internal LANs. Some commercially available firewalls provide a high level of security, whereas others are less secure but more efficient. Firewalls may be grouped into two general types: network-level firewalls and application-level firewalls.

Network-level firewalls provide efficient but low security access control. This type of firewall consists of a **screening router** that examines the source and destination addresses that are attached to incoming message packets. The firewall accepts or denies access requests based on filtering rules that have been programmed into it. The firewall directs incoming calls to the correct internal receiving node. Network-level firewalls are insecure because they are designed to facilitate the free flow of information rather than restrict it. This method does not explicitly authenticate outside users.

Application-level firewalls provide a higher level of customizable network security, but they add overhead to connectivity. These systems are configured to run security applications called proxies that permit routine services, such as e-mail, to pass through the firewall, but they can perform sophisticated functions, such as user authentication for specific tasks. Application-level firewalls also provide comprehensive transmission logging and auditing tools for reporting unauthorized activity.

A high level of firewall security is possible using a dual-homed system. This approach, illustrated in Figure 16-4, has two firewall interfaces. One screens incoming requests from the Internet; the other provides access to the organization's intranet. Direct communication to the Internet is disabled, and the two networks are fully isolated. Proxy applications that impose separate log-on procedures perform all access.

Choosing the right firewall involves a trade-off between convenience and security. Ultimately, organization management, in collaboration with internal audit and network professionals, must come to grips with what constitutes acceptable risk. The more security the firewall provides, however, the less convenient it is for authorized users to pass through it to conduct business.

Controlling Denial of Service Attacks

Chapter 12 described three common forms of denial of service attacks: SYN flood attacks, smurf attacks, and distributed denial of service (DDoS) attacks. Each of these techniques has a similar effect on the victim. By clogging the Internet ports of the victim's server with fraudulently generated messages, the targeted firm is rendered incapable of processing legitimate transactions and can be completely isolated from the Internet for the duration of the attack.

In the case of a smurf attack, the targeted organization can program its firewall to ignore all communication from the attacking site, once the attacker's IP address is determined. SYN flood attacks that use IP spoofing to disguise the source, however, are a more serious problem. Although the attack may actually be coming from a single disguised site, the victim's host computer views these transmissions as coming from all over the Internet. IT and network management can take two actions to defeat this sort of attack. First, Internet hosts must embrace a policy of social responsibility by programming their firewalls to block outbound message packets that contain invalid internal IP addresses. This would prevent attackers from hiding their locations from the targeted site and would assure the management of potential intermediary hosts that no undetected attacks could be launched from their sites. This strategy will not, however, prevent attacks from Internet sites that refuse to screen outgoing transmissions. Second, security software is available for the targeted sites that scan for half-open connections. The software looks for SYN packets that have not been followed by an ACK packet. The clogged ports can then be restored to allow legitimate connections to use them.

DDoS attacks are the most difficult of the three to counter. The victim's site becomes inundated with messages from thousands of zombie sites that are distributed across the Internet. The company is rendered helpless because it cannot effectively block transmissions from so many different locations.

As a countermeasure to DDoS attacks, many organizations have invested in **Intrusion Prevention Systems (IPS)** that employ **deep packet inspection (DPI)** to determine when an attack is in progress. DPI uses a variety of analytical and statistical techniques to evaluate the contents of message packets. It searches the individual packets for protocol noncompliance and employs predefined criteria to decide if a packet can proceed to its destination. This is in contrast to the normal packet inspection that simply checks the header portion of a packet to determine its destination. By going deeper and examining the payload or body of the packet, DPI can identify and classify malicious packets based on a database of known attack signatures. Once classified as malicious, the packet can then be blocked and redirected to a security team and/or network reporting agent.

IPS works in-line with a firewall at the perimeter of the network to act as a filter that removes malicious packets from the flow before they can affect servers and networks. IPS may also be used behind the firewall to protect specific network segments and servers. This provides additional

FIGURE 16-4 Dual-Homed Firewall

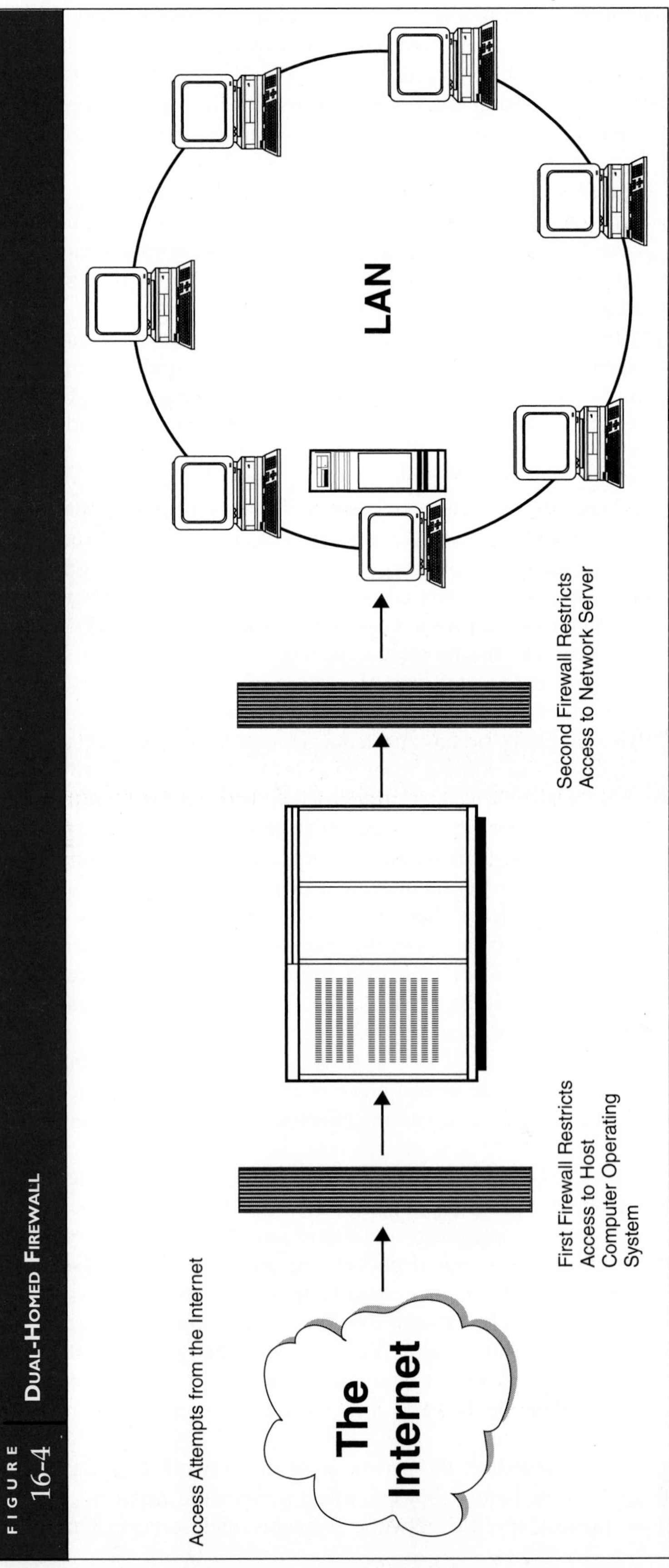

protection against careless laptop users who have been unknowingly infected with a Trojan horse or worm while working outside the protected network environment. IPS techniques can also be employed to protect an organization from becoming part of a botnet by inspecting outbound packets and blocking malicious traffic before it reaches the Internet.

Encryption

Encryption is the conversion of data into a secret code for storage in databases and transmission over networks. The discussion here pertains to transmitted data, but these basic principles apply also to stored data. The sender uses an encryption algorithm to convert the original message, called cleartext, into a coded equivalent, called ciphertext. At the receiving end, the ciphertext is decoded (decrypted) back into cleartext. The encryption algorithm uses a key, which is a binary number that typically is from 56 to 128 bits in length. The more bits in the key, the stronger the encryption method. Today, nothing less than 128-bit algorithms are considered truly secure. Two general approaches to encryption are **private key** and **public key encryption**.

PRIVATE KEY ENCRYPTION. Advanced encryption standard (AES) is a 128-bit encryption technique that has become a US government standard for private key encryption. The AES algorithm uses a single key known to both the sender and the receiver of the message. To encode a message, the sender provides the encryption algorithm with the key, which is used to produce a ciphertext message. The message enters the communication channel and is transmitted to the receiver's location, where it is stored. The receiver decodes the message with a decryption program that uses the same key the sender employs. Figure 16-5 illustrates this technique.

FIGURE 16-5 THE ADVANCED ENCRYPTION STANDARD TECHNIQUE

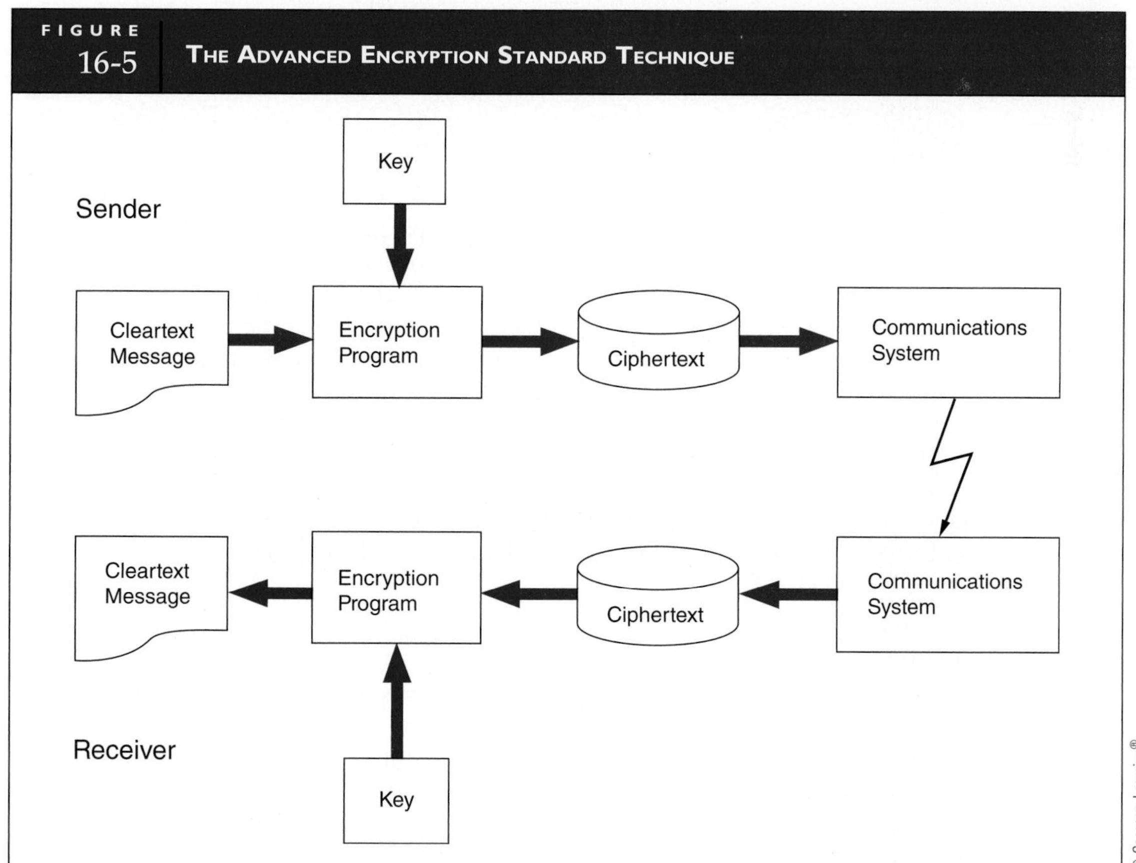

Triple-DES encryption is an enhancement to an older encryption technique called the Data Encryption Standard (DES). Triple DES provides considerably improved security over most single encryption techniques. Two forms of triple-DES encryption are EEE3 and EDE3. **EEE3** uses three different keys to encrypt the message three times. **EDE3** uses one key to encrypt the message. A second key is used to decode it. The resulting message is garbled because the key used for decoding is different from the one that encrypted it. Finally, a third key is used to encrypt the garbled message. The use of multiple keys greatly reduces the chances of breaking the cipher. Triple-DES encryption is thought to be very secure, and major banks use it to transmit transactions. Unfortunately, it is also very slow. The EEE3 and EDE3 techniques are illustrated in Figure 16-6.

All private key techniques have a common problem: The more individuals who need to know the key, the greater the probability of it falling into the wrong hands. If a perpetrator discovers the key, he or she can intercept and decipher coded messages. Therefore, encrypting data that are to be transmitted among large numbers of relative strangers (such as Internet transactions between businesses and customers) require a different approach. The solution to this problem is public key encryption.

PUBLIC KEY ENCRYPTION. Public key encryption uses two different keys: one for encoding messages and the other for decoding them. Each recipient has a private key that is kept secret and a public key that is published. The sender of a message uses the receiver's public key to encrypt the message. The receiver then uses his or her private key to decode the message. Users never need to share their private keys to decrypt messages, thus reducing the likelihood that they fall into the hands of a criminal.

RSA (Rivest-Shamir-Adleman) is a highly secure public key cryptography method. This method is, however, computationally intensive and much slower than standard DES encryption. Sometimes, both DES and RSA are used together in what is called a **digital envelope**. The actual message is encrypted using DES to provide the fastest decoding. The DES private key needed to decrypt the message is encrypted using RSA and transmitted along with the message. The receiver first decodes the DES key, which is then used to decode the message.

Digital Signatures

A **digital signature** is electronic authentication that cannot be forged. It ensures that the message or document the sender transmitted was not tampered with after the signature was applied. Figure 16-7 illustrates this process. The sender uses a one-way hashing algorithm to calculate a **digest** of the text message. The digest is a mathematical value calculated from the text content of the message. The digest is then encrypted using the sender's private key to produce the digital signature. Next, the digital signature and the text message are encrypted using the receiver's public key and transmitted to the receiver. At the receiving end, the message is decrypted using the receiver's private key to produce the digital signature (encrypted digest) and the cleartext version of the message. The receiver then uses the sender's public key to decrypt the digital signal to produce the digest. Finally, the receiver recalculates the digest from the cleartext using the original hashing algorithm and compares this to the decoded digest. If the message is authentic, the two digest values will match. If even a single character of the message was changed in transmission, the digest figures will not be equal.

Digital Certificate

The aforementioned process proves that the message received was not tampered with during transmission. It does not prove, however, that the sender is who he or she claims to be. The sender could be an impersonator. Verifying the sender's identity requires a **digital certificate**, which a trusted third party issues, called a **certification authority (CA)**. A digital certificate is used in conjunction with a public key encryption system to authenticate the sender of a message. The process for certification varies depending on the level of certification desired. It involves establishing one's identity with formal documents, such as a driver's license, notarization, and fingerprints, and

FIGURE 16-6 EEE3 AND EDE3 ENCRYPTION

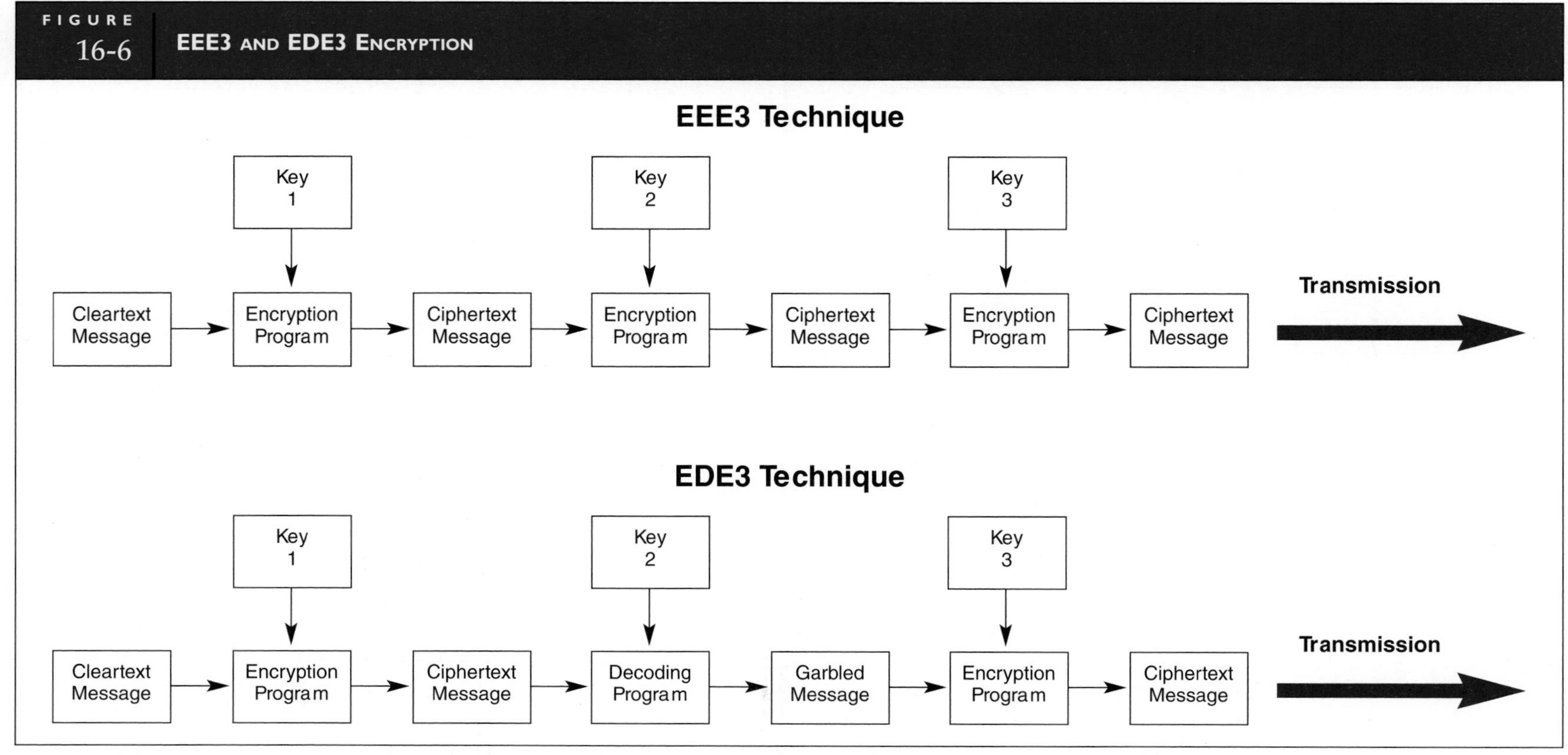

FIGURE 16-7 DIGITAL SIGNATURE

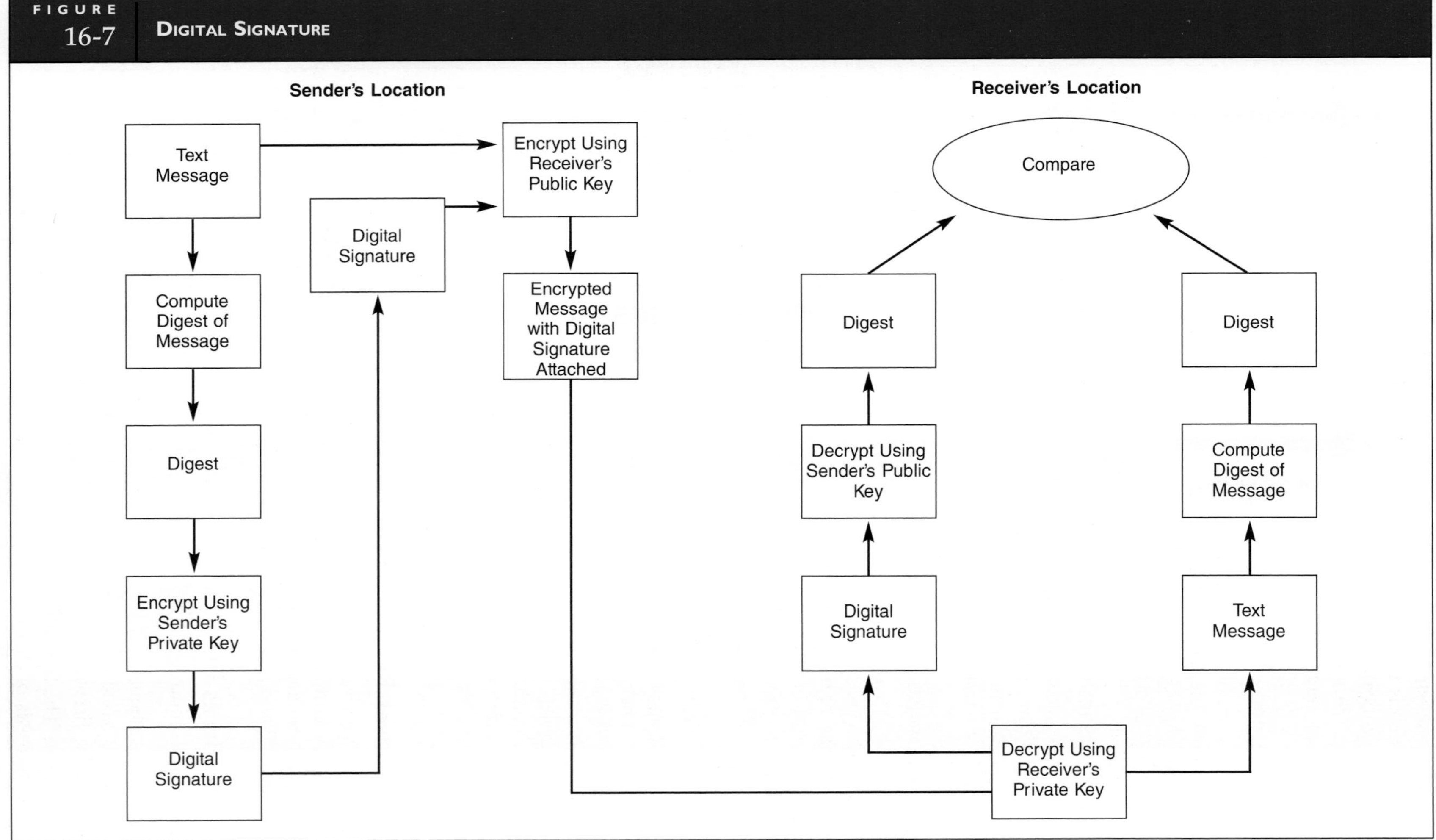

proving one's ownership of the public key. After verifying the owner's identity, the CA creates the certification, which is the owner's public key, and other data the CA has digitally signed.

The digital certificate is transmitted with the encrypted message to authenticate the sender. The receiver uses the CA's public key, which is widely publicized, to decrypt the sender's public key attached to the message. The sender's public key is then used to decrypt the message.

Message Sequence Numbering

An intruder in the communications channel may attempt to delete a message from a stream of messages, change the order of messages received, or duplicate a message. Through **message sequence numbering**, a sequence number is inserted in each message, and any such attempt will become apparent at the receiving end.

Message Transaction Log

An intruder may successfully penetrate the system by trying different password and user ID combinations. Therefore, all incoming and outgoing messages, as well as attempted (failed) access, should be recorded in a **message transaction log**. The log should record the user ID, the time of the access, and the terminal location or telephone number from which the access originated.

Request-Response Technique

An intruder may attempt to prevent or delay the receipt of a message from the sender. When senders and receivers are not in constant contact, the receiver may not know whether the communications channel has been interrupted and messages have been diverted. Using the **request-response technique**, a control message from the sender and a response from the receiver are sent at periodic, synchronized intervals. The timing of the messages should follow a random pattern that will be difficult for the intruder to determine and circumvent.

Call-Back Devices

As we have seen, networks can be equipped with security features, such as passwords, authentication devices, and encryption. The common weakness to all of these technologies is that they apply the security measure after the criminal has connected to the network server. Many believe that the key to security is to keep the intruder off the network to begin with.

A **call-back device** requires the dial-in user to enter a password and be identified. The system then breaks the connection to perform user authentication. If the caller is authorized, the call-back device dials the caller's number to establish a new connection. This restricts access to only authorized terminals or telephone numbers and prevents an intruder masquerading as a legitimate user.

Audit Objectives Relating to Subversive Threats

The auditor's objective is to verify the security and integrity of financial transactions by determining that network controls (1) can prevent and detect illegal access both internally and from the Internet, (2) will render useless any data that a perpetrator successfully captures, and (3) are sufficient to preserve the integrity and physical security of data connected to the network.

Audit Procedures Relating to Subversive Threats

To achieve these control objectives, the auditor may perform the following tests of controls:

1. Review the adequacy of the firewall in achieving the proper balance between control and convenience based on the organization's business objectives and potential risks. Criteria for assessing the firewall effectiveness include:
   - *Flexibility.* The firewall should be flexible enough to accommodate new services as the security needs of the organization change.

- *Proxy services.* Adequate proxy applications should be in place to provide explicit user authentication to sensitive services, applications, and data.
- *Filtering.* Strong filtering techniques should be designed to deny all services that are not explicitly permitted. In other words, the firewall should specify only those services the user is permitted to access, rather than specifying the services that are denied.
- *Segregation of systems.* Systems that do not require public access should be segregated from the Internet.
- *Audit tools.* The firewall should provide a thorough set of audit and logging tools that identify and record suspicious activity.
- *Probe for weaknesses.* To validate security, the auditor (or a professional security analyst) should periodically probe the firewall for weaknesses, just as a computer Internet hacker would do. A number of software products are currently available for identifying security weaknesses.

2. Verify that an Intrusion Prevention Systems (IPS) with deep packet inspection (DPI) is in place for organizations that are vulnerable to DDoS attacks, such as financial institutions.
3. Review security procedures governing the administration of data encryption keys.
4. Verify the encryption process by transmitting a test message and examining the contents at various points along the channel between the sending and receiving locations.
5. Review the message transaction logs to verify that all messages were received in their proper sequence.
6. Test the operation of the call-back feature by placing an unauthorized call from outside the installation.

CONTROLLING RISKS FROM EQUIPMENT FAILURE

Line Errors

The most common problem in data communications is data loss due to **line error**. The bit structure of the message can be corrupted through noise on the communications lines. Noise is made up of random signals that can interfere with the message signal when they reach a certain level. Electric motors, atmospheric conditions, faulty wiring, defective components in equipment, or noise spilling over from an adjacent communications channel may cause these random signals. If not detected, bit structure changes to transmitted data can be catastrophic to the firm. For example, in the case of a database update program, the presence of line errors can result in incorrect transaction values being posted to the accounts. The following two techniques are commonly used to detect and correct such data errors before they are processed.

ECHO CHECK. The **echo check** involves the receiver of the message returning the message to the sender. The sender compares the returned message with a stored copy of the original. If there is a discrepancy between the returned message and the original, suggesting a transmission error, the message is retransmitted. This technique reduces, by one-half, throughput over communications channels. Using full-duplex channels, which allow both parties to transmit and receive simultaneously, can increase throughput.

PARITY CHECK. The **parity check** incorporates an extra bit (the parity bit) into the structure of a bit string when it is created or transmitted. Parity can be both vertical and horizontal (longitudinal). Figure 16-8 illustrates both types of parities. Vertical parity adds the parity bit to each character in the message when the characters are originally coded and stored in magnetic form. For example, the number of 1 bits in the bit structure of each character is counted. If the number is even (for instance, there are four 1 bits in a given eight-bit character), the system assigns the parity bit a value of one. If the number of 1 bits is odd, a 0 parity bit is added to the bit structure.

The concern is that during transmission, a 1 bit will be converted to a 0 bit or vice versa, thus destroying the bit structure integrity of the character. In other words, the original character is incorrectly presented as a different yet valid character. Errors of this sort, if undetected, could alter

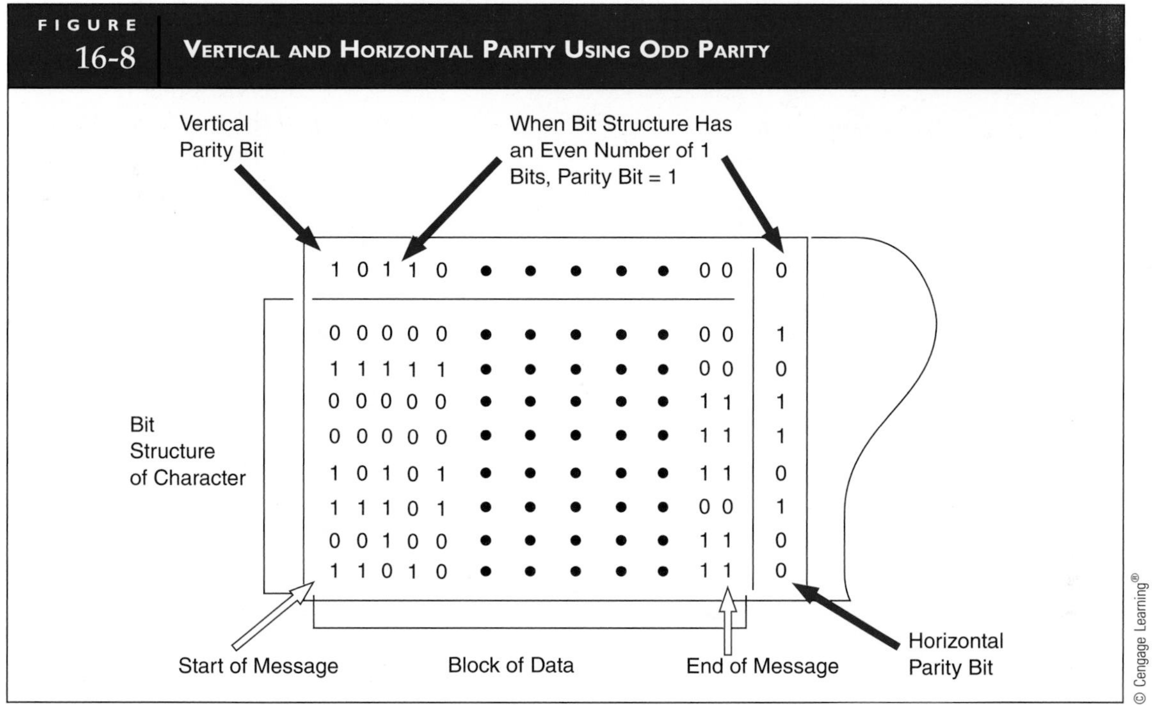

FIGURE 16-8 VERTICAL AND HORIZONTAL PARITY USING ODD PARITY

financial numbers. A parity check can detect errors at the receiving end. The system again counts the 1 bits, which should always equal an odd number. If a 1 bit is added to or removed from the bit structure during transmission, the number of 1 bits for the character will be even, which would signal an error.

The problem with using vertical parity alone is the possibility that an error will change two bits in the structure simultaneously, thus retaining the parity of the character. In fact, some estimates indicate a 40 to 50 percent chance that line noise will corrupt more than one bit within a character. Using horizontal parity in conjunction with vertical parity reduces this problem. In Figure 16-8, notice the parity bit following each block of characters. The combination of vertical and horizontal parity provides a higher degree of protection from line errors.

Audit Objectives Relating to Equipment Failure

The auditor's objective is to verify the integrity of the electronic commerce transactions by determining that controls are in place to detect and correct message loss due to equipment failure.

Audit Procedures Relating to Equipment Failure

To achieve this control objective, the auditor can select a sample of messages from the transaction log and examine them for garbled contents that line noise causes. The auditor should verify that all corrupted messages were successfully retransmitted.

Electronic Data Interchange (EDI) Controls

EDI substantially changes the way companies do business and creates unique control issues that accountants need to recognize. Before examining these issues, let's first review the EDI concept. Figure 16-9 illustrates the data flow through the basic elements of an EDI system that links two trading partners—the customer (Company A) and the vendor (Company B). When Company A wishes to place an order with Company B, Company A's purchases system automatically creates and sends an electronic purchase order to its EDI translation software. The translation software converts the purchase order from Company A's internal format to a standard format, such as

FIGURE 16-9 EDI SYSTEM

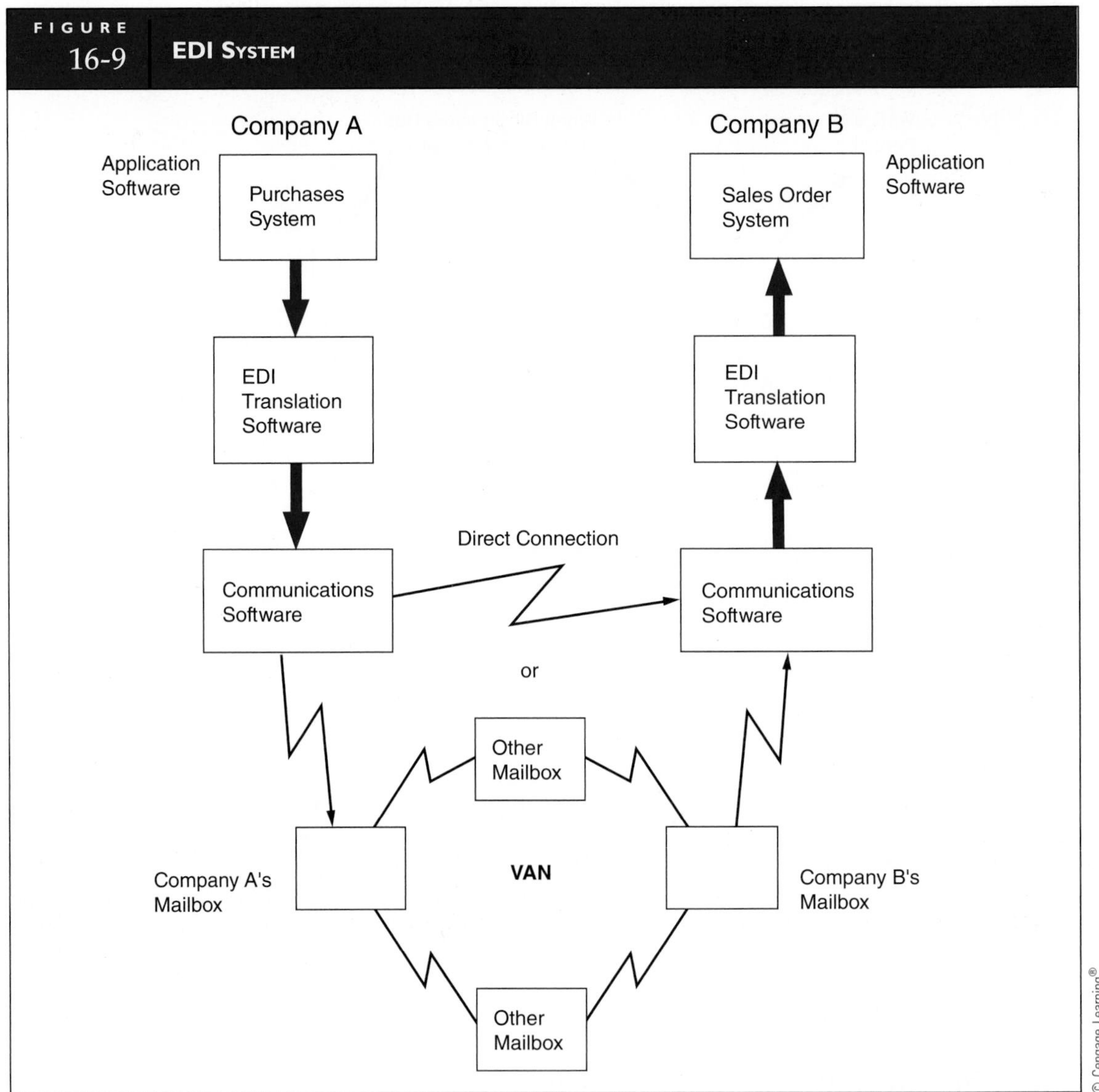

ANSI X.12. Next, the communications software adds the protocols to the message to prepare it for transmission over the communication channel. The transmission may be either a direct connection between the trading partners or an indirect connection through a value-added network (VAN). At Company B, the process is reversed, yielding a sales order in Company B's internal format, which its sales order system processes automatically.

The absence of human intervention in this process presents a unique twist to traditional control problems, including ensuring that transactions are authorized and valid, preventing unauthorized access to data files, and maintaining an audit trail of transactions. The following techniques are used in dealing with these issues.

TRANSACTION AUTHORIZATION AND VALIDATION

Both the customer and the supplier must establish that the transaction being processed is to (or from) a valid trading partner and is authorized. This can be accomplished at three points in the process.

1. Some VANs have the capability of validating passwords and user ID codes for the vendor by matching these against a valid customer file. The VAN rejects any unauthorized trading partner transactions before they reach the vendor's system.

2. Before being converted, the translation software can validate the trading partner's ID and password against a validation file in the firm's database.
3. Before processing, the trading partner's application software references the valid customer and vendor files to validate the transaction.

ACCESS CONTROL

To function smoothly, EDI trading partners must permit a degree of access to private data files that would be forbidden in a traditional environment. The trading partner agreement will determine the degree of access control in place. For example, it may permit the customer's system to access the vendor's inventory files to determine if inventories are available. Also, trading partners may agree that the prices on the purchase order will be binding on both parties. The customer must, therefore, periodically access the vendor's price list file to keep pricing information current. Alternatively, the vendor may need access to the customer's price list to update prices.

To guard against unauthorized access, each company must establish valid vendor and customer files. Inquiries against databases can thus be validated, and unauthorized attempts at access can be rejected. User authority tables can also be established, which specify the degree of access a trading partner is allowed. For example, the partner may be authorized to read inventory or pricing data but not change values.

EDI AUDIT TRAIL

The absence of source documents in EDI transactions eliminates the traditional audit trail and restricts the ability of accountants to verify the validity, completeness, timing, and accuracy of transactions. One technique for restoring the audit trail is to maintain a control log, which records the transaction's flow through each phase of the EDI system. Figure 16-10 illustrates how this approach may be employed.

As the transaction is received at each stage in the process, an entry is made in the log. In the customer's system, the transaction log can be reconciled to ensure that all transactions the purchases system initiated were correctly translated and communicated. Likewise, in the vendor's system, the control log will establish that the sales order system correctly translated and processed all messages that the communications software received.

Audit Objectives Relating to EDI

The auditor's objectives are to determine that (1) all EDI transactions are authorized, validated, and in compliance with the trading partner agreement; (2) no unauthorized organizations gain access to database records; (3) authorized trading partners have access only to approved data; and (4) adequate controls are in place to ensure a complete audit trail of all EDI transactions.

Audit Procedures Relating to EDI

To achieve these control objectives, the auditor may perform the following tests of controls.

TESTS OF AUTHORIZATION AND VALIDATION CONTROLS. The auditor should establish that trading partner identification codes are verified before transactions are processed. To accomplish this, the auditor should (1) review agreements with the VAN facility to validate transactions and ensure that information regarding valid trading partners is complete and correct, and (2) examine the organization's valid trading partner file for accuracy and completeness.

TESTS OF ACCESS CONTROLS. Security over the valid trading partner file and databases is central to the EDI control framework. The auditor can verify control adequacy in the following ways:

1. The auditor should determine that access to the valid vendor or customer file is limited to authorized employees only. The auditor should verify that passwords and authority tables control access to this file and that the data are encrypted.

FIGURE 16-10 EDI System Using Transaction Control Log for Audit Trail

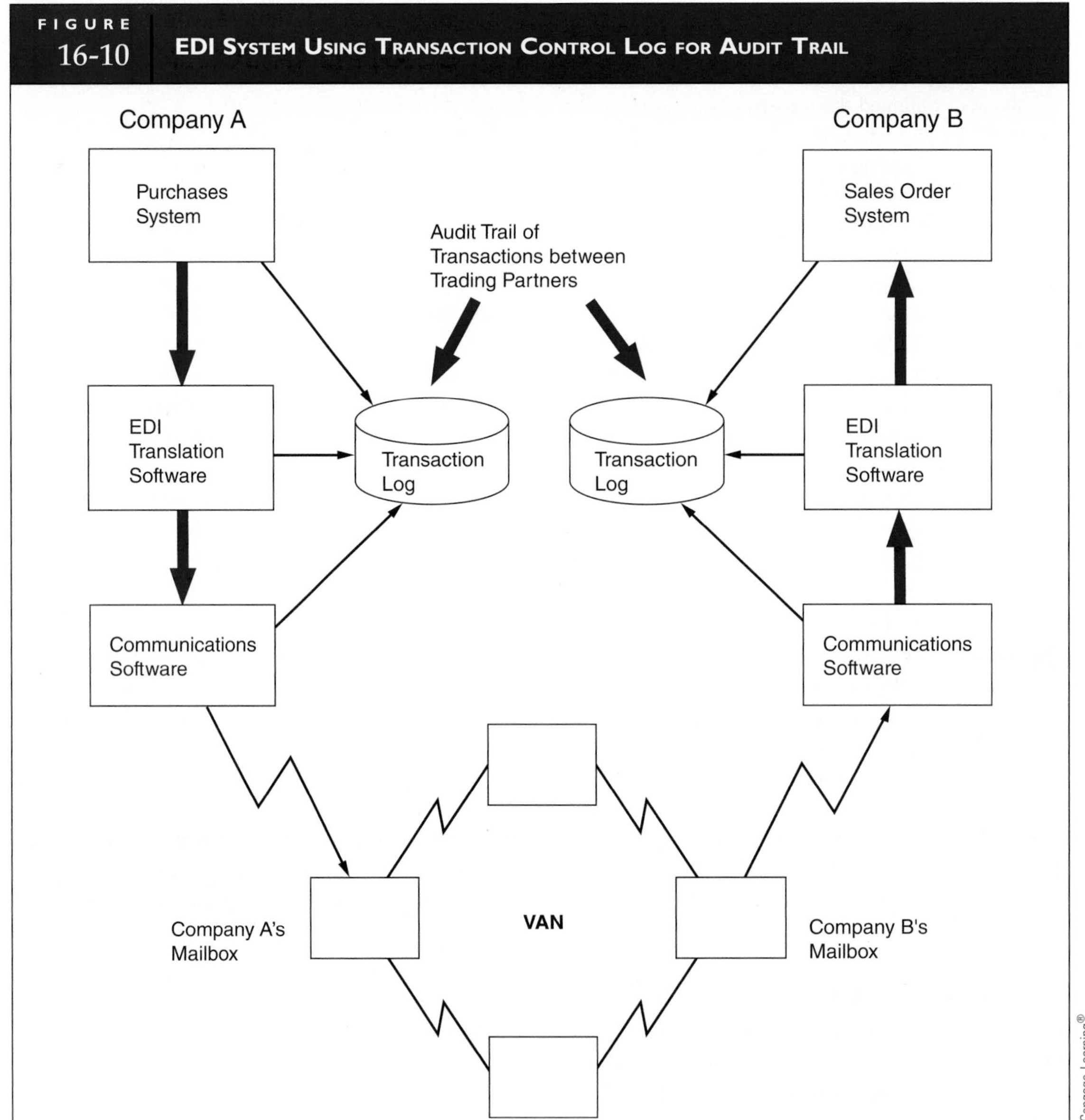

2. The trading agreement will determine the degree of access a trading partner should have to the firm's database records (such as inventory levels and price lists). The auditor should reconcile the terms of the trading agreement against the trading partner's access privileges stated in the database authority table.
3. The auditor should simulate access by a sample of trading partners and attempt to violate access privileges.

TESTS OF AUDIT TRAIL CONTROLS. The auditor should verify that the EDI system produces a transaction log that tracks transactions through all stages of processing. By selecting a sample of transactions and tracing these through the process, the auditor can verify that key data values were recorded correctly at each point.

Summary

This chapter continued the discussion of IT general controls and audit tests begun in Chapter 15. It examined the risks and controls over operating systems, database management systems, networks, and EDI systems. The principal threats to the operating system are (l) unauthorized access, (2) intentional or unintentional insertion of viruses, and (3) loss of data due to system malfunctions.

Unauthorized access to the database can be effectively controlled through the use of well-designed user views, authorization rules, user-defined procedures, and data encryption. Backup and recovery techniques can be used to safeguard data against system malfunctions. Networks and communication links are susceptible to exposures from both criminal subversion and equipment failure. Subversive threats can be minimized through a variety of security and access control measures, including firewalls, IPS, DPI, data encryption, and call-back devices. Equipment failure usually takes the form of line errors, which noise in communication lines causes. These can be effectively reduced through echo checks and parity checks. The discussion then turned to EDI, in which firms are faced with a variety of exposures that arise in connection with an environment void of human intermediaries to authorize or review transactions. Controls in an EDI environment are achieved primarily through programmed procedures to authorize transactions, limit access to data files, and ensure that transactions the system processes are valid.

Appendix

Malicious and Destructive Programs

Virus

A virus is a program (usually destructive) that attaches itself to a legitimate program to penetrate the operating system and destroy application programs, data files, and the operating system itself. An insidious aspect of a virus is its ability to spread throughout the host system and to other systems before perpetrating its destructive acts. Often, a virus will have a built-in counter that will trigger its destructive role only after it has copied itself a specified number of times to other programs and systems. The virus thus grows geometrically, which makes tracing its origin extremely difficult.

Personal computers are a major source of virus penetration. When connected in a network or a mainframe, an infected PC can upload the virus to the host system. Once in the host, the virus can spread throughout the operating system and to other users. Virus programs usually attach themselves to the following types of files:

1. An .EXE or .COM program file
2. An .OVL (overlay) program file
3. The boot sector of a disk
4. A device driver program

Mechanisms for spreading viruses include e-mail attachments, downloading of public-domain programs from the Internet, and using illegal bootleg software. Because of the general lack of control in PC operating systems, microcomputers connected to mainframes pose a serious threat to the mainframe environment as well.

Worm

The term *worm* is used interchangeably with *virus.* A worm is a software program that virtually burrows into the computer's memory and replicates itself into areas of idle memory. The worm systematically occupies idle memory until the memory is exhausted and the system fails. Technically, worms differ from viruses in that the replicated worm modules remain in contact with the original worm that controls their growth, whereas the replicated virus modules grow independently.

Logic Bomb

A logic bomb is a destructive program, such as a virus, that some predetermined event triggers. Often a date (such as Friday the 13th, April Fool's Day, or the 4th of July) will be the logic bomb's trigger. Events of less public prominence, such as the dismissal of an employee, have also triggered these bombs. For example, during the customary two-week severance period, a terminated programmer may embed a logic bomb in the system that will get activated six months after his or her departure from the firm.

Back Door

A back door (also called a trap door) is a software program that allows unauthorized access to a system without going through the normal (front door) log-on procedure. Programmers who want to provide themselves with unrestricted access to a system that they are developing for users may create a log-on procedure that will accept either the user's private password or their own secret password, thus creating a back door to the system. The purpose of the back door may be to provide easy access to perform program maintenance, or it may be to perpetrate a fraud or insert a virus into the system.

Trojan Horse

A Trojan horse is a program whose purpose is to capture IDs and passwords from unsuspecting users. These programs are designed to mimic the normal log-on procedures of the operating system. When the user enters his or her ID and password, the Trojan horse stores a copy of them in a secret file. At some later date, the author of the Trojan horse uses these IDs and passwords to access the system and masquerade as an authorized user.

Key Terms

access control list (683)
access controls (688)
access token (682)
advanced encryption standard (AES) (695)
application-level firewalls (693)
backup controls (688)
biometric devices (690)
call-back device (699)
certification authority (CA) (696)
checkpoint feature (691)
compilers (681)
data encryption (690)
database authorization table (689)
deep packet inspection (DPI) (693)
digest (696)
digital certificate (696)
digital envelope (696)
digital signature (696)
discretionary access privileges (683)
echo check (700)
EDE3 (696)
EEE3 (696)
encryption (695)
event monitoring (687)

firewall (692)
interpreters (681)
intrusion prevention systems (IPS) (693)
keystroke monitoring (687)
line error (700)
log-on procedure (682)
message sequence numbering (699)
message transaction log (699)
network-level firewalls (692)
one-time password (685)
operating system (681)
operating system security (682)
parity check (700)
password (684)
private key (695)
public key encryption (695)
recovery module (691)
request-response technique (699)
reusable password (684)
RSA (Rivest-Shamir-Adleman) (696)
screening router (692)
system audit trails (686)
transaction log (691)
triple-DES encryption (696)
user-defined procedure (690)
user view (688)

Review Questions

1. What are the five control objectives of an operating system?
2. What are the three main tasks the operating system performs?
3. What is the purpose of an access control list?
4. What are the four techniques that a virus could use to infect a system?
5. What is an access token?
6. Explain discretionary access privileges.
7. What is event monitoring?
8. What is keystroke monitoring?
9. What is a vaccine, and what are its limitations?
10. What are the four basic backup and recovery features necessary in a database management system? Briefly explain each.
11. What are the risks from subversive threats?
12. What are the risks from equipment failure?
13. What is a firewall?
14. Distinguish between network-level and application-level firewalls.
15. What are the most common forms of contra-security behavior?
16. What can be done to defeat a DDoS attack?
17. How does public key encryption work?
18. What is a digital envelope?
19. What is a digital signature?
20. Categorize each of the following as either an equipment failure control or an unauthorized access control.
    a. message authentication
    b. parity check
    c. call-back device
    d. echo check
    e. line error
    f. data encryption
    g. request-response technique
21. What is DPI?
22. At what three points in an electronic data interchange transaction and validation process can authorization and validation be accomplished?

Discussion Questions

1. Why is human behavior considered one of the biggest potential threats to operating system integrity?
2. Why would a systems programmer create a back door if he or she has access to the program in his or her day-to-day tasks?
3. Discuss the issues that need to be considered before implementing keystroke monitoring.
4. Explain how an access token and an access control list are used to approve or deny access.
5. Explain how a Trojan horse may be used to penetrate a system.

6. Discuss six ways that threats from destructive programs can be substantially reduced through a combination of technology controls and administrative procedures.
7. Explain the three ways that audit trails can be used to support security objectives.
8. Explain how poorly designed audit trail logs can actually be dysfunctional.
9. Many authorities believe that the employer does not prosecute 90 percent of all computer fraud acts. What do you think accounts for this lack of prosecution? Discuss the importance of the establishment of a formal policy for taking disciplinary (or legal) action against security violations.
10. Why is it risky to allow programmers to create user subschemas and assign access authority to users? What unethical technique do programmers sometimes use when they are not allowed to assign access authority to users?
11. Is access control of greater concern in the flat-file or database file environment?
12. How can passwords actually circumvent security? What actions can be taken to minimize this?
13. Explain how the one-time password approach works.
14. End-user computing has become extremely popular in distributed data processing organizations. The end users like it because they think they can more readily design and implement their own applications. Does this type of environment always foster more efficient development of applications? Explain your answer.
15. Distinguish between data access and access privileges. Design and explain a database authorization table as an example.
16. What are the objectives of auditors in auditing data management?
17. What are some tests of data communications controls?
18. Explain how smurf attacks and SYN flood attacks can be controlled.
19. Discuss the risks from equipment failure and how they can be controlled.
20. Does every organization that has a LAN need a firewall?
21. Describe three ways in which IPS can be used to protect against DDoS attacks.
22. What problem is common to all private key encryption techniques?
23. What is RSA encryption?
24. Explain the triple-DES encryption techniques known as EEE3 and EDE3.
25. Distinguish between a digital signature and a digital certificate.
26. Describe a digest within the context of a digital signature.
27. What is a digital envelope?
28. Why is inadequate segregation of duties a problem in the personal computer environment?
29. Why is the request-response technique important? Discuss the reasons an intruder may wish to prevent or delay the receipt of a message.
30. Is backup redundancy inefficient?
31. Discuss how the widespread use of laptop and notebook computers is making data encryption standards more easily penetrable.
32. Discuss the unique control problems EDI creates.
33. "In an EDI system, only the customer needs to verify that the order being placed is from a valid supplier and not vice versa." Do you agree with this statement? Why or why not?
34. Discuss how EDI creates an environment in which sensitive information, such as inventory amounts and price data, is no longer private. What potential dangers exist if the proper controls are not in place? Give an example.

Multiple-Choice Questions

1. When someone disguises the source of Internet messages to make appear that it is coming from a different source, this is called:
   a. deep packet inspection
   b. message packet switching.
   c. dual-homed signaling
   d. IP screening.
   e. none of the above
2. A program that attaches to another legitimate program but does NOT replicate itself is called a
   a. virus.
   b. worm.
   c. Trojan horse.
   d. logic bomb.
   e. none of the above.
3. The purpose of a checkpoint procedure is to facilitate restarting after
   a. data processing errors.
   b. data input errors.
   c. the failure to have all input data ready on time.
   d. computer operator intervention.
   e. none of the above.
4. A user's application may consist of several modules stored in separate memory locations, each with its own data. One module must not be allowed to destroy or corrupt another module. This is an objective of
   a. EDI controls.
   b. network controls.
   c. Detection Risk controls
   d. application controls.
   e. none of the above
5. An integrated group of programs that supports the applications and facilitates their access to specified resources is called a(n)
   a. operating system.
   b. database management system.
   c. utility system.
   d. facility system.
   e. none of the above.
6. Which of the following is NOT a network control objective?
   a. Preventing illegal access
   b. Correcting message loss due to equipment failure
   c. Maintaining the critical application list
   d. Rendering useless any data that a perpetrator successfully captures
   e. All the above are network control objectives
7. Reviewing database authority tables is an example of a(n)
   a. operating resource control.
   b. organizational structure control.
   c. data resource control.
   d. none of the above
8. The database attributes that individual users have permission to access are defined in the
   a. operating system.
   b. user manual.
   c. database schema.
   d. user view.
   e. application listing.
9. Transmitting numerous SYN packets to a targeted receiver, but NOT responding to an ACK, is
   a. a DES message.
   b. a denial of service attack.
   c. the request-response technique.
   d. a call-back device.
   e. none of the above
10. Which of the following is not an operating system objective?
    a. The operating system must protect itself from users.
    b. The operating system must protect users from themselves.
    c. The operating system must be protected from its environment.
    d. The operating system must protect users from each other.
    e. All of the above are operating system objectives.

Problems

1. NETWORK CONTROL

A manufacturing company has a sales force that works remotely visiting clients in their assigned sales area. The sales staff access the company's central computer system via their laptops to submit sales invoices, access customer credit and sales data, and check e-mail.

Required

Describe the types of control needed to mitigate potential risks in this environment.

2. SYSTEM RISKS AND CONTROLS

Last year ACME Manufacturing commissioned Fly-By-Night Consulting (FBNC) to oversee the implementation of a new information system. Based on FBNC recommendations to establish an "open" environment with a more efficient workflow, the IT professionals at ACME have provided users with relatively free access to the computer center and applications.

Almost since implementation of the system malicious programs, such as viruses, worms, and Trojan horses, have plagued the company and caused minor data corruption. Recently, however, systems problems and hardware failures have caused more severe disruptions and have caused the operating system to crash. The CEO of ACME was also informed that confidential company information may have been printed to hard copy as a result of these crashes and disposed of in the trash. Also, important digital documents appear to have been erased from storage media.

Required

a. Describe operating risks at ACME.
b. Describe the controls that need to be implemented to mitigate the risks.

3. INTERNAL CONTROL AND FRAUD

Mary Scott has a master's degree in computer science and experience as a network engineer. For the past two years, however, she has worked for Hoffman Inc as an accounts payable clerk. She did not disclose her technology background on her resume when she applied for the clerk position. Early on Mary established a reputation as a hardworking, enthusiastic, and reliable employee. She often works late and is dedicated to doing an excellent job. Her late night presence in the company became a common occurrence that was at first appreciated by her boss, and then virtually went unnoticed.

While working late, Mary used her computer skills to install a sniffer program on the intranet to capture employee IDs and passwords. With the information she collected Mary was able to play many roles and establish herself as a vendor, receiving clerk, cash disbursements clerk, and general ledger clerk. With this authority along with her legitimate role of AP clerk Mary implemented a vendor fraud scheme, which she has been perpetrating for over a year at a cost of $250,000 to Hoffman Inc.

Required

Describe the controls that could have prevented Mary from perpetrating this fraud.

4. INTERNAL CONTROL AND FRAUD

Stephanie Baskill, an unemployed accounting clerk, lives one block from Cleaver Manufacturing Company. While walking her dog last year, she noticed some ERP manuals in the dumpsters. Curious, she took the manuals home with her. She found that the documentation in the manual was dated 2 months previous, so she thought that the information must be fairly current. Over the next month, Stephanie continued to collect all types of manuals from the dumpster during her dog-walking excursions. Cleaver Manufacturing Company was apparently updating all of its documentation manuals and placing them online. Eventually, Stephanie found manuals about critical inventory reorder formulas, the billing system, the sales order system, the payables system, and the operating system. Stephanie went to the local library and read as much as she could about this particular operating system.

To gain access to the organization, she took a low-profile position as a cleaning woman, giving her access to all areas in the building. While working, Stephanie snooped through offices, watched people who were working late type in their passwords, and guessed their passwords. She ultimately printed out lists of user IDs and passwords using a Trojan horse virus, thus obtaining all the necessary passwords to set herself up as a supplier, customer, systems operator, and systems librarian.

As a customer, she ordered enough goods to trigger the automatic inventory procurement system to purchase more raw materials. Then, as a supplier, Stephanie would deliver the goods at the specified price. She then adjusted the transaction logs once the bills were paid to cover her tracks. Stephanie was able to embezzle, on average, $125,000 a month. About 16 months after she began working at Cleaver, the controller saw her at a very expensive French restaurant one evening, driving a Jaguar. He told the internal auditors to keep a close watch on her, and they were able to catch her in the act.

Required

a. What weaknesses in the organization's control structure must have existed to permit this type of embezzlement?
b. What specific control techniques and procedures could have helped prevent or detect this fraud?

5. INPUT CONTROLS AND NETWORKING

A global manufacturing company has over 100 subsidiaries worldwide reporting to it each month. The reporting units prepare the basic financial statements and other key financial data on prescribed forms, which are e-mailed or faxed to the corporate headquarters. The financial data are then entered into the corporate database from which consolidated statements are prepared for internal planning and decision making.

Current reporting policy requires that the subsidiaries provide the previous month's reports by the tenth working day of each new month. Accounting department staff log and enter the reports into the database. Approximately 15 percent of the reporting units are delinquent in submitting their reports and three to four days are required to enter all the data into the database. After the data are loaded into the system, data verification programs are run to check footings, cross-statement consistency, and dollar range limits. Any errors in the data are traced and corrected, and reporting units are notified of all errors via e-mail.

The company has decided to upgrade its computer communications network with a new system that will support more timely receipt of data at corporate headquarters. The IT department at corporate headquarters is responsible for the overall design and implementation of the new system. It will use current computer communications technology and install LANs, PCs, and servers at all reporting units.

The new system will allow clerks at the remote sites to send financial data to the corporate office via the Internet. The required form templates will be downloaded to the remote sites, along with the data verification programs. The clerks will enter data into the forms to create a temporary file, which data verification programs will check for errors. All corrections can thus be made before transmitting the data to headquarters. Either the data would be transmitted to corporate headquarters immediately, or the corporate headquarters computer would retrieve it from disk storage at the remote site as needed. Data used at corporate headquarters would therefore be free from errors and ready for consolidation.

The company's controller is pleased with the prospects of the new system, which should shorten the reporting period by three days. He is, however, concerned about security and data integrity during the transmission. He has scheduled a meeting with key personnel from the systems department to discuss these concerns.

Required

The company could experience data security and integrity problems when transmitting data between the reporting units and corporate headquarters.

a. Identify and explain the data security and integrity problems that could occur.
b. For each problem identified, describe a control procedure that could be employed to minimize or eliminate the problem. Use the following format to present your answer.

Problem Identification and Explanation	Control Procedure and Explanation

6. PREVENTIVE CONTROLS

Listed here are five scenarios. For each scenario, discuss the possible damages that can occur. Suggest a preventive control.

a. An intruder taps into a telecommunications device and retrieves the identifying codes and personal identification numbers for ATM cardholders. (The user subsequently codes this information onto a magnetic coding device and places this strip on a piece of cardboard.)
b. Because of occasional noise on a transmission line, electronic messages received are extremely garbled.
c. Because of occasional noise on a transmission line, data being transferred are lost or garbled.
d. An intruder is temporarily delaying important strategic messages over the telecommunications lines.
e. An intruder is altering electronic messages before the user receives them.

7. OPERATING SYSTEM RISKS AND CONTROLS

Listed here are four scenarios. For each scenario, discuss the potential consequences and give a prevention technique.

a. A company has recently installed a new computer network. The operating philosophy adopted by the new network administrator was to establish an open system that would foster work group data sharing, flexible access, and minimal inconvenience to the network users. To accomplish this objective, the data administrator assigned employee access privileges to data based on department and functional affiliation rather than specific tasks.
b. Mary is a system programmer who was told she would be terminated in 3 weeks due to poor performance and was asked to conclude all of her projects during that three-week period. Two weeks later Mary created a logic bomb designed to get activated 3 months after her departure. Subsequently, the bomb destroyed hundreds of records in her previous employer's accounts receivable invoice file.
c. Robert discovered a new sensitivity analysis public-domain program on the Internet. He downloaded the software to his laptop at home, which he also used at his office when connecting to the company's network. The program contained a virus that spread to the company's mainframe.
d. Murray, a trusted employee and a systems engineer, had access to both the network access control list and user passwords. The firm's competitor recently hired him for a large increase in salary. After leaving, Murray continued to browse through his old employer's data, such as price lists, customer lists, bids on jobs, and so on. He passed this information on to his new employer.

8. DATABASE AUTHORIZATION TABLE

The following information is stored in two relational database files:

Employee Master File
Social Security number
Name
Address
Date hired
Hourly wage rate
Marital status
Number of exemptions

Weekly Payroll File
Social Security number
Hours worked
Deductions Bonuses

Required

a. Bogey works in personnel and Bacall works in payroll. Prepare a database authorization table that you think is appropriate for Bogey and Bacall for these two files.
b. Discuss potential risks if the right controls are not in place or if Bogey and Bacall collude.

9. SECURITY AND CONTROL ASSESSMENT

Better Business Company (BBC) is in the process of planning a more advanced computer-based information system. Slavish, & Moore, LLP, BBC's consulting firm, has recently been provided with an overview of their proposed plan:

To ensure that the system functions as needed, the BBC Information System (BBCIS) will be created with input from its employees. System construction will begin with prototyping, computer-aided software engineering (CASE) technology, and Gantt charts. From this point, IT professionals and a systems administrator, who are full-time employees of BBC, will create data models of the business process, define conceptual user views, design database tables, and specify system controls. Users in each department will submit written descriptions of their information needs and business problems to the IT professionals, who will then perform feasibility studies. Each aspect of the system will be documented in accordance with best practices and standards.

The systems administrator will determine access privileges and maintain access control lists and database authorization tables. The administrator will have sole access to the transaction log, which will be used to record all changes made to database tables. A role of the administrator is to detect unauthorized access, reconstruct events, and promote personal accountability. The systems administrator will also be responsible for ensuring that virus protection software is current. Another important task of the administrator is to ensure that adequate backup to databases and applications occur and that disks and tapes are stored in a secure off-site location.

Each employee requiring computer access will be assigned a user ID and password that will be entered when logging onto the system. If a computer terminal is left idle for more than five minutes, the system will close out the session and the user will need to log on again. Furthermore, users will be required to change their passwords once every year.

Hardware will be purchased from Bell Computer Company with the advice of in-house systems developers. With the exception of basic applications, user departments will be allowed to purchase additional software that they need, which will be added to the system.

BBCIS will run on a central server in the computer center located in the company's administration building. Two security guards will be assigned to the entrance to the computer room. To access the computer center, employees will swipe their ID cards on the lock to the main entrance door. The system will record the times of each entry and departure from the center. The data center will employ an advanced air-conditioning and air filtration system to eliminate dust and pollens. There will also be a sprinkler system to minimize damages in case of a fire.

Required

Based on BBC's plans for the implementation of a new computer system, describe the potential risks and needed controls. Classify these according to the relevant areas of the COSO framework.

10. NETWORK ACCESS CONTROL

Ajax Automotive supports retail automotive centers on the east coast by supplying them with quality car and truck parts such as brake pads, oil filters, water pumps, etc. The company's 123 sales representatives work exclusively in the field visiting client company locations and submitting sales orders from laptop computers via an Internet connection to the corporate offices in Delaware. All of Ajax's sales orders are received in this manner. Customer account, sales history, inventory, and cash receipts records are stored on a central server at the corporate site. Customers are billed digitally from the corporate office on a net 30 basis.

Required

Outline the access controls that would be appropriate for this situation. Explain why these controls are necessary.

11. INTERNAL CONTROL AND FRAUD

John Martin, a highly skilled computer technician with a master's degree in computer science, took a low-profile evening job as a janitor at Kent Manufacturing Company. Since the position was of a low-level category, no security clearance or background check was necessary. While working at nights, John snooped through offices for confidential information regarding system operations, internal controls, and the financial thresholds for transaction that would trigger special reviews. He observed employees who were working late type in their passwords and managed to install a Trojan Horse virus onto the system to capture the IDs and passwords of other employees. During the course of several weeks, John obtained the necessary IDs and passwords to set himself up in the system as a supplier, a customer, and systems administrator, which gave him access to most of the accounting system's functions.

As a customer, John ordered inventory that was shipped to a rented building and later sold. As system administrator, he approved his credit sales orders and falsified his customer payment records to make it appear that the goods had been paid for. He also generated purchase orders to himself and created false receiving reports and supplier invoices as part of a vendor fraud scheme. He was thus able to fool the system into setting up accounts payable to himself and writing checks in payment of inventory items that the company never received.

John was careful to ensure that all his transactions fell just below the financial materiality thresholds that triggered special reviews. Nevertheless, his fraud schemes cost Kent Manufacturing approximately $100,000 per month and went undetected for 1½ years. John, however, became overconfident and careless in his life style. Working late one evening, the internal auditor observed John arriving for work in an expensive sports car that seemed out of place for a poorly paid janitor. The auditor initiated an investigation that exposed John's activities. He was arrested and charged with computer fraud.

Required

a. What controls weaknesses allowed John to perpetrate these frauds?
b. Explain the controls that should be in places to reduce the risk of fraud.

12. DATABASE AUTHORIZATION TABLE

Some relevant database tables and attributes are presented in the figure designated Problem 12 on the following page.

Required

a. Create a database authorization table for an Accounts Payable clerk. Structure your response similar to the example below:

Authority Level	Table 1 Name	Table 2 Name	Table .....
Read	Y	Y	Y
Insert	Y	N	N
Modify	Y		
Delete			

Indicate the name of each table the AP clerk may access and the degree of access privilege as defined below:

Read existing records in the table

Insert new record into the table,

Modify or edit existing records in the table

Delete existing attribute values or entire records from the table

b. Explain your answers to part (a) above.

Problem 12	
Customer Table Customer Number Billing Address Shipping Address Available Credit	**Sales Invoice (AR)** Sales Invoice Number Customer Number Product Number Invoice Amount Invoice Date
Inventory Table Product Number Quantity on hand Unit Cost Sales Price Vendor Number	**Cash Receipts Table** Cash Receipts Number Customer Number Check Number Sales Invoice Number Check Amount Date
Vendor Table Vendor Number Vendor Address Tel Number	**Purchase Order Table** PO Number Vendor Number Product Number Quantity Order Date
Receiving Report Table PO Number Product Number Quantity Received Condition Code Received Date	**Vendor Invoice Table (AP)** Vendor Invoice Num Vendor Number Product Number Invoice Amount Invoice Date
Cash Disbursement Table Check Number Vendor Invoice Num Check Amount Date	

13. DATABASE AUTHORIZATION TABLE

Required

a. Using the database table and attribute structures presented in Problem 12 create a database authorization table for a Sales Clerk. Structure your response similar to the example provided in Problem 12.

b. Explain your answer to (a) above.

CHAPTER

17

Auditing IT Controls Part III: Systems Development, Program Changes, and Application Auditing

Learning Objectives

After studying this chapter, you should:

- Be familiar with the controls and audit tests relevant to the systems development process.
- Understand the risks and controls associated with program change procedures and the role of the source program library.
- Understand the auditing techniques (CAATTs) used to verify the effective functioning of application controls.
- Understand the auditing techniques used to perform substantive tests in an IT environment.

This chapter is divided into four main sections. The first concludes our treatment of general IT controls as outlined in the COSO control framework. The focus is on Sarbanes-Oxley (SOX) compliance regarding systems development activities and program change procedures. This section examines the risks, controls, audit objectives, and tests of controls that may be performed to satisfy compliance or attest responsibilities. The other three sections of the chapter address tests of application controls and substantive testing in an IT environment. These sections present several computer-aided audit tools and techniques (CAATTs) for testing application controls and conclude with a discussion of embedded audit modules and generalized audit software used for substantive testing.

Systems Development Controls

Chapters 13 and 14 presented the systems development life cycle (SDLC) as a multiphase process by which organizations satisfy their formal information needs. An important point at this juncture is that specific SDLC steps will vary from firm to firm. In reviewing the effectiveness of a particular systems development methodology, the accountant should focus on the controllable activities that are common to all systems development approaches. These are outlined in the following section.

CONTROLLING SYSTEMS DEVELOPMENT ACTIVITIES

This section and the one that follows examine several controllable activities that distinguish an effective systems development process. The six activities discussed deal with the authorization, development, and implementation of new systems. Controls over application changes are presented in the next section.

Systems Authorization Activities

All systems should be properly authorized to ensure their economic justification and feasibility. This requires a formal environment in which users submit requests to systems professionals in written form.

User Specification Activities

Users need to be actively involved in the systems development process. The technical complexity of the system should not stifle user involvement. Regardless of the technology involved, the user should create a detailed written description of his or her needs. The creation of a user specification document often involves the joint efforts of the user and systems professionals. However, this document must remain a statement of user needs. It should describe the user's view of the problem, not that of systems professionals alone.

Technical Design Activities

The technical design activities translate user specifications into a set of detailed technical specifications for a system that meets the user's needs. The scope of these activities includes systems analysis, feasibility analysis, and detailed systems design. The adequacy of these activities is measured by the quality of the documentation that emerges from each phase. Documentation is both a control and evidence of control, and it is critical to the system's long-term success. We discussed specific documentation requirements, including designer, operator, user, and auditor documentation, in Chapter 14.

Internal Audit Participation

To meet the governance-related expectations of management under SOX, an organization's internal audit department needs to be independent, objective, and technically qualified. As such, the internal auditor can play an important role in the control of systems development activities. The internal auditor can serve as a liaison between users and the systems professionals to ensure an effective transfer of knowledge. An internal audit group, astute in computer technology and possessing a solid grasp of the business problems to be solved, is invaluable to the organization during all phases of the SDLC. Internal auditors should therefore become formally involved at the inception of the systems development process to oversee the definition of user needs requirements and appropriate controls. Furthermore, this involvement should continue throughout all phases of development and maintenance activities.

Program Testing

All program modules must be thoroughly tested before they are implemented. Figure 17-1 shows a program testing procedure involving the creation of hypothetical master files and transactions files. The results of the tests are then compared against predetermined results to identify programming

FIGURE 17-1 PROGRAM TESTING PROCEDURES

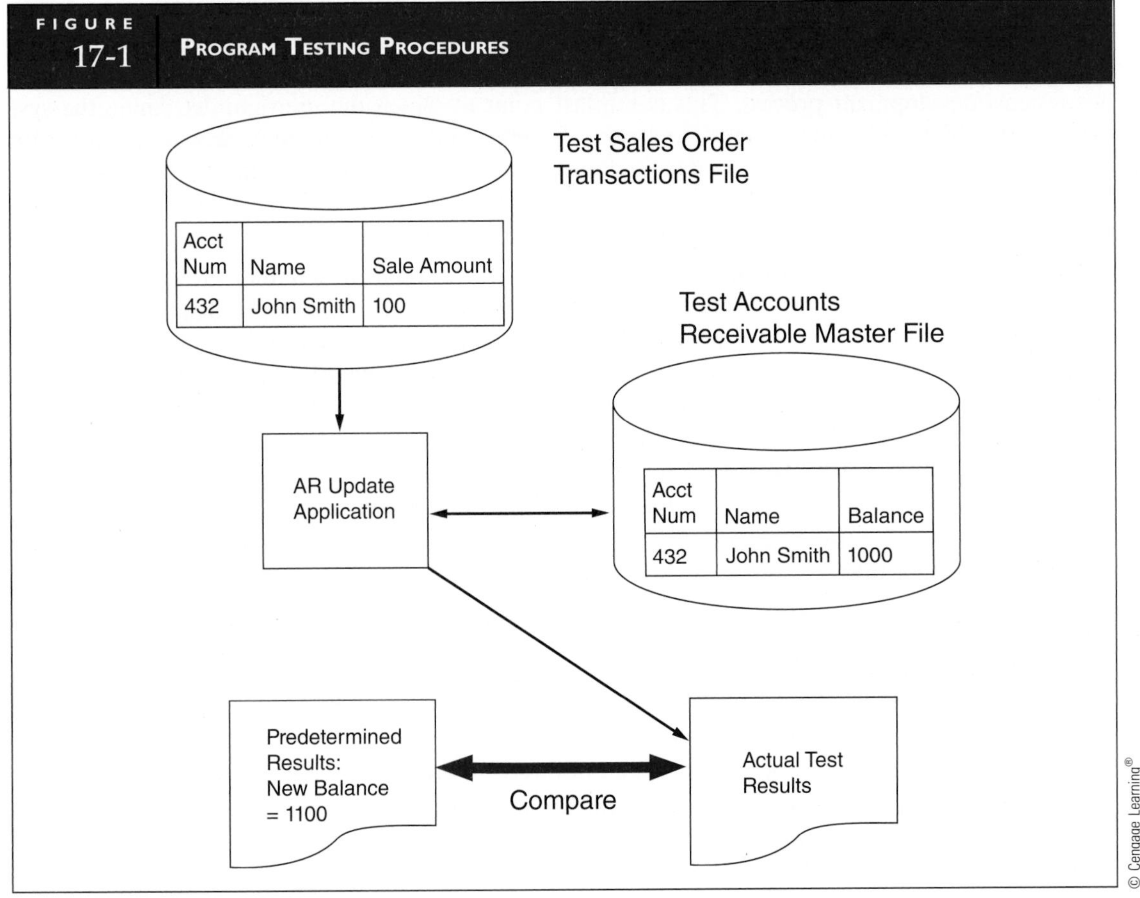

and logic errors. For example, a programmer testing the logic of the accounts receivable update module illustrated in Figure 17-1 might create an accounts receivable master file record for John Smith with a current balance of $1,000 and a sales order transaction record for $100. Before performing the update test, the programmer concludes that a new balance of $1,100 should result. To verify the module's internal logic, the programmer compares the actual results obtained from the test with the predetermined results. This is a very simple example of a program test intended to illustrate the concept. Actual testing would be extensive and involve many transactions that test all aspects of the module's logic.

The task of creating meaningful test data is time-consuming. This should not, however, be considered a single-use activity. As we shall later see, application control testing requires test data. To support future audit needs, test data prepared during systems implementation should be preserved. This will give the auditor a frame of reference for designing and evaluating future audit tests. For example, if a program has undergone no maintenance changes since its implementation, the test results from the audit should be identical to the original test results. Having a basis for comparison, the auditor can thus quickly verify the integrity of the program code. On the other hand, if changes have occurred, the original test data can provide a baseline for assessing the impact of changes. The auditor can thus concentrate tests of application controls on areas where computer logic was changed.

User Test and Acceptance Procedures

Prior to system implementation, the individual modules of the system need to be formally and rigorously tested as a whole. The test team should be composed of user personnel, systems professionals, and internal auditors. The details of the tests performed and their results need to be formally documented and analyzed. Once the test team is satisfied that the system meets its stated requirements, the system can be transferred to the user.

Many consider the formal testing and acceptance event to be the most important control over the systems development process. This is the last point at which the user can determine the system's acceptability prior to it going into service. Whereas discovering a major flaw at this juncture is costly, discovering it later, during day-to-day operations, may be devastating.

Audit Objectives Relating to Systems Development

The auditor's objectives are to ensure that (1) systems development activities are applied consistently and in accordance with management's policies to all systems development projects, (2) the system as originally implemented was free from material errors and fraud, (3) the system was judged necessary and justified at various checkpoints throughout the SDLC, and (4) system documentation is sufficiently accurate and complete to facilitate audit and maintenance activities.

Tests of Systems Development Controls

The auditor should select a sample of completed projects and review the documentation for evidence of compliance with stated systems development policies. Specific points for review should include determining that:

- User and computer services management properly authorized the project.
- A preliminary feasibility study showed that the project had merit.
- A detailed analysis of user needs was conducted that resulted in alternative conceptual designs.
- A cost-benefit analysis was conducted using reasonably accurate values.
- The detailed design was an appropriate and accurate solution to the user's problem.
- Test results show that the system was thoroughly tested at both the individual module and the total system level before implementation. (To confirm these test results, the auditor may decide to retest selected elements of the application.)
- There is a checklist of specific problems detected during the conversion period, along with evidence that they were corrected in the maintenance phase.
- Systems documentation complies with organizational requirements and standards.

CONTROLLING PROGRAM CHANGE ACTIVITIES

Upon implementation, the information system enters the maintenance phase of the SDLC. This is the longest period in the SDLC, often spanning several years. Most systems do not remain static throughout this period. Rather, they undergo substantial changes that often constitute, in dollars, an amount many times their original implementation cost.

Little is served by designing and implementing controls over systems development activities if control is not continued into the maintenance phase. Unrestricted maintenance access to systems increases the risk that application logic will be corrupted either by accident or intent to defraud. To minimize the risk, all maintenance actions should require, as a minimum, four controls: formal authorizations, technical specifications, testing, and documentation updates. In other words, maintenance activities should be given essentially the same treatment as new development. The extent of the change and its potential impact on the system should govern the degree of control applied. When maintenance causes extensive changes to program logic, additional controls, such as involvement by the internal auditor and additional user test, and acceptance procedures may be necessary.

SOURCE PROGRAM LIBRARY CONTROLS

Even with formal maintenance procedures in place, individuals who gain unauthorized access to programs threaten application integrity. The remainder of this section deals with control techniques and procedures for reducing this risk.

FIGURE 17-2 UNCONTROLLED ACCESS TO THE SOURCE PROGRAM LIBRA

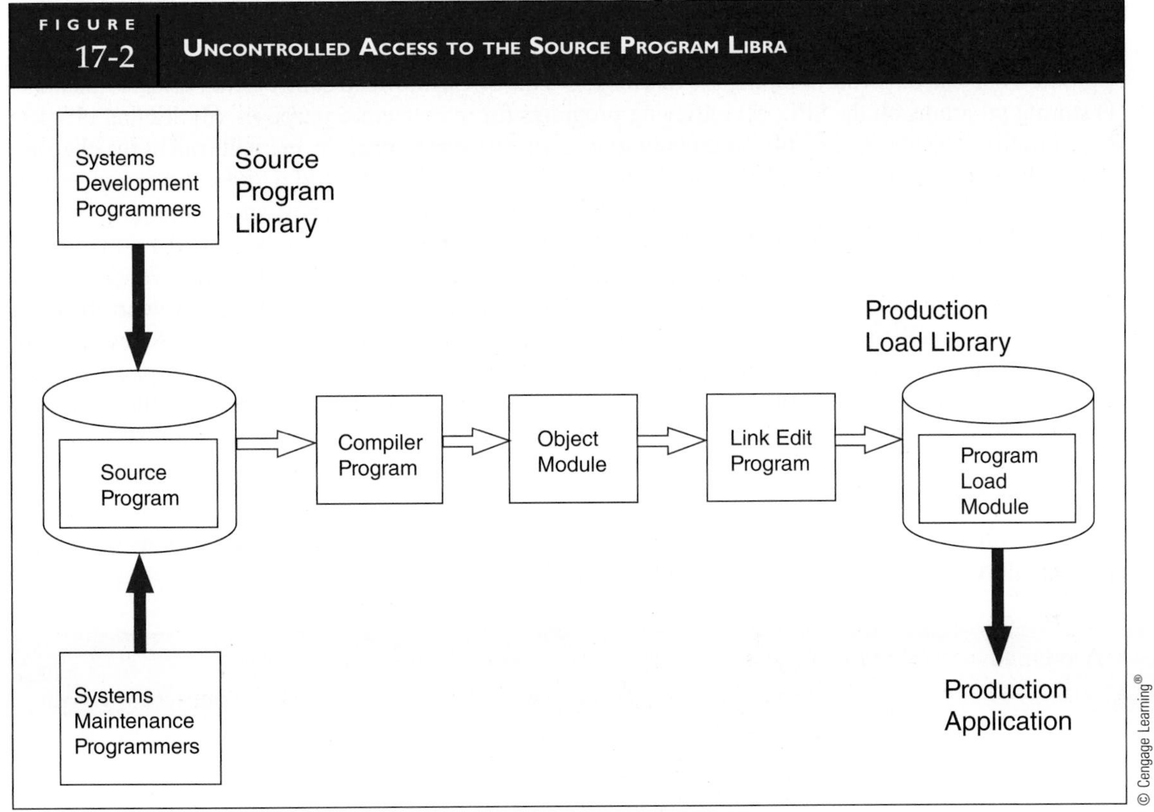

In larger computer systems, application program modules are stored in source code format on a disk repository called the source program library (SPL). Figure 17-2 illustrates the relationship between the SPL and other key components of the operating environment. This material presumes an understanding of the program compilation process. If you are uncertain about the meaning of the terms *source program, compiler,* and *load module,* review the section on language translators on the book's web page, located at www.cengagebrain.com.

Executing a production application requires that the source code be compiled and linked to a load module, which the computer can process. As a practical matter, programs in their compiled state are secure and free from the threat of unauthorized modification. At this point, the source code is not needed for the application to run. In fact, we could destroy it if no future changes to the application were ever to be made. To make a program change, however, requires first changing the logic of the source code on the SPL. This is then recompiled and linked to create a new load module that incorporates the changed code. Clearly, protecting the source code on the SPL is central to protecting the production application.

THE WORST-CASE SITUATION: NO CONTROLS

Figure 17-2 shows the SPL without controls. In this situation, access to application programs is completely unrestricted. Legitimate maintenance programmers and others may access any programs stored in the library, which has no provision for detecting an unauthorized intrusion. Because these programs are open to unauthorized changes, no basis exists for relying on the effectiveness of controls designed into them. Even testing these controls proves only that they work now, but says nothing about how they worked last week or last month. In other words, with no control over access to the SPL, a program's integrity during the period of review cannot be established.

A CONTROLLED SPL ENVIRONMENT

Controlling the SPL requires SPL management system (SPLMS) software. Figure 17-3 illustrates this approach. The black box surrounding the SPL signifies the SPLMS, which controls four critical functions: (1) storing programs on the SPL, (2) retrieving programs for maintenance purposes, (3) deleting obsolete programs from the library, and (4) documenting program changes to provide an audit trail of the changes.

You have probably observed the similarities between the SPLMS and a database management system (DBMS). This is a valid analogy, the difference being that SPL software manages program files and DBMSs manage data files. Computer manufacturers may supply SPLMS software as part of the operating system, or the software may be purchased through third-party vendors.

The mere presence of an SPLMS does not guarantee program integrity. Again, we can draw an analogy with the DBMS. To achieve data integrity, the DBMS must be properly deployed; control does not come automatically—it must be planned. Likewise, an SPL requires specific planning and control techniques to ensure program integrity. The control techniques discussed in the following section address the most vulnerable areas and should be considered minimum SPL controls.

Password Control

Password control over the SPL is similar to password controls in a DBMS. Every financially significant program stored in the SPL can be assigned a separate password. As previously discussed, passwords

FIGURE 17-3 SOURCE PROGRAM LIBRARY UNDER THE CONTROL OF SPL MANAGEMENT SOFTWARE

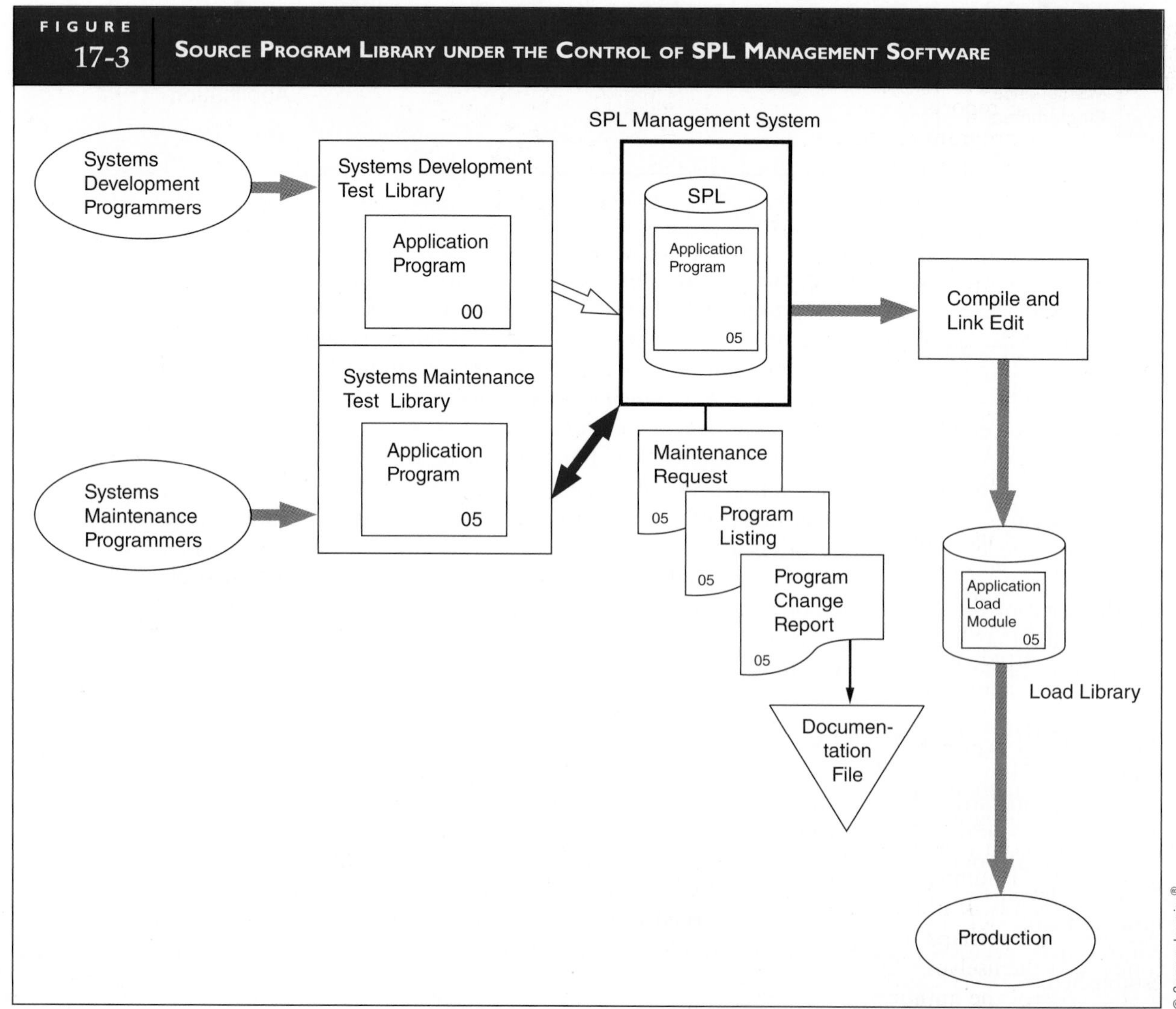

have drawbacks. When more than one person is authorized to access a program, preserving the secrecy of a shared password is a problem. Because responsibility for the secrecy of a shared password lies with the group rather than with an individual, personal accountability is reduced.

Separation of Test Libraries

Figure 17-3 illustrates an improvement on the shared password approach through the creation of separate password-controlled libraries (or directories) for each programmer. Under this concept, a strict separation is maintained between the production programs that are subject to maintenance in the SPL and those being developed. Production programs are copied into the programmer's library for maintenance and testing purposes only. Direct access to the production SPL is limited to a specific librarian group that approves all requests to modify, delete, and copy programs.

An enhancement to this control feature is the implementation of program-naming conventions. The name assigned to a program clearly distinguishes it as being either a test or a production program. When a program is copied from the production SPL to the programmer's library, it is given a temporary test name. When the program is returned to the SPL, it is renamed with its original production name. This technique greatly reduces the risk of accidentally running an untested version of a program in place of the production program.

Audit Trail and Management Reports

An important feature of SPL management software is the creation of reports that enhance management control and support the audit function. The most useful of these are program modification reports, which describe in detail all program changes (additions and deletions) to each module. These reports should be part of the documentation file of each application to form an audit trail of program changes over the life of the application. During an audit, the reports can be reconciled against program maintenance requests to verify that only approved changes were implemented. For example, if a programmer attempted to use a legitimate maintenance event as an opportunity to commit program fraud, the unauthorized code changes would be documented in the program modification report. These reports can be hard copies or digital and can be governed by password control, thus limiting access to management and auditors.

Program Version Numbers

The SPLMS assigns a version number automatically to each program stored on the SPL. When programs are first placed in the libraries (at implementation), they are assigned version number zero. With each modification to the program, the version number is increased by one. For instance, after five authorized maintenance changes, the production program will be Version 05, as illustrated in Figure 17-3. This feature, when combined with audit trail reports, provides a basis for detecting unauthorized changes to the application program. An unauthorized change is signaled by a version number on the production load module that cannot be reconciled to the number of authorized changes. For example, if 10 changes were authorized but the production program is Version 12, then two possible control violations may have happened: (1) authorized changes occurred, which for some reason went undocumented; or (2) unauthorized changes were made, which incremented the version numbers. We will discuss this issue in more detail later.

Controlling Access to Maintenance Commands

Powerful maintenance commands are available for most library systems that can be used to alter or eliminate program passwords, alter the program version number, and temporarily modify a program without generating a record of the modification.

There are a number of legitimate technical reasons why systems designers must sometimes use these commands. If not controlled, however, maintenance commands open the possibility of unauthorized, and perhaps undocumented, program modifications. Hence, access to the maintenance commands themselves should be password controlled, and management or an IT security group should control the authority to use them.

FIGURE 17-4 AUDITING SPL SOFTWARE SYSTEM

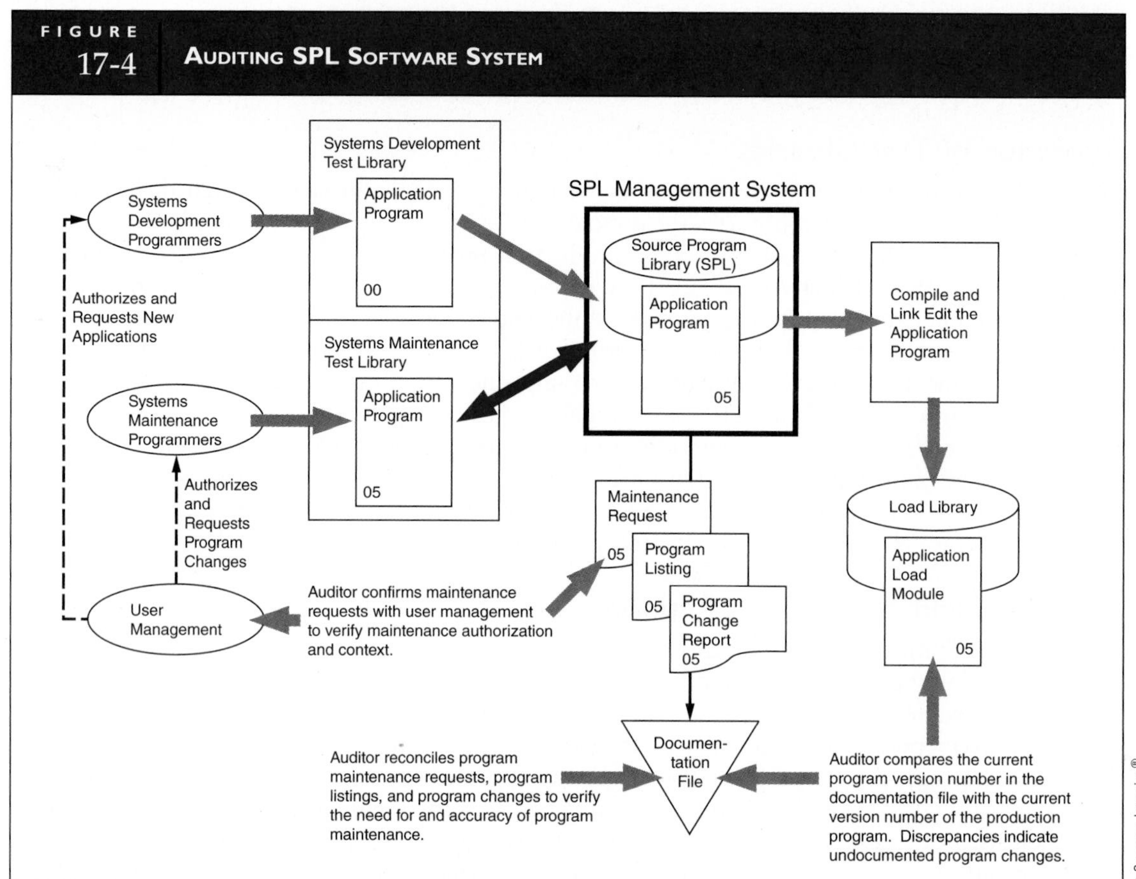

Audit Objectives Relating to Systems Maintenance

The auditor's objectives are to determine that (1) maintenance procedures protect applications from unauthorized changes, (2) applications are free from material errors, and (3) program libraries are protected from unauthorized access.

The **tests of controls** necessary to achieve each of these objectives are examined in the following section. The discussion assumes that the organization employs SPL software to control program maintenance. Without such software, achieving the audit objectives may be impossible. The procedures described here are illustrated in Figure 17-4.

Audit Procedures for Identifying Unauthorized Program Changes

To establish that program changes were authorized, the auditor should examine the audit trail of program changes for a sample of applications that have undergone maintenance. The auditor can confirm that authorization procedures were followed by performing the following tests of controls.

RECONCILE PROGRAM VERSION NUMBERS. The permanent file of the application should contain program change authorization documents that correspond to the current version number of the production application. In other words, if the production application is in its tenth version, there should be ten program change authorizations in the permanent file as supporting documentation.[1] Any

1 In most systems, a program in its original (unmodified) state has a version number of 00. Thus, ten changes will give a version number of 10.

discrepancies between version numbers and supporting documents may indicate that unauthorized changes were made.

CONFIRM MAINTENANCE AUTHORIZATION. The program maintenance authorization should indicate the nature of the change requested and the date of the change. The appropriate management from both computer services and the user departments should also sign and approve it. The auditor should confirm the facts contained in the maintenance authorization and verify the authorizing signatures with the managers involved.

Audit Procedures for Identifying Application Errors

The auditor can perform three types of tests of controls—reconcile the source code, review the test results, and retest the program—to determine that programs are free from material errors.

RECONCILE THE SOURCE CODE. Each application's permanent file should contain the current program listing and listings of all changes made to the application. These documents describe in detail the application's maintenance history. In addition, the nature of the program change should be clearly stated on the program change authorization document. The auditor should select a sample of applications and reconcile each program change with the appropriate authorization documents. The modular approach to systems design (creating applications that comprise many small discrete program modules) greatly facilitates this testing technique. The reduced complexity of these modules enhances the auditor's ability to identify irregularities that indicate errors, omissions, and potentially fraudulent programming codes.

REVIEW THE TEST RESULTS. Every program change should be thoroughly tested before being implemented. Program test procedures should be properly documented as to the test objectives, test data, and processing results. The auditor should review this record for each significant program change to establish that testing was sufficiently rigorous to identify any errors.

RETEST THE PROGRAM. The auditor can retest the application to confirm its integrity. We examine several techniques for application testing later in the chapter.

Audit Procedures for Testing Access to Libraries

The existence of a secure program library is central to preventing errors and program fraud. One control method is to assign library access privileges to system librarians only. Their function is to retrieve applications from the program libraries for maintenance and to restore the modified programs to the library. Thus, maintenance programmers test applications in their private libraries but do not have direct access to the program library. The auditor may perform the following tests of controls to assess program library security.

REVIEW PROGRAMMER AUTHORITY TABLES. The auditor can select a sample of programmers and review their access authority. The programmer's authority table will specify the libraries a programmer may access. These authorizations should be matched against the programmer's maintenance authority to ensure that no irregularities exist.

TEST AUTHORITY TABLE. To test the programmer's access privileges, the auditor may violate the authorization rules in an attempt to access unauthorized libraries. The operating system should deny any such attempt.

IT Application Control Testing and Substantive Testing

In addition to general IT controls, SOX requires management and auditors to consider application controls relevant to financial reporting. These controls fall into three broad categories: input controls, processing controls, and output controls. Several previous chapters examined the application controls pertaining to specific systems, such as sales order processing, purchases, cash disbursements, and payroll systems. Depending upon the system under review and its financial relevance, the auditor will develop specific audit objectives. Once developed, achieving the audit objectives involves performing audit procedures to gather evidence through a combination of tests of application controls and substantive tests of transaction details and account balances. The audit process that relates management assertions, tests of controls, and substantive tests is presented in the appendix to Chapter 15. The remainder of this chapter examines several techniques for performing tests of application IT controls and substantive tests.

DESIGNING TESTS OF APPLICATION CONTROLS

Auditors design tests of IT controls to verify computer logic specific to a particular application. These tests, however, fall into the general categories listed below:

1. **Access tests** verify that individuals, programmed procedures, or messages (such as electronic data interchange [EDI] transmissions) attempting to access a system are authentic and valid. Access tests include verifications of user IDs, passwords, valid vendor codes, and authority tables.
2. **Validity tests** ensure that the system processes only data values that conform to specified tolerances. Examples include range tests, field tests, limit tests, and reasonableness tests. Validity tests also apply to transaction approvals, such as verifying that credit checks and AP three-way-matches are properly performed by the application.
3. **Accuracy tests** ensure that mathematical calculations are accurate and posted to the correct accounts. Examples include recalculations of control totals and reconciliations of transaction postings to subsidiary ledgers.
4. **Completeness tests** identify missing data within a single record and entire records missing from a batch. The types of tests performed are field tests, record sequence tests, and recalculation of hash totals and financial control totals.
5. **Redundancy tests** determine that an application processes each record only once. Redundancy tests include reviewing record counts and recalculation of hash totals and financial control totals.
6. **Audit trail tests** ensure that the application creates an adequate audit trail. Tests include obtaining evidence that the application records all transactions in a transaction log (journal), posts data values to the appropriate accounts, produces complete transaction listings, and generates error files and reports for all exceptions.

Figure 17-5 illustrates the general approach used to test application controls. The steps in this process are listed below:

1) The auditor must first obtain a current version of the application under review or, alternatively, remove the production application from service so that it may be tested directly.
2) Next, the auditor creates test master files containing hypothetical (dummy) records.
3) The auditor then prepares test transactions to be processed through the logic of the application. These transactions should consist of records that are correct, as well as records that contain errors. The error records should be designed such that the internal controls embedded in the application will detect and reject them. If the application processes data in real time, the auditor will submit the transactions via a terminal (option "A" in Figure 17-5). If it is a batch system, then the transaction data will take the form of a transaction file (option "B" in the figure).
4) The next step is for the auditor to calculate the expected results of processing based on the transaction and master file account values assigned to the test data.
5) Finally, the auditor runs the test and reconciles the results obtained with the predetermined results.

Although the above steps seem straightforward in concept, performing them is technically complex and time-consuming. Therefore, to facilitate this activity, several computer-aided auditing

FIGURE 17-5 THE TEST DATA TECHNIQUE

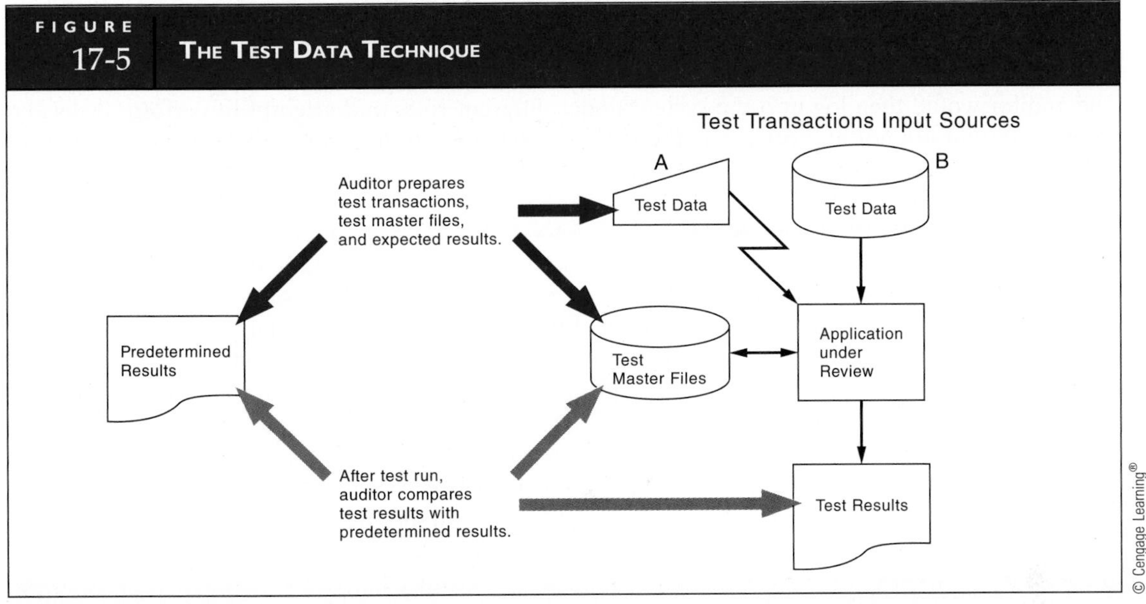

techniques have been developed, which we examine later in the chapter. At this point, we turn our attention to reviewing specific examples of tests of application controls.

Examples of Tests of IT Application Controls

This section presents examples of tests of controls as they apply to specific applications. These tests are representative and not intended to be regarded as a complete set, but the general techniques outlined here may be applied to various transaction-processing tasks.

TESTING CUSTOMER CREDIT APPROVALS. To test credit approval controls in a sales order system, the auditor would create a master file of customer records (AR) with set credit limits. The transactions would consist of sales invoices for amounts that would drive the customer's balances above the credit limit in the master file. If the control is functioning properly, the records will be flagged for management approval or rejected. The sales invoices should also include amounts that do not exceed credit limits. The application should approve and process these transactions against the master file accounts.

TESTING ACCURACY OF POSTINGS TO CUSTOMER ACCOUNTS. This test could be coupled with the previous test with little additional effort and using the same test data. The approved transactions (those that pass the credit limit test) should be accurately posted to the customer accounts in the test master files. The auditor would verify their accuracy by reviewing account balance reports produced by the sales order application and reconcile them with the predetermined results. Discrepancies would indicate a logic error in the math calculation or an error that posts transactions to the wrong accounts.

TESTING THE THREE-WAY MATCH. This test involves creating two test master files: a purchase order file and a receiving report file. The transaction in this case is the supplier's invoice. The test data should be designed to contain discrepancies that fall both within and outside of acceptable limits, based on company policy. When the invoice is entered, the AP system should match the three documents (create a digital AP packet) and reconcile the quantities ordered with those received, and the invoice amount with the expected price. The auditor will reconcile both rejected and accepted invoices to determine that the control is functioning in accordance with company policy.

TESTING MULTILEVEL SECURITY AND ACCESS PRIVILEGES IN THE PURCHASES/AP SYSTEM. This test would involve creating several master files: purchase order file; inventory file; receiving report file; and general ledger accounts for cash, inventory control, and AP control. The auditor would then log into the system under different roles and attempt to perform tasks and access data that are not authorized by the various roles. Failure to detect or prevent such attempts indicates a control weakness in the system.

TESTING ROUNDING ERROR ROUTINES IN FINANCIAL SYSTEMS. Financial systems that calculate interest payments on bank accounts or charges on mortgages and other loans employ special rounding error applications. Rounding errors occur when the level of precision used in a calculation is greater than that used for reporting. For example, interest calculations on bank account balances may have a precision of five decimal places, whereas only two decimal places are reported on balances. If the remaining three decimal places are simply truncated, the total interest reported for the total number of accounts will not equal the sum of the individual calculations.

Figure 17-6 shows the logic for handling the rounding error problem. This technique uses an accumulator to keep track of the rounding differences between calculated and reported balances. Note how the sign and the absolute value of the amount in the accumulator determine how

FIGURE 17-6 ROUNDING ERROR ALGORITHM

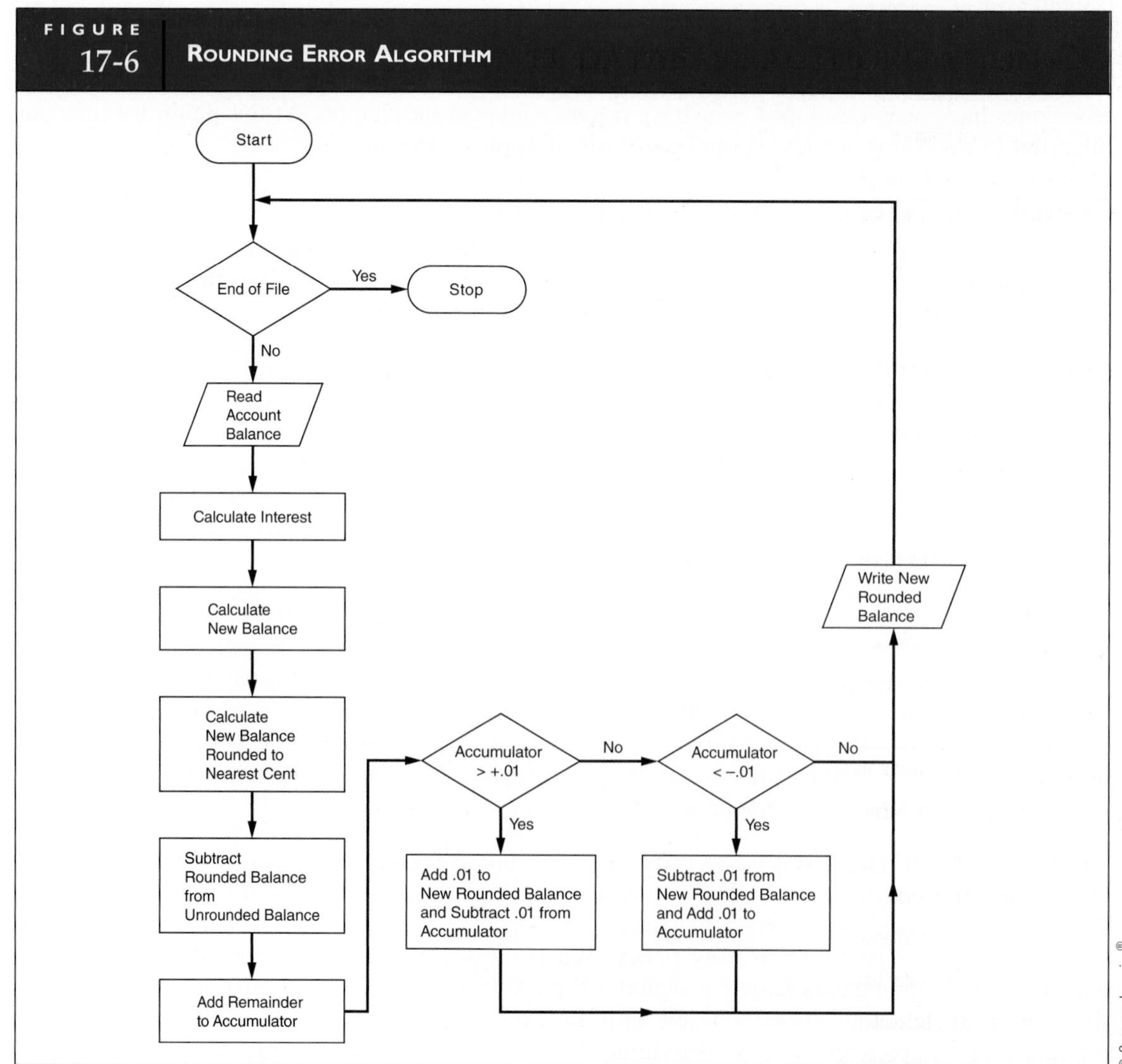

rounding affects the customer account. To illustrate, the rounding logic is applied to three hypothetical bank account balances (see Table 17-1). The interest calculations are based on an interest rate of 5.25 percent.

Failure to properly account for the rounding difference can result in an imbalance between the total (control) figure and the sum of the detail figures for each account. Rounding errors are also an opportunity for fraud.

SALAMI FRAUD. Rounding programs are particularly susceptible to the so-called **salami fraud**. This fraud affects large numbers of victims, but each in a minimal way. The fraud scheme takes its name from the analogy of slicing a large salami (the total fraud) into many thin pieces. Each victim gets one of these small pieces and is unaware of being defrauded. For example, a programmer, or someone with access to the rounding program shown in Figure 17-6, can modify the rounding

TABLE 17-1 SAMPLE DATA

Record 1	
Beginning accumulator balance	.00861
Beginning account balance	2,741.78
Calculated interest	143.94345
New account balance	2,885.72345
Rounded account balance	2,885.72
Adjusted accumulator balance	.01206 (.00345 + .00861)
Ending account balance	**2,885.73 (round up 1 cent)**
Ending accumulator balance	.00206 (.01206 – .01)
Record 2	
Beginning accumulator balance	.00206
Beginning account balance	1,893.44
Calculated interest	99.4056
New account balance	1,992.8456
Rounded account balance	1,992.85
Adjusted accumulator balance	–.00234 (.00206 – .0044)
Ending account balance	**1,992.85 (no change)**
Ending accumulator balance	–.00234
Record 3	
Beginning accumulator balance	–.00234
Beginning account balance	7,423.34
Calculated interest	389.72535
New account balance	7,813.06535
Rounded account balance	7,813.07
Adjusted accumulator balance	–.00699 (–.00234 – .00465)
Ending account balance	**7,813.07 (no change)**
Ending accumulator balance	–.00699

logic to perpetrate a salami fraud as follows: at the point in the process where the algorithm should increase the current customer's account (that is, the accumulator value is > +.01), the program instead adds one cent to the perpetrator's account. Although the absolute amount of each fraud transaction is small, given the hundreds of thousands of accounts processed, the total amount of the fraud becomes significant over time.

The test of the rounding error control would require special audit software to detect excessive file activity. In the case of the salami fraud, there would be thousands of postings to the computer criminal's personal account, which the audit software should detect. A clever programmer, however, may funnel these entries through several temporary accounts to disguise this activity. These accounts are then posted to a smaller number of intermediate accounts and finally to the programmer's personal account. By using many levels of temporary accounts in this way, the activity to any single account is reduced, and the audit software may not detect it. The auditor can also use audit software to review system audit trail logs (Chapter 16) to detect the existence of unauthorized (dummy) files that contain the intermediate accounts used in such a fraud.

Internal Control Testing Techniques

The previous section described the types of application control tests that an auditor may perform. We now examine techniques for performing such tests. We begin by looking at the *black box* approach and then review several *through-the-computer* techniques.

BLACK BOX APPROACH

The **black box approach** (also called *auditing around the computer)* does not require the auditor to create test files or to obtain a detailed knowledge of the application's internal logic. Instead, auditors analyze flowcharts and interview knowledgeable personnel in the client's organization to understand the functional characteristics of the application. With an understanding of what the application is supposed to do, the auditor tests the application by reconciling actual production transactions processed with output results. The output results are analyzed to verify the application's compliance with its functional requirements. Figure 17-7 illustrates the black box approach.

One advantage of this technique is that the application need not be removed from service and tested directly. Black box testing is feasible for applications that are relatively simple, with inputs and outputs that are easily reconciled. More complex applications, however, often draw input data from multiple sources, perform a variety of complex operations, and produce multiple

FIGURE 17-7 AUDITING AROUND THE COMPUTER—THE BLACK BOX APPROACH

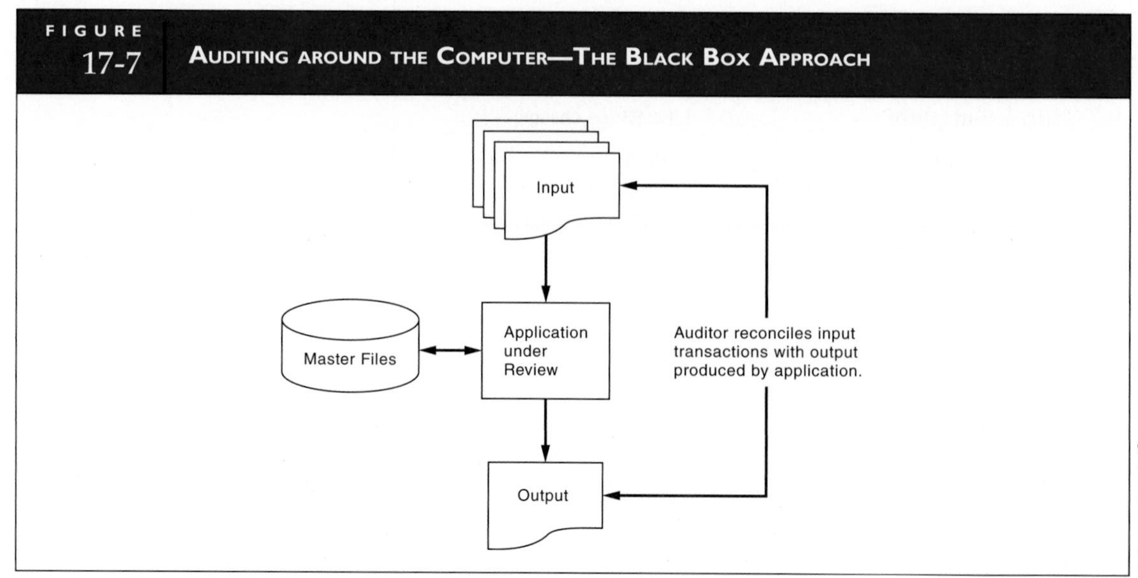

outputs. These applications demand more intensive through-the-computer testing to provide the auditor with evidence of application integrity.

THROUGH-THE-COMPUTER APPROACHES

Through-the-computer testing employs **computer-assisted audit tools and techniques (CAATTs)** and requires an in-depth understanding of the internal logic of the application under review. This section describes the key features of five CAATTs: the test data method, base case system evaluation, tracing, integrated test facility, and parallel simulation.

Test Data Method

The **test data method** was introduced previously (see Figure 17-5) to illustrate the general approach to testing application controls. To employ this approach, the auditor requires detailed and current systems documentation: (1) program flowcharts that describe the application's internal logic and allow the auditor to determine which logic branches to test, and (2) record layout diagrams that describe the structure of transaction and master files, which will allow the auditor to create test data.

CREATING TEST DATA. Test data should consist of a complete set of valid and invalid transactions. Incomplete test data may fail to explore critical branches of application logic and error checking routines. Test transactions should be designed to test all possible input errors, logical processes, and irregularities pertinent to the audit objective.

Gaining knowledge of the application's internal logic sufficient to create meaningful test data represents a considerable investment in time. The efficiency of this task is improved, however, through careful planning during systems development. Systems designers should save for future use the test data created to test program modules during the implementation phase of the SDLC. If the application has undergone no changes since its initial implementation, then the current audit test results should equal the original test results obtained at implementation. If the application has been changed, the auditor need only create additional test data that focus on the areas of the program changes.

Results from testing will be in the form of routine output reports, transaction listings, and error reports that are normally produced by the application. In addition, the auditor must examine the updated master files to determine that account balances have been correctly updated. The test results are then compared with the auditor's expected results to determine if the application is functioning properly. This comparison may be performed manually or through the use of special-purpose software.

Using a sales order system as an example, Figure 17-8 illustrates the sort of hypothetical transactions and accounts receivable records that an auditor would prepare. The figure also shows an error report of rejected transactions (the errors are marked with an "X"), and a listing of the updated AR master file. Any deviations between the actual results and those the auditor has predetermined may indicate a logic error or control problem.

Base Case System Evaluation

Base case system evaluation (BCSE) is a variant of the test data approach. BCSE tests are conducted with a set of test transactions containing all possible transaction types. These are processed through repeated iterations during systems development testing until consistent and valid results are obtained. These validated results become the base case. When subsequent changes to the application occur during maintenance, their effects are evaluated by comparing current results with base case results.

Tracing

Another type of the test data technique called **tracing** performs an electronic walk-through of the application's internal logic. The tracing procedure involves three steps:

1. The application under review first undergoes a special compilation process to activate the trace feature.

FIGURE 17-8 **Example of Test Data and Test Results**

Test Transaction File

REC NUM	CUST NUM	CUSTOMER NAME	PART NUM	DESCRIPTION	QNTY	UNIT PRICE	TOTAL PRICE
1	231893	Smith, Joe	AX-612	Water Pump	1	20.00	20.00
2	231893	Azar, Atul	J-912	Gear	3	15.00	45.00
3	245851	Jones, Mary	123-LM	Hose	20	20.00	400.00
4	256519	Lang, Tony	Y-771	Spacer	5	2.00	10.00
5	259552	Tuner, Agnes	U-734	Bushing	5	25.00	120.00
6	175995	Hanz, James	EA-74	Seal	1	3.00	3.00
7	267991	Swindle, Joe	EN-12	Rebuilt Engine	1	1,220.00	1,220.00

Original Test AR Master File

CUST NUM	CUSTOMER NAME	CUSTOMER ADDRESS	CREDIT LIMIT	CURRENT BALANCE
231893	Smith, Joe	1520 S. Maple, City	1,000.00	400.00
256519	Lang, Tony	18 Etwine St., City	5,000.00	850.00
267991	Swindle, Joe	1 Shady Side, City	3,000.00	2,900.00

Updated Test AR Master File

CUST NUM	CUSTOMER NAME	CUSTOMER ADDRESS	CREDIT LIMIT	CURRENT BALANCE
231893	Smith, Joe	1520 S. Maple, City	1,000.00	420.00
256519	Lang, Tony	18 Etwine St., City	5,000.00	860.00
267991	Swindle, Joe	1 Shady Side, City	3,000.00	2,900.00

Error Report

REC NUM	CUST NUM	CUSTOMER NAME	PART NUM	DESCRIPTION	QNTY	UNIT PRICE	TOTAL PRICE	EXPLANATION OF ERROR
2	231893	Azar, Atul X	J-912	Gear	3	15.00	45.00	CUSTOMER NAME does not correspond to CUST NUM 231893
3	245851 X	Jones, Mary	123-LM	Hose	20	20.00	400.00	Check digit error in CUST NUM field
5	259552	Tuner, Agnes	U-734	Bushing	5	25.00	120.00 X	Price extension error
6	175995 X	Hanz, James	EA-74	Seal	1	3.00	3.00	Record out of sequence
7	267991	Swindle, Joe	EN-12	Rebuilt Engine	1	1,220.00 X	1,220.00 X	Credit limit error

2. Test data transactions are created.
3. The test data transactions are traced through all processing stages of the program, and a listing is produced of all programmed instructions that were executed during the test.

Figure 17-9 illustrates the tracing process using a portion of the logic for a payroll application. The example shows records from two payroll files—a transaction record showing hours worked and two records from a master file showing pay rates. The trace listing at the bottom of Figure 17-9 identifies the program statements that were executed and the order of execution. Analysis of trace options indicates that Commands 0001 through 0020 were executed. At that point, the application transferred to Command 0060. This occurred because the employee number

FIGURE 17-9 TRACING

Payroll Transaction File

Time Card #	Employee Number	Name	Year	Pay Period	Reg Hrs	OT Hrs
8945	33456	Jones, J.J.	2007	14	40.0	3.0

Payroll Master File

Employee Number	Hourly Rate	YTD Earnings	Dependents	YTD Withhold	YTD FICA
33276	15	12,050	3	3,200	873.62
33456	15	13,100	2	3,600	949.75

Computer Program Logic

```
0001  Read Record from Transaction File
0010  Read Record from Master File
0020  If Employee Number (T) = Employee Number (M)
0030       Wage = (Reg Hrs + [OT Hrs x 1.5] ) x Hourly Rate
0040       Add Wage to YTD Earnings
0050       Go to 0001
0060  Else Go to 0010
```

Trace Listing

0001, 0010, 0020, 0060, 0010, 0020, 0030, 0040, 0050

(the key) of the transaction record did not match the key of the first record in the master file. Then Commands 0010 through 0050 were executed.

Advantages of Test Data Techniques

Test data techniques have three primary advantages. First, they employ through-the-computer testing, thus providing the auditor with explicit evidence concerning application functions. Second, if properly planned, tests can be employed with only minimal disruption to the organization's operations. Third, they require only minimal computer expertise on the part of auditors.

Disadvantages of Test Data Techniques

The primary disadvantage of test data techniques is that auditors rely on the client's IT personnel to obtain a copy of the production application under review. The risk here is that the IT personnel may intentionally or accidentally provide the auditor with the wrong version of the application. Audit evidence collected independently is more reliable than evidence the client supplies. A second disadvantage is that these techniques produce a static picture of application integrity at a single point in time. They are not a convenient means for gathering evidence of ongoing application functionality. A third disadvantage is their high cost of implementation. Gaining an understanding of program logic and creating test data is time-consuming. The following section presents techniques designed to resolve these problems.

THE INTEGRATED TEST FACILITY

The **integrated test facility (ITF)** approach is an automated technique that enables the auditor to test an application's logic and controls during its normal operation. ITF involves designing special audit modules into the application during the systems development process. In addition, corporate production databases are designed to include test master file records. During normal operations, test transactions are merged into the input stream of regular (production)

FIGURE 17-10 THE ITF TECHNIQUE

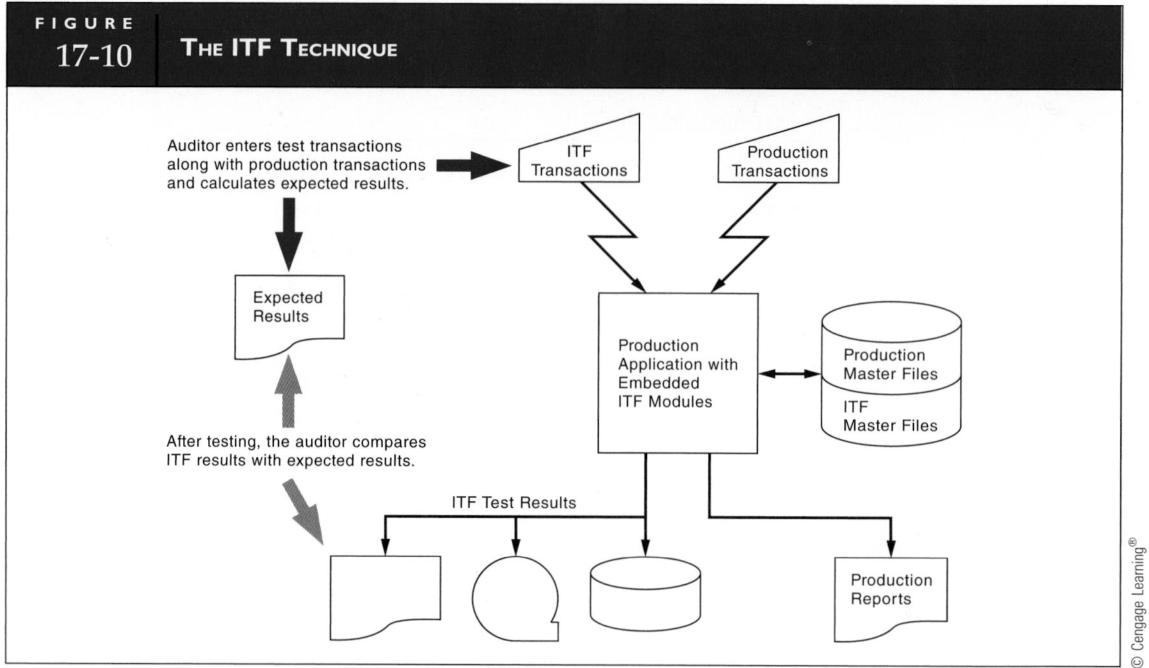

transactions and are processed against the dummy files in the database. Figure 17-10 illustrates the ITF concept.

ITF audit modules are designed to discriminate between ITF transactions and production data. This may be accomplished in a number of ways. One of the simplest and most commonly used is to assign a unique range of key values exclusively to ITF transactions. For example, in a sales order processing system, account numbers between 2000 and 2100 are reserved for ITF transactions and will not be assigned to actual customer accounts. By segregating ITF transactions from legitimate transactions in this way, ITF test data do not corrupt routine output reports. Test results are produced separately in digital or hard-copy form and distributed directly to the auditor. Just as with traditional test data techniques, the auditor analyzes ITF results against expected results.

Advantages of ITF

The ITF technique has two advantages over test data techniques. First, ITF supports continuous monitoring of controls, as recommended by COSO. Second, ITF-enhanced applications can be economically tested without disrupting the user's operations and without the intervention of computer services personnel. Thus, ITF improves the efficiency of the audit and increases the reliability of the audit evidence gathered.

Disadvantages of ITF

The primary disadvantage of ITF is the potential for corrupting corporate databases with test data that may end up in the financial reporting process. Steps need to be taken to ensure that ITF test transactions do not materially affect financial statements by becoming mixed with valid transactions. This problem can be remedied by processing adjusting entries to remove the effects of ITF from general ledger account balances.

PARALLEL SIMULATION

Parallel simulation involves creating a program that simulates key features or processes of the application under review. The simulated application is then used to reprocess the same transactions that the production application previously processed. This technique is illustrated in Figure 17-11. The results

FIGURE 17-11 PARALLEL SIMULATION TECHNIQUE

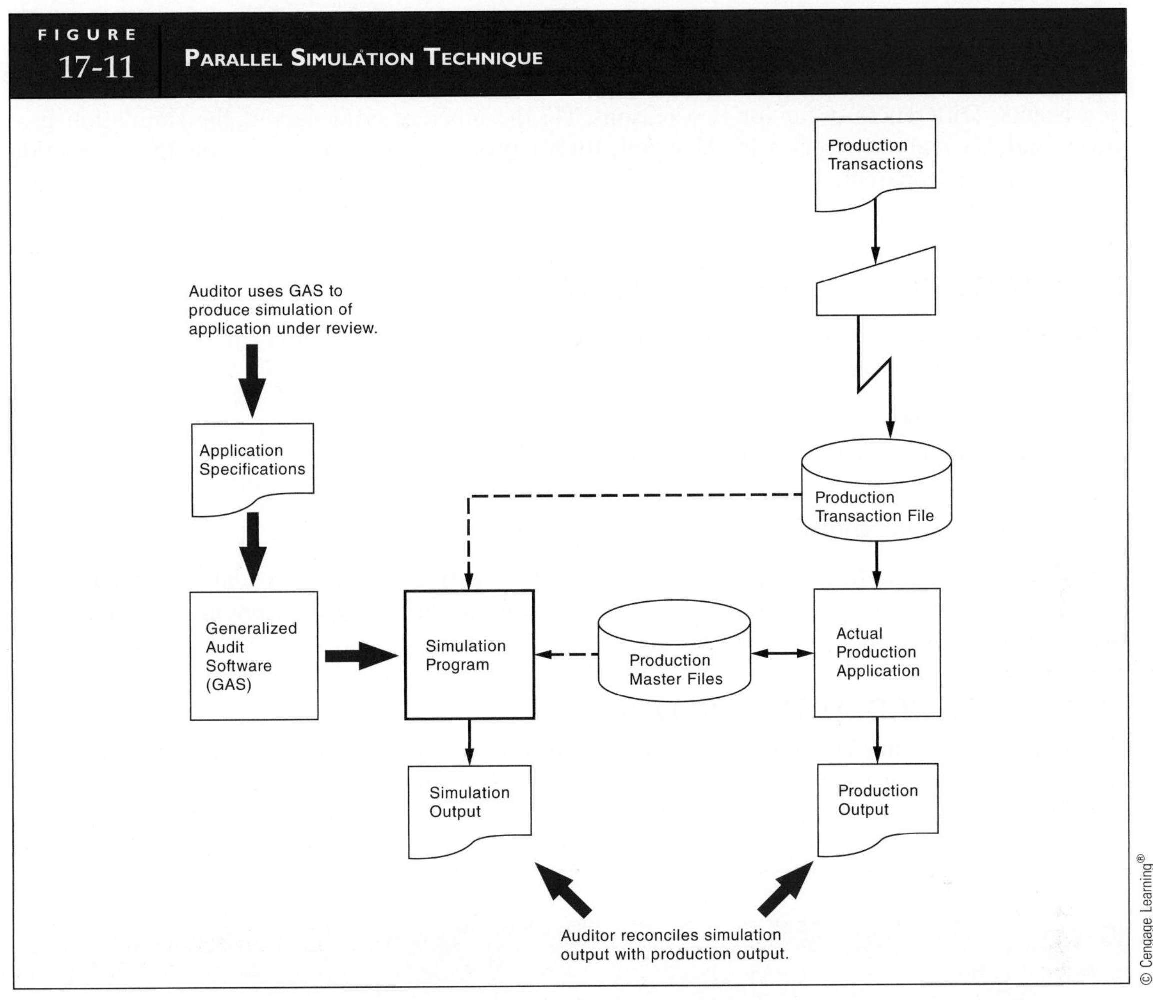

obtained from the simulation are reconciled with the results of the original production run to determine if application processes and controls are functioning correctly.

Creating a Simulation Program

Simulation packages are commercially available and are sometimes a feature of **generalized audit software (GAS)**.[2] The steps involved in performing parallel simulation testing are outlined in the following section.

1. The auditor must first gain a thorough understanding of the application under review. Constructing an accurate simulation requires complete and current documentation.
2. The auditor must then identify those processes and controls in the application that pertain to the audit objective. These are the processes to be simulated.
3. The auditor creates the simulation using special-purpose commercial software.
4. The auditor runs the simulation program using production transactions and master files to produce a set of results.
5. Finally, the auditor reconciles the test results with the previously created production results.

2 Although GAS can be used for testing internal controls, it is primarily a substantive testing technique. For this reason, this technology is discussed in the following section that deals with substantive testing.

Simulated applications are less complex than the production applications they represent because they contain only processes, calculations, and controls relevant to specific audit objectives. The auditor must therefore carefully interpret the discrepancies between test results and production results. Differences occur for two reasons: (1) the inherent crudeness of the simulation program, and (2) real deficiencies in the application's processes or controls, which the simulation program makes apparent.

Substantive Testing Techniques

Substantive tests are so named because they are used to substantiate dollar amounts in account balances. Substantive tests include, but are not limited to, the following:

1. Determining the correct value of inventory.
2. Determining the accuracy of prepayments and accruals.
3. Confirming accounts receivable with customers.
4. Searching for unrecorded liabilities.

To perform substantive tests, the auditor must first extract the account data from corporate databases and files. The two CAATTs examined in this section assist auditors in selecting, accessing, and organizing data for substantive tests.

THE EMBEDDED AUDIT MODULE

Embedded audit module (EAM) techniques use one or more programmed modules embedded in a host application to select transactions that meet predetermined conditions. This approach is illustrated in Figure 17-12.

FIGURE 17-12 EMBEDDED AUDIT MODULE TECHNIQUE

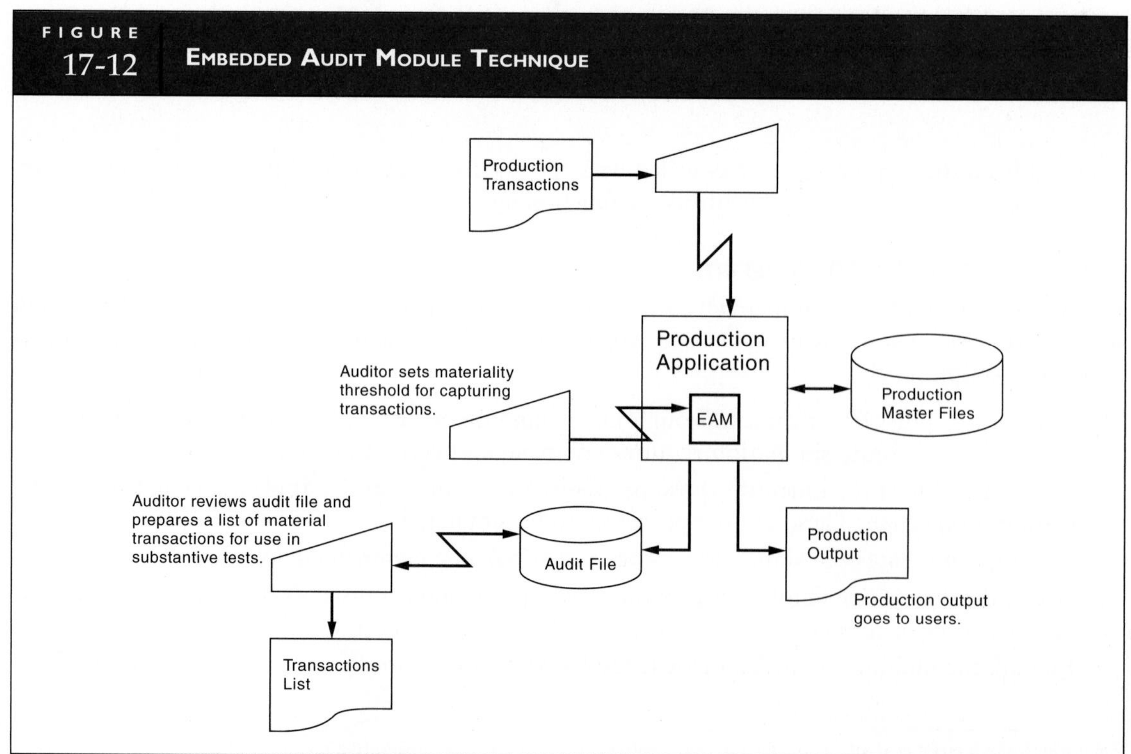

As the host application processes the selected transaction, a copy of it is stored on an audit file for subsequent review. The EAM approach allows material transactions to be captured throughout the audit period. The auditor retrieves captured transactions at period-end or at any point in the period, thus significantly reducing the amount of work the auditor must do to identify significant transactions for substantive testing.

To begin data capturing, the auditor specifies to the EAM the parameters and materiality threshold of the transactions set to be captured. For example, assume that the auditor establishes a $50,000 materiality threshold for supplier invoices in an AP system. Invoices equal to or greater than $50,000 will be copied to the audit file. From this set of transactions, the auditor will select a subset to be used for substantive tests. The EAM will ignore transactions that fall below this threshold.

Although primarily a substantive testing technique, EAMs may also be used to monitor application controls on a continuous basis, as recommended in the COSO framework. For example, selected transactions can be reviewed for proper authorization, completeness and accuracy of processing, and correct posting to accounts.

Disadvantages of EAMs

The EAM approach has two significant disadvantages. The first pertains to operational efficiency and the second to EAM integrity.

OPERATIONAL EFFICIENCY. From the user's point of view, EAMs decrease operational performance. The presence of an audit module within the host application may create processing delays, particularly when the level of testing is high. One approach for relieving this burden from the system is to design modules that the auditor may turn on and off. Doing so will, of course, reduce the effectiveness of the EAM as an ongoing audit tool.

VERIFYING EAM INTEGRITY. The EAM approach may not be a viable audit technique in environments with a high level of program maintenance. When host applications are undergoing frequent changes, the EAMs embedded within the hosts will also require frequent modifications. The integrity concerns raised earlier in the chapter regarding application maintenance apply equally to EAMs. The integrity of the EAM directly affects the quality of the audit process. Auditors must therefore evaluate the EAM integrity. This would be accomplished in the same way as testing the host application controls.

GENERALIZED AUDIT SOFTWARE

Generalized Audit Software (GAS) is a widely used CAATT for IT auditing that allows auditors to access digital data files and perform various operations on the contents. ACL and IDEA are currently the leading GAS products, but others exist with similar features. The following audit tasks can be performed using GAS:

1. Footing and balancing entire files or selected data items.
2. Selecting and reporting detailed data contained on files.
3. Selecting stratified statistical samples from data files.
4. Formatting results of tests into reports.
5. Printing confirmations in either standardized or special wording.
6. Screening data and selectively including or excluding items.
7. Comparing two files and identifying any differences.
8. Recalculating data fields.

FIGURE 17-13 USING GAS TO ACCESS SIMPLE FILE STRUCTURE

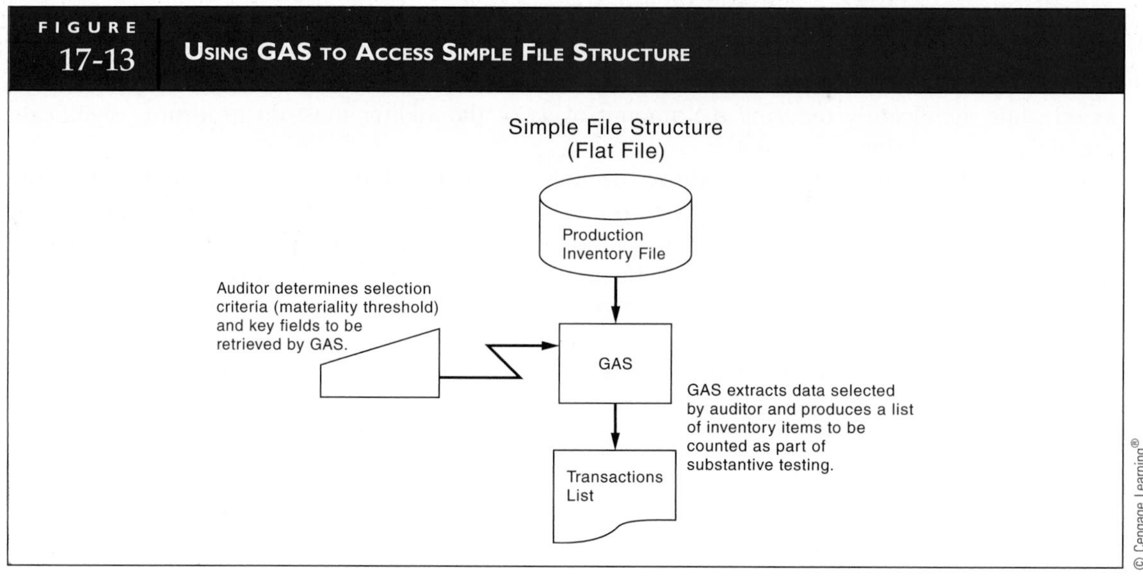

The widespread popularity of GAS is due to four factors: (1) GAS languages are easy to use and require little IT background on the part of the auditor, (2) GAS may be used on any type of computer because it is hardware independent, (3) auditors can perform their tests on data independent of client IT professionals, and (4) GAS can be used to audit the data files of many different applications (in contrast with EAMs, which are application-specific).

Using GAS to Access Simple Structures

Accessing flat-file structures (such as a text file) is a simple process, as illustrated in Figure 17-13. In this example, an inventory file is read directly into the GAS, which is configured to extract key information needed for the audit, including the quantity on hand, the dollar value, and the warehouse location of each inventory item. The auditor's task is to perform a physical count of a representative sample of the inventory on hand to verify the existence and value of the inventory. Thus, on the basis of a materiality threshold that the auditor provides, the GAS selects the sample records and prepares a report with the key information.

Using GAS to Access Complex Structures

Accessing complex structures, such as virtual storage access method (VSAM) files and relational database tables, poses more of a problem for the auditor. Most DBMSs, however, have utility features that will reformat complex structures into flat files or spreadsheets, which the GAS can then access. Figure 17-14 shows this technique.

To illustrate the file-flattening process, consider the complex database structure presented in Figure 17-15. The database structure uses pointers to integrate three related files—Customer, Sales Invoice, and Line Item—in a hierarchical model. Extracting audit evidence directly from a structure of this complexity using GAS would be difficult, if not impossible. A simpler flat-file version of this structure is illustrated in Figure 17-16. The resulting single text file represents the three record types as a sequential structure with variable length records that GAS can easily access.

FIGURE 17-14 USING GAS TO ACCESS COMPLEX FILE STRUCTURE

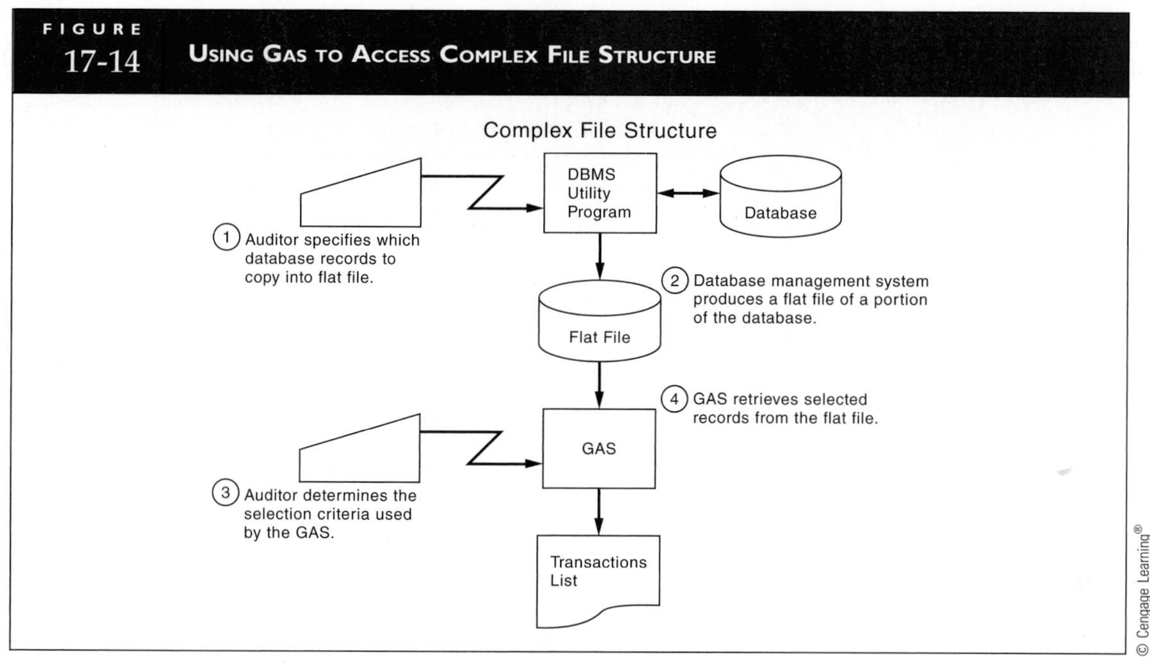

FIGURE 17-15 COMPLEX DATABASE STRUCTURE

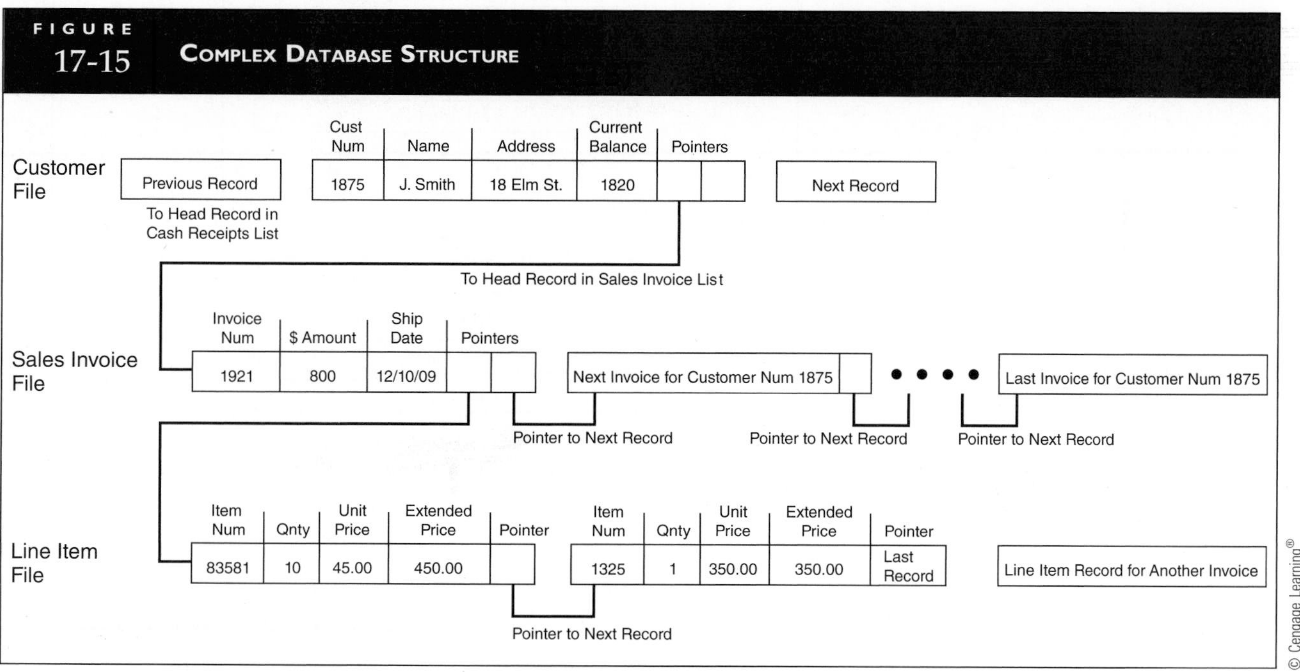

Audit Issue Pertaining to the Creation of Flat Files

When auditors rely on client IT personnel to produce flat files from their databases, they run the risk that database integrity will be compromised. For example, if the auditor is confirming accounts receivable, certain fraudulent accounts in the original database may be intentionally omitted from the flat file provided to the auditor. Auditors skilled in relational and object database technology can avoid this problem. Not surprisingly, public accounting firms are aggressively seeking employees with strong computer skills to accompany their accounting training.

FIGURE 17-16 FLAT VERSION OF A COMPLEX FILE STRUCTURE

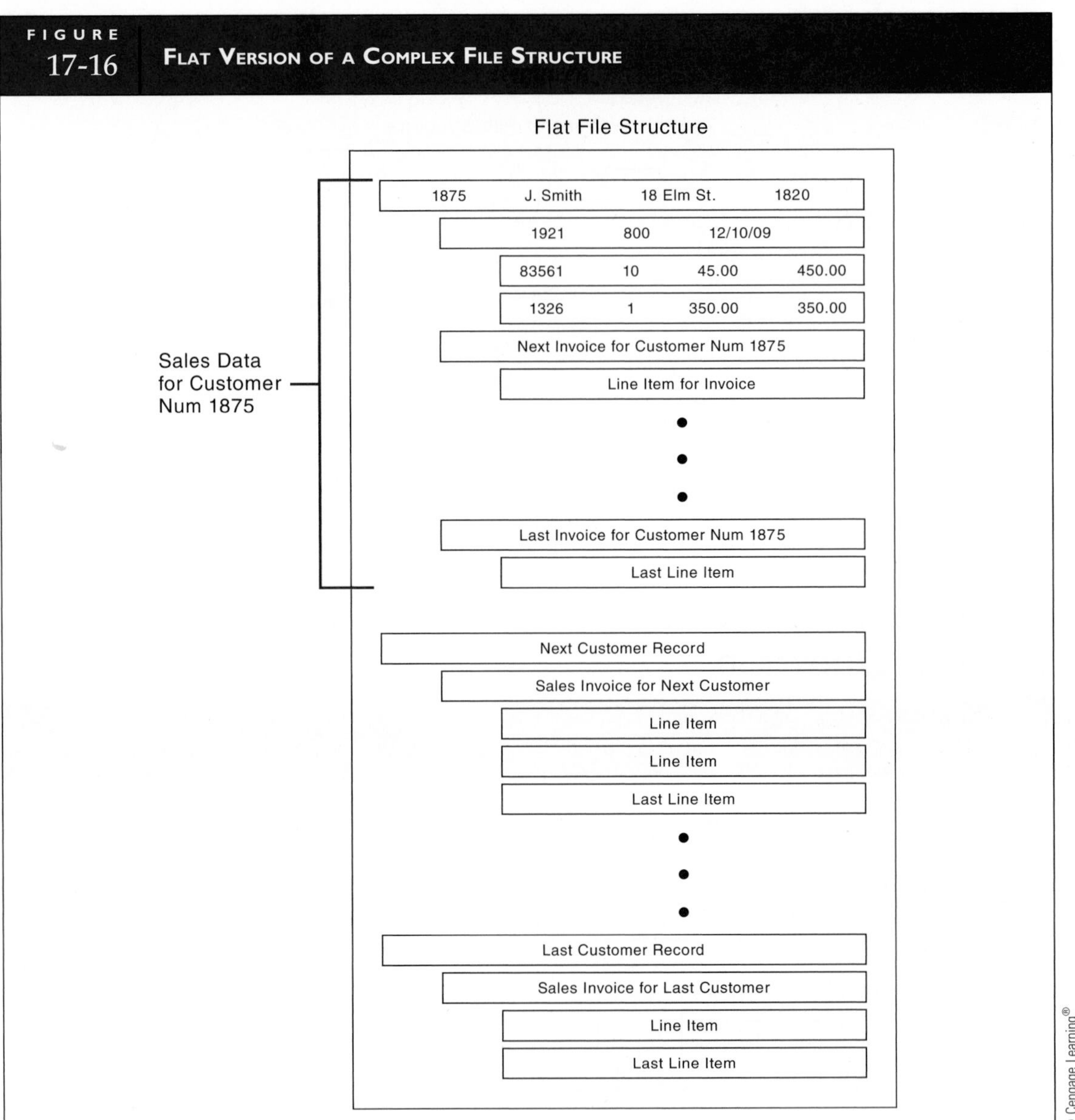

Summary

This chapter dealt with the business risks, IT controls, and test of controls pertaining to three areas of specific concern to SOX: systems development, program change procedures, and computer applications.

The integrity of financial data is directly dependent on the accuracy of the applications that process them. Likewise, the integrity of those applications depends on the quality of the systems development process that produced them and on the program change procedures through which they were modified. Lack of control over these areas, or inconsistency in their function, can result in unintentional application errors and program fraud.

The systems development and maintenance controls and the test of controls described in this chapter apply both to management's SOX-compliance objectives and the auditor's attest responsibility. To test specific application controls, auditors (internal and external) use several types of CAATT, including the test data method, the integrated test facility, and parallel simulation. This chapter concluded with a discussion of two popular CAATTs (embedded audit module and generalized audit software) used for substantive testing.

Key Terms

access tests (724)
accuracy tests (724)
audit trail tests (724)
base case system evaluation (BCSE) (729)
black box approach (728)
completeness tests (724)
computer-assisted audit tools and techniques (CAATTs) (729)
embedded audit module (EAM) (734)
generalized audit software (GAS) (733)
integrated test facility (ITF) (731)
parallel simulation (732)
redundancy tests (724)
salami fraud (727)
substantive tests (734)
test data method (729)
tests of controls (722)
tracing (729)
validity tests (724)

Review Questions

1. List the six systems development controls the chapter addresses. List the two systems maintenance controls.
2. Explain how program testing is conducted, and explain the importance of test data.
3. Why are user specification activities important?
4. What is the role of the internal auditor in systems development?
5. What is the purpose of program testing in the SDLC?
6. Give one example of an error that a check digit control detects.
7. Why are program change procedures important to auditors?
8. What is the importance of the SPL?
9. What functions does the SPLMS control?
10. Why should programs undergoing maintenance be renamed?
11. What is a program version number?
12. What tests may be conducted for identifying unauthorized program changes?
13. What tests may be conducted for identifying application errors?
14. What does *auditing around the computer* mean versus *auditing through the computer*? Why is this so important?
15. What are the through-the-computer techniques?
16. What is an embedded audit module?
17. Explain what GAS is and why it is so popular with larger public accounting firms. Discuss the independence issue related to GAS.
18. Name the general categories of IT application control tests that auditors design.
19. What is the purpose of a range check?
20. What is a reasonableness test?

Discussion Questions

1. Discuss how a controlled SPL environment can help to deter unauthorized changes to programs. Can the use of maintenance commands mitigate these controls?
2. What types of output would be considered extremely sensitive in a university setting? Give three examples, and explain why the information would be considered sensitive. Discuss who should and should not have access to each type of information.
3. What are user test and acceptance procedures?

4. What are rounding error routines, and why are they used?
5. How does the salami fraud get its name, and how does it work?
6. Discuss the black box approach, and explain how it is different from through-the-computer approaches to testing application controls.
7. Discuss the problem associated with creating test data and how it can be alleviated.
8. Why is reliance on the client IT staff to provide a copy of the production application a potential risk?
9. The systems development life cycle is a methodology. Why are auditors responsible for evaluating the controls in this process?
10. What factors do you think might cause an auditing team to spend more time than average on tests to identify application errors? For unauthorized program changes?
11. Explain how an embedded audit module works.
12. Compare and contrast the following techniques based on costs and benefits:
    - test data method
    - base case system evaluation
    - tracing
    - integrated test facility
    - parallel simulation
13. What risks, if any, are associated with reliance on client IT personnel to provide the auditor with flat files from complex data structures?

Multiple-Choice Questions

1. Which of the following statements about test data techniques for testing application controls are NOT correct?
   a. Applications may be tested directly without being removed from service.
   b. The test provides only a static picture of application integrity.
   c. Implementing the test is costly and labor intensive.
   d. The test provides explicit evidence of application functions.
   e. All of the above are correct statements.
2. Which of the following is NOT a common type of through-the-computer tests of controls?
   a. Inference tests
   b. Redundancy tests
   c. Completeness tests
   d. Validity tests
   e. All of the above are through-the-computer tests
3. Which of the following is NOT an SDLC controllable activity?
   a. User specification
   b. Systems authorization
   c. User test and acceptance procedures
   d. External audit participation
   e. All are SDLC controls
4. Which of the following statements is NOT correct?
   a. Executing a production application requires that the source code be compiled and linked to a load module.
   b. As a practical matter, programs in their compiled state are secure and free from the threat of unauthorized modification.
   c. Application logic changes may be made directly to the load module.
   d. Once the application is compiled, the source code is not needed to run the application.
   e. All of the above are correct statements.
5. Which of the following statements is NOT correct?
   a. EAMs have the potential to corrupt corporate databases.
   b. EAMs support continuous monitoring of controls.
   c. EAMs capture transactions during processing without removing the application from service.
   d. EAMs decrease operational performance.
   e. All of the above are correct statements.
6. Tracing is a technique that:
   a. reviews interest calculations to identify a salami fraud.
   b. allows test data to be merged with production data and traces the effects in the database.
   c. performs an electronic walk through of computed logic.
   d. none of the above

7. Which of the following is NOT a test for identifying application control errors?
   a. Access tests
   b. User acceptance tests
   c. Field tests
   d. Range tests
   e. All of the above

8. Which of the following statements about the GAS techniques for substantive testing is NOT correct?
   a. GAS captures data during processing without removing the application from service.
   b. GAS languages are easy to use and require lit tle IT background.
   c. GAS techniques are limited to use with flat files and relational database tables.
   d. Complex file structures need to be flattened before they can be read by GAS.
   e. All of the above are correct statements.

9. Which of the following is NOT an SDLC control issue during an audit?
   a. User and computer services management properly authorized the project.
   b. A preliminary feasibility study showed that the project had merit.
   c. A cost-benefit analysis was conducted using reasonably accurate values.
   d. The detailed design was an appropriate and accurate solution to the user's problem.
   e. All of the above are specific points for review.

10. Which of the following statements about the ITF technique for testing is NOT correct?
   a. Applications may be tested directly without being removed from service.
   b. ITF supports continuous monitoring of controls.
   c. ITF has the potential to corrupt corporate databases.
   d. During normal operations, test transactions are merged into the input stream of regular (production) transactions.
   e. All of the above are correct statements.

Problems

1. DESIGN TESTS OF APPLICATION CONTROLS

Required
Describe the test data (transaction files and master files) the auditor would create, and the tests that an auditor would perform, to evaluate the accuracy of inventory receipts in the receiving department. Assume the following:

- The receiving clerk records receipts from a terminal in the receiving department.
- Inventory is automatically updated by an integrated system.
- The auditor has a current copy of the application and documentation.

Use the examples of tests of IT controls in this chapter as a basis for your responses.

2. COMPUTER FRAUD AND CONTROLS

For many organizations, the security threat from external penetration is significant; however, many fraud threats are internal. These include (1) data input alteration, (2) program alteration, (3) file alteration, (4) data theft, and (5) sabotage.

Required
Explain how each of these five types of frauds is committed. Also, identify a method of protection against each without using the same protection method for more than one type of fraud. Use the following format.

Type of Fraud	Explanation	Description of Protection Methods
a.		
b.		
c.		
d.		
e.		

3. AUDIT PLAN

The CPA firm of True, Blue, and Smith (TBS) has taken on a new audit client. The TBS partner in charge of the audit has concerns in the following areas: system access and security; systems development and program changes; and organization of the IT function.

Required
Outline an audit plan that specifies audit objective and procedures needed to test controls in the areas of concern.

4. AUDIT PLAN

The auditors for Golden Gate Company have a gut feeling that liabilities may be unrecorded. Their initial suspicions stem from a radical decline in accrued liabilities from last year. Golden Gate's records are all computerized.

Required
Devise a plan to search the data files to perform a substantive test for identifying unrecorded liabilities.

5. RISK IDENTIFICATION AND PLAN OF ACTION

Two years ago, an external auditing firm supervised the programming of embedded audit modules for Pre-vits Office Equipment Company. During the audit process this year, the external auditors requested that a transaction log of all transactions be copied to the audit file. The external auditors noticed large gaps in dates and times for transactions being copied to the audit file. When they inquired about this, they were informed that increased processing of transactions had been burdening the Mainframe system and that operators frequently had to turn off the EAM to allow the processing of important transactions in a timely fashion. In addition, much maintenance had been performed during the past year on the application programs.

Required
Outline any potential exposures, and determine the courses of action the external auditors should use to proceed.

6. RISK IDENTIFICATION AND PLAN OF ACTION

The internal auditors of Brown Electrical Company report to the controller. Because of changes made in the past year to several of the transaction processing programs, the internal auditors created a new test data set. The external auditors requested that the old data set also be run. The internal auditors, embarrassed, explained that they overwrote the original test data set.

Required
Outline any potential risks, and determine the courses of action the external auditor should take.

7. SYSTEMS DEVELOPMENT AND PROGRAM CHANGES

Winston Financial Services (WFS), located in Parsippany, NJ provides financial advice to small and mid-sized businesses. Its primary operations are in portfolio management and financial services for clients in the health care industry. Each client has general business and financial information stored on servers in the main office in Parsippany. Client investment information is stored on a separate server in their Tulsa Oklahoma data center. This includes the total value of the portfolio, type of investments made, the income structure of each client, and associated tax liabilities.

WFS had purchase specialized asset management software called VIEW, which allows the company to run analytics on client portfolios and to run simulations of market trends. The customization and implementation of VIEW was performed by a team of IT professionals from the consulting firm of Cutting Edge Solutions (CES).

The contract with CES required them to train a WFS employee to maintain VIEW after the implementation. For this purpose, WFS selected a programmer from their systems maintenance group who was subsequently trained in VIEW's proprietary language and all of its functionality and controls.

Two years after the implementation of VIEW, WFS management is now considering investing in a significant custom upgrade to the system. Furthermore, since their contract with CES has expired, they have decided to assign the upgrade task to their in-house maintenance programmer who had been trained in VIEW by CES. Once the project is completed, the programmer will be redeployed to the maintenance group. This is viewed by the WFS management team to be the most feasible and economic approach.

Required
a. Discuss the risks associated with systems development approach.
b. What controls weaknesses are apparent in this approach?

8. AUDIT OBJECTIVES AND PROCEDURES

You are conducting substantive tests on the accounts receivable file to verify its accuracy. The file is large, and you decide to sample test the records in it. Because of the complexity of the database structure, you cannot access it directly. The client's systems programmer writes a special application that produces a flat file, which he provides for testing purposes.

Required

Discuss any concerns you would have as an auditor and any actions you would take.

9. RISK IDENTIFICATION AND PLAN OF ACTION

As the manager of the external audit team, you realize that the embedded audit module writes material invoices only to the audit file for the accounts receivable confirmation process. You are immediately concerned that the accounts receivable account may be substantially overstated this year and for the prior years in which this EAM was used.

Required

Explain why you are concerned because all "material" invoices are candidates for confirmation by the customer. Outline a plan for determining if the accounts receivable are overstated.

10. COMPUTER-ASSISTED AUDIT TOOLS AND TECHNIQUES (CAATTS)

Required

a. Explain the advantages of using GAS to assist with IT audits, and give five examples of how it may be used.
b. Describe the audit purpose facilitated and the procedural steps to be followed when using the following CAATTs.
   1. ITF
   2. EAM
   3. parallel simulation

11. AUDIT OF SYSTEMS DEVELOPMENT

The Balcar Company's external auditors are developing an audit plan to review the company's systems development procedures. Their audit objectives are to ensure that

1. the system was judged necessary and justified at various checkpoints throughout the SDLC.
2. systems development activities are applied consistently and in accordance with management's policies to all systems development projects.
3. the system as originally implemented was free from material errors and fraud.
4. system documentation is sufficiently accurate and complete to facilitate audit and maintenance activities.

The following six controllable activities have been identified as sources of audit evidence for meeting these objectives: systems authorization, user specification, technical design, internal audit participation, program testing, and user testing and acceptance.

Required

a. Explain the importance of each of the six activities in promoting effective control.
b. Outline the tests of controls that the auditor would perform in meeting audit objectives.

12. PAYROLL APPLICATION CONTROL

Using this supplemental information, analyze the flowchart in the diagram for Problem 12.

- The personnel department determines the wage rate of all employees. To start the process, the personnel department sends the payroll coordinator, George Jones, an authorization form to add an employee to the payroll. After Jones enters this information into the system, the computer automatically determines the overtime and shift differential rates for the individual, updating the payroll master files.
- Employees use a time clock to record the hours worked. Every Monday morning, George Jones collects the previous week's timecards and begins the computerized processing of payroll information to produce paychecks the following Friday. Jones then reviews the timecards to ensure that the hours worked are correctly totaled; the system determines overtime and/or any shift differential.
- Jones performs all other processes displayed on the flowchart. The system automatically assigns a sequential number to each payroll check produced. The check stocks are stored in a box next to the computer printer to provide immediate access. After the checks are printed, an automatic check-signing machine signs them with an authorized signature plate that Jones keeps locked in a safe.

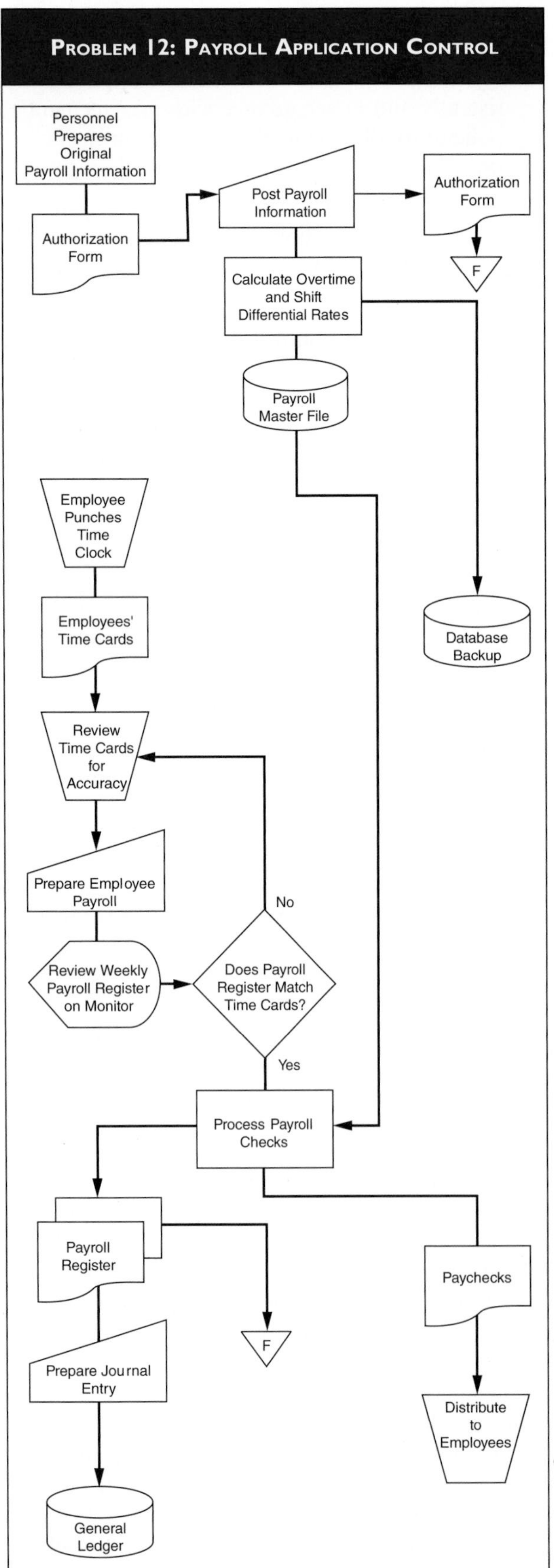

After the check processing is completed, Jones distributes the checks to the employees, leaving the checks for the second- and third-shift employees with the appropriate shift supervisor. Jones then notifies the data processing department that he is finished with his weekly processing, and data processing makes a backup of the payroll master for storage in the computer room.

Required

Identify and describe:

a. areas in the payroll processing system in which the internal controls are inadequate.
b. two areas in the payroll system in which the system controls are satisfactory.

13. ANNOUNCING A NEW INFORMATION SYSTEM

The AJAX Company is considering implementing a new accounting system, which will automate sales processing, cash receipts, accounts payable, and cash disbursement procedures. Roger Moore, AJAX's CIO sent an announcement letter to the AJAX community. In the letter Moore said: "I have contracted with Spartan Consulting Group to do the needs analysis, system selection, and design work. The programming and implementation will be performed in-house using existing IT department staff. The development process will be unobtrusive to user departments because Spartan knows what needs to be done. They will work independently, in the background, and will not disrupt departmental and internal audit work flow with time-consuming interviews, surveys, and questionnaires. This promises to be an efficient process that will produce a system appreciated by all users."

Required

Draft a memo from George Jones, Director of Internal Audits in response to Moore's letter.

14. PROBLEMS VS SYMPTOMS

Being able to distinguish between a symptom and a problem is an important analysis skill. Classify each of the following as a problem or a symptom. If it is a symptom, give two examples of a possible underlying problem. If it is a problem, give two examples of a possible symptom that may be detected.

a. declining profits
b. defective production process
c. low-quality raw materials

d. shortfall in cash balance
e. declining market share
f. shortage of employees in the accounts payable department
g. shortage of raw material due to a drought in the Midwest
h. inadequately trained workers
i. decreasing customer satisfaction

15. SPL RISKS AND CONTROLS

Orben Manufacturing Company has an in-house IT department that incurs a high volume of new development and program maintenance projects. To efficiently manage the workload, the director of IT has combined the systems development and maintenance functions into a single department. This allows the programmers of new applications to also maintain those applications. The immediate effect has been an increase in the work flow by reducing the startup time needed by programmers to become familiar with the systems being modified. It also reduces the time spent on system documentation. Since the designer and the maintenance programmer are the same person, highly detailed and standardized documentation is not needed. To achieve cross training, programmers also maintain applications programmed by other IT personnel. This has resulted in an "open" library policy that allows programmers to access any program stored in the SPL. Programmers download the application undergoing maintenance to their personal computers, perform the necessary maintenance, and then restore the application to the SPL under its original name.

Required

a. Comment on the trade-off between efficiency and control as it pertains in this situation.
b. Discuss the risk potential related to Orben Manufacturing's program change procedures.
c. Discuss the controls that would reduce the risks described in (b) above.

GLOSSARY

A

Access control list (ACL): Lists containing information that defines the access privileges for all valid users of the resource. An access control list assigned to each resource controls access to system resources such as directories, files, programs, and printers.

Access controls: Controls that ensure that only authorized personnel have access to the firm's assets.

Access method: Technique used to locate records and navigate through the database.

Access tests: Tests that ensure that the application prevents authorized users from unauthorized access to data.

Access token: These contain key information about the user, including user ID, password, user group, and privileges granted to the user.

Accounting information systems (AIS): Specialized subset of information systems that processes financial transactions.

Accounting records: Document, journal, or ledger used in transaction cycles.

Accounts receivable (AR) subsidiary ledger: Account record that shows activity by detail for each account type, and containing, at minimum: customer name; customer address; current balance; available credit; transaction dates; invoice numbers; and credits for payments, returns, and allowances.

Accuracy tests: Tests that ensure that the system processes only data values that conform to specified tolerances.

Activities: Work performed in a firm.

Activity driver: Factor that measures the activity consumption by the cost object.

Activity-based costing (ABC): Accounting technique that provides managers with information about activities and cost objects.

Actual cost inventory ledger: A ledger that records inventory values based on actual costs rather than standard costs.

Ad hoc reports: Technology that provides direct-inquiry and report-generation capabilities.

Advanced encryption standard (AES): Also known as Rijndael, a private key (or symmetric key) encryption technique.

Agents: Individuals and departments that participate in an economic event.

Algorithm: Procedure of shifting each letter in the cleartext message by the number of positions that the key value indicates.

Alphabetic codes: Alphabetic characters assigned sequentially.

Alphanumeric codes: Codes that allow the use of pure alphabetic characters embedded within numeric codes.

Anomalies: Negative operational symptoms caused by improperly normalized tables.

AP packet: Reconciled AP supporting documents (PO, receiving report, and invoice).

AP pending file: File containing supporting documents needed to set up an account payable.

AP subsidiary ledger: Records controlling the exposure in the cash disbursements subsystems.

Application controls: Controls that ensure the integrity of specific systems.

Application-level firewall: Provides high-level network security.

Approved credit memo: The credit manager evaluates the circumstances of the return and makes a judgment to grant (or disapprove) credit.

Approved sales order: Contains sales order information for the sales manager to review once the sales order is approved.

Architecture description: Formal description of an information system that identifies and defines the structural properties of the system.

Archive file: File that contains records of past transactions that are retained for future reference.

Asset acquisition: Obtaining a new asset or replacing an existing one.

Asset maintenance: Adjusting the fixed asset subsidiary account balances as the assets (excluding land) depreciate over time or with usage.

Association: Relationship among record types.

Attest function: Independent auditor's responsibility to opine as to the fair presentation of a client firm's financial statement.

Attributes: Equivalents to adjectives in the English language that serve to describe the objects.

Audit objectives: Task of creating meaningful test data.

Audit planning: The first step in the IT audit is audit planning in which the auditor gains a thorough understanding of the client's business. A major part of this phase of the audit is the analysis of audit risk.

Audit risk: Probability that the auditor will render unqualified opinions on financial statements that are, in fact, materially misstated.

Audit trail controls: Ensures that every transaction can be traced through each stage of processing from its economic source to its presentation in financial statements.

Audit trail tests: Ensures that the application creates an adequate audit trail.

Audit trail: Accounting records that trace transactions from their source documents to the financial statements.

Auditor: Expert who expresses an opinion about the fairness of a company's financial statements.

Authority: Right to make decisions pertaining to areas of responsibility.

Automated storage and retrieval systems (AS/RS): Computer-controlled conveyor systems that carry raw materials from stores to the shop floor and finished products to the warehouse.

B

Backbone systems: Basic system structure on which to build.

Back-order: Records that stay on file until the inventories arrive from the supplier. Back-ordered items are shipped before new sales are processed.

Backup controls: Ensure that in the event of data loss due to unauthorized access, equipment failure, or physical disaster, the organization can recover its files and databases.

Balanced scorecard (BSC): Management system that enables organizations to clarify their vision and strategy and translate them into action.

Base case system evaluation (BCSE): Variant of the test data technique inwhich comprehensive test data are used.

Batch controls: Effective method of managing high volumes of transaction data through a system.

Batch systems: Systems that assemble transactions into groups for processing.

Big bang: Attempt by organizations to switch operations from their old legacy systems to a new system in a single event that implements the ERP across the entire company.

Bill of lading: Formal contract between the seller and the shipping company that transports the goods to the customer.

Bill of materials (BOM): Document that specifies the types and quantities of the raw materials and subassemblies used in producing a single unit of finished product.

Billing schemes: Schemes under which an employee causes the employer to issue a payment to a false supplier or vendor by submitting invoices for fictitious goods/services, inflated invoices, or invoices for personal purchases. See *shell company, pass through fraud,* and *pay-and-return.*

Biometric devices: Devices that measure various personal characteristics, such as finger, voice, or retina prints, or other signature characteristics.

Biometric time clocks: Verify employees' identities by using fingerprint or hand-vein scan technology.

Black box approach: An approach that does not require the auditor to create test files or to obtain a detailed knowledge of the application's internal logic. Instead, auditors can analyze flowcharts and interview knowledgeable personnel in the client's organization to understand the functional characteristics of the application.

Blind copy: Purchase order copy that contains no price or quantity information.

Block code: Coding scheme that assigns ranges of values to specific attributes such as account classifications.

Bolt-on software: Software provided by third-party vendors used in conjunction with already purchased ERP software.

Botnets: Collections of compromised computers.

Bribery: Giving, offering, soliciting, or receiving things of value to influence an official in the performance of his or her lawful duties.

Budget: Process that helps management achieve its financial objectives by establishing measurable goals for each organizational segment.

Budget master file: Contains budgeted amounts for revenues, expenditures, and other resources for responsibility centers.

Business ethics: Pertains to the principles of conduct that individuals use in making choices and guiding their behavior in situations that involve the concepts of right and wrong.

C

Caesar cipher: Earliest encryption method; Julius Caesar is said to have used it to send coded messages to his generals in the field.

Call-back device: Hardware component that asks the caller to enter a password and then breaks the connection to perform a security check.

Cardinality: Numerical mapping between entity instances.

Cash disbursement vouchers: Provide improved control over cash disbursements and allow firms to consolidate several payments to the same supplier on a single voucher, thus reducing the number of checks written.

Cash disbursements journal: Contains the voucher number authorizing each check and provides an audit trail for verifying the authenticity of each check written.

Cash larceny: Theft of cash receipts from an organization after those receipts have been recorded in the organization's books and records.

Cash receipts journal: Records that include details of all cash receipts transactions, including cash sales, miscellaneous cash receipts, and cash received.

Centralized data processing: Model under which all data processing is performed by one or more large computers, housed at a central site, that serve users throughout the organization.

Centralized database: Database retained in a central location.

Certification authorities (CAs): Trusted third parties that issue digital certificates.

Changed data capture: Technique that can dramatically reduce extraction time by capturing only newly modified data.

Chart of accounts: Listing of an organization's accounts showing the account number and name.

Check digit: Method for detecting data coding errors in which a control digit is added to the code when it is originally designed to allow the integrity of the code to be established during subsequent processing.

Check register: Record of all cash disbursements.

Check tampering: Forging, or changing in some material way, a check that was written to a legitimate payee.

Checkpoint feature: Feature that suspends all data processing while the system reconciles the transaction log and the database change log against the database.

Client-server model: Form of network topology in which a user's computer or terminal (the client) accesses the ERP programs and data via a host computer called the server.

Closed AP file: Record of all accounts payable that have been discharged by making payment to the creditors.

Closed database architecture: Database management system used to provide minimal technological advantage over flat file systems.

Cloud computing: Location-independent computing variant of IT outsourcing whereby shared data centers deliver hosted IT services over the Internet. These services fall into three categories: software as a service (SaaS), infrastructure as a service (IaaS), and platform as a service (PaaS).

Cohesion: Number of tasks a module performs.

Cold turkey cutover: Process of converting entirely from an existing accounting system to a new system on a particular day rather than phasing in the conversion process over time.

Commercial software: Pre-coded software that a user purchases from a software vendor. Commercial software is available for both general accounting use and for industry specific applications, such as medical billing. Commercial software packages are sometimes called turnkey systems because they can often be implemented by the user with little or no modification.

Committee of Sponsoring Organizations of the Treadway Commission (COSO): A joint initiative of the five private sector organizations listed on the left and is dedicated to providing thought leadership through the development of frameworks and guidance on enterprise risk management, internal control and fraud deterrence.

Commodity IT assets: Assets not unique to an organization and easily acquired in the marketplace (e.g., network management, systems operations, server maintenance, help-desk functions).

Competency analysis: Provides a complete picture of the organization's effectiveness as seen via four strategic filters: resources, infrastructure, products/services, and customers.

Compilers: Language translation modules of the operation system.

Completeness tests: Tests identifying missing data within a single record and entire records missing from a batch.

Composite key: Composed of two attributes: INVOICE NUM and PROD NUM.

Computer ethics: Analysis of the nature and social impact of computer technology and the corresponding formulation and justification of policies for the ethical use of such technology. Includes details about software as well as hardware and concerns about networks connecting computers as well as computers themselves.

Computer fraud: Theft, misuse, or misappropriation of assets by altering computer-readable records and files, or by altering the logic of computer software; the illegal use of computer-readable information; or the intentional destruction of computer software or hardware.

Computer numerical controlled (CNC): Computer-controlled machines that replace skilled labor. The computer contains programs for all parts being manufactured by the machine.

Computer-aided audit tools and techniques (CAATTs): Use of computers to illustrate how application controls are tested and to verify the effective functioning of application controls.

Computer-aided design (CAD): Use of computers to design products to be manufactured.

Computer-aided manufacturing (CAM): Use of computers in factory automation.

Computer-aided software engineering (CASE): Use of computer systems to design and code computer software.

Computer-assisted audit tools and techniques (CAATTs): Use of computers to illustrate how application controls are tested and to verify the effective functioning of application controls.

Computer-integrated manufacturing (CIM): Completely automated environment.

Conceptual system: Production of several alternative designs for a new system.

Conceptual user views: Description of the entire database.

Concurrency control: System that ensures that transactions processed at each site are accurately reflected in the databases at all other sites.

Conflict of interest: Outline of procedures for dealing with actual or apparent conflicts of interest between personal and professional relationships.

Consolidation: Aggregation or roll-up of data.

Construct: Design and building of software that is ready to be tested and delivered to its user community. This phase involves modeling the system, programming the applications, and application testing.

Control activities: Policies and procedures to ensure that appropriate actions are taken to deal with the organization's risks.

Control environment: The foundation of internal control.

Control risk: The likelihood that the control structure is flawed because controls are either absent or inadequate to prevent or detect errors in the accounts.

Controller's: The cash receipts department typically reports to the treasurer, who has responsibility for financial assets. Accounting functions report to the controller. Normally these two general areas of responsibility are performed independently.

Conversion cycle: Cycle composed of the production system and the cost accounting system.

Cookies: Files containing user information that are created by the web server of the site being visited and are then stored on the visitor's own computer hard drive.

Core applications: Applications that operationally support the day-to-day activities of the business.

Core competency theory: Theory underlying outsourcing that posits an organization should focus exclusively on its core business competencies while allowing outsourcing vendors to manage non-core areas such as IT functions efficiently.

Corporate IT function: Coordinating IT unit that attempts to establish corporate-wide standards among distributed IT units.

Corrective controls: Actions taken to reverse the effects of errors detected.

Corruption: Involves an executive, a manager, or an employee of the organization in collusion with an outsider. The ACFE study identifies four principal types of corruption: bribery, illegal gratuities, conflicts of interest, and economic extortion. Corruption accounts for about 10 percent of occupational fraud cases.

Cost center: Organizational unit with responsibility for cost management within budgetary limits.

Cost objects: Reasons for performing activities.

Cost-benefit analysis: Process that helps management determine whether (and by how much) the benefits exceed costs.

Coupling: Measure of the degree of interaction between modules.

Credit memo: Document used to authorize the customer to receive credit for the merchandise returned.

Currency of information: Problem associated with the flat-file model because of its failure to update all the user files affected by a change in status; may result in decisions based on outdated information.

Custom software: Software built to individual specifications. Larger organizations with unique information needs often develop custom software through a formal process called the systems development life cycle. Creating custom software requires the organization to have an in-house team of qualified and experienced IT professionals consisting of systems analysts, programmers, and database designers. Custom systems are more expensive than commercial packages.

Customer order: Document indicating the type and quantity of merchandise being requested.

Cutover: Process of converting from the old system to the new system.

D

Data: Facts, which may or may not be processed (edited, summarized, or refined) and which have no direct effect on the user.

Data attribute: The most elemental piece of potentially useful data in the database.

Data collection: First operational stage in the information system.

Data collision: Collision of two or more signals due to simultaneous transmission that destroys both messages from the transmitting and the receiving nodes.

Data currency: When the firm's data files accurately reflect the effects of its transactions.

Data definition language (DDL): Programming language used to define the database to the database management system.

Data dictionary: Description of every data element in the database.

Data encryption: Use of an algorithm to scramble selected data, making it unreadable to an intruder browsing the database.

Data flow diagram (DFD): Use of a set of symbols in a diagram to represent the processes, data sources, data flows, and process sequences of a current or proposed system.

Data manipulation language (DML): Language used to insert special database commands into application programs written in conventional languages.

Data mart: Data warehouse organized for a single department or function.

Data mining: Process of selecting, exploring, and modeling large amounts of data to uncover relationships and global patterns that exist in large databases but are hidden among the vast amount of facts.

Data model: Blueprint for what ultimately will become the physical database.

Data modelling: Task of formalizing the data requirements of the business process as a conceptual model.

Data processing: Group that manages the computer resources used to perform the day-to-day processing of transactions.

Data redundancy: State of data elements being represented in all user files.

Data sources: Financial transactions that enter the information system from both internal and external sources.

Data storage: Efficient information system that captures and stores data only once and makes this single source available to all users who need it.

Data structures: Techniques for physically arranging records in a database.

Data updating: Periodic updating of data stored in the files of an organization.

Data warehouse: Database constructed for quick searching, retrieval, ad hoc queries, and ease of use.

Database: Physical repository for financial data.

Database administrator (DBA): Individual responsible for managing the database resource.

Database authorization table: Table containing rules that limit the actions a user can take.

Database conversion: Transfer of data from its current form to the format or medium the new system requires.

Database lockout: Software control that prevents multiple simultaneous access to data.

Database management: Special software system that is programmed to know which data elements each user is authorized to access.

Database management fraud: Altering, deleting, corrupting, destroying, or stealing an organization's data.

Database management system (DBMS): Software system that controls access to the data resource.

Database model: Symbolic model of the structure of, and the associations between, an organization's data entities.

Deadlock: "Wait" state that occurs between sites when data are locked by multiple sites that are waiting for the removal of the locks from the other sites.

Decision-making process: Cognitive process leading to the selection of a course of action among variations.

Deep packet inspection (DPI): Program used to determine when a DOS attack is in progress through a variety of analytical and statistical techniques that evaluate the contents of message packets.

Deletion anomaly: Unintentional deletion of data from a table.

Denial of service attack (DoS): Assault on a web server to prevent it from servicing its legitimate users.

Deposit slip: Written notification accompanying a bank deposit that specifies and categorizes the funds (such as checks, bills, and coins) being deposited.

Depreciation schedule: Record used to initiate depreciation calculations.

Design phase: Production of a detailed description of the proposed system that both satisfies the system requirements identified during systems analysis and is in accordance with the conceptual design.

Detailed design report: Set of blueprints that specify input screen formats, output report layouts, database structures, and process logic.

Detailed feasibility study: Step in the system evaluation and selection process where the feasibility factors that were evaluated on a preliminary basis as part of the systems proposal are reexamined.

Detection risk: The risk that auditors are willing to take that errors not detected or prevented by the control structure will also not be detected by the auditor.

Detective controls: Devices, techniques, and procedures designed to identify and expose undesirable events that elude preventive controls.

Digest: Mathematical value calculated from the text content of the message.

Digital certificate: Sender's public key that has been digitally signed by trusted third parties.

Digital envelope: Encryption method in which both DES and RSA are used together.

Digital signature: Electronic authentication technique that ensures the transmitted message originated with the authorized sender and that it was not tampered with after the signature was applied.

Direct access structures: Storage of data at a unique location, known as an address, on a hard disk or floppy disk.

Disaster recovery plan (DRP): Comprehensive statement of all actions to be taken before, during, and after a disaster, along with documented, tested procedures to ensure the continuity of operations.

Discovery model: Model that uses data mining to discover previously unknown but important information that is hidden within the data.

Discretionary access privileges: Grants access privileges to other users. For example, the controller, who is the owner of the general ledger, may grant read-only privileges to a manager in the budgeting department.

Discretionary reporting: A type of reporting in which the organization can choose what information to report and how to present it.

Disseminating: Providing knowledge to recipients in a usable form.

Distributed data processing (DDP): Reorganizing the IT function into small information processing units (IPUs) that are distributed to end users and placed under their control.

Distributed databases: Databases distributed using either the partitioned or replicated technique.

Distributed denial of service (DDoS): A distributed denial of service (DDoS) attack may take the form of a SYN flood or Smurf attack. The distinguishing feature of the DDoS is the sheer scope of the event.

Distribution level: Internet marketing model that sells and delivers digital products to customers.

Document name: A component of the URL that indicates the name of the file/document.

Documentation: Written description of how the system works.

Domain name: Organization's unique name combined with a top-level domain (TLD) name.

Drill-down: Operations permitting the disaggregation of data to reveal the underlying details that explain certain phenomena.

Duality: An economic exchange represented by a give event and a corresponding take event.

Dynamic virtual organization: Electronic partnering of business enterprises sharing costs and resources for the purpose of benefits to all parties involved.

E

Eavesdropping: Listening to output transmissions over telecommunications lines.

Echo check: Technique that involves the receiver of the message returning the message to the sender.

Economic events: Phenomena that affect changes (increases or decreases) in resources.

Economic extortion: Use (or threat) of force (including economic sanctions) by an individual or organization to obtain something of value. The item of value could be a financial or economic asset, information, or cooperation to obtain a favorable decision on some matter under review.

Economic feasibility: Pertains to the availability of funds to complete the project.

Economic order quantity (EOQ) model: Inventory model designed to reduce total inventory costs.

EDE3: Encryption that uses one key to encrypt the message.

EEE3: Encryption that uses three different keys to encrypt the message three times.

Electronic data interchange (EDI): Intercompany exchange of computer-processable business information in standard format.

Electronic input techniques: Forms of electronic data collection. These fall into two basic types: input from source documents and direct input.

Embedded audit module (EAM): Technique in which one or more specially programmed modules embedded in a host application select and record predetermined types of transactions for subsequent analysis.

Embedded instructions: Instructions contained within the body of the form itself rather than on a separate sheet.

Employee fraud: Performance fraud by nonmanagement employee generally designed to directly convert cash or other assets to the employee's personal benefit.

Employee payroll records: System an employer uses to calculate, track, and report employee pay.

Employee records file: Comprises the additions of new employees, deletions of terminated employees, changes in work dependents, changes in withholdings, and changes in job status such as job title and pay rate. Human resources clerks enter data into the employee records file in real time from terminals.

Empty shell: Arrangement that involves two or more user organizations that buy or lease a building and remodel it into a computer site, but without the computer and peripheral equipment.

Encryption: Use of a computer program to transform a standard message being transmitted into a coded (cipher text) form.

End users: Users for whom the system is built.

Enterprise resource planning (ERP): System assembled of prefabricated software components.

Entity: Resource, event, or agent.

Entity relationship (ER) diagram: Documentation technique used to represent the relationship among data entities in a system.

Ethical responsibility: Responsibility of organization managers to seek a balance between the risks and benefits to their constituents that result from their decisions.

Ethics: Principles of conduct that individuals use in making choices that guide their behavior in situations involving the concepts of right and wrong.

Event monitoring: Summarizes key activities related to system resources.

Event-driven languages: Visual Basic or object-oriented programming (OOP) languages such as Java or C++.

Expenditure cycle: Acquisition of materials, property, and labor in exchange for cash.

Expense reimbursement frauds: Claiming reimbursement of fictitious or inflated business expenses.

Exposure: Absence or weakness of a control.

External agent: Economic agents outside the organization with discretionary power to use or dispose of economic resources.

Extranet: Password-controlled network for private users rather than the general public.

F

Fault tolerance: Ability of the system to continue operation when part of the system fails due to hardware failure, application program error, or operator error.

Feedback: Form of output that is sent back to the system as a source of data. Feedback may be internal or external and is used to initiate or alter a process.

File Transfer Protocol (FTP): Protocol used to transfer text files, programs, spreadsheets, and databases across the Internet.

Financial transaction: Economic event that affects the assets and equities of the organization, is measured in financial terms, and is reflected in the accounts of the firm.

Firewall: Software and hardware that provide a focal point for security by channeling all network connections through a control gateway.

First normal form (INF): Low degree of normalization of relational database tables.

Fixed assets: Property, plant, and equipment used in the operation of a business.

Flat-file: File structure that does not support the integration of data.

Flat-file approach: Organizational environment in which users own their data exclusively.

Flat-file model: Environment in which individual data files are not related to other files.

Foreign keys: Key that permits the physical connection of logically related tables to achieve the associations described in the data model.

Formalization of tasks: Subdivision of organizational areas into tasks that represent full-time job positions.

Fraud: False representation of a material fact made by one party to another party, with the intent to deceive and induce the other party to justifiably rely on the material fact to his or her detriment.

Fraud triangle: Triad of factors associated with management and employee fraud: situational pressure (includes personal or job-related stresses that could coerce an individual to act dishonestly); opportunity (involves direct access to assets and/ or access to information that controls assets); and ethics (pertains to one's character and degree of moral opposition to acts of dishonesty).

Fraudulent statements: Statements associated with management fraud. This class of fraud scheme the financial statement misrepresentation must itself bring direct or indirect financial benefit to the perpetrator.

G

Gantt chart: Horizontal bar chart that presents time on a horizontal plane and activities on a vertical plane.

Gathering: Process in knowledge management that brings data into the system.

General computer controls: Specific activities performed by persons or systems designed to ensure that business objectives are met.

General controls: Controls that pertain to entity-wide concerns such as controls over the data center, organization databases, systems development, and program maintenance.

General ledger change report: Report that presents the effects of journal voucher transactions on the general ledger accounts.

General ledger history file: File that presents comparative financial reports on a historic basis.

General ledger master file: Principal file in the GLS database. This file is based on the organization's published chart of accounts.

General ledger/financial reporting system (GL/FRS): System that produces traditional financial statements, such as income statements, balance sheets, statements of cash flows, tax returns, and other reports required by law.

General model for AIS: Model that describes all information systems, regardless of their technological architecture. The elements of the general model are end users, data sources, data collection, data processing, database management, information generation, and feedback.

Generalized audit software (GAS): Software that allows auditors to access electronically coded data files and perform various operations on their contents.

Give event: Economic event mirrored by another event in the opposite direction. These dual events constitute the give event and receive event of an economic exchange.

Goal congruence: Merging of goals within an organization.

Grandfather-father-son (GFS): A back-up technique employed by systems that use sequential master files (whether tape or disk). It is an integral part of the master file update process.

Group codes: Codes used to represent complex items or events involving two or more pieces of related data.

Group memory: The collective knowledge of an organization that makes it more effective, just as human beings become more effective and mature with the accumulation of thoughts and memories.

H

Hard-copy: Traditional paper-based data storage medium used for reports and documentation.

Hash total: Control technique that uses nonfinancial data to keep track of the records in a batch.

Hashing structure: Structure employing an algorithm that converts the primary key of a record directly into a storage address.

Hierarchical indexed direct access method: Method in which the root segment (customer file) of the database is organized as an indexed file.

Hierarchical model: Database model that represents data in a hierarchical structure and permits only a single parent record for each child record.

Home page: Typical point of entry for an Internet website.

Human resource management (HRM) system: Captures and processes a wide range of personnel-related data, including employee benefits, labor resource planning, employee relations, employee skills, and personnel actions (pay rates, deductions, and so on), as well as payroll. HRM systems need to provide real-time access to personnel files for purposes of direct inquiries and recording changes in employee status as they occur.

Hyper Text Markup Language (HTML): Provides the formatting for a web page as well as hypertext links to other web pages. The linked pages may be stored on the same server or anywhere in the world.

Hyper Text Transfer Protocol (HTTP): Communications protocol used to transfer or convey information on the World Wide Web.

Hyper-Text Transport Protocol-Next Generation (HTTP-NG): Enhanced version of HTTP that maintains the simplicity of HTTP while adding important features such as security and authentication.

I

Illegal gratuity: Giving, receiving, offering, or soliciting something of value because of an official act that has been taken.

Implementation: Carrying out, execution, or practice of a plan, a method, or any design for doing something. Shortterm planning involves the implementation of specific plans that are needed to achieve the objectives of the long-range plan.

Inappropriate performance measures: Behavior and performance measures inconsistent with the objectives of the firm.

Independence: Separation of the record-keeping function of accounting from the functional areas that have custody of physical resources.

Indexed random file: Randomly organized file accessed via an index.

Indexed sequential file: Sequential file structure accessed via an index.

Indexed structure: Class of file structure that uses indexes for its primary access method.

Industry analysis: Analysis provided to management of the driving forces that affect the industry and the organization's performance.

Information content: Ability of a report to reduce uncertainty and influence behavior of the user.

Information flows: Flow of information into and out of an organization.

Information generation: Process of compiling, arranging, formatting, and presenting information to users.

Information level: Level of activity in which an organization uses the Internet only to display information about the company, its products, services, and business policies.

Information overload: When a manager receives more information than can be assimilated.

Information system: Set of formal procedures by which data are collected, processed into information, and distributed to users.

Information technology controls: Include controls over IT governance, IT infrastructure, security, and access to operating systems and databases, application acquisition and development, and program changes.

Information: Facts that cause the user to take an action that he or she otherwise could not, or would not, have taken.

Infrastructure as a service (IaaS): The provision of computing power and disk space to client firms who access it from desktop PCs. The client firm can configure the infrastructure for storage, networks, and other computing needs, including running operating systems and data processing applications.

Inherent risk: The risk associated with the unique characteristics of the business or industry of the client.

Inheritance: Programming property that allows each object instance to inherit the attributes and operations of the class to which it belongs.

Input controls: Programmed procedures, often called edits, that perform tests on transaction data to ensure that they are free from errors.

Insertion anomaly: Unintentional insertion of data into a table.

Instance: Single occurrence of an object within a class.

Integrated test facility (ITF): Automated technique that enables the auditor to test an application's logic and controls during its normal operation.

Intelligent control agents: Computer programs that embody auditor-defined heuristics that search electronic transactions for anomalies.

Intelligent forms: Forms that help the user complete the form and that make calculations automatically.

Internal agent: Economic agents inside the organization with discretionary power to use or dispose of economic resources.

Internal auditing: Appraisal function housed within the organization.

Internal control system: Policies a firm employs to safeguard the firm's assets, ensure accurate and reliable accounting records and information, promote efficiency, and measure compliance with established policies.

Internal view: Physical arrangement of records in the database.

International Standards Organization: Voluntary group composed of representatives from the national standards organizations of its member countries. The ISO works toward the establishment of international standards for data encryption, data communications, and protocols.

Internet Message Access Protocol: Protocol for transmitting e-mail messages. Other e-mail protocols are Post Office Protocol (POP) and Simple Network Mail Protocol (SNMP).

Internet Relay Chat (IRC): Interactive Internet service that lets thousands of people from around the world engage in real-time communications via their computers.

Interpreters: Language translation modules of the operation system that convert one line of logic at a time.

Intrusion Prevention Systems (IPS): Use of deep packet inspection (DPI) to determine when an attack is in progress.

Inventory subsidiary ledger: Ledger with inventory records updated from the stock release copy by the inventory control system.

Inverted list: Cross-reference created from multiple indexes.

Investment center: Organizational unit that has the objective of maximizing the return on investment assets.

IP broadcast address: 32-bit number that identifies each sender or receiver of information sent in packets across the Internet.

IP spoofing: Form of masquerading to gain unauthorized access to a web server and/or to perpetrate an unlawful act without revealing one's identity.

Islands of technology: Environment where modern automation exists in the form of islands that stand alone within the traditional setting.

IT auditing: Review of the computer-based components of an organization. The audit is often performed as part of a broader financial audit.

IT outsourcing: Contracting with a third-party vendor to take over the costs, risks, and responsibilities associated with maintaining an effective corporate IT function, including management of IT assets and staff and delivery of IT services such as data entry, data center operations, applications development, applications maintenance, and network management.

J

Job tickets: Mechanisms to capture the time that individual workers spend on each production job.

Join: Builds a new physical table from two tables consisting of all concatenated pairs of rows from each table.

Journal: Record of a chronological entry.

Journal voucher file: Compilation of all journal vouchers posted to the general ledger.

Journal voucher history file: File that contains journal vouchers for past periods.

Journal voucher listing: Listing that provides relevant details about each journal voucher received by the GL/FRS.

Journal voucher: Accounting journal entries into an accounting system for the purposes of making corrections or adjustments to the accounting data. For control purposes, all JVs should be approved by the appropriate designated authority.

Just-in-time (JIT): Philosophy that addresses manufacturing problems through process simplification.

K

Key: Mathematical value that the sender selects for the purpose of encrypting or decoding data.

Keystroke monitoring: Recording both the user's keystrokes and the system's responses.

Knowledge management: Gathering, organizing, refining, and disseminating information.

L

Labor distribution summary: Summarization of labor costs in work-in-process accounts.

Labor usage file: File in which the cost accounting department enters job cost data (real time or daily).

Lapping: Use of customer checks, received in payment of their accounts, to conceal cash previously stolen by an employee.

Lean manufacturing: Improves efficiency and effectiveness in product design, supplier interaction, factory operations, employee management, and customer relations.

Ledger: Book of accounts that reflects the financial effects of the firm's transactions after they are posted from the various journals.

Ledger copy: Copy of the sales order received along with the customer sales invoice by the billing department clerk from the sales department.

Legacy systems: Large mainframe systems implemented in the late 1960s through the 1980s.

Legal feasibility: Ensures that the proposed system is not in conflict with the company's ability to discharge its legal responsibilities.

Line error: Errors caused when the bit structure of the message is corrupted through noise on the communications lines.

Logical key pointer: Pointer containing the primary key of the related record.

Log-on procedure: Operating system's first line of defense against unauthorized access.

M

Magnetic swipe ID cards: Works like a credit card. Each employee is issued an ID card that has a magnetic strip containing employee information. The employee swipes the card through the time clock to record start and end time on the job.

Mail room fraud: Fraud committed when an employee opening the mail steals a customer's check and destroys the associated remittance advice.

Management assertions: Combination of tests of application controls and substantive tests of transaction details and account balances.

Management by exception: Concept that managers should limit their attention to potential problem areas rather than being involved with every activity or decision.

Management control decisions: Technique for motivating managers in all functional areas to use resources as productively as possible.

Management fraud: Performance fraud that often uses deceptive practices to inflate earnings or to forestall the recognition of either insolvency or a decline in earnings.

Management information system (MIS): System that processes nonfinancial transactions not normally processed by traditional accounting information systems.

Management report: Discretionary report used for internal decision making. Management reports are not mandated like income statements, balance sheets, etc.

Management reporting system (MRS): System that provides the internal financial information needed to manage a business.

Management responsibility: Concept under which the responsibility for the establishment and maintenance of a system of internal control falls to management.

Manufacturing flexibility: Ability to physically organize and reorganize production facilities and the employment of automated technologies.

Manufacturing resources planning (MRP II): System that incorporates techniques to execute the production plan, provide feedback, and control the process.

Master file: File containing account data.

Materials requirements planning (MRP): System used to plan inventory requirements in response to production work orders.

Materials requisition: Document that authorizes the storekeeper to release materials to individuals or work centers in the production process.

Message sequence numbering: Sequence number inserted in each message to foil any attempt by an intruder in the communications channel to delete a message from a stream of messages, change the order of messages received, or duplicate a message.

Message transaction log: Log in which all incoming and outgoing messages, as well as attempted (failed) access, should be recorded.

Methods: Actions that are performed on or by objects that may change the objects' attributes.

Mirrored data center: Data center that reflects current economic events of the firm.

Mnemonic codes: Alphabetic characters in the form of acronyms that convey meaning.

Mobile remote devices: Allow employees to clock in using handheld devices (PDA or cell phone) or web browsers from laptop computers. This option is popular among businesses with employees in the field who travel between clients and with companies engaged in global business with foreign-based employees.

Monitoring: Process by which the quality of internal control design and operation can be assessed.

Move ticket: Document that records work done in each work center and authorizes the movement of the job or batch from one work center to the next.

N

Navigational models: Model that possesses explicit links or paths among data elements.

Net present value method: Method in which the present value of the costs is deducted from the present value of the benefits over the life of the system.

Network: A collection of interconnected computers and communications devices that allows users to communicate, access data and applications, and share information and resources.

Network administration: Responsible for the effective functioning of the software and hardware that constitute the organization's network. This involves configuring, implementing, and maintaining network equipment.

Network model: Variation of the hierarchical model.

Network News Transfer Protocol (NNTP): Network used to connect to Usenet groups on the Internet.

Network virtualization: Increases effective network bandwidth by dividing it into independent channels, which are then assigned to separate virtual computers. It optimizes network speed, flexibility, and reliability; most importantly, it improves network scalability. It is especially effective in networks that experience sudden, large, and unforeseen surges in usage.

Network-level firewall: System that provides basic screening of low-security messages (for example, e-mail) and routes them to their destinations based on the source and destination addresses attached.

Non-cash fraud: Theft or misuse of non-cash assets (e.g., inventory, confidential information).

Nondiscretionary reporting: A type of reporting in which the organization has few or no choices in the information it provides. Much of this information consists of traditional financial statements, tax returns, and other legal documents.

Nonfinancial transactions: Events that do not meet the narrow definition of a financial transaction. For example, adding a new supplier of raw materials to the list of valid suppliers is an event that may be processed by the enterprise's information system as a transaction.

Object class: Logical grouping of individual objects that share the same attributes and operations.

Object-oriented design: Building information systems from reusable standard components or modules.

Object-oriented programming (OOP) language: Programming language containing the attributes and operations that constitute the object modules represented in the ER diagram at the implementation phase of the SDLC.

Occurrence: Used to describe the number of instances or records that pertain to a specific entity.

Off-site storage: Storage procedure used to safeguard the critical resources.

On-demand reports: Reports triggered by events.

One-time password: Network passwords that constantly change.

Online analytical processing (OLAP): Enterprise resource planning decision support tool used to supply management with real-time information. It also permits timely decisions that are needed to improve performance and achieve a competitive advantage.

Online documentation: Guides the user interactively in the use of a system. Examples include tutorials and help features.

Online transaction processing (OLTP): Events consisting of large numbers of relatively simple transactions such as updating accounting records that are stored in several related tables.

Open AP file: File organized by payment due date and scanned daily to ensure that debts are paid on the last possible date without missing due dates and losing discounts.

Open purchase order file: File that contains the last copy of the multipart purchase order along with the purchase requisition.

Open purchase requisition file: File that contains a copy of purchase requisitions

Open System Interface (OSI): Provides standards by which the products of different manufacturers can interface with one another in a seamless interconnection at the user level.

Open/closed purchase order file: The last copy that is flied while preparing a purchase order.

Operating system: A computer's control program.

Operating system security: Controls the system in an ever-expanding user community sharing more and more computer resources.

Operational control decisions: Technique that ensures that the firm operates in accordance with pre-established criteria.

Operational feasibility: Pertains to the degree of compatibility between the firm's existing procedures and personnel skills and the operational requirements of the new system.

Operations control reports: Identifies activities that are about to go out of control and ignores those that are functioning within normal limits.

Operations fraud: Misuse or theft of the firm's computer resources.

Organization: Refers to the way records are physically arranged on the secondary storage device (e.g., a disk).

Organizational chart: Shows typical job positions in a manufacturing firm.

Organizing: Associating data items with subjects, giving them context.

Output controls: A combination of programmed routines and other procedures to ensure that system output is not lost, misdirected, or corrupted and that privacy is not violated.

Ownership: State or fact of exclusive rights and control over property, which may be an object, land/real estate, intellectual property, or some other kind of property.

P

Packet switching: Division of messages into small packets for transmission.

Packing slip: Document that travels with the goods to the customer to describe the contents of the order.

Parallel operation cutover: Conversion process in which the old system and the new system are run simultaneously for a period of time.

Parallel simulation: Technique that requires the auditor to write a program that simulates key features of processes of the application under review.

Parity check: Technique that incorporates an extra bit into the structure of a bit string when it is created or transmitted.

Partial dependencies: Occurs when one or more nonkey attributes are dependent on (defined by) only part of the primary key rather than the whole key.

Partitioned database: Database approach that splits the central database into segments or partitions that are distributed to their primary users.

Pass through fraud: Similar to shell company except that a transaction actually takes place. The perpetrator creates a false vendor and issues purchases orders to it for inventory or supplies. The false vendor purchases the needed inventory from a legitimate vendor, charges the victim company a much higher than market price for the items, and pockets the difference. See *shell company*.

Password: Code, usually kept secret, entered by the user to gain access to data files.

Pay-and-return: Scheme under which a clerk with checkwriting authority pays a vendor twice for the same products (inventory or supplies) received, then intercepts and cashes the overpayment returned by the vendor.

Payback method: Variation of break-even analysis. Under the payback method, the break-even point is reached when total costs equal total benefits.

Paychecks: A bank check given as salary or wages.

Payroll fraud: Distribution of fraudulent paychecks to existent and/or nonexistent employees.

Payroll imprest account: Account into which a single check for the entire amount of the payroll is deposited.

Payroll register: Document showing gross pay, deductions, overtime pay, and net pay.

Personnel action forms: Document identifying employees authorized to receive a paycheck; the form is used to reflect changes in pay rates, payroll deductions, and job classification.

PERT chart: Chart that reflects the relationship among the many activities that constitute the implementation process.

Phased cutover: Process of converting an old system to a new system in modules.

Phased-in: Approach for implementing ERP systems in a phased manner.

Physical address pointer: Contains the actual disk storage location (cylinder, surface, and record number) that the disk controller needs.

Physical database: Lowest level of the database containing magnetic spots on magnetic disks.

Physical system: Medium and method for capturing and presenting the information.

Ping: Internet maintenance tool used to test the state of network congestion and determine whether a particular host computer is connected and available on the network.

Pointer structure: Structure in which the address (pointer) of one record is stored in the field on a related record.

Point-of-sale (POS) systems: Revenue system in which no customer accounts receivable are maintained and inventory is kept on the store's shelves, not in a separate warehouse.

Polling: Actively sampling the status of an external device by a client program as a synchronous activity.

Post Office Protocol: Protocol for transmitting email messages. Other e-mail protocols are Internet Message Access Protocol (IMAP) and Simple Network Mail Protocol (SNMP).

Prenumbered documents: Documents (sales orders, shipping notices, remittance advices, and so on) sequentially numbered by the printer that allow every transaction to be identified uniquely.

Preventive controls: Passive techniques designed to reduce the frequency of occurrence of undesirable events.

Primary key: Characteristics that uniquely identify each record in the tables.

Privacy Enhanced Mail (PEM): Standard for secure e-mail on the Internet. It supports encryption, digital signatures, and digital certificates as well as both private and public key methods.

Privacy: Full control of what and how much information about an individual is available to others and to whom it is available.

Private Communications Technology (PCT): Security protocol that provides secure transactions over the World Wide Web.

Private key: One method of encryption.

Proactive management: Management that stays alert to subtle signs of problems and aggressively looks for ways to improve the organization's systems.

Procedural language: Specifies the precise order in which the program logic is executed.

Processing controls: Programmed procedures to ensure that an application's logic is functioning properly.

Product documents: Documents that result from transaction processing.

Product family: Product families share common processes from the point of placing the order to shipping the finished goods to the customer.

Production schedule: Formal plan and authorization to begin production.

Profit center: Organizational unit with responsibility for both cost control and revenue generation.

Program flowchart: Diagram providing a detailed description of the sequential and logical operations of the program.

Program fraud: Techniques such as creating illegal programs that can access data files to alter, delete, or insert values into accounting records; destroying or corrupting a program's logic using a computer virus; or altering program logic to cause the application to process data incorrectly.

Programmed reports: Reports that provide information to solve problems that users have anticipated.

Project: Extracts specified attributes (columns) from a table to create a virtual table.

Project feasibility: Analysis that determines how best to proceed with a project.

Protocol: Rules and standards governing the design of hardware and software that permit network users to communicate and share data.

Protocol prefix: General format for a URL; i.e., http:// is a protocol prefix.

Prototyping: Technique for providing users with a preliminary working version of the system.

Pseudocode: English-like code that describes the logic of a program without specific language systems.

Public Company Accounting Oversight Board (PCAOB): Federal organization empowered to set auditing, quality control, and ethics standards; to inspect registered accounting firms; to conduct investigations; and to take disciplinary actions.

Public key encryption: Technique that uses two encryption keys: one for encoding the message, the other for decoding it.

Public key infrastructure (PKI): Constitutes the policies and procedures for administering this activity.

Pull processing: Principle characterizing the lean manufacturing approach where products are pulled into production as capacity downstream becomes available. Products are pulled from the consumer end (demand).

Purchase order: Document based on a purchase requisition that specifies items ordered from a vendor or supplier.

Purchase requisition: Document that authorizes a purchase transaction.

Purchase requisition file: Comprises purchase requisitions. It is created during the sales activity when the inventories drop to their predetermined reorder point.

Q

Quality assurance group: Independent group of programmers, analysts, users, and internal auditors who simulate the operation of the system to uncover errors, omissions, and ambiguities in the design.

R

REA diagram: Diagram consisting of three entity types (resources, events, and agents) and a set of associations linking them.

REA model: Alternative accounting framework for modeling an organization's critical resources, events, and agents, and the relationships between them.

Reactive management: Management that responds to problems only when they reach a crisis state and can no longer be ignored.

Real-time systems: Systems that process transactions individually at the moment the economic event occurs.

Reasonable assurance: Assurance provided by the internal control system that the four broad objectives of internal control are met in a cost-effective manner.

Receive event: Economic event mirrored by another event in the opposite direction. These dual events constitute the give event and receive event of an economic exchange.

Receiving report: Report that lists quantity and condition of the inventories received.

Receiving report file: File in which a copy of the receiving report (stating the quantity and condition of the inventories) is placed.

Record layout diagrams: Used to reveal the internal structure of the records that constitute a file or database table. The layout diagram usually shows the name, data type, and length of each attribute (or field) in the record.

Recovery module: Uses the logs and backup files to restart the system after a failure.

Recovery operations center (ROC): Arrangement involving two or more user organizations that buy or lease a building and remodel it into a completely equipped computer site.

Redundancy tests: Tests that determine that an application processes each record only once.

Redundant arrays of independent disks (RAID): Use of parallel disks that contain redundant elements of data and applications.

Reference file: File that stores the data used as standards for processing transactions.

Refining: Adding value by discovering relationships between data, performing synthesis, and abstracting.

Register: Often used to denote certain types of special journals. For example, the payroll journal is often called the payroll register.

Relational model: Data model that is more flexible than traditional navigational models. It allows users to create new and unique paths through the database to solve a wide range of business problems.

Reliability: Property of information that makes it useful to users.

Remittance advices: Source document that contains key information required to service the customers account.

Remittance list: Cash prelist, where all cash received is logged.

Reorder point (ROP): Lead time multiplied by daily demand.

Replicated databases: Database approach in which the central database is replicated at each site.

Report attributes: Characteristics of a report. To be effective, a report must possess the following attributes: relevance, summarization, exception orientation, accuracy, completeness, timeliness, and conciseness.

Request for proposal (RFP): Document summarizing system requirements and sent to each prospective vendor.

Request-response technique: Technique in which a control message from the sender and a response from the sender are sent at periodic synchronized intervals.

Resources: Assets of an organization.

Responsibility: Individual's obligation to achieve desired results.

Responsibility accounting: Concept that every economic event affecting the organization is the responsibility of and can be traced to an individual manager.

Responsibility center file: Contains the revenues, expenditures, and other resource utilization data for each responsibility center in the organization.

Responsibility centers: Organization of business entities into areas involving cost, profit, and investment.

Responsibility reports: Reports containing performance measures at each operational segment in the firm, which flow upward to senior levels of management.

Restrict: Command to extracts specified rows from a specified table.

Return slip: Document recording the counting and inspect of items returned, prepared by the receiving department employee.

Reusable password: Network password that can be used more than one time.

Revenue cycle: Cycle composed of sales order processing and cash receipts.

Risk: Possibility of loss or injury that can reduce or eliminate an organization's ability to achieve its objectives. In terms of electronic commerce, risk relates to the loss, theft, or destruction of data as well as the use of computer programs that financially or physically harm an organization.

Risk assessment: Identification, analysis, and management of risks relevant to financial reporting.

Rivest-Shamir-Adleman (RSA): One of the most trusted public key encryption methods. This method, however, is computationally intensive and much slower than private key encryption.

Role: Formal technique for grouping users according to the system resources they require to perform their assigned tasks.

Role-based access control (RBAC): Formal technique for grouping users according to the system resources they require to perform their assigned tasks.

Role-based governance: Systems that allow managers to view current and historical inventory of roles, permissions granted, and individuals assigned to roles; identify unnecessary or inappropriate access entitlements and segregation-of-duties violations; and verify that changes to roles and entitlements have been successfully implemented.

Route sheet: Document that shows the production path a particular batch of products follows during manufacturing.

RSA (Rivest-Shamir-Adleman): One of the most trusted public key encryption methods. This method, however, is computationally intensive and much slower than private key encryption.

Run manual: Documentation describing how to run the system.

Run-to-run controls: Controls that use batch figures to monitor the batch as it moves from one programmed procedure to another.

S

S.O. pending file: File used to store the sales order (invoice copy) from the receive-order task until receipt of the shipping notice.

Safe Harbor Agreement: Two-way agreement between the United States and the European Union establishing standards for information transmittal.

Safety stock: Additional inventories added to the reorder point to avoid unanticipated stock-out conditions.

Salami fraud: Fraud in which each of multiple victims is defrauded out of a very small amount, but the fraud in total constitutes a large sum.

Sales invoice: Document that formally depicts the charges to the customer.

Sales journal: Special journal used for recording completed sales transactions.

Sales order: Source document that captures such vital information as the name and address of the customer making the purchase; the customer's account number; the name, number, and description of the product; the quantities and unit price of the items sold; and other financial information.

Sales order (credit copy): Copy of sales order sent by the receive-order task to the check-credit task. It is used to check the credit-worthiness of a customer.

Sales order (invoice copy): Copy of sales order to be reconciled with the shipping notice,. It describes the products that were actually shipped to the customer.

Sarbanes-Oxley Act (SOX): Most significant federal securities law, with provisions designed to deal with specific problems relating to capital markets, corporate governance, and the auditing profession.

Scalability: Ability of the system to grow smoothly and economically as user requirements increase.

Scavenging: Searching through the trash of the computer center for discarded output.

Schedule feasibility: Relates to the firm's ability to implement the project within an acceptable time.

Scheduled reports: Reports produced according to an established time frame.

Schema: Description of the entire database.

Screening router: Firewall that examines the source and destination addresses attached to incoming message packets.

Second normal form (2NF): Table that is free of both repeating group and partial dependencies.

Secure Electronic Transmission: Encryption scheme developed by a consortium of technology firms and banks to secure credit card transactions.

Secure Sockets Layer (SSL): Low-level encryption scheme used to secure transmissions in higher-level HTTP format.

Security: Attempt to avoid such undesirable events as a loss of confidentiality or data integrity.

Segments: A functional unit of a business organization.

Segregation of duties: Separation of employee duties to minimize incompatible functions.

Semantic models: Models that capture the operational meaning of the user's data and provide a concise description of it.

Sequential access method: Method in which all records in the file are accessed sequentially.

Sequential codes: Codes that represent items in some sequential order.

Sequential files: Files that are structured sequentially and must be accessed sequentially.

Sequential structure: A data structure in which all records in the file lie in contiguous storage spaces in a specified sequence arranged by their primary key.

Shell company: Establishment of a false vendor on the company's books, then manufacturing false purchase orders, receiving reports, and invoices in the name of the vendor and submitting them to the accounting system, creating the illusion of a legitimate transaction. The system ultimately issues a check to the false vendor.

Shipping log: Specifies orders shipped during the period.

Shipping notice: Document that informs the billing department that the customer's order has been filled and shipped.

Simple Network Mail Protocol (SNMP): Protocol for transmitting e-mail messages. Other e-mail protocols are Post Office Protocol (POP) and Internet Message Access Protocol (IMAP).

Skimming: Stealing cash from an organization before it is recorded on the organization's books and records.

Slicing and dicing: Operations enabling the user to examine data from different viewpoints.

Smurf attack: DOS attack that involves three parties: the perpetrator, the intermediary, and the victim.

Software-as-a-Service (SaaS): A software distribution model in which service providers host applications for client organizations over a private network or the Internet.

Sophisticated users: Users of financial reports who understand the conventions and accounting principles that are applied and that the statements have information content that is useful.

Source documents: Documents that capture and formalize transaction data needed for processing by their respective transaction cycles.

Span of control: Number of subordinates directly under a manager's control.

Specific IT assets: Assets unique to an organization that support its strategic objectives. Specific IT assets have little value outside their current use. May be tangible (computer equipment), intellectual (computer programs), or human.

Spooling: Direction of an application's output to a magnetic disk file rather than to the printer directly.

Stakeholders: Entities either inside or outside an organization that have a direct or indirect interest in the firm.

Standard cost system: Organizations that carry their inventories at a predetermined standard value regardless of the price actually paid to the vendor.

Statement on Auditing Standards (SAS) No. 109: The current authoritative document for specifying internal control objectives and techniques. It is based on the COSO framework.

Statement on Auditing Standards (SAS) No. 99: Authoritative document that defines fraud as an intentional act that results in a material misstatement in financial statements.

Steering committee: Organizational committee consisting of senior-level management responsible for systems planning.

Stock flow: Economic events that effect changes (increases or decreases) in resources.

Stock records: Formal accounting records for controlling inventory assets.

Stock release: Document that identifies which items of inventory must be located and picked from the warehouse shelves.

Storage virtualization: The pooling of physical storage from multiple network storage devices into what appears to be a single virtual storage device. This pool is then managed from a central server.

Strategic planning decisions: Planning with a long-term time frame that is associated with a high degree of uncertainty.

Structure diagram: Diagram that divides processes into input, process, and output functions.

Structured design: Disciplined way of designing systems from the top down.

Structured models: The data elements for predefined structured paths.

Structured problem: Problem in which data, procedures, and objectives are known with certainty.

Structured query language: Data processing tool for end users and professional programmers to access data in the database directly without the need for conventional programs.

Subdirectory name: General format for a URL.

Substantive tests: Tests that determine whether database contents fairly reflect the organization's transactions.

Supervision: Control activity involving the critical oversight of employees.

Supplier's invoice: Bill sent from the seller to the buyer showing unit costs, taxes, freight, and other charges.

Supply chain management (SCM): Class of application software that supports the set of activities associated with moving goods from the raw materials stage through to the consumer.

Support events: Control, planning, and management activities that are related to economic events but do not effect a change in resources.

Symmetric key: Single key used in an encryption algorithm to both code and decode a message.

SYN flood attack: Server that keeps signaling for acknowledgement until the server times out.

SYNchronize-ACKnowledge (SYN-ACK): Receiving server that acknowledges the request.

System audit trails: Logs that record activity at the system, application, and user level.

System flowchart: Flowcharts used to show the relationship between the key elements—input sources, programs, and output products—of computer systems.

System survey: Determination of what elements, if any, of the current system should be preserved as part of the new system.

Systems analysis: Two-step process that involves a survey of the current system and then an analysis of the user's needs.

Systems analysis report: Formal report that marks the conclusion of the systems analysis phase.

Systems design: Reflects the analysts' perception of information needs rather than the perception of accountants and other users.

Systems development life cycle (SDLC): Software development process.

Systems evaluation and selection: Optimization process that seeks to identify the best system.

Systems professionals: Analysts, designers, and programmers who have expertise in the specific areas that the feasibility study covers.

Systems project proposal: Proposal that provides management with a basis for deciding whether to proceed with the project.

Systems selection report: Deliverable portion of the systems selection process that will go to the next phase.

Systems strategy: Understanding of the strategic business needs of the organization based on the mission statement.

T

Tactical planning decisions: Planning performed by the middle-level manager to achieve the strategic plans of the organization.

Task-data dependency: User's inability to obtain additional information as his or her needs change.

Technical feasibility: Determination of whether the system can be developed under existing technology or if new technology is required.

TELNET: Terminal emulation protocol used on TCP/IP based networks.

TELOS: Acronym that refers to the technical, economic, *legal*, operational, and schedule feasibility of a project.

Temporary inconsistency: During accounting transactions, account balances pass through a state where the values are incorrectly stated.

Test data method: Technique used to establish application integrity by processing specially prepared sets of input data through production applications that are under review.

Tests of controls: Tests that establish whether internal controls are functioning properly.

Thefts of cash: Direct theft of cash on hand in the organization.

Third normal form (3NF): Normalization that occurs by dividing an unnormalized database into smaller tables until all attributes in the resulting tables are uniquely and wholly dependent on (explained by) the primary key.

Third-generation languages: Procedural languages in which the programmer must specify the sequence of events used in an operation.

Three-tier model: Model in which the database and application functions are separated.

Time and attendance file: Generated by employees directly entering timekeeping data in real time.

Time cards: Tool to capture the time the employee is at work.

Toyota Production System (TPS): Lean manufacturing system based on the just-in-time production model.

Tracing: Test data technique that performs an electronic walkthrough of the application's internal logic.

Trading partner agreement: An agreement that specifies the terms of a strategic business arrangement between buyer and seller in which they agree, in advance, to these terms of their relationship.

Trading partners: Category of external user, including customer sales and billing information, purchase information for suppliers, and inventory receipts information.

Transaction authorization: Procedure to ensure that employees process only valid transactions within the scope of their authority.

Transaction Cost Economics (TCE) theory: Belief that organizations should retain certain specific non-core IT assets in-house; due to their esoteric nature, such assets cannot be easily replaced once they are given up in an outsourcing arrangement. Supports outsourcing of commodity assets, which are easily replaced.

Transaction file: Temporary file that holds transaction records that will be used to change or update data in a master file.

Transaction level: Internet business model that uses the Internet to accept orders from customer and/or to place them with their suppliers.

Transaction log: Listing of transactions that provides an audit trail of all processed events.

Transaction processing system (TPS): Activity composed of three major subsystems—the revenue cycle, the expenditure cycle, and the conversion cycle.

Transaction: Event that affects an organization and that is processed by its information system as a unit of work.

Transcription errors: Type of errors that can corrupt a data code and cause processing errors.

Transfer Control Protocol/Internet Protocol (TCP/IP): Basic protocol that permits communication between Internet nodes.

Transitive dependencies: A transitive dependency occurs in a table where nonkey attributes are dependent on another nonkey attribute and independent of the table's primary key.

Transposition errors: Error that occurs when digits are transposed.

Triple-DES encryption: Enhancement to an older encryption technique for transmitting transactions.

Turnaround documents: Product documents of one system that become source documents for another system.

Turnkey systems: Completely finished and tested systems that are ready for implementation.

Two-tier model: Model where the server handles both application and database duties.

U

Uniform Resource Locator (URL): Address of the target site in the web browser to access the website.

Uninterruptible power supplies: Technologies that prevent data loss and system corruption due to power failure.

Universal Product Code (UPC): Label containing price information (and other data) that is attached to items purchased in a point-of-sale system.

Unstructured problem: Problem for which there are no precise solution techniques.

Update anomaly: Unintentional updating of data in a table, resulting from data redundancy.

User handbook: Reference manual of commands for getting started.

User view: Set of data that a particular user needs to achieve his or her assigned tasks.

User-defined procedure: Procedure that allows the user to create a personal security program. It provides more positive user identification than a password.

Users: Individuals who employ systems, receive information, and act on the information received.

V

Valid vendor file: File containing vendor mailing information.

Validity tests: Ensure that the system processes only data values that conform to specified tolerances. Examples include range tests, field tests, limit tests, and reasonableness tests. Validity tests also apply to transaction approvals, such as verifying that credit checks and AP three-way-matches are properly performed by the application.

Value chain: Activities that use cash to obtain resources and employ those resources for revenues.

Value stream accounting: An accounting technique that captures cost data according to value stream rather than by department.

Value stream map (VSM): Graphical representation of the business process to identify aspects that are wasteful and should be removed.

Value-added network (VAN): Hosted service offering that acts as an intermediary between business partners sharing standards-based or proprietary data via shared business processes.

Variance: Difference between the expected price—the standard—and the price actually paid.

Vendor fraud: See Billing schemes.

Vendor's invoice: Commercial document issued by a vendor to a buyer, indicating the products or services, quantities, and agreed prices for products or services that the vendor has already provided to the buyer. An invoice indicates that payment is due from the buyer to the vendor, according to the payment terms.

Verification model: Drill-down technique to either verify or reject a user's hypothesis.

Verification procedures: Independent checks of the accounting system to identify errors and misrepresentations.

Verified stock release: After stock is picked, verification of the order for accuracy and release of the goods.

View integration: Combining the data needs of all users into a single schema or enterprise-wide view.

View modeling: Determines the associations between entities and document them with an ER diagram.

Virtual private network (VPN): Private network within a public network.

Virtual storage access method (VSAM): Structure used for very large files that require routine batch processing and a moderate degree of individual record processing.

Virtualization: A technology that multiplies the effectiveness of the physical system by creating virtual (software) versions of the computer with separate operating systems that reside in the same physical equipment. In other words, virtualization is the concept of running more than one "virtual computer" on a single physical computer.

Voucher register: Register that reflects a firm's accounts payable liability.

Vouchers payable file: Equivalent to the open AP file.

Vouchers payable system: System under which the AP department uses cash disbursement vouchers and maintains a voucher register.

W

Walk-through: Analysis of system design to ensure the design is free from conceptual errors that could become programmed into the final system.

Wall of code: An object-oriented coding scheme that prevents direct access to the object's internal structure and data.

Web page: Fundamental format for the World Wide Web. Text documents called web pages have embedded Hypertext Markup Language (HTML) codes that provide the formatting for the page as well as hypertext links to other pages.

Websites: Computer servers that support Hypertext–Transfer Protocol (HTTP). The pages are accessed and read via a web browser such as Internet Explorer.

Work order: Document that draws from bills of materials and route sheets to specify the materials and production for each batch.

X

XBRL (extensible Business Reporting Language): XML-based language that was designed to provide the financial community with a standardized method for preparing, publishing, and automatically exchanging financial information, including financial statements of publicly held companies.

XBRL instance documents: Mapping of the organization's internal data to XBRL taxonomy elements.

XBRL taxonomy: Classification schemes that are compliant with the XBRL Specifications to accomplish a specific information exchange or reporting objective such as filing with the Securities and Exchange Commission.

XML (extensible Markup Language): Metalanguage for describing markup languages that can be used to model the data structure of an organization's internal database.

Z

Zombie: A virtual army of so-called bot (robot) computers used to launch a DDoS attack.

Zones: Areas on a form that contain related data.

INDEX

A

B

D

E

G

H

I

J

K

Q

R

S

T

U

V

W

X

Z